THE VICTORIA HISTORY
OF THE
COUNTIES OF ENGLAND

—

A HISTORY OF
SOMERSET

VOLUME III

THE VICTORIA HISTORY
OF THE
COUNTIES OF ENGLAND

EDITED BY R. B. PUGH, D.LIT.

THE UNIVERSITY OF LONDON
INSTITUTE OF
HISTORICAL RESEARCH

Oxford University Press, Ely House, 37 Dover Street, London, WIX 4AH

GLASGOW NEW YORK TORONTO MELBOURNE WELLINGTON
CAPE TOWN IBADAN NAIROBI DAR ES SALAAM LUSAKA ADDIS ABABA
DELHI BOMBAY CALCUTTA MADRAS KARACHI LAHORE DACCA
KUALA LUMPUR SINGAPORE HONG KONG TOKYO

ISBN 0 19 722739 2

Printed in Great Britain
at the University Press, Oxford
by Vivian Ridler
Printer to the University

INSCRIBED TO THE
MEMORY OF HER LATE MAJESTY
QUEEN VICTORIA
WHO GRACIOUSLY GAVE THE TITLE TO
AND ACCEPTED THE DEDICATION
OF THIS HISTORY

LANGPORT FROM THE AIR, 1960

A HISTORY OF THE
COUNTY OF
SOMERSET

EDITED BY R. W. DUNNING

VOLUME III

PUBLISHED FOR

THE INSTITUTE OF HISTORICAL RESEARCH

BY

OXFORD UNIVERSITY PRESS

1974

Distributed by Oxford University Press until 1 January 1977
thereafter by Dawsons of Pall Mall

CONTENTS OF VOLUME THREE

LIST OF ILLUSTRATIONS

Thanks are rendered to the following for permission to reproduce material in their possession and for the loan of photographs: Somerset Archaeological and Natural History Society (illustrations marked S.A.S.), the Royal Commission on Historical Monuments (England) (marked N.M.R.), the National Portrait Gallery, the Department of the Environment, the British Museum, Miss E. G. M. Lock, and Mr. W. B. Denman. Photographs dated 1972 and 1973 are by A. P. Baggs.

LIST OF ILLUSTRATIONS

LIST OF MAPS AND PLANS

The church plans and the plan of Muchelney abbey site were drawn by A. P. Baggs, the street plans and maps by K. J. Wass, of the Department of Geography, University College, London, from drafts by R. W. Dunning and R. J. E. Bush. The maps, street plans, and plan of Muchelney abbey site are based on the Ordnance Survey with the sanction of the Controller of H.M. Stationery Office, Crown Copyright reserved.

EDITORIAL NOTE

VOLUME I of the *Victoria History of Somerset* was published in 1906 and Volume II in 1911. Those two volumes contained all the 'general' articles planned for the county's history, but little progress was made with the 'topographical' volumes that were to present the histories of the individual towns and parishes. It is likely that the First World War put a stop to work on the *History* of Somerset as of many other counties.

Following proposals made in 1963 by the Somerset Archaeological and Natural History Society for the resumption of the *Victoria History* of the county, the Somerset County Council resolved to make funds available for the appointment of a special staff to write and organize the completion of the work. In 1966 a sub-committee of the County Records Committee was formed to superintend the arrangements, presided over by Lt.-Col. C. T. Mitford-Slade, C.M.G., C.V.O., H.M. Lieutenant of Somerset. The result was another of those partnerships between local patrons and the University of London, of which the prototype was that between the University and the Wiltshire Victoria History Committee, described in the editorial note to Volume VII of the *Victoria History of Wiltshire*. The essence of such a partnership is that the local patrons undertake to provide money to meet the expenses of compiling and editing the *History* of their county, and the University agrees to publish what is prepared, provided that it approves the result. The present volume is the first-fruits of the partnership in Somerset. The generous attitude displayed by the Somerset County Council is most sincerely appreciated by the University.

In 1967 Dr. R. W. Dunning was appointed county editor for Somerset, and he was joined in 1970 by Mr. R. J. E. Bush, as assistant editor.

Many people have helped in the preparation of this volume. The help of those who were concerned with particular parishes is acknowledged in the footnotes to the accounts of those parishes. The keeper of the records of the Duchy of Cornwall, the Duke of Devonshire, P.C., M.C., the Duke of Northumberland, K.G., T.D., F.R.S., the Marquess of Northampton, D.S.O., the Dean and Chapter of Bristol, the Dean and Chapter of Wells, Mr. R. J. R. Arundell, Mr. J. Stevens Cox, and Mr. A. R. E. Pretor-Pinney are thanked for making available the records in their possession. Among the public libraries and record offices to whose librarians or archivists and their staff thanks are rendered for their sympathetic co-operation, special mention must be made of the Somerset Record Office.

The structure and aims of the *History* as a whole are outlined in the *General Introduction* (1970).

LIST OF CLASSES OF DOCUMENTS
IN THE PUBLIC RECORD OFFICE
USED IN THIS VOLUME
WITH THEIR CLASS NUMBERS

Chancery

	Proceedings
C 1	Early
C 2	Series I
C 3	Series II
C 44	Placita in Cancellaria, Tower Series
C 47	Miscellanea
C 54	Close Rolls
C 60	Fine Rolls
C 66	Patent Rolls
	Inquisitions post mortem
C 132	Series I, Hen. III
C 133	Edw. I
C 134	Edw. II
C 135	Edw. III
C 136	Ric. II
C 137	Hen. IV
C 138	Hen. V
C 139	Hen. VI
C 140	Edw. IV and V
C 141	Ric. III
C 142	Series II
C 143	Inquisitions ad quod damnum
C 145	Miscellaneous Inquisitions
C 146	Ancient Deeds, Series C
C 260	Chancery Files (Tower and Rolls Chapel), Recorda

Court of Common Pleas

C.P. 25(2)	Feet of Fines, Series II
C.P. 40	De Banco Rolls
C.P. 43	Recovery Rolls

Duchy of Lancaster

D.L. 25	Deeds, Series L
D.L. 42	Miscellaneous Books
D.L. 43	Rentals and Surveys

Exchequer, King's Remembrancer

E 117	Church Goods
E 123	Decrees and Orders, Series I
E 134	Depositions taken by Commission
E 142	Ancient Extents
E 149	Inquisitions post mortem, Series I
E 153	Escheators' Files
E 178	Special Commissions of Inquiry
E 179	Subsidy Rolls, etc.

Exchequer, Augmentation Office

E 310	Particulars of Leases
E 315	Miscellaneous Books
E 317	Parliamentary Surveys, Commonwealth
E 318	Particulars for Grants
	Ancient Deeds
E 326	Series B
E 329	Series BS

Exchequer, Lord Treasurer's Remembrancer's and Pipe Offices

E 372	Pipe Rolls

Home Office

H.O. 129	Census Papers: Ecclesiastical Returns

Justices Itinerant, Assize and Gaol Delivery Justices, etc.

J.I. 1	Eyre Rolls, Assize Rolls, etc.
J.I. 3	Gaol Delivery Rolls

Court of King's Bench (Crown Side)

K.B. 26	Curia Regis Rolls

Exchequer, Office of the Auditors of Land Revenue

L.R. 2	Miscellaneous Books

Prerogative Court of Canterbury

Prob. 11	Registered Copies of Wills proved in P.C.C.

Privy Seal Office

P.S.O. 1	Warrants for the Privy Seal, Series I

Registrar General

R.G. 4	Non-parochial Registers
R.G. 9	Census Returns, 1861

Court of Requests

Req. 2	Proceedings

Special Collections

S.C. 2	Court Rolls
S.C. 6	Ministers' Accounts
	Rentals and Surveys
S.C. 11	Rolls
S.C. 12	Portfolios

Court of Star Chamber

Sta. Cha. 2	Proceedings, Hen. VIII

SELECT LIST OF ACCUMULATIONS
IN THE SOMERSET RECORD OFFICE
AND OTHER COUNTY RECORD OFFICES

Deposited Collections

DD/AB	Lord Ashburton
AH	Acland-Hood family of Fairfield
BT	Bennett & Co. of Bruton (surveyors)
CA	Vaughan-Lee family of Dillington
CC	Church Commissioners
CM	Combe family of Earnshill
DEV	Duke of Devonshire
DN	Dickinson family of Kingweston
DNL	Bailward family of Horsington
ED	Estate Duty copy wills
EDS	Dept. of Education & Science, building grants and plans
ES	Esdaile family of Cothelstone
FS	Foster of Wells (solicitors)
GS	Glastonbury Antiquarian Society
HLM	Helyar family of Poundisford
HN	Harbin family of Newton Surmaville
HW	Hawksworth family of Snitterfield
KW	King, Wilkinson, & Co. of Taunton (surveyors)
LC	Clarke, Louch, Wilmott, & Clarke of Langport (solicitors)
LTR	Fownes-Luttrell family of Edington
MGR	Moger collection of copy wills
MI	Mildmay family of Hazlegrove
MKG	Meade-King & Co. of Bristol (solicitors)
PH	Phelips family of Montacute
PI	Pretor-Pinney family of Somerton Erleigh
PL	Batten-Pooll family of Ivybridge
PLE	Poole & Son of South Petherton (solicitors)
PM	Portman family of Orchard Portman
PR	Parsons family of Misterton
PT	Poulett family of Hinton St. George
SAS	Somerset Archaeological Society
SE	Trustees of Sexey's Hospital, Bruton
SF	Sanford family of Nynehead
SFR	Society of Friends
SH	Strachie family of Sutton Court
SMC	Somerton Charity Trustees
SP	Sheppard family of Taunton
TB	Trollope-Bellew family of Crowcombe
TH THG	} Thring family of Alford
WY	Wyndham family of Orchard Wyndham
YB	Yeatman-Biggs family of Warminster
S/BT	Grenville family of Butleigh
ST	Stradling family of Chilton Polden
X/BB	Bamber family of Castle Hill
DST	Dorset Record Office
KN	Neal family of Kingsdon
ME	Mullings, Ellett, & Co. of Cirencester (solicitors)

DD/BR/ar	Anderson family of London
bs	Baileys, Shaw, & Gillett of London (solicitors)
hmp	Hyde, Mahon, & Pascall of London (solicitors)
lr	Lawrence, Graham, & Co. of London (solicitors)
py	Perry of Brighton (solicitors)
D/P/	Parish Collections
D/PC/	Parish Council Collections

Borough Collections

D/B/ilch	Ilchester
la	Langport

Diocesan Records

D/D/Bg	exchanges of glebe
Bp	presentation deeds
Bo	ordination papers
Ca	act books
Cd	deposition books
P	peculiars
Rg	glebe terriers
Rm	meeting-house licences
Rn	nominations of schoolmasters, etc.
Vc	visitations acts
V rtns	visitations returns

Quarter Sessions Records

CR	Inclosure awards
Q/petns	Petitions, Commonwealth
R	deposited plans, Friendly Society returns, jurors' books
RE	land tax assessments
REr	electoral registers
RL	victuallers' recognizances
RR	recusants' lands, meeting-house licences
SO	order books
SR	sessions rolls

County Council Records

C/C	property deeds
E	education dept.
S	surveyor's dept.

Other Deposits

D/G/SM	Shepton Mallet poor-law union
Y	Yeovil poor-law union
PS/ilm	Ilminster petty sessions
	Turnpike trusts
T/ilch	Ilchester
ilm	Ilminster
lsc	Langport, Somerton, and Castle Cary
T/PH/vch	photostats, Victoria History of Somerset

Devon Record Office

123M	Petre family of Ingatestone
1148	Acland family of Killerton

Dorset Record Office

D 16	Glyn MSS.
54	Weld family of Lulworth
124	Fox-Strangways family of Melbury

Wiltshire County Record Office

383	Hoare family of Stourhead

NOTE ON ABBREVIATIONS

Among the abbreviations and short titles used the following may require elucidation:

Bk. of Fairs	*Authentic Account published by the King's Authority, of all the Fairs in England and Wales* (5th edn. London, 1767)
Collinson, *Hist. Som.*	Collinson, *History and Antiquities of the County of Somerset* (3 vols. Bath, 1791)
County Gazette Dir. (1840)	*General Directory for the County of Somerset, presented gratuitously to the subscribers to the County Gazette Newspaper* (Taunton, 1840)
Darby & Finn, *Dom. Geog. S.W. Eng.*	H. C. Darby and R. Welldon Finn, *Domesday Geography of South-West England* (1967)
D.C.O.	Duchy of Cornwall Office
D.R.O.	Dorset Record Office
Devon R.O.	Devon Record Office
Dioc. Dir.	*Bath and Wells Diocesan Directory* (*and Almanack*) (1908–) (Almanack discontinued 1948)
Dioc. Kal.	(*New*) *Bath and Wells Diocesan Kalendar* (1888–1907)
Finberg, *Early Charters of Wessex*	H. P. R. Finberg, *Early Charters of Wessex* (Leicester University Press, 1964)
Grundy, *Saxon Charters*	G. B. Grundy, *Saxon Charters of Somerset* (*Proc. Som. Arch. Soc.* lxxiii–lxxx)
H.M.C. Wells	Historical Manuscripts Commission, Series 12, *Calendar of the Manuscripts of the Dean and Chapter of Wells* (2 vols. 1907, 1914)
Hunt. Libr.	Huntington Library, San Marino, California
Ilchester Almshouse Deeds, ed. W. Buckler	*Ilchester Almshouse Deeds, 1200–1625,* ed. W. Buckler (Yeovil, 1866)
Pevsner, *South and West Som.*	N. Pevsner, *South and West Somerset* (Buildings of England Series) (London, 1958)
Proc. Som. Arch. Soc.	*Proceedings of the Somersetshire Archaeological and Natural History Society* (from 1968 *Somerset Archaeology and Natural History*)
Rep. Som. Cong. Union (1896)	*Annual Report of the Somerset Congregational Union and of the Evangelist Society presented at the One-Hundredth Anniversary* (Wellington, 1896)
S. & D. N. & Q.	*Somerset and Dorset Notes and Queries*
S.R.O.	Somerset Record Office
S.R.S.	Somerset Record Society (for list of publications used see p. xx)
Som. C.C., Educ. Cttee.	Somerset County Council, Education Committee
Som. Incumbents, ed. Weaver	*Somerset Incumbents,* ed. F. W. Weaver (Bristol, 1889)
Som. Wills, ed. Brown	*Abstracts of Somersetshire Wills etc., copied from the Manuscript Collections of the late Rev. F. Brown* (6 vols. priv. print. 1887–90)
W.R.O.	Wiltshire County Record Office

LIST OF
SOMERSET RECORD SOCIETY PUBLICATIONS
USED IN THIS VOLUME

THE HUNDRED OF KINGSBURY (EAST)

KINGSBURY (East) hundred, belonging to the bishops of Bath and Wells and located in different parts of the county, comprised the parishes of Chard, Combe St. Nicholas, Winsham, Kingsbury Episcopi, and Huish Episcopi. The history of the hundred is deferred, but the history of Huish Episcopi is given below because of the intimate association of the parish with Langport.

HUISH EPISCOPI

THE parish of Huish Episcopi, normally known as Huish until the end of the 18th century, surrounds Langport on three sides. It lies principally in the hundred of Kingsbury (East), of which it forms a detached part. Portions of the parish extended into the neighbouring hundreds of Pitney and Somerton.[1] That part lying in Kingsbury (East) hundred measured 1,780 a. in 1841.[2] Just over 196 a. on King's Sedgemoor allotted to Huish in 1795[3] lay in Whitley hundred, and an area round Paradise in the north-east was in Williton and Freemanors hundred. In 1861 the area of the whole parish was 2,282 a.[4] In 1885 the detached portion of the parish on King's Sedgemoor was transferred to High Ham, and Huish gained small detached parts of High Ham and Pitney.[5] In 1901 the area was 2,314 a.[6]

The parish is highly irregular in shape and its boundaries are dictated largely by natural features, modified by the effects of drainage and inclosure of the 'moors', and by the position of Langport. Much of the western boundary follows the river Parrett, flowing north to Common moor. The original division then probably followed the eastern edge of the 'moor', which was considered extra-parochial and was subject to disputed ownership in 1637 and c. 1718.[7] The division of the 'moor' by agreement between Langport, Aller, and Huish, was made in 1797.[8] From the 'moor' the boundary runs up the scarp to Bowdens (Abovedowne alias Bowden in 1576)[9] through the hamlet of Combe, and then follows the contour round the scarp of Aller hill. The eastern limit of the parish follows the mill brook, the Wernestreme or Wernenstreme of the late-12th- or early-13th-century perambulation

of High Ham,[10] as it flows south. East of Pound Farm, Wearne, however, the boundary takes in a triangular tract, perhaps the thirty strips of ploughland belonging, according to the same perambulation, to the king.[11] This land formed part of the manor of Pitney Wearne which was in the hands of the Crown until c. 1203.[12] The course of the boundary on Ham Down was established under inclosure in 1799.[13] The southern limit is the course of the Yeo and a stream, perhaps marking the earlier channel of either the Yeo or the Parrett, and known in the Middle Ages as Horsies Pyll, the rhine towards Muchelney, and Oldryver.[14] The south-western boundary along Perry moor bank in Perry moor and then over rising ground, formerly the bishop's park, was established, at least as far as the park was concerned, by agreement between the bishop of Bath and Wells and the abbot of Muchelney in 1279.[15] The perambulation attached to a charter of Athelstan granting lands in Curry Rivel to Muchelney includes within the area of the modern parish of Drayton all that part of Huish south-west of the Parrett. The historical evidence suggests a forgery of the perambulation by Muchelney connected with the abbot's dispute over the bishop's park.[16]

South-west of the Parrett Huish Level lies on loam over clay and gravel in the flood plain, but further west the land rises to over 75 ft. In the extreme west over 50 a. were wooded at least until the early 19th century.[17] The centre of the parish, on gently undulating ground, then had a 'dry, good soil'. Further north, however, on Bowdens, and Aller hill above Combe and Wearne where the

[1] S.R.S. iii. 324, 328, 331. This article was completed in 1971.
[2] Census, 1841.
[3] S.R.O., CR 116.
[4] P.O. Dir. Som. (1861).
[5] Local Govt. Bd. Prov. Orders Conf. Order (Poor Law), (No. 2), Act (1885).
[6] V.C.H. Som. ii. 346.
[7] E 178/5621; Cal. Treas. Papers, 1714–19, 408–9.
[8] S.R.O., D/B/la 26.
[9] S.R.O., DD/CC 31523.
[10] Grundy, Saxon Charters of Som. 119.
[11] Ibid.
[12] See p. 51.
[13] S.R.O., CR 108.
[14] Grundy, op. cit. 133; H.M.C. Wells, i. 484; Lambeth Palace MSS., CR 1187; see below, p. 38.
[15] S.R.S. vii. 99; xiv. 56–7.
[16] Grundy, op. cit. 133; S.R.S. xiv. 39.
[17] S.R.O., DD/CC 12461.

land rises to 300 ft., the soil was described as 'very thin and stony'.[18] At Pibsbury, in the south-east, near the 50 ft. contour, the fields are in many places uneven, the result of extensive quarrying for the lias which lies near the surface there.[19]

the edge of this marsh.[21] Littleney, the 'little island' which gave its name to the bishop's estate in the parish at Domesday, provided a limited amount of arable a few feet above the level of the surrounding marsh.[22] By the early 14th century much of the

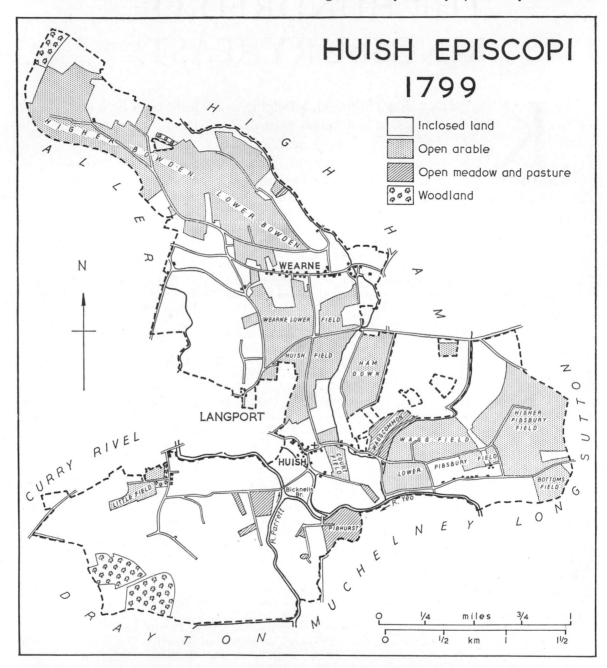

There seem to have been Roman sites on the west bank of the Parrett and at Wearne.[20] The pattern of the later settlement seems to have been Saxon, and was dictated by the irregular terrain and by the stretches of marsh beside the rivers. Huish, Littleney, Pibsbury, and Combe were all established at

marsh had been drained, and the settlement itself virtually deserted.[23] Huish, the 'homestead' or 'hide' settlement,[24] commanded a route to Langport and became the most important in the parish, acquiring the church, court-house, vicarage house, cross, and green.[25] Pibsbury, anciently Pibbesbyrig,[26]

[18] S.R.O., DD/DEV 29: survey 1765.
[19] See p. 7.
[20] V.C.H. Som. i. 328, 364; Proc. Som. Arch. Soc. xcvi. 49. The coins from the Parrett site were dated between A.D. 250 and 350: Isabel Wyatt, The Book of Huish (Yeovil, 1934), 10.
[21] H.M.C. Wells, i. 429; Cod. Dipl. ed. Kemble, iv, p. 164.

[22] V.C.H. Som. i. 456.   [23] See below.
[24] E. Ekwall, Dict. Eng. Place Names.
[25] S.R.O., DD/CC 13322 2/9; 121651. The green was at the junction of the Muchelney road with the lane to Huish bridge; the cross stood at the junction east of the church: S.C. 6/1131/9; S.R.O., CR 131.
[26] Cod. Dipl. ed. Kemble, iv, p. 164.

lay near a fordable point on the Yeo which, from the 15th century, was the loading place for local stone.[27] By the end of the 18th century if not before Pibsbury's houses stood in a neat cluster on the north side of the road a mile east of Huish church, with regular plots stretching behind them. The road there was known as Pibsbury Street in the 18th century, and may have formed some kind of defence against flooding.[28]

Two other hamlets, Combe and Wearne, lie in the northern part of the parish. Combe, on the edge of Poolmead, appears never to have been of much consequence. A mile to the east lies Wearne, the centre of the western part of Pitney Wearne manor.[29] It stretches for half a mile along a road on the southern slope of Bowdens. At Paradise, a name which first occurs in 1562, there is a subsidiary settlement.[30] In the 11th century there was a small arable holding at Wearne, possibly an area of warren forming part of the warren of Somerton.[31] There were two other settlements in the parish: the 'borough' of Southwick or Froglane, perhaps an extension of Littleney, which is treated elsewhere,[32] and the hamlet of Wagg. The second of these resulted from encroachments by cottagers on Wagg common, east of Huish village. Encroachment had started by the end of the 17th century,[33] and had become considerable by the end of the 18th century.[34]

Huish had three open arable fields in the Middle Ages, Court and Littleney fields and Huish Hill.[35] By 1755 they were known as Court, Inner, and Outer fields.[36] Pibsbury, which contained no demesne land, had three fields in 1650,[37] and four by 1755, known as Pibsbury, Pibsbury Farther, Horsey Furlong, and Lower Kinghill fields.[38] In 1799 they were known as Higher and Lower Pibsbury, Wagg, and Bottoms fields.[39] By the end of the 18th century Wearne was served by Higher and Lower Bowdens and Wearne Lower field.[40] Small-scale inclosure by agreement occurred on Aller hill, Ham Down, and Poolmead in the early 18th century,[41] part of Wagg common in 1786–7,[42] and Common moor in 1797.[43] Some 718 a. of arable was divided and allotted between 61 owners under an Award in 1799.[44] Under the same Award 58 a. of common meadow at Wagg and Pibhurst, the latter on the banks of the Yeo at Pibsbury, were divided.[45]

Main roads from Bridgwater, Somerton, and Ilchester to Langport pass through Huish. The Somerton road entered the parish via a ford across the mill brook until after 1823.[46] The present line from Brooklands House was adopted when the railway was constructed in 1906. The road was turnpiked in 1753.[47] The road from Ilchester, through Huish village, was turnpiked in 1792, and the Bridgwater road in 1824. The road from Brooklands House to Huish church was also adopted in 1824 in connexion with the new route south to Muchelney.[48]

There were two important bridges in the south of the parish. Huish bridge, over the Parrett below its confluence with the Yeo, carried a road from Huish village to Huish Level and Frog Lane. It was so named in 1581,[49] and was destroyed by the king's forces in 1646.[50] In 1791 it was described as of wood, standing on four stone piers.[51] The present bridge, called Black bridge, is of iron. Bicknell's bridge, formerly Bickling bridge, carries the road from Huish village to Muchelney.[52] It replaced a footbridge in 1829–30.[53] 'Stenebrugge' occurs in 1369, but its position is not known;[54] Wearne bridge and Pound bridge, found in 1666 and 1803, are probably names for the bridge, now a culvert, crossing the mill brook at Pound Farm.[55] There were at least two medieval fish weirs in the parish. 'Kingswere' was probably on the Parrett below Langport and was attached to a holding in Wearne by 1275–6;[56] the other was owned by the abbot of Muchelney and seems to have been across the Parrett on the Muchelney–Huish boundary. It occurs in 1353 and was still there in 1440, having a weir house near it in 1424.[57]

The present system of embankments and catchwaters was begun in 1795 with measures to improve the navigation of the Yeo.[58] Similar improvements on the Parrett threatened an increase in flooding, and the Long Sutton Catchwater drain, running along the northern bank of the Yeo was dug in 1836 and enlarged c. 1841.[59] It was equipped by 1971 with a pumping station.

The Yeovil–Durston branch of the Bristol and Exeter railway was constructed through the parish in 1853, and a station, known as Langport West, was built south-west of Langport Bridge.[60] The station and line were closed in 1964. Langport East station, partly in Huish parish, was built in 1906 on the link line between Castle Cary and Langport. It was closed to passengers in 1962 and to goods in 1964.[61]

[27] See p. 7.
[28] S.R.O., DD/CC 12428.
[29] See p. 51.
[30] Castle Ashby, Northampton MSS. 810(2).
[31] V.C.H. Som. i. 520; ii. 552–3; W. H. P. Greswell, Forests of Som. 99; Cal. Chart. R. 1226–57, 115, 119, 181; Close R. 1227–31, 304, 330.
[32] See p. 6.
[33] S.R.O., DD/CC 23736.
[34] S.R.O., DD/SAS PR 428.
[35] S.C. 6/1131/9; S.R.O., DD/CC 31559.
[36] S.R.O., DD/CC 24184.
[37] Ibid. 121651.
[38] Ibid. 24184.
[39] S.R.O., CR 131.   [40] Ibid.
[41] S.R.O., DD/DEV 26. There was a case of illegal inclosure in 1464: Lambeth Palace MSS., CR 550.
[42] S.R.O., DD/SAS PR 428; D/B/la 12.
[43] S.R.O., D/B/la 26.
[44] S.R.O., CR 131.
[45] Ibid.
[46] S.R.O., DD/SAS (C/212), map 1823.

[47] S.R.O., D/T/lsc 2.
[48] Ibid.
[49] Lambeth Palace MSS., CR 1192.
[50] S.R.S. xxviii. 2–3, 34.
[51] Collinson, Hist. Som. ii. 470.
[52] S.R.O., DD/CC 13339, 23730.
[53] Ibid. 12460.
[54] Lambeth Palace MSS., CR 1179.
[55] 9th Rep. Com. Char. H.C. 258, pp. 522–4 (1823), ix; S.R.O., D/P/h.ep. 14/5/1.
[56] Rot. Hund. (Rec. Com.), ii. 122; Plac. de Quo Warr. (Rec. Com.), 695.
[57] Lambeth Palace MSS., CR 1177, 1187, 1189.
[58] M. Williams, The Draining of the Somerset Levels, 159. Excommunication was used against breakers of flood banks in the 14th century: Cal. Pat. 1313–17, 412, 417; S.R.S. i. 117.
[59] Williams, op. cit. 159; S.R.O., DD/CC 13296, 13298; Q/R deposited plans 7.
[60] See plate facing p. 32.
[61] C. R. Clinker and J. M. Firth, Reg. Closed Stations, ii and suppl.

Most of the agricultural holdings in the parish were small, and the surviving 17th- and early-18th-century houses, mostly of lias and originally thatched, are generally of three-roomed ground plan. Pound Cottage has the parlour in a cross-wing, where there are two cruck trusses. In the hall, which is probably of late-medieval origin, there are parts of a further cruck truss. Pound Cottage, Huish, and Pound Farm, Wearne, have a cross-passage against the stack. During the 18th century several more sophisticated houses were built, notably Huish House. Of this only fragments, in the grounds of the late-19th-century house of the same name, remain. Wearne House, of 1729, has an unheated central room which is flanked by a larger room with gable stacks. The central room is lit by a vernacular version of a Venetian window with a five-centred middle unit.[62] A survivor of a more humble dwelling is Cornerways, Huish, built as three single-storeyed cottages in rubble and thatch, with brick stacks, in the late 18th or early 19th century. Langport began to extend its built-up area into Huish in the 19th century; Newtown occurs by 1845, the Avenue c. 1877.[63] Local Authority houses were built in Garden City between 1918 and 1929.[64] Similar houses were erected in Huish village after the Second World War, and private development took place north and north-west of the church in the early 1970s.[65]

In 1770 the New Inn was established in the parish.[66] The Rose and Crown, in Huish village, was so named by 1835, and the present building, with Gothic windows and a thatched roof, is contemporary.[67]

Huish seems, in the 19th century if not earlier, to have been a centre of popular entertainments including sports and revels, a ploughing match, and a flower show, the last of which still continued in 1971.[68] The parish proved a fruitful source for folk songs collected by Cecil Sharp.[69]

There were said to be 420 communicants at Huish and Langport together in 1548.[70] In 1563 there were 67 households in Huish.[71] By 1801 the population was 367, and in the next fifty years rose rapidly to 760, evidently owing in part to the development of dwellings at Newtown.[72] In the next half century the total fluctuated between 706 and 637, rose to 733 in 1911, fell in the next two decades, and was 945 in 1961.[73]

MANORS AND OTHER ESTATES. In 1065 Edward the Confessor confirmed to Bishop Giso of Wells the villages of Lytelenige, Hiwisc, Cuma, and Pybbesbyrig.[74] The Domesday survey recorded Giso's holding only as Littelaneia, but its acreage implies that he also held the other properties.[75] By 1179, when a church had been built at Huish, the estate was known as the manor of HUISH.[76] Successive bishops of Bath and Wells held the manor until 1548, when Bishop Barlow was forced to surrender it to the Crown for the benefit of Edward Seymour, duke of Somerset.[77] The bishop recovered it in 1550,[78] and it continued to be part of the endowment of the bishopric of Bath and Wells until 1855, when ownership was transferred to the Ecclesiastical (later Church) Commissioners. In 1858 the estate measured over 977 a. Most of it was sold to the tenants in 1859–60, though the lordship was not included in any sale.[79] The Church Commissioners sold their last holding in 1952.[80]

In 1316 a piece of land in Southmoor was described as lying between 'the bishop's manor of la Hull' and 'the rhine towards Muchelney', and near 'the new close called Lytilnye'.[81] The 'manor' was probably the house and buildings from which the demesne was administered. Buildings on the demesne in 1302 included a hay barton and a cowshed by the park.[82] There were two barns by 1329,[83] and in 1351 land was described as lying between the grange of Hull and the bishop's park.[84] Repairs were made to the manor-house and kitchen in 1458–9, though by that time most of the land was divided and let.[85] There is no further trace of buildings, though pasture grounds included Hill Barton and Derehill, recalling the ancient name of the manor-house.[86] Park farm, the name of the largest single holding on the bishop's estate and embracing the presumed site of the park, included a field called Hill Park.[87]

By 1634 there was a court-house on the manor.[88] At least from that time it was let to a succession of tenants, and stood in a field, adjacent to a dovecot, sometimes known as Court Barton.[89] It was sold by the Ecclesiastical Commissioners in 1858, when it was divided into two dwellings.[90] It was subsequently known as Pound Farm, and in 1971 as Tanyard Cottage. It is a 16th- or early-17th-century structure with lias walls and a thatched roof. The internal walls appear to be later insertions and the Ham stone window surrounds are of various dates.

The manor of Pitney Plucknett or Pitney Wearne included a considerable amount of property in and near Wearne. Its descent has been traced elsewhere.[91] A farm opposite the present Pound Farm in Wearne was described as a capital messuage in 1692.[92] It was a building of the 17th century with three-roomed plan, internal chimney, and cross-passage.

[62] See plate facing p. 193.
[63] S.R.O., D/D/Rm, box 2; DD/LC, conveyance, duke of Devonshire to James Broadmead, 1877.
[64] Garden City was so called from Kelway's Nurseries there. Rail excursions from Taunton to 'peony valley' were popular in the 1930s: S.R.O., DD/SAS PR 54/1, p. 30.
[65] See map, p. 18.
[66] S.R.O., Q/RL, victuallers' recogs.
[67] S.R.O., D/P/h.ep. 9/1/1.
[68] Wyatt, Book of Huish, 92–6.   [69] Ibid. 102.
[70] S.R.S. ii. 116.
[71] B.M. Harl. MS. 594 f. 50v.
[72] S.R.O., D/D/Rm, box 2.
[73] V.C.H. Som. ii. 346; Census, 1911–61.
[74] H.M.C. Wells, i. 429; Cod. Dipl. ed. Kemble, iv, p. 164.
[75] V.C.H. Som. i. 456.
[76] H.M.C. Wells, i. 439; Archaeologia, l. 354.
[77] Cal. Pat. 1548–9, 128.
[78] Ibid. 180; S.C. 6/Ed. VI/257.
[79] Church Commissioners, London, Report 127551/2.
[80] Ibid.
[81] H.M.C. Wells, i. 484.
[82] S.C. 6/1131/3.
[83] S.C. 6/1131/6.
[84] S.R.O., DD/SAS BA/1.
[85] S.C. 6/1131/9.
[86] Ibid.; S.R.O., DD/SAS BA/3.
[87] S.R.O., DD/CC 13324, p. 114.
[88] Ibid. p. 113.
[89] S.R.O., DD/CC 13339, 23726, 27025; CR 131.
[90] Church Commissioners, London, Report 127551/2.
[91] See p. 51.   [92] S.R.O., DD/DEV 21.

The floors and internal walls were removed early in the 20th century when it was converted for use as a barn.

In 1305 John Dammory died in possession of ⅓ hide of land in Wearne held of William le Venour. His heir was his son John, but the subsequent descent of the property has not been found.[93]

In 1305 Robert de St. Clare settled a small estate of 2 messuages, 2 virgates, 17 a. of meadow, and 6 a. of pasture in Long Sutton and Wearne on Reynold de St. Clare.[94] One third of this was given to Sibyl de St. Clare, and the rest was settled in 1360 on Richard, grandson of Sibyl, and on his wife Margaret, with remainder to William Bonville.[95] Bonville succeeded in 1362 to Richard's holding and in 1372 to Sibyl's.[96] He was one of the two free suitors to Huish hundred court in 1373.[97] The subsequent descent of the land has not been traced.[98]

The rectorial estate was held by successive archdeacons of Wells from the end of the 12th century.[99] It was let in 1547 for £28 a year.[1] The same rent was still payable in 1897.[2] In 1650 the whole estate was valued at £142, and comprised tithes and just over 74 a. of land, with 6 beast leazes or 6 a. of meadow in addition.[3] There were still 56 a. remaining in 1897.[4] Most of the tithes were commuted for corn rents worth £278 16s. in 1799, which in turn became a rent-charge of £185 1s. 2d. in 1914.[5] The remaining tithes, in Langport, were commuted to a rent-charge of £15 in 1840,[6] and tithes and moduses in Huish moor to a similar charge of £4 17s. 6d. in 1845.[7] A large proportion of the great tithes of Pitney also belonged to the parsonage of Huish by grant of Athelney abbey c. 1232.[8] These were commuted to corn rents worth £46 3s. 6½d. in 1797, and became a rent-charge of £32 16s. 4d. in 1876.[9]

The estate was normally held on lease from the archdeacons of Wells. Successive members of the Tucker family held it from 1624 at least until 1650.[10] From 1808 until 1897 the lessees were members of the King family, beginning with Walker King, bishop of Rochester, and ending with his son Edward, bishop of Lincoln.[11] In 1897 the latter sold the remainder of his lease of both tithes and glebe to the Ecclesiastical Commissioners, who by 1924 had disposed of the land.[12]

In 1650 the buildings of the estate included two thatched stone barns at the western end of the churchyard, one of five and the other of seven bays.[13] There were also other farm buildings, including some on the south side of Huish Street, opposite the church, the site of which is now occupied by the present vicarage house.[14] One of the two barns survived until 1883.[15]

ECONOMIC HISTORY. Two recognizable parts of Huish were described in the Domesday survey: the estate of the bishop of Wells, then called Litelande or Littelaneia, which T.R.E. gelded for 2 hides, and the 2½-virgate holding at Wearne of Robert de Odburville.[16] Robert's holding had been waste in 1066; by 1086 it was worth 15s., there was arable for half a plough, worked by a bordar and a serf, and the demesne was stocked with 4 beasts and 15 sheep. The bishop's estate had land for 8 ploughs: one hide in demesne was worked by 2 serfs with 2 ploughs, and one hide was cultivated by 3 villeins and 6 bordars. There were 12 a. of meadow, 100 a. of pasture, and 20 a. of wood, but the only beast recorded was a riding-horse. The value of the bishop's holding was 40s.[17]

The size of the bishop's demesne does not seem to have altered significantly during the next five centuries: in 1521–2 the arable measured 149 a., the meadow 30¾ a., and the pasture about 107 a.[18] Drainage work, however, significantly increased the size of the cultivable land in the rest of the manor, and is reflected in the increase in the bishop's rent income: at least 86 a. of meadow and pasture ground, from which overland rents were payable, seem to have been recovered by 1302 in Newmead, Pibhurst, Middlemoor, Russehurst, Southwick, and Little Haymoor, now lying along the banks of the Yeo and Parrett.[19]

The demesne lands of the bishop's manor lay mostly in the south-west of the parish and by 1302 included a cluster of farm buildings around a house, a park, and the small settlement of Southwick, soon to be developed for a short while as a borough, presumably to attract business from the road at the western end of the Parrett crossing into Langport. The farm buildings of the demesne, housing a cowman, a parker, and other workers, included a cowshed and two barns.[20] By 1458 the demesne was entirely let, for £6 4s. 2d.[21] The arable lay mostly in large inclosures called Hill field (75 a.) and Court field (28 a.), with smaller units at Derehill (now Dairy hill) and Lytelnye field (later Little field), and small strips at Huish hill. Between 1504 and 1510 Hill field was divided into two and called Bishop's field.[22] Demesne meadows were let in 1458 for £5 10s. 1½d., and pasture for £14 15s. 10d.[23] These figures remained virtually unchanged at least until the mid 17th century.[24]

The bishop's park originated in a grant of free warren in 1257,[25] confirmed in 1280.[26] Shortly before

---

[93] *Cal. Inq. p.m.* iv, p. 202.
[94] *S.R.S.* vi. 337.
[95] Ibid. xvii. 44–5.
[96] *Cal. Inq. p.m.* xiii, pp. 62, 177.
[97] Lambeth Palace MSS., CR 1180.
[98] See p. 137.
[99] See p. 9.
[1] *H.M.C. Wells.* ii. 252; *Cal. Pat.* 1547–8, 190.
[2] S.R.O., DD/CC 268187.
[3] Ibid. 121651.
[4] Ibid. 268187.
[5] S.R.O., CR 131; tithe award.
[6] S.R.O., Langport tithe award.
[7] S.R.O., Huish tithe award.
[8] *H.M.C. Wells,* i. 47.
[9] S.R.O., CR 116; Pitney tithe award.

[10] S.R.O., DD/CC 121651.
[11] Ibid. 121881, 268187.
[12] Church Commissioners, London, Report 127551/2.
[13] S.R.O., DD/CC 121651.
[14] Ibid.
[15] S.R.O., D/P/h.ep. 6/1/1: faculty to demolish.
[16] *V.C.H. Som.* i. 456, 520.   [17] Ibid.
[18] S.R.O., DD/CC 31559.
[19] S.C. 6/1131/3.
[20] S.C. 6/1131/3–4.
[21] S.C. 6/1131/9.
[22] S.R.O., DD/SAS BA/3; DD/BR/su.
[23] S.C. 6/1131/9.
[24] See below.
[25] *Cal. Chart. R.* 1226–57, 469.
[26] *H.M.C. Wells,* i. 147.

this confirmation an agreement was made with the abbot of Muchelney whereby the bishop, who had built a 'wall' around his park to divide it from the abbot's park of Drayton, should also own a strip of land outside the wall, which the abbot's beasts could, nevertheless, graze.[27] Pasture in the park was let in the 15th century, though the area was still evidently fenced and gated.[28] Thickets and thorns from the park, suggesting lack of recent use, were sold in 1490–1, when oak and ash trees there were still reserved to the lord.[29] Sale of underwood and pasturage continued at least until 1566,[30] but by the mid 17th century the park had become the nucleus of the largest farm in the manor.[31]

The 'borough' of Southwick or Froglane, seems to have emerged very early in the 14th century. In 1302 it was referred to simply in connexion with overland pasture,[32] but in 1308 the Hospitallers of Buckland were in possession of a messuage and arable land 'in the vill of Langport in the street of Froggelane'.[33] By 1351 Southwick was the name of a separate jurisdiction within Huish hundred, and by 1458 it was described as a borough, with 31 burgesses paying a total rent of 32s. 10d.[34] There were still 31 burgages in 'Froglane in Sowthwyke' in 1566,[35] and the rent was still paid in 1592.[36] It seems clear, however, that any urban development had long since disappeared. Properties in Southwick and Froglane Close in 1611 were closes of pasture,[37] though the fiction of burgage lands continued as late as 1809.[38]

The tenants on the bishop's manor in 1458–9 comprised 3 freeholders, 4 virgaters, 16 half-virgaters, 13 'ferdellers', and 4 cottagers.[39] Rents and other income from these tenants amounted to over £37, more than half the total income from the manor. Overland rents accounted for over £16, payments in lieu of works for over £10 8s., and assessed rents and traditional levies of Peter's Pence, 'faldeselver', church scot (churset), and 'larder' rents for over £9 9s.[40] Customary works were valued at only £7 13s. 3d. in 1362–3, and were then owed by 28 tenants.[41] It is not clear when works were last performed, though the final occasion was probably between 1302[42] and 1329.[43] Perquisites of court included payment of chevage in 1492,[44] and a manumission was granted in 1450.[45]

Throughout the 16th and 17th centuries the income from the manor remained virtually stationary at just over £62.[46] The only means of increasing income significantly was to impose large entrance fines and heriots. This practice is particularly

noticeable from 1554 to 1577, after the recovery of the estate from the Crown, and produced an income of £111 10s. 11¼d. in 1554–5[47] and £177 15s. 1½d. in 1572–3.[48] By 1634 the rental was fixed at £56 5s. 'or there abouts', though between then and 1640 this amount was once exceeded but normally not quite achieved.[49] The income from the same sources was virtually the same in 1773.[50] Other small increases were temporarily made by selling underwood in the park, letting a horse-mill, or leasing fowling and fishing rights. These last rights continued to be let by the lord of the manor at least until the end of the 18th century.[51]

Among the early lessees of such minor items as the dovecot and fowling were members of the Gateryn family, which had been established in the parish by the end of the 14th century.[52] Thomas Gateryn (d. 1554) was a prosperous yeoman farmer, and one of the manorial freeholders. At his death he left oxen, cows, sheep, horses, pigs, and bees, growing corn, hay, and beans, and among other effects a boat with fishing and fowling gear.[53]

The pattern of land tenure in the bishop's manor c. 1634 was a roughly equal division between 38 copyholds and 35 properties let on leases for lives. The largest holding was known as the Park, worth £50 and let for £5. Most of the other farms were small.[54] The Park, later known as Park farm, measured nearly 105 a. by 1798,[55] and over 114 a. in 1799.[56] This had been overtaken in size by the farm of the Revd. Lawrence Heard Luxton, which in 1799 measured 164 a.[57] The third substantial holding was that of John Michell, the vicar, who had just over 91 a. in 34 separate units under one lease, and a further 27 a. under three other leases.[58] The remainder of the estate was held in small parcels and tenure was, with two small exceptions, by leases for three lives. Heriots were still payable on 38 holdings, the copyholds of 1634, normally of best beasts or best goods, often with an alternative cash payment and occasionally described as customary. There were also three cases of rents in kind: a fat pullet at Candlemas, a fat turkey, and a large pike at Lady Day.[59] Heriots remained payable on some leases until 1854.[60]

In comparison the Wearne part of Pitney Wearne manor, amounting to some 377 a. of arable, 87 a. of pasture, and 22 a. of meadow, with an annual rental of £34 16s. 10½d. in 1692, was then divided into 47 separate holdings, of which 38 were copyhold. Three were over 50 a. in extent, and one of these included the capital messuage.[61] By 1765 all

[27] S.R.S. vii. 99; xiv. 56–7; see above, p. 1.
[28] S.C. 6/1131/9.
[29] S.C. 6/Hen. VII/575.
[30] S.R.O., DD/CC 31523, 31559.
[31] See below.
[32] S.C. 6/1131/3.
[33] S.R.S. xxv. 90.
[34] S.C. 6/1131/9.
[35] S.R.O., DD/CC 31523.
[36] S.C. 11/951.
[37] C 142/517/66.
[38] S.R.O., DD/CC 13324, pp. 105–15; 13472; D/B/la 49.
[39] S.C. 6/1131/9.
[40] Ibid.
[41] E 153/360/3.
[42] S.C. 6/1131/3.
[43] S.C. 6/1131/6.
[44] S.C. 6/Hen. VII/576.
[45] S.R.S. xlix. 155.
[46] S.C. 6/Hen. VII/575–6; S.C. 6/Phil. & Mary/263; S.C.

6/Eliz. I/2011, 2014; S.C. 11/951; E 318/1412; Lambeth Palace MSS., CR 224b; S.R.O., DD/CC 13324, p. 140; ibid. 31523; DD/SAS BA/5–6; Bristol R.O., AC/M 21/5; H. E. Reynolds, Wells Cathedral, lxix–lxx.
[47] S.C. 6/Phil. & Mary/263.
[48] S.R.O., DD/CC 31523.
[49] Ibid. 13324, pp. 363, 372, 381, 391, 403, 415, 427.
[50] Ibid. 28436.
[51] Ibid. 23630.
[52] Lambeth Palace MSS., CR 1180; S.C. 6/Hen. VII/575.
[53] S.R.S. xl. 174.
[54] S.R.O., DD/CC 13324, pp. 105–15.
[55] Ibid. 12461.
[56] S.R.O., CR 131.
[57] Ibid.
[58] S.R.O., DD/CC 13339.
[59] Ibid.
[60] Ibid. 12425.
[61] S.R.O., DD/DEV 21.

but three houses on the whole estate had been enfranchised.[62] The property measured 588 a. in 1814, divided between 30 occupiers; there were four farms of over 50 a.[63]

It was thought in 1794 that inclosure would increase the value of the Wearne estate by at least a half.[64] Under an Award of 1799 nearly 718 a. of arable and just over 58 a. of meadow and pasture in the parish were inclosed, and 175 a. on King's Sedgemoor were also divided.[65] The size of farming units was comparatively little affected, but the rent roll of the bishop's manor rose to over £229 by 1832–3, an increase of over 250%.[66] In general, however, agricultural capital was diminishing, although in 1834 there were 110 labourers in the parish earning an average of £26 a year, and unemployment was rare.[67]

The substantial tenants on the bishop's manor were absentees. The Parks or Park farm, held by Ambrose Rhodes of Buckland Tout Saints (Devon) by 1798, and by George and Thomas Wolrige of Plymouth from 1801,[68] had no farm-house and even in 1886 only possessed a small group of buildings in Park Lane on the boundary with Drayton.[69] A farm-house for the present Merrick's farm, formerly known as Blakes and leased to the Luxtons of Weacombe in West Quantoxhead, was not built until after 1799, and by 1837 occupied a site once used for lime burning.[70] The third large holding, that of John Michell, the vicar, had buildings scattered around the estate but no central barton. The tenant lived in Huish House. Pound Farm in Wearne is the only survivor from the substantial holdings on Wearne manor. Two other farm-houses stood near the site of the former Langport cattle market, and a fourth was the former capital messuage opposite Pound Farm.[71]

Sales of reversions of leases on the bishop's manor began soon after 1850, shortly before the property was transferred to the Ecclesiastical Commissioners.[72] In 1858 974 a. were held on 110 separate leases for lives, and the average size of each holding was under 10 a.[73] There were, in consequence, few substantial farm buildings, and much of the land, especially near Wearne, was divided into small orchards. Timber was worth only £152, much having been cut down since 1845. The Commissioners were encouraged to sell, and three of the largest units were disposed of in the next few years: 92 a. to Mrs. Julia Stuckey in 1859, 213 a. to Gen. Michell in 1860, and 111 a. comprising Park farm, to the tenants in 1866.[74] Most farming units,

however, remained small, and as late as 1939 there were still 13 farms, 6 smallholdings, and 3 market gardens, besides the nurseries of Kelway and Son, formerly the Royal Nurseries, founded by James Kelway in 1851.[75] The main development in farming has been the continuing contraction of arable: by 1905 grassland, noted in the 18th century for the 'vast' amount of cattle fattened for the London market,[76] accounted for 1,368 a., compared with only 429 a. of arable.[77] A similar balance was retained in the mid 20th century.

Quarrying seems to have been the most important occupation in the parish after farming. Pibsbury quarries provided stone for repairing Bridgwater parish church in 1414–15,[78] and for a slipway at Bridgwater in 1488.[79] The stone was transported by river from a wharf near Pibsbury ford and the wharf continued in use at least until 1858.[80] Most of the later quarrying was indiscriminate and uneven fields bear witness to unsatisfactory reinstatement.[81] In 1858 there were three quarries: one had a large limekiln and lay near Tengore Lane. The others, further south-west, were held by Job Bradford and Mrs. Julia Stuckey.[82] By 1875 the firm of Bradford and Sons was working the quarry at Pibsbury and continued there until the early 1920s.[83] Limekilns had been built in various places by 1886 and quarries with limekilns had been opened in Frog Lane, operated with Merrick's farm.[84] Some of the kilns were in use in 1971.

Minor occupations in the parish in the 19th century included gloving, brewing, withy-growing, and the manufacture of straw hats.[85] A tannery was established in the parish by 1832 and gave its name to Tanyard Lane.[86] The business closed in the 1920s, but the premises were used in 1971 as a slaughter-house.[87]

There was a mill at Huish, let by the lord of the manor, by 1302.[88] Driven by a stream rising in High Ham, it stood north of Huish Street. A pair of millstones were purchased for it in 1503–4.[89] The mill was held by John Wetherell in 1565 and 1572,[90] by members of the Baker family c. 1634 and 1691,[91] and by the Edwards family in the 18th century.[92] Through the marriage of Mary Edwards to John Major c. 1798 it passed to Thomas Major, lessee by 1807.[93] Walter Wheller, who acquired the lease in 1852, subsequently bought the property, and by 1861 combined flour milling with beer retailing.[94] In 1867 a steam engine was installed to supplement water power and to drive a saw mill.[95] The mill closed between 1914 and 1919.[96] Part of

[62] Ibid. 29.
[63] Ibid. 32, 34.
[64] S.R.O., DD/CC 13339.
[65] S.R.O., CR 131; O.S. Map 6″, Som. LXXII. NE.
[66] S.R.O., CR 131; DD/CC 12380/1, 13339, 31525.
[67] S.R.O., DD/DEV 34; CR 131.
[68] S.R.O., DD/CC 13339.
[69] S.R.O., CR 131; O.S. Map 6″, Som. LXXII. NE.
[70] S.R.O., CR 131; DD/CC 12380/1, 13339, 31525.
[71] S.R.O., DD/DEV 34; CR 131.
[72] S.R.O., DD/CC, 12446–52.
[73] London, Church Commrs. Report 127551/2.
[74] Ibid.
[75] Kelly's Dir. Som. (1939); S.R.O., DD/CC 12419.
[76] Collinson, Hist. Som. ii. 470.
[77] Statistics supplied by the then Bd. of Agric.
[78] S.R.S. lviii. 48.
[79] Bridgwater Borough Archives, no. 803.
[80] Church Commrs. Report 127551/2.

[81] S.R.O., DD/CC 13207, 97614.
[82] Church Commrs. Report 127551/2.
[83] P.O. Dir. Som. (1875); Kelly's Dir. Som. (1919, 1923).
[84] O.S. Map 6″, Som. LXXII. NE; Kelly's Dir. Som. (1897).
[85] Rep. Com. Children and Women in Agric. [4202–I] H.C. (1868–9), xiii; Wyatt, Book of Huish, 67–8, 92.
[86] S.R.O., D/P/h.ep. 13/2/4.
[87] Kelly's Dir. Som. (1919, 1923).
[88] S.C. 6/1131/3.
[89] S.R.O., DD/SAS BA/3.
[90] S.R.O., DD/CC 31523.
[91] Ibid. 13324; S.R.O., D/P/h.ep. 13/1/1.
[92] S.R.O., DD/CC 13322, 28436.
[93] Ibid. 12461, 13322.
[94] Ibid. 31525; P.O. Dir. Som. (1861).
[95] Datestone on chimney.
[96] Kelly's Dir. Som. (1914, 1919).

the buildings, including a chimney, was still standing in 1971.

A field called Windmill Hill, on the scarp above Wearne,[97] contains the remains of a mill mound. James Courtenay owned a windmill in Wearne in 1585, and sailcloth was stolen from Col. Stawell's windmill at Wearne in 1664.[98] 'Miltoyt Way' in Wearne occurs in 1620 and may refer to this mill or to Bowdens mill,[99] the site of which is above Combe.[1] Bowden's mill was probably still in use in 1886;[2] Wearne windmill was abandoned by the end of the 18th century.[3] A third windmill stood at Pibsbury, at the junction of Higher Pibsbury Road (later Windmill Lane) with Kinshill Road.[4] It was built by William Wheller between 1797 and 1823 and cost him 'many hundreds of pounds'.[5] It was in use until shortly after 1897,[6] and part of it collapsed in 1915.[7] The remainder was dismantled in 1921.[8]

A horse-mill was erected on Huish manor in 1478, but its site is unknown.[9] It was still working in 1511, but the rent was unpaid in 1522 when it probably ceased production.[10]

LOCAL GOVERNMENT. In the 11th century the southern part of Huish parish, then known as Litelande or Littelaneia, was part of the bishop's fief.[11] By 1327 the bishop's estate of Huish was regarded as part of Kingsbury hundred for fiscal purposes though for judicial purposes it seems to have formed a separate jurisdiction.[12] Some of the more northerly parts of the parish were evidently reckoned as part of Pitney at the same time, and were therefore linked either with the hundred of Somerton or with Pitney hundred until the 19th century.[13]

Medieval records survive only for the bishop's part of the parish. There are hundred court rolls for Michaelmas 1351, Midsummer 1373, and Purification 1464; hallmote court rolls for Michaelmas 1351, Michaelmas 1369, Midsummer 1440, Purification 1464, Michaelmas 1539, and Hockday 1581; and records of both courts together for Purification 1343, Midsummer 1353, Midsummer 1361, and Midsummer 1424.[14] For the year from Michaelmas 1438 there is a roll of fifteen sessions of what is described as a hundred court.[15]

Huish hundred court, in existence by 1329,[16] evidently met at the four normal times in the year often, by the 15th century, on or near the date of the Kingsbury hundred court.[17] It was described as

curia legalis, and retained characteristics of a hundred court by receiving tithing-pennies as late as 1545, although by 1521 it was evidently subservient to Kingsbury hundred[18] and the tithings of Huish and Combe mustered in the same hundred in 1539.[19] By 1351 the hundred court of Huish had jurisdiction over the tithings of Huish and Combe and the borough of Southwick. In that year tithingmen and bailiff presented cases of hue and cry wrongly raised, illegal brewing, unscoured watercourses, and trespass, and the jury for the whole court presented a defective roadway.[20] The courts for 1438–9 dealt mostly with pleas of debt.[21] Free tenants of the manor also appeared as suitors to this court.[22]

The jurisdiction of the hallmote court is less certain, and the practice of holding it with the hundred court probably early blurred the distinction between them. It was held at the four usual terms of the year at least until 1581.[23] When held separately from the hundred in 1351 it dealt with pleas of trespass and detention of goods, and recorded the entry of a tenant.[24] Its territorial jurisdiction cannot be defined. Other separate rolls record its concern for strays, scouring ditches, repair of the pinfold, and illegal inclosures.[25] By 1581, when the hundred had disappeared, it was also taking the suits of free tenants for the manor.[26] Both courts, recorded if not sitting together, covered matters of general economic concern, such as the control of sand digging, the repair of buildings, and licences for serfs to live outside the manor.[27]

There was a reeve and a parker by 1302, a bailiff of Southwick by 1351, as well as a bailiff for the hundred and tithingmen for Huish and Combe.[28] A bailiff and a reeve were charged jointly by the hundred and hallmote courts in 1343 to measure land in demesne and in severalty.[29] A hayward occurs in 1308.[30] At the Michaelmas hallmote in 1539 four men were presented for the office of reeve and three for the office of hayward.[31] A reeve and a hayward were presented for appointment at the Hockday hallmote in 1581.[32]

Wearne was presumably administered by the Pitney Plucknett or Pitney Wearne court during the Middle Ages, and was certainly included within its jurisdiction by the 16th century.[33] A tithingman and a hayward answered for Wearne twice a year at Pitney until 1770, and once a year until 1839.[34]

By the 18th century Huish manor was administered by courts baron and leet, the former sitting irregularly for entries and surrenders, the

[97] O.S. Nat. Grid 424298.
[98] C.P. 25(2)/206/27 & 28 Eliz. I Mich; S.R.O., Q/SR 106/63.
[99] Castle Ashby, Northampton MSS. 810(3); S.R.O., DD/DEV 34.
[1] O.S. Nat. Grid 415286.
[2] O.S. Map 6″, Som. LXXII. NE (1886 edn.).
[3] Wyatt, *Book of Huish*, 82–3, 105.
[4] See plate facing p. 65.
[5] S.R.O., CR 131; DD/CC 13322 9/9.
[6] *Kelly's Dir. Som.* (1897).
[7] Wyatt, *Book of Huish*, 105.
[8] Ibid.
[9] S.R.O., DD/SAS BA/3.
[10] S.R.O., DD/BR/su; DD/CC 31559.
[11] *V.C.H. Som.* ii. 456.
[12] *S.R.S.* iii. 256.
[13] Ibid. 280, 324, 328.
[14] Lambeth Palace MSS., CR 529–30, 1176–80, 1187, 1189, 1191–2; S.R.O., DD/SAS BA/1.

[15] Lambeth Palace MSS., CR 529.
[16] S.C. 6/1131/6.
[17] Lambeth Palace MSS., CR 529–30.
[18] S.C. 6/1131/9; S.R.O., DD/CC 31559.
[19] *L & P. Hen. VIII*, xiv, p. 289.
[20] S.R.O., DD/SAS BA/1.
[21] Lambeth Palace MSS., CR 529.
[22] Ibid. 1176, 1180.
[23] S.R.O., DD/CC 31559; Lambeth Palace MSS., CR 1192.
[24] S.R.O., DD/SAS BA/1.
[25] Lambeth Palace MSS., CR 530, 1179, 1189, 1191.
[26] Ibid. 1192.
[27] Ibid. 1176, 1187.
[28] S.R.O., DD/SAS BA/1; S.C. 6/1131/3.
[29] Lambeth Palace MSS., CR 1176.
[30] S.C. 6/1131/4.
[31] Lambeth Palace MSS., CR 1191.
[32] Ibid. 1192.
[33] D.R.O., D16/M 44.
[34] See p. 54.

latter annually at least from 1758 until 1841. Its place of meeting by 1833 was the Langport Arms.[35] The court leet was concerned mainly with the regulation of agriculture. Its officers were a constable, two tithingmen, a hayward, all appointed in rotation, and from 1825 a bailiff. The two tithings were Huish with Pibsbury and Combe with Westover, presumably the equivalents of the medieval tithings of Huish and Combe.

The parish was divided into Pibsbury, Wearne, Combe, and Huish divisions for poor rates in the 18th century.[36] Until 1818 the open vestry appointed wardens, overseers, and surveyors,[37] and at its monthly meetings also administered the parish charities.[38] After 1818 the vestry, meeting less frequently, remained directly responsible for the repair of roads. Among its additional activities were the payment of an annual subscription for the use of Langport fire engine from 1798, the establishment of bounty payments for the destruction of sparrows from 1802, and the clearance of reeds in the river.[39]

By the end of the 17th century the overseers were supporting the poor either by direct cash grants, especially in cases of sickness or temporary unemployment, by payment of house rents, and by making allowances to those lodging paupers.[40] By 1703 there was a parish house, maintained and repaired regularly by the overseers until 1726.[41] By the end of the 18th century the vestry was making orders for gifts of food, clothing, and money for the poor, and arranged apprenticeships of pauper children.[42] In 1800 the increasing financial burden resulted in an order to the overseers to provide a workhouse where the poor might make stockings, and produce linen and linsey goods with material provided.[43] In 1805 the overseers were ordered to find a poorhouse and, having failed to do so, were in 1808 required to build one. Three additional dwellings adjacent to the house were ordered in 1812.[44] Payment of house rents ceased after 1808, but clothing and blankets were occasionally given and apprentices bound. Apprenticeships were often difficult to arrange and in 1802 the vestry ordered that in such cases boys should be bound to ships' masters and girls to linen- or woollen-manufacturers.[45] After 1814 no more payments were to be made to families refusing to live in the poorhouse, and from 1818 all receiving relief were to attend church every Sunday morning. A nurse and doctor were employed to treat the sick after 1818,[46] and

the vestry was still capable of acts of generosity such as providing a tea kettle or an easy chair for two paupers.[47] The parish became part of the Langport poor-law union in 1836,[48] and two years later the poorhouses, two tenements each with three apartments, were sold.[49] The houses stood opposite the churchyard, south of the present church room, at least until 1933.[50]

CHURCH. There was a church at Huish by 1179, possession of which was then confirmed to Reynold FitzJocelin, bishop of Bath.[51] Both rectorial and vicarial glebe was later found in that part of the parish belonging to the bishops' manor, suggesting that the church was an episcopal foundation. By 1199 the church was granted to the archdeacon of Wells and his successors as part of the endowment of the prebend of Huish and Brent.[52] A vicarage was probably ordained c. 1232.[53] The benefice included the annexed chapelry of Langport from the end of the 14th century, if not *ab origine*;[54] the chapelry was severed from Huish from 1882.[55] In 1970 the living was united with the rectory of Pitney, and the incumbent of the benefice is styled a rector.[56]

Ecclesiastical connexions between Huish and Pitney were both ancient and close. In 1232, at the dedication of Huish church, perhaps after a fire[57] and possibly relating to the ordination of the vicarage, tithes belonging to Athelney abbey in Pitney were given to the vicar of Huish.[58] That Huish was in some sense the mother church of Pitney seems established by the fact that in the 18th and early 19th centuries the Pitney churchwardens contributed to the repair of Huish church tower.[59] Pitney inhabitants, in return, had burial rights at Huish at least in the early 17th century.[60]

The advowson of the vicarage belonged to successive archdeacons of Wells, who occasionally presented by proxy.[61] The Crown presented in 1381 and 1391 during vacancies in the archdeaconry,[62] and the bishop collated in 1413 after a simoniacal presentation.[63] The archdeacon of Wells is the patron of the united benefice.

The vicarage was valued in 1291 at £4 13s. 4d.[64] and at £14 10s. 5d. in 1535.[65] In 1650 it was said to be worth £50,[66] and there were plans to augment it in 1658.[67] By 1668 it was put at only £30.[68] The benefice was augmented in 1719 and 1826, and in 1831 brought in £210.[69] There were further augmentations of £200 each in 1833 and 1834.[70]

[35] S.R.O., DD/CC 13330, 13461–2, 28436: ct. bk. 1711–69, papers 1780–1841, presentments 1758–79.
[36] S.R.O., D/P/h.ep. 4/1/1: chwdns.' accts. 1717–1832; 13/2/1–4: overseers' accts. 1690–1730, 1796–1805, 1815–22, 1832–7; 14/5/1: surveyors' accts. 1792–1830.
[37] Ibid. 9/1/1: vestry mins. 1791–1848.
[38] See p. 12.
[39] S.R.O., D/P/h.ep. 13/2/3.
[40] Ibid. 13/2/1.
[41] Ibid.
[42] Ibid. 9/1/1.
[43] Ibid. 13/2/2.
[44] Ibid.
[45] Ibid. 9/1/1.
[46] Ibid.
[47] Ibid. 13/2/2, 23/5.
[48] *Poor Law Com. 2nd Rep.*, p. 548.
[49] S.R.O., D/P/h.ep. 13/2/3–4.
[50] Wyatt, *Book of Huish*, 55. See below, plate facing p. 16.
[51] *H.M.C. Wells*, i. 439; *Archaeologia*, l. 354.
[52] *Cal. Papal Regs.* i. 7; C. M. Church, *Chapters in Early Hist. of Church of Wells*, 56.
[53] *H.M.C. Wells*, i. 47.
[54] *Cal. Pat.* 1388–92, 379; see below, p. 33.
[55] *Lond. Gaz.* 4 Apr. 1876, p. 2272.
[56] *Dioc. Dir.*
[57] See below.
[58] *H.M.C. Wells*, i. 47.
[59] S.R.O., D/P/h.ep. 4/1/1, 8/4/2, 9/1/1.
[60] Ibid. 2/1/1.
[61] *S.R.S.* x. 608, 620; liv. 64.
[62] *Cal. Pat.* 1377–81, 614; 1381–5, 20, 68; 1388–92, 379.
[63] *S.R.S.* xxix. 143.
[64] *Tax. Eccl.* (Rec. Com.), 199.
[65] *Valor. Eccl.* (Rec. Com.), i. 197: *S.R.S.* ii. 116.
[66] S.R.O., DD/CC 121651.
[67] Lambeth Palace MSS., COMM VIb/2 ff. 131, 134; *Cal. S.P. Dom.* 1658–9, 307.
[68] S.R.O., D/D/Vc 24.
[69] W. Phelps, *Hist. Som.* I. ii. 115; *Aug. Livings*, 1703–1815, H.C. 115 (1813–14), xii; Hodgson, *Queen Anne's Bounty*; *Rep. Com. Eccl. Revenues*, pp. 166–7.
[70] S.R.O., D/P/h.ep. 3/1/1.

Tithes and oblations of the vicarage were worth £14 19s. 4d. in 1535.[71] The most valuable portion were the tithes of Langport, which were commuted to a rent-charge of £70 in 1840.[72] Most of the tithes from Huish were converted to corn rents in 1799,[73] and the remainder, with moduses, became a rent-charge of £2 5s. 6d. in 1846.[74] The corn rents were exchanged for a rent-charge of £53 17s. 2d. in 1914.[75]

Glebe lands of the vicarage were worth 9s. 4d. in 1535.[76] In 1636 they measured c. 7 a., and included a burgage in Langport and an acre in Langport field.[77] The burgage had been held since 1535 at the latest, when the vicar paid a rent to the duke of Richmond, then lord of Langport.[78] Neither property was held by the vicar in 1840.[79] About 49 a. of land in High Ham were purchased in 1723 with augmentation money, and a further 9 a. there in 1833, though only just over 49 a. were apparently held in 1838.[80] Just over 4 a. in Huish were bought from the rectory estate in 1842.[81] There were said to be 75 a. in 1883.[82] Nearly 49 a. in High Ham were sold in 1919,[83] leaving 11 a. by 1923 and c. 6 a. by 1927.[84] In 1948 the glebe was worth £29.[85]

In 1827 the vicarage house, 'in a sad state of dilapidation, wholly unfit for the residence of the spiritual person', was replaced by the present house, built on former rectorial glebe land a little to the north.[86] The former house, an L-shaped building, was apparently converted to piggeries, and has almost disappeared.[87] The present house, of local lias with a slate roof, incorporates fragments of medieval Ham stone masonry, brought either from the older building or more probably from Muchelney.

Thomas Combe (vicar 1413–16) was allowed in 1415 to farm his benefice for ten years in order to study, but his early departure from the parish must have affected the church comparatively little.[88] Most of his successors in the 15th century were graduates, and included two lawyers, Robert Hurst (vicar 1462–5), commissary-general of the diocese, and John Standerwick (vicar 1502–4), proctor-general in the consistory court at Wells,[89] neither of whom could have been regularly resident. Cananuel Bernard, appointed in 1625, was at the same time rector of Pitney.[90] His Huish living was probably sequestrated by 1656, but by 1650 he had been replaced by John Hillman.[91] Hillman was followed by John Jennings (1656), Charles Darby (1658), formerly vicar of Montacute, and John Bush (1659).[92] Bush apparently continued to serve Langport as 'curate' after Bernard was restored to the benefice in 1660, but was ejected two years later.[93]

During the 18th century the church, like much of the parish, was dominated by the Michell family: John Michell was vicar from 1722 to 1744; Thomas Michell was assistant curate for at least 14 years until 1768; another John was curate from 1777 until appointed vicar in 1780. He was a prebendary of Gloucester from 1798, but seems occasionally to have served the cure for his successor, Edward Willes, until 1809. Michell's son William also served Willes as curate in 1812.[94] Edward Willes himself, vicar 1802–24, was given the benefice by his father. He held West Camel at the same time, and lived at Bath; the duty was carried out entirely by assistant curates.[95] George Baily Tuson (vicar 1824–39) lived ten miles from Huish until the new vicarage house was completed.[96] His successors were resident, though Joseph Stubbs (vicar 1882–1923) also held the living of Muchelney from 1902 until 1923.[97]

There is little evidence for the conduct of services before the 19th century, though a parochial chaplain was employed in 1463 and 1468, and a curate served the resident vicars in the 1530s and 1540s, in addition to chaplains at Langport.[98] In the late 18th century the benefice was served largely by assistant curates, most of the incumbents being non-resident.[99] In 1818 the churchwardens approached the bishop, apparently not for the first time, to ask for a service and sermon each Sunday,[1] and by 1827 there was 'full service' at both Huish and Langport, alternately morning and afternoon.[2] This remained the practice at least until 1870, with celebrations of the Holy Communion four times a year.[3] By 1884 two services were held each Sunday, with monthly celebrations.[4] On Census Sunday 1851 340 people attended the morning service, including 90 Sunday school pupils.[5]

A fraternity or brotherhood of Huish was active in 1543 and 1545.[6] A church house was rebuilt by the overseers, apparently the owners, in 1698–9; the new building was of timber on a stone sill, with a thatched roof. It was still standing in 1725.[7] The present church room, to the east of the church, was designed by C. H. Samson of Taunton, and opened in 1896.[8]

The church of the *BLESSED VIRGIN MARY* is of lias with Ham stone dressings and has a chancel with organ chamber, nave with north chapel, south aisle, north vestry, south porch, and west tower.

[71] *Valor. Eccl.* (Rec. Com.), i. 197.
[72] S.R.O., Langport tithe award.
[73] S.R.O., CR 131.
[74] S.R.O., Huish tithe award.　　　[75] Ibid.
[76] *Valor Eccl.* (Rec. Com.), i. 197.
[77] S.R.O., D/D/Rg 215.
[78] *Valor Eccl.* (Rec. Com.), i. 197.
[79] S.R.O., Langport tithe award.
[80] S.R.O., D/P/h.ep. 3/1/1; S.R.O., High Ham tithe award.
[81] S.R.O., D/P/h.ep. 3/1/1; Church Commissioners, London, Report 127551/2.
[82] *Kelly's Dir. Som.* (1883).
[83] S.R.O., D/P/h.ep. 3/1/1.
[84] *Kelly's Dir. Som.* (1923, 1927).
[85] *Crockford.*
[86] S.R.O., D/D/Paw; S.R.O., D/D/V rtns. 1827; S.R.O., D/P/h.ep. 3/4/1–2.
[87] O.S. Map, 6″ Som. LXXII. NE (1886 edn.); Wyatt, *Book of Huish*, 55.
[88] *Cal. Papal Regs.* vi. 495; *S.R.S.* xxix. 183, 266.

[89] Emden, *Biog. Reg. Univ. Oxford*, s.n.; *Proc. Som. Arch. Soc.* cvi. 51, 53.
[90] *Proc. Som. Arch. Soc.* xxxvii. 92–9.
[91] S.R.O., DD/CC 121651.
[92] *Calamy Revised*, ed. Matthews.
[93] Ibid.; see below, p. 36.
[94] S.R.O., D/P/h.ep. 2/1/3–5.
[95] Ibid.; see below, p. 79.
[96] S.R.O., D/D/V rtns. 1827.
[97] See p. 48.
[98] *S.R.S.* xl. 51, 110; xlix. 396; lii. 25; S.R.O., D/D/Vc 20; see below, p. 34.
[99] See above.
[1] S.R.O., D/P/h.ep. 4/1/1; see also ibid. 9/1/1.
[2] S.R.O., D/D/V rtns. 1827.
[3] Ibid. 1870.
[4] S.R.O., D/P/h.ep. 2/5/1.
[5] H.O. 129/317/2/6/19.
[6] *S.R.S.* xl. 51, 110.
[7] S.R.O., D/P/h.ep. 13/2/1.
[8] Ibid. 8/3/2, 18/1/1.

The elaborately decorated south doorway is of the 12th century and apparently *in situ*, but no other part of the building can be attributed to such an early date. The stonework of the doorway is reddened, apparently by fire, which suggests that the rest of the early church may have been destroyed in that way.[9] The north wall of the nave is of the 13th century, perhaps the date of the reconstruction after the fire—a possibility which is strengthened by the recorded dedication of the church in 1232.[10] In the 14th century the church was enlarged by the rebuilding of the chancel and the addition of the

removed before the church was restored by Benjamin Ferrey in 1872–3. Alterations included the removal of monuments from the chancel, re-roofing the nave and re-ceiling the south aisle, and the construction of the vestry.[13] The present tower screen was brought from Enmore church in 1873;[14] the organ chamber was added in 1892. The furniture includes a Perpendicular font, a Jacobean communion table, and a pulpit dated 1625. The glass in the east window of the south aisle, installed in 1899, was designed by Burne-Jones and made by William Morris.

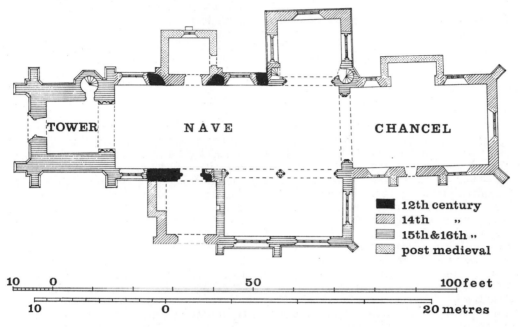

TOWER   NAVE   CHANCEL

■ 12th century
▨ 14th ,,
▤ 15th & 16th ,,
▦ post medieval

10   0   50   100 feet

10   0   20 metres

THE CHURCH OF THE BLESSED VIRGIN MARY, HUISH EPISCOPI

north chapel and south porch. There was presumably a south transept at that date, completing the cruciform plan, but the surviving part of the south aisle which occupies its position is of the 15th century, as are also the nave windows and those in the east and west walls of the north chapel. The ornate west tower,[11] which is more than 100 ft. high, was added at the end of the 15th century and must have replaced one in a central position. Its removal allowed the nave to be extended eastwards and necessitated the rebuilding of the chancel and north and south transept arches. The rebuilding of the south transept may be contemporary with these changes. The south aisle was created early in the 16th century by extending the south transept westwards to meet the porch and by duplicating the south transept arch to form an arcade.

The chancel screen was removed in 1774 and at the same time a singing gallery was erected, probably at the west end.[12] The gallery was evidently

There are eight bells: (i) and (ii) 1956, Taylor of Loughborough; (iii), (iv), and (v) 1902, Taylor of Loughborough; (vi) 1822, John Kingston of Bridgwater; (vii) 1620, Robert Austen I; (viii) 1650, Robert Austen II.[15] The plate includes a cup of *c.* 1689 with a cover of 1571; and a paten of 1700.[16] The registers begin in 1678, but there is a gap between 1727 and 1754.[17]

NONCONFORMITY. The Wesleyan minister of the Glastonbury and Somerton circuit was licensed to use James Sawtell's house in Wearne as a place of worship in 1825.[18] A building attached to James Lovibond's house was similarly licensed in 1828 in the name of the minister from South Petherton.[19] Methodists continued to meet in private houses, including that of Kesia Culliford in 1841,[20] until a chapel was licensed in 1847.[21] The position of this chapel has not been traced. No return has survived

[9] Traces of fire were found in other parts of the church during restoration: *Proc. Som. Arch. Soc.* xl. 80.
[10] *H.M.C. Wells*, i. 47.
[11] See plate facing p. 16. The tower and porch were illustrated on a postage stamp in 1972.
[12] S.R.O., D/P/h.ep. 4/1/1.
[13] Ibid. 8/3/3.
[14] *Proc. Som. Arch. Soc.* xl. 82.
[15] S.R.O., DD/SAS CH 16; ex inf. Mr. R. W. Pitman.
[16] *Proc. Som. Arch. Soc.* xlv. 131.
[17] S.R.O., D/P/h.ep. 2/1/1–7.
[18] S.R.O., D/D/Rm, box 2.
[19] Ibid.
[20] S.R.O., Q/RR, meeting-house lics.
[21] S.R.O., D/D/Rm, box 2.

from Methodists for the 1851 census, and the cause may have lapsed. A new building, at the junction of the Avenue with the then road to Somerton, now known as Eastover, was opened in 1890.[22] It is of lias with stone dressings and a slate roof, and seats 150.[23] The building has been used since *c.* 1943 by a group of Christian Brethren, and is now known as the Gospel Hall.[24]

The tradition of nonconformist meetings in a barn at Newtown and at Combe[25] is partly borne out by a licence granted to the Independent minister of Somerton for use of a house in Newtown in 1845.[26]

EDUCATION. In 1818 there were no schools in Huish, though it was thought that 'the poorer classes' were 'desirous of having the means of education'.[27] By 1826 there were Sunday schools at both Langport and Huish, teaching between them 80 boys and 80 girls.[28] Seven years later the parish had three small day-schools, catering for *c.* 28 children at the expense of their parents.[29] 'Several children' attended the National School, then said to be in Langport, but in fact in Huish parish, a few yards east of the Hanging Chapel.[30] This school was built in 1827,[31] and by 1833 housed both a day- and a Sunday-school for 80 children. It was supported by grant, subscriptions, and school pence, and had a lending library.[32] In 1846–7 the day-school had 67 boys and 78 girls, and the Sunday school 15 boys and 33 girls.[33] The school was closed *c.* 1876 when the Board Schools opened; the semi-detached teachers' houses, in 1971 private dwellings, form an irregular stone building, formerly thatched, in a plain Gothic style.[34] The schoolroom, after closure used as a Sunday school, stood in Bond's Pool Lane, a few yards north-west. It was sold *c.* 1897 and had been demolished by 1903.[35]

In 1874 a School Board was formed, and a building providing two rooms each for 100 boys, 100 girls, and 125 infants, and a residence for a teacher, was erected in 1876 on the east side of North Street, Langport, in the parish of Huish.[36] In 1903 there were 6 trained teachers and 3 pupil teachers; the boys were 'well taught', the girls 'doing well', and the infants 'fairly satisfactory'. The premises were also used for evening continuation classes and parish council meetings.[37]

The Board School, under the County Education Committee from 1903, became known as the Council Schools for the parishes of Langport and Huish Episcopi.[38] The boys' and girls' schools were merged in 1925, and in 1940 the senior pupils were transferred to a new building, north-east of Huish church.[39] This became known as Huish Episcopi Modern Secondary or County School in 1945. In 1969 it had 476 pupils.[40] The junior and infants' school, remaining in the original building, had 201 pupils in 1969.[41]

There are said to have been at least three private schools in Huish in the 19th century. A family school was held at Wagg in winter evenings in the 1850s; a dame's school at Pict's hill in the 1860s; and a girls' school kept by Miss Georgina Stone in 1897.[42]

CHARITIES FOR THE POOR. Before 1666 small properties in Huish and a house in Langport were given in trust for the maintenance of Huish and Wearne bridges, and became known as the Bridge Land charity. By the beginning of the 19th century the income was added to the general rate income.[43] In 1840 Huish bridge, then a footbridge, was taken over by the Parrett Navigation Company, which replaced it by a wooden carriage bridge. Wearne bridge was subsequently converted into a culvert by the local highway authority.[44] The income of the charity therefore accumulated until, in 1894, after various local disputes over its application, a Scheme was established, under which £150 was given to rebuild Huish bridge and up to £100 to enlarge the churchyard.[45] The remaining income was to be 'applied for any public purpose approved by the Charity Commissioners for the benefit of the parishioners'. From 1897 until closure in 1933 the charity provided scholarships for Huish boys at Langport Grammar School; subsequently, and until 1944, financial assistance was given to Huish boys attending Huish's Grammar School, Taunton.[46] Since that time the charity contributed towards the cost of the recreation field, owned jointly by Huish and Langport.[47] In 1894 the real property of the charity was sold and the total income from investments amounted to £21 16*s.* a year.[48] The assets of the charity in 1965 amounted to £245 18*s.* 10*d.* investment shares.[49]

Interest received from a capital sum of £15 lent by the churchwardens for various purposes was occasionally paid by them to the second poor. Such payments were made in 1762, 1772, and 1783, but by 1786 the charity was lost.[50]

By will dated 1797 Martha Bond (d. 1797) bequeathed all money in her possession or at interest to be divided equally between the poor of Huish, Langport, and Aller. In 1801 the share of each parish, £141 19*s.* 1*d.*, was invested, producing £7 15*s.* for each, distributed at Christmas to people chosen by the churchwardens[51] and submitted to

[22] Date stones on building.
[23] *Methodist Church Buildings, Statistical Rtns.* (1940).
[24] Local information.
[25] S.R.O., DD/SAS PR 54 (1), 23; Wyatt, *Book of Huish*, 87.
[26] S.R.O., D/D/Rm, box 2.
[27] *Digest of Returns to Sel. Cttee. on Educ. of Poor*, H.C. 224 (1819), ix (2).
[28] *Rep. B. & W. Dioc. Assoc. S.P.C.K.* (1825–6).
[29] *Educ. Enquiry Abstract*, H.C. 62 (1835), xlii.
[30] Ibid.
[31] Lewis, *Topog. Dict. Eng.* (1833).
[32] *Educ. Enquiry Abstract*.
[33] *Church Sch. Inquiry, 1846–7*.
[34] Wyatt, *Book of Huish*, 92.
[35] O.S. Map 1/2,500, Som. LXXII.8 (1886 edn.); Char. Com. files; D. M. Ross, *Hist. Langport*, 368.

[36] S.R.O., C/E 27.
[37] Ibid.
[38] S.R.O., DD/LC, managers' mins. 1931–48.
[39] Som. C.C. Educ. Cttee. *Schs. List.*
[40] S.R.O., DD/LC, managers' mins. 1940–6; Som. C.C. Educ. Cttee. *Schs. List.*
[41] Som. C.C. Educ. Cttee. *Schs. List.*
[42] Wyatt, *Book of Huish*, 91–2; Kelly's *Dir. Som.* (1897).
[43] *9th Rep. Com. Char.* H.C. 258, pp. 522–4 (1823), ix.
[44] *Langport and Somerton Herald*, 21 Apr. 1894.
[45] Ibid.; Trustees' min. bk. *penes* the clerk.
[46] Trustees' min. bk.
[47] Ibid.; ex inf. Mr. R. W. Pitman.
[48] Trustees' min. bk.   [49] Ibid.
[50] S.R.O., D/P/h.ep. 4/1/1; *9th Rep. Com. Char.* 524–5.
[51] *9th Rep. Com. Char.* 524.

the vestry.[52] In the early 19th century the money was divided annually among the second poor, numbering as many as 161 in 1837, each one receiving in that year 1s.[53]

Under a Scheme of 1919 a capital sum bequeathed under the will of Emma Tilley, dated 1917, was used to purchase £276 1s. 3d. stock. Half this sum, known as the Tilley Charity, was for the purchase and distribution of coal among the 'deserving poor' of Huish of 60 years and over, not in receipt of poor law relief other than medical relief.[54] Under a Scheme of 1964 Bond's and Tilley's charities are administered together, and sums of not less than 5s. are given annually to pensioners.[55]

[52] S.R.O., D/P/h.ep. 9/1/1.
[53] Ibid.
[54] Char. Com. file.
[55] Ex inf. the clerk and Mr. R. W. Pitman.

THE HUNDRED OF PITNEY

T HE hundred of Pitney occupies the Langport Gap, where the Parrett, its waters increased by the Isle and the Yeo, flows north-west in a narrow valley between the Curry Rivel ridge and the lower promontory on which the Saxon burh of Langport was built. The flat 'moors' south and east of Langport, now drained and forming rich pasture land, were formerly subject to severe

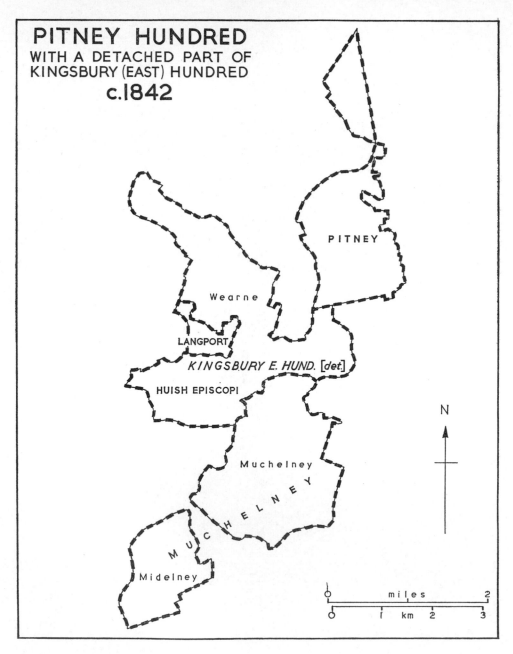

PITNEY HUNDRED
WITH A DETACHED PART OF
KINGSBURY (EAST) HUNDRED
c.1842

PITNEY

Wearne

LANGPORT

KINGSBURY E. HUND. [det.]

HUISH EPISCOPI

Muchelney

M U C H E L N E Y

M U C H E L N E Y

Midelney

N

miles

km

flooding, and are characterized by scattered settlements on small 'islands' of higher ground. In striking contrast are the scarps of the northern parts of Huish and Pitney, once devoted to open-field arable. The rivers have been the key both to the character of much of the surrounding land and to the origin and prosperity of Langport through river-borne traffic.

The hundred is not of ancient foundation and appears to have been a fiscal development of the 16th century from two free manors and a borough which happened to be adjacent to one another. From as early as 1219 the phrase 'free manor' was used to describe land in Pitney, which from 1225 was associated with the manor of Pitney Lorty.[1] Beer, in High Ham, later known as Berelorty, which owed tithe to the rector of Pitney,[2] was considered part of the free manor by 1225.[3] By 1316 the manor also included the hamlet of Knole, in Long Sutton, but only for fiscal, not for jurisdictional purposes.[4] Knole was a possession of Henry Lorty, lord of Pitney.[5] In 1327 Downhead, in West Camel, also Lorty property, was part of Pitney manor.[6] In 1384 the successor of the Lortys, Sir Robert Ashton, died in possession of an estate described as the manor and hundred of Pitney Lorty, a phrase first used a year earlier. It was held of the Crown for the same rent as the manor alone.[7] Ownership of the hundred then descended with the manor of Pitney Lorty.[8]

In 1431 the hundred comprised Pitney Lorty in Pitney, Knole, Bineham, and Corbyns, in Long Sutton,[9] and Beer in High Ham.[10] Pitney, Beer, and Knole tithings made up the hundred in 1522–3.[11] Lands in Somerton were also said to be in Pitney hundred.[12] By 1569 the hundred comprised the tithings of Pitney, Knole, and Muchelney, the last also including Midelney, locally in Drayton parish.[13] The liberty of Muchelney had anciently included the hamlets of Thorney and Ham.[14] The men of Langport were grouped with those of Pitney in 1588,[15] and the borough was included in the 'hundred and liberty' of Pitney by 1624.[16] In a rating dispute in 1635 Pitney and Knole tithings were rated at half the value of the combined tithings of Muchelney, Midelney, and Langport borough.[17] In the mid 18th century parts of Huish, presumably the lands of the manor of Pitney Wearne, were regarded as part of the hundred.[18]

No more than a normal manorial jurisdiction was exercised by Pitney court until 1608. In that year what appears to be the manor court of Pitney Lorty ordered every constable to submit his accounts to the *curia legalis* at the end of each year before the steward 'and the hundred', and at the same time claimed jurisdiction over Pitney Wearne manor.[19] Records of courts leet and views of frankpledge 'in and for the hundred' from 1696 to 1703 form part of the normal run of manorial records for Pitney Lorty manor, and business beyond the appointment of constable of the hundred, who in two cases came from tithings in Muchelney manor, is indistinguishable from normal manorial proceedings.

[1] *Bk. of Fees*, 263; *S.R.S.* xi. 290; *Rot. Hund.* (Rec. Com.), ii. 127, 138.
[2] See p. 55.
[3] *S.R.S.* xi. 290.
[4] See p. 163.
[5] *Feud. Aids*, iv. 327; *S.R.S.* iii. 67.
[6] *S.R.S.* iii. 253–4, 280.
[7] D.R.O., D 124, box 106; *Cal. Fine R. 1383–91*, 58; *Cal. Pat. 1381–5*, 483, 518–19; *S.R.S.* xvii. 127; B.M. Harl. Ch. 58 G 10.
[8] See p. 52.
[9] See p. 154.
[10] *Feud. Aids*, iv. 422.
[11] B.M. Harl. Roll O 6.
[12] D.R.O., D 124, boxes 106, 107.
[13] *S.R.S.* xx. 181–2.
[14] *Feud. Aids*, iv. 327.
[15] E. Green, *Som. at the time of Spanish Armada*, 90.
[16] *S.R.S.* xxiii. 351.
[17] Ibid. xxiv. 242, 252, 264, 275, 280. See also *Cal. S.P. Dom. 1637–8*, 156–7.
[18] *S.R.S.* iii. 304, 328.
[19] B.M. Add. Roll 28281.

LANGPORT

THE town and parish of Langport was formerly a corporate borough and market town, known as Langport Eastover by the 14th century to distinguish it from the manor and borough of Langport Westover in Curry Rivel.[1] It had an area of 171 a. in 1840,[2] of which total 21 a. represented Langport's allotment in Common moor, divided by private agreement between the parishes of Langport, Huish Episcopi, and Aller in 1797.[3] The parish is 5 miles west of Somerton and 13 miles east of Taunton and forms a small irregularly shaped region north and east of a bend in the river Parrett, almost surrounded by Huish Episcopi. The low-lying area beside the river is alluvium over lias, providing rich pasture north-west of the town. Above the flood plain to the east the Rhaetic clays rise to form Langport hill, above 75 ft., with a lias outcrop upon its summit.[4] To the south-west lies Whatley hill, a small spur above the river.

From the Parrett south of the town a ditch, known as the Portlake rhine by 1526[5] and later as the Catchwater, ran through the town and north-west over the Langport 'moors' to rejoin the river. The portion through the 'moors' was filled in 1966[6] and south of the Little Bow bridge it has been covered by a car park. The Back river, known as a common rhine in 1470-1,[7] runs west from the Catchwater south of the town and enters the Parrett above the Great Bow bridge. In 1794 it was proposed to improve the navigation of the Parrett and in the following year an Act was obtained to straighten and deepen the Catchwater through the Langport 'moors' and under the Little Bow, and also to make a new cut inland below Langport hill for ¾ mile upstream to join the river Yeo at Bicknell's bridge in Huish.[8] The work within the parish and part of the cut to Bicknell's bridge had been completed by 1797, but the project was then discontinued.[9] Two Acts obtained in 1836 and 1839 resulted in the formation of the Parrett Navigation Company and in the making of a second cut from the Little Bow, running beside the Parrett and Yeo rivers to Bicknell's bridge, completed in 1840.[10] Locks built in the Parrett opposite the Langport 'moors' as part of this improvement were later used as flood drains.[11]

Archaeological evidence suggests[12] that the crossing of the Parrett at this point was used in Roman times and that the construction of the causeway across the former marshes, along which Bow Street now runs, may have preceded permanent settlement at Langport. The town is first mentioned in the Burghal Hidage and thus was one of the fortified burhs in the defensive network of the south and west in the early 10th century.[13] It possessed a mint by c. 930.[14] By 1066 it was evidently the dependent commercial settlement of the large agricultural estate of Somerton.[15] Physically, however, the settlement had already been separated from Somerton through the grant of Huish, Combe, and Pibsbury to the bishop of Wells by 1065.[16] Langport's ecclesiastical status as a dependent chapelry of Huish presumably dates from the grant to the bishop,[17] though it does not exclude the possibility of an earlier church in the town. The name Langport suggests the use of Bow Street causeway as a trading area by the early 10th century. Possibly quays lay along its southern side which the Back river was cut to serve. The site of the original settlement is indicated by the course of an embankment which surrounds Langport hill, forming a roughly triangular enclosure. To the west of the hill a bank with external ditch ran along the lower slope and its remains may be seen in the gardens of the present Hill House and around Whatley hill. Langport hill is defended on the south by a steep slope and the line of defences probably ran along the southern limit of the churchyard, turning north-west just short of the eastern parish boundary in the area of the Hanging Chapel. It then ran through the grounds of St. Gildas Convent enclosing Dolemans close, now tennis courts. The bank and ditch are again visible at the northernmost point where they form the parish boundary.[18] The regular entrenchment north-east of the early fortifications, which forms the boundary of the present recreation ground, is almost certainly later in date, possibly 17th century. It was within this enclosed area that the initial settlement of the borough took place and the church was built.

The area below Langport hill and its early defences was known as Beneathcliff in 1344[19] and Beneathwall from 1350-1.[20] It was treated separately in the earliest surviving manorial accounts[21] and was probably settled after the available frontages on the hill had already been occupied. The tightly packed burgage tenements along both sides of the causeway,

[1] B.M. Add Ch. 16127; E 149/9/24. This article was completed in 1972.
[2] S.R.O., tithe award.
[3] S.R.O., D/B/la 26; see below, p. 25.
[4] Geol. Surv. Map 1", solid and drift, sheet 296 (1969 edn.).
[5] S.R.O., DD/PH 225/39.
[6] Local information.   [7] S.R.O., DD/PH 225/39.
[8] Yeo Navigation Act, 35 Geo. III, c. 105 (Priv. Act); S.R.O., Q/R, deposited plans, 7; C. Hadfield, *Canals of S. Eng.* 223.
[9] Hadfield, op. cit. 223.
[10] Ibid. 225-6; Parrett Navigation Acts, 6 & 7 Wm. IV, c. 101 (Local and Personal); 2 & 3 Vict. c. 37 (Local and Personal).
[11] Hadfield, op. cit. 225; M. Williams, *Draining of the Som. Levels*, 158-9.

[12] *V.C.H. Som.* i, map, pp. 206-7.
[13] *A.-S. Charters*, ed. A. J. Robertson, 246-8. The identification of Langport as the site of the Arthurian battle of Llongborth (*Proc. Som. Arch. Soc.* iv. 44-59; D. M. Ross, *Langport and its Church*, 40-1) has not been substantiated.
[14] See p. 23.
[15] *V.C.H. Som.* i. 434.
[16] See p. 4.
[17] See p. 33.
[18] S.R.O., tithe award; see *Proc. Som. Arch. Soc.* xi. 194-6, for an early attempt to trace the course of the bank.
[19] B.M. Add. Ch. 16127.
[20] Devon R.O. 1142 B/M 28.
[21] Devon R.O. 1142 B/M 28-39; S.R.O., DD/SAS, CU/1(a-f), 12.

Kingstone Church from the South

Huish Episcopi Church from the East, *c.* 1863

WALTER BAGEHOT (1826–77)

VINCENT STUCKEY (1771–1845)

now Bow Street, with long narrow rear yards or gardens running north and south, were probably the last to be laid out. A deed assigned to the late 12th century but now lost, refers to the reclamation from marsh of 5 a. north of the 'old street' (probably Bow Street) and another 5 a. west of the 'old wall' (probably along North Street) called 'the new land of Langport'.[22] A house 'above the bridge of Langport to the north' is mentioned in 1220.[23] It seems likely that the manor of Langport originally included the settlement known as Langport Westover on the western bank of the Parrett, so that both ends of the crossing were controlled by a single lord. Although the manor and borough which grew up on the opposite bank had developed a separate identity by the 14th century,[24] it continued in common ownership with Langport Eastover until the 16th century.[25]

The street plan of the town has changed little since the Middle Ages. The main thoroughfare from Taunton enters the parish in the west, crossing the Parrett by the Great Bow bridge, and subsequently passes over the Catchwater by the Little Bow bridge to the foot of Langport hill and the site of the former cross.[26] This street is now called Cheapside (Silver Street or Cheapside in 1827)[27] between the site of the cross and the Little Bow, and Bow Street between the two bridges. It did not receive its present names until the early 19th century.[28] North Street enters the town from the north to meet Cheapside at the site of the cross. Three houses there are mentioned in 1251.[29] The road now called the Hill and providing the principal access to the borough from the east passes beneath the Hanging Chapel, over the hill, across the site of the former market-place by St. Gildas Convent, and runs down the hill to meet North Street and Cheapside. This road was formerly known as Cheapstreet (mentioned 1370–1)[30] between the Hanging Chapel and the market-place, and Upstreet (mentioned 1372–3,[31] called Upstreet alias Cheapside in 1596,[32] and Cornhill in 1600)[33] from the market-place to the foot of the hill. By 1659 the whole road was known as Upstreet alias Cheapstreet.[34] Subsequently it was generally called Upstreet[35] but by 1827 was known as Upstreet or the Hill,[36] the last name having persisted to the present day.

Stalls and burgage tenements evidently clustered around the market-place. New rents from plots there are mentioned in 1350–1[37] and areas of waste were

granted for stalls in Cheapstreet in 1373–4.[38] The area of settlement formerly extended northwards from the market-place into the grounds of the convent. Five burgages on the 'upper Roughdich' are recorded in 1372–3[39] and there was a windmill on Rowditch (Roughdiche in 1365–6,[40] Rowediche in 1375–6)[41] by 1344.[42] A market-house on the north side of the market-place was built soon after 1563 and partially demolished c. 1713–14.[43] The whole northern area around the market-place was taken into the grounds of St. Gildas Convent (then Hill House) in the early 19th century.[44]

From the market-place Priest Lane (so called in 1711)[45] runs north-west to meet North Street, and Whatley Lane (probably 'Werelane' mentioned in 1506–7,[46] called Whatley Lane in 1620)[47] drops south-west to the lands by the river known as Whatley (Wartly in 1596).[48] From Cheapside a lane, now also known as Whatley, runs south to meet Whatley Lane near the site of the former pound.[49] The area known as Whatley and lying south of Cheapside was formerly open pasture leased with the Swan Inn (now the Langport Arms) by 1596.[50] There was a Whatley mill in the later 16th century[51] and three borough properties were evidently built there in 1646.[52] The fourth borough fair was also held there in that year,[53] probably on Whatley green. This green was granted out on building leases by the corporation for four cottages erected in 1828.[54] Beyond the 1839–40 canal, but formerly part of Whatley, lies Barley close. Towards the west end of this field an iron foundry had been established by 1819[55] and immediately west of this the Langport Coal Gas Company, founded in 1835, set up its works.[56]

On the eastern boundary of the parish Bennetts Lane runs south from the main road. It formerly served fields known as the Hams beyond the 1795–7 canal.[57] Bonds Pool Lane runs north-east from the main road and forms part of the parish boundary. It may be named after Bond dole in Langport field, mentioned in 1659.[58] Bow and North Streets were adopted by the Langport, Somerton, and Castle Cary turnpike trust in 1753,[59] and the Hill in 1792.[60] Two roads in the parish not positively identified were Mill Lane, mentioned in 1382–3,[61] and Pig Street, mentioned between 1703[62] and 1798.[63] The latter was possibly that part of the Hill immediately west of the Hanging Chapel.[64]

[22] S.R.S. xv. 131.
[23] Ibid. xiv. 62.
[24] B.M. Add. Ch. 16127.
[25] L. & P. Hen. VIII, iv, p. 673 n.
[26] See p. 27.
[27] S.R.O., D/B/la 46.
[28] Ibid.
[29] S.R.S. viii. 65.
[30] Devon R.O. 1142 B/M 33.
[31] S.R.O., DD/SAS, CU/1(b).
[32] S.R.O., D/B/la 6.
[33] S.R.O., DD/SE 38, survey of manor, 1620.
[34] S.R.O., D/B/la 6. The same form is found in 1796: ibid. 3.
[35] Ibid. 49.
[36] Ibid. 46.
[37] Devon R.O. 1142 B/M 29.
[38] Ibid. M 34.
[39] S.R.O., DD/SAS, CU/1(b); Devon R.O. 1142 B/M 34.
[40] Devon R.O. 1142 B/M 31.
[41] Ibid. M 35.
[42] See p. 26.
[43] See p. 27.

[44] S.R.O., D/B/la 3, survey of borough lands, 1796; tithe award; Q/SR 416.
[45] S.R.O., D/B/la 49, lease, 3 Feb. 1710/11.
[46] S.C. 6/Hen. VII/1236.
[47] S.R.O., DD/SE 38.
[48] S.R.O., D/B/la 6.
[49] Ibid. 51.   [50] Ibid. 6.
[51] E 134/42 & 43 Eliz. I/Mich. 27.
[52] S.R.O., D/B/la 6, survey of borough lands, 1659.
[53] Ibid. 81; see below, p. 28.
[54] S.R.O., D/B/la 7, 24 (plan of Whatley green, 1827).
[55] Par. rec., chwdns.' accts. 1779–1842; S.R.O., D/B/la 37, ct. paper, 13 Oct. 1819.
[56] S.R.O., DD/LC, deed of settlement, 28 Apr. 1835.
[57] S.R.O., tithe award.
[58] S.R.O., D/B/la 5.
[59] Langport, Somerton, and Castle Cary Turnpike Act, 26 Geo. II, c. 92 (Priv. Act).
[60] Langport, Somerton, and Castle Cary Turnpike Act, 32 Geo. III, c. 130 (Priv. Act).
[61] Devon R.O. 1142 B/M 36.
[62] S.R.O., D/B/la 6.
[63] Ibid. 49.
[64] Ibid. 3, 46, 49.

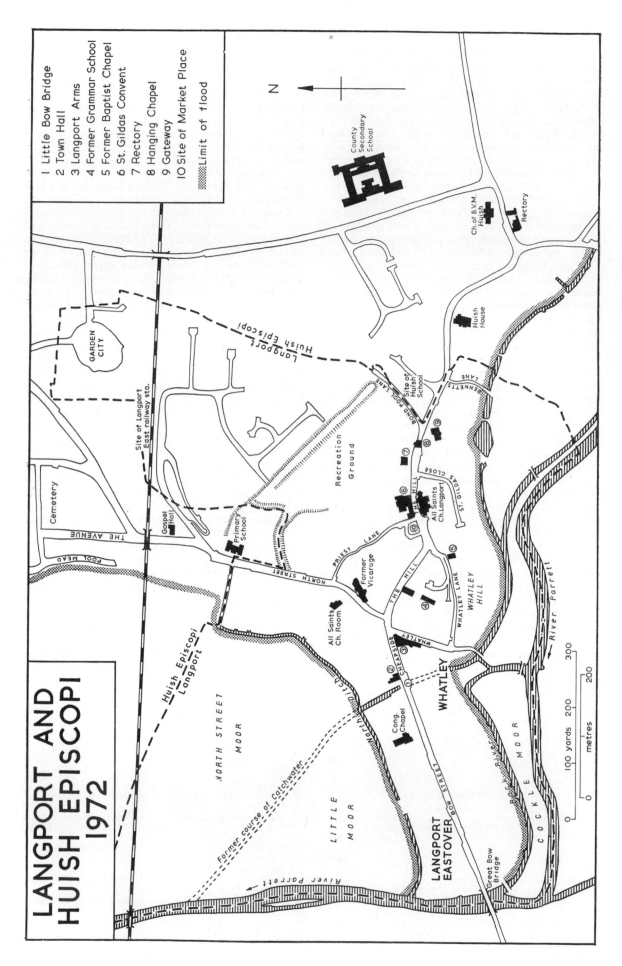

LANGPORT AND HUISH EPISCOPI 1972

1 Little Bow Bridge
2 Town Hall
3 Langport Arms
4 Former Grammar School
5 Former Baptist Chapel
6 St. Gildas Convent
7 Rectory
8 Hanging Chapel
9 Gateway
10 Site of Market Place

Limit of flood

N

County Secondary School

Ch. of B.V.M. Huish

Rectory

Huish House

Langport
Huish Episcopi

Site of Huish School

BENNETTS LANE

BOND POOL LANE

Recreation Ground

GARDEN CITY

Site of Langport East railway sta.

Cemetery

Gospel Hall

THE AVENUE

POOL MEAD

Primary School

THE HILL

All Saints Ch. Langport

ST. GILDAS CLOSE

PRIEST LANE

Former Vicarage

THE HILL

WHATLEY LANE

WHATLEY HILL

River Parrett

Huish Episcopi
Langport

North Millditch

NORTH STREET

All Saints Ch. Room

WHATLEY

CHEAPSIDE

WHATLEY

Cong. Chapel

NORTH STREET MOOR

LITTLE MOOR

Former course of Catchwater

River Parrett

LANGPORT EASTOVER

BOW STREET

Brook River

COCKLE MOOR

Great Bow Bridge

0   100 yards   200   300
0   metres   100   200

18

Langport's trade necessarily depended much on the efficiency of its communications with the surrounding areas and London. About 1793 the London–Taunton coach passed through the town, 'which drops the goods here from London to be carried further by water'.[65] In 1822 coaches left the town daily for London and Barnstaple and three times a week for Bristol and Exeter.[66] Twenty years later, however, the borough was served only by the North Devon coach, running to London and Barnstaple three times a week and passing through Taunton, Ilminster, and Chard.[67] Immediately before the construction of the railway in 1853[68] the town was linked to Bridgwater by an omnibus service and to Yeovil and Taunton by the Fairy Mail coach.[69]

Langport field, first mentioned in 1596[70] and lying in the north-east of the parish beyond the hill, may probably be identified with Horsecroft in which lay 41½ a. of arable burgage land by 1344.[71] The two Langport 'moors', pastures lying north-west of the town and formerly divided by the Catchwater, were described as Langport moor in 1331–2,[72] as Eastmoor and Westmoor in 1476–7,[73] and as Higher and Lower moors by 1600.[74] They are occasionally referred to at the present time as North Street moor and Little moor.[75] Langport Common moor, now meadow and formerly pasture, which lies at the north-western corner of the parish, was called Levermore in 1274[76] and Lyvermore in 1280.[77] In the 13th century it comprised 30 a. of pasture which Somerton manor claimed had been appropriated by the lady of Langport c. 1250.[78] It was first described as Common moor in 1371–2[79] and was referred to as 'Langport Lower Liver moor now called Common moor' in 1756.[80] Cocklemoor, lying south of Bow Street, forms an island bounded by the Parrett on the south and Back river on the north. It is first recorded as Redeham in 1384–5 and as 'Burgesmore, late Redeham, and now Cockell moore' in 1470–1.[81] South and south-west of Langport hill beside the Parrett lie further pasture lands: Barley close and the Hams. All the low-lying lands beside the river, and indeed much of the town, have been subject to regular flooding, particularly in winter, until modern times.

River-borne traffic on the Parrett was a vital factor in the town's economy from an early date, much of the trade being conducted near the Great and Little Bow bridges at either end of Bow Street. A bridge at Langport is recorded in 1220[82] and a reference to John of the little bridge in 1268[83] suggests that both bridges had been erected by that date. A bequest was made to the great bridge of Langport in 1413,[84] and in 1472 indulgences were granted to those contributing to the repair of Langport bridge called Brodebow, which had been damaged by the sea and by flood.[85] In 1499 further indulgences were granted to those helping to rebuild two bridges in the town called the Bredbowe and Lytylbryge.[86] In 1548 the commonalty tried to divert the revenues of two suppressed chantries to the repair of the Great Bow.[87] It was then said to be of stone with 30 arches,[88] a number which presumably included the many arches under Bow Street beneath which passed the drainage ditches serving tenements in that street. The great cost to the borough of bridge repair was ostensibly the motive for securing a grant of markets and fairs in 1563 and a charter in 1616.[89] Little Bow was rebuilt in 1800[90] and widened in 1875.[91] A rail to carry boats and barges under the Great Bow when the river was low was constructed in 1833.[92] By an agreement reached in 1839 the Parrett Navigation Company agreed to demolish the old bridge of nine arches, build a new one of three arches, and subsequently maintain it, on payment of £500 by the corporation towards their costs.[93] The present Great Bow bridge was completed in 1841.[94] It was at the western end of Bow Street by the Great Bow that the principal landing place was sited and around which warehouses were built. There by 1652 stood the Storehouse[95] and by 1657 the thatched Salt House or Rock House.[96] In 1677 the portreeve was ordered to restore the slips there to their former state and the lessee of 'Nomans Plot' was required to allow the boatmen access for their boats.[97] The corporation were indicted in 1772 for not repairing the slip or stone steps at the Great Bow.[98] From this site, too, Stuckey and Bagehot developed their trading business in the 19th century.[99] The coming of the railway in 1853 resulted in an abrupt decline in water-borne traffic and the Navigation Company was taken over by the Somerset Drainage Commissioners in 1878.[1] There was, however, still some barge traffic on a small scale in 1906.[2]

The town was served initially by the Yeovil and Durston branch of the Bristol and Exeter Railway, opened in 1853,[3] which ran west of the parish beyond the Parrett. The line from Curry Rivel junction to Somerton, which passed through the north-east tip of the parish and across the north-west end of

[65] *Univ. Brit. Dir.* iii.
[66] Pigot, *Nat. Com. Dir.* (1822–3).
[67] Ibid. (1842).
[68] See below.
[69] Slater, *Nat. Com. Dir.* (1852–3).
[70] S.R.O., D/B/la 6.
[71] B.M. Add. Ch. 16127.
[72] S.R.O., DD/PH 225/39.
[73] Ibid.
[74] E 134/42 & 43 Eliz. I/Mich. 27.
[75] Local information.
[76] *Rot. Hund.* (Rec. Com.), ii. 122.
[77] *Plac. de Quo Warr.* (Rec. Com.), 702.
[78] *Rot. Hund.* (Rec. Com.), ii. 122.
[79] S.R.O., DD/PH 225/39.
[80] S.R.O., D/B/la 49, leases, 6 & 10 Feb. 1756.
[81] S.R.O., DD/PH 225/39.
[82] *S.R.S.* xiv. 62.
[83] Ibid. vi. 219.
[84] Ibid. xvi. 63.

[85] Ibid. lii. 90–1.
[86] Ibid. liv. 33.
[87] Ibid. ii. 115.
[88] Ibid.
[89] *Cal. Pat.* 1560–3, 496–7; S.R.O., D/B/la 1.
[90] S.R.O., D/B/la 7, 23 (letter, 1807).
[91] Ross, *Langport and its Ch.* 365; S.R.O., D/B/la 82, account, 1875. The Registry was built on its northern side in 1837: D/B/la 8.
[92] S.R.O., D/B/la 8.
[93] Ibid.
[94] Ibid.
[95] S.R.O., DD/LC, deeds of Storehouse.
[96] S.R.O., D/B/la 5, 46 (survey of manor, 1827).
[97] S.R.O., D/B/la 6.   [98] Ibid. 12.
[99] S.R.O., tithe award; see below, p. 26.
[1] Hadfield, *Canals of S. Eng.* 227.
[2] *Rep. of Medical Inspectors of the Local Govt. Bd.* no. 230 (1906).
[3] S.R.O., D/B/la 8.

Higher moor over a viaduct, was opened in 1906.[4] Langport East station, closed in 1962, lay partly in Huish parish.[5]

The water supply has always been plentiful. An upper well, in the area of the market-place, and a lower well, at the western foot of Langport hill, are both mentioned in 1668.[6] The lower well was converted into a pump, known as the Town Pump, between 1709 and 1722,[7] and a second pump, installed on top of the hill in 1830,[8] was still visible on the north side of the former market-place in 1972. Water from the lower well was 'justly boasted of as the best in the county, or even in the kingdom,' in 1842.[9] Many houses in all parts of the town had their own pumps by the 19th century, although those in Bow Street were sometimes fouled as a result of the primitive drainage system.[10]

The Langport Coal Gas Company was formed in 1835,[11] and gas works were erected in Whatley.[12] The plant was closed in 1955.[13] The town was supplied with piped water from a borehole at Compton Durville in 1905,[14] and the town was first lit by electricity in 1932.[15] A cemetery and mortuary chapel were established for the benefit of Langport in 1880, the site in Huish being provided by James Broadmead.[16] Following the First World War a Memorial playing field was laid out in 1920 to the north of the Board school in Huish.[17] This was replaced in 1962 by the present recreation ground lying north of the convent grounds.[18]

There was a music club in Langport as early as 1793, when the corporation contributed to its funds.[19] The Reading Room, built in 1833, was being used by the Langport Literary and Scientific Association in 1861[20] and housed a library revived by the corporation in 1875.[21] Special arrangements were made for the public to bathe in the Parrett at Common moor in 1859.[22] The Langport and District Rifle Club, mentioned in 1906,[23] won the Daily Mail Cup in 1910 as first in the British Isles and second in the Empire.[24]

The earliest secular buildings in the town are the Langport Arms, late-16th-century, and Virginia House, probably 17th-century, both of which stand at the foot of Langport hill just above the point at which the causeway started. The two buildings have been much altered but the moulded timber ceilings of the Langport Arms are of notably good quality for this part of the county. With other buildings, now lost, they show that by the later 16th century the town centre had been transferred hither from Langport hill. The existence of a town hall in Cheapside by 1596 contributes to the same conclusion.[25] Late-17th-century cottages in Bennetts Lane are the only survivals of tenements on the south side of

the Hill east of the Hanging Chapel, most of which were demolished in the early 19th century in order to extend the grounds of the Meadows, now the Gateway, formerly the home of the Broadmead family.[26] The earlier 18th century saw the introduction into the town of national copy-book styles of architecture and the first substantial houses, like Ensor House, to the west of the Little Bow bridge. By the end of the century the lower parts of the Hill and the east end of Bow Street were almost continuously lined by buildings in the Georgian style. Most were newly built but a few, like the Langport Arms, are older structures with new fronts. Brick walling was used occasionally, as in the town hall, but the local lias continued to be used and dressings of Ham stone were common with both materials.

In the late 18th century Sir Richard Colt Hoare, lord of the manor, and the corporation sold much land in the lower part of the town and this resulted in extensive rebuilding of the houses standing upon it, so that it could be said in 1828 that the town wore a 'very different appearance' from that of the preceding century.[27] The earlier 19th century saw the emergence of the area on top of the hill as the most fashionable residential part of the town with several substantial villas which possessed large gardens. The chief of these, Hill House, was built by the banker, Vincent Stuckey, in the early 19th century.[28] By this time Bow Street had been rebuilt almost as far as the Great Bow, mostly in a plain brick but with occasional patches of flamboyance, like the stone-fronted house of 'Atyeo mason and bricklayer' on the south side. Between 1844 and 1879 the corporation subsidized the demolition of projecting buildings in order to widen the streets,[29] and several surviving house fronts of this period result from that policy. Of the earlier warehouses once used for goods brought up river only one, a three-storeyed brick building of the mid 19th century, remains. More recently, with most of the suitable building land in the parish already occupied, the town has been forced to expand north and northeast into Huish parish, where many of the rural district council houses lie. Garden City, part of which occupies the site of the former Langport field, was begun in 1919,[30] and old peoples' bungalows on the site of the old Memorial playing field were completed in 1963.[31] Modern private building within the parish has been principally restricted to the southern slopes of Langport hill, now known as St. Gildas Close, and to sites on the western slope of the hill east of the old grammar school. South of Cheapside a car park, laid out in 1937, was extended in 1970 and a terrace of shops built nearby.[32]

[4] D. St. J. Thomas, *Regional Hist. of the Railways of G.B.* i. 128.
[5] C. R. Clinker & J. M. Firth, *Reg. Closed Stations*, ii and suppl.
[6] S.R.O., D/B/la 5.
[7] S.R.O., DD/CM, box 8, conveyances, 25 Mar. 1709, 28 Oct. 1729.
[8] Par. rec., vestry mins. 1820–49.
[9] Pigot, *Nat. Com. Dir.* (1842).
[10] Local information.
[11] S.R.O., DD/LC, deed of settlement, 28 Apr. 1835.
[12] S.R.O., tithe award.
[13] S.R.O., DD/WI 22.
[14] *Kelly's Dir. Som.* (1906).
[15] Par. cncl. mins. 1923–37.
[16] Par. rec., vestry mins. 1849–1928.

[17] Par. cncl. Town Trust mins. 1920–59.
[18] Par. cncl. mins. 1958–64.
[19] S.R.O., D/B/la 12.
[20] Ibid. 8.
[21] Ibid. 9.
[22] Ibid. 8.
[23] *Kelly's Dir. Som.* (1906).
[24] Ross, *Langport and its Ch.* 366; S.R.O., D/B/la 94.
[25] See p. 31.
[26] Title deeds of the Gateway, *penes* Mr. J. M. Alexander.
[27] S.R.O., D/B/la 23, replies to queries, 1828; see below, pp. 24, 31.
[28] S.R.O., Q/SR 416; tithe award.
[29] S.R.O., D/B/la 8, 9.
[30] Par. cncl. mins. 1894–1954.
[31] S.R.O., DD/WI 22.
[32] S.R.O., D/B/la 94; local information.

For its size Langport has been served by many inns. The Swan is mentioned as 'the inn' in 1596, its rent being nearly twice as much as that paid for any other individual property held by the commonalty.[33] Throughout the 17th and 18th centuries corporation dinners were invariably held there, and borough and manor courts frequently adjourned to its rooms.[34] An Excise office was located there by 1715.[35] The inn was leased by John Michell from the borough in 1653[36] and held by his family for over 150 years. Charles Michell purchased it from the corporation in 1808 and sold it back to the borough for £800 in 1817.[37] It was known as the White Swan in 1800[38] and the Langport Arms from 1818.[39] The corporation added the portico in 1828[40] and sold the freehold in 1901.[41]

The George inn, first mentioned in 1664,[42] formerly stood on the south side of Bow Street near the Little Bow bridge, but had been converted to a dwelling-house before 1775 by Samuel Stuckey.[43] The Red Lion lay on the south side of Cheapside east of Whatley by 1714, when it was acquired by the Bush family,[44] but had been converted to a dwelling by 1752.[45] The Nag's Head, mentioned in 1717 and probably built in 1692,[46] stood on the north side of the Hill near its junction with North Street,[47] had become the White Horse inn by 1726,[48] and a private house by 1779.[49] An Angel inn in North Street is mentioned in 1725 and 1727,[50] but the present Angel on the south side of Bow Street is first recorded in 1787 when a court leet was held there.[51] The Excise office had moved there from the Swan by c. 1793.[52] The Five Bells was mentioned in 1727, as was the Black Swan, now on the west side of North Street.[53] The Bell occurs between 1754 and 1756, and the Carpenters' Arms between 1768 and 1775.[54] The Dolphin, now on the south side of Bow Street, is first mentioned in 1778,[55] and the Lamb is recorded between 1779 and 1821.[56] The White Lion, still standing on the west side of North Street, dates probably from c. 1786,[57] and the Admiral Vernon, near the west door of the church, is recorded between 1800 and 1818.[58] The Castle, formerly on the south side of the Hill west of the old Baptist chapel, is mentioned between 1840 and 1864.[59] In the 19th century there were also five beer houses in Bow Street, the last of which closed in 1960.[60]

Early friendly societies in the town included those held at the Admiral Vernon (1791–1817)[61] and the Black Swan (1815–41).[62] Five other societies occur in the town during the 19th century, including the Langport Friendly which was revived in 1902 and 1960 and still meets annually.[63]

The 1327 subsidy was paid by 28 inhabitants of the borough,[64] and in 1548 Langport and Huish Episcopi together had 420 communicants,[65] of whom about 240 probably belonged to Langport. The town contained 87 households in 1563,[66] but thereafter no figure for the population survives until the beginning of the censuses. In 1801 the parish contained 754 people, a figure which subsequently rose steadily to 1,245 in 1831. The population then declined as steadily as it had risen: to 897 in 1881,[67] 773 in 1911, and 686 in 1931.[68] This fall was occasioned principally by the decline in river-borne traffic, particularly in coal, once the railways had been built. Areas in the neighbourhood of Langport which had formerly used Welsh coal brought up the Parrett now bought coal mined in the north-east of the county. The extension of gardens attached to the more prominent houses by the demolition of adjacent burgage tenements also reduced the number of houses within the borough. The population subsequently grew only slightly, and stood at 777 in 1961.[69]

In the campaign of 1643 Hopton advanced from Cornwall and garrisoned Langport in June, placing it under the governorship of Sir Francis Mackworth.[70] Fortifications were evidently raised around Langport hill and a long rampart was built probably on the north-east side above Langport field. Rivalry between Mackworth and Col. Wyndham, then governor of Bridgwater, led to the borough being deprived of both men and supplies. In 1645 the royalist club-men imprisoned certain officers and soldiers and attacked the garrison, before being driven off by Mackworth. On 10 July 1645 the royalist forces under Goring were routed by the parliamentarians under Fairfax at the battle of Langport. Fighting took place east of the town in High Ham and in consequence of the defeat

[33] S.R.O., D/B/la 6.
[34] Ibid. 12, 37, 81.
[35] S.R.O., DD/SAS (C/1193), 4, p. 129.
[36] S.R.O., D/B/la 6.
[37] Ibid. 3, 6.
[38] Ibid. 57.
[39] Ibid. 7.
[40] Ibid.
[41] Char. Com. files.
[42] S.R.O., D/B/la 81.
[43] Ibid. 49, lease to Stuckey, 9 Sep. 1775.
[44] S.R.O., DD/PL 12, abstract of title. The site is indicated by the marr. settl. of the Revd. W. Pyne, 15 Aug. 1825 (S.R.O., DD/LC).
[45] S.R.O., DD/PL 22. A reference to the Red Lion c. 1793 (Univ. Brit. Dir. iii) probably relates to the White Lion.
[46] S.R.O., D/B/la 42 (presentment, 7 May 1717), 49 (leases, 31 Oct. 1692, 28 Oct. 1712, 1 Nov. 1725).
[47] Devon R.O., add. B/MT 167, plan on deed of 1850.
[48] S.R.O., D/B/la 49, lease, 1 Nov. 1726.
[49] Ibid. lease, 12 Oct. 1779.
[50] S.R.O., D/B/la 6, 12.
[51] Ibid. 37.
[52] Univ. Brit. Dir. iii.
[53] S.R.O., D/B/la 12.
[54] Par. rec., chwdns.' accts. 1753–79.
[55] Ibid.
[56] Ibid.; 1779–1842.
[57] S.R.O., D/B/la 105, conveyance, 1 Nov. 1804; Univ. Brit. Dir. iii.
[58] S.R.O., D/B/la 57; Ross, Langport and its Ch. 345.
[59] County Gazette Dir. Som. (1840); par. rec., chwdns.' accts. 1842–76; local information.
[60] Par. rec., chwdns.' accts. 1779–1842, 1842–76; S.R.O., D/B/la 108; ex inf. Miss E. G. M. Lock.
[61] S.R.O., Q/R, Friendly Soc. rtns.; Poor Law Abstract, 1804.
[62] S.R.O., Q/R, Friendly Soc. rtns.; par. rec., service reg. 1840–61.
[63] Par. rec., service regs. 1840–61, 1861–77; Western Gazette, 30 May 1884; Taunton Castle, Langport Friendly Soc. Rules (1902) (Tite, 95/59).
[64] S.R.S. iii. 276.
[65] Ibid. ii. 116.
[66] B.M. Harl. MS. 594 f. 50v.
[67] V.C.H. Som. ii. 348.
[68] Census, 1911–31.
[69] Rep. of Medical Inspectors of the Loc. Govt. Bd. no. 230 (1906); Census, 1951, 1961.
[70] Sources for the history of Langport during the Civil War are treated fully in Ross, Langport and its Ch. 279–320; Proc. Som. Arch. Soc. xl. 123–40; liii. 150–61. See also H. C. B. Rogers, Battles and Generals of the Civil War, 240–4.

Mackworth quitted Langport. The corporation petitioned the governor and the marquess of Hertford to save the town from devastation and the constables tried to prevent plundering.[71] In their flight, however, Goring's men fired twenty houses in Bow Street in an attempt to hamper pursuit. The victory was commemorated by bestowing the name Langport on a 50-gun vessel in the Commonwealth navy.[72]

The duke of Monmouth evidently drew adherents to his cause from the town in 1685,[73] and Lord Churchill based his forces at Langport in June when harrassing the rebels on their march northwards.[74] Three men, not necessarily natives of the borough, were executed at Langport after the Taunton assizes.[75] George Paviott, a Langport blacksmith, was pardoned in 1686 for his part in the rebellion.[76]

Three sons of William Quekett, master of Langport grammar school 1790–1842, all born and educated in the town, attained a certain renown after leaving it: William (1802–88), divine, Edward John (1808–88), microscopist, and John Thomas (1815–61), histologist.[77] The first was commended by Dickens in *Household Words*.[78] Another son, Edward (d. 1875), a banker in the town, kept a museum in the Hanging Chapel.[79] Walter Bagehot (1826–77), economist and journalist, gained his early experience of banking at Stuckey's Bank and was deputy recorder of the corporation from 1872 until his death.[80]

'The Black (or 'girt') Dog of Langport', one of many Somerset black dogs,[81] occurs in a wassail first printed in 1895[82] and is recorded in a variant version by Cecil Sharp in 1909.[83]

MANOR AND BOROUGH. In the early 10th century when Langport is first recorded as a fortified burh[84] it probably formed part of the royal demesne. By 1066 it was held of the Crown as parcel of the manor of Somerton.[85] Somerton tenants were still claiming common pasture by virtue of this tenure in 1274 and 1280.[86] Before 1156, however, the borough had been granted to Hugh de Gundeville,[87] who last occurs as holding the town in 1181.[88] From then until the early 16th century Langport was held with the manor of Curry Rivel, of which it formed a member and with which its

accounts were rendered.[89] The circumstances in which the Gundevilles relinquished it are not clear, but in 1209 another Hugh de Gundeville bought a writ of *mort d'ancestor* of Langport,[90] and in 1251 Sibyl de Gundeville quitclaimed the manor to Sabina de Lorty for 10 marks.[91]

Richard Revel (I) received a Crown grant of the manor in 1190[92] and by 1212 had been succeeded by his son Richard (II) (d. *c*. 1222).[93] Sabina, daughter of Richard (II), married Henry de Lorty (I), who held the manor in 1230.[94] At her husband's death Sabina's lands were seized by the Crown and Langport was granted to Henry Mare during her widowhood.[95] On her death in 1254 Sabina was succeeded by her grandson Henry (II) (d. 1321), son of Richard de Lorty.[96] In 1331 Henry's son John sold the reversion of the manor expectant upon the death of Sibyl his mother to William de Montacute (cr. earl of Salisbury 1337, d. 1344).[97] By 1344 the property was known as the manor and borough of *LANGPORT EASTOVER*.[98] The first earl's son William, earl of Salisbury (d. 1397), in 1394 conveyed the reversion on his death to John Beaufort (cr. earl of Somerset 1397, d. 1410).[99] Beaufort was succeeded in turn by his sons Henry (d. 1418) and John (cr. duke of Somerset 1443, d. 1444).[1] John's widow continued to hold the manor during the minority of her daughter Margaret, subsequently wife of Edmund Tudor, earl of Richmond, whose heir on her death in 1509 was her grandson Henry VIII.[2]

In 1525 the king granted the manor to his natural son Henry FitzRoy, duke of Richmond (d. 1536).[3] On his death it evidently reverted to the Crown.[4] In 1569 John Milner secured a lease of the borough for 60 years and of the market, fairs, and courts for 21 years.[5] This lease had passed to Tamsin Wilshere by 1576.[6] A fresh grant was made to Hugh Sexey of Bruton in 1584: the borough for 40 years and the courts and fairs for 21 years.[7] Sexey received a new lease in 1590 for the unexpired period of the terms, since there was some doubt whether the earlier grant was valid.[8] The manor itself was conveyed to George Utley, Sexey's cousin, in 1589, and Utley sold it to Sexey in 1604.[9] In 1616 Sexey (d. 1619) conveyed his lands to feoffees in trust to fulfil certain unspecified charitable intentions, and the

[71] S.R.O., D/B/la 81.
[72] *Mariner's Mirror*, iv. pts. 4, 5.
[73] B.M. Add. MS. 30077 f. 36.
[74] B. Little, *Monmouth Episode*, 126.
[75] C. D. Curtis, *Sedgemoor and the Bloody Assize*, 111. The portreeve was allowed his expences for the execution: S.R.O., D/B/la 12.
[76] *Cal. S.P. Dom.* 1686–7, 149, 440.
[77] *D.N.B.*; W. Quekett, *My Sayings and Doings* (1888).
[78] Op. cit. 16 Nov. 1850, 24 Jan. 1852.
[79] Ross, *Langport and its Ch.* 360–1; see below, p. 35.
[80] Mrs. R. Barrington, *Life of Walter Bagehot*; *D.N.B.*; Ross, *Langport and its Ch.* 357–60; S.R.O., D/B/la 9.
[81] Ruth L. Tongue and K. M. Briggs, *Som. Folklore*, 107–10.
[82] W. Raymond, *Tryphena in Love* (1895), 142–5.
[83] C. J. Sharp, *Folk Songs of Som.* 5th ser. no. 130. The significance of the 'Black Dog' is discussed by Sharp, op. cit. p. 96, and Ross, *Langport and its Ch.* 89–90.
[84] See p. 16.
[85] *V.C.H. Som.* i. 434.
[86] *Rot. Hund.* (Rec. Com.), ii. 122; *Plac. de Quo Warr.* (Rec. Com.), 702.
[87] *Red Bk. Exch.* (Rolls Ser.), ii. 677; *Pipe R.* 1156–8 (Rec. Com.), 30.
[88] *Pipe R.* 1181 (P.R.S. xxx), 4.

[89] E 149/9/24; B.M. Add. Ch. 16127; Devon R.O. 1142 B/M 28–41; S.R.O., DD/SAS, CU/1(a–f), 2(e2), 12.
[90] *Pipe R.* 1209 (P.R.S. N.S. xxiv), 102.
[91] *S.R.S.* vi. 151. 'Chory' and 'Langeford' are evidently Curry Rivel and Langport.
[92] *Cart. Ant.* (P.R.S. N.S. xxxiii), 128.
[93] *Bk. of Fees*, i. 78; *S.R.S.* xiv. 62; Sanders, *Eng. Baronies*, 84.
[94] *Pipe R.* 1230 (P.R.S. N.S. iv), 37; *Ex. e Rot. Fin.* i. 92.
[95] *Proc. Som. Arch. Soc.* xlii. 36; *Close R.* 1253–4, 67.
[96] *Cal. Inq. p.m.* i, p.84; vi, p. 184.
[97] Ibid. vi, p. 184; viii, p. 387; *Cal. Inq. Misc.* ii, pp. 187–8; *Cal. Pat.* 1330–4, 116; *S.R.S.* xii. 153.
[98] B.M. Add. Ch. 16127; E 149/9/24.
[99] *Cal. Inq. p.m.* viii, p. 387; *Cal. Pat.* 1391–6, 351, 529; *S.R.S.* xvii. 159–60; C 137/80/44.
[1] *Complete Peerage*, s.v. Somerset; *Feud. Aids*, iv. 372; *Cal. Pat.* 1441–6, 349.
[2] *Cal. Pat.* 1441–6, 349; 1467–77, 339; C 142/25/31; *Cat. Anct. D.* iv, A 6312.
[3] *L. & P. Hen. VIII*, iv, p. 673.
[4] *Complete Peerage*, s.v. Richmond.
[5] S.R.O., DD/SE 18/2; *Cal. Pat.* 1566–9, 342.
[6] S.C. 6/Eliz. I/1975.   [7] E 310/23/124/46.
[8] E 310/23/129/25.
[9] S.R.O., DD/SE 18/4, 38/1, 44.

endowment was used to found a hospital at Bruton.[10] In 1631 the feoffees granted the manor in fee-farm to the portreeve and commonalty of Langport for £12 a year.[11] It is not clear whether the grant took effect, for in 1634 the feoffees made another grant to Sir Charles Berkeley for the same fee-farm rent of £12.[12] This rent continued to be paid by the immediate lords to Sexey's hospital until the sale of the manor in 1808, when the charge was transferred to Bruton manor.[13]

Sir Charles Berkeley (later Viscount Fitzharding, d. 1668) was succeeded in turn by his sons Maurice (d. 1690) and John (d. 1712), successive viscounts.[14] Their estates were encumbered with heavy mortgages, and a suit in Chancery resulted in the sale of the manor to the principal creditor Sir William Brownlowe in 1698.[15] Sir John Brownlowe, his son, sold the manor to William, Lord Berkeley (d. 1741), in 1717.[16] Under Lord Berkeley's will the manor was to have been divided between his four daughters. The two quarter shares held by Ann and Jane, who died unmarried before their father, passed to their brother John, Lord Berkeley (d. 1773). The quarter held by Frances was left to her son William, Lord Byron, who had sold the reversion to Stamp Brooksbank in 1760, and the fourth share, held by Barbara, passed on her death in 1772 to Dr. John Bettesworth.[17]

All four shares were purchased in 1777 by Henry Hoare (d. 1785) and on his death passed to his daughter Anne, wife of her cousin Sir Richard Hoare (d. 1787), and subsequently to their son Sir Richard Colt Hoare, Bt.[18] Sir Richard sold the manor to Uriah and George Messiter for £150 in 1808.[19] The Messiters conveyed it in the following year to Langport corporation for £250, and the corporation held it until the dissolution of the borough in 1886.[20] It was thereafter retained by the Langport town trust, whose members have since 1966 been appointed by the Langport parish council.[21]

There is no express reference to a manor-house in Langport. A pigeon-house and orchard were stated in 1668 to be parcel of the manors of both Langport Eastover and Langport Westover.[22] Their site has not been traced.

The largest single holding within the parish, other than the manor itself, was the lands held by the portreeve and commonalty from the Middle Ages,[23] called 'Prockters burgages' in 1600.[24] They were termed the 'manor intrinsecal' by Collinson in 1791.[25] Courts for the leasing of borough lands were held by 1657,[26] and most of the corporation's property was sold in the early 19th century.[27]

ECONOMIC HISTORY.

The choice of Langport as the site of one of the largest of the 10th-century burhs in the county suggests a strategic importance which was never equalled in the later history of the town.[28] Its security and possibly its economic importance are also suggested by the presence during Athelstan's reign of a mint which was still in production at the time of the Confessor.[29] Langport's status as a borough in 1086 is unquestioned. The third penny rendered by the town was worth 10s. and the 39 burgesses (29 according to the Exeter Domesday) paid an additional 18s. 2d.[30] The town also had links with country estates: five of the burgages belonged to North Curry manor, and Staple Fitzpaine manor held a piece of land (ortus) in return for a rent of 50 eels.[31]

Langport's position as a member of Curry Rivel manor by 1155[32] prevents any separate assessment of the borough's income until the 13th century, though the total income from Curry and Langport together suggests little increase in rent in the century after 1156.[33] The borough was valued at £8 7s. 7½d. in 1254 and at £6 13s. 4d. in 1324,[34] but it is likely that these figures include the manor and borough of Langport Westover in Curry Rivel. The two estates together were valued at £7 19s. 0¾d. in 1344.[35]

In the later 14th century and earlier 15th the lord's gross income from Langport Eastover varied between about £15 and £30; in the long term the fluctuation was governed by the level of assized rents, which yielded £7 3s. 1¼d. in 1350–1, £18 1s. 11¾d. in 1382–3, and £9 9s. 9¼d. in 1410–11, but in any given year a high total might result from a large yield from the perquisites of court, amounting in 1410–11 to £12 7s. 11d. The totals showed in general a fall from the 1380s and a gradual recovery from c. 1410.[36]

Langport occurs as a taxation borough on nine occasions during the period 1306–36.[37] Its general economic position in the early 14th century may be defined in the context of its taxable value, where it stood eighth in the list of the county's towns. By 1340 it had risen to sixth, and seems to have retained that position at least until the 1370s.[38] The basis of its economy in the Middle Ages is difficult to determine, though a number of religious houses and prominent landowners held property within the borough. Glastonbury abbey had a house there by c. 1191;[39] Athelney abbey acquired a tenement and a cottage in 1392[40] and held seven burgages by 1538;[41] Taunton priory had a burgage by 1535.[42] Among the lay owners were Sir William Bonville (d. 1461),[43] Sir Richard Choke (d. 1483) of Long Ashton, justice of Common Pleas,[44] and John

[10] Ibid. 38, 39.
[11] Ibid. 38, feoffees mins. 1628–37.
[12] W.R.O. 383/417.   [13] S.R.O., D/B/la 33.
[14] Complete Peerage, s.v. Fitzharding.
[15] W.R.O. 383/420; G.E.C. Baronetage, ii. 111–12.
[16] W.R.O. 383/417.
[17] Ibid.; S.R.O., D/B/la 33; Complete Peerage, s.v. Byron.   [18] W.R.O. 383/420.
[19] S.R.O., D/B/la 33.   [20] Ibid. 9, 33.
[21] Par. cncl. Town Trust mins. 1960–7.
[22] S.R.O., DD/S/ET, box 1, assignment, 17 Aug. 1668.
[23] See p. 24.
[24] E 134/42 & 43 Eliz. I/Mich. 27.
[25] Collinson, Hist. Som. iii. 132.
[26] See p. 29.   [27] See p. 31.   [28] See p. 16.
[29] British Numismatic Journal, xxix. 65–6.
[30] V.C.H. Som. i. 434, 438, 441.

[31] Ibid. 438, 476.   [32] See p. 22.
[33] Pipe R. 1156–8 (Rec. Com.), 30, 98, 121; 1212 (P.R.S. n.s. xxx), 113.
[34] Close R. 1253–4, 67; Cal. Inq. Misc. ii, pp. 187–8.
[35] E 149/9/24.
[36] Devon R.O. 1142 B/M 28–39; S.R.O., DD/SAS CU/1(a–f), 12.
[37] Hist. Essays in Honour of James Tait, ed. J. G. Edwards, V. H. Galbraith, and E. F. Jacob, 434.
[38] S. & D. N. & Q. xxix. 11–12.
[39] S.R.S. lxiv. 705–6.
[40] Cal. Inq. Misc. vi, pp. 33–4.
[41] S.C. 6/Hen. VIII/3144.
[42] Valor Eccl. (Rec. Com.), i. 206.
[43] Cal. Inq. p.m. (Rec. Com.), iv. 312; Complete Peerage, s.v. Bonville.
[44] Cal. Inq. p.m. Hen. VII, i, pp. 164–5.

Heyron (d. 1501).[45] Dependence on the cloth trade is revealed by Langport's rise, between 1460–1 and 1464–5, from being the eighth to the fourth largest importer of woad through Southampton.[46] Tradesmen in the town included a goldsmith in 1327,[47] dyers in 1416 and 1454–5,[48] a draper or tailor in 1457,[49] and a cloth merchant in 1504.[50] Langport's trade relied to a large extent on the free flow of traffic along the Parrett, and complaints were made in 1280 that the lord of Aller had prevented the towing of boats between the town and Bridgwater.[51] Similarly in the early years of the 14th century it was claimed that a fishery, owned by the lord of Langport, had blocked the river, causing reeds to hinder navigation.[52]

Although primarily a trading community, Langport possessed some agricultural land within its borders. Horsecroft, later known as Langport field, provided the arable, though it was evidently too small for crop rotation; and the meadow and pasture grounds to the north and south of the town subject, as already said,[53] to persistent winter flooding. During the summer, however, they were pastured in common with cattle and pigs.[54] The rivers in return provided fish. One of the two fisheries in 1086 may probably be identified with Poundweir which lay at the north-west end of Common moor.[55] Two other fisheries, 'Lachemere' and 'New Mill', occur from 1350–1,[56] and both were leased in 1362 on condition that the weir was rebuilt.[57] The principal value of the fisheries lay in the abundance of eels to be found in the Parrett.[58]

During the late 15th century the town seems to have somewhat declined. By 1507–8 the income from the manor was £9 14s. 8¾d., and the real value of the assized rents was £5 4s. 2¼d., not much more than half the total a hundred years earlier.[59] Thereafter, until 1569, the net income from the manor generally varied between £6 and £8, except when perquisites of court were unusually high.[60] In 1569 John Milner contracted for a lease of the borough on the following terms: to hold the burgages, shambles, and booths for 60 years at a rent of £5 0s. 2d. and the market, fairs, and courts for 21 years at a rent of £1 16s. 8d.[61] It was then stated that the assized rents, formerly worth £4 18s. 5d., had fallen in value to £2 14s. 3¼d. as the burgages and shambles needed repair. Milner was to pay the full farm of £6 16s. 10d. by reviving the decayed rents.[62] That this policy succeeded may be deduced from the fact that by 1585 the clear yearly value of

the manor had risen to £15 5s. 9½d., and that Hugh Sexey subsequently purchased the manor, which he had leased in 1584.[63] A Bill to rebuild the town, read twice in 1597 but never enacted, suggests that improvements may have been carried out at this time.[64]

The tenure of property held of the manor in the Middle Ages had evidently been for one, two, or three lives,[65] and in 1563 the borough was stated to have practised the custom of borough-English 'beyond the memory of man'.[66] Profits from the manor amounted to £6 17s. 6¼d. in 1625–6 based on a rental of £7 7s. 6¼d.[67] These figures varied little until the end of the 18th century although the value of the manor was eroded by inflation. In 1620 the manor had 54 freehold tenants, 34 copyhold tenants holding for lives, one tenant at will (for a rope and bull collar), and the fishery held for a term of years.[68] By 1727, although the number of copyholders had remained about the same, the number of freeholders had nearly tripled, to 145,[69] indicating considerable subdivision of holdings. The number of copyholds decreased during the 18th and 19th centuries,[70] but there appears to have been no corresponding conversion to leasehold tenure. During the years 1799–1804 the rental fell from £6 11s. 5d. to £3 10s. 4d.,[71] evidently the result of extensive enfranchisements by Sir Richard Colt Hoare. The number of tenants had also fallen by 1804, to 75 freeholders and 18 copyholders.[72] After the manor was purchased by the corporation in 1809 the copyholds were evidently sold to the tenants, and by 1827 the manor comprised 102 freehold tenants paying £1 6s. 9½d. Many of the freehold rents had lapsed owing to the difficulty of identifying the properties to which they related, and during the 19th century the remaining rents were collected only once every six years.[73]

Unlike the manorial tenements the corporation lands were by 1659 entirely leasehold: 30 tenants holding for 99 years or one, two, or three lives, 2 for terms of years (both granted in 1598), and 13 where the tenure was not stated.[74] After 1698, however, grants for 99 years or lives were made only in reversion.[75] Tenure for lives continued until the sale of the corporation lands in the early 19th century.[76]

Apart from the manor itself and the corporation lands, comprising 42½ a. in 1344,[77] and 52 burgages and 51 a. in 1596,[78] there were never any other substantial holdings within the parish. During the

[45] Cal. Inq. p.m. Hen. VII, iii, pp. 446–7; Req. 2/6/176; C 142/25/42.
[46] Brokage Bk. of Southampton, ed. Olive Coleman, ii (Southampton Rec. Soc. vi), 322–3.
[47] S.R.S. iii. 276: Thomas the goldsmith. William le Goldstone is also mentioned. A family named Goldsmith occurs regularly from 1350–1 to 1476 (Devon R.O. 1142 B/M 28; Cal. Close, 1402–5, 476).
[48] Cal. Pat. 1416–22, 15; Ross, Langport and its Ch. 223.
[49] Cal. Pat. 1452–61, 377.
[50] S.R.S. xix. 66.
[51] Ibid. xliv. 119–20.
[52] Ibid. lxiii. 522.
[53] See p. 19.
[54] S.R.O., DD/PH 225/39.
[55] S.R.S. lxiii. 522; Devon R.O. 1142 B/M 28; S.R.O., DD/SAS CU/5; Cal. Treas. Papers, 1714–19, 408–9.
[56] Devon R.O. 1142 B/M 28.
[57] Ibid. M 30.
[58] V.C.H. Som. i. 476; S.R.S. xv. 132; local information.

[59] S.C. 6/Hen. VII/1237.
[60] S.C. 6/Hen. VIII/3044–52; S.C. 6/Edw. VI/418–21; S.C. 6/Ph. and Mary/ 257–62; S.C. 6/Eliz. I/1960–6.
[61] Cal. Pat. 1566–9, p. 342.
[62] E 310/23/126/20.
[63] E 310/23/124/46; see above, p. 22.
[64] E. Green, Bibliotheca Somersetensis, ii. 13.
[65] Devon R.O. 1142 B/M 28–41; S.R.O., DD/SAS CU/ 1(a–f), 2(e2), 12.
[66] C 66/988.
[67] S.R.O., DD/SE 30, accts. of Sexey lands, 1626–9.
[68] Ibid., survey of manor, 1620.
[69] S.R.O., D/B/la 41.
[70] Ibid.
[71] Ibid.
[72] Ibid.
[73] S.R.O., D/B/la 46.
[74] Ibid. 6.
[75] Ibid. 49.
[76] Ibid. 6.
[77] B.M. Add. Ch. 16127.
[78] S.R.O., D/B/la 6.

17th and 18th centuries, however, two important families in the neighbourhood continued to hold property within the town and served as officers of the corporation. Thomas Trevillian of Midelney in Drayton (town clerk 1617–57)[79] held three burgages on the Hill,[80] and John Trevillian served as recorder of the borough between 1699 and 1749.[81] The Phelips family of Montacute held lands in the borough in 1638,[82] and Sir Edward Phelips served as both recorder (1667–99) and portreeve (1679–81, 1689–91).[83]

Pressure on the limited agricultural land around the town was evidently strong in the 17th century. Langport field was still cultivated in strips in 1596[84] but was evidently inclosed in the early and mid 18th century.[85] Barley Close, the Hams, and Whatley hill were probably inclosed and devoted to pasture at an earlier date.[86] Common moor, 60 a. in extent in 1637 and under water for most of the year, was then valued at 40s. It was owned by the Crown and used jointly by Langport, Aller, and Huish.[87] Attempts to procure grants of the 'moor' in the late 17th and 18th centuries suggest that its value had increased.[88] It was inclosed by private agreement between the three parishes in 1797.[89] Langport's allotment of 21 a. was subdivided by order of the vestry in 1832 and the grass has been sold by the parish since that time.[90] Cocklemoor, containing nearly 4 a. in 1839,[91] was formerly larger, for between 1596 and 1802 it was said to be 7½ a.– 8 a.[92] It had been divided into two closes by 1687.[93] Until the 16th century it was regarded as common pasture enjoyed by the burgesses, but in 1528–30 the burgesses' rights were questioned.[94] It was subsequently annexed by the Crown and granted to John Herbert and Andrew Palmer in 1575.[95] By 1596 it had been re-acquired by the corporation and was thereafter leased to private individuals until its sale in 1802.[96]

Higher and Lower moors were administered by the portreeve until the manor was farmed in 1569.[97] Typical breaches of custom by 16th-century tenants included failure to scour ditches, driving pigs over the 'moors' to Common moor, and laying bridges over the North Ditch from tenements directly into the 'moors'.[98] In 1600–1 a suit between the farmer of the manor and the portreeve and commonalty established that occupiers of corporation lands possessed as such no rights of common, but only tenants of the manor.[99] Thus in 1620 ten of 36 copyhold tenants of the manor had common of

pasture for two beasts in the 'moors',[1] and no common rights were claimed in respect of borough lands in 1596 or 1659.[2] By 1657, however, control of the 'moors' had passed to the borough court at which the moorherds made their presentments.[3] In the 17th century these included, among other matters, badger poaching, stocking with horses and geese against custom, and winnowing corn to the damage of the grass.[4] A bull, acquired by the commoners in 1668 for their common use, was sold two years later and the money put towards building a bridge from Higher moor into Common moor.[5] By the 18th century control of the 'moors' had passed to the manor court. According to customs presented in 1808 only married or widowed tenants of the manor were allowed to stock and could exercise only one right of stocking even if more were held. The 'moors' were stocked on the Monday after Old Holy Rood day (3 May) and hayned or unstocked three weeks and three days before Old Christmas day. Each year the commoners swore to stock only with their own beasts.[6] From 1811, after the purchase of the manor by the corporation, the common rights were separated from the tenements to which they belonged and were sold in fee.[7] Those still held for lives by copy were allowed to fall into hand from 1823 to prevent overstocking.[8] By 1850, and probably from an earlier date, the commoners had formed themselves into a body to administer the two 'moors', meeting once a year in April or May.[9] From 1902 the requirement that the 'moors' be stocked with the commoners' own beasts only was discontinued,[10] and subsequently the commoners often leased their grazing rights to local farmers. In 1959, owing to the difficulty of finding moor reeves willing to serve, the stocking of the 'moors' was suspended, the grass sold by auction, and the profits divided between the commoners.[11] In 1960 £214 15s. was divided between 41 commoners, and each received £28 in 1969.[12]

In consequence of the shortage of land it was stated in 1772 that the town, 'being unable to supply itself, is obliged to purchase provisions at an exorbitant rate'.[13] In 1839 of a total acreage of 102 a. not occupied by buildings, gardens, or orchards, nearly 70 a. were pasture, 20½ a. meadow, and less than 12 a. arable.[14] By 1905 there was no arable land and 81¾ a. of permanent grass.[15]

The 'fry of fish' was leased by the lord of the manor in 1563–4[16] and again in 1620.[17] The

[79] Ibid. 1, 5.
[80] Ibid. 6, survey of corp. lands, 1659.
[81] Ibid.
[82] *S.R.S.* li. 272–3.
[83] S.R.O., D/B/la 5, 6, 49.
[84] Ibid. 6.
[85] Ibid. 49, leases, 1 Nov. 1736, 14 Nov. 1752.
[86] Ibid. 6 (survey of corp. lands, 1659), 49.
[87] E 178/5621.
[88] *Cal. S.P. Dom.* 1683–4, 150; *Cal. Treas. Papers,* 1714–19, 408–9; S.R.O., D/B/la 26.
[89] S.R.O., D/B/la 26.
[90] Par. rec., vestry mins. 1820–49, 1849–1928; local information.
[91] S.R.O., tithe award.
[92] S.R.O., D/B/la 6.
[93] Ibid. 49, lease, 10 May 1687.
[94] S.R.O., DD/PH 225/39.
[95] C 66/1125 no. 3.
[96] S.R.O., D/B/la 6.
[97] E 134/42 & 43 Eliz. I/Mich. 27.

[98] S.R.O., DD/PH 225/39.
[99] E 134/42 & 43 Eliz. I/Mich. 27.
[1] S.R.O., DD/SE 38.
[2] S.R.O., D/B/la 6.
[3] Ibid. 5.
[4] Ibid., 19 Oct. 1658, 1 May 1661, 8 May 1666, 19 Apr. 1670.
[5] Ibid., 15 Mar. 1669/70, 31 May 1670; D/B/la 81, accts. 1667–8, 1670–1.
[6] S.R.O., D/B/la 37.
[7] Ibid. 7.
[8] Ibid.
[9] S.R.O., D/B/la 99.
[10] Ibid.
[11] Par. cncl. commoners' mins. 1905 to date.
[12] Ibid.
[13] *The Lady's Magazine,* Oct. 1772.
[14] S.R.O., tithe award.
[15] Statistics supplied by the then Bd. of Agric. 1905.
[16] S.R.O., DD/PH 225/39.
[17] S.R.O., DD/SE 38.

corporation were claiming and leasing the fishery of the river throughout the borough by 1691,[18] the rent for which by 1761 included a dish of fish for the portreeve's feast.[19] The lord of the manor was again leasing the fishing and fowling during the 18th century, and in 1791 had to be dissuaded by Lady Chatham of Burton Pynsent from letting the river to a firm of fishmongers who, she claimed, would clear it of fish.[20] The conflicting jurisdictions over the river of both manor and borough were evidently reconciled with the purchase of the manor by the corporation in 1809.[21] The borough authorities continued to let the fishery during the 19th century,[22] and it was leased to the Langport Angling Society from 1968.[23] The 'game of swans and swan-moat alias swanmark' in the river at Langport was settled by Barnabas Lewis on his son Barnabas in 1618.[24] No subsequent reference has been found to it.

The range of goods for which Langport acted as a clearing-house was considerable. The principal commodities brought up river from Bridgwater in 1616 were herrings, salt, coal, and grain.[25] The plague outbreak at Bridgwater in 1625 caused great loss to the boatmen there because the 'accustomed traffic and commerce' in coal and culm with Langport had been forbidden.[26] Tolls on iron were mentioned in 1637.[27] Some merchants made considerable fortunes. Edith, daughter of a Langport iron-monger, John Blake, married Sir Edward Phelips of Montacute and was left £2,000 by her father in his will proved in 1699.[28] The medieval textile trade continued into the late 17th century when cloth-workers and worsted-combers are mentioned,[29] and feltmaking is referred to frequently in the 18th century.[30] A glover is recorded in 1788[31] and gloving, mentioned again in 1868,[32] was carried on at Ensor House in Bow Street until 1971.[33]

Occupations represented in the town during the 18th century include those of tobacconist in 1693,[34] apothecary and tobacco-tong maker in 1714,[35] nail-maker in 1735,[36] peruke-maker in 1791, soap-boiler[37] and hairdresser c. 1793.[38] There were two auctioneers, six attorneys, two printers and book-binders, an umbrella manufacturer, and a watch-maker in 1822.[39] A land- and timber-surveyor was mentioned in 1830,[40] and a boat-builder, engineer, and soap and candle manufacturer in 1840.[41] By 1859 a brightsmith and bell-hanger, a cheese factor,

three jewellers, and two undertakers had established themselves,[42] and by 1866 three builders and a photographer.[43] The Langport and Mid-Somerset Building Society appears to have been founded in 1859.[44] A seed warehouse was recorded by 1875[45] and two garages and a jam factory by 1927.[46] Industrial enterprises in the town in 1972 included two luggage manufacturers, a woodcraft firm, and Silkolene Lubricants. Until 1966 there was a seed processing and retailing firm, and the cheese factors near the foot of the Hill had in 1972 only recently closed down.[47]

The town's prosperity in the late 18th and 19th centuries depended principally on the trading firm of Stuckey and Bagehot. George Stuckey (I) (d. 1726) came from Kingsdon in the late 17th century as a worsted comber and later a sergemaker.[48] His son George (II) (d. 1774), merchant, went into partnership with Thomas Bagehot, a maltster, who had arrived in the town by 1747.[49] Together they traded in a wide range of goods, particularly corn, timber, and salt,[50] passing the business on to their sons, George Stuckey (III) (d. 1807) and Robert Codrington Bagehot (d. 1836).[51] Samuel Stuckey (d. 1812), younger son of George (II), diversified his trading activities and founded Stuckey's Bank in the town c. 1770.[52] By c. 1793 Stuckey and Bagehot carried on a regular trade with Birmingham, Manchester, Liverpool, and London, both by road and by water.[53] The business increased during the 19th century, and by 1866 they owned 14 East Indiamen and 19 barges.[54] The Somerset Trading Company, established by 1883, subsequently developed out of the old firm.[55]

Stuckey's Bank, with branches at Bridgwater and Bristol, became a joint stock company in 1826 under the chairmanship of Vincent Stuckey (d. 1845). During the 19th century the bank took over thirteen others, principally in Somerset. The family connexion was maintained by Vincent Stuckey's grandson, Vincent Wood, who changed his name to Stuckey and acted as chairman until 1900. The company was itself taken over by Parr's Bank in 1909 and was subsequently absorbed by the Westminster (later the National Westminster) Bank. At the time of its amalgamation Stuckey's Bank had a banknote circulation second only to that of the Bank of England.[56]

A windmill, first mentioned in 1344, stood on the

[18] S.R.O., D/B/la 42.
[19] Ibid. 6.
[20] Ibid. 42.
[21] See p. 23.
[22] S.R.O., D/B/la 8.
[23] Par. cncl. mins. 1964–9.
[24] C 142/467/138.
[25] S.R.O., D/B/la 1.
[26] S.R.S. xxiv. 9. Part of the quay above Bridgwater Bridge was known as the Langport slip: Bridgwater Borough Archives no. 1896.
[27] S.R.O., D/B/la 24.
[28] S.R.O., DD/PH 190.
[29] Ibid. 49.　　　　　　　　　　　[30] Ibid.
[31] S.R.O., Q/SR 251/3.
[32] Rep. Com. on Children and Women in Agric. [4202–I] H.C. p. 478 (1868–9), xiii.
[33] Local information.
[34] S.R.O., D/B/la 49.
[35] S.R.O., Q/SR 251/1, 3; D/B/la 49.
[36] S.R.O., D/B/la 49.
[37] Par. reg. 1728–1812.
[38] Univ. Brit. Dir. iii.

[39] Pigot, Nat. Com. Dir. (1822–3).
[40] Ibid. (1830).
[41] County Gazette Dir. (1840).
[42] Harrison, Harrod, & Co., Dir. Som. (1859).
[43] P.O. Dir. Som. (1866).
[44] S.R.O., D/B/la 8, 17 Dec. 1859; P.O. Dir. Som. (1861).
[45] P.O. Dir. Som. (1875).
[46] Kelly's Dir. Som. (1927).
[47] S.R.O., DD/WI 22; local information.
[48] S.R.O., D/B/la 49, leases, 8 May 1699, 1 Nov. 1710; M. Churchman, 'The Stuckeys of Somerset' (TS. in S.R.O., DD/X/CU), 7.
[49] Churchman, 'The Stuckeys of Somerset', 7; Ross, Langport and its Ch. 352; S.R.O., D/B/la 49, lease, 25 Oct. 1749.
[50] Churchman, 'The Stuckeys of Somerset', 10.
[51] Ibid.
[52] Ibid.; P. T. Saunders, Stuckey's Bank (1928), 1–4.
[53] Univ. Brit. Dir. iii.
[54] Ross, Langport and its Ch. 353.
[55] Ibid.; Kelly's Dir. Som. (1883).
[56] Saunders, Stuckey's Bank, passim.

higher part of Rowditch on the north side of Langport hill, and was held with 2 a. of arable land and ½ a. of meadow in 'Mulleclif'.[57] It was farmed out by the lord from 1349–50 for 26s. 8d.[58] It was blown down by a 'great wind' in January 1362 and was evidently never rebuilt, but the mound on which it stood, known as Windmill Toyt,[59] may be that on which a Calvary has been erected in the grounds of St. Gildas Convent.

A water-mill recorded as new in 1344[60] had ceased to grind by 1352[61] and lay vacant in 1356–7 because the water had been diverted from it.[62] A plot of land between the new mill and 'Wakesham' was leased in 1360,[63] and the fishery of 'la newemulle' occurs regularly from 1350.[64] This mill probably lay on a leat near the Parrett superseded by the present Catchwater.

A water-mill, the property of the lord of the manor, is mentioned in 1351–2, when the grinding of corn was transferred to it from the new mill.[65] It recurs in 1357.[66]

A tenement and horse-mill, acquired by the lord from John Middleney, rector of Charlton Mackrell, were leased to John Ellis, chaplain, in 1382.[67]

In 1596 a burgage, 'being a millhouse', was held by Thomas Weech. It apparently stood on the Hill, although by 1659 it was no longer worked.[68] A house containing a grist mill called Wartley is mentioned in 1600 as having been built by the commonalty of Langport,[69] and presumably lay in the area later known as Whatley. A mill held by Abraham Edwards was included among properties whose rents could not be recovered by the corporation between 1756 and 1763.[70] In 1761 Lucy Bush's malt-mill, with a cog wheel, is mentioned.[71]

MARKETS AND FAIRS. A market, held on Saturdays, was first mentioned in 1344 when it was let to farm by the lord.[72] By 1370 it was being farmed annually to the portreeve then in office.[73] Three new stalls were set up in 1374–5, one in Cheapstreet for the sale of shoes.[74] By 1563 the market was being held on the north side of the Hill, immediately west of the present convent.[75] Here, soon after 1563, a thatched market-house was erected and shortly afterwards a little house adjoining it was built to accommodate a cage, a pillory, and a poor man who cleaned the market-place.[76] In 1568–9 the market-place was pitched,[77] and by 1596 the borough lands included

twelve thatched shambles in the market-place, a number which had decreased to five by 1659.[78]

A tiled market cross stood at the foot of the Hill by 1506.[79] It evidently housed market stalls and was last mentioned in 1778–9.[80] From 1563 there was a court of pie powder[81] and, under the 1616 charter, the portreeve became ex officio clerk of the market.[82]

In the 16th century the market was principally for the sale of corn,[83] although the presence of shambles may indicate that meat also was sold. In 1633 it was also 'well furnished with fowl and full of pecked (speared) eels'.[84] An inventory of borough property in 1659 included the weights and measures.[85] Renewed and repaired as necessary, they remained the responsibility of the portreeve.[86] From 1677 the market bell (mentioned in 1653) was to be rung at noon, when selling might begin.[87] In 1702 a man was employed to set out the standings and tubs from the market-house,[88] a duty performed by the sergeant-at-mace in 1737.[89]

The market-house was partially demolished in 1713–14 and the standings were then stored in the little house adjoining[90] until the present town hall was erected in 1732.[91] Thereafter the ground floor of the new hall was used for storing the market equipment,[92] although markets probably continued to be held on the Hill for a time. In 1823 six new butchers' stalls were erected under the town hall and leased for 10s. a year each.[93] The market was still being held on Saturdays in 1828,[94] but subsequently lapsed.

In 1854 a weekly corn market on Tuesdays was established under the town hall and in 1855 a pig market was set up on the south side of Cheapside, and a cattle market in North Street.[95] A sheep market was built in Whatley Lane in 1871, and after 1873 the cattle market was held on alternate Tuesdays instead of monthly.[96] In 1876 the market had 'of late years considerably increased in importance',[97] and in 1884 it was common for 700 to 800 pigs to be brought to Langport for sale.[98] The cattle market in North Street was held in the roadway until 1890, when land at the north end of the street was given to the town trust by James Broadmead.[99] The pig market became a car park in 1937[1] and the cattle market was discontinued after the Second World War. An attempt to revive the weekly market under the town hall failed in 1970.[2]

In 1563 the borough was granted three fairs: on

[57] B.M. Add. Ch. 16127; S.R.O., D/B/la 49, leases, 1697, 1726, 1744, 1767, 1791.
[58] Devon R.O. 1142 B/M 28.
[59] S.R.O., D/B/la 49, leases, 1697, 1726, 1744, 1767, 1791.
[60] B.M. Add. Ch. 16127; E 149/9/24.
[61] Devon R.O. 1142 B/M 28.
[62] Ibid. M 29.
[63] Ibid. M 30.
[64] Ibid. M 28–41.
[65] Ibid. M 28.
[66] Ibid. M 29.
[67] Ibid. M 36.
[68] S.R.O., D/B/la 6, surveys, 1596, 1659.
[69] E 134/42 & 43 Eliz. I/Mich. 27.
[70] S.R.O., D/B/la 12.
[71] Ibid. 32.
[72] B.M. Add. Ch. 16127; E 149/9/24.
[73] Devon R.O. 1142 B/M 33.
[74] Ibid. M 34.
[75] S.R.O., D/B/la 6; tithe award.
[76] E 134/42 & 43 Eliz. I/Mich. 27; S.R.O., D/B/la 12.
[77] Ross, Langport and its Ch. 269.

[78] S.R.O., D/B/la 6.
[79] S.C. 6/Hen. VII/1236; S.R.O., D/B/la 6, survey, 1596.
[80] S.R.O., D/B/la 5, 11, 12.
[81] C 66/988.
[82] S.R.O., D/B/la 1.
[83] E 134/42 & 43 Eliz. I/Mich. 27.
[84] S.R.S. xv. 132.
[85] S.R.O., D/B/la 6.
[86] Ibid. 6, 12.
[87] Ibid. 6, 81.
[88] Ibid. 6.
[89] Ibid. 12.
[90] Ibid. 12, 49 (lease, 22 Feb. 1714/15).
[91] See p. 21.
[92] S.R.O., D/B/la 6, 15 Oct. 1760.   [93] Ibid. 47.
[94] Ibid. 23, replies to queries, 1828.
[95] Ibid. 8; P.O. Dir. Som. (1861).
[96] S.R.O., D/B/la 9; P.O. Dir. Som. (1861).
[97] S.R.O., D/B/la 9.
[98] Western Gazette, 30 May 1884.
[99] Kelly's Dir. Som. (1899).
[1] S.R.O., D/B/la 94.
[2] Local information.

the eve, day, and morrow of the feasts of St. Peter and St. Paul (28–30 June) and of St. Martin (10–12 November), and on the Monday in the second week of Lent for three days, subject to the payment of a fee-farm rent to the Crown of 30s.[3] To these in 1616 was added a fourth fair on the third day after the feast of St. Matthew for three days (24–26 September) for an additional fee-farm rent of 10s.[4] The rent of 10s. was redeemed in 1788[5] and that of 30s., long held in private hands, discharged in 1954.[6] The fourth fair was held in Whatley[7] and was described as a horse fair in 1810.[8] In 1767 the Lenten fair was principally devoted to fat cattle, that in June to black cattle and lambs, St. Matthew's fair (then altered to 5 October) to fat cattle and sucking colts, and the Martinstide fair to cattle, hogs, and sheep.[9] In 1824 the fair days were altered to the Monday before Lent, the second Wednesday in August, the penultimate Monday in September, and the last Monday in November, all to last for three days.[10] By 1861 these had been reduced to two cattle fairs on the second Tuesdays in March and December,[11] the 'Christmas great market' being altered to the first Tuesday in December in 1874.[12] Both these fairs had been discontinued by 1906.[13] A horse and colt fair on 4 September was established in 1875 (altered to 3 September by 1899) and held in Whatley Lane and North Street.[14] This was still being held in 1939,[15] but was not revived after the Second World War.

LOCAL GOVERNMENT. In 1066 Langport was held in fee farm under Somerton manor,[16] and appears to have been considered as part of Somerton hundred in 1212.[17] The five burgages held under North Curry manor in 1086[18] presumably account for the suit paid to North Curry hundred court by Langport in 1385 and until at least 1528.[19] At various dates between 1303 and 1428, by virtue of its common tenure with Curry Rivel, it formed part of Bulstone hundred,[20] but did not pay suit to its court during the 15th century.[21]

Langport was required to send two members to Parliament in 1305, one or two in 1306, and two in 1307. Those representing the borough were John de Petherton (1305, 1307), Robert Grey (1305), and Richard the Franklin (1306, 1307).[22] All three occur in an inquisition held at Langport in 1310,[23] and were probably local men. No writ was subsequently addressed to the borough.

No charter appears to have been granted to the borough until the 16th century and there are no medieval records of borough administration. The commonalty was headed by bailiffs in 1280,[24] superseded by a reeve or portreeve (*prepositus*) by 1369.[25] There is a reference to a mayor in 1375–6,[26] but the office does not recur. The commonalty held borough lands from the lord for an annual farm by 1344[27] and the tolls of the market were annually leased to the portreeve by 1371.[28] Before the grant of their charter the portreeve and bailiffs acted only as officers of the lord, presiding over the courts and collecting all fines, amercements, and other perquisites.[29] The portreeve then accounted with the lord's receiver for his receipts and expenditure and by 1507 was allowed an annual fee for the execution of his office.[30] The commonalty was also responsible for the repair of the bridges, and in 1548 tried to divert the stipends of two chantry priests to that purpose.[31]

In 1350–1 nine courts were held for the borough and manor, one being Hockday law court, and all were summoned on a Monday.[32] A Michaelmas law court had been added by 1359,[33] and a Hilary law court by 1371.[34] The total number of courts held each year varied. There were 13 in 1360–1,[35] 7 in 1383–4,[36] and 20 in 1405–6,[37] all held on Mondays. By 1506–7 and until at least 1545–6 three law courts and four other courts were being held each year.[38] By 1600 two leets or lawdays were being held annually by the farmer of the borough, summoned by precept directed from the steward to the portreeve. At the Michaelmas leet the portreeve was elected and sworn, and the leet jury chose the constables, bailiffs, sealers of leather, verderers, moorherds, and other officers.[39] The summoning of these leets and the choice of officers were transferred to the corporation under their charter of 1616.[40] Courts were held in the church house until the late 16th century, when the commonalty prevented the use of the building for that purpose.[41] According to depositions taken in 1600, the Crown or the farmer of the borough then kept a court baron 'in the nature of a hundred court from three weeks to three weeks or monthly' for the trial of all actions under 40s.[42] The court was presided over by the portreeve or his deputy who accounted for fines and amercements to the Crown.[43] No rolls for this court have survived, but references to the hundred of Langport are found in 1338 and 1340[44] and to the hundred of Langport Eastover, held with the manor and

[3] *Cal. Pat.* 1560–3, 496–7.
[4] S.R.O., D/B/la 1.   [5] Ibid. 3.
[6] Par. cncl. Town Trust mins. 1920–59.
[7] S.R.O., D/B/la 11, 12.
[8] Ibid. 37.
[9] *Fairs in Eng. and Wales* (1767), 67.
[10] S.R.O., D/B/la 7, 23.
[11] *P.O. Dir. Som.* (1861).
[12] S.R.O., D/B/la 9.
[13] *Kelly's Dir. Som.* (1906).
[14] S.R.O., D/B/la 9; *Kelly's Dir. Som.* (1899).
[15] *Kelly's Dir. Som.* (1939).
[16] See p. 22.
[17] *Bk. of Fees*, i. 78.
[18] *V.C.H. Som.* i. 438.
[19] S.R.O., DD/CC 131904/2, 113569.
[20] *Feud. Aids*, iv. 314, 330, 336, 372; *S.R.S.* iii. 71.
[21] S.R.O., DD/SE 3.
[22] Ross, *Langport and its Ch.* 162.
[23] *Proc. Som. Arch. Soc.* xlii. 42–3.
[24] *Plac. de Quo Warr.* (Rec. Com.), 702.

[25] S.R.O., DD/PH 225/7.   [26] Ibid.
[27] B.M. Add. Ch. 16127.
[28] Devon R.O. 1142 B/M 33.
[29] E 134/42 & 43 Eliz. I/Mich. 27.
[30] Ibid.; S.C. 6/Hen. VII/1236.
[31] *S.R.S.* ii. 115.
[32] Devon R.O. 1142 B/M 28.
[33] S.R.O., DD/SAS CU/1(a).
[34] Devon R.O. 1142 B/M 33.
[35] S.R.O., DD/SAS CU/12.   [36] Ibid. 1(d).
[37] Devon R.O. 1142 B/M 40.
[38] S.C. 6/Hen. VII/1236–7; S.C. 6/Hen. VIII/3044–52.
[39] E 134/42 & 43 Eliz. I/Mich. 27.
[40] S.R.O., D/B/la 1.
[41] E 134/42 & 43 Eliz. I/Mich. 27; S.R.O., DD/SE 18/5.
[42] E 134/42 & 43 Eliz. I/Mich. 27; E 134/43 Eliz. I/East. 16.
[43] E 134/42 & 43 Eliz. I/Mich. 27.
[44] *Proc. before J.P.s Edw. III and Ric. II*, ed. Bertha Putnam, 163, 174.

borough, in 1678 and 1777.[45] By 1624 (and possibly from 1588), however, the borough formed part of Pitney hundred.[46]

In 1563 the portreeve and commonalty obtained a charter acknowledging their status and confirming to them the tolls of the Saturday market and three fairs for the express purpose of repairing the bridges within the borough.[47] In the years which followed this grant the commonalty came into conflict with the farmer of the manor. The portreeves exceeded the limited powers granted to them by their charter by establishing two town courts in the Hanging Chapel, then converted to a town hall, seizing felons' goods, and by claiming the soil of the 'moors', the waste of the manor, the royalties of hunting, hawking, and fishing, and the election of manorial officers.[48] These claims were contested in the Exchequer by Hugh Sexey, farmer of the manor, in 1600, and the commonalty were eventually threatened with the removal of their charter if they exceeded their jurisdiction.[49]

In 1616 the town obtained a charter of incorporation as 'the portreeve and commonalty of the borough of Langport Eastover', which effectively settled the differences between the borough and the lord of the manor. The corporation was to consist of twelve chief or capital burgesses headed by a portreeve, acting also as coroner and clerk of the market, and two bailiffs, all three to be elected annually from the burgesses. There was also to be a recorder, town clerk, and sergeant-at-mace (also described as the portreeve's bailiff in 1663),[50] holding office during the pleasure of the chief burgesses. The inferior burgesses of the town had no powers and, indeed, the chief burgesses were to be elected by the corporation from all the inhabitants of the borough. Borough courts were to be held twice a year for the appointment of officers, the election to take place on All Saints day, and a court of record to be held every Tuesday to determine cases under £40. The charter also added a fourth fair[51] and authorized the corporation to collect tolls on all goods crossing the two Bow bridges or unloaded within 600 ft. of them.[52]

The 1616 charter created a division between manorial and borough jurisdiction. Thereafter the manor courts were summoned and presided over by the lord's officers. Manor court papers survive in a very full series from 1702 to 1829,[53] and court minutes for the period 1766–71.[54] Presentments for isolated years are extant during the 19th century and those from 1908 are entered in the commoners' minute book.[55] During the 18th century the court was generally held twice a year, in spring and autumn, and known as the court leet and court baron, sometimes with the words 'view of frankpledge' added. Business dealt with concerned principally the repair of buildings, particularly chimneys, the causeways or

pavements, the arches under Bow Street, the bridges, and other public structures.[56] Preoccupation with the administration, stocking, and hayning (unstocking) of the two 'moors' eventually became the principal purpose of the court, and in the 19th and 20th centuries leets were generally summoned only when new orders or changes in custom relating to the 'moors' became necessary.[57] The court leet was last summoned in 1959.[58]

Officers regularly elected at the manor courts in the 18th century were two constables, a constables' bailiff, a King's or Queen's bailiff, two verderers (1706–28), two moorherds or moor reeves, four wellwardens (1706), two searchers and sealers of leather, two shambles wardens, a hayward and keeper of the pound (from 1727), and two aletasters (from 1759).[59] In 1877 three moor reeves, a hayward, two aletasters, and two shambles wardens were elected,[60] but in 1906 and 1908 one man served as bailiff and hayward and only two moor reeves were appointed.[61] A steward and deputy steward of the manor were appointed annually by the town trust until 1966.[62]

Records of the borough courts survive intermittently from 1657 to 1808. Sessions were described as 'the court of the portreeve and commonalty of the borough and town', from 1668 as the *curia baronis*, and from 1776 to 1808 usually as the customary court.[63] They were held initially twice a year, as provided for by the charter, in April and October. A single court in October appears to have been held after 1680, and in 1723 the portreeve was ordered to hold court for the borough lands on the Tuesday after Michaelmas. From 1747 courts were held once a year in October, and from 1756 on 1 November. The form of the court was at first that of a court baron with view of frankpledge devoted to the administration of the borough lands and commons. The court was presided over by a steward and presentments made by the homage jury and moorherds. These presentments were concerned with the disrepair of buildings, bridges, and arches, encroachments, abuses of custom, particularly with regard to grazing on the 'moors', and failure to scour ditches. Thus the court had the same functions as the manor court but with jurisdiction only over borough lands and tenants. Subsequently the moorherds ceased to present and during the 18th century the court concerned itself only with leasing the borough lands and recording the homage jury's presentments. The homage invariably presented the new portreeve and bailiffs, but the actual appointments of these and other borough officers were usually made at a corporation meeting on All Saints day.[64] The borough courts ceased to be held after the manor had been purchased by the corporation in 1809.[65]

Officers elected at the borough courts included

[45] C.P. 25(2)/717/29 & 30 Chas. II Hil.; C.P. 25(2)/1399/17 Geo. III Trin.
[46] See p. 15.
[47] C 66/988.
[48] E 134/42 & 43 Eliz. I/Mich. 27; E 123/27; E 123/28, p. 30; S.R.O., DD/SE 18/7.
[49] E 134/42 & 43 Eliz. I/Mich. 27; E 134/43 Eliz. I/Mich. 32; E 134/43 Eliz. I/East. 16; E 123/27–8; S.R.O., DD/SE 18/7.
[50] S.R.O., D/B/la 5.
[51] See p. 28.
[52] S.R.O., D/B/la 1.

[53] Ibid. 37.
[54] Ibid. 32.
[55] Ibid. 37, 94, 99.
[56] Ibid. 32, 37.
[57] Ibid. 94, 99; par. cncl. commoners' mins. 1905 to date.
[58] Par. cncl. commoners' mins. 1905 to date.
[59] S.R.O., D/B/la 32, 37.
[60] Ibid. 37.
[61] Ibid. 94; commoners' mins. 1905 to date.
[62] Par. cncl. Town Trust mins. 1960–7.
[63] S.R.O., D/B/la 5, 6, 44.
[64] Ibid. 5, 6, 44.
[65] See p. 23.

two chief magistrates or justices (usually the then portreeve and his predecessor) and two moorherds from 1657,[66] and a water bailiff to collect tolls in 1665 and 1739–40.[67] A deputy recorder was appointed from 1699, an office usually held by the town clerk.[68] Until 1798 the portreeve rendered the annual accounts, but thereafter a treasurer was appointed.[69] Lists of recorders and town clerks have been printed.[70]

Court rolls of the court of record, established by the 1616 charter and called the *curia placitorum*, survive from 1666 to 1685.[71] It was presided over by the portreeve, recorder, and bailiffs, but the date at which it ceased is not known. The inhabitants petitioned the corporation for its revival in 1833,[72] evidently without success. No records survive relating to the piepowder court.

Records of meetings of the commonalty survive from 1658.[73] The precise distinction between types of business dealt with at these meetings and in the borough courts is not apparent. The leasing of borough tenements and the appointment of borough officers were not restricted to the two (later one) town courts each year, but took place when required. The appointment of Sir Edward Phelips as recorder was made in 1667 at a meeting of the portreeve and 'masters' (as the commonalty sometimes styled themselves), and a case of contempt of the borough court in the following year was also heard at a meeting.[74]

The religious sympathies of the corporation in Charles II's reign are indicated by the decision of 1670 to go to church in procession each week in order 'to give a good example to all persons dissenting the public service on the Lord's day'. John Bush, the Presbyterian minister, was repeatedly fined for refusing to take the oaths of allegiance and supremacy when elected a burgess in 1676,[75] although he was subsequently elected portreeve in 1686.[76] Richard Seward was expelled from the corporation in 1678 because he remained excommunicate and 'doth obstinately refuse and neglect to reconcile himself to the church'.[77] Dismissal from the corporation for other reasons was not unusual. In 1701 a chief burgess was dismissed for irregular behaviour while portreeve,[78] two burgesses were removed in 1745 for leaving the town, and in 1750 one burgess was dismissed for poor attendance and another for leaving the borough for more than 40 days.[79] Thomas Beedall, portreeve in 1761–2, was replaced when he went bankrupt, and William Trevillian was removed from the office of recorder in 1795 for refusing to attend meetings.[80] The last dismissal

noted was that of a burgess in 1802 for leaving the neighbourhood and not paying a fine.[81]

The corporation assumed some responsibility for the welfare of the poor. The burgesses apprenticed a pauper in 1659, bought clothes for the poor in 1665,[82] and baked into bread six pecks or two bushels of wheat a week for distribution to the poor in 1674.[83] The following year they supplied blue or green garments to impoverished inhabitants,[84] and in 1677 gave £7 in clothes and bread.[85] Aid in the form of food or money was also distributed during the winters between 1810 and 1817.[86]

The tolls collected by the corporation under the 1616 charter, known as wheelage and pontage, proved unpopular among the inhabitants of the borough. In 1637 four boatmen prosecuted for nonpayment of pontage claimed that those dwelling within the town were exempt from such dues, and that the corporation collected sufficient money from foreigners to repair the town's bridges.[87] Thereafter the levying of pontage seems to have been suspended, for c. 1687 it was stated that the toll had not been imposed for about 50 years, although wheelage had continued to be collected.[88] A water bailiff was appointed in 1665, efforts were made to reintroduce pontage in 1668,[89] and in the following year a new scale of tolls was introduced, giving preferential treatment to Langport traders over strangers.[90] Prosecutions for failure to pay these tolls between 1671 and 1687 produced claims that the corporation had 'near ruined and undone' the town by demanding pontage and that, as the 4d. carriage charged by boatmen for a barrel of herrings equalled the toll imposed, the carriers would have nothing for their labour.[91] A further attempt to revive pontage with the appointment of a water bailiff in 1740 was evidently unsuccessful.[92] The collection of wheelage was leased out with the market and fair tolls by 1741,[93] and in 1764 George Stuckey (III) was ordered to be prosecuted for assaulting the wheelage collector.[94] Wheelage was not mentioned after 1804–5,[95] although the collection of market and fair tolls was held by Stuckey and Bagehot in 1809.[96]

The corporation lands produced rents of £20 12s. 8d. in 1596.[97] This sum had fallen to £5 10s. 2d. by 1643 but rose again to £20 7s. 6d. by 1660,[98] and to £30 11s. 2d. (including Cocklemoor) by 1684.[99] These sums were considerably augmented by renewal fines and income from corporation money lent on bond, so that in 1709–10 total receipts were £84 14s. 2d.[1]

Among extraordinary items of expenditure the

[66] S.R.O., D/B/la 5; *Rep. Munic. Corps.* H.C. 116, p. 1296 (1835), xxiv.
[67] S.R.O., D/B/la 5, 6.
[68] Ibid. 6, 7.
[69] Ibid. 7.
[70] Ross, *Langport and its Ch.* 370–1.
[71] S.R.O., D/B/la 1, 4.
[72] Ibid. 8, 23.
[73] Ibid. 5–9.
[74] Ibid. 5.
[75] Ibid. 6.
[76] Ibid.
[77] Ibid.
[78] Ibid. 5.
[79] Ibid. 5, 6.
[80] Ibid. 6.
[81] *Rep. Munic. Corps.* H.C. 116, p. 1295 (1835), xxiv.
[82] S.R.O., D/B/la 5.
[83] Ibid. 6.
[84] Ibid. 5.
[85] Ibid. 6.
[86] Ibid. 7.
[87] Ibid. 24.
[88] Ibid.
[89] Ibid. 5.
[90] Ibid. 6.
[91] Ibid. 5, 24.
[92] Ibid. 6.
[93] Ibid. 12.
[94] Ibid. 6.
[95] Ibid. 12.
[96] Ibid. 45.
[97] Ibid. 6.
[98] Ibid. 81.
[99] Ibid. 11.
[1] Ibid. 12.

corporation helped to secure the endowment of the grammar school in 1707–8,[2] rebuilt the town hall in 1732 and Little Bow House in 1774, and discharged in 1740 their enforced contributions towards the repair of Stanmore bridge in Stoke St. Gregory.[3] Towards the end of the 18th century the portreeves' accounts frequently showed a deficit.[4] A hint of attempted economy is found in 1795 when the expense of the portreeve's two feasts on assuming and relinquishing office was temporarily reduced from twenty to ten guineas,[5] and in 1801 the corporation took legal advice on selling the borough lands in fee. Thus in the period 1802–4 nineteen properties were sold for £1,004. The manor of Langport Eastover was purchased in 1809 and the common grazing rights belonging to it were also sold.[6] Having disposed of most of their property, the corporation appear to have reconsidered their position and repurchased the Langport Arms.[7] The surplus profits arising from these and other transactions were invested. Subsequently half of it was devoted to rebuilding the Great Bow bridge and the remainder to purchasing securities in the Langport, Somerton, and Castle Cary turnpike trust.[8] Although the corporation was investigated in 1834, it was not subjected to the 1835 Act.

During the 19th century the corporation tried to improve the town, principally by widening Bow and North Streets.[9] The Reading Room had been built in 1833 and a sewer to serve properties on the Hill, draining into the Catchwater at Little Bow, was begun in 1850.[10] The decline in river traffic, however, the fall in value of the turnpike investments, and the heavy expense of establishing a pig market in 1885[11] all led to financial difficulties for the corporation. In 1868–9 the turnpike bonds were sold for only 75 per cent of the original outlay and 18½ a. of land at Westonzoyland were purchased for £1,800,[12] producing £79 a year in 1875.[13] At this date the corporation tried unsuccessfully to sell the Langport Arms, the repair of which had been a constant drain on the borough finances. The total annual income of the corporation stood at £172 in 1876, giving a surplus over fixed items of expenditure of £41 a year; but this made no allowance for extraordinary sums required, and in 1882 £750 was borrowed to finance flood prevention. By 1884 the treasurer's accounts showed a deficit of £662 and two years later, under the Municipal Corporations Act of 1883, the town lost its charter.[14]

Thereafter, under a Scheme of 1888, the corporate property was taken over by the Langport Town Trust, the objects of which were to maintain toll-free markets, the fire brigade, Reading Room, and other borough properties, and to liquidate the debts incurred by the dissolved corporation.[15] The trust appointed a steward and deputy steward of the manor each year and also a man to serve as hall-keeper and market bailiff.[16] The Westonzoyland lands were mortgaged in 1890 to discharge debts (and subsequently sold in 1919), the Langport Arms was sold in 1901, and four cottages in Whatley in 1933.[17] Having thus disposed of their assets and with no means of securing additional income to meet rising costs and liabilities, the trustees were unable to fulfil the obligations placed on them. Under these circumstances the parish council assumed control of the trust in 1966.[18]

A house 'commonly called the town hall', standing on the site of the present building in Cheapside, is mentioned in 1596. This hall was probably erected soon after the commonalty received the charter of 1563. The same source of 1596 refers to 'the town hall commonly called the chapel',[19] now the Hanging Chapel, and in 1600 it was stated that 'the whole town of Langport do now use the said chapel as a place meet for consultation about such common causes as they have in hand'.[20] The 1616 charter gave the corporation power to 'have, retain, and erect a council house'[21] and it may have been then that the borough authorities again changed the place of their meetings to the hall in Cheapside. The town hall contained a jury chamber in 1658 and a kitchen in 1660.[22] The present hall, with market area beneath, was erected in 1732 with a loan from the then portreeve.[23] A strong-room was added and the kitchen improved in 1836.[24] After the dissolution of the corporation in 1886 the hall was used for parish functions and entertainments.[25] Since 1967 it has been leased to the British Legion.[26] Under a Scheme of 1970 the income from the charity of W. J. Carne-Hill (d. 1906) is to be applied to the repair and maintenance of the town hall.[27] The building has an open ground floor, formerly providing accommodation for the market, and has a Ham stone arcade of three bays in the street front. The first floor is of brick with Ham stone rustications and moulded eaves cornice. The pyramidal roof is surmounted by a bellcot and a weather vane dated 1733.

A prison called the Little Ease with a dwelling over it was erected in the later 16th century 'in the east side of the bridge called the Little Bow and in the north side of the street', sometimes described as being on the bridge itself.[28] Under the 1616 charter this was to be maintained by the bailiffs.[29] A lease of the property in 1630 probably relates to the dwelling over the gaol.[30] The repair of the prison figures regularly in the portreeves' accounts[31] until, in 1732, the site on which the gaol formerly stood was leased for building.[32] The site of the

[2] Ibid.
[3] Ibid. 12, 25.
[4] Ibid. 12.
[5] Ibid. 6.
[6] Ibid. 7.
[7] Ibid.; see above, p. 21.
[8] S.R.O., D/B/la 8.
[9] Ibid. 8, 9; see above, p. 20.
[10] S.R.O., D/B/la 8.
[11] Ibid.; see above, p. 27.
[12] S.R.O., D/B/la 8.
[13] Ibid. 53, draft lease to Tazewell.
[14] Ibid. 9.
[15] Char. Com. files.
[16] Par. cncl. Town Trust mins. 1920–59.

[17] S.R.O., D/B/la 56; Char. Com. files.
[18] Par. cncl. Town Trust mins. 1960–7; par. cncl. mins. 1964–9.
[19] S.R.O., D/B/la 6.
[20] E 134/42 & 43 Eliz. I/Mich. 27.
[21] S.R.O., D/B/la 1.   [22] Ibid. 5.
[23] Ibid. 12; see plate facing p. 49.
[24] S.R.O., D/B/la 8.
[25] Par. cncl. Town Trust mins. 1920–67.
[26] Par. cncl. mins. 1964–9.
[27] Char. Com. files.
[28] E 134/42 & 43 Eliz. I/Mich. 27.
[29] S.R.O., D/B/la 1.
[30] Ibid. 6.   [31] Ibid. 11, 12.
[32] Ibid. 6 (court, 5 Nov. 1731), 49 (lease, 1 Nov. 1732).

new prison, traditionally in Whatley, has not been traced.[33] A general watch was established in 1756, kept by four householders each night between 9 p.m. and 5 a.m.[34] In 1778–9 two men were paid to guard prisoners in the town gaol and locks for the windows and grates were purchased.[35] The prison was improved in 1852 when the sergeant-at-mace was entitled to 6d. nightly for each prisoner.[36] The county authorities were eventually persuaded to accept responsibility for the gaol in 1878. In that year a cottage in Whatley was purchased and cells erected, and a resident police constable was installed in 1879.[37] A new police house, office, and two cells were built in 1904 on the east side of North Street, south of the schools, in Huish parish.[38] These were superseded in 1969 on the completion of the present police station on the site of the old cattle market in North Street.[39]

A fire engine was maintained by the parish in 1768[40] and kept in the church in 1811.[41] In 1824 neighbouring parishes were to have the use of it on paying £1 a year and fetching and returning it, and a building was erected in 1826 on the north side of the church tower to house it.[42] The corporation acquired a fire engine in 1845, stored in a building erected on the north side of the Hanging Chapel,[43] and also took over the parish engine in the following year.[44] The engine was moved to a shed on the old pig market, south of Cheapside, c. 1877[45] and was transferred to the town hall in 1925. The fire-fighting equipment was taken over by Langport R.D.C. in 1939, and the town has since been served from Somerton.[46]

Vestry minutes survive from 1820 and record the appointment of two churchwardens, two overseers of the poor until 1894, a salaried assistant overseer or rate collector from 1827, two waywardens from 1837 (one only 1864–94), a waterer of the streets in 1859, and two lamp inspectors from 1890.[47]

A poorhouse is mentioned in 1743,[48] occupied by a tenant between 1754 and 1756.[49] In 1761 the overseers rebuilt a house belonging to the corporation for use as a poorhouse.[50] This probably lay on the Hill near the church, and was conveyed to the parish by the corporation in 1807.[51] A site for new poorhouses on the west side of North Street was acquired by the overseers in 1817[52] and £200 was borrowed from the corporation to finance their erection.[53] The building was completed c. 1820, and in 1827 there was stated to be much disease among the poor there owing to bad drainage and low

floors.[54] The parish became part of the Langport poor-law union in 1836 and the guardians rented Langport poorhouse until the Union workhouse in High Ham had been completed.[55] The poorhouse was sold in 1837.[56]

ARMS, SEALS, AND INSIGNIA. The earliest badges used by the town were said at the end of the 18th century to have been an embattled and crenellated tower, superseded by a portcullis.[57] No seals bearing these devices have been noted but an embattled tower appeared on the cover of an old borough minute book, no longer extant.[58] The portcullis probably originates from that badge found on the east and west faces of the church tower. A trade token issued by the portreeve in 1667 bears the portcullis,[59] as does the inn sign of the Langport Arms. The borough had a seal in 1600[60] and the charter of 1616 provided for one.[61] The first known impression, attached to a lease of 1682,[62] is oval, showing a blackamoor's head turned to the left, filleted, the neck encircled by a lace collar, with the inscription in Roman SIGILLUM PREPOSITI ET COMVNI BURGI DE LANG. ESTO. The silver matrix survives among the borough records and is 1⅜ in. in diameter.[63] It may date from 1646 when a new seal was purchased.[64]

At least three impressions of a seal used by the portreeve survive, attached to leases dated between 1750 and 1773.[65] They bear the inscription in Roman LANGPORT EASTOVER above a portcullis. The seal is circular, ⅜ in.

The 1616 charter provided that the sergeant-at-mace should bear a gold or silver mace engraved with the royal arms.[66] A mace preserved at the town hall comprises a head 4 in. long and a staff of 14 in., both of silver gilt. The head, crowned by a ring of alternate fleurs de lis and crosses, is divided into four compartments each bearing a crown and the royal monogram 'C.R.', surmounting the rose, thistle, harp, and fleur de lis. The staff bears the repeated device of the portcullis and on the foot the bust of a crowned figure. The head presumably dates from 1625–49. In 1658–9 £7 10s. was expended on the mace when it was sent to London.[67] The expenditure may indicate the renewal of the staff.

CHURCH. The chapel (later church) of Langport is first mentioned in 1318.[68] The carved lintel

[33] Ibid. 12; local information.
[34] S.R.O., D/B/la 8.
[35] Ibid. 12.
[36] Ibid. 8.
[37] Ibid. 9.
[38] Ibid. 63.
[39] Local information.
[40] Par. rec., chwdns.' accts. 1753–79.
[41] Ibid. 1779–1842.
[42] Par. rec., vestry mins. 1820–49.
[43] S.R.O., D/B/la 8.
[44] Par. rec., chwdns.' accts. 1842–76.
[45] S.R.O., D/B/la 9, 18 Aug. 1877.
[46] Par. cncl. Town Trust mins. 1920–59.
[47] Par. rec., vestry mins. 1820–49, 1849–1928.
[48] S.R.O., D/B/la 37.
[49] Par. rec., chwdns.' accts. 1753–79.
[50] S.R.O., D/B/la 6, 49 (leases, 20 May 1760, 14 Apr. 1761); Ross, Langport and its Ch. 362.
[51] S.R.O., D/B/la 7.
[52] Ibid. 40.

[53] Ibid. 7, 6 Jan. 1821.
[54] Par. rec., vestry mins. 1820–49.
[55] Poor Law Com. 2nd Rep. p. 548; par. rec., vestry mins. 1820–49.
[56] Par. rec., vestry mins. 1820–49; S.R.O., D/PS/ilm. box 16, order for sale, 17 Nov. 1837.
[57] Collinson, Hist. Som. iii. 132. He inspected 'ancient seals' and a 'town piece'.
[58] Ross, Langport and its Ch. 265.
[59] Token in Somerset County Museum.
[60] E 134/42 & 43 Eliz. I/Mich. 27.
[61] S.R.O., D/B/la 1.
[62] Ibid. 49, lease, 2 May 1682.
[63] Ibid. 2.
[64] Ibid. 81.
[65] Ibid. 49, leases, 28 Feb. 1749/50, 31 Oct. 1763, 1 Nov. 1773.
[66] Ibid. 1.   [67] Ibid. 81.
[68] Cal. Chanc. Wts. i. 492. A reference to a vicar of Langport in 1302 (S.R.S. vii. 167) is almost certainly a scribal error.

HUISH EPISCOPI: LANGPORT WEST RAILWAY STATION, 1894

LONG SUTTON: FRIENDLY SOCIETY WALK AT KNOLE, *c.* 1912

Muchelney: Priest's House

Aller: Old Rectory

Pitney: former rectory-house

Thorn Coffin: former rectory-house

PARSONAGE HOUSES

above the south doorway probably dates from the 12th century,[69] and may have formed part of an earlier church on this site. The existence of a deputy archdeacon of Langport in 1208 may suggest the foundation of a church before that date.[70] From 1381, and probably from its foundation, Langport formed a chapelry annexed to Huish Episcopi,[71] and continued as such until it became a separate ecclesiastical parish from 1882.[72] The first vicar was instituted in 1883,[73] and the living was united with the rectory of Aller in 1970.[74] The archdeacon of Wells has held the patronage since 1876.[75]

As a dependent chapelry Langport had no endowments and was served by parochial chaplains or assistant curates at least from the 15th century.[76] By 1648 and until 1660 the corporation regularly paid for lectures in the parish church, entertained the ministers who attended, and from 1710 paid for an annual sermon on All Saints Day, when the portreeve was chosen.[77] It was not until 1842 that an endowment fund was established to pay a lecturer for a sermon on a week-day.[78] A capital sum was evidently then employed in the purchase of lands which produced a gross rent of £122 a year in 1907. The lands were administered by trustees of the vicarage endowment charity until their sale for £4,140 in 1919. The investment of this sum then produced £235 a year.[79] The management of this charity was transferred to the Ecclesiastical Commissioners in 1925.[80] The benefice itself was endowed out of the common fund with £230 a year in 1883.[81]

The lands which produced the income for the Langport endowment fund, acquired in 1842, comprised 11 a. in Stoke St. Gregory, 10 a. in Aller, and (in 1868) 23 a. in Chilton Trinity.[82] These were all sold in 1919.[83]

In 1883 £1,500 was given from the common fund to purchase a parsonage house on the east side of North Street near the present Post Office, known as Victoria House in 1972.[84] This property was sold in 1920 and the present vicarage house, known as the Rectory since the benefice was united with Aller, was acquired.[85] It lies on the north side of the Hill, west of the Hanging Chapel, and is a large 19th-century brick house.

The vicars of Huish Episcopi were frequently referred to as vicars of Langport.[86] Assistant curates in the earlier 19th century appear to have been graduates,[87] but there was no curate in 1870.[88] Of those who have served the church since 1883, David Melville Ross (vicar 1896–1919) published an extensive history of Langport.[89]

In 1412 an interdict placed on the churches of Langport, Huish, and Aller, with others, for permitting unlicensed Lollards to preach, was lifted.[90] The churchyard was polluted by bloodshed in 1415 and had to be reconsecrated.[91] Lollardy continued to flourish in the parish during the 15th century. Bishop Bekynton complained in 1447 to Edmund, duke of Somerset, then lord of the manor, that the duke's tenants had forsaken the church, buried their own dead, and prevented their curate and other clergy from saying divine service and administering the sacraments.[92] In 1547 the church lacked a bible.[93] The church organs were mended at a cost of 3s. in 1581,[94] and it was stated in 1600 that there had formerly been 'salary or wages limited and appointed for organ players and singing men in the parish church' paid by the portreeve, but the origin of the grant was not known.[95] The corporation publicly attended church on Sundays from 1670.[96] In 1851 there was only a morning service on Census Sunday, attended by a congregation of 350. There were then 800 sittings, of which 200 were free.[97] A Sunday evening lecture had been established by 1855[98] and was still being given in 1870.[99] In the latter year services were held alternately, morning and afternoon, and Holy Communion was celebrated about five times annually.[1]

A church house existed in 1577 when the churchwardens received £4 from a church ale held there.[2] It had a buttery attached by 1592.[3] The court leet and hundred courts were stated c. 1600 to have been anciently kept 'in a great house called the church house', although the portreeve and commonalty had then forbidden the farmer of the borough to use it for that purpose.[4] It was leased from the corporation in 1646,[5] but in 1661 its kitchen was out of repair.[6] The thatching was replaced in 1701–2 and the house is last mentioned in the portreeve's accounts for 1727.[7] The property may be represented by the Great House, occupied by George Sawtle in 1655[8] and described in 1802 as 'some time since demolished'.[9] The house stood probably on the south side of the Hill between the old grammar school and the turning into Whatley Lane.[10]

[69] See below.
[70] *Mem. R.* 1208 (P.R.S. n.s. xxxi), 44.
[71] *Cal. Pat.* 1377–81, 614.
[72] *Lond. Gaz.* 4 Apr. 1876, p. 2272.
[73] Ross, *Langport and its Ch.* 194, 197.
[74] *Dioc. Dir.* (1971).
[75] *Crockford*; see above, p. 9.
[76] *S.R.S.* xlix. 137, 396; l. 456; S.R.O., D/D/Vc 20; D/D/Rr 242; D/D/Bo; par. rec., par. reg. *passim*.
[77] S.R.O., D/B/la 5, 11, 81.
[78] Ross, *Langport and its Ch.* 364.
[79] Par. rec., Vicar's Stipend Charity, mins. 1907–19.
[80] Char. Com. files.
[81] *Lond. Gaz.* 1 June 1883, p. 2868.
[82] Ross, *Langport and its Ch.* 364; par. rec., Vicar's Stipend Charity, mins. 1907–19, misc. notes.
[83] See above.
[84] *Lond. Gaz.* 1 June 1883, p. 2868; O.S. Map 6″, Som. LXXII. NE. (1886 edn.).
[85] Ex inf. the rector, the Revd. W. E. L. Houlden. Until 1920 it was known as Magnolia House.
[86] e.g. *Cal. Pat.* 1385–9, 540; *S.R.S.* xvi. 123.
[87] Par. rec., par. reg. 1728–1812, notes at end of vol.
[88] S.R.O., D/D/V rtns. 1870.
[89] Ross, *Langport and its Ch.* (1911).
[90] *S.R.S.* xxix. 115–16.
[91] Ibid. 217.
[92] *Corresp. Thomas Bekynton* (Rolls Ser.), ii. 340–1.
[93] S.R.O., D/D/Ca 17, p. 57.
[94] S.R.O., D/P/la.
[95] E 134/42 & 43 Eliz. I/Mich. 27.
[96] S.R.O., D/B/la 5.
[97] H.O. 129/317/2/5/15.
[98] Par. rec., vestry mins. 1849–1928.
[99] S.R.O., D/D/V rtns. 1870.
[1] Ibid.
[2] S.R.O., D/P/la.
[3] Ibid.
[4] S.R.O., DD/SE 18/5; E 134/42 & 43 Eliz. I/Mich. 27.
[5] S.R.O., D/B/la 81.
[6] Ibid. 5.
[7] Ibid. 12.
[8] S.R.O., DD/SAS C/82, 27.
[9] S.R.O., DD/LC, conveyance, Gilbert & Gillett to Warren, 24 Mar. 1802.
[10] Ibid.; S.R.O., D/B/la 8, 41, 46.

All Saints church room, on the west side of North Street, was erected by subscription in 1892 for the Sunday school and other parish purposes.[11] It is a plain lias structure with a bellcot at its eastern gable end.

A chantry of the Holy Cross in the parish church is mentioned in 1349, when it was endowed with 2s. from lands in Long Sutton.[12]

A chaplain mentioned in 1450 served St. Catherine's chantry in 1463.[13] This chantry was probably in the parish church and its chaplain may be identified with one of two 'fraternity' priests paid by the corporation until 1548.[14]

In 1499 John Heyron (d. 1501) secured a licence to found a chantry of the Blessed Virgin Mary in the parish church.[15] By his will he ordered his son John to fulfil his intentions. The priest was to pray for Heyron's parents, wife, and other named persons, to say a *placebo* and dirge with a requiem mass every Wednesday and Friday, and to turn his back to the altar at the ablutions.[16] The testator's son died in 1507 before the chantry had been founded,[17] but it was subsequently established in the south chapel of the parish church.[18] The endowment comprised lands in a number of parishes valued at £7 2s. 1d. in 1548, including a plot of land in Langport 'on which the dwelling house of the cantarist of the said chantry was built'.[19] At its suppression in 1548 the chantry had a silver chalice of 12 oz. and ornaments worth 5s. The priest at that date, John Benet, was a former monk of Glastonbury.[20] The chantry and its lands were granted to Laurence Hyde of London in 1549.[21]

John Witcombe of Martock (d. 1527) by his will devised lands in Langport Eastover and Langport Westover to establish an obit in the parish church for the souls of himself and others, from which 6s. 8d. was to be paid for food and drink for celebrants, and a similar amount to be distributed in bread to the poor.[22]

The church of *ALL SAINTS*[23] lies on the summit of Langport hill on the south side of the road. A move to divert the road in 1318 so that the church could be lengthened or enlarged does not seem to have been carried through.[24] The church is built of lias with Ham stone dressings and has a chancel with north and south chapels and east vestry, aisled and clerestoried nave with south chapel and porch, and west tower, nearly all in the late Perpendicular style. A north porch was mentioned in 1579.[25] Reset above the south doorway is a 12th-century lintel carved with the Lamb of God flanked by angels and figures,[26] which is presumed to have been preserved from an earlier

church on the site. The west wall of the north aisle is the oldest surviving part of the building apparently *in situ*. It contains the base of the reveals of a 13th-century window. The openings of the windows in the north wall of the aisle are probably 14th century and are evidence for the existence by that time of a church with a nave as long as that which exists today (67 ft.). All other traces of this early church were destroyed in the course of the major rebuilding which took place in the late 15th and early 16th century. This began at the north aisle, where new tracery was inserted into the windows and there was a new arcade, progressed to the nave, tower, and south aisle and porch, then the south chapel, the chancel arch, the chancel and vestry, and the north and south chancel chapels. The structural evidence suggests that the building was not conceived as a whole but grew in scale as the work proceeded, and that the total time for construction was quite long, probably more than fifty years. It is known that John Heyron (d. 1501) erected the south chapel and it appears likely that he also built the chancel. In 1633 his arms were to be seen on 'almost . . . all the pillars' in the church.[27] A Heyron tomb, stripped of its brass, stood in the south chapel in 1785,[28] but was removed shortly before 1823.[29] The marble slab from this tomb served as a table top in the vestry in 1972.

In 1822 the vestry, which was ruinous in 1785,[30] was repaired. The whole church was reseated and upper and lower galleries were put into the west end in 1825. Eight years later the top stage of the tower and the stair turret were rebuilt,[31] but the portcullis motif on the battlements, later adopted as the badge of the town, appears on an illustration before that date.[32] It has been suggested that this refers to Margaret Beaufort, lady of the manor, who may have rebuilt the tower,[33] but the badge was also used by her son Henry VII and grandson Henry VIII, and was possibly a loyal allusion to the monarch. The nave roof was destroyed by fire in 1845 and during the repairs part of the chancel arch was rebuilt.[34] The fire may also have destroyed the galleries and the new seating in the nave. The restoration of the chancel, under the direction of W. B. Paul, took place in 1867.[35] Ten years later the rest of the church was restored and in the course of the work the 15th-century rood-stair was uncovered in the north aisle, and the north doorway, still visible from outside, was blocked.[36] The reredos and sedilia were put into the chancel in 1887.[37]

The octagonal font is late-15th-century. All the 15th- and early-16th-century glass remaining in the church was restored and collected into the

---

[11] Par. rec., vestry mins. 1849–1928.
[12] Ross, *Langport and its Ch.* 187.
[13] *S.R.S.* xlix. 137; l. 465.
[14] Ibid. ii. 115.
[15] *Cal. Pat.* 1494–1509, 172; *Cal. Inq. p.m. Hen. VII,* iii, pp. 446–7.
[16] *Proc. Som. Arch. Soc.* xl. 71–3.
[17] Ibid. 74; C 142/25/42.
[18] Collinson, *Hist. Som.* iii. 133.
[19] *S.R.S.* ii. 299–302.
[20] Ibid. 115.
[21] *Cal. Pat.* 1548–9, 288.
[22] *S.R.S.* xix. 262–6.
[23] The dedication was mentioned in 1349: Ross, *Langport and its Ch.* 187.
[24] *Cal. Chanc. Wts.* i. 492.
[25] S.R.O., D/P/la.

[26] Illustrated in Pevsner, *South and West Som.* pl. 7.
[27] *S.R.S.* xv. 132.
[28] Collinson, *Hist. Som.* iii. 133.
[29] Par. rec., vestry mins. 1820–49.
[30] Collinson, *Hist. Som.* iii. 133.
[31] Par. rec., vestry mins. 1820–49.
[32] Taunton Castle, Pigott Colln., water-colour drawing by John Buckler, 1830.
[33] Ross, *Langport and its Ch.* 230; W. E. L. Houlden, *Story of All Saints Church* (n.d.), 5–6.
[34] Par. rec., vestry mins. 1820–49.
[35] Ibid. 1849–1928. Persistent efforts to force the rector of Huish, the archdeacon of Wells, to repair the chancel between 1846 and 1857 and again in 1884–5 were unsuccessful (vestry mins. 1820–49, 1849–1928).
[36] Ross, *Langport and its Ch.* 365.
[37] Par. rec., vestry mins. 1849–1928.

east window in 1867.[38] The pulpit is late-17th- or early-18th-century. Five of the six bells were cast by Thomas Bailey of Bridgwater in 1772; the sixth was added in 1897.[39] The plate includes a large cup and cover by R. Orange of Sherborne, dated 1574, and a large pewter flagon. A modern set of plate was given to the church by Vincent Stuckey in 1839.[40] The registers are complete from 1728.[41]

A chantry of the Blessed Virgin Mary is first mentioned in 1344, when 9s. 8d. a year was paid to it from the farm of the windmill.[42] This sum was

VI's time by the vicar of Huish.[50] The building, described as the 'Hawninge' Chapel, was granted in 1575 to John Herbert and Andrew Palmer,[51] and was subsequently used as the town hall between 1596 and 1600.[52] It was later occupied by Langport grammar school, probably from 1706 until c. 1790,[53] after which it was leased to private individuals.[54] Arms were stored there by the local militia between 1809 and 1816, it was devoted to a Sunday school from 1818 to 1827, and was again leased privately thereafter.[55] In 1834 it was let to Edward Quekett as a museum for stuffed birds and miscellaneous

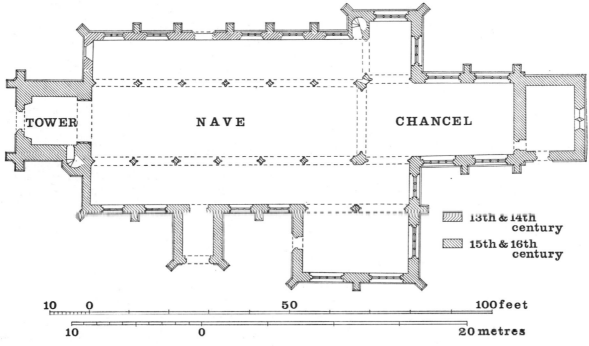

| | 13th & 14th century |
| | 15th & 16th century |

10   0   50   100 feet

10   0   20 metres

THE CHURCH OF ALL SAINTS, LANGPORT

evidently lost after the mill blew down in 1362.[43] In 1374–5 7s. 8d. was paid to the chantry from the rent of a tenement in Langport Westover,[44] and in 1376 a tenement with a curtilage called 'Seyntmariehey', left to the chantry without licence and worth 12s. 6d. a year, was seized by the lord of the manor.[45] Two market stalls late held by the proctor of this chantry are mentioned between 1405 and 1410.[46] The chaplain may be identified with one of two chantry priests mentioned in 1450[47] and 1532,[48] described as 'fraternity' priests receiving £5 6s. 8d. each from the commonalty until 1548.[49] The chantry was located in the Hanging Chapel. A man deposed in 1600 that he had known Latin service said in the chapel in Henry VIII's time and mass said there in Rogation week until Edward

antiquities until 1875.[56] It was first leased to the Portcullis Lodge of Freemasons, the present occupiers, in 1891.[57]

The Hanging Chapel stands at the eastern end of the borough above a gateway with a pointed barrel roof, both of lias stone, and the present building probably dates from the 15th century. There is a small niche in the north wall of the tunnel and a blocked pointed window in the south wall. An external western stair gives access to the chapel by a west door. The chapel itself is a plain rectangular structure with tiled roof, lit by a three-light east window and two north and one south windows of two lights each, all moulded with traceried heads. The east window appears to have been given a debased round arch at a later date. A central southern

[38] Ibid.; Collinson, *Hist. Som.* iii. 133.
[39] Ross, *Langport and its Ch.* 367.
[40] *Proc. Som. Arch. Soc.* xlv. 133.
[41] Par. rec., par. regs.
[42] B.M. Add. Ch. 16127; see above, p. 26.
[43] Devon R.O. 1142 B/M 30.
[44] Ibid. M 34.
[45] Ibid. M 35.
[46] Ibid. M 38–40.
[47] *S.R.S.* xlix. 137.
[48] S.R.O., D/D/Vc 20.

[49] *S.R.S.* ii. 115. Ross's description of the building as a guild chapel (Ross, *Langport and its Ch.* 189–91) rests solely on the reference to fraternity priests.
[50] E 134/42 & 43 Eliz. I/Mich. 27.
[51] C 66/1125/3.
[52] S.R.O., D/B/la 6; E 134/42 & 43 Eliz. I/Mich. 27; E 134/43 Eliz. I/East. 16.
[53] Ross, *Langport and its Ch.* 329–30.
[54] S.R.O., D/B/la 7.
[55] Ibid. 7, 47.
[56] Ibid. 7, 9.   [57] Ibid. 94.

doorway gives access to a room on the south side of the chapel at a lower level, added later, probably when the grammar school was housed there. A third doorway at the south-western corner of the chapel has been blocked. There is a simple niche at floor level towards the east end of the south wall.

ROMAN CATHOLICISM. In 1903 a group of sisters, members of the Order of Christian Instruction, came to Langport to escape political pressures in France. They settled at Hill House, acquired from the daughter of Vincent Stuckey (d. 1902) and renamed St. Gildas Convent, converting the billiard room, later the library, into a chapel. St. Gildas Convent school for girls was founded there in 1914.[58] The church of *ST. JOSEPH*, adjoining the convent on the east, was built in 1929. It is a plain rectangular structure with a low pitched roof. A semi-circular sanctuary, rising above the body of the church to form a tower, was added in 1965. A chaplain serving both the sisters and the church has been resident at the convent since its inception.[59]

PROTESTANT NONCONFORMITY. John Bush (d. 1712), minister in the parish during the Interregnum, subsequently became a Presbyterian preacher in the town.[60] He was licensed to preach in 1672[61] and his house was registered for dissenting worship in 1691.[62] He received a grant from the Common Fund between 1699 and 1706 and was described as 'the most faithful friend, and most desirable enemy that a man could well have'.[63] The house of his son Thomas was licensed for protestant meetings in 1731.[64]

In 1672 the houses of Richard Bennet and Richard Seward were licensed by dissenters.[65] Further licences for worship in private houses in the town were issued in 1689, 1696, 1716, and 1731, the last being in respect of the house of George Stuckey (II), father of the founder of Stuckey's Bank.[66] The house of Edith Bedell was licensed for Quaker meetings in 1731.[67]

Thomas Bagehot was trained in the nonconformist ministry and is supposed to have established a Socinian chapel in North Street at some date after 1747, attended by many of the borough's leading inhabitants.[68] The site was stated c. 1860 to have been occupied by cottages for many years,[69] and the chapel may possibly be identified with the house

in that street occupied by Mary Bobbett and licensed for worship in 1818.[70]

The Independents rented premises known as Parks's Buildings in 1807,[71] but their efforts within the town initially met with little success. The Revd. Mr. Prankerd of Somerton preached in the town hall at some date before 1821 and subsequently leased a slaughter-house for his meetings.[72] James Moreton, Independent minister of Kingsdon, registered a house in the parish in 1824, and in 1828 instigated the building of the present chapel on the north side of Bow Street, opened the following year.[73] The site was bought from Vincent Stuckey, who wished to prevent the Independents from building in Priest Lane near his home.[74] The Independent (later Congregational) chapel was originally a plain rectangular building, the façade comprising a pediment with date stone, and three round-headed upper, and two lower, windows.[75] On Census Sunday in 1851 the services were attended by 63 persons in the morning and 166 in the evening.[76] The building was restored and largely rebuilt in 1874–5 and an internal gallery removed.[77] The present building is of lias and has a brick and stone front in gothic revival style. The manse abutting on the east wall of the chapel, was built in 1850, a vestry was erected in 1858, and a schoolroom, added at the rear of the chapel in 1874, was enlarged in 1885.[78] The Independents used another building in the town for worship in 1837[79] but its site has not been identified.

The Christian Brethren occupied a room over a warehouse in Bow Street in 1845, holding about 200 people.[80] Their congregation in 1851 totalled 40 in the morning and 45 in the evening.[81] After meeting in a number of houses in the town, they moved c. 1943 to the former Wesleyan chapel in Huish, now known as the Gospel Hall.[82]

The Particular Baptists registered a house in the parish in 1847[83] and erected a chapel on the south side of the Hill in 1851,[84] which still survived in 1972. In 1851 there was an attendance of 29 in the morning, 34 in the afternoon, and 60 in the evening.[85] It was known as Zion Chapel in 1880, and in 1912, when there had been no service for ten years or more, it was sold. It was used by Langport grammar school from 1928 to 1933, when it was known as the Stone Building,[86] and it had been converted to a private garage by 1972. It is a plain rectangular building of lias with Classical façade.

Jehovah's Witnesses met in the Reading Room from 1968[87] and established 'Kingdom Hall' in Beard's Yard, off Bow Street, in 1970.[88]

[58] See p. 37. The former home of the first sisters was St. Gildas des Bois, Loire Inférieure, France, after which the convent was named.
[59] Ex inf. Sister Marie, St. Gildas Convent; conveyance of Hill House, 17 Oct. 1903, *penes* St. Gildas Convent.
[60] *Calamy Revised*, ed. A. G. Matthews; also see above, p. 30. [61] *Cal. S.P. Dom.* 1672, 237, 575.
[62] S.R.O., Q/RR, meeting-house lics.
[63] *Calamy Revised*, ed. Matthews.
[64] S.R.O., Q/RR, meeting-house lics.
[65] *Cal. S.P. Dom.* 1672, 579.
[66] S.R.O., Q/RR, meeting-house lics.; M. Churchman, 'The Stuckeys of Somerset' (T.S. in S.R.O., DD/X/CU), 7, 12.
[67] S.R.O., Q/RR, meeting-house lics.
[68] Ross, *Langport and its Ch.* 346–7, 356.
[69] J. Moreton, *Home Missionary Memorials* (n.d.) (MS. transcript *penes* Mr. W. B. Denman).

[70] S.R.O., D/D/Rm, box 2.   [71] Ibid.
[72] Moreton, op. cit.
[73] Ibid.; S.R.O., D/D/Rm, boxes 2, 6.
[74] Moreton, op cit.
[75] Photographs *penes* Mr. W. B. Denman.
[76] H.O. 129/317/2/5/16.
[77] Ex inf. Mr. W. B. Denman.
[78] Ibid.; *Rep. Som. Cong. Union* (1896).
[79] S.R.O., D/D/Rm, vol. 2.
[80] Ibid.; H.O. 129/317/2/5/17.
[81] H.O. 129/317/2/5/17.
[82] Local information.
[83] S.R.O., D/D/Rm, vol. 2; H.O. 129/317/2/5/18.
[84] H.O. 129/317/2/5/18.   [85] Ibid.
[86] Deeds of former Baptist chapel, *penes* Dr. P. W. Henderson, Virginia House, Langport.
[87] Par. cncl. mins. 1964–9.
[88] Local information.

EDUCATION. Nicholas Hurtnell was licensed to teach Latin in the town in 1604.[89] After John Bush had been ejected from his situation as curate of Langport c. 1662 he kept a grammar school in the borough.[90] There is, however, no positive evidence that this was Langport grammar school.[91] Sarah Hurtnell, who died in 1840 aged 90, had formerly kept a dame school at which Vincent Stuckey (b. 1771) was first educated.[92] In about 1793 there was a girls' boarding school in the town run by Elizabeth and Ann Lake.[93] A Sunday school, mentioned from 1792,[94] was attended in 1818 by about 80 children[95] and was held in the Hanging Chapel from that year until 1827.[96] In 1818 there were two day-schools,[97] probably private. The National school, founded in 1827, like its successor, the Board school of 1876 in North Street, lay in Huish parish.[98]

An infant school was founded in 1830 in a house on the south side of Bow Street towards its west end.[99] In 1833 it had 70 pupils paying 2d. a week each and was aided by private subscription.[1] The school is mentioned in 1875[2] but was probably closed in the following year when the Board school, which included an infant department, was built.[3] The building, a rectangular lias structure of two storeys with Ham stone mullioned windows, was occupied as three private dwellings in 1972.

A Sunday school was established in 1832 at the Congregational chapel in Bow Street, attended by 90 pupils in 1833.[4] A day-school in the vestry there had been established by c. 1860.[5]

In 1833 there were three private boarding schools in the parish educating 34 children.[6] By 1859 this number had increased to four, comprising a preparatory school and three girls' schools, and the master of the grammar school was also taking private pupils.[7] Demand for private education in the town declined thereafter; there was one day-school, in Bow Street, in 1886, and a girls' school there in 1899.[8]

St. Gildas Convent school for girls was established in 1914 by nuns of the Order of Christian Instruction.[9] Part of the stable block at the Convent was converted c. 1920 to form two additional classrooms, and in 1931 the school was attended by 66 pupils, of which only six were drawn from Langport itself.[10] Two further classrooms were erected at the rear of the house in 1958 and a laboratory and art room added there in the following year. Three classrooms were built on the north side of the stables in 1965, a swimming pool in 1968, and a home economics building in 1969. The school had about 200 pupils in 1972 and was divided into senior, junior, and infant departments.[11]

CHARITIES FOR THE POOR. Matthew Jefford of Langport Westover by will dated 1578 gave £20 to the borough of Langport Eastover for interest free loans to poor persons, repayable yearly.[12] Traces of this charity may survive in the loan of £5 in 1674 to a man to set up his looms for coverlet weaving, £10 to the sergeant-at-mace in 1677,[13] £1 to a man to build a boat in 1700,[14] and £12 to a blacksmith in 1721.[15] No subsequent reference to this charity has been noted.

Martha Bond of Langport by will dated 1797 left the residue of her estate to be divided equally between the parishes of Langport Eastover, Aller, and Huish Episcopi, the income to be distributed to the poor.[16] The proceeds were initially employed in defraying the cost of the inclosure of Common moor.[17] The share of each parish, £141 19s. 1d., produced an income of £7 15s.,[18] which in 1821 was distributed amongst the second poor.[19] In 1954 the income of £6 9s. 4d. was divided between 26 persons in varying amounts.[20]

John Prankerd, a Langport surgeon (d. 1896),[21] devised a capital sum the interest from which was distributed to the poor in coal. The income was £4 9s. in 1954, and was employed according to the donor's wishes.[22]

In 1915 William Gough, formerly manager of Stuckey's Bank, left £300, the income to be distributed annually at Christmas to the deserving poor. By will proved in 1926 William Rowe bequeathed £200 to the vicar and churchwardens, who were to devote the interest to buy coal and other material benefits to be given to the aged and other deserving poor of the parish on 26 March annually.[23] The Gough and Rowe charities were subsequently united, and in 1954 the income stood at £16 1s. 2d., distributed to 32 persons.[24]

The Annie Tite charity was founded by Charles Tite of Taunton (d. 1933),[25] who left £2,000 to the Langport town trust in memory of his first wife, Hannah Sophia (d. 1879), a native of the borough. The interest was to be divided between members of his family during their lives and thereafter applied in assisting the higher education of Langport children, in granting marriage portions to young girls, and in augmenting the income of poor or

---

[89] S.R.O., D/D/Vc 68.
[90] Calamy Revised, ed. Matthews, 92.
[91] For the grammar school see V.C.H. Som. ii. 456–7.
[92] Par. rec., par. reg., burials 1813–60.
[93] Univ. Brit. Dir. iii.
[94] S.R.O., D/B/la 12.
[95] Digest of Returns to Sel. Cttee. on Educ. of Poor, H.C. 224 (1819), ix (2).
[96] S.R.O., D/B/la 7, 47.
[97] Digest of Returns to Sel. Cttee. on Educ. of Poor, H.C. 224 (1819), ix (2).
[98] See p. 12.
[99] Educ. Enquiry Abstract, H.C. 62 (1835), xlii; S.R.O., tithe award.
[1] Educ. Enquiry Abstract, H.C. 62 (1835), xlii.
[2] S.R.O., D/B/la 9.
[3] See p. 12.
[4] Educ. Enquiry Abstract, H.C. 62 (1835), xlii.
[5] W. B. Denman, 'Hist. of Congregationalism in Langport' (TS. penes the author, Taunton), ii. 22.

[6] Educ. Enquiry Abstract, H.C. 62 (1835), xlii.
[7] Harrison, Harrod, & Co., Dir. Som. (1859).
[8] P.O. Dir. Som. (1866); Kelly's Dir. Som. (1899).
[9] Ex inf. Sister Marie, St. Gildas Convent; see p. 36.
[10] S.R.O., C/E 60.
[11] Ex inf. Sister Marie.
[12] Ross, Langport and its Ch. 270.
[13] S.R.O., D/B/la 6.
[14] Ibid. 5.
[15] Ibid. 6.
[16] 11th Rep. Com. Char. 440–1.
[17] S.R.O., D/B/la 26; see p. 25.
[18] 11th Rep. Com. Char. 440–1.
[19] Par. rec., vestry mins. 1820–49.
[20] Char. Com. files.
[21] M.I. in churchyard.
[22] Char. Com. files.
[23] Par. rec., vestry mins. 1849–1928.
[24] Char. Com. files.
[25] Proc. Som. Arch. Soc. lxxix. 120–2.

retired tradesmen of the town.[26] The charity, administered by the parish council, became payable in 1967 under a Scheme of that year.[27] The income has been used principally to provide marriage portions of about £10 each,[28] the charity's investments producing about £93 in 1968.[29] In recent years it has been difficult to find qualified recipients for the charity.

MUCHELNEY

THE parish of Muchelney, lying on loam above clay and gravel between the converging rivers Yeo and Parrett, 1½ mile SSE. of Langport, is just over 2 miles from north to south and 1¾ mile from east to west, and measured 1,591 a. in 1901.[1] The extreme north-western boundary falls short of the confluence of the two rivers, but follows an irregular watercourse known in the Middle Ages as Horsies Pyll and Oldryver,[2] evidently the original line of one of the two rivers which later changed its course in time of flood. Part of the southern boundary of the parish also follows a stream known as Oldriver brook,[3] indicating a change in the course of the Parrett.

Much of the land between the Yeo and the Parrett, constituting the extreme north-western part of the Saxon royal estate of Martock,[4] lies below the 25 ft. contour. Settlements developed on some of the 'islands' of slightly higher ground rising from the marsh, three of which, Muchelney (Great Island), Midelney, and Thorney, were named by the 11th century.[5] Midelney later became part of Drayton parish, itself once a dependency of Muchelney,[6] though in 1569 the churchwardens of Muchelney still claimed that its people should not attend Drayton church.[7] Horsey, in the north of the parish, was a medieval farm site,[8] but other 'islands' including Nidney or Netney (Litney or Littleney in the later Middle Ages)[9] and Ilsey,[10] both in Thorney moor, and the Down,[11] north-east of the church, were cultivated but not occupied. Only in times of flood were all these 'islands' apparent, but flooding was frequent and Muchelney itself was often known as an island rather than as a parish until the 17th century.[12]

Permanent settlement probably resulted from the foundation of the abbey early in the 8th century.[13] The position of Muchelney, Thorney, and Ham, and of the site of the abbey was governed by their relative immunity from flooding. The abbey complex included in the 16th century not only the abbey church and claustral buildings but also the demesne farm barton, the almonry,[14] the parish church and vicarage, and the 15th-century cross.[15] This group lay in some isolation, which may explain why the church house, normally near the parish church, stood further to the south, in Lower Muchelney,[16] more accessible to the rest of the parish.

Before turnpike extensions in 1829–30 created the direct road link between Muchelney and Huish Episcopi, the main routes from Lower Muchelney ran as now south and south-east to Thorney and to Ham.[17] A third route ran due west, past the Court House and over the Parrett by Bage bridge, known as Bougkebrygge in 1474, Banckbridge in 1553, and Barge bridge in 1667.[18] In 1768 this was a wooden structure of three arches,[19] and the route was still used in 1842.[20] The bridge was replaced by Westover bridge, formerly known as Muchelney Ford bridge or Muchelney bridge, on the line of the present Drayton road. It was built in 1840 on the site of Muchelney ford by the Parrett Navigation Company, and was probably of stone and timber.[21] It was rebuilt c. 1882, and was replaced by the present bridge in 1948–9.[22] The turnpike road which joined Huish with Muchelney was built in 1829–30, and its route continued through Thorney to Kingsbury Episcopi.[23] It formed an extension to the roads of the Langport, Somerton, and Castle Cary Trust.[24] The new road in the north replaced a grass track known as Langport Wall.[25] A single-storeyed brick toll-house was still standing in 1971 where the new road entered the village.[26] The only cart route northwards was along Horsey Lane, known in the 18th century as Chambers's drove, which skirted the southern and eastern edges of Muchelney Level and crossed the Yeo at Pibsbury ford.[27]

Droves and lanes serving the open fields and 'moors' included Strap drove and New Mead drove, south-east of Ham, in existence by 1239 when an earlier agreement was confirmed which

[26] S.R.O., D/B/la 22; M.I. to Annie Tite in churchyard.
[27] Char. Com. files.
[28] Par. cncl. Town Trust mins. 1920–59.
[29] Ex inf. Mr. S. H. Bennett.
[1] V.C.H. Som. ii. 348. This article was completed in 1970.
[2] See p. 1.
[3] O.S. Map 6″, Som. LXXII. SE. (1886 edn.).
[4] See p. 255.
[5] V.C.H. Som. i. 468.
[6] Cal. Papal Regs. v. 300; see below, p. 47.
[7] S.R.O., D/D/Ca 40.   [8] S.R.S. iii. 254.
[9] V.C.H. Som. i. 468; S.R.O., DD/PR 78, map 1768; tithe award; DD/AB 4; DD/PH 156, survey 1553.
[10] S.R.O., DD/AB 5.
[11] S.R.O., DD/PH 156.
[12] Rot. de Ob. et Fin. (Rec. Com.), 202; S.R.S. iii. 254–5; xiv. 93; xxiii. 381; Feud. Aids, vi. 507; Cal. Pat. 1558–60, 218; Longleat House, Entry Bk. of Henry Gold, 1629–30.

[13] S.R.S. xiv. 4; V.C.H. Som. ii. 103–4; Jnl. Royal Arch. Inst. cvii. 120. Roman fragments were found in 1889: H. M. Page, Muchelney Abbey and Church, 6.
[14] S.R.O., DD/PH 156; see below, p. 49.
[15] The cross was moved in 1829–30: S.R.O., DD/X/EE (N/137).
[16] See p. 48.
[17] S.R.O., DD/AB 5.
[18] Ibid. 6; DD/PH 156; S.R.S. xxxiv. 31.
[19] S.R.O., DD/PR 78.
[20] S.R.O., tithe award.
[21] Somerset River Authority, Bridgwater, General Cttee. Mins. 1837–78; plan and estimate, 1839; ex inf. Messrs. E. L. Kelting and G. Thomson.
[22] Ex inf. Mr. G. Thomson.
[23] S.R.O., DD/X/EE (N/137).
[24] S.R.O., D/T/lsc 2; Q/R, deposited plan 73.
[25] S.R.O., DD/PR 78.
[26] See plate facing p. 65.
[27] S.R.O., DD/PR 78.

allowed corn to be transported from Stapleton in Martock parish to Muchelney abbey.[28] Others, such as Bethune's drove which gave access to parts of Thorney moor, probably disappeared after inclosure in 1826.[29] Another route went through the farmyard of Abbey farm south-west to join the road to Bage bridge. It served Gally farm, and both buildings and lane had virtually disappeared by 1886.[30]

There was a coal yard on the bank of the Parrett at Thorney by 1841–2.[31] Also at Thorney was a halt

the south side of the Muchelney–Ham road.[35] The fourth field in the medieval arable complex was North field. Its exact position is not clear, but it was probably north of Ham, between Eastmoor and Whetmoor. The name was still retained in 1723.[36] South field and Seven Acres were created after the surrender of the abbey in 1538. Part of the former was still in strips in 1842; the latter was partially inclosed shortly before 1741.[37]

Common pastures and meadows occupied the surrounding levels. To the north was Muchelney

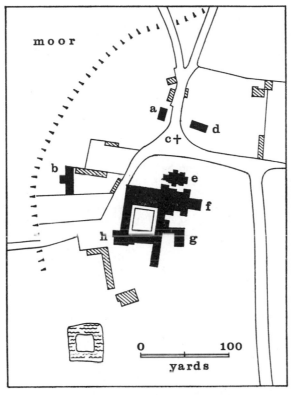

SITE PLAN OF MUCHELNEY ABBEY

a, Almonry; b, Barn; c, Cross; d, Priest's House; e, Parish Church;
f, Monastic Church; g, Infirmary; h, Abbot's House.

on the Yeovil–Durston branch of the Bristol and Exeter railway. The track was opened in 1853, but Thorney and Kingsbury Halt, later known simply as Thorney Halt, was constructed later. Both halt and line were closed in 1964.[32]

Before 1538 there were six common arable fields, on the relatively higher ground near the main settlements. West and Hill, later Tout, fields served Thorney, and lay on either side of the hamlet.[33] The tithings of Muchelney and Ham appear to have shared four fields. By the mid 16th century one of these, Hamond field, had virtually disappeared. Ham field lay between Hill field and the hamlet of Ham.[34] Muchelney field lay to the north-west, on

Level, formerly known as Barramores, by the end of the 15th century part of the inclosed demesne of the abbey.[38] Drainage had also produced small inclosed meadows in the south of the parish by the end of the 15th century: Reedmead and Stonemead had been created by 1411, New mead by 1451.[39] To east and west of the 'great island' lay much larger tracts of low-lying land not fully brought into use until inclosure in 1826. To the west was Thorney moor, which included a piece of ground called High Alders in the 19th century, and three hundred years earlier had been divided into small withy beds.[40] The 'moor' was commoned until 1826, and measured then c. 155 a.[41] In the east of the parish

[28] *S.R.S.* xiv. 66–7.
[29] S.R.O., DD/PR 78.
[30] Ibid.; O.S. Map 6″, Som. LXXII. SE. (1886 edn.).
[31] S.R.O., tithe award.
[32] E. T. Macdermot, *Hist. G.W.R.*, ii. 155–6; C. R. Clinker & J. M. Firth, *Reg. Closed Stations* ii.
[33] S.R.O., DD/PH 156.
[34] Ibid.

[35] Ibid; tithe award.
[36] S.R.O., DD/AB 1; DD/PH 156; DD/PR 78; DD/ SAS (C/909a) 9.
[37] S.R.O., DD/PH 156; DD/BR/lr (C/1835).
[38] S.C. 6/974/5.
[39] S.R.O., DD/AB 1, 4.
[40] S.R.O., tithe award; DD/PH 156.
[41] S.R.O., CR 102.

lay the much larger tract of land stretching with ill-defined boundaries into Martock. Eastmoor, the area nearest Muchelney, was divided into closes of meadow and pasture by the early 16th century.[42] The surviving name Black Withies suggests other uses for wetter ground to the north.[43] Further west is Whetmoor, occupying a third of the parish and uninclosed until 1826.[44] It was partly fenced in the early 18th century, but cattle from Martock often came across the 12 ft. 'lake' and fed on Muchelney soil 'through neglect of tenants in not keeping up fences'.[45]

In 1205 Muchelney abbey had licence to inclose a wood on their 'island' and make it into a park.[46] The park, which was arable in the 15th century, lay at the northern end of Netney in Thorney moor.[47] It was divided into Kine Park and Clarkenparke in the 16th century, when it comprised 12 a. of meadow and pasture.[48] The tenant of Abbey farm in the 16th century had fishing rights from Load to Hambridge on the river Isle, and thence to the 'longe draughts'.[49] By 1553 a fishery called 'Barrymore fishing' was let for 2s. a year, and there were two other fisheries, each worth 1s. 4d.[50] Fowling in the manor was then let for 2s.[51] Both fowling and fishing on the manor in 1727 were said to be good.[52]

No part of the abbey church has been left standing. Excavations on the site in the 1950s[53] revealed the remains of an early-8th-century church, having a semicircular apse with a polygonal external face, which was incorporated in the 12th-century church as a crypt under the choir. The Norman church had an apsidal east end with bubble chapels on its east, north, and south sides. A similar chapel stood from the south transept. A rectangular Lady Chapel was later added, probably the chapel of St. Mary atte stone for which an indulgence to visitors was issued in 1360.[54] The whole building, 247 ft. long, was evidently ornamented in the 15th century, fragments of casing still being *in situ*.

The main cloister lay to the south of the church. Judging by its surviving southern alley and the adjoining abbot's lodging the whole was largely rebuilt in the late 15th or early 16th century. Fragments of 12th-century masonry were incorporated in its walls. The cloister alley is two-storeyed with chambers above and an arcade, formerly filled with tracery, below. The lodging, which is remarkably complete, includes a kitchen and a hall or anteroom on the ground floor and several upper chambers.[55] The finest of these, the abbot's parlour, has an elaborately carved fireplace with two recumbent lions surmounting the now blank panel above it. One wall is occupied by an oak settle with linenfold panels. The windows contain fragments of glass bearing the initials of Abbot Thomas Broke (1505–22). The refectory adjoined the lodging to the east.

Its surviving north wall, backing on the cloister alley, is carved with stone panelling, evidently to match the windows in the missing wall opposite. The sites of warming house, chapter house, and infirmary have been located, and the reredorter still stands.

To the west and south-west of the abbey church was the barton of the demesne farm, now divided by the present road to Drayton, and includes a 9-bay barn, probably dating from the early 16th century.[56] It is of lias with Ham stone dressings, some original slit openings to the ground floor, and a four-centred doorway near the south end. The structural evidence suggests that it was always at least partly two-storeyed, although the present floors are not the original ones. The tie-beam roof trusses have collars and curved raking struts. There are three purlins to each roof slope and a few curved windbraces survive. The almonry, further north, was converted to a domestic dwelling after the surrender of the abbey.[57] The present Almonry farm-house replaced the original in 1902.[58] It was then a small thatched building of two storeys adjoining a larger brick farm-house.[59] Over the door, in a round-headed niche, was the carved figure of an ecclesiastic, with hand raised in blessing.[60] The figure remains over the door of the present farm-house.

Many houses in the village bear witness to their builders' use of the abbey ruins as a stone quarry. Before the mid 16th century timber was evidently the more usual building material. The Tudor House in Lower Muchelney is an example of a timber-framed structure with crucks, dating probably from the early 16th century, and subsequently cased in stone.[61] Lias rubble and thatch were the chief materials in the 17th and 18th centuries, several houses in Silver Street, Lower Muchelney, and in the more scattered settlements of Thorney and Ham, showing their use with mullioned windows and hood moulds. Two substantial brick houses, Manor Farm and School Farm, both in Lower Muchelney, show the same features persisting in the different medium of brick, and probably date from the early 18th century. The Court House in Silver Street, used as a vicarage in the later 19th century,[62] apparently originated as an early-18th-century stone farm-house consisting of a single range with a stair projection at the rear. It was extended eastwards in 1874 when 15th-century fragments from the abbey were incorporated in the building and buttresses were added to the older range.

In 1840 the churchwardens reported that there was neither inn nor beer house in the parish, but they had heard of, and hoped to suppress, the clandestine sale of cider.[63] A beer house, in business by 1861,[64] was closed in 1878.[65]

[42] S.R.O., DD/PH 156.
[43] S.R.O., tithe award.
[44] S.R.O., CR 102.
[45] S.R.O., DD/SP, box 1, sale cat. 1727.
[46] *Rot. de Ob. et Fin.* (Rec. Com.), 202; *Rot. Chart.* (Rec. Com.), 157.
[47] S.R.O., DD/AB 4.
[48] S.R.O., tithe award.
[49] S.R.O., DD/PH 156.
[50] Ibid.
[51] Ibid.
[52] S.R.O., DD/SP, box 1.
[53] *Jnl. Royal Arch. Inst.* cvii. 120.
[54] *Cal. Papal Pets.* 352.

[55] See p. 42.
[56] S.R.O., DD/PH 156.
[57] Ibid.
[58] H. M. Page, *Muchelney Abbey and Church*, 30.
[59] T. Hugo, *Muchelney Abbey* (extra-illustrated copy in Taunton Borough Libr.).
[60] Taunton Castle, Braikenridge Colln., sketch by W. W. Wheatley, 1850.
[61] *Proc. Som. Arch. Soc.* cxiv. 56.
[62] See p. 48.
[63] S.R.O., D/D/V rtns. 1840.
[64] *P.O. Dir. Som.* (1861).
[65] S.R.O., D/P/much 23/4: diary of the Revd. S. O. Baker, vicar, 1872–99.

Men of the parish in the 19th century shared a friendly society with Drayton, holding their annual feast on Whit Wednesday.[66] Muchelney women were admitted to the Drayton women's club in 1880.[67] Parishioners were from 1879 eligible for membership of the Drayton and Curry Rivel Agricultural Association.[68]

The population of the parish in 1801 was 283. After four decades of fluctuation the total of 349 was reached in 1841, followed by 340 in 1851. The total then fell each decade to 103 in 1911 and then, after a slight recovery to 213 in 1931, fell to 164 in 1961.[69]

MANOR AND OTHER ESTATES. At the time of the Domesday survey the Benedictine community of Muchelney owned the 'islands' of Muchelney, Midelney, and Thorney which had formed part of the demesnes of the abbey presumably from the time of its foundation, possibly by the early 8th century.[70] The monks surrendered their house and possessions early in 1538, and the whole property, described as the manor, rectory, and advowson, was granted almost immediately to Edward Seymour, earl of Hertford, later duke of Somerset.[71] The Crown recovered the property on Seymour's execution in 1552,[72] and in the following year leased the manor and the site of the monastery for 21 years to John Penne, a groom of the Privy Chamber.[73] Some few days later Penne made over his lease to Robert King, gentleman usher of the Queen's Chamber.[74] In 1557 King received from the Crown a further 21-year lease, to take effect after the expiry of the original lease in 1574.[75] In 1562 King sold his interest to John Walshe, then a serjeant-at-law and later a justice of Common Pleas, who was a native of Cathanger in Curry Rivel.[76] On Walshe's death in 1572 the lease reverted to King, who retained the property until 1580, when his title was declared void.[77]

The manor, divided since the surrender of the monastery into separate holdings, was thenceforward leased by the Crown in these units. The largest, a holding of over 200 a. largely of inclosed pasture known as the Old Demesnes,[78] together with the 'residue' of the manor and the rents of free and customary tenants, was let to Sir Edward Phelips, his wife, and son for their lives, the Old Demesnes in 1586, the 'residue' in 1592.[79] The site of the monastery and adjacent closes were leased to Robert Cole alias Plume in 1575;[80] the New Demesnes were leased to William Symes of Poundis-

ford in 1581;[81] and Horsey farm was in the hands of the Phelips family by 1587.[82]

Edward Phelips was tenant of the 'residue' of the manor, including the manor rents and presumably the courts, when Robert King's lease was declared void in 1580.[83] By Exchequer decree he was allowed to have the property as Crown lessee for the unexpired term of King's lease. Early in 1591 he in turn made a lease to Robert Redhead, his tenant, and early in 1592 the manor was let by the Crown to Redhead and to Edward and Robert Phelips for their lives.[84] In 1628, in return for the sale of the manor of Broadway to the Crown, Sir Robert Phelips acquired the freehold of the manor.[85] He sold it to his son Edward, for the payment of his debts, in 1638.[86]

By 1654 the manor belonged to Edward Davenant, D.D., treasurer of Salisbury Cathedral.[87] It was probably settled in that year on his son John (d. 1671). His grandson, also John, of Landford (Wilts.), in 1680 allowed it to stand as security for payments under his father's will,[88] but it did not have to be sold, and passed eventually to his three daughters each of whom, Rebecca, Catherine, and Elizabeth, had one third share of the property, between 1717 and 1719.[89] The whole manor was evidently put up for sale in 1727, and was probably then purchased by Walter Long of Salisbury and Preshaw (Hants).[90]

Walter Long died in 1769 and his son, also Walter, died unmarried in 1807. William, a younger son (d. 1818), was followed by Walter, son of another son John (1728–97). Walter Long died in 1871 and was succeeded by his son Walter Jervis Long (d. 1891), and then by his grandson Walter Long (d. 1919), whose trustees sold the manor and other property, amounting to nearly all the land in the parish, to the tenants in 1921.[91]

The site of the monastery and adjacent closes, amounting to about 140 a., were leased to Robert Cole alias Plume for 21 years from 1575; William Symes of Poundisford was granted the reversion in 1581.[92] In 1592, before Cole's lease had expired, the Crown granted a 31-year lease to Arthur Worliche of Leighs (Essex), who immediately assigned it to a London goldsmith and then sold it to Hugh Portman of Orchard Portman (d. 1603).[93]

In 1614 Sir Edward Phelips purchased the site and the farm from the Crown, and two years later his son Sir Robert settled it upon Anne Portman, widow of Sir John Portman (d. 1614), Hugh Portman's brother.[94] The Portman family owned the farm until 1825 when Edward Berkeley Portman

[66] Margaret Fuller, *West Country Friendly Socs.* 146.
[67] S.R.O., D/P/much 23/4.
[68] Ibid.
[69] *V.C.H. Som.* ii. 348; *Census*, 1911–61.
[70] *V.C.H. Som.* i. 468; see above, p. 40.
[71] *L. & P. Hen.* VIII, xiii(1), pp. 10, 14, 64. Original grant in Wilts. R.O., Ailesbury MSS.; copies in S.R.O., DD/SAS (C/77), 24.
[72] C 142/115/38.
[73] *Cal. Pat.* 1557–8, 293.
[74] S.R.O., DD/PH 29.
[75] *Cal. Pat.* 1557–8, 293; S.R.O., DD/PH 29.
[76] S.R.O., DD/PH 29; E. Foss, *Judges of Eng.* v. 542–3. In 1564 Walshe was said to hold only a moiety: C 2/Eliz. I M7/6.
[77] E 310/23/126/2.
[78] See p. 44.

[79] E 310/23/126/2.
[80] S.R.O., DD/PM, box 3, OB 3, Worliche to Portman.
[81] E 310/23/126/2.
[82] E 134/29 Eliz. I/East. 13.   [83] E 310/23/126/2.
[84] Ibid.; *Cal. S.P. Dom.* 1591–4, 205.
[85] *Cal. S.P. Dom.* 1628–9, 223.
[86] C 142/486/151; *S.R.S.* li. 273–4.
[87] C.P. 25(2)/616/Hil. 1654.
[88] *V.C.H. Hants*, iv. 569; S.R.O., DD/SAS (C/77), 24.
[89] *V.C.H. Hants*, iv. 569; C.P. 25(2)/1056/4 Geo. I Trin.;/6 Geo. I Mich.;/1087/3 Geo. I Hil.
[90] S.R.O., DD/SP, box 1.
[91] Burke, *Land. Gent.* (1906), 1040; *Kelly's Dir. Som.* (1923). Settlements 1839–71 in Hants R.O. 8M49 E31.
[92] S.R.O., DD/PM, box 3, OB 3, Worliche to Portman.
[93] Ibid.
[94] S.R.O., DD/PH 29; DD/PM, box 3, FL 3.

exchanged it with Walter Long for the manor of Gussage St. Michael (Dors.).[95] With the rest of the Long family holding it was sold in 1921.[96]

The farm, the only demesne lands retained by the monastery at the surrender, was let to John Smythe and his wife in 1547 for £11 12s.[97] It then comprised the site of the monastery and its remaining buildings, and adjoining closes containing c. 140 a.[98] William Witcombe was tenant of the farm in 1592.[99] Muchelney farm, as it was called in the 18th century, measured nearly 178 a. by 1763, and c. 185 a. in 1825.[1] It was let to John Pitt, an Ilchester maltster, from 1742,[2] and later to Robert Gatcombe and the Stuckey family.[3] By 1841 it was tenanted by Isaac Young;[4] the Westlake family took the tenancy in 1850–1 and remained at least until 1897.[5]

The former farm-house was originally the lodging of the abbot of Muchelney. The buildings were described in 1547 as of three roofs, namely a hall, kitchen, larder-house, and buttery, with a chamber over the hall and 'beyond and by the sides thereof' three other chambers.[6] The building dates from the late 15th or early 16th century.[7] With the adjoining abbey church site it was taken into the guardianship of the Crown in 1927.[8]

The Old Demesnes, some 200 a. largely of inclosed pasture grounds, let by the monks before their surrender, were in 1586 leased to Edward Phelips, Margaret his wife, and Robert their son for their lives.[9] Sir Edward, as he then was, still held the property, including Barramores, in 1609,[10] but he or his son seem to have disposed of the property before 1638. The descent of the New Demesnes is also not clear. In 1581 they were leased to William Symes for 21 years;[11] in 1594 the Crown granted them to Robert Smythe and his sons John and Gervase.[12] By 1601 they were in the hands of Sir Thomas Neale of Warneford (Hants), who was still tenant in 1609.[13]

By 1667–8 two estates, later known as the 'manors' of Neales and Barramores, were owned by a Mr. Goodwin, probably John Goodwin of Bletchingley (Surr.).[14] His grandson Deane succeeded him in 1674 and added to his holding in the parish the so-called 'manor' of Knowles's, acquired from Stephen Knowles in or after 1679.[15] Deane Goodwin was succeeded in 1692 by his brother Charles who died, probably in 1726, and then by John Goodwin,

described in 1729 as of St. James's, Westminster.[16] Goodwin held courts baron until 1739, and his estate was variously described as the 'manor' of Muchelney or as three separate 'manors'.[17]

Goodwin's widow Mary, formerly of Worth (Suss.), wife of Andrew Bethune of East Grinstead (Suss.), held courts until 1748 as guardian of her daughter Mary Goodwin.[18] The daughter had come of age by 1752, but is not found after 1761.[19] Certainly her mother had succeeded her by 1768, and still held courts in 1772.[20] By 1777 her daughters by her second husband, Catherine and Anna Bethune, were 'ladies of the manors', the former being married to the Revd. Dr. George Bethune of Worth (d. 1803).[21] Catherine survived both her sister and her husband until at least 1808, and her four children retained possession until 1824.[22] By 1826 the property had been acquired by Walter Long, lord of Muchelney manor.[23]

In 1586 tenements and a sheephouse at Horsey and 100 a. of land, formerly tenanted by John Seymour and Thomas Phelips under Robert King's lease of the manor, were let by the Crown to Richard Phelips of Winterborne Whitchurch (Dors.).[24] A further lease to Phelips was granted in 1588.[25] Both grants were for the lives of Phelips, his wife Mary, and Richard, son of John Phelips. In 1607 the latter, described as of Corfe Mullen (Dors.), leased the property, then called Lanes Horsey, to Sir Robert Phelips of Montacute.[26] The freehold was purchased from the Crown in 1614, and Horsey was part of the estate sold by Sir Robert to his son Edward for the payment of his debts in 1638.[27] The subsequent descent of the land has not been traced with certainty, but a survey of the manor in 1670 includes holdings known as Horsey leases.[28]

The benefice estate, formally separated from the vicarage in 1308,[29] amounted in 1334 to pasture worth 24s. and tithes and oblations worth 76s.[30] By 1535 the income was from tithes alone, assessed at £11;[31] but in 1560 they were said to be worth only 20s. to the Crown grantees.[32] A number of tithe suits in the late 16th and early 17th centuries suggest a much higher potential value from moduses and tithes in kind.[33] Just over 990 a. were still titheable in kind in 1841, and a modus of 2d. an acre was payable on a further 455 a. As many as 113 a. were exempt by prescription.[34] Under the

[95] S.R.O., DD/BR/lr (C/1893); G.E.C. Baronetage; Complete Peerage, s.v. Portman.
[96] Kelly's Dir. Som. (1923).
[97] S.R.O., DD/PH 156, survey, 1553.
[98] Ibid.
[99] S.R.O., DD/PM, box 3, OB 3.
[1] S.R.O., DD/PM, box 24, survey and reference bk.; DD/BR/lr (C/1893), Portman to Long.
[2] S.R.O., DD/PM, box 17.
[3] S.R.O., DD/BR/lr (C/1893), Portman to Stuckey (1800), Portman to Long (1825).
[4] S.R.O., tithe award.
[5] S.R.O., D/P/much 13/1/1; Kelly's Dir. Som. (1897).
[6] S.R.O., DD/PH 156.
[7] See p. 40.
[8] Ministry of Works, Guide.
[9] E 310/23/126/2; S.R.O., DD/PH 156.
[10] E 134/7 Jas. I/Mich. 48.
[11] E 310/23/126/2.
[12] E 310/23/126/1; Cal. S.P. Dom. 1591–4, 483.
[13] C 2/Eliz. I/P5/43, P10/39; E 134/7 Jas. I/Mich. 16.
[14] S.R.O., DD/BR/lr (C/1835), survey, 1667–8; J. Comber, Suss. Genealogies (Ardingly Centre), 226–7.
[15] S.R.O., DD/BR/lr (C/1835), survey, 1741; Comber, Suss. Genealogies, 226–7.

[16] Uvedale Lambert, Bletchingley, ii. 450–1; S.R.O., DD/BR/lr (C/1835), survey, 1741; DD/CA, box 96, Goodwin to Bosgrove.
[17] S.R.O., DD/BR/lr (C/1835), 'a count of the estates . . . late of John Goodwin'; Suss. N. & Q. iv. 185.
[18] S.R.O., DD/CA, box 96; Suss. N & Q. iv. 185.
[19] S.R.O., DD/CA, box 96; DD/BR/lr (C/1835), survey, 1777.
[20] S.R.O., DD/PR 78: map, 1768; DD/BR/lr (C/1835), survey, 1777.
[21] S.R.O., DD/CA, box 96; Suss. Arch. Collns. lxix. 196.
[22] S.R.O., Q/RE, land tax assessments.
[23] Ibid.
[24] E 310/23/129/12; E 134/29 Eliz. I/East. 13.
[25] E 310/23/126/2.
[26] S.R.O., DD/PH 29.
[27] Ibid.; S.R.S. lii. 273–4.
[28] S.R.O., DD/BR/lr (C/1835).
[29] See below.
[30] E 179/169/14.
[31] Valor Eccl. (Rec. Com.), i. 194.
[32] Cal. Pat. 1558–60, 276–7.
[33] C 2/Eliz. I/P 15/43; E 134/29 Eliz. I/East. 13; E 134/7 Jas. I/Mich. 16.
[34] S.R.O., tithe award.

tithe award a rent-charge of £336 11s. was established, all but £2 payable to the lord of the manor. At the same time just over 12 a. of land were reckoned part of the rectorial estate, and formed part of Parsonage farm.[35]

At the surrender of the monastery in 1538 the rectory property was granted to Edward Seymour, earl of Hertford.[36] It reverted to the Crown on his execution in 1552, and was granted in 1560 to Robert Davye and Henry Dynne, both of London.[37] The lands and tithes were in practice in the control of lessees, members of the Smythe family. John Smythe was probably farming the tithes from the abbot in 1535–6, and he certainly held the profits under the duke of Somerset from 1547.[38] These profits are said to have included glebe.[39] Smythe was still receiving tithes at least until 1564–5.[40] His son Robert was still alive in 1594,[41] and Robert's elder son John was described as farmer of the rectory in 1606.[42]

By 1607 John Pyne of Curry Mallet was lay rector; he left the parsonage to his wife Juliana who presented to the benefice in 1619.[43] Her second son Hugh, of Cathanger (d. 1628), devised the rectory to his son Arthur.[44] Christabel, Arthur's sister, wife of Sir Edmund Wyndham, succeeded on her brother's death in 1639.[45] It is possible that the family lost the property during the Interregnum, but Sir Charles Wyndham (d. 1706), of Cranbury (Hants), son of Sir Edmund and Christabel, left the parsonage to his wife James.[46] She died in 1720 and her heirs sold the property, including some land recently added to the holding, in 1725 to John Collins of Ilminster (d. 1741).[47]

Collins's son John, of Hatch Beauchamp, died in 1792 heavily in debt, and his widow and son sold the property to Henry Tripp of Orchard Wyndham in 1803.[48] Tripp sold the rectory and 27 a. of land to Walter Long, lord of the manor, in 1825 for £2,275.[49]

ECONOMIC HISTORY. In 1086 there were only four carucates of arable on the three 'islands' of Muchelney, Midelney, and Thorney, apparently divided equally between demesne and tenants. There were also 25 a. of meadow, 12 a. of wood, 100 a. of pasture, an arpent of vineyard, and two fisheries paying 6,000 eels.[50] The surrounding 'moors' were clearly not included in the survey, and the whole estate was worth only £3. Frequent

flooding continued to hamper the economy of the parish: in 1243 the abbey was 'distressed for water';[51] in 1317 the abbot was allowed to combine his office with that of sacristan to save money.[52] At the same time there was a continuous process of drainage and recovery of meadow and pasture grounds, at least from the mid 13th century, notably on the southeastern boundary with Martock.[53]

There were 3 villeins, 18 bordars, and 4 serfs on the estate in 1086, cultivating their lands with two ploughs.[54] This high ratio of customary holdings persisted throughout the Middle Ages. There were only three small freeholdings on the manor, producing in 1484–5 a rent of 2s. 5d., and in 1535 8s. 11d. for a total of 36½ a.[55] The largest, in Thorney, belonged in 1412 to Sir William Bonville, and by c. 1525 measured 27 a.[56] A man of villein status was presented at the manor court in 1411 for leaving the manor.[57] Another died in 1450 as tenant of a house and two cows were payable as heriot.[58] Between the freeholders and the serfs were the customary tenants. By 1484–5 customary works had virtually ceased, though some were but newly commuted,[59] and as late as 1451 three tenants were presented for not coming with their oxen and ploughs to the lord's park.[60] Customary payments amounted to about a sixth of the income of the manor. Payments in lieu of works rose from 9s. 6d. in 1434 to 10s. 3d. in 1444, and to £3 7s. 1d. in 1484–5.[61] Other customary payments comprised *auxilium villani*, levied at Martinmas, and worth over £4 throughout the 15th century; 'rypesylver', a total of 9s. from 36 customary tenants; 4s. 8d. in lieu of 14 'slabs' of iron paid by 14 tenants at Whitsun and commuted for 4d. each; 3s. 2d. for Peter's Pence; and church-scot.[62] By the mid 16th century none but church-scot remained. In 1407 this had comprised gifts to the abbot of 70 chickens at Martinmas, of 84 geese at Lammas, and 3 capons at Michaelmas.[63] In the mid 16th century these payments were still reckoned in geese and chickens but were paid in cash and amounted to 16s. 7d.[64]

By the end of the 15th century the demesne lands actually cultivated by the abbey included 97 a. of arable. In 1484–5 41 a. were sown with wheat, 39½ a. with oats, 12 a. with beans, and 4½ a. with barley. The wheat yield was nearly twice as great as the oats.[65] By 1484–5 the abbot was employing a shepherd, two ploughmen, two drovers, and a keeper of the barton.[66] In 1440 the demesne livestock comprised 60 cattle, including 19 cows but no

[35] Ibid.
[36] L. & P. Hen. VIII, xiii, p. 64.
[37] Cal. Pat. 1558–60, 276–7.
[38] E 134/7 Jas. I/Mich. 16; S.R.O., DD/PH 156, survey, 1553.
[39] S.R.O., DD/PH 156.
[40] E 134/7 Jas. I/Mich. 16.
[41] Cal. S.P. Dom. 1591–4, 483.
[42] S.R.O., D/D/Ca 150.
[43] Som. Wills, ed. Brown, i. 3–4; Som. Incumbents, ed. Weaver, 149.
[44] C 142/448/96; Som. Wills, ii. 71–2.
[45] C 142/764/3.
[46] S.R.O., DD/BR/lr (C/1893), Symes to Shuter; will of Sir Chas. Wyndham.
[47] Ibid., will of John Collins; fine, 1725; Som. Wills, ii. 44.
[48] S.R.O., DD/BR/lr (C/1893), will of John Collins; conveyance, Collins to Tripp.
[49] Ibid., conveyance, Tripp to Long.

[50] V.C.H. Som. i. 468–9.
[51] S.R.S. vii. 29.
[52] Ibid. i. 168.
[53] Ibid. xiv. 60–1, 96–7.
[54] V.C.H. Som. i. 468–9.
[55] S.C. 6/974/5; S.R.O., DD/PH 156, survey 1553.
[56] S.R.O., DD/AB 2; S.C. 6/974/5; E 315/385 f. 79. For earlier owners see S.R.S. xvii. 153–4; xxii. 24; xlii. 110.
[57] S.R.O., DD/AB 1–2.
[58] Ibid. 4.
[59] S.C. 6/974/5.
[60] S.R.O., DD/AB 4.
[61] Ibid. 11–12; S.C. 6/974/5.
[62] S.R.O., DD/AB 10–12; S.C. 6/974/5.
[63] S.R.O., DD/AB 10. 'Churs' appears at the head of the rental.
[64] S.R.O., DD/PH 156.
[65] S.C. 6/974/5.
[66] Ibid.

oxen, and 25 horses.[67] A tenant in 1411 had a flock of 100 sheep.[68] A levy on pigs was paid at the manor court early in the 15th century and 53 were counted in 1412.[69] Figures for the rest of the century are much lower.[70] There was an eel fishery on the Yeo in 1475; it was let for 31½ 'sticks' of eels, and the lord had to find timber to make and repair the weir.[71]

There are indications during the later 15th century of a systematic exploitation of the estate, a policy probably connected with the large-scale rebuilding of the abbey.[72] Exploitation took the form of letting hitherto unused land for grazing, mostly for life; of building cottages to be rented out; and of turning into cash such small items as ash bows, hides, and boughs of trees.[73] The extra land and new cottages produced an income in 1484–5 of £2 19s. 4d. More significant in terms of income in that year were the sales of meadow and pasture from the demesne. Occasional sales of grazing in closes, amounting to only a few pence, dated from the 1450s,[74] but rose to 18s. 9d. in the summer court of 1475,[75] and to £8 18s. 4d. in 1484–5.[76] This still represented under-exploitation, for some pastures remained unsold.[77]

The policy was carried a stage further between 1511 and the surrender of the abbey in 1538, during which time well over 200 a. of largely inclosed pasture grounds were granted out in copyholds for terms of lives.[78] Just over half lay in the north and east of the parish at Barramores and Eastmoors, and the whole came to be known during the 16th century as the Old Demesnes. By 1553 the Old Demesnes produced an income of £24.[79]

By the time of the surrender of the abbey in 1538 the demesne farm amounted to c. 390 a., of which c. 70 a. were arable.[80] It produced an income of £8 6s. in 1535, less than a tenth of the value of the whole manor.[81] The farm staff comprised only a shepherd and a ploughman.[82] Division of the demesne continued after the Dissolution: the New Demesnes, some 250 a. of land, two-thirds uninclosed meadow and pasture, were divided between copyholders on leases for lives, and by 1560 produced an additional £27 8s. 4d.[83]

The severe contraction of the demesne holding increased the economic significance of the new tenants. In 1484–5 payments by customary tenants for assessed rent, commuted works, new rents, and traditional dues amounted to £30 0s. 10d.[84] In the next fifty years rents rose to £73 9s. 4d.[85] Tenant farms varied considerably in size: by 1560 there were 112 separate holdings, with rents ranging between 1s. and £5 13s. 4d., besides the abbey site and farm of c. 140 a., let for £11 12s.[86] 'Horsey Place', the nucleus of Horsey farm, was the largest

single holding, an inclosed pasture farm, including a sheephouse, stretching to 100 a.[87] Some holdings were grouped into the hands of a single tenant: John Larcombe, probably bailiff of the manor under the abbey in 1535,[88] had four copyhold tenements totalling over 94 a.[89]

The pattern of cultivation changed as a result of the policy of demesne leasing. By c. 1511, when leasing began, much of the demesne meadow and pasture was already inclosed. Well over 50 a. of Eastmoor, for example, were shared between 15 closes, and these small grounds were the first to be let. After 1538 larger areas came to be divided into small units for the same purpose. Rodmead, later Reedmead, which before 1538 amounted to 21 a., was divided between 14 holdings. Similar divisions took place elsewhere, including Seven Acres, where an 18-a. field became 14 strips mostly of pasture.[90] Arable lands were affected less. Hamond field, one of the six common fields, used only by the tenants of Muchelney hamlet, had virtually disappeared by 1553, but was evidently replaced by South field, where 47 a. were shared between Muchelney and Ham.[91] South field had originally been part of the abbey arable demesne, and a witness in a later tithe suit testified that in his youth he 'did often times go into the said South field when the abbot's own ploughman did plough the arable lands there'.[92] Another witness implied that the original field extended to c. 100 a.[93]

The whole estate thus leased was in 1553 worth over £88, of which the former demesnes accounted for over £51.[94] It remained, subject to reversionary grants, in the hands of a single Crown lessee until 1580.[95] Thenceforward it was divided into several units. By 1614 the Phelips family were holding the 'residue' of the manor with the remaining demesne farm, the Old Demesnes, and Horsey farm, together valued at £116 16s. 5d. a year.[96] The pattern of holdings changed in the 17th century, the property falling into three main divisions: the manor, which included Horsey, the 'manors' of Neales, Knowles's, and Barramores, which probably originated from the Old and New Demesnes, and the site of the abbey with its farm. These three estates, all owned by absentee landlords, were brought together c. 1825, when the whole parish was again under one owner, a state of affairs which continued until just after the First World War.[97]

By 1670[98] the manor was an estate of over 566 a., fairly evenly divided between arable and meadow. Including Horsey Leases there were 84 separate tenements, most having a share in the commons as well as beast leazes on Thorney moor. The tenants themselves comprised three freeholders and the rest

[67] *Penes* Mr. J. S. Cox, St. Peter Port, Guernsey. Photocopy in S.R.O., D/PH/vch 12.
[68] S.R.O., DD/AB 1.
[69] Ibid. 2.
[70] Ibid. 3–6.
[71] Ibid. 6.
[72] See p. 40.
[73] S.R.O., DD/AB 5; S.C. 6/974/5.
[74] S.R.O., DD/AB 4–5.
[75] Ibid.
[76] S.C. 6/974/5.
[77] Ibid.
[78] S.R.O., DD/PH 156.
[79] Ibid.
[80] Ibid.
[81] *Valor Eccl.* (Rec. Com.), i. 193.

[82] S.C. 12/14/38.
[83] S.R.O., DD/PH 156.
[84] S.C. 6/974/5.
[85] *Valor Eccl.* (Rec. Com.), i. 193.
[86] S.R.O., DD/PH 156.
[87] Ibid.; see above, p. 42.
[88] *Valor Eccl.* (Rec. Com.), i. 193.
[89] S.R.O., DD/PH 156.
[90] Ibid.
[91] Ibid.
[92] E 134/7 Jas. I/Mich. 16.
[93] Ibid.
[94] S.R.O., DD/PH 156.
[95] See p. 41.
[96] E 310/23/128/33.
[97] See p. 41.
[98] S.R.O., DD/BR/lr (C/1835).

copyholders for lives, 55 of whom paid heriots or an equivalent in cash. The total rental was £36 15s. 2d. The common on Whetmoor, shared between Muchelney and Martock, was thought to be of great benefit to both lords and tenants 'if it happen to be divided'.[99]

In 1727 the manor measured just over 662 a., divided into 68 tenements, of which 11 were leasehold and the rest copyhold.[1] The estate was then up for sale, and was worth over £946 a year. Improvements were expected by the inclosure of Whetmoor and Thorney moor, which by that time provided 52 commons and 230 beast leazes respectively for the tenants. Inclosure intended 'this year' would have provided an additional 600 a. of 'very good pasture', bringing the yearly value to nearly £1,717. At the time many holdings were near surrender and it was declared that 'no manor was ever more abused, neglected', or 'underlet'.[2] The manor was probably sold in that year, but inclosure did not take place for another century.[3]

Barramores 'manor' in 1668 was a holding of c. 200 a. of pasture divided into 38 holdings, two of which were leasehold and the rest copyhold.[4] At the same date Neales 'manor', of c. 120 a. in 31 holdings, was by contrast under mixed cultivation and was all held by lease.[5] By 1740 the combined 'manors' of Knowles's, Neales, and Barramores amounted to 506 a., of which 133 a. were in hand.[6] The agent of the absent owner in 1731 had complained of 'four times the trouble . . . in letting, managing, and taking care of the estates', and the amount of land in hand underlined the difficulty of finding tenants at the time.[7] Changes from copyholds to leaseholds and some consolidation of holdings on these estates are evident during the 18th century. On Barramores in 1741 there were still 38 holdings but as many as 18 were leasehold; and by 1777 23 were so held. The number of holdings on Neales had been reduced to 20 by 1777; on Knowles's there was still little change: heriots were no longer payable, and there was a slight reduction in the number of separate holdings.[8]

Little is known of the third estate in the parish in the 18th century. It comprised Muchelney, now Abbey, farm, and Raymond's Tenements, all fenced in 1763 and amounting to nearly 203 a., with beast leazes in Thorney moor and common on Whetmoor.[9] From 1742 it was let for 21 years for £160 a year to an Ilchester maltster, the tenant agreeing to let 23 a. lie fallow each year, ploughing it three times.[10] Subsequent tenants paid higher sums: Robert Gatcombe £200 a year and Thomas Stuckey £440.[11] In 1800 a new tenant took the farm for 14 years, paying £330 for the first seven and £340 for the remainder. A levy of £20 an acre was to be paid if

grassland put down in the previous seven years was ploughed, and grass was to be mown only once a year. There was also a restriction on the amount of potatoes and other garden produce grown and the tenant was to keep sheep penned at night, attend to and pay for all repairs, manure the land adequately, and keep 23 a. fallow each year.[12]

An act for the inclosure of c. 60 a. of common arable land, the remaining areas of Thorney West field, Thorney Hill or Tout field, and Muchelney field, c. 155 a. of Thorney moor, and pasture on Whetmoor, shared between Martock and Muchelney, was passed in 1819.[13] Only two landowners, Walter Long and Edward Berkeley Portman, were involved, but the award was not completed until 1826.[14]

By 1841 a pattern of farming had emerged in the parish which has largely persisted to the present day. The largest holding, a combination of the present Manor and Daws farms, was of nearly 323 a. Two farms at Thorney were over 200 a. and four others, Abbey with Gally farm, Almery (now Almonry), Horsey, and Parsonage farms, were between 125 a. and 170 a. The largest farm at Ham was just over 92 a.[15] During the 19th century the amount of arable land in the parish, always small, contracted still further. In 1801 there were 337 a. under plough, of which 207 a. produced wheat, 63½ a. beans, 42 a. barley, 12 a. peas, and 10½ a. potatoes.[16] By 1841 293 a. were arable,[17] and by 1905 only 222¼ a.[18]

Grassland thus remained of paramount importance for sheep and other stock and, from the later 19th century, for dairying. Two men renting dairies were in business at Ham by 1861, and a third dairy had been established by 1866.[19]

In 1821 53 out of 63 families in the parish were engaged in agriculture;[20] and in the 1840s an expanding population required new cottages.[21] Later in the century the effects of flooding accentuated the more general effects of the agricultural depression. In 1879 and 1880, for example, there was a reduction of a tenth in all rents because of floods, and sheep had to be sold or slaughtered because of disease.[22] In 1891 the labourers were said to be 'much on the move', and six cottages stood empty in 1892.[23] The farmers relying on grass and not on corn were less seriously affected by the national depression, and farms changed little in size up to the mid 1970s. The only major unit to disappear, Parsonage or Rectory farm, was divided in 1855.[24]

In the 19th century the demands of farmers created ancillary trades in the community. In 1861 there were two carpenters and a stone-mason; and a few years later a blacksmith and a thatcher.[25] Pottery and corn-dolly making were revived in the

[99] Ibid.
[1] S.R.O., DD/SP, box 1, sale partics.
[2] Ibid.
[3] See below and p. 41.
[4] S.R.O., DD/BR/lr (C/1835).
[5] Ibid.
[6] Ibid.
[7] Ibid.
[8] Ibid.
[9] S.R.O., DD/PM, box 24, survey and reference bk.
[10] Ibid. box 17, Portman to Pitt.
[11] S.R.O., DD/BR/lr (C/1893), Portman to Long, 1825.
[12] Ibid., Portman to Stuckey.
[13] 59 Geo. III, c. 12 (priv. act).

[14] S.R.O., CR 102.
[15] S.R.O., tithe award.
[16] S.R.O., D/P/much 2/1/2: par. reg. 1722–1813, inside front cover.
[17] S.R.O., tithe award.
[18] Statistics supplied by the then Bd. of Agric., 1905.
[19] P.O. Dir. Som. (1861, 1866).
[20] C. &. J. Greenwood, Som. Delineated.
[21] S.R.O., D/P/much 4/1/1: chwdns'. accts. etc. 1791–1941, rate, 1844.
[22] S.R.O., D/P/much 23/4.
[23] Ibid.
[24] S.R.O., D/P/much 13/1/2: overseers' rate bk. 1855–7.
[25] P.O. Dir. Som. (1861); Kelly's Dir. Som. (1883).

parish in the mid 20th century. Stock raising and dairying remained the centre of the economy, and some corn was grown solely for use as thatching material.

About 1280 the abbot of Muchelney had fairs on 29 June and 1 August.[26] They did not survive the 15th century.[27]

There is no direct evidence for a mill, but Mill Close drove, on the south side of the present Drayton road, survived as a field-name until the 19th century.[28] Closes called 'Millhey' and 'Millese', part of Abbey farm in 1547, also lay probably in that area.[29]

LOCAL GOVERNMENT. The abbot of Muchelney claimed to hold a liberty at Muchelney, indicated at the time of Domesday when he paid no geld for his holding.[30] This liberty, confirmed c. 1280,[31] was evidently still enjoyed in the 15th century, and surviving court rolls illustrate how it was exercised.[32] When defined c. 1290 the abbot enjoyed return of writs and quittance of the common summons; and his own rights within the manor comprised infangthief, chattels of felons, amercements from pleas there, gallows, assizes of bread and ale, tumbrel, pillory, view of frankpledge, waifs and strays, and free warren.[33]

The manorial court in the 15th century had jurisdiction over the four tithings of Muchelney, Thorney, Ham, and Midelney.[34] Four courts were held each year, at Michaelmas and Hockday described usually as *curia legalis* with view of frankpledge,[35] and at Christmas and Midsummer described simply as *curia*. No clear division of function between the courts is evident, and procedure seems to have varied, though presentments of each tithing and presentments of the jury of freemen for the whole manor usually followed proceedings between parties.

Business in the court was varied. Pleas of debt and trespass between parties were common. Both tithings and jury reported houses, roads, causeways, and ditches in need of repair, breaches of the assizes and of the peace, illegal snaring and fishing, and the production of bad ale, though the jury in some ways acted as a counter-check on the tithings. Thus in May 1411 Muchelney and Thorney tithings reported breaches of the assize of ale, and Thorney in addition a woman who had raised the hue against a neighbour. Ham tithing told of a breach of the peace and of a lane in need of repair. The jury of the manor presented several tenants to mend the bars controlling access to Thorney moor, and four people for keeping dogs which chased and killed

geese.[36] The court acted upon these and similar presentments, ordering repairs or fines; and it initiated action against escaped *nativi*, or against a man keeping company with another's wife.[37]

In the early 15th century there were separate haywards for Muchelney and Midelney, but by 1454 each of the four tithings elected both a hayward and a reeve.[38] Tithingmen were apparently chosen annually by virtue of their holdings, though in 1451 the tithingman of Ham successfully resisted a second year in office in respect of a second holding.[39] Other officers included a man to oversee Thorney moor to ensure that no outsiders' beasts grazed there, and by 1455 there were scavengers to report and remove dead animals.[40] The haywards, who collected fines and attached goods as well as selling grazing, were also responsible for selling ash bows, hides, and strays.[41]

The court was held in the church house early in 1547,[42] but the subsequent division of the manor probably resulted in its suspension. The right to hold courts leet and baron and views of frankpledge was retained in law in the early 18th century,[43] and the lord was certainly holding courts by 1744.[44] The representative of the lord normally headed the signatories to vestry decisions during the 18th century, and the vestry seems by that time to have taken over the functions of the earlier court.[45] Extracts from courts baron for entries survive for the 'manors' of Knowles's, Neales, and Barramores between 1718 and 1761.[46] The only local officers known in the 17th and early 18th centuries are constables. Muchelney and Midelney had one each in 1637–8,[47] and the constable of Muchelney occurs in 1710.[48]

By 1740 parish affairs were controlled by the vestry. Two waywardens or surveyors of highways were appointed in 1747 and 1765, and from 1852 until 1894 the names of those liable for office as waywarden and overseer were recorded annually.[49] A salaried assistant overseer was appointed from 1791. In the 1740s there were four haywards responsible for the grazing control of Thorney moor.[50] Clothing and cash payments to the poor were often supplemented at times of crisis. In 1768 bread and peas were given, and in 1796 barley and bacon were purchased to be sold at a loss. Allowances of bread were also made in 1796. Coal was bought for the poor in 1799, potatoes in 1800, 1801, and 1809, and bread in 1846–8.[51] The vestry was also concerned with the construction and maintenance of sluices, the prevention of pigs from grazing on Whetmoor, and the rewards for the destruction of vermin.[52]

In 1744 the vestry agreed to lease the parish house, probably the old church house, from the

26 *S.R.S.* xiv. 93.
27 No mention of fairs in court rolls or bailiff's acct.: S.R.O., DD/AB 1–6; S.C. 6/974/5.
28 S.R.O., tithe award.
29 S.R.O., DD/PH 156.
30 *V.C.H. Som.* i. 468.
31 *S.R.S.* xiv. 93.
32 C 260/112/19: copy of liberties, 1 Henry IV; S.R.O., DD/AB 1–6: ct. rolls 1411–12, 1433–4, 1450–1, 1454–5, 1474–5.
33 *S.R.S.* xiv. 93.
34 Midelney is reserved for treatment in Drayton parish; see p. 15.
35 The courts for 1433–4 were also called hundred courts: S.R.O., DD/AB 3.
36 S.R.O., DD/AB 1.

37 Ibid. 1, 4–5.
38 Ibid. 2, 5.
39 Ibid. 4.
40 Ibid. 1, 4.
41 See p. 44.
42 S.R.O., DD/PH 156.
43 C.P. 25(2)/1056/4 Geo. I Trin.;/6 Geo. I Mich.; /1087/3 Geo. I Hil.
44 S.R.O., D/P/much 9/1/1.
45 Ibid.
46 S.R.O., DD/CA 96.
47 *Cal. S.P. Dom.* 1637–8, 156–7.
48 S.R.O., Q/SR 256/6–8.
49 S.R.O., D/P/much 9/1/1.   50 Ibid.
51 Ibid. 4/1/1, 9/1/1.
52 Ibid. 9/1/1; see above, p. 45.

lord of the manor, presumably to house the poor.[53] A further lease was taken in 1777.[54] In 1801 it was agreed to repair the house, then called the poor-house, and to 'have chambers over the great hall and little room and make three dwellings'.[55] The poorhouse in use in 1829, presumably the same building, stood on the site later occupied by the school in Muchelney village.[56] It had been demolished by 1842.[57] The parish became part of the Langport poor-law union in 1836.[58]

CHURCH. Until 1400 Muchelney was the mother church of Drayton, and such a relationship suggests an early foundation, perhaps preceding the Conquest.[59] The church was appropriated to Muchelney abbey before 1228, when a vicar is first found.[60] A vicarage was ordained in 1308, though the vicar received no glebe beyond a residence, an orchard, and a garden, and was dependent for his food and stipend upon the monastery.[61] After the Dissolution a small rent-charge was made upon the lay rectory.[62] While still occasionally described as vicar in the 17th century, the incumbent was more usually known during the 18th century as a curate. From 1824, after a Parliamentary grant, the benefice was commonly called a perpetual curacy.[63] It was united with the vicarage of Drayton in 1924.[64]

The patronage of the living belonged to Muchelney abbey until 1538. After the surrender of the house it passed to Edward Seymour, earl of Hertford.[65] On his attainder in 1552 the property reverted to the Crown, which presented in 1555, 1557, and 1575.[66] Robert Smythe, lessee of the lay rectory, presented in 1582.[67] By 1619 the lay rector herself was in possession of the advowson, and subsequent owners of the parsonage, and from 1825 of the manor, presented. The Long family continued as patrons after the sale of the manor in 1921. Walter Long's son W. V. Campbell-Wyndham-Long was patron in 1923. A. W. Long, who had succeeded him by 1945, transferred the patronage to the bishop about 1950.[68]

The church was taxed at £6 in 1291.[69] Under the ordination of 1308 the vicar received bread and ale daily from the monastery, meat on Sundays and Tuesdays, and eggs and fish on other days. In addition the abbey sacrist paid him £4 a year to support the charges of his vicarage. Sunday offerings at both Muchelney and the daughter church at Drayton, oblations at burials, offerings of bread and eggs at Easter, and oblations at confessions, wed-

dings, and churchings were payable to the vicar, who had to find a chaplain for Drayton and to support all charges of his cure except procurations.[70] Subsequent alterations of these arrangements probably occurred when Drayton became virtually independent of the mother church in 1400.[71] Certainly in the years immediately preceding the surrender of the monastery the vicar was receiving a 'pension' of £10 from the abbey,[72] and also 40s. as 'wages'.[73] The second sum may have been in return for personal services to the abbot, for only the larger sum was considered part of the benefice income.[74]

In 1560 the lay rectors were charged to pay the sum of £10 to the vicar, together with unspecified sums to support the cure.[75] By 1635 the vicar received in addition fees for weddings and churchings.[76] The reputed value was still only £10 in c. 1668.[77] By 1831 the income had improved to £93, the result of a succession of endowments and grants,[78] and twenty years later comprised £74 from land in other parishes, £7 10s. from glebe in Muchelney, and £10 7s. from the lay rector.[79] A further augmentation was made in 1879.[80]

The glebe in 1635 comprised an orchard and garden.[81] Royal Bounty of £200 in 1741 purchased c. 10 a. of meadow in Aller in 1746. Further similar sums from the same source in 1775 and 1783, the latter met by two grants of £100 each from the Horner and Pincombe trustees, were laid out in 18 a. of land in South Petherton in 1785. Grants from the same trusts and from the patron, Henry Tripp, in 1819, and from the Pincombe trustees and the incumbent, Samuel Alford, in 1824, totalling £400, purchased just over 7 a. in Aller and nearly 8 a. in Long Load. In 1879 the patron, W. J. Long, added 22 a. of land in Muchelney, producing £50 a year, which was met by a grant of £45 a year from the Ecclesiastical Commissioners. This grant brought the glebe estate to about 55 a., producing an income of £157 12s. 6d.[82] Most of this land was attached to the benefice in 1970.[83]

The house and buildings occupied by the vicar in 1308 were formally assigned to him and his successors under the terms of the ordination.[84] The vicarage-house was described as 'ruinous' in 1606,[85] and as 'much decayed in timber and thatching' in 1623.[86] In 1815 the non-resident curate described it as 'small, and yet an incumbent may live in it, but equally as large as it has been for ages'.[87] His successor found it 'only a small cottage', and lived in another parish.[88] By 1840 the house was used

[53] S.R.O., D/P/much 9/1/1, *sub anno*; see below, p. 48.
[54] S.R.O., D/P/much 9/1/1, *sub anno*.
[55] Ibid.
[56] S.R.O., D/T/lsc 2: bk. of maps, 1830; DD/X/EE (N/137), poster inside cover.
[57] S.R.O., tithe award.
[58] *Poor Law Com. 2nd Rep.* p. 548.
[59] *Cal. Papal Regs.* v. 300.
[60] *S.R.S.* xiv. 53.
[61] Ibid. 108–9; xlii. 46.
[62] See below.
[63] *Rep. Com. Eccl. Revenues*, pp. 172–3.
[64] *Dioc. Dir.*; see below.
[65] *L. & P. Hen. VIII*, xiii, p. 64.
[66] *Cal. Pat.* 1554–5, 253; 1555–7, 365; *Som. Incumbents*, ed. Weaver, 149.
[67] *Som. Incumbents*, ed. Weaver, 149.
[68] *Dioc. Dir.*
[69] *Tax. Eccl.* (Rec. Com.), i. 194.

[70] *S.R.S.* xlii. 46.
[71] *Cal. Papal Regs.* v. 300.
[72] *Valor Eccl.* (Rec. Com.), i. 194.
[73] S.C. 12/14/38.
[74] *Valor Eccl.* (Rec. Com.), i. 198.
[75] *Cal. Pat.* 1558–60, 276–7.
[76] S.R.O., D/D/Rg 226.
[77] S.R.O., D/D/Vc 24.
[78] *Rep. Com. Eccl. Revenues*, pp. 172–3; see below.
[79] H.O. 129/317/2/7/20.
[80] *Lond. Gaz.* 14 March, 1879, p. 2144; see below.
[81] S.R.O., D/D/Rg 226.
[82] S.R.O., D/P/much 3/1/2–3, 3/3/1–2, 5/2/1, 23/4; Hodgson, *Queen Anne's Bounty*; *Lond. Gaz.* 14 March, 1879, p. 2144.
[83] Ex inf. Mr. J. U. White, churchwarden.
[84] *S.R.S.* xlii. 46.
[85] S.R.O., D/D/Ca 150.
[86] Ibid. 236.
[87] S.R.O., D/D/V rtns. 1815.
[88] Ibid. 1827.

as a cellar and later as a school; and in the later 19th century it was rented by a local farmer.[89] Resident incumbents lived at the Court House until after 1902, when the benefice was held in plurality.[90] The medieval vicarage-house was acquired by the National Trust in 1911.[91]

The building stands north of the church and is of stone with a thatched roof. When originally constructed in the early 14th century, it comprised a two-bay open-roofed hall, with a parlour and solar at the east end, and a service room and a guest room above at the west end, beyond the screens passage, with a narrow room over the screens passage, possibly for a servant. Later alterations include two windows of the solar, dating from the mid 14th century, and the two large hall windows, the panelled ceiling of the parlour, and perhaps the roof, of c. 1475. The inserted floor in the hall and a large stone fireplace on the screens passage are of c. 1550.[92] From its date it seems likely that the house was built as a direct result of the ordination of the vicarage in 1308, replacing the older house then in existence.

Nicholas Gillet (vicar from 1512 until at least 1545) was persuaded by a party within the community to declare Thomas Ive, Cromwell's candidate for the vacant abbacy in 1532, under canonical age.[93] Services were not 'in due time' in 1569, and the curate did not catechize nor read the Injunctions.[94] By 1606 divine service had not been held for three years, and for want of a minister the children were not catechized nor Holy Communion celebrated.[95] In 1623 the vicar was involved in scandalous behaviour with a former female parishioner.[96] The church was served from 1655 by James Jolliffe, appointed by the Lord Protector, but there was apparently no minister in the parish for several years after the Restoration.[97]

Thomas Powell (vicar 1782–1816) was non-resident after 1792, and Christopher Winter was appointed stipendiary curate from 1813.[98] By 1815 Powell was living in Wales because of 'illness and infirmity'. Winter lived at Stoke sub Hamdon and served East Lambrook, but conducted at Muchelney a 'full service' and preached once every Sunday, and celebrated Holy Communion four times a year.[99] Samuel Alford (vicar 1820–43) lived at Curry Rivel in 1827 and also served Drayton. Services at Muchelney were held once every Sunday, alternately morning and afternoon.[1] The average congregation in 1851 was 130 in the morning and 200 in the afternoon, each figure including 50 Sunday school pupils, but services were still held as before on alternate Sundays.[2] Two services each Sunday were introduced in 1858,[3] and by 1870 the resident curate celebrated Holy Communion six times a

year 'immediately after morning prayer'.[4] Monthly celebrations were introduced by S. O. Baker in 1873.[5]

A church house, the property of the lord of the manor, is first mentioned in 1547, when it was being used for a session of the manor court.[6] In 1553 it was held 'in the name of the parish'.[7] It was still in existence in 1670, but was then in hand.[8] Almost certainly it was used in the 18th century as a poorhouse.[9]

The parish church of *ST. PETER AND ST. PAUL*, apparently dedicated to St. Peter only in 1543,[10] and clearly taking its dedication from that of the abbey church, stands immediately to the north of the ruins of the abbey. It consists of a chancel, with north and south chapels extending from the aisles; a nave of 3 bays with north and south aisles; a two-storeyed north porch, balanced on the south side by a 19th-century vestry; and a west tower. The north side of the church, always the more important entrance front, has embattled parapets with quatrefoil ornament to the merlons. The whole building is in the later Perpendicular style, but it is likely that the chapels and the tower were the last parts to be built. The embattled and pinnacled tower, of three lofty stages, has set-back buttresses, windows flanked by canopied niches to the middle stage, and two belfry windows on each face. There is a pillar stoup outside the west door. The chapels are more ornate than the aisles and are slightly wider. Any earlier features in the church, notably the tiles in the sanctuary and around the font, were discovered on the site of the abbey church in 1873, and the four canopied niches in the east wall of the south chapel were found elsewhere in the parish.[11] The internal jambs of the south chancel window are carried down to accommodate three canopied sedilia. Both the lower stage of the north porch and the space below the tower are stone-vaulted. The font has an octagonal bowl with carved panels and four square attached shafts. There are four original poppy-head bench-ends. Fragments of glass in the east window date from the later 15th century; three roundels in the north window of the chancel are Netherlandish, dating in part from the 17th century.[12] An outstanding feature of the church is the waggon roof of the nave, with painted panels depicting angels and cherubs, surrounded by clouds and stars in a firmament with a sun in the centre. The work is thought to be of the early 17th century.

The pulpit and lectern, made for the Lord Mayor's chapel in Bristol in 1830, were given to the parish by Sir Charles Wathen in 1889 and 1892 respectively.[13] In the gallery above the 19th-century south vestry is a contemporary barrel organ.[14] The tomb

[89] Ibid. 1840; D/P/much 4/3/1, 13/1/1–2: rate bks.
[90] See above and p. 40.
[91] *Rep. of the Council of the National Trust 1911–12*, p. 19.
[92] *Medieval Arch.* i (1957), 121–4.
[93] *L. & P. Hen. VIII*, v, p. 535.
[94] S.R.O., D/D/Ca 40.
[95] Ibid. 150.
[96] Ibid. 236.
[97] Lambeth Palace MSS., COMM II. 508; S.R.O., D/D/Rr 289.
[98] S.R.O., D/P/much 1/2/1.
[99] S.R.O., D/D/V rtns. 1815.
[1] Ibid. 1827.
[2] H.O. 129/317/2/7/20.

[3] S.R.O., D/P/much 9/1/1.
[4] S.R.O., D/D/V rtns. 1870.
[5] S.R.O., D/P/much 23/4.
[6] S.R.O., DD/PH 156.
[7] Ibid.
[8] S.R.O., DD/BR/lr (C/1835), survey, 1670.
[9] See p. 47.
[10] *S.R.S.* xl. 48.
[11] S.R.O., D/P/much 23/4.
[12] C. Woodforde, *Stained Glass in Som.*, 50–1, 120, 265–6.
[13] S.R.O., D/P/much 23/4. The Revd. S. O. Baker was also minister of Low Ham, a benefice in Sir Charles Wathen's patronage.
[14] By Gray and Davison, c. 1835–40: TS guide to ch.

CHARLTON MACKRELL: LYTES CARY FROM THE SOUTH

TINTINHULL HOUSE FROM THE WEST

LANGPORT TOWN HALL

STOKE SUB HAMDON: FORMER SCHOOL

MUCHELNEY: FORMER SCHOOL

in the churchyard at the east end of the church, incorporating the headless effigy of an abbot, was discovered during excavations at the abbey site in 1873.[15]

The plate includes a cup and cover, dated 1633, made by 'R.S.', and a chalice, paten, and flagon given in 1873 by William Long of Westhay, Wrington.[16] There are five bells: (i) 1692, Thomas Knight of Closworth; (ii) 1707, Thomas Knight; (iii) and (iv), 1847 and 1872, Mears; (v) 1626, Thomas Pennington of Exeter.[17] The registers begin in 1702 and the series is complete.[18]

NONCONFORMITY. A Quaker lived in the parish in 1684[19] and two others were imprisoned for refusing to pay the church rate between 1699 and 1713.[20]

The house of Richard Scott at Ham was licensed for worship in 1708, but no denomination was specified.[21]

EDUCATION. In 1787 the vestry agreed to support from the poor rate a Sunday school to teach poor children reading and the catechism. This school continued at least until 1792.[22] In 1818 a day-school and a Sunday school, the latter supported by subscription, taught between 20 and 30 children.[23] By 1825–6 the Sunday school had 20 boys and 20 girls, and the old vicarage-house was being suggested as suitable for a permanent day-school and residence for a mistress. The Lord of the manor was already giving £10 annually, and the use of the house 'would enable the incumbent to keep up a daily school, and be . . . the fulfilment of his earnest wish'.[24] By 1833 there were two day-schools in the parish, teaching 27 children at their parents' expense, and a Sunday school, supported by Lady Mary Long, for 52 children. The vicar and the lord of the manor selected and supported a lending library.[25]

By 1846–7 there was only one day-school, for 14 children, supported both by subscriptions and school pence. There were, however, two Sunday schools, with a combined total of 60 pupils, supported by subscription.[26] They were probably held under the same roof at the old vicarage-house, and continued at least until the 1880s.[27] A private day school continued at least until 1866.[28]

In 1870 the vestry agreed to establish an elementary school, and early in 1872 the Muchelney Parochial School was opened. Built by the lord of the manor, it was at first controlled by a committee of the owner, the vicar and churchwardens, and three 'principal ratepayers'. Children over the age of three years were taken, and costs were shared equally between the lord of the manor and a rate. School pence were payable until a Parliamentary grant was received.[29] The school building was extended in 1878 and again in 1883.[30] Average attendance was 53 in 1894 and 43 in 1903.[31]

The school was normally staffed by two mistresses. The new head teacher in 1888 undertook also to superintend the Sunday school, play the harmonium in church, and train the choir.[32] In 1903 the school was described as a 'pleasantly conducted and well-taught school'.[33] It remained a National school with voluntary status until 1930, and from 1931 accepted only junior pupils.[34] Numbers in the school fell rapidly during the Second World War, and from 1948 there was only one teacher. The school was closed in 1960 and the pupils transferred to Huish Episcopi.

The school building, of local lias rubble, includes copies of details found in the old vicarage-house.[35] The building was in 1970 a private dwelling.

In 1892 lectures on nursing were organised by the vicar and were 'fairly well attended by the wives and daughters of labourers'.[36]

CHARITIES FOR THE POOR. By 1484 Muchelney abbey owned a house, distinct from the Almonry,[37] described as the 'Bedehouse'.[38] The 'almeshouse' in 1535 gave shelter to four poor people, and was supported by an annual payment of £6 13s. 4d. from the abbey.[39] Payments ceased at the surrender of the monastery and the house was presumably closed.

By will proved 1910 Rhoda Stuckey Reeves bequeathed £300, the residue to be distributed at Christmas to aged poor of 60 years and more.[40] The Revd. Samuel Ogilvy Baker Memorial Fund was established under a trust in 1945 by Baker's nephew and niece. The sum of £600 was invested to provide clothes for poor parishioners. In 1965 four persons each received £4 from the charity.[41] Both charities were in existence in 1970.[42]

[15] Photograph in extra-illustrated copy of T. Hugo, *Muchelney Abbey*, in Taunton Bor. Libr.
[16] S.R.O., D/P/much 23/4.
[17] S.R.O., DD/SAS CH 16.
[18] S.R.O., D/P/much 2/1/1–6.
[19] Besse, *Sufferings*, 642.
[20] *S. & D. N. & Q.* v. 233, 294, 350.
[21] S.R.O., Q/SO, 1688–1708, Midsummer 1708.
[22] S.R.O., D/P/much 9/1/1: vestry bk. 1740–1894, sub annis.
[23] *Digest of Returns to Cttee. on Educ. of Poor*, H.C. 224 (1819), ix(2).
[24] *Rep. B. & W. Dioc. Assoc. S.P.C.K.* (1825–6).
[25] *Educ. Enquiry Abstract*, H.C. 62 (1835), xlii.
[26] *Church Sch. Inquiry, 1846–7*.
[27] *P.O. Dir. Som.* (1861, 1866); see below.
[28] *P.O. Dir. Som.* (1861, 1866).
[29] S.R.O., D/P/much 18/7/1, 23/4.
[30] *Kelly's Dir. Som.* (1883); S.R.O., D/P/much 23/4.
[31] *Return of Schs. 1893* [C 7529] H.C. (1894), lxv; S.R.O., C/E 27.
[32] S.R.O., D/P/much 18/7/1: agreement with teacher, 1888; C/E 40, log bk. 1916–60.
[33] S.R.O., C/E 27.   [34] Ibid. 40.
[35] See plate facing p. 49.
[36] S.R.O., D/P/much 23/4.
[37] See p. 38.
[38] S.C. 6/974/5.
[39] *Valor Eccl.* (Rec. Com), i. 194.
[40] Char. Com. file.
[41] Ibid. Baker was vicar of Muchelney 1872–96.
[42] Ex inf. Mr. J. U. White, churchwarden.

PITNEY

THE ancient parish of Pitney in 1876 was said to be just over 1,303 a. in extent,[1] which included 262 a. of Pitney moor, part of King's Sedgemoor, awarded to the parish in return for its proportion of common rights in the whole 'moor' in 1795.[2] The detached meadows in Kingsmoor, east of Knole, were transferred to Long Sutton in 1885.[3] The present area of the parish is 1,341 a.[4]

The parish, including Pitney moor, is over three miles from north to south, and about a mile from east to west at its widest point. Pitney moor forms a roughly triangular area in the north, joined to the remainder by Pitney Steart bridge, and is wedged between the parishes of High Ham and Somerton. The irregular eastern boundary interlocks with Somerton, suggesting that in origin at least part of the settlement belonged to that manor.[5] The southern boundary with Long Sutton interlocks in similar fashion and for similar reasons at its eastern end.[6] Its relation to the present Langport–Somerton road suggests that the original course may have formed the boundary between the two parishes. The western boundary, with High Ham, largely follows the course of the Low Ham rhine, flowing southwards from King's Sedgemoor.

Pitney village lies in a valley on each side of a stream flowing westwards into the Low Ham rhine. From this valley the ground rises eastwards and southwards, reaching 150 ft. along the Langport–Somerton road. To the north, near Pitney wood, it reaches 225 ft., forming a spur at the end of the scarp running westwards from Somerton, overlooking King's Sedgemoor. The arable land of the parish lay on this clayey ground rising from the village. Meadow lay largely along the western boundary, on the narrow ledge between the foot of the scarp and the Low Ham rhine.

There was no large-scale quarrying, but there is evidence of private digging for lias from the 16th century.[7] A quarry was opened on Stowey hill in the 1830s to provide stone for road mending.[8]

The origin of the settlement implied by the evidence of the place name suggests an island.[9] An earlier interpretation, deriving from the Saxon word for soft dirt, seemed to Gerard appropriate 'being seated in a very miry country'.[10] The two Roman villas, one at the foot of the northern scarp overlooking King's Sedgemoor, the other on the southern slope, both on the promontory north of the present village,[11] may point to this topographical feature as the 'island'. Settlement in the present parish thus dates from the Roman period, though an earlier object, a Bronze Age sword of c. 200 B.C., was discovered on Pitney moor.[12]

The village lies along and between two roads, lying parallel to and on each side of a small stream which is crossed at intervals to form a grid pattern. The church stands near the western end of the village, and the original farms have their houses in the village centre, the yards often divided by the stream. Farms established outside the village developed as a result of inclosure or the division of the main estate at the beginning of the 20th century.[13]

Three roads run directly north of the village, parallel to each other; they were known in the early 19th century as Laneing End (now Rectory Hill), Chessills Road, and Stowey Road and served the arable fields. South field was reached by similar roads and tracks, the present road from the Langport–Somerton road at Halfway House being known as Hermitage Lane nearest the village and then as Pitney Road.[14] The east of the parish, with earlier closes, was similarly served by tracks. Leazemoor Lane, which runs from Gore Road west of the church along the valley following the Low Ham rhine, gives access to Pitney moor. The Langport–Somerton road only served to by-pass the parish.

The close connexions between Pitney and Wearne in Huish parish[15] clearly made Gore Road of importance as the direct link across the Low Ham rhine. Frequent references to bridges from the 15th century onwards suggest additional links with High Ham. 'Whytewillbrygge', then broken down, occurs in 1423,[16] and again in 1538.[17] It may well be the predecessor of the footbridge which takes a path parallel and south of Gore Road, near the present Whitewell. 'Halberstonesbryge' occurs in 1520 evidently joining the parish with the abbot of Glastonbury's lands.[18] Stembridge, where a strip of Pitney crosses the Low Ham rhine in the north-west of the parish, leads directly through High Ham East field to Stembridge mill.[19] Pitney Steart bridge, formerly Pitney Door bridge, rebuilt in 1807, crosses the Cary and serves Pitney moor.[20]

Until the parish was inclosed in 1807 there were three substantial open arable fields in Pitney. North field and Middle field occupied the rising ground north of the village, the northern boundary being marked by Pitney wood, and the division between them by Middle Hedge road.[21] South field lay between the village and the southern boundary.[22] The earliest reference to these fields is in 1745.[23] There is some evidence to suggest an earlier and different arrangement, implying the existence of

[1] S.R.O., tithe award. This article was completed 1971.
[2] S.R.O., CR 116.
[3] *Local Govt. Bd. Prov. Orders Conf. Order (Poor Law), (No. 2), Act* (1885), 48 & 49 Vict. c. 5.
[4] *Census*, 1961.
[5] See below, p. 134.
[6] D.R.O., D 16/M 44.
[7] Ibid. M96; B.M. Add. Roll 28281; S.R.O., DD/CM, box 11, Pyne to White, 1746.
[8] S.R.O., D/P/h.ep. 9/1/1.
[9] E. Ekwall, *Dict. Engl. Place Names* (4th edn.), 368.
[10] *S.R.S.* xv. 210.

[11] *V.C.H. Som.* i. 326–8, 366; *Proc. Som. Arch. Soc.* xcvi. 48; B.M. Add. MS. 33712.
[12] *Proc. Som. Arch. Soc.* xlvii. 230–3.
[13] See p. 54.
[14] S.R.O., CR 57.
[15] See p. 3.
[16] B.M. Harl. Roll K 25.
[17] D.R.O., D 16/M 44.
[18] B.M. Harl. Roll K 27.
[19] S.R.O., CR 57.
[20] Ibid.
[21] Ibid.
[22] Ibid.
[23] S.R.O., DD/DEV 18.

only one field, known as Pitney field, in the 15th and 16th centuries,[24] and of an Eastern field, by 1807 divided into a number of closes in the south-east of the parish.[25]

Commonable pasture, which after 1807 was entirely absorbed into existing holdings, was largely on King's Sedgemoor, but also on Leazemoor and Pitney Steart moor, in the north of the parish, and on Gore common, north of Gore Road.[26] The detached meadows comprised an area on Kingsmoor in Long Sutton parish, known as Chestermead or Chestlemead and later as Pitney Western, Pitney Eastern, and Pitney Knole meads;[27] and small shares in Poolmead in Huish Episcopi.[28] Poolmead occurs as Pylmede in 1423 when a new sheep-house was built on Pitney land there.[29] Parts of Leazemoor were apparently inclosed c. 1583, when the 'moor' was claimed as waste.[30]

Most of the older buildings in the village have lias outer walls and thatched roofs. Brick is first found in the 18th-century Rookery, where it may be the casing of an older stone wall. Window frames are of wood, as in the 17th-century example at Estate Farm,[31] or more commonly of Ham stone which may sometimes be a replacement for wood. Except for those which incorporate the chimney stack, internal walls are of lapped planks or timber frame and wattle until the 18th century. Two buildings which have been demolished had cruck truss roofs.[32] The 17th- and early-18th-century farmhouses are generally of three-roomed ground plan. They include East End Farm, which has a cross-passage between the hall chimney and the kitchen screens, and which leads into a 'linhay' alongside a low service wing; Estate Farm, which has been partly rebuilt after a fire but retains its cross-passage plan and has a panel on the front wall with the name of John Pyne and the date 1694; and Butterwell Farm, which has a central pantry with principal rooms at each end of the range.

By 1756 there was an inn in the village, known by 1759 as the Horse and Jockey. From 1788 it was called the Crown, and from 1795 the Rose and Crown. It survived until 1808.[33] The Half Way House inn on the Langport–Somerton road was so named in 1817, having formerly been called the Hermitage.[34]

The population of Pitney in 1801 was 243. The total nearly doubled, to 465 by 1841, but there followed an irregular decline to 199 by 1931. In 1951 there were 216 inhabitants and in 1961, 192.[35]

MANORS. The later manors in Pitney were made up from a succession of Crown grants, mostly from Somerton manor, to Richard Revel the elder between c. 1190 and 1203. The first grant appears to have been described as a soke, held at a rent of 72s. 6d., confirmed to Revel in 1190.[36] Richard Revel the younger still held this in 1219 and probably until his death in 1222.[37] The second was a gift by Richard I to the elder Revel of rents of 60s. in Somerton in return for a quit rent.[38] The third, made before 1203, was of land for £12 a year, to which was added in 1203 a further estate in the same manor comprising land worth 50s. a year, and described under the form 'Pettewurth'.[39] The larger of these estates was subsequently described as at Pitney and at Wearne.[40]

Part of Richard Revel's land was granted to his son William in 1205.[41] This holding was given in 1217 to Geoffrey de Craucumbe, and by 1219 he had evidently succeeded as tenant to the other former Revel property.[42] In that year he was holding 12 librates of royal demesne in Pitney and Wearne in Somerton manor.[43] The estate, assessed at ¼ fee, was granted to Geoffrey and his heirs in 1230, together with land and rents in Langport and free warren for hares in Pitney.[44]

Geoffrey evidently died without heirs in or before 1249 and the manor was kept in hand and administered for the Crown by farmers.[45] In or shortly before 1266 this estate, described as the 'manors' of PITNEY and WEARNE, and subsequently as the manor of PITNEY WEARNE PLUCKNETT, PITNEY PLUCKNETT, or PITNEY PLUCKNETT and WEARNE,[46] was granted to Eleanor of Castile, wife of Prince Edward.[47] In 1270 the property, described as West Pitney and Wearne, was given in exchange for lands in Hampshire to Sir Alan de Plucknett.[48]

Alan died in 1298 holding half the hamlet of Pitney of the Crown by a quit rent.[49] He was succeeded by his son, also Alan (d. 1325), and then by his daughter Joan (d. 1327), possibly the Joan de Bohun of Kilpeck (Herefs.) who granted lands in Pitney and Wearne to Sir Thomas de Marlebergh in 1327.[50] Thomas settled this property in or before 1341 on Sir Henry de Haddon (d. 1348) and on Eleanor, his wife (d. 1361), with reversion to William FitzWaryn (d. 1360) and his wife Amice, daughter of Henry and Eleanor.[51] Sir Ives Fitz-Waryn, son of Amice, succeeded his mother and died in 1414.[52] His sole surviving daughter Eleanor married successively Sir John Chidiock (d. 1415)

[24] *Cal. Pat.* 1401–5, 108; B.M. Add. Roll 28281; C 3/15/9.
[25] S.R.O., CR 57.
[26] Ibid.
[27] S.R.O., DD/CM, box 11, Pyne to White, 1746; B.M. Add Roll 28281.
[28] S.R.O., CR 57.
[29] B.M. Harl. Roll K 25.
[30] *S.R.S.* lxix. 28–9.
[31] See below.
[32] *Proc. Som. Arch. Soc.* xcvii. 79–89; Taunton Castle, photographic slide of cottage, demolished 1905.
[33] S.R.O., Q/RL, victuallers' recogs.
[34] S.R.O., CR 57; O.S. Map 1", sheet 18 (1st edn.).
[35] *V.C.H. Som.* ii. 348; *Census*, 1911–61.
[36] *Cart. Ant.* (P.R.S. n.s. xxxiii), p. 128; *Red Bk. Exch.* (Rolls Ser.), ii. 549.
[37] See p. 73.
[38] *Bk. of Fees*, i. 79; see below.

[39] *Rot. Lib.* (Rec. Com.), 56; *Pipe R.* 1205 (P.R.S. n.s. xix), 133; *Red. Bk. Exch.* ii. 549.
[40] *Red. Bk. Exch.* ii. 780. For the origin of the Wearne estate see above, p. 1.
[41] *Rot. Litt. Claus.* (Rec. Com.), 51.
[42] Ibid. 296.   [43] *Bk. of Fees*, i. 263.
[44] *Cal. Chart. R.* 1226–57, 115, 119, 181; *Close R.* 1227–31, 304, 330.
[45] *Close R.* 1247–51, 160; *Cal. Lib.* vi. 281.
[46] *Cal. Inq. p.m.* ix, pp. 94–5; *Feud. Aids*, iv. 428.
[47] *Cal. Pat.* 1258–66, 555, 580.
[48] Ibid. 1266–72, 484; *Cal. Chart. R.* 1257–1300, 149–50; *Rot. Hund.* (Rec. Com.), ii. 122.
[49] C 133/91/1; *Cal. Inq. p.m.* iii, p. 416.
[50] Hook Manor, Donhead St. Andrew, Arundell MSS. G/1098–9; Sanders, *Eng. Baronies*, 73–4.
[51] *Cal. Pat.* 1340–3, 194; *Cal. Inq. p.m.* ix, pp. 94–5; xi, pp. 58, 64; *Cal. Close*, 1346–9, 482–3; 1360–4, 304.
[52] *Feud. Aids*, iv. 507; C 138/9/1.

and Ralph Bush.[53] Pitney and Wearne were settled on Eleanor's son William Bush and on his wife Joan in 1433, but a later agreement gave Sir John Chidiock a reversionary interest in 1439, and he succeeded on Bush's death in 1441.[54]

Sir John died in 1450 leaving two daughters. The younger, Catherine, married successively William Stafford (d. 1450) and Sir John Arundell of Lanherne (Cornw.) (d. 1473) and died in 1479. Her son and heir Sir Thomas Arundell, K.B., died in 1487, when the manor was said, clearly in error, to have been held of the abbot of Glastonbury.[55] Thomas was followed by his son Sir John (d. 1545), and by his grandson, also Sir John, who in 1546 sold the manor to Leonard Chamberlayne of Woodstock (Oxon.).[56]

Chamberlayne conveyed the manor shortly afterwards to Sir William Essex (d. 1548), of Lambourn (Berks.), who left successive life interests to George, Edward, Thomas, Edmund, and Humphrey Essex. The last was evidently in possession in 1559.[57] George Essex (d. 1588), then of North Street, Langport, was lord of the manor by 1562.[58] Another George settled the property in 1599 on his 'cousin german', Robert Essex of Ashdown (Berks.).[59] Robert sold the manor in 1610 to William Compton, Lord Compton, later earl of Northampton (d. 1630).[60]

The manor descended, like the manor of Sutton in Long Sutton, in the Compton family to George Compton, the 6th earl (d. 1758).[61] His widow, then wife of Claudius Amyand, held it until her death in 1800, when it passed to Lord George Cavendish, third son of William Cavendish, duke of Devonshire (d. 1764), through his marriage with Elizabeth (d. 1835), heir of Charles, earl of Northampton (d. 1763).[62] George, created earl of Burlington in 1831, died in 1834; his grandson and heir William (d. 1891) succeeded as duke of Devonshire in 1858. Victor (d. 1938), the 9th duke, sold his estate in Pitney, amounting to 641 a., in 1919, though the lordship of the manor was not included in the sale.[63]

In 1441 and 1450 the manor-house was described as an ancient hall.[64] Its site may well have been in the field later called Court Hay at the eastern end of the village, though there is a tradition which links the site with the present Manor Farm.[65]

By 1227 Henry Lorty, husband of Sabina, daughter of Richard Revel the younger, was holding lands in Pitney and Somerton by a quit rent.[66] In

1242 he and his wife accounted together for land worth 72s. in Pitney and Wearne, and Henry paid a total of £12 5s. for a soke in Somerton and other lands.[67] Sabina died in 1254, having settled her estate, described as the manor of *PITNEY*, and later known as *PITNEY LORTY*, on her son Richard (d. *c.* 1253) and his wife Maud, both minors.[68] The manor, held in chief, passed to Sabina's grandson Henry, who came of age *c.* 1273, and who was summoned to Parliament as Lord Lorty in 1299.[69] Lorty died in 1321 leaving the manor, with the advowson of the chapel, to his son John.[70]

After John's death in 1340 the descent becomes confused owing to the attempt by Ralph de Middleney, husband of John's sister Elizabeth, to obtain control of the property by illegally marrying his son to John Lorty's heir Sibyl.[71] Ralph held the manor until his death in 1363, and his widow, who had a joint interest for life, succeeded as sole owner.[72] By 1374 Elizabeth had married Sir Robert de Ashton, and he held the manor in right of his wife until his death ten years later.[73]

Maud, wife of John Langrich, and Elizabeth, wife of John Gunter, heirs of Sibyl Lorty, established their claim to the manor on Sir Robert's death,[74] and gave a life interest to Philippe, Sir Robert de Ashton's widow.[75] Sir John Tiptoft, Philippe's third husband, held the manor in her name until her death in 1417.[76] It then passed to Elizabeth, wife of John Andrewe and widow of John Gunter, sole surviving heir of Sibyl Lorty; and on her death in 1422 the manor then devolved on Roger Gunter of Racton (Suss.) (d. 1436), son and heir by her first husband.[77] John Gunter died in 1474, leaving his brother William as his heir.[78] William Gunter was succeeded in 1484 by his nephew Edmund who sold the manor in 1484–5 to trustees for Robert Morton.[79]

By will dated 1486 Morton devised a life interest in his manors, including Pitney, to his widow Agnes. On her death in 1517 she was succeeded by her son and heir Robert, who held them until his death in 1559. He paid the ancient quit rent for the manor of Pitney at least until 1534.[80] The estate, subject to the jointure of his son's widow, passed to his grandson George Morton who in 1579 sold it to John (later Sir John) Popham, serjeant-at-law.[81] Pitney then passed to the Hanham family, of Deans

[53] *Cat. Anct. D.* vi. C 6977; *Complete Peerage*, v. 458.
[54] *S.R.S.* xxii. 191, 194–5; B.M. Harl. Roll C 32; Harl. Ch. 58 D 42; C 139/107/26.
[55] C 139/139/26; *Cal. Inq. p.m. Hen. VII*, i. 83; *Complete Peerage*, s.v. Fitzpayn; Wedgwood, *Hist. Parl. Biogs.*
[56] D.R.O., D 16/M 114; C.P. 40/143 rot. 11 d.
[57] Req. 2/168/34; C 142/88/4; C.P. 40/189 rot. 707.
[58] Castle Ashby, Northampton MSS. 810; Collinson, *Hist. Som.* ii. 470.
[59] Northampton MSS. 805.
[60] C.P. 25(2)/345/8 Jas. I Mich.
[61] See p. 157.
[62] *Complete Peerage* s.v. Northampton; C.P. 43/886 rot. 399; 889 rot. 312.   [63] S.R.O. DD/X/DST.
[64] C 139/107/26; C 139/139/26.
[65] *Local Legends and Fragments of History* (1894) (priv. print.), 80; S.R.O., tithe award.
[66] *Pat. R.* 1225–32, 150.
[67] *Pipe R.* 1242 (ed. H. L. Cannon), 325, 327.
[68] *Abbrev. Rot. Orig.* (Rec. Com.), i. 13; *Close R.* 1253–4, 90; 1254–6, 46; *Ex. e Rot. Fin.* (Rec. Com.), ii. 188–9, 295; *Cal. Inq. p.m.* i. 84; Sanders, *Eng. Baronies*, 84.
[69] *Complete Peerage*, s.v. Lorty.

[70] *Cal. Inq. p.m.* vi, p. 184.
[71] *Cal. Inq. p.m.* viii, p. 180; *Cal. Pat.* 1340–3, 9; 1338–40, 560; 1345–8, 139; *Cal. Close*, 1339–41, 551–2; *S.R.S.* xii. 249; C 260/97/11.
[72] *Cal. Pat.* 1361–4, 426.
[73] C 136/30/3; C 260/97/11; *Cal. Fine R.* 1383–91, 58.
[74] C.P. 40/533 rot. 78.
[75] *Cal. Pat.* 1381–5, 483, 518–19; B.M. Harl. Ch. 58 G 10; *S.R.S.* xvii. 127.
[76] C 260/129/5; *Cal. Fine R.* 1413–22, 208; *Feud. Aids*, vi. 504.
[77] C 139/1/22; C 139/81/39; *S.R.S.* xiv. 196; *Feud. Aids*, iv. 422.
[78] C 140/47/61; *Cal. Fine R.* 1471–85, 76, 95–6.
[79] C 141/5/6; B.M. Harl. Roll K 26; MS. *penes* J. S. Cox, St. Peter Port, Guernsey (*Sotheby's Cat.* (Philipps Colln. (1936)), lot 420); *Cal. Close*, 1476–85, 393; 1485–1500, 13; B.M. Harl. Ch. 51 A 24, 30.
[80] C 142/32/89; B.M. Harl. Ch. 45 D 4, 50 H 57, 55 D 48, 56 F 17, 57 D 19.
[81] C 142/128/70; C.P. 25(2)/77/660/4 & 5 Phil. & Mary Mart.; C.P. 25(2)/205/21 Eliz. I Hil.; *Cal. Pat.* 1557–8, 333.

Court, Wimborne Minster (Dors.), through the marriage of Sir John Popham's daughter Penelope with Thomas Hanham (d. *c.* 1593).[82] Their son John died in 1625 leaving as heir to the property his daughter Eleanor, later wife of John Pyne.[83] Their son, also John, died in 1699, and was succeeded by his nephew Francis, third son of his brother Charles. By 1704 Charles Pyne, evidently heir to his son Francis, was owner of the manor, and settled it in 1715 in trust on his wife Frances.[84] She held it for at least the next ten years, but by 1746 it had passed to her eldest son John, of Curry Mallet (d. 1764). His son, also John, of Charlton Mackrell, died in 1791 leaving it to his eldest son Anthony, a clergyman, who presented himself to the rectory in the following year.[85]

Anthony died in 1819. By 1824 at least until 1839 William Uttermare of Curry Rivel and his sister Hannah Michell of Taunton were jointly lord and lady of the manor. By 1843 they had been succeeded by William Pyne (d. 1881), second son of Anthony Pyne and rector from 1824 until 1851.[86] By 1876 the holding amounted to just over 179 a., and no manorial rights were then claimed. The Pyne family survived until the death of Charlotte Uttermare, widow of B. Nathan Smith, in 1925.[87]

The capital messuage of the manor was known in the 15th century as Courteplace.[88] A house at the foot of Rectory Hill, now called Court House, possibly the successor to this building, incorporates fragments of 16th-century timbering.

ECONOMIC HISTORY. Pitney Lorty does not appear as a separate estate in the Domesday survey, though by 1254 there were $1\frac{1}{2}$ carucate in demesne, gardens, a dovecot, and a mill, and the whole manor was extended at just over £18 17s.[89] Free and customary tenants together paid rents totalling £9 15s. 9d., and works were assessed at just over 29s.[90] Rents had fallen to £7 3s. by 1423.[91] The manor of Pitney Wearne was formed in part by $2\frac{1}{2}$ virgates held by Robert de Odburville in 1086 in Huish parish.[92] This property became linked with land in Pitney formerly part of Somerton manor. By 1260–1 the estate, then in royal hands, was charged for a tallage at 20 marks.[93] In 1270 West Pitney and Wearne was said to be worth £23 and about ten years later £20 18s.[94] By 1298 the estate included half the hamlet of Pitney. The demesne farm then comprised 195 a. of arable, 6 a. of meadow, 4 a. of wood, a small piece of common pasture, gardens attached to the capital messuage, and a dovecot. There was one free tenant holding

a virgate, 3 customary tenants each with a virgate, 5 with $\frac{3}{4}$ virgate, 9 with $\frac{1}{2}$ virgate, 10 with $\frac{1}{4}$ virgate or 'ferdell', and 4 cottagers. The customary tenants owed labour services and paid small rents known as 'wodeschep' at Hockday and church-scot (chursutt) at Martinmas. The cottagers paid money rents. The whole land held by the tenants produced £7 9s. 11d. rent and services worth £8 17s.[95] The estate was let to farm in 1369 for £33 14s. 2½d.,[96] and by 1412 was assessed at £44.[97]

By the end of the 15th century the revenues of the manor, based on assessed rents of £25 9s. 6½d., increased by 20s. from 1513–14. Arrears and defective rents mounted between 1518 and 1528, occasionally to a fifth or more of the total income, though fines and perquisites usually amounted to very much more.[98]

In 1327 33 taxpayers in the two manors together were assessed at a total of 51s. 3d., both totals larger than those of the neighbouring town of Langport, though lower than Aller and Muchelney.[99] Any economic decline suggested by increasing arrears and defective rents at the beginning of the 16th century seems to have been reversed on Pitney Wearne manor by 1610, when the rental amounted to £35 12s. 6d., together with 21 capons and 3 hens.[1] This figure remained fairly constant for the rest of the 17th century.[2] Exchanges of land to consolidate holdings, presumably in connexion with small-scale inclosure, were common on Pitney Lorty manor by the end of the 16th century, and its economy, too, may well have benefited.[3]

About 1625 the manor of Pitney Wearne was estimated at 1,114 a. in extent.[4] Some 616 a. lay in Pitney parish in 1692, and of these 458 a. were arable, 112 a. pasture, and 33 a. meadow.[5] The farming units were small, the largest amounting to 84 a. There were 24 copyhold tenements and 30 held on lease; heriots were still payable on 12 holdings.[6] By 1765 only one farm, one cottage, and the site of the dovecot were copyhold.[7] No such details have been found for Pitney Lorty manor, though both clearly depended on their share of King's Sedgemoor, a scheme of *c.* 1625 allotting 318 a. to Pitney Wearne and 251 a. to Pitney Lorty.[8] The failure of the scheme prevented any significant improvement of the 'moor' until it was finally divided in 1795.[9]

There is some evidence of inclosure for pasture at the beginning of the 18th century,[10] but over 463 a. remained in open-field cultivation until 1807.[11] The small detached areas of common 'moor' on Kingsmoor, amounting to just over 30 a., had been previously sold to pay the inclosure expenses.[12]

[82] Hutchins, *Hist. Dors.* iii. 217, 231; *Som. Wills*, ed. Brown, v. 108.
[83] C 142/424/85; S.R.O., DD/CM, box 11.
[84] S.R.O., DD/CM, box 11.
[85] Ibid.; *Som. Incumbents*, ed. Weaver, 168.
[86] S.R.O., DD/LC, marr. settlements and leases; see below, p. 55.
[87] S.R.O., tithe award; M.I. in Pitney churchyard.
[88] C 139/1/22.
[89] C 132/16/10; *Ex. e Rot. Fin.* (Rec. Com.), ii. 188–9.
[90] C 132/16/10.
[91] *S.R.S.* xiv. 196.
[92] *V.C.H. Som.* i. 520; see above, p. 4.
[93] *Close R.* 1264–8, 539.
[94] *Cal. Chart. R.* 1257–1300, 149–50; *Rot. Hund.* (Rec. Com.), ii. 122; S.C. 6/1089/13.
[95] C 133/91/1.

[96] *Cal. Inq. p.m.* xi, pp. 58, 65.
[97] *Feud. Aids*, vi. 507.
[98] D.R.O., D 16/M 60, 66–7, 79, 83, 87, 89–90, 92–4, 96–100, 102–7, 109–10, 114. See also B.M. Harl. Ch. 58 F 11.
[99] *S.R.S.* iii. 253–4, 280.
[1] Castle Ashby, Northampton MSS. 811–12.
[2] Ibid. 813; S.R.O., DD/DEV 21.
[3] B.M. Add. Roll 28281.
[4] D.R.O., D 124, box 18.
[5] S.R.O., DD/DEV 21.
[6] Ibid.   [7] Ibid.
[8] D.R.O., D 124, box 18.
[9] S.R.O., CR 116.
[10] S.R.O., DD/MI, box 5, Cecil to Lovell.
[11] S.R.O., CR 57; DD/CM, box 11.
[12] S.R.O., CR 57.

Throughout the 19th century, as before, half the parish was held by one landlord; in 1876 the duke of Devonshire owned 575 a., and by 1919 641 a.[13] The largest farm in 1876 measured 214 a., and incorporated the present Manor and Brookside farms. There were two others of 137 a. and 127 a. on the Devonshire estate, and one of 134 a. on the Pyne estate. The largest freeholding, 54 a., is now represented by Estate farm.[14] Within the next forty years these units were divided, and by 1919 there were seventeen named farms, only one of which, Manor farm, was over 100 a.[15] By 1939 there were twelve farms in the parish,[16] a number which had decreased by 1971.

Pitney was thus an exclusively agricultural community, 66 of its 70 families in 1821 being engaged in agriculture.[17] This pattern survived until after the Second World War, the village having before then attracted few private residents.[18] Trades were largely confined to those ancillary to farming, though some gloving was carried on.[19] The decline of population began in the 1840s, and at least three families were helped to emigrate either to the Colonies or to the United States.[20]

There was a mill belonging to Pitney Lorty manor by 1254,[21] and two mills in 1579.[22] Two millers regularly appeared at the manor court between 1596 and 1604.[23] In 1605 a third miller, Edward Clawsey, was said to have recently erected a windmill.[24] In 1691 Pitney Lorty manor included a water-mill and a windmill.[25] It is not known where these mills stood, though the long narrow field, terminating in an irregular plot in the southwestern part of the parish, and known as Mill Close, may well, despite its position in a valley, be the site of a windmill.[26]

LOCAL GOVERNMENT. Summaries and fragments of court rolls for Pitney Plucknett or Pitney Wearne survive intermittently for the period 1553–1639,[27] court books for 1534–8,[28] 1612,[29] and 1745–1839.[30] For Pitney Lorty there are extracts from court rolls for 1423 and 1520–1,[31] and rolls for 1596–1609,[32] 1693–6, and 1701–3.[33]

The courts for Pitney Plucknett or Pitney Wearne, in the 16th century described as *curie legale* and *curie manerii* for the usual twice-yearly sessions in April and October, and as *curie baronis* for additional meetings largely concerned with entries, were regularly called views of frankpledge and courts baron from 1620 onwards. In the 18th century the winter court was described as court leet and court baron, the Spring session as court baron only. Spring sessions ceased after 1770. The officers of this manor were a tithingman and two haywards, one for Wearne and one for Pitney. The tithingman evidently was answerable for Wearne only. These officers were appointed until 1839.

Pitney Lorty courts were also held twice a year, and were usually described as courts leet and manor courts or as courts leet and views of frankpledge. The officers were a constable, a tithingman, and a hayward, the first chosen by the steward from names submitted by the court, the others holding by rotation. The distinction between this and the hundred court was not always clearly drawn,[34] and in 1697 the officers were apparently chosen in the hundred court. Conversely, an order of Lorty manor court in 1608 was to apply to both manors, though perhaps only as they concerned Pitney parish.[35]

Both courts made repeated and evidently unsuccessful attempts to improve the standard of buildings in the 16th and early 17th centuries, and were also concerned with the more usual prevention of sub-letting and the control of agricultural practice. Fines for allowing strays, always very common, extended to asses and a swarm of bees.[36] Stocks were maintained by each court.[37]

Part of the poor rate in the 18th century was occasionally allowed to the waywardens.[38] Besides the normal parish officers was the Sedgemoor expenditor, whose original responsibility for the drainage of the 'moors' in the parish was extended by the vestry to supervising grazing in the droves, mole catching, the sale of parish road-scrapings, and paying bounties for the destruction of sparrows.[39] From 1850 until 1872 names of inhabitants eligible for office as constable were submitted to the vestry. The workhouse, in existence by 1815, was not used in 1834, and was sold in 1838.[40] The parish became part of the Langport poor-law union in 1836.[41]

CHURCH. A reference in 1225 to William, parson of Pitney, is the first indication of a church there.[42] It was described as a chapel as late as 1321,[43] and the close link with Pitney Lorty manor suggests that it originated as a foundation of one of the lords of that manor.[44] Traditional claims by the parishioners of Pitney to right of burial in Huish Episcopi, and the complementary assumption that Pitney should contribute towards the maintenance of Huish church tower, is evidence of the close connexion

[13] S.R.O., tithe award; DD/X/DST.
[14] S.R.O., tithe award.
[15] S.R.O., DD/X/DST.
[16] *Kelly's Dir. Som.* (1939).
[17] C. & J. Greenwood, *Som. Delineated.*
[18] *Kelly's Dir. Som.* (1883–1939).
[19] *Rep. Com. Children and Women in Agric.* [4202–I] p. 478, H.C. (1868–9), xiii.
[20] S.R.O., D/P/pitn. 9/1/1–2: vestry bks. *sub. annis* 1841, 1848, 1851.
[21] C 132/16/10.
[22] C.P. 25(2)/205/21 Eliz. I Hil.
[23] B.M. Add. Roll 28281. The millers could, however, have come from other parishes in the hundred.
[24] B.M. Add. Roll 28281.
[25] C.P. 25(2)/869/3 Wm. & Mary East.
[26] S.R.O., tithe award.
[27] Castle Ashby, Northampton MSS. 803–6, 810.
[28] D.R.O., D 16/M 44.

[29] Northampton MSS. 810.
[30] S.R.O., DD/DEV 18–19.
[31] B.M. Harl. Rolls K 25, 27; Harl. Ch. 58 F 12–13.
[32] B.M. Add. Roll 28281.
[33] S.R.O., SAS PD 102, 105.   [34] See p. 15.
[35] B.M. Add. Roll 28281.
[36] Northampton MSS. 810, 26 Oct. 1639; S.R.O., DD/DEV 19, *sub anno* 1782.
[37] B.M. Add. Roll 28281; Northampton MSS. 810, 21 Oct. 1631.
[38] S.R.O., D/P/pitn. 13/2/1: overseers' accts. 1700–34.
[39] Ibid. 13/2/2: Sedgemoor expenditors' accts. 1813–1902.
[40] Ibid. 9/1/2: vestry bk. 1844–98; *Rep. Com. Poor Laws*, H.C. 44 (1834), xxx–xxxiv.
[41] *Poor Law Com. 2nd Rep.* p. 548.
[42] *S.R.S.* xi. 73.
[43] Ibid. i. 170; *Cal. Inq. p.m.* vi, p. 184.
[44] See above p. 52.

between the two parishes through the lands of the manor of Pitney Wearne, and may also be evidence that Pitney was a daughter church of Huish.[45] This last claim seems to have been the origin of the peculiar jurisdiction exercised by the archdeacon of Wells, rector of Huish, in the parish of Pitney in the 19th century.[46] The benefice of Pitney has always been regarded as a rectory, though the incumbent formerly received the great tithes of only a part of his parish.[47] From 1962 the rectory was held in plurality with Aller, but in 1970 it was united with the vicarage of Huish Episcopi.[48]

The advowson of Pitney belonged to the Lorty family and to their successors as lords of the manor of Pitney Lorty from the early 14th century at the latest[49] until the mid 19th century, though the archdeacon of Wells presented in 1624 and the bishop in 1699.[50] The vicar of Huish made an unsuccessful claim in 1541.[51] William Pyne, lord of the manor, and John Williams were patrons in 1819.[52] The right of presentation was acquired from the Pynes by Capt. Joseph Dudman by 1857.[53] On his death in 1864 it passed to his son Lumsden Shirreff Dudman of Pitney House (rector 1851–78),[54] and then to his grandson J. L. S. Shirreff Dudman (d. 1930) of Hove, also a clergyman.[55] The last was followed as patron by his widow Beatrice (d. 1955), and then by Miss G. M. S. Dudman, his daughter, who presented in 1970.[56] The patron of the united benefice in 1971 was the archdeacon of Wells.

The church was not included in the *Taxatio* of 1291, though in 1445 it was assessed at £5 6s. 8d.[57] The net value in 1535 was £9 14s. 8½d.[58] About 1668 it was said to be worth £50, and in 1815 about £153.[59] By 1831 the average net income was £170.[60]

The rector of Pitney received predial and personal tithes and tithes of wool, which in 1535 amounted to £9 13s. 2d.[61] By 1634 all meadow and pasture in the parish was charged with a modus of 1d. an acre, and the rector also received tithe hay from the detached meadows by the Yeo east of Knole and of a small area in Pitney 'Yeards' and Broad Poolmead; tithes of West wood, and in Pitney wood 'tithe in kind at felling thereof'.[62] All parishioners paid 3d. for cow white and 1½d. for each heifer, and at Easter payments of 3d. were made by every married couple, 1d. by every single person born in the parish, and 2d. by every servant.[63] At the same time the rector had the great tithes of some 114 a., in High Ham, largely at Beer, and of just over 29 a. in Huish Episcopi.[64]

Under the inclosure award of 1807 the rector of Pitney was assigned corn rents in lieu of tithe over 807 a. of the parish, valued at £110 13s. 2¾d. Moduses still payable to him, amounting to 30s. 9d., were confirmed.[65] Corn rents worth £5 4s. 9¾d. were awarded to the rector of Pitney in lieu of tithe from Huish in 1799,[66] and the tithes in High Ham were converted to a rent-charge of £21 in 1838.[67] The Pitney corn rents were converted to a rent-charge in 1876 and were then worth £85 19s. 8d.[68] By 1916 these rents had risen to £97 11s. 10d.[69] The total rent-charge from the three sources in 1923 was £122.[70]

The glebe lands were valued at 4s. 6d. in 1535.[71] By 1634 there were 13 a., and by 1807 just over 18 a.[72] The second figure included an augmentation of 2 a. of pasture, the origin of which was not known in 1705.[73] The glebe was sold in 1921.[74] The former rectory-house stood on the north side of the churchyard. It was a stone building with thatched roof, of two storeys, with three- and four-light Perpendicular windows with quatrefoil tracery to the ground floor.[75] The house was no longer occupied by the rector in 1827, and was soon afterwards described as unfit.[76] It was still standing in 1840, but had been demolished by 1876.[77] By 1869 a new house had been built further to the north, probably by Lumsden Shirreff Dudman, the rector.[78] This house, copying some of the features of the old, was occupied by succeeding rectors until 1970.

During the 15th century the benefice was held by at least two rectors in minor orders;[79] and the rector in 1467 was among others accused of counterfeiting money.[80] In 1463 the rector was employing a parochial chaplain.[81] Cananuel Bernard (rector 1624–68) accused in 1634 of celebrating clandestine marriages of people from Langport, appears to have retained his benefice without interruption during the Interregnum, and to have continued to celebrate marriages according to the rites of the Established church throughout the district.[82] A young clerk, probably Faithful Cape, was c. 1693 ordained 'to read prayers for an ancient minister, or officiate at a little place called Pitney'.[83] Anthony Pyne (rector 1792–1819) was also rector of Kingweston and both patron and lord of the manor of Pitney Lorty.[84] His son William succeeded him as patron and lord of the manor in 1819, and was rector from 1824 until 1851, when he became rector of the sinecure benefice of Sock Dennis.[85] In 1827 he was living at Langport and serving as assistant curate at Compton

[45] See pp. 1, 9.
[46] S.R.O., D/D/Paw; *V.C.H. Som.* ii. 67.
[47] *Proc. Som. Arch. Soc.* cxii. 86.
[48] *Dioc. Dir.* (1962–70).
[49] e.g. *S.R.S.* i. 170.
[50] *Som. Incumbents*, ed. Weaver, 167–8.
[51] B.M. Harl. Ch. 58 G 15.
[52] S.R.O., D/D/Bp.
[53] *Clergy List* (1857).
[54] *Crockford* (1874).
[55] Ibid. (1910).
[56] M.I. in church; *Dioc. Dir.* (1970).
[57] *S.R.S.* xlix. 32.
[58] *Valor Eccl.* (Rec. Com.), i. 198.
[59] S.R.O., D/D/Vc 24; D/D/V rtns. 1815.
[60] *Rep. Com. Eccl. Revenues*, pp. 174–5.
[61] *Valor Eccl.* (Rec. Com.), i. 198.
[62] S.R.O., D/D/Rg 231.
[63] Ibid.
[64] Ibid.
[65] S.R.O., CR 57.
[66] Ibid. 131.

[67] S.R.O., tithe award.
[68] Ibid.
[69] S.R.O., D/P/pitn. 5/2/1.
[70] *Crockford* (1923).
[71] *Valor Eccl.* (Rec. Com.), i. 198.
[72] S.R.O., D/D/Rg 231; CR 57.
[73] *Proc. Som. Arch. Soc.* cxii. 86.
[74] S.R.O., D/P/pitn. 5/2/1.
[75] B.M. Add. MS. 36439 f. 271.
[76] S.R.O., D/D/V rtns. 1827; *Rep. Com. Eccl. Revenues*, pp. 174–5.
[77] B.M. Add. MS. 36439 f. 271; S.R.O., tithe award.
[78] S.R.O., D/P/pitn. 13/1/1.
[79] *S.R.S.* xiii. 40; lii. 180.
[80] *Cal. Pat.* 1467–77, 53.
[81] *S.R.S.* xlix. 396.
[82] S.R.O., D/D/Ca 300 ff. 40–40v; D/P/pitn. 2/1/1; *Proc. Som. Arch. Soc.* xxxvii. 92–9.
[83] *S.R.S.* xxxvii. 88.
[84] See p. 53.
[85] See pp. 53, 234.

Dundon.[86] Pyne's successor as rector, Lumsden Shirreff Dudman, was presented to the benefice by his father.[87]

In 1815 only one service was held each Sunday, alternately morning and evening.[88] This was still the practice in 1827.[89] 'Few' attended the morning service on Census Sunday 1851, but the church, seating 256, was 'generally full' in the afternoon.[90] At the beginning of the incumbency of Charles Powell Berryman (rector 1879–85) two services for adults and one for children were held each Sunday, each with a sermon, Holy Communion was celebrated fortnightly and at festivals, and there were also weekday services. In 1880 the rector introduced an embroidered altar frontal, a pulpit fall, and a stole.[91]

The church of *ST. JOHN THE BAPTIST* is built of lias with Ham stone dressings and consists of a chancel with north vestry, nave with south chapel and porch, and west tower. The earliest part of the building is the early-13th-century chancel which has been extensively rebuilt but retains a two-centred doorway and formerly had an east window of three stepped lancets.[92] Presumably there was a contemporary or earlier nave, and a southern transeptal chapel may be inferred from a rib-vaulted squint in the south respond of the chancel arch. The arch, the four-bayed nave, the porch, and the tower are all of mid- to late-14th-century origin. All are or were of relatively plain character with continuous chamfers to the chancel and tower arches, a plain rectangular tower with projecting stair turret, and a cusped outer south doorway. The existing south chapel was built in the 15th century when the two south windows in the nave were enlarged, two new windows were placed in the south wall of the chancel, and the tower was heightened.

The chancel was restored in 1853 when most of the windows were altered and a small vestry was built against the north wall. The restoration of the nave took place in 1874,[93] when the north wall was rebuilt, a new roof incorporating four medieval bosses was put on, and the east window of the chapel altered. The plinth of the font is 14th century. The pulpit and parts of the reading desk are early 17th century.

There are five bells: (i) 1897; (ii) *c.* 1350, Thomas Hey,? of Shaftesbury (Dors.); (iii) *c.* 1350, Dorset foundry; (iv) and (v) 1705, Thomas Knight of Closworth.[94] The plate includes a cup of 1572 by 'I.P.' and a paten given in 1738.[95] The registers begin in 1623 and the series is complete.[96]

NONCONFORMITY. By 1668 Quakers were meeting regularly in Pitney, jointly with Friends from Somerton, but their numbers were so small that in 1674 the meeting was united with that of Long Sutton.[97] Thomas Willis (d. 1682), ejected from Heathfield, was licensed to preach to Congregationalists in his house in 1672.[98] It is not clear whether this group has a continuous history to the present day; the house of William Chard was used as a meeting-house in 1693, and there is a tradition that George Whitefield (d. 1770) preached in the parish at a house called the Old Meeting.[99] No further licences for Independent meetings have been traced until 1798 and 1799.[1] These cottage meetings apparently continued until 1842 when a chapel was erected. In 1851 services were held every Sunday evening for adults, and on Census Sunday the congregation numbered 60. There were Sunday schools in the morning and afternoon for 50 and 45 respectively.[2] The chapel, which seated 150,[3] was rebuilt in 1874, and is called Hope Chapel.[4] It is a simple lias building with a tile roof, and stands at the eastern end of the village.

EDUCATION. There was a day-school in the parish by 1818; possibly the same school in 1833 had 20 pupils, and was supported by contributions from parents. A Sunday school, started in 1823, had 30 pupils ten years later, and was financed by the rector.[5] By 1838 it was evidently housed in a room owned by the duke of Devonshire, and by 1846–7 had 24 day pupils.[6] There was also a dame school with 18 pupils and a Sunday school, held in the Independent chapel, which in 1851 had a morning session with 50 pupils and an afternoon one with 45 pupils.[7]

The day-school probably continued without interruption, and in 1875 the duke of Devonshire conveyed a site for a new building to the archdeacon of Wells.[8] The school was affiliated to the National Society and was supported, though sometimes reluctantly, by voluntary contributions. The building was extended in 1887, and by 1894 had accommodation for 87 pupils and an average attendance of 59.[9] By 1903 there were 43 boys and girls and 25 infants on the books, and the premises were sometimes used for evening continuation classes, for the Sunday school, and for parochial entertainments.[10] The school took juniors and infants only from 1930, and was closed in 1963.[11] The building is now leased for use as the village hall.[12]

CHARITIES FOR THE POOR. None known.

[86] S.R.O., D/D/V rtns. 1827.
[87] M.I. in church.
[88] S.R.O., D/D/V rtns. 1815.
[89] Ibid. 1827.
[90] H.O. 129/317/2/2/5.
[91] S.R.O., D/P/pitn. 23/1.
[92] Taunton Castle, water-colour by J. Buckler, 1840.
[93] S.R.O., D/P/pitn. 6/1/1–2, 6/3/1. The architect was C. Knowles of Bridgwater.
[94] S.R.O., DD/SAS CH 16, pp. 17, 99.
[95] *Proc. Som. Arch. Soc.* xlv. 136.
[96] S.R.O., D/P/pitn. 2/1/1–7.
[97] S.R.O., DD/SFR 1/1, p. 47.
[98] *Cal. S.P. Dom.* 1672, 196, 202; *Calamy Revised,* ed. Matthews.
[99] S.R.O., Q/RR, meeting-house lics.; *Rep. Som. Cong. Union* (1896), 72–3.
[1] S.R.O., D/D/Rm, box 1, 201; box 2. The house of

Samuel Andrews was used 1812–17 by Wesleyan Methodists who then moved to Aller: S.R.O., D/N/sp.c. 1.
[2] H.O. 129/317/2/2/6; *Rep. Som. Cong. Union* (1896), 72–3.
[3] H.O. 129/317/2/2/6.   [4] Inscription on building.
[5] *Digest of Returns to Sel. Cttee. on Educ. of Poor,* H.C. 224 (1819), ix (2); *Educ. Enquiry Abstract,* H.C. 62 (1835), xlii.
[6] D.R.O., D 124, Som. estates general, sale cat. 1838; *Church Sch. Inquiry, 1846–7.*
[7] *Church Sch. Inquiry, 1846–7;* H.O. 129/317/2/2/6.
[8] S.R.O., D/P/pitn. 18/8/1. Managers' mins. 1903–62 are D/P/pitn. 18/7/1–2.
[9] *Return of Schs. 1893* [C 7529], H.C. (1894), lxv; inscription on wall of building.
[10] S.R.O., C/E 27.
[11] Som. C.C. Educ. Cttee. *Schs. List.*
[12] Char. Com. files.

THE HUNDRED OF SOMERTON

THE hundred lies in the southern central area of the county, principally on the Lower Lias which provides the main building stone for the district. It is bisected by the river Cary and, with the exception of East Lydford, is bounded on the south-east by the Foss Way and on the south by the river Yeo. Its economy has always been agrarian, although the market town of Somerton provided an early focus for the cloth trade and was the county's administrative centre for a brief period in the 13th and 14th centuries.[1] The landscape of the lias areas is composed largely of nucleated villages with scattered hamlets, mainly of manorial origin, subsisting originally on open-field arable agriculture. At Aller and in parishes bordering the rivers Yeo and Cary the drainage of low-lying 'moors' provided rich tracts of pasture. Conversion from arable to grassland following 18th- and 19th-century inclosure has also contributed to the current predominance of dairy farming.

The hundred evidently originated in the pre-Conquest royal estate at Somerton and its members. As a hundred it first occurs in contemporary indices of the geld rolls, although the inquest itself is missing.[2] If the early area coincided with that of Somerton warren it included the parishes of Somerton (south and west of the Cary), Kingsdon, Northover, Long Sutton, Pitney, and parts of Huish Episcopi and High Ham.[3] Suit to the forest court in the 13th century was required of Somerton, Kingsdon, Pitney, and Knole (in Long Sutton).[4] It has also been suggested that the hundred may formerly have included the manors which comprised the later hundred of Pitney.[5]

The hundred was mentioned as an administrative unit in 1168[6] and in 1212 its jurisdiction evidently included Langport and Curry Rivel, Newton Placy (in North Petherton), Hurcot (in Somerton), Steart (in Pitney ?), and West Camel.[7] To these may be added Wearne (in Pitney and Huish) and Kingsdon, mentioned in 1225.[8] By c. 1243 Aller, Northover, Charlton Mackrell, and Bineham (in Long Sutton) also lay within the hundred,[9] as did Nether Somerton and Long Sutton in 1251–2,[10] and Bridgehampton (in Yeovilton), Queen Camel, and Littleton (in Compton Dundon) in 1265.[11] The jury of the out-hundred (*hundredum forinsecum*) presented in 1274 that the manor and hundred had been much 'alienated and dismembered', but had formerly included Ilchester, East (or Queen) Camel, Pitney and Wearne, Curry Rivel and Langport, North Curry, Aller, a moiety of Northover, and Sedgemoor, besides smaller areas of land.[12] In 1286 the hundred comprised Queen Camel, West Camel, Yeovilton (with Bridgehampton and Speckington), Kingsdon, Long Sutton, Aller, Littleton, Charlton Adam, Charlton Mackrell (with Cary Fitzpaine and Lytes Cary), and East Lydford.[13] In the course of the 14th century Queen Camel was removed, Charlton Adam and

[1] See pp. 138–9, 142.
[2] R. W. Eyton, *Dom. Studies, Som.* i. 90–1, 207–9; ii. 9, 37–8.
[3] See *V.C.H. Som.* ii. 552, for perambulation of the warren. 'Modresford' and 'Monkesham' both lay in High Ham (*S.R.S.* lix, pp. (xi), 230).
[4] *V.C.H. Som.* ii. 553.
[5] R. W. Eyton, *Dom. Studies, Som.* i. 207–9.
[6] *Pipe R.* 1168 (P.R.S. xii), 151.
[7] *Bk. of Fees,* i. 78–9.
[8] *S.R.S.* xi. 41, 57.
[9] Ibid. 257.
[10] *Bk. of Fees,* ii. 1265.
[11] *Cal. Inq. Misc.* i, p. 267.
[12] *Rot. Hund.* (Rec. Com.) ii. 121.
[13] *Feud. Aids,* iv. 285–6.

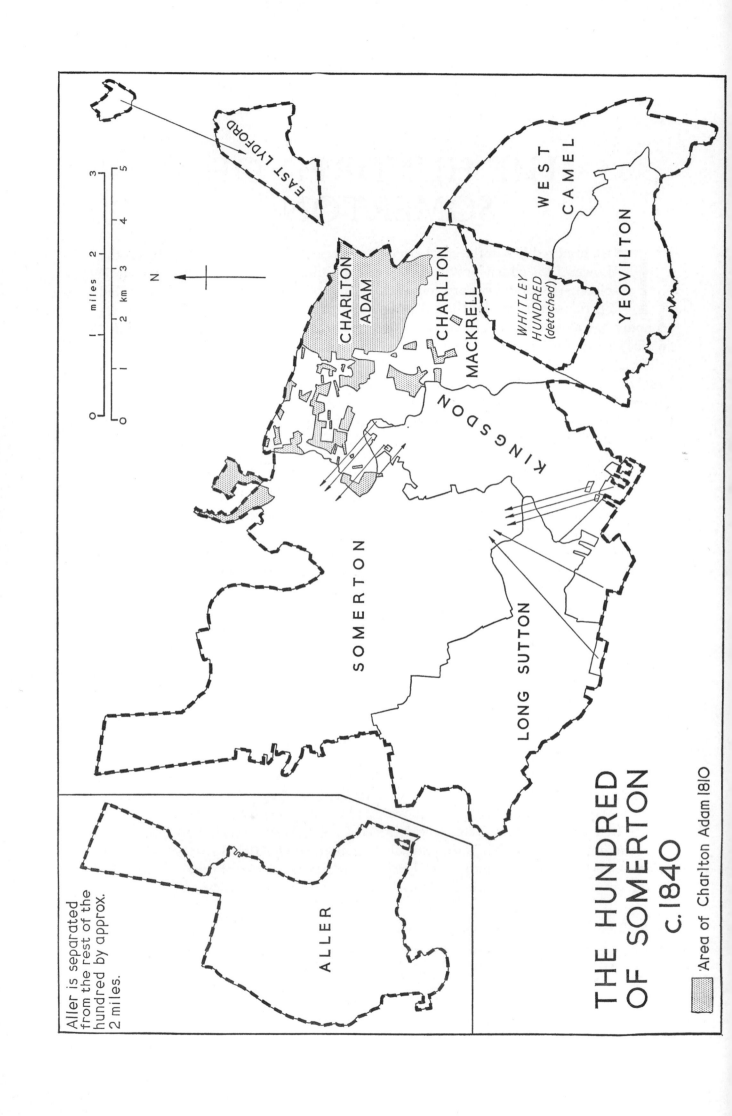

THE HUNDRED
OF SOMERTON
C.1840

Area of Charlton Adam 1810

Aller is separated
from the rest of the
hundred by approx.
2 miles.

EAST LYDFORD

WEST
CAMEL

YEOVILTON

WHITLEY
HUNDRED
(detached)

CHARLTON
ADAM

CHARLTON
MACKRELL

KINGSDON

SOMERTON

LONG SUTTON

ALLER

N

miles

km

0 1 2 3

0 1 2 3 4 5

Charlton Mackrell were united to form a single tithing, and Cary Fitzpaine in Charlton Mackrell was transfered to Whitley hundred.[14] In 1327 the tithings of Hurcot and Pitney Wearne were taxed with Somerton borough.[15] From 1376 at least until 1762 eleven tithings owed suit to the hundred court: East Lydford, Bridgehampton, Yeovilton, Charlton, Kingsdon, Long Sutton, Demi Sutton (in Long Sutton), Littleton, and Somerton Erleigh.[16] Throughout this period Kingsdon paid suit with the tithing of Cary (Lytes Cary and Tuckers Cary) in Charlton Mackrell.[17] In 1569 the administrative hundred was made up of the borough of Somerton and the tithings of Long Sutton, West Camel, East Lydford, Littleton, Yeovilton, Aller, Hurcot, Somerton Erleigh, Charlton, and Kingsdon.[18] To these Pitney Plucknett (or Pitney Wearne) had been added by 1582.[19] During the 18th century Bridgehampton was often considered an individual fiscal tithing, as were Charlton Adam and Charlton Mackrell.[20] These divisions continued at least until 1832.[21]

In the medieval period Somerton borough was evidently considered to form the in-hundred and all other tithings the out-hundred. In 1262 the hundred was granted to Eleanor of Provence, queen of Henry III, and thereafter it descended with Somerton manor.[22] In 1318 it was committed with the bailiwick to John de Countevill during pleasure.[23] Sir John Carew was appointed steward by the Crown in 1509,[24] and a further grant of the stewardship was made to Carew and William Compton in survivorship in 1512.[25]

Court records for the out-hundred survive for the years 1376–7, 1392–3,[26] 1436–7,[27] 1539–40, 1542–4,[28] 1562–3, 1565–6, 1573–4,[29] 1617–20, 1730–62.[30] There were originally three courts in and for the out-hundred, all held within Somerton borough: a *tremure* court, the equivalent of an early view of frankpledge, the lawday court, and a three-weekly court, which balanced the three-weekly court of Somerton borough.

The *tremure* court was held three times a year, at Michaelmas, Hilary, and Hockday (later Easter), until the 18th century when generally only the two latter courts met. In January 1377 it was combined with the lawday court, and in Michaelmas 1392 and Hockday 1393 with the view of frankpledge. The court was known simply as *tremura* or *Somerton forinsecum, curia tremura*. Its business comprised the appearance of the eleven tithingmen, their presentments, and the payment of customary fines. The presentments included default of suit, breach of the assize of ale, unjust tolls taken by millers, and the disrepair of roads, bridges, and ditches. The customary fines included tithing silver and payments for failure to keep watch at night. *Tremure* courts are also recorded for three Devon hundreds. The term *borh-treming* for view of frankpledge is found in Suffolk, and there was a 'triming day' at Leighton Buzzard (Beds.).[31] It has thus been argued that the trimming of the tithings represents the Anglo-Saxon counterpart of the Norman view of frankpledge.

The hundred lawday court was held twice a year at Michaelmas and Hockday (later Easter), including in 1392–3 the sheriff's tourn and view of frankpledge, and in 1437

[14] Ibid. 321, 343–4, 388; *S.R.S.* iii. 124, 201–3.

[15] *S.R.S.* iii. 279–80.

[16] Hunt. Libr., HA Manorial, hundred ct. rolls 1376–7; D.R.O., D 124, hundred ct. bk. 1730–62.

[17] Hunt. Libr., HA Manorial, hundred ct. rolls 1376–7; D.R.O., D 124, hundred ct. bk. 1730–62.

[18] *S.R.S.* xx. 228–35.

[19] S.R.O., DD/SF 3948.

[20] *S.R.S.* iii. 303; S.R.O., Q/RE, land tax assessments.

[21] *Plac. de Quo Warr.* (Rec. Com.), 689; *Bk. of Fees*, ii. 1251–2; *Rot. Hund.* (Rec. Com.), ii. 121.

[22] See p. 134.

[23] *Cal. Fine R.* 1307–19, 361.

[24] *L. & P. Hen. VIII*, i (1), p. 80.

[25] Ibid. p. 535.

[26] Hunt. Libr., HA Manorial, hundred ct. rolls 1376–7, 1392–3.

[27] S.C. 2/200/33.　　　　[28] S.C. 2/200/34.

[29] Hunt. Libr., HA Manorial, hundred ct. rolls 1562–6, 1573–4.

[30] D.R.O., D 124, hundred ct. bks. 1617–20, 1730–62. All subsequent details of courts are taken from these records unless otherwise stated.

[31] *E.H.R.* lxxi. 428–33.

and from 1573 the view of frankpledge alone. Until 1731 it was held within a few days of the *tremure* court but thereafter it met on the same day. By the mid 17th century the Michaelmas court was customarily adjourned to St. Simon and St. Jude's day (28 October) for the swearing-in of officers.[32] The court was known usually as the *curia legalis* of either Somerton hundred or Somerton *forinsecum*, but after 1731 as the court leet. The tithingmen appeared, presented, and paid further customary fines, including those for not bringing their measures. A jury was empanelled and presented instances of disrepair, assaults, and other minor offences. Pleas, mainly of debt and trespass, were heard, and the freeholders of the hundred paid fines for release of suit to the Michaelmas lawday. In 1376 there were 18 freeholders, generally representing manors within the hundred. This number increased to 24 in 1392 and to 27 between 1543 and 1562. Thereafter persistent default reduced the suitors to 25 between 1573 and 1617 and to 20 or 21 between 1730 and 1762. By the 18th century the lawday court was concerned almost wholly with the maintenance of roads and bridges and the collection of customary payments.

The three weeks court was devoted to pleas, again mainly of debt and trespass. In 1376 East Lydford was paying for release of suit to it and by the 16th century only five tithings, Kingsdon, Charlton, Long Sutton, Somerton Erleigh, and Littleton, were appearing. Courts were known simply as *hundreda* or *curiae hundredi* for Somerton *forinsecum*. No rolls survive for this court after 1574 but it was still being held in the mid 17th century when it dealt with actions for debt or damage under 40s. and was usually held on Mondays.[33]

The only officers appointed by these courts, apart from the tithingmen presented by their tithings, were two constables elected at the Michaelmas lawday from 1565. During the 18th century the hundred was split into two divisions and a constable was selected from each of them. The eastern division comprised Bridgehampton, Yeovilton, Kingsdon, Charlton, East Lydford, and West Camel, and the western Somerton Erleigh, Aller, Long Sutton, Demi Sutton, and Littleton. References to the hundred bailiff occur as late as the 18th century, but he was not elected in any of the three hundred courts.

A reference to the unlawful imprisonment of a clerk by the hundred court in 1436[34] suggests the existence of a gaol for the hundred at Somerton.

---

[32] D.R.O., D 124, box 117, bk. of hundred cts. *c.* 1664–6.   [33] Ibid.   [34] S.C. 2/200/33.

ALLER

THE ancient parish of Aller, known often in the 14th century as King's Aller,[1] had an area of 3,605 a. in 1901,[2] of which 555 a. were allotted to Aller from King's Sedgemoor in 1792.[3]

The parish lies $2\frac{1}{2}$ miles west from Langport and 9 miles south-east from Bridgwater. It is highly irregular in shape, stretching $4\frac{1}{2}$ miles from north to south, $2\frac{1}{2}$ miles from east to west, but is only $\frac{1}{3}$ mile in breadth at the edge of King's Sedgemoor in the north. The boundary to the south and south-west with Curry Rivel and Stoke St. Gregory is formed by the river Parrett, with the exception of Oath, an elliptical addition across the river. The original northern boundary at Beer Wall follows the river Cary, and that to the north-east and east a ridgeway along the summit of Aller hill.

The high ground in the parish known as Aller hill lies on the Keuper Marl along its eastern limit, the highest point being 325 ft. near Beer. Aller 'island' in the centre of the parish and Oath hill across the Parrett to the south are outcrops of Keuper Marl, but most of the parish, comprising the 'moors', lies on the alluvium.[4]

In addition to the Cary and Parrett the 'moors' are drained by a complex system of rhines, the construction of which dates from the 14th century.[5] The parish is protected from flood by the Great Wall or Aller Wall along its southern boundary, by Callis Wall on the west, and Beer Wall to the north, all evidently medieval in origin.[6] Standing on the edge of the 'moors', the parish presents a somewhat bleak and isolated aspect, particularly in winter with periodic flooding. In c. 1583 Francis Hastings found 'no great cause of commendation of the site because it standeth low and unsavoury by reason of the ditches of the moor'.[7] A rector, Ralph Cudworth, wrote in 1618 that 'the air is very bad, especially in the spring, so that I have been often in danger of death by reason of agues, etc., which makes me desirous to remove'.[8] To Camden it was 'a little village of few small huts'.[9]

The original settlement was probably made in the area of Aller Court Farm on Aller 'island', where the parish church also stands, but the village developed along the lower slopes of Aller hill between the 25 ft. and 50 ft. contours. By the later 16th century much of its present area was already built up,[10] further expansion being restricted by the open arable fields, the 'moors', and the steepness of Aller hill. By the 19th century improved drainage

had led to the erection of houses south-west of the village along Church Path, and cottages were also built on the steep slope at Penny Hill,[11] although a number of these were derelict in 1972. Most of the manorial tenement farms lay on either side of the main street in the village.[12] On the south side at the Cross Tree stands the White Lion public house. This was first built on a plot of waste in 1571,[13] had become one of two tippling houses in the parish by 1653,[14] and was known by its present name in 1756.[15]

At Oath settlement had developed around the north-western and south-eastern limits of the hill by the 16th century,[16] although none of the present dwellings exhibits any early features. Two farms at Beer are recorded from the early 14th century,[17] and references in 1322 to Nicholas and William of Bagenham and Robert le Coumbe[18] suggest that the sites of Bagenham Farm, on the western boundary with Othery, and Combe Farm, on the eastern boundary with Huish, had already been settled. From a tenement called the Boathouse near Bagenham there was a ferry by 1561 across the rhine dividing Aller from Othery.[19] In 1653 it was stated that a temporary bridge was annually laid over this rhine at Pathe for the removal of hay from Aller moor, but that at all other times the ferryman might charge for passages.[20] Improved drainage during the 19th century also enabled the building of Withybed (now Willow) Farm on the banks of the Parrett opposite Stathe to the south, and also Longstone Farm in Aller Great drove.[21] Modern dwellings have been erected on individual plots in the village, principally in Beer Road.

The main road through the parish, known initially as the Street in c. 1577, and in the 19th century as South Street or Langport Street,[22] enters Aller in the east from Langport, runs below Aller hill through the site of South field and the village to the Cross Tree. Thence as Beer Road it turns north-east through the former North field towards Beer. Finally it bears west from Beer Cross beside Beer Wall, leaving the parish for Othery. This road was turnpiked throughout its length in 1828, a toll-gate and house being erected at Plotstream, near the eastern end of the parish, and another soon after at Beer Cross.[23] Only the former survives. Church Path runs south-west from the Cross Tree, crossing Weir bridge (mentioned in 1761)[24] to the church and Aller Court Farm. A ridgeway along the summit of

[1] Between 1314 (*S.R.S.* xii. 42) and 1373 (*Cal. Papal Regs.* iv. 189). This article was completed in 1972.
[2] *Census*, 1901.
[3] S.R.O., CR 116.
[4] Geol. Surv. Map 1", solid and drift, sheet 296 (1969 edn.).
[5] See below and p. 66.
[6] See p. 66.
[7] *S.R.S.* lxix. 28.
[8] Bodl. MS. Rawl. Lett. 89 f. 25.
[9] Camden, *Britannia* (1695), 59.
[10] Hunt. Libr., HA Manorial, survey of manor, c. 1577.
[11] S.R.O., tithe award.
[12] Hunt. Libr., HA Manorial, survey of manor, c. 1577.

[13] Ibid. ct. roll.
[14] S.R.O., DD/SAS (C/124), manor customs, 1653.
[15] S.R.O., Q/RL.
[16] Hunt. Libr., HA Manorial, survey of manor, c. 1577.
[17] See p. 65.
[18] E 142/28.
[19] Bodl. MS. Top. Som. c. 1 f. 30.
[20] S.R.O., DD/SAS (C/124), manor customs, 1653.
[21] S.R.O., tithe award; O.S. Map 1/2,500, Som. LXII. 14, 15 (1885 edn.).
[22] Hunt. Libr., HA Manorial, survey of manor, c. 1577; S.R.O., D/P/all. 13/10/2.
[23] S.R.O., DD/X/EE; D/T/lsc. 1, 2.
[24] S.R.O., DD/SAS (W/51), map of Aller manor, 1761.

Aller hill was described as a procession way in 1572 and 1653,[25] and was known as Wood Lane by 1885.[26] Penny Hill Lane runs north-east from the northern end of the village up Aller hill. An elaborate network of droves, all established by c. 1577,[27] serves the entire area of the 'moors' and also links the village with Pathe and Oath. Oath is reached by a footbridge, mentioned in 1808 and 1811 when it was swept away by floods.[28]

Arable land within the parish was largely restricted to the Keuper Marl. Of the two open fields attached to Aller manor North field lay immediately north of the village, forming an elongated rectangle on either side of Beer Road. South field lay immediately south-east of the village, stretching from the summit of Aller hill to the north to below the Langport road southwards.[29] There was a single open field, Beer Court field, in the area of Beer Farm in the north of the parish,[30] and Oath hill was divided into two open fields, East and West, which served Oath manor by c. 1577.[31] Early meadowland was more scattered. Open meadows known as Landmeads, mentioned in 1322,[32] lay along the western edge of the North field and in the South field.[33] Other meadows mentioned in 1322 but not located were known as 'Nywelond-mede' and 'Mormede'.[34] The remainder of the parish, comprising the low-lying 'moors', was devoted to pasture. The area south of Aller Great drove formed Aller moor; North moor lay south of Beer Wall and west of North field; Leaseway (Lesfee in c. 1577) extended west of North moor and north of Aller Great drove.[35] Aller wood lies between the former North field and Wood Lane on the upper slopes of Aller hill.

In 1676 a decoy pool was made in Aller moor by five tenants. The lord gave materials for its construction and allowed those tenants royalty for fowling over the 'moor'. In return they were to stock the decoy and render a quarter of all birds taken.[36] The pool was still there in 1838.[37]

The houses in the village are principally of 18th and 19th century date, of lias or brick, with thatched or tiled roofs. The Manor House and Chantry Farm have mansard roofs and are both of the 18th century.

Aller Friendly Society, known also as the Aller Schoolhouse Benefit Society, was founded in 1849 and reformed in 1870. It held its annual dinner and club walk on Whit Monday,[38] but was disbanded in 1940.[39] The society's banner was held in the church in 1972.

There were 124 communicants in the parish in 1548.[40] The population was 389 in 1801 and rose gradually to 559 in 1841. It remained relatively stable until 1871 and thereafter, in common with other rural parishes, fell steadily from 533 in that year to 347 in 1911.[41] The number of inhabitants has changed little during the present century, amounting to 339 in 1961.[42]

During the Interregnum John Northover, tenant of Aller Court and an ardent royalist, was accused of having supplied two men for the King's army and, on a Sunday evening after church, of inciting the parishioners to join Goring's forces at the siege of Taunton.[43] After the battle of Langport on 9 July 1645 the royalist army fled to Bridgwater across Aller moor, making a brief stand at Aller Great drove. There they were routed. Many horses 'were lost in the ditches . . . and the riders got into the meadows hoping to escape, but could not'.[44] Northover was accused of laying a bridge over a rhine to aid their flight.[45] Sir Thomas Fairfax spent the night after the battle at Aller before proceeding towards Bridgwater.[46]

Ralph Cudworth (1617–88), son of an Aller rector, was born in the parish and educated by his stepfather, John Stoughton, who had succeeded Cudworth's father as rector. He subsequently became the leader of the Cambridge Platonists and served as Regius Professor of Hebrew from 1645 until his death. His principal work, *The True Intellectual System*, was published in 1678.[47]

MANORS. The manor of *ALLER* was held by Ulward in 1066 but by the time of Domesday had passed to Ralph de Limesy.[48] The overlordship evidently descended with the barony of Cavendish (Suff.) to Ralph de Limesy (II) (d. c. 1129) and Ralph's son Alan (d. by 1162).[49] Alan was succeeded by Gerard (d. by 1185), whose son John de Limesy died without issue in 1193.[50] The overlordship of the manor passed to his sister Basile, wife of Hugh de Odingselles (d. 1239), for in 1284–6 and 1303 it was held by her grandson Hugh (II) (d. 1305), son of Gerard de Odingselles (d. 1267).[51] Hugh's son John (I) (d. 1336) held it in 1312,[52] but subsequently it passed from the Odingselles family to John de Stouford, to whose daughter Joan and her husband William FitzWarren of Brightleigh (Devon) the immediate lord of Aller manor did homage in 1363.[53] In 1408 homage for the manor was done to Sir Thomas Brook, then stated to have purchased the Odingselles fees in Somerset formerly held by

[25] Hunt. Libr., HA Manorial, ct. roll; S.R.O., DD/SAS (C/124), manor customs, 1653.
[26] O.S. Map 1/2,500, Som. LXII. 15 (1885 edn.).
[27] Hunt. Libr., HA Manorial, survey of manor, c. 1577.
[28] S.R.O., D/P/all. 4/1/1.
[29] S.R.O., CR 106; see below, p. 67.
[30] S.R.O., DD/SAS (C/124), manor customs, 1653.
[31] Hunt. Libr., HA Manorial, survey of manor, c. 1577.
[32] E 142/28.
[33] S.R.O., DD/SAS (C/124), manor customs, 1653; tithe award.
[34] E 142/28.
[35] Hunt Libr., HA Manorial, survey, c. 1577; S.R.O., tithe award.
[36] S.R.O., DD/MI, box 5, agreement, 20 Mar. 1675/6; the pool was sited at O.S. Nat. Grid 402282.
[37] S.R.O., tithe award.
[38] Taunton Castle, *Articles of the Aller Schoolhouse*

Benefit Soc. (1870), *Aller Friendly Soc. Rules* (1905); Margaret Fuller, *West Country Friendly Soc.* 143.
[39] Ex inf. Mr. W. G. Mitchell.
[40] *S.R.S.* ii. 106.
[41] *V.C.H. Som.* ii. 348; *Census*, 1911.
[42] *Census*, 1921–61.
[43] S.P. 23/G 179 f. 716.
[44] J. Sprigge, *Anglia Rediviva* (1647), 65–6.
[45] S.P. 23/G 179 f. 716.
[46] *Coppie of a letter . . . concerning the great battle . . . at Langport* (1645).
[47] *D.N.B.*   [48] *V.C.H. Som.* i. 511.
[49] Sanders, *Eng. Baronies*, 29–30.
[50] Ibid. 30.
[51] Ibid.; *Feud. Aids*, iv. 285, 300.
[52] Sanders, *Eng. Baronies*, 30; *Cal. Inq. p.m.* v, pp. 229–30.
[53] *Sotheby's Cat.* 1936, 415 (2); *Trans. Devon. Assoc.* xxxiv. 691; xciv. 249; *Cal. Close*, 1385–9, 484.

John Brightleigh (d. 1407) son of William Fitz-Warren.[54] Brook (d. 1418) still held the overlordship in 1412,[55] but by 1462 it had passed to John Launcy, evidently in right of his wife Joan, who also held it in 1478.[56] By 1489 the manor was stated to be held in chief[57] and by 1496 of the honor of Somerton.[58] The overlordship has not been traced thereafter.

It is not known when the manor was subinfeudated, but Raher of Aller, whose family subsequently owned the manor, is mentioned between 1166 and 1187,[59] as is his son Ralph of Aller between 1201 and 1232.[60] Ralph's son Sir John of Aller (d. c. 1272) presumably held the manor which after his death was divided between his daughters Margaret and Elizabeth.[61] Margaret married John de Acton (I) and was succeeded by John (II) (d. 1312).[62] In 1335 John (III) (d. after 1360), son of John (II), granted the remainder, failing male heirs, of his moiety, then known as the manor of *ALLER ACTON*, to his cousin John of Clevedon,[63] owner of the second moiety.[64] Elizabeth, second daughter of Sir John of Aller, married Raymond of Clevedon (d. by 1280) and held the other moiety of the manor in her own right in 1284–6.[65] By 1303 she had been succeeded by her son Matthew (II) of Clevedon (d. by 1332), during whose tenure the moiety was known as the manor of *ALLER CLEVEDON*.[66] Sir Matthew's son Sir John (III) (d. c. 1373), who reunited the two moieties, was succeeded by his granddaughter Margaret (d. 1412), daughter of John of Clevedon (d. before 1348),[67] and wife successively of Sir John St. Lo (d. 1375) and Sir Peter Courtenay (d. 1405).[68] She was succeeded by her grandson William, Lord Botreaux (d. 1462), son of her daughter Elizabeth (d. 1389).[69] Botreaux's widow Margaret (d. 1488) and her second husband Sir Thomas Burgh (d. 1496) retained a life interest in the manor, which passed on their deaths to her great-granddaughter Mary, daughter of Sir Thomas Hungerford and wife of Edward, Lord Hastings (d. 1506).[70] Lady Hastings subsequently

married Richard Sacheverell, who received a life interest in the manor and was still holding it in 1545.[71]

The manor was known by 1532 as *ALLER AND ALLERMOOR*,[72] and from 1589 as *ALLER AND ALLER CHANTRY*.[73] The reversion descended to George Hastings (cr. earl of Huntingdon 1529, d. 1545), son of Edward, Lord Hastings, and then to his son Francis (d. 1560).[74] Thence the manor passed in turn to Francis's sons Henry (d. 1595) and George (d. 1604), the latter being succeeded by his grandson Henry, earl of Huntingdon (d. 1643).[75] The last sold it to Sir John Davis in 1612, excluding the manor-house, demesne lands, Combe farm, and Aller moor,[76] and Davis conveyed it to John (later Sir John) Stawell of Cothelstone in 1623.[77] During the Interregnum Stawell's estates were sequestered, *ALLER* manor being purchased by Maj.-Gen. Thomas Harrison in 1653.[78] From Harrison the manor evidently passed to John Aubrey of Low Ham, who conveyed it in 1658 to Walter Long, possibly his father-in-law, and Mary Long, widow.[79] Sir John Stawell's lands were restored to him at the Restoration,[80] and after his death in 1662 the manor descended in turn to his sons George (d. 1669) and Ralph (cr. baron Stawell of Somerton 1683, d. 1689).[81] Ralph's son John, Lord Stawell (d. 1692), encumbered his estates with heavy mortgages and the manor was vested in trustees.[82] Under a Chancery decree of 1697 it was sold in 1706 to Anne Mowrie of Low Ham and William Harrison of North Petherton.[83] Many of the manorial lands were sold off soon after this conveyance, the lordship and residue of the estate descending to William Mowrie (d. 1745), son of Anne.[84] William devised his estate to his nephew John Pyne of Charlton Adam (d. 1791), whose sons William and John sold it to James Hyde in 1793.[85] Hyde was evidently uncertain whether or not he possessed the manor and in 1830 procured a conveyance of the lordship from John, Lord Sherborne, heir of the Stawell family.[86] This grant included no lands but led to the

[54] B.M. Add. Ch. 25886; *Cal. Pat.* 1405–8, 261, 289, 305; *Cal. Inq. p.m.* (Rec. Com.) iii. 313; *Trans. Devon. Assoc.* xciv. 251.
[55] C 137/86/30. [56] C 140/7/15; C 140/67/40.
[57] *Cal. Inq. p.m. Hen. VII*, i, pp. 195–6.
[58] Ibid. 532–3.
[59] *S.R.S.* xiv. 161; *Pipe R.* 1187 (P.R.S. xxxvii), 27.
[60] *S.R.S.* xi. 6; *Bracton's Note Bk.* ed. Maitland, ii. 515.
[61] *Bracton's Note Bk.* ed. Maitland, ii. 515; *S.R.S.* xliv. 108; lxiii. 302; *Feud. Aids*, iv. 285; E 142/28; *Proc. Som. Arch. Soc.* lxxi. 13–15.
[62] *S.R.S.* vi. 273; xliv. 108; *Cal. Inq. p.m.* v, pp. 229–30.
[63] *Cal. Inq. p.m.* v, p. 230; *S.R.S.* xii. 177; E 142/28; *Feud. Aids*, iv. 343; *H.M.C. Wells*, i. 502. [64] See below.
[65] *S.R.S.* xliv. 108; *Feud. Aids*, iv. 285; *Proc. Som. Arch. Soc.* xli. 5–8.
[66] *Feud. Aids*, iv. 300, 321; *S.R.S.* ix. 111; E 142/28; *Proc. Som. Arch. Soc.* xli. 9–10.
[67] *Proc. Som. Arch. Soc.* xli. 10–17; lxxi. 15–26.
[68] Ibid. xli. 17–20; lxxi. 26–30; *S.R.S.* xvii. 142–3; *Cal. Close*, 1402–5, 445–6; C 137/50/38; C 137/86/30; *S. & D. N. & Q.* vi. 243–5.
[69] C 137/86/30; *Proc. Som. Arch. Soc.* xli. 20; *Complete Peerage*, s.v. Botreaux; *Cal. Close*, 1413–19, 436–7, 439–40; *Feud. Aids*, iv. 388, 428; C 140/7/15.
[70] *S.R.S.* xxii. 126–7; Bodl. MS. Chart. Som. a. 1 f. 1; *Cal. Close*, 1468–76, 62–3; C 140/7/15; C 140/67/40; *Cal. Inq. p.m. Hen. VII*, i, pp. 195–6, 532–3; *Complete Peerage*, s.v. Botreaux.
[71] *Complete Peerage*, s.v. Botreaux, Hastings; Bodl. MS. Chart. Som. a. 1 f. 3; C 142/56/36; C 142/70/1.
[72] Bodl. MS. Chart. Som. a. 1 f. 5.

[73] Ibid. ff. 11–14, 17.
[74] C 142/70/1; *Complete Peerage*, s.v. Huntingdon; Bodl. MS. Chart. Som. a. 1 ff. 3–5.
[75] Bodl. MS. Chart. Som. a. 1, ff. 6–19; *Complete Peerage*, s.v. Huntingdon.
[76] Bodl. MS. Carte 289 f. 64; *Cal. Charters, etc. at Sherborne House, Glos.* (1900, priv. print.), 190.
[77] Bodl. MS. Chart. Som. a. 1 ff. 36–8; S.R.O., D/PC/all. 5/1–2.
[78] G. D. Stawell, *A Quantock Family* (1910), 97–9, 419.
[79] S.R.O., DD/MI, box 6, notes on Sir John Stawell's estate; C.P. 25 (2)/593/1658 East.
[80] G. D. Stawell, *A Quantock Family*, 97–9, 419.
[81] *Complete Peerage*, s.v. Stawell; S.R.O., DD/MI, box 5, deeds 9 June 1666, 20 Mar. 1675/6; *S.R.S.* xxxiv. 28.
[82] D.R.O., D 124, box 108, conveyance, 15 May 1707; S.R.O., DD/HLM, box 1, conveyance, 15 May 1707.
[83] D.R.O., D 124, box 108, conveyance, 15 May 1707; S.R.O., DD/HLM, box 1, conveyance, 15 May 1707.
[84] S.R.O., D/PC/all. 5/1–2; DD/ES, box 18, survey of manor, c. 1740.
[85] S.R.O., DD/CM, box 8, abstr. of will of William Mowrie, 10 May 1745; DD/LC, box 14, schedule of deeds, 1880.
[86] S.R.O., D/PC/all. 5/1–2. The manor of Aller, although relinquished by the Stawells in 1706, continued to be included in some of their family settlements (ibid., covenant to produce deeds, 12 Oct. 1830). In c. 1740 their 'manor' of Aller comprised 82 a. held by 9 leaseholders (S.R.O., DD/ES, box 18, survey bk.), and Lord Sherborne 'enfranchised' lands in 1828 (John Hodge & Co., solicitors, Weston-super-Mare, deed of Aller lands).

Hyde family naming their residence the Manor House.[87] On James Hyde's death in 1832 his lands in the parish passed to his five sons and eventually to his son Charles.[88] After the death of Charles's widow in 1879 the 'Aller manor estate' was split up and auctioned in 1880.[89] The lordship was sold in the following year to T. H. Gent (d. 1898) for £5, and his sons, T. C. and W. F. Gent, conveyed it in 1910 to Aller parish council, the present lords of the manor.[90] The only property allied to the title from 1880 was the village pound.[91]

The manor-house is first mentioned in 1312,[92] and was held with the moiety of Aller Acton in 1322.[93] The house and demesne lands, known as Aller Court by 1533, were then leased for 70 years to Nicholas Thorne (d. 1546), a Bristol merchant.[94] Thorne bequeathed the lease to his widow Bridget,[95] and by 1559 it had passed to Mary, widow of his son Robert Thorne.[96] Before 1565 it had been assigned to John Wake who transferred it in that year to William Northover.[97] The Northover family continued to occupy the property during the 17th century.[98] The freehold was evidently acquired by the Stawell family and sold by their trustees to Sir Thomas Wroth (d. 1721) of North Petherton, being then known as the manors or reputed manors of *ALLER AND OATH*.[99] On Wroth's death his estates were divided between his two daughters, the Aller property passing to Elizabeth, wife of Thomas Palmer of Fairfield, Stogursey.[1] She was succeeded in 1737–8 by her sister Cecily, married first to Sir Hugh Acland (d. 1728) and second to Thomas Troyte.[2] Thence the manor passed to Cecily's second son, Arthur Acland (d. 1771), and subsequently to his son Sir John Palmer Acland (d. 1823) and to his grandson Sir Peregrine P. F. P. Acland (d. 1871).[3] Sir Peregrine had evidently settled the property on his son-in-law Sir Alexander Acland-Hood by c. 1860.[4] Acland-Hood with the Acland trustees sold the farm to the occupier, Henry Munckton (d. 1890) in 1872.[5] The manorial status of the estate was not mentioned in the conveyance. By Order in Chancery of 1893 the premises were awarded to the surviving holders of Munckton's undischarged mortgage, B. B. Greene and Sir William J. W. Baynes, Bt., who sold the farm to C. R. Morris of North Curry in 1894.[6] In 1918 Morris's executors conveyed it to their tenant T. H. Jeanes, who sold it to L. S. Garner

in 1947.[7] A year later it was purchased by Mrs. E. M. Haywood who conveyed the farm to the present owner, Mr. P. C. Maltby, in 1969.[8]

The house was described in 1633 as 'an ancient castlelike house, highly seated in a low place',[9] but the old building was largely demolished in 1812 and 'a modern farm' built for the tenant.[10] Both wings of the present farm-house are at least of 17th-century origin, but the principal range which connects them dates from the Acland rebuilding. The earliest element of the group is the great barn, originally a large medieval domestic building, part at least of two storeys. An outbuilding west of the farm is of c. 1500 and was probably a self-contained house.

There was a manorial chapel dedicated to the Blessed Virgin Mary in which a chantry was founded in 1263 by Sir John of Aller where masses were to be said daily for the souls of his late wife and other members of his family.[11] The patronage descended with the lordship of Aller manor, passing during the early 14th century with the moiety of Aller Clevedon.[12] The bishop collated by lapse in 1463,[13] and the last presentation was made in 1533 by the lessee of Aller Court.[14] In 1546 the incumbent had a silver chalice, parcel gilt, a pair of vestments, and a corporal with case.[15] In 1548 the chantry was dissolved, its possessions then being a chalice weighing 19 oz., ornaments, and 40 lb. of bell metal.[16] The chapel was then roofed with stone.[17] The lands belonging to the chantry, valued at £6 a year, comprised 42 a. of pasture, 18 a. of arable, and a dwelling-house, all leased. A parlour and chamber in the same house, evidently at one time occupied by the chaplain, were also leased.[18] The chapel was described as lying 'in the manor of Aller' in 1473,[19] 'in the base court of the manor place' in 1548,[20] and was still standing in 1561.[21] The chantry and its lands were granted in 1550 to Francis, earl of Huntingdon, and Thomas Hazlewood and subsequently formed a leasehold estate within Aller manor now known as Chantry farm.[22]

Lands in 'Oht' held with Aller property by the Acton family were mentioned in 1288, and Oath hermitage lay in Aller parish in 1328.[23] A moiety of *OATH* manor was held by Sir John de Acton (III) in 1346,[24] indicating that it was then held

[87] S.R.O., tithe award.
[88] S.R.O., DD/BR/hmp, will of Marianne Hyde, proved 1879; DD/LC, box 14, schedule of deeds, 1880.
[89] S.R.O., DD/LC, box 14, schedule of deeds, 1880.
[90] S.R.O., D/PC/all. 5/1–2.
[91] Ex inf. Mrs. F. McNelly.
[92] C 134/30/11.
[93] E 142/28.
[94] Bodl. MS. Chart. Som. a. 1 f. 6.
[95] *Great Orphan Bk. and Bk. of Wills at Bristol*, ed. T. P. Wadley (1886), 184.
[96] Req. 2/39/90.
[97] C.P. 40/1234 rot. 49.
[98] *S. & D. N. & Q.* iv. 255.
[99] Devon R.O. 1148 add/bay 15, box 2, partition, 22 Nov. 1723; S.R.O., DD/SH 107.
[1] Devon R.O. 1148 add/bay 15, box 2, partition, 22 Nov. 1723.
[2] J. L. Vivian, *Visit. of Devon*, 5; *Som. Wills*, ed. Brown, ii. 85–9.
[3] *Som. Wills*, ed. Brown, ii. 86; S.R.O., tithe award; D/P/all. 4/1/1.
[4] Burke, *Peerage* (1949), 1761; S.R.O., D/P/all. 13/10/2.
[5] John Hodge and Co., solicitors, Weston-super-Mare, deeds of Aller Court farm (1894–1969).

[6] Ibid.
[7] Ibid.
[8] Ibid.
[9] *S.R.S.* xv. 214.
[10] S.R.O., DD/AH, Aller bundle, letters from J. Richards, 25 July 1812, and J. House, 3 Sept. 1812; B.M. Add. MS. 33691 f. 126.
[11] *S.R.S.* ix. 185–6.
[12] See p. 63.
[13] *S.R.S.* xlix. 380.   [14] Ibid. lv. 100.
[15] E 117/8/23b.
[16] *S.R.S.* ii. 105; E 117/12/21.
[17] *S.R.S.* ii. 105.
[18] Ibid. 105, 290; *Valor Eccl.* (Rec. Com.), i. 197.
[19] *S.R.S.* lii. 48.
[20] Ibid. ii. 106. The statement that in 1523 the chapel lay within the parish church is presumably erroneous (*S.R.S.* lv. 28).
[21] Bodl. MS. Top. Som. c. 1 f. 125.
[22] Hunt. Libr., HA Manorial, surveys.
[23] *S.R.S.* i. 284; vi. 273; C 260/118/12.
[24] C 260/118/12. Oath may possibly be identified with a virgate of land 'taken away' from Curry Rivel between 1066 and 1086 and held at the latter date by Bretel under the count of Mortain (*V.C.H. Som.* i. 435).

Somerton: 'Somerton Castle'

Ilchester: Cordelyon House

MEDIEVAL TOWN HOUSES

HUISH EPISCOPI: PIBSBURY MILL, c. 1895

STOKE SUB HAMDON: MASONS' WORKSHOP, 1952

LONG SUTTON: KNOLE MILL

MUCHELNEY TOLL-HOUSE

with Aller. William Mowrie of Low Ham, described as lord of Oath in 1725,[25] sold the manor to trustees of John and Mary Webb of Wilton in 1732.[26] Two years later it was held by the widowed Mary Webb for life with remainder to James Syndercombe of Stratton (Dors.).[27] Syndercombe held the manor in 1741, but by 1743 it had passed to John Broadway of Oath and Langport.[28] There is evidence of enfranchisement by Broadway in 1743,[29] although most of Oath remained in possession of his family. No subsequent reference to the manor has been found, but John Broadway held property there in 1791 and was succeeded by Susannah Michell of Langport, probably his daughter, who died c. 1822.[30] She left her lands at Oath to her nephew Joel Broadway Horsey, with remainder to his sons Joel Broadway and John Horsey.[31] These sons were holding Oath farm jointly in 1838, when it comprised 99 a.[32] No manor-house has been traced. Oath Farm, the only likely property, was a copyhold tenement c. 1577.[33]

Lands in the north-east of the parish probably formed part of the estate or manor of Beer in High Ham in the 13th century. In 1314 Gilbert of Beer, whose family had held lands in High Ham for at least three generations, conveyed to John de Knolton a messuage and two carucates of land in Aller and Beer.[34] This grant appears to relate to the manor of *BEER* held by John de Knolton in 1316 and 1322.[35] John de la Slo conveyed another messuage and two carucates to John de Knolton in 1324, also stated to lie in Aller and Beer.[36] In 1338 Knolton's son John (II) was stated to hold tenements in Aller of Sir John of Clevedon by knight service, and Beer continued to be held as a freehold of Aller manor at least until c. 1665.[37]

By 1369 the manor of *BEER NEXT ALLER* was held by Sir William Bonville.[38] On Bonville's death in 1408 it passed to his grandson William (cr. Lord Bonville 1449, d. 1461), who settled the manor on his daughter Margaret, wife of Sir William Courtenay (I).[39] Their eldest son Sir William (II) (d.1512) defended his title to the manor or manors, then known as *BEER AND BURGH* or *BEER WITH BURGH* against his younger brother Peter Courtenay, *temp.* Henry VII.[40] The double place-name possibly has its origin in the two separate acquisitions made by John de Knolton (I).[41] The property passed to James Courtenay (d. 1546), a younger son of Sir William (II), and in 1548 was

held by his son James (II) (d. 1592).[42] On the latter's death his heir was given variously as his son James (III), or brother Edward Courtenay.[43] By 1599 it was held jointly by James and Sir William Courtenay,[44] and in 1617 by Sir William Courtenay of Powderham (Devon) and his son Francis.[45] In 1617 the estate was mortgaged to Simon (later Sir Simon) Leach (I) of Cadleigh (Devon) and others.[46] By 1630 the freehold had evidently passed to Leach who, at his death in 1637, devised it to his grandson Simon (II) (d. 1660), son of Sir Walter Leach.[47] The manor was held in 1691 by Sir Simon Leach (III) (d. 1708), son of Simon (II).[48] It is not mentioned thereafter, although lands formerly of the manor are referred to as late as 1772.[49]

The two messuages mentioned in the early 14th century formed part of the manor in 1384 and 1391.[50] One of these probably became the manor-house known as Beer Court Farm in 1747,[51] more recently as Beer Farm, and now as Nightingale Farm. By 1747 the farm had been acquired by James Smith (d. 1748) of St. Audries, who left it to his daughter Lavinia, wife of William Fellows.[52] It was subsequently purchased by William James of Forton, Chard, probably before 1770,[53] and in 1832 the farm was held by Mrs. James, probably his widow.[54] By 1838 it had passed to Richard Bridge,[55] and c. 1860 was owned by George Jeremy of Lea Combe House, Axminster (Devon).[56] On his death in 1874 Jeremy left the farm to his first cousin, Charlotte Ann, wife of the Revd. A. H. F. Luttrell of Minehead.[57] It was purchased by W. J. Lockyer from the Luttrells in 1925 and was held by his son Mr. W. E. G. Lockyer in 1972.[58] The farm-house is a long stone building with a thatched roof. It is at least of 17th-century origin but appears to have been considerably altered internally in the 19th century.

ECONOMIC HISTORY. At the time of Domesday Aller manor comprised two hides, of which three virgates were held in demesne and five were cultivated by the tenants. The figures given for the land use of the demesne, 15 a. of meadow, 200 a. of pasture, and 10 a. of wood, indicate that Aller moor was not included in the assessment. There were then 5 villeins, 12 bordars, and 2 serfs on the manor, with 12 beasts, 6 swine, and 16 sheep.[59]

[25] S.R.O., DD/SW, box 1, lease, 24 Apr. 1725.
[26] S.R.O., DD/NW 6/11.
[27] Ibid.
[28] Ibid.; DD/SW, box 1, assignments, 4 Oct. 1743, 3 June 1754.
[29] S.R.O., DD/NW 6/11; DD/SW, box 1, assignment, 4 Oct. 1743.
[30] S.R.O., Q/RE; DD/LC, box 5, probate of Susannah Michell, 1823.
[31] S.R.O., DD/LC, box 5, probate of S. Michell.
[32] S.R.O., tithe award.
[33] Hunt. Libr., HA Manorial, survey c. 1577.
[34] *S.R.S.* v. 164; xii. 42; lxiii, pp. clxix, 494.
[35] *Feud. Aids,* iv. 321; E 142/28. John de Knolton occurs as a free tenant of Aller Clevedon.
[36] *S.R.S.* xii. 96–7.
[37] Ibid. lxiii. 490–2; C 137/68/42; S.R.O., DD/MI, box 9, survey, c. 1665.
[38] Devon R.O. 123 M/TB 478–80, 483–6; *S.R.S.* xvii. 200; *Cal. Close,* 1389–92, 538.
[39] *Complete Peerage,* s.v. Bonville; *S.R.S.* xxvii. 52.
[40] *S.R.S.* xxvii. 50–5.   [41] See above.

[42] C 142/234/84; C 142/236/99; *S.R.S.* ii. 105–6; *Cat. Anct. D.* v. A 12609.
[43] C 142/234/84; C 142/236/99.
[44] C.P. 25(2)/262/41–2 Eliz. I Mich.
[45] *S.R.S.* li. 209–10.   [46] Ibid.
[47] C.P. 25(2)/526/5 Chas. I Mich.; C 142/482/101; J. L. Vivian, *Visit. of Devon* (1895), 526.
[48] C.P. 25(2)/869/2 Wm. & Mary Hil.; J. L. Vivian, *Visit. of Devon,* 526.
[49] S.R.O., DD/LC, box 13, conveyance, 1772.
[50] S.R.S. xvii. 200; *Cal. Close,* 1389–92, 538.
[51] S.R.O., D/P/all. 7/1/1.
[52] Ibid.; Devon R.O. 146 B/F 20; 74 B/MT 2006.
[53] S.R.O., Q/RE; DD/LTR, box 4, lease, 1 Sept. 1770.
[54] S.R.O., Q/RE.
[55] S.R.O., tithe award.
[56] S.R.O., D/P/all. 13/10/2.
[57] S.R.O., DD/LTR, box 5, copy will of George Jeremy, 1874.
[58] Ibid. sale account, 1925; Devon R.O. 547 B/P 3670; ex inf. Mr. W. E. G. Lockyer.
[59] *V.C.H. Som.* i. 511.

By 1322, when the manor was held in divided moieties, the number of tenants had increased to 7 freeholders (one holding Beer manor), 22 villeins or customary tenants, and 24 cottars.[60] Apart from Beer the freeholds were small, producing total rents of 39s. 8d.[61] By 1573 the number of freeholders had fallen to two,[62] and by c. 1665 only Beer manor remained.[63] Of the villeins of 1322 19 held one ferdel each and 3 held half a ferdel. Their customary payments and works accounted for nearly one sixth of the total value of the manor. These works comprised principally labour on the demesne lands for between two and four days a week, although one tenant was obliged to cart the lord's corn in autumn and another carted for the lord up to 20 miles from the manor. Villeins also paid Peter's Pence at Lammas, a rent called beaupleader, and church scot at Martinmas rendered in chickens. The cottars paid rent for their holdings but owed no services.[64]

The demesne was considerably extended in the years following Domesday. In 1312 the Acton moiety of the demesne comprised the capital messuage, 60 a. of arable, 20 a. of meadow, pasture in severalty, and a granary, valued together at £5 19s. 4d.[65] By 1322 this moiety had increased in value to £6 11s. 2d., its total extent being estimated at 316 a.[66] The Clevedon demesne in 1322 totalled 624 a., of which 390 a. represented pasture in the 'moors', the whole being valued at £13 13s.[67] The income derived from both moieties of the manor at this date totalled £38 1s. 2d.[68] In 1489 the value is given as 200 marks.[69]

The recovery and exploitation of the 'moors' is the principal feature of the economy of the parish in the Middle Ages. Until 1234 Aller moor evidently extended westwards into the present parish of Othery, but in that year the abbot of Glastonbury secured a moiety of the 'moor' from Ralph of Aller. Ralph attempted to forestall the inclosure by bribing the abbey steward with 'a most noble cockerel'.[70] The erection of the Great Wall around Aller moor along the Parrett was probably taking place in 1280, when John de Acton obstructed the towing of boats up river.[71] Drainage of pasture land evidently began at about that time with the construction of Pathelake, a rhine between Aller and Othery, the maintenance of which was the joint responsibility of Glastonbury abbey and the lord of Aller.[72] Beer Wall is thought to date from the same period.[73] Aller moor and North moor were described in c. 1310 as recently inclosed and divided by rhines.[74] By the 16th century an elaborate

system had evolved whereby wall works and fixed sums of wall money for the repair of the Great Wall had been allotted to each individual close of pasture.[75] A series of 71 leases of closes in Aller moor for 21 years were granted in 1552, all of which placed upon the tenants the responsibility for maintaining rhines around and through their inclosures and for paying a workman to repair the wall for one day each year.[76] Surveys of the 'moor' at this time show that a significant proportion of the pasture was held by out-dwellers, in many cases from adjacent parishes, but also from as far afield as Ilchester and Chard.[77]

From 1533 the manor-house and demesnes were let on long leases,[78] and by 1577 the manor and 'moors' were being administered as separate entities. At that date the manor comprised 612 a., principally arable in the open fields, let for £61 7s. 2½d., and the 'moors' totalled a further 2,028 a. let for £211 16s.[79] The tenants of the 'moors' were then paying £11 15s. 8d. in wall money and owed 53 days wall work.[80] In c. 1583 Sir Francis Hastings, representing the interests of his brother the 3rd earl of Huntingdon, stated that the demesne was 'good and large'. The 'moor' he considered 'a very commodious thing', although dependent on the strength of the river wall, which was being repaired after being seriously damaged in the preceding winter.[81] When the earl's debts mounted in 1592 Hastings so valued the manor that he hoped the earl would 'never so much as once imagine of the sale of Aller'.[82] But the desperate state of the Huntingdon finances led to the sale of Chantry farm in 1608[83] and the manor in 1612,[84] excluding the 'moor' and other properties which were sold piecemeal in the years up to 1620.[85]

The manor as purchased by Sir John Davis in 1612 had suffered from neglect owing to delay in completing the transaction.[86] The 'moor' held with the manor had been reduced to 377 a. although the manorial income, despite enfranchisement, still stood at £274 7s. 0½d.[87] One of the largest purchasers from the earl of Huntingdon was Sir Edward Hext (d. 1624) of Low Ham, who acquired about 400 a. of meadow and pasture in 1620.[88] On Hext's death this passed to his son-in-law Sir John Stawell[89] and was thus reunited with the manor. Most of the 'moor' was subsequently held in fee by the former occupiers, although 626½ a. were still held with the Stawell manor in c. 1665.[90] This period also saw the rise of the fortunes of the Northover family, occupiers of Aller Court farm by 1565[91] and of Chantry farm by c. 1577.[92] In the absence of

60 E 142/28.
61 Ibid.
62 Hunt. Libr., HA Manorial, ct. roll, 13 July 1573.
63 S.R.O., DD/MI, box 9, survey c. 1665.
64 E 142/28.
65 C 134/30/11.
66 E 142/28.
67 Ibid.   68 Ibid.
69 Cal. Inq. p.m. Hen. VII, i, pp. 195–6. This figure included the advowson.
70 Adam de Domerham, ed. T. Hearne (1727), ii. 486–7; John de Glastonbury, ed. T. Hearne (1726), ii. 311.
71 S.R.S. xliv. 119–20.
72 Ibid. lxiii. 522.
73 M. Williams, Draining of the Som. Levels, 54.
74 S.R.S. lxiii. 522.
75 Hunt. Libr., HA Manorial, survey of Aller moor, 1576.

76 Ibid. note of leases.
77 Bodl. MS. Top. Som. c. 2 f. 31.
78 See p. 64.
79 Hunt. Libr., HA Manorial, survey, c. 1577.
80 Ibid.
81 S.R.S. lxix. 28.
82 Ibid. 51.
83 Bodl. MS. Chart. Som. a. 1 f. 25.
84 See p. 63.
85 Hunt. Libr., HA Manorial, note of fines; Bull. Inst. Hist. Res. xl. 34–49.
86 Bodl. MS. Carte 289.
87 Ibid.
88 Hunt. Libr., HA Manorial, note of fines.
89 Som. Wills, ed. Brown, ii. 57.
90 S.R.O., DD/MI, box 9, survey, c. 1665.
91 See p. 64.
92 Hunt. Libr., HA Manorial, survey, c. 1577.

resident lords the Northovers became recognized as leaders of the community, purchasing Chantry farm with lands of 252 a. in 1608 and receiving a grant of arms in 1614.[93]

In c. 1665 the extent of the manor and those parts of the 'moor' held with it totalled 1,441 a., producing an income of £1,430.[94] The holdings of individual tenants were relatively small, the only tenements over 45 a. in area being Combe farm (107 a.) and Bagenham farm (60 a.). Conversion to leasehold had been slight, a mere 11 holdings compared with 48 copyholds, including the whole of Oath.[95] The sale of the manor to pay Stawell's debts in 1706 was followed by extensive enfranchisements. In 1707 at least fifteen tenements with over 400 a. of land were sold.[96] Oath manor was sold in 1732[97] and subsequently split into two farms of about 100 a. each with a number of smallholdings.[98] Beer manor also became a smaller farm in the earlier 18th century, losing much of its lands by enfranchisement.[99]

The principal farming unit in the parish by the early 18th century was Aller Court. The land attached to this property c. 1583 had comprised about 207 a.[1] and between 1706 and 1709 Sir Thomas Wroth added a further 185 a. from Aller manor to form an estate of nearly 400 a.[2] The Aclands further augmented the farm and by 1799 owned 720 a. in the parish, of which 596 a. were held with Aller Court.[3] The gross annual value of the estate increased from £330 in c. 1766[4] to £675 in 1806.[5] The rent from the farm alone rose from £214 in c. 1766,[6] to £660 in 1806,[7] and to £1,150 in 1817.[8] By 1838 the extent of Aller Court had fallen to 362 a. and that of the estate to 465 a.[9] This diminution was probably due to the sale of isolated plots which in 1755 had been leased on lives to 21 tenants.[10]

By 1838[11] Beer farm was the second largest holding, comprising 275 a., followed by Chantry farm with 180 a. There were two farms in the village with lands of 174 a. and 167 a., but the other six farms in the parish all had between 40 a. and 100 a. of land. There was little regular pattern to the ownership of the 'moor', much of it held in small scattered closes as in the 16th century, the largest group comprising 112 a. owned by the Trevillians of Midelney.[12] The herbage of the droveways, in 1653 enjoyed by the occupiers of the 'moors',[13] was let out by the vestry during the 19th century.[14]

The predominance of grassland in the parish has continued, and in 1905 of 2,895 a. only 483½ a. were cultivated as arable.[15] The creation of new farming units has reduced the average acreage attached to individual holdings and in 1939 there were only four farms of more than 150 a.[16] Thus Nightingale (formerly Beer) farm comprised only 130 a. in 1972, 94 a. having been taken to form Dairy House farm.[17] In contrast the lands attached to Aller Court were extended and totalled 437 a. in 1972.[18]

The only major change in the agrarian pattern of the parish was the inclosure of the former open fields and those 'moors' formerly beyond the parish limits. In 1322 there were 106 a. of arable land on the demesne of one moiety of the manor and 80 a. on the demesne of the other.[19] A two-field system was practised by 1552.[20] Customs recorded in 1653 imply that each field lay fallow every other year.[21] Under an Act of 1797 the two fields, then including 280 a., were inclosed and allotted the following year.[22] In c. 1577 Oath manor included 127 a. in the two fields on Oath hill.[23] By 1642 the breach of these fields traditionally belonged to the tenants of Curry Rivel manor whose cattle were subsequently driven off once the crop of grass had been eaten.[24] Oath fields were probably inclosed privately shortly before 1820.[25] In the mid 17th century the one arable field belonging to Beer manor was breached by a land reeve appointed in Aller manor court, who then took a prey or drive through both it and Aller North field.[26] No reference to its inclosure has been noted.

Meadow lands totalled 190 a. in 1322, all on the demesne.[27] Only the Landmeads remained uninclosed by c. 1577, when they comprised 24 a. in the North field and 23 a. in the East field, leased to a number of individual tenants.[28] By the mid 17th century these meadows were mown annually at Lammas and thereafter were thrown open with the arable fields for common grazing.[29] Efforts to inclose them and so double their value were made between 1614 and 1616, but were forcibly resisted by the tenants.[30] In 1615 James Northover and others, claiming ancient custom, broke down the gates and hedges and put their cattle into the meadows.[31] The steward suggested that the lord should convert the copyholds to leaseholds, thus extinguishing their common rights, 'and then their custom will never be worth a button'.[32] The

[93] Bodl. MS. Chart. Som. a. 1 f. 25; S. & D. N. & Q. iv. 255.
[94] S.R.O., DD/MI, box 9, survey c. 1665.
[95] Ibid.
[96] S.R.O., DD/HLM, box 1, conveyance, 15 May 1707; Hunt. Libr., HA Manorial, abstr. of indenture, 15 May 1707.
[97] See p. 65.
[98] S.R.O., tithe award.
[99] See p. 65.
[1] Hunt. Libr., HA Manorial, survey of demesne, c. 1583.
[2] Devon R.O. 1148 add/bay 15/2, partition, 22 Nov. 1723; S.R.O., DD/AH, survey bk. 1720–55.
[3] S.R.O., DD/AH, Aller bdl., schedule, 1799.
[4] Ibid. survey bk. 1720–55 (notes on back cover).
[5] Ibid. accts. 1806.
[6] Ibid. survey bk. 1720–55.
[7] Ibid. accts. 1806.
[8] Ibid. accts. 1817.
[9] S.R.O., tithe award.
[10] S.R.O., DD/AH, survey bk. 1720–55.
[11] S.R.O., tithe award.

[12] Ibid.
[13] S.R.O., DD/SAS (C/124), manor customs, 1653.
[14] S.R.O., D/P/all. 9/1/1.
[15] Statistics supplied by the then Bd. of Agric. (1905).
[16] Kelly's Dir. Som. (1939).
[17] Ex inf. Mr. W. E. G. Lockyer.
[18] Ex inf. Mr. P. C. Maltby.
[19] E 142/28.
[20] Hunt. Libr., HA Manorial, lease to John Collens 7 Nov. 1552.
[21] S.R.O., DD/SAS (C/124), manor customs, 1653.
[22] S.R.O., CR 106.
[23] Hunt. Libr., HA Manorial, survey c. 1577.
[24] S.R.O., DD/SAS CU 10, presentments, 1642–54.
[25] S.R.O., CR 111.
[26] S.R.O., DD/SAS (C/124), manor customs, 1653.
[27] E 142/28.
[28] Hunt. Libr., HA Manorial, survey, c. 1577.
[29] S.R.O., DD/SAS (C/124), manor customs, 1653.
[30] Bodl. MS. Carte 289 ff. 7–8, 22, 29–30, 36, 38, 42, 45.
[31] Ibid. f. 30.
[32] Ibid. f. 29.

Landmeads evidently remained open with the arable fields until 1797.[33]

The inhabitants of Aller had common of pasture in King's Sedgemoor by the early 17th century.[34] Tenants of Beer manor paid 8d. and a pair of gloves to the tithingman of Aller for their pasture there.[35] When King's Sedgemoor was inclosed under an Act of 1791 the parish was allotted 555 a. in respect of 82 rights of common.[36] The tenants of Aller manor had common pasture in Common moor with Langport and Huish,[37] which was inclosed by private agreement between the three parishes in 1797.[38] Aller was allotted nearly 24 a., subsequently leased by the vestry with the droves.[39] The tenants of Oath had common of pasture in West Sedgemoor and Week moor in 1653,[40] although their enjoyment of the latter was regulated by Curry Rivel manor court during the 17th century.[41] At the inclosure of Week moor in 1820 freeholders at Oath received an allotment of 7 a. in return for 180 ft. of wall maintenance along the southern bank of the Parrett and the repair of Oath clyse.[42] When West Sedgemoor was inclosed in 1822 the parish was allotted 14 a. in respect of common rights exercised by the inhabitants of Oath.[43]

The fishery of the Parrett and fowling within the manor were leased by the lord of Aller manor in 1552, and were thereafter generally held with copyhold grants of withybeds lying between the Great Wall and the Parrett.[44] Leases of the 16th and 17th centuries invariably reserved ground birds and swans for the lord.[45]

A shipmaster or mariner, mentioned in 1555 and 1559,[46] witnesses to trade along the Parrett with Bridgwater and Langport, but the parish has always been principally concerned with agrarian pursuits. In 1821 72 families out of 85 were employed in agriculture[47] and few earlier references to occupations unconnected with the land have been noted. A road contractor and a machinist occurred in 1906, and an insurance agent in 1910.[48] A milk factory had been set up by 1926, as had tea-rooms by 1939.[49] A small pottery had been established in the village by 1972.

In 1322 the lords of Aller manor shared a horsemill worth 26s. 8d.[50] A mill which had ceased to grind was mentioned in 1437.[51] A mill occurs in c. 1583,[52] and in 1614 and 1623 two water-mills.[53]

The manor of Beer with Burgh also included two mills between 1678 and 1691.[54] No mill sites in the parish can be identified, but a close called Windmill Ground in Aller moor was mentioned in 1796.[55] Closes on the east bank of the Parrett south of Callis Wall were known as Stathe Mill in 1838,[56] and Thomas Baker owned and occupied Stathe Mill in Aller from 1868 to 1884.[57]

LOCAL GOVERNMENT. Courts for the manors of Aller and Oath were held jointly by the 16th century, although Oath's presentments were made by its own homage jury. Rolls survive for the years 1563, 1566, 1571–3,[58] 1576–7,[59] 1589–91,[60] 1632.[61] The court was generally held twice, sometimes three times, a year and was described principally as *curia manerii* but very occasionally as *curia baronis*. The chief business was the scouring of rhines, the observance of grazing customs in the 'moors', and the repair of clyses and buildings. Other concerns included the maintenance of the river walls, grants of timber for the repair of tenements, and the ringing of pigs. A hayward, mentioned in 1338,[62] was elected annually by the 16th century, with two housewardens to report on dilapidations. A land reeve, mentioned in 1653, breached Beer Court field.[63]

Suit to the manor court of Beer with Burgh was mentioned in 1548,[64] as was suit to Oath court baron in 1743, after the separation of Oath manor from Aller.[65] The owners of Aller Court were evidently holding courts in respect of their property in the early 18th century.[66]

Churchwardens and 'posts' are mentioned in 1554[67] and lists of churchwardens and overseers survive for the period 1719–50. These served for their estates in rotation.[68] In 1750 it was agreed that four permanent overseers should serve annually for £1 10s. a year each.[69] By the mid 19th century the vestry was appointing two overseers, with a salaried assistant, two waywardens, two wall-wardens, an expenditor for Sedgemoor (appointed from 1797), and a molecatcher.[70] The two rate-collectors were assisted by a salaried collector from 1858.[71]

In 1730 a cottage was leased by the parish, probably as a poorhouse.[72] In 1807 the poorhouse 'having lately fallen down', a newly-built cottage on the

33 S.R.O., CR 106.
34 S.R.O., DD/MKG, box 4, division and allotment of King's Sedgemoor, c. 1618–27; DD/SAS (C/124), manor customs, 1653.
35 S.R.O., DD/SAS (C/124), manor customs, 1653.
36 S.R.O., CR 116.
37 S.R.O., DD/SAS (C/124), manor customs, 1653.
38 S.R.O., D/B/la 26.
39 S.R.O., D/P/all. 9/1/1.
40 S.R.O., DD/SAS (C/124), manor customs, 1653.
41 Ibid. CU 10, presentments, 1642–54.
42 S.R.O., CR 111.
43 Ibid. 85.
44 Hunt. Libr., HA Manorial, note of leases, 1552; ct. roll, 8 Oct. 1571; lease, 8 Oct. 1571; Bodl. MS. Chart. Som. a. 1 f. 19.
45 e.g. S.R.O., DD/BR/py 42; DD/NW 6/11, lease, 1 Dec. 1675.
46 Cal. Pat. 1554–5, 296; 1558–60, 175.
47 C. & J. Greenwood, Som. Delineated.
48 Kelly's Dir. Som. (1906, 1910).
49 Ibid. (1926–7, 1939).
50 E 142/28.
51 S.C. 2/1864/18.
52 Hunt. Libr., HA Manorial, survey of the demesne, c. 1583.

53 C.P. 25(2)/346/11 Jas. I Hil.; C.P. 25(2)/347/21 Jas. I Mich.
54 C.P. 43/382, rot. 199; C.P. 25(2)/869/2 Wm. & Mary Hil.
55 S.R.O., DD/LC, box 30, release, 2 Feb. 1796.
56 S.R.O., tithe award.
57 S.R.O., Q/REr.
58 Hunt. Libr., HA Manorial.
59 Bodl. MS. Som. Roll 3.
60 Ibid. 2.
61 B.M. Add. Ch. 28279.
62 Proc. before J.Ps. Edw. III and Ric. II, ed. Bertha Putnam, 157.
63 S.R.O., DD/SAS (C/124), customs of manor, 1653; D/P/all. 23/2.
64 Cat. Anct. D. v, A 12609.
65 S.R.O., DD/CM, box 7, lease, 4 Oct. 1743; see above, p. 65.
66 Devon R.O. 1148 add/bay 15, box 2, deed of partition, 22 Nov. 1723.
67 S.R.O., D/D/Ca 22.
68 S.R.O., D/P/all. 23/2.
69 Ibid.
70 Ibid. 9/1/1, 23/1.
71 Ibid. 9/1/1.
72 Ibid. 13/10/1.

west of the lane leading to the church was purchased.[73] This was still in use in 1815.[74] The parish joined the Langport poor-law union in 1836.[75]

CHURCH. The baptism of Guthrum, king of the Danes, at Aller in 878[76] is strong presumptive evidence for the existence of a church in the parish at that date. Possession of a baptistry and the later payments of church scot by the tenants of the manor[77] suggest that in origin the church was a minster, probably of royal foundation. A rector was mentioned in *c.* 1200.[78] By 1325 the advowson was held with the Clevedon moiety of Aller manor and descended with that estate.[79] Margaret, countess of Richmond and Derby, and Sir Reynold Bray presented in 1497 after a grant of that presentation.[80] In 1586 the patronage was conveyed by the lord of Aller manor to Emmanuel College, Cambridge, although the title to the advowson was in dispute with the earls of Huntingdon in the early 17th century.[81] The college continued to present until 1947.[82] The Crown presented in 1809 and 1954 and the bishop in 1958 and 1961, in all cases by lapse.[83] The benefice was sequestered in 1969 and was united with Langport in the following year. The archdeacon of Wells became patron of the new benefice.[84]

The church was valued at £13 6s. 8d. in 1291[85] and the first fruits were sold for £15 13s. 4d. a year in 1329–30.[86] By 1535 the income had risen to £36 14s. 10d.,[87] and by *c.* 1668 to £120.[88] It was estimated at about £300 in the late 18th century,[89] and the net income in 1835 was £623.[90] The predial tithes were worth £11 6s. in 1535 and the personal tithes and oblations £21.[91] The great and small tithes were commuted for £608 in 1838.[92]

The glebe was worth £5 in 1535.[93] In 1623 it comprised 3 a. attached to the parsonage house, 25¾ a. of arable and 40 a. of meadow.[94] It amounted to nearly 67 a. in 1838[95] and was valued at £120 a year in 1840.[96] All but 4 a. was sold in 1920.[97] There was no glebe in 1972.[98]

The parsonage house was in decay in 1554,[99] and the rector was presented in 1606 for not sufficiently repairing it.[1] A dovecot was mentioned in 1783–5.[2] The house is set back from the west side of Beer Road and is a predominantly stone building

of *c.* 1500. The main range was originally of two storeys with the parlour and the principal chamber at the north end. Projecting from the north-west corner is a turret containing a stair and garderobes, and at the north end of the east wall a short wing containing a room on the ground floor which was formerly connected to the parlour by an open stone arch, and above it a chamber with timber-framed walls. The central and southern parts of the house were extensively altered in the 19th century but presumably once contained the hall and service rooms. The south-east block, which has been largely rebuilt, may have been the original kitchen. The house passed into private hands in 1957.[3]

Raher of Aller (rector *c.* 1200) and Matthew of Clevedon (rector from 1330) were evidently both related to lords of Aller manor.[4] During the later 15th and earlier 16th centuries the benefice was served by a succession of distinguished clergy. Thomas Mannyng (rector 1453–62), a noted pluralist, was chaplain and secretary to Henry VI and dean of St. George's Chapel, Windsor.[5] He was attainted in 1461 and charged with holding the rectory in plurality without sufficient dispensation.[6] John Amersham (rector from 1475) was a monk and former archdeacon and sacrist of Westminster abbey.[7] Richard FitzJames (rector 1485–97), who was warden of Merton College, Oxford, chaplain to Edward IV and Henry VII, and held many other preferments while at Aller, resigned to become bishop successively of Rochester, Chichester, and London.[8] His successor was Christopher Bainbridge (rector 1497–1506), who held a number of appointments during his incumbency, including that of Master of the Rolls, and later became bishop of Durham and archbishop of York.[9] He was followed by William Hone (rector 1506–22), former fellow of All Souls, Oxford, who held many other livings in plurality,[10] and John Chamber (rector 1522–?49), warden of Merton College, Oxford, and personal physician to Henry VII and Henry VIII.[11] From 1609 until 1905 every incumbent presented by Emmanuel College was a former fellow of that house.[12] Walter Foster (rector 1633–*c.*1646, 1660–7), a mathematician, remained in the parish after his deprivation and replacement by John Moore (rector *c.* 1646–60).[13] Foster served as parish clerk from 1646[14] and as parish register from 1654, but was

[73] Ibid.
[74] S.R.O., D/P/all. 2/1/7.
[75] *Poor Law Com. 2nd Rep.* p. 548.
[76] *A.–S. Chron.* ed. Dorothy Whitelock (1961), 49–50.
[77] C 134/30/11; E 142/28.
[78] *H.M.C. Wells*, i. 57; *S.R.S.* xiv. 161.
[79] *S.R.S.* i. 292–3; E 142/28; see above, p. 63.
[80] Wells Dioc. Registry, Reg. King, 4.
[81] Cambridge, Emmanuel College, box 1.A.2, conveyance, 19 Jan. 1585/6; Bodl. MS. Tanner 75 f. 339; MS. Carte 289 ff. 18, 22.
[82] *Som. Incumbents*, ed. Weaver, 4; ex. inf. Diocesan Registrar.
[83] S.R.O., D/P/all. 1/1/1; ex. inf. Diocesan Registrar.
[84] S.R.O., D/P/all. 11/1; ex. inf. the rector, the Revd. W. E. L. Houlden.
[85] *Tax. Eccl.* (Rec. Com.), 197.
[86] *S.R.S.* ix. 60–2.
[87] *Valor Eccl.* (Rec. Com.) i. 197; *S.R.S.* ii. 106.
[88] S.R.O., D/D/Vc 24.
[89] Burnham-on-Sea parish recs., 'Ecton's Thesaurus Improved', MS. by Richard Locke.
[90] *Rep. Com. Eccl. Revenues*, pp. 150–1.
[91] *Valor Eccl.* (Rec. Com.), i. 197.
[92] S.R.O., tithe award.

[93] *Valor Eccl.* (Rec. Com.), i. 197.
[94] S.R.O., D/D/Rg 205.
[95] S.R.O., tithe award.
[96] *County Gazette Dir.* (1840).
[97] S.R.O., DD/LC, box 13, sale partics. 1920.
[98] Ex inf. Dioc. Secretary.
[99] S.R.O., D/D/Ca 22.
[1] S.R.O., D/D/Vc 150.
[2] S.R.O., D/P/all. 3/1/1.   [3] Ex inf. Dioc. Secretary.
[4] *H.M.C. Wells*, i. 57; *S.R.S.* i. 292–3; ix. 57; xiv. 161.
[5] Emden, *Biog. Reg. Univ. Oxford*.
[6] Ibid.; *S.R.S.* xlix. 204, 368–9.
[7] Emden, *Biog. Reg. Univ. Oxford*; *S.R.S.* lii. 104.
[8] Emden, *Biog. Reg. Univ. Oxford*; *Cal. Papal Regs.* xiv. 12; *S.R.S.* liv. 5.
[9] Emden, *Biog. Reg. Univ. Oxford*; *S.R.S.* liv. 5, 114–15.
[10] Emden, *Biog. Reg. Univ. Oxford*; *S.R.S.* liv. 114–15; lv. 22.
[11] Emden, *Biog. Reg. Univ. Oxford*; *S.R.S.* ii. 106; lv. 22; S.R.O., D/D/Vc 20; *Valor Eccl.* (Rec. Com.), i. 197.
[12] *Som. Incumbents*, ed. Weaver, 4; ex. inf. Diocesan Registrar; Venn, *Alumni Cantab.*
[13] *D.N.B.*; *Som. Incumbents*, 4; *Calamy Revised*, ed. A. G. Matthews; S.R.O., D/P/all. 2/1/1.
[14] *S.R.S.* xxviii. 208.

replaced the following year 'having absented himself'.[15] He successfully petitioned for restoration in 1660[16] and died in 1667 'in opposition to all popish corruptions and fanatical enormities so rife now amongst us'.[17]

The tenure of the benefice by nationally-known figures in the 15th and 16th centuries suggests that the living was probably served by assistant clergy. Curates are mentioned regularly from 1528 until 1633[18] although some rectors, such as William Radberd (rector from 1556 at least until 1575)[19] and Ralph Cudworth (rector 1609–24)[20] were occasionally resident. 'I am seated', said Cudworth in 1618, 'in a barren place where my neighbour ministers either want skill and cannot, or have some skill and will not, confer together about matters of learning. If they chance to be questioned they think they are posed'.[21] Curates recur during the years 1716–18[22] and 1782–1809,[23] but rectors appear to have been generally resident during the 19th century.[24]

A light founded within the parish church and mentioned in 1548 was endowed with 10lb. of wax or 5s. from the manor of Beer, then unpaid for three years.[25]

In 1554 there was no altar stone, and the fortieth part of the income had not been distributed to the poor for four years.[26] The parish lacked the *Paraphrases* of Erasmus in 1568;[27] in 1612 Bishop Jewell's *Works* were missing, prayers were not said on Wednesdays or Fridays, and there had been no perambulation.[28] Until after 1840 there was only one service each Sunday,[29] but by 1851 there were two, attended on Census Sunday by 30 in the morning and 60 in the afternoon, with 39 Sunday-school pupils.[30] By 1870 Holy Communion was celebrated monthly.[31]

A church or parish house, dilapidated in 1566,[32] was held of the manor by copy for the use of the lord's tenants in *c.* 1577.[33] It lay immediately east of Chantry Farm on the north side of the street, and its lands comprised the 2½ a. plot on which it stood with 5¼ a. of arable in the open fields.[34] It was called the town house in 1576, when the inhabitants of the village were deemed liable for its repair,[35] and it was last mentioned in 1591.[36]

The church of *ST. ANDREW* stands on the 'island' of Aller immediately east of the former manor-house, Aller Court Farm. It is of lias ashlar with some Ham stone dressings and has a chancel with north vestry, nave with north aisle and north and south porches, and west tower. The nave probably retains its 12th-century dimensions, although the only feature of this date is the south doorway.[37] The earliest feature in the chancel is a 13th-century window in the north wall. Considerable alterations would appear to have taken place in the late 14th century when the south porch and the tower were built[38] and new windows were put into the east and south walls of the chancel. The lowest stage of the tower is within the church and is carried on open arches to the north, east, and south. The diagonal buttresses are carried on to the nave walls by short butting arches below the nave roof. The west window and that on the south side of the nave were both renewed in the 15th century. The vestry, north porch, and aisle were erected in 1861–2 when the rest of the church was restored.[39] The north aisle is in a 13th-century style and is connected to the nave by an arcade of three bays. The chancel arch is in a similar style and was probably enlarged or much restored at this time. The roofs of both the nave and chancel also date from 1861–2.[40]

There is a font with a 12th-century bowl at the west end of the nave and an octagonal font dated 1663. The defaced effigy of a cross-legged knight, dated 1270–80, may represent Sir John of Aller (d. *c.* 1272).[41] In the north wall of the chancel there is a cusped recess enclosing the effigy of a knight, dated 1370–5, probably representing Sir John of Clevedon (d. *c.* 1373).[42] The pulpit is dated 1610 and is notably elaborate for that date. The reredos was designed by J. D. Sedding.[43]

The plate includes a cup and cover of 1630, a plain paten on foot of 1710 by Richard Bayley, and a pewter flagon.[44] There are three bells: (i) 1638, Robert Austen (I); (ii) 1640, Robert Austen (II) (recast 1883); (iii) 1663, Robert Austen (II) of Compton Dundon.[45]

The registers date from 1561 and are complete.[46]

A hermitage housing two hermits at Oath was mentioned in 1328. The vicar of Muchelney was to serve as confessor to the occupants and to have a key to the door for his visits.[47] John de Lorty left one mark to the brothers of Oath in 1340,[48] and the

[15] S.R.O., D/P/all. 2/1/2.
[16] Hist. MSS. Com. 6, *7th Rep.*, p. 101; *Calamy Revised*, ed. A. G. Matthews.
[17] Prob. 11/325 (P.C.C. 168 Carr), f. 168.
[18] *S.R.S.* xix. 268; S.R.O., D/D/Vc 20; *S.R.S.* ii. 106; S.R.O., D/D/Ca 22; *S.R.S.* xxi. 156; *S. & D.N. & Q.* xiv. 107; B.M. Harl. MS. 594 f. 46; *S.R.S.* xl. 75; S.R.O., D/P/all. 2/1/1.
[19] *S. & D. N. & Q.* xiv. 107.
[20] S.R.O., D/P/all. 2/1/1.
[21] Bodl. MS. Rawl. Lett. 89 f. 25.
[22] S.R.O., D/P/all. 2/1/3.
[23] Ibid. 2/1/5.
[24] S.R.O., D/D/V rtns. 1815, 1827, 1840, 1870; *Rep. Com. Eccl. Revenues*, pp. 150–1.
[25] *S.R.S.* ii. 106, 290.
[26] S.R.O., D/D/Ca 22.
[27] Ibid. 40.
[28] Ibid. 177.
[29] S.R.O., D/D/V rtns. 1815, 1827, 1840.
[30] H.O. 129/317/2/4/25.
[31] S.R.O., D/D/V rtns. 1870.
[32] Hunt. Libr., HA Manorial, ct. roll, 20 June 1566.
[33] Ibid. survey, *c.* 1577.
[34] Ibid.
[35] Bodl. MS. Som. Roll 3.
[36] Ibid. 2.
[37] A semi-circular wooden carving of a pelican feeding her young, preserved in the church in 1972, was above the south doorway in 1791 (Collinson, *Hist. Som.* iii. 189) and 1847 (Taunton Castle, Braikenridge Colln., watercolour by W. W. Wheatley).
[38] The arms of Courtenay and Courtenay impaling Clevedon appear on the corbels of the label of the west window and confirm the date of the tower: see p. 63.
[39] S.R.O., D/P/all. 6/1/1; 9/1/1.
[40] S.R.O., D/P/all. 6/1/1; 9/1/1.
[41] See p. 63; *Proc. Som. Arch. Soc.* lxii. 73–4; Pevsner dates the effigy as *c.* 1315 (*South and West Som.* 76), which would suggest John de Acton (II) (d. 1312).
[42] *Proc. Som. Arch. Soc.* lxvii. 29; Pevsner, *South and West Som.* 76.
[43] *Builder*, 25 June 1887.
[44] *Proc. Som. Arch. Soc.* xlv. 129–30.
[45] S.R.O., DD/SAS CH 16.
[46] S.R.O., D/P/all. 2/1/1.
[47] *S.R.S.* i. 284.
[48] *Proc. Som. Arch. Soc.* lxi. 52.

cell may be identified with a chapel there in need of repair in 1373.[49] It stood in Oath East field[50] and by 1559 was evidently no longer used for worship.[51] The enclosure within which it formerly stood, known as Chapel Hay *c.* 1665[52] and Chapel Orchard in 1838, lay towards the south-eastern end of Oath hill.[53] Members of the Broadway family of Oath were buried there between 1747 and *c.* 1822.[54] No trace of the building now remains.

NONCONFORMITY. James Courtenay, lord of the manor of Beer with Burgh, was recorded as a recusant in the period 1591–1606, when he was evidently resident in the parish.[55] Quakers were resident in the parish between 1699 and 1705, the parents of a child baptized in the latter year being described as 'Quakers or heathens'.[56] A house was registered for Dissenting meetings in 1816[57] and Independents worshipped at James Kiddle's house from 1840.[58] Kiddle, a blacksmith, was evidently persecuted for his beliefs and the publicity given to his sufferings secured the aid of the Revd. A. Morris of Holloway Chapel, London. Premises were purchased on the west side of Beer Road and converted into the Holloway Chapel (named after its London counterpart) in 1844.[59] The Congregational chapel in use in 1972 was erected on a near-by site in 1886.[60] On Census Sunday 1851 the evening congregation numbered 80.[61] There were 140 sittings and a Sunday school was attended by 30 in the morning and 30 in the evening.[62] A string band was a feature of the services in 1896.[63]

An Independent chapel at Oath, evidently part of a private house, was opened in 1848, had 40 sittings, and was served from Holloway Chapel.[64]

Services were held only on week-day evenings, the average congregation in 1851 being 30, with a bible class of 13.[65]

EDUCATION. There was no school in the parish in 1818,[66] but by 1825–6 there was a Sunday school attended by 70 children.[67] In 1834 a day-school was erected by subscription on the south-east side of the church path.[68] In 1972 this building was a dwelling-house called Laurel Farm.

A National school containing two rooms was built in 1871 on the east side of Beer Road, north of the Cross Tree.[69] This was attended by about 60 pupils in 1894 and supported chiefly by subscriptions.[70] There were 66 children on the books in 1903,[71] and the school was then described as 'distinctly well managed and efficient'.[72] An evening continuation school was occasionally held there and the rooms were used for all parish meetings and entertainments.[73] Numbers fell to 27 in 1914–15 and after 1925 only juniors were admitted.[74] In 1934–5 there were 26 pupils and in 1944–5 nineteen.[75] The school was closed in 1946 and the pupils transferred to Huish Episcopi.[76]

CHARITIES FOR THE POOR. Martha Bond by will dated 1797 bequeathed the residue of her estate equally between the parishes of Aller, Langport, and Huish Episcopi, the income to be distributed to the poor.[77] Land in Aller was purchased and the parish's share of the profits amounted to £7 15*s.* in 1848.[78] This was paid to poor persons selected by the churchwardens and overseers, who in 1871 used the charity to provide blankets.[79] In 1964 £6 9*s.* 4*d.* was paid out.[80]

WEST CAMEL

THE parish of West Camel, some 3½ miles long and 1¾ mile wide at its broadest, lies 3 miles north-east of Ilchester, and comprised 1,995 a.[1] The boundary with Podimore follows a green way known as Eastmead Lane, that with Babcary the road known as Steart Lane. A footpath marks the division between Queen Camel and West Camel from the Lambrook almost to the church, and the limits of the southern part of the parish, the ancient estate of Little Marston, are formed by a road on

the east and streams on the north and west. The 'ditch' of Lambrook was regarded as the boundary between Little Marston and West Camel in 1241.[2]

West Camel is bisected by the western part of a ridge of Middle Lias, rising to 216 ft. at West Camel hill. There is evidence of quarrying and lime-burning at West Camel hill, Steart hill, and Annis hill during the 19th century.[3] North of the hill the land falls away abruptly to meadow land on the stiff loam of the Lower Lias; to the west Annis hill

[49] *Cal. Papal Regs.* iv. 189.
[50] Hunt. Libr., HA Manorial, survey, *c.* 1577.
[51] Bodl. MS. Top. Som. c. 1, p. 113.
[52] S.R.O., DD/MI, box 9, survey *c.* 1665.
[53] S.R.O., tithe award.
[54] S.R.O., D/P/all. 2/1/3; DD/LC, box 5, probate of Susannah Michell of Langport, 1823.
[55] *S. & D. N. & Q.* v. 112.
[56] S.R.O., D/P/all. 2/1/2.
[57] S.R.O., D/D/Rm, box 2. Evidently Wesleyan: S.R.O., D/N/sp.c. 1.
[58] Ibid. vol. 2.
[59] *Rep. Som. Cong. Union* (1896); S.R.O., D/D/Rm, box 2; tithe award.
[60] *Rep. Som. Cong. Union* (1896).
[61] H.O. 129/317/2/4/14.
[62] Ibid.
[63] *Rep. Som. Cong. Union* (1896).
[64] H.O. 129/317/2/4/13.
[65] Ibid.

[66] *Digest of Returns to Sel. Cttee. on Educ. of Poor,* H.C. 224 (1819), ix (2).
[67] *Educ. Enquiry Abstract,* H.C. 62 (1835), xlii.
[68] S.R.O., DD/BR/hmp, conveyance, 9 June 1834.
[69] S.R.O., DD/EDS (C/1404); C/E, box 26.
[70] *Rtns. of Schs.* [C 7529] H.C. (1894), lxv.
[71] S.R.O., C/E, box 26.
[72] Ibid.
[73] Ibid.
[74] Som. C.C. Educ. Cttee. *Schs. List.*
[75] Ibid.
[76] S.R.O., C/E, box 1, log bks. 1890–1946.
[77] Char. Com. files.
[78] S.R.O., D/P/h.ep. 9/1/1; D/P/all. 9/1/1.
[79] Char. Com. files; S.R.O., D/P/all. 9/1/1.
[80] Char. com. files.
[1] *Census*, 1901. This article was completed in 1969.
[2] *S.R.S.* xiv. 74.
[3] S.R.O., tithe award; Sherborne, Digby Estate Office, rent bk. 1861–2; O.S. Map 6", Som. LXXIV. SW. (1886 edn.).

rises to 122 ft. but the land on the extreme boundary is only 58 ft. above sea level. South of the ridge the land falls to the valley of the river Cam, around which most of the main settlement is concentrated. Further south, again on the Lower Lias, the road from Queen Camel to Yeovilton (the 'rigeweye' of 1305)[4] follows the contour at just over 100 ft., though the land still further south falls to below 75 ft.

Apart from the river Cam, flowing south-west in the valley below the lias ridge, there are two streams from Marston Magna flowing through Little Marston. The more northerly has been called Lambrook at least since the 13th century.[5] The northern half of the parish is less well watered, Dyke brook and a tributary in the extreme north being the only streams of size, forming part of the boundary of the Stock mead. Repeated orders for cleansing ditches and waterways in surviving court rolls[6] emphasise the value of man-made drainage in the area.

The road pattern in West Camel is complex. The parish is bisected by the Exeter–London road which gradually climbs the dip slope of West Camel hill and finally crosses the ridge in the adjoining parish. This road was turnpiked in 1753 and came under the Ilchester trust.[7] Several roads lead from it north and west: the road through Podimore to Langport and Taunton branches west at a small green formerly called Cob Door Cross, and later Camel Cross;[8] northwards two roads serve Downhead, converging above the settlement, and thence lead to Newclose farm and the fields. A fourth road leads north over Steart hill from Conegore Corner towards Babcary and the Charltons. Steart hill is linked to Downhead by Slate Lane, now a green track, which runs along the ridge to West Camel hill, and served both the fields and later the quarries. The roads in the southern half of the parish are more influenced by adjoining settlements; three lead into the Cam valley, the one from Plowage formerly creating a triangular green where it joined the London road, known as Ploughage Green in 1826.[9] These three roads continue the line of those serving the north of the parish. Roads within the village and further south along the slight ridge meet these at right angles, forming a rough grid. The main settlement of the parish is found scattered rather loosely around this grid.

Fore Street, and its westward extension Keep Street (Kip Street in 1752),[10] were evidently the principal streets of the village, modern houses between the older farms and cottages still reflecting this position. Roughly parallel, on the southern side of the Cam, is Back Street, having two old established farm-houses[11] at its western end and

more modern development to the east. These two parallel roads are joined by the narrow Frog Lane in the west and by the road from Conegore Corner southwards leading eventually to Yeovil, and for that reason the busiest thoroughfare of the village. For some yards southward from its junction with Back Street this road divides, forming parallel ways around a small green. This road now contains the inn, the former school, the Rectory, and the church.

There are several small clusters of farms and private houses distant from the main settlement. The largest of these, probably dating back beyond Domesday, is Downhead,[12] which at the end of the 18th century comprised eleven houses.[13] This is the only ancient settlement in the northern half of the parish, though late in the 18th century 'many bodies regularly arranged in rows' were discovered in two 'catacombs', evidently in this area.[14] Downhead is now much smaller, but includes the substantial farm-houses of Downhead Manor farm and Glebe farm. Urgashay is a settlement west of the main village. As 'Orgishie' it occurs in 1618,[15] and at the end of the 18th century was a group of nine houses.[16] Slowcourt farm represents another such isolated settlement, dating from the early 13th century.[17] At the junction of Plowage Lane and Keep Street is a later group, evidently a development on the manorial waste, once including the pound, the Second Poor house, and a carpenter's shop with Methodist chapel above it.[18] Buildings along the London road reflect the importance of this line of communication: there were scattered houses along its route early in the 19th century at Ploughage Green, Conegore Corner, and later around the site of the Methodist chapel, post office, and bakery.[19] Twentieth-century building in West Camel includes local authority housing at Howell hill, erected in 1926,[20] houses at Steart hill and South Street, and caravans at Plowage.

Little Marston appears to have had two open fields: East field, in the 13th century reaching the Lambrook to the north-east of Little Marston farm;[21] and West field, still so named in the 19th century.[22] By the same date there were still traces of one open field, Hill field, near Downhead, on the southern slopes of West Camel hill, which may originally have occupied the triangle between Slate Lane, the London road, and the road to Downhead from Plowage.[23] There are also traces of a Middle field, a West field, and an East field at Downhead. Middle field seems to have occupied the area between Downhead Manor Farm and Annis hill.[24] West field in the 18th century probably lay between Middle field and the Langport road.[25] There are also traces of furlongs, suggesting an open field, on Steart hill.[26] These furlongs may have formed

---

[4] *Cal. Pat.* 1391–6, 497; *S.R.S.* xlii. 68.
[5] *S.R.S.* xiv. 74.
[6] S.R.O., DD/AB 7; see below, p. 77.
[7] S.R.O., D/T/ilch. The road was called Great New Western Road in the early 19th century: S.R.O., DD/CC 13347 (sale partics. 1825).
[8] S.R.O., D/T/ilch.
[9] Ibid.
[10] S.R.O., D/P/w. ca 13/10/1.
[11] M. W. Barley, *The English Farmhouse and Cottage*, 104.
[12] See p. 73.
[13] Collinson, *Hist. Som.* iii. 189.
[14] Ibid. 189–90.
[15] *S.R.S.* li. 220.

[16] Collinson, *Hist. Som.* iii. 189.
[17] See p. 74.
[18] See pp. 77, 80.
[19] O.S. Map 1″, sheet XVIII (1811 edn.); O.S. Map 6″, Som. LXXIV. SW. (1886 edn.); S.R.O. tithe award.
[20] S.R.O., D/G/Y 160.
[21] *S.R.S.* xiv. 71.
[22] S.R.O., tithe award.
[23] S.R.O., tithe award, nos. 108–17; perhaps the same as 'Pynehill', two open fields in 1436–7: S.R.O., DD/AB 7.
[24] S.R.O., DD/YB 2; tithe award.
[25] S.R.O., DD/YB 2, 216, 218.
[26] S.R.O., tithe award.

part of the East field mentioned in 1437.[27] West Camel manor had a South field in 1392; it lay south of the road from Queen Camel to Yeovilton and in the 17th century included Warris hill.[28]

There were 43 inhabited houses in the parish about 1822.[29] Most of these probably still survive as the rubble-and-tile or thatched farm-houses scattered throughout the parish. The largest single dwelling to survive is probably the so-called Manor House, north of the Rectory, a five-bay stone building of two storeys and attics, with a slate roof and pedimented doorway. It probably dates from the 17th century, but has been much altered and enlarged, having later sash windows. Its only connexion with the manor was as the residence of the tenant of West Camel farm about 1825.[30]

The population of West Camel in 1801 was 224; there was a gradual rise to 376 in 1851, and then a decline to 224 in 1911. Since the Second World War, and particularly since 1951, the rise has been rapid, reaching 378 in 1961.[31]

MANORS AND OTHER ESTATES. Between 939 and 975 three thegns, Aelfar, Cinric, and Brihtric each held lands in 'Cantmell' or 'Cantmel' by grants from Saxon kings, but the lands themselves cannot positively be identified with either West or Queen Camel.[32] More certain is the grant by Ethelred in 995 to Muchelney abbey. The somewhat suspicious charter purports to confirm to the monastery the land at Cantmael purchased by Abbot Leofric, together with four *cassati* of land adjoining, given by the ealdorman Aethelmaer.[33] The abbey certainly held the estate called Camelle in 1086 which afterwards became the manor of CAMEL ABBOTS or WEST CAMEL.[34] The property gelded T.R.E. for ten hides.[35]

Muchelney abbey retained the manor until 1538.[36] Almost immediately the property was granted to Edward Seymour, earl of Hertford and later duke of Somerset.[37] After his execution and attainder in 1552 his estates were forfeited, but were restored to his son Edward (cr. earl of Hertford 1559, d. 1621) in 1554.[38] Edward's heir was his grandson William (cr. marquess of Hertford 1641, duke of Somerset 1660), though Camel was in the hands of Edward's widow Frances, then duchess of Richmond and Lennox, in 1629.[39] William died in 1660 and was succeeded first by his grandson William (d. 1671)

and then by his own second son John. John died without issue in 1675 and the estate passed to his niece Elizabeth (d. 1697), wife of Thomas Bruce, earl of Ailesbury.[40]

Charles Bruce, Lord Bruce, their eldest son, together with his brothers, sold the manor, with the manor of Downhead, to William Player of Hadspen and John Russe of Castle Cary in 1709.[41] Player died in 1719; his lands were settled on his two sons, one of whom, Thomas, in 1731 procured an Act of Parliament to break the settlement.[42] Francis Newman of North Cadbury, surviving trustee and devisee of Thomas Player, was lord of the two manors by 1752[43] and was holding courts in 1760.[44] By 1766 his property in West Camel seems to have come to Charles Bragg, who had acquired other parts of the Player estates.[45] By 1775 the owner was Francis Kingston of Blandford (Dors.).[46] He was in 1787 succeeded by his great-nephew Francis Kingston Galpine.[47] Galpine sold the property in 1825 to Richard Webb.[48] There is no separate reference to the manor of West Camel after that date.

The manor of DOWNHEAD probably originated in the estate held by Dodeman in 1086.[49] Possibly, though not certainly, it was held in 1166 by Richard Revel.[50] He or another of the same name was certainly holding two fifths of a fee there of the abbot of Muchelney in 1211.[51] Richard Revel the younger had succeeded by 1213 but died in 1222, leaving as his heir a daughter Sabina, wife of Henry (I) de Lorty.[52] She was succeeded in 1254 by her grandson Henry (II) de Lorty.[53] He held two fifths of a fee of the abbot of Muchelney at Downhead in 1297.[54] John de Lorty succeeded his father in 1321 and died in 1340, leaving a daughter Sibyl, wife of Robert Holme.[55]

John du Boys (d. 1309) held the manor of Henry Lorty for a third of a fee, and was succeeded as under-tenant by his daughter Margery.[56] Walter de Thornhull and his wife Margery sold their interest to Ela, wife of Robert FitzPayn, in 1329.[57] Walter still claimed rights there in 1340,[58] though Robert and Ela were clearly in possession in 1354, when they sold the manor to Richard de Acton and John of Somerton.[59] Four years later Richard made the manor over to Alexander Camel and William Derby; they in turn, acting as feoffees, granted it to Muchelney abbey to provide a chaplain to celebrate in the abbey church.[60] From that date Robert and Sibyl ceased to be mesne lords.[61]

[27] S.R.O., DD/AB 7.
[28] D.L. 43/14/3 ff. 71–71v; S.R.O., DD/YB 2, 216, 218; tithe award.
[29] C. & J. Greenwood, *Som. Delineated*.
[30] S.R.O., Q/RE, land tax assessments; D/P/w. ca 3/2/4.
[31] *V.C.H. Som.* ii. 348; *Census, 1911–61*.
[32] Finberg, *Early Charters of Wessex*, pp. 134, 139, 144.
[33] S.R.O., DD/SAS PR 502; Finberg, op. cit. p. 147; *S.R.S.* xiv. 43–5.
[34] *V.C.H. Som.* i. 469; ii. 104.
[35] Ibid. i. 469.
[36] Ibid. 106.
[37] *L. & P. Hen. VIII*, xiii (1), p. 64; xv, p. 219.
[38] *Complete Peerage*, s.v. Somerset.
[39] *Acts of P.C.* 1628–9, 399.
[40] *Complete Peerage*, s.v. Ailesbury.
[41] S.R.O., DD/SAS (C/120) 8.
[42] W. Phelps, *Hist. Som.* i. 258; 4 Geo. II, c. 26 (Priv. Act).
[43] S.R.O., D/P/w. ca 13/10/1; see *Proc. Som. Arch. Soc.* xxxvi. 156–7.

[44] S.R.O., DD/SAS (C/120) 8, extract of court baron.
[45] S.R.O., Q/RE, land tax assessments; Collinson, *Hist. Som.* ii. 56.
[46] S.R.O., D/P/w. ca 3/2/1, receipt for tithe (at end).
[47] S.R.O., Q/RE, land tax assessments; DD/FL 99, Withers and Galpine to Petty; Hutchins, *Hist. Dors.* i. 223.
[48] C.P. 43/967 rot. 251.
[49] *V.C.H. Som.* i. 469.
[50] *Red Bk. Exch.* (Rolls Ser.), 224; *Proc. Som. Arch. Soc.* xlii. 34.
[51] *S.R.S.* xiv. 62, 97–8.
[52] Ibid. 61–2; *Complete Peerage*, s.v. Orty.
[53] *Complete Peerage*, s.v. Orty.
[54] *S.R.S.* xiv. 98.
[55] *Complete Peerage*, s.v. Orty.
[56] *Cal. Inq. p.m.* v, p. 109.
[57] *S.R.S.* iii. 254; xii. 135; xiv. 109.
[58] *Year Bk. 1340* (Rolls Ser.), 24.
[59] *S.R.S.* xiv. 110; xvii. 25.
[60] Ibid. xiv. 110; xlii. 27–34; *Cal. Pat. 1358–61*, 116.
[61] *S.R.S.* xvii. 44; xlii. 34.

The manor then descended with that of West Camel until 1825. Richard Webb, who in that year purchased the manors of Camel and Downhead or West Camel, died before 1839. A namesake living at Melchet Park (Hants) was owner until 1847 when he was succeeded by Francis Webb of Doughty Street, London.[62] Ten years later he sold it to G. D. Wingfield-Digby of Sherborne Castle (Dors.). The latter was succeeded in 1883 by his nephew John (d. 1888) and then by John's son J. K. D. Wingfield-Digby (d. 1904). His son F. J. B. Wingfield-Digby sold most of the property in 1919.[63]

The manor of *LITTLE MARSTON* may originally have been part of the parish of Marston Magna. Until the 19th century it was, like Marston Magna, in the hundred of Horethorne.[64] It may well have been one of the estates at Marston held by a thegn in the Confessor's time.[65] The manor of Marston was held by the count of Mortain in 1086,[66] and Little Marston was said to have been held of Robert, count of Mortain.[67] It was in the hands of John as count of Mortain before he came to the throne in 1199,[68] and was thereafter held in chief as parcel of the manor of Barwick.[69] The connexion with Barwick was retained at least until 1462.[70]

William son of John held the estate of Robert, count of Mortain.[71] By 1199 the tenant was Fulk de Cauntelo.[72] He was evidently succeeded by Sir William Haket, who may have married Fulk's heiress; Haket was certainly lord of Little Marston in 1214, though evidently not in his own right, since in 1245 he became tenant for life of William de Cauntelo (II).[73] William de Cauntelo died in 1251 and his son William in 1254. The heir was his grandson George (d. 1273). George's successor was John (I) de Hastings (later Lord Hastings (d. 1313)), son of his sister Joan.[74]

John de Hastings had livery of his lands in 1283.[75] He was succeeded by his second son John (II) (d. 1325), and then by his grandson Laurence (cr. earl of Pembroke 1339).[76] Laurence died in 1348, his son John in 1375, and his grandson, also John, in 1389. The heir to the estate was Reynold Grey, Lord Grey of Ruthin.[77] Grey, however, secured only the reversion, Little Marston forming part of the dower of Philippe, second wife of John (IV).[78] Philippe died in 1400 and Little Marston passed to the feoffees of Lord Grey.[79] Two years later Grey sold it to William Stourton (d. 1413).[80]

John Stourton (cr. Baron Stourton 1448) succeeded on his father's death, and the manor was then held by successive barons Stourton until 1641.[81] In the time of William, Lord Stourton (d. 1524), the estate, measuring 490 a., was let to the Barbour family, who held it until the middle of the century.[82] In 1615 the manor was settled on William, son of Edward, Lord Stourton (d. 1633), and William and his sons Edward and Thomas made over the property to a group of trustees headed by Sir Henry Compton.[83]

The subsequent descent of the manor has not been traced until 1766, though in 1687 Robert Brent and Francis Bagshaw were concerned in a recovery, possibly for this property.[84] By 1766 it was no longer described as a manor but usually as Little Marston farm. In that year it was owned by Henry Seymour (d. 1805) of Redland Court (Glos.);[85] it passed to his son Henry (d. 1849), of East Knoyle (Wilts.) and Trent (Dors.), and then to his grandson Henry Danby Seymour (d. 1877) of Trent. Alfred Seymour, brother of Henry, then succeeded, followed successively by his widow and their daughter Miss J. M. Seymour, who sold the land between 1915 and 1921.[86]

By 1841 the total holding was 271 a., divided into two farms. By 1863 the holdings had been reunited, but were divided again when the Seymours disposed of the property into Little Marston farm and Springside now Spring farm.[87]

In 1392 the manor-house at Little Marston consisted of a thatched hall and chamber.[88] The present house, of lias with a slate roof, probably originated in the 17th century, but was extensively remodelled in the 19th century.

A freehold estate of at least $1\frac{1}{2}$ virgate, held of Muchelney abbey, had been established at 'the Slo' by a family of the same name by 1238. Simon de la Slo, possibly a former owner, occurs in 1211.[89] Gillian, widow of Simon, was assigned dower in 1238, the rest of the holding being occupied for her life by Wymara de la Slo.[90] Between 1251 and 1274 Roger de la Slo died holding the property.[91] At the beginning of the 14th century the estate was variously assessed at a messuage and 2 virgates[92] or $1\frac{1}{2}$ virgate, and was held by knight service in 1316 and 1328 by John de la Sloo or Slou.[93] In 1353 John atte Sloo and Margery his wife settled their estate in West Camel, together with Slough Court in Stoke St. Gregory, on their sons John and William in tail.[94] By 1412 John Montague was holding the West Camel lands.[95] His family had acquired land elsewhere from Margery atte Sloo in 1366.[96] Agnes Montague became owner in or before 1436.[97]

[62] See above; S.R.O., tithe award; Q/REr: register of electors, western divn.
[63] Sherborne, Digby Estate Office, rent bks. and sale cat.; Burke, *Land. Gent.* (1906), 465–6.
[64] S.R.O., Q/RE, land tax assessments; see above, p. 59.
[65] *V.C.H. Som.* i. 482. [66] Ibid.
[67] *Pipe R.* 1194 (P.R.S. n.s. v), 186.
[68] Ibid. 1200 (P.R.S. n.s. xii), 98.
[69] *S.R.S.* vi. 126; *Cal. Inq. p.m.* ii, p. 18; xi, p. 70; xiv, pp. 144–5; *Cal. Close, 1396–9,* 178.
[70] C 140/2/18.
[71] *Pipe R.* 1194 (P.R.S. n.s. v), 186.
[72] Ibid. 1200 (P.R.S. n.s. xii), 98.
[73] B.M. Harl. Ch. 47 G 33; *S.R.S.* vi. 126; xiv. 71, 74; *L. & P. Hen. VIII,* xiii (1), p. 64; Sanders, *Eng. Baronies,* 39–40.
[74] *Cal. Inq. p.m.* ii, p. 18; *Cal. Fine R. 1272–1307,* 18.
[75] *Cal. Close, 1279–88,* 212.
[76] *Complete Peerage,* s.v. Pembroke; *Feud. Aids,* iv. 361; *Cal. Inq. p.m.* xi, p. 70.
[77] C 136/30/61–3; C 137/25/54.
[78] C 136/4/1; *Cal. Close, 1396–9,* 178.
[79] *Cal. Close, 1399–1402,* 242; *S.R.S.* xxii. 157–8.
[80] *Cal. Close, 1402–5,* 300.
[81] *Complete Peerage,* s.v. Stourton.
[82] Req. 2/20/128; C 3/191/54.
[83] C.P. 25(2)/528/17 Chas. I Trin.
[84] C.P. 40/418 rot. 169.
[85] S.R.O., Q/RE, land tax assessments.
[86] S.R.O., D/G/Y 160; Burke, *Land. Gent.* (1906), 1509.
[87] S.R.O., D/P/w. ca 13/1/1; D/G/Y 160.
[88] D.L. 43/14/3 ff. 71–71v.
[89] *S.R.S.* vi. 106; xiv. 98. [90] Ibid. vi. 106.
[91] Ibid. xlii. 13–14.
[92] Ibid. 95.
[93] Ibid. 83, 91.
[94] Ibid. xvii. 23.
[95] *Fued. Aids,* vi. 504.
[96] *S.R.S.* xvii. 62; xlii. 83.
[97] S.R.O., DD/AB 7.

William Montague (d. by 1481) was succeeded by his son Robert (d. 1509). Robert's heirs were his sister Emme, wife of Thomas Clundell, and his nephews John Bevyn and John Moleyns.[98] The property, described at this time as a manor, was held in 1536 by John Montague.[99] In 1573, two years before his death, Montague settled the property, described as 'Sloo Abbattes and Camell', on his elder son George.[1] The settlement involved Montague in a Chancery suit through an attempt by another party to deprive Montague, 'a very simple man and of very slender judgment', of his lands. Montague believed that he had lost the estate and 'presently languished and shortly after took his bed and for very sorrow died'.[2] George Montague was still in possession in 1579.[3]

Ownership passed to the Cheeke family.[4] Andrew Parsons of West Camel, his wife, and her sister Elizabeth Cheeke sold the property, then called Slow Court farm, to John Cox of Yeovilton and Nicholas Gullye of Urgashay in 1618.[5] William Parsons was living there in 1629 and it was owned by the Kirton family in the 1630s.[6] In 1754 it was occupied by 'Farmer' Snook;[7] Dr. Drummond owned it by 1780 until c. 1810, when he was succeeded by the Palmer family, who retained it until c. 1822.[8] The farm in 1840 was a little under 80 a.;[9] it was only 28 a. by 1863 and 21 a. by 1895.[10]

The house, now called Slowcourt, stands on low-lying ground at the foot of Slowcourt Lane. Gerard considered it appropriately named 'for in winter time the very house stands as it were in a slough or mire'.[11] It was then 'lately new built'.[12] The house is of two storeys, of rubble, with a tiled roof and brick and rubble stacks. It appears to be the house Gerard saw.

Before 1709 a substantial copyhold estate of over 450 a. had developed from the demesne holding of West Camel manor, and was known as West Camel farm. The fee simple was sold in that year for over £1,100 to John Hody of Middlestreet (Dors.).[13] Shortly before 1770 Elizabeth Hody sold the farm to William Taunton of Stratton (Dors.).[14] Taunton died in 1788 and was succeeded by his son the Revd. Dr. Robert Taunton (d. 1796) and then by his grandson W. L. T. P. Taunton (d. 1850).[15] The latter left as his heirs two daughters. They sold the farm in 1874 to Capt. H. G. St. John-Mildmay of Hazlegrove House, Queen Camel (d. 1882). His brother and heir, the Revd. C. A. St. John-Mildmay, died in 1904; his second son Major G. St. John-Mildmay sold the family estate in 1929.[16]

By 1825 the farm, the largest in the parish, was described as part of Manor farm and measured 320 a.[17]

By 1841 it was 346 a.[18] About 1895 the estate was divided: just over 100 a. became Steart South farm, and West Camel farm was reduced to 186 a.[19] The northern properties were again rearranged in 1912 to create Steart farm, now Steart Hill farm.

The farm-house of West Camel farm stood immediately north-west of the church. It was a rubble and stone building with a tiled roof, and was built probably in the 18th century.[20] An adjacent house by the present church path was probably an outbuilding belonging to the farm-house complex. Also of rubble, it incorporates a pigeon loft at its western gable end. The farm-house itself was probably demolished at the end of the 19th century when the farm was divided.

ECONOMIC HISTORY. The estate of Muchelney abbey in West Camel in the 11th century was assessed at 10 hides; there was land for 16 ploughs, though only 12 are recorded. Nine hides were held by the abbot himself, half in demesne and half worked by 7 villeins and 8 bordars with 6 ploughs. The demesne farm was worked by 5 serfs with 4 ploughs. There were 60 a. of meadow and a similar area of pasture attached to the abbot's holding; and stock included 2 pack-horses, 7 cows, 1 swine, and 91 sheep.[21]

An estate of 1 hide, possibly the origin of the settlement at Downhead, was held of Muchelney by Dodeman. The demesne farm there, measuring a virgate, had one plough.[22] The estate supported 4 beasts and 100 sheep though no meadow or pasture is recorded.

The value of the abbot's land was £9, a figure which probably did not include the mill; Dodeman's holding was worth 10s. when he received it and had doubled in value by 1086.[23]

Little Marston is probably not included in the West Camel assessment, but may well be entered as part of Marston Magna.[24] By the middle of the 13th century it was closely linked with Barwick and Stockwood (Dors.), other properties of the lordship then temporarily out of the hands of the Cauntelos.[25] During the 6½ winter months when it was in the hands of the Crown the income, largely from sales of hay, pasture, and stubble was 54s. 5d. including over 30s. arrears. The arable on the estate was cultivated that winter and spring with three ploughs and a harrow, two ploughs coming from Stockwood, and one being lent for part of the time to Barwick. Wheat was sown on 45 a. and oats on 24 a.[26] Downhead manor at the beginning of the 14th century was predominantly arable. The property

[98] C 142/25/36; *S.R.S.* xxii. 152.
[99] C.P. 25(2)/36/239/28 Hen. VIII Mich.
[1] C 142/183/63, 68; C 2/Eliz. I/C 13/56.
[2] C 2/Eliz. I/C 13/56.
[3] C.P. 25(2)/260/15 Eliz. I Trin.;/260/21 Eliz. I Hil.
[4] C 142/201/90; *Visit. Som. 1531, 1573*, ed. Weaver, 121; *S.R.S.* li. 103.
[5] *S.R.S.* li. 220.
[6] Ibid. xv. 199; xxiv. 96.
[7] S.R.O., D/P/w. ca 3/2/1.
[8] S.R.O., Q/RE, land tax assessments.
[9] S.R.O., tithe award.
[10] S.R.O., D/G/Y 160.
[11] *S.R.S.* xv. 194.
[12] Ibid. 199.
[13] S.R.O., DD/SAS (C/120) 8, Player and Russe to Hody.

[14] S.R.O., DD/RS 9.   [15] Ibid.
[16] Ibid.; R. P. A. Lankester, *A History of Hazelgrove House* (1958).
[17] S.R.O., D/P/w. ca 3/2/4.
[18] Ibid. 13/1/1; D/G/Y 160.
[19] S.R.O., D/G/Y 160.
[20] S.R.O., tithe award; Taunton Castle, photograph c. 1890; photograph *penes* the rector.
[21] *V.C.H. Som.* i. 469.
[22] The Exeter Domesday says 1½ plough: *V.C.H. Som.* i. 469.
[23] Ibid.
[24] See p. 74.
[25] S.C. 6/1094/11 rot. 7d.
[26] Ibid. There were 44 a. of arable and 8½ a. of meadow on the holding of Eve Haket there in 1273: *Cal. Inq. p.m.* ii. p. 18.

included 100 a. of arable in demesne, but only 8 a. of meadow. Six tenants in villeinage held a fardel of land each, and rendered for every fardel 5s. for all services. Four cottars paid 1s. each for their holdings.[27] Little Marston demesne contained 173 a. of arable in 1392, compared with about 12 a. of pasture. The whole manor was then worth £9 17s. 10d., including rents of 24s. 4d., and a dovecot worth 6s. 8d.[28]

At least until the 15th century, therefore, the parish seems to have been predominantly under arable cultivation, meadow and pasture playing a relatively minor role in the economy. Annis hill (Aneyshill in 1436–7) was evidently pasture attached to Downhead manor; and Old Land, in the extreme north of the parish, was subject to certain common rights.[29] As late as 1754 the meadow at Old Land was breached on 30 June, the time of Sherborne fair, and remained common until Candlemas.[30] The only known woodland was 'Hawksbere', which in 1298 was considered to be part of Neroche forest as a result of illegal extensions of that forest made since 1154.[31]

Inclosures around West Camel village are probably of medieval origin, and the process was certainly in train on a small scale at the beginning of the 14th century.[32] How far this process had reached by the end of the Middle Ages is not clear, but it seems from the evidence of field names at Little Marston that by 1503 the arable fields had given place to pasture for sheep.[33] The glebe terrier, by showing a modus from Little Marston unless corn were grown, confirms this evidence.[34]

The net value of the Muchelney properties in 1484–5 was just over £25. Assessed rents in West Camel, in a rental of 1462, amounted to £18 10s. 6d., to which were added 3s. 4d. for a dovecot and increased rent for meadow at 'Chestermede'. Assessed rents in Downhead were worth £4 1s. 10d. The demesne, probably of West Camel and Downhead combined, had normally been let for £9, but tenants, holding a nine-year lease, had their farm lowered to £8 for the current year. Decayed rents, including that for the water-mill, amounted to £2 6s. 1d.[35]

By 1535 the Muchelney properties, the manors of West Camel and Downhead, were worth just over £40, including rents from copyhold and freehold tenants amounting to £28 4s. 5d.[36] These were slightly higher by 1671, freehold rents amounting to 25s. and copyhold to £28 18s. 6d. The total net income in 1671, including arrears, was £39 12s. 4d.[37] The regularity of fields in the north-west of the parish, and the frequent use of the names Pindle and Breach, the former for a narrow inclosure, the latter for an inclosure ready for sowing or uncultiva-

ted land, suggests some fairly large-scale inclosure, possibly during the 17th century. There is no direct documentary evidence for such a process, but the field-name Pindle occurs in 1710.[38]

The sale of the former Muchelney manors by Lord Bruce in 1709 marked the beginning of the dispersal of the ancient holdings in the parish. West Camel farm, with over 450 a., was sold in 1709, and another copyhold farm of over 100 a. to John Chalcroft in 1710.[39] The second farm was formed from four smaller units, mostly in the north of the parish, and passed from John Chalcroft in 1763 to his nephew, John Beaton. The Beatons still retained the property at least until 1801, but Henry Beaton's holding in 1839 was only some 59 a.[40] Other small farms, such as that of George Vincent, of 50 a., one fifth arable, also emerged during the 18th century.[41]

Among the farmers in West Camel at the beginning of the 19th century was J. W. Parsons whose farm, probably Parsonage farm, was the subject of a survey by the Bath and West of England Society in 1803. Parsons's views on land and cattle improvements and on cider were given publicity by the same society between 1796 and 1810.[42]

By 1840 there were six farms in the parish of more than 100 a.: the largest, West Camel farm, measured 406 a., followed by Downhead farm with 349 a. The holdings of Robert Welsh, including Parsonage farm, and of Henry Seymour (Little Marston), were of almost equal size, just over 270 a. There were several smaller holdings of between 50 a. and 100 a., including Urgashay farm. By the end of the 19th century some of these larger units had begun to split. By 1897 the largest was Downhead farm with 278 a., followed by Little Marston with 271 a., West Camel farm with 186 a., and 'No. 2 Back Street farm', now Parsonage farm, with 158 a. Lower farm (134 a.) and Steart Hill farm (101 a.) were next in order of size. Further division had evidently taken place by 1921, for there were then only three farms of over 150 a., though by 1939 there were four.[43]

In 1086 there was a mill at West Camel worth 10s.[44] It belonged to Muchelney abbey, who still owned it in 1305.[45] Robert the miller occurs in 1327,[46] and in 1437 the miller was accused of demanding excessive toll.[47] This mill may be identified with Old Mill or Higher Mill, on the river Cam, north of the church. By 1825 it belonged to the Way family, and as Way's Mill it occurs in 1863. It was then owned by the Feaver family,[48] but between 1883 and 1889 passed to the Mildmays.[49] It seems to have continued in use as a mill until soon after 1927.[50] A second mill, called New Mill in 1825, stood on the north bank of the Cam

[27] C 134/16/3.
[28] D.L. 43/14/3 ff. 71–71v.
[29] S.R.O., DD/AB 7.
[30] S.R.O., D/P/w. ca 3/2/1: tithe bk. 1754.
[31] V.C.H. Som. ii. 562.
[32] Cal. Pat. 1391–6, 497.
[33] Req. 2/20/128.
[34] S.R.O., D/P/w. ca 3/1/1: attested copy glebe terrier.
[35] S.C. 6/974/5.
[36] Valor Eccl. (Rec. Com.), i. 193–4.
[37] S.R.O., DD/AB 14. [38] S.R.O., DD/YB2.
[39] S.R.O., DD/SAS (C/120) 8; DD/YB 2. Another small farm was sold in 1714: DD/BR/rb, Player and Russe to Gannett.

[40] S.R.O., DD/YB 216, 218, 239; tithe award.
[41] S.R.O., DD/TCW 21.
[42] Proc. Bath and West of England Soc. viii, x, xii.
[43] S.R.O., tithe award; D/G/Y/160; Kelly's Dir. Som. (1939).
[44] V.C.H. Som. i. 469.
[45] Cal. Pat. 1391–6, 497.
[46] S.R.S. iii. 201.
[47] S.R.O., DD/AB 7.
[48] S.R.O., D/P/w. ca 3/2/4, 13/1/1; tithe award; D/G/Y 160.
[49] S.R.O., D/G/Y 160.
[50] Kelly's Dir. Som. (1927). There was no miller in 1931: ibid. (1931).

west of Frog Lane.[51] Its usual name was Lower Mill and was also known as Beaton's Mill. The Beaton family held it until 1843.[52] It seems to have ceased production between 1875 and 1883.[53] There may have been a mill on the estate at Little Marston, though the only indication is a field called 'Mulle-hay' in 1392.[54]

LOCAL GOVERNMENT. Muchelney abbey claimed the assize of ale, tumbrel, and rights of waif and stray in West Camel by 1280.[55] Downhead, not then in the hands of the monks, owed separate suit to the hundred court, and separate courts continued to be held in the two manors after 1358 when both were owned by Muchelney.[56] Court rolls have survived for Michaelmas 1436 and for Christmas and Hockday 1436–7; there are entries for Camel Abbots manor for each session and for Downhead for Michaelmas and Christmas.[57] There was then only one bailiff for the two manors, chosen from four nominees at the Michaelmas court,[58] though each manor was represented by its tithingman chosen at the same court.

Business at the courts in 1436–7 included orders against individuals for illegal breach of fields and for excessive toll at the mill. In 1436 compensation was required of four dyers who had allowed what was called 'flor' and other poisons to enter the river.[59]

No further court rolls have been found.[60] By the 18th century the vestry was in control of the parish, making decisions on labour and haulage, probably for the repair of roads, and on payments from the overseers' rate.[61] Before 1744 the vestry decided to negotiate with the lord of the manor for the purchase of a poorhouse.[62] In 1752 the lord leased to the rector and overseers a cottage built on the waste in Keep Street for the use of 'the second poor who received no alms'.[63] This was presumably the 'small old tenement' in 'consider-able decay' which by 1823 was called the Second Poor house. The parish had paid rent for the house for many years up to that time, and it had usually been occupied by the parish poor. Small rents were taken from such occupants as could pay, who were few.[64] By 1839–40 the rector and overseers owned the house which was divided into two tenements.[65] It stood near the junction of Plowage Lane and Keep Street.

Between 1804 and 1825[66] a poorhouse was erected in the centre of the village. By 1839 it was occupied by a local farmer.[67] It was demolished in or before 1869 when a house for the schoolmistress was built on or near the same site.[68] The parish became part of the Yeovil poor-law union in 1836.[69]

CHURCH. If the fragment of decorated cross-shaft, influenced by the Jellinge style and now mounted in the north transept, originated in the parish, then the church must date from the late 9th or early 10th century.[70] The earliest written evidence yet traced is from 1219,[71] but the Norman font, if not the cross-shaft, is evidence of a church build-ing at an earlier date. The church may well have been founded by Muchelney abbey, owners of the manor from the 10th century, and, physically, it is close to the remaining buildings of the former demesne farm.[72]

The rectory was in the patronage of Muchelney abbey until 1239 when Bishop Jocelin of Bath and Wells acquired the advowson.[73] Thenceforward the patronage was in the hands of successive bishops, though appointments were also made by papal pro-vision or by the Crown during the voidance of the see.[74] In 1574 the duchess of Somerset and her second husband, Francis Newdigate, jointly pre-sented,[75] and Henry Albin was presumably in-truded about 1646.[76] The benefice has been held in plurality with Queen Camel since 1944.[77]

The value of the living in 1291 was £13 6s. 8d.[78] The fruits were sold for the same sum in 1329–30,[79] and the assessment remained constant through-out the 15th century.[80] The clear value was given as £13 8s. 8d. in 1535.[81] By c. 1668 the benefice was worth some £80;[82] the average net income by 1831 was £275,[83] rising to £323 in 1851.[84]

The tithes of corn were valued at 25s. 4d., and oblations, obventions, and other small tithes at £4 in 1334.[85] Predial tithes were worth £8, tithe wool and lambs 20s., and oblations and personal tithes 6os., making a total of £12 in 1535.[86] By the beginning of the 17th century a modus of 42s. was usually paid by the occupier of Little Marston, though tithe corn was payable there whenever it was sown. Some 25 a. in Marston Lancs, possibly in Marston Magna parish, were also charged with tithe by the rector of West Camel.[87] By the middle

[51] S.R.O., D/P/w. ca 3/2/4.
[52] Ibid. 13/1/1.
[53] S.R.O., D/G/Y 160. It was still so called in 1895 but not thereafter.
[54] D.L. 43/14/3 ff. 71–71v.
[55] S.R.S. xiv. 94.
[56] Rot. Hund. (Rec. Com.), ii. 134; see below.
[57] S.R.O., DD/AB 7.
[58] S.C. 12/14/38; Valor Eccl. (Rec. Com.), i. 193; S.R.O., DD/AB 7.
[59] S.R.O., DD/AB 7. The dye was probably copper oxide.
[60] Extract of court baron 1760: S.R.O., DD/SAS (C/120) 8.
[61] S.R.O., D/P/w. ca 13/2/2.
[62] Ibid. 4/1/1: chwdns' accts. and rates 1793–1903.
[63] Ibid. 13/10/1.
[64] 11th Rep. Com. Char. H.C. 433, pp. 441–2 (1823), xiv.
[65] S.R.O., tithe award.
[66] Poor Law Abstract, 1804, where all expenditure was for out relief; S.R.O., D/P/w. ca 3/2/4.
[67] S.R.O., tithe award.

[68] See p. 80.
[69] Poor Law Com. 2nd Rep. p. 550.
[70] Dates between the 9th and 11th century have been given: Jnl. Royal Arch. Inst. xv. 144–51; D. Talbot-Rice, English Art, 871–1100, 128; Pevsner, South and West Som. 337.
[71] Cal. Papal Regs. i. 65.
[72] See p. 75.
[73] S.R.S. xiv. 51–2.
[74] Cal. Pat. 1330–4, 242; 1367–70, 7.
[75] S.R.O., D/D/Bp, 2 Sept. 1574.
[76] Walker Revised, ed. Matthews, s.v. Richardson.
[77] Dioc. Dir.
[78] Tax. Eccl. (Rec. Com.), 197.
[79] S.R.S. ix. 61.
[80] Feud. Aids, iv. 400; S.R.S. xlix. 32.
[81] Valor Eccl. (Rec. Com.), i. 204.
[82] S.R.O., D/D/Vc 24.
[83] Rep. Com. Eccl. Revenues, pp. 156–7.
[84] H.O. 129/319/5/11/13.
[85] E 179/169/14.
[86] Valor Eccl. (Rec. Com.), i. 204.
[87] S.R.O., D/P/w. ca 3/1/1: attested copy glebe terrier.

of the 18th century some tithes had been commuted for cash payments: people not resident in the parish paid 20*d.* in the pound for agistments, and the parishioners paid 4*d.* for offerings and 1*d.* for each garden. Most tithes were still paid in kind: the rector received every seventh calf, or, if one was killed, the left shoulder; milk was also paid in kind 'if not agreed for'; and the rector claimed the third of a litter of seven or more pigs, and the eighth best lamb and thereafter a share, amounting to three lambs in every twenty-five. The whole tithe of shorn wool was also claimed.[88] By 1775 a modus of 2½*d.* a cow, 1½*d.* a heifer, and 2*d.* an acre was payable in lieu of great and small tithes on just over 140 a. at the northern edge of the parish, known as North moor or Stock mead.[89] The moduses of 42*s.* for Little Marston and of 2*d.* an acre at North moor were still paid in 1839.[90] The tithes were valued at £254 3*s.* 10¾*d.* in 1830, and were commuted in 1839 for a rent-charge of £264.[91]

In 1305, in addition to property he already possessed in right of his church, the rector was allowed common rights over the demesne lands of Muchelney abbey in his parish 'according to the extent of his holding'. He was permitted to pasture six oxen with those of the abbot, except in the abbot's gardens and in the 'grove'. Further, he was assigned 8 a. of inclosed land between the 'rigeweye' and his own farmyard. This agreement was ratified in 1394.[92] By 1334 the rector's total holding was thus substantial, amounting to a virgate of arable, worth 20*s.*, 6 a. of meadow, and rents worth 8*s.*[93] The glebe was worth 40*s.* in 1535,[94] but by 1606 it amounted to 70 a., together with a small farm of 18 a. let by copy and a small plot in Chilton Cantelo.[95] There was still 70 a. of glebe at the end of the 18th century, though by 1830 some 5 a. had been sold. The glebe was then valued at £88.[96] The small holding, now represented by Glebe farm, Downhead, was also still retained.[97] Some 25 a. of glebe were sold in 1912, and by 1961 there remained just over 38 a.[98]

The rectory house and buildings covered 2 a. in 1606, and comprised the dwelling-house, together with barn, stable, garden, and orchard.[99] Edward Willes found the house 'very small' for his large family in the 1820s,[1] and in 1836 it was enlarged.[2] The present house is a T-shaped building and clearly comprises two distinct parts: the south wing, of two storeys and attics, has sash windows and deep eaves. This is presumably the 1836 addition. The range at right angles to it on the north side is built of stone and appears to represent the solar wing of the medieval rectory house. It is

of two storeys with 16th- or early-17th-century mullioned windows and other alterations of this and later periods. Near the east end of the south wall are the remains, visible both outside and in, of a blocked stone doorway with a pointed head. The range is now of five bays but the westermost bay is a later addition; in the former west gable end, now concealed, is the head of a pointed window. The roof over the original range has four arch-braced collar-beam trusses, the collars supporting crown posts with two-way struts. The chamfered braces below each collar meet in the centre, forming a depressed arch with a small ogee at the apex. The timbers are not smoke-blackened and it may be assumed that the formerly open roof covered a long upper room or solar in a range that was always two-storeyed. The medieval hall may have been on the site of the 19th-century wing.

To the west of the rectory house is a stone-built tithe barn with five compound cruck trusses, probably dating from *c.* 1500.[3] A circular dovecot, standing south-west of the house, may also be of late-medieval date. It has buttressed stone walls and a conical roof crowned by a central cupola.

Throughout the history of the benefice there has been a tradition of absenteeism, the result of the appointment of men who were on the staffs of successive bishops. Master Stephen Tripp, rector by 1329 and then only in subdeacon's orders, was an active member of Bishop Ralph of Shrewsbury's administration[4] and in his time and later there was a resident chaplain at West Camel.[5] Master John Sidenhale, rector by 1351, was also one of Bishop Ralph's clerks.[6] Thomas Cosyn was licensed to absent himself from the benefice in 1402, but employed a chaplain to carry out his duties.[7] Andrew Grantham (rector 1472–92) and Thomas Shelyngford (rector 1492 to 1535 or later) were both resident at Wells, the former as a vicar-choral and cathedral chantrist, the latter as a chantrist.[8] By 1532 Shelyngford was employing two clergy at West Camel.[9]

The benefice in 1554 was vacant owing to the deprivation of rector John Smith for marriage.[10] He was succeeded by William Finch (d. 1559), formerly prior of Breamore (Hants), and from 1538 the first suffragan bishop of Taunton.[11] The rector from 1574 was the Northamptonshire Puritan Eusebius Pagett.[12] Anthony Richardson, appointed in 1614, lost the benefice about 1646 having, among other things, failed to keep the fast imposed by Parliament, and having continued to use the Prayer Book.[13] He was replaced by Henry Albin, later a widely-known Nonconformist preacher.[14] Richardson was restored in 1660.[15] Dr. John Vannam

88 Ibid. 3/2/1, tithe bk. 1754.
89 Ibid., receipt for tithe, 1775; tithe award, 1839.
90 S.R.O., tithe award.
91 Ibid.; D/P/w. ca 3/2/5: tithe valuation, 1830.
92 *Cal. Pat.* 1391–6, 497; *S.R.S.* xlii. 68.
93 E 179/169/14.
94 *Valor Eccl.* (Rec. Com.), i. 204.
95 S.R.O., D/P/w. ca 3/1/1.
96 Ibid. 3/2/2: tithe bk. 1789–1805; 3/2/5.
97 S.R.O., tithe award; par. rec., correspondence.
98 Par. rec., inventory.
99 S.R.O., D/P/w. ca 3/1/1.
1 Ibid. 1/1/1.
2 Ibid. 3/1/2.
3 *Proc. Som. Arch. Soc.* cxiv. 51.
4 *S.R.S.* ix. 17, 36, 40, 285, 320; x. 447, 507; *Abbrev. Rot. Orig.* (Rec. Com.), ii. 198.

5 *S.R.S.* ix. 242; xix. 313; xlix. 395; lii. 24.
6 *Cal. Papal Regs.* iii. 424; *Cal. Papal Pets.* 246; Emden, *Biog. Reg. Univ. Oxford.*
7 *S.R.S.* xiii. 25; xix. 313; Le Neve, *Fasti, 1300–1541, Bath and Wells*, 26.
8 S.R.O., D/D/Vc 20; *H.M.C. Wells*, ii. 101, 104, 107, 111, 113, 119, 207, 694, 696; *S.R.S.* xix. 145, 224; lii. 174; liv. 129.
9 S.R.O., D/D/Vc 20.   10 *S.R.S.* lv. 121.
11 Ibid.; Foster, *Alumni Oxon.*; *Handbk. of Brit. Chron.* ed. Powicke and Fryde, 272.
12 S.R.O., D/D/Bp; *S.R.S.* lxix. 27.
13 *Walker Revised*, ed. Matthews; *Proc. Som. Arch. Soc.* iv. 69–71.
14 *Calamy Revised*, ed. Matthews; *D.N.B.* See also *S.R.S.* xxviii. 300.
15 *Walker Revised*, ed. Matthews.

(rector 1665–1721) was chaplain-in-ordinary to the king and vicar of Bibury (Glos.) from 1673 to 1721.[16]

The later years of the 18th century saw a return to the practice of appointing diocesan staff to the benefice, as well as a certain amount of nepotism. Francis Potter (rector 1757–67)[17] was successively archdeacon of Taunton (1758–60) and of Wells (1760–7). Edward Aubery (rector 1784–86) was grandson of the patron, Bishop Edward Willes.[18] Charles Moss, only son of Bishop Willes's successor, became subdean of Wells shortly after his father's translation in 1774, and held West Camel for about a year from 1787.[19] On Moss's resignation William Willes, archdeacon of Wells and son of the former bishop, became rector. He, in turn, resigned the benefice in favour of his son Edward in 1797.[20] Edward Willes's failure to reside at West Camel led to sequestration and cession in 1824,[21] in favour of Henry Law, son of the then bishop, and archdeacon of Richmond (Yorks.). In 1826 Law was appointed archdeacon of Wells and two years later a residentiary canon at Wells, though retaining West Camel until 1836.[22]

At a visitation in 1554 the wardens and posts reported that service books required for the restored liturgy were missing.[23] In 1559 the rector lived in Gloucester diocese, and in 1568 was reported for non-residence and for failing to preach the quarterly sermons.[24] There seems to have been some trouble during Henry Albin's intrusion in the 17th century: one parishioner was accused of 'very ill behaviour' towards him,[25] and in 1654 the bell-ringers forcibly prevented the removal of a dog from the pulpit.[26]

During the mid 19th century the Holy Communion was celebrated six times a year, but in 1870 there were eight celebrations 'at about noon'.[27] Two and sometimes three sermons were preached on a Sunday by 1840, though by 1851 only two services, morning and afternoon, were normally held. On Census Sunday 1851 the general congregation in the morning numbered 54, and in the afternoon 105; Sunday-school pupils, regularly catechized in the schoolroom, numbered 20 and 18 respectively.[28]

A church house was rented from the lord of the manor at least until 1671, but was not by that date necessarily used by the parish.[29]

There was a chapel at Little Marston by 1403, though no mention of it was made in the survey of the manor eleven years earlier.[30]

The church of *ALL SAINTS* consists of chancel, nave, north and south transepts,[31] and south porch.

The south transept forms the base of the unbuttressed tower. The present cruciform building dates from the late 13th and earlier 14th centuries with some 15th-century alterations. The arches leading to both transepts, the trefoiled rere-arch of the east window, the narrow north window in the north transept, and traces of roll-moulded string-course outside the north wall of the nave, all belong to the earlier phase of the building. The 13th-century trefoil-headed sedilia and double piscina on the south side of the chancel were completely renewed in the 19th century; to the west of them is a bracket which formerly supported the Lenten veil. The east and side windows of the chancel, one window in the nave, and the belfry windows of the tower have tracery of the earlier 14th century. In the 15th century the west window and a south window were inserted in the nave. The fine tie-beam roof of the nave, low pitched and with carved angel brackets, is of the same period, as are the external parapets and prominent gargoyles. There is also a 15th-century stone pulpit which formerly stood west of the tower arch.[32]

Before the extensive restoration of 1866–7 the chancel arch was similar in size and style to the surviving arches into the transepts, supported on moulded corbel brackets.[33] The chancel itself in the 1830s and 1840s was unfurnished save for the surviving Norman font, which is decorated with intersecting arches.[34] There are traces of secondary altars in both transepts, one of which must have been 'Our Lady yelde' mentioned in 1545.[35] The north transept contains a 16th-century chest holding a collection of books including the *Paraphrases* of Erasmus (1523) and Jewel's *Works* (1609).

There are five bells: (i) 1951, Taylor; (ii) 1737, Knight of Closworth; (iii) c. 1500, a Dorset founder; (iv) 1737, Knight of Closworth; (v) 1617, Purdue.[36] The medieval plate included a chalice given by the rector in 1413.[37] He gave, in addition, a pair of vestments, a surplice, and a corporal and case. A rector in 1493 gave a printed missal (*de le preynte*).[38] The plate was stolen in 1855 and the present modern plate replaced it.[39] The registers of burials begin in 1678 but there is a gap for 1704–9; the registers of baptisms and marriages begin in 1710, but there is a gap in the marriage registers for 1751–3.[40]

NONCONFORMITY. From the early 1590s until at least 1629 there was a group of recusants in the parish. Richard Dampier, tailor, Agnes his wife, and their children were regularly reported by the

[16] Venn, *Alumni Cantab.*
[17] A Francis Potter was rector 1746–57, probably the same man.
[18] S. H. Cassan, *Lives of Bishops of Bath and Wells*, 173. John Willes (rector 1768–84) may have been a relative of Bishop Willes. [19] *D.N.B.*
[20] R. Locke, *Survey of Som.*, ed. Ward, 56; Foster, *Alumni Oxon.*
[21] S.R.O., D/P/w. ca 1/1/1.
[22] *D.N.B.* Law resided at Yeovilton, where he was rector 1830–4: *Rep. Com. Eccl. Revenues*, pp. 156–7.
[23] S.R.O., D/D/Ca 22.
[24] Corpus Christi Coll., Cambridge, MS. 97, p. 120; S.R.O., D/D/Ca 40.
[25] *S.R.S.* xxviii. 300. [26] Ibid. pp. xliii–iv.
[27] S.R.O., D/D/V rtns. 1840, 1843, 1854, 1870.
[28] H.O. 129/319/5/11/13; S.R.O., D/D/V rtns. 1840–70; *P.O. Dir. Som.* (1861).

[29] S.R.O., DD/AB 14.
[30] *Cal. Close*, 1402–5, 300; D.L. 43/14/3 ff. 71–71v.
[31] Said to belong to the proprietor of Slow Court: Collinson, *Hist. Som.* iii. 190.
[32] Taunton Castle, Pigott Colln., drawing by Buckler (1832). The pulpit then stood on a circular pedestal and had a Jacobean sounding board.
[33] *S.R.S.* xl. 199–200; *P.O. Dir. Som.* (1866); S.R.O., D/P/w. ca 3/1/2.
[34] Taunton Castle, Pigott Colln., drawing by Buckler (1832); Braikenridge Colln., drawing by W. W. Wheatley (1847).
[35] *S.R.S.* xl. 199–200.
[36] S.R.O, DD/SAS CH 16.
[37] *S.R.S.* xix. 313.
[38] *H.M.C. Wells*, ii. 694.
[39] S.R.O., D/P/w. ca 4/1/1.
[40] Ibid. 2/1/1–3.

churchwardens, and Richard Smart, yeoman, Richard Mogg, and Anne, wife of Edward Mullyns the younger, were also similarly accused.[41]

Preaching licences were issued to nonconformists meeting in the houses of John Harris in 1692, of Henry Parsons in 1708, and of Hannah Langdon in 1710, though there is no indication of the denomination of any of these groups.[42] No further activity has been traced until 1800, when the house of Wilton Tally was licenced for use, though again the denomination of the group is not known.[43] One of the signatories of the petition for the licence was Richard Mitchell, and in 1817 the house of a Richard Mitchell became the meeting-place of a group of Independents who had their own minister.[44] This group continued at least until 1833, when the then minister had his own house licensed,[45] though there is no further trace of them after this date.

The group meeting in Wilton Tally's house, however, seems in origin to have been Methodist, one of the signatories of the petition being Thomas Connock, a native of the parish and founder of Methodism in Somerton.[46] Connock had been appointed a class-leader by John Wesley, and seems to have taken part in the establishment of a group in his native parish. The Methodist cause may then be traced to the house of Thomas Bennett, licensed in 1809 and again in 1814, perhaps on rebuilding.[47] Certainly, later worshippers dated the origin of their chapel from the year 1814.[48] The chapel was the upper storey of a carpenter's shop opposite the pound, at the western end of Keep Street. It was still owned by the Bennett family in 1840,[49] but later passed to the Digby Estate. J. K. Wingfield-Digby sold it to Thomas Martin in 1892.[50]

This 'upper room' had sittings for 84 people, of which 60 were free. In 1851 there were three services each Sunday, and on Census Sunday the congregations were 6 in the morning, 12 in the afternoon, and 45 in the evening.[51]

The present chapel, on the London road, was erected on a site given by Mr. A. E. Clothier. The building, of Keinton stone with brick dressings, was designed by James Spire and was opened in 1908. There is accommodation for 140, and an adjoining hall houses the Sunday school. Since 1934 the chapel has been part of the Somerset Mission, and was formerly in the Glastonbury Circuit and then the Mid-Somerset Mission.[52]

EDUCATION. A boarding school and a Sunday school for about 30 pupils had been established in the parish by 1818, but there were no endowments,

and the assistant curate reported that 'the poor would be glad of more sufficient means for educating their children'.[53] By 1825–6 there was a small daily school, and a Sunday school 'particularly worthy of notice'.[54] Two day-schools, one of which was kept by a dissenter, between them taught 25 children in 1833, all at their parents' expense. There were also two Sunday schools, one said to have been started in 1824; the latter, supported by the rector, taught 21 boys and 19 girls. The other, for 11 boys and 7 girls, was financed by pupils' fees.[55] A 'village school' for Sunday, day, and evening classes, was founded in 1837,[56] and was united to the district board of the National Society. In 1846–7 there were 26 pupils who attended on weekdays and Sundays, and 24 on weekdays only. Three boys and two girls attended on Sunday and weekday evenings, 7 boys and 2 girls on weekday evenings only. The staff consisted of a paid master and two paid mistresses, and 2 masters and 3 mistresses served voluntarily. The school was housed in one room and was supported both by subscriptions and by payments by pupils.[57] A house was added for a schoolmistress in 1869.[58]

There was accommodation for 67 pupils in this school by 1894, but the average attendance was only 31.[59] One teacher and a monitress were the sole staff by 1903, though it was reported that 'distinctly good work' was being done. The school was taken over by the County Education Authority in that year, though the buildings remained under the control of the rector and churchwardens, who used it for parochial and other meetings when required.[60] The numbers in the school declined in the 1920s and from 1926 juniors and infants only were taken: in 1921 there were 29 pupils on the books, but by 1938 the average attendance was only 15.[61] The school was closed in 1948 and the pupils were transferred to Queen Camel.[62] The school building reverted to the Digby Estate, and was purchased by the Parochial Church Council for use as a parish hall.[63]

CHARITIES FOR THE POOR. Richardson's Gift was probably founded by Anthony Richardson (d. 1665), rector from 1614.[64] In 1787 the capital sum of £10 produced 8s. a year. In 1799 the principal passed to Edward Willes (rector 1797–1824), and money was distributed by him in small sums to 'those who may appear to stand most in need of relief'.[65] By 1781 Richardson's Gift was evidently combined with the income from a cottage in Keep Street, formerly the Second Poor house.[66] The

---

[41] S.R.O., D/D/Ca 150 (pp. 230–1), 177, 236, 237; S. & D. N. & Q. v. 116.
[42] S.R.O., Q/RR, meeting-house lics.
[43] S.R.O., D/D/Rm, box 2.
[44] Ibid.   [45] Ibid.
[46] Ibid.; E. G. Marley, The Story of the Methodist Church in West Camel (1958). For Methodism in Somerton, see p. 151.
[47] S.R.O., D/D/Rm, box 2.
[48] H.O. 129/319/5/11/14.
[49] S.R.O., tithe award.
[50] Glastonbury, Lambrook St. Methodist Church, trust deeds etc.
[51] H.O. 129/319/5/11/14.
[52] Marley, Methodist Church in West Camel.
[53] Digest of Returns to Sel. Cttee. on Educ. of Poor, H.C. 224 (1819), ix (2).

[54] Rep. B. & W. Dioc. Assoc. S.P.C.K. (1825–6).
[55] Educ. Enquiry Abstract, H.C. 62 (1835), xlii.
[56] Kelly's Dir. Som. (1897).
[57] Acct. of Church Educ. among Poor (1846).
[58] S.R.O., DD/EDS, plan of house; the architect was Henry Hall of London. Also S.R.O., D/P/w. ca 18/1/1, correspondence. The house is now called Bridge Cottage.
[59] Return of Schs. 1893 [C 7529], H.C. (1894), lxv.
[60] S.R.O., C/E 28. See D/P/w. ca 18/7/1 for log bk. 1868–96; C/E 52 for log bk. 1921–48; D/P/w. ca 18/7/2 for managers' min. bk. 1903–48.
[61] S.R.O., C/E 52; Som. C.C. Educ. Cttee. Schs. List; Bd. of Educ., List 21, [1938] (H.M.S.O.), 353.
[62] S.R.O., C/E 52.
[63] Ex inf. the Rector.
[64] 11th Rep. Com. Char. H.C. 433 (1824), xiv.
[65] Ibid.   [66] See p. 77.

total income of £7 13s. 10d. was distributed in cash.[67] The charity is now merged with the Feaver Charity.

Silas Feaver in 1859 bequeathed the sum of £100, the interest to be paid to poor unrelieved parishioners.[68] By 1871 the income was £3 3s. 10d.[69] The charity is now governed by a body of trustees under a Scheme of 1935.[70] Its capital was increased by £50 in 1962, and for many years it has been administered with the Second Poor House Charity and Richardson's Gift. The income of the combined charities, still distributed in cash, amounted to £7 8s. in 1968–9.[71]

CHARLTON ADAM

THE ancient parish of Charlton Adam, often known as East Charlton, had an area estimated at 1,458 a. in 1810[1] and at 1,476 a. in 1861,[2] but no accurate assessment of its area survives. The many detached portions of the parish lying dispersed in Charlton Mackrell, some at Wellham on its western boundary, may represent tenements originally granted to Bruton priory, together with their holdings in the common fields, which were subsequently administered from Charlton Adam.[3] Two irregularly shaped areas, totalling 132 a., lay detached in Copley wood, about 2 miles north-west of the parish.[4] When the civil parishes of Charlton Adam and Charlton Mackrell were amalgamated under the name of Charlton Mackrell in 1885, the western portion was transferred to Compton Dundon and the eastern to Kingweston.[5]

The parish is situated 3 miles east of Somerton, extending 1½ mile from north to south and nearly 2 miles from east to west, excluding the detached areas. It abuts north-east on Kingweston and Keinton Mandeville, east on Babcary, and south and west on Charlton Mackrell.

The soil of the parish is clay over limestone and lias.[6] The land rises above the 150 ft. contour at Bulland in the north-west, and above 125 ft. by the Foss Way in the north-east, and falls away gradually to the river Cary in the south-west. South and west of Manor Farm the ground rises steeply above 100 ft. and 150 ft. respectively. The area is poorly watered; a single small stream, known as Matford brook ('Modford broke' in 1327),[7] runs immediately east of Withybed Lane under the new course of the Foss Way at Sticklebridge, passes south-east of the old road and west of Midney, and flows into the parish of Keinton Mandeville in the north-east. A small stream which formerly served Peck Mill, south of Manor Farm, is dry for much of the year.

The road pattern is irregular. The Foss Way (A 37) runs north-east through the south-western end of the parish, with a diversion to the north at Sticklebridge. It seems evident that this is not original and that its course was formerly straight.

It has been suggested[8] that this alteration was to avoid an area of low-lying marshy ground, and the change of route may have been permanently effected when the common pasture there was inclosed in 1634.[9] Part of the former road survives as a lane south-west of Sticklebridge, indicating that a less abrupt diversion was once used, possibly until the Foss was adopted by the Ilchester turnpike trust in 1753.[10] 'The way which is called Fos' occurs in a Charlton Adam charter of c. 1258.[11] From the Foss at Sticklebridge a lane, probably once known as Eastwell Lane[12] but now as Broadway, runs west to the north end of the village. A bend in the lane and the position of two fields named Cornish Way[13] suggest that its course once lay further south to meet the Foss at its shorter diversion, presumably crossing the stream there by means of Matford.[14] The village itself is formed by a rectangle of four lanes: Broad Street runs south from the western end of Broadway to meet first Station Road, sometimes known as Court Lane, and then George Street, both on the west. The rectangle, known as the Penning or Square in 1832,[15] is completed by Church Lane which links Station Road and George Street. Apart from Church Lane which occurs in 1836,[16] none of these names is mentioned before the late 19th century. Front Street and Quay Lane, which occur in the early 19th century,[17] can probably be identified with George Street and Broad Street respectively. Broad Street continues north and then north-east as Combe Lane to Keinton Mandeville, and an irregular track known as Balls Lane, probably from a 16th-century family of that name,[18] proceeds eastwards from George Street and subsequently north to Broadway, evidently to provide access to fields along its course. Station Road runs west and then north-west to that part of Charlton Mackrell around Charlton House, and subsequently to Kingweston. A lane, originally known as Chessells Lane from the adjoining field, goes south from George Street to the south-western limit of the parish at Tout. Thence three roads run north-west to Charlton Mackrell, and south and south-west to the Foss in Charlton Mackrell. Ten Acre Lane

---

[67] Dig. End. Chars. 1869–71, H.C. 25 (1873), li.
[68] Ex inf. the Revd. M. P. Ralph-Bowman, rector.
[69] Dig. End. Chars. 1869–71.
[70] Ex inf. the rector.
[71] Ibid.
[1] S.R.O., CR 92. This article was completed in 1970.
[2] P.O. Dir. Som. (1861).
[3] See map, p. 59.
[4] S.R.O., CR 92.
[5] Local Govt. Bd. Order 19,585.
[6] Geol. Surv. Map 1″, solid and drift, sheet 296 (1969 edn.).
[7] S.R.S. viii. 92; Devon R.O. 123 M/TB 139.

[8] I. D. Margary, Roman Roads in Britain, i. 115.
[9] S.R.O., DD/X/HO, ct. roll; see below, p. 90.
[10] Ilchester Turnpike Act, 26 Geo. II, c. 71 (Priv. Act).
[11] S.R.S. viii. 45.
[12] S.R.O., DD/DN, box 38, deeds of cottage in Eastwell Lane; CR 92. 'Estewell' occurs in a charter of 1327: S.R.S. viii. 92.
[13] S.R.O., CR 92.
[14] Suggested by Mr. C. F. Hamilton.
[15] S.R.O., DD/ED 166/306.
[16] S.R.O., Q/REr.
[17] Ibid.
[18] Devon R.O. 123 M/E 31.

runs north from Station Road just west of its junction with Church Street, then east across Combe Lane and north-east, originally for access to the open fields in that part of the parish. Two lanes run north-west from the Foss Way at Sticklebridge: Withybed Lane runs into Combe Lane at the northern limit of the parish, for the latter part of its course forming the parish boundary, and Common Lane links Sticklebridge with Keinton Mandeville. In the east of the parish a lane runs south-east from the Foss, across the Cary at Steart bridge to Steart in Babcary.

The Great Western rail link between Castle Cary and Charlton Mackrell, running through the north-west of the parish, was opened in 1905, and from Charlton Mackrell to Somerton in the following year.[19] Charlton Mackrell station, which lay just within the western boundary of Charlton Adam, was closed to all traffic in 1962.[20]

The early inclosure of the common fields makes it difficult to trace their extent with certainty. Of the two medieval arable fields,[21] North field appears to have stretched from Bulland on the north-western boundary to Red Holes ('Revedol Furlong' c. 1258),[22] possibly bordering Withybed Lane in the north and east, and crossing the Broadway in the south at Withyhays ('Witheheye' c. 1258).[23] It is not certain whether North field included Walkmoor lying across Combe Lane in the north of the parish. South field lay south of Balls Lane, adjoining the parish boundary on the south, Chessels Lane on the west, and possibly including most of the area known as the Slades between Balls Lane and the Foss.[24] The four-field system, formed by c. 1564–6,[25] was created by the subdivision of North field and South field. North-east field, sometimes inexplicably called West field, occupied the area south-west of Withybed Lane between Walkmoor and Red Holes. South-east or East field lay between Balls Lane and the Foss, south of Matford, possibly including lands further west. The medieval common pasture and meadows are represented by sixteen field names,[26] but of these only one can be located: 'Middelnyemed', occurring in 1340.[27] This can be identified with Midney in the south-east corner of the parish. It seems likely that most of the early pasture and meadows lay in this area on the land beyond the Foss dropping down towards the river Cary. The common pastures inclosed in 1634 lay further north. Matford extended south of Broadway, between Balls Lane and the Foss. The Lains ('Laynes and Brokes' in c. 1564–6, 'Mackerise Layne' in 1634) occupied the extreme eastern corner of the parish in the area of the Foss diversion, with Hale ('Hayle' in c. 1564–6, 'Heale' in 1634) and Heaples to the south, and Turdhills to the north-west.[28]

Archaeological evidence for Romano-British settlement in Charlton Adam includes potsherds, coins, slab graves, and traces of building found in Perrin's Quarry at Bulland in the north-west of the parish, which suggest occupation and possible quarrying activity during the 3rd or 4th century.[29] The field name Chessels (Cheshull in c. 1238),[30] which is found south of the village, may indicate another site of Roman settlement, as has been shown to be the case elsewhere.[31] The parish church and 'the Abbey', formerly the lay rectory, lie in the south-east corner of Station Road and Church Lane. Settlement in the village appears originally to have been restricted to both sides of Broad Street and the south side of George Street, established round lands held with 'the Abbey'. The earliest buildings in this area date from the 16th century, although most are lias houses and cottages of the 18th and 19th centuries. Four cottages were erected on the waste in Eastwell Lane between 1595 and 1611.[32] A row of houses on the north side of Broadway is dated 1842 and modern houses have been built to the south, towards its western end. In the 19th century the school and former Methodist chapel were erected on the south-west corner of Station Road and Broad Street. Just south of the school lies the Temperance Hall, first mentioned in 1902[33] and used in 1970 as a youth club. The principal village shops stand on the east side of Broad Street at this junction. The farm-houses lie generally within the village itself. East Farm is sited on the east side of Broad Street with its farm buildings opposite. Just north of the junction of Broadway and Combe Lane stands the Barton, formerly known as Walters' Barton from the family which owned it in the early 19th century.[34] On the north side of the lane leading west from George Street stood the farm-house held in turn by the Willes and Thring families, probably to be identified with a dwelling-house now called 'the Laurels', east of which cottage development has taken place. 'Pleasant Spot', lying north of Broadway, and Sticklebridge, on the south side of the Foss Way diversion, were small farms, both erected in the middle or late 19th century.[35] Priory Farm and Manor Farm both lie in a detached part of the parish in Charlton Mackrell, on the east side of Peck Mill Lane, running north from the hill on which Charlton Mackrell church stands.

A public house called the New Inn occurs between 1745[36] and 1764,[37] and in 1765 appears to have changed its name to the Old Inn.[38] It is not mentioned thereafter and its site has not been traced. The Blue Boy inn is recorded in 1769.[39] During the 19th century the parish appears to have been served by beer shops, one of which, the George, gave its name to George Street.[40] The

[19] E. T. MacDermot, rev. C. R. Clinker, *Hist. G.W.R.* ii (1964), 322–3.
[20] C. R. Clinker & J. M. Firth, *Reg. Closed Stations,* ii and suppl.
[21] Devon R.O. 123 M/TB 119.
[22] *S.R.S.* viii. 44.
[23] Ibid. 45; S.R.O., CR 92.
[24] 'Eldeputteslade', 'Laverslade', and 'la Slade' are described as lying in South field in the 13th century: Devon R.O. 123 M/TB 119, 121; *S.R.S.* viii. 45.
[25] Devon R.O. 123 M/E 31.
[26] Ibid. TB 113, 119, 134, 145; *S.R.S.* viii. 42–4, 50, 91.
[27] Devon R.O. 123 M/TB 145.

[28] Ibid. E 31; S.R.O., DD/X/HO, ct. roll, 1634.
[29] Ex inf. Som. County Museum.
[30] *S.R.S.* viii. 48.
[31] *Field Archaeology* (H.M.S.O. 1963), 9–10.
[32] Devon R.O. 123 M/E 35.
[33] *Kelly's Dir. Som.* (1902).
[34] S.R.O., Q/ERr; CR 92.
[35] S.R.O., CR 92; O.S. Map 6″, Som. LXIV. SW. (1885 edn.).
[36] S.R.O., DD/DN, box 40, lease, 29 Jan. 1744/5, Strangways to Withey.
[37] S.R.O., Q/RL.
[38] Ibid.   [39] Ibid.
[40] c. 1890, ex inf. Mr. C. F. Hamilton.

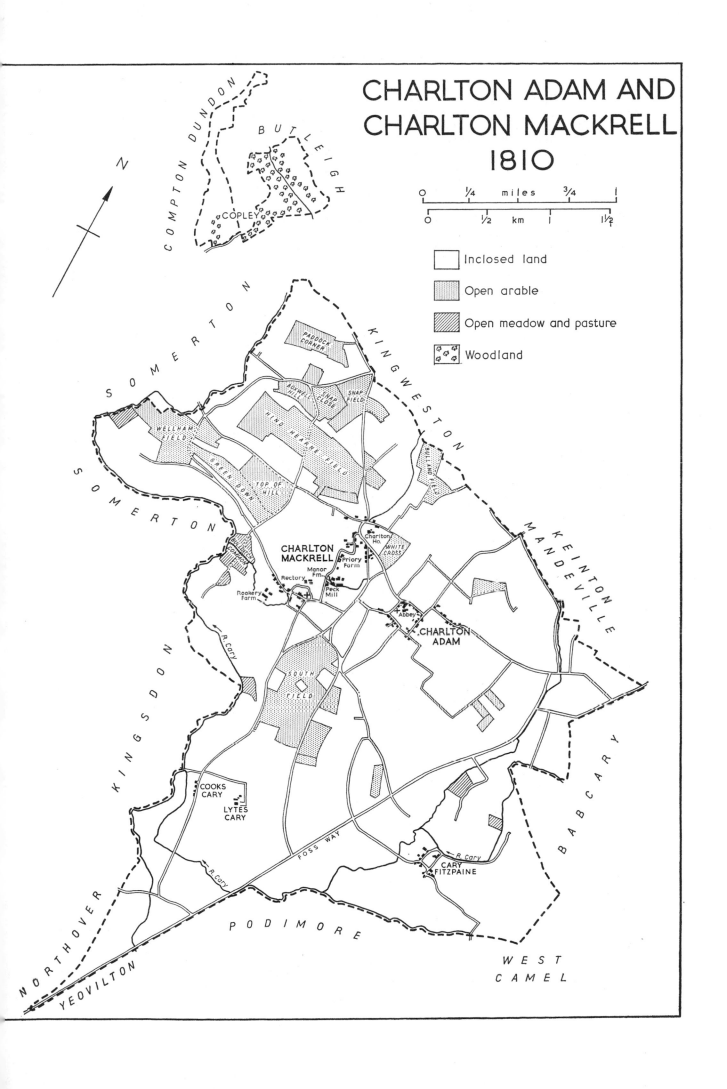

CHARLTON ADAM AND CHARLTON MACKRELL
1810

N

0 ¼ miles ¾ 1

0 ½ km 1 1½

☐ Inclosed land

▦ Open arable

▨ Open meadow and pasture

▢ Woodland

COMPTON DUNDON

BUTLEIGH

COPLEY

SOMERTON

KINGWESTON

PADDOCK CORNER

BOXWELL HILL

SNAP CLOSE

SNAP FIELD

WELLHAM FIELD

HIND HEANE FIELD

BULLAND FIELD

GREEN DOWN

TOP OF HILL

KEINTON MANDEVILLE

Charlton Ho.

WHITE CROSS

CHARLTON MACKRELL

Priory Farm

COMMON

Manor Fm.

Rectory

Peck Mill

Rookery Farm

Abbey

CHARLTON ADAM

SOMERTON

R. Cary

KINGSDON

SOUTH FIELD

BABCARY

COOKS CARY

LYTES CARY

FOSS WAY

R. Cary

R. Cary

CARY FITZPAINE

NORTHOVER

YEOVILTON

PODIMORE

WEST CAMEL

former Fox and Hounds, on the south side of Broadway, was converted to an inn in the 19th century, possibly when the north wing was added in 1866.[41] There was no public house in the parish in 1970.

Most of the buildings in the village date from the early and mid 19th century. They are of the local blue lias stone, probably quarried in Charlton Adam or Charlton Mackrell, with thatched or tiled roofs; one or two have classical porches of Ham stone. On the west side of Broad Street, just north of East Farm buildings, is a plain lias house of two storeys, standing at right angles to the road and probably built c. 1700. In the south wall are four Ham stone mullioned windows with hood moulds, the moulding on the ground floor being continuous. 'Cedar Lodge' at the south end of Broad Street is a larger L-shaped house of lias with thatched stables and a coach-house, bordering the lower east end of the street. It is probably of 18th-century origin. The range abutting on the road was formerly thatched but was gutted by fire and largely rebuilt with a tiled roof in the 20th century. The history of the house is poorly documented, but in 1810 it was occupied by the Revd. Anthony Pyne,[42] a member of the family formerly resident at Charlton House in Charlton Mackrell.[43] 'Court Hay' in George Street, with a Ham stone porch, was also owned by the Pyne family in 1810.[44]

The population of the parish was given as 210 in 1791.[45] In 1801 it had risen to 254, but fell slightly to 251 in 1811. Thereafter it rose to 550 in 1851. Subsequently a steady decline set in: 530 in 1861, 416 in 1881, and an abrupt drop to 295 in 1891, due no doubt to the general agricultural depression. The last available total, indicating a slight recovery, is 322 in 1901, after which Charlton Adam was included with Charlton Mackrell for census purposes. The cumulative totals show a small rise in 1911, dropping again after the First World War, with a gradual increase thereafter.[46]

MANORS AND OTHER ESTATES. In 1066 the manor was held by three thegns and one clerk 'in parage', but by 1086 had passed to Robert, count of Mortain.[47] Robert was probably succeeded in 1090 by his son William, until William forfeited his estates in 1106.[48] The Mortain overlordship appears subsequently to have been retained by the Crown.

In 1086 Reynold de Vautort held under the count,[49] but by 1160–1 John son of Hamon, whose family had been Domesday tenants of the count at Buckhorn Weston (Dors.), was holding the church and manor.[50] John had been succeeded before 1166 by his son William, who appears to have died without issue by 1211.[51] The manor then passed to John son of Richard, grandson of John son of Hamon, who was succeeded by his brother Henry son of Richard in 1226.[52] He was stated to hold two fees in Charlton of the Crown in 1242–3.[53] On his death in c. 1243 his lands were divided between five coheirs, Thomas le Breton, Matthew Wake, Walter de Esselegh, William son of Walter, and Henry Walleram.[54] Nothing further is known of Walleram's share. William son of Walter sold his interest to Thomas le Breton, who conveyed the resultant two shares or moiety to Geoffrey de Mandeville.[55] In 1249 Mandeville's holding was itself described as two fees in Charlton; the mesne lordship of one of these he sold to Bruton priory.[56] By 1268–9 Geoffrey had been succeeded by his son John de Mandeville,[57] who in 1286 occurs as lord of the latter fee and another, of which ¾ was held by John de Perham and ¼ by Humphrey de Kail.[58] The Mandevilles were lords of East Coker manor until 1305–6,[59] and in 1321 the prior of Bruton was stated to hold Charlton Adam of the lord of East Coker.[60] The tenure is again recorded in 1431–2,[61] but has not been noted thereafter.

Matthew Wake gave his share in marriage with his daughter Joan to Philip Lucyen, who quitclaimed lands in Charlton held by Thomas de Perham to Berengar de Welles and Richard de Wyggeber and their wives, the other two daughters of Matthew Wake.[62] Walter de Esselegh's share passed to Geoffrey of the marsh, who gave it in marriage with his niece to Emery de Gardino.[63] No further reference to their lordship has been traced. By 1305 the Mortimer earls of March were claiming the lordship of lands in Charlton including the fee held by Bruton priory.[64] They continued to claim it until 1399,[65] but by what right is not known.

In the early 13th century William son of Adam held one fee in Charlton Adam,[66] but by 1249 he had been succeeded by his son William.[67] In 1258 William FitzAdam sold his manor of *CHARLTON ADAM* to Bruton priory for 120 marks and a life interest in Brewham manor, held by the priory.[68] The priory (later an abbey) retained the manor until the Dissolution.[69] It received many small grants of lands in the parish during the 13th and 14th centuries.[70] These lands were probably united with the manor of Charlton Adam held by the

[41] Date under window. References to Lydia and Arthur Sweet, and William C. Gaylard, beer retailers, relate to the Fox and Hounds: *Kelly's Dir. Som.* (1883–1939).
[42] S.R.O., CR 92.
[43] See p. 103.
[44] S.R.O., CR 92.
[45] Collinson, *Hist. Som.* iii. 191.
[46] *V.C.H. Som.* ii. 348; *Census, 1911–61.*
[47] *V.C.H. Som.* i. 479.
[48] Sanders, *Eng. Baronies,* 14, 60, 136.
[49] *V.C.H. Som.* i. 479.
[50] *Red. Bk. Exch.* (Rolls Ser.), i. 27, 33, 223, 764; *V.C.H. Dors.* iii. 84; Hutchins, *Hist. Dors.* iv. 115; *S.R.S.* viii. 41.
[51] *S.R.S.* viii. 41; *Red Bk. Exch.* (Rolls Ser.), i. 44, 223; *Pipe R. 1211* (P.R.S. N.S. xxviii), 230.
[52] *Pipe R. 1211,* 230; *Rot. Litt. Claus.* (Rec. Com.), i. 310; *Ex e Rot. Fin.* (Rec. Com.), i. 145; *Bk. of Fees,* i. 91.
[53] *Bk. of Fees,* ii. 752.
[54] Ibid. ii. 1269; *Ex. e Rot. Fin.* (Rec. Com.), i. 401.
[55] *Bk. of Fees,* ii. 1269.
[56] *S.R.S.* viii. 43–4; xi. 368.
[57] *Ex. e Rot. Fin.* (Rec. Com.), ii. 495.
[58] *Feud. Aids,* iv. 285.
[59] *Cal. Inq. p.m.* iv, p. 164.
[60] S.R.O., DD/WHh, 656, extent of E. Coker manor; J. Batten, *Early Hist. of South Som.* 124–5, 164.
[61] Batten, *op. cit.,* 124–5, 164.
[62] *Ex. e Rot. Fin.* (Rec. Com.), ii. 41; *S.R.S.* vi. 370.
[63] *Bk. of Fees,* ii. 1269.
[64] *Cal. Close, 1302–7,* 275; *Cal. Inq. p.m.* iv, p. 164.
[65] *Cal. Close, 1396–9,* 454.
[66] Devon R.O. 123 M/TB 110, 115–17, 119; *S.R.S.* viii. 42–50.
[67] *S.R.S.* xi. 377–8, 405–6, 408; *Cal. Close, 1247–51,* 365.
[68] *S.R.S.* viii. 43; Devon R.O. 123 M/TB 116.
[69] *Valor Eccl.* (Rec. Com.), i. 149.
[70] Devon R.O. 123 M/TB 111, 115, 124, 126–8, 131, 134, 137–8, 144, 149, 151, 152; *S.R.S.* viii. 42–50.

priory, and other plots initially located in Charlton Mackrell may be represented by detached lands there later belonging to Charlton Adam parish. In 1560 the manor was granted to Francis Walsingham who sold it in that year to Sir William Petre (d. 1572).[71] He was succeeded by his son John, Lord Petre (d. 1613), who settled the manor on his third son Thomas Petre of Cranham (Essex).[72] Thomas entailed the manor upon his sons John (d. 1623) and Francis successively, and died in 1625.[73] Francis Petre (d. c. 1660) appears to have sold it during the Interregnum to Nathaniel Wright, a London merchant, who compounded for it in 1648 on Petre's recusancy, and held court in 1649.[74] By 1662 Francis's son, Sir Francis, Bt. (d. between 1670 and 1679), had recovered the manor.[75] He was succeeded by Anthony Petre, claimant to the baronetcy,[76] who in 1682 sold the manor to Edmund Gregory of Thorne in Castle Cary.[77] Gregory left it by will proved in 1697 to his nephew Edmund Seaman.[78] Seaman sold it to his niece's husband, Thomas Gapper of Sutton in Wincanton in 1705,[79] who left it to his son Edmund Gapper of Baltonsborough.[80] The last was succeeded by his son the Revd. Edmund Gapper (d. 1773), and by his grandson the Revd. Edmund Gapper (d. 1809).[81] The second was followed by his widow Mary, and son William Southby Gapper, who in 1819 subdivided and sold it.[82] In 1832 the lordship was claimed by Edward Richards Adams of Elmer Lodge, Beckenham (Kent),[83] who appears to have acquired lands on Walkmoor from Mary Gapper c. 1829.[84] Adams was still holding these lands in 1856.[85] The lordship was claimed in 1861 by Francis Henry Dickinson,[86] and subsequently by his son William, and by his grandson William Francis Dickinson.[87] However, the Dickinson claim may rest on the ownership of Manor farm, which formed a separate estate.[88]

The second fee in Charlton Adam, held under Henry son of Richard, was by 1286 divided between John de Perham, who held ¾ of a fee, and Humphrey de Kail, who held the remaining ¼ fee.[89] In the early 13th century Thomas de Perham received lands in Charlton Adam from William son of Adam and his sons totalling 120 a. of arable and 15 a. of meadow.[90] In 1249 Isabel, widow of William son of Adam, claimed dower in 3 virgates there held by Thomas de Perham,[91] and in the same year Thomas is shown holding lands in Charlton from the heirs of the Mandevilles.[92] In 1254 Thomas exchanged a caru-

cate in Charlton Adam for a carucate in Charlton Mackrell with Thomas son of John de Perham, possibly his nephew.[93] By 1286 he had been succeeded by John de Perham (I), who granted 4s. rent from 3 virgates in the manor to Bruton priory.[94] He was also stated to hold 2 virgates from Robert son and heir of Robert de Netherton, who held from the priory.[95] John de Perham (I) appears to have died by 1302, for in that year his widow Joan brought an action for dower against the Staunton family.[96] His successor appears to have been John de Perham (II), probably his son,[97] who died in 1327, in which year Robert de Netherton assigned to the priory his claim to overlordship of the Perham property, and the priory granted dower in the lands to John's widow, Joan de Perham.[98] John held 160 a. of arable and 24 a. of meadow in Charlton Adam from Bruton priory, and other lands in Charlton Mackrell from John de Lorty.[99] The origin of this lordship is unknown, but it was illegally seized on John's death by Roger Mortimer, earl of March, whose claims were subsequently disallowed.[1] John de Perham's son and heir John (III) was dead by 1332, his heir being his sister Thomasia, wife of William Paulet.[2] William died between 1349 and 1353 and was succeeded by his son Nicholas Paulet, then a minor.[3] The custody of his son's lands had been granted by William Paulet to Thomas and Nicholas de Panes who conveyed it to Bruton priory in 1358.[4] In the same year the priory granted the wardship to Sir John FitzPayn and Peter de Wenyete.[5] Nicholas Paulet was still living in 1412,[6] but these lands appear to have been united with those held by the Kail and Paulet families treated below.

The ¼ fee held in 1286 by Humphrey de Kail under John de Mandeville was held by the former with $\frac{1}{10}$ fee in Charlton Mackrell from Robert FitzPayn.[7] As Kail also held the advowson of the chantry of the Holy Ghost, founded by Henry son of Richard in c. 1238 and adjacent to the latter's manor-house,[8] this ¼ fee probably represents the capital messuage and demesne lands of the whole fee retained by Henry son of Richard.[9] In 1346 Humphrey de Kail and William Paulet jointly held ¼ fee in Charlton Adam,[10] and the latter twice presented to the chantry in 1349.[11] Humphrey de Kail appears to have been succeeded by William Kail (d. 1348).[12] During the minority of William's son his lands were held by Thomas de Panes, and

[71] Cal. Pat. 1558–60, 248, 377; D.N.B. xlv. 94.
[72] S.R.S. lxvii. 191–3; Visit. of Essex, 1552–1634 (Harl. Soc. xiii), 469; Devon R.O. 123 M/TP 27–9.
[73] S.R.S. lxvii. 191–3; C 142/418/78.
[74] Cal. Cttee. for Compounding, iii. 1667; S.R.O., DD/X/HO, ct. roll.
[75] C.P. 43/317 rot. 110.
[76] S.R.O., DD/TH, box 7, conveyance, 14 Feb. 1679/80.
[77] Ibid. conveyance, 2 Feb. 1681/2.
[78] Prob. 11/437 (83 Pyne).
[79] Ibid.; S.R.O. DD/TH, box 7, conveyance, 2 Apr. 1705.
[80] S.R.O., DD/DNL 3, copy will of Thomas Gapper, 1703; DD/TH, box 7, release, 25 Mar. 1714.
[81] M.I in church; S.R.O., DD/TH, box 7, marriage settl. 1 July 1752, will of Edmund Gapper, proved 1773.
[82] S.R.O., DD/DN, box 40, sale cat. 1819.
[83] S.R.O., Q/REr.
[84] S.R.O., Q/RE.
[85] S.R.O., Q/REr, 1856–7.
[86] P.O. Dir. Som. (1861).
[87] Ibid. (1866–75); Kelly's Dir. Som. (1883–1927).

[88] See below.
[89] Feud. Aids, iv. 285.
[90] Devon R.O. 123 M/TB 119–22.
[91] S.R.S. xi. 378.
[92] Ibid. vi. 370.
[93] Ibid. 158.
[94] Devon R.O. 123 M/TB 133.
[95] Ibid. TB 137–8; S.R.S. viii. 90–1.
[96] C.P. 40/148 rot. 172d.
[97] Ibid.
[98] S.R.S. viii. 90–3; Devon R.O. 123 M/TB 137–9.
[99] Cal. Inq. p.m. vii, pp. 297–8.
[1] Ibid. pp. 297–8, 466.
[2] Ibid. p. 466; Devon R.O. 123 M/TB 140–1.
[3] S.R.S. x. 591, 729; Devon R.O. 123 M/TB 154.
[4] Devon R.O. 123 M/TB 155.   [5] Ibid.
[6] S.R.S. xxix. 122.
[7] Feud. Aids, iv. 285.
[8] See below.   [9] See above.
[10] Feud Aids, iv. 362.
[11] S.R.S. x. 583–4, 591.
[12] Cal. Inq. p.m. xiii, p. 15.

in 1360 and 1399 the overlordship was claimed by the Mortimers.[13] William was succeeded by his son John Kail (d. c. 1383–4), and grandson Thomas Kail (d. c. 1394–5).[14] Thomas Kail was followed by his sister Idony, wife of John Paulet, who had issue two sons, John and Thomas Paulet. Both of them died in 1413, the premises reverting to a feoffee, John Kaynes.[15] Idony Paulet evidently held the advowson of the chantry of the Holy Ghost until her death in c. 1401–2,[16] which thereafter passed to Nicholas Paulet. The lands appear to have descended with the patronage of the chantry, which was held in 1423 and 1448 by John Lymington.[17] He was succeeded by William Brytte, patron between 1452 and 1486, in right of his wife Elizabeth.[18] In 1476 Brytte settled his lands on Hugh Larder on his marriage with his daughter Alice,[19] and by 1509 John Larder, probably their son, was presenting to the chantry.[20] John Larder and Ursula his daughter and heir, wife of Thomas Baskett, both died in 1556, leaving Ursula's two daughters as coheirs.[21] Thomas Baskett (d. 1592) occurs in 1564–6 as holding 140 a. of freehold land from the Petre manor of Charlton Adam,[22] and this passed to his daughter Mary (d. 1628–9), wife of Thomas Hussey of Shapwick (Dors.), and to her son Hubert Hussey (d. 1659).[23] Thereafter the latter's lands were divided between his daughters and coheiresses.[24]

The bulk of the lands held by the Larder family, lying both in Charlton Adam and Charlton Mackrell, descended to Baskett's second daughter Mabel, wife of John Bonham.[25] These lands appear to have formed the nucleus of a manor known subsequently either as that of *CHARLTON ADAM* or *CHARLTON ADAM WITH CHARLTON MACKRELL*, the owners of which enjoyed the right of burial in the south chapel of Charlton Adam church, and lived at what is now known as Manor Farm. John Bonham's daughter and heir, Anne, married Thomas Strangways of Winterborne Muston in Winterborne Kingston (Dors.).[26] An interest in the manor of Charlton Adam with Charlton Mackrell, held in 1609 by Mabel wife of Andrew Walton of Low Ham,[27] who was possibly related to the Baskett or Bonham family, was conveyed in 1635 and 1649 to Thomas and Anne Strangways.[28] The manor then descended from father to son in the Strangways family, Thomas (d. 1648), Giles (d. 1677), Bonham (d. 1719), Giles (d. 1744), Giles (d. 1777), and Thomas Littleton Strangways.[29] In 1796 the last sold the manorial lands, then comprising Manor farm, Peck Mill, and 421 a. of land, to John White

Parsons of West Camel,[30] and the lordship separately to an unknown purchaser.[31] In 1798 the manorial lands were sold by Parsons to James King of Cranborne (Dors.), later of Stowey, who conveyed them to William Dickinson of Kingweston in 1805,[32] after which they formed part of the Dickinson estate. The farm-house, now known as Manor Farm, with the lands immediately adjacent to it, were sold to Major Charles Jackson by William Francis Dickinson in 1930,[33] and the house was held by his widow in 1970.

Manor Farm is a long low lias building of two storeys with tiled roof.[34] The walls contain traces of timber-framing and the plan, originally one room deep and consisting of parlour, hall, screens-passage, and kitchen, suggests that the house may have had a medieval or 16th-century origin. Among its older features are the two gable-end chimneys, that at the west, or parlour, end having a newel stair beside it. The house was altered early in the 18th century when a square dining room was formed out of part of the hall. The room is handsomely fitted with bolection-moulded panelling, the upper panels being painted with real and imaginary landscapes. One portrays Glastonbury Tor and another the second Eddystone lighthouse. The inclusion of the latter, built in 1709 and destroyed in 1755, suggests an approximate date for the work. The dining room chimney on the south front may be contemporary, but, if so, the four-centred arches to the Ham stone fireplaces on both floors are somewhat archaic in design.[35] A narrow addition along the north side of the house may date from the early 19th century. It contains the principal staircase and is housed under a low-pitched extension of the main roof. All the windows, both casements and sashes, appear to belong to this or later periods. In the 20th century a new entrance hall was formed at the north-west corner of the house when the front door was moved there from the screens-passage site on the south side.

In the early 13th century Bruton priory granted to Henry son of Richard the right to have a free chapel in 'his court of Charlton', to be served by chaplains from the priory.[36] They were to receive all oblations except those due from the free serjeant of the manor, when resident, and from the lord's household.[37] In return Henry granted 6 a. of arable and 1 a. of meadow from his demesne to the priory.[38] The grant was confirmed in 1238.[39] The chapel was dedicated to the Holy Ghost and in 1548 was stated to adjoin the house of John Larder, probably

[13] Ibid. x, p. 538; *Cal. Inq. p.m.* (Rec. Com.), iii. 59, 181; *Cal. Close*, 1396–9, 454.
[14] *Cal. Inq. p.m.* (Rec. Com.) iii. 240.
[15] *Cal. Close*, 1413–19, 28–9; *Cal. Inq. p.m.* (Rec. Com.), iv. 6.
[16] *Cal. Inq. p.m.* (Rec. Com.), iii. 282; *Cal. Pat.* 1401–5, 7.
[17] *S.R.S.* xxx. 443; xlix. 103.
[18] Ibid. xlix. 195, 367; lii. 40, 128, 135–6.
[19] C.P. 25(1)/202/16 Edw. IV East.
[20] *S.R.S.* liv. 134.
[21] C 142/114/50; Hutchins, *Hist. Dors.* iii. 608.
[22] M.I. in church; Devon R.O. 123 M/E 31, survey.
[23] Devon R.O. 123 M/E 31, 32, 35, surveys; S.R.O., DD/X/HO, ct. roll; Hutchins, *Hist. Dors.* iii. 163, 711.
[24] Hutchins, *Hist. Dors.* iii. 163; S.R.O., DD/DN, box 52, conveyance, 1 June 1670.
[25] Hutchins, *Hist. Dors.* ii. 149; iii. 163; S.R.O., DD/DN, box 39, Strangways pedigree.

[26] Hutchins, *Hist. Dors.* ii. 149; M.I. in church.
[27] C.P. 25(2)/345/7 Jas. I East.
[28] C.P. 25(2)/480/11 Chas. I East.; C.P. 43/264 rot. 2.
[29] S.R.O., DD/DN, box 39, abstract of title 1783, Strangways pedigree; Hutchins, *Hist. Dors.* ii. 149; M.I. in church.
[30] S.R.O., DD/DN, box 39, abstract of title, 1783, Strangways pedigree; box 51, conveyance, 29 Sept. 1796.
[31] S.R.O., DD/THG, box 8, sale cat. 1796.
[32] S.R.O., DD/DN, box 51, conveyances, 24 Mar. 1798, 16 Apr. 1805.
[33] Sale cat. Kingweston Estate, 1930, *penes* Mrs. J. Burden, the Dower House, Kingweston.
[34] For views see *Country Life*, 20 Jan. 1950.
[35] The upper fireplace has been moved to the drawing room: ex inf. Mrs. H. Jackson.
[36] *S.R.S.* viii. 48.   [37] Ibid.
[38] Ibid.; Devon R.O. 123 M/TB 111.
[39] *S.R.S.* viii. 48.

Manor Farm.[40] The earliest reference to the patronage of the chapel is in 1302 when Joan, widow of John de Perham, sued William de Staunton and his family for her dower, which included the advowson of the chapel.[41] It appears to have descended with the fee formerly held by Henry son of Richard, which by 1286 had been divided between the Perham and Kail families.[42] In 1348 Humphrey de Kail presented,[43] and in the following year William de Paulet.[44] The patronage continued in the hands of the Paulet family until 1412,[45] Nicholas Panes presenting as guardian of Nicholas Paulet in 1353,[46] and Sir John Beauchamp of Lillesdon in 1362.[47] The Crown presented in 1401 and 1403 during the minority of the heir of Idony, wife of John Paulet.[48] John Chicheley held the advowson in 1415,[49] and was succeeded by John Lymington, who presented in 1423 and 1448.[50] Thereafter the presentation descended through the Brytte and Larder families until the chantry was dissolved in 1548.[51] It was stated at that time that no mass had been celebrated there for the past 20 or 30 years, Robert Bysse (chaplain 1509–44) having been Vicar-General of the diocese and a notorious pluralist.[52] In 1545 the penultimate incumbent, Thomas Russell (chaplain 1544–7), leased the chantry and its lands to the patron, John Larder, at a rent of 26s. 8d.[53] There were no ornaments nor plate in 1548 and no incumbent, although a chaplain had been presented in the previous year.[54] In 1548 the chantry was granted to Sir Thomas Bell of Gloucester and Richard Duke of London,[55] but its subsequent descent has not been traced. No description of its lands survives and no vestiges of the building remain in the vicinity of Manor Farm, its probable site.

The manor of East Lydford included lands in Charlton Adam which in the late 14th century, before the tripartite division of East Lydford manor in c. 1394, are occasionally referred to as the manor of CHARLTON.[56] It was probably this holding that led William de Reigny, lord of East Lydford manor, to quit claim his rights in the manor of Charlton Adam to Bruton priory in 1320.[57] When one third of East Lydford manor was partitioned in 1775, 105 a. of land were found to lie in Charlton Adam.[58] The major part of this property comprised a farm and 86 a. of land which were sold to Samuel Pitt (d. 1790) in 1777.[59] The lands subsequently

passed to his son Charles Pitt, and then to his granddaughter Eliza Jane, wife of George Augustus Hennesy of Northover, who sold the farm to William Dickinson in 1825.[60] It subsequently formed the nucleus of East farm, the largest agricultural unit in the parish in 1939.[61]

The rectory estate was included in a grant of the church to Bruton priory by John son of Hamon between 1142 and 1166, and was retained by the priory (later an abbey) until the Dissolution.[62] The rectory was valued at £6 in 1291,[63] and in 1334 the tithes were worth 18s. 4d., oblations and obventions £4 1s. 4d., and the lands £1 0s. 4d.[64] In 1535 these lands comprised closes adjoining the rectory house totalling 10 a., with a dovehouse and barn. The total income from the estate was then still £6, although by that date the lands were subject to a customary payment of £2 13s. 4d. to the vicar,[65] a sum still paid in 1809 when the tithes were commuted.[66] The rectory estate was leased to Thomas Tucker in 1527 for 40 years,[67] and both were granted to John Bellowe and John Broxolme in 1546.[68] William Hodges of Middle Chinnock was given money to purchase the rectory for his father, but secured a grant to himself in 1546 and forged a conveyance to his father to satisfy him.[69] The subterfuge came to light on the son's death in 1553, when he was succeeded by his son Bartholomew.[70] William Hodges, the father, conveyed his interest in the property to Giles Hodges of Curry Rivel in 1566,[71] when it was valued at £10 a year or under.[72] Giles had evidently occupied the rectory house by 1576, in which year he is described as of Charlton Adam.[73] He died in 1591 and was succeeded by his eldest son William.[74] In 1626 John Hodges died holding the rectory and was followed by his son, also John.[75] In 1635 Stephen Hodges was farmer of the rectory,[76] and in the following year John, Stephen, and Theophilus Hodges, with others, conveyed it to William Strode.[77]

The Strodes still held the rectory in 1695[78] but sold it c. 1700 to John Bond of Combe St. Nicholas.[79] The latter's son, also John, conveyed the rectory to Edmund Gapper of Baltonsborough in 1716,[80] after which it descended with the Gapper manor of Charlton Adam.[81] The Bonds augmented the rectory lands by purchasing 141 a., of which 14½ a. lay in Charlton Mackrell.[82] By the time of the 1809 inclosure this had been reduced to 82 a., the

40 Ibid. ii. 112.
41 C.P. 40/148 rot. 172d.
42 Feud. Aids, iv. 285.
43 S.R.S. x. 557.
44 Ibid. 583–4.
45 Ibid. xxix. 122.
46 Ibid. x. 729.
47 Ibid. 769.
48 Cal. Pat. 1401–5, 7, 192.
49 S.R.S. xxi. 208.
50 Ibid. 443; xlix. 103.
51 See above.
52 S.R.S. ii. 112; Emden, Biog. Reg. Univ. Oxford.
53 S.R.S. ii. 112.
54 Ibid. lv. 118.
55 Cal. Pat. 1548–9, 41.
56 C 136/30/3; C 136/37/1; Cal. Fine R. 1383–91, 149; S.R.S. xvii. 190; Cal. Close, 1392–6, 27–8; see below, p. 123.
57 Devon R.O. 123 M/TB 135.
58 S.R.O., DD/DN, box 39, partition, 20 Mar. 1775.
59 Ibid. abstract of title, c. 1825.
60 Ibid. conveyance, 31 Dec. 1825.
61 Kelly's Dir. Som. (1939).
62 S.R.S. viii. 41; Valor Eccl. (Rec. Com.), i. 198.
63 Tax. Eccl. (Rec. Com.), 197.
64 E 179/169/14.
65 Valor Eccl. (Rec. Com.), i. 198.
66 S.R.O., CR 92.
67 S.C. 6/Hen. VIII/3137.
68 L. & P. Hen. VIII, xxi (2), p. 242.
69 Ibid. p. 346; C 3/97/66.
70 C 3/97/66; C 142/104/84.
71 Cal. Pat. 1563–6, p. 519; S.R.S. li. 115–16.
72 Devon R.O. 123 M/E 31.
73 S.R.S. li. 115.
74 C 142/231/70.
75 C 142/436/27.
76 S.R.O., D/D/Ca 300 ff. 238, 242.
77 C.P. 25(2)/480/12 Chas. I East.
78 S.R.O., DD/SFR 8/2.
79 S.R.O., DD/TH, box 7, conveyance, 13 Dec. 1716; DD/DT 3, 4.
80 S.R.O., DD/TH, box 7, conveyance, 13 Dec. 1716.
81 See p. 85.
82 S.R.O., DD/TH, box 7, conveyance, 13 Dec. 1716.

Charlton Mackrell and other lands having been sold off by the Gappers.[83] The rectorial tithes were converted into corn rents assessed on the average price of wheat over the previous 14 years and yielded about £116.[84] Mary, widow of Edmund Gapper (d. 1809), sold further rectory lands[85] and in 1823 leased the rectory house to John Hopkins Bradney (vicar 1825–40).[86] The house was sold to J. G. D. Thring of Alford House (d. 1874) for £7,500 in 1831.[87] Thring was succeeded by his son Theodore (d. 1891) and by his grandson John Huntley Thring.[88] The Thrings extended the estate attached to the house, which amounted to 151 a. in 1876.[89] The property was leased to Claude Neville of Butleigh Court (d. 1944) for 21 years in 1902, and he purchased it with 48 a. of land in 1905.[90] It was held in 1970 by his son Cdr. Edward Neville.

The large rectory house, lying immediately north-east of the church and known as the Abbey or Abbey Farm by 1849,[91] is described as a 'mansion' in 1549.[92] Although the present house has several pre-Reformation features, including external buttresses, it has been so much altered that the original plan is obscure.[93] Major changes were probably the work of the Hodges family in the late 16th century. The building is mainly two-storeyed, of lias stone with tiled roofs. Projecting from the west end, now the entrance front, is a small buttressed wing of three storeys with a two-light mullioned window, apparently of late medieval date, on the ground floor and traces of a relieving arch on the floor above. The wing contains an Elizabethan oak staircase and a coved ceiling to the top room. The ceiling was renewed after an extensive fire in 1960.[94] Behind the wing and stretching across the house from north to south is the main Elizabethan structure, housed under its own roof. It may represent an earlier solar wing. The south room on the ground floor is the parlour or drawing-room which has contemporary oak panelling, an enriched frieze, and a carved chimney-piece. Above was a lofty 'great chamber' which probably occupied the whole upper floor with a tall mullioned and transomed window at each end. The northern half was later divided horizontally and only the south room retains its original coved ceiling. In the eastern part of the house some of the medieval fabric may have survived. There is a stone doorway with a two-centred head in the north wall of the present kitchen, traces of an early stair, and a pointed oak doorway in one of the attics.

The east end of the building has been much altered and extended, notably in the early 20th century when Claude Neville built extra service rooms at the north-east corner. Another 20th-century addition is an entrance lobby with a new front door on the west front.

The holding now known as Priory farm was an ancient freehold held of the lord of Somerton hundred by payment of a fine. It appears to have been held by the heirs of John Maunsell in 1543,[95] probably father of John Maunsell, who was in possession in 1565,[96] and grandfather of Richard Maunsell, who owned the property in 1617 and 1619.[97] By 1634 it had been conveyed to John Wroth of North Petherton, who died in that year, when the premises passed to Sir Thomas Wroth.[98] The property continued in the Wroth family until the death of another Sir Thomas Wroth in 1721.[99] His daughter Cecily married Sir Hugh Acland of Columbjohn (Devon),[1] and the latter sold the property, then described as 'the remaining parts of the manors of Charlton Adam and Charlton Mackrell', to John Bryan of Charlton Adam in 1732.[2] He was succeeded by his son John and his grandson John Bryan of Redland, Bristol.[3] The daughter of the last, Mary Anne, married W. N. Tonge (d. 1844) of Alveston (Glos.) in 1804.[4] They were succeeded in turn by their sons A. H. Tonge (d. 1867) and L. C. H. Tonge (d. 1895).[5] On the latter's death, or soon after, the property appears to have been purchased by Frank Percy Pitman, who held it in 1902 and whose family still owned and occupied the farm in 1970.[6]

The farm-house originally lay south of the present outbuildings, but was described as being in ruins in 1902 and was demolished when the railway was built.[7] The present house, to the north-east of the farm buildings, was built in the 19th century and in 1886 evidently formed part of a holding known as Folly farm.[8] It has served as the farm-house for Priory farm since at least 1904.[9]

The estate of 196 a. held by J. G. D. Thring in 1810,[10] and dispersed after the sale in 1905 of the Thring lands in Charlton Adam,[11] had its origin in the amalgamation of two properties by the Willes family. As a result of his marriage with Frances daughter of Thomas Freke, a Bristol merchant, John Willes of Astrop (Northants.) received lands in Charlton Adam and Charlton Mackrell purchased by Freke in 1730 from Bridget, widow of Henry

[83] S.R.O., CR 92. [84] Ibid.
[85] S.R.O., DD/TH, box 7, deeds of rectory.
[86] Ibid. memorandum of lease, 29 Apr. 1823; Wells Dioc. Regy., Beadon, 208; S.R.O., D/P/cha. a. 2/1/5.
[87] S.R.O., DD/TH, box 7, agreement, 25 Mar. 1831.
[88] Burke, Land. Gent. (1937), 2247–8.
[89] S.R.O., DD/TH, box 7, reconveyance, 10 July 1876.
[90] Ex inf. Mr. C. F. Hamilton.
[91] S.R.O., D/P/cha. a. 9/1/1.
[92] Cal. Pat. 1548–9, 398.
[93] It is possible that some of the buttresses were added later for decorative reasons. For illustrations of the house see Country Life, 13 Jan. 1950.
[94] Ex inf. Mrs. E. Neville; photographs of fire at National Monuments Record.
[95] S.C. 2/200/28. It may possibly be identified with lands described in 1480 as lying in Charlton Mackrell and held of Cary Fitzpaine manor by John Maunsell: Alnwick Castle, Northumberland MSS. XII. 12. 3b, ct. roll Cary Fitzpaine, 1480.
[96] Hunt. Libr., HA Manorial, Somerton hundred ct. roll, 8 Oct. 1565.
[97] D.R.O., D 124, Somerton hundred ct. bk. 1617–20, ff. 2, 90; Visit. Som. 1531–91, ed. Weaver, 49.
[98] C 142/526/12.
[99] S.R.O., DD/MI, box 9, note of fines, Somerton hundred, c. 1660; D.R.O., D 124, Somerton hundred ct. bk. 1730–62, f. 1; Som. Wills, ed. Brown, ii. 86.
[1] Som. Wills, ii. 86.
[2] S.R.O., DD/DN, box 39, contract for sale, 25 July 1732. This description suggests a link with the reputed manor of Charlton Adam and Charlton Mackrell held by Sir William Willoughby in 1486: see below, p. 102.
[3] S.R.O., DD/DN, box 44, abstract of title, n.d.
[4] Ibid.
[5] Burke, Land. Gent. (1937), 2261; S.R.O., Q/REr.
[6] Ex inf. Mrs. J. P. Pitman; S.R.O., Q/R, deposited plans 539.
[7] S.R.O., Q/R, deposited plans 539.
[8] S.R.O., CR 92; O.S. Map 6", Som. LXIII. SE. (1886 edn.).
[9] O.S. Map 6", Som. LXIII. SE. (1904 edn.).
[10] S.R.O., CR 92.
[11] Ex inf. Mr. C. F. Hamilton.

Dampier and only child of Richard Kellaway, and held during the late 17th century by John Wilcox.[12] To these Willes added lands in Charlton Adam acquired from the heirs of Dr. William Logan of Bristol in 1771, which the latter had purchased from Robert Houlton in 1732 and which had formerly been held by Richard Eggerdon of Whatley.[13] John Willes was succeeded by his son John Freke Willes, who left his lands to his cousin William Shippen Willes of Cirencester (Glos.).[14] The latter sold the property to Richard Selfe of Cirencester in 1805, who conveyed it to John Thring of Warminster (Wilts.) in 1807.[15] On the latter's death in 1830 he was succeeded by his son J. G. D. Thring.[16] The farm-house, an 18th-century lias building, was in 1970 a dwelling-house called 'the Laurels'.

ECONOMIC HISTORY. In 1086 Charlton Adam was assessed at 5 hides; there was land for 6 ploughs, although only 4½ are recorded. Two hides were held in demesne by Reynold de Vautort under the count of Mortain, and 2½ were worked by 5 villeins, 6 bordars, and 2 cottars with 1½ plough. The additional ½ hide is not accounted for in the Exeter Domesday. There were 50 a. of meadow, 60 a. of pasture, and 20 a. of underwood. Stock included 1 pack-horse, 5 beasts, 30 swine, and 60 sheep. The manor was then valued at £6, the same figure as before the Conquest.[17]

Early grants from the demesne indicate the presence of a number of substantial freeholders: Robert Frаunceis, who gave 18 a. of arable and 3 a. of meadow to Bruton priory in 1257–8;[18] William de la Lade under whom Thomas de Reigny held a ½ virgate of land and 2½ a. of meadow, which he gave to the priory c. 1273;[19] Ralph de la Purie, who married Isabel, widow of William son of Adam, and his son Robert, all three of whom granted lands and rents to the priory at the end of the 13th century.[20] The largest grants from the demesne, however, were those made by William son of Adam and his sons, William and Adam, to Thomas de Perham in the early 13th century, totalling 120 a. of arable and 15 a. of meadow, with common of pasture for 14 oxen and 40 sheep.[21] Grants to the priory by Henry son of Richard from his demesne at about the same period comprised 4 a. and 9 selions on Chessels, 1 a. of meadow below 'Childebereg', and 2 a. near Hurcot,[22] the latter presumably represented by parts of Charlton Adam lying detached in Charlton Mackrell. By the Dissolution the demesne lands, totalling 237 a., had been leased to four tenants for lives, and were subsequently treated as copyhold.[23]

The 13th- and 14th-century charters of Bruton priory show that a two-field system, based on North field and South field, had already developed and that the meadows were generally stinted.[24] By the mid 16th century a four-field system had emerged, North-east field or West field having been divided from North field, and East or South-east field from South field.[25] Strips of arable farmed by tenants of the Petre manor in c. 1564–6 comprised 102 a. in North field, 38 a. in South field, 91 a. in East field, and 106 a. in North-east field. These figures probably indicate the areal relationship of the open fields at that time.[26] The manor then comprised 295 a. held by four freeholders and 540 a. by customary tenants, paying a total rent of £11 10s. 2d.[27] Of the customary lands 337 a. were arable in the common fields.[28]

These totals do not include a further 200 a. of common pasture. The Lains and Brooks comprised 120 a., stated to be dry ground, Hale and Matford 50 a., adjudged better ground, and 30 a. at Midney hill devoted to cattle, being the best pasture.[29] Over these commons 18 customary tenants claimed stinted grazing rights for 113 beasts and 780 sheep.[30] The manor court carefully regulated grazing, particularly in the arable fields after harvest.[31] In 1616 it was ordered that no pigs were to be allowed in the common fields before the feast of St. Simon and St. Jude (28 Oct.); from 1617 no horse was allowed loose in the fields or on the highways; and in 1618 those tenants holding grazing rights on Midney hill and Matford were permitted to pasture one beast for every 2 a. they held in the common meadows, a rother beast for every 2 a. in the stubble fields, and a horse beast for every 4 a. there.[32] From 1627 the tenants were allowed to pasture one sheep for each acre they held, and two for each acre on Lains Common. These customs were later altered in detail.[33] Severe fines for the breach of grazing rights were imposed, assessed on a basis of the number of days each animal had been illegally pastured. Thus in 1627 one tenant was amerced 33s. 4d. for wrongly depasturing a cow on Midney hill and Matford for 5 months.[34] Fences, gates, and ditches around the common fields were repaired jointly by tenants claiming common rights.[35] All customary estates were subject to widows' estate and heriots and were described as 'metely fineable'.[36]

Until the late 16th century copyhold for 1, 2, or 3 lives was the invariable tenure.[37] Conversion to leases for 99 years or 3 lives began in 1599[38] and proceeded slowly during the 17th century. When the manor was conveyed to Edmund Gregory in 1682 there was only one copyhold estate excepted from the grant, and seven leasehold tenements were

[12] S.R.O., DD/TH, box 7, deeds of land in Charlton Adam; DD/DN, box 55, abstract of title to lands in Tuckers Cary.
[13] Ibid.
[14] Ibid.
[15] Ibid.
[16] Burke, *Land. Gent.* (1937), 2247.
[17] *V.C.H. Som.* i. 479.
[18] *S.R.S.* viii. 44–5.
[19] Ibid. 45–6; Devon R.O. 123 M/TB 126, 128.
[20] Devon R.O. 123 M/TB 124, 134; *S.R.S.* viii. 46–7, 49–50.
[21] Devon R.O. 123 M/TB 119–22.
[22] *S.R.S.* viii. 48–9.
[23] Devon R.O. 123 M/E 31.

[24] Ibid. TB 110–51; *S.R.S.* viii. 42–50.
[25] Devon R.O. 123 M/E 31.
[26] Ibid.
[27] Ibid.
[28] Ibid.
[29] Ibid.
[30] Ibid.
[31] S.R.O., DD/X/HO, ct. rolls.
[32] Ibid.
[33] Ibid.
[34] Ibid.
[35] Ibid.
[36] Ibid; Devon R.O. 123 M/E 31.
[37] Devon R.O. 123 M/E 31, 32.
[38] Ibid. E 35, L 1454–5.

mentioned.[39] Seven of the 18 customary tenants in c. 1564–6 farmed 90 per cent of the total customary lands within the manor, the sizes of their holdings ranging from 110 a. to 48 a.[40] By c. 1612 the erection of five cottages on the waste and the subdivision of some of the larger holdings had increased the number of customary tenants to 22.[41] By the early 18th century, owing principally to enfranchisements executed by the Petres, there were only twelve customary holdings, all in reversion, of which half were cottagers.[42]

By 1535 the value of the manor had risen to £12 19s. 6d., based on a rental of £11 5s.[43] By 1559 the total had fallen slightly to £10 6s. 8d., but only because perquisites were low and no fines had been levied that year.[44] The rental rose to £11 14s. 11d. by c. 1612, owing partly to rents from cottages recently erected on the waste.[45] In 1625 the manor was stated to be worth only £7, although annual receipts from lands in Charlton Adam of £11 12s. 9d. suggest that this was an underestimate.[46] In the early 18th century the total rents from the manor, which had undergone considerable enfranchisement, were £11 15s. 11d. and the value of the manor for sale was put at £1,941.[47]

Surviving charters of the 13th and early 14th century make virtually no reference to inclosed lands in Charlton Adam,[48] and even by c. 1564–6 such lands were generally limited to curtilages and orchards adjoining dwelling-houses.[49] In 1565 it was stated that the inclosure of lands within the manor, 'being already begun, shall further proceed the next year'.[50] A tentative move to inclose common meadow and pasture was made in 1614,[51] and in 1634, by agreement with the lord, 132½ a. of pasture in Midney hill, Mead Ditch, Hale, Little Turdhill, and Mackerise Lain, were inclosed and allotted to 13 customary tenants; a further 53½ a. at Matford, Heaples, and Turdhill were allotted to two freeholders.[52] Inclosure of the arable lands seems to have taken place gradually during the earlier 18th century by private agreement,[53] and by 1781 the estate of Edmund Gapper, including both the manor and the rectory, lay entirely in closes.[54] By award of 1810 112 a. in Charlton Adam were inclosed, but most of this comprised land belonging to the parish lying dispersed in Charlton Mackrell common fields.[55] Barely 12 a. lay in Charlton Adam itself.

At the time of the inclosure the largest estate in the parish was that of William Dickinson, then containing 370 a.;[56] 224 a. of this were land attached to Manor farm, acquired in 1805.[57] Edmund Gapper held 317 a., of which 82 a. represented the lands of the lay rectory, and the remainder the remnants of Charlton Adam manor.[58] J. G. D. Thring possessed a further 196 a., the former estate of the Willes family,[59] purchased from Richard Selfe in 1807,[60] and Charles Pitt owned 97 a.,[61] formerly part of East Lydford manor and later known as East farm.[62] Priory farm, held by Maria Bryan, was 131 a. in extent, but only 74 a. lay in Charlton Adam parish.[63] Similarly James Sutton held 67 a. in Charlton Adam, but this formed part of his 458 a. estate at Cary Fitzpaine. Some smaller holdings were also farmed from Charlton Mackrell.[64] Subsequently the Dickinsons increased their estate by purchase, acquiring the Pitt property in 1825,[65] so that by c. 1835 they owned about 600 a. in the parish.[66] At that time 171 a. were farmed from East farm (of which 36 a. lay in Charlton Mackrell) and 246 a. were farmed from Manor farm (of which 40 a. lay in Charlton Mackrell).[67] J. G. D. Thring's purchase of the rectory lands in 1831, and the subdivision and sale of the Gapper estate,[68] made the Thring family the only other prominent landowners in the parish during the later 19th century. Since the break-up of the Dickinson estate in 1930 most of the lands have been owned by the farmers.[69] Manor Farm, formerly part of the largest farm in the parish, was sold with only 24½ a. of land in 1930.[70] Dairy farming has continued to predominate within the parish.

The quarrying of blue lias stone for building purposes appears to have been carried on in the Charltons at least since Roman times,[71] but never on a very large scale. In c. 1564–6 the manor included a lias quarry of 'small value'.[72] The field name Quarry Close occurs in 1810 on the east side of the lane running south from the village to Tout,[73] and may indicate the site of much earlier workings. Stonemasons are mentioned regularly during the 19th century;[74] by 1897 there were two quarries in operation and by 1906 three.[75] Since that time the industry has continued to expand and is still an important feature of the economy of the parish. The quarries, several now abandoned, lie generally in the north-west of the parish beyond the railway, north of Broadway near the Barton, and in the south-west in the area of Tout House, which formed the centre of quarrying operations by the Cary family in the late 19th and early 20th centuries.[76]

There is evidence that gloving as a cottage industry was pursued by the women of the village

---

[39] S.R.O., DD/TH, box 7, conveyance, 2 Feb. 1681/2.
[40] Devon R.O. 123 M/E 31.
[41] Ibid. E 35.
[42] S.R.O., DD/DN, box 39, rental (n.d.).
[43] Valor Eccl. (Rec. Com.), i. 149.
[44] Devon R.O. 123 M/E 89.
[45] Ibid. E 35.
[46] S.R.S. lxvii. 192.
[47] S.R.O., DD/DN, box 39, rental (n.d.).
[48] S.R.S. viii. 42–50; Devon R.O. 123 M/TB 110–51.
[49] Devon R.O. 123 M/E 31.
[50] Exeter R.O., DD/49/26/4/3.
[51] S.R.O., DD/X/HO, ct. rolls.
[52] Ibid.
[53] e.g. S.R.O., DD/CC 102403, 102411, 102426; DD/TH, box 7, conveyances, 29 Sept. 1704, 13 Dec. 1716.
[54] S.R.O., DD/THG, box 3, map of Gapper estate, 1781.
[55] S.R.O., CR 92.
[56] Ibid.

[57] See p. 86.
[58] S.R.O., CR 92.
[59] Ibid.
[60] See p. 89.
[61] S.R.O., CR 92.
[62] See p. 87.
[63] S.R.O., CR 92.
[64] Ibid.
[65] See p. 87.
[66] S.R.O., DD/DN, box 38, particular of estates, c. 1835.
[67] Ibid.
[68] See pp. 85, 88.
[69] Kelly's Dir. Som. (1931, 1935).
[70] Sale cat. Kingweston estate, 1930, penes Mrs. J. Burden, the Dower House, Kingweston.
[71] See p. 82.
[72] Devon R.O. 123 M/E 31.
[73] S.R.O., CR 92.
[74] S.R.O., D/P/cha. a. 2/1/4.
[75] Kelly's Dir. Som. (1897, 1906).
[76] Ibid. (1883–1906).

during the 19th century, the finished products being taken to Glastonbury for sale.[77] By 1868 the Dickinson estate at Kingweston was providing employment for Charlton men, and the Dickinsons had erected new cottages at Charlton Adam on ¼ a. plots to supplement existing accommodation, which was generally poor.[78] Allotments, also of ¼ a., were let by the vicar to the parishioners for 7s. 6d. a year, where they grew potatoes and beans for their pigs.[79] In the later 19th century some new trades were introduced. A few shopkeepers had established themselves by 1861, including a draper and grocer, a butcher, and a basketmaker.[80] By 1866 a baker, tailor, and coal merchant had settled here, and by 1883 a general store had been opened.[81] A cycle agent, bootmaker, hairdresser, and motor-car proprietor occur in 1923, a chemist in 1927, a music teacher in 1931, and a dog food manufacturer in 1939.[82]

A stream running along the southern boundary of Manor Farm garden was described as the 'Mullbroke' in 1257–8.[83] It evidently supplied the water grist mill known as Peck Mill in 1810.[84] This may also be the mill called Bydelmyll in 1376,[85] and was probably one of the two mills in Charlton tithing mentioned between 1392 and 1437, when their millers were presented for taking excessive tolls.[86] John Larder was presented for the same offence in 1539.[87] When William Brytte settled his lands in Charlton Adam and Charlton Mackrell on his daughter Alice and her husband Hugh Larder in 1467, two mills formed part of the estate.[88] They were probably the water-mill and windmill which occur in 1616 as part of the Manor farm lands.[89] Thereafter Peck Mill appears always to have descended with the latter property. In 1780 the mill was stated to be out of repair and without water,[90] and in 1785 most of its fixtures, including the ironwork and millstone, were sold by Thomas Littleton Strangways.[91] It was evidently renovated and in c. 1800 was leased to Farmer Hockey.[92] When the Manor farm estate was leased to John Knight in 1802 he covenanted to maintain the thatch of the mill-house.[93] The mill does not appear to have been worked to any great extent during the later 19th century, when grain was regularly taken to West Lydford for grinding.[94] It was demolished during the first quarter of the 20th century.[95]

LOCAL GOVERNMENT. Manor courts appear to have been held only for the manor owned by Bruton priory and later by the Petre family. Court rolls for this manor survive for the years 1612–20, 1623–9, 1632–8, and 1649.[96] Courts were generally held twice a year in April and October, and were described principally as curie manerii, but occasionally as curie baronis or curie legalis. The use of the last title may imply the vestiges of a former leet jurisdiction. Considerable attention was paid in the courts to the erection and maintenance of fences, scouring ditches, and the observance of grazing customs in the common pastures. Other business included licences to live outside the manor, strays, pound breach, and the repair of houses. A hayward was appointed annually, usually in October.[97] A single tithingman served for both Charlton Adam and Charlton Mackrell[98] and in 1756 the cost of his housing a prisoner was equally divided between the two parishes.[99] The vestry appointed two churchwardens from 1843 to 1911, and two overseers from 1845 to 1885, except between 1871 and 1873, when three were appointed. Four were appointed in 1886.[1] The vestry also elected one or two waywardens (1843–83) and a hayward (1871, 1873).[2]

References to a poorhouse occur in 1797 and 1803.[3] During the 18th century various houses were rented for the accommodation of paupers,[4] and it is doubtful whether there was ever any permanent building for their reception. The parish became part of the Langport union in 1836.[5]

CHURCH. A clerk was holding lands within the manor at the time of the Norman Conquest,[6] although the church of Charlton Adam is not mentioned until between 1142 and 1166.[7] During this period the church was granted to Bruton priory by John son of Hamon,[8] and this grant evidently included lands which later formed the rectory estate. No reference to the ordination of a vicarage has been traced, but this had evidently taken place by 1291.[9] By 1535 the incumbent was in receipt of a pension from the rectory lands, a pension still being paid in 1809.[10] The benefices of Charlton Adam and Charlton Mackrell were united in 1921.[11]

The advowson descended with the rectory and its lands at least until 1626.[12] By 1635 John Hodges had conveyed the advowson to Robert Hammon, mercer, who in that year presented William Hammon to the vicarage.[13] The latter succeeded to the patronage and conveyed the next presentation to John Rock, vicar of Butleigh, and Simon Whetcombe, rector of Charlton Mackrell. Whetcombe

[77] MS. notes on the Charltons by W. Small, 1928, p. 23, penes Mr. C. F. Hamilton, Wells; Rep. Com. Children and Women in Agriculture [4202–I] H.C. p. 426 (1868–9), xiii.
[78] Ibid.   [79] Ibid.
[80] P.O. Dir. Som. (1861).
[81] Ibid. (1866); Kelly's Dir. Som. (1883).
[82] Ibid. (1923–39).
[83] S.R.S. viii. 44; Devon R.O. 123 M/TB 113.
[84] S.R.O., CR 92.
[85] Hunt. Libr., HA Manorial, Somerton hundred ct. roll, 1376–7.
[86] Ibid. 1392–3; S.C. 2/200/33.
[87] S.C. 2/200/34.
[88] C.P. 25(1)/202/16 Edw. IV East.
[89] C.P. 25(2)/346/14 Jas. I Mich.
[90] S.R.O., DD/DN, box 22, letter from W. Reynolds to W. Dickinson, 30 June 1780.
[91] Ibid. box 39, notes by W. Dickinson, n.d.
[92] Ibid. box 18, particular of Manor farm, c. 1800.

[93] Ibid. box 18, agreement, 12 Jan. 1802.
[94] MS. notes on the Charltons by W. Small, 1928 (loose sheet enclosed), penes Mr. C. F. Hamilton.
[95] Ex inf. Mrs. H. Jackson.
[96] S.R.O., DD/X/HO.
[97] S.R.O., DD/X/HO, 25 Oct. 1625.
[98] D.R.O., D 124, Somerton hundred ct. book, 1730–62.
[99] S.R.O., D/P/cha a. 13/2/1.
[1] Ibid. 9/1/1.   [2] Ibid.
[3] S.R.O., D/P/cha. a. 13/2/1.
[4] Ibid.
[5] Poor Law Com. 2nd Rep. p. 548.
[6] V.C.H. Som. i. 479.
[7] S.R.S. viii. 41.
[8] Ibid.
[9] Tax. Eccl. (Rec. Com.), 197.
[10] Valor Eccl. (Rec. Com.), i. 198; S.R.O., CR 92.
[11] Lond. Gaz. 14 Oct. 1921, p. 8076.
[12] See p. 87.
[13] Som. Incumbents, ed. Weaver, 47.

having died in 1657, Rock presented Robert Hammon in 1664.[14] The bishop collated by lapse in 1678, although the Hammons appear to have retained the advowson after this date.[15] The patronage was evidently acquired by Alexander Starke (vicar 1678–1700) as his widow, Maria, presented in 1700.[16] In 1709 the patron was Thomas Clare, and in 1719 Sarah Cridland of Staplegrove.[17] The latter presented her son-in-law, Benjamin Kebby (vicar 1719–66),[18] who subsequently succeeded to the advowson.[19] By 1766 the patronage had been acquired by William Sealy Strangways, who also presented in 1770.[20] In 1808 Thomas Strangways presented himself, his executors held the advowson in 1823,[21] and the family was still enjoying it in 1840.[22] It was then acquired by John Barney (vicar 1840–61),[23] but between 1859 and 1861 it passed to Guy Bryan, rector of Woodham Walter (Essex).[24] Between 1875 and 1883 Bryan was succeeded by the Revd. Henry Guy Bryan, and in 1897 by the Revd. Henry Percival Bryan of Askerswell (Dors.).[25] Wilmot Lee Bryan of South Godstone (Surr.) held the advowson between 1899 and 1906,[26] but in 1910 the bishop collated by lapse,[27] and by 1912 the Diocesan Trustees were patrons.[28] They continued to present until the union of the benefices of Charlton Adam and Charlton Mackrell in 1921.[29] The subsequent descent of the advowson is treated under Charlton Mackrell.[30]

The vicarage was valued at £5 in 1291,[31] but this figure had fallen to 5 marks by 1445.[32] In 1535 it was worth £6 14s. 11d.,[33] and in c. 1668 the common reputed value was £30.[34] In 1793 the living was augmented by lot with £200,[35] and in 1811 by a further £200 from the Horner trustees.[36] Thus by 1814 the income had risen to £115,[37] and by 1831 to £137 net.[38] In 1851 it stood at £119 19s. 0d.[39]

The predial tithes and tithes of wool belonging to the vicar were valued at 38s. 2d. in 1535, and oblations and personal tithes at 36s. 5d.[40] In 1626 the vicar claimed tithe hay from specified meadows at Midney, and from others in detached areas of Charlton Adam at Wildmoors and Southwells situated in Charlton Mackrell. He also held the tithes of calves, kine, white wool, lambs, pigs, geese, eggs, pigeons, colts, honey, fruit, hemp, flax, teazles, and withies. He received the tenth penny of meadow or pasture leased to outdwellers, the left shoulder of each slaughtered calf, ½d. for each weaned calf, 3d. for a cow, 1½d. for a heifer, and the tithe of underwood in Copley wood whenever it was cut. He was also to keep a bull and a boar for the use of his parishioners.[41] The vicarial tithes, like those paid to the lay rector, were converted into corn rents in 1810,[42] and were valued at £57 in 1851[43] and in 1874.[44] They had dropped to £41 in 1902,[45] and in 1920 were converted to a tithe rent-charge fixed at £43 0s. 10d.[46]

The vicarial glebe was worth 7s. in 1535.[47] In 1626 it comprised 7 a. of arable land attached to the vicarage house, the herbage of the churchyard and trees there, and a messuage and tenement with 10½ a. of arable land, 1 a. of meadow, two hedge plots, and two beast leazes in Midney and Matford.[48] These lands probably included the 2 a. of arable and 1 a. of meadow which William son of Adam gave to Bruton priory for the increase of the tenement of Charlton church in the early 13th century, and a further grant of 1 a. of land made by him at about the same time.[49] In 1810 the glebe lands totalled just over 19 a.,[50] but by 1874 these had been increased to 24 a., and by 1902 to 28 a.[51] In 1913 certain glebe lands were sold for £845.[52] There were c. 37 a. of glebe in 1972.[53]

The old parsonage house lay on the east side of a short lane running south from George Street.[54] It was 'in decay' in 1557,[55] but in 1626 was described as 'well builded', with a barn, stable, curtilage, and garden.[56] In 1734 the vicar, Benjamin Kebby, stated that he had spent £50 in repairing the house, and over £30 some years before.[57] In 1815 the house was stated to be too small and 'fit only for a labourer',[58] and by 1827 the vicar was living in 'the Abbey'.[59] The house was described as being in good repair in 1840, but was not occupied by the vicar nor his curate.[60] A new vicarage house was built in 1862 to the south of the old building, which was demolished, at a total cost of £555, of which £500 was provided by Queen Anne's Bounty.[61] It is a two-storeyed structure of three bays, built of blue lias with a tiled roof. A new rectory house was built to the west of the vicarage house in 1955.[62]

John Donneslegh (vicar by 1405–7), 'broken down by old age and not having judgement of

[14] Ibid.; M.I. to Whetcombe in Charlton Mackrell church.
[15] S.R.O., D/D/Vc 24.
[16] Som. Incumbents, 37.
[17] Ibid.
[18] Ibid.; S.R.O., DD/SP, box 39, Staplegrove surrender, 12 Oct. 1717; Cannington par. reg., 26 May 1715.
[19] S.R.O., DD/SH 107.
[20] Wells Dioc. Regy., Reg. Willes, ii, 67, 76.
[21] Wells Dioc. Regy., Reg. Beadon, 42, 208.
[22] County Gazette Dir. Som. (1840).
[23] Clergy List (1857, 1859).
[24] Ibid.; P.O. Dir. Som. (1861).
[25] Kelly's Dir. Som. (1897); S.R.O., D/P/cha. a. 2/5/1.
[26] Kelly's Dir. Som. (1906).
[27] Ex inf. Dioc. Registrar.
[28] S.R.O., D/P/cha. a. 2/5/1.
[29] Crockford.
[30] See pp. 107–8.
[31] Tax. Eccl. (Rec. Com.), 197.
[32] S.R.S. xlix. 32.
[33] Valor Eccl. (Rec. Com.), i. 198.
[34] S.R.O., D/D/Vc 24.
[35] Aug. Livings, 1703–1815, H.C. 115 (1814–15), xii.
[36] Hodgson, Queen Anne's Bounty.
[37] S.R.O., D/D/V rtns. 1815.
[38] Rep. Com. Eccl. Revenues, pp. 156–7.
[39] H.O. 129/317/1/7/15.
[40] Valor Eccl. (Rec. Com.), i. 198.
[41] S.R.O., D/D/Rg 207.
[42] S.R.O., CR 92.
[43] H.O. 129/317/1/7/15.
[44] Crockford.
[45] Ibid.
[46] S.R.O., D/P/cha. a. 2/5/2.
[47] Valor Eccl. (Rec. Com.), i. 198.
[48] S.R.O., D/D/Rg 207.
[49] Devon R.O. 123 M/TB 115; S.R.S. viii. 42–3.
[50] S.R.O., CR 92.
[51] Crockford.
[52] S.R.O., D/P/cha. a. 2/5/2.
[53] Ex inf. Dioc. Secretary.
[54] S.R.O., CR 92.
[55] S.R.O., D/D/Ca 27.
[56] S.R.O., D/D/Rg 207.
[57] S.R.O., D/P/cha. a. 2/1/1.
[58] S.R.O., D/D/V rtns. 1815.
[59] Rep. Com. Eccl. Revenues, pp. 156–7; S.R.O., DD/TH, box 7, memorandum of lease, 29 Apr. 1823.
[60] S.R.O., D/D/V rtns. 1840.
[61] S.R.O., DD/CC C/1942, 185.
[62] Ex inf. the Revd. Hugh Knapman, rector.

mind', was in 1405 given a curate to assist him, initially appointed for one year only.[63] Owen Smyth (vicar 1463–5), a canon of St. John's, Carmarthen, obtained papal dispensation to hold the benefice.[64] In 1511 Thomas Griffith (vicar from 1506 at least until 1535) was ordered to pay 26s. 8d. to John Larder of Manor Farm for having publicly slandered him, and they were ordered 'to live together charitably as good Christian men should do, and as nigh as God shall give them grace'.[65] William Abbott (vicar 1545–58) was evidently non-resident in 1557.[66] William Hammon (vicar 1635–64) appears to have survived the Interregnum.[67] Of the ten vicars between 1678 and 1861, all were graduates except one,[68] Thomas Strangways (vicar 1808–23), and four occupied other benefices in plurality: Thomas Kemp (vicar 1700–9), Benjamin Kebby (vicar 1719–66), James Minifie (vicar 1766–8), and Samuel Gatehouse (vicar 1770–1808).[69] Both Gatehouse and Strangways appear to have been non-resident and employed curates to serve the church in their absence.[70] Percival Wilmot Bryan held the vicarage for 48 years until his death at the age of 92 in 1909.[71]

In 1554 the churchyard was insufficiently enclosed and the chancel windows needed repair.[72] Three years later the church wall was stated to be in decay.[73] The poor state of the churchyard wall was again presented in 1568, and also the lack of a table of the Ten Commandments.[74] The latter was still wanting in 1606, and the pews were found to be dilapidated.[75]

In 1827 services were held alternately, morning and evening, each Sunday,[76] and in 1843 Holy Communion was being celebrated six times a year.[77] On Census Sunday in 1851 morning service was attended by 36, and the afternoon by 90 persons.[78] By 1895 the celebration of Holy Communion had been increased to once a week and there were two services every Sunday.[79]

A church house is mentioned in 1548, when it was stated to have been given for the maintenance of obits in the parish church.[80] It was then worth £3 and had been let for 12d.[81] In 1549 it was granted to Thomas Marshe of London and Roger Williams of Usk (Mon.) and was described as adjoining the rectory.[82] William Hodges claimed it as parcel of the rectory purchased by him in 1546,[83] and it appears to have been held with that property by the Hodges family in 1591 and 1626, and by the Bond family in 1715.[84] No reference to it has been traced thereafter.

An annual payment of 2s. 2d. from the manor to the churchwardens, to maintain the church and

lights before the high altar there, is mentioned in 1539.[85]

The church of *ST. PETER AND ST. PAUL* lies immediately to the north-west of the village, on the east side of Church Lane. It is described as the church of St. Peter the Apostle in the early 13th century[86] and in 1543,[87] and it is not known when the double dedication was adopted. The building comprises chancel, nave, south transeptal chapel, south porch, and west tower. It dates from the 13th, 14th, and 15th centuries. The east window in the chancel has Perpendicular panel tracery, two low lancet 13th-century windows in the north wall, and a 15th-century window in the south wall, possibly in an earlier opening. There is a shallow piscina in a niche in the south wall of the sanctuary. The chancel arch is 14th century, as are the nave and south door. The nave has Perpendicular windows, original roof corbels, and against the north wall a rood loft stair turret. There are reset 14th century niches in the east-wall of the porch and over the south door, the latter containing a grotesque figure. The plain west tower is of three stages with diagonal buttresses, a pyramidal roof behind embattled parapets, and a prominent north-east stair turret. There are early Perpendicular windows to the belfry and a large renewed Perpendicular window in the west wall. The south chapel, known as the Strangways aisle, was added in the 16th century. It is separated from the nave by a three-centred arch and has mullioned windows of four segmental-headed lights. An oblique passage with a smaller window and an external door communicates with the chancel. The chapel contains a wall monument to Thomas Baskett (d. 1592) and one across the north-east angle to Giles Strangways (d. 1638). Other inscribed slate tablets commemorate members of the Bonham and Strangways families. Francis Henry Dickinson, as owner of the Manor Farm estate, renounced his right to the chapel in 1889.[88] The font, with round bowl and shaft, is c. 1200, and the pulpit Jacobean. The chancel was restored c. 1860 and the remainder of the church in 1892.[89] The barrel roof of the nave probably dates from this time, and the restoration included the removal of a gallery which had accommodated the choir.[90] In the churchyard to the west of the south porch is the base of a cross, formerly consisting of two octagonal steps with a shallow socket, possibly late 13th century in date.[91] The third step and shaft are modern.

The plate includes an Elizabethan cup of c. 1573 and a small paten of 1718.[92] There are five bells: (i) 1714, Edward Bilbie; (ii) 1738, Bilbie; (iii)

[63] *S.R.S.* xiii. 54, 71.
[64] *Cal. Pat.* 1461–7, 283.
[65] *S.R.S.* liv. 149–50.
[66] S.R.O., D/D/Ca 27.
[67] S.R.O., D/D/Rr 87, burial of Mr. William Hammon, 19 July 1664.
[68] Foster, *Alumni Oxon.*; Venn, *Alumni Cantab.*
[69] S.R.O., Clergy index (Fitzroy-Jones).
[70] S.R.O., D/D/Bo, Bp; D/D/V rtns. 1815.
[71] *Crockford*; S.R.O., D/P/cha. a. 2/1/5.
[72] S.R.O., D/D/Ca 22.
[73] Ibid. 27.
[74] Ibid. 40.
[75] S.R.O., D/D/Vc 150.
[76] S.R.O., D/D/V rtns. 1827.
[77] Ibid. 1843.

[78] H.O. 129/317/1/7/15.
[79] S.R.O., D/P/cha. a. 2/5/1.
[80] *S.R.S.* ii. 112.
[81] Ibid. 112, 296.
[82] *Cal. Pat.* 1548–9, 398.
[83] *S.R.S.* ii. 112; *L. & P. Hen. VIII*, xxi(2), p. 346.
[84] C 142/231/70; C 142/436/27; S.R.O., DD/DT 3, mortgage, 20 Apr. 1715.
[85] S.C. 6/Hen. VIII/3137.
[86] *S.R.S.* viii. 42.
[87] Ibid. xl. 29.
[88] S.R.O., D/P/cha. a. 8/2/1.   [89] Ibid.
[90] E. G. Freeman, *A Little Guide to the Parish Church of Charlton Adam* (n.d.), 15.
[91] C. Pooley, *Old Stone Crosses of Som.* (1877).
[92] *Proc. Som. Arch. Soc.* xlv. 130.

c. 1480–1500, Bristol foundry; (iv) 1714, Edward Bilbie; (v) 1832, T. Mears of London.[93] The fourth bell bears the inscription:

'I am not now as wonce I was,
Sq: Straingwing was the caus'.[94]

This presumably refers to Giles Strangways (d. 1744).

The registers are complete from 1704.[95]

NONCONFORMITY. John Cappes and eight other members of his family were presented as recusants in 1612,[96] followed by Jane, widow of John Fitzjames, and her son George at intervals between 1620 and 1626.[97] Joan wife of Thomas Hodges was cited in 1626,[98] and William Fawkner and his wife in 1629,[99] both families being prominent landowners in the Charltons.

The houses of John Lewis and Samuel Cossens were licensed in 1690 for Dissenting meetings, as were those of Elizabeth Strode in 1698, and Richard Kellaway in 1700 and 1709.[1] John Walter's house was licensed for Independent worship in 1789 on petition from eight inhabitants of the Charltons and a minister of Martock.[2] It was licensed again in 1809 and John Reynold's house, possibly as a temporary replacement for the former, in 1796.[3] Licences were also granted for Protestant meetings in the houses of Samuel Grinham in 1815 and of Charles Seymour in 1843,[4] but their denominations are unknown.

A Bible Christian chapel, erected 'since 1820', with 200 free sittings, had two services each Sunday in 1851. On Census Sunday the congregations numbered 50 in the morning and 45 in the evening.[5] No subsequent reference to this chapel has been found, and its site has not been traced.

A Wesleyan Methodist chapel was founded in 1841, the license being granted for services to be held in a schoolroom owned by Robert Barrett.[6] In 1851 the building was still being used as a day school, there were 150 free sittings, two services each Sunday, and a Sunday school with 30 pupils. On Census Sunday there were 15 worshippers in the afternoon and 50 in the evening.[7] The small stone chapel stands on the west side of Broad Street near its junction with Station Road, and was closed in 1970.[8]

In 1897 the vicar was concerned lest the management of the school should be taken out of the hands of the Church and 'thrown open to the Dissenters, who in this parish are very numerous'.[9]

EDUCATION. In 1818 there was a school for small children, and a Sunday school for 30 to 40 pupils;[10] the latter was attended by 27 boys and 38 girls in 1825.[11] In 1830 a day-school was begun for about 30 children, supported by subscription and parental payments of 1*d.* a week.[12] By 1833 there was another day-school attended by 10 boys and 7 girls, and an evening school for 5 boys and 3 girls, supported wholly by school pence.[13] There were also two Sunday schools, one run by the Church of England for 19 boys and 17 girls and supported by voluntary contributions, and the other founded in that year and attended by 24 boys and 15 girls, taught gratuitously by dissenters, probably Wesleyans.[14] In 1841 a schoolroom was licensed for dissenting meetings,[15] and this was still being used as a day school in 1851.[16] By 1846–7 there was only a dame school for 10 boys and 12 girls who paid for instruction, taught by one mistress, having one room and a teacher's house.[17]

In 1864 a parochial schoolroom building fund was started to replace the school 'lost to the parish some years previously', and this led to the foundation of the Charlton Adam Infants School, probably in 1865.[18] The declared object of the school was to provide education for children of the parish who, at the age of 7 or 8, would be transferred to the Charlton Mackrell school.[19] A cottage and garden were purchased by public subscription and a small 'gothic' schoolroom erected on the south side of Station Road near its junction with Broad Street. The school was subject to governmental and diocesan inspection.[20] There was one mistress, generally certificated, assisted by a stipendiary monitress.[21] In 1903 the school was stated to be 'unusually well taught' and there were 38 children on the books with an average attendance of 25.[22] It was closed in 1917 and the 15 remaining pupils were transferred to Charlton Mackrell school.[23] The building is now (1970) used as a storeroom.

CHARITIES FOR THE POOR. None known.

[93] S.R.O., DD/SAS CH 16.
[94] Ibid.
[95] S.R.O., D/P/cha. a. 2/1/1–2.
[96] S.R.O., D/D/Ca 177.
[97] Ibid. 218, 236, 244.
[98] Ibid. 244.
[99] Ibid. 267.
[1] S.R.O., Q/RR, meeting-house lics.
[2] S.R.O., D/D/Rm, vol. 1, pp. 63, 72.
[3] Ibid. vol. 2, p. 168; box 2.
[4] Ibid. box 2.
[5] H.O. 129/317/1/7/16.
[6] S.R.O., D/D/Rm, box 2; H.O. 129/317/1/7/17.
[7] H.O. 129/317/1/7/17.
[8] Local information.

[9] S.R.O., DD/DN, box 6, letter from P. W. Bryan to Wm. Dickinson, 11 Dec. 1897.
[10] *Digest of Returns to Sel. Cttee. on Educ. of Poor*, H.C. 224 (1819), ix.
[11] *Ann. Rep. B. & W. Dioc. Assoc. of S.P.C.K.* (1825–6).
[12] *Educ. Enquiry Abstract*, H.C. 62 (1835), xlii.
[13] Ibid.   [14] Ibid.
[15] S.R.O., D/D/Rm, box 2.
[16] H.O. 129/317/1/7/17.
[17] *Church Sch. Inquiry, 1846–7*.
[18] S.R.O., D/P/cha. a. 18/1/1.   [19] Ibid.
[20] S.R.O., C/E, box 26.
[21] Ibid. box 5, log bk.
[22] Ibid. box 26.
[23] S.R.O., C/E, box 5, admission reg., log bk.

CHARLTON MACKRELL

THE ancient parish of Charlton Mackrell, often known as West Charlton, had an area estimated at 2,021 a. in 1861,[1] but no accurate assessment for its earlier extent survives. Within its boundaries lie many detached areas formerly belonging to Charlton Adam, which were absorbed when the civil parish was united with that of Charlton Adam in 1885.[2] In the same year two small detached areas in the north-west of the parish were transferred from Somerton,[3] giving a total area for the civil parish of 3,499 a. in 1901.[4] The parish lies 2½ miles east of Somerton and nearly 4 miles north of Ilchester, being bounded on the north by Kingweston, on the east by Charlton Adam and Babcary, on the south-east by West Camel and Podimore Milton, on the south by Ilchester and Yeovilton, on the south-west by Kingsdon, and on the west by Somerton. It extends for 4 miles from north to south and nearly 3½ miles from east to west, although its irregular shape gives it a breadth of only ½ mile at its centre.

The soil of the parish is generally clay, the sub-soil limestone and lias. Traces of Keuper Marl are found in the extreme west of the parish, and alluvium along the banks of the Cary.[5] On the northern boundary the land lies above the 225 ft. contour. This falls away slightly to form a small plateau known as Windmill or Snap hill in the north-west of the parish; the land drops sharply at Green Down on its southern side to the Somerton road and the river Cary, and more gradually on the east towards the village around Charlton House. The ground rises steeply again above 100 ft. further south in the area of the church and more gently to the south-east beyond Rookery Farm. A ridge runs south from Tout above the 100 ft. contour, sloping gradually to the river Cary in the south and the Foss Way in the south-east. The southern point of the parish and its south-eastern area are flat and low-lying. The river Cary enters the east of the parish on its boundary with Charlton Adam and flows north and east of Cary Fitzpaine to the south-eastern boundary, passing under the Foss Way at Popple bridge, across the southern point of the parish. Thereafter it forms the south-western boundary until it passes into Somerton at Willmoors. Two small streams flow into the Cary in the area of Cary Fitzpaine: one from Charlton Adam in the north meets it just north-west of the farm, and the other, forming the south-eastern parish boundary, just before Popple bridge. Park brook runs into the southern extremity of the parish from Podimore, entering the river at Cary bridge.

Another stream from Kingweston runs south through the village around Charlton House and flows north of, and below, the church, past Rookery Farm, to join the Cary below the Somerton road. It formerly drove Peck Mill in Charlton Adam. Chalkbrook or Chabrick Mill Stream ('Chalbrouke' in 1393),[6] marking the western boundary of the parish, also flows into the same river.

The road system is irregular. The Foss Way from Ilchester forms the extreme south-western boundary of the parish, and runs north-east into Charlton Adam, severing Cary Fitzpaine from the remainder of the parish. It was turnpiked in 1753.[7] The road linking Somerton and Castle Cary, known as Butwell Road in 1757,[8] the Glaston highway in 1787,[9] and more recently as Snap Hill, passes through the north-western corner of the parish, leaving it at Christians Cross, referred to in the 13th century as 'Crispine Croy'.[10] It was also turnpiked in 1753.[11] From this road, at its point of entry, Somerton Lane, called Windmill Hill Road in 1757,[12] crosses Windmill hill to the village around Charlton House. From the same starting point Somerton Road skirts the southern extremity of Windmill hill and Green Down to the area of medieval settlement around the church. Until the 19th century this continued south-west to Tout and Cary Fitzpaine,[13] but subsequently that portion lying within the village was stopped up, leaving the present road which runs west past the church. From this road two lanes run north to the area around Charlton House, the western one known as West Charlton Road and the eastern one formerly running through the grounds of Charlton House, from which it was diverted in the 18th century,[14] to Christians Cross, known as Kingweston Road. A small lane running south-west then south from Snap Hill Road across Windmill hill is called Green Down Road in 1810,[15] and in 1970 was known as Boxhill Lane up to the crossing of Somerton Lane, and as Sug Hill thereafter. Originally it continued beyond the Somerton road into Summerleaze common beside the river Cary.[16] Two lanes run east to Charlton Adam, one from Charlton House and the other further south. Ridgeway Lane formerly ran south from a field between the parishes known as Twixt Towns to join the Foss Way,[17] but the portion forming the boundary with Charlton Adam, before it crosses the road to Cary Fitzpaine, is now closed. A lane running east from Lytes Cary crosses the river at Cary bridge and continues to Kingsdon village. Rag Lane, mentioned in 1664,[18] serves

---

[1] *P.O. Dir. Som.* (1861). This article was completed in 1970.
[2] *Local Govt. Bd. Order* 19,585.
[3] *Local Govt. Bd. Prov. Orders Conf. Order (Poor Law), (No. 2), Act* (1885).
[4] *Census*, 1901.
[5] Geol. Surv. Map 1″, solid and drift, sheet 296 (1969 edn.).
[6] Hunt. Libr., HA Manorial, Somerton hundred ct. roll, 1392–3.
[7] Ilchester Turnpike Act, 26 Geo. II, c. 71 (Priv. Act).
[8] S.R.O., DD/DN, box 40, map of Charlton Mackrell manor, 1757.

[9] Ibid. box 44, marriage settl. 2 Feb. 1787.
[10] Devon R.O. 123 M/TB 125.
[11] Langport, Somerton, and Castle Cary Turnpike Act, 26 Geo. II, c. 92 (Priv. Act).
[12] S.R.O., DD/DN, box 40, map of Charlton Mackrell manor, 1757.
[13] S.R.O., CR 92.
[14] See p. 103.
[15] S.R.O., CR 92.
[16] Ibid.
[17] Ibid.
[18] S.R.O., DD/DN, box 39, ct. roll, Cary Fitzpaine, 25 Oct. 1664.

fields north-east of Cary Fitzpaine, and two other lanes link that settlement with the Foss Way to the west, and the Langport–Wincanton road to the south. A footpath ran south-west from Rookery Farm to Kingsdon. It crossed the Cary at Pimple bridge, mentioned in 1752[19] and rebuilt in 1790.[20]

Of the two medieval open arable fields in Charlton Mackrell manor, East field appears to have lain in the north-east of the parish on both sides of the Kingweston road, and West field evidently stretched from Wellham in the west to Boxwell and Christians Cross in the north, and Windmill hill in the south.[21] The 16th-century four-field system which developed from this cannot be traced precisely. North field appears to have included lands at Paddock hill and Boxwell hill beyond Snap Hill Road in the north-west of the parish, and also areas north-east of the Kingweston road at Rush Plot, Fatmoor, and Bulland. West field included most of the lands in the area of Windmill hill and Green Down, and at Wellham. South field lay between Cary Lane and Ridgeway Lane, south-west of the old village. East field was largely inclosed by this time but had lain north-east of Ridgeway Lane and north-west of the Foss Way, being known as Easter field by 1810.[22] Apart from South field, the arable fields had been divided into smaller units by 1810, the largest being Wellham, Green Down, Top of Hill, and Hind Hearne, all formerly part of West field, and Snap field, Boxwell Hill, Paddock Corner, and Bulland, all in the area of North field.[23]

There was common meadow at Willmoors and Upmead along the river Cary in the extreme west of the parish from the 13th century,[24] and common pasture at Summerleaze, known as Bullditch common in 1810, stretching south from Somerton Road along the east bank of the Cary.[25] Former open fields in Cary Fitzpaine manor may be represented by the field names Great Cary field and Little Cary field to the east of the farm there, and West field between the Foss Way and the Cary, all mentioned in 1810.[26] Common pasture within the same manor probably lay in Great Broad Leaze and Little Broad Leaze south-west of the farm, and over East Leaze in the extreme east of the parish.[27]

Evidence of Roman and Romano-British occupation rests chiefly on two villa sites:[28] the first evidently lay at the south-western edge of Windmill hill, where finds included 'herringbone' walls, tiles, a hoard of coins, and three stone coffins.[29] The second was sited near the river Cary, north-west of Lytes Cary, where a hypocaust was uncovered.[30] Miscellaneous small finds of pottery, implements,

and burials have also been unearthed north and south of the area around Charlton House.[31] Medieval settlement was probably concentrated in the area between the church and the manor-house (Rookery Farm) on both sides of the Somerton road where, in 1810, many of the small tenements of the manor were sited.[32] These were largely demolished during the 19th century, those on the south side of the road (including the poorhouse) by the Dickinson family of Kingweston and by fire,[33] and those on the north side by the extension of the churchyard and rectory house grounds.[34] There remains a group of cottages in the area of the chantry farm, to the east of which modern housing has been erected, and the 19th-century school, lying east of the church.

A second village grew up about ½ mile north of the church, separated from the latter by a detached area formerly belonging to Charlton Adam which includes Manor Farm and Priory Farm.[35] This second village now forms the principal area of settlement in the parish, centred upon Charlton House. A number of the tenements which comprised the rectory manor were sited here, some of which were demolished when the grounds of Charlton House were extended in the late 18th century.[36] The buildings in this area date from the 17th century and include Georgian Cottage, the Reading Room, the Woods, Sheppards Orchard, and the Greyhound inn. Modern housing development extends north-west along the eastern side of the Kingweston road, and along a short lane north-east of Charlton House. The medieval settlements of Lytes Cary and Tuckers (now Cooks) Cary lie close together on opposite sides of Cary Lane, and Cary Fitzpaine, formerly a hamlet but now little more than a single large farm, is situated in the south-east corner of the parish. Wellham farm, in the extreme west of the parish, and Withy farm, south-east of the church, are both 19th-century creations.[37]

The Greyhound inn, lying south-east of Charlton House, is mentioned by name in 1861,[38] but was probably first licensed by the Hockey family in c. 1837, having previously served as a beer shop.[39] In 1970 it was the only public house in the parish.

The West Charlton Friendly Society was founded in 1855 and was discontinued c. 1912.[40] The Reading Room was built in the 19th century by the Brymer family for the use of parishioners.[41] The building is mentioned in 1855, although the present structure is dated 1859.[42] The room was given to the parishes of Charlton Mackrell and Charlton Adam by W. J. Brymer in 1937.[43]

[19] D.R.O., D 124, Somerton hundred ct. bk. 1730–62.
[20] S.R.O., D/P/cha. ma. 4/1/2.
[21] Devon R.O. 123 M/TB 125.
[22] S.R.O., CR 92.
[23] Ibid.; DD/DN, box 39, ct. roll, Cary Fitzpaine, 29 Aug. 1628; marriage settl. 26 Nov. 1737; box 54, conveyance, 10 Feb. 1758; box 40, map of Charlton Mackrell manor, 1757; D.R.O., D 78/2.
[24] Devon R.O. 123 M/TB 125; S.R.O., CR 92.
[25] S.R.O., CR 92; DD/DN, box 40, map of Charlton Mackrell manor, 1757.
[26] S.R.O., CR 92.
[27] Ibid.
[28] V.C.H. Som. i. 323, 326.
[29] Ibid. 323.
[30] Ibid. 326.

[31] Ex inf. Som. County Museum.
[32] S.R.O., CR 92.
[33] MS. notes on the Charltons by W. Small, p. 43, penes Mr. C. F. Hamilton, Wells.
[34] O.S. Map 6″, Som. LXXIII. NE. (1888 edn.).
[35] See pp. 86, 88.
[36] See p. 103.
[37] S.R.O., CR 92; O.S. Map 6″, Som. LXXIII. NE. (1888 edn.).
[38] P.O. Dir. Som. (1861).
[39] S.R.O., DD/DN, box 10, letter, R. Page to W. Dickinson, Aug. 1837.
[40] S.R.O., D/P/cha. ma. 23/2; A. Fitzgerald, Five years . . . of . . . Charlton Friendly Soc. (1861).
[41] Ex inf. Mr. C. F. Hamilton.
[42] S.R.O., D/P/cha. ma. 9/1/1; date on chimney breast.
[43] S.R.O., D/P/cha. a. 9/1/1; D/P/cha. ma. 4/1/1.

Apart from the major houses in the parish, treated subsequently,[44] Sheppards Orchard, occupied by Ann Sheppard in 1810[45] and lying east of the Greyhound inn, is of two storeys, rubble, and thatched, with brick and stone stacks. The casements are modern but the building probably dates from the 17th century. The Woods, occupied by William Woods in 1810,[46] lies west of West Charlton Road, comprising two storeys of rubble and rough ashlar, with thatch, wooden casements, and stone stacks, and is 18th-century in date. Most of the houses in the parish are constructed of the local lias and are thatched or tiled.

The population of Charlton Mackrell stood at 268 in 1801, but after a small drop to 239 in 1811 rose steadily to 405 in 1841 and, after a brief recession, to 419 in 1871. It then plummeted to 290 in 1881 and to 231 in 1891.[47] The last available figure, for 1901, showed a small rise to 288,[48] but the cumulative totals for Charlton Mackrell and Charlton Adam together indicate that the parishes are only now returning to the population which they possessed in 1911.[49]

Henry (I) Lyte (c. 1529–1607) of Lytes Cary is remembered as the translator and editor of Dodoens' *Cruydeboeck* or *Herbal*, known subsequently as *Lyte's Herbal*, which he first published in 1578.[50] The work included references to 'the Cary Bridge Pear' and 'the Somerton Pear, an excellent pear, ripe before Kingsdon's feast'.[51] His son Thomas (III) Lyte (c. 1568–1638) compiled a fanciful pedigree deriving James I from Brutus the Trojan, for which the king presented him with a jewel containing the royal portrait in miniature.[52]

Charles Summers (1827–78), the sculptor, was born at Higher Sandpits in the parish and came of a family of Charlton masons. He left the parish in his youth and his most celebrated works were executed in Australia and Italy.[53]

MANORS AND OTHER ESTATES. The manor of *CHARLTON MACKRELL*[54] was held T.R.W. by Roger Arundel, the Saxon owner of 1066, Alverd, having been dispossessed.[55] No further reference to the ownership of the manor has been traced until 1220, when it appears as parcel of the Arundel barony,[56] centred upon Powerstock (Dors.), which was held by Roger Arundel in 1086.[57] Roger was succeeded by Robert Arundel, living in 1135, and subsequently by Roger (II) (d. 1165),

who left as heir his sister Maud, wife of Gerbert de Percy (d. 1179). Maud left two daughters, Sibyl and Alice, who divided the barony and manor between them.[58]

Sibyl married first Maurice de Pole, whose son Roger died without issue on the crusade of 1190. Roger's brother Robert also died childless in 1198, when he was succeeded by his half brother Robert (I) FitzPayn, presumably by a second husband of Sibyl. Robert died c. 1217–22, and was followed by his son Roger FitzPayn (d. 1237).[59] In 1224 Roger quitclaimed his rights in the other moiety of the manor and advowson to Roger de Newburgh, husband of his father's cousin Maud, and to Roger's sister, Margery Belet.[60] Roger FitzPayn was succeeded by his son Sir Robert (II) (d. 1281), who held a carucate of land in the manor of Charlton in 1251–2.[61] This moiety of the manor was described in 1284–5 as ⅛ fee, and in 1303 as ½ fee.[62] Robert (III), Lord FitzPayn, son and heir of Robert (II), died in 1315, when he was said to hold the hamlet of Charlton under John Apadam,[63] although no other reference to this overlordship has been found. Robert (III) was succeeded by his son Robert (IV), Lord FitzPayn (d. 1354), who in 1354 settled the moiety on his nephew Robert Grey of Codnor (Essex) (d. 1393), who subsequently took the name FitzPayn.[64] The latter's daughter Isabel (d. 1394) married Richard de Poynings, Lord Poynings,[65] and was followed by her son Robert, Lord Poynings (d. 1446).[66] His son Sir Richard de Poynings (d. 1429) left a daughter Eleanor, heir to her grandfather, who married Henry Percy, earl of Northumberland.[67] After the latter's attainder in 1461, the moiety was granted to the king's brother George, duke of Clarence, in 1463.[68] Clarence was attainted in 1478, and the moiety was apparently restored to Eleanor, countess of Northumberland, who held it at her death in 1484.[69] It then passed to her son Henry, earl of Northumberland (d. 1489),[70] and continued in the family until 1536, when Henry, earl of Northumberland (d. 1537), granted it to the Crown.[71] Thereafter it was probably amalgamated with the manor of Cary Fitzpaine which, with the moiety of the advowson, was evidently granted to Henry, marquess of Exeter, attainted in 1538.[72] In 1539 Henry VIII granted it to John, Lord Russell,[73] who conveyed it in the following year to Sir John Horsey, owner of the other moiety.[74]

The second moiety apparently passed to Alice, daughter of Gerbert de Percy, wife of Robert of

[44] Rookery Farm, see p. 99; Lytes Cary, see p. 100; Cooks Cary, see p. 102; Charlton House, see p. 102; the Cottage, see p. 103; Georgian Cottage, see p. 104; Charlton Mackrell Court, see p. 108.
[45] S.R.O., CR 92. [46] Ibid.
[47] V.C.H. Som. ii. 348.
[48] Ibid.
[49] Census, 1911–61.
[50] Proc. Som. Arch. Soc. xxxviii. 44–59.
[51] Ibid. xxxviii. 44–50.
[52] Ibid. 59–73; civ. 124–5.
[53] D.N.B. lv. 165; Langport & Somerton Herald, 26 May 1928.
[54] The suffix 'Mackrell' is probably derived from an unrecorded tenant of the mesne lordship in the 12th century. The surname 'Makerel' occurs in connexion with lands in Somerton in 1243: Bk. of Fees, ii. 1384.
[55] V.C.H. Som. i. 495.
[56] Rot. de Ob. et Fin. (Rec. Com.), 91.
[57] Sanders, Eng. Baronies, 72.

[58] Ibid.
[59] Ibid.
[60] S.R.S. vi. 362. See below, p. 98.
[61] C.P. 40/277 rot. 43; Cal. Inq. p.m. ii, p. 232; Bk. of Fees, ii. 1265.
[62] Feud. Aids, iv. 285, 299.
[63] Cal. Inq. p.m. ii, p. 232; v, p. 389; Complete Peerage, v. 448.
[64] Complete Peerage, v. 451–5, 463–4; S.R.S. xvii. 182–3.
[65] C 136/82/2; Complete Peerage, x. 662.
[66] C 139/220/24; Complete Peerage, x. 662.
[67] Complete Peerage, x. 662; ix. 716.
[68] Cal. Pat. 1461–7, 226; 1467–77, 457, 530.
[69] C 140/67/46; C 141/2/26.
[70] Cal. Inq. p.m. Hen. VII, i, pp. 228–9.
[71] C.P. 25(2)/52/371/27 Hen. VIII Hil.
[72] E 149/928/18 & 19.
[73] L. & P. Hen. VIII, xiv(2), p. 156.
[74] Ibid. xv, p. 103; see below, p. 98.

Glastonbury, whose heir was her daughter, Maud, wife of Roger de Newburgh (d. 1194).[75] Their son Robert de Newburgh (d. 1246), who held the moiety in 1220,[76] was succeeded by his son Henry de Newburgh, who sold the manor of Hurcot, in Somerton, and other lands to Queen Eleanor in 1276.[77] By virtue of this grant the Queen evidently took the overlordship of the Charlton Mackrell moiety, which she claimed to hold in 1286.[78] In 1305 John de Newburgh, son of Henry, recovered $\frac{1}{2}$ fee in Charlton Mackrell held by the Queen,[79] but no further reference has been found to this overlordship.

In 1194 Robert Belet purchased the wardship of Robert de Newburgh, then a minor,[80] and subsequently arranged a marriage between his son William Belet, and Margery de Newburgh, Robert's sister.[81] In 1227 Robert de Newburgh granted the mesne lordship of the moiety to his sister Margery Belet, to be held of him for the service of $\frac{1}{5}$ fee.[82] In the same year she further subinfeudated the property by granting the moiety, described as $\frac{1}{2}$ hide, to William (I) de Horsey, to be held under her by the same service.[83] William purchased the mesne lordship from William Belet, son of Robert and grandson of Margery Belet, at a date given variously as 1239–40 and 1256–7.[84] John (I) de Horsey, son of William, held the moiety, described as $\frac{1}{5}$ fee, in 1286[85] and died in or before 1294, when the moiety was held as $\frac{1}{2}$ fee.[86] His son William (II) de Horsey held it in 1316, but died in or before 1327, leaving a son John (III).[87] On the latter's death without issue in or before 1337 the moiety passed to his brother Ralph de Horsey (d. 1354),[88] succeeded in turn by his son John (IV) (d. 1375), and grandson John (V).[89] In 1415 John (V) Horsey granted the moiety to his son William (III) (d. c. 1420), and the latter's wife Joan,[90] later wife of John Tretheke.[91] On her death in 1430 the moiety passed in turn to William's brothers Henry Horsey (d. 1460), who died childless,[92] and Thomas Horsey (d. 1468).[93] It was then inherited by Thomas's son John (VI) (d. 1531),[94] and grandson Sir John (VII) Horsey (d. 1546), who acquired the other moiety of the advowson and probably the rest of the manor in 1540.[95]

Sir John (VII) Horsey left the manor to his second

son Roger,[96] but it nevertheless passed to his eldest son Sir John (VIII) Horsey, who settled the property for life on his intended wife Dorothy, widow of Sir George Speke, in 1589 and died the same year. The manor, presumably on Dorothy's death, was divided between Sir John's coheirs, his sister Mary, wife of Richard Arnold, and his nephew Reginald (later Sir Reginald) Mohun.[97] The undivided moiety held by Mary Arnold (d. 1611) was inherited successively by her son Robert (d. 1626),[98] and grandson Ralph of Armswell in Buckland Newton (Dors.) (d. 1657).[99] On the death of Ralph Arnold's two sons George and Hubert, without issue, the freehold of the moiety vested in their two sisters Ann, wife of John Henley of Armswell, and Mary, wife of Thomas Green of Motcombe (Dors.), who conveyed it to Sir John Cutler of Westminster, Bt., in 1689.[1] On Cutler's death in 1693, the moiety passed to his daughter Elizabeth (d. 1697), wife of Charles Bodville, earl of Radnor.[2] Radnor sold it to James Samson of Podimore Milton in 1710,[3] who left it in 1713 to his son James Samson of Cary Fitzpaine.[4] In 1733 the latter conveyed the moiety to Thomas Lockyer, who subsequently purchased the rest of the manor.[5]

The other moiety, held by Sir Reginald Mohun, was conveyed in 1613 to Robert Henley (d. 1614) of Leigh, Winsham,[6] who was succeeded by his son Henry (d. 1639).[7] The moiety continued in the Henley family until in 1717 Henry Henley sold it to John Hardy of Charlton Mackrell,[8] who conveyed it to Charles Lockyer of London in 1718.[9] On his death in 1752, the latter left the moiety to John Lockyer of Colehall in Ealing (Mdx.), who sold it in 1759 to Thomas Lockyer of London (later of Ilchester),[10] owner of the second moiety. Thomas died in 1785, leaving the reunited manor to his daughter Mary, wife of Samuel Smith, for life, with remainder to his grandson Thomas Smith of Sunninghill (Berks.).[11] Thomas and Mary Smith conveyed it to trustees for sale in 1799,[12] and it was purchased by William Dickinson of Kingweston in 1802.[13] On his death in 1837 the manor passed first to his son Francis Henry Dickinson (d. 1890), and then to his grandson William Dickinson (d. 1914).[14] The latter's son, William Francis Dickinson, subdivided and sold the estate

---

[75] Hutchins, *Hist. Dors.* ii. 858–9; Sanders, *Eng. Baronies*, 72; *Pipe R.* 1194 (P.R.S. N.S.), 190.

[76] *Ex. e Rot. Fin.* (Rec. Com.), i. 460; *Rot. de Ob. et Fin.* (Rec. Com.), 91.

[77] *Cal. Pat.* 1266–72, 515, 673; Sanders, *Eng. Baronies*, 72–3; *S.R.S.* vi, 381.

[78] *Feud. Aids*, iv. 285.

[79] Sanders, *Eng. Baronies*, 73; *Abbrev. Plac.* (Rec. Com.), 256.

[80] *Pipe R.* 1194 (P.R.S. N.S. v), 190.

[81] *Bk. of Fees*, i. 260; *Rot. de Ob. et Fin.* (Rec. Com.), 8.

[82] *S.R.S.* vi. 61.

[83] Ibid. 52–3.

[84] C.P. 40/277 rot. 43; *S.R.S.* xv. 228; B.M. Harl. MS. 4120 f. 4.

[85] C.P. 40/277 rot. 43; *Feud. Aids*, iv. 285.

[86] *Cal. Inq. p.m.* iii, p. 142.

[87] C.P. 40/277 rot. 43; *Feud. Aids*, iv. 321; *Cal. Inq. p.m.* vii, p. 29.

[88] *Cal. Inq. p.m.* viii, p. 63; *Abbrev. Rot. Orig.* (Rec. Com.), ii. 157.

[89] *Cal. Inq. p.m.* viii, p. 63; xiv, p. 142.

[90] *Cal. Pat.* 1413–16, 349; C 139/48/19; *Cal. Inq. p.m.* (Rec. Com.), iv. 40.

[91] *Cal. Close*, 1419–22, 92; C 139/48/19.

[92] C 139/79/7; *Cal. Close*, 1435–41, 82–3; 1454–61,

69–70; *Cal. Fine. R.* 1430–7, 330; *S.R.S.* xxii. 202; C 140/2/25.

[93] C 140/28/32.

[94] Hutchins, *Hist. Dors.* iv. 427.

[95] *L. & P. Hen. VIII*, xv, p. 103; C 142/84/37.

[96] C 142/84/37.

[97] C 142/221/102.

[98] C 142/439/52.

[99] Ibid.; Hutchins, *Hist. Dors.* iii. 711.

[1] S.R.O., DD/DN, box 55, assignment, 10 July 1701; DD/CC 102402.

[2] G.E.C. *Baronetage*, iii. 128; S.R.O., DD/CC 102402; *Complete Peerage*, x. 715.

[3] S.R.O., DD/CC 102407.

[4] Ibid. 102408.

[5] Ibid. 102417; see below.

[6] C.P. 25(2)/346/11 Jas. I East; Prob. 11/124 (P.C.C. 67 Lawe); Prob. 11/125 (P.C.C. 15 Rudd).

[7] *Som. Wills*, ed. Brown, i. 14.

[8] S.R.O., DD/DN box 52, conveyance, 29 Mar. 1717.

[9] Ibid. conveyance, 1 Oct. 1718.

[10] Ibid. conveyance, 17 Feb. 1759.

[11] Ibid, box 44, abstract of title, c. 1801.

[12] Ibid.

[13] Ibid. box 59, conveyance, 10 Jan. 1802.

[14] Burke, *Land. Gent.* (1937), 616–17.

in 1922 and 1930,[15] but the lordship itself was retained and in 1970 was held by his daughter, Mrs. J. Burden of Kingweston.[16] In 1970 the manor farm was held with Charlton Mackrell Court by Mr. I. L. Phillips.[17]

The manor-house is first mentioned in 1327, when it formed part of the moiety held by the Horsey family.[18] During the second subdivision of the manor the property was initially held in divided moieties,[19] but by 1717 was held entirely with the Henley moiety.[20] In 1757 it was identified with Rookery Farm, which then comprised 162 a.[21] By 1800 it had been combined with all lands within the manor not previously enfranchised, to form a farming unit of 344 a. leased to Hugh Penny.[22] The buildings were stated to be in a 'bad plight' in 1802,[23] and the house was probably rebuilt by the Dickinsons in the early 19th century. The present farm-house is a plain two-storeyed lias building with a slated roof.

The manor of *CARY FITZPAINE*, sometimes called *LITTLE CARY*,[24] was held in 1066 by two thegns, Alinc and Lovinc, who by 1086 had been dispossessed by Roger Arundel, of whom the manor was held by Robert.[25] It is possible that the latter may be identified with Robert de Gatemore, who held other lands in Somerset under Roger Arundel.[26] The Gatemore family held lands in Charlton Mackrell c. 1271.[27] The overlordship of the manor was held in 1281 by Anselm de Gournay,[28] and in 1284–5 by Robert FitzPayn.[29] By 1315 it had passed to John Apadam,[30] who had married Anselm de Gournay's granddaughter,[31] but in 1323 and thereafter the manor was stated to be held in chief.[32] A mesne lordship held by Robert of Aumale is mentioned in 1284–5.[33]

In 1281 the manor was held by Sir Robert (II) FitzPayn as ½ fee,[34] suggesting that it had descended with that moiety of Charlton Mackrell manor held by the FitzPayns, as part of the Arundel lands allotted to Sibyl de Pole.[35] Subsequently it descended with that moiety, and was granted to Sir John Horsey, owner of the second moiety of Charlton Mackrell manor, by John, Lord Russell, in 1540.[36] Like Charlton Mackrell it was split into moieties between the coheirs of Sir John (VIII) Horsey (d. 1589).[37] The moiety formerly held by the Arnold family was sold by the earl of Radnor to James Samson (d. 1713) in 1710,[38] who was succeeded by

his son James.[39] In 1733 the latter partitioned the manor with Thomas Lockyer, owner of the other moiety.[40] By this agreement Samson secured those lands belonging to Cary Fitzpaine which lay largely south-east of the Foss Way and formed the major part of the manor. Lockyer received the remainder of Cary Fitzpaine manor and Samson's moiety of Charlton Mackrell manor.[41] Those areas of Cary Fitzpaine manor taken by Lockyer were probably combined with the latter's manor of Charlton Mackrell. Samson died without issue in 1763, leaving the manor to his sister, Hester.[42] On her death in 1765 it passed in turn to her nieces Grace (d. c. 1768) and Elizabeth Shute.[43] By Elizabeth's will, proved in 1783, her lands were to be divided between Thomas Harris, a Bristol merchant, and the Revd. Henry Shute of Stapleton (Glos.),[44] and all the Shute lands in the Charltons passed to Harris when the estate was partitioned.[45] Thomas Harris died in 1797, stating in his will that, as his son, Thomas, had 'manifested an utter dislike' of the manor and hamlet of Cary Fitzpaine, if the latter lived in the mansion there more than 60 days in any one year the property was to pass to the Revd. Henry Shute.[46] The son survived his father by only two years, and his mother, Mercy Harris (d. 1819), married James Sutton of Bristol. Sutton retained and occupied the property until his death in 1824.[47] The manor then passed to the Revd. Henry Shute (d. 1841), who was succeeded by his son Henry, of Winterbourne (Glos.) (d. 1864).[48] The Shute trustees sold the manor in 1865 to the present owners, the Ecclesiastical (now Church) Commissioners.[49]

The manor-house, known as Phippens (i.e. Fitzpaine's) Cary in the 16th century, and Cary Farm or Little Cary Farm in the 17th and 18th centuries, is first mentioned in 1551, when it was granted as a copyhold with 252 a. within the manor to the Creech *alias* Powell (later Creech) family.[50] This family continued to occupy the property until the late 16th century, despite a succession of Chancery suits between 1564 and 1620.[51] The freehold of the moiety of the farm was granted by Henry Henley of Colway in Lyme Regis (Dors.), to his grandson Thomas Henley in 1694, when the property was held under lease by James Samson.[52] Samson purchased both moieties of the farm in 1700 and 1701,[53] and reunited it with the manor in

[15] Ibid.; S.R.O., DD/X/PHL, sale cat. 1922; sale cat. Kingweston estate, *penes* Mrs. J. Burden, Kingweston.
[16] Ex inf. Mrs. J. Burden.
[17] Ex inf. Mr. I. L. Phillips.
[18] C 135/3/6.
[19] S.R.O., DD/DN, box 39, survey, 1626; *S.R.S.* xxiii. 142–3.
[20] S.R.O., DD/DN, box 52, conveyance, 29 Mar. 1717.
[21] Ibid. box 40, map of manor, 1757.
[22] Ibid. box 18, sale cat. 1800.
[23] Ibid. endorsement, 1802.
[24] *S.R.S.* xxii. 196.
[25] *V.C.H. Som.* i. 495.
[26] Ibid. 494–5.
[27] B.M. Cott. Ch. xxv, 34; *S.R.S.* vi. 232.
[28] *Cal. Inq. p.m.* ii, p. 232.
[29] *Feud. Aids*, iv. 285.
[30] *Cal. Inq. p.m.* v, p. 389.
[31] Sanders, *Eng. Baronies*, 14.
[32] *Cal. Pat.* 1321–4, 244; *Cal. Fine R.* 1319–27, 244. A claim that the manor was held under the abbot of Glastonbury in 1490 (*Cal. Inq. p.m. Hen. VII*, i, pp. 228–9) cannot be substantiated.

[33] *Feud. Aids*, iv. 285.
[34] *Cal. Inq. p.m.* ii, p. 232.
[35] See above.
[36] *L. & P. Hen. VIII*, xv, p. 103.
[37] See p. 98.
[38] S.R.O., DD/CC 102407.
[39] Ibid. 102408.
[40] Ibid. 102417.
[41] Ibid.
[42] Ibid. 102440.
[43] Ibid. 102441–2, 102444–7.
[44] Ibid. 102459.
[45] Ibid. 102460.
[46] Ibid. 102480–1.
[47] Ibid. 102479–80.
[48] Ibid. 102482, 102500.
[49] Ex inf. Church Commissioners.
[50] S.R.O., DD/DN, box 39, survey, Cary Fitzpaine, 1626.
[51] C 3/39/73; C 3/63/67; C 3/95/11; C 3/139/86; C 3/310/10.
[52] S.R.O., DD/CC 102401.
[53] Ibid. 102401–2.

1710.[54] The house was still standing in 1810,[55] but had been demolished by the late 19th century.[56]

The manor of *LYTES CARY*[57] is first mentioned in 1284–5 as 'Kari',[58] but the present form of the name, adopted from its owners, has not been traced before 1333.[59] It may possibly be identified with the larger of two Domesday manors called Cary, both owned in 1086 by Humphrey the chamberlain.[60] Before the Conquest this had been held 'in parage' by Leving, who may be identified with Living, one of the two brothers who held the smaller manor, under Brihtric son of Alfgar, and with Lovinc who held part of Cary Fitzpaine.[61] Brihtric's lands appear to have been bestowed by William I on his queen Maud, who gave many of them to Humphrey the chamberlain.[62] His successor was probably Henry de Orescuilz, whose son Ellis left a son Richard and two daughters, Maud and Alice. On Richard's death his lands were divided between his sisters.[63] Maud married William son of John of Harptree (d. 1232) and was succeeded by her grandson Robert de Gournay, son of Thomas of Harptree.[64] Their descendant, Anselm de Gournay (d. 1286), was stated to hold the overlordship of Lytes Cary in 1284–5.[65] The second sister Alice married Roger (I) de Vilers, whose grandson Roger (III), son of Roger (II) de Vilers, was overlord of lands in Tuckers Cary in 1265.[66] Roger (III) died without surviving issue, and his lands were divided between his sisters, Mabel and Maud.[67] The former married Roger (I) de Studecumb and either he or his son Roger (II) occurs in 1284–5 as mesne lord of Lytes Cary under Anselm de Gournay.[68] The overlordship is not mentioned again until 1523, when it was held by Leonard Knoyle (d. 1532).[69] It occurs again in 1566, when it was held by Leonard's son, Edward Knoyle,[70] and finally in 1638, when it was owned by Edward Knoyle.[71] It is not referred to thereafter, nor is the mesne lordship mentioned again.

It is not known when the subinfeudation of the manor occurred. The manor was held in 1284–5 by William de (or le) Lyte by service of ¼ fee.[72] William is mentioned as witness to a deed of land in Tuckers Cary in 1255–6,[73] and he held a carucate of land there in 1265, when he was declared to be a rebel adherent of Brian de Gouvis, lord of Kingsdon.[74] On his death *c.* 1316 the manor passed either to his son Robert (I) le Lyte or to his grandson Robert

(II) le Lyte.[75] Robert (II) appears to have been succeeded by his son Peter le Lyte (d. 1348), and subsequently by his grandson Edmund Lyte (d. 1418).[76] Edmund's son John (I) Lyte (d. after 1453) left a son Thomas (I) Lyte, on whose death *c.* 1468–9 the manor passed to his son John (II).[77] The latter's son Thomas (II) Lyte had succeeded his father by 1512 and died in 1523,[78] being followed by his son John (III) (d. 1566), whose arms and initials with those of his wife Edith Horsey are to be found throughout the house at Lytes Cary.[79] The manor then passed to their son Henry (I) (d. 1607)[80] and grandson Thomas (III) Lyte (d. 1638).[81] It was then inherited in turn by Thomas's son Henry (II) (d. 1666) and grandson Henry (III) Lyte (d. 1711).[82] The latter's son Henry (IV) (d. 1685) left issue Henry (V) Lyte, living in 1706, but in 1711 the manor evidently passed to Thomas (IV) Lyte, son of John (d. 1698), and grandson of Henry (III).[83] Thomas (IV) secured heavy mortgages on the estate and in 1755, with his son John (to whom he had conveyed his interest in return for an annuity in 1748), sold the manor to Thomas Lockyer of Il-chester.[84] Lockyer died in 1785, leaving the manor to his daughter Mary Smith and to her son Thomas.[85] They sold it to William Dickinson of Kingweston in 1802.[86] Thereafter it descended with the manor of Charlton Mackrell until 1907 when it was sold by William Dickinson to Sir Walter Jenner (d. 1948).[87] Sir Walter left the manor to the National Trust, the present owners.[88]

The manor-house of Lytes Cary is probably of 14th-century origin. The presentation of a chaplain to a chapel at Tuckers Cary by Peter le Lyte in 1341, and the fact that before this date the Lytes are referred to in connexion with lands lying at Tuckers Cary, suggests that they were originally tenants of the FitzPayn family there.[89] The institution of a chaplain to Lytes Cary chapel in 1343[90] probably indicates that the house was originally built by Peter le Lyte shortly before this date. Thereafter it was evidently occupied continuously by the Lyte family until the 18th century, with the exception of a lease for 5 years to Robert Mere in 1583.[91] At least part of the house was rebuilt in the 15th century, perhaps by Thomas (I) Lyte (d. *c.* 1468–9), and it was much altered and extended by John (III) Lyte nearly 100 years later. The medieval and Tudor building formed a rectangle

---

[54] Ibid. 102407.
[55] S.R.O., CR 92.
[56] S.R.O., D/P/cha. ma. 3/2/1.
[57] The descent of this manor is based on two papers by Sir Henry Maxwell-Lyte: *Proc. Som. Arch. Soc.* xxxviii. 1–100; lxxvii. 115–35.
[58] *Feud. Aids*, iv. 285.
[59] *Proc. Som. Arch. Soc.* xxxviii. 11–12.
[60] *V.C.H. Som*, i. 519–20.   [61] Ibid.
[62] R. W. Eyton, *Domesday Studies, Dors.* 77, 137.
[63] *Proc. Som. Arch. Soc.* lxix. 39–40.
[64] Ibid.
[65] *Feud. Aids*, iv. 285.
[66] *Proc. Som. Arch. Soc.* lxix. 45–6; *Cal. Inq. Misc.* i, p. 267.
[67] *Proc. Som. Arch. Soc.* lxix. 46–7.
[68] Ibid.; *Feud. Aids*, iv. 285.
[69] The overlordship descended with the manor of Sandford Orcas: *Proc. Som. Arch. Soc.* lxix. 38–48.
[70] C 142/152/132.
[71] C 145/528/74.
[72] *Feud. Aids*, iv. 285.
[73] *Proc. Som. Arch. Soc.* xxxviii. 5–6.

[74] *Cal. Inq. Misc.* i, p. 267.
[75] *Proc. Som. Arch. Soc.* xxxviii. 10–11.
[76] Ibid. 11–20. A reference to Sir Ellis FitzPayn as lord of Lytes Cary in 1359 (ibid. 14) probably relates to his lordship of Tuckers Cary.
[77] Ibid. 20–8.
[78] Ibid. 28–32.
[79] Ibid. 35–42.
[80] Ibid. 44–59.
[81] Ibid. 59–75. Thomas Lyte's 'Book', *penes* J. M. Maxwell-Lyte, was located after this article had gone to press.
[82] *Proc. Som. Arch. Soc.* xxxviii. 76–81.
[83] Ibid. 78–82.
[84] S.R.O., DD/DN, box 53, deeds of Lytes Cary; box 52, agreement, 2 May 1784.
[85] Ibid. box 59, conveyance, 10 Jan. 1802.
[86] Ibid.
[87] *Lytes Cary* (Nat. Trust Guide) (1950).
[88] Ibid.
[89] *S.R.S.* x. 436; see below, p. 102.
[90] *S.R.S.* x. 464.
[91] *Proc. Som. Arch. Soc.* xxxviii. 55.

around a small courtyard with the chapel, initially detached, joined to the house at its eastern corner since the 15th century. Today only the north-east and south-east ranges and the chapel remain, a late-18th-century farm-house having been erected in place of the north-western range, and a 20th-century south-west wing built by Sir Walter Jenner on the site of buildings demolished before 1810.[92] The house is built of the local lias with Ham stone dressings.[93] With the exception of the chapel the oldest part is the north-east range which contains a 15th-century hall with a screens-passage across its north-west end. The building of the 18th-century farm-house beyond the passage has obliterated any medieval service rooms which may have stood there. The hall retains an original fireplace and roof. The latter is of four bays and has arch-braced collar-beam trusses, three tiers of cusped windbraces, and a cornice of pierced quatrefoils with carved angels at the base of the principal rafters. Nearly all the other features of the hall represent alterations carried out by John Lyte in the second quarter of the 16th century. Large three-light mullioned windows with four-centred heads to the lights were inserted and a two-storeyed porch and a projecting bay or 'oriel' were added to the front. The latter, at the dais end of the hall, consists of a small room on each floor, the lower one divided from the hall by a wide stone arch, carved with panelling, in which there was formerly a wooden screen. Both porch and oriel have bay windows resting on moulded corbels on the upper floors and their gables are surmounted by heraldic finials of the Lyte and Horsey families. Another stone-panelled arch leads to the staircase in the angle between the hall range and the south-east, or solar, wing. A small cusped window at the foot of the stair may have belonged to an earlier stair-turret. The solar wing, together with other, now vanished, buildings round the courtyard, was the work of John Lyte. At the centre of the south-east front is a two-storeyed bay window of eight lights with an embattled parapet pierced with quatrefoils. The bay is dated 1533 with the arms of Lyte impaling Horsey. Windows on this front originally contained heraldic glass recording the various marriages of the Lyte family.[94] The principal ground floor room, lit by the central bay and two flanking windows, is the great parlour. It was later enriched with Jacobean panelling and Ionic pilasters, and includes a fine chimneypiece. Immediately above, the great chamber is lit by windows identical with those on the ground floor. The barrel ceiling has plaster decoration in a geometrical design of moulded ribs, ornamented alternately with the arms of Lyte and Horsey, a very early example of such work. The frieze at one end carried the arms of Henry VIII. Entrance to the room is gained through an inner porch of linenfold panelling. The range to the south-west of the courtyard,

built by Sir Walter Jenner after 1907, is mainly in the style of the later 17th century. Its elaborate internal fittings include carving from one of Wren's city churches.[95]

A chantry chapel in the court of Tuckers Cary, mentioned in 1341,[96] had evidently been transferred to Lytes Cary manor-house by 1343,[97] as in the 15th century it is referred to as the chantry of Lytes Cary *alias* Tuckers Cary.[98] The patronage descended with the manor of Lytes Cary, though the bishop collated in 1343,[99] and John de Draycot presented in 1351.[1] The last presentation was made in 1433,[2] although the chalice, vestments, altar cloths, and cruets are mentioned in 1546 and 1559.[3] The chaplain in 1421 was given leave to serve a cure elsewhere for a year in consideration of the poverty of the chantry.[4] The chapel, comprising three bays, is of lias with Ham stone dressings, and the style agrees with the date of *c.* 1343 supplied above. It has an arch-braced roof with collar trusses and is lit by late Decorated windows. The east window is pointed, of three lights, filled with 19th-century glass in 13th-century style, and there are two square-headed two-light windows in the side walls, all three having reticulated tracery. The building is entered by a door in the north wall with two-centred head, and a small window in the west wall contains some medieval glass inserted by Sir Walter Jenner. Fragments of an early piscina may have been brought from the former chapel at Tuckers Cary. The chapel was restored in 1631 by Thomas (III) Lyte. It was he who initiated the painted coats of arms forming a frieze round the west, north, and south walls to commemorate marriages made by his family. He also erected two tablets, one recording the restoration of the building, and the other a copy of a medieval window formerly in the north aisle of the parish church, depicting his earliest known ancestors, William and Agnes le Lyte. Most of the woodwork dates from Lyte's restoration, but the screen at the west end was evidently inserted by Jenner.[5] Besides restoring the house and chapel in the early 20th century, Sir Walter Jenner laid out the gardens in their present form. His work included a water-tower in the guise of a circular dovecot, closing the vista from the north-east front of the house.

The manor of *TUCKERS CARY, TUCKS CARY,* or *LITTLE CARY* later known as *COOKS CARY* or *LOWER LYTES CARY,* is first mentioned in 1321,[6] but occurs as a place name from 1255–6 ('Towkerekary').[7] It may possibly be identified with the smaller of two Domesday manors called Cary, both owned in 1086 by Humphrey the chamberlain.[8] In 1066 this had been held 'in parage' by two brothers, Ordric and Living, and, like other of Humphrey's manors, had formed part of the estate of Brihtric son of Alfgar.[9] By 1480 and at least until 1638 the manor was held under that of

[92] S.R.O., CR 92.
[93] For external and internal views see *Country Life*, 18, 25 July, 1 Aug. 1947.
[94] S.R.O., D/P/cha. ma. 2/1/8; *Proc. Som. Arch. Soc.* xxxviii. 86–9.
[95] *Country Life*, 1 Aug. 1947, 229.
[96] *S.R.S.* x. 436.
[97] Ibid. 464.
[98] Ibid. xxx. 409; xxxi. 151.
[99] Ibid. x. 464.

[1] Ibid. 650.
[2] *S.R.S.* xxxi. 151.
[3] *Proc. Som. Arch. Soc.* xxxviii. 40–1.
[4] *S.R.S.* xxx. 409.
[5] For full description of chapel and fittings see *Proc. Som. Arch. Soc.* xxxviii. 70–2, 86–94, 101–3.
[6] *S.R.S.* xii. 86.
[7] *Proc. Som. Arch. Soc.* xxxviii. 5.
[8] *V.C.H. Som.* i. 416, 519–20.
[9] Ibid.

Cary Fitzpaine by fealty, suit of court, a rent of 12*d.*, and ½ lb. of cummin.[10]

Richard de Gatemore, whose family may have held Cary Fitzpaine in 1086,[11] granted his lands in Tuckers Cary to Sir Roger FitzPayn in *c.* 1271.[12] In 1280 John de Gatemore, Richard's son, failed in an attempt to recover land and rent there from Sir Roger.[13] By 1321 the manor was held by Ellis FitzPayn and Gillian his wife,[14] but by 1345–6 his lands had passed to his widow and to their son John.[15] They were succeeded by Sir John FitzPayn and his wife Eleanor before 1380–1,[16] and in 1384 the manor was settled on their son Ellis.[17] In 1412 it was held by Sir Thomas FitzPayn,[18] but by 1428 had passed to his son John,[19] and by 1439 to John Austell, husband of Margaret FitzPayn.[20] In 1439 Austell conveyed his lands in 'Lytilkary *alias* Tokeryskary', then held for life by John Plasman, to his daughter Agnes, wife of Thomas Burton.[21] Agnes married Sir Nicholas St. Lo (d. 1486)[22] and was succeeded in turn by her son Sir John (d. 1499),[23] and grandson Nicholas St. Lo (d. 1508).[24] The latter's son, Sir John, sold the manor to John (III) Lyte (d. 1566) of Lytes Cary in 1540,[25] and thereafter the manor descended with that of Lytes Cary.[26] In 1720 Thomas (IV) Lyte sold it to his step-father Thomas Cooke, husband of Catherine Lyte;[27] it has been known since then as Cooks Cary. Cooke's widow and children conveyed the manor to Thomas Freke of Bristol in 1732,[28] from whom it passed to his daughter Frances and her husband John Willes of Astrop (Northants.).[29] Their son John Freke Willes, by will dated 1799, left the manor to his cousin the Revd. William Shippen Willes of Cirencester (Glos.), who sold it to William Dickinson of Kingweston in 1803.[30] Thereafter it descended with the manor of Charlton Mackrell,[31] although Cooks Cary farm was sold to the Dickinson tenant, Mr. F. Attwell, in 1930.[32]

It may be presumed that the manor-house, now Cooks Cary farm-house, existed in 1341, when a priest was instituted to the chantry 'in the court of Toukereskary'.[33] The present two-storey house is built of lias and tiled, but includes no identifiable features earlier than the 19th century.

An estate held in 1317 by Richard Lovel and Muriel his wife was described then as the manor of *CHARLTON MACKRELL*.[34] Lovel's heir was his granddaughter Muriel, wife of Sir Nicholas de Seymour (d. 1361).[35] The Seymours also held a house and land in Charlton Adam under Thomas Horsey, which was granted to Henry Power (d. 1361) during the minority of Richard, son of Sir Nicholas Seymour.[36] Both Richard Seymour (d. 1401) and his son Richard (d. 1409) were stated to hold two houses and lands in Charlton Mackrell and Charlton Adam under Nicholas Paulet,[37] suggesting that the two estates had been combined. These lands descended to Alice, wife of William, Lord Zouche (d. 1463), and subsequently to their son William (d. 1469), when they were described as the manors of *CHARLTON ADAM AND CHARLTON MACKRELL*.[38] In 1480 they were held of Cary Fitzpaine manor and known as Knyghtysplace.[39] John, Lord Zouche, William's son, was attained after Bosworth, and the manors were granted in 1486 to Sir William Willoughby.[40] The Zouche attainder was reversed in 1489, and it seems likely that their estate in the Charltons was restored, for in 1540 Richard, later Lord Zouche, sold lands and tenements called Lanchers and Clearkes in the two parishes to John (III) Lyte of Lytes Cary (d. 1566).[41] Thereafter the estate descended with the manor of Lytes Cary,[42] and in 1626 and 1637 a farm called 'Lanchsheare' was acknowledged to be held as a freehold of Cary Fitzpaine manor by fealty, suit of court, and a rent of 1*d.* or a pair of gloves.[43] In 1702 the lands, then comprising two amalgamated tenements of 100 a. known as Lanchers farm and Bellamys tenement, were settled on Thomas Lyte (d. 1748), third son of Henry (III), before his marriage.[44] It was he who rebuilt the house attached to Bellamys tenement, subsequently known as Charlton House, in 1726.[45] In that year the premises were settled on his daughter Silvestra on her marriage with Thomas Blackwell, rector of St. Clement Danes, London, whose two daughters Silvestra, wife of James Monypenny, and Mary sold them to John Pyne of Low Ham in 1758.[46] On his death in 1791 John Pyne left the

[10] Alnwick Castle, Northumberland MSS. X II 12 3b, ct. roll, Cary Fitzpaine, 1480; *Cal. Inq. p.m. Hen. VII*, iii, pp. 335–6; S.R.O., DD/DN, box 38, ct. roll, Cary Fitzpaine, 7 Sept. 1626, 20 Sept. 1637; C 145/528/74.
[11] See p. 99.
[12] B.M. Cott. Ch. xxv, 34; *S.R.S.* vi. 232.
[13] *S.R.S.* xliv. 303.
[14] Ibid. xii. 86.
[15] *S. & D. N. & Q.* vii. 72.
[16] Ibid. 103.
[17] *S.R.S.* xvii. 124.
[18] *Feud. Aids*, vi. 503.
[19] Ibid. i. 490, 497; *S. & D. N. & Q.* vii. 104.
[20] B.M. Harl. Ch. 111 D 5; *S.R.S.* xxii. 196–7; *S. & D. N. & Q.* vii. 104.
[21] B.M. Harl. Ch. 111 D 5.
[22] *S. & D. N. & Q.* vii. 104; *Cal. Inq. p.m. Hen. VII*, i, p. 37.
[23] *Cal. Inq. p.m. Hen. VII*, ii, pp. 125–6.
[24] Ibid. iii, pp. 335–6. Nicholas St. Lo was stated to hold only a moiety of the manor, presumably because Austell had been succeeded by two coheirs, but the grant of 1439 (B.M. Harl. Ch. 111 D 5) indicates that the whole manor passed to the St. Lo family.
[25] C.P. 40/119 rot. 4; C.P. 25(2)/240/32 Hen. VIII Trin.
[26] See p. 100.
[27] S.R.O., DD/DN, box 55, abstract of title, 1803; *Proc. Som. Arch. Soc.* xxxviii. 78–82.

[28] S.R.O., DD/DN, box 53, assignment, 18 May 1732.
[29] Ibid. box 55, abstract of title, 1803.
[30] Ibid. box 59, conveyance, 17 Dec. 1803.
[31] See above.
[32] Sale cat. Kingweston estate, 1930, *penes* Mrs. J. Burden, Kingweston.
[33] *S.R.S.* x. 436.
[34] Ibid. xii. 69.
[35] *Complete Peerage*, xi. 358–62.
[36] *Cal. Inq. p.m.* xi, p. 159; xiv, p. 82.
[37] C 137/26/55; C 137/72/38; *Complete Peerage*, xi. 358–62.
[38] *Complete Peerage*, s.v. Zouche; C 140/30/53.
[39] Alnwick Castle, Northumberland MSS. X II 12 3b, ct. roll, Cary Fitzpaine, 1480.
[40] *Complete Peerage*, s.v. Zouche; *Cal. Pat.* 1485–94, 127–8.
[41] *Complete Peerage*, s.v. Zouche; C.P. 25(2)/240/32 Hen. VIII Trin. Walter Lanscher of Charlton is mentioned in 1393: Hunt. Libr., HA Manorial, Somerton hundred ct. roll, 1392–3.
[42] See p. 100.
[43] S.R.O., DD/DN, box 39, ct. roll. 7 Sept. 1626, 20 Sept. 1637.
[44] Ibid. box 54, abstract of title, *c.* 1810; *Proc. Som. Arch. Soc.* xxxviii. 79–80.
[45] Date on rainwater-heads.
[46] S.R.O., DD/DN, box 54, abstract of title, *c.* 1810.

house and lands to his son William, who conveyed them to Robert Clarke of Castle Cary in 1794.[47] Clarke sold the estate to John Jerritt in 1800; it was resold to Lionel Lukin in 1806, to John Whitelocke in 1809, and finally to William Dickinson in 1811.[48] It subsequently descended in the Dickinson family with the manor of Charlton Mackrell, until its sale by William Francis Dickinson in 1930.[49]

When John Pyne acquired Charlton House in 1758 it was held with the original estate of 100 a.[50] Pyne purchased three houses adjoining the house, Jerritt a further nine, and Whitelocke two more. These were demolished and the lands added to the gardens.[51] Jerritt also used the acquired lands to divert the road running from Charlton Adam to Kingweston further to the west, and to convert the old road into a carriage drive past the house.[52] The farm buildings adjoining the house were demolished, new cottages erected in their place, and much of the farm lands sold off.[53] Thus by 1806 the gardens had been extended from 2 a. to 15 a.[54] and by 1810 the total lands held with the house had been reduced to 64 a., farmed from a house on the north side of Somerton Lane towards its eastern end.[55] When Charlton House was sold in 1930 only the gardens remained.[56] The size and character of the property led to its occupation under the Dickinsons by a succession of prominent inhabitants of the parish. These included Capt. Robert Page (1819–52),[57] the Revd. William Pyne (1853–81),[58] Edwin Langdale Christie (1891–1905),[59] and Sir Arthur Theodore Thring (1905–32).[60] The house is a large building of stone and slate, having two storeys with an attic above. The largely unaltered front, seven bays wide, has rusticated quoins, bolection-moulded architraves, a heavily moulded stringcourse, and a parapet cornice swept up in the centre and at the angles. Niches flank the central bay on both floors. Lead rainwater-heads are dated 1726, one bearing the Lyte swan, the other blank. The Tuscan porch is a later addition. Of the two slightly recessed flanking wings, one is of the original date and the other appears to have been rebuilt or remodelled in the early 19th century. Internally there is a staircase of c. 1726. At the north-east corner of the house stands an 18th-century dovecot, two storeys high, with nesting boxes on the upper floor.

The lands of the chantry in the south aisle of the parish church, founded by Ralph Horsey in 1342, originally comprised 2 virgates (80 a.) of land and 12 a. of meadow within the parish.[61] A house

had been built there by 1374,[62] and the lands appear to have been retained by the chaplains until the chantry was dissolved in 1548.[63] At that date the estate was estimated to contain 30 a. of land and 8 a. of meadow.[64] A grant of the chantry and lands to Sir Thomas Bell of Gloucester and Richard Duke of London in 1548[65] never appears to have taken effect. The lands had evidently formed part of the manor of Cary Fitzpaine and at the dissolution reverted to the lord of that manor, Sir John Horsey.[66] In 1548 the lessee had been John Drewe, probably father of the last incumbent, and Drewe purchased them from Horsey in 1553, when they comprised two messuages, a cottage, and 107 a. of land.[67] John Drewe died in 1570 and was succeeded by his grandson Henry.[68] The latter entered on the premises in 1582 when the lands were valued at 29s. 8d. and the chantry at 26s. 8d.[69] The Drewe family continued to hold the property until it was sold by John Drewe to John Eastment of Sherborne (Dors.) in 1664.[70] The latter's granddaughter and heir, Dorothy Eastment (d. 1742), married Carew Hervey Mildmay of Hazlegrove in 1718. On his death in 1784 Mildmay left his estates to his great-niece Jane, wife of Sir Henry Paulet St. John-Mildmay.[71] They sold the farm and 97 a. of land to John Jerritt in 1807,[72] and he conveyed them in the same year to William Dickinson.[73] The buildings were sold in 1922[74] and in 1970 were held with Rookery farm and Charlton Mackrell Court by Mr. I. L. Phillips.[75] Included with the estate in 1588 was a building called the Chantry House,[76] which can possibly be identified with a two-storeyed lias cottage, set back from the south side of Somerton Road. Its eastern half, which has a large chimney and the remains of a smoke chamber at the gable-end, may date from the early 16th century. The ground floor formerly consisted of a single room with a panelled screen dividing it from a cross passage. Beyond the passage the west end of the cottage has been rebuilt as a separate dwelling. Against the south, or back, wall of the original room, and entered from it by a stone doorway with a four-centred head, is a staircase projection. The back wall also has a moulded stone-mullioned window of three slightly pointed lights. There is a similar four-light window in the front wall and, further west, a reset two-light window. The latter probably replaces the original front doorway of the screens-passage.

A farm-house and lands of 93 a. in the parish formed the principal estate held by Young's School

[47] Ibid.
[48] Ibid.; DD/DN, box 50, conveyance, 29 Oct. 1811.
[49] See above; sale cat. Kingweston estate, 1930, penes Mrs. J. Burden, Kingweston.
[50] S.R.O., DD/DN, box 54, abstract of title, c. 1810.
[51] Ibid.
[52] Ibid.; DD/DN, box 40, map of Charlton Mackrell manor, 1757.
[53] S.R.O., DD/DN, box 54, abstract of title, c. 1810.
[54] Ibid.
[55] S.R.O., CR 92.
[56] Sale cat. Kingweston estate, 1930, penes Mrs. J. Burden, Kingweston.
[57] S.R.O., Q/RE; Q/REr.
[58] S.R.O., Q/REr.
[59] S.R.O., DD/DN, box 7, letter, 28 Mar. 1903.
[60] Ibid. box 6, letter, 16 June 1905; D/P/cha. ma. 4/1/1.
[61] Cal. Pat. 1340–3, 476; Cal. Close, 1377–81, 271–2; see below, p. 109.

[62] C 260/107/35.
[63] S.R.S. ii. 113, 297.
[64] Ibid.
[65] Cal. Pat. 1548–9, 41.
[66] S.R.O., DD/MI, box 5, quitclaim, 28 Oct. 1553.
[67] Ibid.; Cal. Pat. 1553–4, 191.
[68] S.R.O., DD/MI, box 5, general livery, 17 Apr. 1583; deed to lead uses of fine, 31 Mar. 1588; C142/159/51.
[69] S.R.O., DD/MI, box 5, covenant and valor, 16 Nov. 1582.
[70] Ibid. lease, 3 May 1656; bond, 20 Oct. 1664; final concord, 1664.
[71] S.R.O., DD/X/WN, abstract of title, c. 1807; Burke, Peerage (1949), 1384.
[72] S.R.O., DD/X/WN, draft conveyance, 19 Mar. 1807.
[73] S.R.O., DD/DN, box 59, conveyance, 8 Apr. 1807.
[74] S.R.O., DD/X/PHL, sale cat. 1922.
[75] Ex inf. Mr. I. L. Phillips.
[76] S.R.O., DD/MI, box 5, deed to lead uses of fine, 31 Mar. 1588.

in Trent (Dors.) evidently purchased by the trustees between 1678 and 1705 from Thomas Hodges.[77] The inclosure award of 1810 reduced the acreage to 76 a., and the farm was exchanged for lands in Trent with Edward Newman in 1846.[78] Newman sold the property to William Dickinson in the same year.[79] The farm-house, dated 1791, is now known as Georgian Cottage.

ECONOMIC HISTORY. In 1086 Charlton Mackrell manor was assessed at 3 hides; there was land for 6 ploughs, although only 4 were mentioned. A ½ hide was held in demesne by Roger Arundel with 1 plough, and there were 3 villeins, 9 bordars, and 4 serfs who worked the remaining 2½ hides with 3 ploughs. There were 30 a. of meadow and 2 a. of wood, and stock comprised only 1 packhorse, 14 swine, and 15 sheep. At the same date Cary Fitzpaine was wholly held in demesne by Robert under Roger Arundel. It gelded for 1 hide less 1 ferling, worked by 1 plough, and was evidently farmed as a single unit. There were 4 cottars there, 20 a. of meadow, 10 beasts, and 9 swine. Of the two other Cary manors, the larger, possibly Lytes Cary, was assessed at 2 hides and there was land for 3 ploughs. The demesne comprised 1 hide and 1 virgate, and 24 a. of meadow, with 2 ploughs, and the remaining land was farmed by 3 villeins and 3 bordars with 1 plough. The smaller Cary manor, possibly Tuckers Cary, gelded for 1 hide and 1 ferling, with 1 ploughland. Like Cary Fitzpaine it was all held in demesne, with 1 bordar and 2 cottars holding 7 a. of land. There were 20 a. of meadow, 12 beasts, and 100 sheep.[80]

In 1327 the demesne lands of Charlton Mackrell manor comprised a capital messuage, 60 a. of land, and 12 a. of meadow.[81] Ralph Horsey granted 85 a. of land and 12 a. of meadow to found a chantry in 1342,[82] but this property was evidently not part of the demesne. His remaining lands, constituting half of the manor, then totalled 244 a. of land and 41 a. of meadow.[83] In the early 17th century the demesne lands contained 56 a. and were leased on lives in separate moieties to Hugh Ball and John Fawkner.[84] The property was physically subdivided between these men, for in 1615 Ball claimed that Fawkner had neglected his own moiety and entered upon Ball's lands.[85] By 1757 the farm had been extended to include 162 a. of the manor,[86] and by 1800 the whole manor, comprising 344 a., had been combined to form a single farm.[87]

The manor of Cary Fitzpaine was initially culti-vated as a demesne farm. In 1733 most of the lands within the manor which lay north-west of the Foss Way were conveyed to Thomas Lockyer,[88] and were probably united with Charlton Mackrell manor. The manor-house was leased out on lives by the mid 16th century[89] and in 1616 was held with lands of 252 a.[90] Lytes Cary and Tuckers Cary both appear to have been cultivated as single farms, and no significant expansion or diminution of their lands has been traced.

No comprehensive figures are available for medieval land use within the parish; nor does the inclosure award supply details of cultivation. In the 17th and 18th centuries the impression is given of a preponderance of arable land in the area of Charlton Mackrell manor, and of grassland in the three Cary manors. In 1690 Lytes Cary and Tuckers Cary together contained 126 a. of arable, 120 a. of meadow, and 248 a. of pasture,[91] and in 1757 Cary Fitzpaine comprised 93 a. of arable, 108 a. of meadow, and 163 a. of pasture.[92] After the inclosure of 1810 much of the arable land was evidently con-verted to meadow or pasture, and by 1905 exactly ⅔ of the total acreage in Charlton Mackrell and Charlton Adam parishes was permanent grassland.[93] When 696 a. of the Dickinson estate were sold in 1930 only 116 a. were then arable land.[94] This trend has continued to the present.

The income from Charlton Mackrell manor fell from £6 in 1066 to £5 in 1086,[95] and this had risen only to 102s. by 1327.[96] Subsequent figures relate to a moiety of the manor: £2 9s. 11d. in 1330,[97] £10 in 1490,[98] £39 12s. 11d. in 1670,[99] and £58 12s. in 1680.[1] The total rental of the moiety, which stood at £4 12s. 11d. in 1626,[2] continued at about the same level, falling slightly to £4 12s. 3d. in 1670.[3] Cary Fitzpaine's Domesday value was £1, the same figure as in 1066.[4] It was valued at £5 in 1490,[5] but no estimate is available thereafter. The total rental in 1616 was £10 7s. 2½d., and in 1626 £10 6s. 10½d.[6] The larger of the two Cary manors mentioned in Domesday, possibly Lytes Cary, had increased in value from £1 to £2 between 1066 and 1086, and the smaller, possibly Tuckers Cary, from 30s. to 40s.[7] A moiety of Tuckers Cary manor was valued at £5 in 1508,[8] but no other estimates for the two manors have been found.

In Charlton Mackrell manor in 1327 there were two free tenants paying £1, four *nativi* paying 32s. and holding a fardel of land each, and six cottars paying 6s.[9] Customary labour was then valued at 5s. but no subsequent reference to such service has been found.[10] In 1626 the manor comprised 232 a.

[77] *11th Rep. Com. Char.* H.C. 433, pp. 430–2 (1824), xiv; D.R.O., D 78/2.
[78] S.R.O., CR 92; DD/DN, box 50, conveyance, 24 June 1846.
[79] S.R.O., DD/DN, box 50, conveyance, 24 June 1846.
[80] *V.C.H. Som.* i. 495, 519–20.
[81] C 135/3/6.
[82] *Cal. Inq. p.m.* x, p. 160.
[83] Ibid.
[84] S.R.O., DD/DN, box 39, survey, 1626; rental, n.d.; *S.R.S.* xxiii. 142–3.
[85] *S.R.S.* xxiii. 142–3.
[86] S.R.O., DD/DN, box 40, map of manor, 1757.
[87] Ibid. box 18, sale cat. 1800.
[88] S.R.O., DD/CC 102417.
[89] C 3/39/73; C 3/63/67; C 3/139/86.
[90] S.R.O., DD/DN, box 39, survey, 1616.
[91] Ibid. box 52, conveyance, 23 Dec. 1690.

[92] S.R.O., DD/CC 102434.
[93] Statistics supplied by the then Bd. of Agric. (1905).
[94] Sale cat. Kingweston, estate, 1930, *penes* Mrs. J. Burden, Kingweston.
[95] *V.C.H. Som.* i. 495.
[96] C 135/3/6.
[97] C 135/50/21.
[98] *Cal. Inq. p.m. Hen. VII,* i, pp. 228–9.
[99] S.R.O., DD/DN, box 39, rental, 1670.
[1] Ibid. rental, 1680.
[2] Ibid. survey, 1626.
[3] Ibid. rental, 1670.
[4] *V.C.H. Som.* i. 495.
[5] *Cal. Inq. p.m. Hen. VII,* i, pp. 228–9.
[6] S.R.O., DD/DN, box 39, surveys, 1616, 1626.
[7] *V.C.H. Som.* i. 519–20.
[8] *Cal. Inq. p.m. Hen. VII,* iii, p. 336.
[9] C 135/3/6.
[10] Ibid

of land, of which 146 a. were held by four copyhold tenants, 29 a. were overland held under lease by six tenants, and there were four cottagers holding by copy.[11] At the same date Cary Fitzpaine manor contained 728 a. of land, of which 686 a. were held by nine tenants in holdings varying in size from 91 a. to 28 a., and one cottager.[12] There were also free-holders of both manors, six owing suit of court to Cary Fitzpaine in 1613.[13]

Both of these two manors had similar customs, probably by virtue of their common descent. All tenements paid heriots, were held on 1, 2, 3, or 4 lives, and widows estate was recognized in respect of copyholds not composed of overland.[14] Tenants were forbidden to lease their pasture to outdwellers if any tenant or parishioner was willing to pay an equal price.[15] By the late 17th and early 18th century those tenements in the two manors which had not been enfranchised were generally held on leases for 99 years or 2 or 3 lives.[16]

In 1613 the rectorial manor comprised 130 a., let in 9 tenements.[17] The fact that three of these had an area of about 21½ a. each,[18] and that in 1670 the manor was stated to comprise 6 tenements,[19] suggests that the holding was originally leased to 6 tenants each farming 21½ a. In 1724 tenements were leased for a single life, tenants paying heriots and entry fines, and admission and surrender were performed by delivery of a 'mote' or pen.[20] All tenants owed one day's labour to the rector at harvest-time, and had common rights in Summerleaze and 'Powditch'.[21] During the 18th century as customary tenants died their holdings were granted to members of the families of successive rectors, and by 1794 98 a. had been repossessed in this manner.[22] Further tenements were enfranchised in 1802 and 1810 to extend the gardens of Charlton House.[23]

In the early 13th century there were two common arable fields, East and West; and there was common meadow at Willmoors.[24] By c. 1564–6 a four-field system had emerged, based on North, South, East, and West fields.[25] Piecemeal inclosure had already begun, and by 1690 East field had been almost completely inclosed, and the parish reduced to a three-field system.[26] In 1637 Thomas Strangways was presented for pasturing sheep in the South field when he had already inclosed the lands there to which he was entitled.[27] Field-name evidence indicates that Cary Fitzpaine may have possessed a three-field system and Cary North field remained in

strips as late as 1758, but early inclosure and common descent with Charlton Mackrell manor led to the tenure of arable holdings in the common fields of the latter.[28] The manors of Lytes Cary and Tuckers Cary never appear to have developed open-field systems of their own and also possessed small holdings in the fields of Charlton Mackrell manor.[29] Common pasture in Summerleaze was held by the tenants of Charlton Mackrell manor and the rectory manor in the form of beast leazes belonging to each tenement.[30] Most of the remaining common meadow and pasture was inclosed by the early 17th century.[31] The inclosure of both Charlton Mackrell and Charlton Adam parishes, together with the conversion of tithes into corn-rents, was first proposed in 1802, in consequence of a tithe dispute between the rector and landowners of Charlton Mackrell.[32] At inclosure there were 28 common fields in the two parishes, varying in size from 93 a. to 3 a. They totalled 447 a., about 100 a. of which were detached areas of Charlton Adam parish lying in Charlton Mackrell.[33] The parishes were inclosed simultaneously because their common boundary was very complicated. For the same reason it took 8 years to complete the process of allotment.[34]

At the time of the 1810 inclosure about half the parish, 1,090 a., was owned by William Dickinson, and included the manors of Charlton Mackrell, Lytes Cary, and Tuckers Cary, leased to three farmers.[35] By c. 1835 the Dickinson lands had been reorganized to form more viable farming units.[36] The principal improvement was the creation of a new farm in the former open fields at Wellham to which were allotted 106 a. from Charlton Mackrell manor, of which 45 a. lay in Charlton Adam.[37] Lytes Cary farm contained 336 a. and Cooks (formerly Tuckers) Cary farm 176 a. (of which about 20 a. lay in Charlton Adam).[38] The rest of the lands which formed Charlton Mackrell manor farm (later Rookery farm) had been combined with the farm formerly held by the Mildmays and acquired in 1807 to form a new farm of 228 a.[39] A farm of 116 a. adjoining the church, purchased from Thomas Bryan in 1805, was increased in size to 151 a., of which 32 a. lay in Charlton Adam.[40] With the exception of the last these holdings were still dairy farms in 1970. The only other large property in 1810 was Cary Fitzpaine, comprising 526 a., of which 67 a. lay in Charlton Adam.[41] During the 18th century the estate had included four small farms,[42] but

[11] S.R.O., DD/DN, box 39, survey, 1626.
[12] Ibid.
[13] Ibid. ct. roll, 15 Dec. 1613.
[14] Ibid. survey, 1626.
[15] Ibid. ct. roll, Cary Fitzpaine, 7 Sept. 1626.
[16] Ibid. box 40, leases 1690–1799.
[17] S.R.O., D/P/cha. ma. 3/1/1.
[18] Ibid.
[19] S.R.O., DD/DN, box 39, survey, 17 Jan. 1669/70.
[20] S.R.O., D/P/cha. ma. 3/1/1.
[21] Ibid.   [22] Ibid. 3/1/1–2.
[23] S.R.O., DD/DN, box 54, conveyances, 21 July 1802, 6 Mar. 1810.
[24] Devon R.O. 123 M/TB 125.
[25] Ibid. E 31.
[26] S.R.O., DD/DN, box 52, conveyance, 23 Dec. 1690; D.R.O., D 78/2.
[27] S.R.O., DD/DN, box 39, ct. roll, Charlton Mackrell, 20 Sept. 1637.
[28] S.R.O., CR 92; DD/CC 102434, 102436. West field, Cary field, and Little Cary field are mentioned.

[29] S.R.O., DD/DN, box 52, conveyance, 23 Dec. 1690.
[30] Ibid. box 39, ct. roll, Charlton Mackrell, 28 Aug. 1628; D/P/cha. ma. 3/1/1.
[31] S.R.O., DD/DN, box 39, surveys, 1626.
[32] Ibid. box 18, survey uninclosed lands, 1802; agreement, 2 May 1803.
[33] S.R.O., CR 92.
[34] S.R.O., DD/DN, box 39, letter, G. Tuson to W. Dickinson, 12 Apr. 1810.
[35] S.R.O., CR 92; DD/DN, box 18, particular of Mrs. Smith's farm, 1800.
[36] S.R.O., DD/DN, box 38, particular of Dickinson estate, c. 1835.
[37] Ibid.
[38] Ibid.
[39] Ibid.; see above, p. 103.
[40] S.R.O., DD/DN, box 18, estimate of Thomas Bryan's lands, 1805; box 38, particular of Dickinson estate c. 1835.
[41] S.R.O., CR 92.
[42] S.R.O., DD/CC 102417.

by 1842 and until 1885 the lands were held by two tenants.[43] Since 1885 it has been farmed as a single unit.[44] The glebe with the rectory manor had measured 153 a. in 1810,[45] 145 a. in c. 1840,[46] and 171 a. when sold in 1922.[47] The Charlton House estate and the farm held by Trent school trustees, together totalling 140 a. in 1810 (of which 23 a. lay in Charlton Adam), were acquired by the Dickinsons in 1811 and 1846 respectively.[48] The small farm held by the York family in 1810, comprising 76 a. (of which 14 a. lay in Charlton Adam),[49] was still owned by them c. 1840.[50] It was later purchased by the Dickinsons and the farm-house leased as a cottage holding.[51]

Few parishioners followed non-agrarian pursuits. Lias building stone was evidently quarried in the Charltons from Roman times,[52] but most of this activity was confined to Charlton Adam. In the 19th century quarries in Charlton Mackrell were sited near Tuckers Batch and south of Tout, and masons, stonecutters, and allied craftsmen occur regularly in the parish registers from 1814.[53] The common arable field called Sandpits in the extreme north of the parish probably indicates the site of earlier excavations.[54] A poultry packing station existed by 1930, and a haulage business based on Cooks Cary farm was established in 1931.[55]

MILLS. A water-mill was held in moieties with the manor of Charlton Mackrell in 1294.[56] Two millers in Charlton tithing were presented for taking excessive tolls at their mills in 1392, one of which, owned by John FitzPayn, probably lay in Charlton Mackrell.[57] Walter the miller of Charlton was presented for a similar offence in 1393,[58] as were John Donfoll and Edmund Rose, millers, in 1436 and 1437,[59] and John Larder and Richard Ball in 1452 and 1456.[60] The last probably occupied the mill known as Chalkbrook mill, evidently held by Edward Ball in 1573 and 1574,[61] and by Hugh Ball in 1619.[62] In 1613 the joint tenants of Charlton Mackrell manor-house and lands were ordered to repair the water-mill,[63] and a Charlton Mackrell miller was mentioned in 1621.[64] Between 1680 and 1687 'Chalbrooks' mill was occupied by Richard Bartlett,[65] and in 1717 by Thomas Bartlett, when a moiety of the mills, described as a water grist mill, was conveyed with a moiety of the manor.[66] By 1738 it had been acquired by James Samson,[67] lord of Cary Fitzpaine manor and of a moiety of

Charlton Mackrell manor. It descended with the manor of Cary Fitzpaine until 1783, when it was evidently purchased by the occupier, Thomas Bryan.[68] He sold it to Thomas Harris c. 1795, and it continued to be held with Cary Fitzpaine until at least 1832.[69] It is doubtful whether the mill was still being worked at this date, since no buildings are shown on the inclosure map of 1810.[70]

A windmill on the summit of the present Windmill hill is first mentioned in 1616, when it was conveyed with other lands held by Andrew and Mabel Walton to trustees.[71] It may, however, be one of two mills settled by William Brytte on his daughter and son-in-law in 1476.[72] In 1626 it was described as 'Mr. Thomas Baskett's windmill', Baskett having died in 1592,[73] and the mill evidently descended with the Manor farm estate in Charlton Adam from Baskett to the Strangways family.[74] It still existed in 1757,[75] but had been demolished by 1810.[76]

LOCAL GOVERNMENT. Charlton Mackrell and Charlton Adam were always regarded as a single tithing within Somerton hundred, but Cary Fitzpaine was considered to be a tithing of Whitley hundred in 1327,[77] and owed suit of court there as late as 1821.[78] Lytes Cary and Tuckers Cary both formed part of Kingsdon tithing.[79]

There is a 1480 court roll for Cary Fitzpaine manor.[80] Draft manor court rolls survive for the Henley moieties of Charlton Mackrell and Cary Fitzpaine: in respect of the former for the years 1613–14, 1626–38, and 1653–75, and for the latter, 1610–14, 1626–39, 1653–96, and 1719, although in 1633, 1660, and 1664 joint courts were held for both moieties of the two manors.[81] The court met at varying dates once or twice a year for each manor, and was generally described as curia baronis, but occasionally as curia manerii or simply as curia.[82] The breach of the fields was made at the court from 1637, by agreement between Thomas Lyte and Thomas Strangways for the freeholders, the rector for himself and the tenants of the rectory manor, and John Fawkner and Henry Creech for the tenants of Charlton Mackrell and Cary Fitzpaine manors respectively.[83] The same bailiff appears to have served for the moieties of both manors for the period for which court rolls survive. A hayward was appointed for Charlton Mackrell in 1613 and 1653,

[43] Ibid. 102500–3; ex inf. the Church Commissioners.
[44] Ex inf. the Church Commissioners.
[45] S.R.O., CR 92.
[46] S.R.O., D/P/cha. ma. 3/2/1.
[47] S.R.O., DD/X/DST, sale cat. rectory, 1922.
[48] S.R.O., CR 92, see above, pp. 103, 104.
[49] S.R.O., CR 92.
[50] S.R.O., D/P/cha. ma. 3/2/1.
[51] S.R.O., DD/X/PHL, sale cat. 1922.
[52] See p. 82.
[53] S.R.O., D/P/cha. ma. 2/1/7.
[54] S.R.O., CR 92.
[55] Kelly's Dir. Som. (1930, 1931).
[56] E 149/2/4.
[57] Hunt. Libr., HA Manorial, hundred ct. roll, 1392–3.
[58] Ibid.
[59] S.C. 2/200/33.
[60] S.C. 2/200/34.
[61] Hunt. Libr., HA Manorial, hundred ct. roll, 1573–4.
[62] D.R.O., D 124, Somerton hundred ct. bk. 1617–20.
[63] S.R.O., DD/DN, box 39, ct. roll, Charlton Mackrell.

[64] S.R.S. xxiii. 289.
[65] S.R.O., DD/DN, box 39, rentals, 1680, 1687.
[66] Ibid. box 52, conveyance, 29 Mar. 1717.
[67] S.R.O., D/P/cha. ma. 4/1/1.
[68] S.R.O., Q/RE; see above, p. 99.
[69] S.R.O., Q/RE.
[70] S.R.O., CR 92.
[71] C.P. 25(2)/346/14 Jas. I Mich.
[72] C.P. 25(1)/202/16 Edw. IV East.
[73] S.R.O., DD/DN, box 39, survey, 1626; M.I. in Charlton Adam church.
[74] See p. 86.
[75] S.R.O., DD/DN, box 40, map, 1757.
[76] S.R.O., CR 92.
[77] S.R.S. iii. 124.
[78] S.R.O., DD/S/BT, box 1, estreat roll, 1763–1821.
[79] S.R.O., D 124, Somerton hundred ct. bk. 1617–20; S.R.O., Q/RE.
[80] Alnwick Castle, Northumberland MSS. X II 12 3b.
[81] S.R.O., DD/DN, box 39, composite draft ct. rolls.
[82] Ibid.   [83] Ibid.

and another for Cary Fitzpaine in 1628 and 1635. A keeper of the fields was elected for Cary Fitzpaine manor in 1664.[84]

Court rolls for the rectory manor of Charlton Mackrell survive for 1672[85] and 1724–1854.[86] Courts were held at very irregular intervals, presided over by the steward or his deputy, and described throughout as 'court baron'. Business conducted by the court almost wholly comprised admissions and surrenders, with isolated orders to repair tenements. A hayward was appointed in 1808 and 1834.[87] There is nothing to show that courts were ever held for the manors of Lytes Cary or Tuckers Cary.

By the 19th century the vestry appointed one or two parish surgeons (1819–34), two churchwardens (1825–97), two overseers (1837–94), one or two waywardens (1837–94), two or more constables (1842–72), and a hayward (1864).[88] The vestry subsidized the emigration of poor families to New Zealand in 1841 and to Canada in 1842 and 1848.[89]

A poorhouse is mentioned in 1789, and was built probably at about that date.[90] Surviving plans show a long two-storey building divided vertically into four units, each with a separate entrance, comprising ground-floor room and bedroom above.[91] The house was sold to Francis Henry Dickinson in 1838[92] and subsequently demolished.[93] The parish became part of the Langport union in 1836.[94]

CHURCH. The church of Charlton Mackrell is first mentioned in 1217.[95] A vicarage then existed, charged with an annual payment of 50s. to a rector instituted in that year.[96] No further reference to a vicar has been found, and from 1248 the benefice was always a rectory.[97] The benefices of Charlton Mackrell and Charlton Adam were united in 1921.[98]

The advowson descended initially with that moiety of Charlton Mackrell manor held by the FitzPayn family. Robert FitzPayn (I) presented Robert de Meisy as vicar between 1198 and 1217, and was described in 1329 as the first to exercise patronage.[99] The right of alternate presentation was conveyed by Roger FitzPayn to Margery Belet, owner of the second moiety of the manor, in 1224,[1] and subsequently passed with that moiety to the Horsey family. A dispute in 1329 between Sir Robert FitzPayn (IV) and John Horsey (III) as to which of them held the next presentation was

resolved in favour of FitzPayn.[2] In 1426 John Tretheke presented as second husband of Joan, widow of William Horsey (III),[3] and in 1472 and 1477 the feoffees of Thomas Horsey (d. 1468) held the advowson.[4] The moieties were reunited in the person of Sir John Horsey in 1540.[5] In 1567 John Sprynt presented, and in 1571 Henry Bayly, both by grant of the Horsey family.[6] The advowson, like the manor, was again divided after 1589 between the coheirs of Sir John Horsey.[7]

In 1609 William Lockett presented his son Giles, on behalf of Reginald Mohun,[8] and Giles's brother the Revd. William Lockett, with Robert and John Whetcombe, presented Simon Whetcombe in 1646, the latter having married Constance Lockett in 1644.[9] This moiety had reverted to Henry Henley by 1684,[10] who reserved his right to the advowson when he sold his moiety of the manor in 1717.[11] Henry presented William Dodd (rector 1718–60) in the following year.[12]

The second moiety was held by Hubert Arnold in 1670,[13] and the next presentation was granted to William Raven, whose executor presented Richard Carter (rector 1686–1718).[14] Carter purchased this moiety from the earl of Radnor in 1704,[15] and it was acquired from his family by his successor, William Dodd, in 1731.[16] Dodd was reinstituted in that year, although the patron was again described as Henry Henley.[17]

Dodd apparently acquired the Henley moiety, and was sole patron at his death in 1790.[18] The advowson then passed to his eldest daughter Jane and her husband, Edward Cheselden (rector 1760–80) of Somerby (Leics.), and Cheselden himself was instituted at their joint presentation.[19] Their daughter Wilhelmina Jane Cheselden was patroness in 1780.[20] Lydia Munday of Andover (Hants) acquired it from her, and presented her future husband Richard Ford in 1783.[21] At his death in 1817 Ford left the patronage to his sister-in-law Harriet Munday, who evidently sold it to Alexander Brymer of Bathwick, patron in 1818 and 1821.[22] He was succeeded by his son John Brymer, who held the patronage between 1861 and 1875.[23] His trustees held it between 1883 and 1906.[24] John George Brymer, rector of Ilsington (Devon), was patron between 1914 and 1919,[25] but on the union of the benefice with Charlton Adam in 1921 it was agreed that the Brymer family should have

84 Ibid.
85 S.R.O., DD/MC N/71.
86 S.R.O., D/P/cha. ma. 3/1/1, 2.
87 Ibid.
88 S.R.O., D/P/cha. ma. 9/1/1, 2.
89 Ibid. 9/1/2.   90 Ibid. 13/4/1.
91 Ibid. Plans and estimate are undated.
92 S.R.O., DD/DN, box 45, conveyance, 11 Dec. 1838; D/PS/ilm. box 16, order for sale, 1837.
93 O.S. Map 6″, Som. LXXIII. NE. (1888 edn.).
94 Poor Law Com. 2nd Rep. p. 548.
95 S.R.O., DD/CC 110025, 34/44; H.M.C. Wells, i. 404.
96 S.R.O., DD/CC 110025, 34/44; H.M.C. Wells, i. 404.
97 Cal. Papal Regs. i. 248.
98 Lond. Gaz. 14 Oct. 1921, p. 8076.
99 See p. 97; S.R.O., DD/CC 110025, 34/44; C.P. 40/277 rot. 43.
1 S.R.S. vi. 362.
2 C.P. 40/377 rot. 43; S.R.S. ix. 50–1.
3 S.R.S. xxxi. 34; see above, p. 98.
4 S.R.S. lii. 72, 94.
5 L. & P. Hen. VIII, xv, p. 103.

6 Som. Incumbents, ed. Weaver, 50.
7 See p. 98.
8 Som. Incumbents, 50; S. & D. N. & Q. ix. 63.
9 Som. Incumbents, 50; S. & D. N. & Q. ix. 63; S.R.O., D/P/cha. ma. 2/1/1.
10 Som. Incumbents, 50.
11 S.R.O., DD/DN, box 52, conveyance, 29 Mar. 1717.
12 Som. Incumbents, 50.
13 Ibid.
14 Ibid.
15 S.R.O., DD/YB, box 3, conveyance, 12 Aug. 1704.
16 C.P. 25(2)/1194/4 & 5 Geo. II Trin.
17 Som. Incumbents, 50.
18 M.I. in church.
19 Wells Dioc. Registry, Reg. Willes, i. 70.
20 Wells Dioc. Registry, Reg. Moss, 42.
21 Ibid. 60.
22 Copy will of Richard Ford, proved 1818, penes Mr. C. F. Hamilton, Wells; Wells Dioc. Registry, Reg. Beadon, 131, 181.
23 P.O. Dir. Som. (1861–75).
24 Kelly's Dir. Som. (1883–1906).
25 Ibid. (1914, 1919).

two presentations and the Bath and Wells Diocesan Trustees one.[26] The last presentation made by the Brymers was in 1950. Since that time the Diocesan Board of Patronage has been sole patron.[27]

The rectory was valued at £16 13s. 4d. in 1291,[28] at '£20 to bide on and 20 marks to let out' in 1521,[29] and £16 0s. 1½d. in 1535.[30] By c. 1668 the common reputed value was £80,[31] although the true figure was probably nearer that of £120 supplied by a survey of 1670.[32] By 1831 the income had risen to £499 net, a figure which remained steady until at least 1875.[33]

Small tithes, oblations, and obventions produced £5 8s. 8d. in 1334.[34] Predial tithes and tithes of wool were valued at £9 13s. 4d. in 1535, oblations and personal tithes being worth £4 11s. in that year.[35] In 1613 the rector took all tithes in kind, receiving 2d. an acre for the first share of 'stock' meadow.[36] A series of law suits brought by the rector for non-payment resulted in an agreement in 1803 to give him not less than £300 in corn rents, though the allotment of 1810 was only £280 12s. 0¾d.[37] The income from corn rents fell to £264 in 1874, and to £160 in 1902.[38]

In 1334 the rector held a close, 4 bovates of land, and 5 a. of meadow which, with rents and perquisites, were valued at £4 4s. 8d.[39] The demesne lands were worth 40s. in 1535 and perquisites of court from the rectory manor produced a further 6s. 8d.[40] The glebe lands in 1613, including the rectory manor, comprised 129 a. of arable in the common fields, 26½ a. of meadow, and 24 a. of pasture, with common in Summerleaze, the manor producing an annual rental of 51s. 10d.[41] In 1810 the total glebe comprised 154 a.,[42] was reduced by 6 a. in 1823,[43] and stood at 145 a. by c. 1840.[44] The rectory manor was last mentioned in 1858.[45] In 1919 there were 130 a. of glebe, in 1923 50 a., and between 1931 and 1939 37 a.[46] There was no glebe in 1972.[47]

The rectory house is first mentioned in 1521, when it was stated that John Walgrave (rector 1504–c. 1541) had 'builded a fair mansion place out of the ground of stone and slated, very well finished and glazed, with goodly orchards about it, walled close round about'.[48] Richard Ford (rector 1783–1817) found the house 'very ruinous' and had it 'completely repaired'.[49] This repair evidently involved much reconstruction and may probably be ascribed to c. 1792.[50] The house was sold in 1922

after the union of the benefice with Charlton Adam, and has since been known as Charlton Mackrell Court.[51] It is a large, three-storeyed house, retaining in part the thick walls and basically medieval plan of the early-16th-century building. In 1922 it appears to have consisted of a two-storeyed range, one room deep, from which the screens-passage, hall, and parlour have survived along the present south front. At the east end of the house a single-light stone window in a deep reveal, part of the original parlour, was opened up in the 1960s.[52] There is evidence that extensions had been made at the rear before Richard Ford's major alterations of c. 1792. Ford rebuilt the south front of the house as a nearly symmetrical three-storeyed elevation, giving it an embattled parapet, sash windows with Gothic glazing bars, and a double centred porch with Tudor arches. Because of the off-centre position of the original screens-passage entrance, he was forced, in the interests of symmetry, to include one of the hall windows beneath the porch. The Gothic taste of the period is again evident in the delicate three-bay screen across the entrance hall and in the cast-iron balustrade of the curved staircase behind it.[53] Alterations were made at the west or service end of the house by Mr. I. L. Phillips in the mid 20th century.

The high value of the rectory led to its tenure by a succession of distinguished men, a number of the earlier ones holding in plurality. In 1248 William de Warneford was authorized to hold the church with two other benefices,[54] and William of Charlton, rector in 1297, was succentor and later canon of Wells.[55] William Bykenell (rector 1426–44) held four canonries while at Charlton, and enjoyed other smaller livings at the same time.[56] His successor, John Perch (rector 1444–6), was a fellow of Magdalene Hall, Oxford, and while rector was canon and chancellor in South Malling college (Suss.).[57] Thomas Markham (rector 1451–72) was granted leave to hold a second benefice in 1457,[58] and John Joy (rector 1473–7) was prior of Boxgrove (Suss.).[59] William Horsey (rector 1499–1502) was principal of Peckwater Inn, Oxford, and held other livings in Somerset and Dorset while at Charlton.[60] In 1554 William Squire was deprived as he 'was married and doth not minister'.[61] Since 1609 all incumbents have held degrees, with the exception of Thomas Jarvis (rector c. 1657–70) who left Oxford without one.[62] W. T. P. Brymer (rector 1821–52) was

[26] Crockford.
[27] Ibid.
[28] Tax. Eccl. (Rec. Com.), 197.
[29] L. & P. Hen. VIII, Add i (1), pp. 90–1.
[30] Valor Eccl. (Rec. Com.), i. 198.
[31] S.R.O., D/D/Vc 24.
[32] S.R.O., DD/DN, box 39, survey, 17 Jan. 1669/70.
[33] Rep. Com. Eccl. Revenues, pp. 156–7; Crockford; P.O. Dir. Som. (1866–75).
[34] E 179/169/14.
[35] Valor Eccl. (Rec. Com.), i. 198.
[36] S.R.O., D/P/cha. ma. 3/1/1.
[37] S.R.O., DD/DN, box 18, agreement, 2 May 1803; CR 92.
[38] Crockford.
[39] E 179/169/14.
[40] Valor Eccl. (Rec. Com.), i. 198.
[41] S.R.O., D/P/cha. ma. 3/1/1.
[42] S.R.O., CR 92.
[43] S.R.O., D/D/Bg 30.
[44] S.R.O., D/P/cha. ma. 3/2/1.
[45] Ibid. 3/1/1–2.

[46] Kelly's Dir. Som. (1919–39).
[47] Ex inf. Dioc. Sec.
[48] S.P. 1/233 f. 44.
[49] S.R.O., D/D/V rtns. 1815.
[50] 'R.F. 1792' on outbuilding. The house is described as 'new' in 1800 (photostat, Sun Insurance policy, penes Mr. I. L. Phillips, Charlton Mackrell Court).
[51] Ex inf. Mr. C. F. Hamilton.
[52] Ex inf. Mr. I. L. Phillips.
[53] For views of interior and exterior see Country Life, 20 Jan. 1950.
[54] Cal. Papal Regs. i. 248; he may possibly be identified with William de Berdesle, presented to the rectory by Roger FitzPayn (C.P. 40/277 rot. 43).
[55] Cal. Pat. 1292–1301, 274; S.R.S. lix. 184.
[56] Emden, Biog. Reg. Univ. Oxford.   [57] Ibid.
[58] Cal. Papal Regs. xi. 154.
[59] S.R.S. lii. 48–9.
[60] Emden, Biog. Reg. Univ. Oxford.
[61] S.R.O., D/D/Ca 22; D/D/Vc 66 f. 16.
[62] Som. Incumbents, ed. Weaver, 50; Foster, Alumni Oxon.

archdeacon of Bath, and both his successors, A. O. Fitzgerald (rector 1853–76) and F. A. Brymer (rector 1877–1917), were archdeacons of Wells.[63]

In 1815 services were accustomed to be held once every Sunday, but as the rector held no other benefice at that time he gave his parishioners 'double service'.[64] The two services held on Census Sunday in 1851 were attended by 66 in the morning and 118 in the evening.[65] Holy Communion was celebrated monthly by 1870.[66]

A curate was mentioned in 1532[67] and another occurs during the years 1601–7.[68] Thereafter rectors were generally resident, but assistant curates are found regularly from the mid 18th century.[69]

In 1593 it was stated that there had been a church house in the parish from 'time immemorial', held by successive trustees for the benefit of the church.[70] In that year a Chancery suit was begun by the churchwardens to recover the building from Richard Arnold, lord of a moiety of Charlton Mackrell manor, to whom the house had been surrendered to discharge the personal debts of the surviving trustee.[71] The property was evidently recovered, for it was held by the parish in 1613,[72] although its site and subsequent history have not been traced.

Ralph Horsey received a licence in 1342 to alienate lands valued at 16s. a year to a chaplain to celebrate daily in the parish church for the souls of Ralph and his ancestors.[73] These were seized by the Crown in 1374 but restored seven years later,[74] and it is evident that a chantry had been founded in a chapel called 'Horsiesele', now the south transeptal chapel.[75] A chaplain was presented by the Crown in 1378, after the chantry had been seized,[76] but the first incumbent was restored to his position and lands in 1381.[77] The chantry was dissolved in 1548, but there were no ornaments nor plate, and the last incumbent, John Drewe the younger, received a pension.[78] The lands of the chantry, stated to be worth 26s. 8d. in 1535,[79] were granted in 1548 to Sir Thomas Bell and Richard Duke,[80] and their subsequent descent has already been traced.[81] After the Dissolution Horsey's aisle descended jointly with the manors of Cary Fitzpaine and Charlton Mackrell, for in 1639 responsibility for the repair of its windows was attributed to Henry Creech and John Fawkner, then occupiers of the two manor-houses.[82] Similarly in 1805 it was divided equally between William Dickinson and James Sutton as owners of the two manors.[83]

Roger Roundel granted 2 a. of land to the rector

in c. 1358 to ring the curfew every night and early in the morning, 8 a. of land to supply lights to burn in two cressets within the church on every double feast, and 10 a. of land and 2 a. of meadow to provide a lamp to burn daily before the high altar.[84] These lands were seized by the Crown in 1374 because they had been alienated without licence.[85] The brothers and sisters of the 'sepulture light' there occur in 1541,[86] and a further 8 a. of land and 1 a. of meadow, given to maintain seven lights 'called a beam light' in the church, are mentioned between 1568 and 1572.[87] A parcel of land in the parish, formerly given to provide a light in the church, was granted to John and William Mershe of London in 1574.[88]

The church of *ST. MARY THE VIRGIN* lies on the north side of the road from Somerton, near the summit of a small hill in the centre of the old parish. Claims that the church was originally dedicated to St. Martin cannot be substantiated.[89] The building comprises chancel, nave, north and south transepts, and central crossing tower. It underwent very considerable renovation between 1792 and 1794, when the roof was wholly replaced,[90] and again in c. 1847, when the porch, windows, and probably much of the fabric were reconstructed, and a vestry added on the north side of the chancel, replacing one on the south side. The church contains an early 13th-century font with a circular bowl and a 'water-holding' base, but the fabric itself dates from the 14th and 15th centuries. The oldest surviving work is at the crossing and in the north transept. The chancel is also 14th century in style but appears to have been largely rebuilt in 1847. The north transept has an original north window of c. 1330–40 containing five lights, the tracery consisting of reticulations and a large circle. This transept was originally held by the owners of Lytes Cary and known as Lytes aisle;[91] the north window formerly contained medieval glass depicting the Five Joys of Our Lady and the kneeling figures of William le Lyte and his wife. The latter's Purbeck marble tomb, now a shapeless mass in the churchyard, was formerly sited here, but this, the glass, and other monuments of the family were removed at the restorations.[92] The trussed-rafter roof of the north transept has unusual trefoil-headed arcading above the wall plates. A squint, combined with a piscina, is cut through into the reveal of a chancel window. There is a corresponding squint in the south transept. A tomb recess, now behind the

[63] M.I. in church; *Crockford*.
[64] S.R.O., D/D/V rtns. 1815.
[65] H.O. 129/317/1/8/18.
[66] S.R.O., D/D/V rtns. 1870.
[67] S.R.O., D/D/Vc 20.
[68] S.R.O., D/D/Rr 89; D/D/Vc 60.
[69] S.R.O., D/P/cha. ma. 2/1/3–7.
[70] C 3/235/2.   [71] Ibid.
[72] S.R.O., D/P/cha. ma. 3/1/1.
[73] *Cal. Pat.* 1340–3, 476; C 44/10/18; *Cal. Inq. p.m.* x. 160.
[74] C 260/107/35; *Cal. Close,* 1377–81, 271–2; *Cal. Fine R.* 1377–83, 275.
[75] C 260/107/35.
[76] *Cal. Pat.* 1377–81, 263.
[77] C 44/10/18; C 85/38/39.
[78] *S.R.S.* ii. pp. xx, 113, 297.
[79] *Valor Eccl.* (Rec. Com.), i. 198.
[80] *Cal. Pat.* 1548–9, 41.
[81] See p. 103.
[82] S.R.O., D/D/Ca 327.

[83] S.R.O., D/P/cha. ma. 4/1/1.
[84] C 260/107/35; *Cal. Inq. Misc.* iii, p. 386.
[85] C 260/107/35.
[86] S.R.O., DD/SAS SE/30 f. 34.
[87] E 310/23/127 f. 6; S.C. 6/Eliz. I/1970.
[88] C 66/1119 m. 12.
[89] Ecton, *Thesaurus Rerum Ecclesiasticarum* (1742); *Som. Incumbents*, ed. Weaver, 50. References to the present dedication occur from 1341: *Cal. Pat.* 1340–3, 476; *Procs. before J.P.s Edw. III and Ric. II*, ed. Putnam, 186.
[90] S.R.O., D/P/cha. ma. 4/1/1, 3; 8/2/1.
[91] The transept was excepted from the grant of Lytes Cary manor to Lockyer in 1755 (S.R.O., DD/CC 102433) and conveyed by John Lyte, then of Pilton, to Giles Strangways of Charlton Adam, reserving the right of burial there for himself and his children (DD/CC 102437). Giles's son, Thomas Littleton Strangways, sold it to Thomas Harris of Bristol, owner of Cary Fitzpaine, in 1789 (DD/CC 102464), and thereafter it descended with that manor: see above, p. 99.
[92] *Proc. Som. Arch. Soc.* xxxviii. 7–9.

organ, probably once held a Horsey effigy. The nave and embattled central tower may have been completed in the 15th century. The latter has two-light openings filled with Somerset tracery at the belfry stage and a south-west stair-turret crowned by a modern spirelet.

A singing gallery, mentioned from 1750,[93] was probably removed at the second restoration. A number of 16th-century bench ends survive, mostly straight-headed but some with poppy-heads. They include a representation of the Percy arms and a figure identified as Titivillus. The cover of the 13th-century font lies in the church-yard by the south wall of the church. Also in the churchyard, near the south porch, stands a 15th-century cross raised on three steps, the octagonal base bearing the symbols of the four Evangelists and having four square attached shafts. The cross was restored in 1800, and again in 1923 when the shaft and figures were added.[94]

The plate includes an Elizabethan cup and cover of 1570 given to the church in 1822.[95] There are six bells: (i) 1833, T. Mears of London; (ii) 1788, William Bilbie of Chewstoke; (iii) 1912, Taylor of Loughborough; (iv) 1665(?), 'T.C.'; (v) 1855, Taylor of Loughborough; (vi) 1833, Mears.[96] The registers are complete from 1575.[97]

NONCONFORMITY.
William Fawkner and Edith his wife, who had been presented for not attending service nor taking communion in 1623,[98] were again presented in 1626 as 'popish recusants' with William Nipp.[99] Edith Fawkner was presented in 1639 as a 'popish recusant' and for standing 'ex-communicated and aggravated'.[1]

The manor-house of James Samson at Cary Fitzpaine was licensed for Dissenting worship in 1697.[2] A house was registered for Quaker meetings in 1738,[3] and Charlton Mackrell inhabitants were among those petitioning for an Independent meeting-house at Charlton Adam in 1787.[4] The dwelling-house of Henry Thomas Woodward was licensed by the Baptists in 1816[5] but nonconformity seems to have been stronger in Charlton Adam, and most dissenters probably met in that parish.

EDUCATION.
In 1818 there were two Sunday schools in the parish, supported by voluntary contributions and attended by 41 pupils.[6] By 1826 the numbers had risen to 65, and it was stated that liberal provision had been made for schools by local landowners and the rector.[7] An infant and daily National school for 70 children was started in 1830, supported by subscriptions.[8] A single weekly payment of 1d. entitled a family to send any number of children to the school.[9] By 1846 the numbers had increased to 82 pupils, and the school comprised a single room and teacher's house.[10] The Sunday school was attended by 65 children in 1833[11] and was probably held in the same premises.

W. T. P. Brymer (d. 1852), rector, left £1,500 in trust to pay £30 a year to the master or mistress of the Sunday and day-school and the residue to the rector to defray the expenses of running the schools.[12] A new school building was erected in 1853 on land given by Francis Henry Dickinson, subsequently known as the West Charlton National School.[13] In 1868 the endowment produced £105, of which the schoolmaster received £90. The school was then educating children from outside the parish, including tradesmen's sons from Ilchester.[14] An evening school was also held during the winter.[15] Pupils were received from Charlton Adam Infants school when they reached the age of 7 or 8.[16] In 1894 the average attendance was 70,[17] and by 1903 there were 100 children on the books, of which 17 were infants.[18] It was then described as 'an excellent county school' where great attention was paid 'to personal cleanliness and to the neatness and arrange-ment of the schoolroom'.[19] The establishment be-came a junior school in 1940 and was attended by 62 children in 1969.[20]

CHARITIES FOR THE POOR.
In 1810 the parish owned lands, the income from which was applied by the overseers to the general relief of the poor.[21] In 1823 it was not known when, nor under what circumstances, the lands had been given.[22] Part was sold in 1838,[23] but the remainder con-tinued to be let until at least 1879.[24] No subsequent reference to the charity has been traced.

93 S.R.O., D/P/cha. ma. 4/1/1.
94 Ibid.
95 *Proc. Som. Arch. Soc.* xlv. 130–1.
96 S.R.O., DD/SAS CH/16.
97 S.R.O., D/P/cha. ma. 2/1/1–7.
98 S.R.O., D/D/Ca 236.
99 Ibid. 244.
1 Ibid. 327.
2 S.R.O., Q/RR, meeting-house lics.
3 S.R.O., D/D/Rm, vol. 1, p. 7.
4 Ibid. p. 63; see above, p. 94.
5 S.R.O., D/D/Rm, box 2.
6 *Digest of Returns to Sel. Cttee. on Educ. of Poor*, H.C. 224 (1819), ix.
7 *Ann. Rep. B. & W. Dioc. Assoc. S.P.C.K.* (1825–6).
8 *Educ. Enquiry Abstract*, H.C. 62 (1835), xliii.
9 Ibid.
10 *Church Sch. Inquiry, 1846–7.*
11 *Educ. Enquiry Abstract*, H.C. 62 (1835), xliii.
12 Plaque in ch.
13 S.R.O., D/P/cha. ma. 18/1/1, 18/7/1; C/E 26.
14 *Rep. Com. Children and Women in Agric.* [4202–I] H.C. p. 479 (1868–9), xiii.
15 Ibid.
16 S.R.O., D/P/cha. a. 18/1/1.
17 *Rtns. of Schs.* [C 7529] H.C. (1894), lxv.
18 S.R.O., C/E 26.
19 Ibid.
20 Som. C.C. Educ. Cttee., *Sch. List.*
21 S.R.O., CR 92; *11th Rep. Com. Char.* H.C. 433, p. 442 (1824), xiv.
22 *11th Rep. Com. Char.* H.C. 433, p. 442 (1824), xiv.
23 S.R.O., DD/DN, box 45, conveyance, 11 Dec. 1838.
24 S.R.O., D/P/cha. ma. 9/1/1–2.

KINGSDON

THE ancient parish of Kingsdon, sometimes known in the 16th and 17th centuries as Kingsdon Cary,[1] had an area given as 1,870 a. in 1841.[2] Evidently this total did not account for the inclosure of Southmead c. 1803, which amounted to 194 a. in the parish.[3] In 1885 parts of Kingsmoor and two small areas in the east of Somerton were added,[4] and the parish was estimated at 2,330 a. in 1901.[5] The parish lies 2½ miles south-east of Somerton and 2 miles north of Ilchester, being bounded by Charlton Mackrell on the north and east, Ilchester and Northover on the south, and Long Sutton and Somerton on the west and north-west. It is of irregular shape: 3½ miles from north to south, 1½ mile wide in the north, and 2 miles at its widest point in the south.

The soil is principally clay over lias with Rhaetic clay and Keuper Marl in the extreme north and estuarine alluvium along the banks of the river Cary to the east.[6] The highest point in the parish is 287 ft. in the north-west on Kingsdon hill, from which the parish probably takes its name. To the north and north-east to Kingsdon wood, and east to Nut hill and Hally hill, the ground slopes gradually downwards and then drops more sharply to the river Cary. The village, on the south-west side of Kingsdon hill, lies between the 175 ft. and 125 ft. contours. Further south the land falls away towards Southmead and apart from a slight rise at Bondip hill the south of the parish lies generally at about 50 ft. Apart from rivers bounding the parish, it is watered only by shallow rhines and ditches.

The eastern and northern boundary of the parish is formed by the river Cary and its tributary, Park brook; the extreme southern boundary beyond Southmead by the river Yeo. A stretch of the western boundary follows Lime Pit Lane, a medieval road.

The principal road through the parish runs from Somerton to Ilchester, entering Kingsdon in the north-west, crossing Kingsdon hill, passing west of the village to Red Post Cross, over Bondip hill, and out of the parish in the south. From Red Post Cross southwards the road formed part of the Ilchester turnpike from 1753.[7] The remainder was adopted by the Langport, Somerton, and Castle Cary turnpike trust from 1777–8.[8] The Langport–Wincanton road enters the parish in the west near Catsgore, runs south of the village to Red Post Cross and over the eastern boundary. The western section to Red Post Cross was turnpiked in 1792, the eastern in 1824, also by the Langport, Somerton, and Castle

Cary trust.[9] Turnpike gates formerly stood at the northern approach to Kingsdon hill and at Catsgore.[10] Kingsdon village now lies east of the Somerton–Ilchester road, although it seems likely that the main route once passed through the village. Wood Lane or Quarry Lane and Underwood Road, subsequently Nuthill Lane, both run north from the village to Kingsdon wood and Nut hill respectively, and Henley Road runs north-east from the village to Cary bridge and Lytes Cary. Mill Lane leaves the Somerton road on the north side of Kingsdon hill and runs south-east, crossing Wood Lane at the old quarry, meeting Henley Road at a point known as Halley or Holy Cross,[11] and continuing beyond as Park Lane, mentioned in 1608.[12]

The village is roughly triangular in shape, its western limit formed by High or Top Street, the northern by Pound Street at North Town, and the south-eastern by Bottom Street (Tarrs Lane in 1861)[13] and Manor Close. Middle Street runs south through the centre of the village to Chapel Street, the latter crossing from east to west and meeting High Street at Pie or Pike Corner. At its eastern end Chapel Street leaves the village and turns south, passing Langlands Farm to become Frog Lane.[14] Another lane south of Chapel Street links Manor Close and High Street. Originally Chapel Street ran along the southern edge of Bondip Farm but in the 19th century it was turned south to meet High Street near the church.[15] Similarly Frog Lane formerly continued south from Langlands Farm through the grounds of Kingsdon Manor to meet Lodge Road, but the lanes in this area were diverted in 1833 to avoid Kingsdon Manor and its gardens.[16]

In the earlier 19th century the whole parish was intersected by a maze of tracks and footpaths serving the common fields, particularly in the south and south-west,[17] but many of these have been closed.

Of the three open arable fields of the 16th century,[18] North field comprised most of the north and north-east of the parish, bounded on the south-west by the Somerton–Ilchester road, Mill Lane, and Park Lane, excluding most of Kingsdon wood and Huish in the extreme north and parts of Ruttle ('Ruttle Hyll' or 'Reddelhyll' in 1563)[19] and Groundhams ('Gromeham' or 'Gromonham' in 1563),[20] but including North Town furlong immediately north of the village, Nut Hill, Hally Hill ('Halowyll' in 1563, 'Hallow Hill' in 1598–9)[21] and Okey Land. West field was bounded on the north and north-east by the Somerton–Ilchester road and Mill

[1] S.R.O., DD/SAS (C/73), 9, conveyances, 10 Sept. 1542, 13 Aug. 1614; C 2/Eliz. I/H 1/39; C 2/Jas. I/P 9/5; see below, pp. 114–15. This article was completed in 1971.
[2] Census, 1841.
[3] S.R.O., CR 43.
[4] Local Govt. Bd. Prov. Orders Conf. Order (Poor Law), (No. 2), Act (1885), 48 & 49 Vict. c.5.
[5] Census, 1901.
[6] Geol. Surv. Map 1″ solid and drift, sheet 296 (1969 edn.).
[7] S.R.O., D/T/ilch.
[8] S.R.O., D/T/lsc.
[9] Ibid.
[10] S.R.O., tithe award.
[11] Ibid.

[12] Hook Manor, Donhead St. Andrew, Arundell MSS. MS. bk. 53, Aug. 1608.
[13] R.G. 9/1628.
[14] Ibid.
[15] S.R.O., tithe award; O.S. Map 1/2,500, Som. LXXIII.8 (1887 edn.).
[16] S.R.O., Q/SR, 470.
[17] S.R.O., DD/SAS (C/212), map and survey of Kingsdon, 1827; tithe award.
[18] Sources used to reconstruct the open field pattern include: D.R.O., D 54/M 8, 9; S.R.O., D/D/Rg 217; DD/SAS (C/73), 9; DD/BR/ar (C/1056); DD/S/ST 19/1; Arundell MSS. MS. bks. 47, 49, 51–6, 58, ct. bks. 14–20.
[19] D.R.O., D 54/M 8.   [20] Ibid.
[21] Ibid. M 8, 9.

Lane, on the east by Wood Lane, the village, Lodge Road, and the Somerton–Ilchester road again, to Red Post Cross, on the south by the Langport–Wincanton road, and on the west by the parish boundary. South or East field[22] cannot be precisely located but appears to have lain south-east of the village, bounded on the north and east by Park Lane and the parish boundary, stretching south of the Langport–Wincanton road to Wheatland.[23] Open pasture lay at Huish in the extreme north and generally in the south of the parish, including Witch, Dark Pits ('Derpitte' in 1508),[24] Nidens ('Nethon' in 1563, 'Neythen' in 1587),[25] Middle moors, Brinshill ('Brounshulle' in 1321),[26] Edmonds Hill ('Eadmoreshulle' in 1321),[27] Chinnocks Hill, Southmoor, and Bondip ('Bondelypp' in 1563).[28] Open and common meadow lay at Southmead ('Brodemeade' *alias* South mede' in 1563, 'of old called Pill meade' in 1617)[29] and Middle moors in the south of the parish, at Huish in the north, and in smaller plots elsewhere. There was also common pasture at 'Northmore', probably by the Cary beyond the north-western boundary, and common waste at the northern end of the village known as North Town in 1656[30] and as Kingsdon green in 1810.[31]

Kingsdon wood in the north of the parish was 60 a. in extent in 1353[32] but had shrunk to 40 a. by 1563.[33] It was this depletion which probably led to the regulation of tree felling there. In 1608 the tenant of the wood was ordered to fell a certain agreed quantity of timber in each year and the price at which this was to be sold had to be assessed by the other tenants.[34] In 1592 and 1639 occupiers of the wood were presented for cutting too much[35] and by the 18th century saplings were being planted to replace timber that had been felled.[36] The wood remained relatively stable in extent, comprising 38 a. in 1783,[37] and was let for shooting in 1971.[38]

The principal evidence for Roman settlement in the parish is provided by two villas recorded by Sir Richard Colt Hoare and probably discovered by Samuel Hasell in the 19th century,[39] the first supposed to lie west of the village and the Somerton–Ilchester road, and the second located in the north-east of the parish at Hally hill, near the banks of the river Cary.[40] Kingsdon village lies in the centre of the parish on the south-eastern slopes of Kingsdon hill, and remains the only area of settlement. Initial development probably took place along High Street,

subsequently spreading further downhill to the south-east. The earliest surviving domestic architecture dates from the early 17th century and references to the building of cottages at the northern and southern extremities of the village occur in the manor court rolls of that period.[41] All the farmhouses lie in the village, with the exception of Springfield farm to the south-west, created out of the open fields in the mid 19th century.[42] The Congregational chapel[43] and school[44] both stand on the south side of Chapel Street, Kingsdon Cary manor-house[45] lay on the eastern edge of the village, and Kingsdon Manor[46] to the south. Modern houses have been built along Underwood Road north of the village, and to the south-west near Kingsdon Manor.

There was an alehouse in the parish in 1694[47] and between 1736 and 1738.[48] Another was closed in 1748 because of disorderly conduct there.[49] An inn mentioned in 1755 was known as the Black Swan from 1763 to 1769, the Swan in 1776, and the White Swan in 1778.[50] A second public house, the Malt Shovel, was licensed during the years 1763–5, and the New Inn occurs in 1769.[51] Beer retailers in the parish are mentioned from 1859[52] and the present Kingsdon inn in Middle Street is first recorded in 1897.[53]

The building stone is generally the local blue lias, formerly quarried in the parish.[54] The village retains a number of 17th- and early-18th-century houses with lias walls, most of which also have thatched roofs. There is a variety of two and three-roomed plans, similar to those which occur in Pitney and Huish, with both internal and gable chimneys. Of particular interest is Oak Cottage which has two rooms on the ground floor, each with a gable fireplace, and a central passage flanked on one side by a plank and muntin wall and on the other by a wall of lapped planks. Park Cottage retains many of its ovolo moulded wooden window-frames of the early 18th century. Many of the present outbuildings in the village were once cottages and others are now derelict, illustrating the effects of 19th-century depopulation. In 1868 more cottages were needed; many were allowed to fall down and their occupants moved to Somerton, 'where women would rather they lived'.[55]

A bowling green is mentioned in 1777[56] and lay south of the rectory and churchyard.[57] The pastime was popular in the parish as early as 1619, when

[22] S.R.O., D/D/Rg 217. 'Langefuland' in the South field was mentioned in the early 14th century: B.M. Harl. Ch. 52 E 19.
[23] D.R.O., D 54/M 9.
[24] Alnwick Castle, Northumberland MSS., X II 12 3c, ct. roll, 8 May 1508.
[25] D.R.O., D 54/M 9; C 2/Eliz. I/H 1/39. 'Nithendiche' was mentioned in 1508: Northumberland MSS., X II 12 3c, ct. roll, 8 May 1508.
[26] B.M. Harl. Ch. 45 F 22.
[27] Ibid.
[28] D.R.O., D 54/M 8.
[29] S.R.O., D/D/Rg 217.
[30] Arundell MSS. rentals & surveys, 65.
[31] S.R.O., CR 94.
[32] C 135/123/3.
[33] D.R.O., D 54/M 8.
[34] Arundell MSS. MS. bk. 53, 18 Aug. 1608.
[35] Ibid. ct. bk. 16, 28 Sept. 1592; MS. bk. 56, 20 Aug. 1639.
[36] Ibid. MS. bk. 167, 1779–80.
[37] S.R.O., DD/X/KN.

[38] Ex inf. Mr. B. J. Mann.
[39] V.C.H. Som. i. 325–6.
[40] Ibid.; Proc. Som. Arch. Soc. xcvi. 50.
[41] Arundell MSS. MS. bks. 52–3, 56; ct. bks. 16–19; S.R.S. xxiii, 206–7.
[42] S.R.O., tithe award; O.S. Map 1/2,500, Som. LXXIII.7,8 (1887 edn.).
[43] See p. 119.
[44] See p. 120.
[45] See p. 115.
[46] See p. 114.
[47] S.R.O., Q/SR 197/19.
[48] S.R.O., Q/RL.
[49] S.R.O., DD/X/PR, bond, 29 Nov. 1748.
[50] S.R.O., Q/RL.
[51] Ibid.
[52] Harrison, Harrod, & Co. Dir. Som. (1859); P.O. Dir. Som. (1861–75); Kelly's Dir. Som. (1883).
[53] Kelly's Dir. Som. (1897).
[54] See pp. 116–17.
[55] Rep. Com. on Children and Women in Agric. [4202–I] H.C. p. 477 (1868–9), xiii.
[56] D.R.O., D 128A/T 1, mortgage, 21 Nov. 1777.
[57] S.R.O., tithe award.

six men were fined 6*d*. each at the hundred court for playing bowls.[58] There was a miniature rifle club in the village in 1914.[59] The Kingsdon Friendly Society was founded in 1834.[60] The former infant school on the church path was used as a reading room in the early 20th century.[61]

In 1624 there were 216 communicants in the parish.[62] The population was about 450 in 1791,[63] and 455 in 1801. Thereafter the figure rose to 610 in 1831 but subsequently declined to 252 in 1901.[64] After the First World War the population remained stable, but since 1931 has risen slightly, reaching 313 in 1951, and 312 in 1961.[65]

After the Civil War Thomas Hurd and his son Thomas compounded for their estates in the sum of £186 for 'adhering to the King's party'.[66] At the time of Monmouth's rebellion the churchwardens paid 11*s*. 6*d*. for the relief and quartering of the King's soldiers, and 2*s*. 6*d*. to the pressmaster to redeem a horse plough.[67]

MANORS.[68] At the time of Domesday *KINGSDON* appears to have formed part of the royal manor of Somerton,[69] although there is no positive evidence to identify the manor with one of three estates mentioned as members of Somerton in 1066[70] or to indicate when the separation from the royal manor took place. The overlordship may have been held with the honor of Gloucester *c*. 1284–6,[71] but the descent has not been traced thereafter.

The senior branch of the Gouvis family probably held the mesne lordship by 1194, at which date their cadet branch was in possession of the lordship itself.[72] William (I) de Gouvis (d. *c*. 1194) was elsewhere succeeded in turn by his son Robert (I) (d. by 1229) and grandson Robert (II) (d. by 1241).[73] The mesne lordship is first recorded in 1265 when it was held by Robert's son William (II) de Gouvis (d. 1298–9).[74] Thence it passed to the elder of William's two daughters, Joan wife of Sir John de Latimer (d. 1326),[75] whose son Sir Robert (I) (d. 1361)[76] and grandson Sir Robert (II) occur as mesne lord in 1353 and 1407 respectively.[77] The subsequent descent has not been traced precisely but the mesne lordship was held by the earl

of Salisbury in 1436,[78] by William Carent in 1458,[79] and by the prior of St. Swithun's, Winchester, in 1502.[80]

The lordship of the manor was evidently granted by the senior branch of the Gouvis family to their cousins,[81] although the exact relationship has not been determined. In 1194 the manor was seized by the Crown from Brian (I) de Gouvis, possibly son and successor of Richard de Gouvis (d. 1176–7), in consequence of his revolt against Richard I in 1193.[82] The Gouvis estates were probably restored on John's accession in 1199. Brian was succeeded in turn by his sons, Brian (II) and Roger de Gouvis (d. 1231).[83] Brian (III), son of Roger, leased Kingsdon to Geoffrey de Fanacourt for 12 years, and Avice, countess of Devon, claimed it in 1280 by assignment.[84] The case was resolved by a grant to the countess for one year (1280–1).[85] A substantial grant from the manor, if not the manor itself, comprising 7 carucates, was made in 1283 by Brian (III) to his second son Brian (IV), in return for a pension of £60 a year.[86] Richard de Gouvis, eldest son of Brian (III), predeceased his father,[87] leaving an only daughter Margery, wife of Robert du Boys.[88] On the death of Brian (IV) *c*. 1293 Robert and Margery du Boys took possession but were ejected by the mesne lord when Brian's widow produced a posthumous heir, Brian (V) de Gouvis.[89] Subsequent efforts by the du Boys family to secure the child's person and his wardship were unsuccessful.[90] In 1345 Brian (V) leased the manor for 12 years to Roger Turtle, a Bristol merchant (d. *c*. 1347).[91] Turtle's executor, Robert de Gyen of Bristol (d. 1353), succeeded to the term,[92] but his estates were seized by the Crown in 1352 for his withholding money from the King.[93] The remainder of the lease was granted to Sir Guy Brien in 1353,[94] and he purchased the fee in that year from Brian (VI) de Gouvis.[95]

In 1386 Brien (d. 1390) settled the manor on his son William, who died in 1395.[96] The Brien estates were then divided between Sir Guy's granddaughters and Kingsdon passed to Philippe, wife successively of Sir John de Ros (d. 1396) and Henry Scrope of Masham (Yorks.).[97] On Philippe's death in 1406 her lands passed to her sister Elizabeth,

[58] D.R.O., D 124, Somerton hundred ct. bk. 1617–20.
[59] *Kelly's Dir. Som.* (1914).
[60] S.R.O., Q/R, Friendly Soc. rtns.
[61] Local information.
[62] S.R.O., D/P/kingsd. 2/1/1, 2.
[63] Collinson, *Hist. Som.* iii. 195.
[64] *V.C.H. Som.* ii. 348.
[65] *Census*, 1911–61.
[66] *Cal. Cttee. for Compounding*, iii. 1722.
[67] S.R.O., D/P/kingsd. 2/1/1, chwdns'. accts. 1686.
[68] The descent of the manors is treated by A. W. Vivian-Neal in *Proc. Som. Arch. Soc.* ciii. 22–71.
[69] Ibid. 25–6; see below, p. 134.
[70] *V.C.H. Som.* i. 434–5.
[71] *Feud. Aids*, iv. 285.
[72] *Pipe R.* 1194 (P.R.S. n.s. v), 19.
[73] *Proc. Som. Arch. Soc.* ciii. 28–30; Hutchins, *Hist. Dorset*, iii. 694–9.
[74] *Cal. Inq. Misc.* i, p. 267; *Feud. Aids*, iv. 285; *Cal. Pat.* 1292–1301, 50; *Proc. Som. Arch. Soc.* ciii. 30–2.
[75] *Proc. Som. Arch. Soc.* ciii. 32–3.
[76] Ibid.; *Cal. Inq. p.m.* x, pp. 89–90.
[77] Hutchins, *Hist. Dorset*, iii. 704–7; C 137/59/54.
[78] C 139/81/39.
[79] C 139/165/16.
[80] *Cal. Inq. p.m. Hen. VII*, ii, p. 328.

[81] *Proc. Som. Arch. Soc.* ciii. 29, 34–5.
[82] *Pipe R.* 1194 (P.R.S. n.s. v), 19, 194; 1195 (P.R.S. n.s. vi), 39, 54; *Proc. Som. Arch. Soc.* ciii. 34–5.
[83] *Proc. Som. Arch. Soc.* ciii. 35–6.
[84] Ibid. lxii. 77; ciii. 36–43; *Cal. Pat.* 1292–1301, 50; *S.R.S.* xliv. 132–4, 271–3.
[85] *S.R.S.* xliv. 132–4, 271–3.   [86] Ibid. vi. 258.
[87] *S. & D. N. & Q.* xvi. 258; *Proc. Som. Arch. Soc.* ciii. 41–2.
[88] *Proc. Som. Arch. Soc.* ciii. 41–2; *S.R.S.* xliv. 3; *Knights of Edw.* I, i. (Harl. Soc. lxxx), 115.
[89] Hutchins, *Hist. Dorset*, iii. 701; C.P. 40/105 rot. 103.
[90] C.P. 40/105 rot. 103; *Cal. Pat.* 1292–1301, 50; *Abbrev. Plac.* (Rec. Com.), 290; *Proc. Som. Arch. Soc.* ciii. 44–5.
[91] *Cal. Inq. p.m.* x, pp. 89–90; *Proc. Som. Arch. Soc.* ciii. 46.
[92] *Cal. Inq. p.m.* x, pp. 89–90.
[93] *Cal. Pat.* 1350–4, 522.
[94] *Cal. Fine R.* 1347–56, 365; *Abbrev. Rot. Orig.* (Rec. Com.), ii. 227.
[95] *S.R.S.* xvii. 24, 182, 184, 186; *Cal. Close*, 1354–60, 340–1, 642–3.
[96] *S.R.S.* xvii. 202; *Proc. Som. Arch. Soc.* ciii. 53–4.
[97] *Proc. Som. Arch. Soc.* ciii. 54–5; *Complete Peerage*, s.v. Brien.

wife of Robert Lovell,[98] and in 1407 this couple settled a life interest on Henry Scrope (d. 1415).[99] Lovell's only child Maud (d. 1436) married first Sir Richard Stafford (d. c. 1427), leaving an only daughter Avice, and secondly John d'Arundel, earl of Arundel (d. 1435), by whom she had a son Humphrey.[1] On Humphrey's death in 1438 the manor passed to his half-sister Avice, wife of James Butler, earl of Ormond (cr. earl of Wiltshire, 1449), who in 1445 settled it on their issue with remainder to the right heirs of James.[2] Avice died childless in 1457 and the manor was forfeited to the Crown after the earl of Wiltshire's execution in 1461.[3] In 1462 it was granted to William Neville, earl of Kent, who died in the following year. It was then conveyed to George, duke of Clarence, subject to a pension granted as jointure in 1470 to Eleanor, countess of Wiltshire.[4] On Clarence's attainder in 1478 a life interest was granted to Eleanor, then wife of Sir Robert Spencer.[5]

In 1488 an agreement was reached between the surviving descendants of Sir Guy Brien for the partition of the estate between them, by which the reversion of Kingsdon was allotted to Thomas Butler, earl of Ormond, Eleanor's brother-in-law.[6] Ormond succeeded on Eleanor's death in 1501,[7] and by his will the manor passed in 1515 to Henry Percy, earl of Northumberland (d. 1527), husband of Eleanor's daughter and coheir Catherine.[8] In 1528 the manor was sold by the earl of Northumberland to Thomas Arundell, later of Wardour (Wilts.).[9] On Arundell's execution in 1552[10] it was granted to Edward Fiennes, Lord Clinton and Saye (d. 1585), who sold it back to the Crown only eight months later.[11] Arundell's widow received a life grant of the manor in 1553,[12] the reversion going to her son Matthew (later Sir Matthew) Arundell in the following year.[13] His son Thomas (cr. lord Arundell of Wardour, 1605) succeeded him in 1598,[14] and his grandson Thomas, Lord Arundell, in 1639.[15] The latter died in 1643 fighting for the royalist cause, but Kingsdon was saved from sequestration by its sale to trustees in 1653.[16] It was regranted to the Arundells at the Restoration[17] and thereafter continued in the family. It was sold by Henry, Lord Arundell (d. 1808), to Aaron Moody (d. 1829) of Southampton in 1801,[18] and his son C. A. Moody

conveyed it to William Neal of London in 1864.[19] On Neal's death in 1890 the manor passed in turn to his sons Capt. William Neal (d. 1901) and the Revd. John Neal (d. 1916).[20] The latter was succeeded by his son J. F. Neal (d. 1919) and by his grandson J. S. Neal (d. 1942).[21] The lordship was held by the trustees of the Neal estate in 1971.[22]

The medieval manor-house probably stood immediately north of the churchyard in a field called Culverhay.[23] A dovecot belonging to the lord of the manor, mentioned in 1353,[24] stood in a field of that name in 1598–9[25] and 1773.[26] The house was burnt down probably shortly before 1552 when the demesne lands were split up and leased to the tenants.[27] In 1827 Kingsdon House, occupied by the lord of the manor, stood at the south-western edge of the village.[28] C. A. Moody rebuilt the house further south before 1833, when the village roads were diverted around the grounds.[29] The architect was believed to have been William Wilkins and the lias stone used was quarried on the site.[30] Shortly after the purchase of the estate in 1864 William Neal 'reconstructed and greatly enlarged' the building, known as Kingsdon Manor from c. 1902.[31] It was sold to Bristol Corporation in 1952 and was occupied by Kingsdon Manor school in 1971.[32] The present house is built of stone with slate roof. It has two and three storeys, having two slightly projecting wings with pediments and an open parapet to the centre of the building.

The Cary family appear to have held lands in Kingsdon from the 12th century. Henry son of Gormund of Cary owned property there in the time of King John, and was succeeded in turn by Adam of Cary and his son John (I) of Cary.[33] John (II) of Cary held lands in Kingsdon in 1308,[34] and it was probably his son John (III) who paid 5s. for his lands there in 1327, when the Gouvis holding was taxed at 6s.[35] John's son William died without issue and was succeeded by his uncle Thomas (d. 1356).[36] He was followed in turn by his sons Sir Thomas (d. 1361)[37] and John (IV), of Bluntshay in Whitchurch Canonicorum (Dors.).[38] In 1375 John (IV) sold his lands in Kingsdon to Sir John Mautravers of Hooke (Dors.) (d. 1386).[39] Mautravers was followed by his daughters and coheirs Maud (d. 1406) and Elizabeth, the latter succeeding her sister

[98] C 137/59/54.
[99] S.R.S. xxii. 25–6.
[1] Proc. Som. Arch. Soc. ciii. 55–6; Feud. Aids, iv. 429; Cal. Close, 1435–41, 11; C 139/81/39.
[2] S.R.S. xxii. 198; Proc. Som. Arch. Soc. ciii. 56–7.
[3] Proc. Som. Arch. Soc. ciii. 57–8; Cal. Pat. 1476–85, 106.
[4] Cal. Pat. 1461–7, 225–6, 454; 1467–77, 211, 457, 518, 557.
[5] Cal. Pat. 1476–85, 106; Proc. Som. Arch. Soc. ciii. 59.
[6] Cal. Close, 1485–1500, 111–12, 114–16.
[7] Cal. Inq. p.m. Hen. VII, ii, p. 328.
[8] Ibid.; L. & P. Hen. VIII, iv(2), p. 1421.
[9] Hooke Manor, Donhead St. Andrew, Arundell MSS. deeds, gen. ser. K 628; E 315/47/102.
[10] C 142/97/77.
[11] Cal. Pat. 1550–3, 363–4.
[12] Ibid. 1553, 31–2.
[13] Ibid. 1553–4, 339–40.
[14] C 142/257/83.
[15] C 142/495/17; Complete Peerage, s.v. Arundell.
[16] Arundell MSS. rentals & surveys, 63; Cal. Cttee. for Compounding, ii. 1223; Proc. Som. Arch. Soc. ciii. 64.
[17] C 66/2931 no. 16.

[18] Ibid.; Proc. Som. Arch. Soc. ciii. 66; M.I. in church.
[19] Proc. Som. Arch. Soc. ciii. 67.
[20] Ibid.; Burke, Land. Gent. (1952), 1861.
[21] Proc. Som. Arch. Soc. ciii. 68–9; Burke, Land. Gent. (1952), 1861.
[22] Proc. Som. Arch. Soc. ciii. 69.
[23] S.R.O., DD/SAS C/212, map & survey, 1827.
[24] C 135/123/3.
[25] D.R.O., D 54/M 9.
[26] Arundell MSS. deeds, Kingsdon, 168.
[27] D.R.O., D 54/M 8.
[28] S.R.O., DD/SAS C/212, map & survey, 1827.
[29] S.R.O., Q/SR 470.
[30] Proc. Som. Arch. Soc. ciii. 67. The attribution to Wilkins is considered doubtful.
[31] Ibid. 67–9.
[32] Ibid. 69; see below, p. 120.
[33] S.R.S. xv. 226; xli. 36.
[34] Cal. Inq. p.m. v, pp. 27–8.
[35] S.R.S. iii. 201–2.
[36] Cal. Inq. p.m. x, p. 260.
[37] Ibid. xi, p. 34.
[38] D.R.O., D 124, box 17, grants, 1367, 1368.
[39] S.R.S. xvii. 87–8; Cal. Close, 1385–9, 164–5; Hutchins, Hist. Dorset, iii. 315.

and marrying Sir Humphrey Stafford of Hooke (d. 1442).[40] In the 15th century the estate was known as the manor of *KINGSDON* or *KINGSDON CARY*.[41] On Sir Humphrey's death the manor passed to his third son William[42] but at William's request was conveyed in 1444 to his niece Avice, countess of Ormond, then owner of the larger manor of Kingsdon.[43] On her death without issue in 1457 the manor evidently passed in turn to Humphrey (d. 1461), son of Sir John Stafford, and to Humphrey (cr. earl of Devon, 1469, d. 1469), son of William Stafford.[44] The earl was succeeded by his cousin and coheir Eleanor, wife of Thomas Strangways of Stinsford (Dors.) (d. 1484).[45] Their grandson Sir Giles Strangways (d. 1547) was owner in 1543,[46] and his grandson Sir Giles held Kingsdon Cary at his death in 1562.[47] The manor then passed successively to John (d. 1593), Sir John (d. 1666), Giles (d. 1675), and Thomas (d. 1713).[48] Thomas Strangways, son of the last, died without issue in 1726 and the manor descended to his surviving daughter Susanna, wife of Thomas Horner of Mells (subsequently known as Thomas Strangways Horner).[49] In 1783 it was held by her grandson Henry Thomas Fox-Strangways, earl of Ilchester (d. 1802).[50] It continued to be held by that family until 1864 when the 4th earl conveyed the property to William Pinney of Somerton Erleigh.[51] By this date the estate had long ceased to enjoy manorial status.

Kingsdon Cary manor-house is first mentioned in 1356.[52] It lay at the south-eastern edge of the village near Langlands Farm[53] and is now derelict. The house was known as Cariescourt in 1454,[54] Kingsdon Farm in 1787,[55] and later as the Old Manor. It was evidently a rectangular two-storeyed building of lias with Ham stone dressings, and includes a fire-place with a four-centred head which masks an earlier wooden bressummer.

At his death in 1308 Sir John Meriet held the overlordship of two virgates of land each held under him as $\frac{1}{16}$ of a fee by Brian (V) de Gouvis and John (II) of Cary.[56] On the death of Sir John's grandson, Sir John Meriet, in 1369[57] the same lands were described as a virgate of land held as $\frac{1}{8}$ of a fee by Sir Guy Brien and a carucate of land held as a $\frac{1}{4}$ of a fee by John (IV) Cary.[58] The origins and subsequent descents of these holdings have not been traced, but they probably merged with the above two manors.

ECONOMIC HISTORY. In 1284–6 the manor of Kingsdon was stated to be held for one 'forthurtha' of the mesne lord,[59] possibly meaning an outlying area of open land and referring to the former status of the manor in relation to Somerton. The word may survive in the field name Great Forehead in Kingsdon North field, first noted in 1625.[60] The manor produced an income of £16 in 1194,[61] and £30 in 1265, the Michaelmas rents then totalling 60s.[62] The value of the manor in 1353 was £31 8s. 7d of which rents accounted for £24;[63] demesne lands comprised 305 a. of arable land, 47 a. of meadow, and 60 a. of wood.[64] When the custody of the manor was granted to Sir Guy Brien in that year, however, deductions from the income amounted to £20 13s. 4d.[65] By 1502 the value had fallen to £20,[66] although the rental rose to £43 7s. 3½d. in 1514–15, of which £10 11s. 8d. was derived from the farm of the demesne.[67]

In 1552 demesne land totalling 233 a. of pasture, 76½ a. of arable, and 23 a. of meadow was parcelled out among 11 leaseholders and 17 copyholders to produce a total rent of £11 7s.,[68] and continued thereafter to be farmed by tenants of the manor. In 1563, discounting the recently divided demesne, there were 8 freeholders with about 170 a., 10 lease holders with 595 a., and 26 copyholders with 817 a., paying total rents of £34 1s. 11d.[69] Thereafter the income from rents remained stable: £46 3s. 7d. in 1643,[70] £46 7s. 8½d. in 1711,[71] and £47 5s. 8½d. in 1783.[72] Enfranchisements made by the Arundells were probably responsible for a reduction in the rental to £39 7s. 2½d. by 1798.[73]

In 1563 there were 1,060 a. of arable (all in the three open fields), 528 a. of pasture, and 153 a. of meadow within the manor.[74] The extent of pasture is significant. In 1615 the inhabitants were pasturing at Northmore in common with the men of Somerton Erleigh, and also in Southmead.[75]

In the early 17th century Southmead, then about 200 a. in area, was held in common with 14 other lords and freeholders. The lord of Kingsdon held the right to strays, preys, and drifts both there and in Northmore.[76] In 1610 it was found that 30 years earlier the Pitney tenants of Sir John Hanham had illegally inclosed 9 a. in Southmead, and that 40 years before a further 40 a. there had been inclosed by Somerton tenants. The bailiff and tenants of Kingsdon were therefore ordered to pull down

[40] *S.R.S.* xxii. 156, 165; Hutchins, *Hist. Dorset.* iii. 315.
[41] *S.R.S.* xxii. 156, 165; C 140/32/30; D.R.O., D 124, box 17, grant, 9 Sept. 1442.
[42] D.R.O., D 124, box 17, grant, 9 Sept. 1442.
[43] Ibid. grant, 12 Feb. 1443/4; lease, 16 Sept. 1454; see above.
[44] *Proc. Som. Arch. Soc.* ciii. 57, 70–1.
[45] Hutchins, *Hist. Dorset,* ii. 179, 662–3.
[46] Ibid. 662–3; Hunt. Libr., HA manorial, Somerton hundred ct. roll, 1562.
[47] Hutchins, *Hist. Dorset,* ii. 662–3; D.R.O., D 54/M 8.
[48] Hutchins, *Hist. Dorset,* ii. 662–3; Arundell MSS. MS. bk. 55; ct. bks. 15, 17–20; rentals & surveys 90, 95.
[49] D.R.O., D 124, box 96, lease, 1 Mar. 1731/2; Hutchins, *Hist. Dorset,* ii. 662–3.
[50] Hutchins, *Hist. Dorset,* ii. 662–3; S.R.O., DD/X/KN, survey, 1783.
[51] Hutchins, *Hist. Dorset,* ii. 662–3; S.R.O., DD/SAS C/212, survey of Kingsdon, 1827; tithe award; Burke, *Peerage* (1969); D.R.O., D 124, box 82, conveyance, 29 Sept. 1864.
[52] *Cal. Inq. p.m.* x, p. 260.
[53] S.R.O., tithe award.

[54] D.R.O., D 124, box 17, lease, 16 Sept. 1454
[55] Ibid. box 96, lease, 10 Nov. 1787.
[56] *Cal. Inq. p.m.* v, pp. 27–8.
[57] *Proc. Som. Arch. Soc.* xxviii. 101 (pedigree).
[58] *Cal. Inq. p.m.* xiv, p. 188.
[59] *Feud. Aids,* iv. 285.
[60] Arundell MSS. MS. bk. 55; S.R.O., tithe award.
[61] *Pipe R.* 1194 (P.R.S. n.s. v), 19.
[62] *Cal. Inq. Misc.* i, p. 267.
[63] C 135/123/3.   [64] Ibid.
[65] *Cal. Fine R.* 1347–56, 365.
[66] *Cal. Inq. p.m. Hen. VII,* ii, p. 328.
[67] Alnwick Castle, Northumberland MSS., X II 12 3b, compotus, 1514–15.
[68] D.R.O., D 54/M 8.   [69] Ibid.
[70] Arundell MSS. ministers' accts. ser. I, 19.
[71] Ibid. rentals & surveys, 95.
[72] S.R.O., DD/X/KN.
[73] Arundell MSS. ministers' accts. ser. II, 37.
[74] D.R.O., D 54/M 8.
[75] Arundell MSS. MS. bk. 54, 12 Sept. 1615.
[76] Ibid. MS. bk. 54, 12 Sept. 1615; MS. bk. 58, 3 Oct. 1654.

the hedges.[77] After the breach of Southmead, pasture there was apportioned among the tenants from St. Giles's day (1 September) to Martinmas by the rate of 2 rother beasts, 1 horse, or 4 sheep for each acre held there. Holders of only a yard of ground in the meadow or poor cottagers with no land there were permitted to pasture a rother beast or horse.[78] All such customs, however, were subject to agreement with the lord of Somerton manor and his tenants.[79] Various abuses were reformed as they came to light, and an elaborate scale of fines for the breach of many different customs was drawn up in 1616.[80] A move to inclose Southmead in 1597 to resolve territorial anomalies seems to have come to nothing.[81]

By 1563 about 250 a. had been inclosed within Kingsdon manor.[82] Thirty acres of common pasture called Nidens ('Nethon' in 1563) appears to have been inclosed by the lord in the early 16th century, possibly without the consent of his tenants.[83] Inclosures within Kingsdon manor during the late 16th and early 17th century were generally resisted by the manor court,[84] and encroachments on the common fields may probably be attributed to the late 17th and early 18th centuries. By the early 19th century only West field (103 a.) of three open arable fields preserved its identity, North field was composed of more scattered plots totalling 111 a., and South or East field had been almost entirely inclosed.[85] It was stated c. 1800 that the land here was 'of an inferior quality, yet very much improveable and capable of being much better laid out and the common fields divided'.[86] Meadow and pasture totalling 119 a. and principally in Southmead was inclosed c. 1803 by an award made in 1829.[87] The Kingsdon Inclosure Award of 1810 regulated the inclosure of 294 a., of which nearly 259 a. were arable.[88] Conversion to grassland evidently took place during the earlier 19th century and by 1839 the parish contained 1,057 a. of meadow and pasture and only 780 a. of arable.[89] This trend continued during the 19th century and by 1905 grassland had increased to 1,243 a., and arable had shrunk still further to 451 a.[90]

Medieval land tenure was principally on three lives.[91] By 1563 copyhold tenements were held on 1, 2, 3, or 4 lives, but in 1552 ten leases for 99 years absolute were granted.[92] Conversion to leasehold

continued during the 17th century, and by 1726 only 32 tenements were copyhold and 61 leasehold.[93] Of these leasehold tenements 25 were held on lives and 36 on 99 years or lives.[94] However, by 1761 the trend had been reversed, for although copyholds had shrunk to 26, there were 41 leases on lives and only 25 on 99 years or lives.[95]

The dominant holding within the parish has always been the Kingsdon manor estate. In 1563 it comprised about 1,784 a.,[96] in 1656 1,976 a.,[97] in 1839 1,649 a.,[98] and in 1971 about 1,500 a.[99] In 1563 within the manor there were 3 holdings over 100 a. (the largest of 121 a.), 20 between 20 a. and 100 a., and 13 tenants holding less than 20 a.[1] By 1783 there were 2 farms of 355 a. and 135 a., 17 tenements between 60 a. and 100 a., and 26 tenants holding less than 20 a.[2] By 1734 the principal occupier of lands within the parish was George Hilborne (d. 1741).[3] His family occurs at Kingsdon in the late 13th century as 'Hillebrond',[4] and received a grant of arms in 1708.[5] George's tenements passed to his sister Dorothy (d. 1749), wife of James Hare of Bristol,[6] whose only child Mary married Christopher Jolliffe (d. 1799).[7] Jolliffe occupied 355 a. on the manor estate in 1783 and was the most prominent freeholder.[8] His son, James Hare Jolliffe (d. 1836), temporarily occupied the manor-house.[9]

Kingsdon Cary manor comprised 125 a. in 1454,[10] 120 a. in 1563,[11] and 107 a. in 1864.[12] The only other sizable holding in 1598–9 was that of Thomas Browning, which contained 50 a.[13] By 1827, the Jolliffes having left the parish, the manor estate had been reorganized and contained three farms of over 200 a. and four farms of between 100 a. and 200 a.[14] By 1839, apart from Kingsdon manor itself, there were four farms of over 200 a. and one of 176 a.[15] Springfield farm, created in the mid 19th century, which the Neals kept in hand under a bailiff,[16] included about 400 a. in 1861 and was sold early in the 20th century.[17] In 1971 the manor estate comprised Bondip farm (285 a.), Sunnyside farm (264 a.), Langlands farm (242 a.), Park farm (183 a.), Cottage farm (150 a.), and Stoneleigh farm (119 a.). Lands of 185 a. attached to Manor farm were split up among the other estate farms in 1971.[18]

In 1552 there was a common quarry for lias in the parish,[19] although taking stone was restricted by the manor court, which in the early 17th century

[77] Ibid. MS. bk. 53, 10 Sept. 1610.
[78] Ibid. MS. bk. 52, 25 Sept. 1598; MS. bk. 53, 18 Aug. 1608.
[79] Ibid. MS. bk. 52, 25 Sept. 1598; MS. bk. 53, 18 Aug. 1608.
[80] Ibid. ct. bk. 20, 11 Sept. 1616.
[81] Ibid. ct. bk. 17, 10 Aug. 1597.
[82] D.R.O., D 54/M 8.
[83] Ibid.
[84] Arundell MSS. MS. bks. 47, 49–56, 58; ct. bks. 14–20, 27–8.
[85] S.R.O., CR 94.
[86] Locke's Additions to Collinson, ed. Ward, 99.
[87] S.R.O., CR 43.
[88] Ibid. 94.
[89] S.R.O., tithe award.
[90] Statistics supplied by the then Bd. of Agric. (1905).
[91] B.M. Add. Ch. 17658.
[92] D.R.O., D 54/M 8.
[93] S.R.O., Q/RR, papists' estates, rolls 9, 10.
[94] Ibid.
[95] Ibid. (1761).
[96] D.R.O., D 54/M 8.
[97] Arundell MSS. rentals & surveys, 65.

[98] S.R.O., tithe award.
[99] Ex inf. Mr. B. J. Mann.
[1] D.R.O., D 54/M 8.
[2] S.R.O., DD/X/KN.
[3] S.R.O., DD/SAS (C/73), 9, land tax assessment, 1734.
[4] B.M. Add. Ch. 54936.
[5] Proc. Som. Arch. Soc. xxxvii. 50.
[6] S.R.O., DD/MGR, Hilborne wills; D/P/kingsd. 2/1/2.
[7] S.R.O., D/P/kingsd. 2/1/3; Q/RE.
[8] S.R.O., DD/X/KN.
[9] S.R.O., D/P/kingsd. 2/1/3; M.I. in Bathford church.
[10] D.R.O., D 124, box 17, lease, 16 Sept. 1454.
[11] D.R.O., D 54/M 8, 9.
[12] D.R.O., D 124, box 82, conveyance, 29 Sept. 1864.
[13] D.R.O., D 54/M 9.
[14] S.R.O., DD/SAS (C/212), map and survey, 1827.
[15] S.R.O., tithe award.
[16] Proc. Som. Arch. Soc. ciii. 69.
[17] Ex inf. Mr. B. J. Mann.
[18] Ibid. None of these farm names occur before the late 19th century. Bondip and Langland farms take their names from the areas in which their principal holdings lie.
[19] D.R.O., D 54/M 8.

granted licences to dig on the payment of fines.[20] Elizabeth Hilborne (d. 1750) left her quarries at Pitts, south-east of Kingsdon Green, to her sons,[21] one of whom rendered a fine to the lord for selling stones out of the manor in 1775.[22] James Sansom paid regularly for licence to quarry stone on Kingsdon Green between 1780 and 1798.[23] Masons in the parish occur regularly during the 19th century,[24] but the stone has not been extensively worked in the 20th century. The principal quarry evidently lay at the western corner of the junction between Mill Lane and Wood Lane.[25]

Linen-weavers are found regularly in the parish during the 18th century,[26] amongst whom was Christopher Dampier (d. 1784), the most prominent nonconformist in Kingsdon.[27] Apart from masons and weavers, agriculture provided employment for most of the inhabitants, and 79 out of 111 families were thus engaged in 1821.[28] During the 19th century many of the women were employed in gloving,[29] although in 1868 it was stated that 'the pay is very bad, about a day and a half's work for a day's pay'.[30] A machine-maker was working in the parish in 1843,[31] a builder in 1902, a horse trainer and a traction engine proprietor in 1923,[32] and a motor mechanic in 1926.[33]

A mill formed part of property conveyed by John and Joan Cary to John Mautravers in 1375[34] and the following year a miller was taking unjust tolls.[35] John Reynolds was presented for the same offence in 1573 and 1574,[36] and two other millers in 1618 and 1619.[37] In 1628 a windmill formed part of the estate held by Thomas Browning (d. 1626),[38] and was probably the windmill in North field mentioned in 1694.[39] Field names indicate that this stood towards the north-western end of Mill Lane on the summit of Kingsdon hill.[40] A miller occurs in the parish in 1829.[41]

LOCAL GOVERNMENT

LOCAL GOVERNMENT. Kingsdon, a tithing in Somerton hundred, included both the parish of Kingsdon and the manors of Lytes Cary and Tuckers Cary, in Charlton Mackrell.[42]

No court records survive before 1502, although suit to Kingsdon manor court at Michaelmas and Hockday is mentioned in 1345.[43] Rolls are extant for certain years in the period 1503–13,[44] and in broken series for 1574–1663.[45] The court, described as *curia manerii*, met generally twice a year usually in spring and in autumn.[46] Two haywards were appointed annually at the autumn court, each holding serving by rotation,[47] and two sheep-tellers occur in 1602 and 1605.[48] A body known as 'the Seven Men' is mentioned between 1590 and 1639, its duties generally comprising the settlement of boundary disputes. During the 16th and 17th centuries the court seems to have been unusually vigilant in dealing with misdemeanours or, conversely, to have suffered from extremely unruly tenants. Thus in years when many presentments were made against tenants of dilapidated buildings or to prevent illegal sub-letting the perquisites were high. In other years, once the *status quo* had been restored, the income from this source fell abruptly.

Churchwardens and 'posts' occur in 1554[49], two churchwardens were being appointed annually by 1587,[50] and two collectors for the poor are mentioned in 1654.[51] Between 1760 and 1832 two overseers were elected annually, serving in rotation for their holdings.[52] The church house had been converted for use as a poorhouse by 1762 and continued to be so used until 1836,[53] when the parish became part of the Langport poor-law union.[54]

CHURCH

CHURCH. The church is first mentioned in 1242.[55] The advowson descended with the manor from at least 1343,[56] but the bishop of London presented in 1521 by grant of Henry, earl of Northumberland (d. 1527).[57] Thomas Arundell, who bought the manor in 1528,[58] evidently also acquired an interest in the advowson; the presentation in 1556 was made by the executor of Anne Tydder, widow of Nicholas Tydder, of Shaftesbury (Dors.), to whom Arundell had granted the living.[59] Arundell's widow presented in 1558 and 1562.[60] The Crown presented in 1582,[61] but after 1589, when Matthew Arundell was patron,[62] members of the family, because of their adherence to Roman Catholicism, leased successive presentations to others: Edward Kirton of Castle Cary in 1641 and 1642,[63] Nicholas Ingram in

[20] Arundell MSS. MS. bk. 53, 18 Sept. 1605; ct. bk. 19, 2 Sept. 1613; MS. bk. 54, 12 Sept. 1615.
[21] S.R.O., DD/MGR, copy will, Elizabeth Hilborne, 1750.
[22] Arundell MSS. ministers' accts. ser. II, 30.
[23] Ibid. 31–7; MS. bk. 167.
[24] S.R.O., D/P/kingsd. 2/1/5.
[25] O.S. Map 1/2,500, Som. LXXIII. 8 (1887 edn.).
[26] e.g. S.R.O., D/P/kingsd. 2/1/4; 13/3/3; 13/6/1; DD/X/PR, settlement examn. 14 May 1810.
[27] D.R.O., D 128A/L 1; S.R.O., DD/X/KN.
[28] C. & J. Greenwood, *Som. Delineated.*
[29] S.R.O., D/P/kingsd. 2/1/8.
[30] *Rep. Com. on Children and Women in Agric.* [4202–I] H.C. (1868–9), xiii.
[31] S.R.O., D/P/kingsd. 2/1/5.
[32] *Kelly's Dir. Som.* (1902, 1923).
[33] S.R.O., D/P/kingsd. 2/1/9.
[34] *S.R.S.* xvii. 87–8.
[35] Hunt. Libr., HA Manorial, Somerton hundred ct. roll, 1376–7.
[36] Ibid. hundred ct. roll, 1573–4.
[37] D.R.O., D 124, hundred ct. bk. 1617–20.
[38] C 145/535/116.
[39] S.R.O., DD/SAS (C/73), 9, conveyance, 19 May 1694.
[40] S.R.O., tithe award.
[41] S.R.O., D/P/kingsd. 2/1/5.
[42] D.R.O., D 124, Somerton hundred ct. roll, 1617–20; S.R.O., Q/RE.
[43] B.M. Add. Ch. 17658.
[44] Alnwick Castle, Northumberland MSS., X II 12 3c.
[45] Arundell MSS. MS. bks. 47, 49–56, 58; ct. bks. 14–20, 27–8.
[46] Ibid.
[47] Arundell MSS. MS. bk. 58, 3 Oct. 1654.
[48] Ibid. ct. bk. 18, 31 Aug. 1602; MS. bk. 53, 18 Sept. 1605.
[49] S.R.O., D/D/Ca 22.
[50] S.R.O., D/P/kingsd. 2/1/1.
[51] Ibid. 2/1/2.
[52] Ibid. 13/2/1.
[53] Ibid.; D/PS/ilm. box 16; see below, p. 119.
[54] *Poor Law Com. 2nd Rep.* p. 548.
[55] Devon R.O. 123 M/TB 112.
[56] *S.R.S.* x.491; see above, pp. 113–14.
[57] Ibid. lv. 18.
[58] See p. 114.
[59] *S.R.S.* lv. 147.
[60] Ibid. 153; *Som. Incumbents*, ed. Weaver, 118.
[61] *Som. Incumbents*, 118.
[62] Ibid.
[63] Ibid.; *S. & D. N. & Q.* iii. 48.

1690,[64] and John Bush of Burnett in 1719.[65] The form of these grants is probably indicated by a lease of the advowson dated 1735 to the Revd. William Dodd and Edward Clothier for 14 years, with a covenant to renew the same for a similar period if the resident incumbent survived the initial term.[66] The widow of William Cox (rector 1719–40) joined these lessees in presenting in 1741, as did the widow of Edward Mervin (rector 1741–4) in 1744 and 1745.[67] All the 18th-century rectors appear to have had a personal interest in the patronage. Robert Tucker presented Thomas Tucker (rector 1767–94),[68] and John Tucker subsequently presented Thomas's son Thomas Tucker (rector 1794–1827), and his successor.[69] When the Arundell family put the manor up for sale in 1779 the advowson 'after two lives' was included, and the patronage also formed part of the sales held in 1783 and 1787.[70] It was probably on the latter occasion that the Tucker family, holders of the lease, purchased the advowson which was sold to University College, Oxford, by John Tucker of Taunton in 1829.[71] The college presented in 1835,[72] but sold the patronage to William Neal between 1888 and 1891.[73] It continued in the Neal family until the union with Podimore in 1943; thereafter the Neals had two turns and the bishop one.[74] The united benefice has been held with Babcary and Yeovilton since c. 1965.[75]

The church was valued at £14 in 1291[76] and 1334,[77] at £26 3s. 1d. in 1535[78] and at over £80 in 1656.[79] The common reputed value c. 1668 was £100,[80] and rose to £190 in 1787.[81] In 1815 the income exceeded £150[82] and had risen to £432 by 1831.[83]

In 1242 the rector agreed to pay rent for land in Charlton Mackrell in return for tithes owned by Bruton priory in the parish.[84] In 1334 the tithes of corn and pasture were valued at £2 6s., and oblations and small tithes at £4 9s. 4d.[85] By 1535 the predial tithes were assessed at £16, personal tithes, oblations, and other profits at £6 7s. 2d., and tithes of wool and lambs at £2 6s. 2d.[86] In 1839 the rector received a tithe rent-charge of £342.[87] A modus of 2d. an acre in lieu of great and small tithes had previously been paid on some land.[88] In 1841 the rent-charge was reduced to £326.[89]

In 1334 the rector held 60 a. of arable land valued at 30s.,[90] a figure which had risen to £2 by 1535.[91] In 1606 he had 46 a. of arable, 8 a. of meadow, and 8 a. of pasture, excluding the lands attached to the parsonage house.[92] The rector was allotted 21 a. under the inclosure award of 1810,[93] and his holding in 1839 totalled 62 a.[94] It was increased by 8 a. in 1841,[95] and was 70 a. in 1939.[96] The value of the glebe was given as £90 15s. in 1851,[97] and the lands were leased in 1918 for £67 a year.[98] In 1971 most of the glebe, including the site of the derelict rectory,[99] formed part of Western farm, lying immediately west and south of the churchyard,[1] and comprised nearly 48 a.[2]

The parsonage house was described in 1521 as 'a very goodly mansion place and well apparelled',[3] but by 1557 it was 'ruinous and in decay and part thereof fallen down'.[4] In 1617 the rector had the house, a barn of 6 'poles', stable, stall, 'grunter' house (pig house), hay house of 5 'poles', and 2 cottages, one occupied by the parish clerk.[5] The old rectory, standing immediately west of the church, was burnt down in 1925[6] and was derelict in 1971. A new house was erected in 1925 at the north end of the village.

At least three of the 14th-century rectors, Adam Hildebrond (rector by 1310), Peter Pyk (rector 1319–43), and Hugh Erlegh (rector by 1389) were not in priest's orders when serving the parish.[7] John Trewargh (rector by 1402 until 1451) had licence to absent himself and farm his church in 1402,[8] and Christopher Twynyow (rector until 1509), James FitzJames (rector from 1509), and James Gilbert (rector 1521–56) all held the benefice in plurality.[9] John Dunster (rector 1556–8) was a former canon of Bruton abbey.[10] John Dotin, M.D. (rector 1558–61), another pluralist, was rector of Exeter College, Oxford, and a noted astrologer.[11] Alexander Westerdale (rector 1642–89) was incumbent throughout the Interregnum, having been appointed parish register in 1654.[12] Richard Carter (rector 1690–1718) held the benefice with Charlton Mackrell where he evidently lived.[13] Peter Hansell (rector 1835–97) was fellow and bursar of University College, Oxford, until 1836 and was rector for 62 years until his death at the age of 91.[14] His

[64] *Som. Incumbents*, 118.
[65] Ibid.
[66] Hook Manor, Donhead St. Andrew, Arundell MSS. advowsons, box 41, lease, 1735.
[67] Wells Dioc. Regy., Reg. Wynne f. 41; Reg. Willes, i ff. 9, 11.
[68] Wells Dioc. Regy., Reg. Willes, ii f. 49.
[69] Wells Dioc. Regy., Reg. Moss f. 131; Reg. Law f. 53.
[70] S.R.O., DD/X/KN.
[71] Ex inf. Mr. A. D. M. Cox, University College, Oxford.
[72] *Rep. Com. Eccl. Revenues*, pp. 168–9.
[73] *Dioc. Kal.* (1888, 1891).
[74] S.R.O., D/P/kingsd. 2/8/1; *Crockford*.
[75] *Dioc. Dir.* (1966–70).
[76] *Tax. Eccl.* (Rec. Com.), 197.
[77] E 179/169/14.
[78] *Valor Eccl.* (Rec. Com.), i. 198.
[79] Arundell MSS. rentals & surveys, 65.
[80] S.R.O., D/D/Vc 24.
[81] S.R.O., DD/X/KN.
[82] S.R.O., D/D/V rtns. 1815.
[83] *Rep. Com. Eccl. Revenues*, pp. 168–9.
[84] Devon R.O. 123 M/TB 112.
[85] E 179/169/14.
[86] *Valor Eccl.* (Rec. Com.), i. 198.
[87] S.R.O., tithe award.
[88] Ibid.

[89] S.R.O., D/P/kingsd. 13/1/2.
[90] E 179/169/14.
[91] *Valor Eccl.* (Rec. Com.), i. 198.
[92] S.R.O., D/D/Rg 217.
[93] S.R.O., CR 94.
[94] S.R.O., tithe award.
[95] S.R.O., D/P/kingsd. 13/1/2.
[96] *Kelly's Dir. Som.* (1883–1939).
[97] H.O. 129/317/1/9/19.
[98] S.R.O., D/P/kingsd. 13/1/2.
[99] See below.
[1] Ex. inf. Mr. B. J. Mann.
[2] Ex inf. Dioc. Secretary.
[3] S.P. 1/233 f. 45.
[4] S.R.O., D/D/Ca 27.   [5] S.R.O., D/D/Rg 217.
[6] Ex inf. the rector, the Revd. J. H. H. Williams.
[7] *S.R.S.* i. 30, 34; *Reg. Thomas Brantingham*, ed. F. C. Hingeston-Randolph, ii. 62; Hunt. Libr., HA Manorial, Somerton hundred ct. roll, 1392–3.
[8] *S.R.S.* xiii. 25.
[9] Emden, *Biog. Reg. Univ. Oxford*; Foster, *Alumn Oxon.*
[10] *S.R.S.* viii, p. lv.
[11] Foster, *Alumni Oxon.*; brass in church.
[12] S.R.O., D/P/kingsd. 2/1/2.
[13] *Som. Incumbents*, 50, 118; S.R.O., D/P/cha. ma. 2/1/1.
[14] Foster, *Alumni Oxon.*; M.I. in church.

tenure was interrupted for a period of 7 years from 1844, which he spent in France, after suspension and sequestration for immoral behaviour with a parishioner.[15]

A parish chaplain occurs in 1450,[16] and curates are mentioned between 1532 and 1575[17] and in 1745, 1792,[18] and 1831.[19] In 1610 Holy Communion was celebrated five times and the annual figure fluctuated between four and seven times until the Civil War when it fell to three.[20] After the Restoration it fluctuated between one and five times, falling as the rector grew older.[21] The figure varied between two and five during the years 1767–1828, rose to six in 1829, and to nine in 1833. There were monthly celebrations between 1834 and 1836.[22] By 1843 there were two sermons every Sunday and communion was celebrated six times a year,[23] but by 1870 the sacrament was again being administered monthly.[24] On Census Sunday 1851 the morning service was attended by a congregation of 80 and the afternoon by 134, although the minister maintained that the normal figure had been reduced by the absence of the squire's establishment and by 'a prevailing epidemic'.[25]

A church house was rented from the lord by 1563;[26] it was in disrepair in 1613 and 1614.[27] In 1623, in consequence of the movement against church ales, brewing lead, two spits, and a rack were sold and the house sub-let.[28] By 1762 it had been converted into a poorhouse.[29] It lay south-west of the junction of the path to the church and High Street,[30] and the enclosure in which it stood is still (1971) extant.

The church of *ALL SAINTS* stands at the western edge of the village. In 1461 the dedication feast was changed from 4 September to the Sunday after the Decollation of St. John the Baptist (29 August) to avoid harvest time.[31] The building is of lias with Ham stone dressings and has a chancel with north vestry and organ chamber, nave with transeptal north and south chapels and south porch, and west tower. The nave is of 12th-century origin and there is a niche of that date over the south door, but the only other early features are two 13th-century window openings in the north wall. The chancel was rebuilt in the 14th century and has no evidence of the enlargement which was recorded in 1521 as having taken place in the 15th century.[32] The north chapel was formerly the base of a 14th-century tower. Windows were inserted and the arch into the nave enlarged in the 15th century when the tower was replaced by one at the west end. The

porch and the south chapel, formerly known as St. Catherine's aisle,[33] were also added. A new window was put into the south side of the nave and new tracery into those on the north.

The floor of the chancel was raised in 1636.[34] The church was restored in 1869 when the chancel is said to have been rebuilt and the organ chamber added, and again in 1906, when the vestry may have been built.[35]

The bowl of the font is of the 12th century and some late medieval bench-ends are reset in the screen to the north chapel. The Ham stone effigy of a cross-legged knight under the north window of the north chapel was originally in the chancel but was removed into the churchyard in the 15th century, where it lay in 1521.[36] It has been dated 1270–80 and may portray Brian (III) de Gouvis.[37] The three-lock register coffer is mentioned in 1605[38] and probably dates from 1538. The early-17th-century pulpit is probably that made by William Squier in 1627.[39]

The plate dates from 1831.[40] There are six bells: (i) *c.* 1400, probably William Dawe of London; (ii) 1607, Robert Wiseman of Montacute, recast 1952; (iii) *c.* 1450, Roger Landen of Wokingham; (iv) 1782, recast 1936, William Bilbie; (v) 1861; (vi) 1946.[41] From 1830 a morning labour bell was rung in the church at 5 a.m. during the summer and 7 a.m. in the winter.[42]

The registers, complete from 1538, comprise both the original paper register and a parchment copy from 1558.[43]

NONCONFORMITY. A private house was licensed for Presbyterian worship in 1749.[44]

A chapel 'now erected' was licensed in 1759, probably succeeding a house licensed by the Independents in 1756,[45] although the congregation preserved traditions of an earlier foundation given variously as 1664,[46] 1676,[47] and *c.* 1710.[48] In the early 19th century it was served by resident ministers,[49] but has generally been supplied by visitors since that time.[50] On Census Sunday 1851 the congregation totalled 65 in the afternoon and 112 in the evening, and the Sunday school was attended by 6 in the morning and 6 in the afternoon.[51] The chapel, on the south side of Chapel Street, is a plain rectangular building of lias with a vestry at its eastern end. The manse lies on the west side of Middle Street.

[15] S.R.O., D/D/Cm, papers in causes.
[16] *S.R.S.* xlix. 137.
[17] S.R.O., D/D/Vc 20; B.M. Harl. MS. 594 f. 47; *S. & D. N. & Q.* xiv. 106.
[18] S.R.O., D/D/Bo.
[19] *Rep. Com. Eccl. Revenues*, pp. 168–9.
[20] S.R.O., D/P/kingsd. 2/1/1.
[21] Ibid. Alexander Westerdale died in 1689 aged *c.* 74; Foster, *Alumni Oxon.*; S.R.O., D/P/kingsd. 2/1/2.
[22] S.R.O., D/P/kingsd. 4/1/1.
[23] S.R.O., D/D/V rtns. 1843.
[24] Ibid. 1870.
[25] H.O. 129/317/1/9/19.
[26] D.R.O., D 54/M 8.
[27] Arundell MSS. ct. bk. 19, 2 Sept. 1613; MS. bk 54, 20 Sept. 1614.
[28] S.R.O., D/P/kingsd. 2/1/1.
[29] Ibid. 13/2/1.
[30] S.R.O., DD/SAS (C/212), map & survey, 1827.
[31] *S.R.S.* xlix. 359.

[32] S.P. 1/233 f. 44.
[33] S.R.O., D/P/kingsd. 2/1/2, list of seats, 1603.
[34] Ibid. 2/1/1.
[35] Ibid. 4/1/2; 8/2/1.
[36] S.P. 1/233 f. 44.
[37] *Proc. Som. Arch. Soc.* lxxii. 77; see above, p. 113.
[38] S.R.O., D/P/kingsd. 2/1/1.
[39] Ibid.
[40] *Proc. Som. Arch. Soc.* xlv. 133.
[41] S.R.O., DD/SAS CH/16; information in church.
[42] S.R.O., D/P/kingsd. 4/1/1.
[43] Ibid. 2/1/1–10.
[44] S.R.O., Q/RR, meeting-house lics.
[45] Ibid.
[46] Details in vestry.
[47] *Rep. Som. Cong. Union* (1896).
[48] R.G. 4/2349.
[49] Ibid.
[50] *Rep. Som. Cong. Union* (1896).
[51] H.O. 129/317/1/9/20.

A house was licensed for dissenting worship in 1815,[52] but the denomination was not stated.

EDUCATION. A schoolmaster was teaching in the rectory in 1606,[53] and another was licensed in 1631.[54] In 1818 there were day-schools for c. 40 children and a Sunday school, supported by subscription, attended by c. 80 pupils.[55] In 1833 there was an infant school for 70 children started c. 1826,[56] and two segregated day-schools for 40 children, supported by subscription and payments from pupils. There were also two Sunday schools for 50 children.[57] The day- and infants'-schools were supported by the National Society by 1846.[58] The boys' school was then attended by 22 during the week, by 37 on Sundays, and by 8 during the evenings. The girls' school had 59 pupils during the week and on Sundays, and the infants' school had a complement of 31 children.[59] A local farmer stated n 1868 that he preferred to employ boys who had not been to school and that, although he 'does not mind reading and writing', he 'dislikes too much education'.[60]

The National day-schools subsequently combined and the present building on the south side of Chapel Street was opened in 1872.[61] The Sunday school was later held in a separate property on the west side of High Street below the church.[62] In 1894 the average attendance at the National school was 41,[63] and in 1903 the number on the books was 58.[64] The school then comprised two rooms (also used by the Sunday school) and a cottage for the mistress.[65] The school had been 'in a bad condition' but the mistress was then 'working it up with some success'.[66] In 1907 the name was changed from the Kingsdon Voluntary school to the Kingsdon Church of England school.[67] The attendance fell to 42 in 1914–15 and the establishment became a junior school in 1925.[68] In consequence the numbers dropped to 16 in 1934–5, rising thereafter to 22 in 1944–5, and 39 in 1954–5.[69] The school had 34 pupils in 1969.[70]

A school, administered by the Bristol education authority, was moved to Kingsdon Manor in 1948.[71] The school is for handicapped boys and in 1971 had 60 pupils.[72] The manor-house, originally leased from the manor estate, was purchased by the authority in 1952.[73]

CHARITIES FOR THE POOR. William Neal (d. 1890) left £300 to the rector and churchwardens, the income to be applied every Christmas in the distribution of meat among the deserving poor of the parish.[74] The income in 1970 amounted to £7 15s. 4d. and was employed according to the donor's wishes.[75]

EAST LYDFORD

THE irregularly shaped parish of East Lydford lies 5 miles east of Somerton, extending about 1½ mile from north to south, and from east to west. The course of the Foss Way forms the whole of its north-western boundary; its northern boundary is marked by the river Brue and a small stream, and the southern by the river Cary and an old road to Foddington, now overgrown and represented in part by Hook Lane. The western boundary with Wheathill and Lovington runs NNW. from the Cary in a straight line which becomes irregular north of the Somerton to Castle Cary road. The ancient parish contained 708 a. in 1838.[1] A detached part of the parish, known as Fourfoot and situated about 2 miles north-east, was transferred to West Lydford in 1884.[2] By 1901 the parish contained 644 a.[3] The civil parishes of East and West Lydford were amalgamated in 1933.[4]

The soil of the parish is clay over lias with estuarine alluvium along the banks of the Brue and Cary.[5] Most of the land lies below the 100 ft. contour, falling away slightly towards the river Brue on the north. The ground rises to 120 ft. in the area of Cross Keys, and to about 130 ft. on the boundary with Wheathill. Apart from the Brue and Cary the parish is watered only by a small stream running north from Cary Road, marking the eastern boundary of fields and orchards in Church Lane and entering the Brue near the old church in the north.

Until the 19th century the principal route through the parish was the Somerton–Langport road, adopted by the Langport, Somerton, and Castle Cary turnpike trust in 1753,[6] and known as Cary Road from the 19th century.[7] The Foss Way subsequently became of more importance and the hamlet of Cross Keys, now known also as Lydford-

[52] S.R.O., D/D/Rm, box 2.
[53] S.R.O., D/D/Vc 150 f. 281.
[54] S.R.O., D/D/Vc 58.
[55] Digest of Returns to Sel. Cttee. on Educ. of Poor, H.C. 224 (1819), ix(2).
[56] Educ. Enquiry Abstract, H.C. 62 (1835), xlii.
[57] Ibid.
[58] Church Sch. Inquiry, 1846–7.
[59] Ibid.
[60] Rep. Com. on Children and Women in Agric. [4202–I] H.C. p. 477 (1868–9), xiii.
[61] Log book, Kingsdon school.
[62] O.S. Map 1/2,500, Som. LXXIII. 8 (1887 edn.).
[63] Rtns. of Schs. [C 7529] H.C. (1894), lxv.
[64] S.R.O., C/E, box 27.
[65] Ibid.   [66] Ibid.
[67] S.R.O., D/P/kingsd. 18/7/1.
[68] Som. C.C., Educ. Cttee., Schs. List.

[69] Ibid.   [70] Ibid.
[71] Log book, Kingsdon Manor school.
[72] Ex inf. the headmaster.
[73] Proc. Som. Arch. Soc. ciii. 69.
[74] S.R.O., D/P/kingsd. 4/1/2.
[75] Ex inf. Mr. E. C. G. Marrow.
[1] S.R.O., tithe award. This article was completed in 1970.
[2] Local Govt. Board Order 16,340.
[3] Census, 1901.   [4] Som. Review Order, 1933.
[5] Geol. Surv. Map 1", solid and drift, sheet 296 (1969 edn.).
[6] Langport, Somerton, and Castle Cary Turnpike Act, 26 Geo. II, c. 92 (Priv. Act). Side gates erected from Cary Road into the Foss Way in the 18th century indicate that the former was then the principal road (S.R.O. D/T/lsc., map, 1832).
[7] S.R.O., D/G/SM, 160/30.

on-Foss, grew up around an inn at the junction. The older village lies along Church Lane, leading from Cary Road northwards to the site of the old parish church on the banks of the Brue. This may have been the area of early settlement in the parish, deserted because of persistent flooding. Church Farm, Manor Farm, and Home Farm are all in Church Lane, as are the Old Rectory and Old Schoolhouse. A number of cottages and modern houses lie in the area of its junction with West Lane, so called by 1544,[8] which runs west to the Foss Way. Lydford Lane, known as Cross Keys or West Field Drove in 1838,[9] runs south from Cross Keys to Babcary. A parallel road, known as Honeypot Lane by 1744,[10] also ran south into West field. Perry Road, known as Perry Mead Lane in 1725,[11] runs south-west from Cary Road near its junction with Church Lane. It cuts off part of East field, crosses the Cary at Perry bridge, mentioned in 1481,[12] and continues to Foddington in Babcary. From this road runs Rubbery Lane, serving Rubbery Farm, and a lane dividing East field from Perry mead, known as Wheathill Drove in 1838.[13] Large numbers of ox shoes found on the banks of the Cary south of Rubbery Farm suggest a watering place for oxen and a droveway north over lands belonging to the farm.[14]

The Cross Keys hotel lies on the south side of Cary Road just east of its intersection with the Foss Way. The inn was first mentioned by name in 1759.[15] It served both as tavern and small farm during the 19th century,[16] and a weighbridge was installed behind it c. 1899.[17] Eighteenth- and nineteenth-century buildings developed along Cary Road from the inn. Amongst these were two cottages built on the north side of the road in 1711,[18] and a rectory house was erected to the west of them soon after 1872.[19] Two inns in the parish whose sites have not been located were the Lamb or Royal Lamb, 1755–9, and the Buck in 1778.[20]

Lydford Hall on the north side of West Lane was owned and occupied in 1838 by the rector, James Hooper (d. 1849),[21] and J. J. Moss, a former rector, lived there in 1872.[22] Cecil Henry Paulet purchased it before the First World War[23] and it was held by a member of his family in 1970. Rubbery farm takes its name from Rowborough, a medieval common pasture field, and lies south of Cary Road. The first buildings on the site were erected shortly before 1688.[24]

The detached part of the parish at Fourfoot was originally demesne woodlands, known as Raynes wood in 1587[25] and Reynolds wood in 1639,[26] presumably after the Reigny family, lords of East Lydford manor by the 13th century.[27] It is now known as Park wood. In 1669 a house had been recently erected there,[28] and it was probably this that by 1732 had become an inn called the Maiden Head.[29] It was subsequently known as the Three Horseshoes in 1759–60,[30] the White Swan in 1763–5,[31] and the Nut Tree in 1769–78.[32] The inn was known as the Blue Boy from 1783 until 1787,[33] and the Buffalo's Head between 1808 and 1832.[34] By 1838 it had been acquired by Edward Francis Colston,[35] lord of West Lydford manor, and by 1859 was known as the Colston's Arms after its owner.[36] Between 1872 and 1875 it became a farm-house,[37] and the property is now known as Fourfoot Farm. Cottages were built along the Foss Way, south-west from the farm.

Most of the buildings in the parish date from the 18th century and are principally of lias with tiled roofs.

There were two arable open fields mentioned in 1396 and inclosed in 1838:[38] West field, formerly south of Cross Keys, and East field, south-west of Cary Road and east of Perry Road.[39] Apart from Lydford moor, there were three common pastures; Herbrooks, called Hurtebrok in 1396,[40] lay in the south-western corner of the parish. Rowborough, occasionally called South field in the late 14th century,[41] may represent the original third field of a three-field system. It lay between East field and West field and formed the present site of Rubbery farm. Broad mead, called Bordemed in 1396,[42] lay south-west of East field and may originally have included the lands later known as Perry mead.

The Great Western rail link between Castle Cary and Charlton Mackrell, running through the south of the parish, was opened in 1905.[43] Keinton Mandeville station, which lay in the south-western corner of East Lydford, was closed to both passengers and freight in 1962.[44]

In 1801 the population of the parish was 143. This figure increased to 194 in 1841. Thereafter it fell to 130 in 1901. A recovery to 156 in 1911 was followed by a further decline to 113 in 1931.[45] No individual population statistics are available for East Lydford after its union with West Lydford.

[8] S.C. 2/200/34.
[9] S.R.O., CR 28.
[10] S.R.O., D/P/e. lyd. 13/2/1.
[11] Ibid.
[12] B.M. Harl. Ch. 55 E 8.
[13] S.R.O., CR 28.
[14] Ex inf. Mr. M. G. Vearncombe.
[15] S.R.O., Q/RL. It was known as the Duke's Head in 1763–5 (ibid.).
[16] P.O. Dir. Som. (1861).
[17] S.R.O., D/G/SM, 160/30.
[18] S.R.O., DD/WG, box 13, bk. of grants.
[19] S.R.O., D/P/e. lyd. 23/1.
[20] S.R.O., Q/RL.
[21] S.R.O., tithe award.
[22] Morris & Co. Dir. Som. (1872).
[23] Kelly's Dir. Som. (1906, 1914).
[24] S.R.O., DD/X/ME, lease, Foyle to Chapman, 1688.
[25] S.R.O., DD/WG, box 16, rental, 1587.
[26] S.R.O., DD/HN A II, 32, I.P.M. of John Harbin, 1639.
[27] See p. 122.

[28] S.R.O., DD/WG, box 13, bk. of grants.
[29] S.R.O., DD/PH 34, lease, Phelips to Lyde, 1732.
[30] S.R.O., Q/RL.
[31] Ibid.
[32] Ibid.
[33] S.R.O., DD/BR/bs; Q/RL.
[34] S.R.O., DD/BR/bs; Q/RL; Q/RP.
[35] S.R.O., tithe award.
[36] Harrison, Harrod, & Co. Dir. Som. (1859).
[37] Morris & Co. Dir. Som. (1872); P.O. Dir. Som. (1875).
[38] S.C. 2/198/58; S.R.O., CR 28.
[39] An enclosure in West field is called Costelorum in the 17th century (S.R.O., D/D/Rg 112) and Costeloe in 1838 (S.R.O., tithe award).
[40] S.C. 2/198/58.
[41] Ibid.   [42] Ibid.
[43] E. T. MacDermot, rev. C. R. Clinker, Hist. G.W.R. ii (1964), 322–3.
[44] C. R. Clinker & J. M. Firth, Reg. Closed Stations, ii & suppl.
[45] V.C.H. Som. ii. 348; Census, 1911–31.

MANOR AND LESSER ESTATES. The manor of *EAST LYDFORD* was held in 1066 by Alward, a thegn, under Glastonbury abbey, 'nor could he be separated from the church'. In 1086 it was held by Roger de Courcelles under the abbey,[46] but no further reference to the abbey's overlordship has been found, and by 1342 the manor had never rendered homage or service to Glastonbury within memory.[47] Thereafter the manor formed part of the honor of Curry Mallet. Roger de Courcelles was succeeded in the honor by Robert Malet (possibly before the death of Henry I), and before 1156 had been followed successively by William Malet (I) (d. 1169), Gilbert Malet (d. 1194), and William Malet (II) (d. c. 1216).[48] The last left three daughters and coheirs, Helewise, Mabel, and Bertha. Bertha died unmarried before 1221; Mabel's half share descended to William Forz, her son by her second husband Hugh de Vivonia. William died in 1259 and his four daughters received ⅓ of the barony each.[49] Helewise Malet married Hugh Pointz (I) (d. 1220), and the moiety of the overlordship descended to her son Nicholas Pointz (I) (d. 1273), who acquired the other moiety rated as a whole fee.[50] The overlordship passed through successive generations of the Pointz family until Sir Nicholas Pointz (III) sold it to Sir Matthew de Gournay in 1358.[51] On the latter's death it was granted by Gournay's assignees to John Tiptoft for life with remainder to the duchy of Cornwall, to which it passed on his death in 1443.[52] It was held by members of the royal family[53] until 1566 when it was granted to Sir Hugh Paulet (d. 1573).[54]

In 1600 the manor was stated to be held of the heir of Sir Hugh's grandson Anthony Paulet (d. 1600).[55] Thereafter the honor reverted to the duchy of Cornwall which leased Curry Mallet manor to Thomas Cary in 1627–8.[56] In 1631 a third of East Lydford manor was held of Thomas Cary as of his manor of Curry Mallet.[57]

It is not known when the manor was subinfeudated, but Thomas de Reigny was concerned in litigation with the incumbent over rights of pasture on Lydford moor in 1230.[58] In 1278 Richard de Reigny was trying to replevy his lands in East Lydford, confiscated by the Crown.[59] William de Reigny occurs in 1286 and 1312 as holding one fee in East Lydford, described as ¼ fee in 1303, and in 1316 was holding Lydford with William Martin, lord of West Lydford.[60] In 1329 William de Reigny, possibly son of William, and Elizabeth his wife, settled a messuage and lands in East Lydford on

their son Walter,[61] and in 1332 the manor, with the exception of this property, was settled on John son of William de Reigny, probably their grandson, with remainder to their younger children, to be held by William and Elizabeth for their lives.[62] William de Reigny appears to have died by 1336 and to have been succeeded by Sir Ralph de Middleney, probably husband of the widowed Elizabeth de Reigny.[63] In 1346 Sir Ralph (d. 1363) held ¼ fee in East Lydford.[64] Elizabeth his widow still held a life interest in the manor, which she brought to her third husband Sir Robert de Ashton.[65] In 1368 Sir Robert and his wife settled the manor on Robert's daughter Eleanor and her husband, John son of Thomas de Berkeley.[66] On Ashton's death in 1384 Sir William of Windsor (d. 1384) entered the manor under a conveyance from Ashton to his wife Alice Perers, mistress of Edward III.[67] The manor was committed to John of Windsor in 1386, but the heirs of the Reigny family successfully proceeded against him for its recovery in 1388 and 1392–3.[68] The manor was thereafter divided between the descendants of three daughters of William and Elizabeth de Reigny: William Banastre (II), John Montfort, and Catherine wife of John Wykyng.[69]

William Banastre (II) (d. 1395) was succeeded by his daughter Joan, wife of Robert de Affeton.[70] After Robert's death Joan married John Stourton of Preston Plucknett, who held with others ¼ fee in East Lydford in 1428.[71] Stourton died in 1439, leaving a daughter Cecily, wife first of John Hill of Spaxton (d. 1434), and secondly of Sir Thomas Keriell.[72] In 1472 this third of the manor passed to Genevieve, wife of Sir William Say and daughter of John Hill son of Cecily.[73] Sir William Say survived his wife and died without issue in 1529.[74] Genevieve's coheirs were the descendants of her father's sister Elizabeth, wife of John Cheney of Pinhoe (Devon). Elizabeth's son John Cheney had issue Joan, who by her two husbands, Thomas Say and Sir Richard Pudsey, left four daughters, whose children succeeded jointly to the Hill estate.[75]

One moiety and a third of another moiety of his portion of the manor were held by John Waldegrave, grandson of Thomas and Joan Say, at his death in 1543.[76] He was succeeded by his son Sir Edward Waldegrave (d. 1561), and the third of the manor evidently continued intact in the Waldegrave family until James, Earl Waldegrave (d. 1741), sold it to Edward Phelips of Montacute (d. 1734) between 1725 and 1730.[77] In time the lands in East Lydford which made up this third were considered to form

46 *V.C.H. Som.* i. 461.
47 *S.R.S.* xxvi. 114.
48 Sanders, *Eng. Baronies*, 38.   49 Ibid. 39.
50 Ibid.; *Rot. Hund.* (Rec. Com.), ii. 277.
51 *S.R.S.* xvii. 39.
52 C 139/110/45.
53 C 139/160/38; *Cal. Inq. p.m. Hen. VII*, i, p. 353.
54 C 142/221/119; *Cal. Pat.* 1563–6, 372; C 142/167/78.
55 C 142/260/143; C 142/260/141.
56 C 66/2420.
57 C 145/534/155.
58 *Cur. Reg. R.* xiv. 129, 228, 290, 395.
59 *Cal. Close*, 1272–9, 501.
60 *Feud. Aids*, iv. 285, 303, 321; *Cal. Inq. p.m.* v, p. 196.
61 *S.R.S.* xii. 136.   62 Ibid. 161.
63 *Cal. Pat.* 1334–8, 219.
64 *Feud. Aids*, iv. 344.
65 *Cal. Inq. p.m.*, xi. p. 393; S.R.O., DD/WG, box 7, proceedings in Common Pleas.

66 *S.R.S.* xii. 190–1.
67 C 136/30/5; *Cal. Pat.* 1377–81, 503; C 136/30/3; *Cal. Pat.* 1381–5, 376; C 136/37/1.
68 *Cal. Fine R.* 1383–91, 149; S.R.O., DD/WG, box 7, proceedings in Common Pleas.
69 S.R.O., DD/WG, box 7, proceedings in Common Pleas; *S.R.S.* xii. 195–6.
70 C 136/86/6; S.R.O., DD/WG, box 18, ct. roll.
71 C. J. B. Stourton, Lord Mowbray, Segrave and Stourton, *Hist. Noble House of Stourton*, i. 80, 84–5; *Feud. Aids*, iv. 388.
72 *Hist. Noble House of Stourton*, i. 80, 84–5; C 139/71/36; *S.R.S.* xvii. 95–6.
73 *Cat. Anc. D.* ii, A 3222.
74 C 142/51/35.
75 Ibid.; *S.R.S. extra series*, 314–15; C 1/406/37.
76 C 142/68/54.
77 S.R.O., DD/WG, box 13, bks. of grants; DD/HN A VI, 4, 5.

part of Wheathill manor, as indeed was the third presentation to East Lydford rectory.[78] In 1761, in accordance with a wish contained in the will of his mother,[79] Edward Phelips (d. 1797) conveyed Wheathill manor to his brother the Revd. John Phelips of Yeovil, at which time its value was increasing and, 'from the age and condition of the tenants on life, likely every day to become more considerable'.[80] On his death in 1766 John Phelips left the manor to his wife Mary,[81] who in turn left it in 1803 to her niece Rhoda, daughter of Edward Phelips and wife of William Harbin of Newton Surmaville.[82] Rhoda Harbin survived her husband and died in 1846, leaving all her lands to her son George Harbin, who had sold Wheathill manor by 1849.[83] In 1838 lands held by Rhoda Harbin in East Lydford totalled only 30 a.[84]

A further third of the manor passed to John Montfort, described as a tenant in fee of a third of the manor in 1400,[85] and he was holding lands there in 1412.[86] He was succeeded by his daughter Eleanor, wife of Geoffrey Rokell of Wormingford (Essex), and she and her husband were granting leases there in 1431.[87] By the late 15th century, like other former properties of the Montforts of Nunney, it was held by Simon Wiseman of Essex,[88] who claimed to have descended in the fifth generation from John Wiseman and his wife Magdalen Rokell.[89] In 1494 Wiseman sold his third of the manor to Richard Mawdeley of Nunney (d. 1509),[90] from whom it descended successively to John (d. 1531),[91] Roger, Richard (d. 1600),[92] and Roger Mawdeley (d. 1630).[93] Under a settlement of 1630 the property passed to Roger's daughter Frances, wife of Robert Clarke,[94] who conveyed it to Thomas Coteel in 1637.[95] Coteel appears to have been succeeded by Susan, wife of Thomas Garrard of Lambourn (Berks.), and Jane, wife of Calvert Wright of Nuneham Courtnay (Oxon.), apparently daughters and coheirs of Sir John Blagrave of Southcote in Reading (Berks.) (d. 1655), husband of Coteel's sister Magdalen.[96] The two couples presented jointly to the rectory in 1660,[97] but by 1669 the lands had evidently descended to Robert Wright of Windsor (Hants), son of Calvert and Jane.[98] An interest in the share was also held by John Deane of Oxenwood in Shalbourne (Wilts.), whose wife Magdalen was daughter of Magdalen, wife

of John Stroughill of Barkham (Berks.), another daughter and coheir of Sir John Blagrave.[99] By 1679 Deane held the whole third, which he described as the manor of East Lydford,[1] In 1681 he mortgaged an undivided third part of his share to George Duke of Sarson (Hants), who obtained the freehold from James Deane of Salisbury (Wilts.), son of John, in 1696.[2] George Duke (d. c. 1721) was succeeded by his son John (d. 1744), who mortgaged the share to John Allen Pusey of Pusey (Berks.) in 1742.[3] The share was sold by an Order in Chancery in 1771 to pay off the mortgage and other debts of John Duke's estate, and conveyed in the following year to John Blake of St. Clement Danes, London, and Ralph Etwall of Andover (Hants).[4]

The remaining two thirds of John Deane's share were mortgaged to Elizabeth Low of London in 1686, whose representatives assigned it in 1738 to John Allen Pusey as trustee for Thomas Deane, rector of Witchampton (Dors.), grandson of John and Magdalen Deane.[5] Thomas Deane secured the freehold from Edward Deane, great-grandson and heir of John and Magdalen Deane, in 1739, and the following year, with his father John, conveyed the share to John Allen Pusey.[6] Pusey died in 1753 and was succeeded by his two sisters Elizabeth (d. 1757) and Jane Allen.[7] Jane presented to the rectory in 1763,[8] but sold her share to Thomas Wyld of Speen (Berks.) in 1772.[9]

In 1775, by agreement between Thomas Wyld, John Blake, and Ralph Etwall, the Deane share was divided between them. Wyld, as owner of two thirds, secured 56 a. in East Lydford, 91 a. in Foddington and Charlton Adam, and a third of the advowson.[10] Blake and Etwall received 86 a. in Charlton Adam in respect of their third.[11] By will proved 1789 Wyld left his share to his son George Wyld, who evidently sold it to John Davis between 1789 and 1791.[12] Thereafter it appears to have formed part of the Davis estate sold in 1848.[13]

The final third of the manor passed to the Knoyle family of Sandford Orcas (Dors.), possibly by marriage with the Wykyng family or their descendants. Thomas Knoyle, son of Robert (d. c. 1412) and Joan Knoyle, held lands in East Lydford in 1412 and died in 1416.[14] William Knoyle (d. 1502) held it by 1475,[15] and thereafter the property descended successively to Peter (d. 1508),[16] Leonard

---

[78] S.R.O., DD/HN A II; DD/PH 34, Phelips to Lyde, 1732; Q/RR, papists' estates, 1.

[79] S.R.O., DD/PH 224/114.

[80] Ibid.; DD/HN A VI, 4, 5.

[81] S.R.O., DD/PH C/709, box 3, copy will of Revd. John Phelips.

[82] S.R.O., DD/HN A I, 12, will of Mary Phelips.

[83] Ibid. box 9, k, will of Rhoda Phelips.

[84] S.R.O., tithe award.

[85] S.R.O., DD/WG, box 18, ct. rolls.

[86] Feud. Aids, vi. 510.

[87] S.R.S. xlix. 297; B.M. Harl. Ch. 55 E 8.

[88] V.C.H. Wilts. viii. 104; C 142/25/40.

[89] Visit. of Essex, 1552–1634 (Harl. Soc. xiii), 326.

[90] C 142/25/40.   [91] C 142/51/54.

[92] C 142/260/141.

[93] C 145/534/155.

[94] Hist. MSS. Com. 63, Egmont, i, p. 85; C 145/534/155.

[95] C.P. 25(2)/480/13 Chas. I Mich.

[96] Visit. of London, 1633–35 (Harl. Soc. xv), 192; Visit. of Berkshire, 1532–1666 (Harl. Soc. lvi), 291; Ibid. (Harl. Soc. lvii), 71; S.R.O., DD/DN, box 39, covenant, 1774; C.P. 25(2)/528/23 Chas. II Mich.

[97] Som. Incumbents, ed. Weaver, 133.

[98] S.R.O., DD/DN, box 39, covenant 1774.

[99] Ibid.; Visit. of Berkshire, 1532–1666 (Harl. Soc. lvi), 291.

[1] S.R.O., DD/DN, box 39, covenant, 1774, abstract of title from 1686.

[2] Ibid. box 39, abstract of title from 1681.

[3] Ibid.; R. E. H. Duke, Family of Duke of Lake (1916), pedigree C.

[4] S.R.O., DD/DN, box 39, abstract of title from 1681.

[5] Ibid. box 39, abstract of title from 1686.

[6] Ibid.   [7] Ibid.

[8] Wells Dioc. Regy., Reg. Willes, ii f. 15.

[9] S.R.O., DD/DN, box 39, abstract of title from 1686; DD/CC 102465.

[10] S.R.O., DD/DN, box 39, deed of partition, 1775.

[11] Ibid.; see p. 87.

[12] S.R.O., DD/CC 102462–3; Q/RE.

[13] See below.

[14] Prob. 11/2A (P.C.C. 24 Marche, will of Robert Knoyle); Feud. Aids, vi. 506; Prob. 11/2B (P.C.C. 31 Marche, will of Thomas Knoyle).

[15] S.C. 6/977/16, 21, 22; Visit. of Somerset, 1623 (Harl. Soc. xi), 123; Cal. Inq. p.m. Hen. VII, ii, p. 383.

[16] C 142/25/33.

(d. 1532),[17] and Edward Knoyle.[18] John Parham of Poyntington (Dors.) married Edward's eldest daughter in 1571,[19] and Edward Knoyle and his son William conveyed the third to Parham in 1583.[20] John Parham and his son, Sir Edward, sold it to John Foyle (I) of Shaftesbury (Dors.) in 1620.[21] Foyle was succeeded in 1647–8 by his grandson John Foyle (III) of Chute (Wilts.), son of John Foyle (II) of Kympton (Hants).[22] The latter's son Edward (d. 1720), who was granting leases in East Lydford in 1692, left a son, Edward Foyle of Somerford Keynes (Wilts.).[23] Edward entered on his father's East Lydford property in 1730,[24] and 'Mr. Foyle' was stated to be one of the three lords of the manor c. 1736.[25] The descent after this date is confused, but this was evidently the third which John Ryall devised to his nephew the Revd. Narcissus Ryall in 1781, together with a third of the advowson.[26] It is not apparent when or from whom he acquired it. Narcissus Ryall died in 1829,[27] but the subsequent descent of this final third has not been traced.

The manor-house, probably still in existence when the manor was divided in the late 14th century,[28] has not been located. It may have stood near the field called Court Orchard in 1476[29] and Court Close by 1587,[30] which was divided equally between the owners of each third of the manor.[31]

The freehold settled by William de Reigny on his son Walter in 1329, described then as a messuage, a carucate of arable, 10 a. of meadow, 60 a. of wood, 11s. rent, and pasture for 60 oxen on Lydford moor, may represent the demesne land.[32] This can be identified with a messuage, a carucate of arable, and 10 a. of meadow, held in fee by John Reigny in the late 14th century.[33] By 1587 this was held by the heirs of James Smyth,[34] and John Smyth occurs as a free tenant of the manor between 1588 and 1599.[35] In the early 17th century it was held by the Goodwin family of Bower Hinton in Martock. From Thomas Goodwin it passed to John Goodwin, who died before 1674.[36] He was succeeded by his widow Mary, and son William, who conveyed it in that year to Richard Duke of Otterton (Devon).[37] In 1679 Duke sold the property to Henry Scrase (I) of Blatchington (Suss.), who was succeeded by his son Henry (II) and grandson Henry (III).[38] The assignee of a mortgage on the property, Caleb Dickinson of Kingweston, proceeded against Scrase in Chancery for repayment, and in 1747 the property

was conveyed to him.[39] During the 18th century the holding was known simply as 'the Farm' or as East Lydford farm,[40] the name Manor farm not being attached to it until the 19th century.[41] The Dickinsons still held the premises in 1931, but appear to have sold them by 1935.[42]

The estate which John Ryall of South Cadbury built up during the 18th century in East Lydford was devised by him in 1781 to his nephew John Davis, and to Davis's daughter Elizabeth.[43] Davis died in 1836, leaving his property to be divided equally between his five children, but giving his elder son, M. J. Davis, the option of taking the East Lydford estates with the exception of the cottages.[44] In 1838 the estate, then comprising 190 a., was held jointly by M. J. Davis and his mother.[45] The former died in 1846,[46] the latter in 1848,[47] but a suit in Chancery between the descendants of John Davis, begun during the lifetime of his elder son, led to the sale of the estate by auction in 1848 and to the subdivision of the property.[48]

The prior of St. John's hospital, Wells, occurs as holding land in East Lydford manor between 1396[49] and 1476.[50] The tenement was probably held with the hospital's lands in the adjacent parishes of Keinton Mandeville and Babcary.[51]

ECONOMIC HISTORY. Roger de Courcelles's estate, acquired after the Conquest, was rated for geld at 4 hides; 3 hides and $\frac{1}{2}$ virgate were held in demesne, which 6 serfs worked with 2 ploughs. The remainder of the land, $3\frac{1}{2}$ virgates, was tilled by 6 villeins and 3 bordars with $1\frac{1}{2}$ plough, although there was land for 5 ploughs. Only 40 a. of meadow are mentioned, but the number of stock, one riding-horse, 6 cows, 13 pigs, and 160 sheep, suggests a large amount of unrecorded pasture, probably in Lydford moor.[52]

In 1319 William de Reigny held 169 a. of arable, 12 a. of meadow, 40 a. of pasture, 60 a. of wood, and 10s. 4d. rent in East Lydford, Foddington, and Babcary,[53] and in 1329 a messuage, a carucate of arable, 10 a. of meadow, 60 a. of wood, 11s. rent, and pasture for 60 oxen.[54] By the late 14th century the manor had been reduced to about 248 a. of land.[55] The physical subdivision of the manor between the Reigny heirs took place c. 1394,[56] but as the pattern of the manor was evidently one of open fields and

[17] C 142/54/86.
[18] Cal. Pat. 1553, 371.
[19] Sandford Orcas, parish reg.
[20] C.P. 25(2)/205/25 Eliz. I East.
[21] C.P. 25(2)/387/18 Jas. I East.; C.P. 25(2)/526/5 Chas. I Hil.; S.R.O., DD/SAS C/82, 34.
[22] Prob. 11/206 (P.C.C. 167 Essex, will of John Foyle); S.R.O., DD/X/ME; Reg. Adm. Middle Temple, ed. H. A. C. Sturgess, i. 90, 132, 171.
[23] S.R.O., DD/X/ME; Reg. Adm. Middle Temple, i. 185, 261.
[24] S.R.O., DD/HN A VI, 2, 3.
[25] S.R.O., DD/SH 107.
[26] Prob. 11/1095 (P.C.C. 467 Gostling, will of John Ryall).
[27] M.I. in ch.   [28] See above.
[29] S.C. 6/977/6.
[30] S.R.O., DD/WG, box 16, rental, 1587.
[31] Ibid.
[32] S.R.S. xii. 136.
[33] S.C. 2/198/58; S.R.O., DD/WG, box 18, ct. roll.
[34] Ibid. box 16, rental, 1587.
[35] Ibid. box 16, composite ct. rolls.

[36] D.R.O., D 203/B 85.
[37] Ibid.
[38] S.R.O., DD/DN, box 46, deeds of Manor farm.
[39] S.R.O., DD/DN, box 46.
[40] S.R.O., D/P/e. lyd. 13/2/1, 2; DD/DN, box 46, map of E. Lydford farm (n.d.).
[41] P.O. Dir. Som. (1875).
[42] Kelly's Dir. Som. (1931, 1935).
[43] Prob. 11/1095 (P.C.C. 467 Gostling, will of John Ryall).
[44] S.R.O., DD/ED 145B/705, will of John Davis.
[45] S.R.O., tithe award.
[46] S.R.O., DD/ED 222/43, will of Morgan John Davis.
[47] Ibid. 226/431, will of Mary Bradford Davis.
[48] S.R.O., DD/SAS SE/25, sale cat.
[49] S.C. 2/198/58.
[50] S.C. 2/200/55.
[51] H.M.C. Wells, i. 531; Valor Eccl. (Rec. Com.), i. 140.
[52] V.C.H. Som. i. 461.
[53] S.R.S. xii. 119.
[54] Ibid. 136.
[55] S.C. 2/198/58.   [56] Ibid.

common pastures, scattered rather than consolidated holdings were thus created.

The value of the manor at Domesday was £4, the same figure as before the Conquest.[57] The income from the whole manor was £14 5s. in 1396, most of which was derived from leasing pasture.[58] Between 1475 and 1494 the income from the third held by the Say family varied between £4 19s. 3d. in 1475,[59] and £13 1s. 5d. in 1476,[60] decreasing to £6 18s. 2d. in the years 1489–90 and 1493–4.[61] The third share held by the Knoyle family was stated to be worth £2 in 1502,[62] but had risen to £6 18s. 2d. in 1551.[63]

The principal income of the manor came from leasing summer and winter pasture. By 1397 for pasture in the 'moor' and East field the lord received 2d. a week for a horse, 1½d. a week for an ox, and 1d. a week for a calf. Nineteen acres of meadow in Broadmead were leased for 2s. 8d. an acre, and 18 a. of meadow in Herbrooks for 2s. 6d. an acre. Summer pasture in the Garden, West field, Herbrooks, and Rowborough was leased for composite sums. Other tenants took pasture for their animals by the season; 1s. 8d. for a horse, 1s. for an ox, and 8d. for a calf. The total income derived in 1397 from pasture was £15 0s. 5d.[64]

In 1394 there were twelve tenants, comprising one freeholder, three holding ½ virgate, five holding a fardel, one holding ⅓ fardel, one holding 30 a., and one holding a single close. Their properties included land in Babcary and Foddington.[65] A few years later there were three freeholders and 16 other tenants, including one *nativus* holding 13½ a.,[66] whose daughter was sold for £1 in 1398.[67] Two other *nativi* were noted to have fled from the manor in the following year.[68]

There were at least two open fields, East and West, by 1396.[69] Arable was also held in closes by 1394,[70] and closes of pasture had been made in Herbrooks by 1466.[71] Lydford moor was described as 'lately enclosed' in 1732, evidently by mutual agreement among the proprietors.[72] Moves were made in 1803 to inclose East and West fields. They were opposed among others by the rector and the principal landowner, John Davis, who claimed that the arable lands could not be 'too open nor too much exposed to the sun and air'.[73] The East and West fields were inclosed in 1838 and involved the inclosure of 173 a. of arable, just under one quarter of the total area of the parish.[74] References to inclosed pasture near Reynyslese in 1394,[75] and to the leasing of pasture in the lord's wood in 1399,[76] suggest that clearance and inclosure were already taking place there. Twenty-five oak trees were carried away without the licence of the lord in 1604,[77] and a covenant in a lease of 1732 enforced the planting of twelve oak saplings for every acre of timber felled.[78]

By the late 14th century grants of manorial land appear to have been either for one life or three lives,[79] although a lease for two lives was granted in 1431.[80] In the late 16th century a conversion from copyhold to leases for 99 years or two or three lives becomes evident,[81] and this was standard practice during the 17th and 18th centuries.[82] Progressive enfranchisement appears to have taken place during the late 17th and early 18th centuries, particularly on the Foyle holdings.[83]

The largest 18th-century property in the parish, later known as Manor farm, was acquired by the Dickinsons of Kingweston in 1747,[84] when it comprised 166 a., of which 37 a. were leasehold.[85] Lands were purchased in Herbrooks c. 1762,[86] and between 1838 and 1889 the farm comprised nearly 177 a.[87] The Dickinsons sub-let the property at rents rising from £95 in 1748[88] to £150 in 1794.[89] The net income derived from the farm rose from £92 in 1794 to £138 in 1804.[90] The lands acquired by John Ryall from 1744 onwards,[91] which largely passed to the Davis family in 1781,[92] totalled 190 a. in 1838, and included Church farm and Home farm.[93] In 1838 the Davis family were also leasing Manor farm from the Dickinsons,[94] and were therefore personally farming more than half the total acreage of the parish. On the sale of the Davis property in 1848[95] the estate was divided, and by 1889 Church farm (86 a.) and Home farm (43 a.) were in separate ownership and occupation.[96] Rubbery farm originated from 4 closes of leasehold land and pasture in 1688,[97] and had grown to 70 a. in 1838[98] and to 108 a. by 1889.[99] Thus in 1889 414 a. were occupied by four farmers, and there were no other holdings in excess of 30 a.[1] By 1838 there were 276½ a. of arable and 365 a. of meadow.[2] During the

[57] *V.C.H. Som.* i. 461.
[58] S.C. 2/198/58.
[59] S.C. 6/977/14.
[60] S.C. 6/977/16.
[61] S.C. 6/Hen. VII/557–60.
[62] *Cal. Inq. p.m. Hen. VII,* ii, p. 383.
[63] *Cal. Pat.* 1553, 371.
[64] S.R.O., DD/WG, box 18, ct. roll.
[65] S.C. 2/198/58.
[66] Ibid.
[67] S.R.O., DD/WG, box 18, ct. roll.
[68] Ibid.
[69] S.C. 2/198/58.
[70] Ibid.
[71] S.C. 2/200/55.
[72] S.R.O., DD/DN, box 46, lease, 1747.
[73] S.R.O., D/P/e. lyd. 9/1/1.
[74] S.R.O., CR 28.
[75] S.C. 2/198/58.
[76] S.R.O., DD/WG, box 18, ct. roll.
[77] Ibid. box 16, ct. roll.
[78] S.R.O., DD/PH 34, lease, Phelips to Lyde, 1732.
[79] S.C. 2/198/58; S.C. 2/200/55; S.C. 6/977/14, 24; S.R.O., DD/WG, box 18, ct. roll.
[80] B.M. Harl. Ch. 55 E 8.

[81] S.R.O., DD/X/ME. First noted in 1587 in a lease of 1623.
[82] Ibid.; DD/WG, boxes 9, 13; Q/RR, papists' estates, roll 3.
[83] S.R.O., DD/X/ME; DD/DN, box 46; DD/HN A VI, 2, 3.
[84] S.R.O., DD/DN, box 46.
[85] Ibid. box 45.
[86] Ibid. box 34, ledger C.
[87] S.R.O., tithe award; D/G/SM, 160/30.
[88] S.R.O., DD/DN, box 34, ledger C.
[89] Ibid. box 36, ledger C.
[90] Ibid.
[91] S.R.O., D/P/e. lyd. 13/2/1.
[92] Prob. 11/1095 (P.C.C. 467 Gostling, will of John Ryall).
[93] S.R.O., tithe award.
[94] Ibid.
[95] S.R.O., DD/SAS SE/25.
[96] S.R.O., D/G/SM, 160/30.
[97] S.R.O., DD/X/ME.
[98] S.R.O., tithe award.
[99] S.R.O., D/G/SM, 160/30.
[1] Ibid.
[2] S.R.O., tithe award.

19th century conversion from arable to pasture on a large scale took place, and by 1905 85 per cent of the parish was permanent grass.[3] Notes made for tithe purposes in 1772 show that on seven holdings with 109½ a. of arable, wheat accounted for 51½ a., beans for 46 a., and barley (grown only on Rubbery farm) for 12 a.[4]

In 1821 there were only 16 out of 30 families employed in agriculture,[5] and the proximity of the parish to both the Foss Way and to the Somerton to Castle Cary road encouraged tradesmen. In 1859 there were a chemist and druggist, baker, shoemaker, coal merchant, grocer, and wheelwright,[6] a marine store dealer in 1875,[7] a road contractor in 1883,[8] a butcher and poultry dealer in 1897,[9] a threshing machine proprietor and a steam haulier in 1919,[10] and a motor engineer in 1931.[11] A dairy was established on the Foss Way near the railway station shortly before the First World War;[12] in 1970 it was a garage and scrapyard.

At the time of Domesday there was a mill paying 10s.[13] Nothing is known of its site or subsequent history.

LOCAL GOVERNMENT. Court rolls have been found only for that third of the manor held successively by the Banastre, Stourton, Hill, Say, and Waldegrave families. Court rolls survive for the years 1394–1400, 1457, 1466–7, and intermittently from 1588 to 1605.[14] During the late 14th and 15th centuries the manor court for this third, described as a *curia legalis*, was generally held twice a year and always once in the autumn. By the late 16th and early 17th centuries it met once a year in April or May. By 1433 it was held with that of Wheathill.[15] Leases of properties formerly held of East Lydford manor and later of Wheathill owed suit of court to Wheathill in the 18th century.[16] Leasehold tenements forming part of the third held by the Knoyle, Parham, and Foyle families owed suit of court to East Lydford at intervals between 1579 and 1688.[17] Apart from tenurial business and minor offences, the chief concern was the annual leasing of summer and winter pasture.

No appointments of manorial officials have been noted, probably because of the division of the manor. Two churchwardens were appointed by 1554,[18] but between 1724 and 1815 the vestry generally appointed only one, together with one overseer of the poor,[19] and from 1742 to 1803 one or two surveyors of the highways,[20] all of whom

served for their estates in rotation and took parish apprentices in the same manner. In 1871–89 and 1905 both a rector's warden and parish warden were appointed. Two overseers were appointed between 1854 and 1891, and four between 1892 and 1894. The vestry also appointed a waywarden between 1854 and 1893, and a hayward to impound strays in 1862.[21]

There was a poorhouse by 1756.[22] A house for the poor was rented from Mary Phelips in 1775 and 1778, and from John Davis between 1783 and 1815.[23] The parish became part of the Shepton Mallet poor-law union in 1836.[24]

CHURCH. The church of East Lydford is first mentioned in 1230, although reference was made at that date to the then parson's predecessors.[25] By 1323 the advowson was held by the Reigny family, lords of the manor.[26] It continued in their hands until, like the manor, it passed to Sir Ralph de Middleney, who presented in 1343 and 1362.[27] The Crown presented in 1388 while the Reigny family was attempting to regain the manor from the Windsors.[28] Thereafter the advowson, like the manor, split into three parts and descended with them, the owner of each share presenting at every third vacancy. In 1415, after an inquisition to determine the right of patronage, three chaplains, probably as feoffees, presented for the Montforts.[29] Robert Erlegh presented in 1435, presumably for the Wykyng and Knoyle share,[30] and Robert More in 1504, probably during the minority of Peter Knoyle.[31] Frances, widow of Giles Paulet, and others presented in 1580 for the Waldegraves.[32] The Bishop collated by lapse in 1691,[33] and in 1730 mistakenly granted the presentation to Jeremy Cray.[34] Cray's incumbent resigned when Edward Foyle claimed the patronage, and Foyle presented his own candidate in the same year.[35]

John Ryall appears to have acquired the Foyle share for his nephew, Narcissus Ryall, and on the former's death in 1781 it was left in trust to another nephew John Davis, and the latter's daughter Elizabeth, on condition that they presented Narcissus on his taking holy orders.[36] Between 1789 and 1791 Davis also appears to have acquired from Thomas Wyld the third formerly held by the Deane and Duke families.[37] William Harbin of Sherborne (Dors.) (d. 1823), appears to have purchased two-thirds of the advowson, which he left to his wife Rhoda, who had inherited the remaining third.[38]

[3] Statistics supplied by the then Bd. of Agric. (1905).
[4] S.R.O., D/P/e. lyd. 14/5/1.
[5] C. & J. Greenwood, *Som. Delineated*.
[6] Harrison, Harrod, & Co. *Dir. Som.* (1859).
[7] *P.O. Dir. Som.* (1875).
[8] *Kelly's Dir. Som.* (1883).
[9] Ibid. (1897).
[10] Ibid. (1919).
[11] Ibid. (1931).
[12] Ibid. (1914).
[13] *V.C.H. Som.* i. 461.
[14] S.C. 2/198/58 (1394–96); S.R.O., DD/WG, box 18 (1397–1400); S.C. 2/200/57 (1433–4); S.C. 2/200/55 (1457, 1466–7); S.R.O., DD/WG, box 16 (1588–1605).
[15] S.C. 2/200/57.
[16] S.R.O., DD/PH 34, lease, Phelips to Lyde, 1732.
[17] S.R.O., DD/X/ME.
[18] S.R.O., D/D/Ca 22.
[19] S.R.O., D/P/e. lyd. 4/1/1, 13/1/1, 2.

[20] Ibid. 14/5/1, 2.
[21] Ibid. 9/1/2.
[22] S.R.O., D/P/e. lyd. 13/2/1.   [23] Ibid.
[24] *Poor Law Com. 2nd Rep.* p. 549.
[25] *Cur. Reg. R.* xiv. 129, 290.
[26] *S.R.S.* i. 222, 288, 303; ix. 151.
[27] Ibid. x. 722, 759.
[28] *Cal. Pat.* 1385–8, 533.
[29] *S.R.S.* xxix. 202; xiii. 31.
[30] Ibid. xxxii. 184.
[31] Ibid. liv. 80, 103.
[32] *Som. Incumbents*, ed. Weaver, 132, 174, 214.
[33] Ibid. 133; Wells Dioc. Regy., Reg. Kidder f. 1.
[34] *Som. Incumbents*, 133.
[35] Ibid.; Wells Dioc. Regy., Reg. Wynne f. 10.
[36] Prob. 11/1095 (P.C.C. 467 Gostling, will of John Ryall).
[37] S.R.O., Q/RE.
[38] S.R.O., DD/HN, box 9, k.

She presented in 1829, 1833, and 1839, and on her death in 1846 the patronage was sold.[39] It appears to have been purchased by P. J. Newell, instituted in 1849, and succeeded in both patronage and rectory by the Revd. P. S. Newell in 1853.[40] It was purchased from the latter by J. J. Moss, who presented himself in 1864 and another in 1870.[41] Moss died in 1887,[42] the Bishop collating by lapse the following year,[43] and both patronage and rectory were acquired by G. S. Henning in 1895.[44] The National Church League Trustees, now the Church Society, have presented since 1916.[45] In 1905 the rectories of East Lydford and Wheathill were united,[46] and in 1965 were combined with West Lydford to form a united benefice called the Lydfords.[47] The rector in 1970 also held the united benefice of Alford and Hornblotton, and lived at West Lydford.[48]

The church was valued at £6 13s. 4d. in 1291.[49] In 1535 the net value was £7 16s. 7d.[50] By c. 1668 it was said to be worth £40[51] and in 1742 £39 12s. 9d.[52] By 1831 the net income had risen to £135.[53] J. J. Moss (rector 1864–70) evidently bequeathed stock to augment the living, and this was transferred to the Governors of Queen Anne's Bounty in 1889.[54]

The tithes were valued at £6 5s. 3d. in 1535.[55] By 1672 the rector claimed tithes of corn and grain, and specified 2d. an acre for mown grass (6d. if let to an outsider), 2d. for an orchard, 1d. for a garden, 3d. for a cow's milk, 2d. for the milk of heifers under 4 years old; 2d. a month for every 20 sheep or tithe of wool if kept the whole year; 1d. for the fall of a colt, ½d. for the fall of each calf, lamb, or pig; one egg for each hen and 2 eggs for the master cock; 1d. in the shilling from all rents paid by outsiders for grazing land in the parish; the tenth faggot cut in Raynes wood, and a customary payment of 6s. 8d. in respect of 20 a. of meadow and pasture by Raynes wood.[56] In 1838 a rent-charge of £106 16s. 3d. was assigned to the rector.[57]

In 1230 the parson held a virgate of land formerly given to the church, in respect of which he claimed common grazing in Lydford moor for four oxen, two cows, and one draught beast.[58] In 1334 the glebe comprised 40 a. of arable and 3 a. of meadow which, with oblations, obventions, and small tithes, was valued at 53s. 10d.[59] In 1535 the glebe was valued at 31s. 4d.,[60] and in 1606 the

rector possessed 36 a. of which 27 a. were arable in the two open fields.[61] By 1838 the rector held a total of 32 a.,[62] reduced by 1875 to 26 a.[63] and to 23 a. by 1894.[64] There were nearly 25 a. of glebe in 1972.[65]

Before the 19th century the site of the parsonage house was probably always in Church Lane. The property was described as unfit in 1831,[66] and was used as a farm-house in 1840,[67] although it had been occupied by the previous incumbent.[68] The building, known as the Old Rectory, was occupied as a private dwelling-house in 1970. It is a two-storeyed building of lias with three bays and a slate roof. In 1872 the rector exchanged parcels of glebe with Moss, the former rector, for 3 a. on the north side of Cary Road, on which a large rectory house was built.[69] This house was sold c. 1965 on the union of the benefices of East and West Lydford,[70] and in 1970 was known as the Rookery.

In 1568 the parson was reported for not preaching the quarterly sermons and was adjudged 'not a man able to serve for the parish'.[71] In 1623 there was no catechizing and only irregular services, and James Smith, the assistant curate, was presented as 'a man of dissolute life and conversation, an ale house haunter', and unfit for the ministry.[72] In 1827 and 1840 morning and evening services were held alternately,[73] but by 1870, although there was no resident rector nor curate, there were two services every Sunday and Holy Communion once a month.[74] By 1893 the Sunday services had been increased to three and there were 23 communicants on the roll.[75] By 1920 there was a return to two Sunday services, although communion was administered weekly.[76]

Edward Wareham (rector from 1613) held West Lydford in plurality[77] and employed assistant curates to serve East Lydford.[78] It is not known if he retained East Lydford during the Interregnum. Thomas Horsey (rector c. 1657–90) had been accused of being 'a drunkard, quarreler, a railer, a malignant for contemning of authority and vilifying of Acts of Parliament, a constant gamester, a prophaner of the Lord's day, a breaker down of fences, an encourager of idle loose livers and swearers, a false swearer, an abusive man in language, with much more wickedness'.[79] His personal influence among the Justices apparently prevented a trial and also obtained for him the living of East Lydford between 1656 and 1658.[80] He secured the

[39] Ibid.; list in church.
[40] List in church; *P.O. Dir. Som.* (1861).
[41] List in church.
[42] S.R.O., D/P/e. lyd. 23/3, death cert.
[43] *Kelly's Dir. Som.* (1889).
[44] Ibid. (1897).
[45] *Dioc. Dir.* (1916–70); *Crockford.*
[46] Order in Council, 11 Dec. 1905.
[47] Ex. inf. the rector, the Revd. R. Gregory.
[48] Ibid.
[49] *Tax. Eccl.* (Rec. Com.), 197, 201.
[50] *Valor Eccl.* (Rec. Com.), i. 153.
[51] S.R.O., D/D/Vc 24.
[52] *Compleat Hist. of Som.* (1742), 200.
[53] *Rep. Com. Eccl. Revenues,* pp. 170–1.
[54] S.R.O., D/P/e. lyd. 23/2, 3.
[55] *Valor Eccl.* (Rec. Com.), i. 153.
[56] S.R.O., D/D/Rg 112.
[57] S.R.O., tithe award.
[58] *Cur. Reg. R.* xiv. 290.
[59] E 179/169/14.
[60] *Valor Eccl.* (Rec. Com.), i. 153.
[61] S.R.O., D/D/Rg 112.
[62] S.R.O., tithe award.
[63] *P.O. Dir. Som.* (1875).
[64] Ibid. (1894).
[65] Ex inf. Dioc. Secretary.
[66] *Rep. Com. Eccl. Revenues,* pp. 170–1.
[67] S.R.O., D/D/V rtns. 1840.
[68] Ibid. 1827.
[69] S.R.O., D/P/e. lyd. 23/1.
[70] Ex inf. the rector, the Revd. R. Gregory.
[71] S.R.O., D/D/Ca 40.
[72] Ibid. 236.
[73] S.R.O., D/D/V rtns. 1827, 1840.
[74] Ibid. 1870.
[75] S.R.O., D/P/e. lyd. 23/2.
[76] Ibid. 2/5/2.
[77] *Som. Incumbents,* ed. Weaver, 134.
[78] S.R.O., D/D/Rr 112: 1620, 1628, 1630
[79] S.R.O., DD/SFR 8/1 f. 21.
[80] Ibid.; Q/SR 95, ii, 196.

imprisonment of many East Lydford Quakers for non-payment of tithes, interrupting services, and non-attendance at church.[81] In 1661 he forcibly prevented the removal of a Quaker's coffin which was being carried from Alford to Limington via East Lydford and secured its burial in the churchyard.[82]

A number of subsequent incumbents held in plurality, including Phipps Weston (rector 1763–84) who, while incumbent here, was fellow of Magdalen College, Oxford, rector of Rushall (Wilts.), and vicar of Shabbington (Bucks.).[83] Curates were employed regularly at least from Weston's time,[84] and both Edward Harbin (rector 1829–33) and James Hooper (rector 1839–49) held the living of Kingweston in plurality.[85]

The medieval church of St. Peter lay isolated at the northern end of the village on the banks of the Brue. The site is marked by the remains of the churchyard wall, a heap of rubble around the remains of the porch, and a few scattered gravestones. It was a small stone building comprising chancel and nave with a large south porch and small square bellcot, possibly of wood, on the west gable end. There were two square-headed mullioned windows of two lights each in the south wall of the chancel and nave, and also a Decorated window in the south chancel wall. Inside the porch was a heavy carved door, surmounted by a canopied niche with corbel under, and to the right of the door a Decorated stoup.[86] Reference is made to a tower in 1756 and 1761.[87] The proximity of the church to the river evidently led to periodic flooding; in 1786 a wall was swept away by the 'late great flood',[88] and in 1799 the church was cleaned after an 'inundation'.[89] In 1864 the parishioners decided to rebuild the church on a new site, the old building being dilapidated, damp, and inconvenient.[90]

The present church of the *BLESSED VIRGIN MARY* was erected nearer the centre of the village, the site and cost of the building being provided by J. J. Moss (rector 1864–70) in memory of his deceased wife.[91] It was designed by Benjamin Ferrey and consecrated in 1866.[92] It is generally in 14th-century style and consists of a chancel and nave, with an octagonal north tower and spire. The walls are of Keinton stone with Doulting stone dressings. The Jacobean oak pulpit and a plain font, possibly 13th century, were taken from the old church. In the west wall are set two inscriptions

brought by Moss from catacombs in Rome, and between them a 15th-century alabaster relief of St. George, acquired by him in the north of England.[93] The east window by C. E. Kempe was installed in 1879.[94]

The plate includes a paten of 1725 and chalices of 1776 and 1796, only the second of which belonged to the old church.[95] There is one bell dated 1865.[96] The registers begin in 1730, but the marriages are incomplete.[97]

NONCONFORMITY. The Quaker, John Clothier, was one of the 'first receivers of those that first published the Gospel' in Somerset, *c.* 1656, and many meetings were held at his house.[98] Persecution of the Quakers by the post-Restoration rector seems to have led to a gradual diminution in their numbers,[99] although Clothier's house was licensed for meetings in 1689[1] and a bequest to poor Quakers was made in the will of Henry Scrase of Manor Farm, dated 1694.[2]

The house of William Paige, Independent minister, was licensed for meetings in 1846, but he moved to Castle Cary in the following year.[3]

EDUCATION. A schoolmaster was mentioned in 1813,[4] and in 1818 there were weekly schools for small children.[5] A free Sunday school for 8 boys and 14 girls is recorded in 1835,[6] which by 1846 was supported by subscriptions.[7] A schoolmaster, mentioned in 1852 and 1856,[8] probably taught in the day- and Sunday school supported by the rector, which survived until at least 1861.[9]

A school, erected by subscription on the west side of Church Lane in 1875, was endowed with £400 by J. J. Moss, the rector, owner of the site.[10] Thirty children were admitted in 1876.[11] The school comprised a small teacher's house, single schoolroom, and porch.[12] The first mistress was certificated and a stipendiary monitress was appointed in 1880.[13] The children of the 'labouring classes' were charged 2*d.* a week for the first child from each family, 1*d.* a week for each subsequent child, and 2*d.* a week if over 9 years of age. All other children paid 3*d.* a week.[14] The school was administered by managers but was subject to governmental and diocesan inspection.[15] In 1903

[81] S.R.O., DD/SFR 8/1, *passim.*
[82] Ibid. f. 10.
[83] Foster, *Alumni Oxon.*
[84] S.R.O., D/D/Bo, 1781, 1784.
[85] S.R.O., D/P/kingw. 2/1/4.
[86] Taunton Castle, Pigott Colln., water-colour by J. Buckler, 1833; Braikenridge Colln., water-colours by W. W. Wheatley, 1846.
[87] S.R.O., D/P/e. lyd. 4/1/1.
[88] Ibid.
[89] Ibid.
[90] S.R.O., D/P/e. lyd. 8/3/1.
[91] Ibid.
[92] *Langport Herald*, 7 Apr. 1866.
[93] S.R.O., D/P/e. lyd. 23/2.
[94] Pevsner, *South and West Som.*, 163.
[95] *Proc. Som. Arch. Soc.*, xliii. 181.
[96] S.R.O., DD/SAS CH/16, p. 237.
[97] S.R.O., D/P/e. lyd. 2/1/1, 2.
[98] S.R.O., DD/SFR 8/1.
[99] See above.

[1] S.R.O., Q/RR, meeting-house lics.
[2] S.R.O., DD/DN, box 46, will of Henry Scrase, 1694.
[3] S.R.O., D/D/Rm 2. The Wesleyan chapel, licensed in 1833 and attributed to East Lydford, is probably the chapel on the Foss Way near Cross Keys, which lies in West Lydford (ibid.).
[4] East Lydford par. reg. *penes* the rector.
[5] *Digest of Returns to Sel. Cttee. on Educ. of Poor*, H.C. 224 (1819), ix.
[6] *Educ. Enquiry Abstract*, H.C. 62 (1835), xlii.
[7] *Church Sch. Inquiry*, 1846–7.
[8] East Lydford par. reg. *penes* the rector.
[9] *P.O. Dir. Som.* (1861).
[10] S.R.O., D/P/e. lyd. 9/1/2, 18/7/1, 23/2; *Kelly's Dir. Som.* (1875).
[11] *Kelly's Dir. Som.* (1875); S.R.O., C/E, box 13, admission reg.
[12] S.R.O., DD/EDS, East Lydford.
[13] S.R.O., D/P/e. lyd. 18/7/1.
[14] Ibid.
[15] Ibid.

there were 31 pupils on the books and it was stated to be 'a neatly kept and carefully taught little school'.[16] The attendance having dwindled to two by 1949, the school was closed and the remaining pupils transferred to West Lydford school.[17] The

buildings are now (1970) occupied as a dwelling-house called the Old Schoolhouse.

CHARITIES FOR THE POOR. None known.

SOMERTON

SOMERTON parish, the largest in the hundred, shares with Pitney and Kingsdon the 200 ft. Lower Lias ridge between the valleys of the Yeo and the Cary.[1] It is over $6\frac{1}{4}$ miles from the Eighteen Feet Rhine in King's Sedgemoor in the north-west to Catsgore in the south-east, and is up to 4 miles from east to west. The river Cary forms the natural boundary with Compton Dundon and Charlton Mackrell in the north and east and, before the loss of Kingsmoor at the end of the 19th century, the southern limit was the Yeo. Elsewhere the boundaries follow no natural features and those with Pitney and Kingsdon interlock in a manner suggesting relatively late formation.[2] Even later are the limits of Somerton on King's Sedgemoor, suggested c. 1625[3] but not finally defined until inclosure of the 'moor' in 1795.[4] In 1841 the total area was 6,928 a.[5] In 1885 the detached parts of the parish were absorbed by neighbours: Kingsmoor went to Long Sutton and Kingsdon, and two smaller areas to the east were added to Charlton Mackrell and Kingsdon.[6] In 1901 the area was 6,610 a.[7]

The parish came within the 'wealthy corn-growing hinterland' of Roman Ilchester and was evidently cultivated by farmers who in the 1st century were purely native but later increasingly Romanized. At least eight such farms and a larger settlement at Catsgore have been identified, not necessarily occupied at the same time.[8] The position of these sites has had no obvious effect on later settlement with the possible exception of Hurcot, north-east of the town beyond the Cary, where alabaster was quarried on the Keuper marl.[9] There a Romanized farmstead site was succeeded by a medieval manor with its own field system.[10] There was a population there in 1604–5 of 18 adults and 22 youths,[11] and in 1765 there were 16 houses.[12]

The suggested origin of the name Somerton as 'summer dwelling' is at variance with the physical position of the town and of most of the parish.[13] The town itself has two main suburbs: Lower Somerton, the manorial settlement of Somerton Erleigh[14] south-east of the town, and West End

or Western Town, until the 20th century an irregular group of small cottages between the Langport and Long Sutton roads, probably settled in the 17th century.[15] In 1630 complaints were made against the 'great number' of cottages erected about the town and occupied by poor people liable at any time to fall a burden on the rates.[16] Points of early settlement elsewhere in the parish include St. Cleers farm, Melbury, and Highbrooks. St. Cleers, traditionally the site of a Saxon royal dwelling,[17] was a farm complex in 1336.[18] Melbury seems to have originated as the site of a windmill, and a settlement, probably with a chapel, grew up around a green.[19] Buildings there were in decay in the early 18th century, and the settlement had disappeared by the 19th century.[20] Highbrooks, on the southern boundary of the parish, was a small farm at least from the 14th century.[21]

The parish had three field systems centred on the three main manors. Hurcot had one common field in the 17th and 18th centuries; Somerton Erleigh had East, South, West, and Lower Somerton fields at the beginning of the 17th century, though the last two may have been the same.[22] Somerton manor had four fields, named after the cardinal points, in the Middle Ages, which were rearranged in the 16th century.[23] By 1806 North field occupied the plateau north of the town, including Bancombe, Bradley, and Brockle hills. North-west field was in the angle formed by the Langport road, extending to Somerton hill, and the High Ham road. South-west field lay immediately south of the Langport road, to the west of St. Cleers Farm. South field occupied South hill and the southern slopes of the parish. These fields were inclosed in 1806.

Grassland was largely on the alluvium of the Yeo and Cary valleys, but Hibroc, now Highbrooks, occurs as meadow in the 12th century.[24] By 1484 Somerton manor alone had at least 62 a. of meadow in demesne at 'Blakmore', 'Newdich', 'Rodehampe', and 'Lowdeche'.[25] New moor in Somerton Erleigh occurs in 1597,[26] and Somerton New mead in 1672.[27]

In 1352 woodland attached to Somerton manor

[16] S.R.O., C/E 26.
[17] S.R.O., D/P/e. lyd. 18/7/2; C/E, box 13, log bks.
[1] Geol. Surv. Map 1", solid and drift, sheet 296 (1969 edn.). This article was completed in 1971.
[2] See pp. 50, 134.
[3] D.R.O., D 124, box 18.
[4] S.R.O., CR 116.   [5] Census, 1841.
[6] Local Govt. Bd. Prov. Orders Conf. Order (Poor Law), (No. 2), Act (1885).
[7] Census, 1901.
[8] Proc. Som. Arch. Soc. xcvi. 41–77; ex inf. Mr. R. H. Leech.
[9] Collinson, Hist. Som. iii. 182.
[10] Proc. Som. Arch. Soc. xcvi. 47.
[11] S.R.O., D/P/som 4/1/1, pp. 176–87.
[12] S.R.O., DD/DN, box 43.
[13] E. Ekwall, Dict. Eng. Place Names (4th edn.), 430; see below, p. 138.

[14] See p. 135.
[15] S.R.O., D/P/som 4/1/1, p. 17: D.R.O., D 124, box 1, ct. papers, 1809; box 17, ct. bk. 1702.
[16] S.R.S. xxiv. 141; see below, p. 142.
[17] See p. 138.
[18] C 135/49/18.
[19] D.R.O., D 124, boxes 109, 110; S.R.O., D/P/som 4/1/1, pp. 73, 338, 346; see below, pp. 144, 150.
[20] D.R.O., D 124, boxes 109, 116; S.R.O., tithe award.
[21] S.R.S. xii. 31.
[22] S.R.O., T/PH/vch 11; D.R.O., D 124, box 2; Hunt. Libr., HA Manorial, box 22, survey 1581.
[23] S.R.O., T/PH/vch 11.
[24] K.B. 26/158 rot. 4; Ilchester Almshouse Deeds, ed. W. Buckler, no. 62; S.R.S. xxv. 1–2, 27.
[25] S.C. 6/974/6.
[26] S.R.O., DD/SAS (C/114), 6.
[27] D.R.O., D 124, box 110.

amounted to 64 a., 'from which nothing can be carried in winter owing to the depth of the road there'.[28] This was known in the 16th century as West wood or Westwood Park.[29] Under West wood the present Park farm recalls the position of a park which in the 13th century was used to impound stock.[30] Copley wood above Hurcot covers a field known as Parks, and adjoins others which may have formed another area for stocking game.[31] Most of the wood on the Somerton Erleigh estate is of 19th-century origin, though ornamental planting was begun by William Howe in the late 18th century.[32] The total amount of wood in the parish increased from 219 a. in 1841 to 322 a. in 1905.[33]

The parish is not well watered, only two streams draining the whole area south of the town. The town itself was supplied by four common wells and by Pound Pools, a spring near the pound at the western end of the town, which fed a stream running through the streets.[34] The Cary did not drive a mill, but fishing rights produced a small income. There was a ruined fish house near the river bank in 1484 and rights to fish between Cary bridge and Pitney Steart (Stertewethy) allowed the tenant to use a fish weir and instruments called 'elesperes', 'shybbes', and 'stryngas piscare'.[35]

The road system of the parish, as of several of its neighbours, demonstrates the importance of the east–west market routes, though the centre of the town is now so placed as to make all but its western access indirect. The eastern and northern routes converge at the north end of Cary bridge, which was in existence by 1258.[36] The medieval route from Ilchester via Kingsdon entered from the east. Its course, passing close to the north side of Somerton Randolph manor-house, was diverted by John Frederick Pinney in stages between 1824 and 1846 in order to improve his own property.[37] The direct western route from Langport entered the town by the long slope from Somerton hill and joined the built-up area at Shorn Tree.[38] The western limit of the town proper was marked by a cross, first referred to c. 1225.[39] The west, north, and east routes into the town were turnpiked by the Langport, Somerton, and Castle Cary trust in 1753, the stretch from Cary bridge to Kingsdon in 1777–8, and a road south to Catsgore Farm in 1856–7.[40] The last was one of several which criss-crossed the southern part of the parish, serving the former open fields. North of the town the roads were fewer in number and now serve only the 'moors'.

There was a ford through the Cary below Bradley hill, known in 1447 as Stonyford, and now as Grove Steining ford.[41] Pitney Steart, Park, Somerton Door, and Etsome bridges are modern and comparatively new structures crossing the Cary.[42] Earlier bridges in the parish included Stonebrugge in 1447,[43] Lady bridge in Lower Somerton by 1484,[44] Levorum and Sedgemoor's bridges in 1599,[45] and Miss bridge in 1760.[46]

Somerton was gradually isolated in the 19th century because of the development of the more southerly route eastwards from Langport through Long Sutton, and by the absence of a railway. The Southern Junction Railway was mooted in 1881 and again in 1898 and 1901, all schemes taking roughly the same route as the present course of the railway.[47] The link between Castle Cary and Langport was constructed in 1906, involving a viaduct over the Cary,[48] a deep cutting in the centre of the town, where the station was built, and a tunnel under South hill. The station was closed to passengers in 1962 and to goods in 1964.[49] Plans for a tramway linking the town with Keinton Mandeville, Castle Cary, and Evercreech were put forward in 1891, 1892, and 1894.[50]

The town itself seems to have originated as a short-lived Saxon burh in the area north-west of the church, known as Bury by 1349.[51] The abandonment of the original settlement centre probably dates from the creation of the new market and surrounding burgage properties south of the church before 1290.[52] A new alignment of streets involving the creation of West Street and Broad Street gradually obliterated the original network, which comprised a direct east–west route north of the Vicarage and church, with a junction or crossroads later providing access to the new market place. There were 'ancient burgages' north of the churchyard in the 17th century in a street then referred to as East Street,[53] now represented by the road between Cow Square and the Vicarage. New Street, so named by 1349,[54] was a continuation of East Street, and serves as further evidence of the town's expansion in the 13th and early 14th centuries.

North Street first occurs in 1624–5,[55] Pig or Swine Street, Long Acre Lane, and Kircombe Street by 1664–6.[56] Pig Street became known as Broad Street in the late 18th century. Kircombe Street probably derives its name from the Kirkham family: Robert Kirkham occurs in 1447,[57] and Nicholas Kirkham of Winchester, lunatic, held 100 a. in the

[28] *Cal. Inq. p.m.* x, p. 44.
[29] *S.R.S.* lxix, p. 29.
[30] *Rot. Hund.* (Rec. Com.), ii. 123, 141.
[31] S.R.O., tithe award.
[32] Bristol Univ. Libr., Pinney papers, letter bk.
[33] S.R.O., tithe award; statistics supplied by the then Bd. of Agric. (1905).
[34] D.R.O., D 124, boxes 1, 111; S.R.O., D/P/som 4/1/2, p. 447.
[35] S.C. 6/974/6.
[36] K.B. 26/158 rot. 4.
[37] S.R.O., DD/PI 7/7, 9/10, 10/1, 16/1. The present approach to New Street was evidently cut at the same time and Old Hill was abandoned: D.R.O., D 124, box 285.
[38] S.R.O., DD/S/BT 96, Ilchester to Scriven 1772.
[39] *S.R.S.* xiv. 66.
[40] S.R.O., D/T/lsc 2: bk. of maps, 1830; Langport, Somerton, and Castle Cary Turnpike Act, 26 Geo. II, c. 92 (Local and Personal); Extension Act, 18 Geo. III, c. 100 (Local and Personal); Extension Act, 20–1 Vict. c. 56 (Local and Personal).

[41] Hunt. Libr., HA Manorial, box 22, ct. roll 1447; O.S. Nat. Grid 476305.
[42] S.R.O., D/P/som 13/2/1, p. 302.
[43] Hunt. Libr., HA Manorial, box 22, ct. roll 1447.
[44] S.C. 6/974/6.
[45] S.R.O., D/P/som 4/1/1, p. 145.
[46] D.R.O., D 124, box 17, manor ct. bk. 1754–1814.
[47] S.R.O., Q/R, deposited plans 393, 507, 533.
[48] S.R.O., DD/PI 16.
[49] C. R. Clinker and J. M. Firth, *Reg. Closed Passenger Stations*, ii and suppl.
[50] S.R.O., Q/R, deposited plans 445, 448, 463; Somerton and Evercreech Tramway Act, 56–7 Vict. c. 8 (Local Act).
[51] Hunt. Libr., HA Manorial, box 22, ct. roll.
[52] See p. 143.
[53] D.R.O., D 124, box 17, manor ct. bk. 1701–16, *sub anno* 1703; box 111, Stawell to Collins 1672.
[54] Hunt. Libr., HA Manorial, box 22, ct. roll.
[55] C 3/444/62. [56] D.R.O., D 124, box 117, survey.
[57] Hunt. Libr., HA Manorial, box 22, ct. roll.

parish in 1486.[58] Other features of the town plan include the old pound at the end of West Street, so named in 1572,[59] on which three houses had been built by 1661;[60] Pye Corner (by 1700), Webber, Warber, or Pollum Lane (1656); and Pester's Lane (by 1739).[61]

and Ham stone as building materials has preserved the unity and scale of the older town. The Market Place, with its buildings irregularly disposed round the 17th-century Town Hall and Market Cross, has been called 'one of the most happily grouped urban pictures in Somerset'.[63] From its north-east

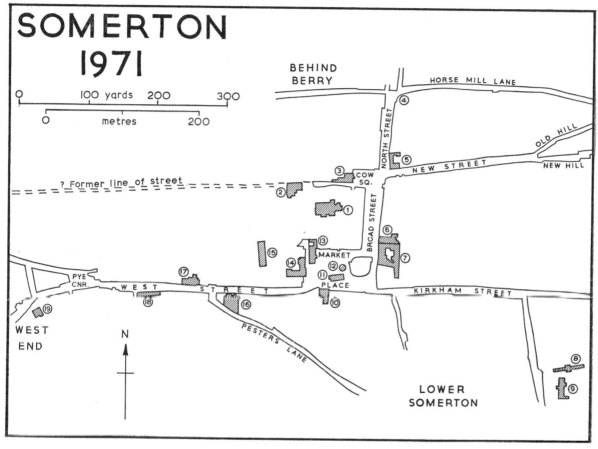

1. St. Michael's Church
2. Vicarage
3. Old Hall
4. Site of Horse Mill
5. Scott Gould Homes
6. Former Free School
7. Red Lion Inn
8. Tithe Barn
9. Old Parsonage
10. White Hart Inn
11. Town Hall
12. Market Cross
13. Lady Smith Memorial Hall
14. Bank House, Site of Great House
15. Methodist Chapel
16. Congregational Chapel
17. Unicorn Inn
18. Hext Alms-houses
19. Former Bible Christian Chapel

Houses in and near the Market Place were among the most substantial in the town in the 17th century. They were followed by several dignified 18th-century residences and by the re-fronting of earlier houses. By the end of the 18th century Somerton had an 'air of neatness and respectability'[62]—a description which could still be applied to the town centre in the 1970s. No wholesale redevelopment has taken place and few shop-fronts have been inserted. At the same time the continued use of lias

corner runs the tree-lined Broad Street with Cow Square opening out of it. In this area Somerton's better 18th-century houses are situated, several of them still occupied as residences. Beyond, in North Street, the houses are rather smaller and date mostly from the earlier 19th century.

Several domestic buildings in Somerton, including the Vicarage,[64] contain medieval features. The present White Hart inn (formerly the Bear), which stands on the south side of the Market Place, was

[58] Cal. Inq. p.m. Hen. VII, iii, p. 558.
[59] Hunt. Libr., HA Manorial, box 22, ct. roll.
[60] S.R.O., DD/MI, box 9, survey.
[61] D.R.O., D 124, box 17, survey 1700; box 106, Applyn to Strangways 1656; box 108, Horner to Hacker 1739.

[62] W. G. Maton, Observations on Western Counties (1797), ii. 28.
[63] Pevsner, South & West Som. 290; see pl. facing p. 192.
[64] See p. 148.

re-fronted in the mid 19th century. It contains an open roof of late-medieval date on the upper floor of what was originally a gable cross-wing. The presence of very thick walls and other masonry in outbuildings behind the inn has often been quoted in support of a tradition that a castle once occupied the site. This tradition dates from the late 18th century, and evidently arose from a confusion with Somerton (Lincs.), where there is a castle.[65] The name 'Somerton Castle' was also at one time applied to a large house which formerly stood further east on the south side of the Market Place.[66] It was evidently a late-medieval building with a single-storeyed hall lit by mullioned and transomed windows with traceried heads. To the west of the hall was an imposing two-storeyed porch with Perpendicular windows and an embattled parapet. When the house was demolished in 1842 the porch was removed to Chilton Polden and re-erected as a garden feature.[67] It is possible that the 'castle' remains associated with the White Hart represent parts of the medieval or Tudor outbuildings belonging to this house. The remains were much more extensive in 1828, when they were assumed to be the walls of 'Somerton Castle', and included what appeared to be several incomplete stone buildings. One contained a small round-headed doorway, described as 'Anglo-Norman', and another had, high up, two very small pointed windows.[68]

The Unicorn in West Street, recorded as an inn of that name from 1756,[69] is also a building of late-medieval or 16th-century origin. A formerly open roof of seven bays covers the long range fronting the street. The roof trusses are of jointed cruck construction and have cambered collars with chamfered arch-braces. The timbers are not smoke-blackened, suggesting that the range, although having a basically medieval plan, was always two-storeyed. At its east end a large walled-up fire-place has a former smoke chamber beside it. The front of the house was remodelled in the mid 17th century and given a two-storeyed gabled porch with a semi-circular outer arch and an inner doorway with a four-centred head. The former Nag's Head, also in West Street and recorded as an inn from 1672 onwards,[70] is a timber-framed structure. It was divided into two dwellings and largely faced with lias in the 19th century. There are remains of a moulded bressummer of the late 15th or 16th century to the former jettied upper floor and the side wall in the yard entry is of stud and panel construction.

The increasing prosperity of Somerton in the 17th century is reflected by the number of substantial houses which were built or improved at that time. The largest was the Great House. With its out-buildings it occupied the whole west side of the Market Place, covering six ancient burgage plots. It was built by Sir John Strangways (d. 1666) who had acquired the manor of Somerton St. Cleers in 1638.[71] The plots, on some of which buildings were already standing, were leased by Sir John from several owners. By 1661 his 'great dwelling house', which included his hall, was described as 'new'. There was also 'a stable, anciently a barn', a 'gate court', garden, and orchard. Old buildings which survived had 'a little court' amongst them.[72] At the south end of the block, on the corner of West Street, was a burgage called Lady House.[73] After Sir John's death the Great House was divided, tenants at subsequent periods including an apothecary, a post-master, and a grocer.[74] Lady House was rebuilt after a fire in 1671 and later became a shop.[75] During the 18th century most of the remaining property was occupied by an inn called the White Hart.[76] The inn was afterwards sub-divided. The southern half was rebuilt in 1786[77] and evidently re-fronted in the 19th century; it is now occupied as a bank. The northern half became a shop and, by 1841, the Crown inn.[78] The only part of Sir John's house to survive apparently corresponds with this northern half and is now known as Bank House. The two-storeyed stone front was probably rebuilt in the 18th or early 19th century. The ground floor contains the original hall, divided by later partitions, with a parlour to the north of it. Both rooms have Ham stone fire-places and several stone doorways, some with moulded arches and jambs. At the back is a projecting wing which probably housed a large staircase, but no trace of this remains. A cellar below had evidently been used by the inn. The service rooms of the Great House are likely to have been in the rebuilt portion to the south, now the bank. The first-floor room above the hall has an enriched plaster ceiling with a geometrical design of moulded ribs, panel ornaments, and pendants. Its style is surprisingly early for a mid-17th-century house. Above the fire-place is an elaborate overmantel incorporating the arms of the Doddington family.[79]

In front of the Great House, on part of the site now occupied by the Lady Smith Memorial Hall (built 1901),[80] a barn and other buildings which had belonged to the White Hart survived at least until 1841.[81] There were also houses, now demolished, at the southern entrance to the churchyard.[82] Cross House, so called by 1661, was a 17th-century building forming part of the island site east of the Town Hall and Cross.[83] It was apparently rebuilt in its original style by William Pinney in the 19th century and bears his initials.[84] The 'Market House' on the north side of the Market Place, has

[65] *S. & D. N. & Q.* xii. 215; R. Warner, *Walk Thro' Western Counties* (1800), 204; W. G. Maton, *Observations on Western Counties* (1797), ii. 28; Collinson, *Hist. Som.* iii. 182.   [66] See pl. facing p. 64.
[67] S.R.O., DD/S/ST 17/6; *Hist. Somerton* (W.I. hist.), opp. p. 34.   [68] B.M. Add. MS. 33702 ff. 90–2.
[69] S.R.O., Q/RL, victuallers' recogs.
[70] S.R.O., D/P/som 4/1/2, p. 226.
[71] See below, p. 137.
[72] S.R.O., DD/MI, box 9, survey c. 1661; D.R.O., D 124, box 117, survey 1664–6.
[73] D.R.O., D 124, box 106, Strangways to Fisher.
[74] Ibid. box 17, survey 1676; box 286, survey 1770; S.R.O., tithe award.

[75] D.R.O., D 124, box 17, survey 1676; box 110, Strangways to Fisher.
[76] Ibid. box 109, Strangways to Jacques 1701.
[77] Ibid. box 286, survey 1770.
[78] Ibid.; S.R.O., tithe award.
[79] The arms presumably refer to occupants of the house before Strangways.
[80] Named after Frances, wife of Sir John Smith and elder daughter of J. F. Pinney.
[81] D.R.O., D 124, box 286, survey 1770; S.R.O., tithe award; see pl. facing p. 192.
[82] B.M. Add. MS. 36383 f. 176. See plate facing p. 144.
[83] S.R.O., DD/MI, box 9, survey c. 1661.
[84] S.R.O., DD/PI, 16/1.

a mid-17th-century stone front. There are, however, indications of timber construction internally. The front has two oriel windows on the first floor with attic gables above them; all the windows have ovolo-moulded mullions. The roof of the house next to the east has curved windbraces.

In the 17th century William Taylor had a 'fair dwelling house' on the east side of North Street which had been divided by 1714.[85] It occupied several burgage plots, one formerly known as the 'Star'.[86] Another divided house is now represented by Medwyn and Stockers House on the east side of Broad Street. Together they form an L-shaped building with a long wing, now part of Medwyn, at the rear. The room at the far end has a large open fire-place flanked by a spiral stone stair on one side and a former smoke-chamber on the other. There is a decorative plaster frieze of late-16th- or early-17th-century date in an upper room,[87] and some re-set panelling dated 1623 in the entrance passage. The original front doorway is of Ham stone with a four-centred head. The Jacobean overmantel now at the Old Parsonage is said to have come from Medwyn.[88] Stockers House, with a later addition at the rear, appears to incorporate the parlour and former staircase wing of the original house.

Craigmore, adjoining Stockers House, dates from c. 1700. The front was altered later, perhaps in the mid 18th century when a new wing, now called Narrow House, was added. Narrow House has a pedimented gable facing the road, below which is a round-headed window. The present Westminster Bank on the same side of Broad Street was built as a house in 1708.[89] The two-storeyed front of five bays has rusticated quoins to the angles and to the window openings, a moulded string-course, and a bolection-moulded doorway. At the south end of Broad Street stands the Red Lion, which has the most ambitious 18th-century façade in the town. The south end of the range may be of 17th-century origin but the northern end, including the stable-yard of the inn and a house which was formerly the post office, was built c. 1770.[90] The whole frontage, which has uniform three-light sash windows, was remodelled at this time. The central feature is a segmental-headed archway to the yard, surmounted by a Venetian window and flanked by stone pilasters supporting an open pediment; in the tympanum are the arms of the earls of Ilchester, carved in relief. The southern half of the building contains a large Ham stone fire-place with a baking oven, perhaps part of the earlier Red Lion inn. A square stone column supporting a lion, said in 1828 to have been 'carved in good style by a medical person residing in the town who had never had any in-

struction in the sculptor's art', stood in front of the building until 1897.[91]

Donisthorpe in Cow Square is said to have been built in 1770.[92] It has a symmetrical front of seven bays with moulded window surrounds and a classical porch. The forecourt is bounded by contemporary wrought-iron railings, gate, and gate-piers. Hopefield next door is of similar date and may represent a converted stable range. The Georgian group in Cow Square is completed by the Old Hall which has a mansard roof and a late-18th-century front with a central porch.

On the western outskirts of Somerton a few scattered 17th- and 18th-century cottages survive. Pipers Green, in the Langport road, is one of two identical detached stone cottages with steeply-pitched thatched roofs. They are L-shaped in plan and have two small rooms to each floor, the upper rooms being in the roof. Each cottage has an open fire-place on the ground floor with a spiral stone stair beside it. They probably date from c. 1700 and are said to have been built for lime-burners in connexion with the nearby stone quarry.[93]

In 1604–5 a rating assessment of Somerton parish revealed the names of 348 inhabitants.[94] In 1801 the population was 1,145, a figure which rose gradually to a peak of 2,302 in 1871. It then fell to 1,797 in 1901, rose temporarily, and then fell again, to 1,776 in 1921. It had recovered to 2,182 in 1961, and has risen rapidly in the last decade.[95]

As a royal possession until the 14th century, visits to the town by Saxon kings and their successors may not have been unusual. Ethelred was almost certainly there in 860,[96] and Edward I from 12 to 15 December 1285.[97] The town was used as a temporary base both in the Civil War and during Monmouth's rebellion. The marquess of Hertford was there with troops in 1643, and it was probably one of these soldiers who was buried in the church in that year.[98] Charles I came to Kingsmoor, a popular place for musters,[99] to meet the *posse comitatus* in an abortive attempt to raise troops in July 1644.[1] Parliamentary horse were reported marching to the town in September 1644, and Goring was there with Royalist foot in May 1645.[2] Only two months later Parliamentary troops came to the town just before Goring was defeated near Langport.[3] The militia commissioners used the town for their meetings during the Interregnum.[4] The earl of Feversham used the town as a base from which to 'observe the rebels' in July 1685 on the three days before the battle of Sedgemoor.[5] During the 18th century Kingsmoor was 'considered by sportsmen as one of the best coursed in the Kingdom'.[6]

Distinguished natives of the town include

[85] D.R.O., D 124, box 117, survey 1664–6.
[86] Ibid. box 1, survey 1718.
[87] Similar in style to a frieze in the chancel of the church probably added in 1564: see p. 150.
[88] Local information.
[89] *11th. Rep. Com. Char.* H.C. 433, p. 449 (1824), xiv.
[90] D.R.O., D 124, box 114, Ilchester to Reeves, Jan. 1770, when it was described as 'new built'.
[91] B.M. Add. MS. 33702 f. 105v. Sketched by the Revd. John Skinner at the request of Sir Richard Colt Hoare from their room in the inn: ibid. f. 109.
[92] *Hist. Somerton* (W.I. hist.), 31.   [93] See p. 143.
[94] S.R.O., D/P/som 4/1/1, pp. 176–86.
[95] *Census*, 1801–1961.
[96] Finberg, *Early Charters of Wessex*, p. 75.
[97] *Cal. Pat.* 1281–92, 213; *Cal. Close*, 1279–88, 380.

[98] *S.R.S.* xviii. 48; S.R.O., D/P/som 4/1/1, p. 29.
[99] *Earl of Hertford's Lieutenancy Papers*, 1603–12 (Wilts. Rec. Soc. xxiii), 106.
[1] *Richard Symonds' Diary* (Camden Soc. lxxiv), 36.
[2] *Cal. S.P. Dom.* 1644, 495; 1644–5, 493.
[3] Hist. MSS. Com. 29, *13th Rep. II, Portland*, ii, p. 232.
[4] *Cal. Cttee. for Compounding*, i. 410; *Cal. S.P. Dom.* 1659–60, 379.
[5] *Lond. Gaz.* 2048–9, 2, 6, and 9 July 1685; *Cal. S.P. Dom.* Feb.–Dec. 1685, 250; Hist. MSS. Com. 29, *13th Rep. II, Portland*, ii, p. 158; Hist. MSS. Com. 8. *9th Rep. III*, Stopford-Sackville, 3b.
[6] S. Simpson, *Agreeable Historian* (1746); Spencer, *Complete English Traveller* (1772); *New Display of Beauties of Eng.* (1776), 319; *Univ. Brit. Dir.* s.v. Ilchester.

Humphrey Philips (1633-1707), a Presbyterian divine, Marmaduke Cradock (1660?-1716), a painter of animals and birds, and Joseph Sams (1784-1860), the orientalist.[7] Richard Newcourt (d. 1679), the topographical draughtsman, lived in the town and was buried there.[8] The barony of Stawell of Somerton, granted to Ralph Stawell in 1683 in consideration of the loyal services of his father, Sir John Stawell (d. 1662), took its name from the family's estates in and near the town.

MANORS AND OTHER ESTATES. In 733 Ethelbald of Mercia occupied the 'royal town' of Somerton, formerly in the possession of the West Saxon kings.[9] The kings of Wessex re-established themselves there by the early 9th century,[10] and continuous ownership by them may thereafter be assumed. By the time of Domesday parts of the original estate had been alienated,[11] but the manor included most, if not all, of the present parishes of Kingsdon and Pitney.[12] The area of the estate was later contracted in consequence of the separation of Somerton Erleigh by 1176, of Hurcot by 1207 and, in the 13th century, of Pitney Lorty and Pitney Plucknett.[13] The remainder, known as the manor of *SOMERTON*, was granted during pleasure to a succession of royal servants: Hugh de Neville in 1215, William de Torinton in 1217.[14] By 1242 the men of Somerton were holding the manor at farm for £60,[15] but ten years later they were superseded by Adam Wymer, king's serjeant.[16] From 1262 the farm was assigned to Queen Eleanor in dower,[17] and from 1265 was paid by Eleanor of Castile, wife of the lord Edward, first as keeper, in February 1266 as farmer, and later in the year as tenant for life.[18]

On her death in 1290 it was resumed by the Crown, until settled as dower on Edward I's second wife, Margaret of France (d. 1318), in 1299.[19] On her death the manor, town, and hundred, with Kingsmoor, were given to her second son Edmund of Woodstock (cr. earl of Kent 1321, d. 1330).[20] The earl's heirs were his two infant sons Edmund and John.[21] William de Montacute (cr. earl of Salisbury 1337, d. 1344) was given the property for life,[22] but Kent's rehabilitation in 1331 gave Montacute custody only during the minority of the heir.[23]

Edmund, the elder son, died in 1331; John took possession in 1351 but died in the following year.[24] His widow retained the manor as dower until her death in 1411.[25] Her successor was Eleanor Holand, grand-daughter of Joan, countess of Kent (d. 1385), sister and heir of John, earl of Kent.[26] Eleanor's husband, Thomas de Montacute, earl of Salisbury, held the manor in 1412.[27]

Montacute (d. 1428) was succeeded by his only daughter Alice, wife of Richard Neville, earl of Salisbury (d. 1460).[28] From his son Richard, earl of Warwick (d. 1471) Somerton passed through his elder daughter Isabel to George, duke of Clarence (d. 1478). Their son Edward, earl of Warwick (d. 1499), succeeded as a minor to his mother's lands which remained in Crown custody.[29] Warwick's attainder was reversed in 1513-14,[30] and his lands were given to his sister Margaret, countess of Salisbury, wife of Sir Richard Pole. Her estates were, in their turn, forfeited in 1539, and remained in the hands of the Crown until 1552 when they were restored in favour of her grand-daughter Catherine, wife of Francis Hastings, earl of Huntingdon (d. 1560).[31] Their son Henry (d. 1595) sold the Somerton property to his brother Francis and to Sir Edward Hext (d. 1626) of Low Ham in 1592.[32] Later in the same year Hastings sold his share to Hext.[33]

The estate passed to Hext's only daughter Elizabeth, wife of Sir John Stawell, K.B. (d. 1662).[34] It was sequestrated in 1646 because of Sir John's political activities but was discharged in 1653.[35] The manor was settled in 1661 on Sir John's eldest son George, and it passed on George's death in 1669 to his brother Ralph (cr. Lord Stawell of Somerton 1683).[36] Lord Stawell's elder son John succeeded in 1689, but the estate was so heavily encumbered at his death in 1692 that a trust was established which sold the whole property in 1700 to Col. (later Sir) Thomas Strangways, already owner of the manor of St. Cleers.[37]

Strangways died in 1713 leaving a son Thomas (d. 1726) and two daughters Susanna (d. 1758), wife of Thomas Strangways Horner of Mells, and Elizabeth (d. 1729), wife of James Hamilton, duke of Hamilton and Brandon (d. 1743).[38] The younger Thomas died without issue, and on the death of the duchess of Hamilton in 1729 the property passed

[7] D.N.B.
[8] Ibid.
[9] Anglo-Saxon Chron. ed. Dorothy Whitelock, 28; Chron. of Aethelweard, ed. A. Campbell, 21; F. M. Stenton, Anglo-Saxon Eng. (3rd edn.), 203.
[10] Stenton, op. cit. 229.
[11] V.C.H. Som. i. 521; Rot. Hund. (Rec. Com.), ii. 122, 128; Proc. Som. Arch. Soc. xcix and c. 46; see above, p. 16.
[12] See pp. 51, 113.
[13] See pp. 51-2
[14] Rot. Litt. Claus. (Rec. Com.), i. 214, 303; Pat. R. 1216-25, 65. A grant to Robert Burgate, also in 1217 (Rot. Litt. Claus. (Rec. Com.), i. 298), may not have taken effect.
[15] Pipe R. 1242, ed. H. L. Cannon, 339.
[16] Bk. of Fees, ii. 1265; Cal. Pat. 1247-58, 165.
[17] Cal. Pat. 1266-72, 737.
[18] Ibid. 1258-66, 420, 555, 580. She was also given arrears owed by the men of Somerton: Close R. 1264-8, 347.
[19] Cal. Chart. R. 1257-1300, 143; Cal. Pat. 1292-1301 452; 1307-13, 217; S.C. 6/1090/4 m. 12; 1090/6.
[20] Cal. Pat. 1317-21, 187; Cal. Chart. R. 1300-26, 416.

[21] Cal. Inq. p.m. vii, p. 227.
[22] Cal. Pat. 1327-30, 523; 1330-4, 31; Cal. Fine R. 1327-37, 175-6; Cal. Close, 1337-9, 225.
[23] Cal. Pat. 1330-4, 113.
[24] Cal. Inq. p.m. x, p. 44.
[25] Cal. Close, 1349-54, 531, 594; C 137/83/35.
[26] Cal. Fine R. 1405-13, 211; C 137/83/34; Complete Peerage, s.v. Kent.
[27] Feud. Aids, vi. 508.
[28] Ibid. iv. 429.
[29] C 142/28/22; Cal. Pat. 1476-85, 142.
[30] 5 Hen. VIII c. 12.
[31] Cal. Pat. 1553-4, 186.
[32] C.P. 25(2)/206/34 Eliz. I Hil.; Cal. S.P. Dom. 1591-4, 172; Hunt. Libr., HA Manorial, draft indenture, Hastings to Hext.
[33] S.R.S. li. 151.
[34] G. D. Stawell, A Quantock Family: a history of the Stawell family, 86, 374.
[35] Cal. Cttee. for Compounding, ii. 1430.
[36] D.R.O., D 124, box 113, abstract of title.
[37] Ibid. boxes 17, 113.
[38] Hutchins, Hist. Dors. ii. 662-3; Complete Peerage, s.v. Hamilton.

entire to Susanna. Susanna's only daughter Elizabeth married Stephen Fox. He took the additional name of Strangways and in 1741 was created Lord Ilchester and Baron Strangways. He became earl of Ilchester in 1756.[39] On his death in 1776 the property passed successively to Henry Thomas his eldest son (d. 1802), and to two grandsons Henry Stephen (d. 1858) and William Thomas Horner (d. 1865), successively earls of Ilchester.[40] Henry Edward, the 5th earl, nephew of the last, sold 2,500 a. of the estate as separate farms in 1874.[41] His son, who succeeded in 1905, sold the remainder in 1913, 1920, and 1921.[42] The lordship of the manor was not included in any of these sales.

The estate of *HURCOT* occurs in 1205 when it was to be given by the Crown to Ralph de Forz in exchange for land in Puckington.[43] The exchange was evidently not made, but a similar one with Robert de Newburgh for Powerstock (Dors.) in 1207 seems to have been effective, though at least until 1214 Robert appears only as tenant of Hurcot and continued to hold his Dorset lands.[44] Robert died in 1246 holding an estate at Hurcot valued at £9 12s.[45] Eleanor, queen of Edward I, acquired it from Henry de Newburgh in 1276.[46] On her death in 1290 the property, described as a manor, was resumed by the Crown, and was administered directly by Crown officials.[47] In 1302 it was given to the king's daughter Mary, a nun at Amesbury (Wilts.), 'for the maintenance of her chamber'.[48] Its subsequent descent is not clear, but it seems probable that the grant of dower lands in Somerset to William de Montacute in 1330 included Hurcot.[49] Montacute's holding was evidently smaller than Queen Eleanor's, nearly 100 a. having been alienated by 1302.[50]

In or before 1337 William de Montacute gave the manor to his newly-founded priory at Bisham (Berks.).[51] The priory was dissolved in 1536 but was refounded as an abbey in the following year, when the estates were given to it.[52] The abbey was dissolved two years later, and in 1541 the manor of Hurcot was given to Anne of Cleves.[53] After her death in 1557 it was resumed by the Crown and then in 1559 settled in tail male on Sir John Grey (d. 1564), son of Thomas Grey, marquess of Dorset (d. 1530).[54] Grey's son Henry, Lord Grey of Groby (d. 1614), left Hurcot to his own son also Henry (cr. earl of Stamford 1628).[55] The earl sold

it in 1629 to Thomas Bennet (cr. Bt. 1660), whose son Levinus (d. 1693) was succeeded by Richard, of Babraham (Cambs.) (d. 1701).[56] Richard's daughter Judith died under age in 1713 and the property was therefore divided between his five sisters.[57] In 1765 it was reunited in the hands of Richard Henry Alexander Benet of St. James's Street, London, and later of Beckenham (Kent), son of Benet Alexander (later Benet), son of Richard's sister Levina.[58]

In 1798 Benet sold the manor to Joseph Bradney of Ham (Surr.).[59] Bradney's son, the Revd. John Hopkins Bradney, sold it to Francis Henry Dickinson (d. 1890) of Kingweston about 1839.[60] The estate was then just over 600 a. in area.[61] Capt. W. F. Dickinson sold his holding in Hurcot, then consisting of Hurcot farm and other lands, amounting to over 540 a., to the tenant in 1930.[62]

The 'court house' in Hurcot in 1297 included a hall and chamber, with associated stall and barn.[63]

William de Erleigh paid 100s. in 1176 for lands in Somerton which may have been alienated from the royal estate in that year.[64] His grandson John (II) de Erleigh, who had succeeded in 1199, held the estate in 1210–12 as a royal chamberlain;[65] the serjeanty service was later the duty of carrying a towel (*tuellam*) before the king at Pentecost.[66] Lands late of William Peverell in Somerton were added to John's holding in 1217.[67] John de Erleigh was still alive in 1231.[68] Henry de Erleigh, his brother, succeeded by 1251–2 to an estate then known as Little Somerton,[69] and is said to have died in 1272.[70] His heir, Philip de Erleigh, succeeded by 1280 but was dead by 1284–5 when his own son was still a minor. The property, then called East Somerton, was in the custody of William de Montfort.[71] John (III) de Erleigh, who came of age by 1299, died in 1324.[72]

John (IV), his heir, died in 1337, when the estate was first described as a manor, later known as the manor of *SOMERTON ERLEIGH*.[73] John (V) succeeded as a minor and his lands were held by his mother Elizabeth until 1361.[74] In 1371–2 John (V) made over the manor to his father-in-law Sir Guy Brien, providing the tenants, Richard Brice and Edith his wife, with a life interest.[75] This settlement was altered in 1386 in favour of Sir William Brien and Philip Brien,[76] and again in 1388 in favour of Sir Guy's eldest son's, children.[77] A disputed

[39] *Complete Peerage*, s.v. Ilchester.
[40] Ibid.   [41] S.R.O., DD/PI 12/14.
[42] S.R.O., C/C, Knole Estate sale cat. 1913; DD/KW, sale cat. 1921; *Hist. Somerton* (W.I. hist.), 93.
[43] *Rot. Litt. Claus.* (Rec. Com.), i. 50.
[44] Ibid. i. 95; *Bk. of Fees*, i. 79; *Red Bk. Exch.* (Rec. Com.), ii. 549; *Pipe R.* 1210 (P.R.S. n.s. xxvi), 68; 1211 (P.R.S. n.s. xxviii), 221; 1212 (P.R.S. n.s. xxx), 113; 1214 (P.R.S. n.s. xxxv), 96; *Rot. Hund.* (Rec. Com.), ii. 121.
[45] *Cal. Inq. p.m.* i, p. 18; C 133/4/15.
[46] *S.R.S.* vi. 381; *Cal. Memo. R.* 1326–7, no. 815.
[47] S.C. 6/1090/4 m. 8; 1089/25; 1090/6.
[48] *Cal. Pat.* 1301–7, 52, 327; *Cal. Fine R.* 1272–1307, 457; *Cal. Inq. p.m.* iv, p. 202.
[49] *Cal. Pat.* 1327–30, 523.
[50] *Cal. Inq. p.m.* iv, p. 67; *Cal. Fine R.* 1272–1307, 455.
[51] *Cal. Close*, 1337–9, 276; Dugdale, *Mon.* vi. 526–34.
[52] *L. & P. Hen. VIII*, xii, p. 469.
[53] Ibid. xvi, p. 717.
[54] *Cal. Pat.* 1558–60, 82.
[55] C 142/346/170.
[56] S.R.O., DD/DN, box 43; G.E.C. *Baronetage*, iii. 130–1.

[57] S.R.O., DD/DN, box 43.   [58] Ibid.
[59] Ibid. boxes 43–4.
[60] Ibid. box 43.
[61] Ibid.
[62] Sale cat. (1930) *penes* Mrs. J. Burden, Kingweston.
[63] S.C. 6/1090/4 m. 8.
[64] *Pipe R.* 1177 (P.R.S. xxvi), 24.
[65] *Red Bk. Exch.* ii. 547.
[66] *Rot. Hund.* (Rec. Com.) ii. 121.
[67] *Rot. Litt. Claus.* (Rec. Com.), i. 304.
[68] *Close R.* 1227–31, 255, 346, 517–18; *Cur. Reg. R.* xiv. 394.
[69] *Bk. of Fees*, ii. 1265.
[70] *S.R.S.* xxv, p. xviii.
[71] *Rot. Hund.* (Rec. Com.), ii. 121; *Feud. Aids*, iv. 285.
[72] *S.R.S.* xiv. 106; *Cal. Inq. p.m.* vi, p. 297.
[73] *Cal. Inq. p.m.* viii, p. 58.
[74] Ibid.; *Cal. Pat.* 1334–8, 466; *S.R.S.* ix. 386; *Cal. Inq. p.m.* xi, p. 52; *Cal. Close*, 1360–4, 320.
[75] *Cal. Pat.* 1370–4, 117, 193; *Ilchester Almshouse Deeds*, ed. W. Buckler, no. 62; *Proc. Som. Arch. Soc.* ciii. 51.
[76] *Cal. Pat.* 1385–9, 162; *S.R.S.* xvii. 202–3.
[77] *Cal. Close*, 1385–9, 604, 628.

succession followed the death of Guy the elder in 1390, and the manor passed to his elder grand-daughter Philippe, wife successively of John de Ros and Henry le Scrope of Masham.[78] She died in 1406 and her heir was her sister Elizabeth, wife of Robert Lovell.[79] The manor was said to be held of the countess of Kent as of her manor of Somerton.[80] Scrope held it of the Lovells until his execution in 1415.[81]

Maud, sole heir of the Lovells, died in 1436 leaving as heir her son Humphrey by John d'Arundel, earl of Arundel (d. 1435).[82] Humphrey's death two years later brought the manor to his half-sister Avice, daughter of Maud by Sir Richard Stafford. Shortly afterwards Avice (d. 1457) married James Butler, earl of Ormond (cr. earl of Wiltshire 1449, d. 1461).[83] Butler's estates were forfeited to the Crown in 1461 and a year later the manor was given to William Neville, earl of Kent (d. 1463). On his death the manor was granted to George, duke of Clarence, already lord of the capital manor.[84] Eleanor, countess of Wiltshire, received part of the estate as jointure in 1470,[85] but Clarence retained the remainder until his death in 1478, when possession of the whole reverted to Eleanor, then wife of Sir Robert Spencer.[86] Eleanor died in 1501 and was succeeded by Thomas Butler, earl of Ormond.[87] Under his will the former Brien estates passed in 1515 to Henry Algernon Percy, earl of Northumberland (d. 1527) whose wife, Catherine, was one of Eleanor's heirs.[88] Their son Henry (d. 1537) sold the estate in 1530 to Thomas (later Sir Thomas) Johnson, though apparently he retained an interest at least until 1531.[89] Johnson sold the manor to William Popley in 1536, though he was still credited with property in the parish in 1538.[90] Popley, of Chitterne All Saints (Wilts.), sold the manor with Somerton Randolph to John Wysse, founder, in 1546.[91]

John Wysse (d. 1554) was succeeded by his son Thomas; his grandson, also Thomas, of Longhope (Glos.) inherited in 1585,[92] but sold both properties in 1597 to James Fisher (d. 1636), whose father Richard had been tenant of part of the estate since 1587.[93] Almost immediately the Fishers began leasing parts of the estate for long terms of years, and thereafter claimed no manorial rights.[94] Those parts retained by the family were held by James Fisher c. 1661, followed by a John Fisher who occurs between 1662 and 1719, and another John in 1730; James Fisher occurs in 1732 and his brother John in 1748.[95] The death of John Fisher in 1752 revealed the complications of the long leases.[96] Fisher's heirs, Samuel and Jane Barnard and

Joseph Gill, contested their respective shares. The whole property was in 1785 made the subject of a fine in which it was described as 'the manor of Somerton Erle alias Somerton Erle and Rendall'. The estate, then comprising over 355 a. of land, was vested in Joseph Gill and Jane his wife, John Fisher Barnard and Mary his wife, and William Cornish Barnard.[97]

Gill's share, 'late Mr. Fisher's farm', included the capital messuage of the estate. Some of the land was sold in 1796 and the house and remainder, called Gill's farm, were absorbed into John Barnard's holding.[98] Barnard put the property, described as the manors of Somerton Erleigh and Randall, up for sale in 1800,[99] but in the same year described himself as lord of the manor of Lower Somerton.[1] Some of the land was acquired by John Frederick Pinney in 1802,[2] but Barnard retained the house and most of the estate until 1807. From 1808 until 1812 the house was owned by John Jacobs and in 1812 was first called the Court. In 1813 it was acquired by Edward Stephenson,[3] and was occupied by his successors, later Hall-Stephenson, until 1933.[4]

Somerton Court, the former manor-house, is a stone building of two storeys, basement, and attics. A tablet on the porch is dated 1641 with the initials of, presumably, James Fisher and his wife. Fisher's house consisted of a long range, one room deep, perhaps having a staircase wing at the rear. The seven-bay entrance front was symmetrical with a central two-storeyed porch and three-light mul-lioned windows with hood-moulds. Two canted bay windows terminated in attic gables resting on angle corbels.[5] The entrance arch to the surviving porch is round-headed with prominent keystone and imposts, but the doorway inside has a four-centred head—a combination which seems to have been standard practice in the area for much of the 17th century. Early in the 19th century the house was gothicized, perhaps at the time it became known as Somerton Court. The parapets were raised and embattled, hiding the attic windows and destroying the gables. The porch became a tower-like feature with angle turrets and a rose window, while the other windows were given diagonal glazing bars. A new range, with front and back staircases, was built along the back of the house in a similar style. Further extensions were made later in the 19th century.

The origin of the manor or reputed manor of *SOMERTON RANDOLPH* or *RANDALL* seems to lie in certain lands and tenements held by Richard Mucheldevre of Sir Guy Brien in 1384.[6] The hold-

78 *Complete Peerage*, s.v. Bryan.
79 C 137/59/54.   80 Ibid.
81 *S.R.S.* xxii. 25, 177.
82 C 139/71/37; *Cal. Close, 1435–41*, 11.
83 C 139/81/39; 164/16; *S.R.S.* xxii. 198.
84 *Cal. Pat. 1461–7*, 225–6, 454.
85 Ibid. 1467–77, 211.
86 C 140/67/46; *Cal. Pat. 1476–85*, 106.
87 C.P. 40/907 rot. 354; *Cal. Close, 1485–1500*, 111, 114–15; *Cal. Inq. p.m. Hen. VII*, ii. 328.
88 *L. & P. Hen. VIII*, iv(2), p. 1421.
89 C.P. 25(2)/35/237, 22 Hen. VIII Trin.; C.P. 40/1071 rot. 144; *L. & P. Hen. VIII*, iv(2), p. 3050.
90 C.P. 25(2)/52/371/28 Hen. VIII Mich.; *L. & P. Hen. VIII*, xiii(1), p. 366.
91 C.P. 25(2)/36/242, 38 Hen. VIII Trin.; C 54/447 no. 27; *L. & P. Hen. VIII*, xx(1), p. 428.

92 C 142/104/106; 207/96; *Cal. Pat. 1554–5*, 247.
93 C 142/479/38; S.R.O., DD/PI 2/1; D/P/som 4/1/1, rates 1587.
94 S.R.O., DD/SAS (C/127), 1; ibid. (C/114), 6; DD/PI 2/1; DD/S/BT, box 25.
95 D.R.O., D 124, box 1, ct. bks. 1617–20, 1730–62; box 17, ct. bk. 1732–53; S.R.O., DD/MI, box 9.
96 S.R.O., DD/DN, box 52.   97 Ibid.
98 S.R.O., Q/RE, land tax assessments.
99 S.R.O., DD/PI 12/11.
1 S.R.O., DD/S/BT 96.
2 S.R.O., DD/PI 5/7.
3 S.R.O., Q/RE, land tax assessments.
4 S.R.O., D/P/som 4/1/4.
5 Drawing of front before early-19th-century altera-tions *penes* Col. Bray, Somerton Court.
6 B.M. Add. Ch. 29250.

ing was described as a manor four years later.[7] Its descent followed that of the manor of Somerton Erleigh, though in 1457 it was said to be held of Sir William Paulet,[8] and in 1489 and 1501 of the prior of St. Swithun's, Winchester.[9]

The whole property, including the capital messuage, was let at least by 1538 when Sir William Sydney was occupier.[10] By 1597 the tenancy had been acquired by John Still, bishop of Bath and Wells,[11] and he later apparently purchased the freehold. The property passed to his son Thomas (d. 1640).[12] Thomas's successor, John Still of Shaftesbury (Dors.), who acquired more lands from the owners of Somerton Erleigh on lease in 1657,[13] assigned his rights in 1662 to John Howe, late of Berwick St. Leonard (Wilts.).[14] Howe's holding in 1664 amounted to just over 148 a.[15] He died about 1672[16] and was succeeded by William Howe, who added the tenancy of Cranes farm to his holding.[17] William died in 1742 and his son John in 1764.[18] George Howe, son of John, died in 1768 leaving his estate to his brother William, subject to the life interest of his sister-in-law.[19] William Howe sold the estate to John Pretor Pinney (d. 1818) in 1799.[20] It then comprised a house and pleasure grounds with some 40 a. of surrounding land, and a farm of 49 a.[21] Pinney's son and grandson John Frederick (d. 1845) and William (d. 1898) considerably increased this estate by the purchase of adjoining farms: Midney farm was acquired by 1837[22] and Catsgore farm in 1865.[23] The latter originated in a lease by the Fisher family in 1665 and was thus part of the manor of Somerton Erleigh.

William Pinney was succeeded in 1898 by his cousin Frederick Wake Pretor-Pinney (d. 1909), who in 1906 made over the estate to his eldest son Charles Frederick. The latter died of wounds in 1917 and his heir was his brother Robert Wake (d. 1950). Giles Robert took over the estate in 1935 and was killed in action in 1942. The present owner of the estate, in 1971 comprising some 880 a., is Robert's grandson, Mr. A. R. E. Pretor-Pinney.[24]

The capital messuage of the manor, then known as the Farm, was occupied by the Stills by 1597.[25] It was described as newly built, evidently by Thomas Still, about 1633.[26] William Howe rebuilt it, and it was described as 'newly erected' in 1789.[27] It was a large L-shaped building with detached wash house, stables, and other offices to the east. About 1846 the house was extensively remodelled if not entirely rebuilt to form the present square block of two tall storeys and attics in grey lias ashlar, with

a plain garden front of seven bays.[28] The new north entrance front has a projecting bay with Tuscan portico of Ham stone, surmounted by a Venetian window and pediment. The house was extended eastwards to include the 18th-century stable block, and a new stable court with entrance archway and ornate tower was erected to the north east about 1860.[29] The house has been known as Somerton Erleigh since the early 19th century.

In 1223 Robert de St. Clare entered on two virgates of freehold land in Somerton, held of the manor, probably in succession to Geoffrey de St. Clare his father.[30] Another Robert died in 1336 and his estate was charged with dower for both his mother and his widow.[31] His son, also Robert, died in 1359 and in the following year the estate was settled on his grandson Richard and on Richard's wife Margaret, with remainder to William Bonville.[32] Bonville succeeded to Richard's property in 1362, and to the dower holding of Sibyl de St. Clare ten years later.[33] William, Lord Bonville (d. 1461), grandson of William, settled the property on his daughter Elizabeth, on her marriage with William Tailboys (d. 1464).[34] It descended through the Tailboys family like the manor of Yeovilton, and during the 16th century acquired manorial status as the manor of *SOMERTON ST. CLEERS*.[35] It was acquired by Thomas Cary of Cockington (Devon) in 1560,[36] and probably passed from him directly to James Hodges.[37] Hodges died in 1601 leaving a daughter Mary, wife of John Rosse.[38] Their son James, of Shepton Beauchamp, sold it in 1638 to Sir John Strangways of Melbury Sampford (Dors.).[39] Sir John died in 1666 and his property passed to his son Giles (d. 1675) and then to his grandson Col. Thomas Strangways (d. 1713) owner of the capital manor from 1700.[40] St. Cleers manor thenceforward descended with the capital manor.

There was no manor-house attached to St. Cleers manor, but Sir John Strangways built a large dwelling, known as the Great House, on the west side of the Market Place, mostly on land which he leased from other owners.[41] After his death in 1666 the house was abandoned by the family and was divided among tenants; much of it was later rebuilt.

About 1280 the men of Somerton finally won their dispute with Ilchester for possession of Kingsmoor, some 1,000 a. of land stretching along the north bank of the Yeo from Pill Bridge in the east to Load Bridge in the west.[42] Ilchester had evidently gained control by 1242, but when its claims were

---

[7] C 143/407/27.
[8] C 139/164/16.
[9] C.P. 40/907 rot. 354; *Cal. Inq. p.m. Hen. VII*, ii. 328.
[10] *L. & P. Hen. VIII*, xiii(1), p. 366.
[11] S.R.O., DD/SAS (C/127), 1; D/P/som 4/1/1, pp. 176–87.
[12] C 142/495/83.
[13] S.R.O., DD/SAS (C/127), 1.
[14] Ibid. (C/114), 6; (C/127), 1; DD/PI 4/8, 9/7.
[15] S.R.O., DD/SAS (C/96), 20.
[16] S.R.O., D/P/som 4/1/2, p. 231.
[17] Ibid. p. 547.
[18] S.R.O., DD/PI 1/5.
[19] Ibid.
[20] Ibid. 5/7.
[21] Ibid. 6/6.
[22] Ibid. 3/11.
[23] Ibid. 8/5.
[24] Burke, *Land. Gent.* (1952), 2036–7; ex inf. Mr. A. R. E. Pretor-Pinney.

[25] S.R.O., DD/SAS (C/127), 1.
[26] *S.R.S.* xv. 233.
[27] S.R.O., DD/PI 1/4.
[28] Ibid. 16/1, plan of house and grounds c. 1846.
[29] Ibid., elevations of stable block.
[30] *Ex. e Rot. Fin.* (Rec. Com.), 97; *Cur. Reg. R.* xii. 20–1; *S.R.S.* xiv. 66.
[31] *Cal. Inq. p.m.* viii, pp. 23–4, 45.
[32] Ibid. xii, p. 233; *S.R.S.* xvii. 44–5.
[33] *Cal. Inq. p.m.* xiii, pp. 62, 177.
[34] See p. 169.
[35] *Cal. Pat.* 1554–5, 268.
[36] C.P. 40/1136.
[37] See p. 160.
[38] *Som. Wills*, ed. Brown, i. 30.
[39] C 3/419/72; C.P. 25(2)/480/14 Chas. I East.; D.R.O., D 124, box 106, Wyndham to Strangways.
[40] Hutchins, *Hist. Dors.* ii. 662–3; see above, p. 134.
[41] See p. 132.
[42] See p. 146.

disallowed ownership of the 'moor', described as warren and pasture, lay with successive lords of the manor of Somerton.[43] It was separately administered until inclosure in 1797.[44]

By 1499 William Strode held some property in Somerton and in that year was succeeded by his son Richard.[45] John Strode (d. 1581) of Parnham (Dors.) and later his son Robert were tenants of Somerton manor in respect of land in Lower Somerton.[46] Robert, later Sir Robert, increased his holding and by 1597 it was described as a manor.[47] In the following year he settled it on his daughter Catherine and on her husband Sir Richard Strode of Newnham (Devon) (d. 1669).[48] Sir Richard's son and grandson, William and Richard Strode, sold the manor to Robert Burridge of Lyme Regis (Dors.), merchant, in 1661.[49] Burridge sold it in 1665 to Solomon Andrews of Lyme, also a merchant,[50] and Andrews conveyed it to John Stocker of Somerton in 1672.[51] Stocker settled it in 1702 on his daughter Frances, wife of Henry Norton of Somerton. The property then comprised 23 houses and just over 20 a. of land, and was described as a manor or reputed manor.[52] Thereafter it was never given manorial status, was absorbed into the rest of the Norton holdings, and was divided on the death of John Stocker Norton, Henry Norton's son, in 1785.[53]

The rectorial estate granted to Muchelney abbey in the early 12th century[54] and increased by a pension confirmed in 1191 and by the tithes of Somerton Erleigh in 1254,[55] was valued at £20 in 1291 and at £37 13s. 4d. in 1535.[56] The glebe amounted to 149 a. in the 15th century.[57] On the surrender of the abbey in 1538 the estate was granted to Edward Seymour, earl of Hertford,[58] who in 1542 exchanged it for other land with the newly-founded chapter of Bristol.[59] In 1649 the property was said to be worth £262 but the chapter normally leased it for £38.[60] Humphrey Worth, the first lessee, was followed by Hugh Worth in 1602–4.[61] Hugh assigned his lease in or before 1614 to Thomas Preene of London, and Preene's family held the lands, comprising 220 a. by c. 1625,[62] until 1665.[63] George Clarke of Swainswick had the lease from 1665,[64] and in 1674 began the long tenure of the Wyndham family, beginning with John Wynd-

ham of Norrington, in Alvediston, (Wilts.).[65] He was followed in 1724 by his younger son Thomas (cr. Lord Wyndham of Finglass 1731, d. 1745) and then by his elder son John (d. 1750).[66] John's daughter and sole heir Anne, wife of James Everard Arundell, succeeded as lessee.[67] Their son James, Lord Arundell of Wardour (d. 1817), farmed the parsonage until 1812, when the earl of Ilchester acquired the lease.[68] In 1841 the holding measured just over 196 a.[69] Lord Ilchester purchased the fee simple of the rectory from the Ecclesiastical Commissioners in 1907 and 1911,[70] and it was absorbed into the rest of his holding. Parts, including the parsonage house and tithe barn, were sold in 1913 and the remainder in 1920 and 1921.[71]

The parsonage house, known as the Old Parsonage, seems to have been built or substantially altered by Thomas Preene 'within four years' of 1619.[72] It is a long two-storeyed stone building, one room deep, having stone-mullioned windows with hood moulds and a frontage of five bays. The central two-storeyed porch has a semi-circular outer arch and an inner doorway with a four-centred head; a stone balustrade has been added above the parapet which at one time was embattled.[73] The house has been extended at the rear and altered internally, but retains several original fire-places of Ham stone. There was formerly a spiral stair at the north-east corner. A Jacobean overmantel and oak panelling are said to have been brought from the house called Medwyn in Broad Street.[74] To the north stands the tithe barn, a very long stone building with buttressed walls; the original roof has been replaced.

COUNTY TOWN. The claim that Somerton was 'capital' of Wessex[75] is based on a belief dating from the 16th century that the West Saxon kings had a residence at St. Cleers, the ruins of which were said to be visible in 1579.[76] The county name has been interpreted as being the people who looked to Somerton as their centre.[77] There is written evidence for only one meeting of the witan at Somerton, in 949,[78] and the etymology of the name of the town has been taken to suggest only temporary settlement for summer grazing.[79] The choice of Somerton as the

[43] *Plac. de Quo Warr.* (Rec. Com.), 701; *Rot. Hund.* (Rec. Com.), ii. 126, 128; *Cal. Pat.* 1281–92, 24; *S.R.S.* xi. 259; xiv. 128–9.
[44] S.R.O., CR 43, 45; see p. 147.
[45] *Cal. Inq. p.m. Hen. VII*, ii. 202–3.
[46] *S.R.S.* lxix, p. 29.
[47] C.P. 25(2)/262/39 Eliz. I Hil.
[48] C 142/764/3.
[49] D.R.O., D 124, box 117; J. L. Vivian, *Visit. Devon*, 718–19.
[50] D.R.O., D 124, box 117.
[51] Ibid.
[52] Ibid.
[53] Ibid.; S.R.O., DD/S/BT, box 25.
[54] See p. 147.
[55] *S.R.S.* xiv. 49–51; *Valor Eccl.* (Rec. Com.), i. 207.
[56] *Tax. Eccl.* (Rec. Com.), 197; *Valor Eccl.* (Rec. Com.), i. 194.
[57] *S.R.S.* xlii. 115.
[58] *L. & P. Hen. VIII*, xiii(1), p. 64.
[59] Ibid. xvii, p. 322.
[60] Bristol Cath., Dean and Chapter MSS., Parl. Survey f. 181; *S. & D. N. & Q.* xiv. 52, 312; Bristol R.O., DC/E/1/10, p. 353.
[61] Bristol R.O., DC/E/1/1; Bristol Cath., MSS. accts. 1550–1, 1560–1, 1571–2, 1591–2; *S.&D. N.&Q.* xiv. 52.

[62] Bristol Univ. Libr., DM 177, lease 19 June 1614; D.R.O., D 124, box 18, allotment of King's Sedgemoor.
[63] Bristol R.O., DC/E/1/2 ff. 104–106v; Bristol Cath. MSS. accts. 1619–21, 1640–1, 1660; *S. & D. N. & Q.* xiv. 52, 312.
[64] Bristol R.O., DC/E/1/2 ff. 213–15.
[65] Bristol R.O., DC/E/1/3 f. 32v.
[66] Bristol R.O., DC/E/1/5, pp. 97–9, 113–15.
[67] C.P. 25(2)/1197/26 Geo. II Mich; S.R.O., DD/SAS (C/114), 6.
[68] D.R.O., D 124, boxes 117–18.
[69] S.R.O., tithe award.
[70] S.R.O., C/C, Knole estate sale cat. 1913.
[71] Ibid.; DD/KW, sale cat. 1921; *Hist. Somerton* (W.I. hist.), 93.
[72] Bristol Cath. MSS., Dean Chetwynd's survey f. 15.
[73] Taunton Castle, Braikenridge Colln., water-colour by W. W. Wheatley, 1845.
[74] Local information; see p. 133.
[75] In modern tourist literature.
[76] *S. & D. N. & Q.* xii. 173.
[77] E. Ekwall, *Oxford Dict. Eng. Place Names* (4th edn.), 430.
[78] *Cart. Sax.* ed. Birch, iii. 27; see F. M. Stenton, *Anglo-Saxon Eng.* (3rd edn.), 291, 332.
[79] Ekwall, op. cit. 410.

county town in the 13th century may have been made in the knowledge of its ancient status.

Somerton's brief period as a county town began in 1278 when the shire courts were transferred there from Ilchester.[80] The county gaol was established in the town in 1280, and itinerant justices began to deliver it in the same year.[81] Early in 1366 the justices met again at Ilchester and, later in that year, in order to relieve Ilchester's economic depression, both shire and circuit courts were again permanently established there.[82] By 1371 the gaol at Somerton was no longer holding county prisoners.[83]

The gaol and its adjacent hall of pleas, where a riot had taken place in 1344,[84] then went out of use. In 1434 John Harper leased a parcel of the house formerly called the court hall (*aula curie*), probably the hall of pleas, which stood 'by the churchyard of the church of Somerton'.[85] Four years later Richard Smyth held a waste site within the lord's gaol on the west of this hall.[86] The burgage known as the 'gayle' was by 1507–8 a total ruin, and was still so described in 1537,[87] though in 1529–30 money had been spent on the court-house (*domus curie*) to provide 'barrez' for the safe keeping of prisoners during sessions,[88] presumably in connexion with the last visit of the circuit judges to the town in 1530.[89]

In 1579 'an old tower embattled about castle-like' was thought to be the remains of the gaol.[90] A house in Cow Square, near the north-eastern corner of the churchyard, has been known as the Old Hall since at least 1661, and may stand on the site of the former hall of pleas.[91]

ECONOMIC HISTORY. Although for much of its history Somerton was the site of a weekly market it has never been other than a town on the smallest scale. The cloth industry made an impression upon it in the 17th century but until the 20th century the main occupation of its inhabitants was agriculture. The failure to develop lasting urban characteristics was due in part to the proximity of Ilchester and in part to the fragmented manorial holdings in the parish.

AGRICULTURE. Somerton was royal demesne and paid no geld, but was linked with Cheddar to provide the *firma unius noctis*; Somerton paid roughly four fifths of the required sum.[92] In 1086 there was land for 50 ploughs, but it is likely that this area included the later parishes of Pitney and Kingsdon.[93] The main features of the estate were its extensive arable land and small demesne. On the

main holding then held directly by the Crown, 45 ploughs were recorded, but only 5 were on the demesne, which was farmed by 4 serfs. The remainder was divided between 80 villeins and 28 bordars. There were 100 a. of meadow, pasture measuring a league by half a league, and wood of a league by a furlong. Stock on the demesne comprised 2 riding-horses, 9 pigs, and 500 sheep. An additional estate, possibly the origin of Pitney parish, was held in parage by three thegns T.R.E. and by 1086 was divided into three holdings. Together they amounted to 5½ hides, and were worked by 7 villeins and 5 bordars with 4 ploughs.[94]

In 1176 King's Somerton was required to contribute 20 marks towards an aid,[95] and from that time it regularly paid tallages and scutages: in 1189 £4 16s. 9d.;[96] in 1198 £20, the same as Ilchester and more than any other town in Somerset and Dorset;[97] in 1199 20 marks, the same as Bath and more than Ilchester;[98] but thereafter at a lower level.[99] In 1234 a tallage of 10 marks was reduced by half.[1] The last such imposition was in 1260–1.[2] It was thus a large and valuable property, and seems to have been regarded as the centre of royal estate administration in the area. Until the mid 13th century there was a chequer there for the receipt of royal rents,[3] and in 1285 a quantity of the king's silver was held there.[4] The king's park at Somerton was used for keeping stock taken as distresses for debts to the Crown.[5] Somerton was also a base for the king's serjeants by 1239, and in 1255–6 buildings were erected to house them and to store the king's corn.[6]

The estates at Somerton T.R.E. were 'in various ways alienated and dismembered' by Crown grants beginning before 1086 and continuing until the early 14th century.[7] By 1246 Hurcot comprised 2 carucates in demesne worth £4, rent worth £3, and services valued at £2 12s.[8] By 1296–7 income from the manor amounted to £24 16s. 8½d., of which rents accounted for just over £3. Services, worth £4 3s. 1d., were mostly commuted, though labour charges of a similar amount were incurred, largely for harvest work. The demesne estate was predominantly arable: in 1297 120 a. were sown with wheat and 17½ a. with oats. Sales of corn were relatively high, amounting to £16 5s. 4d. in that year and to £30 16s. 4d. in 1300–1.[9] Barley, beans, and vetches for the *familia* had to be purchased outside the manor. Grassland and wood were limited in area; sales were low and stock, mostly draught animals, included neither cows nor sheep. The permanent staff of the manor, however, included a hayward and a 'repreve' besides the bailiff,

[80] *Cal. Close*, 1272–9, 468.
[81] R. B. Pugh, *Imprisonment in Medieval Eng.* 66.
[82] *Cal. Pat.* 1364–7, 235; see below, p. 185.
[83] Pugh, op. cit. 67; see below, p. 185.
[84] *Cal. Pat.* 1343–5, 270.
[85] S.C. 6/974/6.
[86] Ibid.; see p. 133.
[87] S.C. 6/Hen. VII/1363; Hen. VIII/3043.
[88] D.R.O., D 124, box 10.
[89] *L. & P. Hen. VIII*, iv (3), p. 2921.
[90] *S. & D. N. & Q.* xii. 173.
[91] S.R.O. DD/MI, box 9, survey; D.R.O., D 124, box 1, survey 1752; box 285, survey 1835.
[92] *V.C.H. Som.* i. 434–5; *Dom. Geog. South West Eng.* ed. Darby and Welldon Finn, 150, 151n, 170–1.
[93] See above, pp. 51, 113.
[94] *V.C.H. Som.* i. 434–5.

[95] *Pipe R.* 1177 (P.R.S. xxvi), 24.
[96] Ibid. 1189 (Rec. Com.), 149.
[97] Ibid. 1198 (P.R.S. N.S. ix), 223.
[98] Ibid. 1199 (P.R.S. N.S. x), 240.
[99] Ibid. 1205 (P.R.S. N.S. xix), 141–2; 1210 (P.R.S. N.S. xxvi), 71; 1214 (P.R.S. N.S. xxxv), 103.
[1] *Close R.* 1231–4, 389.
[2] Ibid. 1264–8, 539.
[3] *Bk. of Fees*, i. 263; *Rot. Hund.* (Rec. Com.), ii. 122.
[4] *Cal. Inq. Misc.* i, p. 393.
[5] *Rot. Hund.* (Rec. Com.), ii. 123, 141.
[6] *Cal. Lib.* 1226–40, 387; 1251–60, 291.
[7] *Rot. Hund.* (Rec. Com.), ii. 121–2, 128; *V.C.H. Som.* i. 434–5, 521; *Proc. Som. Arch. Soc.* xcix and c. 46; see above, pp. 51, 113.
[8] C 133/4/15.
[9] S.C. 6/1090/4, 6.

four ploughmen, and a woman who kept the courthouse and made their pottage.[10]

Somerton Erleigh was predominantly arable. In 1324 the estate comprised 200 a. of arable, compared with 20 a. of meadow and 20 a. of old pasture. There were 6 free tenants, 10 'ferdellers', and 5 'half-ferdellers'.[11] By 1337 the same property was described as 220 a. of arable, half sown, half fallow, 40 a. of meadow subject to commons after haymaking, 15 a. of wood, and rents worth £10.[12] On the other side of the town the St. Cleers estate demesne comprised 152 a. of arable, 17 a. of meadow, and 7 a. of pasture, the last used only in alternate years. The tenants were 3 'ferlingers', 2 'half-ferlingers', and 5 cottagers. Only the 'ferlingers' performed boon works. The whole estate was worth £3 10s. 6d.[13] There were several smaller freeholds also predominantly arable.[14]

Nearly as large as the other holdings combined was Somerton manor. In 1331 it comprised 430 a. of arable, just over 48 a. of meadow, and extensive pastures including Kingsmoor. The agricultural as distinct from the urban tenants were 3 freeholders, 9 'virgaters', 5 'tresferdellers', an unspecified number of 'half-virgaters', 10 'ferdellers', 3 'half-ferdellers', and 10 cottagers, all rendering rents and works, probably commuted. The total valuation of the manor was just over £88.[15] The manor retained this pattern well into the 16th century, though customary payments like church scot and 'wodeshope' were being absorbed into the category of assessed rents in the late 15th century.[16] By 1484 the demesnes were let to the manorial tenants, producing an income of £17 9s. from 425 a. of arable and 62 a. of meadow and pasture.[17] The Hastings family continued the same policy, and in 1583–4 had a net income from the manor of just over £130.[18]

Much of the improvement in the economy of the town in the 17th century was due to the division and allotment of King's Sedgemoor about 1625. The landowners of Somerton acquired an additional 1,505 a. of rich pasture land where cattle for the market could be fattened.[19] The pasture in the parish was already extensive: about 1,000 a. at Kingsmoor[20] and over 250 a. at Staplemoor, Southmoor, Goosemoor, Stertmoor, and Waggmoor, some intercommoned with Kingsdon, Long Sutton, and Huish Episcopi.[21] The lord of Somerton manor also had a prey or right to levy a charge on pigs on West Sedgemoor around Midsummer.[22]

Small parcels of open arable were being inclosed out of East field in Somerton Erleigh and South field in Somerton in the late 17th century.[23] The process continued on Somerton Erleigh manor, and was complete before 1806.[24] Hurcot, evidently an estate of consolidated farms at least a century earlier, still had a common field c. 1661[25] and 1765.[26] St. Cleers and Somerton manor continued traditional patterns, though the former was better managed and its value rose from £6 10s. 10d. in 1602 to £25 5s. 3d. in 1676.[27] Total rents from over 240 holdings on Somerton manor about 1661 amounted to £98 2s.; by 1700 the value was £104 9s. 8d., and during the next twenty years the net income did not rise much above £80.[28] The holdings themselves were divided between 102 copyholders sharing 2,623 a., and 125 leaseholders with 905 a.[29] Elsewhere in the parish the farms were relatively small: Ralph Stawell's holding c. 1661, amounting to 678 a., was divided into three farms and smaller units, and Somerton Randolph farm was only 148 a. in 1664.[30]

Inclosure in the south of the parish continued by agreement in the 18th century, and spread into North field.[31] The remaining open fields, North, Northwest, South, and Southwest, and the common 'moors' and meadows were inclosed in 1806.[32] Some 1,363 a. of arable, 938 a. of King's Sedgemoor, 83 a. of Southmead, 13 a. at Catsgore, and 415 commons on Kingsmoor were allotted among 52 owners, principally to the earl of Ilchester.[33] In 1796 William Marshall commented unfavourably on the uninclosed land he passed on his way from Langport, though he noted 'large, good oxen' and 'good horned wedders'.[34] There was no immediate improvement after inclosure, and rents in arrear on Lord Ilchester's estate alone in 1815 totalled £1,757.[35] Later in the 19th century consolidated farming units were formed. By 1841 Hurcot was being worked as a single farm, and the Pinney estates were being rapidly made into compact units. The latter then measured 855 a., of which 254 a. formed Midney farm and 258 a. Cranes farm.[36] In contrast the farms on the Ilchester estate were widely dispersed. The most compact was St. Cleers farm, measuring 341 a., the largest single unit after Hurcot. Others on the estate had been affected by inclosure: in 1802 there were at least eight farms, including Park, Vagshurst, Whitfield, Eastmoors, Grove, and Kingsmoor farms, some of which were altered or absorbed after 1806.[37] By 1841 there were four holdings of between 180 a. and 190 a. including Park and Vagshurst farms, and four of between 107 a. and 115 a. Mowries farm, in 1841 in independent ownership, illustrates the

---

[10] In 1300–1 there was a shepherd instead of a repreve but there were no sheep on the demesne: S.C. 6/1090/6.
[11] C 134/81/20.   [12] C 135/158/16.
[13] C 135/47/15.
[14] *Cal. Inq. p.m.* ii, p. 119; iv, p. 67; *S.R.S.* iii. 202; vi. 288; xii. 31.
[15] C 135/24/31. There were 22 'semi-virgaters' in 1484–5: S.C. 6/974/6.
[16] S.C. 6/974/6; Hen. VIII/3043.
[17] S.C. 6/974/6.
[18] Bodl. MS. Top. Som. c. 2 ff. 7–7v.
[19] D.R.O., D 124, box 18.
[20] *S.R.S.* xiv. 128–9; S.R.O., DD/MI, box 9, survey c. 1661; Sta. Cha. 4/2/71–2, 4/10/60; D.R.O., D 124, box 117, survey 1664–6.
[21] *Ilchester Almshouse Deeds*, ed. Buckler, nos. 62–3; Hook Manor, Donhead St. Andrew, Arundell MSS. MS. bk. 54, Kingsdon manor ct. 12 Sept. 1615.

[22] S.R.O., DD/MI, box 9, survey.
[23] S.R.O., DD/SAS (C/127), 1; ibid. (C/96), 20; DD/PI 9/2.
[24] B.M. Harl. MS. 608 f. 73v.
[25] S.R.O., DD/MI, box 9, survey.
[26] S.R.O., DD/DN, box 43.
[27] S.R.O., T/PH/vch 11; D.R.O., D 124, box 17.
[28] S.R.O., DD/MI, box 9; D.R.O., D 124, box 17.
[29] S.R.O., DD/MI, box 9.
[30] Ibid.; DD/SAS (C/96), 20.
[31] D.R.O., D 124, box 110, Ilchester to Donisthorpe; S.R.O., DD/S/BT 96.
[32] S.R.O., CR 45.
[33] Ibid.
[34] W. Marshall, *Rural Econ. of West of Eng.* ii. 197–8.
[35] D.R.O., D 124, box 18.
[36] S.R.O., DD/DN, box 43; tithe award.
[37] S.R.O., D/P/som 13/2/3; CR 45.

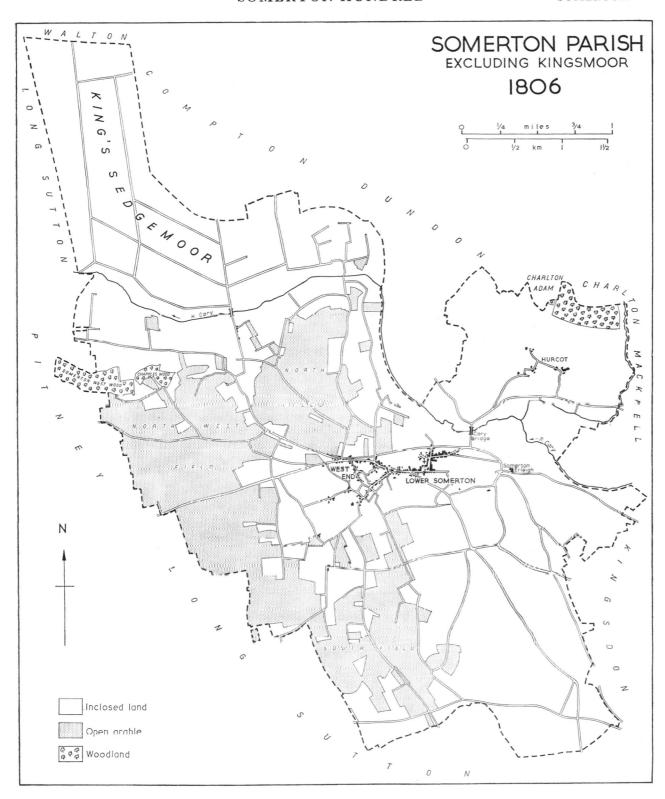

SOMERTON PARISH
EXCLUDING KINGSMOOR
1806

Inclosed land
Open arable
Woodland

dispersed character of the holdings: most of its land lay on and below Brockle hill, while its barton and buildings were in Pound Pools, just north of West Street, a mile away.[38]

Amalgamation of holdings continued during the 19th century. By 1874 St. Cleers farm measured 420 a.; Home farm was a new creation from twelve separate holdings; Somerton Door farm, its farmhouse the capital messuage of the earlier Whitfield farm and later known as Sedgemoor Folly House, and Etsome farm absorbed holdings on and near the northern 'moors'.[39] These new farms on the Ilchester estate were put up for sale from 1874 onwards: just over 2,400 a. were offered in 1874,

[38] S.R.O., tithe award.

[39] S.R.O., DD/PI 12/14: sale cat. 1874.

and only 587 a. remained by 1921.[40] Most of this was then sold. There remained in the parish a considerable number of smallholders, who in 1897 founded the Somerton Cottagers Horticultural Society to add to the agricultural society already in being.[41] In the sixty years from 1841 there was a substantial increase in the amount of grassland in the parish, and the trend continued in the 20th century.[42] Another distinctive feature from the 1920s was the creation of small poultry farms, nine of which were concentrated on South hill by 1939.[43] Grassland predominated in 1971.

TRADE AND INDUSTRY. In the late 13th century the prosperity of Somerton was increased not only by the acquisition of Kingsmoor in 1275 and by the transfer of the county and assize courts and county gaol in 1278–9,[44] but also by the market grant of 1255,[45] and by burgages and newly-built ovens and a windmill, worth in all £46 by 1275–6.[46] By 1290 the number of burgages had been increased to form a 'new borough', probably around the market-place, which then accounted for a third of the income from the manor.[47] By 1296–7 borough and manor together produced £80, and just over that sum was paid by the inhabitants when they were farming the property in 1309–10.[48] The new borough alone produced rents of £6 14s. in 1331.[49] Further physical expansion of the town along New Street took place before 1349,[50] and by that time the town had several shops and its craftsmen included dyers, skinners, webbers, shearers, and smiths.[51] The withdrawal of the assize and county courts in 1366 must have damaged the rather narrow economy[52] but the market continued and in 1447 7 butchers, 2 tailors, a tanner, and a baker were presented for breaking trading regulations there.[53] The income from the borough rose slightly by the end of the 15th century, half the increase being due to the conversion of a burgage into the 'Neutaverne' and the erection of a pair of shackles for shoeing horses.[54] Rents rose from £8 3s. 4½d. in 1485–6 to £9 3s. 11½d. by 1507–8, but were thereafter stable until at least 1537.[55]

In 1540 Somerton was one of the towns to be 're-edified' under Act of Parliament, but there is no evidence of action or economic recovery.[56] In the early 17th century neighbouring parishes were required to support its poor, many of whom had moved into the town because of the great number of cottages built there.[57] There were said to be 360 paupers there in 1616,[58] compared with only 348 rated inhabitants in 1604–5,[59] and by 1631 the number of paupers was said to have increased threefold.[60] By 1635 the town was described as 'very poor, having no trade to subsist on, and having many poor people inhabiting'.[61] Yet by 1630 it was evidently a cloth town, and leases of property in the next fifty years show clothiers, mercers, linen-drapers, woollen-drapers, haberdashers, and craftsmen in wool, linen, silk, serge, and felt concentrated in the town.[62] This narrow range was supplemented by a few glovers, tanners, masons, and two tobacconists.[63]

Buildings, especially in the Market Place, suggest that the 17th century was a period of prosperity in Somerton, and the social life of the town in the first decades of the 17th century does not suggest a depression. The parish house was a frequent resort of strolling players and entertainers such as Lord Chandos's men in 1605–6, the 'interlude players' in 1607–8, and the traveller 'showing of his child' in 1615–16.[64] Other similar activities left their mark as place-names in the parish: a cockpit, west of the churchyard, a bowling green behind the Red Lion, and Bull-baiting Close in Lower Somerton.[65]

Markets and fairs saved the town, and a reflection of increased business is the growing number of inns in and around the market place.[66] In 1620 6 innholders and 5 tipplers were licensed to trade there, and by the 1660s there were a number of substantial inns including the Red Lion, the Bear, the Swan, and the Angel in the Market Place, the Three Cups in North Street, the Bell in West Street, and the Dog or Greyhound in New Street.[67] By 1760 the number of inns had risen to at least sixteen to cater for the traders, including London drovers who came to the town to buy lean cattle.[68]

The range of trades seems to have widened slightly during the 18th century and included fellmongers, braziers, gunsmiths, a pewterer, clockmakers, and a succession of apothecaries and surgeons. During the same period the cloth industry was evidently abandoned: no clothier occurs after 1740, no mercer after 1730, no serge-weaver after 1710.[69] In 1796 the western suburbs of the town were described as in ruins and the whole town as a 'decaying place'.[70] Some recovery was made in the 19th century. Somerton Brewery, later Somerton Steam Brewery, in West Street, was established by 1840 and by 1883 supplied an area of 40 miles radius.[71] By 1866

[40] S.R.O., DD/KW, sale cat. 1921.
[41] Kelly's Dir. Som. (1897).
[42] S.R.O., tithe award; statistics supplied by the then Bd. of Agric. (1905).
[43] Kelly's Dir. Som. (1923, 1927, 1939).
[44] See pp. 137, 139.   [45] See below.
[46] Rot. Hund. (Rec. Com.), ii. 128.
[47] S.C. 6/1089/25.
[48] S.C. 6/1090/4, 7.
[49] C 135/24/31.   [50] See p. 130.
[51] Hunt. Libr., HA Manorial, box 22, ct. roll 1349.
[52] See p. 139.
[53] Hunt. Libr., HA Manorial, box 22, ct. roll 1447.
[54] S.C. 6/974/6. The 'Nywewyntaverne' occurs in 1394: S.C. 2/200/31.
[55] S.C. 6/Hen. VII/1355, 1363; Hen. VIII/3043.
[56] 32 Henry VIII c. 19.
[57] S.R.S. xxiii. 33, 167, 190, 195, 210–11, 347; xxiv. 14, 140.
[58] Ibid. xxiii. 175.
[59] S.R.O., D/P/som 4/1/1, pp. 176–86.
[60] S.R.S. xxiv. 140.   [61] Ibid. 241–2.
[62] D.R.O., D 124, boxes 106–11, 115–17; S.R.O., D/P/som 4/1/2, pp. 15, 17; DD/SAS (C/127), 1; S.R.S. xxxiv. 144, 218.
[63] D.R.O., D 124, boxes 106–7, 109–11, 115; S.R.O., DD/SAS (C/96); 20; Cal. S.P. Dom. 1639–40, 40.
[64] S.R.O., D/P/som 4/1/1, pp. 193, 211, 217, 271, 308.
[65] D.R.O., D 124, box 111; S.R.O., DD/PI, 2/9.
[66] See p. 131.
[67] S.R.O., D/P/som 4/1/2, pp. 167–8; DD/MI, box 9; D.R.O., D 124, box 117.
[68] D.R.O., D 124, boxes 17, 115–16; S.R.O., Q/RL, victuallers' recogs.
[69] D.R.O., D 124, boxes 108–11, 116–17; S.R.O., DD/SAS (C/96), 20; DD/SAS (C/127), 1; DD/S/BT 96; D/P/som 4/1/2, p. 627; 13/2/20: min. 19 Aug. 1778; 13/3/6; H. H. Cotterell, Bristol and West Country Pewterers.
[70] W. Marshall, Rural Econ. of West of Eng. ii. 197–8.
[71] County Gazette Dir. Som. (1840); Kelly's Dir. Som. (1883).

Edward Welsh (later Welsh and Clark) had a factory for linen shirt collars in Broad Street which by 1868 employed 100 girls.[72] Rope, twine, and straw bonnets were manufactured in the town by 1840,[73] and twenty years later women and girls were employed in gloving and binding shoes.[74] Market gardening was a common means of livelihood.[75] Later in the century there were three booksellers, a printer, a professor of music, and a photographer.[76] By 1897 a cardboard box factory had been established, and by 1902 the patentee and manufacturer of the 'celebrated "Wee Wee" liver pills' was in business at 'Apothecaries Hall' in the town.[77] Somerton was, indeed, the natural focus of a wide community until the railway was brought to Langport. In 1840 there were two auctioneers, four attorneys, three surgeons, and three veterinary surgeons, and by 1859 two banks had been established there.[78] The town was also the headquarters of a division of the county police force, the meeting-place for magistrates, and the headquarters of a volunteer battalion of the Somerset Light Infantry.[79]

During the same period the town's communications were virtually cut by the development of the railways. Until the 1840s Somerton was served by coaches to London, Barnstaple, Bristol, Bath, Chard, Axminster, Wincanton, and Langport.[80] A daily van went to Bridgwater, the nearest railway station.[81] By 1859 there were only carriers, travelling merely to Langport, Glastonbury, and Castle Cary.[82] Somerton had no railway station until 1906.[83] The town's industry could not compete with larger concerns; the brewery closed soon after the First World War and the shirt factory in the late 1930s. Some new employment was provided by a milk factory established in 1926, and by the Beam Radio Station, in 1971 part of the External Communications Executive, set up about the same time. Increasing use of road transport is reflected in the growth of motor businesses from 1919, and during the 1920s two restaurants and an antique dealer came to the town.[84] Tourism and local shopping remain important in Somerton's economy.

Building stone was accessible in many parts of the parish, and several quarries were opened in North field in the early 18th century. They were later filled and either built on or converted to orchards.[85] During the 19th century quarries were opened further south at Ashen Cross and Highbrooks, both of which were in use until the early 20th century.[86]

MARKET AND FAIRS. In 1255 a weekly market on Monday was established in Somerton for the improvement of the manor.[87] The grant was said to have damaged the market at Ilchester, but Somerton's market was itself later harmed by a rival at Queen Camel.[88] A market-place was established south of the church and was surrounded by newly-created burgage plots, the whole area being described by 1290 as a new town or new borough.[89] By 1331 the market and fairs combined were valued at only 30s. but by the late 15th century the market alone was let for £5.[90] Its existence was threatened c. 1583 and it may have ceased shortly afterwards.[91] A new grant was made by the Crown in 1606,[92] and in 1688 market day was changed to Tuesday.[93]

An eight-day fair was also granted in 1255, to be held on the eve, feast, and morrow of All Saints and on the five days following (31 Oct.–7 Nov.).[94] A second fair, for nine days from the eve of St. Andrew (29 Nov.–7 Dec.), was granted in 1320.[95] Only the first fair survived until 1485, but it was then of little consequence and does not thereafter occur.[96]

By the 1630s there were weekly fairs from Palm Sunday until the middle of June,[97] described in 1664–6 as on Palm Monday, Hock Monday, Procession Monday, Trinity Monday, and St. Simon and St. Jude's Day (28 Oct.).[98] All but the last were probably, in effect, augmented markets. In 1686, on the petition of Lord Stawell, the Crown granted a horse fair, a fair for cattle and other commodities for ten days before Michaelmas, and a similar one for ten days before Christmas.[99] The lease of all these fairs and markets in 1688 included new fairs on 24 February and 19 September or on the Mondays after these dates as well as the October fair.[1] About 1665 the fairs and market, valued at £100, were leased for £13 6s. 8d.[2] Seven 'fairs' in 1700 were valued at £60, and the rent in 1731–3 was £90 a year and in 1768 £110.[3]

About 1740 the spring fairs for fat cattle, 'the great resort even of London drovers', had been recently changed from Mondays to Fridays because 'Sabbatical notions' had prevailed 'to prevent dealers from driving their cattle . . . on the Sundays'.[4] By 1840 the market was still held every Tuesday and fairs on the last Monday in January, on the Tuesday in Passion week and the third, sixth, ninth, and twelfth Tuesdays following, all for cattle; and on September 30th and November 8th for cattle,

[72] P.O. Dir. Som. (1866); Rep. Com. Children and Women in Agric. [4202–I], p. 476, H.C. (1868–9), xiii.
[73] County Gazette Dir. (1840).
[74] Ibid.; P.O. Dir. Som. (1861); Rep. Com. Children and Women in Agric. p. 476.
[75] P.O. Dir. Som. (1861).
[76] Harrison, Harrod, & Co. Dir. (1859); P.O. Dir. Som. (1866).
[77] Kelly's Dir. Som. (1897, 1902).
[78] County Gazette Dir. Som. (1840); Harrison, Harrod, & Co. Dir. (1859).
[79] Harrison, Harrod, & Co. Dir. (1859); Kelly's Dir. Som. (1897); S.R.O., DD/PI, 11/1, 14/1.
[80] County Gazette Dir. Som. (1840).
[81] Pigot, Nat. Com. Dir. (1842).
[82] Harrison, Harrod, & Co. Dir. (1859).
[83] See p. 130.
[84] Kelly's Dir. Som. (1919, 1923, 1927); Hist. Somerton (W.I. hist.), 85.
[85] Hunt. Libr., HA Manorial, box 22, ct. roll 1572; D.R.O., D 124, boxes 17, 110, 112, 114.

[86] Kelly's Dir. Som. (1910, 1927, 1935, 1939); O.S. Map 6", Som. LXXIII. NE. (1886 edn.).
[87] Close R. 1254–6, 146.
[88] Rot. Hund. (Rec. Com.), ii. 128–9, 139.
[89] S.C. 6/1089/25; 1090/4, 7; see above, p. 130.
[90] C 135/24/31; S.C. 6/Hen. VII/1329; Hen. VIII/3043.
[91] S.R.S. lxix, p. 29.
[92] C 66/1708.
[93] Cal. S.P. Dom. Jan. 1686–May 1687, 74–5, 305; D.R.O., D 124, box 115.
[94] Close R. 1254–6, 146.
[95] Cal. Chart. R. 1300–26, 434.
[96] Cal. Inq. p.m. x, p. 44; S.C. 6/974/6.
[97] S.R.S. xv. 231–2.
[98] D.R.O., D 124, box 117.
[99] Cal. S.P. Dom. Jan. 1686–May 1687, pp. 74–5, 305.
[1] D.R.O., D 124, box 111.
[2] S.R.O., DD/MI, box 9.
[3] D.R.O., D 124, box 17, survey 1700; box 18, abstract accts.
[4] S.R.O., DD/SH, 107.

sheep, hogs, and pedlary.[5] The market was 'quite obsolete' by 1897, and by that time fairs were largely for entertainment only.[6] The spring fair, presumably the Palm Tuesday fair, survived longest for the sale of stock.[7]

The market was under the control of a bailiff by 1485 at least until 1530.[8] In the mid 17th century the borough court held a special piepowder session during fairs.[9]

Goods and cattle were sold not only immediately around the High Cross or market cross;[10] the eastern end of the market-place, at its junction with Kircombe Street, was the site of the sheep market by 1664–6, and beasts were exhibited for sale in the present Broad Street, known as Pig or Swine Street, North Street, and Cow Square.[11] Some householders paid increased rents for the privilege of erecting posts and rails to protect their property during fairs and markets.[12]

The lease of the markets and fairs in 1688 included a shambles house, a tolsey house, and a shed to store sheep hurdles.[13] The position of the tolsey is unknown; it occurs in 1669–70 but not after 1688.[14] The hurdle house in the Sheep Market was later separately leased and survived until after 1767.[15] The shambles house is the building later known as the Market House or Town Hall. It was extensively repaired in 1719[16] and by 1841 was used by the town's butchers.[17] The borough court jury in 1855 asked the owner, Lord Ilchester, to rebuild it 'because of its delapidated condition as not adapted for its purposes'.[18] A further suggestion to rebuild was made in 1887.[19] In 1913 the Town Hall, used until the 1870s by local magistrates, was sold by Lord Ilchester.[20] It then comprised a billiard hall and other rooms on the ground floor and an assembly room above. In 1970 it was owned by the Somerton Club, and the upper floor used as a furniture store. The building is a rectangular structure of lias with Ham stone dressings. It is of 17th-century or earlier origin but has undergone much alteration. Surviving buttresses along the north and south sides do not reach the eaves, suggesting that the walls have been raised. Several features appear to date from the improvements of 1719, including a large round-headed mullioned and transomed window at the east end. A floor which cuts across both this window and one in the north wall was inserted later to provide an upper room for public assemblies.

In the early 19th century the building had arched entrances at the centre of each long side and a bellcot above the west gable.[21] There was a porch-like structure against the west wall, said to have been used as a lock-up.[22] Outside it a well-head, later replaced by a pump, belonged to one of the common wells.[23] Late-19th-century and subsequent alterations included the insertion of a large west window to the upper floor with a corresponding lowering of the 'lock-up' roof, the construction of a chimney on the north side, and other modifications.

There was a cross at the market by 1390.[24] In 1799 traders were presented for putting carts and waggons in the cross, and the borough crier was ordered to give notice that butter and cheese should be sold there.[25] Lord Ilchester sold the cross to the parish council in 1916.[26] The present cross is dated 1673 and was restored in 1925 and 1950.[27] It is an open octagonal structure of lias with a central pier resting on a stepped base. The eight segmental arches are separated by low angle buttresses. The octagonal roof has an embattled parapet and terminates in a ball finial. Sparse Ham stone dressings include a string course, parapet coping, gargoyles, and keystones.

MILLS. By 1275–6 a windmill *de novo levatum* was part of Somerton manor;[28] it was still in existence in 1330.[29] By 1334 there was also a windmill on the parsonage estate, standing at Mileburgh, now Melbury; it had gone out of use by 1484.[30] In 1575 Thomas Wysse sold a grain mill to James Hodges.[31] By 1619 it was described as a windmill and stood in South field.[32] It presumably passed with the St. Cleers estate to Sir John Strangways in 1638, and was let by him in 1657 to Richard Applin of Shepton Mallet.[33] It may be the 'old mill near St. Cleers Pitts' mentioned in 1715,[34] and probably stood in a field called Mill Close, later cut by the railway and the new road north of Wasps Nest.[35] Elizabeth Moore of Shepton, sister of William Applin, became tenant in 1721, and the mill, still called Applin's mill, passed to James Bown or Brown by 1745 and to John Edwards in 1770.[36] Ten years later it was let to George Nutt, but had evidently gone out of use by 1802.[37]

By 1616 there was a windmill on Crane's farm.[38] It was described in 1674 as near Lower Somerton field, and passed with the farm to Henry Parsons.[39]

[5] *County Gazette Dir. Som.* (1840).
[6] *Kelly's Dir. Som.* (1897).
[7] *Hist. Somerton* (W.I. hist.), 83.
[8] S.C. 6/Hen. VII/1329, 1355; D.R.O., D 124, box 10, acct. 1529–30.
[9] D.R.O., D 124, box 117, survey 1664–6.
[10] See below.
[11] D.R.O., D 124, box 108, Stawell to Stocker 1688; box 117, survey 1664–6.
[12] D.R.O., D 124, box 17, bailiffs' accts.
[13] D.R.O., D 124, box 111.
[14] S.R.O., D/P/som 4/1/2, p. 217.
[15] D.R.O., D 124, box 110.
[16] Ibid. box 17: acct. bk. 1714–24.
[17] S.R.O., tithe award.
[18] D.R.O., D 124, box 1: ct. bk. 1845–60.
[19] *Life Thoughts of the late Edwin Gunning*, ed. T. B. Clark (Yeovil, n.d.).
[20] S.R.O., C/C, sale cat. Knole Estate, 1913.
[21] Ashmolean Mus., Sutherland Colln., water-colour by Geo. Shepherd, 1823 (reprod. in Hist. Somerton (W.I. hist.), opp. 88); B.M. Add. MS. 33702 ff. 85–6: sketch by Revd. John Skinner, 1828; Taunton Castle, Braikenridge Colln., water-colour by W. W. Wheatley, 1845.

[22] Local information.
[23] See p. 146.
[24] Hunt. Libr., HA Manorial, box 22, ct. roll 1390.
[25] D.R.O., D 124, box 1, ct. bk. 1799–1827; repeated 1800, 1816.
[26] Par. Council recs., conveyance.
[27] Inscription on cross.
[28] *Rot. Hund.* (Rec. Com.), ii. 128.
[29] C 135/24/31.
[30] E 179/169/14; S.C. 6/974/5.
[31] C.P. 25(2)/204/17 Eliz. I Hil.
[32] C.P. 25(2)/346/17 Jas. I Trin.; D.R.O., D 124, box 110; see above, p. 129.
[33] D.R.O., D 124, box 110.
[34] S.R.O., DD/SAS (C/114), 6.
[35] S.R.O., tithe award; the site is O.S. Nat. Grid 476278.
[36] D.R.O., D 124, boxes 109, 286; S.R.O., D/P/som 13/2/1.
[37] D.R.O., D 124, box 18, rents in arrear; S.R.O., D/P/som 13/2/3.
[38] C.P. 25(2)/346/13 Jas. I Mich.
[39] S.R.O., DD/SAS (C/96), 20; D/P/som 4/1/2, p. 547; 13/2/1–2.

Somerton, later school-house, 1830

Stoke sub Hamdon, later Fleur de Lis inn, 1848

CHURCH HOUSES

EAST LYDFORD OLD CHURCH FROM THE SOUTH-WEST, 1833

STOKE SUB HAMDON: 'THE PRIORY' FROM THE NORTH-EAST, 1836

By 1737 it had been acquired by Adam Pitman, though it retained the name Crane's mill.[40] Pitman still held it in 1779, but it had been dismantled by 1802.[41] It evidently stood south-east of the cross-roads on Perry hill, near fields called Crane's Mill Close, Mill Ground, and Mill Close.[42] A windmill in the parish was devised by William Champion of Shapwick in 1650–1;[43] its site is unknown. Another mill, on South hill, was owned and occupied by John Coolin in 1685;[44] it was called Cullen's mill in 1692 and was still standing in 1749.[45]

There was apparently only one water-mill in Somerton, which stood east of the town.[46] It first occurs in 1513.[47] By the mid 17th century it was known as Tanckers mill, later Tankins or Tanketts mill.[48] By 1732 it belonged to John Fisher, and passed with a share of the Fisher estate to Joseph Gill by 1778.[49] Gill sold it in 1785 to Robert Chappell who occupied it until 1810.[50] John Jacobs, owner of Somerton Court, acquired it in that year, and sold it to John Pinney in 1814.[51] It was known as Somerton Flour Mill in the 19th century.[52] A steam engine was installed there by 1910 and the mill continued in use until soon after 1935.[53] The buildings were still visible in 1970.

By 1330 there was a horse-mill in the town, then part of the estate of the earl of Kent.[54] By 1484–5 it was held with 3 a. of meadow to provide grazing for the tenants' horses.[55] Thereafter, for a time, it was let with the common oven in the town, but in 1529–30 it produced no income and was in need of repair.[56] Ownership remained with the lord of the capital manor, and the Stawells leased it to John Stocker in 1673.[57] By 1701 it was described as a customary malt mill, and was evidently still in use in 1766.[58] The mill stood on the east side of North Street at its northern end, and gave its name to Horse Mill Lane.[59]

There was at least one other mill in the town in the 15th century, presumably horse-driven, and occupied from 1438 by Richard Smyth.[60] By 1841 there was a steam mill on the south side of the Market Place,[61] and the owner of the brewery in West Street was described as a miller in 1859.[62] In 1914 there was an oil mill called Bury Mill in the north of the town.[63]

LOCAL GOVERNMENT AND PUBLIC SERVICES.
Successive alienations from the Domesday

manor of Somerton led to the creation of independent manorial jurisdictions both within and outside the parish.[64] Within the parish there developed courts for Somerton, Somerton Erleigh, and Hurcot manors, for Somerton Borough, and for Kingsmoor.

The men of Somerton achieved some kind of autonomy within Somerton manor by 1242 when they farmed it from the Crown for £60 a year.[65] They were superseded by a royal keeper in 1252, but farmed it again in 1296 and 1310.[66] Before 1275–6 a piece of ground by Cary bridge, formerly used for trials by combat and including an ordeal pit succeeded by gallows, had been taken from the manor.[67] New urban development, complete by 1290, gave rise to a separate jurisdiction which by the mid 14th century had its own court and common seal.[68] The borough, however, was always in the hands of the lord of the capital manor, and the distinction between the two jurisdictions is not easy to define.

There are court rolls for the borough for one session in 1349,[69] for the years 1390–1,[70] 1394–5,[71] 1413–14,[72] 1447–8,[73] for one session in 1542, and for the years 1543–4,[74] 1565–6, and 1571–2.[75] They record the business of a court held every three or four weeks, described normally as a *curia*, but in 1391 as a halmote, and the twice-yearly sessions or lawdays of Michaelmas and Hockday. During this period the court dealt with cases of debt, trespass, breaches of the peace, and breaches of the assize of bread and ale, and recorded entries into burgage property. At the same time it exercised control over the haywards of the arable fields of the manor, and much of its business concerned the maintenance of ditches and roads.

By the early 17th century the three-week courts had in practice disappeared, though they survived nominally until the mid 17th century to try cases under 40s. between party and party for both borough and manor.[76] The twice-yearly lawdays became at the same time the borough courts, in theory held jointly with the manor and attended by all inhabitants of 12 years and over.[77] Records survive as court books for 1617–20, 1701–16, 1730–96, and 1799–1860, and as court papers for 1617, 1693–1800, and 1830–63.[78] Two courts continued to be held each year until 1765, when it became the practice to adjourn the October session for a month and then appoint officers.

The presentments of the borough court in the

[40] S.R.O., D/P/som 13/2/1.
[41] Ibid. 13/2/2–3.
[42] S.R.O., tithe award.
[43] *Som. Wills*, ed. Brown, iii. 100.
[44] S.R.O., Q/SR 160/6.
[45] S.R.O., DD/DEV 5, 13.
[46] O.S. Nat. Grid 497285.
[47] Alnwick, Northumberland MSS. X II 12 3c.
[48] S.R.O., DD/MI, box 9; DD/PI 9/6–7, 10.
[49] S.R.O., D/P/som 4/1/2, p. 547; 13/2/2.
[50] S.R.O., Q/RE, land tax assessments; DD/PI 3/14.
[51] S.R.O., DD/PI 3/14.
[52] Harrison, Harrod, & Co. *Dir.* (1859); *Kelly's Dir. Som.* (1885); O.S. Map 6″, Som. LXXIII. NE. (1886 edn.).
[53] *Kelly's Dir. Som.* (1910, 1935, 1939).
[54] C 135/24/31.
[55] S.C. 6/974/6.
[56] D.R.O., D 124, box 10, acct. 1529–30.
[57] Hunt. Libr., HA. Manorial, box 18, demesne valn. f. 6v.; D.R.O., D 124, box 17, surveys 1700–1.
[58] D.R.O., D 124, box 17, survey 1701; S.R.O., D/P/som 13/2/1.
[59] D.R.O., D 124, box 111, Stawell to Dymond, 1685.
[60] S.C. 6/974/6.
[61] S.R.O., tithe award.
[62] Harrison, Harrod, & Co. *Dir.* (1859).
[63] *Kelly's Dir. Som.* (1914).
[64] See p. 134.
[65] *Pipe R.* 1242, ed. H. L. Cannon, 339; *Bk. of Fees*, ii. 1265.
[66] *Cal. Pat.* 1247–58, 165; *Close R.* 1264–8, 347, *Rot. Hund.* (Rec. Com.), ii. 122; S.C. 6/1090/4, 6, 7.
[67] *Rot. Hund.* (Rec. Com.), ii. 121–2, 128.
[68] S.R.O., DD/PI 8/7; Hunt. Libr. H.A. Manorial, box 22, ct. roll 1349; see above, p. 143.
[69] Hunt. Libr., HA Manorial, box 22, ct. roll 1349.
[70] Ibid.
[71] S.C. 2/200/31.
[72] S.C. 2/200/32.
[73] Hunt. Libr., HA Manorial, box 22, ct. roll 1447–8.
[74] S.C. 2/200/35.
[75] Hunt. Libr., HA Manorial, box 22, ct. rolls 1565–6, 1571–2.
[76] D.R.O., D 124, box 117, survey 1664–6.
[77] Ibid.
[78] D.R.O., D 124, boxes 1, 286; S.R.O., DD/SAS M5.

early 17th century were concerned almost exclusively with the removal of tenants and lodgers. A century later there were no presentments and the only business apart from the appointment of officers was the occasional change of tenancy of a burgage. The jury began to take more interest in local affairs after 1726, though presentments repeated annually over a period of more than a century suggest that the court was powerless to prevent people from tying their horses to the Market House windows or to the sheep racks, or to ensure that the pillory and stocks were kept in repair. Detailed presentments of nuisances in the 19th century reveal a greater interest in the conduct of the market and of shopkeepers, in the condition of streets and buildings, and in the need for some kind of lock-up.[79]

During the 15th century the officers of the borough court were a constable, a bailiff, a reeve, aletasters, and five haywards each for the north and south fields. The bailiff was evidently nominated by the steward and the reeve chosen by the steward from three nominees of the jury. The steward himself had a residence in West Street, let permanently by the mid 15th century.[80] By the mid 17th century there were two constables, one for the manor and one for the borough but both answerable to the borough court; a bailiff to collect chief rents, fines, and reliefs and to attend the constables when they tried offenders; two assizers of weights and measures and of bread and ale, two searchers and sealers of leather, and a street warden.[81] With the exception of the street wardens and the assizers of weights and measures, these offices were retained at least until 1863. By 1617 the eastern common well of the borough was controlled by a surveyor. From 1720 onwards two wardens were appointed annually for each of the three, and from 1736 the four common wells in the town, with power to levy rates for maintenance.[82] From time to time committees for viewing gutters and streams in the town were set up or persons appointed to keep pigs from churchyard and marketplace.[83]

Somerton manor court met three times a year by 1484.[84] Its records survive as extracts from 1562, 1565–6, and 1572;[85] as more continuous series for 1617–20 and 1694–7;[86] as court books 1701–1860; and as presentments 1757–89 and 1832–63.[87] In the early 17th century the court met twice a year, in March and September. By the early 18th century it was described as a court baron, and was held in April and October, usually a day or two after the borough court. Annual sessions in October only began in 1748.

At the end of the 15th century the manor was administered by a reeve.[88] By 1617 the reeve and two haywards each for the north and south fields, and a variable number for the 'moors' served the court. By the mid 18th century one man seems to have performed the duties of hayward for the whole manor, though four continued to be appointed each year for the fields and one for the borough and the 'moors' together. The court concerned itself almost exclusively with farming matters; as late as 1860 it was reporting beasts straying in the streets, horses and carts left standing to cause a nuisance, and farmers burning grass in the 'moors'.

Hurcot formed a small and unremunerative jurisdiction by 1290, and in 1296–7 the court employed a reeve, a hayward, and a 'repereve'.[89] No courts were mentioned in an extent of the holding in 1246.[90]

Courts were held at Somerton Erleigh manor by 1324.[91] Court rolls survive for single sessions in 1508, 1513, 1527, and 1530, of what is described simply as *curia*.[92] No officers occur, and business was confined largely to entries and orders to repair houses.

The parsonage estate was administered by a bailiff in the early 16th century, but courts in 1484–5 provided no income.[93] Farmers under the chapter of Bristol held courts baron at will for the admission of copyholders 'by the rod according to custom'. Court books survive for the period 1742–1910, and sessions were described variously as courts baron, special courts baron, and private courts baron.[94] Copies of court roll exist for 1718[95] and 1768,[96] and admission and surrender papers for 1838–58 and 1879–88.[97]

Courts baron for entries in the 'manor' of St. Cleers were held in the 17th century, but no separate records seem to have been kept for the manor after 1700, when the Strangways family acquired the main manor.[98]

Kingsmoor was administered by the borough court in the 14th century, but by 1484 a separate session of the court was held for the 'moor' alone.[99] Courts were held twice a year by the 1540s, but the borough bailiff was still in control, assisted by the manorial reeve and two moor reeves.[1] Court rolls survive from 1543,[2] 1563, and 1572,[3] court books for the periods 1618–20 and 1701–96, and papers for 1730 and 1765–97.[4] By 1701 the 'moor' was described as a liberty, administered through a legal court and view of frankpledge. The court met twice a year, in April or May and October, and until 1706 was staffed by a reeve, a bailiff, and two haywards. From 1706 only one hayward was appointed, and from 1775 the offices of reeve and bailiff were combined. In the 16th century the court

[79] See p. 144.
[80] S.C. 6/974/6.
[81] D.R.O., D 124, box 117, survey 1664–6.
[82] The wells were Church Hatch, under Prankard's house, end of the Market House, and Ringers Well.
[83] Hunt. Libr., HA Manorial, box 22, ct. roll 1565; D.R.O., D 124, box 1, ct. bk. 1730–96, *sub anno* 1741.
[84] S.C. 6/974/6.
[85] Hunt. Libr., HA Manorial, box 22.
[86] D.R.O., D 124, boxes 1 (1617–20), 17 (1694–7).
[87] Ibid. boxes 17 (ct. bks. 1701–1814 and presentments), 286 (ct. bks. 1815–60).
[88] S.C. 6/Hen. VII/1329, 1355, 1363; Hen. VIII/3039, 3043.
[89] S.C. 6/1089/25; 1090/4 (m. 8), 6.

[90] C 133/4/15.
[91] C 134/81/20.
[92] Alnwick, Northumberland MSS., X II 12 3c, 3d.
[93] S.C. 6/974/5; *Valor Eccl.* (Rec. Com.), i. 194.
[94] D.R.O., D 124, box 18.
[95] S.R.O., DD/DN, box 23.
[96] S.R.O., DD/SAS (C/114), 6.
[97] D.R.O., D 124, boxes 108–9; S.R.O., DD/PI 9/11.
[98] Ibid. box 10, gen. ct. bk. 1656–66, pp. 163, 219; 17, copy 1677.
[99] Hunt. Libr., HA Manorial, box 22, ct. roll 1390; S.C. 6/974/6.
[1] S.C. 2/198/35.   [2] Ibid.
[3] Hunt. Libr., HA Manorial, box 22.
[4] D.R.O., D 124, boxes 1, 18.

controlled pasturage and the maintenance of bridges and banks; its income was from fines for encroachments including 'weyne silver' and 'lever silver', fines on non-commoners for using the 'moor' as a thoroughfare, and on commoners for cutting too much grass. Control of sheep, cattle, and geese on the 'moor' was the main business of the 18th century, together with fines on coal-barge owners for using the river bank at Pill Bridge as a wharf, and for allowing their horses to stray from the towpath. The 'moor' was inclosed in 1797 and allotments were made in respect of 415 commons.[5]

Parochial administration developed slowly in face of strong manorial and borough courts. The annual 'general day of account', forerunner of the Easter vestry, was the only regular assembly of the parish in the 17th century. This body in 1678 decided that of the four men put forward as overseers, two should be churchwardens.[6] By 1687 a salaried parish clerk was employed.[7] The 'parish meeting for the town and borough of Somerton' continued in the early 18th century, passing the wardens' accounts and approving the sale of pews.[8] From 1746 onwards it was known as the vestry, and was open in character.[9] Its interest gradually widened to include the destruction of vermin from 1754,[10] the provision of a ladder 'for the use of the town in case of fire or any other accident' in 1775,[11] payments to men raised for the local militia by the overseers in 1813,[12] and in the same year the appointment of a committee to discuss 'the various burglaries, felonies, and depredations' committed in the town.[13] Regular payments to paupers were supplemented by grants to those 'in necessity'; gifts of food and clothing were frequently made, and work was occasionally found at favourable rates.[14] From 1782 the vicar established the right to choose one of the two churchwardens. The number of overseers varied: there were usually four in the 18th century and two in the nineteenth. A salaried assistant overseer was employed by 1817.[15] Waywardens occur from 1772.[16]

The overseers rented a house in West Street as a poorhouse by 1824.[17] The parish became part of the Langport poor-law union in 1836.[18]

The borough court seems to have won back many of its public functions in the 19th century, though the vestry from 1838 housed and later regularly supported the town's fire engine.[19] The abandonment of the manorial courts after 1863 left the vestry the sole governing body of the town. From that date the public officers comprised two churchwardens, two overseers, two constables, two waywardens, an assistant overseer and vestry clerk, and

three inspectors of public lights.[20] The constables, who survived only until 1872, and the overseers were chosen from lists of ten names submitted annually by the vestry. A poll of the town was taken in the event of two or more names for the same office. The vestry concerned itself with minor roads and pavements, lighting and drainage, and, from 1880, with the accounts of local charities. A Burial Board was formed in 1871, a sanitary rate was levied from 1878, and a School Board was established in 1888.[21]

The parish council constituted in 1894 continued the work of the vestry. Early activities included an improved sewage system and the formation in 1896 of a parish council fire brigade.[22] The Somerton Gas Company Limited was formed in 1857 and acquired a site for its works in Horse Mill Lane in the following year.[23] The centre of the town was immediately supplied, and by 1890 the main streets were so lighted.[24] Electricity replaced gas for public lighting in 1930.[25]

Only one impression of the seal of the medieval community of Somerton survives, attached to a surrender of 1355.[26] It is vesica-shaped, 6 cm. × 3.8 cm. Legend, lombardic: SIGILLUM COMU[NITATIS BU]RG[I] . . . ON; device a winged mailed figure, probably St. Michael, his left hand holding a spear piercing a dragon beneath his feet, his breast protected by a shield charged with a cross.

CHURCH. Until the time of the Empress Maud a chapel at Somerton was a daughter of the church of Queen Camel and belonged to the Crown.[27] There was probably also a chapel at Somerton Erleigh, the tithes there having been given by King Ethelred to the monks of Athelney in 894.[28] The growth of Somerton in the early 12th century must have produced pressure to improve the inferior status of its church, and resulted in a grant c. 1140 by the Empress which allowed it burial rights and made it, in its turn, a mother church.[29] The monks of Muchelney claimed that the Empress's grant gave the church to them, though the advowson was also said to have been given to them by Henry I and by John.[30] The monks established their right before 1205, and between 1198 and 1205 a vicarage in their gift was ordained, though in 1212 the king presented to the living, possibly during a vacancy at Muchelney.[31] A further confirmation of Muchelney's rights was therefore necessary in 1239.[32] Thereafter the monks remained appropriators until their house was surrendered in 1538.[33]

Like most of the abbey's property the rectory

[5] S.R.O., CR 43, 45.
[6] S.R.O., D/P/som 4/1/2, pp. 273, 284.
[7] Ibid. p. 311.
[8] Ibid. p. 567.
[9] Ibid. p. 619.
[10] S.R.O., D/P/som 13/2/5.
[11] Ibid. 4/1/3, sub anno.
[12] Ibid. 13/2/12, vestry min. 25 Feb. 1813.
[13] Ibid. 13/2/3: min (at end) 11 Nov. 1813.
[14] Ibid. 13/2/1-2, 5-12; 13/2/6, min. 24 June 1755.
[15] Ibid. 13/2/3.
[16] D.R.O., D 124, box 1, sub anno.
[17] 11th Rep. Com. Char. 460.
[18] Poor Law Com. 2nd Rep. p. 548.
[19] S.R.O., D/P/som 4/1/4.
[20] Somerton, Par. Cncl. rec. (penes Clarke, Louch, Willmott, and Clarke, solrs.), vestry min. bk. 1862-91.

[21] Ibid. vestry min. bk. 1862-91; conveyance of land for burial ground 1873.
[22] Hist. Somerton (W.I. hist.), 64-7, 79-80. The brigade was taken over by Langport R.D.C. in 1939.
[23] D.R.O., D 124, box 112.
[24] Par. Cncl. rec. vestry min. bk. 1862-91.
[25] Hist. Somerton (W.I. hist.), 80-1.
[26] S.R.O., DD/PI 8/7.
[27] Rot. Hund. (Rec Com.), ii. 122.
[28] Collinson, Hist. Som. iii. 186, quoting a register now lost.
[29] Rot. Hund. (Rec. Com.), ii. 122.
[30] S.R.S. xiv. 91-2; Rot. Hund. (Rec. Com.), ii. 122, 128.
[31] S.R.S. xiv. 49; H.M.C. Wells, i. 57, 387; Rot. Litt. Pat. (Rec. Com.), 95.
[32] S.R.S. xiv. 49-50.   [33] V.C.H. Som. ii. 106.

passed to Edward Seymour, earl of Hertford (d. 1552).[34] Hertford exchanged the land in 1542,[35] but the advowson was retained by his family until the death of William, duke of Somerset, in 1671. It then passed to his sister Elizabeth (d. 1697), wife of Thomas Bruce, earl of Ailesbury (d. 1741).[36] Her sons Charles, Robert, and James sold it in 1722 to Edmund Bower of Somerton, who in the same year sold it to Thomas Dickinson of Somerton. Dickinson gave it to his son John in 1729, and John sold it a month later to William Dodd, rector of Charlton Mackrell. The Dickinsons still retained an interest for, despite a further transfer from Dodd to William Keat, later rector of Kingweston, Keat presented John Dickinson to the vicarage in 1732 and was party to a settlement of the patronage on Dickinson's wife in 1738. William Dickinson, their son and heir, sold the patronage to Stephen Fox-Strangways, earl of Ilchester (d. 1776), in 1762.[37] Successive earls exercised the right until 1921, when it was transferred to the bishop of Bath and Wells, patron in 1970.[38]

By 1205 the vicarage was endowed with arable lands, altarage, all obventions, and small tithes.[39] In 1239 the income was further defined to give him the demesnes 'as well of the mother church . . . as of the chapels',[40] though he was charged with the 'ordinance' of the church, proportionately with the abbots of Muchelney and Athelney.[41] By the end of the 13th century the vicarage was valued at £5.[42] In 1334 it was assessed at £9 3s. 4d. and in 1535 at £16 0s. 7d.[43] In 1650 the income of £40 was augmented to £66 12s.[44] About 1668 it was said to be worth £60,[45] but in 1705 'not under £30 nor truly much above'.[46] By 1831 the income was £259.[47] This was the value of the tithes only in 1851, the whole benefice income amounting to £341 5s.[48]

Oblations and small tithes in 1334 were worth £7 3s. 4d.[49] In 1535 this income was divided between personal tithes and casuals at £10 13s. 4d., and tithes of wool and lambs at £4 10s.[50] By 1705 the vicar claimed a modus of 1d., 1½d., or 2d. an acre 'for most of the water meadow', 1d. for each garden, and 1d. 'cow white'.[51] By 1841 he received 2d. for every cow in lieu of tithe milk and in lieu of tithes of meadow and pasture when fed with cows. Tithe hay was payable from grounds when mown. He also claimed 2d. for offerings and garden tithes, 2d. for each cottage, and the same sum for every calf. For the keep of sheep if not shorn he received 4d. a score monthly.[52] In 1841 the tithes were commuted for a rent-charge of £259.[53]

Land and pasture attached to the vicarage were

worth 20s. in 1334 and £2 8s. 4d. in 1535.[54] In area this was just over 51 a. in 1613, rising to 57¾ a. in 1633, and to 60½ a. in 1639.[55] By 1841 it measured 40 a.[56] The glebe was sold by the earl of Ilchester in 1920.[57]

The vicarage house at the north-east corner of the churchyard was isolated in the early 17th century, the vicar having no right of way to it except through the churchyard.[58] A settlement reached before 1672 gave him wayleave for horse and waggon through a plot of land east of the vicarage barn and a detached kitchen.[59] The vicarage house, described as 'very good' in 1815,[60] perhaps soon after its present south wing had been built, is an L-shaped stone building of two storeys, incorporating on its north side a late medieval range which may have been built as the solar wing of an even earlier house. The range retains an original timber roof of four bays, now ceiled in. It has arch-braced collar-beam trusses, two chamfered through-purlins to each slope, and three tiers of windbraces, the top one with the curves of the braces reversed. The bay at the east end is divided by a partition truss from what was evidently a fine upper room of three bays with an open roof. On the ground floor the easternmost bay is entered by a south doorway of Ham stone with a depressed pointed arch. A large chimney, perhaps inserted in the 16th or 17th century, is built against the south wall of the range. Externally at the west gable-end are the remains of a Ham stone window with two relieving arches in the wall above; the stone-mullioned window on the upper floor may be a 17th-century replacement. The south wing of the house, containing the staircase, hall, and drawing-room, was built or rebuilt early in the 19th century, and an eastern extension of the medieval range is an even later addition.

The medieval incumbents include Richard Tewkesbury, king's clerk, presented by the Crown in 1400 when the abbacy of Muchelney was vacant, who was allowed to farm the benefice on his absence in the following year.[61] Thomas Shortrugg, presented in 1450, was ordered to study for a year in view of his lack of learning.[62] William Rodbard was deprived in 1554 for being married, but was restored to the benefice under Elizabeth I.[63] John Seward, vicar from 1621, was also rector of Kingston Seymour; he was removed in 1649 and was replaced by Roger Derby, who held the benefice for ten years.[64] At least one of the 18th-century vicars, Benjamin Kebby, was a pluralist, and most employed assistant curates.[65]

The parishioners in 1554 had failed like many of

---

34 L. & P. Hen. VIII, xiii(1), p. 64.
35 Ibid. xvii, p. 322; see above, p. 138.
36 Complete Peerage, s.v. Somerset.
37 D.R.O., D 124, box 109.
38 Lond. Gaz. 14 Oct. 1921, pp. 8074–5; S.R.O., D/P/som 1/1/1.
39 S.R.S. xiv. 49.
40 Ibid. 49–50.
41 Ibid.
42 Ibid. 91–2; Tax Eccl. (Rec. Com.), 197.
43 E 179/169/14; Valor Eccl. (Rec. Com.), i. 198.
44 Lambeth Palace MSS., COMM VIa/6 ff. 646–7; VIb/2 f. 132.
45 S.R.O., D/D/Vc 24.
46 Proc. Som. Arch. Soc. cxii. 89.
47 Rep. Com. Eccl. Revenues, pp. 178–9.
48 H.O. 129/317/1/2/3.
49 E 179/169/14.

50 Valor Eccl. (Rec. Com.), i. 198.
51 Proc. Som. Arch. Soc. cxii. 88.
52 S.R.O., tithe award.   53 Ibid.
54 E 179/169/14; Valor Eccl. (Rec. Com.), i. 198.
55 S.R.O., D/D/Rg 233.
56 S.R.O., tithe award.
57 S.R.O., DD/SMC 19, sale cat. 1920.
58 S.R.O., D/D/Rg 233; D/D/Ca 177.
59 D.R.O., D 124, box 111, Stawell to Collins.
60 S.R.O., D/D/V rtns. 1815.
61 Cal. Pat. 1399–1401, 338, 382; Cal. Papal Regs. v. 467.
62 S.R.S. xlix. 154.
63 S.R.O., D/D/Ca 22; S.R.S. lv. 115; S & D. N. & Q. xiv. 107.
64 Walker Revised, ed. Matthews; S.R.O., D/P/som 4/1/2, pp. 53, 132.
65 Par. reg. passim.

their neighbours to replace the vestments sold or destroyed during Edward VI's reign.[66] An organ, acquired by 1637, was dismantled shortly before 1653.[67] From 1639 the assistant curate said morning prayer daily at 6 o'clock.[68] By 1815 morning and afternoon services, with a sermon in the afternoon, were held every Sunday, and prayers were said every Wednesday.[69] Prayers every Friday and on Saints' and Holy Days were discontinued in 1828 'in consequence of the advancing age and infirmities' of the incumbent.[70] Five years later, under a new vicar, morning prayers on Wednesdays and Fridays were discontinued because of the 'very small number indeed' who attended.[71] In 1836 the vestry agreed that the duties of the vicar, namely two sermons on each Sunday, should stand in lieu of week-day duties.[72] The same pattern continued until 1870 when Holy Communion was celebrated monthly and at festivals.[73] On Census Sunday 1851 the morning congregation was 449 including 178 Sunday-school children, and 608 with 189 children in the afternoon. The attendance was said to be 'not so good as in the summer months'.[74]

In 1349 Richard of Somerton gave a burgage in the town to the churchwardens to provide an obit for himself, his wife, and his parents.[75] By the mid 17th century the church owned 20 burgages with a total rental of 11s. 7½d.[76] In 1705 the income was £7 12s. 10½d., and by 1869 the income from the church lands comprised rent of nearly £127 and interest from securities.[77] This income is devoted to the fabric of the church.[78] Somerton Church Lands were established as a charity under a Scheme of 1889.[79]

A church house was rebuilt in 1581–2. It was of stone, with a tiled roof, and included a hall, kitchen, and cellar.[80] Part of the building was let as a shop in 1615, but at least until 1636 it was used for public functions,[81] and was still kept in repair by the parish in 1679–80.[82] Its site is not known. In 1581–2 the churchwardens bought a house known as the parish house.[83] It was rebuilt in 1582–3 to provide a hall on the first floor and a shop and kitchen beneath.[84] The shop, kitchen, and other chambers were normally leased, and the hall, approached by an external stair from the churchyard, was at first used for parish ales and other feasts.[85] It was occasionally let to outsiders.[86] By 1617–18 part of the building was used as a school,[87] part as a vestry room, and part for storing arms for the militia.[88] The house, which stood by the southern entrance to the churchyard, was demolished c. 1840.[89]

By 1510 there was a fraternity of the Holy Trinity attached to the church.[90] It was probably the brotherhood still in existence in 1544.[91]

By 1355 there was a chantry, probably in the parish church, dedicated to the Virgin, with property in the town.[92] The chantry continued until after 1381.[93] Its property evidently included pasture in Lower Somerton, known as 'chauntrie' in 1657.[94]

The parish church of *ST. MICHAEL AND ALL ANGELS*, dedicated to St. Michael alone by 1349,[95] is a large church of grey stone with Ham stone dressings. It consists of chancel with north vestry, north transept and south tower in the transeptal position, and nave with north and south aisles and south porch. The oldest remaining parts date from the earlier 13th century when it appears to have been a cruciform building with an aisleless nave. The arches to both transepts are of that date as well as several features in the south transept. They include two lancet windows (one blocked), a former west doorway, and a trefoil-headed piscina; a tomb recess in the south wall with a much-worn female effigy may also be of the 13th century. The upper part of the tower is octagonal, the transition from the square base being made by large plain broaches. Timber for the repair of the belfry was given by the king in 1278.[96] The present belfry windows and the embattled parapet are additions of the Perpendicular period when a new window was also inserted lower down in the south wall. The north window of the north transept has enriched forking tracery of c. 1300. The church was enlarged towards the middle of the 14th century by the rebuilding of the nave and the addition of north and south aisles, each with an arcade of four bays. Two consecration crosses are still visible, one near each end of the south arcade. The construction of the south aisle, which evidently had an altar at its east end, possibly the altar of the St. Mary's chantry, enclosed part of the west wall of the tower and its stair turret within the church. The south aisle has three 14th-century windows with reticulated tracery and there is one similar window in the north aisle and one in the north transept. The large west window of the nave contains flowing tracery. The chancel, which has Perpendicular windows, was probably rebuilt in the 15th century. A clerestory was added to the nave at the same period. The nave roof, one of the finest in Somerset, dates from c. 1510.[97] It is of low pitch with short king-posts above the tie beams. The timbers are richly moulded and ornamented, the roof slopes being divided into small square panels containing carved quatrefoils. A unique feature is the treatment of the spandrels above the tie beams which are filled with carvings of dragon-like beasts.

In 1563–4 the chancel roof was re-leaded;[98] some of its present features, including an ornamental

66 S.R.O., D/D/Ca 22.
67 S.R.O., D/P/som 4/1/1, p. 400; 4/1/2, pp. 13, 91.
68 S.R.O., D/P/som 4/1/1, p. 426.
69 S.R.O., D/D/V rtns. 1815.
70 S.R.O., D/P/som 4/1/4, vestry min. 8 July 1828.
71 Ibid. vestry min. 10 Nov. 1833.
72 Ibid. vestry min. 30 Nov. 1836.
73 S.R.O., D/D/V rtns. 1870.
74 H.O. 129/317/1/2/3.
75 Hunt. Libr., HA Manorial, ct. roll 1349.
76 S.R.O., DD/MI, box 9, survey.
77 Proc. Som. Arch. Soc. cxii. 89.
78 S.R.O., D/D/V rtns. 1870.
79 S.R.O., DD/SMC 7.
80 S.R.O., D/P/som 4/1/1, pp. 8, 10–13.
81 Ibid. pp. 190–1, 194, 269, 312, 390.

82 Ibid. 4/1/2, p. 287.
83 Ibid. 4/1/1, p. 7.
84 Ibid. pp. 20–1.
85 Ibid. pp. 17–18, 80, 91, 95, 160, 194–5, 199, 357.
86 See p. 142.   87 See p. 151.
88 S.R.O., D/P/som 4/1/2, p. 551; 4/1/3, passim.
89 Ibid. 4/1/3, vestry min. 28 Mar. 1839.
90 S.R.S. xix. 142.   91 Ibid. xl. 74.
92 S.R.O., DD/PI 8/7.
93 Proc. Som. Arch. Soc. cxiv. 94.
94 S.R.O., DD/SAS (C/127), 1, Still to Howe, 1662.
95 Hunt. Libr., HA Manorial, ct. roll 1349.
96 Cal. Close, 1272–9, 451.
97 A. K. Wickham, Churches of Som. 51, 139.
98 Bristol Cathedral, Dean and Chapter MSS., acct. 1563–4.

plaster frieze, may be the result of these repairs. A new window, possibly one of the Perpendicular windows in the chancel, was inserted *c.* 1581, and at the same time the rood loft stair was removed;[99] the doorway to the loft is still visible. The vestry on the north side of the chancel was added in 1770, the gift of Harbin Arnold (d. 1782), who also gave two of the three brass chandeliers in the nave.[1]

The church was restored in 1889, when the galleries erected in the previous three centuries were taken down and the double-gabled south porch, incorporating a stair to the south gallery, was rebuilt.[2] At the restoration bench-ends of the late 15th or early 16th century were added to modern pews. The carved pulpit is dated 1615, and the communion table with bulbous legs is dated 1626. Parts of the reredos, of domestic origin and installed when the chancel was restored in the 20th century, are also Jacobean. The pew opposite the pulpit at the chancel step was known as the archdeacon's pew, used by him during visitations.[3] The font, in the south aisle, is octagonal on a circular pedestal; it has a Jacobean cover.

There are eight bells: (i) and (ii) 1970, Taylor of Loughborough; (iii) 1914, Warner; (iv) 1874, Warner; (v) 1760, Thomas Bilbie; (vi) 1808, James Wells, Aldbourne (Wilts.); (vii) and (viii) 1914, Warner.[4] The oldest piece of plate is a cup and cover by 'I.P.' dated 1573. There is a set of cup, paten, flagon, and almsdish of 1692, probably by Ralph Leeke, and an earlier paten, probably given by Mrs. Mary Rosse, daughter of James Hodges (d. 1601) of St. Cleers.[5] The registers date from 1697 and the series is complete.

By 1280 there was a chapel at Hurcot which had probably been in existence from *c.* 1200. It may have originated in a grant of land made by the Crown to Muchelney abbey to celebrate mass there three times a week. There were at least two chapels dependent on the parish church by 1205, and from 1207 the Crown ceased to have a direct interest in Hurcot.[6] By 1280 the land supporting the chaplain, amounting to half a virgate, was annexed to the parish church, and the chaplain must, therefore, have been directly under the control of the vicar of Somerton.[7] The chapel was dedicated to St. James by 1457, and bequests were made to it in the late 15th century.[8] It had ceased to be used for worship by 1572 when the Crown granted it to Henry Middlemore; it was then valued at 4*d.*[9] It was

granted by the Crown to John Cook and others in 1613, and by 1617 was owned by Hugh Worth.[10] Worth sold it to Sir Edward Hext in the same year, and Hext sold it in 1618 to Humphrey Were.[11] No further trace of the chapel has been found. Its site may have been at the junction of two 'ancient' roads, north-west of Hurcot Farm, a small plot of ground which formed an isolated part of Somerton manor until 1921.[12]

There was probably a chapel at Somerton Erleigh in the late 9th century.[13] A violent scene took place there in 1319 between the bishop and the proctor of the chapter of Wells.[14] The chapel was still in existence in 1371 when the advowson passed, with the manor of Somerton Erleigh, from Sir John (V) de Erleigh to Richard Brice.[15] The later history of the chapel is unknown.

There was a chapel near Melbury, south-west of the town, associated with the settlement of Melbury Green.[16] In 1572 'Maide Milboroughes' chapel, valued at 2*d.*, was granted by the Crown to Henry Middlemore.[17] 'The Maid of Milboroughes chappell alias Milborough' passed, like Hurcot chapel, into the hands of Humphrey Were,[18] and has not been traced further.

ROMAN CATHOLICISM. A wooden church, dedicated to St. Dunstan and standing on the north side of Langport Road, was opened in 1927. It was served from Glastonbury.[19] The present church, on the same site, was opened in 1965, and is served from Langport.[20] It is a square lias building, with a pyramidal tiled roof and a central lantern.

PROTESTANT NONCONFORMITY. A group of Baptists was meeting at Somerton by 1653, and probably continued at least until 1658.[21] In 1672 a group of Presbyterians was licensed to use a barn for worship.[22] In 1719 a barn adjoining Pester's Lane, already called the 'Meeting House' and sometimes known as 'Serjeant's Barn', evidently the building the Presbyterians had used,[23] was given in trust for use by Baptists.[24] Between 1798 and 1802 the congregation, evidently led by the Revd. Richard Herdsman of South Petherton, became for a time Presbyterian.[25] In 1803, however, the premises were being used by Independents, who had worshipped in the house of Thomas Barnard since 1798.[26] The present Congregational chapel was erected on the same site in 1803, and was enlarged in 1822 and

[99] S.R.O., D/P/som 4/1/1, p. 9.
[1] M.I. in chancel.
[2] S.R.O., D/P/som 6/1/1; Taunton Castle, Piggott Colln., drawing by J. Buckler, 1834; Braikenridge Colln., water-colour by W. W. Wheatley, 1845; B.M. Add. MS. 33702 f. 82.
[3] S.R.O., D/P/som 4/1/2, pp. 590–1; DD/SMC 19, seating survey, 1806.
[4] Ex inf. Mr. H. E. G. Jeanes.
[5] *Proc. Som. Arch. Soc.* xlv. 137.
[6] *S.R.S.* xiv. 92–3; *H.M.C. Wells,* i. 57, 387; see above, p. 135.
[7] *S.R.S.* xiv. 92–3.
[8] Ibid. xvi. 175, 270, 358.
[9] E 310/23/127/90; *Cal. Pat.* 1569–72, pp. 389–90.
[10] C 66/1993; C.P. 25(2)/346/15 Jas. I East.
[11] C.P. 25(2)/346/15 Jas. I East., Hil.
[12] S.R.O., DD/KW, sale cat. 1921.
[13] Collinson, *Hist. Som.* iii. 186.

[14] H. E. Reynolds, *Wells Cathedral,* 135–6.
[15] *Cal. Pat.* 1370–4, 117.
[16] See above, p. 129.
[17] E 310/23/127/90; *Cal. Pat.* 1569–72, pp. 389–90.
[18] C.P. 25(2)/346/15 Jas. I Hil.
[19] Ex inf. Mr. S. Dean.
[20] Ex inf. Fr. J. G. Byrne.
[21] D. Jackman, *Baptists in the West Country,* i; *Confession of the Faith of Several Churches of Christ in Somerset* (1656); *Bibliotheca Somersetensis,* ed. E. Green, iii. 117.
[22] G. L. Turner, *Rec. Early Nonconf.* ii. 1105.
[23] D.R.O., D 124, box 1, rentals, 1718, 1752; box 17, acct. book, 1714–24; box 107, Bennett to Biddell. The barn was there by *c.* 1667: S.R.O., DD/MI, box 9.
[24] Taunton, Somerset Congregational Union, Somerton chapel deeds.
[25] Ibid.
[26] Ibid.; S.R.O., D/D/Rm, box 1.

again in 1865, when the present frontage was constructed.[27] The Lecture Hall was added in 1873. Attendance at the chapel on Census Sunday 1851 comprised a general congregation of 130 in the morning; in the afternoon there were 70 children and 23 young people, and in the evening 200 people. The average attendance was usually higher.[28]

A number of Quakers in the parish suffered persecution in the 17th century.[29] By 1668 Friends from the town were evidently meeting at Pitney,[30] but in 1674 numbers had fallen so that the meeting-house there closed, and all went to Long Sutton.[31] As a result of 'large meetings' at Somerton and 'very good service' there, it was decided to open a meeting-house in 1691.[32] William Penn addressed Friends there in 1694, possibly in the house of Henry Maber, which had been licensed in 1692.[33] The house of another Quaker, Eleanor Peddle, was licensed in 1703.[34] From 1753 Elizabeth Piddle's house was used.[35] By 1824 no Quaker families remained in the parish, and four years later the meeting-house at the Lynch was sold.[36] In 1876 a new meeting-house, on the north side of New Street, was opened, the result of the arrival in the town of Messrs. Welsh and Clark, the collar manufacturers.[37] It was closed in 1935.[38]

It is possible that a house near the Unicorn inn, West Street, licensed in 1788, may have been used by the first Methodists in Somerton.[39] The earliest certain date is the licence granted in 1810 to Thomas Connock for the use of his house in West Street. The licence was transferred in 1828 to a former carpenter's shop behind the house.[40] Connock, described as a druggist and a farrier, was born in West Camel in 1761, and was in 1788 appointed a class leader by John Wesley.[41] The present chapel in West Street was erected on or near the site of the shop in 1845, with seats for 224. The congregations on Census Sunday 1851 comprised 154 in the afternoon, including 57 Sunday-school pupils, and 123 in the evening.[42]

Five licences were issued to Dissenting groups in the period 1816 to 1825; three were almost certainly for Methodists, though it is not clear whether the same or several groups are involved.[43]

Probably the Bible Christians in the town originated from one of these. Zion Chapel was built by them in 1841, and was licensed in 1844.[44] By 1851 services were held there twice each Sunday, and attendances averaged 33 in the morning and 60 in the evening.[45] The congregation became affiliated to the United Methodist Church in 1907, but the chapel was used by the Methodists until 1949.[46]

The Salvation Army began work, against considerable opposition, in 1885.[47] They occupied a hall on the north side of Langport Road, near the present Roman Catholic church,[48] and then took over Zion Chapel in West End, in succession to the Methodists. Their work ceased in c. 1964.[49]

In 1933 meetings of the Brethren began in a house known as 'Valeside', and were continued in another called 'Ringers Well', both in West Street. A building called St. Cleers Chapel was opened for worship in 1949.[50]

EDUCATION. In 1577 Benet Parker was licensed to teach boys grammar in Somerton, and in 1593–4 William Odeams was teaching in the town without licence.[51] By 1617–18 part of the parish house was being used as a schoolroom, though the master was not supported by the parish.[52] In 1691, however, the schoolmaster was appointed to serve as sexton.[53]

In 1675 Thomas Glover, a London ironmonger whose father was born in Somerton, gave the Three Cups inn in Broad Street in trust to establish and maintain a school and schoolmaster to teach boys of the town and parish.[54] The school continued throughout most of the 18th century,[55] and was known for teaching Latin, Greek, and Hebrew.[56] By the early 19th century, however, it was said to be 'greatly in want of some interference':[57] its income, despite an increase in endowment of £5 a year in 1716 'for educating at an English school twelve poor children', given by Mrs. Alice Yeates of Hurcot,[58] had to be augmented by donations. The school had only 12 pupils in 1818,[59] though perhaps then and certainly in the 1840s the master took boarders to increase his income.[60]

By 1850 the Free Grammar School was under the

[27] Inscr. on building; Som. Cong. Union, Somerton chapel deeds; Rep. Som. Cong. Union (1896), 55. The records of the chapel include accts. 1805–39 and mins. 1826–1911. See also A. Braine, Brief Hist. of Somerton Cong. Ch. (1878).
[28] H.O. 129/317/1/2/5. Part of the house of John Meech was licensed for Independents in 1815: S.R.O., D/D/Rm, box 2.
[29] J. Whiting, Persecution Exposed (1791), 40, 203, 219; S. & D. N. & Q. v. 263; Besse, Sufferings, i. 585–6, 613.
[30] S.R.O., DD/SFR 1/1, 1.
[31] Ibid. 1/1, 47.
[32] Ibid. DD/SFR 1/2, 57.
[33] Whiting, Persecution Exposed, 203, 504; S.R.O., Q/RR, meeting-house lics.
[34] S.R.O., Q/RR, meeting-house lics.
[35] Ibid.
[36] Street Meeting-house, Somerset Monthly Meeting mins. 1793–1839, mins. 7 Oct. 1824, 30 Jan. 1828.
[37] Ibid. mins. 1839–79, min. 9 Nov. 1876.
[38] Ibid. mins. 1923–43, 145.
[39] S.R.O., Q/RR, meeting-house lics. See P. Davies, Wesleyan Methodism in Somerton, 1814–1945 (priv. print.).
[40] S.R.O., D/D/Rm, box 2.
[41] Davies, Wesleyan Methodism in Somerton.
[42] H.O. 129/317/1/2/4. The chapel was enlarged in 1905.

[43] S.R.O., D/D/Rm, box 2, 1816, 1817, 1819, 1822, 1825.
[44] H.O. 129/317/1/2/6; S.R.O., DD/Rm, box 2.
[45] H.O. 129/317/1/2/6.
[46] Ex inf. Mr. A. O. Locke.
[47] Life Thoughts of . . . Edwin T. Gunning, ed. T. B. Clark (Yeovil n.d.), 66–7, 89; ex inf. Mr. F. S. Mundy.
[48] O.S. Map 6", Som. LXIII. SW. (1886 edn.).
[49] Ex inf. Mr. A. O. Locke.
[50] Ibid.
[51] S.R.O., D/D/ol 5; D/D/Ca 98.
[52] S.R.O., D/P/som 4/1/1, pp. 284, 359; 4/1/2, pp. 11, 48, 149, 206, 241–2, 284, 310.
[53] S.R.O., D/P/som 4/1/2, p. 327. Two schoolmasters mentioned in 1717 probably had private schools, evidently in West St.: D.R.O., D 124, box 1, borough ct. papers.
[54] 11th Rep. Com. Char. H.C. 433, p. 443 (1824), xiv; Somerton ch. M.I.
[55] 11th Rep. Com. Char. pp. 443, 447; S.R.O., D/D/Rn, certif. for John Banbury, 1739–40.
[56] New Display of Beauties of Eng. (1776), 323.
[57] Digest of Returns to Sel. Cttee on Educ. of Poor, H.C. 224 (1819), ix(2).
[58] Somerton ch. M.I.; S.R.O., DD/SMC 12, 13.
[59] Digest of Returns to Sel. Cttee on Educ. of Poor.
[60] Pigot & Co. Dir. (1842). There were only 27 boys on the foundation in 1846–7: Church Sch. Inquiry, 1846–7.

control of the trustees of the parish charities, and from 1858 was known as the Somerton Free School.[61] By the 1870s the income of the school was being augmented by subscriptions, by government grants, and by the payment of fees for pupils not on the foundation.[62] From 1868 a night school for adults was held on the premises, evening classes under the County Technical Education Committee were held there from 1891, and the 'Somerton Adult School' used the rooms on Sundays from 1894. The school assumed aided status under the County Education Committee in 1903, and its endowment fund was later widened to be applied 'to education purposes for the parish'.[63] Somerton Free Church of England School, as it was known after 1903, remained a boys' school, with an average attendance in 1904–5 of 102.[64] Juniors only were taken from 1940, and numbers fell below 50. The school was closed in 1963, and was merged with Monteclefe (see below).[65]

The school occupied the former parish house at least until 1830; it moved to a room in Broad Street, next to the Bank House, successor to the Three Cups of the original endowment. A second room was added in 1878.[66] The property is now a youth club.

In the early 19th century there were several other schools in the town. In 1806 a Sunday school was established by the vestry in Broad Street, supported by subscriptions.[67] It had 126 pupils in 1818,[68] and was probably one of the 'large' Sunday schools in the town in 1825, one with a library attached.[69] In 1833 there were 113 pupils.[70] By 1841 the schoolroom was occupied by the master of the Free School,[71] and by 1889 was in use as a vestry room.[72]

By 1833 there was an infants' school, founded in 1828, for 70 children, three day-schools, apart from the Free School, for 121 pupils, and two Sunday schools for 183 pupils. The day-schools were maintained at parents' expense and the smallest, with 24 pupils, was taught by Independents. The second Sunday school was also attached to the Independent chapel.[73] By 1840 there were private schools for girls in West Street and for boys in New Street.[74] Three Sunday schools by 1846–7 had 208 pupils.[75]

Monteclefe National School, now known as Monteclefe Church of England Junior School, was built in 1851 by Miss Anna Maria Pinney, daughter of J. F. Pinney of Somerton Erleigh. It was enlarged in 1888 by Lady Smith, her sister, and in 1894 provided accommodation for 226 girls and infants, with an average attendance of 124.[76] Juniors

only were taken from 1940, and since the closure of the Free School in 1963 it has been a junior mixed school. In 1969 the average attendance was 147.[77]

West Street National Infants' School was built in 1870 by Col. William Pinney of Somerton Erleigh.[78] In 1873 the vestry was required by the government to provide a school for infants in the town, and Col. Pinney leased his school for the purpose in 1875.[79] Voluntary rates for its support proved difficult to collect in the 1880s and a school board was consequently formed in 1888.[80] In 1894 there was accommodation for 63 children, with an average attendance of 58.[81] The school was taken over by the County Education Committee in 1903, and was closed in 1966. It was replaced by Somerton County Infants School, Etsome Terrace, which in 1969 had an attendance of 126.[82]

Private establishments in the 19th century included a boy's school in West Street in 1859, a girls' school in Kirkcombe Street in 1861, and a school run by a Miss Dredge, in West Street in 1866, and in Broad Street in 1872 and 1875.[83] By 1897 there was a girls' school in Broad Street, transferred to North Street by 1902, which continued until after 1914; and by 1910 the Misses Brown held a preparatory school at Selwood House, in the Market Place, which continued until after 1923.[84]

CHARITIES FOR THE POOR. Between 1604 and 1642 a number of small sums were bequeathed to the vicar and churchwardens for the use of the poor, amounting to a capital sum of £50 6s. 8d.[85] Shortly after 1642 the disposition of this poor stock was placed in the hands of two men, not churchwardens.[86] From this capital, small sums were lent throughout the 17th century, the interest presumably being distributed for the benefit of the poor.[87] No further trace of this stock has been found.

In 1675 Thomas Glover, a London ironmonger, gave in trust a house called the 'Passage House', in Broad Street, the income to be used in bread for the poor. By Chancery decree in 1744 a capital sum paid as an entry fine for this property was consolidated with Churchey's charity, and the rent of the house was subsequently distributed in bread with that charity.[88] In 1869–71 the combined annual value was £21 7s. 11d.[89] Bread was distributed in 1970.[90]

Thomas Churchey of London, goldsmith, a native of Somerton, by will dated 1690, gave £150 in trust to purchase land, the income to be used to

61 S.R.O., DD/SMC 15, accts. and mins. 1850–1928.
62 Ibid.
63 Ibid.; S.R.O., C/E 28.
64 Som. C.C. Educ. Cttee. Schs. List; S.R.O., DD/SMC 3, 5, 18, managers' mins. and letter bks.
65 Som. C.C. Educ. Cttee. Schs. List.
66 S.R.O., DD/SMC 15, accts. and mins. 1850–1928.
67 S.R.O., D/P/som 18/8/1.
68 Digest of Returns to Sel. Cttee on Educ. of Poor.
69 Rep. B. & W. Dioc. Assoc. S.P.C.K. (1825–6).
70 Educ. Enquiry Abstract, H.C. 62 (1835), xlii.
71 S.R.O., tithe award.
72 S.R.O., D/P/som 18/8/1.
73 Educ. Enquiry Abstract.
74 County Gazette Dir. Som. (1840).
75 Church Sch. Inquiry, 1846–7.
76 Kelly's Dir. Som. (1897); Return of Schs. 1893 [C 7529], H.C. (1894), lxv. For records of the school see S.R.O., DD/SMC, 3, 5, 18. The name Monteclefe derives

from a misreading of St. Cleers: Collinson, Hist. Som. iii. 182; S. & D. N. & Q. xii. 215.
77 Som. C.C. Educ. Cttee. Schs. List.
78 S.R.O., C/E 28; DD/SMC 1–4.
79 Par. Cncl. rec. vestry bk. 1862–91.
80 Ibid.; S.R.O., DD/SMC 2.
81 Return of Schs. 1893.
82 Som. C.C. Educ. Cttee. Schs. List.
83 Harrison, Harrod, & Co. Dir. Som. (1859); P.O. Dir. Som. (1861, 1866, 1875); Morris & Co. Dir. Som. (1872).
84 Kelly's Dir. Som. (1897, 1902, 1910, 1914, 1923.)
85 S.R.O., D/P/som 4/1/2, p. 12.
86 Ibid. p. 20.
87 Ibid. pp. 339, 352.
88 S.R.O., DD/SAS (C/127), 1; 11th Rep. Com. Char. H.C. 433 pp. 458–9, (1824), xiv.
89 Dig. End. Chars. 1869–71, H.C. 25 (1873), li.
90 S.R.O., DD/SMC 15, accts. and mins. 1850–1928.

buy bread to distribute each Sunday after morning service.[91] The capital sum was consolidated in 1744 with funds from Glover's bread charity, and the income applied to unrelieved parishioners.[92] From 1768 the income was further augmented to produce £10 8s. a year, to provide bread for 13 poor families or persons in 4d. loaves.[93] This charity was further augmented with Coombs's and Pittard's charities, and continues to be distributed in bread.[94]

Jerrard Newcourt, of Ivythorn, by will proved 1704, gave the interest on £100 to provide ten coats annually for the poor of the town. There is no evidence that the bequest was effective.[95]

Mrs. Susannah Fisher, of Somerton, by will dated 1716, bequeathed £200, the interest to bind poor children as apprentices.[96] The vicar and church-wardens became trustees in 1761.[97] So much of the capital as could be recovered from a defaulting trustee was used in 1772 towards the purchase of land in Street.[98] Mrs. Fisher also gave a house and land, the rents from which were to provide gowns for second-poor widows.[99] In 1824 the income from the gown charity was £13, and by 1845 was applied in the purchase of blankets.[1] The income in 1869–71 was £12, enough to buy up to 30 pairs each year in the late 19th century. Blankets were last distributed in 1938, and since that time coal has been given instead.[2]

Part of the accrued income of the Free School charity was used in 1772 towards the purchase of an estate at Street, one third of the income from which, it was decided in 1811, was to apply to the school.[3] Other purchase money came from Susannah Fisher's apprentice charity funds.[4] In 1869–71 the apprentice charity had an income of £16, and apprentices were bound to tradesmen as funds allowed until 1887.[5] Thereafter funds seem to have been applied exclusively to the school. The estate was sold in 1936.[6]

Harbin Arnold (d. 1782) gave an annual rent-charge of £8 8s. on land in North Wootton to buy loaves for distribution on Sunday afternoons among four of the oldest and poorest unrelieved families. The rent-charge ceased to be paid in 1821.[7]

A further bread charity was founded under the will of Thomas Pittard in 1849, and comprised the income from £161 stock.[8] From 1886 the charity was administered by the trustees of the Somerton Charities, and was used to provide coal for 20 people.[9] The charity was so administered in 1971.[10]

The Edith Coombs charity was founded under will proved 1854. The capital sum of £100 was to augment the Glover and Yeates charities to provide help in kind.[11] By 1887 the charity was administered with Churchey's and Pittard's, and their combined income in 1893 was £12. Coal and bread were still provided by these charities in 1971.[12]

Sir Edward Hext (d. 1624), of Low Ham, shortly before his death, built an almshouse for eight men at the western end of West Street.[13] His widow Denise endowed it with a rent-charge of £50 on the manor of Middlezoy, and drew up orders for its government. The almsmen, of 50 years and over, were to be chosen, four from Somerton, two from High and Low Ham, and two from Langport Eastover, by Denise Hext and her successors as owners of Nether Ham House, together with two justices of the peace from the neighbourhood. Failing them, selection was to be by the incumbents of the three parishes concerned.

Each of the inmates was to receive 2s. weekly, a coat at Christmas, and an allowance of coal. A small sum was originally reserved to the man, preferably an inmate, who should 'read the common prayers of the church used for Divine Service, Catechism and other godly books or treatises, unto the said poor'. Prayers were to be said at the almshouse each morning when none were said in the parish church. An expected annual surplus of 40s. was to be lent free of charge for a year to poor artificers of the three parishes.

By the early 19th century no surplus was achieved and, in the absence of any funds for the maintenance of the building, places were left vacant in order to provide a repair fund. Under a Scheme of 1883 the number of almsmen was reduced to four, from the same parishes, and the premises were remodelled. The rent-charge was redeemed in 1908.

The Hext Almshouses, dated 1626, comprise a single-storeyed range, originally containing 8 one-room dwellings. The range is of lias with Ham stone dressings and has a stone bellcot at the west gable-end. The doorways along the front are grouped in pairs with, between them, double niches for use as seats. In 1967 the former sculleries at the rear were replaced by new kitchens and bathrooms.[14]

Mrs. Sophia Scott Gould, of North Curry, built and endowed the 'Homes for Widows', situated at the junction of North Street with New Street, in 1866. They were for widows or single women of 60 years or more, and consist of six dwellings around a courtyard. The charity also provides coal and a monthly cash payment.[15]

[91] *11th Rep. Com. Char.* 457–8. Churchey's father was a native of Somerton.
[92] S.R.O., DD/SMC 12–13; D/P/som 4/1/3, vestry min. 1744.
[93] S.R.O., D/P/som 4/1/3, vestry min, 1768; DD/SMC 15.
[94] S.R.O., DD/SMC 14(d), 15.
[95] *Som. Wills*, ed. Brown, iii. 110.
[96] *11th Rep. Com. Char.* 459–60; S.R.O., DD/SMC 12.
[97] S.R.O., D/P/som 4/1/3, vestry min. 1761.
[98] S.R.O., DD/SMC 12.
[99] *11th Rep. Com. Char.* 459–60.
[1] Ibid.; S.R.O., DD/SMC 16.
[2] *Dig. End. Chars. 1869–71*; ex inf. Mrs. M. M. Marshall, clerk to the Somerton Charities.
[3] S.R.O., D/P/som 4/1/3, vestry min. 1772; DD/SMC 13, 15; *11th Rep. Com. Char.* 450–1, 454–5.
[4] See above.

[5] *Dig. End. Chars. 1869–71*; S.R.O., DD/SMC 15, accts. and mins. 1850–1928.
[6] Ex inf. Mrs. Marshall.
[7] *11th Rep. Com. Char.* 455, 466–7; S.R.O., DD/SMC 12, 15.
[8] S.R.O., DD/SMC 12.
[9] Ibid. 15, accts. and mins. 1850–1928. The town's charities were administered by one body of trustees from 1823: *11th Rep. Com. Char.* 479.
[10] Ex inf. Mrs. Marshall.
[11] S.R.O., DD/SMC 12, 14(c). The Glover and Yeates charities supported the Free School, and did not supply general help to the parish.
[12] S.R.O., DD/SMC 15, accts. and mins. 1850–1928; ex inf. Mrs. Marshall.
[13] *11th Rep. Com. Char.* 461–6; S.R.O., DD/MI, box 5; DD/SAS (C/114), 6; DD/SMC 10, 11.
[14] Ex inf. Mrs. Marshall.
[15] *Hist. Somerton* (W.I. hist.), 39; ex inf. Mr. A. O. Locke.

LONG SUTTON

THE parish of Long Sutton, on the north bank of the river Yeo, 3 miles south-east of Langport, is well over 4 miles long from east to west, and nearly 2½ miles at its widest point. It includes the hamlet of Knole and the deserted village of Bineham in the east, the scattered hamlet of Upton in the north-west, and traces of a medieval settlement and a 19th-century wharf at Little Load and Load Bridge in the south. Apart from the inclusion of part of Kingsmoor in the east the present boundaries are thought to be those established by 1300,[1] though intercommoning with Somerton, Huish, and Pitney cannot have produced definite boundaries at some points until inclosure, finally completed in 1814.[2] At least from the 17th century the parish had rights on King's Sedgemoor, and nearly 606 a. were allotted in respect of 69 shares in 1795.[3] The total acreage was 3,956 a. in 1844.[4] The detached area on Sedgemoor was exchanged for parts of Kingsmoor in 1885.[5] In 1901 the parish measured 3,859 a.[6]

The soil is divided between clay over lias on the land around and above the 50 ft. contour, largely arable, and alluvial deposits bordering the river.[7] To the north the parish covers the western scarp of South hill, rising to over 225 ft. The 'moors' of the south are all below 50 ft., and Ablake and Haymoor in the south-west are below 25 ft. In the east are harder rocks forming the isolated outcrops of Knole hill (over 150 ft.) and the lower ridge including Knole Knap, features which probably gave the name to the hamlet of Knole.

The settlement names are all Saxon in origin, though traces of Roman occupation have been found.[8] Sutton itself was presumably named in relation to Somerton. Knole became the centre of a manor in the mid 13th century but Upton remained a settlement of small tenant farmers.[9] Bineham and Little Load also occur in the 13th century. The former, known as Little Benham in 1249 and Esterebenham in 1280,[10] lay on the southern slope of Knole Knap. The site, now known as Bineham City, was still occupied in 1720, though it had probably been in decline from the 16th century.[11] Little Load, absorbed into Long Sutton manor in 1431, had become two inclosed farms by the 17th century.[12] The buildings of the smaller, known in 1970 as Little Load Farm, incorporated features of the 16th century. The other farm stood north-east of

Load Bridge by the Knole millstream, and had been partially demolished by 1886.[13]

The parish lies at the junction of two ancient routes linking three towns of considerable importance in the early Middle Ages, Langport, Somerton, and Ilchester. The Somerton–Martock road probably follows the original route, entering the parish at Load Bridge. This road was turnpiked in 1760–1 by the Martock trust.[14] The Ilchester–Langport route crossed Kingsmoor from Pill Bridge. It survives only as a footpath and a series of lanes, including Hammocks, Knole Hill, and Ilchester lanes, emerging in Knole Causeway near the Vicarage. From there it followed Cross Lane to the village green and proceeded along Shute Lane to the Langport road. The route across Kingsmoor was gradually abandoned, partly because of the decline of Ilchester and partly, at a later date, because the owner of Kingsmoor in the 18th century levied fines on traffic.[15]

The settlement pattern of Sutton village around its large, originally triangular, green was governed by the convergence of these routes. The village cross, near the junction of Knole causeway with the route from Ilchester, marked the entrance to the village from this direction until the 19th century, and its position implies subsequent shrinkage of population.[16] Development along Shute Lane and the Langport road, including the 14th-century Court House,[17] indicates the growth of settlement from the central green to the north-west, and could well have been the reason for the prefix 'Long', which was in use by the 15th century.[18] The closure of the route across Kingsmoor allowed the more northerly route from Langport eastwards towards Kingsdon and the Foss Way to become the principal thoroughfare of the parish, thus by-passing the centre of the village.[19]

The maintenance of bridges and causeways was of considerable importance in the low-lying terrain of the parish. Load Bridge is probably medieval in origin and was certainly in existence by 1543.[20] In 1676 it was 'greatly broken and decayed'.[21] Little bridge and 'Stonybrygge' occur in 1479–80 and 1543 respectively.[22] The former was in Knole manor and still existed by that name in 1733–4.[23] 'Chappel bridge', also in Knole manor, occurs in 1647,[24] and Drayway now Driveway bridge in 1720.[25]

[1] G. B. Grundy, *Saxon Charters of Som.* 127. This article was completed in 1970.
[2] S.R.O., DD/DEV 5; CR 84.
[3] S.R.O., DD/DEV 5; CR 116.
[4] S.R.O., tithe award.
[5] *Local Govt. Bd. Prov. Orders Conf. Order (Poor Law), (No. 2), Act* (1885), 48 & 49 Vict. c. 5.
[6] *Census,* 1901.
[7] Geol. Surv. Map 1", solid and drift, sheet 296 (1969 edn.).
[8] *Proc. Som. Arch. Soc.* xl. 272.
[9] See p. 159.
[10] *S.R.S.* vi. 149; xliv. 333.
[11] D.R.O., D 124 Som. manorial, Knole ct. bk. 1624–48; S.R.O., DD/X/BB, survey 1719–20; M. W. Beresford, *Lost Villages of Eng.* 98, 385, 416. The site is O.S. Nat. Grid 501249.
[12] *Cal. Close,* 1435–41, 166; see below, p. 161.

[13] S.R.O., tithe award; O.S. Map 6", Som. LXXIII. SW. It was then called Load Farm.
[14] S.R.O., D/T/yeo, Act 1 Geo. III, c. 29.
[15] D.R.O., D 124 Som. manorial, Kingsmoor ct. bks.; see above, p. 147.
[16] Par. rec. notebk. of Revd. G. S. Henning. Parts of the cross are in the churchyard. Aerial photographs show building platforms SE of the church.
[17] See p. 160.
[18] *Cal. Close,* 1435–41, 166.
[19] S.R.O., D/T/yeo, Act 32 Geo. III, c. 130.
[20] S.C. 2/198/53.
[21] *S.R.S.* xxxiv. 192.
[22] B.M. Harl. Ch. 58 E 46; S.C. 2/198/53.
[23] Par. rec. overseers' accts. 1728–45.
[24] D.R.O., D 142 Som. manorial, Knole ct. bk. 1624–48.
[25] S.R.O., DD/X/BB, survey 1719–20.

'Harneys way' at 'Wiggemore' near Bineham was sinking because its ditches were blocked in 1443, and complaints reached the hundred court.[26] John Person in 1552 left money for mending the causeway between the church and his house.[27]

The Yeo was used for transport in the Middle Ages,[28] and the farmer of Sutton rectory from 1537 sent his tithes to Athelney by boat, either from the river bank at Rodmoor or, if there was insufficient water, from Langport.[29] A wharf was established at Load Bridge by the mid 18th century, where sand, culm, and coal were unloaded.[30] The wharf was virtually abandoned by 1886.[31]

Long Sutton and Pitney halt was established at Upton on the rail link between Langport and Castle Cary in 1906; it was closed to passengers in 1962 and to goods in 1964.[32]

By the early 17th century there were three open arable fields around Upton known as West, East, and Little fields.[33] By 1720 they were known as West or North-west, East or North-east, and Lower Little fields.[34] Little field was still in existence in 1756 but had virtually disappeared by 1814.[35] By that time East field was called North field. Long Sutton village had two fields, Harding field in the north-east, largely uninclosed until 1814, and the small Cod field, still held in common in 1720 but inclosed before 1814.[36] By the 17th century there were eight small open fields around Knole, including Knapfield which first occurs in 1521.[37] Only three, Knole Hill, Knole Middle, and Knole Hither fields were still in existence by 1760, and by 1814 only small areas of Knole Hill field survived and were then inclosed.[38]

Land along the bank of the Yeo was drained for pasture and meadow from early times. Games marsh in the west is named after Robert Gyen of Bristol (d. 1353) and occurs as Gyensmershe in 1541 and as Geanesmershe in 1602.[39] Littlemoor, by Load Bridge, occurs in 1253,[40] Rothcmorc, later Rowmoor, below Knole Knap, in 1280,[41] Ablake and Swanmore before 1300,[42] and Rodmoor in 1431.[43] Some of these 'moors' were inclosed c. 1620,[44] but Rowmoor remained subject to common rights until the early 18th century, and Ablake and other scattered areas of 'moor' were not inclosed until 1814.[45] Drainage of these areas depended on the regular scouring of ditches and the maintenance of the river bank: each tenant of Hammocks in 1631 was made responsible for the repair of 20 ft. of bank.[46]

The large-scale drainage schemes of the 19th century and the attempt to improve the navigation of the Yeo to Ilchester were largely unsuccessful until the completion of the works at Langport and in the lower reaches of the Parrett.[47]

Almost all the houses in Long Sutton and Upton are built of local lias, the older ones and those with more pretensions having Ham stone windows and dressings. At Knole there are several groups of lias cottages with thatched roofs, including West Knole House and Knole Cottage, both 'yeomen's' houses apparently dating from the late 16th century. One double-fronted house in Long Sutton near the churchyard gate is faced with red brick and carries the date 1782. Long Sutton House is of the early 19th century, with a portico porch in the three-bay front and deep eaves. On the north side of the green stands the unexpectedly imposing Devonshire Arms Hotel with a long five-bay front of lias with Ham stone dressings. Its windows match those of the school at the opposite end of the green, suggesting that, like the school, it was built c. 1870.[48]

The Devonshire Arms was known as the Blue Ball by 1756 and by 1787 until the 1860s it was called the Buck's Head.[49] The Hare and Hounds stood on the west side of the green by 1737 and remained until c. 1870.[50] The Green Dragon had a short life in the 1770s.[51] The Lime Kiln inn on the Kingsdon road at Rock was first licensed in 1814.[52]

The Long Sutton Friendly Society was founded in 1818, and refounded as the Long Sutton New Friendly Society in 1845.[53] The society, which formerly held its club day on Trinity Monday, transferred to Trinity Saturday before 1972. A women's club, founded in 1889–90, ceased well before 1914.[54]

During the Civil War Fairfax marched his troops across Kingsmoor from Ilchester in July 1645 in his attempt to reach Bridgwater. The Royalist troops under Goring, stationed at Load Bridge, withdrew towards Langport, occupying the high ground in High Ham each side of the Somerton road. Skirmishing took place in Upton West field, then lying fallow, as the Parliamentary troops made their way along Tengore Lane. Most of the fighting known as the battle of Langport took place in High Ham parish, but Cromwell described it as the 'Long Sutton mercy' and compared it in importance with Naseby. Long Sutton itself he found 'extremely wanting in provisions' largely owing to the interference

[26] S.R.S. xiv. 197.
[27] Ibid. xxi. 134.
[28] See p. 181.
[29] S.C. 6/Hen. VIII/3144.
[30] Par. rec. chwdns' accts. 1728–43; S.R.O., tithe award; Story of Long Sutton comp. E. A. Smith (W.I. hist. 1953), 6.
[31] O.S. Map 6″, Som. LXXIII. SW.
[32] C. R. Clinker and J. M. Firth, Reg. Closed Stations, ii and suppl.
[33] D.R.O., D 124 Som. manorial, survey 1602.
[34] S.R.O., DD/X/BB, survey 1719–20.
[35] Ibid., contract bk.
[36] Ibid., survey 1719–20; CR 84.
[37] D.R.O., D 124 Som. manorial, Knole ct. bk. 1624–48; B.M. Harl. Roll K 27. The fields were: Knole Hill, Knole Pits, Hither and Middle Knole, Woodlands, Pulpit, Knole Knap, and Bineham.
[38] D.R.O., D 124 Som. manorial, survey 1602.
[39] Cal. Inq. p.m. x, p. 91; Cal. Close, 1354–60, 41; S.R.O., DD/WY W/CR 3; D.R.O., D 124 Som. manorial, survey 1602.
[40] S.R.S., xi. 411.
[41] Plac. de Quo Warr. (Rec. Com.), 688.
[42] Cal. Close, 1435–41, 166; Valor Eccl. (Rec. Com.), i. 102.
[43] B.M. Harl. Ch. 58 E 46.
[44] See p. 161.
[45] S.R.O., D/D/Cd 77; DD/X/BB, survey 1719–20; CR 84.
[46] D.R.O., D 124 Som. manorial, Knole ct. bk. 1624–48.
[47] M. Williams, Draining of Som. Levels, 244–5.
[48] See p. 166.
[49] S.R.O., Q/RL, victuallers' recogs.; P.O. Dir. Som. (1866).
[50] Par. rec. overseers' accts. 1728–45; P.O. Dir. Som. (1866, 1875).
[51] S.R.O., Q/RL.
[52] Ibid.
[53] Ex inf. Mr. R. Burt; S.R.O., Q/R, Friendly Soc. rtns.
[54] Story of Long Sutton, comp. E. A. Smith (W.I. hist. 1953), 25–6.

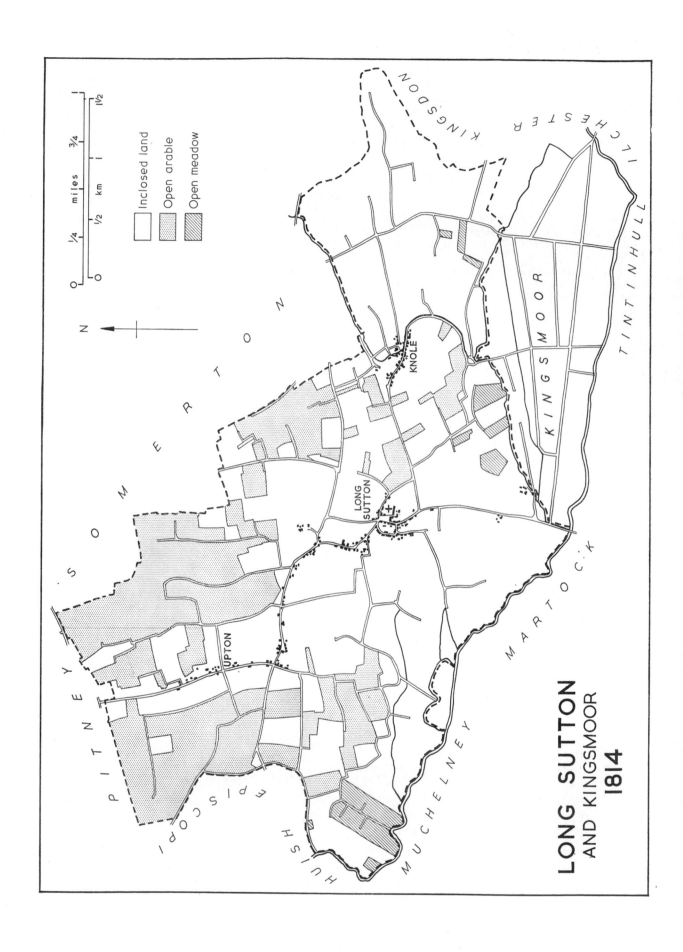

LONG SUTTON
AND KINGSMOOR
1814

Inclosed land
Open arable
Open meadow

N

miles
0   1/4   1/2   3/4

km
0   1/2   1   1 1/2

KINGSDON

ILCHESTER

TINTINHULL

KINGSMOOR

KNOLE

LONG
SUTTON

MARTOCK

UPTON

SOMERTON

PITNEY

EPISCOPI

HUISH

MUCHELNEY

of the Clubmen.[55] Perhaps at this time the army burnt a house at Knole.[56]

In 1327 Sutton tithing was second in wealth and size to Aller in the hundred, 22 taxpayers contributing a total of 52s. Knole had 17 payers.[57] In 1563 Knole had 17 households, Upton 23, and Long Sutton 52.[58] In 1801 the population numbered 735. This rose to 1,050 in 1851 but thereafter declined, reaching 716 in 1901. Recovery by 1911 was followed by fluctuations, but in 1961 the population was 712.[59]

George Palmer (d. 1897), biscuit manufacturer, was born in the parish in 1818 and established a factory at Reading in 1841.[60]

MANORS AND OTHER ESTATES. In 871 or 886 King Alfred gave to Athelney abbey ten *cassatae* in 'Suthtun' free of all but the three customary dues.[61] Athelney's holding there gelded for ten hides T.R.E., but by 1086 for eight hides.[62] Known as the manor of *ABBOT'S SUTTON* or *LONG SUTTON*, it was held by Athelney abbey until the Dissolution in 1539.

At the Dissolution the manor, except the manor-house, was leased to Robert Golde.[63] In 1547 the reversion was granted to Thomas Wriothesley, earl of Southampton (d. 1550) who was in possession in the following year.[64] Ownership passed to his son Henry (d. 1581); in 1600 the manor, described as Long Sutton or *SUTTON VALENCE*, was bought from Henry's son, also Henry, by Sir John Spencer of Canonbury, Lord Mayor of London.[65] Spencer's only daughter Elizabeth succeeded her father in 1610 and brought the manor to her husband William, Lord Compton (cr. earl of Northampton 1618).[66] On her death in 1632 the estate passed to her son Spencer, earl of Northampton (d. 1643),[67] and it descended successively in the Compton family to George Compton (d. 1758), who held the property by 1745 before succeeding his brother as earl in 1754.[68] George's widow, later wife of Claudius Amyand, held the manor until her death in 1800, when it passed to Lord George Cavendish, third son of William, duke of Devonshire (d. 1764), through his marriage with Elizabeth (d. 1835), heir of Charles, earl of Northampton (d. 1763).[69] George, created earl of Burlington in 1831, died in 1834. His grandson and successor William (d. 1891) became duke of Devonshire in 1858. Victor, duke of Devonshire, William's grandson, sold the property, amounting to over 2,000 a., in 1919, but no claims to manorial rights were involved.[70]

By the mid 17th century the demesne included three holdings, based on Manor farm-house, Higher house, next to the vicarage house on the green, and Lower house. In 1674 the Manor farm-house and adjoining land were let to John Stocker and the others to Mary Jeanes.[71] Robert Banbury became lessee of Manor farm in 1695 and in 1717 held 106 a.[72] The family remained lessees throughout the 18th century.[73] In 1919 the farm measured 303 a.[74]

In 1538 the manor-house comprised a hall, kitchen, buttery, and three chambers.[75] The present two-storeyed building, known as Manor Farm, stands immediately south of the churchyard. It appears to date largely from the 16th or 17th century but may incorporate part of an earlier house. The plan is E-shaped, having two projecting wings and a central porch on the north side. There are traces of timber-framing behind the stone facing in both wings and the west wing formerly had its own external doorway. Elsewhere the walls are of lias with Ham stone dressings. Several of the stone-mullioned windows have arched heads to the lights which could belong to a major reconstruction of the mid 17th century. The porch, originally two-storeyed but now with a lean-to roof, has a round-headed outer arch and is of this period. An eastward extension of the main range, containing the present kitchen, may have been added at the same time or somewhat earlier. Alterations, including the insertion of several sash windows with segmental heads, were carried out early in the 18th century. About 100 years later the older part of the south front was re-faced with lias and made into a symmetrical elevation with sash windows and a central doorway and porch. Inside the house is some stained glass thought to have come from the church.[76] It incorporates the initials 'I.M.', either for John Moss, vicar from 1521, or John Major, abbot of Athelney 1531-3.[77] In 1571 a barn, called a shippen, and a gatehouse, associated with the manor-house, were reported as ruinous.[78]

An estate of two hides was held of Athelney abbey before the Conquest by two thegns and in 1086 against the abbot's will by Roger de Courcelles.[79] Most of Roger's estates passed to the Malet family and, on the death of William Malet (II). c. 1216, were divided between two daughters.[80] Hugh Pointz (I) (d. 1220), husband of Helewise Malet, succeeded to two carucates at Sutton by 1219.[81] On the death of Helewise's second husband in 1253-4 the property passed to Nicholas Pointz (I) (d. 1273). His grandson Nicholas (II) (d. 1311) held $\frac{1}{5}$ fee in Sutton at his death;[82] and his grandson

[55] *A More Full Relation of the great Battell fought betweene Sir Tho: Fairfax & Goring* (London 1645); *Letters of Oliver Cromwell*, ed. Carlyle, iii. 245.
[56] D.R.O., D 124 Som. manorial, Knole ct. bk. Apr. 1647.
[57] *S.R.S.* iii. 203, 253.
[58] B.M. Harl. MS. 594 f. 50.
[59] *V.C.H. Som.* ii. 348; *Census*, 1911-61.
[60] *D.N.B.*
[61] Finberg, *Early Charters of Wessex*, pp. 123-5; *S.R.S.* xiv. 126-8.
[62] *V.C.H. Som.* i. 469-70.
[63] S.C. 6/Hen. VIII/3144; *L. & P. Hen. VIII*, xix(1), p. 649.
[64] *Cal. Pat.* 1547-8, 24; Castle Ashby, Northampton MSS. 332.
[65] Northampton MSS. 361-70.
[66] C 142/318/165; 467/189.
[67] C 142/467/189.

[68] S.R.O., DD/X/BB, contract bk. 1744-59.
[69] Ibid., contract bk. 1760-97; *Complete Peerage*, s.v. Northampton.
[70] *Complete Peerage*, s.v. Devonshire; S.R.O., DD/X/DST, sale cat. 1919.
[71] S.R.O., DD/DEV 4.
[72] Ibid. 5, 6.　　[73] Ibid. 17.
[74] S.R.O., DD/X/DST, sale cat. 1919.
[75] S.C. 6/Hen. VIII/3144.
[76] *Story of Long Sutton*, comp. E. A. Smith (W.I. hist. 1953), 9.
[77] *S.R.S.* lv. 17; *V.C.H. Som.* ii. 103.
[78] Northampton MSS. 338.
[79] *V.C.H. Som.* i. 469, 493.
[80] Ibid. i. 413; *V.C.H. Wilts.* viii. 36; Sanders, *Eng. Baronies*, 38-9.
[81] E 372/63 m. 14d.
[82] *Cal. Inq. p.m.* v, p. 196; Sanders, *Eng. Baronies*, 38-9.

Nicholas was overlord in 1354.[83] Further descent of the lordship has not been traced.

The other moiety of William Malet's estate, belonging to Mabel, wife successively of Nicholas Avenel and Hugh de Vivonia (d. 1249), descended to Hugh's son William (d. 1259). It passed to Cecily (d. 1320) wife of John de Beauchamp (I) by 1287.[84] After her death it was added to the Beauchamp estates and was retained by the family until the death of Margaret, widow of John de Beauchamp (III), in 1361.[85] No further trace of the Beauchamp interest has been found.

Roger de Courcelles' tenants in 1086 were Dodman and Warmund, both possibly Englishmen and successors to the two thegns of the Confessor's time.[86] Dodman was probably the occupier of the Pointz moiety. By 1311 the tenant was William Bossard, perhaps descendant of Richard Boschard who held ¼ fee in Sutton in 1208.[87] John Bossard, William's successor, died by 1354 and was followed by a minor.[88] This holding has not been traced further, but it may have been divided to form the several freeholds of the main manor in 1538–9.[89]

Warmund, tenant of the Beauchamp moiety, was succeeded by 1249 by Ralph Huse or Hose, from whom the property became known as the manor of *SUTTON HOSEY*.[90] Ralph Huse held part of a fee in 1287 and 1303, and was succeeded by his son Reynold after 1312.[91] Reynold Huse did homage for a 'great' knight's fee in Long Sutton and Butleigh in 1337 and still held it in 1361.[92] Under settlements of 1341 and 1343 the reversion was granted in fee to Nicholas and Isabel Montacute.[93] Robert and Alice Montacute were in possession by 1366, when the estate was described as a messuage, two carucates of arable, and 18 a. of meadow.[94] The Montacutes or Montagues remained in possession until the death of William Montague the younger.[95] In 1482 the property was settled on Catherine, William's widow, and on her second husband John Bevyn of Lufton.[96] Subsequently it was divided between another John Bevyn, John Moleyns, and James Duporte, husband of William Montague's youngest daughter Emme.[97]

The third share of John Bevyn (d. 1554), described as Mountaguyscourt in 1538–9,[98] descended to his daughter Ursula (d. 1608), wife of John Sydenham of Leigh in Old Cleeve, and from her to her nephew Henry Keymer of Pendomer.[99] Keymer sold it to James Arnewood in 1612.[1] John Moleyns had

by 1554 been succeeded by Henry Moleyns of Sandhill in Fordingbridge (Hants);[2] he sold his share to James Arnewood in 1611.[3] The third share, held by James Duporte in 1524–6,[4] passed to Thomas Duporte and in 1583 to his son Henry, of Shepshed (Leics.).[5] This share was sold to James Arnewood before 1613, when the united property was conveyed to John Tucker.[6]

Tucker already possessed a holding known as Dudleys, held in 1568 by Thomas and in 1572 by John Dudley.[7] It seems earlier to have been held by the St. Lo family: Edmund St. Lo (d. 1541) held property in Long Sutton by 1505 and this estate certainly by 1538–9;[8] he was succeeded by Thomas St. Lo (d. by 1546).[9] Sir John St. Lo succeeded Richard St. Lo by 1550.[10] John Tucker was still in possession of both estates in 1639.[11] By 1665 he was succeeded by Reginald Tucker who, in respect of Sutton Hosey, was responsible for the repair of an aisle in the parish church.[12] He was imprisoned for supporting Monmouth and apparently lost his lands to Sir Theophilus Oglethorpe who, in 1688, transferred the holding to William Hall.[13] In 1695 Tucker brought a successful action against Oglethorpe and Hall for recovery of the manor and the capital messuage and farm of Sutton Hosey or Mitchell's farm.[14]

William Steele of St. Martin's in the Fields, London, purchased the property from Tucker in 1704.[15] Part of it, including Mitchell's farm and the aisle in the parish church, was sold to Robert Banbury, lessee of Manor farm, in 1707.[16] The Banbury family remained in possession of Mitchell's or Tucker's farm, otherwise called the manor-house of Sutton Hosey, until the early 19th century.[17] In 1842 it was owned by Anne Chard and came to be known as Chard's farm.[18] It was called Manor House farm in 1969.

Manor House farm, standing north of the Langport road, is mostly faced with lias and consists of a front range and a rear service wing. The front range may be of 16th-century origin. There are indications of former timber-framing at both ends and the remains of moulded ceiling beams in the hall. At the west end is a large Ham stone fire-place with a stone-mullioned window beside it, both recently uncovered; there is evidence that the massive chimney at the gable-end originally projected externally. It may have been this house, therefore, which was damaged by the king's troops in 1685.[19]

[83] *Cal. Inq. p.m.* x, p. 149.
[84] Sanders, *Eng. Baronies*, 38–9; *S.R.S.* xxxv. 30.
[85] *Cal. Inq. p.m.* xi, p. 22.
[86] *S.R.S. extra ser.* 178–9, 306.
[87] *Cal. Inq. p.m.* v, p. 196; *Pipe R.* 1208 (P.R.S. N.S. xxiii), 110. [88] *Cal. Inq. p.m.* x, p. 149.
[89] S.C. 6/Hen. VIII/3144.
[90] *S.R.S.* xi. 149. He succeeded Warmund at N. Cheriton: *V.C.H. Som.* i. 507; *S.R.S.* xi. 79. The property was first called a manor in 1593: C 142/234/51.
[91] *S.R.S.* vi. 328; xxxv. 30, 67; *Feud. Aids*, iv. 300; *Cal. Close*, 1307–13, 549; *H.M.C. Wells*, i. 561.
[92] *S.R.S.* xxxv. 85; *Cal. Inq. p.m.* xi, p. 22.
[93] *S.R.S.* xii. 211. [94] Ibid. xvii. 62.
[95] Wedgwood, *Hist. Parl. Biogs.* s.v. Montague.
[96] *S.R.S.* xxii. 152–3.
[97] Ibid.; *Som. Incumbents*, ed. Weaver, 209.
[98] S.C. 6/Hen. VIII/3144; the name survives as Monday's Court.
[99] *Som. Wills*, ed. Brown, i. 70–1.
[1] C.P. 25(2)/346/9 Jas. I Hil.
[2] *Som. Incumbents*, 196, 209; *V.C.H. Hants*, iv. 573.

[3] C.P. 25(2)/345/8 Jas. I Hil.
[4] *Som. Incumbents*, 196, 209.
[5] C 142/234/51; *Som. Incumbents*, 196, 209.
[6] C.P. 25(2)/346/11 Jas. I Mich.; C.P. 43/123 rot. 5.
[7] Northampton MSS. 335, 339; D.R.O., D 124, Somerton hundred ct. bk. 1617–20, f. 90.
[8] C.P. 25(2)/207/36/21 Hen. VII Mich.; S.C. 6/Hen. VIII/3144; S.R.O., DD/WY W/CR 3.
[9] Northampton MSS. 331.
[10] Ibid. 332–4; C.P. 40/1144 rot. 21.
[11] Northampton MSS. 360.
[12] S.R.O., DD/MI, box 9, survey c. 1665; DD/GS, box 2, 'Autographs, Som. etc.'.
[13] C.P. 25(2)/795/4 Jas. II Mich.; S.R.O., Q/SR 162 f. 16; *Lond. Gaz.* 11–15 Mar. 1685; *Cal. S.P. Dom.* Jan. 1686–May 1687, pp. 233, 366, 372.
[14] E 134/7 Wm. III Mich./7.
[15] C.P. 25(2)/961/3 Anne Mich.
[16] C.P. 25(2)/962/6 Anne East.
[17] S.R.O., DD/LC, boxes 2, 10.
[18] S.R.O., tithe award.
[19] J. Whiting, *Persecution Exposed* (1791), 300.

In the early 19th century the range was re-roofed and the eaves were raised. At the same time it was given a symmetrical plastered front with sash windows and a classical porch. The back wing probably dates from the 18th century, as do the gate-piers with ball finials at the entrance to the forecourt. The farm buildings include a medieval rectangular dovecot, originally with about 650 nest holes, but increased by about 130 by the insertion of a dividing wall.[20]

The remainder of the Sutton Hosey estate was devised by William Steele on his death in 1715 in trust for the support of poor Somerset Quakers.[21] Known as Charity farm, Upton, it remained part of the endowment of the Friends' Somerset Charities until 1921, when most of it was sold to the tenant.[22]

Before 1254 Sabina Lorty, daughter of Richard Revel and heir of the St. Clare properties, was holding an estate in Long Sutton, part of which may have descended from the Domesday tenant of Athelney abbey, Roger Brito.[23] Some of Sabina's estate, in 'Little Benham' and 'Lade', was held of Ralph Huse and part, at Knole, of Huse and the abbot of Athelney.[24] Sabina died in 1254 and her heir was her grandson Henry Lorty, then a minor.[25] The estate, called a vill in 1254, was described three years later as the manor of *KNOLE*.[26] From 1280 onwards it was held of the lord of Long Sutton for $\frac{1}{5}$ knight's fee.[27]

The manor then followed the descent of the manor of Pitney Lorty until the death of Sir Robert de Ashton in 1384.[28] It then passed to Sir William Windsor and after his death a few months later to his son John.[29] In 1392 Maud Langrich and Elizabeth Gunter recovered the property as heirs of Sibyl Lorty.[30] Maud, who later married William Horslegh, died without issue, and when Elizabeth died in 1422 she left the whole manor to her son Roger Gunter (d. 1436).[31] The manor passed to his son John (d. 1474) and then to John's brother William, and continued like the manor of Pitney Lorty to the Mortons.[32]

In 1578 George Morton conveyed the manor to John Chafin.[33] Two years later it was in the hands of Thomas Chafin of Folke (Dors.), and by 1601 he was succeeded by his son Bampfield, of Chettle (Dors.) (d. 1644).[34] Bampfield's son Thomas died before 1657 and his son, also Thomas, in 1691.[35] George Chafin, Thomas's third son, succeeded him and died in 1766. His sons George and William

sold the manor in 1768 to Stephen Fox-Strangways, earl of Ilchester (d. 1776).[36] Knole thereafter formed part of the Ilchester estates until 1913, when it was sold as separate farms.[37]

In 1326 Richard de St. Clare granted to Henry Power an estate of 184 a. in Long Sutton and Martock.[38] This holding was settled in 1344 on Joan, Henry's daughter, and on her husband William Shareshull the younger.[39] Power died in 1361 leaving an estate of 45 a. held of the earl of Salisbury, lord of Martock.[40] It is possible that this holding was the origin of the reputed manor of *SUTTON ST. CLEERS* or *BOURNE'S MANOR*, a freehold estate settled by John Bourne in 1528 on his son William, on William's marriage with Mary Poure.[41] William Bourne (d. 1552) was succeeded in turn by his son Francis, of Bath (d. 1601), and by his grandson John (d. 1625).[42] John's estate comprised 100 a. of arable, 20 a. of meadow, and 20 a. of pasture in Long Sutton, Somerton, and Martock, held of the lord of Long Sutton.[43] The property was tenanted for her life by his mother Bennett, wife of the lawyer and wit John Hoskins.[44] John Bourne, son or grandson of John, survived until c. 1706.[45]

The property was then divided into three parts, one third passing to Dorothy, his daughter, and to her husband Walter Nourse.[46] The other two thirds were held in 1710 by Mary Clarke, possibly Bourne's other daughter Mary, and by John Smith.[47] Dorothy, Walter, Mary, and John held courts at least until 1714.[48] From 1720 until 1729 Walter and Dorothy Nourse shared the lordship with John Holder and Elizabeth his wife, and by 1738 with Elizabeth Holder only.[49] Elizabeth Nourse, spinster, and Elizabeth Holder, widow, held the manor jointly in 1756.[50] Ten years later the property was held by John Lewis.[51] Richard Lewis was owner between 1780 and 1806, followed for two years by Richard Welsh.[52] By 1809 one Thomson held the property, which was usually known as Thomson's farm until 1832.[53] By 1838 the owner was C. E. Poulett Thomson (cr. Baron Sydenham and Toronto 1840, d. 1841) then President of the Board of Trade.[54] He was still charged with the payment of 4s. 6d. to the lord of Long Sutton as his predecessor, John Bourne, had been in 1539.[55] The property seems to have been sold after Thomson's death. Between 1832 and 1845 it was known as Demas Sutton farm, recalling the medieval tithing name of Demi Sutton.[56]

20 E. Horne, 'Som. Dovecots' (TS. in Taunton Castle); *S. & D. N. & Q.* xxiv. 9.
21 Street, Friends' Meeting-house, acct. bk. of trust properties, 1720–1830; S.R.O., DD/SFR 4/1: Half-year's Meeting mins. 1719–84, p. 3.
22 *Bristol and Som. Quarterly Meeting Trust Property Bk.* (revised 1936).   23 *V.C.H. Som.* i. 469.
24 *S.R.S.* vi. 149; xiv. 132; *Cal. Inq. p.m.* i, p. 84.
25 *Cal. Inq. p.m.* i, p. 84; *Cal. Pat.* 1247–58, 539.
26 *Cal. Inq. p.m.* i, p. 84; *Cal. Pat.* 1247–58, 539.
27 *Plac. de Quo Warr.* (Rec. Com.), 688; *S.R.S.* xiv. 196–7; B.M. Harl. Ch. 58 H 14; S.C. 6/Hen. VIII/3144.
28 See p. 52.
29 C 136/30/5, 37/1; B.M. Harl. Ch. 54 I 5: *Cal. Fine R.* 1383–91, 149.
30 C.P. 40/533 rot. 78; B.M. Harl. Ch. 49 G 13, 58 D 8; see also *V.C.H. Wilts.* viii. 64–5.
31 B.M. Harl. Ch. 52 C 32; C 138/27/40; C 139/1/22.
32 See p. 52.   33 Northampton MSS. 344.
34 Ibid. 346; Hutchins, *Hist. Dors.* iii. 565.
35 D.R.O., D 124 Som. manorial, ct. papers, abstract of title.
36 D.R.O., D 124 Som. deeds, Knole.
37 S.R.O., C/C, sale cat. Knole Estate 1913.
38 *S.R.S.* xii. 106–7.
39 Ibid. 221.
40 *Cal. Inq. p.m.* xi, p. 159; *Cal. Close,* 1360–4, 311.
41 C 142/97/78.
42 S.C. 6/Hen. VIII/3144; C 142/97/78; *Som. Wills,* ed. Brown, i. 29.
43 *S.R.S.* lxvii. 11.
44 C 142/429/115; *D.N.B.*
45 S.R.O., DD/SAS PR 191.
46 C.P. 25(2)/987/4 Anne Mich.
47 S.R.O., DD/SAS PR 191.
48 Ibid.   49 Ibid.
50 S.R.O., DD/S/BT, box 20, bundle 92, Hodges to Notley, 1764.
51 Ibid., extract of ct. roll.
52 S.R.O., Q/RE, land tax assessments.   53 Ibid.
54 D.R.O., D 124 Som. estates general, sale cat.
55 S.C. 6/Hen. VIII/3144.
56 See p. 59. Called Sutton Damer in 1791: Collinson, *Hist. Som.* iii. 197.

The farm-house attached to this property in 1844 is now known as the Court House. It is the oldest domestic building in the village and may be of 14th-century origin. It is built of lias with Ham stone dressings and consists of a single range on an approximately north–south axis with porches of different dates projecting from the two long sides. The northern half of the range contains a formerly open hall, later divided by a floor, with a screens-passage and gallery across its south end. Beyond the passage the building appears always to have been two-storeyed, but this part of the house has been altered and re-roofed. There are indications of timber-framing in the end wall to the south; it contains a window with closely-set diagonal mullions, blocked by the insertion of a later chimney. The former hall has retained its smoke-blackened open roof, though some of the timbers were replaced in the 1930s. The roof has three main bays, divided by arch-braced collar-beam trusses with raised base-cruck principals. Braced crown-posts support a collar purlin and each main bay has two tall but slender wind-braces, slightly curved. Lighter intermediate trusses have no crown-posts. The trusses on the two end walls are of the 'aisled' type and other features of the roof, notably the main through-purlins which are set square in the manner of arcade-plates, are reminiscent of aisled-hall construction. The same early characteristics, also associated with base-cruck principals, have been found in several other roofs in the West of England; comparison with dated examples suggests that they may belong to the late 13th and 14th centuries.[57]

The front entrance of the medieval house was evidently at the west end of the screens-passage where there is a wooden pointed arch. The two-storeyed stone porch outside it has diagonal buttresses. The outer opening has been walled up but what appears to be its relieving arch is still visible; in the south wall of the porch is a primitive two-light stone window. A pointed stone doorway on the south side of the screens-passage has been blocked by a 17th-century stair. The house was evidently altered at various dates and contains an assortment of mullioned windows, both of wood and stone. The most drastic reconstruction seems to have been carried out in 1658 by the tenant, Thomas Spigurnell, gentleman.[58] It included the insertion of stone-mullioned windows in the north gable-end and the east front which have archaic four-centred heads to the lights. Spigurnell evidently renewed much of the masonry and built the large chimney against the west wall of the hall. The removal of the main entrance from the west side of the house, which entailed adding an east porch, is also likely to be

his work. The porch, which may originally have been two-storeyed, has a semi-circular outer arch and an inner doorway with a four-centred head.

The Court House, including the hall roof, was carefully restored in the 1930s and vested in a trust by the Society of Friends.[59] A dovecot, forming part of a barn south-west of the house, probably dates from the 17th century.

In 1538–9 a freehold estate was held by John Porter of the lord of Long Sutton manor.[60] Thomas Porter owned it in 1546, and William Porter in 1557–60.[61] Robert Cary was in possession by 1566, but two years later it was in the hands of James Hodges.[62] Hodges died in 1601 leaving land in Upton and Somerton to his daughter Mary and her husband John Rosse.[63] Their son James conveyed the Upton property, then described as the 'manor' of Upton, to Samuel Spalding in 1637.[64] Augustine Spalding sold it to Arthur Fortescue in 1661.[65] Fortescue was still owner in 1692, but by 1729 it had come into the hands of the Langfield family.[66] Sylvester Langfield (d. 1746) was succeeded by his son Sylvester; the son seems to have held the property until 1774, and Elizabeth Langfield, apparently his mother, until 1791.[67] John Laver held it from that time at least until 1838.[68]

The rectory of Long Sutton, created a prebend in Wells Cathedral c. 1200,[69] was held by successive abbots of Athelney until after the Dissolution, the last abbot retaining it until 1554 or later.[70] In that year the reversion was granted to the chapter of Wells, but Dr. John Lloyd of Owlswick (Bucks.) held it by 1583 and Thomas Butler of London had a Crown lease in 1591.[71] In that same year it passed to the newly-constituted chapter of Wells,[72] who leased it throughout the 17th and 18th centuries. From 1703 if not earlier the lessees were successive lords of Long Sutton manor.[73] Between 1822 and 1831 it was sold to the then lessee, Lord George Cavendish.[74] About 1920 a large portion was given by the duke of Devonshire to augment the vicarage, and the remainder was transferred to the Church Commissioners in 1923.[75]

The rectory was taxed at £23 6s. 8d. in 1291.[76] In 1535 the net value was £6 16s. 10d. and the income of over £11 was entirely from tithe corn.[77] Between 1538 and 1546 it was farmed for £26 13s. 4d.,[78] and in the 17th and 18th centuries was let for £40, though its value was assessed in 1650 at £100.[79] In 1721 it was worth £120.[80] The tithes were commuted in 1844 for £400.[81] The only buildings belonging to the rectory were a nine-bay stone barn and a garner house.[82] The barn stood between the manor-house and the churchyard and was demolished in the late 19th century.[83]

[57] Trans. Devon Assoc. xviii. 135–8; see also Vernacular Archit. i. 7–8.
[58] Tablet in N. gable; par. rec. burial reg. 31 Aug. 1663.
[59] Country Life, 17 Oct. 1968, 974.
[60] S.C. 6/Hen. VIII/3144.
[61] D.R.O., D 124 Som. manorial, survey 1602.
[62] Ibid.; Northampton MSS. 335.
[63] D.R.O., D 124 Som. manorial, survey 1602; Som. Wills, ed. Brown, i. 30.
[64] C.P. 25(2)/480/12 Chas. I Hil.
[65] C.P. 25(2)/715/13 Chas. II Mich.
[66] S.R.O., DD/DEV 5; par. rec. overseers' accts. 1728–45.
[67] S.R.O., DD/DEV 2, 3.
[68] D.R.O., D 124 Som. estates general, sale cat.

[69] H.M.C. Wells, i. 57, 68.
[70] Cal. Pat. 1553–4, 399–400.
[71] Req. 2/269/2; C 66/1366 mm. 1–6.
[72] H. E. Reynolds, Wells Cathedral, 249.
[73] S.R.O., DD/CC 111371–5, 111377, 111379, 114081, 114086.
[74] Ibid. 111379; Rep. Com. Eccl. Revenues, pp. 180–1.
[75] Par. rec., conveyance, 1 Feb. 1923; Dioc. Dir. (1920).
[76] Tax. Eccl. (Rec. Com.), 200.
[77] Valor Eccl. (Rec. Com.), i. 207; S.C. 12/14/40.
[78] S.C. 6/Hen. VIII/3144–50.
[79] e.g. S.R.O., DD/CC 131910a.   [80] Ibid. 111381.
[81] S.R.O., tithe award.
[82] S.R.O., DD/CC 111380.
[83] Ibid. 110001, p. 204.

KINGSDON CHURCH FROM THE NORTH-EAST

ALLER CHURCH: INTERIOR

MUCHELNEY ABBEY: CLOISTER

LONG SUTTON: PULPIT

ECONOMIC HISTORY. Eight of the ten hides in Sutton were in 1086 held by Athelney abbey, and the remainder, formerly abbey property, by Roger de Courcelles. Four hides were held by the abbey in demesne, 3½ were farmed by 8 villeins and 6 bordars, and ½ hide was occupied by Roger Brito. The demesne of de Courcelles' holding was worked by 4 villeins and 3 bordars. There were 4 serfs on the abbey demesne and one on de Courcelles'.[84] There was said to be land for 16 ploughs but only 11 were recorded, 6 on the villein holding under Athelney, and only 2 on the abbey demesne. Pasture was clearly of importance: the abbey demesne comprised 40 a. of meadow and 100 a. of pasture, and there were 6 beasts (*animalia*), 15 pigs, and 102 sheep. Only 6 a.[85] of meadow were recorded on de Courcelles' holding, but his tenants had between them a cow, 9 pigs, and 214 sheep. The abbey estate was valued at £8, de Courcelles' estate 50s.[86]

By the mid 13th century customary rents on Knole manor, worth £4 7s. 6½d., were larger than the value of works, either still performed or commuted.[87] Commutation had evidently taken place on Long Sutton manor by 1349,[88] and on a small freeholding by 1305.[89] By 1539 the bailiwick of Sutton, the whole of Athelney's estate in the parish, comprised 61 customary holdings, worth over £57, and 7 freeholdings.[90] Some of these freeholds later acquired some of the attributes of manorial status, but ancient rents were still paid until the 19th century.[91]

The abbey demesne in Long Sutton manor in 1349 comprised 100 a. of arable, 20 a. of meadow, and 12 a. of pasture.[92] One or two small holdings were added after that date and by 1538 the demesne farm included 145 a. of arable in the common fields.[93] Knole manor comprised a carucate in demesne *c.* 1254, together with meadow worth 34s., and withybeds.[94] The freehold estate of Edmund St. Lo, later known as the 'manor' of Upton, was 120 a. in 1541.[95] The total extent of Athelney's demesne in 1349 was £8 1s. 11d., and in 1486 £8 0s. 7d.[96] Total rents of the bailiwick in 1538–9 were £59 3s. 8¾d.[97] Rents at Knole were £6 5s. 8½d. *c.* 1254 and £19 1s. 4d. in the later 15th century, with an extra sum of 31s. 7½d. described as *donum Sancti Martini*.[98]

The importance of pasture land is illustrated by the frequency of disputes over ownership and common rights,[99] which reveal complicated grazing regulations. Rights in Little moor, near Load Bridge, were disputed between the abbot of Athelney, the Crown, and a number of commoners from 1364

until 1383. The proceedings revealed how part was held in severalty by the owner of Knole manor from February until August each year for hay; by the abbot as chief lord from then until Michaelmas; and was then open to various commoners for the rest of the year, the share of Knole manor being pasture for 8 oxen and a 'beast of the plough'.[1] The conveyance of a small holding at Little Load to the abbot in 1431 included common of pasture for 8 oxen, a mare, and a colt in Rodmoor.[2]

Despite the importance of pasture, arable land accounted for a considerably larger area. A three-year rotation was practised by 1349 on Long Sutton manor.[3] Part of the rent for the rectory, the only income of which was tithe corn, amounted to 66 quarters of wheat and 14 quarters of dredge in 1538–9. The lessee of the manor at the same time had to sow 40 a. of wheat and 46 a. of spring corn in the last year of his tenancy, and the farm had to be stocked with 6 oxen, 6 cows, a bull, and 2 sheep.[4]

Early in the 17th century the income from Long Sutton manor was £90 10s. 4d. and in 1663 £85 6s. 6d. At the earlier date there were 119 copyholders on one, two, or three lives, and 7 leaseholders, also for lives. By 1663 there were 66 copyholders and 40 life leaseholders.[5] Within the next thirty years the number of copyholders fell to 56 but there was evidently some fragmentation of leaseholds for lives, which had risen in number to 92,[6] Rents, however, remained stable, and were £90 15s. 9d. in 1765.[7]

Cattle grazing was of some importance in the 17th century. Landmoors, West Landmoors, and Haymoors in the west of the parish were inclosed *c.* 1620, and had doubled in value by *c.* 1633.[8] Between 1627 and 1637 two brothers supplied the London market with stock from the parish.[9] Consolidated farms also began to emerge including Little Load farm by 1674 and another in the same area by 1692.[10] By 1720 there were 55 tenants on Long Sutton manor with over a hundred separate holdings, but one farmer had over 200 a., three over 100 a., and seven over 60 a.[11] Some forty years later there were three farms at Knole with *c.* 60 a. or over.[12] Leases for lives persisted: in a total of 3,993 a. for the whole parish 2,232 a. were so held *c.* 1815.[13] By 1838 freehold tenure had been increased by over 670 a. on Long Sutton manor, and by 1844 only 102 a. were held for lives on Knole manor, a reduction of nearly three quarters.[14]

The remaining commonable land was inclosed in 1814 under an Act of 1809. Just over 1,418 a., mostly arable land in the north-west of the parish, were

[84] *V.C.H. Som.* i. 469–70, 493.
[85] Given as 8 a. elsewhere in the Survey: ibid. 493.
[86] Ibid. 469–70.
[87] C 132/16/10.
[88] B.M. Add. MS. 6165, p. 13.
[89] *Cal. Inq. p.m.* iv, p. 202.
[90] S.C. 6/Hen. VIII/3144.
[91] See pp. 158, 160.
[92] B.M. Add. MS. 6165, p. 13.
[93] S.C. 6/Hen. VIII/3144.
[94] C 132/16/10.   [95] S.R.O., DD/WY W/CR 3.
[96] B.M. Add. MS. 6165, p. 13; *Cal. Inq. p.m. Hen. VII,* iii, p. 548.
[97] S.C. 6/Hen. VIII/3144.
[98] C 132/16/10; B.M. Harl. Ch. 58 F 11.
[99] *Plac. de Quo Warr.* (Rec. Com.), 688; *S.R.S.* xli. 189; *Cal. Pat.* 1446–52, 503.

[1] S.C. 6/974/12; C 260/94/34; *Cal. Fine R.* 1377–83, 180; *Cal. Pat.* 1381–5, 266; *S.R.S.* xiv. 131.
[2] *Cal. Close,* 1435–41, 166.
[3] B.M. Add. MS. 6165, p. 13.
[4] S.C. 6/Hen. VIII/3144.
[5] Northampton MSS. 824–6.
[6] S.R.O., DD/DEV 5.
[7] Ibid. 13.
[8] S.R.O., D/D/Cd 77.
[9] *S.R.S.* xxiv. 59, 108, 185; li. 270.
[10] S.R.O., DD/DEV 4, 5.
[11] S.R.O., DD/X/BB, survey 1719–20; DD/DEV 11.
[12] D.R.O., D 124 Som. manorial, MS. sale partics. 1767.
[13] S.R.O., DD/DEV 17.
[14] D.R.O., D 124 Som. estates gen. sale partics. 1838; S.R.O., tithe award.

allotted among 20 owners, principally to Lord George Cavendish.[15] Subsequently improved drainage in the south and east of the parish enhanced the quality of the grassland around Knole, and in the years after 1840 dairying became important. Farm buildings were often extended to house more cows and new sets of buildings were erected. In 1844 Lower Knole farm had its buildings concentrated around the farm-house on the southern side of Stone Mead Lane.[16] By 1886 stalls, calving pens, two cattle yards, and other buildings had been added on the opposite side of the lane as the tenant farmer concentrated his efforts on dairying.[17] A similar development took place at Bineham House, subsequently Bineham Dairy farm, also on the Ilchester estate.[18] Three new farms, Bineham, Plot Dairy, and Upton, complete with buildings, were established during the same period on the Devonshire estate.[19] In 1859 twelve men were described as farmers in the parish, in 1866 31 including two dairymen, and in 1875 30 including five dairymen.[20] Many of the farms were sold to the sitting tenants when the Ilchester and Devonshire estates were sold in 1913 and 1919, but there followed a certain amount of consolidation, so that by 1919 there were only 17 farms and a dairy.[21] Dairy farming continues to be of major importance.

A tucking-mill was working in the parish in 1715, and cloth was made on a small scale at the end of the century: there was a silk-house in 1798, and the manufacture of Dowlas, Teck, and sail-cloth employed many people.[22] There was also a 'tobacco manufactory with a snuff mill',[23] and gloving was done by women at home.[24] For a short time in the 1920s the Wessex Shirt and Collar Co. Ltd. had a factory producing shirts, collars, pyjamas, and gloves.[25] Quarrying was also important. Shallow workings in the lias for local use gave way to systematic exploitation in the 1890s which continued until 1939.[26] Lime burning was carried on at Upton from the mid 18th century until the 1930s.[27]

The number of shops in the village in the late 19th century was larger than that of many neighbouring villages, and included one retailer who described himself as draper and grocer who also sold patent medicines and kept a shoe warehouse.[28] A post office was established by 1861.[29] The first garage was opened by 1923 and the increasing traffic along the Langport road was catered for at the Court House where meals were served in the 1930s.[30]

In 1616 the parish refused to help to support the poor of Somerton because 60 of its own poor, many of whom were children, needed daily relief, and 80 more had 'neither house, nor anything else but their hands to relieve them', and the rates were producing but half of their former return.[31] A century later between 20 and 25 people were being regularly relieved at a cost of c. £95.[32] Expenditure by 1744–5 was a little lower and was similar in 1776.[33] It rose sharply by 1803, when 27 people including 10 children were supported.[34] This high level remained a permanent feature.[35]

In 1267 the monks of Athelney were granted an annual fair on the eve, feast, and morrow of St. James (25 July).[36] No further trace of this fair has been found. A 'pedlary' fair was held in the village on Trinity Monday by 1791, and continued in connexion with the annual walk of the friendly society until 1970.[37]

A mill was held by Reynold Huse in 1341.[38] Paul Tucker, who held the same estate in the 17th century, occupied a mill in 1678.[39] He was succeeded by the Gillett family, John Gillett in 1715 holding the former water grist mill as a tucking mill.[40] The family still held the property in 1767.[41] A mill on Long Sutton manor in 1349 was worth only 2s. because it could not grind in summer for want of water.[42] This mill was still working in 1679.[43] By 1844 only its site and the site of the pond were known, immediately west of Manor Farm.[44] Athelney abbey had a windmill in 1349.[45] It was let for 10s. in 1538–9, and may have stood in a field, formerly known as Mill Toit, to the north of the Langport road in the west of the parish.[46] There was a mill at Knole by 1479–80.[47] It occurs in 1520–1, and occupiers are traceable throughout the 18th century.[48] About 1870 it was moved to its present position in the centre of the hamlet from a site higher upstream. It then became an overshot mill, driven by means of an iron wheel placed at the end of the long, two-storeyed lias building. It seems to have gone out of use by 1883.[49]

LOCAL GOVERNMENT. Rolls and books of the manor court of Long Sutton or Sutton Valence survive for 1541–2,[50] intermittently for the period 1546–1669,[51] and regularly between 1671 and 1694

15 S.R.O., CR 84.
16 S.R.O., tithe award.
17 O.S. Map 6″, Som. LXXIII. SW. (1886 edn.).
18 Ibid. 19 Ibid.
20 P.O. Dir. Som. (1859, 1866, 1875).
21 Kelly's Dir. Som. (1919); see above, pp. 157, 159.
22 S.R.O., D/D/Rm 2; R. Locke, Additions to Collinson, ed. Ward; see below, p. 165.
23 Locke, Additions to Collinson.
24 Story of Long Sutton, comp. E. A. Smith (W.I. hist. 1953), 3–4.
25 Kelly's Dir. Som. (1923, 1927).
26 S.R.O., tithe award; D.R.O., D 124, Som. estates gen., lease of quarry; P.O. Dir. Som. (1866); Kelly's Dir. Som. (1894, 1897, 1939).
27 S.R.O., DD/X/BB, contract bk. 1754; Kelly's Dir. Som. (1897–1935).
28 P.O. Dir. Som. (1861); Kelly's Dir. Som. (1883).
29 P.O. Dir. Som. (1861).
30 Kelly's Dir. Som. (1923, 1935, 1939).
31 S.R.S. xxiii. 175–6.
32 Par. rec. overseers' accts. 1728–45.

33 Ibid.; Poor Law Abstract, 1804.
34 Poor Law Abstract, 1804.
35 Rep. Sel. Cttee. Poor Rate Rtns. H.C. 556 (1822), v; Poor Rel. Rtns. H.C. 83 (1830–1), xi.
36 Cal. Chart. R. 1257–1300, 85.
37 Collinson, Hist. Som. iii. 197.
38 S.R.S. xii. 311. 39 S.R.O., DD/DEV 4.
40 S.R.O., DD/X/BB; DD/DEV 7.
41 S.R.O., DD/X/BB, contract bk.
42 Cal. Inq. Misc. iii, p. 15; B.M. Add. MS. 6165, p. 13.
43 S.R.O., DD/DEV 1, 4; DD/X/BB, survey 1719–20.
44 S.R.O., tithe award.
45 Cal. Inq. Misc. iii, p. 15; B.M. Add. MS. 6165, p. 13.
46 S.C. 6/Hen. VIII/3144; S.R.O., tithe award.
47 B.M. Harl. Ch. 58 E 46.
48 B.M. Harl. Roll K 27; D.R.O., D 124 Som. deeds; S.R.O., Q/RE, land tax assessments.
49 P.O. Dir. Som. (1866, 1875); Kelly's Dir. Som. (1883). See above, plate facing p. 65.
50 S.R.O., DD/WY W/CR 3.
51 Castle Ashby, Northampton MSS. 331–47, 349–60, 810, 824–5.

and between 1745 and 1839. There is no further record until the last court in 1885.[52] The court, described as a manor court until the late 17th century and from 1745 as a court baron, met twice a year, in spring and autumn, until 1784, and thereafter only in autumn. From the 16th century and probably earlier its jurisdiction was divided into two parts, wards, or ends, each apparently coinciding with a tithing, and each part made separate presentments through its tithingman.[53] A hayward was appointed for each part until 1745 and again, though less regularly, from 1756 until 1839; there were three haywards between 1787 and 1800 and one in 1885. About 1602 the haywardship of the east part carried a salary of 5s. a year, while in the west part the office was held in rotation by eight tenants of certain arable plots.[54] There were apparently no other officers of the court, but particular orders of the court were regularly supervised by committees. Courts in the 17th century were held in the upper room of the church house.[55] The last court was held in the Devonshire Arms.[56]

The lord of Knole owed suit to the court at Sutton and his tenants in 1541–2 were presented there for overcharging the common fields there.[57] The chief concerns of the Sutton court were the maintenance and repair of houses, river banks, and ditches, and the administration of the fields. It claimed jurisdiction over pleas of debt of customary tenants in the 16th century,[58] and issued orders that, among other things, the churchwardens in 1547 should choose their successors,[59] in 1639 that dyed wool should not be washed in streams,[60] and, from 1760, that horses of coal-carriers found straying from the towing-path should be impounded.[61]

Courts were held at Knole by c. 1254.[62] Rolls, books, and other papers survive for 1479–80[63] and 1521,[64] and intermittently for 1625–65, 1728–91, and 1830–63.[65] In the early 17th century the courts were described as views of frankpledge but from 1657 the regular twice-yearly sittings in April and October were usually called collectively courts leet and baron. A tithingman occurs by 1479 and a tithingman, a constable, and a hayward in 1664. No constable was appointed after 1740, but the tithingmanship continued until 1841 and a hayward was appointed until 1863.[66]

A court-house stood in Knole until after 1844; it was demolished before 1912.[67] Repairs to ditches, roads, and bridges were the main concern of the

court until the 18th century, when its main business was the control of the common fields.

The owners of the reputed manor of Sutton St. Cleers held courts for the admission of tenants between 1662 and 1728.[68] The farmer of the rectory held courts in 1616–17.[69]

From the early 18th century a 'public vestry or parish meeting', summoned by 'warning . . . from house to house', administered the parish, the overseers serving in rotation in respect of their holdings.[70] Overseers' rates financed not only generous cash payments for maintenance, clothing, and rents for all badged paupers, but also paid for repairs to river banks, roads, and gates. Surveyors of highways, one for each tithing, occur by 1730.[71] The vestry became more select during the early 19th century and by 1839 the parish was effectively controlled by the two churchwardens, one of whom was responsible for the administration of the Sedgemoor allotment.[72] From 1867 until 1870 waywardens were appointed by the vestry.[73]

By 1674 the ground floor of the church house was leased to the churchwardens for the use of the poor.[74] By 1692 the house was held by the overseers, and in 1737 was established as a workhouse.[75] A poorhouse was established at Upton by 1782.[76] The former church house was replaced by a poorhouse in Back Lane, which remained in use until 1852.[77] The parish became part of the Langport poor law union in 1836.[78]

CHURCH. Fragments of Norman masonry preserved beneath the pulpit precede the earliest documentary evidence for the church.[79] About 1200 Athelney abbey, which had owned an estate at Sutton from the 9th century, gave the church to Bishop Savaric (bishop 1192–1205) to form a prebend in Wells Cathedral, to be held by successive abbots. In return the church was appropriated, and before 1227 a vicarage was ordained.[80]

The patronage was initially also granted to the bishop[81] but, except in 1342 when he 'conferred' the benefice by apostolic authority,[82] the monks presented to the vicarage.[83] Sir Thomas Dyar presented in 1564 and the farmer of the prebend in 1596.[84] The chapter of Wells were patrons in 1574 and from the 17th century to the present day.[85]

The vicarage was taxed at £5 in 1291.[86] In 1535

[52] S.R.O., DD/DEV 1–3.
[53] Northampton MSS. 331; DD/DEV 5; S. & D. N. & Q. xxiv. 96–7. The tithings were known as Sutton and Demi Sutton.
[54] S.R.O., DD/DEV 2; S. & D. N. & Q. xxiv. 96–7.
[55] S.R.O., DD/DEV 4.
[56] Ibid. 3.
[57] S.R.O., DD/WY W/CR 3.
[58] Northampton MSS. 334, 343.
[59] Ibid. 331.
[60] Ibid. 360.
[61] S.R.O., DD/DEV 2.
[62] C 132/16/10.
[63] B.M. Harl. Ch. 58 E 46.
[64] B.M. Harl. Roll K 27.
[65] D.R.O., D 124, passim.
[66] Two haywards served 1840–5.
[67] S.R.O., tithe award; C/C, sale cat. Knole estate 1913.
[68] S.R.O., DD/SAS PR 191.
[69] S.R.O., DD/CC 131910a/3.
[70] Par. rec. overseers' accts. 1728–45, chwdns'. accts.

1728–43. The vol. includes a list of overseers 1703–44 and of chwdns. 1703–34, 1739, 1741–4.
[71] Par. rec. overseers' accts.
[72] Par. rec. chwdns'. accts. and vestry mins. 1830–80.
[73] Ibid.
[74] S.R.O., DD/DEV 4.
[75] Ibid. 5; par. rec. overseers' accts. vestry min. 8 June 1737.
[76] S.R.O., DD/DEV 3.
[77] Par. rec. chwdns'. accts. and vestry mins. 1830–80. Now used as dwellings.
[78] Poor Law Com. 2nd Rep. p. 548.
[79] See p. 165.
[80] H.M.C. Wells, i. 57, 68; S.R.S. xxxix, 64; lvi. 97; V.C.H. Som. ii. 67. The date of grant is 1198 × 1205.
[81] H.M.C. Wells, i. 487: date of grant 1206 × 1227.
[82] S.R.S. x. 441.
[83] Som. Incumbents, ed. Weaver, 195.   [84] Ibid.
[85] Ibid. In 1825 the bishop of Coventry and Lichfield presented jointly: S. & D. N. & Q. iv. 216.
[86] Tax. Eccl. (Rec. Com.), 199.

the net value was £8 18s. 0d.; an allowance of 6 qr. of wheat and 6 qr. of dredge payable from the rectory and valued at £2 3s. 4d. was probably not included.[87] By 1613 this allowance, described as 6 qr. of wheat, 4 qr. of dredge, 2 qr. of beans, and 16s. or a winter gown, had not been paid for 20 years.[88] The sum of £8 in lieu was paid by the impropriator from 1703 until 1923.[89] The benefice was temporarily augmented to £40 during the Interregnum,[90] but the reputed value c. 1668 was £30.[91] The net income in 1831 was £229.[92]

Tithes payable to the vicar were worth £13 8s. in 1535.[93] They were commuted to a rent-charge of £232 in 1844. By composition all meadow land, some 656 a., paid a modus of 3d. an acre; 3d. was paid for each cow and 1d. for the fall of calf or colt in lieu of tithes of milk, calves, and colts. Just under 200 a. paid five farthings an acre for all vicarial tithes.[94]

In 1535 the glebe was worth 10s.[95] By 1613 it measured ½ a. of inclosed arable and pasture, 3 a. of meadow, and c. 10 a. in the common fields, together with a garden and barton.[96] By 1844 the glebe measured just over 17 a., which by 1948 was reduced to 14 a.[97] The former vicarage house stood on the west side of the green in the centre of the village.[98] Early in 1663 it was reported to have been 'down' for some time, and in 1681 the hall, porch, and buttery with a chamber above were in need of rebuilding.[99] In 1815 the house was considered unfit for residence 'being very old'.[1] It was demolished by 1840.[2] The present Vicarage, on the eastern outskirts of the village, replaced it.

William Underhill, vicar in 1397, was licensed to farm the benefice for seven years while studying.[3] John Towkere (vicar 1429–36) was deprived for farming the glebe without licence and leaving the cure unserved.[4] Pluralism was common in the 17th century. Paul Godwin (vicar 1596–1607) was also vicar of Burnham and rector of Rampisham (Dors.).[5] John Norris, vicar from 1639, was replaced by Gabriel Ball, who served the parish between 1647 and 1654.[6] For much of the 18th century the benefice was held by Moses Foster (vicar 1738–53) and his son Aaron (vicar 1753–76).[7]

In 1815 services were held once every Sunday, alternately morning and evening.[8] Two services were held by 1851, the average congregation being 100 in the morning and 210 in the afternoon, including 55 Sunday-school pupils at each service.[9] Holy Communion was celebrated monthly by 1870.[10]

The churchwardens rented a church house from the lord of the manor by 1539–40.[11] By 1674 it was in use as a poorhouse.[12]

There was a chapel at Upton, founded probably by Henry III, who granted to Athelney abbey four messuages and 158 a. of land to support a chantry priest to celebrate on three days each week.[13] The endowment was still attached to the chapel in 1381,[14] but most seems to have been lost by 1535 when the curate of the parish serving the chapel was paid a composition from the vicarage income.[15] In 1548 its land was worth 4d.[16] It was serving 23 households in 1563[17] but probably went out of use soon afterwards. It was leased in 1572 and has not been traced thereafter.[18] Its site is not known.

A chapel at Knole was also under the care of the assistant curate in 1535.[19] It was endowed with lands worth 4d. and in 1563 served 17 households.[20] It was leased in 1572 with Upton chapel.[21] A field called Chapel Hays at the eastern end of Bineham field may be either its site or its endowment.

The parish church of the *HOLY TRINITY* is a large building of lias with Ham stone dressings. It consists of a chancel with north and south chapels extending from the aisles, aisled and clerestoreyed nave with north and south porches, and west tower. The building dates almost entirely from the late 15th century, an order to dedicate the work having been issued in 1493.[22] The tower, which dominates the rest of the church by its height, appears from its style to be of the same period. An analysis of the various features in comparison with those of other notable Somerset towers, however, has suggested a building date as early as 1440.[23] It has set-back angle buttresses, intermediate vertical shafts, a south-west stair-turret, and an embattled parapet with pinnacles. The west doorway has a stoup beside it and is surmounted by a large Perpendicular window. Two stages higher there are central windows flanked by niches. The belfry stage has three openings to each face, the central one with Somerset tracery, the others blind. On the west side the central opening is dated 1622, suggesting that the tracery may have been renewed at that period. On the other hand there is plenty of evidence that quite elaborate Perpendicular work was being carried out in the county in the earlier 17th century[24] and it is possible that the upper stages of the tower were not completed until 1622.

In the rest of the church the windows, nave arcades, and other features are in a uniform Per-

[87] *Valor Eccl.* (Rec. Com.), i. 198, 207; S.C. 6/Hen. VIII/3144; S.C. 12/14/40.
[88] S.R.O., DD/CC 131910a; it was still not paid in 1635: D/D/Rg 219.
[89] S.R.O., DD/CC 111379–80, 114086.
[90] Lambeth MSS. COMM. VIb/2 f.133.
[91] S.R.O., D/D/Vc 24.
[92] *Rep. Com. Eccl. Revenues*, pp. 180–1.
[93] *Valor Eccl.* (Rec. Com.), i. 198.
[94] S.R.O., tithe award.
[95] *Valor Eccl.* (Rec. Com.), i. 198.
[96] S.R.O., DD/CC 111380.
[97] S.R.O., tithe award; *Crockford*.
[98] S.R.O., DD/DEV 1, *sub anno* 1679.
[99] S.R.O., DD/GS, box 2, 'Autographs, Som. etc.', presentment; *S.R.S.* lxxii. 193.
[1] S.R.O., D/D/V rtns. 1815.
[2] See p. 166.
[3] *Cal. Papal Regs.* v. 24.
[4] *S.R.S.* xxxii. 194–5.
[5] Foster, *Alumni Oxon.*

[6] Par. reg.; Lambeth MSS. COMM. VIb/2 f. 133; *S.R.S.* lxxi. 62.
[7] Foster, *Alumni Oxon.*
[8] S.R.O., D/D/V rtns. 1815.
[9] H.O. 129/317/2/1/1.
[10] S.R.O., D/D/V rtns. 1870.
[11] S.C. 6/Hen. VIII/3144.   [12] See p. 163.
[13] C 260/94/34; *Cal. Close*, 1377–81, 434.
[14] *Cal. Close*, 1377–81, 434.
[15] S.R.O., D/D/Vc 20; *Valor Eccl.* (Rec. Com.), i. 198.
[16] *S.R.S.* ii. 113, 297.
[17] B.M. Harl. MS. 594 f. 50.
[18] *Cal. Pat.* 1569–72, pp. 389–90; E 310/23/127 no. 90. Either this or Knole chapel was dedicated to St. Mary Magdalene, the other to St. Peter.
[19] *Valor Eccl.* (Rec. Com.), i. 198.
[20] *S.R.S.* ii. 113, 297; B.M. Harl. MS. 594 f. 50.
[21] *Cal. Pat.* 1569–72, pp. 389–90; E 310/23/127 no. 90.
[22] *S.R.S.* lii. 183.
[23] Ex inf. Mr. P. Poyntz-Wright.
[24] Pevsner, *South and West Som.* 59.

pendicular style. The tower-arch and the arches to both chapels are panelled and it is likely that these parts of the church were the last to be built. In the chancel the sedilia have four-centred heads and there is a trefoil-headed piscina. That the two porches are later additions is suggested by the fact that the buttresses on the nave walls have been cut back to accommodate them.

There is little evidence of the earlier churches on the site. The plain jambs and rear-arch of one of the south aisle windows may indicate that an older opening was adapted for the insertion of Perpendicular tracery. The richly-carved wooden pulpit carries the initials 'I.P.' and 'W.S.' It may therefore date from the time of abbot John Petherton (1424–58) and William Singleton (vicar 1455–62), in which case it would have been made between 1455 and 1458; the figures in the niches were added in 1910.[25] The nave roof, with carved tie-beams and supporting angels, is contemporary with the rest of the building. The fine wooden screen, of the Devon type, stretches across the church, dividing nave from chancel and aisles from chapels. The upper part, including carved fan-vaulting supporting the former rood loft, has been restored. The rood loft stair is housed in a projecting turret on the south side of the church. The 15th-century octagonal font, carved with quatrefoils, has a Jacobean cover. The aisle roofs are 17th-century replacements, that on the north being dated 1691, their repair was the responsibility of the owners of two freeholds in the parish as late as 1798.[26] Outside the church is what appears to be the base of a 15th-century cross, similar to that at Charlton Mackrell;[27] it has much-weathered carved panels and, on the diagonal sides, square attached shafts.

The church has six bells: (i) 1961; (ii) 1618; (iii) 15th century, Exeter foundry; (iv–vi) 1863, Mears. The plate includes a cup and cover of 1781.[28] The registers begin in 1559, but there are gaps for the periods 1654–9 and 1666–1710.

NONCONFORMITY. A Friends' meeting was being held in the parish by 1662.[29] A group of twenty 'sectaries', many if not all Quakers, were presented at a visitation in 1663 for refusing to attend public worship, and marriages without banns and unlicensed burials were reported.[30] There was a permanent meeting-house by 1669, when Robert Ford's house was licensed for use by 100 Quakers under three teachers.[31] In the next year meetings were held in the house of Richard Nowell, one of the 'sectaries' of 1663 and one of the 19 people fined a total of over £153 in that year alone.[32]

Further licences were issued in 1689 for meetings in the house of Richard Nowell, and in 1699 for Samuel Langfield's house.[33] The meeting-house in use in 1970 was erected in 1717.[34]

The Quaker community decreased in numbers in the 18th century and by 1793 only one family was living in the parish. The meeting-house was therefore closed and members went to Somerton.[35] It was re-opened in 1795, alternating with Somerton, was closed again in 1798, and alternated with Somerton again from 1801.[36] This arrangement must have been discontinued by 1828, when the Somerton meeting-house was sold.[37] The Sutton meeting continued and was considerably revived at the end of the 19th century after a series of missions and the establishment of a school.[38]

The house now divided into two dwellings opposite the meeting-house is traditionally the site of Richard Nowell's house.[39] The present meeting-house, dating from 1717[40], stands in a small graveyard. It is a plain rectangular building of local lias, divided horizontally by a Ham stone string-course. The hipped slate roof has stone slates along the eaves and a coved cornice. Sash windows with plain wooden shutters are set in Ham stone frames. Across one end of the building is a passage with a gallery above it, entered from both front and rear by doorways surmounted by segmental hoods on brackets. Internally the original benches survive, as well as the wooden partitions with movable shutters which divide both passage and gallery from the main meeting-room. Ancillary buildings include stabling with a mounting block.

In 1798 a silk-house was licensed for use by a group of Independents.[41] In 1839 a house was licensed on the application of George Lilley, minister.[42] Cottage services were held at Knole by Congregationalists from 1860, and a house was later converted into a chapel. The building, which stood on the south side of Gore Lane, was abandoned by 1896.[43]

Wesleyans held services between 1812 and 1841.[44] In 1844 Francis Masters, Bible Christian minister at Somerton, applied for licence to use a house occupied by John Gould. Gould signed the 1851 return in respect of part of a dwelling-house, which had room for 30 people. Attendances numbered 12 in the afternoon and 23 in the evening of Census Sunday.[45]

In 1850 Samuel Ralls of Load Bridge was licensed to use a building there for worship.[46] Possibly deriving from this licence a group of Brethren were meeting in a chapel holding 120 people by the following year. An average of 15 attended each Sunday morning, but no figure was available for

[25] *Proc. Som. Arch. Soc.* xl(i). 37–40, which makes the pulpit contemporary with the rebuilding.
[26] S.R.O., DD/GS, box 2, 'Autographs, Som. etc.': presentments 1676–80; DD/CC 111365: presentments 1797–8.
[27] See p. 110.
[28] *Proc. Som. Arch. Soc.* xlv. 134.
[29] Besse, *Sufferings* (1753), i. 582, 589.
[30] S.R.O., DD/GS, box 2, 'Autographs, Somerset etc.': chwdns'. presentments.
[31] Turner, *Orig. Recs. Early Nonconformity*, ii. 1126.
[32] Beese, *Sufferings*, i. 603, 609; J. Whiting, *Persecution Exposed*; Street, Friends' Meeting-house, Monthly Meeting mins. 1668–87.
[33] S.R.O., Q/RR, meeting-house lics.

[34] Datestone on building.
[35] S.R.O., DD/SFR 2/1, p. 128.
[36] Street, Friends' Meeting-house, Monthly Meeting mins. 1793–1839, mins. 2 Dec. 1795, 2 Apr. 1798, 3 Apr. 1801.
[37] See p. 151.
[38] See p. 166.
[39] Ex inf. Mr. S. C. Morland.
[40] Datestone on building.
[41] S.R.O., D/D/Rm, box 2.   [42] Ibid.
[43] *Rep. Som. Cong. Union* (1896); S.R.O., C/C, sale cat. Knole estate 1913.
[44] S.R.O., D/N/Sp. c. 1, 2.
[45] S.R.O., D/D/Rm, box 2; H.O. 129/317/2/1/4.
[46] S.R.O., D/D/Rm, box 2.

the evening service.⁴⁷ By 1886 their chapel stood on the south side of Shute Lane, west of the junction with Back Street.⁴⁸ The congregation later transferred to a building on the Langport road west of the Court House. This chapel was used until *c.* 1943, when the members moved to Somerton.⁴⁹

EDUCATION. There were unlicensed schoolmasters in the parish in 1634 and 1663, the former the assistant curate, and another schoolmaster was married there in 1650.⁵⁰ A Quaker school, first proposed in 1700, was established in the old meeting-house in 1719–20, but continued only until 1722.⁵¹

In 1818 there was a Sunday school for 100 pupils and two day-schools for 45 pupils.⁵² A day-school there in 1825–6 was of ill repute, the money for its support being 'utterly thrown away'. A night-school then kept by the assistant curate did 'much good'.⁵³ The Sunday school, financed by subscription, was re-established in 1828 and by 1833 had 41 boys and 58 girls. The day-school then had 24 boys and 16 girls, whose parents paid for their schooling. There were also three infants' schools with some 72 pupils between them. The largest, started in 1832, was supported both by subscriptions and school pence.⁵⁴

In 1840 the vicar conveyed to trustees a plot of land on the west of the green, formerly the site of the vicarage house, on which to erect a schoolroom.⁵⁵ The school was affiliated to the National Society and was financed by government grant, school pence, and a voluntary rate. The building was replaced in 1871 by the present school on the south side of the green, on a site given by the duke of Devonshire. The old buildings became the master's residence.⁵⁶ By 1903 the school could accommodate 125 boys and girls and 70 infants, though average attendances were 92 in the mixed school and 37 in the infants'.⁵⁷ From 1941 the school ceased to take senior pupils and in 1944–5, when it took voluntary aided status, there were 54 children on the books. In 1969 there were 72 children.⁵⁸

A Sunday school was held in the National schoolroom by 1861 and a night-school was established by 1866.⁵⁹ In 1890 a school for nonconformists was opened in a cottage opposite the Friends' meeting-house. Two years later it was transferred to a schoolroom next door known as Temperance Hall. The school continued until 1939.⁶⁰

CHARITIES FOR THE POOR. None known.

YEOVILTON

IN 1901 the parish of Yeovilton, including the hamlets of Bridgehampton and Speckington, measured 1,787 a.¹ It lies 1 mile east of Ilchester on the north bank of the Yeo, and is over 3 miles from east to west and well over 1 mile from north to south. Its southern boundary is formed by the Yeo, by mill streams encircling the parish's meadows, Olam and Bineham, and by Hornsey brook. The short western boundary from Hainbury northwards is the Foss Way; the northern boundary, with Podimore and West Camel, bisects the Puddi moor and then follows two roads. The remainder of the boundary with West Camel interlocks in a complicated fashion, implying a more recent division than the natural or more rational bounds of the rest of the parish. This may be where an estate was added to the original manor in the 11th century.²

The parish lies partly on the alluvium of the Yeo and Cam valleys and partly on clay loam on the Lower Lias. The landscape is flat, lying mostly between the 50 ft. and 75 ft. contours, a natural site for the airfield which now dominates the area. An

exception is Puddi moor in the north-west, a roughly circular area of marsh below 50 ft., divided by drainage channels into the narrow strips in which it was tenanted jointly with the farmers of Podimore.

Tenurial rather than topographical reasons account for the settlement pattern of the parish. Bridgehampton and Speckington, though evidently Saxon in origin, were the centres of two estates which combined in the late 13th century, but were totally independent of the other half of the parish.³ Bridgehampton lies very near the eastern boundary, only 500 yd. from Urgashay in West Camel. Yeovilton, also evidently a Saxon settlement, lies on the southern boundary, with the church at its north-eastern end. Smaller settlements in the parish are at Hainbury, at the extreme western edge, where a mill occurs at the end of the 14th century;⁴ at Rag or Wrag, where labourers' cottages were built by 1838;⁵ and at Stockwitch.⁶ The buildings of the Royal Naval Air Station, H.M.S. Heron, begun in 1940, cover a complex of several acres both north and south of the London road.⁷

⁴⁷ H.O. 129/317/2/1/3.
⁴⁸ O.S. Map 6″, Som. LXXIII. NW. (1886 edn.).
⁴⁹ Ex inf. Mr. A. O. Locke.
⁵⁰ S.R.O., D/D/Ca 297; DD/GS, box 2, 'Autographs, Som. etc.'; par. rec., marr. reg. 4 July 1650.
⁵¹ S.R.O., DD/SFR 1/3: 24 Oct. 1719, 12 Oct. 1722; SFR 4/1: 23 Oct. 1719; Street, Friends' Meeting-house, Monthly Meeting mins. 1687–1723, 31 Aug. 1700, 25 Nov. 1720.
⁵² *Digest of Returns to Sel. Cttee. on Educ. of Poor*, H.C. 224 (1819), ix (2).
⁵³ *Ann. Rep. B. & W. Dioc. Assoc. S.P.C.K.* (1825–6).
⁵⁴ *Educ. Enquiry Abstract*, H.C. 62 (1835), xlii.
⁵⁵ Par. rec., Managers' mins. 1888–1908, *sub anno* 1893.

⁵⁶ S.R.O., DD/EDS: plans by Benj. Gillett of Langport.
⁵⁷ S.R.O., C/E 27.
⁵⁸ Som. C.C. Educ. Cttee, *Schs. List.*
⁵⁹ *P.O. Dir. Som.* (1861, 1866).
⁶⁰ Street, Friends' Meeting-house, Monthly Meeting mins. 1923–43, p. 190; *Kelly's Dir. Som.* (1897).
¹ *Census*, 1901. This article was completed in 1970.
² *V.C.H. Som.* i. 507.
³ See p. 170.
⁴ See p. 172.
⁵ S.R.O., tithe award; D/G/Y 160.
⁶ S.R.O., tithe award.
⁷ A. H. & R. C. Bell, *Account of Parish of Yeovilton* (1949) (hereafter Bell, *Hist. Yeovilton*), 13.

The road pattern, like the tenurial, reflects a clear division between the eastern and western parts of the parish, a division which the airfield further emphasized. Roads from Speckington and Bridgehampton run north, east, and south, and only one route, partly a lane called Box Hedge Lane through inclosed pastures, partly a track across Yeovilton's East or Great field, connected them with Yeovilton until the mid 19th century.[8] Thereafter a footpath formed the link until the airfield was constructed. Yeovilton village lay on a loop from the London road, part of which, Pyle Lane, formed the boundary between the two manors. Until 1952 the only links with Limington across the Yeo were by footpaths through the meadows and footbridges at Squire's gate or Woodbridge.[9] In that year a road was built linking Weir Lane with Limington.[10]

The London road, perhaps Roman in origin,[11] does not seem to have been much used until the early 19th century, and has not affected the settlement pattern.[12] The main route through the parish in the Middle Ages and later was at or near Bridgehampton, the name implying a crossing place of the Cam in Saxon times. One of the assets of Speckington manor in the early 14th century was a toll bar,[13] and as late as the 17th century the road was the main link between the markets of Sherborne (Dors.) and Somerton.[14]

There seem to have been three open fields belonging to Speckington manor in the Middle Ages. West or Western field occurs in 1448 and 1548, and lay probably between the London road, the Bridgehampton road, and Speckington Lane.[15] South field occurs in 1451, and East field, between the roads to Chilton Cantelo and Marston Magna, in the early 18th century.[16] By 1722 both West field and Bridgehampton field, further north, had been reduced to small closes.[17] In contrast Yeovilton retained open fields under strip cultivation until the mid 19th century.[18] Three fields were in use in 1613 and a fourth was named in 1665.[19] West field, bestriding the London road, was divided into Bramble or Brimble Hill, Sun Rush or Sandrush, and Bineham fields by the mid 18th century; Middle field became Harput and Pond fields; East or Great field was undivided until after 1863.[20] The main areas of meadow were Olam, Bincham, Puddi moor, and North mead, the last retaining the boundary stones marking strips until after 1886.[21]

Yeovilton, though not the largest settlement, retains the earliest buildings, mainly lias rubble and thatch cottages of the 17th and 18th centuries. More substantial are Manor and West Farms, both

of lias with Ham stone dressings. Manor Farm has stone-mullioned windows with cavetto mouldings and a continuous string course, indicating early-18th-century origin. Among its buildings is a brick barn.

In 1548 there were 141 communicants in the parish.[22] By 1801 the population was 200. As in most of the neighbouring parishes there was a rise, to a peak of 342 in 1861, and then a rapid decline to 164 in 1901 and 132 by 1921. The increase to 1,285 by 1951 and to 1,319 by 1961 reflects the advent of the air station, though living quarters are largely confined, in the parish, to the station itself, and the ancient settlements have not greatly increased in size.[23]

MANORS AND OTHER ESTATES. An estate in Yeovilton was granted by King Edward to an unnamed thegn between 899 and 925.[24] King Edwy gave a holding of five hides there to Brihtric between 955 and 959.[25] T.R.E. most of Yeovilton formed part of the extensive holding of the king's thegn Aelfstan of Boscombe (Wilts.) and, like his other lands, passed to William, count of Eu, by 1086.[26] The counts probably retained the overlordship until the beginning of the 13th century, when it passed to the Earl Marshal.[27] The marshal was still overlord of part of the estate in 1284–5, and the wardship in respect of property there was certainly disputed in 1318–19 between Aymer de Valence and Thomas de Brotherton, each owner of half the Marshall properties.[28] There is no further trace of the claims of either party, though by 1411 the manor of Yeovilton was said to be held of John Rogers, as of his manor of Barwick, and in 1602 of Henry Lyte, as of the same manor.[29]

Ralph Bluet was tenant under the count of Eu in 1086;[30] the Bluets held land in Hampshire under the counts.[31] William Bluet held a knight's fee in Yeovilton in 1284–5 as mesne tenant, and by 1303 was succeeded by John Bluet.[32] After John's death c. 1317 the family's mesne tenancy seems to have disappeared.

The occupiers of the later manor of YEOVILTON begin with Hugh son of Richard, who held a fee there from 1179 at least until 1183.[33] He may have been the ancestor of the Yeovilton family, a Hugh of Yeovilton having granted some meadow there to the canons of Bruton, probably early in the 13th century.[34] Hugh's grandson William held the property by 1251.[35] William died c. 1280 and was succeeded by his son, also William.[36] In 1284–5 the holding at Yeovilton was assessed at 2 fees, of which William of Yeovilton held three parts; by

[8] S.R.O., DD/X/WDC, map of Speckington and Bridgehampton 1722; tithe award.
[9] S.R.S. xxviii. 161.
[10] S.R.O., D/P/yeon 17/3/1.
[11] See p. 179.   [12] See p. 182.
[13] Cal. Inq. p.m. v, p. 389.
[14] S.R.S. xxiv. 99.
[15] S.R.O., DD/CC 12462; DD/X/WDC; tithe award.
[16] S.R.O., DD/X/WDC; Alnwick Castle, Northumberland MSS., XII 12 3b; S.R.S. ii. 299.
[17] S.R.O., DD/X/WDC.
[18] See p. 172.
[19] S.R.O., D/D/Rg 235; DD/PH 60.
[20] S.R.O., DD/PH 60; DD/FS, box 31; D/G/Y 160; tithe award.
[21] O.S. Map 6", Som. LXXIII. SE. (1885 edn.).
[22] S.R.S. ii. 114.

[23] V.C.H. Som. ii. 348; Census, 1911–61.
[24] Finberg, Early Charters of Wessex, p. 129.
[25] Ibid. p. 139.
[26] V.C.H. Som. i. 507; Stenton, Anglo-Saxon Eng. 480.
[27] V.C.H. Hants, iv. 52–3.
[28] Feud. Aids, iv. 285; Year Bk. 1318 (Selden Soc.), 123 et seq.; 1319, 5–6; V.C.H. Hants, iv. 52–3.
[29] C 137/82/23; C 142/268/142.
[30] V.C.H. Som. i. 507.
[31] V.C.H. Hants, iv. 52–3.
[32] Feud. Aids, iv. 285, 300.
[33] Pipe R. 1179 (P.R.S. xxviii), 71; 1183 (P.R.S. xxxii), 28.
[34] S.R.S. viii. 74. The manor there appears to belong to Bruton.
[35] Cal. Pat. 1247–58, 265; S.R.S. viii. 74.
[36] S.R.S. xliv. 192, 346

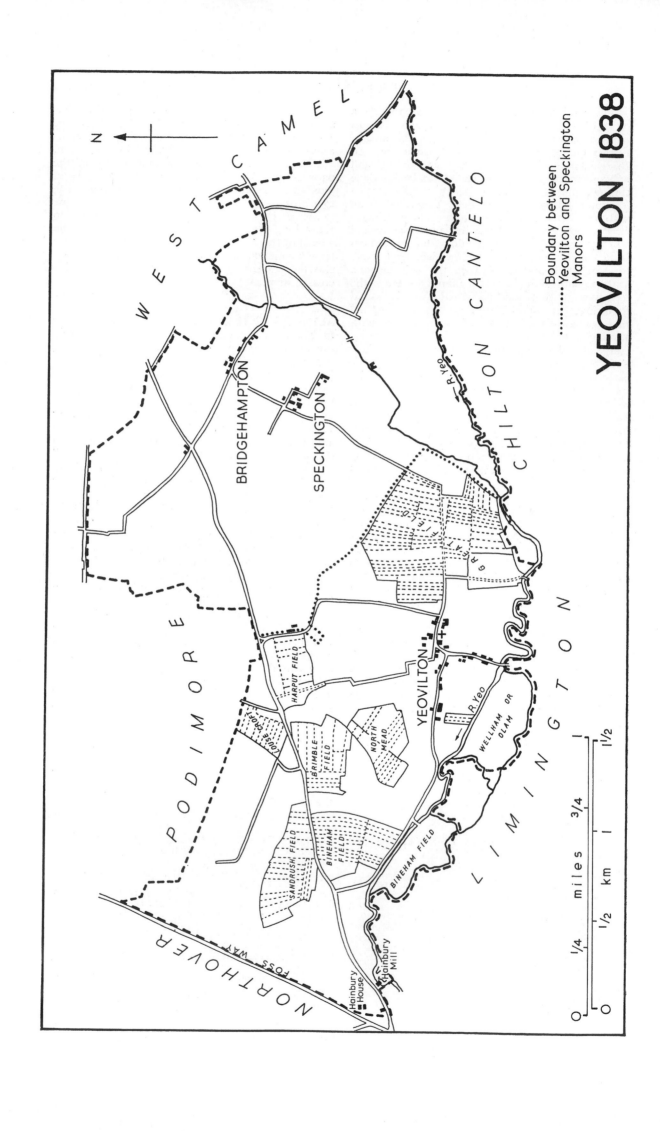

YEOVILTON 1838

Boundary between Yeovilton and Speckington Manors

1303 the assessment was only 1 fee, of which William of Yeovilton held three quarters.[37]

The estate was further divided during the 14th century. By 1316 the holder seems to have been Robert Martin of Athelhampton (Dors.), to whom it may have passed by marriage;[38] Robert Martin and Ralph of Yeovilton shared one fee there in 1346.[39] Martin's estate had by 1377 passed to John Cobham of Blackborough (Devon) (d. 1389) and to his wife Catherine, daughter of Sir William Bonville, and in that year was settled on Cobham's heir's, with remainder to Bonville and his son.[40] John Wyke of Nynehead (d. 1410), Catherine's second husband, held the property in her right at his death, and in 1412 her third husband Humphrey Stafford was returned as owner.[41] On Catherine's death in 1417 the property reverted to William Bonville, grandson of Sir William and Catherine's nephew.[42] Bonville (cr. Lord Bonville 1449) settled Yeovilton on William Tailboys (d. 1464) on his marriage with Bonville's daughter Elizabeth.[43] Elizabeth died in 1491, and her son Sir Robert Tailboys in 1495.[44] Sir Robert's son George died in 1538, outliving his own son Gilbert (cr. Lord Tailboys 1529).[45] Gilbert's son George died in 1540 and his eventual heir was his sister Elizabeth (d. c. 1563), Baroness Tailboys, wife successively of Thomas Wymbish (d. 1552–3) and Ambrose Dudley.[46] George, Lord Tailboys, had held Yeovilton jointly with his wife Margaret; she lost it temporarily through the implication of her second husband Sir Peter Carew of Luppitt (Devon) in Wyatt's rebellion, but it was restored after his pardon in 1556, subject to the reversionary interest of Elizabeth, Lady Tailboys, then wife of Ambrose Dudley.[47]

Elizabeth and her husband sold their interest to the Carews in 1557, shortly before the manor was purchased by Thomas Southcott of Shillingford (Devon).[48] Just over two years later, early in 1560, Southcott sold it to Thomas Cary of Cockington (Devon).[49] The Carys remained owners until debt forced them to sell early in the 18th century. Thomas Cary sold the property to his brother Robert (d. 1586), of Clovelly (Devon), in 1560–61.[50] Robert was succeeded by his son George (d. 1601), and by his grandson William (d. 1652).[51] William was followed by his sons Sir Robert (d. 1675) and George, dean of Exeter (d. 1680), and then by George's eldest son Sir George (d. 1685).[52] William Cary, Sir George's brother, under Act of Parlia-

ment of 1704, was allowed to break settlement of the estate to pay his late brother's debts,[53] and the land was sold in 1715 to William Cleveland of Tapeley in Westleigh (Devon).[54] Cleveland still held it in 1721,[55] but it seems to have come into the possession of Sir William Dodwell of Sevenhampton (Glos.) (d. 1727), whose trustees sold it in 1762 to Thomas Lockyer of Ilchester.[56]

On Lockyer's death in 1785 Yeovilton passed to his daughter Elizabeth, wife of Edward Phelips the younger (d. 1792).[57] She disposed of the estate to Samuel Rodbard of Evercreech in 1794–5,[58] and he retained it until 1822–3 when it passed to Mrs. Mary Brettingham.[59] She still held it in 1838.[60] The property was then no longer described as a manor, but it comprised virtually the whole of the tithing of Yeovilton. The holding was purchased by G. D. W. Digby of Sherborne Castle (Dors.) in 1857, and remained with the Digby family until 1919.[61] It was then sold to the tenants of the constituent farms.[62]

Part of the holding of William of Yeovilton in the early 14th century passed by 1346 to Ralph of Yeovilton.[63] Ralph married the heiress of the Somerton family, and their son Peter in 1386 settled a considerable estate in Yeovilton, Speckington, Bridgehampton, and elsewhere on Margery, wife of Thomas Payn, probably his daughter.[64] Catherine, daughter of Margery and Thomas, married successively John Stourton of Preston Plucknett (d. 1439), John Beynton, and William Carent (d. 1476), and died in 1473 leaving as her heir Giles Daubeney, grandson of John Stourton.[65] Land in Speckington was settled by Henry, Lord Daubeney (d. 1548), on his wife Catherine in 1532, but its subsequent history as a separate estate has not been traced.[66]

The fourth part of a fee in Yeovilton was held in 1284–5 by Elizabeth of Clevedon and Baudry of Nonnington.[67] Matthew (II) of Clevedon had succeeded by 1303, and John (III) of Clevedon by 1332.[68] The second died c. 1373,[69] and was succeeded by his grand-daughter Margaret (d. 1412), wife successively of Sir John St. Lo (d. 1375) and Sir Peter Courtenay (d. 1405). Her heir was her grandson William, Lord Botreaux (d. 1462).[70] In 1458 Botreaux gave his estate, described as a manor, in Yeovilton to Bath priory.[71] By 1545 the property, described as a messuage and lands in Bridgehampton, five messuages in Yeovilton, and a quarter of

[37] Feud. Aids, iv. 285, 300.
[38] Ibid. 321; Hutchins, Hist. Dors. ii. 582; S.R.S. xv. 183–4.
[39] Feud. Aids, iv. 344. See also Cal. Pat. 1338–40, 352–4; 1340–3, 302; 1343–5, 110; Cal. Fine R. 1337–47, 510; S.R.S. viii. 75.
[40] S.R.S. xvii. 194; Cal. Close, 1389–92, 18; C 136/54/11.
[41] C 137/82/23; Feud. Aids, vi. 508.
[42] Cal. Fine R. 1413–22, 206; Cal. Close, 1413–19, 467–8.
[43] Cal. Inq. p.m. Hen. VII, i, p. 299; Wedgwood, Hist. Parl. Biogs. 835; Complete Peerage, s.v. Kyme.
[44] Cal. Inq. p.m. Hen. VII, i, pp. 299, 451.
[45] Complete Peerage, s.v. Tailboys.
[46] Ibid.
[47] Cal. Pat. 1555–7, 534–5, 552–3.
[48] S.R.O., DD/PH 60.
[49] Ibid.
[50] Ibid.
[51] C 142/268/142; Som. Wills, ed. Brown, ii. 216; iii. 93.
[52] J. L. Vivian, Visit. of Devon.

[53] House of Lords Papers, v. 356; 2–3 Anne, c. 33.
[54] S.R.O., DD/PH 60.
[55] Ibid.
[56] C.P. 43/715 rot. 59.
[57] S.R.O., Q/RE, land tax assessments.
[58] Ibid.   [59] Ibid.
[60] S.R.O., tithe award.
[61] Sherborne, Digby Estate Office, rent bks.
[62] Ibid.
[63] Feud. Aids, iv. 344.
[64] S.R.S. xv. 183; xvii. 133–4; xlii, pp. xiii–iv, 98.
[65] C 140/44/30; Proc. Som. Arch. Soc. lxxxi, suppl. 85–6, 90, 108.
[66] C 54/401 m. 14.
[67] Feud. Aids, iv. 285.
[68] Ibid. 344; Proc. Som. Arch. Soc. xli. 9 and opp. 36; Hist. MSS. Com. 78, Hastings, i. 247.
[69] Proc. Som. Arch. Soc. xli. 9; lxxix, suppl. 29.
[70] C 137/86/30; S.R.S. xvii. 142–3; Feud. Aids, vi. 507; Cal. Close, 1402–5, 445–6.
[71] Maclean, Hist. Trigg Minor, i. 638n; Cat. Anct. D. iii. A 5499, 5506.

Hainbury mill, was granted by the Crown to two agents.[72]

It may have been this small estate which, described as a quarter of the manor of Yeovilton, was sold by Thomas Cogan of Montacute to John Brome of Wigborough in 1553.[73] Brome (d. 1558) devised his property jointly to his daughter Elizabeth, wife of James Compton, and to Brome Johnson (d. 1586), his grandson by his daughter Joan.[74] Half the property, therefore, descended from Elizabeth (d. 1579) to her son Henry, and then to her grand-daughter Alice.[75] Brome Johnson's half descended to his son Emorb (d. 1615), on whose marriage to his cousin Alice Compton in 1610 the two halves were re-united.[76] Emorb's heirs were his daughters Penelope, Elizabeth, and Frances. The last did not survive to majority, and the estate descended jointly to Penelope, wife of Sir Thomas Hele (d. 1630), and Elizabeth (d. 1631), wife of John Harris, both of whom died shortly after childbirth.[77] The descent of the properties has not been further traced.

An estate, sometimes described as a manor, at Bridgehampton, was held as ½ fee of William Bluet as of the Earl Marshal in 1284–5, and probably therefore had originally been part of the holding of Aelfstan of Boscombe.[78] In 1303 it was said to be held in chief, but in 1315 to be held of William of Yeovilton for ¼ fee.[79] In 1354 and again at the end of the 15th century it was said to be held of the Crown.[80]

By 1281 the tenant was Sir Robert FitzPayn, who in that year was succeeded by his son Robert, Lord FitzPayn (d. 1315).[81] The younger Robert by his death in 1315 added to his holding the adjoining estate of Speckington and the combined holding was normally known as the manor of *SPECKINGTON AND BRIDGEHAMPTON*.[82] Previously, in 1284–5, Speckington had been held by a different tenant of a different honor from the rest of the parish: it was held of the earl of Gloucester, the actual tenant, Robert de Mere, holding ½ fee of Walter de Tornhull,[83] Walter of John Mautravers, and John of the earl.[84] By 1315 Robert, Lord FitzPayn, held an estate of 80 a. in Speckington of John Mautravers in socage, and the manor of Bridgehampton for ¼ fee of William of Yeovilton. Speckington was held of the heir of John Mautravers in 1446, and of the king in 1484.[85]

Under a settlement made in 1324 Robert, Lord FitzPayn (d. 1354) and his wife Ela were to retain this and other properties for their lives, with remainder to Robert Grey of Codnor, their nephew,[86] subject to the life interest of John de Vere, earl of Oxford, through his wife, the widow of Robert FitzPayn's heir.[87] Grey, who took the name Fitz-Payn, acquired the estate from Vere in 1359.[88] FitzPayn died in 1393, leaving as his heir his daughter Isabel, wife of Richard, Lord Poynings; her death a year later left her son Robert Poynings, a minor, to succeed.[89] Robert, who was said in 1431 to hold the manors of Bridgehampton and Specking-ton for a tenth of a fee,[90] died in 1446, when his heir was his grand-daughter Eleanor, wife of Sir Henry Percy, later earl of Northumberland (d 1461).[91] The countess died in 1484,[92] and the property seems to have reverted to the Crown, being granted in that year to trustees for the payment of the duke of Buckingham's debts, and then in 1485 to John Howard, duke of Norfolk.[93]

Henry, earl of Northumberland (d. 1527), re-covered the property in 1501,[94] but his son sold it in 1535 to Henry Pole, Lord Montague, and two others, probably acting as feoffees for Henry Courtenay, marquess of Exeter.[95] Courtenay cer-tainly acquired the land, though a fine in 1536 gave the holding, with the rest of the Northumberland estates, to the Crown.[96] The Crown certainly held it from Courtenay's attainder and execution in 1539 until 1545.[97] In that year the 'manor and lord-ship of Bridgehampton cum Speckington' was sold to William Hodges of Middle Chinnock and to his second son, also William, of London.[98]

Shortly before his death in 1565 William Hodges the elder settled the property on a younger son William with contingent remainders, though half of the capital messuage of Speckington was in the hands of John Hodges.[99] On the death of William the elder the manor passed to Bartholomew his grandson who in 1570 sold it to William Hodges of Speckington.[1] William died in 1580, leaving as his heirs his brother John and his nephews William and Thomas.[2] In 1597 John Hodges of Lufton, perhaps the brother, sold his interest to William Hodges of Speckington.[3] In 1618 William sold it to John Hunt (d. 1660).[4]

The property was held by the Hunt family of Speckington and Compton Pauncefoot until the 19th century. John Hunt was succeeded by his son Robert (d. 1679), sheriff and M.P. for Ilchester and the county,[5] and it passed from father to eldest son in succession, through John Hunt (d. 1721), John (d. 1740), and John (d. 1807) to John Hubert, who in 1827 sold the estate, then comprising over 615 a.

[72] *L. & P. Hen. VIII*, xx(2), p. 544.
[73] *S.R.S.* li. 45–6.
[74] C 142/214/241; *Som. Wills*, ed. Brown, iv. 23.
[75] C 142/228/55; *Som. Wills*, ed. Brown, iv. 24.
[76] *S.R.S.* lxvii. 121.
[77] C 142/761/128, 130.
[78] *Feud. Aids*, iv. 285.
[79] Ibid. 299; *Cal. Inq. p.m.* v, p. 389.
[80] *Cal. Inq. p.m.* x, p. 150; *Cal. Pat.* 1354–8, 156; C 141/2/26.
[81] *Cal. Inq. p.m.* ii, p. 232.
[82] Ibid. v, p. 389; *Feud. Aids*, iv. 321, 429; *S.R.S.* xii. 93. Perhaps this originated as the two hides held by the thegns T.R.E.: *V.C.H. Som.* i. 507.
[83] Or Thornhull.
[84] *Feud. Aids*, iv. 285.
[85] *Cal. Inq. p.m.* v, p. 389; C 139/126/24; C 141/2/26.
[86] *S.R.S.* xii. 93; *Complete Peerage*, s.v. Grey of Codnor.
[87] C.P. 40/273 rot. 45d; 291 rot. 165d; 292 rot. 335; *Cal. Pat.* 1350–4, 202; 1354–8, 156; *Cal. Inq. p.m.* x, p. 150.

[88] *Cal. Fine R.* 1391–9, 84; *Complete Peerage*, s.v. Grey of Codnor; *S.R.S.* xvii. 42.
[89] C 136/75/12, 82/46, 106/37.
[90] *Feud. Aids*, iv. 429.
[91] C 139/126/24.
[92] C 141/2/26.
[93] *Cal. Pat.* 1476–85, 497.
[94] C.P. 40/955 rot. 311.
[95] C.P. 25(2)/51/370/26 Hen. VIII East.
[96] C.P. 325(2)/71/27 Hen. VIII Hil.; E 329/421; *Stat. R.* 27 Hen. VIII, c. 47.
[97] S.C. 6/Hen. VIII/3062–3, 6164–7.
[98] *L. & P. Hen. VIII*, i, p. 660.
[99] C 142/142/77, 193/78; *Cal. Pat.* 1563–9, p. 518.
[1] C 60/391 m. 35; *S.R.S.* li. 115–16.
[2] C 142/193/78; *Som. Wills*, ed. Brown, iii. 69.
[3] C.P. 25(2)/207/39 Eliz. I East.
[4] C.P. 25(2)/346/16 Jas. I Trin.; *Proc. Som. Arch. Soc.* lxxxiv, suppl. 171.
[5] *Proc. Som. Arch. Soc.* lxxxiv, suppl. 171; cviii, suppl. 40.

to G. H. Law, bishop of Bath and Wells, when it became part of the property of the See.[6] The estate was transferred to the Ecclesiastical Commissioners in 1866–7, and large parts of it were taken over by the Royal Naval Air Station in 1940.[7]

In its present form Speckington Manor is probably early 19th century, but it incorporates many features of a substantial 17th-century house, some of which appear to be *in situ*, and there are traces of a moat.

An endowment of 62 a. of arable, meadow, and pasture in Bridgehampton and Speckington was given in 1315 by Robert, Lord FitzPayn, to the 'parson' of the chapel of Speckington, to celebrate daily for the grantor, his ancestors, and his heirs.[8] In 1548, when the chapel was dissolved, the estate amounted to 55 a. and various tithes.[9] The chapel, except the lead, bells, and advowson, was sold in 1549 to Edward Bury of Eastwood (Essex).[10] Giles Hodges held it before 1565, and William his son succeeded in 1592.[11] Hodges sold the chapel, together with its estate of just over 53 a., in 1606 to the trustees of Ilminster school.[12] The Church Commissioners bought the land from the school in 1948.[13]

ECONOMIC HISTORY. The Domesday estate of Ralph Bluet in Yeovilton, together with the additional holding of the five thegns, paid geld for 10 hides. The 4-hide demesne farm at Yeovilton was cultivated by 4 serfs with 3 ploughs, and the other 4 hides by 6 villeins and 6 bordars with 5 ploughs. There are no details for the additional 2 hides. There were 90 a. of meadow and 40 a. of pasture with 4 horses, 12 beasts (*animalia*), 16 pigs, and 100 sheep.[14] The predominance of arable continued until the 14th century and probably throughout the Middle Ages. There was three times as much arable as meadow and pasture on the demesne at Speckington in 1315,[15] and the rector received no tithes of wool in 1334 and very few in 1535.[16] Yet between 1448 and 1456 there were three flocks each of 200 sheep at Speckington,[17] and some inclosure had taken place there by the mid 14th century.[18]

Agricultural works had been commuted on Speckington manor by 1315 for a payment of 19s., and the manor included a freehold worth 12s. and a cottar holding worth 52s. 11d.[19] By 1538 the demesne was farmed for £8 and freeholders and tenants at will together paid fixed rents totalling £8 15s. 3d.[20] This was a decrease from the income a century earlier; in 1439 the new rental amounted to £10 2s. 8d., but by 1451 at least three sixty-acre holdings, complete with farmsteads, were let at reduced rents 'until better tenants should come'.[21]

By the early 17th century Yeovilton manor measured 530 a., of which 254 a. were arable, mostly in open-field cultivation. Pasture amounted to 185 a.,

and there were some 60 a. in the common meadows as well as the unspecified area of Bineham mead. Ten acres in 1619 were described as arable, recently inclosed for pasture, and by 1665 other small areas, formerly arable and pasture, were completely converted to pasture.[22] A small amount of the rectory estate was similarly inclosed from an open arable field, together with a piece of common meadow.[23]

In 1619 most of Yeovilton manor was divided among 16 tenants, 7 holding farms of between 52 a. and 64 a.; by 1665 two holdings had been combined, making a total of 79 a. These 16 tenants in 1619 held either for lives or by copyhold, and all were subject to heriots of the best goods. In addition there were 6 small freeholds, a close in Puddi moor held by suit of court only, and land in Bridgehampton held for the payment of a red rose on the farm door once a year. By 1665 a distinction was made between 13 holdings, almost unchanged from the largest of those of 1619 and half still held by the same families, and 6 holdings, one copyhold and the rest held on leases for lives, amounting to some 170 a., which had evidently been added to the manor since 1619. The total acreage of the manor was thus just over 700 a., of which about 315 a. were arable and 260 a. pasture.

Two of the large meadows in the manor, Bineham and Olam, were subject to complicated common rights. Rights in Bineham were reckoned in terms of beasts allowed to graze there. Seven of the 16 main tenants of 1619 were permitted to run 118 sheep and a variable number of cows, four tenants between them having 18 cow leazes each year, and three being allowed 4½ leazes normally and 5 leazes every second or third year. Olam was usually reckoned in units of acres, and tenants acquired extra parcels every second, third, or fourth year. The land added to the manor by 1665 had 12¼ leazes in Bineham but no rights in Olam. Bineham was therefore subject to 44¼ leazes for cattle in 1665, to be compared with the 45½ claimed in the 19th century.[24] North mead was also subject to common rights and the rector, at any rate, could not pasture his sheep on common arable after the breach, but only 6 oxen and 2 horses.

There is no direct evidence of the prosperity of the parish in the 17th century, though the rental of the manor in 1619 of £24 7s. 4d. may be compared with the valuation of nearly £377 for the same properties in 1665, and £538 for the whole estate.[25] The general economic improvement is reflected in the rebuilding of three farm-houses by 1619 and a further two by 1665.[26]

Details of stock and produce in the 17th century are confined largely to the indirect evidence of grazing rights for sheep, oxen, horses, and cows.[27] In the early 18th century two farmers working the inclosed pasture lands of Speckington and Bridgehampton specialized in stock raising. 'Colonel' Hunt in 1719 paid tithe for 28 young beasts,

[6] S.R.O., DD/CC 12462–3, 12473, 13344.
[7] Ex inf. Church Commrs.
[8] *Cal. Pat.* 1313–17, 210.
[9] *S.R.S.* ii. 114, 299.
[10] *Cal. Pat.* 1549–51, 121.
[11] C 142/142/77.
[12] R. T. Graham and F. S. Carpenter, *Ilminster Grammar School*, 34; Bell, *Hist. Yeovilton*, 9.
[13] Bell, *Hist. Yeovilton*, 9.
[14] *V.C.H. Som.* i. 507.
[15] C 134/48/5.

[16] E 179/169/14; *Valor Eccl.* (Rec. Com.), i. 199.
[17] Alnwick Castle, Northumberland MSS., X II 12 3b.
[18] *Cal. Pat.* 1350–4, 202.
[19] C 134/48/5.
[20] S.C. 6/Hen. VIII/3062–3, 6164–7.
[21] Northumberland MSS., X II 12 3b, 9a VI.
[22] S.R.O., DD/PH 60.
[23] S.R.O., D/D/Rg 235.
[24] S.R.O., tithe award.
[25] S.R.O., DD/PH 60.
[26] Ibid.   [27] Ibid.; D/D/Rg 235.

3 heifers, and 15 oxen for the whole year, and for 80 sheep for five months and 40 more for seven weeks. 'Farmer' Hunt in the same year paid on 30 milking cows, 14 oxen, and 40 ewes. In 1725 the latter's herd was only 26, but his flock increased to 50 ewes and 30 wethers.[28] Arable still remained of greater importance in Yeovilton manor, where the three-year rotation of wheat, Lent crop, and clover, potatoes, or fallow was strictly adhered to.[29] Apples were also grown in considerable quantities and provided an important source of income for the rector.[30]

The development of consolidated farming units came early to the inclosed lands of Speckington and Bridgehampton. Speckington was already a 'farm place' by 1580,[31] and in 1700 there was a substantial holding there of 236 a.[32] The property in the 18th century was divided between 'Hodges' farm', the slightly smaller 'Great House Estate', and a third farm held by one Pitman.[33] By 1825 the division was between 'Upper farm' (315 a.), 'Lower farm' (162 a.), and other lands totalling in all 615 a.[34] 'Upper farm' soon became known as Speckington farm. By 1845 it measured nearly 500 a. and was let for £835 a year.[35] 'Lower farm' buildings were shortly afterwards disused, the acreage of the farm having been radically reduced, and evidently later merged with the larger farm.[36] By 1867 Speckington farm was just over 599 a.[37] By the same date 244 a. were attached to Courtry House, Bridgehampton, and there was another small holding, making a total of c. 275 a.[38] Stockwitch farm increased from 26 a. in 1838 to over 61 a. by 1885.[39] Manor farm, Bridgehampton, emerged from a regrouping of holdings about 1890,[40] and Hills and Springfield farms were created by 1923 and 1939 respectively.[41]

In the other half of the parish the largest unit was Manor farm, with over 300 a.[42] By 1867 regrouping of the Digby estate left most of the manor, some 642 a., in the hands of one farmer, who held a further 86 a. of other owners, including most of the rectory estate.[43] By 1885 his holding had increased to over 708 a. The main farm was divided in 1897 to form West and Manor farms.

In 1838 there were 1,067 a. of meadow and pasture in the parish compared with 604 a. of arable.[44] By 1905 grass had increased to 1,251 a.[45] Dairying and stock raising were of importance in Bridgehampton and Speckington and one farmer there was well-known as a breeder of shire horses.[46] Arable played a more significant part in the mixed farming of the western half of the parish until

inclosure in the mid 19th century. East or Great field in 1838 amounted to 94 a. in 70 strips; Bineham and Sandrush fields, each only a third of the area, had 20 and 22 strips, and Brimble, Louse Croft, Harput, and Hills were similarly fragmented.[47] Exactly when these strips were consolidated is not clear. There were still traces of East field and Sunrush in 1863,[48] and inclosure probably began after 1857 when the Digbys acquired the estate. Later improvements in farming conditions included sixteen new cottages on the Digby estate and seven erected by the Ecclesiastical Commissioners in 1885.[49]

The pattern of farming remained stable until 1940 when large areas were sold to the Admiralty for the airfield. The Church Commissioners sold some 210 a. in Speckington in that year and a further 42 a. in 1950. Sales in Yeovilton included most of West farm and some 29 a. of glebe.[50]

There were two mills in 1086, together paying 30s., one sixth of the value of the whole estate.[51] One belonged to the manor of Bridgehampton in 1315 and was worth 30s.[52] This was known as Baymylle or Raylemylle in 1448,[53] and probably stood on the Cam in a field later known as Mill Ham, between Bridgehampton and Urgashay.[54] Hainbury mill stood on the Yeo at the western end of the parish. As Hayneberghmyll it occurs in 1392[55] and in 1545 one quarter of it, formerly part of the manor of Yeovilton and later belonging to Bath priory, was granted by the Crown to two agents.[56] Three quarters descended with the rest of Yeovilton manor to the Carys, and John Hodges held it of them in 1619.[57] It was evidently still part of the manor during the 18th century.[58] By 1826 it was known as Hainbury Factory, and it continued in use until c. 1920.[59] The mill-house was occupied in 1970 but the mill was a roofless shell.

In 1254 William of Yeovilton was granted an annual fair at Yeovilton, to be held on the eve, feast, and morrow of St. Bartholomew (24 Aug.).[60] No further trace of the fair has been found.

LOCAL GOVERNMENT. Court rolls for the manor of Speckington and Bridgehampton survive for the periods 1447–52, 1455–9, and 1480–1,[61] but for Yeovilton only for 1674.[62] At least from 1710 until 1874 successive rectors held courts, described as manor courts and courts baron, in respect of their glebe.[63] The Speckington manor court met twice a year, at Michaelmas and Hockday. A reeve was

[28] S.R.O., D/P/yeon 3/2/2.
[29] Ibid. 3/2/1.
[30] Ibid.
[31] C 142/193/78.
[32] S.R.O., DD/CC 12462.
[33] S.R.O., Q/RE, land tax assessments, 1766, 1780.
[34] S.R.O., DD/CC 12473, 13347.
[35] Ibid. 12479.
[36] Ibid. 12477, 12479.
[37] Ibid. 12476; D/G/Y 160.
[38] S.R.O., D/G/Y 160.
[39] S.R.O., tithe award; D/G/Y 160.
[40] S.R.O., D/G/Y 160.
[41] Kelly's Dir. Som. (1923, 1939).
[42] S.R.O., tithe award.
[43] S.R.O., D/G/Y 160.
[44] S.R.O., tithe award.
[45] Statistics supplied by the then Bd. of Agric.
[46] Bell, Hist. Yeovilton, 13.
[47] S.R.O., tithe award.

[48] S.R.O., D/G/Y 160.
[49] Ibid.
[50] Ibid.; ex inf. Church Commrs.
[51] V.C.H. Som. i. 507.
[52] C 134/48/5.
[53] Northumberland MSS., X II 12 3b.
[54] S.R.O., DD/X/WDC: map 1722; tithe award.
[55] Hunt. Libr., HA Manorial, Somerton hundred ct. roll, 1392–3.
[56] L. & P. Hen. VIII, xx(2), p. 543.
[57] S.R.O., DD/PH 60.
[58] S.R.O., D/P/yeon 3/2/1–2.
[59] S.R.O., D/T/ilch: bk. of maps, 1826; Kelly's Dir. Som. (1919, 1923).
[60] Cal. Pat. 1247–58, 265.
[61] Northumberland MSS., X II 12 3b.
[62] S.R.O., DD/PH 60.
[63] S.R.O., DD/FS, box 31, copy court baron 1784. The manor ct. bk. 1710 to 1874 and other manorial papers of the rectory cannot be traced: Som. Par. Docs. ed. J. E. King, 399.

chosen annually at Michaelmas from one or more nominees of the homage; a hayward was evidently appointed by the lord. Yeovilton manor court employed a hayward, the office probably shared between nine tenants each holding a 'hayward's leaze' in Bineham mead.[64]

The two tithings of Bridgehampton or Speckington and Yeovilton probably followed the manorial divisions of the parish. Each tithing was separately assessed for poor rate by the beginning of the 19th century but the overseers, one each year until 1844 and then two, acted for both tithings together. Their accounts were submitted annually to the vestry. The vestry appointed a paid constable from 1842 and a paid assistant overseer from 1866.[65]

The overseers were renting a poorhouse by 1822.[66] Thereafter they not only provided relief in cash but regularly paid rents, bought coal, and in 1829 sent a man and his family to Weymouth for a holiday after illness.[67] The poorhouse was given up in 1835[68] and in 1970 was a private house known as Manor Cottage. The parish became part of the Yeovil poor-law union in 1836.[69] The church supported a clothing club, a boot club, and a sick and aged poor fund as late as 1912.[70]

CHURCH. Architectural evidence places the foundation of the church in Norman times but documentary evidence dates only from the end of the 13th century: the advowson of the rectory was granted by Sir William of Yeovilton to Montacute priory at some date between 1272 and 1282, probably in 1275.[71] Before August 1291 the monks sold it to Robert Burnell, bishop of Bath and Wells,[72] who apparently intended to give it to the chapter of Wells. The Burnell family retained it at least until 1294,[73] and the chapter still had hopes of acquiring it as late as 1307.[74] The then bishop, however, secured it from the Burnell family, and the patronage has since that time remained with the diocesan, except in the case of vacancies,[75] the result of lapse,[76] and when the episcopal estates and other properties were out of the bishop's hands.[77] The presentation in 1616 was made by Jasper and John Bourne by grant of the bishop,[78] and that in 1656 by the Lord Protector.[79] The Crown presented in 1897.[80] The rectory was sequestrated in 1952 and became a

curacy-in-charge held since c. 1965 with Kingsdon, Podimore, and Babcary.[81]

The benefice was assessed at £23 6s. 8d. in 1291[82] and at £26 9s. 1½d. net in 1535.[83] About 1549 it was said to be worth £32[84] and about 1668 £100.[85] The average net income by 1831 was £445[86] and tithes, glebe, and fees together were worth £542 in 1851.[87] The serious fall in the value of the tithe rent-charge in the later 19th century brought the net value of the benefice down to £278 in 1902.[88]

Tithe corn was worth 20s. in 1334 and oblations and small tithes £4 8s. 8d.[89] By 1535 predial tithes were worth £16, tithe wool and lambs £2, and oblations and personal tithes £5.[90] By the 18th century much of the tithe hay had been exchanged for holdings of meadow in the parish, but corn, wool, lambs, and Easter dues, principally apples, were still payable.[91] An early modus gave the rector 3d. a year for every milking cow. By the mid 18th century compositions were in force covering what were known as vicarial tithes, some of them negotiated by George Swayne when he was both lessee of the rectory and curate of the parish between 1662 and 1671. The final composition abolishing tithes in kind was made in 1762.[92] The rector had, from the 16th century, received only half the tithes due from certain fields formerly attached to Speckington chapel.[93] A rent-charge of £462 was awarded in 1838 in lieu of compositions.[94]

By 1334 the glebe comprised 80 a. of arable and 14 a. of meadow, worth together 103s. 6d., assessed rents of 24s., and pasturage worth 15s.[95] The rector's demesne was said to be worth only £4 in 1535.[96] By 1613 there were over 83 a. in hand and four separate holdings, one in Bridgehampton and three in Yeovilton, amounting to over 69 a., let to tenants.[97] By 1838 the estate had been reduced to 65 a.,[98] and in 1862, after several exchanges, it was just over 66 a.[99] Some 40 a. were sold between 1919 and 1923,[1] and all but 4 a., with a house and gardens, were sold to the Admiralty for the airfield in 1940.[2]

The former Rectory was in origin small and rectangular but was extended to form an H-shaped building in the late 16th century. Thereafter there was a hall, parlour, three butteries with chambers over, a study, a kitchen with an adjoining bunting-house, a dairy with two chambers over, and various outbuildings.[3] Substantial reconstruction took place

[64] S.R.O., DD/PH 60, survey 1619.
[65] S.R.O., D/P/yeon 4/1/1.
[66] Ibid.   [67] Ibid.
[68] S.R.O., tithe award.
[69] Poor Law Com. 2nd Rep. p. 550.
[70] S.R.O., D/P/yeon 17/3/1.
[71] S.R.S. viii. 151. Witnessed by Sir William de Mohun (1254–82) who would not have been knighted until 1272 at the earliest: H. Maxwell-Lyte, Hist. Dunster, i. 33. Sir William of Yeovilton answered the prior of Montacute in the King's court in 1275 concerning the advowson: C.P. 40/9 rot. 2.
[72] Cal. Chart. R. 1257–1300, 404.
[73] Cal. Inq. p.m. iii, p. 124.
[74] H.M.C. Wells, i. 204; ii. 583–4; S.R.S. vii. 116.
[75] Cal. Pat. 1385–9, 207; 1422–9, 255.
[76] Ibid. 1569–72, p. 209.
[77] Ibid. 1563–9, p. 164.
[78] Som. Incumbents, ed. Weaver, 230.
[79] Lambeth Palace MSS., COMM A/5/36.
[80] Dioc. Kal.
[81] Dioc. Dir. (1966–70).
[82] Tax. Eccl. (Rec. Com.), 197.
[83] Valor Eccl. (Rec. Com.), i. 199.

[84] S.R.S. ii. 114.
[85] S.R.O., D/D/Vc 24.
[86] Rep. Com. Eccl. Revenues, pp. 186–7.
[87] H.O. 129/319/5/5/7.
[88] S.R.O., tithe award; D/G/Y 160.
[89] E 179/169/14.
[90] Valor Eccl. (Rec. Com.), i. 199.
[91] S.R.O., D/D/Rg 235: glebe terriers 1613 and 1640, partially transcribed and with early-18th-century additions in S. & D. N. & Q. xxii. 253–7. Also S.R.O., D/P/yeon 3/2/1–2, tithe accts. and papers.
[92] S.R.O., D/P/yeon 3/2/1.
[93] Ibid.; S.R.S. ii. 229.
[94] S.R.O., tithe award.
[95] E 179/169/14.
[96] Valor Eccl. (Rec. Com.), i. 199.
[97] S.R.O., D/D/Rg 235.
[98] S.R.O., tithe award.
[99] Ibid.
[1] Ex inf. Church Commrs.
[2] S.R.O., D/P/yeon 17/3/1; ex inf. Church Commrs.
[3] S.R.O., D/D/Rg 235; glebe terriers 1613, 1640; S. & D. N. & Q. xxii. 253–7; R. M. Betham, 'The Family House' (A.R.I.B.A. thesis, 1944).

between 1640 and 1716, presumably in 1713. In 1716 the house comprised a hall 'within which' was a buttery and cellar, a kitchen, and a parlour on the ground floor; four chambers and a closet 'in the middle floor'; and two garrets and a study above. The 'table board' in the hall in the 17th century was converted into a 'lodging room'. The house was extensively repaired in 1867 and extended in 1874.[4]

The house, derelict in 1969, is built of lias with Ham stone dressings and a slate roof. It has a symmetrical five-bay front of two storeys and attics, with shallow projecting wings. The central square-headed doorway has bolection-mouldings with an ornate semi-circular pediment bearing the date 1713 and the arms of the then rector, George Sandys. The rear of the house is irregular and includes a drawing room added in 1874. The only surviving outbuildings are a coach-house and stable; the tithe barn was demolished c. 1868.[5]

Among the rectors who were evidently absentees were Walter (or William) de Harpham (rector 1320–25) who was licensed to travel abroad in 1320 and 1324;[6] Nicholas Trivet, appointed before receiving even minor orders, who was given leave for study in 1331 and who two years later was allowed to farm his church to the rector of Ditcheat;[7] Richard Swan (rector 1458 until 1486 or 1487), a member of Bishop Bekynton's household and provost of Wells;[8] and Richard Addams (rector 1619–34) who was reported absent in 1629.[9] Thomas Day, chaplain and clerk of the kitchen to Bishop Clerk, was deprived in 1554 for being married.[10] He was restored in 1559 and lived to be a 'very aged and impotent man'.[11] Richard Sterne, chaplain to Laud and master of Jesus College, Cambridge, was rector from 1634. He was imprisoned on a ship at Wapping as a royalist but was allowed to attend Laud in the Tower in 1645.[12] His benefice was sequestrated but he was not apparently replaced until 1647.[13] His successor, John Evans, was ejected in 1656.[14] Sterne reclaimed the benefice in 1660.[15] Gilbert Ironside, bishop of Bristol, was rector by 1661 until 1671 and leased the rectory to his curate, George Swayne.[16] Edwin Sandys (rector 1671–1705) was accused of taking little care of his parishioners and, as a Jacobite sympathiser, refused to recognize the authority of Bishop Kidder.[17] He was succeeded by his son George (d. 1716).

Robert Woodforde (rector 1716–62) became a residentiary canon of Wells in 1732.[18] His successor, Daniel Dumaresq, D.D. (rector 1762–1806),

went to St. Petersburg shortly after his appointment to advise the Empress Catherine on education. He held the rectory of Limington in plurality from 1790 until 1802.[19] Henry Law (rector 1830–34), son of the bishop of Bath and Wells, was at the same time rector of West Camel and archdeacon of Wells.[20]

In consequence of such constant absenteeism additional clergy were regularly appointed both in the Middle Ages and later,[21] most continuously in the later 18th and early 19th centuries.[22] The resident rector in 1815 also served the curacy of Limington and took services at Yeovilton alternately morning and evening, with a second service on alternate Sundays in summer.[23] By 1827 he was doing duty at Ilchester but was holding two services at Yeovilton regularly.[24] By 1843 Holy Communion was celebrated eight times a year.[25] The average congregation in 1851 amounted to 50 adults and 35 Sunday-school children in the morning and 85 adults and 35 children in the afternoon.[26]

By 1619 the parishioners were leasing a church house from the manor.[27] The house still stood in 1674.[28]

There was a chapel at Speckington by 1315 when the parson was given land by the lord of the manor to endow a chantry.[29] The incumbents, known variously as rectors of the parish church of Speckington, chaplains of the perpetual chantry, and wardens or masters of the free chapel, were normally appointed by the lords of the manor until the Dissolution in 1548.[30] The chapel, except lead, bells, and the advowson, was sold in 1549.[31] Its site may have been in a field called Chappel Hay opposite the former mission church in Bridgehampton; the residence of the priest may have been further east, at or near the present Chantry House.[32]

The small brick mission church of *ST. LUKE*, Bridgehampton, was opened in 1889.[33] It accommodated 70 people and in 1891 services were held there every Sunday evening, with Holy Communion once a month and a service every Friday evening in winter.[34] It was used until c. 1930 and again from 1936 until 1965.[35] It was sold in 1971.

The parish church of *ST. BARTHOLOMEW* consists of a chancel, nave with north porch and south vestry, and west tower. The vestry, added in 1872, incorporates some fragments of decorative Norman work apparently damaged by fire. Most of the architectural details of the building are Perpendicular, but the rear-arches of windows in both nave and chancel date from the late 13th or early

[4] S.R.O., D/P/yeon 3/1/1; Bell, *Hist. Yeovilton*, 10.
[5] S.R.O., D/P/yeon 18/1/1.
[6] *Cal. Pat.* 1317–21, 450; 1324–7, 49.
[7] *S.R.S.* ix. 49, 67, 170.
[8] Ibid. xlix. 309; Emden, *Biog. Reg. Univ. Oxford*.
[9] S.R.O., D/D/Ca 267.
[10] Phyllis M. Hembry, *Bishops of Bath and Wells, 1540–1640*, 71; *S.R.S.* lv. 121; S.R.O., D/D/Ca 22.
[11] C 3/138/30.
[12] *Walker Revised*, ed. Matthews; *D.N.B.*
[13] Lambeth Palace MSS., COMM A/5/36.
[14] Ibid.; *Calamy Revised*, ed. Matthews. He was replaced by Richard Marton.
[15] *Walker Revised*, ed. Matthews.
[16] *D.N.B.* See above, p. 173.
[17] *S.R.S.* xxxvii. 90–4, 131, 194; *Som. Wills*, ed. Brown, iv. 47.
[18] *H.M.C. Wells*, ii. 512, 523; Bell, *Hist. Yeovilton*, 17–18.
[19] *Registrum Collegii Exon.* ed. Boase (Oxford Hist.

Soc. xxvii), 142; Foster, *Alumni Oxon.*; Bell, *Hist. Yeovilton*, 18–19.
[20] *Rep. Com. Eccl. Revenues*, pp. 186–7.
[21] *Cal. Pat.* 1350–4, 202; *S.R.S.* xlix. 137, 395; S.R.O., D/D/Vc 20, 42; *S. & D. N. & Q.* xiv. 105.
[22] S.R.O., D/P/yeon 2/1/1–5.
[23] S.R.O., D/D/V rtns. 1815.
[24] Ibid. 1827.
[25] Ibid. 1843.
[26] H.O. 129/319/5/5/7.
[27] S.R.O., DD/PH 60.
[28] Ibid.
[29] *Cal. Pat.* 1313–17, 210.
[30] C 136/82/46, 117/12; *S.R.S.* ii. 114, 299; x. 687, 769; xii. 93; xxix. 69, 214; xxxii. 160; lii. 123–4; *Valor Eccl.* (Rec. Com.), i. 200; S.R.O., D/D/Vc 20.
[31] *Cal. Pat.* 1549–51, 121.
[32] S.R.O., tithe award; Bell, *Hist. Yeovilton*, 8.
[33] S.R.O., D/P/yeon 4/1/1.
[34] *Dioc. Kal.* (1891).
[35] S.R.O., D/P/yeon 17/3/1; *Dioc. Dir.* (1936–65); Bell, *Hist. Yeovilton*, 8; ex inf. Mrs. J. R. Stewart.

14th centuries, as do the double lancet and the sexfoil openings in the porch and probably the grotesque outside the south door of the chancel. The ogee-headed piscina over a crude corbel of a human figure is also of the 14th century. Other details include, in the chancel, carved heads on each side of the sanctuary to hold the Lenten veil, a possible wafer oven incorporated in the south door-way, and a Perpendicular font removed from the west end of the nave. Details in the nave include a piscina on the south side of the chancel arch and a carved bracket with a grotesque supporting it, the bracket pierced at the top probably to secure a statue. The lights in the windows of the whole church were renewed in the Perpendicular style, probably by rector Richard Swan, whose initials and motto remain in the east window.[36] The west window contains medieval fragments including the arms of Bishop Thomas Bekynton (d. 1465) and the sun in splendour.[37] The tower, described as new in 1486,[38] but not necessarily then finished, has small bell openings of Somerset tracery, diagonal buttresses, and a stair turret on the south side. The west doorway has carved spandrels, and there is a statue niche on the north side of the tower wall. Restoration in 1871–2 removed all but the bosses of the nave roof and all the Jacobean furniture.[39]

The church has five bells: (i) 1628, Richard or Roger Purdue; (ii) 1820, John Kingston of Bridg-water; (iii) 15th century, Exeter; (iv) 1591, Robert Wiseman of Montacute; (v) 1872.[40] The plate includes a cup and cover by Lawrence Stratford of Dorchester, dated 1574, and a shallow dish or paten of 1700.[41] The registers begin in 1710 and the series is complete.[42]

NONCONFORMITY. The house of Charlotte Hatkins, shopkeeper, was licensed for worship in 1826, but the denomination was unspecified.[43]

EDUCATION. There were two schools in the parish by 1802, one in Yeovilton and one in Bridge-hampton, both supported by the rector and prob-ably administered by the curate.[44] In 1818 there were two schools, a Sunday school with c. 40 pupils, and a day-school with six. The rector thought the day-school was adequate for teaching poor children to read but complained that 'their parents neglect to send them to Sunday school'.[45] By 1825–6 the Sunday school had 16 boys and 30 girls[46] and by 1833 25 boys and 33 girls. A day-school for infants, opened two years earlier, then had 10 boys and 18 girls. Both schools were almost entirely supported by the rector.[47] Both continued, under the same salaried mistress, though total numbers had fallen by 1846–7.[48]

In 1868 a schoolroom was built on the site of the tithe barn between the Rectory and the church. It was conveyed to the archdeacon of Wells to be run in union with the National Society, under the sole management and control of the rector.[49] The build-ing at first comprised one classroom; a further room was added in 1893 when there were 40 children on the books.[50] In 1903, when the school came under the County Education Committee, it was described as 'a capital little school doing very careful and accurate work'.[51] Attendance remained just below 30 until 1932, when senior pupils were transferred elsewhere.[52] The number of pupils rose, however, from 13 in 1934–5 to 26 ten years later and to 58 in 1964–5. The school was closed in 1969 and the pupils were transferred to Northover.[53]

CHARITIES FOR THE POOR. By will dated 1817 Samuel Brown of Bridgehampton (d. 1819), at the request of his daughter Flora, bequeathed the sum of £200 in trust. The interest, to be known as Flora Brown's Charity, was to provide bread twice a year for the poor of Yeovilton, Bridgehampton, and Speckington. It was said in 1824 that 'too narrow a construction' had been put on the terms of the trust; there were few paupers in the parish and the rector had given one loaf to deserving parents and half a loaf to each child.[54] In 1831 43 men, 44 women, and 96 children were each given a loaf at the first distribution, 41 men, 46 women, and 104 children at the second, at a total cost of £8 6s. 8d.[55] The capital was increased slightly in 1895[56] and by that time it had become the custom to distribute loaves on the two Sundays immediately before and after Christmas. In 1893 253 loaves were given.[57] From 1953 the income was divided equally between Bridgehampton and Yeovilton.[58] About the same time grocery vouchers rather than bread were dis-tributed, but c. 1967 the principal was withdrawn and divided between deserving cases.[59] The charity has thus ceased to exist.

[36] S.R.S. xv. 184.
[37] Ibid. xlix, p. xli.
[38] Ibid. xvi. 261.
[39] Photographs in vestry.
[40] S.R.O., DD/SAS CH 16, pp. 40–2, 68, 89, 115.
[41] Proc. Som. Arch. Soc. xlv. 138; S.R.O., D/P/yeon 17/3/1.
[42] S.R.O., D/P/yeon 2/1/1–5. In 1939 there was a register 1653–1710: Som. Par. Docs. ed. J. E. King, 399.
[43] S.R.O., D/D/Rm, box 2.
[44] S.R.O., D/P/yeon 13/2/1, acct. of vicarial tithe 1802.
[45] Digest of Returns to Sel. Cttee on Educ. of Poor, H.C. 224 (1819), ix (2).
[46] Rep. B. & W. Dioc. Assoc. S.P.C.K. (1825–6).
[47] Educ. Enquiry Abstract, H.C. 62 (1835), xlii.
[48] Church Sch. Inquiry, 1846–7.
[49] S.R.O., D/P/yeon 18/1/1.
[50] Return of Schs. 1893 [C. 7529], H.C. (1894), lxv; S.R.O., C/E 28.
[51] S.R.O., C/E 28.
[52] Som. C.C. Educ. Cttee. Schs. List.
[53] Ibid.
[54] 11th Rep. Com. Char. H.C. 433, pp. 470–1 (1824), xiv.
[55] S.R.O., D/P/yeon 17/2/1, charity papers, 1817–1940.
[56] Ibid. 17/3/1, chwdns' accts. and minutes, incl. charity accts. 1871–96.
[57] Ibid.   [58] Ibid.
[59] Ex inf. Mrs. J. R. Stewart, churchwarden.

THE HUNDRED OF TINTINHULL

TINTINHULL hundred lies in the south of the county, partly in the alluvial plain of the Yeo, partly in the irregular landscape of the Yeovil sands. Ilchester, the Roman cantonal capital and the county town of Somerset from the 12th century, was the most important settlement. Several hamlets of manorial origin in the south and one village in the plain, Sock Dennis, had disappeared by the early 17th century. Conversion from arable to grassland began in parishes near the Yeo in the 16th century, but arable remained predominant further south until the nineteenth.

Tintinhull hundred is not mentioned in the geld rolls. Its lands were included under Yeovil hundred. It has been thought that nevertheless it existed by 1084 and that its exclusion was due to the wish to group the count of Mortain's manors, of which Tintinhull was one, into a larger unit. The dubious charters whereby the count granted his Tintinhull and Montacute lands to his newly-founded priory at Montacute refer to Tintinhull hundred and also, under names thought to be interchangeable, to Montacute and Bishopstone hundreds. All three names were used at least until 1184.[1]

Clearly Montacute and Tintinhull were early members of the hundred. In 1187 the lord of Kingstone acknowledged that he and his men owed suit thrice yearly, i.e. on the octaves of Michaelmas, Epiphany, and Hockday.[2] Stoke, Kingstone, and possibly Athelney were included in the hundred by 1212.[3] By 1284–5 the hundred was said to consist of Tintinhull, Stoke, Stokett (East Stoke), Kingstone, and the two detached areas of Hescombe (in West Coker) and Draycott (in Ashington).[4] Montacute, which had been called a 'free manor' in 1275–6,[5] is not expressly mentioned, but recurs in 1316.[6] Hescombe had been part of the hundred since 1265.[7]

The hundred remained thus constituted until at least 1327.[8] By 1416 Ilchester and Sock Dennis were included in it for taxation.[9] Northover, a 'free manor' in the Middle Ages[10] and deemed part of Stone hundred in 1539,[11] was, with Ilchester and Sock, embraced in Tintinhull hundred by 1569.[12] So the hundred remained until the 19th century, though it was disputed whether for ship money assessments Northover was an appendage of Ilchester or a separate township in Tintinhull hundred, and whether Sock and Draycott lay within it at all.[13] Further doubts concerned Thorne. The estate, later called Thorn Prior, owed suit to Stone hundred in the 14th century,[14] but by 1539 was part of Bishopstone tithing in Montacute; it therefore owed suit to Tintinhull hundred.[15] The other part of Thorne parish remained within Stone hundred, though by 1841 it was tabulated under Tintinhull.[16]

[1] *S.R.S.* viii. 119–26.
[2] Ibid. 146–7.
[3] *Bk. of Fees*, 85–6.
[4] *Feud. Aids*, iv. 286.
[5] *Rot. Hund.* (Rec. Com.) ii. 129.
[6] *S.R.S.* iii. 67.
[7] *Cal. Inq. Misc.* i, p. 266; *Rot. Hund.* (Rec. Com.), ii. 140.
[8] *S.R.S.* iii. 67, 223–5.
[9] S.R.O., DD/PH 223/106.
[10] *Rot. Hund.* (Rec. Com.), ii. 127.
[11] *L. & P. Hen. VIII*, xiv (1), p. 289; *S.R.S.* xx. 225–6.
[12] *S.R.S.* xx. 225–6.
[13] For the ship money dispute see T. G. Barnes, *Somerset, 1625–40*, 203–43; *S.R.S.* lxv. 44n.
[14] *S.R.S.* iii. 211; *Feud. Aids*, iv. 320.
[15] See p. 253.
[16] *S.R.S.* iii. 329, 332.

The hundred was held with Tintinhull manor from the 11th century until its jurisdiction lapsed.[17] It was administered with the manor in a court leet and view of frankpledge for both,[18] which met twice a year at Tintinhull until the late 17th century and
afterwards once yearly.[19] A hundred constable was elected at the spring court, and in

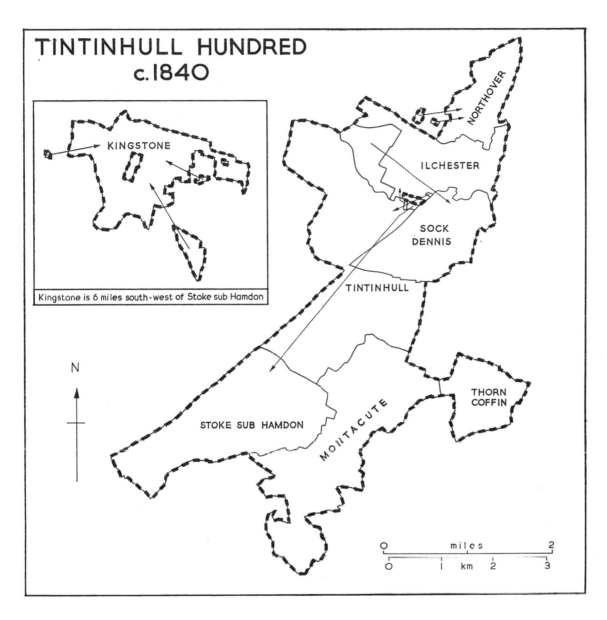

TINTINHULL HUNDRED
c.1840

KINGSTONE

Kingstone is 6 miles south-west of Stoke sub Hamdon

NORTHOVER

ILCHESTER

SOCK
DENNIS

TINTINHULL

N

THORN
COFFIN

STOKE SUB HAMDON

MONTACUTE

miles

km

the early 17th century the tithings of Allowenshay (in Kingstone), Stokett, Draycott,
and Tintinhull were regularly represented.[20] Attendance was commonly released after
1662, and the last joint court was apparently held in 1702.[21] In 1703 but never again
a 'leet of hundred or lawday court' sat.[22] Draycott tithing was represented at the manor
court from 1790 onwards, and there is some evidence for the re-establishment of the
hundredal organization.[23] A constable for the 'out hundred' was appointed in 1801,
a title suggesting bogus antiquarianism, and Northover and Draycott were represented
by their tithingmen in 1805. Tithingmen for Lufton and Sock were appointed in 1818,

[17] See below.
[18] Devon R.O. 123 M/M 108–9; S.R.O., DD/X/HO,
ct. rolls 1612–38, 1649, and ct. bks. 1662–1723, 1770–
1878.
[19] See p. 261.
[20] S.R.O., DD/X/HO.
[21] Ibid. ct. bk. 1662–1723 f. 116v.
[22] Ibid. 118v.
[23] Ibid. ct. bk. 1770–1878.

and by 1827 there was both a hundred bailiff and a constable, and five tithingmen. About 1837 the out-hundred of Tintinhull was said to comprise Tintinhull, Stoke, part of Montacute, Lufton, part of Thorne, Northover, Draycott, Sock Dennis, and Kingstone.[24] Tithingmen were last appointed in 1843, but the hundred constable was elected each year until 1869.[25]

[24] Ibid. entry on flyleaf.   [25] Ibid. ct. bk. 1770–1878.

ILCHESTER

THE ancient parish of Ilchester,[1] about 4½ miles NNW. of Yeovil, lay on the southern bank of the Yeo or Ivel. Before 1838, and probably as a result of the establishment of the county gaol in Northover, the northern boundary of the parish crossed the river to embrace its site.[2] Its other boundaries also follow watercourses, to create an area nearly two miles wide at its widest point between Pill Bridge in the west and the boundary stone on the Limington road in the east, and just over a mile from Ilchester Bridge in the north to the southern boundary of Ilchester mead. The land is alluvium over lias, and provides rich pasture grounds to the west and south of the town, all below the 50 ft. contour. The area of the ancient parish was 653 a.;[3] since 1957 the civil parish has included Northover and part of Sock Dennis, giving a total acreage of 1,550 a. in 1961.[4]

Ilchester probably owed its early importance to its position as a crossing-point of a navigable river. A paved ford, possibly Roman, was still visible west of Ilchester Bridge in the late 18th century,[5] but was largely obscured when obstructions in the river under the gaol wall were removed and used to fill up a hollow in the debtors' court in 1804–5.[6] The Foss Way from Bath, a road from the Bristol Channel, either from Dunball or Uphill, and another from the east converged north of the river and divided below the crossing for Dorchester and Exeter.[7] A Durotrigian settlement was established south of the ford in the 1st century A.D., probably surrounded by a ditch and an earthen bank.[8] It was Romanized from the mid 1st century, perhaps as successor to the fort on Ham Hill,[9] and took on a typical Roman layout, extending well beyond the limits of the original defences, which were therefore levelled. A simple glacis bank of clay formed in the late 2nd or early 3rd century was later reconstructed with a palisade, tied back to posts set in the rear of the rampart. This in turn was succeeded by a wall in the 4th century. By A.D. 369 the town was the *civitas* of the northern division of the Durotriges, and bore the name Lendinis.[10]

Visitors in the 17th and 18th centuries noticed a double wall in places,[11] and William Stukeley claimed to have seen traces of stone and brick walls enclosing a rectangle 300 paces long and 200 broad.[12] A ditch could also be traced in the 19th century.[13] Excavation has established the course of the wall in the north, where Stukeley saw it, in the west, and in the south, where the position of a gateway over the Dorchester road has been found.[14] Evidence of Roman occupation outside the defences was plentiful in the fields south and east of the town in the 17th century.[15] There were burials along both sides of the Foss Way and the Dorchester road, and a villa stood in Ilchester mead.[16]

Roman occupation can be traced to the early 5th century, but there is only scattered evidence for continuity.[17] The defences of the town were potentially adequate to provide protection for moneyers by the end of the 10th century, though the possible removal of the mint to Cadbury might suggest little faith in them.[18] By 1087–8, however, the town was able to withstand attacks from Robert Mowbray.[19] An onslaught in John's reign was, however, more successful, Peter de Mauley and Walerand le Tyeis managing to throw down the walls, taking away the iron bound gates to Sherborne castle (Dors.).[20]

The medieval town had four gates. East Gate, by which the Limington road left the town, was mentioned in 1242, and still stood in 1426.[21] North Gate, presumably at the southern end of the bridge, occurs in 1304.[22] West Gate is first mentioned in 1200, and was apparently still standing in 1605; it spanned the Foss Way and gave access both to the Exeter road and to the route to Pill Bridge and Langport.[23] South Gate, with St. Michael's church above it, was known as Michell's Bowe.[24] It was 'the greatest token of ancient building' which Leland saw in the town.[25] It first occurs *c.* 1230–40, and was probably still standing in 1576.[26]

The principal streets formed an A-shaped plan, the apex at the market-place, the bases at the west and south gates. The western arm, the Foss Way, was called West Street in 1318 and in the early 16th century, and High Street by 1390.[27] High

[1] This article was completed in 1970. It owes much to J. S. Cox, *A History of Ilchester*, issued in continuously paginated monographs between 1947 and 1958 and continuing in Ilchester and District Occasional Papers, from 1972.

[2] S.R.O., tithe award; see below, p. 186.

[3] *Census*, 1901.

[4] *Som. Review Order, 1933*; *Somerset (Parishes in the Rural District of Yeovil) Confirmation Order, 1957*; *Census*, 1961.

[5] Collinson, *Hist. Som.* iii. 298; Cox, *Hist. Ilch.* 205.

[6] S.R.O., D/B/il 9/2, corp(oration) accts. 1788–1889, 33.

[7] I. D. Margary, *Roman Roads in Britain*, i. 114–15; ex inf. Mr. J. S. Cox. For the suggestion of Uphill see *Proc. Som. Arch. Soc.* xcvi. 189.

[8] *Jnl. Royal Arch. Inst.* cvii. 94–5; ex inf. Mr. J. S. Cox.

[9] *Proc. Som. Arch. Soc.* xcvi. 189.

[10] Council for Brit. Arch., Groups 12 and 13, *Arch. Review*, iv. 46; v. 27; ex inf. Messrs. J. S. Cox and J. Casey; *Proc. Som. Arch. Soc.* xcvi. 189–92.

[11] Defoe, *Tour Through England and Wales* (7th edn.), ii. 27; T. H. B. Oldfield, *Hist. Boroughs*, ii; *Univ. Brit. Dir.*; *S.R.S.* xv. 204–6.

[12] W. Stukeley, *Itinerarium Curiosum* (2nd edn.), i. 154.

[13] Collinson, *Hist. Som.* iii. 298; Cox, *Hist. Ilch.* opp. 194; Lewis, *Topog. Dict. Eng.* (1833); *Ilchester Almshouse Deeds*, ed. W. Buckler, pp. 173–4.

[14] Council for Brit. Arch. *Arch. Review*, iv. 46; v. 27; ex inf. Messrs. J. S. Cox and J. Casey.

[15] *S.R.S.* xv. 204.

[16] Ex inf. Mr. J. S. Cox. The site of the villa was known in the Middle Ages as Casteler or Chastell: *S.R.S.* vi. 57; *An Ilchester (Somerset) Rent Roll*, ed. G. S. Cox (Ilchester and District Occas. Papers), 91.

[17] *Jnl. Royal Arch. Inst.* cvii. 94–5.

[18] Cox, *Hist. Ilch.* 37–68.   [19] *V.C.H. Som.* ii. 181.

[20] *Rot. Hund.* (Rec. Com.), ii. 139.

[21] Ibid. 131; *S.R.S.* xi. 323; *Almshouse Deeds*, ed. Buckler, no. 121.

[22] *S.R.S.* xiv. 88; *Almshouse Deeds*, ed. Buckler, no. 14.

[23] *Rot. Chart.* (Rec. Com.), 71; *S.R.S.* lxvii. 116.

[24] *S.R.S.* ii. 107, 292.

[25] Leland, *Itin.* ed. Toulmin Smith, i. 156.

[26] *S.R.S.* xiv. 186; see below, p. 198.

[27] B.M. Harl. Ch. 56 H 23; *Almshouse Deeds*, ed. Buckler, no. 76; *Ilchester Rent Roll*, ed. Cox, 89.

Street was the usual name from the 16th century, though since c. 1900 the name West Street has been used for the southern portion.[28] The eastern arm, including the road from the bridge to the market-place, was known as Cheap Street, the principal trading street in the Middle Ages.[29] The name occurs late in the 13th century in connexion with a shop, a stall, and a goldsmith's tenement.[30] Church Street was an alternative name from the end of the 17th century and the sole one from the later 18th century.[31]

At the junction of the two streets is the market-place, known as Cornhill and Market Hill in the late 18th and early 19th century, when it was levelled, gravelled, and enclosed with chains.[32] Part of it was called the Parade, and it was the site of the stocks and the town well.[33] At the southern end of the green thus formed stands the Town Hall, formerly known as the Shire Hall or Sessions House,[34] successor to the 'king's house . . . where the pleas of the county' were held, which had to be repaired in 1266.[35] Almshouse Lane or Street, or South Street connects the two principal roads further south.[36] Its original course was south-east from High Street, emerging near the site of the present Rectory.[37] As an unnamed lane it occurs in the 13th century,[38] as Abbey Lane in 1424,[39] and after the foundation of the Almshouse at its north-western end in 1426 as Almshouse Lane.[40] It seems also to have been known as Horse Mill Lane in the 16th and 17th centuries.[41]

West of High Street and apparently following the course of the town ditch was Yard Lane. It occurs in 1607 and was still visible in 1742.[42] It was connected to the market-place by Shire Path Lane, probably the site of the first county gaol.[43] The lane disappeared during the rebuilding of the western side of High Street in the early 19th century.[44] East of Church Street are Back Lane, Free Street, and Limington Road. Back Lane, the 'way leading towards New Mill' in 1349,[45] was Mill Street or Mill Lane in the 15th and 17th centuries,[46] and was thereafter extended southwards, east of the churchyard, towards Borough Green. By the end of the 17th century the whole road was known as Back Lane,

but later as Back Street or Mill Lane.[47] Free Street was the name given to the southern part of the street from 1839 when twelve cottages were built on the glebe there.[48]

At the southern end of Back Lane was the triangular Borough Green.[49] As manorial waste it was gradually whittled away during the 18th century: one plot had been 'lately walled in' by 1725; in 1742 a tenant was allowed to rail in a piece of the green and plant a row of trees before his house; and in 1773 a lease for a new cottage and garden formerly taken from the green was given by the corporation.[50] Many of the houses there were let to labourers.[51] The last traces of the green disappeared when buildings on it were demolished and the road realigned between 1826 and 1838.[52] Pye corner, perhaps part of the green, occurs in 1781 and 1798 when eight newly-built houses stood there.[53] Other streets or lanes in the town included Gloverstret, found before 1212,[54] and Marrimore Street in 1709;[55] their positions are not known. Green Lane occurs in 1741, Brown's and Mill Path lanes in 1791–2, and Cock Lane in 1822.[56] The town also had a number of alleys, known as drings, leading from streets to buildings behind the street frontage.[57]

Outside the town was the road leading from the Foss Way to Pill Bridge and Langport, called Moorway or Moorstreet until the 18th century and later known as Langport Way or Pillbridge Lane.[58] Some attempts were made in the 18th century to develop the road in view of the trade to the warehouses and quay at Pill Bridge,[59] and the corporation sold building sites along it including one in 1723 to be built on within five years, the house to consist of 'two good lower rooms and chambers in proportion'.[60] One of the houses, converted into a farm building, remained in 1969.

Ilchester seems to have had one open arable field, known as Ilchester field in the 13th century and as West field in the late 14th century.[61] Parts were inclosed for both arable and pasture by the end of the 13th century.[62] Common meadows were also permanently divided from the 13th century, and

[28] Cox, *Hist. Ilch.* 201.
[29] Ibid. 198–9.
[30] *Almshouse Deeds*, ed. Buckler, nos. 3, 5.
[31] S.R.O., D/B/il 2 (1784); 5 (1696, 1752, 1764); 8 (1693, 1731, 1750). It was called South Street in 1841: S.R.O., D/P/ilch 4/1/1.
[32] S.R.O., D/B/il 8; 9/2, corp. accts. 12–13, 23, 37.
[33] Ibid. 9/2, corp accts. 7, 13, 15, 27, 37.
[34] *Ilchester Rent Roll*, ed. Cox, 89; S.R.O., D/B/il 5 (1700); 8 (1734).
[35] *Cal. Lib.* 1260–7, p. 212.
[36] Cox, *Hist. Ilch.* 197; *Ilchester Rent Roll*, ed. Cox, 87.
[37] *Almshouse Deeds*, ed. Buckler, p. 171.
[38] Ibid. no. 3.
[39] S.R.O., D/B/il 1/115.   [40] See p. 202.
[41] *Ilchester Rent Roll*, ed. Cox 87; S.R.O., D/D/Rg 216. For the mill see below, p. 191.
[42] *S.R.S.* li. 180; S.R.O., D/B/il 8. Perhaps the southern end of the lane had been taken over by the Dominicans: *Cal. Chart. R.* 1257–1300, 285.
[43] *Almshouse Deeds*, ed. Buckler, no. 129; see below, p. 185.
[44] S.R.O., D/B/il 9/2, corp. accts. 1; *Almshouse Deeds*, ed. Buckler, p. 168.
[45] *Almshouse Deeds*, ed. Buckler, no. 37.
[46] *Ilchester Rent Roll*, ed. Cox, 91; S.R.O., D/D/Rg 216; *S.R.S.* li. 213.
[47] S.R.O., D/B/il 2 (1780); 5 (1707, 1716, 1728, 1742); 7 (1716); 8 (1693, 1731, 1764, 1768).

[48] S.R.O., D/P/ilch 13/1/2: poor rate assessment 1839.
[49] C 3/350/39; *Almshouse Deeds*, ed. Buckler, map at end; inset in Strachey's map of Som. (1736). The Limington road was formerly known as East Street: *Ilchester Rent Roll*, ed. Cox, 91.
[50] S.R.O., D/B/il 2 (1725); 5 (1754); 8 (1742, 1773, 1777, 1785).
[51] S.R.O., D/B/il 8.
[52] *Almshouse Deeds*, ed. Buckler (1866), p. 171, says 'some fifty years ago'. The green is shown on a map of 1810 (S.R.O., CR 95), and the roads were not in their present position in 1826 (S.R.O., D/T/ilch: bk. of maps). They had been altered by 1838: S.R.O., tithe award.
[53] S.R.O., D/B/il 8 (1781); D/P/ilch 4/1/1.
[54] *S.R.S.* xxv. 100.
[55] D.R.O., D 203/B 81.
[56] S.R.O., D/B/il 8; 9/2, corp. accts. 7; D/P/ilch 4/1/1; W. Stukeley, *Itinerarium Curiosum* (2nd edn.), i. 154; *Almshouse Deeds*, ed. Buckler, map at end.
[57] S.R.O., D/B/il 2; D/P/ilch 4/1/1; Cox, *Hist. Ilch.* 198.
[58] S.R.O., DD/PH 52, rental etc. ff. 19–19v; D/B/il 5 (1723, 1727, 1751); *Almshouse Deeds*, ed. Buckler, map at end.
[59] S.R.O., D/B/il 2, 5; *S.R.S.* xv. 209; see below.
[60] S.R.O., D/B/il 5 (1723).
[61] *Almshouse Deeds*, ed. Buckler, nos. 22, 74; *Ca . Close*, 1385–9, 622; *S.R.S.* lxiii. 497.
[62] B.M. Harl. Ch. 56 C 21.

further inclosure took place early in the 16th century.[63] Great mead was subject to commoners' rights until 1810.[64] The practice of dividing meadow into units of a sixth of an acre (*sesters*) in the 13th century evidently gave rise to the name Chestermead, an area which, judging by interlocking tenures,

times stopped short of the ford just west of Ilchester Bridge, and traces of Roman quays have been found there.[67] Ilchester Bridge, while superficially a structure of 1797 is, however, of late-12th- or early-13th-century origin.[68] The old bridge was of seven arches, the centre resting on a island in the

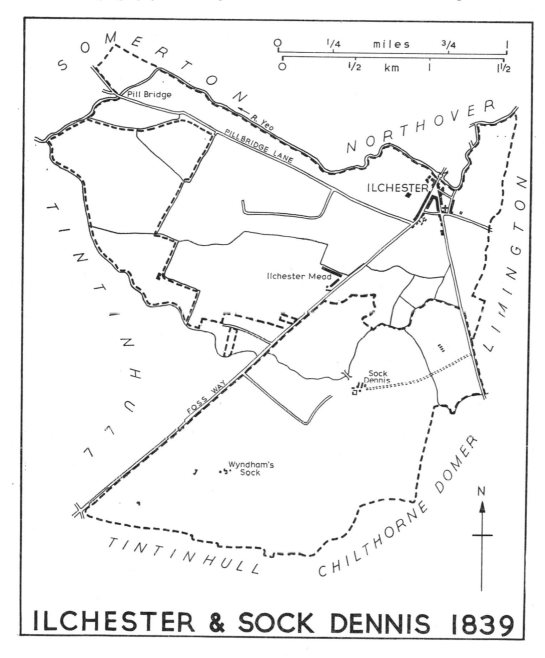

ILCHESTER & SOCK DENNIS 1839

was originally intercommoned between Ilchester and Sock Dennis.[65] By 1354 the estate of Whitehall hospital included grassland described as a park, perhaps the area bounded by a bank and known as 'intrenchments' behind Castle Farm.[66]

Ilchester and Northover together formed a bridgehead settlement. River traffic in Roman

river; the three arches between the island and the town were on a different alignment from the other four.[69] Further downstream, on the north-western boundary, Pill Bridge was built by the early 13th century.[70] The present high and narrow packhorse bridge was built in the 17th century. The lessees of Brook Ilchester in 1530 agreed to maintain

[63] *S.R.S.* lxiii. 497; *Ilchester Rent Roll*, ed. Cox, 95–7.
[64] S.R.O., CR 95.
[65] *Almshouse Deeds*, ed. Buckler, nos. 1, 22–3, 73–4; *S.R.S.* lxvii. 116–17; *Rot. Hund.* (Rec. Com.), ii. 126; S.R.O., DD/TB 20, transcripts of charters of St. John's hospital, Bath.

[66] *Cal. Pat.* 1321–4, 455.
[67] Collinson, *Hist. Som.* iii. 298; Cox, *Hist. Ilch.* 201.
[68] Cox, *Hist. Ilch.* 205–7.
[69] For other references to the bridge see Cox, *Hist. Ilch.* 203–5.
[70] T. Hugo, *Whitehall in Ilchester*, 71–2.

the bridge during their tenancy,[71] and their successor in the mid 18th century was being required to make repairs.[72] A warehouse was established at Pill Bridge by 1699, and a house there, known as Pill Bridge House, survived until shortly before 1805.[73] The Lockyer family leased the house and warehouse and took tolls of all traffic between their wharves below the bridge and the town until trade disappeared at the end of the 18th century.[74] Plans to improve the Ilchester–Langport navigation in 1794 involved cuts below Pill Bridge at Great Yard and, though they were never entirely achieved, obstructions were removed and banks straightened so that coal barges could ply between Langport and Ilchester Bridge until the very end of the 19th century.[75]

Three small bridges carry roads from the south and east of the town across streams. Chear Bow, carrying the Foss Way over a brook at Ilchester mead, is mentioned in 1611. It is known as Spittle Bow or Mead Bow.[76] Bridges known as Cole Bow and Ilchester or Yeovil Bow respectively span streams on the Limington and Yeovil roads.[77] The Foss Way and the Yeovil road were turnpiked in 1754.[78]

At the end of the 18th century Ilchester was badly served by road traffic. No coach apparently passed through the town; there was only one waggon to and from Bristol each week, and goods from London were left at Yeovil.[79] The diversion of the Great Western Road brought London traffic, and by 1822 five coaches visited the town regularly, to London twice daily, to Exeter twice daily, to Bath every week-day, and to Bristol and Weymouth three times a week. Two carriers also served the town, one to London and Exeter three times a week, one to Bristol on Tuesdays, and to Yeovil on Fridays.[80] The number of coaches was even greater by 1839, but a year later some of the services had been abandoned in face of railway competition. There was only one coach on the London–Exeter run on five days of the week, and a summer service from Bath to Lyme Regis on three days.[81] The nearest railway station at Sparkford was no substitute for regular coach services, and Ilchester's short-lived revival was soon over.[82] Until the advent of regular omnibus services about 1926 no public transport served the town.[83]

Apart from the church of St. Mary Major[84] there is no building of medieval origin remaining in Ilchester. Leland remarked the 'wonderful decay'

of the town,[85] but by the early 17th century it had been 'of late beautified in many places with good buildings',[86] and a house called Torrell's Court was singled out.[87] Part of the Dominican friary was still visible at the end of the 18th century,[88] and Cordelyon House, south of the Town Hall, evidently of medieval origin, survived until 1844.[89] One of the earliest surviving domestic buildings is the so-called 'Manor House' at the junction of West Street and Almshouse Lane. It is an L-shaped building of two storeys, basement, and attics, having rendered stone walls with Ham stone mullioned windows and dressings. It was evidently built in the mid 17th century but was partly remodelled about a hundred years later. The main block, facing West Street, has a symmetrical front crowned by three small gables. The pedimented doorway, approached by a double flight of steps, and the Venetian window above it, are 18th-century additions. The east wing was altered in the 18th century to accommodate a new staircase and subsequently appears to have been shortened. The ground-floor room at the angle of the house has fine Jacobean oak panelling with Corinthian pilasters and an enriched frieze. Elsewhere the internal fittings, including panelling, doors, and staircase, are of the mid 18th century. The long service wing south of the main block was extended in the 19th century. A stable range in the yard is an early-18th-century structure of red brick with Ham stone dressings. The central bay is faced with stone and contains an archway surmounted by a semi-circular window and a pediment; flanking it are mullioned and transomed windows and stone doorways with key-blocks.

West and High streets are continuously built up on both sides, mostly with smaller terrace houses of which the earliest date from c. 1820. At the north end of High Street, at the triangular market-place, there are a few slightly larger and older houses. A feature of the town in the 1830s, when, with few exceptions, its houses were 'indifferently built', was the several tenement blocks 'consisting of several storeys, and comprising on each different small tenements inhabited by burgage tenants at a nominal rent, and erected for their accommodation by the parliamentary patrons of the borough'.[90] Among these were two blocks of twenty or thirty tenements erected by the Whig, Lord Darlington, one of which, known as Cleveland Buildings or Row, stood in Back Lane.[91] The name was retained

[71] B.M. Harl. Ch. 46 I 6; for Brook Ilchester see p. 184.

[72] D.R.O., D 124, box 18, Kingsmoor ct. bk. 1757–96, f. 10.

[73] S.R.O., D/B/il 5 (1699); D/P/ilch 4/1/1. The house was rated in 1803 but the entry was cancelled by 1805.

[74] S.R.O., D/B/il 2, 5: leases of property and tolls 1699–1779.

[75] S.R.O., Q/R, deposited plans 7; Cox, Hist. Ilch. 202. The plot known as the coal wharf, now part of Castle farm, was first rated in 1814: D/P/ilch 4/1/1.

[76] S.R.S. xxiii. 55. The entry is somewhat ambiguous, and the name may refer to a bridge further south, now known as Victoria Bow. Spittle Bow occurs in the 19th century: S.R.O., C/S, bridge plans, western divn. It is also called Chard Bow in 1723–5: S.R.O., D/B/il 2, 8.

[77] S.R.O., C/S, bridge plans; Cox, Hist. Ilch. 203. Yeovil Bow was called Galeis or Gallows Bow in 1789: S.R.O., D/B/il 9/2, corp. accts. 1.

[78] Cox, Hist. Ilch. 214.

[79] Univ. Brit. Dir.

[80] Pigot, Nat. Com. Dir. (1822–3).

[81] Ibid.

[82] Lewis, Topog. Dict. Eng. (1833).

[83] Cox, Hist. Ilch. 208–9.

[84] See p. 200.

[85] Leland, Itin. ed. Toulmin Smith, i. 156.

[86] S.R.S. xv. 205.

[87] Ibid. 207.

[88] W. G. Maton, Observations in the Western Counties of Eng. (1797), ii. 24. For the friary see Cox, Hist. Ilch. 17–35; V.C.H. Som. ii. 150–1.

[89] Lewis, Topog. Dict. Eng. (1833). See plate facing p. 64, and below, p. 194.

[90] Lewis, Topog. Dict. Eng. (1833); 11th Rep. Com. Char. H.C. 433, p. 478 (1824), xiv.

[91] Lewis, Topog. Dict. Eng. (1833); S.R.O., D/P/ilch 4/1/1. Lord Darlington became marquess of Cleveland in 1827 and duke of Cleveland in 1833.

until 1841, and the tenements were also known as Trent's or Lower Barton.[92] They still stood in the late 19th century.[93] By 1822, and judging by their name built a few years earlier, were the tenements of Waterloo Double Building or Waterloo Court; and another such block, known as Castle Rookery, had been built behind the present Castle Farm by 1823.[94] A much larger complex, known as the Mead and containing 61 dwellings, was erected by Lord Darlington south of the town in 1818–19.[95] They survive as an isolated group of two terraces at right angles to one another. Each house is double-fronted and of two storeys. The range parallel to the road has a central pediment and the other a pedimented gable-end. They are otherwise plainly built of lias with dark-red tiled roofs and brick chimneys.

In the early 1840s, when Ilchester still benefited from its position on regular, if less frequent, coach routes, there were at least seven inns in the town. None appears to have had a continuous history from the 17th century, though the Bull is on the site of the Sun, in business between 1669 and 1734.[96] Other establishments in the town in the late 17th century were the Red Lion, probably also in the market-place, in existence by 1657 but closed before 1700;[97] the George later Swan, in Church Street by 1686; and the Bell, also in Church Street by 1690.[98] Several new inns, including the Ark, the Blue Bell, the Castle, the New Swan, the White Horse, and the Chough, had appeared by the 19th century, probably connected with the election struggles in the town.[99] In the 19th century the largest inn was the Castle; in 1840 coaches called there, but by 1854 it was converted to a farm-house.[1] The Cow, the Dolphin, and the Victoria were opened by 1859.[2] Only the Bull and the Dolphin survived until 1969.

Seventeen friendly societies, some in existence for only a short time, appeared in the town between 1788 and 1845. The first was the Ilchester Benevolent (1788), followed by the Ilchester Benevolent Friendly (1788), the Ilchester Old Friendly (1798), the Ilchester Guardian, and the Ilchester Female Guardian (both 1801).[3]

Ninety-five communicants were recorded in 1548,[4] and c. 1750 there were said to be some 127 houses in the town.[5] A considerable increase in population must therefore have occurred during the later 18th century. In 1801 the figure was 942; it fell to 745 in 1811, owing at least partly to the

eviction of his political opponents by Sir William Manners.[6] The population then rose steeply, to 994 in 1821 and 1,095 in 1831, again partly due to Manners, who offered houses and grazing to potential voters in his interest.[7] The figure remained at a high level in 1841, but for the rest of the century declined, reaching its lowest point, 433, in 1901. In the 1840s, when some 200 people left the town, several applications were made to the parish for assistance to emigrate to Australia and Tasmania.[8] The population remained at between 400 and 500 until the Second World War, but rose to 552 in 1951. The altered boundaries of the area obscure subsequent comparative figures, though new housing development has taken place within the limits of the ancient parish. There were 1,401 inhabitants in the civil parish in 1961.[9]

The town took a small part in the Civil War. The king stayed there in July 1644 during his campaign against the earl of Essex.[10] The Parliamentary forces planned to garrison it in January 1645,[11] but the Royalist forces remained, under the governorship of Col. Edward Phelips, until the summer of that year, when Fairfax manoeuvred them out of the town just before the battle of Langport.[12]

Roger Bacon, born c. 1214, is generally thought to have been a native of the town or its immediate neighbourhood.[13] John Hoskins (1566–1638), lawyer and wit, taught at a school in the town c. 1592, while compiling his Greek Lexicon.[14] Mrs. Elizabeth Rowe (1674–1737), the authoress, was the eldest daughter of Walter Singer, a nonconformist minister in the town.[15] Edmund Waller, the poet, was M.P. for the borough in 1624–5, and Richard Brinsley Sheridan, the dramatist, was returned in 1807.[16]

MANOR AND OTHER ESTATES. Ilchester was originally part of the royal Saxon estate of Somerton.[17] In 1066 it formed part of the holding of Queen Edith,[18] and in 1086 was held by the Crown.[19] Queen Eleanor, widow of Henry II, had the farm of the town (£28) from 1194 until 1203, and probably until her death in the following year.[20] King John granted the farm to Queen Isabel in 1204,[21] though it was later said to have formed part of the dower of Richard I's widow, Queen Berengaria.[22] The farm was confirmed to Isabel in 1216,[23] and she retained it until her death in 1246.[24] Her

[92] S.R.O., D/P/ilch 4/1/1.
[93] Ibid.
[94] Ibid.
[95] S.R.O., D/B/il 9/2, corp. accts. 64. Payment for the lease was made between Mich. 1818 and Mich. 1819. 36 dwellings were rated in 1822, 61 by 1839: D/P/ilch 4/1/1.
[96] S.R.O., D/B/il 8; Q/SR 112/86–7.
[97] S.R.S. xxviii. 332; S.R.O., D/B/il 5.
[98] S.R.O., D/B/il 5; Cox, Hist. Ilch. 232–3.
[99] Cox, Hist. Ilch. 232–3; see below, p. 196.
[1] County Gazette Dir. Som. (1840); S.R.O., D/B/il 4, highway rate bk. 1846–54.
[2] Harrison, Harrod & Co. Dir. Som. (1859).
[3] Margaret Fuller, West Country Friendly Socs. 140, 161; S.R.O., Q/R, Friendly Soc. rtns.; Cox, Hist. Ilch. 253–5.
[4] S.R.S. ii. 107.
[5] Browne Willis, Notitia Parliamentaria, iii. 45–6.
[6] V.C.H. Som. ii. 349; see below, p. 196.
[7] V.C.H. Som. ii. 349; Bath and Cheltenham Gazette, 18 Oct. 1825; see below, p. 196.

[8] V.C.H. Som. ii. 349; S.R.O., D/P/ilch 4/1/1, sub annis 1842–3, 1849.
[9] Census, 1921–61.
[10] V.C.H. Som. ii. 208; Diary of Richard Symonds (Camden Soc. 74), 35.
[11] Cal. S.P. Dom. 1644–5, 251. Earthworks south of the town have been assigned to the Civil War period: Council for Brit. Arch., Groups 12 and 13, Arch. Review, iv. 46.
[12] V.C.H. Som. ii. 213; see above, p. 21.
[13] D.N.B.
[14] Ibid.   [15] Ibid.
[16] Official Return.
[17] Rot. Hund. (Rec. Com.), ii. 122.
[18] V.C.H. Som. i. 441.
[19] Ibid. 437.
[20] Pipe R. 1194 (P.R.S. n.s. v), 184, 186; 1203 (P.R.S. N.S. xvi), 150.
[21] Rot. Chart. (Rec. Com.), 128.
[22] Cal. Papal. Regs. i. 33.
[23] Rot. Chart. (Rec. Com.), 213.
[24] Rot. Litt. Claus. (Rec. Com.), i. 293.

property was then granted to Richard, earl of Cornwall (d. 1272).[25] The farm of the town passed to his son Edmund (d. 1300), and then to Edmund's widow, Margaret.[26] It seems then to have passed to Piers Gaveston (d. 1312) on his creation as earl of Cornwall in 1307, and Margaret de Clare, Gaveston's widow, was given the farm for her life in 1316.[27] It was given to her second husband, Hugh de Audley, in 1317,[28] was lost and regained in the following year,[29] and was resumed by the Crown in 1319.[30] Thereafter it was held by Queen Isabel in dower from 1327, probably until her disgrace in 1330,[31] and from 1333 to 1336 was parcel of the duchy of Cornwall.[32] It then remained in hand, the farm being from time to time assigned to royal creditors,[33] until 1556 when it was given in fee farm to the burgesses, becoming what was later called the manor of ILCHESTER.[34] The corporation sold the manor to Sir William Manners in 1810 in return for land in Ilchester mead and the discharge of the fee farm rent.[35] Manners's son succeeded in 1833,[36] but sold it in 1834. The sale included about 70 private houses and 'almost . . . the entire . . . parish'.[37]

After the sale the property was divided into a number of holdings, the lordship of the manor passing to successive owners of Ivel House. Charles Boydell sold it to Harriet Shorland in 1843; Charles Harris (d. 1875) purchased it from Mrs. Shorland in 1847. It is thought that Mr. Harris was the last to hold a court. Harris's trustees sold it to Henry Mends, and in the following year it became the property of George Daunt. Mr. James Stevens Cox, who purchased the manor from Mr. Foy in 1937, also acquired Ivel House and the remaining manorial property, comprising the island on which the centre of Ilchester Bridge rests, a small piece of land in Pillbridge Lane, formerly used as a pound, and the freehold of part of the market-place. Until c. 1948 Mr. Cox collected tolls for the use of the market-place.[38]

An estate created in the 13th century by Henry de la Brooke, partly through his marriage to the daughter of Roger de Gouvis, lord of Kingsdon,[39] and partly through purchase,[40] was in 1325 a substantial property known as BROOK ILCHESTER, and later BROOKE'S COURT. Held of the Crown, it contributed a substantial sum to the fee farm of the borough,[41] and by 1331 comprised

84 a. of arable land, and 46 a. of meadow.[42] John le Brooke, who succeeded to the property in 1325, died in 1348 leaving a son, Thomas, as his heir.[43] Sir Thomas Brooke, Thomas's son, who succeeded as a minor in 1367,[44] was one of the county's leading political figures. He was succeeded by his son, also Sir Thomas, in 1418, and the property was shortly afterwards described for the first time as a manor, held in chief in free burgage.[45]

Edward Brooke, Lord Cobham, succeeded his father in 1439 and died in 1464. His son John (d. 1512) let the site of the manor and 150 a. of land to John Hodges of Long Sutton and his son for their lives in 1481.[46] The Hodges family were succeeded as tenants in 1518 by William Rayment and others, and Rayment and three sons had a lease for lives in 1530.[47] Subsequent tenants have not been traced, but the manor was still in the hands of William, Lord Cobham (d. 1597), great-grandson of John, Lord Cobham, at his death.[48] William's son Henry (d. 1619) was attainted in 1603 for his part in the Main Plot. His estate in Ilchester was granted to Joseph Earth of High Holborn, London (d. 1609), from whose brother Roger it appears to have come into the possession of Sir Henry Berkeley of Yarlington.[49] His daughter Dorothy brought it to her husband Francis Godolphin (d. 1666),[50] and in 1759 it was in the hands of her grandson Francis, Earl Godolphin (d. 1766).[51] By this time the estate appears to have comprised little more than ownership of Pill Bridge.

The exact site of the manor-house of Brook Ilchester or Brooke's Court is not known. Its lands lay chiefly in Ilchester mead, and Henry de la Brooke certainly had some land 'near the meadow of Sock and Martock'.[52] The family may, indeed, derive its name from the brook which separates Ilchester from Sock. The land presumably extended to Pill Bridge, and the tenants of 1530 were responsible for its repair and maintenance.[53] This responsibility was later put on the owner.[54] By 1633 traces of the manor-house itself could barely be seen.[55]

An estate called Torrells, thought to be so named from a family 'of eminent note' in Richard I's time and later, was held by Cecily, marchioness of Dorset (d. 1530), heir of William, Lord Bonville. In 1523–6 it comprised some 156 a. of land.[56] The Bonvilles had certainly been acquiring land in Ilchester since the late 14th century.[57] Before

---

[25] *Pat. R.* 1216–25, 302, 329–30; *Cal. Chart. R.* 1226–57, 129.

[26] *Cal. Inq. p.m.* iii, p. 459; *Cal. Close,* 1296–1302, 426.

[27] *Cal. Pat.* 1313–17, 577–8, 624.

[28] Ibid. 664.

[29] *Cal. Fine R.* 1307–19, 365, 374.

[30] Ibid. 1319–27, 4; S.C. 6/1148/2, 8, 15.

[31] *Cal. Pat.* 1327–30, 68; *Cal. Memo. Rolls,* 1326–7, no. 52.

[32] *Cal. Chart. R.* 1327–41, 302–3; *Cal. Fine R.* 1327–37, 494.

[33] e.g. Sir William FitzWaryn, 1336–45: *Cal. Pat.* 1334–8, 320, 427; 1343–5, 497; *Cal. Close,* 1343–6, 612; S.C. 6/1094/13; *Rot. Parl.* v. 174; vi. 303, 499.

[34] *Cal. Pat.* 1555–7, 528–9. A Mr. Rhodes was paid the fee farm until 1798 (S.R.O., D/B/il 9/2, corp. accts. 21), and payments from 1800 until 1805 were to Thomas Gould (ibid. 33).

[35] S.R.O., CR 95. Sir William Manners acquired the fee farm from Gould.

[36] *Complete Peerage,* s.v. Dysart.

[37] S.R.O., DD/SAS, PR 478; sale notice illus. Cox, *Hist. Ilch.* 178–9.

[38] Ex inf. Mr. J. S. Cox, and deeds *penes* Mr. Cox.

[39] B.M. Harl. Ch. 49 G 26.

[40] Ibid. 50 E 30, 56 H 42; B.M. Add. Ch. 25879; *S.R.S.* vi. 238.

[41] *Cal. Inq. p.m.* vi, p. 376; vii, p. 17; *Cal. Fine R.* 1319–27, 336.

[42] *S.R.S.* xii. 157.

[43] *Cal. Inq. p.m.* vi, p. 376; ix, p. 89.

[44] Ibid. xi, pp. 12, 92; *Proc. Som. Arch. Soc.* xliv. 13.

[45] *Cal. Close,* 1435–41, 87–8; B.M. Harl. Ch. 50 E 6.

[46] B.M. Harl. Ch. 46 H 33.

[47] Ibid. 46 H 43, 46 I 6.

[48] C 142/248/24.

[49] T. E. Rogers, *Records of Yarlington,* 40–4.

[50] Ibid.

[51] D.R.O., D 124, box 18, Kingsmoor ct. bk. 1757–96 f. 10.

[52] B.M. Harl. Ch. 49 G 26.

[53] Ibid. 46 I 6.

[54] D.R.O., D 124, box 18, Kingsmoor ct. bk. f. 10.

[55] *S.R.S.* xv. 207–8.

[56] Ibid. 207; E 315/385 f. 48v.

[57] *S.R.S.* xvii. 142.

1538, however, the 'heirs of Bonville' had disposed of some of the property, but still held 16 burgages and over 66 a. of land in fee.[58] It was held of Charles Brandon, duke of Suffolk, by John Cuffe in 1553.[59]

In the 1520s the property included a dovecot, stable, 'shepit', and a garden by 'Torrelles Corwate'.[60] A house called Torrells Court was still standing, near the site of the Dominican friary, in the 1630s.[61]

COUNTY TOWN, GAOL, AND HOUSE OF CORRECTION.

The presence of the county gaol from 1166 and the regular meetings of the shire and circuit courts in the town gave Ilchester the status of the county town of Somerset.[62] Property in and around the town acquired by the county's leading landowners and at least one sheriff indicate the importance attached to the centre of county government at least during the 13th century.[63] The removal of gaol and courts to Somerton in the 1280s seriously harmed the town, but their return between 1366 and 1371, in an attempt to bolster Ilchester's economy, did not again attract investment. Thenceforward first the circuit courts and then the sessions forsook Ilchester. Thus the gaol was delivered at Somerton in 1530,[64] and at Crewkerne in 1547.[65] More often gaol sessions were held at Chard, though Ilchester was again chosen in 1569.[66] The spring meeting of the quarter sessions was regularly held at Ilchester during the 17th century, but only intermittently in the early 18th century. The last was held there in 1766. Magistrates disliked the town because of its poor accommodation.[67]

The gaol and county court remained to provide a living for the inhabitants who gave 'entertainment' to those visiting or attending.[68] The court still sat monthly for the recovery of small debts, and was summoned by the sheriff for parliamentary elections and other duties of the shrievalty. The town's position as the place for county elections was questioned in 1702: Wells and Taunton were suggested as alternatives, since Ilchester was 'such an odious place that there is neither meat, drink, nor

lodging to be had'.[69] Ilchester itself was disfranchized in 1832,[70] and a writer, looking forward to this event, asserted that it would thus lose 'its last remaining claim to the distinction of a County Town'.[71] The redistribution of seats after the Reform Act set up electoral courts in Taunton and Wells, Ilchester being merely a polling place in the Western Division.[72] The closure of the county gaol in 1843 and the abolition of the county court at Ilchester in 1846 finally ended its claims as the county town.[73]

Complying[74] with the order made in 1166 to build gaols in counties where no gaols were to be found, the sheriff in 1166–7 planted a gaol for Somerset at Ilchester,[75] or at least then caused work to be done on an existing gaol there. In the 13th century it was used not only for felons but for forest trespassers,[76] and, at times at any rate, served Dorset as well as Somerset.[77] Orders for delivery began in 1233.[78] The building was expensively repaired in 1186–7[79] and repaired again on ten occasions between 1194–5 and 1213–14.[80] Further works upon it were ordered four times between 1225 and 1272.[81] When surveyed in 1283 it was of both wood and stone.[82] It was abandoned in the 1280s. The last orders for delivery were issued in 1281–2[83] and in 1283 there was a plan to give the building materials to the Dominican friars of the town. This plan was probably not carried out,[84] for in 1429 a recognizable tenement in or near the market-place, perhaps near St. John's church, was said to be one in which the gaol was wont to be of old (ab antiquo).[85] By 1280 a gaol, to replace Ilchester, had been established at Somerton, where it remained until 1371.[86]

It was decided in May 1366 that Ilchester should again become the meeting-place of shire and circuit courts.[87] But even before this, in March of the same year, Ilchester had already become the place for delivering Somerton gaol, and this practice continued until 1370.[88] By 1371 a gaol had once again been established at Ilchester,[89] and there it remained until 1843. In Leland's time it stood in the middle of Ilchester Bridge on the west side.[90] On a prison

[58] S.R.O., DD/PH 52.
[59] *S.R.S.* xxi. 137–8.
[60] E 315/385 f. 48v.
[61] *S.R.S.* xv. 207.
[62] See below.
[63] See p. 187.
[64] *L. & P. Hen. VIII.* iv(3), p. 2921.
[65] *Cal. Pat.* 1547–8, 74.
[66] Ibid. 1553–4 30, 32; 1554–5, 105; 1560–3, 5, 387; 1563–6, pp. 37, 104; 1566–9, p. 350.
[67] *S.R.S.* xxiii–iv, xxviii, xxxiv, *passim*; T. G. Barnes, *Somerset, 1625–40*, 9, 69; S.R.O., *Interim Handlist of Q.S. Rec.* 22.
[68] S.R.O., DD/PH 223/55. The earliest surviving court record is the Entry Book of Henry Gold (1629–30), now at Longleat House.
[69] Hist. MSS. Com. 51, *Leyborne-Popham*, p. 251.
[70] See p. 196.
[71] *Taunton Courier*, 6 July 1831.
[72] 2 & 3 William IV, c. 64.
[73] 9 & 10 Victoria, c. 95.
[74] The history of the medieval gaol is by Professor R. B. Pugh.
[75] *Pipe R.* 1167 (P.R.S. xi), 149.
[76] *Close R.* 1231–4, 205; *Cal. Close*, 1279–88, 9, 104, 159.
[77] e.g. in 1248 and 1252: *Close R.* 1247–51, 32, 68; 1251–3, 140. Also in delivery of July 1280: J. I. 1/1267 m.9.
[78] C 66/43 m. 7d.

[79] *Pipe R.* 1187 (P.R.S. xxxvii), 159.
[80] *Pipe R. passim.*
[81] *Rot. Litt. Claus.* ii. 22; *Cal. Lib. R.* 1226–40, 40; 1251–60, 60; 1260–7, 147; 1267–72, 222.
[82] C 143/6/16.
[83] C 66/101 m. 20d.
[84] C 143/6/16. This is an inq. *a.q.d.* Another of the same date resulted in a licence for the Dominicans to acquire land: *Cal. Pat.* 1281–92, 91.
[85] *Almshouse Deeds*, ed. Buckler, no. 129.
[86] See p. 139.
[87] *Cal. Pat.* 1364–7, 235.
[88] J. I. 3/156 mm. 20–5.
[89] This is the first certain date for the delivery of Ilchester: J.I. 3/156 m.26. Most of the cases heard in Somerset in March 1370 (m. 25) are entered under a heading that declares that the delivery was at Ilchester and the gaol at Somerton. One case (m. 28d), however, states that the gaol was at Ilchester. Since the entry follows the entries for March 1373, when the gaol was certainly at Ilchester, it is not unlikely that the descrepancy is due to scribal carelessness. Note, too, *Cal. Inq. Misc.* iv, p. 82 where a man indicted in Nov. 1368 is said to have been committed 'thereafter' to Ilchester. It does not seem likely that a man indicted late in 1368 would have remained uncommitted until 1371 or even 1370. On the other hand the inquisition embodying this information is dated Dec. 1380, by which time it could have been forgotten that a prison ever existed in Somerton.
[90] Leland, *Itin.* ed. Toulmin Smith, i. 156.

breach in 1533 it was found that the building had contained 22 prisoners, many chained.[91]

By an arrangement which has no exact parallel in England the revenues of St. Katharine's chantry in Ilminster church stood charged, at the time of dissolution, with a small annual payment to the prisoners.[92] This was continued by order of the charity commissioners in 1548, but has not been traced further.[93] By about 1586 an acre of ground in the common mead of Ilchester, called Gayle Acre or Begman's Acre, was set aside to provide for a horse, to be used by the begman 'to beg the county for the relief of the poor prisoners there', and from about the same time the justices authorized official collections for their benefit.[94]

Because the gaol house was thought too small and weak and was noisome, a new gaol was built in Northover parish about 1599.[95] At least by 1615 it was sharing premises with the house of correction,[96] though from 1624 onwards the two were divided, each having separate entrances.[97] Generally one man was in charge of both establishments.[98]

The site of the gaol, on land adjoining the river, was frequently flooded, and partly for that reason the gaol itself was unhealthy.[99] The buildings were fortified by Goring in 1645, and, on his retreat towards Langport, were fired by the governor of the town.[1] Accommodation became an acute problem when large numbers of Quakers and other non-conformists were confined there during the persecutions of the late 17th century. Other quarters, including the Friary, the Nunnery, and private houses were used. There were, for example, 212 Quakers imprisoned between December and March 1660–1; some were lodged with felons and on occasion held in irons, while at other times they were able to move freely in the town and even outside.[2] John Whiting, the Quaker, was imprisoned there 1679–86.

Unhealthy conditions continued to prevail throughout the 18th century, and there are records of none but minor repairs and improvements to the fabric.[3] Howard's criticism after his visit was not severe, his main point being that, though the apartments were roomy, the courtyards were too small, and the male felons were without a day room. The number of prisoners in February 1774 was 31 debtors and 22 felons.[4] An extension to the

buildings was completed in 1789 and included 26 cells each with staples and rings fixed in the floor for chaining prisoners.[5] Large alterations were said to have been made between 1808 and 1821 by the governor William Bridle.[6] They included the division between the quarters for female felons and convicts, and the construction of 'refractory' and 'misdemeanor' wards. Yards were provided with covered arcades, dominated by the two-storeyed cell blocks. Until Bridle's time the prisoners had no opportunity for work, but prison labour provided many of the new buildings, a cloth manufactory was set up, and tailoring and shoemaking were practised. The extended buildings could house well over 200 prisoners, 238 being present in May 1818.[7]

William Bridle's conduct as governor was denounced by the radical politician Henry Hunt (1773–1835), imprisoned there for his part in the Peterloo demonstrations in 1819.[8] Hunt's strictures resulted in both a local and a parliamentary enquiry, and Bridle was dismissed on grounds of brutality.[9] The gaol continued in use until 1843, when it was replaced by Wilton gaol, Taunton. The site of the former gaol was purchased by the Tuson family, and converted into gardens. Two cottages, once part of the laundry and bakehouse, remain.[10] Until 1811 executions took place in a field known as Gallows Five Acres, on the west side of the Yeovil road. A new drop was subsequently erected above the front lodge of the gaol.[11]

The erection of a house of correction had been ordered by 1607, but there was some difficulty in levying money to finance the work.[12] It had certainly been built by 1613.[13] Two years later it is known to have comprised two rooms and a court in the buildings which housed the county gaol.[14] Although usually under the control of the keeper of the gaol,[15] the house was in 1624 clearly divided from the gaol and given a separate entrance.[16] It was occupied by troops in 1645 and damaged by fire.[17] In 1666 it was ordered to be reopened after some years of disuse, but thereafter it seems to have become simply a department of the gaol.[18] From 1691 the county gaoler was no longer paid a separate fee as keeper of the bridewell. Less serious offenders were certainly lodged at Ilchester in the late 18th century.[19]

[91] L. & P. Hen. VIII, vi, pp. 391–3; vii, pp. 23, 149. For earlier escapes see P.S.O. 1/12/643 and Cal. Pat. 1436–41, 569; 1441–6, 314; 1446–52, 268; 1467–77, 39; L. & P. Hen. VIII, iii (2), p. 1264.
[92] S.R.S. ii. 2.
[93] S. & D. N. & Q. xix. 13.
[94] E 178/4450: from about 1594 the land was alienated.
[95] E 178/4450 says about seven years ago in Jan. 1606. By 1838 the boundary of Ilchester parish had altered to embrace the gaol: S.R.O., tithe award.
[96] S.R.S. xxiii. 128–9. The old gaol was still in the hands of the Crown in 1671: Cal. Treas. Bks. iii. 1130.
[97] S.R.S. xxiii. 349, 351; Cox, Hist. Ilch. 77–8.
[98] e.g. S.R.S. xxiii. 307; xxiv. 66; xxviii. 60, 111.
[99] Cox, Hist. Ilch. 78–81; Hist. MSS. Com. 2, 3rd Rep. Northumberland, p. 100.
[1] Joshua Sprigge, Anglia Rediviva (1647), 63, says only the bridewell was fired, though since bridewell and gaol occupied the same building, this may mean that only one wing was burnt. A More Full Relation of the Great Battell [Langport] (1645), 2, says Goring 'fortified both the County Jayles which stood just upon the "Passe"'. Perhaps he occupied the old gaol buildings on the bridge.
[2] Besse, Sufferings, i. 587–8, 595, 612, 629, 633, 647;

Cox, Hist. Ilch. 81. See also Cal. S.P. Dom. 1658–9, 148, 199; 1663–4, 266.
[3] V.C.H. Som. ii. 324, 326–7; Cox, Hist. Ilch. 82–4. A lodge for the turnkey was built in 1733: S.R.O., Q/S rough mins. 1733.
[4] J. Howard, State of the Prisons, 387–9.
[5] Cox, Hist. Ilch. 85.
[6] William Bridle, Narrative of the Improvements Effected at Ilchester Gaol (1822); Cox, Hist. Ilch. 85–8.
[7] Bridle, Narrative; Cox, Hist. Ilch. 86–7 and plans. Plans of the gaol in 1814 and of the infirmary in 1820 are in S.R.O., Q/R, deposited plans 44a, 62.
[8] Henry Hunt, A Peep into a Prison (1821).
[9] Investigation at Ilchester Gaol . . . with an address by Henry Hunt (1821); Rep. Com. on Ilchester Gaol, H.C. 7 (1822), and appendix, H.C. 54 (1822), xi.
[10] Cox, Hist. Ilch. 89–92.   [11] Ibid. 88.
[12] Hist. MSS. Com. 62, Lothian, p. 79.
[13] S.R.S. xxiii. 109, 110.   [14] Ibid. 128–9.
[15] See above.
[16] S.R.S. xxiii. 349, 351.
[17] See above.
[18] S.R.S. xxiv. 1.
[19] S.R.O., Q/FAw 1: hospital bk. 1656–1735.

ECONOMIC HISTORY. The existence of a mint at Ilchester in the late 10th century is the strongest indication of both the economic and defensive strength of the town. A mint was established there in 973 which, though perhaps temporarily moved to South Cadbury late in the reign of Ethelred II in the early 11th century, continued to produce coins until *c*. 1250.[20] Ilchester had all the appearances of a borough by 1086; the third penny payable by the town was worth £6, its 108 burgesses paid a further 20*s*., and a market, evidently very thriving, was worth £11.[21] As in other parts of Somerset one burgess was connected with an outside estate, in this case Castle Cary,[22] and it has been suggested that the borough had similar links with the royal estates at Bedminster and Milborne Port.[23] The later claims of links with Somerton suggest rather that Ilchester, like Langport, lay within the orbit of that extensive royal manor.[24]

The original farm of the borough was £30, to which a rural estate, a mill, and Stone hundred contributed £10 10*s*.[25] In 1204 the Crown resumed Stone hundred and granted the estate in fee to William the Dane of Sock Dennis, but no reduction was made in the farm demanded of the burgesses for the loss of William's estate, and only occasionally for the loss of the hundred.[26] The community was thus from early times burdened with heavy financial responsibilities, made even heavier by the impositions of Richard, earl of Cornwall, in the mid 13th century.[27]

The town, however, bore all the marks of a thriving community. As early as 1200 there were houses outside the walls, suggesting an expanding population, and by 1276 there were at least six parishes.[28] The monastic houses of Glastonbury, Muchelney, Montacute, and Cerne (Dors.) acquired ecclesiastical patronage there, Montacute by 1180, Glastonbury by 1191, the others by 1242.[29] Muchelney had at least one house by 1227–8, Athelney had a rent, and by the end of the century Montacute, Bruton, and Sherborne (Dors.) had similar holdings.[30] In addition the Order of St. John of Jerusalem and St. John's hospital, Bath, had a stake there, the former by 1212, the latter by 1236.[31] There was also a leper hospital by 1212, a hospital, later a nunnery, by 1220, and a Dominican friary by 1261.[32]

In contrast lay families seem to have been less

interested in the town's potential. The Beauchamps had some property there, with which they later endowed their college at Stoke sub Hamdon, but there are no traces of other families of similar eminence until later, when the Bonvilles and the Daubeneys acquired burgages and land.[33] The Brookes, much later to be lords Cobham, probably originated in the parish in the 13th century,[34] but others, such as William the Dane, William of Yeovilton, and the de Gouvises, lords of Kingsdon, were of little more than local importance.

Ilchester's administrative and judicial position rather than its economic potential is almost certainly the reason for the interest shown by the religious houses, though their holdings of burgage properties were nominal, perhaps designed to provide lodgings during sessions. The apparent lack of interest by laymen is therefore the more remarkable. Ilchester's position as the administrative centre of the county certainly accounts for the prominence of Thomas of Cirencester in the third and fourth decades of the 13th century. His landed interests cannot be unconnected with his service as sheriff of the county almost continuously from 1228 until 1237,[35] and as collector of the farm of the borough in 1224 and 1227.[36] His daughter married into the de Gouvises of Kingsdon, and his grandson Thomas had about 180 a. of land in the town and suburbs in 1280.[37]

Apart from the existence of a fair and the weekly market, there is little evidence of trade or industry in Ilchester in the 13th century. Four goldsmiths[38] and two dyers[39] then occur, and there are scattered references to shops and stalls.[40] There were a few Jews in the town led by Solomon of Ilchester and Isaac son of Cresse, with business connexions in Canterbury, Wilton, Exeter, and the Midlands, but they seem to have left the town during the later 13th century.[41] The town as a whole, however, lacked satisfactory trading links even at the height of its prosperity. Roman roads were not necessarily medieval trade routes, and although hospitals in and near the town imply travellers, the one disappeared and the other became a nunnery.[42] Judging by complaints against neighbouring fairs and markets from 1260 onwards the stability of Ilchester's trade was evidently precarious. It may still have been the market where, by ancient custom, tenants of manors such as Taunton and Kimpton took their corn,[43] but competition from Yeovil,

[20] *Anglo-Saxon Coins*, ed. R. H. M. Dolley, 131, 144, 146, 173; Cox, *Hist. Ilch*. 37–68.
[21] Darby and Finn, *Dom. Geog. S.W. Eng*. 141, 197–8; *V.C.H. Som*. i. 437, 441.
[22] *V.C.H. Som*. i. 198.
[23] *Wilts. Arch. Mag*. lviii. 11; J. Tait, *Medieval English Borough*, 54.
[24] See p. 16.
[25] e.g. *Pipe R*. 1188 (P.R.S. xxxviii), 159; 1194 (P.R.S. N.S. v), 186; *Bk. of Fees*, i. 79; *Cal. Close*, 1360–4, 193.
[26] A. Ballard, *British Borough Charters*; *Bk. of Fees*, i. 79; *Rot. Hund*. (Rec. Com.), ii. 126, 139; *Cal. Close*, 1360–4, 193; *Cal. Pat*. 1377–81, 93; *Rot. Parl*. iii. 619; *Pipe R*. 1204 (P.R.S. N.S. xviii), 175; 1206 (P.R.S. N.S. xx), 125; 1207 (P.R.S. N.S. xxii), 54; 1208 (P.R.S. N.S. xxiii), 102–3; 1209 (P.R.S. N.S. xxiv), 96.
[27] *Close R*. 1234–7, 215; 1237–42, 110, 404; 1251–3, 110; 1254–6, 34; 1264–8, 463.
[28] *Rot. Chart*. (Rec. Com.), 71.
[29] See below, pp. 197–8.
[30] *S.R.S*. xiv. 88–9, 186; viii. 74; xlii. 57–8; *Tax. Eccl*. (Rec. Com.), 204.
[31] *Bk. of Fees*, i. 79; *S.R.S*. xxv. 99–100; S.R.O.,

DD/TB 20, transcript of charters of St. John's hosp., Bath.
[32] M. D. Knowles and R. N. Hadcock, *English Medieval Religious Houses*, 185, 232, 280; *V.C.H. Som*. ii. 150–1, 156–8.
[33] *S.R.S*. xvii. 142; xxxv. 11; S.R.O., DD/PH 52, rental etc.; see below.
[34] See p. 184.
[35] *Sheriffs of Som*. ed. S. W. Rawlins, 8–9.
[36] *Pat. R*. 1216–25, 444–5; 1225–32, 134.
[37] *S.R.S*. xliv. 74–5, 134, 333; *S. & D. N. & Q*. xvi. 258.
[38] B.M. Harl. Ch. 56 C 21; *S.R.S*. xxxvi. 110; xli. 116, 142–3; *Almshouse Deeds*, ed. Buckler, no. 5; S.R.O., DD/TB 20, St. John's hosp. Bath, charters.
[39] B.M. Harl. Ch. 56 H 23, 42; *Almshouse Deeds*, nos. 5, 16.
[40] *Almshouse Deeds*, nos. 2, 3, 5.
[41] S.C. 6/1089/10–12; *Cal. Inq. p.m*. iii, p. 459; *Close R*. 1234–7, 141, 151; 1237–42, 354–5; *Cal. Plea Rolls Exch. Jews*, ed. Rigg, i. 56, 64; ii. 193; iii. 226; *S.R.S*. lxviii, p. xvi.
[42] *V.C.H. Som*. ii. 156.   [43] *S.R.S*. lxvi. 32, 80.

Tintinhull Shepton Beauchamp, and Montacute was evidently unwelcome.[44]

The town's difficulties were further increased by the loss of grazing rights in a large tract of land north and west of the Yeo at Kingsmoor.[45] After disputes between Ilchester and Somerton in 1223 and 1242–3 it seems that Ilchester had assumed control, the men of Somerton being allowed limited pasturage there.[46] Richard, earl of Cornwall, lord of Ilchester, seems to have been responsible for the acquisition of the area some 1,000 a. in extent, which the burgesses rented from the Crown.[47] Their rights to Kingsmoor, and also to 10 a. of pasture called King's Furlong, were challenged in 1275,[48] and by 1280 both areas were deemed part of the ancient demesne of the manor of Somerton, to which Ilchester had no right.[49] Almost at the same time as the loss of these grazing rights came the loss, also to Somerton, of the county and circuit courts and the gaol.[50]

Any prosperity the town enjoyed was evidently over by the 1280s: Cerne, Glastonbury, and Muchelney had abandoned their ecclesiastical patronage; the mint had ceased; the income from trade could no longer successfully be supplemented by extensive agricultural interests and commerce coming in the wake of administration and justice. After 1313 the town was not even taxed as a borough,[51] and its history throughout the rest of the Middle Ages is of successive attempts to regain its position as the county town of Somerset, and to ease the burdens of the farm on a contracting population.

A petition to Parliament in 1314–15 only succeeded in getting an enquiry into the relative merits of Ilchester and Somerton as the administrative centre of the county.[52] Somerton retained its position until 1366 when 'for the relief' of the town 'greatly impoverished and distressed by divers adversities', the county and circuit courts were ordered to be moved back to Ilchester.[53] Efforts, eventually successful, to reduce the town farm are a further proof of Ilchester's economic decline. The farm set in 1183 was payable in 1242 but in practice between 1275 and 1325 only c. £20 was collected.[54] In 1369, after a Parliamentary petition of eight years before, arrears of £669 were written off, but by 1377 further arrears of £109 had been accumulated.[55] The farm was then reduced to £8 for eleven years, later extended by a further six.[56] At length, after a further petition in 1407, the farm was finally set at £8, which had been declared in 1399 to be the town's income.[57] It remained unchanged until the charter of 1556 fixed it for good.[58] Contem-

poraries partly justified the reduction of 1369 by the effect of 'mortal pestilences' and that of 1377 by the allegation that the 'greater number' of the inhabitants had left the town and that more proposed to follow them.[59] Certainly in 1377 the inhabitants of Northover outnumbered those of Ilchester by 8 per cent.[60]

Continuing poverty and a contracting population are reflected in the end of Ilchester's parliamentary representation in 1361 and in the 15th century in the union of the town's three remaining parishes in 1502.[61] Similar factors probably contributed to the end of Whitehall nunnery as a religious community between 1436 and 1463.[62] It is unlikely that the Act of 1540–1 for rebuilding decayed houses in Ilchester and other towns had any significant effect;[63] such stimulation of the town's economy as is indicated in the later 16th century almost certainly stems from inclosure and from an expansion of the land market following the Dissolution.

A rental of the town, dated between 1525 and 1538 but based on one of 1476, gives an indication both of the size of the town and of the pattern of land ownership near by.[64] Real property in the town comprised 86 burgages and two or three other houses and cottages. Sixteen of the burgages were held by William Bonville's heirs, nine each by the alms-house estate and by the chaplain of the Whitehall chapel, eight by a burgess, Nicholas Abbot, five each by Thomas Baker and John Strowde, and four by the rector of St. Mary Major. The ancient interest of neighbouring monastic houses was still represented: Muchelney held three burgages, Sherborne, Bruton, and Montacute two each. Sir Edward Brooke and Sir Giles Daubeney each had one to give them a nominal stake in the county town. Of the actual tenants, the most substantial were Thomas Baker with 12 burgages, John Burges with five, and William Golight with four.

Outside the borough the rental reveals that the lands of the parish had recently undergone large-scale inclosure from the common pasture. The largest holding among the ancient inclosures was the Bonville estate known as Torrells, of some 156 a., let for a total rent of over £3.[65] Brooke's Court, in comparison, paid only 14s. 5½d., the Whitehall holding 9s. 6d., the college of Stoke sub Hamdon 5s. 1d. Walter Yarcombe or Yartecombe, the most substantial tenant, held Torrells, the Stoke college land, and a burgage for 30s. 1½d.[66]

This medieval pattern of agriculture was considerably changed when more than 245 a. of common pasture were inclosed before 1538,[67] producing a rent of over £2 10s., or rather more than a third

[44] *Plac. Abbrev.* (Rec. Com.), 153; *S.R.S.* viii. 207; *Rot. Hund.* (Rec. Com.), ii. 139.
[45] See p. 137.
[46] *Rot. Litt. Claus.* (Rec. Com.), i. 540; *S.R.S.* xi. 259.
[47] *Rot. Hund.* (Rec. Com.), ii. 122.
[48] *Plac. de Quo Warr.* (Rec. Com.), 690, 701; *Rot. Hund.* (Rec. Com.), ii. 126, 128, 134.
[49] *S.R.S.* xlii. 34–5; *Cal. Pat.* 1281–92, 24.
[50] See p. 139.
[51] *Hist. Essays in Honour of James Tait,* ed. J. G. Edwards, V. H. Galbraith, and E. F. Jacob, 433.
[52] *Rot. Parl.* i. 307.
[53] *Cal. Pat.* 1364–7, 235; and see above, p. 185.
[54] *Pipe R.* 1242 (ed. H. L. Cannon), 327; *Rot. Hund.* (Rec. Com.), ii. 126, 128; C 260/58/79; S.C. 6/1148/2, 8, 15. The Exchequer still claimed £30 in 1345: C 260/56/31.

[55] *Cal. Close,* 1360–4, 193; *Cal. Pat.* 1367–70, 238.
[56] *Cal. Pat.* 1377–81, 93; 1388–92, 72.
[57] *Rot. Parl.* iii. 619; *Cal. Pat.* 1413–16, 322.
[58] S.C. 6/1089/3; *Cal. Pat.* 1555–7, 528–9.
[59] *Cal. Pat.* 1367–70, 238; 1377–81, 93.
[60] *S. & D. N. & Q.* xxix. 12.
[61] See p. 197.
[62] M. D. Knowles and R. N. Hadcock, *English Medieval Religious Houses,* 232.
[63] Hist. MSS. Com. 8, *9th Rep. I, Corpn. of Plymouth,* p. 277. It was, however, chosen in 1494 as a town for the safe custody of weights and measures, presumably because it was still the county town: 11 Hen. VII, c.4.
[64] *An Ilchester (Somerset) Rent Roll,* ed. G. Stevens Cox (Ilchester and District Occas. Papers 3), (1972).
[65] E 315/385 f. 48v; see p. 184.
[66] *Ilchester Rent Roll,* ed. Cox, 91–3.   [67] Ibid. 95–7.

of the total income of the burgesses.[68] Walter Yarcombe was again the largest tenant, holding 84 a., followed by Whitehall chapel with 54 a., Thomas Baker with 49 a., and William Golight with 48 a.

Further land came on the market when the estate of Whitehall chapel was sold. The burgesses received from the holdings which emerged from the estate a small increase in rent;[69] some families, notably the Hodgeses, benefited directly as lessees and grantees, replacing such men as Walter Yarcombe and Thomas Baker, who had evidently dominated the town earlier in the century. William Hodges (d. 1554) left freeholds and leases in Chestermead and Bearley, common grazing rights, and a flock of sheep, as well as much cash.[70] His son, also William (d. 1605), left a much greater estate, including the 180 a. Torrells farm, held of the corporation, a further 184 a. and other lands described but not measured, and a number of houses in the town including his own residence, the former friary.[71]

In the absence of any continuous series of borough records, evidence of trade and industry in the town in the 16th and 17th centuries depends largely on casual references to individual occupations. Thus there occurs one Henry Adams, described as a coverlet weaver, who died in 1589 leaving over £70 in goods.[72] Stalls in the shambles outside the market hall were prepared for glovers, merchants, linen-drapers, hosiers, and woollen-drapers, as well as butchers, chandlers, and bakers, though in 1614–15, at any rate, the corporation received no rent from these tradesmen. Only leather sellers and the market hall itself proved profitable.[73] Nearly contemporary is a group of tradesmen in the town comprising a whitebaker, a cutler, a victualler, a roper, and a mason.[74]

If the prosperity of the town in the 16th century cannot absolutely be proved,[75] decline is clear enough in the 17th century. A petition of about 1630 asserting that brewing was virtually the only activity, 'trading or travelling being very rare and of small use', though exaggerated, cannot be entirely without foundation.[76] Brewing, it was said, had hitherto employed a hundred people; the grant of a monopoly to a particular brewer would tend to 'the utter destruction of all the rest', since the town consisted of poor men and widows supporting themselves by accommodating visitors to the prison and the monthly courts.[77] This petition was not very successful, the brewer, William Dawe, and his associate George Smith, mercer, remaining dominant in the business of the town for several years.[78]

Some reforms were certainly effected in agriculture, where detailed instructions on the exercise of common rights in Grass Spittle and the Lammas lands were reduced to writing in 1629.[79] One hundred and four individuals with rights ranging from one to six leazes, 'fretted' and 'hayned' the commons with cattle and sheep between given dates, under supervision.[80] For the benefit of the poor this system was modified in 1686, the corporation refraining from stocking their common or Lammas meadow until a later date than hitherto.[81] These two orders were unlikely to have been achieved without pressure from below on men who held most of the land in the town. The cause of the evident economic decline, however, is more difficult to trace: plague was certainly rife in 1641, and neighbouring villages, though rated to support the suffering inhabitants, failed to pay, making the war their excuse.[82]

Though farming remained of much importance to many families in the 18th century, craftsmen and traders were evidently working for a wider market than the town itself provided. Chief among them was Thomas Lockyer, parliamentary patron of the borough, whose family had been mercers in the town and prominent members of the corporation since the early 17th century, and were possessed of an estate of £2,000 there by 1645.[83] Thomas Lockyer's commercial interests centred upon the warehouse at Pill Bridge and the tolls taken along the road which led to it.[84] His lands were valued at c. £3,000. No other businessman could compete on such a scale, though by 1822 nearly half the families in the town were engaged in trade, manufactures, and handicrafts.[85] Most, during the 18th century at least, were concerned with domestic crafts such as shoemaking, woodworking, thatching, tiling, or malting.[86] A minority, for a more sophisticated clientèle, made perukes, buttons, and chairs.[87] An intermediate group was engaged in gloving, net-making, and linen manufacture. A Stoke glover, Joseph Winter, leased a house in the town in 1747, and William Chaffey, glover, occurs in 1777.[88] During the 19th century most of this work was done at home by women and girls for Yeovil and Stoke manufacturers.[89] Net-making was carried on by the Harvey family between 1781 and 1830.[90] More extensive was the linen industry. Two linen-weavers, William Sevior and John West, were active in the town in the 1760s.[91] Sevior's son John apparently had a large business which was in production between 1780 and 1805, and a flax-house, perhaps owned by him, was burnt in 1803.[92] Flax-workers occur at least until 1838.[93] There was

[68] The total was £7 7s. 2½d.
[69] *Ilchester Rent Roll*, ed. Cox, 95–7.
[70] C 142/106/80; *S.R.S.* xxi. 151.
[71] *S.R.S.* li. 213; lxvii. 116–17.
[72] Req. 2/207/7.
[73] S.R.O., DD/PH 52, rental etc. ff. 9–9v.
[74] S.R.O., D/B/il 2 (1617).
[75] In 1633 the town was described as 'of late beautified in many places with good buildings': *S.R.S.* xv. 205. See below p. 191 for the revival of fairs.
[76] S.R.O., DD/PH 223/55.
[77] Ibid.
[78] *Cal. S.P. Dom. 1637–8*, 271; *Cal. Cttee. for Money*, ii. 1159.
[79] S.R.O., DD/PH 223/48.
[80] See p. 192.
[81] S.R.O., DD/PH 223/109. See also ibid. 223/110.
[82] S.R.O., Q/petns.

[83] C 3/452/36; see below, p. 193.
[84] S.R.O., D/B/il 5 (1699); see above, p. 180.
[85] C. & J. Greenwood, *Som. Delineated.*
[86] S.R.O., D/B/il 2, 5, 7, 8; S.R.O., Q/R, jurors' bk. 1697–1766.
[87] S.R.O., D/B/il 2, 5, 7, 8.
[88] S.R.O., D/B/il 6: 'manor of Stocklinch' bk. 26; D/B/il 8.
[89] Lewis, *Topog. Dict. Eng.* (1833); *County Gazette Dir.* (1840); *Rep. Com. Children and Women in Agric.* [4202–I], H.C. p. 472 (1868–9), xiii; *P.O. Dir. Som.* (1866).
[90] S.R.O., D/B/il 8; D/P/ilch 2/1/5.
[91] S.R.O., D/B/il 8: 1762, 1765.
[92] S.R.O., D/B/il 2; D/P/ilch 4/1/1; *Univ. Brit. Dir.*; Neast Greville Prideaux, 'Diary' (TS. in S.R.O., DD/SAS FA 185), 139.
[93] S.R.O., D/P/ilch 2/1/5.

also a small silk-mill in the town in the 1790s,[94] an industry which was still in being in the 1830s;[95] and there was said to have been a 'considerable' manufacture of thread lace,[96] though no local evidence has been found. The north transept of the otherwise ruined friars' church was at the end of the 18th century in use as a spinning-house, though its products are not known.[97]

By about 1822 nearly a third of the town's families was engaged in agriculture, mostly as tenants or labourers on the Manners estate.[98] The dominance of the successive parliamentary patrons, Thomas Lockyer, Richard Troward, and Sir William Manners, was firmly based on the ownership or occupation of a considerable estate in the parish.[99] Troward held nearly 500 a. out of a total of 664 a. in 1798, the rest being divided between five other owners.[1] This property included 61 out of 85 houses in the town. By 1805 Sir William Manners held nearly 606 a., and in 1825 claimed to own all but three houses in the town and every close but one.[2] Most of the land was by now inclosed, the remainder of Ilchester mead, the subject of an Act in 1797, being officially apportioned in 1810.[3] By 1812 Manners's estate was worked in three main units, the largest based on the present Manor Farm, then called Great House. A second holding, the present Castle farm, was based on the then Bell inn, later the Castle inn. The third farm centred upon Kingshams.[4] Manor farm was divided about 1822, and again in 1835 when it belonged the Wyndhams.[5] By 1863 it measured 139 a.[6] In contrast Castle farm, then owned by John Brymer and held by Edward Lock, was nearly 400 a. Kingsham farm amounted to just over 46 a.[7] Slight alterations in size followed during the second half of the century: by 1916 Castle farm was 412 a. and Manor farm 102 a. These two farms and Spittle farm survived in 1970.

Ilchester's farms did not, apparently, suffer noticeably in the depression of the early 19th century.[8] The land was, as Sir William Manners claimed, 'of the best land in Somersetshire', excellent for fattening cattle and sheep.[9] Only 120 a. were arable in 1838,[10] and three-quarters were grazing, with no dairying, in 1868–9.[11] Grazing and fattening were still of importance in the 1960s.[12]

It was firmly stated in 1822 that the principal support for the inhabitants was provided by those who attended the monthly county court, apart from which 'there is no trade here whatever, the greater part of the inhabitants going to Yeovil . . . for almost every article they want'.[13] Luxury articles could probably not be purchased there, but the statement is evidently exaggerated, for there were four bakers, three boot- and shoe-makers, three grocers and tea dealers, and three tailors as well as carpenters, masons, and plumbers. A more urban character was given by the presence of an attorney and a surgeon, a linen-draper, a basket-maker, and an insurance agent.[14] The decline of population during the 19th century does not seem to have altered the range of the town's traders. The growing popularity of motor travel in the early 1930s is reflected in the establishment of a private hotel, a boarding house, and tea rooms. Increasing road traffic and the influx of families attached to Yeovilton Naval Air Station have given a fresh impetus to shops and restaurants, and a small factory now produces 'beer cheese'.

MARKETS AND FAIRS. Ilchester had a very thriving market at the time of Domesday, paying 'with its attached members' as much as £11.[15] The charter of 1204, probably repeating the earlier one granted by Henry II, did not establish a particular day for trading. That day was Wednesday at least from 1556.[16] King John's charter declared that all saleable articles which crossed the town bridge, presumably coming from the north, should be offered for sale in the town and not elsewhere.[17] Shambles are mentioned in 1427, but by the early 16th century there were only four permanent stalls, the property of the burgesses.[18] After the expansion of the town's economy in the second half of the century, trade somewhat increased. By about 1615 the town possessed a market hall,[19] a tolsey hall, sheep pens, and stalls for various traders. Only the market hall, however, seems to have produced any income.[20] The tolsey hall was still in use in 1669 when, together with part of the market hall, it was let.[21] The profits of fairs and the market, including the use of the stalls, were usually let in the late 17th century,[22] though the corporation undertook to keep the market-place and the stalls in repair.[23] This practice was continued in the 18th century: a house and shambles were let to the borough's patron, Thomas Lockyer, in 1765 for 99 years,[24] and John Harcourt's attempt to wrest control from Lockyer included acquisition of a lease of the tolls and fees from the market and fairs as well as the use of the stalls and market-place, for cutting and placing timber.[25] The corporation recovered their rights to tolls by 1793–4, but, having decided to remove stalls from the market hall, their income temporarily ceased.[26] The shambles on Market Hill continued to be used, though from 1814 the standings for

94 Univ. Brit. Dir.
95 S.R.O., D/P/ilch 2/1/6.
96 Nightingale, Beauties, 55.
97 W. G. Maton, Observations on the Western Counties of Eng. (1797), ii. 24.
98 C. & J. Greenwood, Som. Delineated.
99 See p. 196.
1 S.R.O., D/P/ilch 4/1/1.
2 Ibid. 13/2/2; Bristol and Cheltenham Gazette, 18 Oct. 1825.
3 S.R.O., CR 95.
4 S.R.O., D/P/ilch 4/1/1.
5 Ibid.
6 S.R.O., D/G/Y 160.
7 Ibid.
8 As did many farms in the neighbourhood: Agric. State of the Kingdom (1816), ii. 12–13.
9 Bath and Cheltenham Gazette, 18 Oct. 1825.
10 S.R.O., tithe award.
11 Rep. Com. Children and Women in Agric. [4202-I], H.C. p. 472 (1868–9), xiii.
12 Cox, Hist. Ilch. 193.
13 Pigot, Nat. Com. Dir. (1822–3).
14 Ibid.
15 V.C.H. Som. i. 437.
16 Cal. Pat. 1555–7, 528–9.
17 A. Ballard, British Borough Charters.
18 Almshouse Deeds, ed. Buckler, no. 124; S.R.O., DD/PH 52, rental etc. f. 6.
19 See p. 194.
20 S.R.O., DD/PH 52, rental etc. ff. 9–9v.
21 S.R.O., DD/PH 223/108.
22 Ibid.
23 Ibid. 223/110.
24 S.R.O., D/B/il 8.
25 Ibid.
26 S.R.O., D/B/il 9/2, corp. accts. 12, 16–18.

butchers were no longer occupied.[27] The butchers apparently returned and, although the market was 'little attended' by 1822,[28] their standings were rebuilt in 1823 and were not finally abandoned until 1834.[29] The whole market was said to be 'disused' by 1833.[30]

The charter of 1204 confirmed to the town a one-day fair at Midsummer granted by Henry II, probably in 1183.[31] This had evidently been discontinued by the 16th century, and in 1556 the town was granted one on the Monday before Palm Sunday and the two following days, and one on the feast of St. Mary Magdalene (22 July) and the two days after.[32] By 1615 there were three fairs on unspecified days.[33] By 1725 there was a fair for fat oxen held on 30 August.[34] Two fairs, on 2 July and 2 August 'for all sorts of cattle', were noted in 1767,[35] and these and the spring fair survived into the 19th century, for cattle, pigs, and 'sundries'. By 1833 the two summer fairs were said to be 'rapidly falling into neglect'.[36] The spring fair, held for only one day, the Monday before Palm Sunday, survived until after 1875, but had ceased by 1883.[37]

The market cross, a Tuscan column raised on a high base and surmounted by an entablature and finial, was erected on the site of an earlier one in 1795.[38]

MILLS. Richard of Ilchester, a chancery clerk and subsequently bishop of Winchester, held Ilchester mill from the Crown by 1155 until his death in 1188.[39] By 1204 he had been succeeded by William the Dane, who granted this and another mill between 1212 and 1217 to his hospital foundation, later Whitehall priory.[40] Richard's mill, known as New Mill from 1275, perhaps as an indication of rebuilding, remained part of Whitehall's estate until the priory, then a free chapel, was finally dissolved, when it passed to the Hodges family.[41] William Hodges died in 1605 possessed of the 'watermill called New Mill' and Mill Hams.[42] William Hodges, probably his son, sold the mill and other property to John Bendbowe in 1623,[43] and he, in the same year, transferred it to Thomas Freke.[44] In 1702 it passed from John Hartnow to Thomas Smith.[45] By 1798 it was in the hands of Richard Troward, patron of the borough;[46] in 1805 it was owned and occupied by James Masters, who was succeeded in 1811–12 by Robert Corry. Joel Ousley was miller from 1812 until 1814, James

or Joseph Salisbury in 1814–15, and William Sweeting from 1815 for a year. The mill was rated until March 1818, but had probably been abandoned two years earlier.[47]

New Mill lay on the north-eastern edge of the town, where the Yeo turns westwards to flow beneath the north wall and under Ilchester Bridge. It was driven by water channelled from a point on the river midway between Northover weir and Hainbury Mill. Faint traces of the channel and of masonry on the mill site were visible in 1969.

In 1200 Nicholas, son of Richard of Wiltshire, was granted by the Crown, inter alia, a mill held by William the Dane of the Queen's dower estate. This mill stood 'next the west gate', apparently on a small water-course, possibly part of the town's defences.[48] This may have been one of the two mills granted by William to his hospital between 1212 and 1217.[49] The hospital still held two mills in 1223.[50]

By 1268 there was a horse-mill probably in the lane later known as Almshouse Lane.[51] A successor, probably on the same site, at the eastern end of the almshouse, was rebuilt in 1486.[52] The lane was still called Horsemill Lane in 1626.[53]

LOCAL GOVERNMENT. It is not known what measure of autonomy the Domesday burgesses of Ilchester enjoyed, but in or before 1180 they seem to have formed themselves into a guild, and in 1183–4 made payments to the Exchequer for 'new pleas and new agreements', probably the purchase fees for a charter.[54] The charter, which gave them liberties like those of Winchester, 'was afterwards burnt by misfortune'.[55] It was reissued in 1204 and under its terms the burgesses had liberties of sa-ke and so-ke, tholl and theam, and infange-thief, of trial and judgement such as those claimed in Winchester, and exclusive rights to be impleaded only within the town for tenements held there.[56] The burgesses held the borough in fee farm and before 1204 also rented a rural estate and Stone hundred.[57] The borough, despite the economic expansion of the town, ceased to develop thereafter, and was able to make little headway against claims by Edmund, earl of Cornwall, to have the return of writs, view of frankpledge, and the right to appoint a coroner.[58] Similar claims were still being made in 1300 when the burgesses had their liberties temporarily suspended by the lord of the town for a trespass.[59]

[27] Ibid. 60.
[28] C. & J. Greenwood, Som. Delineated.
[29] S.R.O., D/B/il 9/2, corp. accts. 66, 70, 96; S.R.O., D/P/ilch 4/1/1.
[30] Lewis, Topog. Dict. Eng. (1833).
[31] A. Ballard, British Borough Charters.
[32] Cal. Pat. 1555–7, 528–9.
[33] S.R.O., DD/PH 52, rental etc. ff. 9–9v.
[34] S.R.O., D/P/yeon 13/2/2.
[35] Bk. of Fairs.
[36] Pigot, Nat. Com. Dir. (1822–3), 445; Lewis, Topog. Dict. Eng. (1833).
[37] Kelly's Dir. Som. (1875, 1883).
[38] It was the work of Thomas Trask: S.R.O., D/B/il 9/2, corp. accts. 11, 13.
[39] Red Bk. Exch. (Rolls Ser.), 677; Pipe R. 1156–8 (Rec. Com.), 30, 98, 122; Pipe R. 1176 (P.R.S. xxv), 154; 1188 (P.R.S. xxxviii), 156; 1189 (Rec. Com.), 146.
[40] Pipe R. 1204 (P.R.S. n.s. xviii), 177; V.C.H. Som. ii. 156–7.
[41] Rot. Hund. (Rec. Com.), ii. 126.

[42] S.R.S. lxvii. 116–17.
[43] C.P. 25(2)/347/20 Jas. I Hil.; disputed sale by Hodges to Thomas Handover, c. 1622: C3/359/11.
[44] C.P. 25(2)/347/21 Jas. I East.
[45] C.P. 43/476, rot. 204.
[46] S.R.O., D/P/ilch 4/1/1.   [47] Ibid. 13/2/2.
[48] Rot. Chart. (Rec. Com.), 71.
[49] V.C.H. Som. ii. 156–7.
[50] S.R.S. vi. 45.   [51] Ibid. lxiii. 498.
[52] Almshouse Deeds, ed. Buckler, nos. 141–2.
[53] S.R.O., D/D/Rg 216; Cox, Hist. Ilch. 165.
[54] Pipe R. 1180 (P.R.S. xxix), 111; 1183 (P.R.S. xxxii), 30; 1184 (P.R.S. xxxiii), 125.
[55] Rot. Chart. (Rec. Com.), 130.
[56] A. Ballard, British Borough Charters, 1042–1216; Pipe R. 1204 (P.R.S. n.s. xviii), 183; Rot. Hund. (Rec. Com.), ii. 126.
[57] See p. 187.
[58] Cal. Chart. R. 1226–57, 129; Plac. de Quo. Warr. (Rec. Com.), 690.
[59] S.C. 6/1089/13.

The borough court established under the charter seems to have remained in existence throughout the Middle Ages.[60] The town was governed by two bailiffs by the later 13th century.[61] From 1477 the bailiffs and burgesses became trustees of the estate of Ilchester Almshouse, and the administrative machinery set up to run the property gave quasi-corporate structure to the town. By 1538 the estate was administered by a surveyor, a chief steward, and a bailiff, and the town by two bailiffs and a constable.[62]

The town was incorporated by charter in 1556[63] partly, it was said, to revive old rights and liberties, the loss of which had brought the borough 'near to ruin', and partly because of increased burdens on a community which found itself having to support families of prisoners in the county gaol.[64] The corporation was to comprise a bailiff and twelve capital burgesses, the bailiff to be elected annually by the capital burgesses from among their own number. New capital burgesses were to be chosen by those already members of the corporation. The new body was to meet in a room in a guildhall to make 'statutes and ordinances for the governance of the borough' and to lay down 'pains and penalties for the observance of the same'. It was also to hold manorial courts, and traces of a 'manor court' or 'court baron' and of a regular view of frankpledge survive, the courts only during the 18th century.[65] The view was to be held twice yearly, but in the years immediately after 1556 one 'lawday' was held every two years.[66] A view was held regularly twice a year in the later 17th century, but by that time it had become an excuse for holding a town feast.[67] An annual 'town court' was still meeting regularly at the end of the 18th century, perhaps only for conviviality, but was discontinued after 1810 when the corporation sold the lordship of the manor.[68] Courts leet were said in 1833 still to be held,[69] but two years later this was denied, and no courts were thought to have been held since 1810.[70] In 1840 the court was said to have been neglected for three years.[71] Charles Harris, lord of the manor from 1847 until 1875, is thought to have been the last to hold a court.[72]

In the early 17th century there was also a more general court, corresponding closely with the view of frankpledge but described as a meeting of the bailiff, burgesses, and other inhabitants or as the 'accustomable court'. In 1629 this court issued orders about the use of the common lands of the parish,[73] and in 1635 was summoned in the dispute with the high steward, Sir Robert Phelips.[74] The 1556 charter also gave the bailiff and burgesses the right to hold a piepowder court for its markets and fairs, and the assize of bread, wine, ale, and other victuals.[75] The establishment of a borough gaol was permitted by the charter.[76]

No officers of the corporation were mentioned in the 1556 charter, although a number were implied. The office of constable was continued into the 17th century, and in 1629 the holder and the bailiff were given two beast leazes each for administering the common lands.[77] An 'ordinary constable' was in office in 1835, and a headborough and an under-constable were said to have been elected before 1840.[78] A steward appears intermittently in the 17th and 18th centuries holding the courts of the alms-house estate.[79] An under-bailiff occurs by 1669 and the office continued until the dissolution of the corporation.[80] Assizers of bread and ale and a viewer of flesh are mentioned in 1635,[81] a scavenger in 1735,[82] two men to examine weights and measures in 1811.[83] An overseer of the fields occurs in 1629[84] and a hayward about 1636.[85] A crier over the years had a variety of tasks: in 1635 to summon a court, in 1792 to keep strays, and in 1797 to act as constable.[86] The only permanent officials of the corporation in 1835 were the bailiff, the under-bailiff, and the town clerk.[87] These offices ceased when the corporation was dissolved in 1889.[88]

One office lay outside the corporation and was not mentioned in the 1556 charter, that of high steward. It was said to have existed before the charter was granted and the incumbent was chosen by 'the whole body of the burgesses'.[89] Sir Robert Phelips succeeded his father in the office in 1615, and a present of two sheep sent to Montacute in 1683-4 suggests that his grandson Sir Edward still maintained the family connexion.[90] This was no doubt brought to an end soon afterwards, the family having lost all political influence in the borough by 1715.[91] The office of high steward seems to have disappeared at the same time. The office was exercised by Sir Robert Phelips in the 1630s for political reasons during the ship money crisis, and a settlement in Sir Robert's favour resulted in the bailiff having to submit his annual accounts to the high steward for approval.[92] This practice evidently continued at least until 1686.[93]

60 *Proc. Som. Arch. Soc.* xiii. 54.
61 *S.R.S.* xliv. 4, 6; *Rot. Hund.* (Rec. Com.), ii. 126.
62 *Almshouse Deeds*, ed. Buckler, nos. 139, 143.
63 The original charter was thought in 1835 to be at the Tower: *Rep. Munic. Corps.* H.C. 116, pp. 1289-91 (1835), xxiv. A copy, of *c*. 1300, is C 146/9798. The 1556 charter is calendared in *Cal. Pat.* 1555-7, 528-9; annotated copy in S.R.O., DD/PH 52, rental etc. ff. 11-14, and copy in Hist. MSS. Com. 29, *13th Rep. II, Portland*, ii, p. 10. The town only possessed a copy in 1835.
64 Glastonbury had been proposed as the county town in 1554, and the charter may have been an attempt to prevent the move: *C.J.* i. 36.
65 S.R.O., D/B/il 8: 1725, 1751, 1754, 1781.
66 S.R.O., DD/PH 52, rental etc. f. 16.
67 Ibid. 223/108.
68 S.R.O., D/B/il 9/2, corp. accts. 33.
69 Lewis, *Topog. Dict. Eng.* (1833).
70 *Rep. Munic. Corps.* H.C. 116, p. 1291 (1835), xxiv.
71 *County Gazette Dir. Som.* (1840).
72 Ex inf. Mr. J. S. Cox.
73 S.R.O., DD/PH 223/48.

74 Ibid. 223/59.
75 *Cal. Pat.* 1555-7, 528-9.
76 Ibid.
77 S.R.O., DD/PH 223/48; *Cal. Cttee. for Money*, ii. 1159.
78 *County Gazette Dir. Som.* (1840).
79 S.R.O., DD/PH 223/108; D/B/il 9/2, corp. accts. 3 sqq.
80 S.R.O., DD/PH 223/108; D/B/il 9/2, corp. accts.
81 S.R.O., DD/PH 223/59.
82 S.R.O., D/B/il 5.
83 Ibid. 9/2, corp. accts. 49.
84 S.R.O., DD/PH 223/48.
85 Ibid. 223/96.
86 Ibid. 223/59; D/B/il 9/2, corp. accts. 6, 17.
87 *Rep. Munic. Corps.* H.C. 116, p. 1290 (1835), xxiv.
88 Char. Com. file.
89 S.R.O., DD/PH 223/35, 43.
90 Ibid. 223/35, 108.
91 See p. 195.
92 S.R.O., DD/PH 223/73.
93 Ibid. 223/108, 225/29, 30.

SOMERTON MARKET-PLACE, 1834

ILCHESTER MARKET-PLACE, 1847

Kingstone: 'Old Manor House', Allowenshay

Huish Episcopi: Wearne House

Muchelney: 'Tudor House'

Stoke sub Hamdon: 'The Gables'

VILLAGE HOUSES

The position of the 'inferior burgesses' whose cause Sir Robert championed is difficult to determine. Their complaints that their common rights were being taken away by the corporation were upheld, and three such men thenceforward were to sit on a committee of six to administer part of the common. The hayward was chosen from their ranks.[94]

During the 17th century there is some slight evidence that the corporation recognized its public functions, and money was spent, for example, on cleaning the market-place, providing fire buckets, and mending the ducking stool.[95] Already, however, the Phelips family had demonstrated how such a corporation could be manipulated in parliamentary elections, and the patrons of the borough in the 18th century were to demonstrate this still further. Control was made easier because Ilchester's charter was not altered, as were many others in the 1680s, largely owing to Sir Edward Phelips, though another attempt in 1698 seems almost to have succeeded, Sir Francis Wyndham probably saving it.[96] The old charter provided no check on the activities of the corporation, and the history of Ilchester in the 18th century, particularly after the death of Thomas Lockyer in 1785, is of the attempts of successive would-be patrons of the borough's two parliamentary seats to control the personnel of the corporation and thereby the bailiff, the returning officer at parliamentary elections.[97]

Successive parliamentary patrons exercised their power by ensuring the support of the corporation and then by acquiring a stranglehold on its property. The influence of Thomas Lockyer (1699–1785) was achieved through his economic control of the town, and the members of the corporation were either his relatives or tradesmen owing him their livelihood.[98] From 1766 until 1784 no election to the corporation was contested, vacancies being apparently in the patron's gift.[99] The acquiescent corporation then gave Lockyer control over its own property, and by 1788 its income was less than £20.[1] Lockyer's successors as patrons, John Harcourt, a London banker, and Richard Troward, a London attorney, packed the corporation with their adherents, and Troward in 1792 acquired all its properties in the borough in exchange for an estate at Odcombe.[2] Thereafter the income of the corporation almost doubled, but its interest in the town as landlord was lost and it thus temporarily ceased to be an important factor in parliamentary elections.[3] Sir William Manners acquired the patronage of the borough in 1802, and his agent, George Tuson, clerk of the county court since 1794, acquired a financial stranglehold over the corporation. He was probably responsible for the sale of the lordship of the manor to Manners in 1810.[4] An expensive tithe suit over the Odcombe estate,[5] followed by the leasing of corporation land at the Mead to Manners's

rival, Lord Darlington, in 1818–19[6] reduced the corporation's normal income to £6 10s.[7] Heavy spending on the Town Hall and conviviality produced a deficit, wiped out by Lord Darlington in another attempt to beat Manners.

The loss of the franchise in 1832, however, ended outside interest in the corporation. There are no surviving deeds of election after 1818, but the succession of bailiffs indicates that the corporation was dominated by local men, principally by William Shorland, surgeon, who was bailiff ten times between 1821 and 1843.[8] This period proved that a corporation with few public responsibilities was able, even with a limited budget, to keep its property in repair and still remain solvent. It had, it is true, ceased to support the school after 1818, but the craftsmen's bills which usually made up the expenditure were almost certainly for paving, fencing, and cleaning the streets. Yet, almost inevitably, between 1837 and 1843 a credit of £190 became a deficit of £22, and within a year a lawsuit increased the debt to £340. Thereafter one crisis followed another and the situation was not settled until 1868–9 when the Odcombe estate was sold.[9]

From 1870 onwards, after a period when expenditure was largely confined to paying off debts, the corporation in a modest way began spending in the public interest, towards lighting the town, repairing pavements, and providing a public weighbridge in the market-place. The weighbridge and lettings from the Town Hall provided the largest part of its income, which in 1888 amounted to over £27.[10] The membership of the corporation was not, of course, in any sense representative: judging by the bailiffs it reflected the population less accurately than at the beginning of the century. A surgeon, two farmers, two road engineers, and local clergy seem to have dominated the body. In the last twenty years of its life it became even more exclusive and its membership smaller. There were five vacancies in 1883 and only five members petitioned against the dissolution of the corporation: the incumbents of Ilchester and Northover, the town clerk, a surgeon, and a farmer.[11]

The corporation was dissolved in 1889 and its assets were the subject of a Scheme of the Charity Commissioners. The Ilchester Town Trust was established, its income thereafter being devoted to the maintenance of the Town Hall, contributions towards the cost of lighting the town, and to other public benefits.[12]

The division between the jurisdictions of corporation and parish is not easily defined, but it seems clear that the parish officers, expecting no help from the corporation, were responsible for most aspects of poor relief. In the 17th century, when 'by means of the late wars' the borough was 'so much impoverished' as to be unable to maintain its poor, petition for relief came from the

[94] Ibid. 223/73, 96.
[95] Ibid. 223/108.
[96] *Cal. S.P. Dom.* 1698, 440.
[97] See below, p. 195.
[98] S.R.O., D/B/il 5, 8; *Hist. Parl., Commons,* 1754–90, iii. 51.
[99] S.R.O., D/B/il 5, 8.
[1] Ibid. 9/2, corp. accts.
[2] Ibid. 6, alms-house accts. 1745–1852, 184; 'manor of Stocklinch' bk. 33; D/P/ilch 4/1/1: chwdns.' accts. and rates.

[3] See p. 196.
[4] See p. 184.
[5] S.R.O., D/B/il 9/2, corp. accts. 41, 43, 49.
[6] Ibid. 9/2, corp. accts. 64.
[7] The income was often less, since the lessees paid much in arrear: D/B/il 9/2, corp. accts. 80, 91, 111–12.
[8] S.R.O., D/B/il 9/2, corp. accts. *passim.*
[9] Ibid.   [10] Ibid. 165, 167, 169, 204.
[11] S.R.O., D/B/il 9, min. bk. 1873–89, min. 27 July 1882; *Kelly's Dir. Som.* (1883).
[12] Char. Com. file.

inhabitants as a whole and not from the corporation, in an effort to have Chestermead, New mead, and Burlinghams, parts of Sock Dennis,[13] rated for support of the town's poor.[14] The vestry appointed both wardens and overseers until 1800, but from that year one warden was chosen by the rector.[15] The vestry also appointed a parish surgeon.[16] A salaried assistant overseer was employed from 1833, and a collecting overseer from 1836.[17] Late in 1848 the vestry established a committee for nuisances.[18]

In the 18th century the obligation to take parish apprentices lay with a group of substantial occupiers in a known and accepted rotation.[19] A workhouse had been established by 1689 but its name, the Town House, suggests that it was maintained by the corporation.[20] By 1805 the parish was paying Sir William Manners £20 a year rent for the 'old workhouse' and £10 for ten poorhouses, provided after Manners had dispossessed many of his political opponents.[21] In 1806 the poorhouses, occupied by 25 paupers, were given back to Manners, and the inhabitants removed to a new poorhouse.[22] This house may have been the medieval building south of the Town Hall, known as Cordelyon House, which was still used as a poorhouse in 1833.[23] The parish retained the old workhouse at least until 1816.[24]

Ilchester became part of the Yeovil poor-law union in 1836. It is governed by a parish council which since 1933 has had jurisdiction over the civil parish of Northover, and since 1957 over part of the civil parish of Sock Dennis.[25]

The present Town Hall may be of 17th- or early-18th-century origin. A disused courtroom at the west end rises through two storeys and has a Ham stone mullioned window overlooking High Street. The building was remodelled in 1812–16 when the shambles were removed and a large upper room was provided for meetings.[26]

ARMS, SEALS, AND INSIGNIA. The only device used by the borough was an étoile within a crescent, similar to the device on the second Great Seal of Richard I. The tradition of that king's visit to Ilchester has been linked with the town's assumption of the device.[27] The details of the étoile have varied, but on the bailiff's staff it appears as an étoile of sixteen points, alternately straight and wavy, within a silver cresent, on a blue field.

The earliest seal, dating from the 13th century,

is circular, 1¾ in. in diameter, and was in use in 1315.[28] The device is an étoile of eight points wavy, within a crescent, surrounded by the inscription, lombardic, S. BURGEN*SIBUS* BURGI DE IVELCESTRIE. The second seal, dating from the 14th or 15th centuries, is 1 1/10 in. in diameter. The étoile has sixteen points, alternately straight and wavy, with the inscription, roman, SIGNUM BURGI DE YEVELECESTER.[29] It was in use at least until 1695.[30] The third seal dates from the 17th century and measures 1¾ in. in diameter. The device is the same as on the second seal, the inscription, roman, SIGILLUM BURGI DE IVELCHESTER.[31] It is found in use between 1695 and the 19th century.[32] A counterpart seal, ⅖ in. in diameter, with the étoile and crescent surrounded by a circle of pellets but without inscription, occurs early in the 18th century.[33] None of the matrices has survived.

The only survival from the town's insignia is the bailiff's staff, the head of which dates from the mid 13th century or earlier. The head is of latten, formerly gilded, 7½ in. high. An inscription, which has provoked a variety of interpretations,[34] is surmounted by a zig-zag design and then by four shafts, forming an arcade of moulded and trefoil-headed arches, each filled with a figure. The figures are an angel and three kings, and one interpretation of the inscription involves identification of the kings as the magi. The rest of the staff, the whole 7 ft. 4 in. long, probably dates from 1816–37, the date of the royal arms painted thereon.

There is a list of bailiffs of the borough from 1280 to 1886.[35]

PARLIAMENTARY REPRESENTATION. Ilchester was required to send two members to most Parliaments between 1298 and 1361, though only one was sent in 1347–8 and 1351–2, and no returns were made in 1311 and for several assemblies in the early 1330s.[36] Few of the members can be identified, though Robert of Shepton and Reynold of Frome may have been lawyers, the former evidently in the service of the Beauchamp family.[37] Several witnessed local deeds;[38] Robert Cole was described as 'of Ilchester' in 1308,[39] and Roger Page, Thomas Cole, and John Brewton were resident in the town in 1327.[40] The names of John and Richard of Chitterne (or Chilthorne), Hugh and John of Draycote, and Roger of Sock suggest local origins.[41]

[13] See p. 234.
[14] *S.R.S.* xxviii. 77, 276; S.R.O., Q/petns. 1649, 1655.
[15] S.R.O., D/P/ilch 4/1/1, 13/6/1.
[16] Ibid. 13/2/2–4.
[17] Ibid. 13/2/4.
[18] Ibid.
[19] Ibid. 13/6/1.
[20] *C.J.* x. 124.
[21] S.R.O., D/P/ilch 13/2/2; 39 *Parl. Deb.* 1st ser. 1353.
[22] S.R.O., D/P/ilch 13/2/2.
[23] Lewis, *Topog. Dict. Eng.* (1833). See plate facing p. 64.
[24] S.R.O., D/P/ilch 13/2/2.
[25] *Poor Law Com. 2nd Rep.* p. 550; *Som. Review Order, 1933; Somerset (Parishes in the Rural District of Yeovil) Confirmation Order, 1957.*
[26] S.R.O., D/B/il 9/2, corp. accts. 48, 57.
[27] Cox, *Hist. Ilch.* 183; *Almshouse Deeds,* ed. Buckler, p. 170.
[28] S.R.O., DD/SAS/BK 11; W. de G. Birch, *Cat. of Seals in B.M.* ii. 95.

[29] Cox, *Hist. Ilch.* 183 and illus. opp. p. 187.
[30] Ibid. 184.   [31] Ibid. 183.
[32] S.R.O., D/B/il 2, 5.
[33] Cox, *Hist. Ilch.* 184; S.R.O., D/B/il 5.
[34] Ll. Jewitt and W. H. St. J. Hope, *Corp. Plate and Insignia of Office,* ii. 304–6; *Archaeologia,* lii. 762–4; Cox, *Hist. Ilch.* 181–3; Collinson, *Hist. Som.* iii. 299; *Gent. Mag.* 1794, pt. ii. 1001. The staff head is illustrated in: *Archaeologia,* lii, pl. XXXVI; Cox, *Hist. Ilch.* opp. p. 176; Pevsner, *South and West Som.* pl. 37b; Taunton Castle, Braikenridge Colln.
[35] Cox, *Hist. Ilch.* 185–7.
[36] *Official Return.*
[37] *Cal. Pat.* 1292–1301, 448, 538; 1301–7, 182; 1307–13, 111, 212, 281, 324, 584; 1313–17, 229, 334; 1330–4, 350.
[38] *Almshouse Deeds,* ed. Buckler, nos. 14–16, 22–3, 30, 38.
[39] Ibid. nos. 15–16.
[40] *S.R.S.* iii. 273.
[41] Chilthorne Domer and Sock Dennis are neighbouring parishes; Draycott is in Limington, also adjoining.

The town sent no members to Parliament from 1361 until 1621.[42] It was enfranchised again on the petition of Sir Robert Phelips to provide him with a borough seat should he fail at a county election.[43] The election was 'popular':[44] in 1689 the franchise was declared to be in all inhabitants paying scot and lot, known as pot wallers;[45] in 1703 in all inhabitants not receiving alms.[46] There were c. 140 voters in 1688,[47] c. 110 in 1689,[48] c. 150 for most of the 18th century, in 1795 c. 173,[49] c. 119 in 1802,[50] and in 1818 about ninety.[51]

Ilchester produced at least nineteen controverted elections between 1621 and 1832, though not all petitions against returns were proceeded with.[52] The reputation of Ilchester voters, as a result, was low; in 1756 they were said to be 'poor and corrupt, without honour, morals, or attachment to any man or party'.[53] The price of a vote rose from two guineas in 1702 to £30 by 1784.[54] John Harcourt (M.P. 1785–6, 1790–6) found that the electors 'drank out fifty hogsheads of his cider in the course of one year', though several of them 'were so staunch to their party that they requested on their death bed to be buried in true blue coffins'.[55]

The pressure that Sir Robert Phelips was able to bring on the corporation as high steward of the borough resulted in the election of courtiers in 1624–5 and 1625, but Phelips influence was less evident in 1628–9 and 1640–1,[56] and was entirely absent in 1646.[57] The family's power was restored by 1661 in the Tory interest, Edward Phelips the younger being one of the members.[58] Phelips and his fellow member lost their seats in 1679 to William Strode of Barrington and John Speke of Whitelackington, both Whigs and dissenters. Two moderate Tories were returned in 1681, probably with Phelips's support, and Phelips and Sir Edward Wyndham beat Strode and another Whig in 1685.[59] The 'great treats in town and large invitations of his party to his house in Barrington' late in 1681 availed Strode nothing, as the expected election did not then take place.[60]

It was confidently predicted in 1687 that Strode, then a government supporter for Toleration, would be returned at the next election.[61] Phelips was evidently unpopular at Court for persuading the corporation not to surrender their charter, but his influence in the borough was strong.[62] Ilchester chose Sir Edward Wyndham and another Tory for the Convention; Strode and Speke were defeated.[63] Wyndham was elected again in 1690, and Sir Francis Wyndham succeeded to his seat in 1695. The Phelipses still retained an interest in the other seat until 1715 when both Tory members were turned out.

From 1727 until about 1790 elections in the borough were controlled by the Lockyer family, prosperous dissenting merchants.[64] Charles Lockyer (d. 1752) represented the town from 1727 until 1747, and brought with him at the three elections a government nominee. His brother Thomas (1699–1785), succeeded to his patronage, holding one seat from 1746 until 1761. 'Lockyer', wrote Lord Egmont, 'may absolutely have the command of this borough'.[65] After his retirement from the seat he exercised his influence on behalf of the government either for his own relatives—his son Joseph Tolson Lockyer (M.P. 1756–65), or his son-in-law, Samuel Smith (M.P. 1780–4)—or for government supporters. Elections in the later years of Lockyer's control were bitterly disputed: that of 1774 was declared void a year later, the bailiff Christopher Lockyer, having 'shown great partiality' in favour of the members returned by admitting non-voters to the poll.[66] Lockyer's control was by then less complete: two of his candidates were defeated in elections to the corporation in 1784,[67] and by April 1785 John Harcourt, a London banker, had built up an interest in the town by acquiring reversionary interests in much of the corporation's property.[68] Harcourt stood at the election in 1784, but came third in the poll with 70 votes against Lockyer candidates. His strength, however, forced Lockyer to give £30 for votes for his party.[69] Harcourt was elected in the following year, but was unseated for 'gross and illegal' malpractices by the returning officer.[70]

In 1784 the borough was said to be 'open',[71] but Samuel Smith, Lockyer's heir, claimed the 'opportunity of arranging matters', so that the nomination would revert to himself, and offered a seat to Lord Liverpool.[72] In 1789 Smith sold a seat to Francis Baring for £1,500,[73] but in the election of the following year Harcourt's interest proved too strong, and Harcourt himself was returned. Either just before or just after the election Harcourt

---

[42] Browne Willis, *Notitia Parliamentaria*, iii. 45–6, followed by *V.C.H. Som.* ii. 184, states that members were sent to the 1472 Parliament. No foundation for these statements has been discovered.
[43] *Official Return*, i. 453; T. H. B. Oldfield, *The Representative History of Great Britain and Ireland*, iv. 447–8; *Proc. Som. Arch. Soc.* cx. 42; T. G. Barnes, *Somerset*, *1629–40*, 9.
[44] G. Duckett, *Penal Laws and the Test Act*, ii. 230.
[45] *C.J.* x. 124.
[46] Ibid. xiv. 147–8.
[47] Duckett, op. cit. 230.
[48] *C.J.* x. 124.
[49] *Hist. Parl., Commons, 1754–90*; B.M. Add. MS. 37875 f. 41.
[50] Neast Greville Prideaux, 'Diary' (TS in S.R.O., DD/SAS FA 185) under date 5 June 1802.
[51] History of Parliament files. Thanks are due to Mr. E. L. C. Mullins and Mr. R. G. Thorne of the History of Parliament Trust.
[52] *V.C.H. Som.* ii. 233–4; Oldfield, *Representative Hist.* iv. 448–61; *Proc. Som. Arch. Soc.* cx. 40–51 *Hist. Parl., Commons, 1754–90*; Hist. Parl. files.
[53] *Hist. Parl., Commons, 1754–90.*

[54] *A Key to Both Houses* (1832), 341; *C.J.* xiv. 147–8; *Reps. Cttees. of House of Commons upon Controverted Elections*, ed. A. Luders, i. 465–6. It was still £30 in 1802: S.R.O., DD/SAS FA 185.
[55] J. Wilson, *Biog. Index to House of Commons*, 1808.
[56] M. F. Keeler, *The Long Parliament.*
[57] *Proc. Som. Arch. Soc.* cx. 40–51.
[58] *Official Return.*
[59] Hist. Parl. files; *C.J.* ix. 707, 727.
[60] *Cal. S.P. Dom.* 1680–1, 514.
[61] Duckett, *Penal Laws and the Test Act*, ii. 18.
[62] Ibid. 230, 244; for the charter see above, p. 192.
[63] *C.J.* x. 14, 124.
[64] See p. 189.
[65] Hist. Parl. files.
[66] *Hist. Parl., Commons, 1754–90*; Oldfield, *Representative Hist.* iv. 454–5.
[67] S.R.O., D/B/il 5.   [68] Ibid. 8.
[69] Oldfield, *Representative Hist.* iv. 455–7; *Reps. upon Controverted Elections*, ed. Luders, i. 465–6.
[70] *Hist. Parl., Commons, 1754–90.*
[71] Ibid.
[72] B.M. Add. MS. 38458 f. 157.
[73] B.M. Add. MS. 38220 f. 252.

disposed of his interest in the borough, allegedly for £40,000,[74] to Richard Troward the 'celebrated attorney' of Norfolk Street, London. Troward had begun to create an interest in the corporation before the election, and during the 1790s half its members were his nominees.[75] His own position was strengthened by his acquisition of corporation property within the town in exchange for lands outside.[76]

At a by-election in 1799 Lewis Bayly, afterwards Lewis Bayly Wallis, was returned. He was the ward and sole heir of Troward's wealthy partner Albany Wallis who, early in 1800, purchased half Troward's property in Ilchester.[77] Wallis died in the same year in Troward's debt. It was said that the two seats could be bought for 8,000 guineas, £1,500 down,[78] but Bayly Wallis, either for himself or for Troward, sold the patronage of the borough in 1802 to Sir William Manners of Hanby Hall (Lincs.), the Tory borough-monger, for £53,000.[79] The investment did not immediately show a good return. Manners, addressing the electors, could not think they would be misled by 'designing borough agents', and pointed out that 'the whole of that parish . . . with a very small exception and that of no importance' was his property.[80] In the event, opposition from a borough agent proved too strong in 1802, but on petition the whole election was declared void because of corruption before voting, and the arrest of the agents of the returned candidates was ordered.[81] At a second election in the following year Charles Brooke and Sir William Manners were returned, Brooke succeeding to the interest opposed to Manners. A petition against Brooke failed, but Manners himself was unseated on another petition, his brother John being returned in his place in 1804.[82]

Manners certainly controlled the next three elections,[83] but his power was not absolute and, probably after the 1812 election, he demolished about a hundred houses in the town, leaving about sixty standing. Those people rendered homeless were housed in a 'workhouse', hired from him by the corporation, where as lodgers they were automatically disfranchised.[84] 'In consequence of the continued political dissensions which prevailed in the town' Manners even threatened to pull the 'workhouse' down, leaving the evicted homeless.[85] Ilchester, it was said, would have been a 'close' borough in any hands but those of Manners, whose 'insane intolerance provoked the people of the place past all endurance'.[86]

To counter these moves, Lord Darlington, the Whig borough-monger, in 1818–19 leased land in the Mead from the corporation for a large sum to ease their financial difficulties,[87] and erected cottages there to house his potential supporters.[88] The result of the next two elections were victories for Darlington.[89] Sir William Manners, who took the name Talmash and was styled Lord Huntingtower after 1821,[90] secured the return of two of his sons in 1826 after a disputed election, the result of highly successful advertising by which he offered houses, pasture, and work to any voter prepared to qualify by six months residence in the town.[91] Darlington's son-in-law was one of two elected in 1830.[92] Two Whigs returned in 1831 voted for the Reform Bill which abolished Ilchester's franchise.[93] The town then became a polling place in the Western Division of the county, and later in the Middle Division. Since 1885 it has been in the Southern or Yeovil Division.

CHURCHES. At the height of its prosperity in the 13th century Ilchester was divided between at least six parishes. The town may earlier have come within the *parochia* of St. Andrew's church, Northover, in origin evidently a minster of Saxon date.[94] In addition to the parish churches the town contained a house of Dominican friars[95] and, by the late 15th century, two chapels.

The church of St. John the Baptist is first mentioned in 1207.[96] It continued to serve an independent parish until 1502, when it was united with St. Mary Major and St. Mary Minor.[97] It probably ceased to be used soon afterwards.[98] The advowson was in the hands of the Crown by 1207;[99] the Crown also presented in 1221,[1] but it was later said that the advowson was granted to Richard, earl of Cornwall, in 1231.[2] The Crown was clearly patron in 1243,[3] but on his death in

[74] J. Wilson, *Biographical Index to House of Commons* (1806), 440; *Univ. Brit. Dir.* (1791–8), 414; Oldfield, *Hist. Boroughs*, ii.

[75] S.R.O., D/B/il 5.   [76] See p. 193.

[77] Prob. 11/1348 (P.C.C. 691 Adderley). I owe this reference to Mr. R. G. Thorne.

[78] B.M. Add. MS. 37880 f. 197.

[79] Oldfield, *Representative Hist.* iv. 447; B.M. Add. MS. 37880 f. 197; S.R.O., DD/SAS FA 185: transcript of Prideaux diary.

[80] *Morning Chronicle*, 24 June 1802, printed in Cox, *Hist. Ilch.* 219.

[81] *C.J.* lviii. 29–30, 301–2, 425; Oldfield, *Representative Hist.* iv. 457–60, 463–4. For details of the 1802 election see S.R.O., DD/SAS FA 185.

[82] Oldfield, *Representative Hist.* iv. 460–1; *C.J.* lviii. 339, 345; lix. 138, 221.   [83] Hist. Parl. files.

[84] Oldfield, *Representative Hist.* iv. 464; 39 *Parl. Deb.* 1st. ser. 1353, a petition presented in 1819, related to houses demolished after the 1818 election. This is corroborated by C. & J. Greenwood, *Som. Delineated.* Oldfield, however, wrote in 1816, so Manners must have demolished houses after each election. He had also evicted many tenants after the 1802 election: S.R.O., DD/SAS FA 185, under date 9 Aug. 1802, and the supplement to 1802.

[85] 39 *Parl. Deb.* 1st. ser. 1353.

[86] R. W. Ward, *Letters to Ivy*, 305.

[87] S.R.O., D/B/il 6: corp. accts. 63–4, 80; see above, p. 193.

[88] The development at the Mead originally contained 38 dwellings. Lord Darlington also erected 'two piles of building' in the town, each comprising 20–30 tenements: C. & J. Greenwood. *Som. Delineated.* See also *11th. Rep. Com. Char.* H.C. 433, p. 478 (1824), xiv, for the effect of the increased number of buildings, and above, p. 183.

[89] *C.J.* lxxiv. 91.

[90] *Complete Peerage*, iv. 566.

[91] *Bath and Cheltenham Gaz.* 18 Oct. 1825.

[92] *Key to Both Houses* (1832), 341.

[93] 40 *Parl. Deb.* 3rd ser. 782; 2 & 3 Wm. IV, c. 45, schedule A.

[94] See p. 228.

[95] *V.C.H. Som.* ii. 150.

[96] *Rot. Litt. Pat.* (Rec. Com.), 75.

[97] *S.R.S.* liv. 78.

[98] See below.

[99] *Rot. Litt. Pat.* (Rec. Com.), 75.

[1] *Pat. R.* 1216–25, 318.

[2] *Cal. Chart. R.* 1226–57, 129; *Rot. Hund.* (Rec. Com.), ii. 139.

[3] *Bk. of Fees*, ii. 1385; *S.R.S.* xi. 323.

1300 Edmund, earl of Cornwall, certainly held the advowson, and his wife held it in dower.[4] The Crown presented from 1315 until 1433, the bishop collated by lapse in 1458 and 1463, and the Crown presented the last recorded incumbent in 1486.[5]

In 1212 the glebe, let to William the Dane, amounted to 12½ a. and rent from the house called *alba aula*, the whole worth 20¾d.[6] By 1217–20 William had acquired the house and given it to his hospital foundation, later known as Whitehall.[7] John the Dane, William's son, was still holding 10 a. of glebe in 1235: a dispute between him and the then rector of St. John's resulted in a settlement whereby John gave 9 marks for the repair of the church and promised for himself and his successors to pay two pounds of wax to the church every Easter. The glebe was therefore virtually lost.[8] By 1301 the church was said to be worth 5 marks, but by 1445 only 4 marks.[9]

Such a small benefice attracted few identifiable clergy and only two graduates, Thomas Cace (rector 1458) and Thomas Purvyour (rector 1463). Purvyour is unlikely to have been resident and the presence of parochial chaplains there in 1450 and 1463 suggests that his predecessors were similarly absentees.[10] The unification of the remaining town parishes in 1502 was foreshadowed in the appointment of the rector of St. Mary Major to the benefice in 1486.[11] His predecessor was also chaplain of Whitehall.[12]

The site of the church is not known, though it may have been near the old gaol.[13] The building was in ruins in Leland's time.[14]

In 1476 there was a chapel on Ilchester Bridge dedicated to St. Leonard.[15] It was then owned by the corporation and was evidently not used for worship, though it was still recognizable as a chapel in the 17th century.[16] It was then thought to have been built for prisoners in the gaol.[17] At least until 1769 the name 'chapple' was given to a building on the island on which the bridge rested.[18] The property probably disappeared when the bridge was reconstructed in 1797.[19]

The church known as St. Mary the Less or St. Mary Minor, founded by 1227–8, became the property of the hospital of Holy Trinity, or Whitehall, in 1242 as the result of two grants. By the first, made between 1232 and 1242 and presumably at the end of that period, Cerne abbey (Dors.), then

patron of the rectory, transferred the advowson to the bishop of Bath and Wells. A pension of 2s., payable by the rector to the monks, was to be retained during the lifetime of the then rector. The rectory was then granted to the hospital in 1242, the appropriators having to provide a suitable chaplain to serve the church. The pension to Cerne was to be continued, and after the cession or death of the then rector was to be increased to a mark. These changes were designed to give the hospital, which lay in the parish of St. Mary the Less, a separate chapel and burial ground on their own premises, a matter not easy to arrange when their parish church was in other hands.[20]

The church possessed a tenement 'towards the North Gate' by 1227–8,[21] but the income of the benefice was always small, amounting to only 3 marks in 1445.[22] In 1324 its churchyard needed reconciliation after bloodshed.[23] Apart from Thomas, rector of St. Mary's in 1241, the name of only one incumbent, collated to the benefice by lapse in 1498, is known.[24] The parish was united with that of St. Mary Major and St. John in 1502.[25]

The church stood on the east side of Cheap Street opposite Whitehall, just inside the northern entrance to the town.[26] Foundations of a simple building in the grounds of the former Ivel House, now a car park, have been identified as those of St. Mary's church.[27] The building was still standing in Leland's time, but had evidently disappeared a century later.[28]

Among the plate of St. Mary's was a pair of censers and a latten incense-boat, given in 1457.[29]

In 1311 Philip de Courtenay granted the advowson of the church of St. Michael to Thomas de Cirencester for life.[30] The benefice was a rectory, though it was clearly a poor living, and by 1350 vacant and 'destitute'.[31] In that year it was temporarily united with St. Mary Major, the rector of St. Mary's having to continue the services in St. Michael's until the bishop should order otherwise.[32] The church seems to have regained its independence by 1372,[33] but by 1445 its value was only 2 marks.[34] It seems to have lost its parochial status by the late 15th century, and did not figure in the scheme to unite the surviving parishes of the town.[35]

From 1311 at least until 1392 the advowson was held by the Courtenay family, and was associated with a small holding in Sock Dennis.[36] Roger

[4] *Cal. Inq. p.m.* iii, p. 459; *Cal. Close,* 1296–1302, 438.
[5] *Cal. Pat.* 1313–17, 223; 1429–36, 284; 1485–94, 48; *S.R.S.* xlix. 302, 387.
[6] *Bk. of Fees,* i. 79.
[7] T. Hugo, *Whitehall in Ilchester,* 71–2.
[8] *S.R.S.* vi. 83.
[9] *Cal. Close,* 1296–1302, 438; *S.R.S.* xlix. 32.
[10] Emden, *Biog. Reg. Univ. Oxford; S.R.S.* xlix. 137, 395.
[11] *S.R.S.* lii. 136.
[12] Ibid. 134.
[13] See p. 185.
[14] Leland, *Itin.* ed. Toulmin Smith, i. 156.
[15] S.R.O., DD/PH 52, rental etc. It was still let by the corporation in 1614–15.
[16] *S.R.S.* xv. 206.
[17] Ibid. It is possible that it may have been the town gaol.
[18] S.R.O., D/B/il 7: lease of 1742; D/B/il 8: leases of 1747, 1766, 1769.
[19] *Univ. Brit. Dir.* (1791–8); Cox, *Hist. Ilch.* 205.
[20] Hugo, *Whitehall in Ilchester,* 72–5; *S.R.S.* i. 68;

vii. 55. *V.C.H. Som.* ii. 157, places the original grant by the abbot of Cerne *c.* 1237. The abbot's letter refers to a hospital of St. John the Baptist, but the bishop's ordination clearly calls it Holy Trinity hospital.
[21] *S.R.S.* xiv. 88–9.
[22] Ibid. xlix. 32. The benefice was *valde exilis* in 1417, worth 20s. in 1426: *S.R.S.* xxix. 273; xxxi. 23.
[23] *S.R.S.* i. 232.
[24] Ibid. liv. 12–13.
[25] Ibid. 78.
[26] *Almshouse Deeds,* ed. Buckler, no. 30, and p. 182.
[27] Cox, *Hist. Ilch.* 156–8.
[28] Leland, *Itin.* ed. Toulmin Smith, i. 156; *S.R.S.* xv. 205.
[29] *S.R.S.* xvi. 173.
[30] Ibid. vi. 113.
[31] Ibid. x. 625.
[32] Ibid.
[33] *Cal. Pat.* 1370–4, 194.
[34] *S.R.S.* xlix. 32.
[35] Ibid. liv. 78.
[36] Ibid. vi. 113; *Cal. Inq. p.m.* xiv, p. 321; *Cal. Inq. p.m.* (Rec. Com.), iii. 133.

Torel, holder of land in Chilthorne Domer, presented in 1339,[37] and the bishop, apparently, later in the same year.[38] The Crown was patron in 1372,[39] and Sir William Bonville, lord of Sock, in 1424 and 1433.[40] By 1487 the advowson had fallen to the bishop by lapse, and he collated in 1487, 1490, and also in 1494, the last recorded presentation.[41]

St. Michael's was built over the south gate of the town, and during the early 16th century was known as St. Michael's Bowe or St. Michael's at Bowe.[42] Its position and its connexion with land in Sock, to the south of the town, suggests that its ancient parish may have been that area to the south and west of the town outside the walls. By 1548 its glebe land and a dovecot were together worth only 4d.[43] The chapel, described by Leland, was regarded as a chantry, and was taken by the Crown in 1548. It was granted to John Dudley and John Ayscough in 1576, but has not been further traced.[44]

The church of St. Olave, by its dedication probably of pre-Conquest origin, was confirmed to Montacute priory between 1174 and 1180, and a pension of a pound of pepper was then payable by the incumbent.[45] The church was still in existence in 1276 when a thief, removed from the gallows for burial in its churchyard, recovered and took sanctuary there.[46] Its probable site was still known in the 1590s.[47]

The church of St. Peter existed by c. 1191, and was a rectory in the patronage of Glastonbury abbey.[48] From 1191 a pension of ½ mark was payable from the rectory to the precentorship of Glastonbury.[49] In 1281, having acquired the patronage of the church, Bishop Burnell of Bath and Wells, on account of its poverty, united St. Peter's to the rectory of St. Mary Major.[50] The rector remained charged with the pension to Glastonbury until the Dissolution.[51] There is no clear evidence for the site of the church, but St. Peter's Cross was still standing in Cheap Street in 1405.[52]

Presumably soon after Whitehall hospital acquired the patronage of St. Mary the Less in 1242, a chapel was built on the premises.[53] From about 1281 the character of the hospital foundation changed, becoming a nunnery, possibly under Augustinian rule,[54] and the chapel therefore became the focal point of the community. At some date between 1436 and 1463 the community ceased to exist, and the foundation became a free chapel, at

first in Crown patronage.[55] In 1519 a chaplain or rector was appointed by a group of feoffees headed by the bishops of London and Salisbury, at the request of Henry Stafford, earl of Wiltshire (d. 1523).[56] By 1525 the remaining feoffees had granted the advowson to a further group, headed by Sir Richard Grey.[57] Both groups were representatives of Cecily Bonville, marchioness of Dorset (d. 1530), the heir of Sock Dennis and successor of the founder of Whitehall.[58] In 1545 the presentation was made by Michael Mallett, who apparently had received it for that turn only, but from whom is unknown.[59] The Crown presented in 1555, when the Sock properties had been confiscated from the Greys, and again in 1561, the date of the last known appointment.[60]

Two Crown presentees in 1485, Thomas Harryes and William Elyott, were graduates and respectively king's chaplain and assistant Master of the Rolls.[61] Both were almost certainly absentees. William Soper (d. 1519) was a considerable pluralist in East Anglia, and George Carew, archdeacon of Totnes, held the benefice from 1545 together with livings elsewhere in Somerset, Devon, and Wiltshire.[62]

The chapel itself was dedicated to the Holy Trinity, the dedication of the original foundation, and had more than one altar.[63] In 1415 land was given to maintain a chantry at the high altar.[64] In 1546 goods of the chapel, delivered to George Carew the incumbent, included a bell, vestments, two candlesticks and two cruets, a sacring bell, and a coffer, together worth 16s. 8d.[65] The bell was then taken, and the goods had gone two years later, when the incumbent was pensioned and the buildings, already let to Thomas Duporte from 1545, came to the Crown.[66] It is not clear exactly when the chapel was secularized, but its sale by the Crown in 1600 indicates the completion of this process.[67]

The church of St. Mary the Greater, now St. Mary Major, is the only church in the town to survive to the present day. The benefice is a rectory, until 1239 in the patronage of Muchelney abbey. In that year the bishop of Bath and Wells acquired the advowson in return for allowing the monks to appropriate other churches in their patronage.[68] He remained patron and, except in 1560 and 1655, presented until 1852, when the advowson was transferred to the present patron, the bishop of London.[69]

[37] S.R.S. ix. 353; Almshouse Deeds, ed. Buckler, no. 39.
[38] S.R.S. ix. 361.
[39] Cal. Pat. 1370–4, 194.
[40] S.R.S. xxx. 451; xxxi. 151
[41] Ibid. lii. 148, 166, 189–90.
[42] Ibid. ii. 107, 292; C 66/1148.
[43] S.R.S. ii. 107, 292.
[44] Leland, Itin. ed. Toulmin Smith, i. 156; S.R.S. ii. 107, 292; C 66/3348.
[45] S.R.S. viii. 191–2.
[46] Cal. Pat. 1272–81, 175; S.R.S. xli. 34; Cox, Hist. Ilch. 161.
[47] Devon R.O. 123 M/E 33, 91.
[48] S.R.S. lix. 68.
[49] Ibid. xiii. 5; lix. 68–9.
[50] Ibid. lix. 70–1.
[51] H.M.C. Wells, i. 296; Cal. Papal Regs. v. 350 (where the date should be 1385); Dugdale, Mon., i. 15.
[52] Almshouse Deeds, ed. Buckler, no. 94; Cox, Hist. Ilch. 162. The Cross was within (infra) the walls, not underneath, and therefore not necessarily near the south gate.
[53] See above.

[54] M. D. Knowles and R. N. Hadcock, Medieval Religious Houses, 232.
[55] Hugo, Whitehall in Ilchester, 45; Rot. Parl. (Rec. Com.), vi. 349; Cal. Pat. 1485–94, 31; S.R.S. lii. 52.
[56] S.R.S. lv. 8.
[57] Ibid. 40.
[58] Cal. Close, 1500–9, 171.
[59] S.R.S. lv. 109.
[60] Cal. Pat. 1555–7, 110; T. Rymer, Foedera, xv. 618; and see below, p. 232.
[61] S.R.S. lii. 52; Rot. Parl. vi. 349; Cal. Pat. 1485–94, 31; Emden, Biog. Reg. Univ. Oxford.
[62] Emden, Biog. Reg. Univ. Oxford; Foster, Alumni Oxon.
[63] Cal. Pat. 1370–4, 419; 1413–16, 371; Knowles and Hadcock, Med. Relig. Houses, 280.
[64] Cal. Pat. 1413–16, 371.
[65] E 117/8/23b.
[66] E 117/12, no. 21; S.R.S. ii, pp. xx, 107; C 66/1110.
[67] C 66/1110, 1535.
[68] S.R.S. xiv. 51.
[69] Cal. Pat. 1558–60, 267; Lambeth Palace MSS. COMM II. 374; Lond. Gaz. 4 June 1852.

The advowson of the present united benefice is held jointly by the bishop, who has two turns, and the patron of Northover, who has one.[70] At the request of the then rector the churches of St. Mary the Less and St. John were united with St. Mary Major in 1502.[71] The incumbent of St. Mary Major was instituted to 'four or five' churches in the 17th century,[72] and procurations and paschals were still paid by the rector in respect of St. Mary the Less and St. John's in 1952.[73]

A plan in 1656 to unite the benefice with Northover and part of Sock Dennis, and another in the following year to unite Ilchester with Montacute, Lufton, and Sock were dropped.[74] The union of the vicarage of Northover with the rectory took effect in 1936.[75]

During the Middle Ages the benefice income was small. About 1350 the rector was licensed to unite the income of the chantry in his church to his own benefice, provided that the services of the chantry were continued.[76] The living was assessed at £5 6s. 8d. in 1445, and the combined incomes of the three united churches at £7 16s. 9½d. in 1545.[77] It was said to be worth £9 2s. 6d. in 1548, probably gross, and by c. 1668 its value was £30.[78] In 1721 it was augmented by Dame Rebecca Moyer and Queen Anne's Bounty,[79] and by 1809 it was said to be worth £74 11s. 2d.[80] The rector in 1851 declared that the gross income did not exceed £148, and the deduction of the curate's salary left only about £70.[81]

Tithes and oblations of the benefice in 1545 amounted to £8 17s. 10d., almost the whole of the benefice income.[82] By 1838 a modus of 4d. an acre was payable on all meadow and pasture which was fed, and of 8d. on that which was mown. The rector received £52 as a rent-charge in lieu of tithes.[83]

By 1272 the rector had glebe in Podimore Milton parish.[84] Within the town there were four burgages, and in the parish 15½ a. in the open fields and inclosed land called 'Personesham',[85] by the end of the 15th century. The united benefice had glebe worth 16s. in 1545, and presumably included the glebe of St. Mary the Less.[86] By 1621 the rector held 5 burgages in Ilchester and arable, meadow, and pasture in Ilchester, Sock Dennis, Chilton (?Cantelo), Northover, Chilthorne Domer, and Podimore Milton.[87] An estate at Urgashay in West Camel was

purchased in 1725 with £400 provided as an augmentation of the benefice.[88] In 1838 the glebe in Ilchester parish alone measured nearly 18 a., in 1810 consolidated by exchange and inclosure, and situated in Ilchester mead.[89] The West Camel estate was just over 17 a.,[90] but the glebe in the other parishes had apparently been alienated. The property in West Camel was sold in 1911,[91] and the remainder is now combined with the glebe of Northover to give a total of 26 a.[92]

A rectory house formerly stood in the northwest corner of the churchyard, very close to the church itself.[93] Thomas Ebrey (rector 1813–21) found it 'in a very bad state'.[94] Though repaired it was said to be unfit for residence in 1831.[95] Its garden was taken into the churchyard in 1836, the rector receiving in exchange the former parish pound.[96] In 1841 the house was sold and demolished, and the present Rectory was purchased in the following year.[97]

Both church and churchyard had to be reconciled in 1311 after being polluted by bloodshed.[98] Chancel and churchyard were said to be in decay in 1554, and the parson had cut down the trees in the churchyard without consulting the churchwardens.[99]

Plurality and non-residence seem to have been common among the rectors of Ilchester. John Reynolds (rector until 1342) was allowed to leave his cure for a year in 1336 to serve William de Montacute.[1] Joseph Collier (rector 1590–1607) resided on his other living at Nunney.[2] Edward Dyer, appointed in 1643, was ejected in 1646, and there is no trace of an incumbent until John Powell occurs in 1654–5. William Oak was appointed by Cromwell in 1655.[3] Dyer was evidently restored and was instrumental in closing the Quakers' school at the Friary in 1662.[4] Between 1672 and 1713 the benefice was held in plurality with Northover. Pluralism continued into the 19th century: Thomas Ebrey (rector 1813–21) served as curate in Northover in 1815;[5] his successor, Richard Thomas Whalley (rector 1822–30), lived at Yeovilton and employed the vicar of Northover as his curate at Ilchester.[6]

The parson was reported for failing to do the duty in 1554, and for declaring in the pulpit that there was no true word in the Gospel nor in any chapter of the Bible.[7] John Ravens was one of

[70] *Crockford* (1968).
[71] *S.R.S.* liv. 78.
[72] Ibid. xv. 205.
[73] Cox, *Hist. Ilch.* 153, 159.
[74] *Cal. S.P. Dom.* 1655–6, 329; 1657–8, 81.
[75] The parishes were united on the death of the vicar of Northover in 1936, according to the terms agreed in 1924: *Lond. Gaz.* 1 July 1924; *Dioc. Dir.* (1936). The rectory of Limington has been held with the benefice since 1965.
[76] *S.R.S.* x. 627.
[77] Ibid. xlix. 32; liv. 78; *Valor Eccl.* (Rec. Com.), i. 199.
[78] *S.R.S.* ii. 107; S.R.O., D/D/Vc 24.
[79] Hodgson, *Queen Anne's Bounty*; *Augmentation of Livings, 1703–1815*, H.C. 115 (1814–15), xii.
[80] *Aug. Livings, 1703–1815*.
[81] H.O. 129/319/5/2/2.
[82] *Valor Eccl.* (Rec. Com.), i. 199.
[83] S.R.O., tithe award.
[84] *S.R.S.* lxiii. 481.
[85] S.R.O., DD/PH 52, rental etc.
[86] *Valor Eccl.* (Rec. Com.), i. 199.
[87] S.R.O., D/D/Rg 216, transcribed in Cox, *Hist. Ilch.* 163–5.
[88] S.R.O., D/P/ilch 2/1/1, note on flyleaf; printed in

Almshouse Deeds, ed. Buckler, p. 184; S.R.O., DD/SAS (C/120), 8.
[89] S.R.O., tithe award; CR 95.
[90] S.R.O., West Camel tithe award.
[91] MSS. *penes* the rector of Ilchester.
[92] *Crockford* (1948).
[93] *Almshouse Deeds*, ed. Buckler, p. 184. A drawing by J. Buckler in 1836 (B.M. Add. MS. 36382 f. 62) shows an L-shaped building of 2 storeys with mullioned windows.
[94] S.R.O., D/D/V rtns. 1815.
[95] *Rep. Com. Eccl. Revenues*, pp. 166–7.
[96] S.R.O., D/P/ilch 3/5/2.
[97] Ibid. 3/4/1–2.
[98] *S.R.S.* i. 45.
[99] S.R.O., D/D/Ca 22.
[1] *S.R.S.* ix. 300; x. 445–6.
[2] S.R.O., D/D/Vc 150.
[3] *Walker Revised*, ed. Matthews; *Calamy Revised*, ed. Matthews; Lambeth Palace MSS. COMM II. 374; *S.R.S.* lxxi. 60–1.
[4] *Jnl. Friends' Hist. Soc.* viii. 16–19.
[5] S.R.O., D/D/V rtns. 1815.
[6] Ibid. 1827; M.I. in Yeovilton ch.
[7] S.R.O., D/D/Ca 22.

several clergy who refused to read the Book of Constitutions in 1623.[8] One service was held every Sunday by 1815 and occasionally on other days.[9] Two were held by 1827; by 1840 there were still two, in the morning or noon alternately, and every Sunday evening. The churchwardens attended 'when convenient', and the church was cleaned 'when necessary'.[10] On Census Sunday 1851 there was a general congregation of 113, together with 74 Sunday-school children; and in the evening 235 with 60 children. This was also the average attendance figure.[11] By 1870 Holy Communion was celebrated about eight times a year, and the church was said to be cleaned 'occasionally'.[12]

A chantry was established by 1312[13] and was in the bishop's collation.[14] In 1350 its income was merged with that of the rectory, although the services of the chantry had to be continued.[15]

The church of ST. MARY MAJOR comprises a chancel, a nave with a north chapel and south aisle, and a western tower, which also serves as an entrance porch. The chancel dates from the earlier 13th century and has an east window consisting of three graded lancets under a single arch, the spandrel pierced to form a primitive type of plate tracery; internally the rear-arch is moulded and has jamb-shafts with shaft rings and foliated capitals. The nave is evidently of similar date but all its windows have been replaced and its roof line lowered. The massive west tower, square at the base and octagonal above, is rather later than the chancel. The lowest stage is supported by angle buttresses and the upper ones have lancet bell openings and a plain parapet. The stair turret is at the north-east corner. The former chantry chapel, projecting as a transept on the north side of the nave, is entered through an arch carved with Perpendicular panelling. It was built in the late 15th or early 16th century. There are remains of springers at the angles to support a fan-type vault and also remains of two elaborately canopied niches. The windows are late Perpendicular in style, that to the north containing fragments of contemporary glass. Among other Perpendicular windows in the church is one of five lights in the north wall of the chancel which is also very late in style; it has a depressed four-centred arch under a square head and foliage carving in the spandrels.

The present south aisle was added in 1879–80. The destruction of the south wall of the nave for this purpose revealed four circular piers of an early-13th-century arcade; one of the piers is preserved in the churchyard. The present church may thus correspond in size to the medieval plan, probably contracted in the late 15th century. The north chapel may have been added at this time to replace a chantry chapel formerly housed in the south aisle.

Traces of a 13th-century wall painting on the north side of the nave were recorded in the 1950s[16] but have since disappeared. The carved oak pulpit is Jacobean, but stands on a low modern base.

There are five bells: (i) 1783, William Bilbie; (ii) 1854, Mears; (iii) 1612, Robert Wiseman of Montacute; (iv) 1783, William Bilbie; (v) 1609, Roger Purdue of Bristol.[17] The plate includes a silver cup and cover of 1573, made by 'I.P.', a silver paten given in 1628, and a silver-gilt and jewelled chalice and silver-gilt paten of 1897.[18] The registers date from 1690 but are incomplete. The earliest volume was returned to the church in 1827 by Lord Huntingtower's solicitor, and is supposed to have been used in evidence in an election dispute in the previous year.[19] After a report in 1805 that the registers had not been kept since 1794 the bishop was informed, and some of the entries made up from a memorandum book.[20]

NONCONFORMITY. The imprisonment of Quakers in the town in Charles II's reign fostered Quaker activities there. There was a school in 1662, George Fox attended a general men's meeting in 1668 and 'settled' the Monthly Meeting, and Quarterly Meetings seem to have been held for some years before 1680, usually at the Friary, where Friends were then in prison. In 1680 those Friends who were not prisoners were barred from the Friary, and moved to the George, whose landlord, however, was fined for sheltering them. The meetings did not continue after the Quakers ceased to be imprisoned and the meeting was probably transferred to Northover.[21]

Licences for Presbyterian preachers and meeting-houses were issued from 1669. In that year Hester Dawe's house was the meeting-place for the following of John Clement, and in the same year John Baker, possibly the ejected minister of Curry Mallet, was licensed to preach. The chamber 'over the school-house', and the house of Mary Moore were similarly recognized for use by Presbyterians.[22] Four other licences were issued between 1691 and 1702; one of these, in 1698, was for meetings in the Priory. No denomination is known for these groups.[23] A group, either Presbyterian or Independent, was active between 1718 and 1727.[24]

It cannot be shown that these meetings continued throughout the 18th century, but in 1798 services were being held by a group of Independents either in the open air or in the Town Hall. In the same year land was purchased and a chapel, later known as Providence chapel, was built in 1799.[25] The early history of the congregation was 'a source of painful concern', the chapel being forsaken because of doctrinal disputes. A Home Missionary revived the

8 S.R.O., D/D/Ca 236.
9 S.R.O., D/D/V rtns. 1815.
10 S.R.O., D/D/V rtns. 1827, 1840.
11 H.O. 129/319/5/2/2.
12 S.R.O., D/D/V rtns. 1870.
13 S.R.S. i. 52.
14 Ibid. i. 152; x. 549.
15 Ibid. x. 627. The history of its status as a proprietary chapel attached to Manor farm (Cox, Hist. Ilch. 9) has not been traced.
16 Pevsner, South and West Som. 204; J. S. Cox, St. Mary Major Church and Ilchester. For descriptions of the church see Pevsner, 204, and Cox, Hist. Ilch. 4–9.

17 Cox, Hist. Ilch. 4.
18 Ibid. 13.
19 S.R.O., D/P/ilch 2/1/1.
20 Ibid. 4/1/1, vestry Jan. 1805.
21 J. Whiting, Persecution Exposed; Jnl. Friends' Hist. Soc. viii. 16n; George Fox, Jnl., ed. Penney, ii. 123; Besse, Sufferings, i. 615; J. Whiting, Memoirs (2nd edn.), 37, 66, 303–5.
22 G. L. Turner, Rec. Early Nonconf. ii. 1105–6; Cal. S.P. Dom. 1672, 239, 402.
23 S.R.O., Q/RR, meeting-house lics.
24 Rep. Som. Cong. Union (1896), 62.
25 S.R.O., D/D/Rm box 1.

cause, and in 1851 an average congregation of 50 in the afternoon and 100 in the evening attended the 400-seat chapel. The meeting was then described as Independent Calvinist.[26] There was no Sunday school in 1851, but in 1865 Thomas Henry Rio (d. 1867), of Chard, gave £400 for the encouragement of teachers and pupils there.[27] By the end of the 19th century the chapel was under the care of the meeting at Bower Hinton.[28] Meetings having ceased at Ilchester, the chapel was sold in 1961.

Standing in Chapel Dring or Chapel Court to the east of High Street, the former Providence Chapel is a simple brick building with a hipped roof. The interior was galleried, and there was an added vestry and cloakroom.[29]

In 1819 the house of James Coward, glove cutter, was licensed for worship, probably for Methodists.[30] In 1844 a room in the present Castle farm-house, in the Market Place, then occupied by Edward Look, was licensed for use by Wesleyans.[31] The present stone chapel, in Church Street, was erected in 1850 and enlarged in 1861.[32] In 1851 it contained 100 sittings; on Census Sunday the congregation numbered 50 at both afternoon and evening services though the more usual single service of the day, held in the evening, attracted an average of 80.[33]

Three tenements at the Mead were described as a chapel in 1885; four years later they were occupied by two tenants. By 1903 at least until 1916 a cottage and garden, evidently one of these tenements, was occupied by Primitive Methodists and used for worship.[34]

EDUCATION. A school-house in the town is mentioned in 1672,[35] and it may have been the premises repaired by the corporation in 1684–5.[36] A school with corporation support was being held in the Almshouse by 1747,[37] but this was evidently discontinued shortly afterwards. In 1794, however, the corporation established a free school for teaching poor children to read, write, and cast accounts. The school was held in the Almshouse, and a master was paid £10 a year.[38] This survived until about 1802, but probably not thereafter.[39] In 1814 the corporation, at the expense of the almshouse charity, fitted up part of the Town Hall for a school for poor children in place of that in the Almshouse. The master was paid apparently only for holding a Sunday school, though the return made in 1818 described only a day-school for 60 children

and a Sunday school for 35 pupils 'under the direction of some ladies'.[40] The room usually used by the boys was then occupied by poor families turned out of their homes by Sir William Manners.[41] The corporation continued to pay the master's salary until 1827, apparently only for a Sunday school.[42] The same master also kept a private day-school in the Town Hall, later transferred to Church Street.[43] The Sunday school in 1825 was attended by 49 boys and 36 girls.[44]

The corporation ceased to support the school after 1827, and two others took its place, one for Dissenters and one supported by the Church. The former, founded in 1828, had 34 boys and 23 girls in 1833;[45] the latter, begun two years later and superintended by the rector, was free, and was attended by 8 boys and 8 girls. There were also in 1833 two private day-schools, one for 18 boys and 15 girls, the other (founded in 1831) for 13 boys and 16 girls.[46] The first was probably that of William and Sarah Baker of Church Street, probably the successor of the one in the Town Hall.[47]

Ilchester National School, later known as the Infants' school, was founded in 1837, and occupied a building in Church Street adjoining the south-west corner of the churchyard.[48] By 1846–7 it housed two schools within its walls. The first, held on both Sunday and week-days, had 41 boys and 31 girls under a paid mistress; the second, a Sunday school under a paid master, had 12 boys and 27 girls. The two schools were supported by subscriptions, and by payments from pupils.[49] A Sunday school was still held there in 1866.[50]

On the opening of Ilchester Board School in 1878, the National School took infants only.[51] By 1894, though there was accommodation for 105 children in two rooms, the average attendance was only 32.[52] In 1903 the number of children was 41 and the average attendance 31.[53] In that year the school was taken under the control of the County Council and became known as Ilchester Church of England School. It continued under the control of managers, who received Board of Education building grants[54] and also benefited, from about 1860 onwards, from an annual grant from the alms-house charity.[55]

In 1902 it was described as 'a well organised, healthy little school', but its numbers always remained very small, and about 1928 there was an attempt to close it.[56] Numbers rose in the 1930s, and in 1938 there were 42 children, though the attendance

[26] H.O. 129/319/5/2/5.
[27] Char. Com. file.
[28] *Rep. Som. Cong. Union* (1896), 62.
[29] Char. Com. file.
[30] S.R.O., D/D/Rm box 2.
[31] Ibid.; S.R.O., Q/RR, meeting-house lics.
[32] H.O. 129/319/5/2/5; *P.O. Dir. Som.* (1861).
[33] H.O. 129/319/5/2/5.
[34] S.R.O., D/G/Y 160.
[35] *Cal. S.P. Dom.* 1672, 239.
[36] S.R.O., DD/PH 223/108.
[37] S.R.O., D/B/il 6, alms-house acct. bk. 1744–1852, *sub anno* 1747–8.
[38] Ibid. 199.   3 Ibid. 240.
[40] Ibid. 281–2, 286; *Digest of Returns to Sel. Cttee on Educ. of Poor*, H.C. 224 (1819), ix(2). The school was set up 'on the plan of the Central School at Wells'.
[41] *Digest of Returns to Sel. Cttee. on Educ. of Poor*; see p. 196.
[42] S.R.O., D/B/il 9, corp. accts. 1789–1883, 65, 67,

69, 73, 75, 77, 81; *11th Rep. Com. Char.* H.C. 433, p. 482 (1824), xiv.
[43] *11th Rep. Com. Char.* p. 482; Pigot, *Nat. Com. Dir.* (1822–3); see below.
[44] *Rep. B. & W. Dioc. Assoc. S.P.C.K.* (1825–6).
[45] *Educ. Enquiry Abstract*, H.C. 62 (1835), xlii.
[46] Ibid.
[47] Pigot, *Nat. Com. Dir.* (1822–3, 1830).
[48] S.R.O., D/P/ilch 4/1/1: chwdns.' accts. and rates, note in front cover.
[49] *Church Sch. Inquiry, 1846–7.*
[50] *P.O. Dir. Som.* (1866).
[51] S.R.O., C/E 68: Nat. Sch. log bk. 1872–1962.
[52] *Return of Schs. 1893* [C 7529], H.C. 1894, lxv.
[53] S.R.O., C/E 27. The monitress, Miss Annie Beal, was on the staff from 1897 until 1957: S.R.O. D/P/ilch 18/7/2: managers' min. bk. 1904–62.
[54] e.g. *Bd. of Educ. List 21* [1908] (H.M.S.O.), 413.
[55] *P.O. Dir. Som.* (1859, 1861); see p. 203.
[56] S.R.O. C/E 27; C/E 68, log bk., p. 254.

averaged only 18.[57] Some of the school's income, in view of the small number of pupils, was diverted to support boys awarded free places at the County senior school in Yeovil.[58] Dwindling numbers finally forced the closure in 1962, when the buildings were sold to the Parochial Church Council.[59] It was replaced by a new school in Northover.

A school board was formed compulsorily for Ilchester and Northover together in 1875.[60] A school site was also purchased in the same way in the following year,[61] and buildings for 87 pupils were erected in 1877, together with a master's house.[62] There were three classes, for boys, girls, and infants, and fees of 2d. a week were payable.[63] By 1883 the school was crowded, having 111 children on the books, with an average attendance of 89.[64]

In 1902, the year before it became Ilchester County School, it was described as 'a capital school', where 'exceptionally good work is being done'.[65] There was accommodation for 60 juniors and 27 infants, but the numbers had fallen to 66.[66] From about 1909 the school took juniors only, all infants being taught at the Church school, and numbers therefore continued to fall. In 1914–15 average attendance was 48,[67] but had risen to 59 in 1954–5.[68] The buildings were closed in 1962, when the school was transferred to new premises in Northover.[69]

John Hoskins, the lawyer and wit, after graduating from Oxford, taught at a school in the town 'for a year or more' c. 1592.[70] Quakers imprisoned in the Friary in 1662 had a school for about 70 children, where they taught reading, writing, and accounts. Some pupils 'gained more in two weeks there than in half a year elsewhere', but opposition from the rector brought it to an end late in 1662.[71] There is evidence for several private schools during the 19th century, beginning with the day-schools of William Baker in the Town Hall and of Baker and his wife in Church Street in 1830.[72] By 1840 there was a day- and boarding school for boys in Church Street run by J. B. Chant.[73] The teachers at the National School were taking boarders by 1859, and by the same date there were schools in the Market Place taught by Philip Handover and by the postmistress, Mary Morey. The latter continued at least until 1866 if not later.[74] There were two schools for girls and one for boys and girls in the town in the 1870s. Miss James had a boarding school for girls in West Street by 1872; the Misses Bennett had a day-school for girls in High Street, taking about 20 pupils at a fee of 10s. a quarter; and Miss Simpson had a mixed school opposite Manor Farm in West Street.[75]

CHARITIES FOR THE POOR. In 1426 Robert Veel, burgess of Ilchester, settled in trust the manor of Stocklinch Magdalen and lands in Stocklinch Ottersay, Ilchester, Sock Dennis, Limington, Northover, and Somerton, to support an almshouse. The house, evidently then recently built, stood opposite the east gate of the friary, at the junction of what is now Almshouse Lane and West Street. The foundation was to support five to seven poor, infirm, and aged men.[76] Half the income was to be used for maintenance; the rest was to accumulate for 50 years, when it was to be used to purchase a mortmain licence. The surviving trustees were then to vest the estate in the bailiffs of Ilchester, who were to manage the foundation and account annually. The lands were so vested in 1477.[77]

From the end of the 17th century, at the latest, women as well as men were supported on the foundation. In 1796, for example, there were 12 men and 4 women. In 1823 13 men were receiving 4s. a week there, and a woman was paid 3s. 6d. a week for acting as nurse and cleaning the house.[78] Under a Scheme of 1858 up to 18 men, but no women, were to be admitted, and were to receive 4s. weekly. Rooms in the house not required for the almspeople could be allotted, rent free, to single men or women or childless couples.[79] Under a Scheme of 1882 the total number on the foundation was reduced to 14, and the weekly allowance raised to 6s. From 1915 the Almshouse was no longer used, and the foundation became a pension charity only. From 1922 weekly pensions of up to 15s. were payable to poor men of good character over 50 years of age, who had lived in the town for not less than three years.[80]

The alms-house estate c. 1550 was probably worth some £27,[81] and in 1744–5 over £38.[82] It had increased to nearly £104 in 1791.[83] In the following year the properties in Ilchester were exchanged for an estate in Odcombe, an exchange justified by the fact that since the town properties were old, the cost of putting them in adequate repair would have been prohibitive.[84] The income in 1794–5, shortly after the exchange, was £121 19s. 7d. and the outgoings £117 5s. 5d.[85] Fifty years later income was £425 and expenditure £250.[86]

[57] Bd. of Educ., List 21 [1938] (H.M.S.O.), 348.
[58] S.R.O., D/P/ilch 18/7/2: managers' min. bk. sub anno 1937.
[59] Ibid. sub anno 1962.
[60] Lond. Gaz. 12 Mar. 1875, 158.
[61] 39 & 40 Vict. c. cliii (local act).
[62] S.R.O., C/E 27; Returns of Schs. 1893 [C. 7529], H.C. 1894, lxv.
[63] Cox, Hist. Ilch. 235–7, for extracts from the school log bk.
[64] Ibid.
[65] S.R.O., C/E 27.   [66] Ibid.
[67] Som. C.C. Educ. Cttee. Schs. List.
[68] Ibid.
[69] Ibid. The buildings became a depot for an ice-cream manufacturer. See p. 230.
[70] See p. 183.
[71] Jnl. Friends' Hist. Soc. viii. 16–19.
[72] 11th Rep. Com. Char. H.C. 433, p. 482 (1824), xiv; Pigot, Nat. Com. Dir.
[73] County Gazette Dir. (1840).

[74] P.O. Dir. Som. (1859, 1866).
[75] Morris & Co. Dir. Som. (1872); Kelly's Dir. Som. (1883); Cox, Hist. Ilch. 238. The school of the Misses Bennett, in West St. in 1883, remained in being until c. 1890.
[76] Almshouse Deeds, ed. Buckler, no. 121. See Cox, Hist. Ilch. 103–23.
[77] Almshouse Deeds, nos. 139–40; Cal. Pat. 1476–85, 17.
[78] S.R.O., D/B/il 6, alms-house acct. bk. 1744–1852, Cox, Hist. Ilch. 111–12.
[79] Char. Com. file; Cox, Hist. Ilch. 112–13.
[80] Char. Com. file.
[81] S.R.O., D/B/il 7. The rental appears to be for six months only. Printed, and dated c. 1570, in Cox, Hist. Ilch. 118.
[82] S.R.O., D/B/il 6, alms-house acct. bk.
[83] Ibid.
[84] Ibid. 184; 11th Rep. Com. Char. H.C. 433, pp. 477, 811–13 (1824), xiv.
[85] S.R.O., D/B/il 6, alms-house acct. bk.
[86] Ibid.

The Scheme of 1858 raised the number of alms-men and the rate of payment; any surplus money was to be used for promoting education in the parish.[87] The Scheme of 1882 limited the amount to be spent on the almsmen, leaving the rest for the maintenance of the property and for education. In 1905 the Almshouse Educational Trust Founda-tion was established to pay £50 each year to support the Church School, together with any additional sums available beyond the pension fund.[88]

Meanwhile some of the capital was invested and in 1869–71 the total income included a small amount of interest from stock.[89] The Ilchester Town Trust, successors to the dissolved corpora-tion, became trustees of the charity in 1915. The estate then comprised some 175 a. of land in Stock-linch and over 22 a. elsewhere, together with £670 stock.[90] Its income in 1944 was c. £567, of which over £81 came from investments. Two pen-sioners during that year were paid 10s. a week and

ten pensioners 6s. a week for the whole year, two received 6s. for 48 weeks, and one 6s. for one week,[91] making a total of £237 2s., rather less than the sum established by the governing Scheme.[92] By 1961 the gross income of the charity and the educational foundation was about £700.[93]

The house when virtually rebuilt in 1810 included a room on the first floor approached by an external flight of stairs and used as a schoolroom, and possibly earlier as a chapel.[94] Fines from the Stocklinch properties allowed the trustees to 'alter and en-large' the house in 1810 according to the plans of Mr. Beard.[95] The new building provided separate rooms for each inmate, with a common kitchen and two rooms for the sick. The charity provided medical care, a certain amount of furniture, and uniforms. In 1860 the blue clothing was changed for dark grey. Uniforms continued to be worn until closure in 1915. The house itself was sold in 1922 and converted into a private dwelling.[96]

KINGSTONE

KINGSTONE parish was 1,000 a. in extent in 1901.[1] A detached part of the ancient parish, known as Radletts in Hinton Park in Dinnington parish, was absorbed by Dinnington in 1885.[2] Further detached parts, around the Rose and Crown inn at Dinnington and in West Dowlish, were also lost to the parishes which adjoined them, while in turn Kingstone absorbed two fields north and south of the road to the west of Allowenshay, known as Castle estate, which in 1842 belonged to Dinnington.[3]

The boundaries of Kingstone and Dinnington suggest that the two places once formed a single unit, probably when Glastonbury abbey held both in the 10th and early 11th centuries.[4] The deeply-cut Longforward Lane, known in the 16th century as Longforehed Lane,[5] forms much of the two-mile northern boundary of the parish with White-lackington and Seavington St. Mary. The irregular western limit, bordering Ilminster and Dowlish-wake, follows a tributary of the Isle, and subsequently the road south and west of the church. Near the Butts it leaves the road and turns south to Dowlish brook, which then forms part of the southern boundary. The south-eastern boundary, with Din-nington, is highly irregular and in places interlocking, both parishes sharing Allowenshay mead.[6] The ex-treme eastern part of the parish crosses the Foss Way to include Paul's mill.

Most of the parish lies on undulating Yeovil sands, its eastern half being characterized by deep-cut lanes, its western higher and more open. It lies mostly between the 175 ft. and 350 ft. contours, but its highest point, just over 375 ft., is on the western boundary overlooking Dowlishwake. A junction bed of limestone is found around and to the north-east of the parish church; and eastwards, at the foot of the scarp below Longforward Lane, continuing beyond the parish, is a belt of inferior oolite. Limestone and sandstone were quarried at least from the 17th century.[7]

The parish is not well watered: a spring below Longforward Lane sends a stream eastwards below the scarp through the former Allowenshay mead, the largest area of meadow land in the parish.[8] Dowlish brook forms part of the southern boundary, and a tributary of Lopen brook drove Paul's mill.

The settlement pattern of the parish, with its three scattered hamlets, is typical of the south-west of the county. With few exceptions the parish and the small hamlet around the church are consistently referred to by the name they had in the 10th century, though the Domesday form, Chingestone, provides an important variant.[9] The position of this settle-ment, in an irregular protrusion at the extreme western end of the parish, and the later close con-nexion with the former parish of West Dowlish,[10]

[87] Char. Com. file; see above, p. 201.
[88] Char. Com. file.
[89] Dig. End. Chars. 1869–71, H.C. 25(3), p. 34 (1873), li.
[90] Ibid.; Cox, Hist. Ilch. 116.
[91] S.R.O., D/B/il 13: printed accts.
[92] Char. Com. file.
[93] Ibid.
[94] 11th Rep. Com. Char. 482. For its use as a school see above p. 201.
[95] S.R.O., D/B/il 6, alms-house acct. bk. 266, 269. 'Alms House Rebuilt 1810' is carved over the entrance: Cox, Hist. Ilch. 110.
[96] Cox, Hist. Ilch. 115–17.
[1] V.C.H. Som. ii. 349. This article was completed in 1968.

[2] 47–8 Vict. c. 45 (local act).
[3] S.R.O., tithe award.
[4] Finberg, Early Charters of Wessex, p. 133; V.C.H. Som. i. 467, 474.
[5] D.R.O., D 54/M 8, survey of manor of Allowenshay, 1563.
[6] See below.
[7] Hook Manor, Donhead St. Andrew, Arundell MSS. misc. bk. 55 (unfoliated), 12 Sept. 1626; Quarry Ground and Further and Hither Quarry Ground near Dozen's Corner: S.R.O., tithe award; Longforward (ST 396138) and Kingstone quarries were being worked in the 19th century: S.R.O., D/P/kstone 14/5/1, sub anno 1804.
[8] See below.
[9] V.C.H. Som. i. 474.
[10] See p. 205.

suggests that the original estate of which Kingstone church may have been the focus extended further north and west. The settlement at Allowenshay, in the centre of the present parish, is mentioned by 1280.[11] Its early form, Alwynesheye, with its many variants, somewhat supports the theory, expressed by Thomas Gerard in the 17th century, that the name derives from Alwine, a Saxon.[12] After 1300 the name is normally used for the manor which comprised most of the parish, and Allowenshay became the largest settlement. A chapel is thought to have stood there,[13] but apparently no manor-house. Just north of Allowenshay, however, are the remains of a park, represented by fields called the Park, Lower, Higher, and Middle Park, surrounded by the remains of a bank and ditch.[14] This may perhaps date from 1260 when John de Burgh (I) was given free warren in Kingstone.[15]

The third settlement in the parish, at Ludney, probably dates from the end of the 13th century,[16] and a fourth, known as 'Netherton', is mentioned in the 15th and 17th centuries.[17] The last has not positively been identified, though it was clearly the name of a tithing and may have been part of Dinnington.

The principal road through the parish enters at the top of Kingstone hill from Ilminster, and forms the parish boundary through Kingstone hamlet. At the Butts it branches south-east to Ludney Cross, then east to Dozen's Corner, and then south, again forming the parish boundary, towards Crewkerne. This road was adopted by the Ilminster turnpike trust in 1758–9.[18] In 1968 a turnpike house stood in Kingstone hamlet, but just inside the parish of Dowlishwake.[19] Allowenshay, in the centre of the parish, is reached by narrow, deep-cut lanes from the Butts in the west, from Dozen's Corner in the south, from Longforward Lane in the north, and from Dinnington. Longforward Lane and, for a short section Park Lane, form the northern boundary of the parish. The Foss Way cuts diagonally through the eastern end of the parish, and from it Mill Lane runs eastwards to Paul's mill, and Northfield Lane northwards towards Allowenshay mead.

It seems that the arable fields lay around Allowenshay, with a subsidiary one at Ludney. North field in Allowenshay manor is mentioned in 1537, but had disappeared by 1563.[20] Its position is not known, but Northfield Lane at the eastern end of the parish probably refers to the North field of Dinnington.[21] Small parts of West field, or Western field, survived until the 19th century, to the north-east of Boyton hill.[22] The field was still large enough

in 1773 to be called a common field.[23] Ludney field, traceable in c. 1548, was still so called in the 19th century, lying to the north of the settlement.[24] Field names such as Metfordland, Woolverland, and Delverland had 16th-century equivalents in Metefurlong, Wulverlong, and Dulverlong which establish them as parts of open arable fields.[25] In the 16th century there was common meadow land at Allowenshay mead and Allowenshay moor. The former was shared with Dinnington, and the tenants usually held strips of 1½ a. each.[26]

Most of the buildings in the three settlements are of rubble and ashlar, with thatched or tiled roofs, and date from the 18th century. Exceptions are the five-bay Allowenshay Farm, in 1972 known as Old Manor House, with mullioned and labelled windows, which probably dates from the 17th century;[27] and Kingstone Farm which is medieval in origin.[28] Behind the barn at Ludney Farm is a semi-circular thatched addition, probably built to house a horse-mill.

In 1801 the population of the parish was 197. This figure increased steadily to 301 by 1841, but then fell each decade until 1891, when it was 199. A recovery to 231 in 1901 has been followed since 1911 by rapid decline, to 99 in 1961.[29]

MANOR AND OTHER ESTATES. King Edmund gave to Dunstan, abbot of Glastonbury, an estate of eight hides called Kingestan in 940.[30] The abbey retained the property until Edward the Confessor's time, but had lost it by 1086 to the count of Mortain, under whom it was held by Hubert de St. Clare.[31] Hubert's successors held directly from the Crown on the confiscation of the Mortain estates in 1106.

By the end of the 13th century the manor formed part of the barony of Walkern (Herts.),[32] and the manor of Walkern was held c. 1120 by Hamon de St. Clare.[33] His son Hubert, living in 1155, was succeeded by an only daughter, Gunnore, wife of William de Lanvalai (I) (d. 1180).[34] Her son, William, was still a minor in 1185, and Oliver de Lanvalai, described as lord of Kingstone two years later, probably held in his right.[35] William (II) died in 1204 leaving a son William (III).[36] In 1194–5, however, Kingstone was held by William de Vilers,[37] and Roger de Vilers was returned as holder of a ½ fee of Mortain there in 1212.[38] This was presumably a temporary seizure, since in 1215 the manor was returned, 'as his right', to William de Lanvalai (III).[39] William died in the same year leaving a daughter, Hawise, in the wardship of

[11] *Cal. Inq. p.m.* ii, p. 198; Arundell MSS. charters, general series, 588, is an undated charter of John de Burgh, which can be no later than 1280, the year of the death of John de Burgh (II), but may well be some years earlier.
[12] *S.R.S.* xv. 90–1.
[13] See p. 209.
[14] S.R.O., tithe award.
[15] *Cal. Chart. R. 1257–1300*, 27.
[16] *Cal. Inq. p.m.* iii, pp. 89–90.
[17] D.R.O., D 16/A 71; D 54/M 8; Arundell MSS. ct. bk. 4 f. 32; misc. bks. 53 f. 14 (1st nos.), f. 22 (2nd nos.); 55 (unfold.); *S. & D. N. & Q.* xxix. 91–2.
[18] 32 Geo. II, c. 39 (local act).
[19] S.R.O., D/T/ilm.
[20] D.R.O., D 16/M 44; D 54/M 8.
[21] O.S. Map 6", Som. LXXXVIII. NE. (1886 edn.).
[22] S.R.O., tithe award.

[23] S.R.O., DD/PT 18, no. 68.
[24] E 310/23/127, no. 90; S.R.O., tithe award.
[25] D.R.O., D 54/M 8; S.R.O., tithe award.
[26] D.R.O., D 54/M 8.
[27] See plate facing p. 193.
[28] See p. 206.
[29] *V.C.H. Som.* ii. 349; *Census, 1911–61.*
[30] Finberg, *Early Charters of Wessex*, p. 133.
[31] *V.C.H. Som.* i. 474.
[32] *Cal. Inq. p.m.* ii, p. 198.
[33] Sanders, *Eng. Baronies*, 92.
[34] Ibid.; *V.C.H. Herts.* iii. 152.
[35] Sanders, op. cit. 92; *S.R.S.* viii. 146–7.
[36] Sanders, op. cit. 92.
[37] *Pipe R.* 1194 (P.R.S. n.s. v), 19.
[38] *Bk. of Fees*, i. 86.
[39] *Rot. Litt. Claus.* (Rec. Com.), i. 216.

the justiciar Hubert de Burgh.[40] Hubert married her to his son John (I), and their son John (II) succeeded on his father's death in 1275.[41]

Hitherto the property had been called the manor of Kingstone. On the death of John de Burgh (II) in 1280, however, the manor was called Halwenesheye, the origin of the subsequent name of *ALLOWENSHAY*.[42] John's heirs were his two daughters. Allowenshay formed part of the share of Hawise, wife of Robert de Grelley.[43] Sir Robert FitzPayn (Lord FitzPayn from 1299) was certainly lord of the manor by 1311.[44] At his death in 1315, however, he was said to hold Allowenshay and Kingstone hamlets of John de Burgh's heirs.[45] In 1382 the advowson, and presumably the manor, were said to be held of the Crown as of the honor of Wallingford,[46] and in 1445 the manor was held of Richard, duke of York.[47] John de Burgh's heirs were said to be overlords in 1599.[48]

The manor continued in the possession of the barons FitzPayn until 1450. Robert (d. 1315) was succeeded by his son Robert (d. 1354). Sir John de Chidiock (I) (d. 1388), who married Isabel, the FitzPayn heir, succeeded to the barony including Allowenshay.[49] Sir John de Chidiock (II) died in 1390; Sir John (III) (d. 1415) succeeded as a minor, and his wardship was held by Sir Ives FitzWaryn.[50] Allowenshay was held by Sir John's widow in dower until her death in 1434, and it then reverted to her son Sir John (IV).[51] He died in 1450, but Allowenshay was held jointly with his wife, who survived until 1461.[52] The estates were then divided, Allowenshay passing to Catherine, wife of Sir John Arundell of Lanherne (Cornw.) (d. 1473).[53] She died in 1479 and was succeeded by her son Sir Thomas Arundell, K.B. (d. 1487). His son John settled it on his wife in 1495.[54] It passed in 1531 to his second son Thomas, of Wardour (Wilts.) (executed 1552),[55] and then successively to Thomas's son Matthew (d. 1598) and to his grandson Thomas (cr. Lord Arundell of Wardour 1605).[56] Henry, Lord Arundell (d. 1694), grandson of the first baron, sold Allowenshay and other lands in Kingstone to John Poulett, Lord Poulett (d. 1665) in 1663.[57]

The estate remained in the Poulett family, held successively by the lords Poulett (after 1706 earls Poulett) until 1941, when most of the farms were

sold to Oxford University, and then in 1958 to Messrs. Showerings or to the tenants.[58] The lordship of the manor was not, however, included in these sales.

From 1385, when the vicars choral of Wells acquired the rectory, the glebe lands were let to farm: to John Hewet by 1416 until at least 1428, to William Doget between 1450 and 1456.[59] Between 1460 and 1477 the vicars choral administered the property through a bailiff, but from 1480 letting was resumed.[60] The farmers included members of local families, notably Sir Hugh Poulett, lessee from 1547,[61] and William and Roger Long.[62] Nicholas Osborne had a lease from 1568, and his descendants still held the property in 1651, Henry Osborne purchasing the rectory in that year as confiscated church land.[63] By 1669 the Tripp family held the tenancy from the vicars choral,[64] and it passed on the death of Henry Tripp in 1730 to his son-in-law Henry Palmer of Clapton.[65] The Revd. Edmund Lovell of Wells acquired the tenancy in 1754.[66] His son George sub-let the holding to John Hanning of Dowlishwake in 1791 and Hanning's son William acquired the lease in 1807. William's son, John Lee Lee of Dillington House, was lessee until his death in 1874, some eight years after ownership had been transferred from the vicars choral to the Ecclesiastical Commissioners.[67] Capt. A. V. H. Vaughan Lee purchased the estate in 1899 and in 1968 his heirs, the Dillington Estates, owned the property.[68]

The rectory estate comprised tithes and glebe. Its net value was £15 6s. 6½d. in 1535[69] and was assessed at over £76 in 1650.[70] Tithes of land in West Dowlish were commuted in 1838 for £22,[71] and from Kingstone in 1842 for £370.[72] Glebe was worth £4 in 1535, and amounted to 60 a. by 1636,[73] It was increased slightly in the later 18th century, but was just under 58 a. in 1858.[74]

The rectory buildings in 1636 were described as a dwelling-house, orchard and garden, two barns, a stable with outhouses, and a great court with a pigeon-house in it.[75] The house itself in 1650 comprised a hall, kitchen, buttery, and several 'lodging rooms' over them. One of the barns was of stone, with a thatched roof.[76] The lay rector or his under-tenants then lived in the house. The existing farm-house of Kingstone farm evidently incorporates

[40] Ibid. i. 337; *Bk. of Fees*, i. 263.
[41] Sanders, op. cit. 92; *Cal. Fine R.* 1272–1307, 41.
[42] *Cal. Inq. p.m.* ii, p. 198; see above, p. 204.
[43] *Cal. Inq. p.m.* ii, p. 198; *Cal. Fine R.* 1272–1307, 126.
[44] Arundell MSS. charters, general series, 591.
[45] *Cal. Inq. p.m.* v, pp. 387–8.
[46] *Cal. Pat.* 1381–5, 177.   [47] C 139/119/26.
[48] C 142/257/83; S.R.O., DD/PT 18, no. 4.
[49] *Complete Peerage*, s.v. FitzPayn; *S.R.S.* xvii. 18; *Cal. Close*, 1354–60, 125; *Cal. Inq. p.m.* x, p. 151; *Cal. Fine R.* 1383–91, 245.
[50] *Cal. Close*, 1413–19, 259.
[51] C 139/65/38; *S.R.S.* xxii. 185; *Feud. Aids*, iv. 426; *Cal. Close*, 1413–19, 259; 1429–35, 328–9.
[52] *Cal. Fine R.* 1445–52, 160; 1461–71, 2.
[53] *Complete Peerage*, s.v. FitzPayn.
[54] *Cal. Inq. p.m. Hen. VII*, i. 83; *Cal. Close*, 1485–1500, 277–8.
[55] C 142/97/77.
[56] C 142/257/83; S.R.O., DD/PT 18, no. 4.
[57] Arundell MSS. deeds various, 1; S.R.O., DD/PT 17; 18, nos. 2, 2a.
[58] *Sale Cat. University Estate* (1958), *penes* Messrs. T. R. G. Lawrence, Crewkerne; ex inf. Mrs. M. E. Chapman, Ludney Fm.

[59] Wells Cathedral, Vicars Choral MSS. accts (series B), 11, 16–17, 31–2, 36.
[60] Ibid. 41, 43–6, 50, 52, 55, 59, 62, 64, 111, 139, 161–2, 166, 169, 177.
[61] Ibid. 186.
[62] Ibid. 137, 139, 145; see p. 207.
[63] Vicars Choral MSS. 188, 208a, 209–10; C 54/3579, no. 8.
[64] E 134/23 Chas. II/East. 21.
[65] Vicars Choral MSS. Lease Bk. A. 396; S.R.O., DD/CC 115317.
[66] Vicars Choral MSS. Lease Bk. B. 153; S.R.O., DD/CC 115317.
[67] Vicars Choral MSS. Min. Bk. 1845–81, 357 sqq.
[68] Ex inf. the Church Commissioners.
[69] *Valor Eccl.* (Rec. Com.), i. 134.
[70] S.R.O., DD/CC 116013.
[71] S.R.O., Dowlishwake and West Dowlish tithe award.
[72] S.R.O., Kingstone tithe award.
[73] *Valor Eccl.* (Rec. Com.), i. 134; S.R.O., D/D/Rg 311.
[74] Vicars Choral MSS. Lease Bks. B. 153, and F. 174; S.R.O., DD/CA 5, lease, Lovell to Hanning, 1791.
[75] S.R.O., D/D/Rg 311.
[76] S.R.O., DD/CC 116013.

the 1650 building. Although by then it was a two-storeyed structure there may formerly have been a medieval open hall, floored over in the 16th or early 17th century. The present building consists of an east range, containing the service rooms, and a cross wing to the west. There are indications that the floor above the kitchen is an insertion. In the west wing, which may represent the two-storeyed solar wing of the original house, an open collar-beam roof with curved wind-braces is visible. A large stone barn to the west of the farmyard has a similar roof near its south end and a medieval doorway with a pointed head.

Lands in Ludney are first clearly mentioned in 1316. They formed part of property let to the lord of the manor, Robert FitzPayn, which had once been demesne land and were again to be united to the demesne in 1323.[77] Earlier, in 1293, Humphrey de Kail held lands at Lodehaye.[78] Thomas, son of John Kail, who was found in 1413 to have held a carucate in Ludney as parcel of Cudworth manor, may perhaps have been a descendant.[79] John Browne of Frampton (Dors.), owner of a freehold messuage and land in Ludney in 1563, formerly held by William Speke and then Thomas Sydenham, also held land in Netherton tithing known as Kayles Gore.[80]

By the end of the 17th century Ludney farm, occupied by the Longs, included lands in Chillington, and was bought in 1698 by Bernard Hutchings from Robert Browne of Frampton.[81] Hutchings died in 1728 leaving the farm to Vere Poulett, and it was thus merged with the rest of the Poulett holding in the parish.[82] By 1744 the farm measured 90 a. in Kingstone parish; about 1811 it had increased to 152 a. though by 1842 it was only 109 a.[83]

The Mauncell or Maunsell family, of Maunsel in North Petherton, were freeholders in Kingstone by 1486, and held an estate by knight service of the manor of Allowenshay.[84] This was claimed as a manorial holding: a lessee in 1560 was required to do suit at John Maunsell's court at Kingstone.[85] The property then comprised a capital messuage, buildings, and land in Allowenshay, Kingstone, and Dowlishwake. The tenants were the Masters family.[86] Robert Masters bought the farm from Richard Maunsell in 1620 on the latter's failure to repay a mortgage; it was sold by Mary Masters, widow, and another, to William Walden of Dowlishwake in 1661.[87] At the beginning of the 18th century it was owned by the Bacons of Harpford in Langford Budville, who mortgaged and then apparently sold it to John Collins of Ilminster and

Hatch Court. Described then as Kingstone farm, and comprising some 46½ a., it was sold by Collins's widow to John Hanning of Dowlishwake in 1792, and thus descended to John Lee Lee of Dillington House.[88]

ECONOMIC HISTORY. The ancient parish corresponded very closely in size with the 8 hides of the 10th-century estate at Kingstone held by Glastonbury, and with its Domesday successor.[89] It seems likely, however, that the manor as it later developed lay partly in Dinnington.[90] The size of the demesne holding at Domesday, 4 hides, shrank considerably during the next two centuries. At some date between 1215 and 1280 some 143 a., apparently of demesne land, were granted away, leaving only 108 a. in 1315.[91] About 138 a. were bought back about 1319, and by 1563 the demesne estate was over 320 a., most of which was held by copyhold tenants.[92]

There were 3 serfs on the demesne at Domesday with 11 villeins and 13 bordars on the rest of the estate, evidently a highly-populated holding.[93] Twelve *nativi* were attached to the demesne estate of 143 a. granted away before 1280, so that the remaining demesne in 1315 included 16 customary tenants, one cottar, and one free tenant, all paying rent. Labour services were worth 12s. 4d. only, comprising 3s. for ploughing, 16d. for haymaking, and 8d. for harvest.[94] By the mid 15th century the manor yielded rent only.[95]

Arable land predominated in Kingstone in the 11th century, when there were 7 ploughs on land for eight. There were 41 a. of meadow, and woodland 6 by 3 furlongs. Thirty-eight pigs and 61 sheep were supported on the estate.[96] Of the holding granted from the demesne in the 13th century 127 a. were arable and only 16 a. meadow;[97] the demesne in 1315 amounted to 90 a. of arable, 10 a. pasture, and 8 a. of meadow.[98] By the mid 16th century, however, the manor was fairly evenly divided between arable and grassland.[99]

The value of the manor at Domesday was £9, the same as the figure before the Conquest.[1] The depleted demesne in 1315 was worth £8 4s. 6d., and rents formed half that total.[2] Between 1465 and 1530 the income from the manor varied between £33 15s. 5d. in 1488–9, and £43 1s. 7½d. in 1495–6, based on a rental worth over £35.[3] There was evidently a crisis during the period 1519–23 and at its height, in 1519–20, arrears amounted to over £20, more than half the usual income.[4] The same

[77] Arundell MSS. charters, general series, 592–601; *S.R.S.* xii. 90.
[78] *Cal. Inq. p.m.* iii, pp. 89–90.
[79] *Cal. Close*, 1413–19, 29; also *Cal. Close*, 1385–9, 353–4; *Cal. Inq. p.m.* xv, p. 392.
[80] D.R.O., D 54/M 8; see C 3/54/18.
[81] S.R.O., DD/MR 51; DD/PT 16.
[82] S.R.O., DD/PT 16.
[83] S.R.O., DD/MR 51, mortgage, Poulett and Browne; DD/PT 44; tithe award.
[84] D.R.O., D 16/M 71; S.R.O., DD/CA 93, receipt, Arundell to Maunsell, 1521.
[85] S.R.O., DD/CA 93, lease, Maunsell to Masters.
[86] Ibid.
[87] S.R.O., DD/CA 93.
[88] Ibid.
[89] Finberg, *Early Charters of Wessex*, p. 133; *V.C.H. Som.* i. 474; S.R.O., tithe award.

[90] D.R.O., D 54/M 8, survey of manor of Allowenshay, 1563.
[91] Arundell MSS. charters, general series, 588; C 134/48/5.
[92] Arundell MSS. charters, general series, 592, 596; *S.R.S.* xii. 79; D.R.O., D 54/M 8.
[93] *V.C.H. Som.* i. 474.
[94] Arundell MSS. charters, general series, 588; C 134/48/5.
[95] D.R.O., D 16/M 60, 66–7.
[96] *V.C.H. Som.* i. 474.
[97] Arundell MSS. charters, general series, 588.
[98] C 134/48/5.
[99] D.R.O., D 54/M 8.
[1] *V.C.H. Som.* i. 474.
[2] C 134/48/5.
[3] D.R.O., D 16/M 60, 66–7, 71–3, 77–9, 87, 89–93, 96–108; S.C. 6/Hen. VIII/5725.
[4] D.R.O., D 16/M 98.

rental was used in the 17th and 18th centuries, with a further crisis in 1644 when arrears of fines were high and total arrears were over £62.[5] The rectory estate showed a declining income in the 15th century, the annual farm falling from £20 8s. between 1416 and 1428 to £15 between 1450 and 1456.[6] The farm varied between £14 and £22 from 1480 until the mid 16th century.[7] Thereafter, until 1754, the rent was £17, though the real value was £76 in 1650.[8]

When surveyed in 1563 more than half Allowenshay manor was inclosed, several holdings recently, and there is evidence of consolidation in both common arable fields and meadow land.[9] Inclosure continued during the rest of the century: in 1574 and 1579 committees were chosen in the manor court to supervise the division of land for the purpose.[10] There were no traces of common fields beyond names by the time of the tithe award in 1842. Not unconnected with this movement, but whether cause or effect, was the high number of dilapidated tenements in the manor in 1563.[11]

By 1563 the property was divided into the three main settlements of Allowenshay, Kingstone, and Ludney, and the tenures into free, copyhold, and customary, with copyholds and leaseholds on the former demesne.[12] There were 26 copyholds and one leasehold on the former demesne, and 7 freeholds and 16 customary on the rest of the manor. Many of these holdings, one or two described by their ancient names of 'ten acre tenements' or 'twenty acre tenements', were held by a small number of families. The Chapells, for example, had over 220 a. between them, the Longs nearly 200 a. The fortunes of the Longs had probably been founded on the work of William Long, bailiff and rent collector in Kingstone and Pitney for the Arundells.[13] The Drewes held just over 80 a., and Thomas Drewe (d. ante 1579) left goods and farm implements valued at over £200.[14] Another tenant of the manor was Sir Hugh Poulett, whose 100 a. were largely in the detached part of the parish which was later absorbed into Hinton Park.[15]

The history of the next two centuries is of the gradual consolidation of the Poulett holding in the parish and of the growth of that of the Hannings, later of the Lees of Dillington.[16] Farming seems to have been carried on, at least in the 17th and 18th centuries, in units of between 30 a. and 70 a., held on leases for three lives. Dairies were occasionally let for much shorter periods.[17] By 1842 Lord Poulett's holding in Kingstone amounted to nearly 786 a.,

divided between three farms in Allowenshay and Ludney farm, measuring between 60 a. and 109 a., and many smaller holdings.[18] Still in 1935 only two farms were over 150 a. in area.[19]

Farming has always been the dominant activity in the parish: 42 families out of 58 were engaged in it in 1821.[20] The occupations of the 19th-century inhabitants were usually closely related to farming and included, by 1861, a 'machine owner'.[21] In 1872 there was a 'threshing machine proprietor'.[22] Less usual was a 'marine store dealer', in business by 1897.[23] The fairly even balance between arable and grass at the beginning of the 20th century[24] was still apparent in 1968, though a substantial acreage was devoted to fruit growing.

There was a mill in Kingstone parish by 1280, attached to the manorial demesne. It was granted at an unknown date to John de Skeggleton, to whom the miller, Henry de Beaulieu, paid 33s. 4d.[25] The mill became part of the manorial demesne again in 1319.[26] This mill, the precursor of Paul's mill, was repaired in 1494–5 with Ham and local stone and timber.[27] John Sampford was miller in 1538.[28] The holding of William Isham, miller by 1563, comprised the corn mill called 'Pawles mylle', an acre of arable, and an acre of meadow. Customary tenants of the manor had to scour the mill-pond each year on the morning of Thursday in Pentecost week.[29] Christopher Isham was miller by 1573 and was still there in 1581. The sluices were said to be ruinous, and he was ordered to repair them in the latter year.[30] In 1615 the customary tenants were presented for their failure to scour the mill-pond, and the miller, Thomas Pyke, for allowing the floodgates above the mill to decay.[31] During the 18th century the mill was held on lease, in 1706 by Thomas Owsley of Merriott, in 1728 by George Gummer of Hinton St. George, and in 1743 by Gummer's widow.[32] About 1796 Maximilian Brice bought it from the lord of the manor and some three years later there was a dispute between Brice and the tenant of land near the sluice above the mill-pond.[33] The Brices continued to hold the mill until at least 1897, but thereafter it probably ceased to be used.[34] The mill-house was still occupied in 1968, but the mill-pond had been drained, and the water now flows at some distance from the mill, probably in the course of the original stream.

There seems to have been a mill at Ludney by the late 15th century: from 1486 at least until 1530 the lord of the manor received a rent of 40s. from the tenant of this mill.[35]

[5] Arundell MSS. receivers-general accts. 16–19; S.R.O., DD/PT 41 (rental, 1754); DD/PT 44 (rentals, 1729, 1747, 1770–1, 1781).

[6] Wells Cathedral, Vicars Choral MSS. accts. (series B), 11, 16–17, 31–2, 36.

[7] Ibid. 41–186.

[8] Ibid. 188–210; Lease Bk. A, 396; S.R.O., DD/CC 116013.

[9] D.R.O., D 54/M 8.

[10] Arundell MSS. misc. bks. 49; 50 f. 29v.

[11] D.R.O., D 54/M 8.

[12] Ibid.

[13] D.R.O., D 16/M 102–5, 108.

[14] C 3/56/92; see also C 3/54/18.

[15] See p. 203.

[16] See p. 205.

[17] S.R.O., DD/PT 18, nos. 17, 20, 22, 30; DD/PT 46 (17th-cent. survey). DD/PT 18, no. 18 is a 3-year lease of a dairy.

[18] S.R.O., tithe award.

[19] Kelly's Dir. Som. (1935).

[20] C. & J. Greenwood, Som. Delineated, 124.

[21] Kelly's Dir. Som. (1861).

[22] Morris & Co. Dir. Som. (1872).

[23] Kelly's Dir. Som. (1897, 1902).

[24] Statistics supplied by the then Bd. of Agric. (1905).

[25] Arundell MSS. charters, general series, 588.

[26] Ibid. 596; S.R.S. xii. 79.

[27] D.R.O., D 16/M 78.

[28] Ibid. D 16/M 44.   [29] Ibid. D 54/M 8.

[30] Arundell MSS. ct. bk. 4 f. 32; 8 f. 24v; misc. bk. 50 f. 64v.

[31] Ibid. misc. bk. 54 f. 66.

[32] S.R.O., DD/PT 18, nos. 41–3.

[33] S.R.O., DD/PT 18.

[34] S.R.O., D/P/kstone 4/1/1, 14/5/1; Morris & Co. Dir. Som. (1872); Kelly's Dir. Som. (1883, 1897).

[35] D.R.O., D 16/M 71, 108.

LOCAL GOVERNMENT. Kingstone was regarded as a tithing of the hundred of Tintinhull by the end of the 12th century.[36] The tithingman was elected in the manorial court of Allowenshay, though his appointment was not regularly recorded by the 16th century.[37] Allowenshay manor court, described as *curia legalis* and view of frankpledge for general administration and manor court for tenurial business, was meeting twice a year, in April and September, according to the earliest surviving court rolls of 1537–8.[38] From the 1570s onwards only one meeting was held, in September or October, though the manor court for surrenders, recorded separately, met at other times when required. Apart from the tithingman no other manorial official seems to have been appointed by the court, though there are occasional references to a bailiff and a hayward, and inclosures carried out in 1574 and 1579 were supervised by a committee of four.[39]

Books of court proceedings survive intermittently from 1537 to 1679.[40] Apart from matters relating to holdings, a frequent concern was the scouring of ditches. Other business included orders against subleasing and against lodgers in the 1570s and 1580s, the repair of houses, and items of general farming policy. Thus in 1574 pigs were ordered to be kept within their sties or bartons after the corn had been carried, warning having been given by the hayward in church.[41] Customary tenants, it was agreed in 1580, could obtain fuel and wood from Allowenshay mead and Allowenshay moor at any time except between hay and corn harvest.[42]

John Maunsell required the tenant of his farm at Kingstone in 1560 to attend his court and do suit. Maunsell held the property as of the manor of Allowenshay in fee, his grandfather having paid relief in 1521.[43] No court records survive.

The Hearth Tax exemptions of 1674 were signed by the churchwardens, two overseers, and the tithingman.[44] The last office still existed in 1693.[45] In the later 18th century the parish was divided into two units for the purposes of poor-relief, though the two overseers returned figures for a single unit in the early 19th century.[46] There were two surveyors of the highways by the end of the 18th century;[47] they and the overseers were appointed by the vestry.[48] The parish became part of the Chard poor-law union in 1836.[49]

CHURCH. There was a church at Kingstone by 1291.[50] The advowson belonged to the FitzPayns, lords of the manor, by 1311, and descended with the manor until 1382 when Sir John Chidiock gave the rectory with the advowson to the chapter of Wells for the benefit of the vicars choral of the cathedral. A portion was reserved for a parochial chaplain and the rest of the income divided between specified masses in the cathedral and the vicars' common fund.[51] Chaplains were found by the vicars choral until 1568. The responsibility was then transferred to the successive farmers of the rectory, though the vicars choral had to approve their nominees and appointed if the lay rectors failed to do so.[52] Capt. A. V. H. Vaughan Lee was the last lessee of the rectory to be patron when he presented in 1905.[53] The vicars choral presented in 1916 and by Order in Council the patronage was transferred to the chapter of Wells in 1935.[54]

The benefice, which is technically a perpetual curacy, has since 1873 been held in plurality, until 1905 with Lopen, from then until 1916 with Ilminster, and from 1916 until 1969 with Dowlishwake.[55] In 1971 it was a curacy-in-charge with Dowlishwake and Chillington.[56]

The church was valued at £13 6s. 8d. in 1291,[57] but at only £6 8s. 4d. in 1334.[58] When first mentioned in 1533–4 the curate's stipend was £6.[59] From 1552 this sum was gradually raised to £10 10s. in 1559, but from 1565–8 the curate was paid only £10.[60] By 1705 the lessees paid the curate £16,[61] a sum still charged upon the rectory estate in 1968.[62] The benefice was, however, augmented in 1727, 1811,[63] and 1819, in the last year partly by the then incumbent.[64] By 1831, therefore, the income had increased to £53.[65]

During the 17th century the curate had 'a little dwelling-house with a garden'.[66] In 1815 there was said to be a house, but 'unfit for residence, having never been inhabited by a clergyman from its meanness and age'.[67] The then incumbent lived in Ilminster, and he reported 'no glebe house' in 1831.[68] His successors, at least since 1875, have lived outside the parish.[69]

A number of curates in the later 18th century were local men: Nicholas Vere (occurs 1755–69) was a native of Ilminster, John Templeman (occurs 1778–81) came from Merriott, and John Fewtrell

[36] *S.R.S.* viii. 146–7.
[37] Arundell MSS. misc. bks., 50 f. 29v (1579); 53 f. 14, first nos. (1605); 55 (unfol.) (1628).
[38] D.R.O., D 16/M 44.
[39] Arundell MSS. misc. bks. 49; 50 f. 29v.
[40] D.R.O., D 16/M 44; Arundell MSS. ct. bks. 4 (1573), 7 (1577–8), 8 (1581), 9 (1584), 14 (1588–9), 15 (1590), 18 (1602), 19 (1611), 20 (1616); misc. bks. 49 (1574), 50 (1579–80), 51 (1583), 52 (1598), 53 (1605), 54 (1614–15), 55 (1623–8), 58 (1654–8); S.R.O., DD/SAS (C/2072). The court was still functioning in 1730: S.R.O., DD/PT 18, nos. 11–17.
[41] Arundell MSS. misc. bk. 49.
[42] Ibid. 50 f. 64v.
[43] S.R.O., DD/CA 93; see above, p. 206.
[44] Dwelly, *Dir. Som.*
[45] S.R.O., Q/SR 195/5, 13.
[46] *Poorhaw Abstract, 1804.*
[47] S.R.O., D/P/kstone 14/5/1.
[48] Ibid. min. of vestry, 1842.
[49] *Poor Law Com. 2nd Rep.* p. 547.
[50] *Tax. Eccl.* (Rec. Com.), 199. The reference to a church in the Domesday entry probably refers to Glastonbury abbey: *V.C.H. Som.* i. 474.

[51] *H.M.C. Wells*, i. 296, 380; ii. 637–41; Arundell MSS. charters, general series 588a, 591; *Cal. Pat.* 1381–5, 177.
[52] *Proc. Som. Arch. Soc.* cxii. 83; Wells Cathedral, Vicars Choral MSS. Lease Bk. A. 396.
[53] S.R.O., DD/CA 95; *Dioc. Kal.* (1905).
[54] Ex inf. Diocesan Registrar.
[55] *Dioc. Kal.* (1888–1907); *Dioc. Dir.* (1908–68).
[56] *Dioc. Dir.* (1971).
[57] *Tax. Eccl.* (Rec. Com.), 199.
[58] E 179/169/14.
[59] *H.M.C. Wells*, i. 380; ii. 641; Vicars Choral MSS. accts. (series B), 144.
[60] Vicars Choral MSS. accts. (series B), 162, 177, 185–7.
[61] *Proc. Som. Arch. Soc.* cxii. 83.
[62] Ex inf. the Revd. H. D. Cave.
[63] *Augmentation of Livings, 1703–1815*, H.C. 115 (1814–15), xii.
[64] Hodgson, *Queen Anne's Bounty.*
[65] *Rep. Com. Eccl. Revenues*, pp. 168–9.
[66] S.R.O., D/D/Rg 311.
[67] S.R.O., D/D/V rtns. 1815. This entry was later erased and replaced by 'none'.
[68] *Rep. Com. Eccl. Revenues*, pp. 168–9.
[69] See above.

Montacute House from the South-east

Montacute House: the Great Hall, *c.* 1942

Tintinhull

Stoke sub Hamdon

CHURCH INTERIORS

(occurs 1784–90) from Broadway.[70] The most distinguished curate during this period was Septimus Collinson (1777–8), who became rector of Dowlishwake in 1778 and was later to be Lady Margaret Professor of Divinity and Provost of the Queen's College, Oxford.[71] The parish was often served by assistant curates, particularly during the incumbency of John Hawkes Mules the younger (1815–58), who held the benefice with Ilminster, Isle Abbotts, and Thorn Coffin.[72]

It was reported in 1576 that only two sermons had been preached in the previous year, and the farmer of the rectory was cited to answer the charge.[73] In 1815 'alternate service' was 'duly and regularly performed'.[74] Services, alternately morning and evening, were reported in 1840 and 1843.[75] In 1843 it was stated that Holy Communion was celebrated four times a year and that the curate, non-resident by licence, catechized before and after services.[76] Congregations averaged between 70 and 90 in 1850–1, and the morning service attendance on Census Sunday 1851 was 84, including 34 Sunday-school children.[77]

In 1560 the lord of the manor leased a church house to three men,[78] and the manor court in 1602 ordered the churchwardens to repair it.[79] By 1383 a piece of land was attached to the church, known as St. John's acre.[80] Another piece of land, in Ludney field and known as the church acre, given for a light on the high altar, had formerly been part of the church's estate.[81] By 1563 it had become manorial property, though the tenant still paid 2s. a year to the church.[82]

Until 1450 the dedication festival of the church was observed on the eve of the Purification, namely, on the feast of St. Bridget of Kildare.[83] The church, however, was said in 1383 to be dedicated to St. John the Evangelist and All Saints.[84] There was apparently a chapel in Allowenshay;[85] land called 'Chapelhay' in 1563 may have marked its site.[86] The dedication festival of the parish church may have been changed after the chapel had ceased to exist. After 1450, however, the festival was changed to the first Sunday in October 'in order that it may be observed with more solemnity and devotion'.[87]

The parish church of *ST. JOHN THE EVANGELIST AND ALL SAINTS* stands in a prominent position which contributes to the impressive appearance of a comparatively small building. It is built of Ham stone and consists of a chancel with later north vestry, a central tower, and a nave with south porch. The existence of a central tower without transepts is unusual and may indicate the persistence of a Norman plan. The oldest part of the present church, however, is the early-14th-century porch, which incorporates a cusped ogee-headed window, now blocked. The chancel also belongs to the 14th century. The 15th-century tower preceded the nave, the north wall of which was later realigned, at the time when the roof was renewed at a different pitch and the parapet added. The nave has large three-light Perpendicular windows in its side walls and at the west end. Below the west window is a richly-decorated doorway. The angle stair-turret of the tower rises above the parapet and on the south side both the two-light opening at the belfry stage and the opening below are filled with pierced Somerset tracery. The church possesses a Perpendicular font, and there are fragments of glass in the nave windows incorporating the blazing sun emblem.

There are six bells: (i) 1930, Mears and Stainbank; (ii) 1930, Mears and Stainbank; (iii) 1696, Thomas Purdue; (iv) 1930, Mears and Stainbank; (v) 1693, Thomas Purdue; (vi) 1930, Mears and Stainbank.[88] The plate includes a silver cup and cover of 1573, a pewter flagon dated 1633, and a pewter bowl of 1722.[89] The marriage and burial registers begin in 1715, the baptisms in 1717; they appear to be complete.[90]

NONCONFORMITY. In 1825 the house of William Membury in Allowenshay was licensed for use by a group of Bible Christians. The group continued until 1829 and was revived between 1840 and 1843.[91]

EDUCATION. A Sunday school, supported by subscription, with about 30 pupils, was the only school in the parish in 1818.[92] A day-school opened in 1830, and in 1833 there were 17 boys and 19 girls attending it. The school was partly supported by the curate and partly by payments of 1d. by the pupils. At the same time there was a Sunday school, with the same number of pupils, wholly supported by the curate, who also provided a lending library 'amply supplied with religious and useful books'.[93] By 1859 the day-school had been united with the National Society.[94] The school was still active in 1875, but by 1883 the children of the parish went to Dowlishwake, the school at Kingstone having closed.[95]

CHARITIES FOR THE POOR. None known.

[70] Foster, *Alumni Oxon.*
[71] Ibid.
[72] S.R.O., D/P/kstone 2/1/1–3; *Rep. Com. Eccl. Revenues*, pp. 168–9; see below, p. 253.
[73] S.R.O., D/D/Ca 57.
[74] S.R.O., D/D/V rtns. 1815.
[75] Ibid. 1840, 1843.
[76] Ibid. 1843.
[77] H.O. 129/318/1/7.
[78] D.R.O., D 54/M 8.
[79] Arundell MSS. ct. bk. 18 f. 75v.
[80] *H.M.C. Wells*, ii. 637.
[81] E 310/23/127, no. 90; D.R.O., D 54/M 8.
[82] D.R.O., D 54/M 8; *Cal. Pat. 1569–72*, p. 389.
[83] *S.R.S.* xlix. 149.
[84] *H.M.C. Wells*, ii. 637.
[85] The site (ST 391134) is marked by the Ordnance Survey who, however, no longer have the evidence for the ascription. Its existence is also known through local folklore.
[86] D.R.O., D 54/M 8.
[87] *S.R.S.* xlix. 149.
[88] S.R.O., DD/SAS CH 16.
[89] *Proc. Som. Arch. Soc.* xlv. 144–5.
[90] S.R.O., D/P/kstone 2/1/1–5.
[91] S.R.O., D/D/Rm, box 2; D/N/sp.c 31, 32.
[92] *Digest of Returns to Sel. Cttee. on Educ. of Poor*, H.C. 224 (1819), ix (2).
[93] *Educ. Enquiry Abstract*, H.C. 62 (1835), xlii.
[94] Harrison, Harrod & Co. *Dir. Som.* (1859).
[95] *Kelly's Dir. Som.* (1875, 1883).

MONTACUTE

THE ancient parish of Montacute, four miles west of Yeovil, was 1,485 a. in extent before the addition of a detached portion of Norton sub Hamdon was made about 1898.[1] Thereafter the area was 1,518 a. until 1957, when the whole of the detached portion of the parish around Bagnell farm was transferred to Norton sub Hamdon,[2] leaving 1,304 a.[3]

The parish is irregular in shape, and before 1957 was some 3 miles in length, from the Tintinhull boundary to the top of Chiselborough hill. It is only a little more than 1 mile wide at most. The boundary with Stoke sub Hamdon on the west divides Hedgecock hill in two, and was marked by a ditch until Sir Edward Phelips (d. 1614) built a wall along it.[4] It then follows the line of the Iron Age earthworks on the northern edge of Ham or Hamdon Hill. These defences also form part of its boundary with Norton sub Hamdon on the south-west, the rest formerly marked by a ditch, and then by another wall, also built by Phelips.[5] The land around Bagnell farm at the southern end of the parish formed an island including Beacon hill itself[6] and the land stretching up the scarp slope of Chiselborough hill, where the boundary is marked by a deep ditch. This area is divided from the rest of the parish by a road linking Norton sub Hamdon with its East field.[7]

Geologically and topographically the parish falls into two distinct parts, separated by Wellham's brook and the village. To the north and east, on the Pennard sands,[8] the land rises from the narrow strip of alluvium in the valley to over 250 ft. in open country. It seems likely that the lands of the four knights holding half the manor at Domesday were concentrated in this area; the priory certainly had very little land north of the brook,[9] and the two manors of Hide and Brook Montacute were located there.[10] A settlement on the south side of Wellham's brook east of Brook farm survived until the 19th century. South of the village, on the Yeovil sands, the landscape and land-use are in striking contrast. To the west is the 400 ft. mass of Ham Hill, and to the south the irregular and steep scarps around Pit wood and Bagnell farm. The site of the deserted hamlet of Witcombe lies in a valley in the centre of the area.[11] A park, known as Old Park by 1617,[12] lay on the rising ground between the southern end of the village and Park Lane. It was created, apparently, by one of the counts of Mortain before the end of the 11th century, and was granted to the monks of Montacute by King John, when count of Mortain, in 1192.[13] The warren, immediately east of Stroud's hill and including part of the defences of the Iron Age camp, was confirmed to the monks in 1252.[14] Woodland along the earthworks was known as Warren covert, and had at its southern end a small piece of land called the Dog Trap.[15] When the manor was granted to the new monastery in the parish, c. 1102, the property included orchards and vineyards.[16] The southern slopes of St. Michael's hill seem to be the only suitable place for vines. Orchards still dominated the immediate environs of the village in the 19th century.[17] Woodland is found in the south of the parish. Pit wood, with its 18th-century artificial lake,[18] and High wood, on a spur north of Bagnell farm, are the largest. At the beginning of the 20th century there were 94 a. of woodland in the parish.[19]

Apart from the large area inside the Iron Age Camp, divided in the 17th century between Hamdon within and without the walls,[20] the southern part of the parish was anciently inclosed. Montacute's open fields lay in the north, and in the 16th century were known as West, Middle, and East fields.[21] These were later renamed, and evidently divided. Issakell[22] and Higher fields lay respectively west and east of the road to Tintinhull, with Short Kemsicall Close field immediately south of Higher field. Issakell field seems to represent the position of the demesne lands of Brook Montacute.[23] Similarly Great Hide, east of Gaundle farm, is indicative of the Hide manor demesnes. Gaundle field, near Gaundle farm, survived until 1802, and nearer the north-eastern boundary of the parish lay Yonder field.[24]

The road system in the north of the parish was formed to serve these fields by three roughly parallel tracks and lateral lanes. Kissmedown[25] Lane ran through Tintinhull and Sock Dennis to Ilchester. The remainder of the parish was crossed by three east–west roads, the most important being that through the village via Townsend, the Borough, and Middle Street, and thence south of St. Michael's hill to Ham Hill, part of the London–Exeter coach road. At Batemoor a track, known as Green Lane

[1] S.R.O., tithe award; C. Trask, *Norton sub Hamdon*, 4.
[2] *Somerset* (*Parishes in the Rural District of Yeovil*) *Confirmation Order, 1957*.
[3] *Census*, 1901–61.
[4] S.R.O., DD/PH 225/78.
[5] Ibid.
[6] Devon R.O. 123 M/E 91, survey of 1566 referring to Beakenhill; S.R.O., DD/HW 1, will of Thomas Rodbard, 1712, referring to 'Begnell alias Beacon hill'.
[7] Trask, *Norton sub Hamdon*, map facing p. x.
[8] Geol. Surv. Map 1″, solid and drift, sheet 312 (1958 edn.).
[9] See p. 216. The former abbey demesnes are the non-tithable areas of the parish: S.R.O., tithe award.
[10] See p. 215.
[11] See p. 216.
[12] E 134/15 Jas. I Trin./5.
[13] *S.R.S.* viii. 129–30; *Rot. Chart.* (Rec. Com.), 4.

[14] *S.R.S.* viii. 131.
[15] S.R.O., DD/SAS, H/528, map of Montacute, 1825; S.R.O., tithe award.
[16] *S.R.S.* viii. 119; *Reg. Regum Anglo-Norm.* ii, pp. 50, 180.
[17] S.R.O., tithe award.
[18] Llewelyn Powys, *Som. and Dors. Essays*, 89. The name 'Pyte' occurs in the 17th cent.: S.R.O., DD/PH 163; there is thus no connexion with William Pitt.
[19] Statistics supplied by the then Bd. of Agric. (1905).
[20] S.R.O., DD/PH 225/43.
[21] Devon R.O. 123 M/E 91.
[22] The name is preserved in Icicle Barn. It was known as Isaile field in 1739: S.R.O., DD/PH 142.
[23] Brook field occurs in 1657: S.R.O., DD/PH 80.
[24] S.R.O., DD/PH 159, bk. of reference, 1782; S.R.O., tithe award.
[25] Kissmeredown in 1649: S.R.O., DD/PH 80.

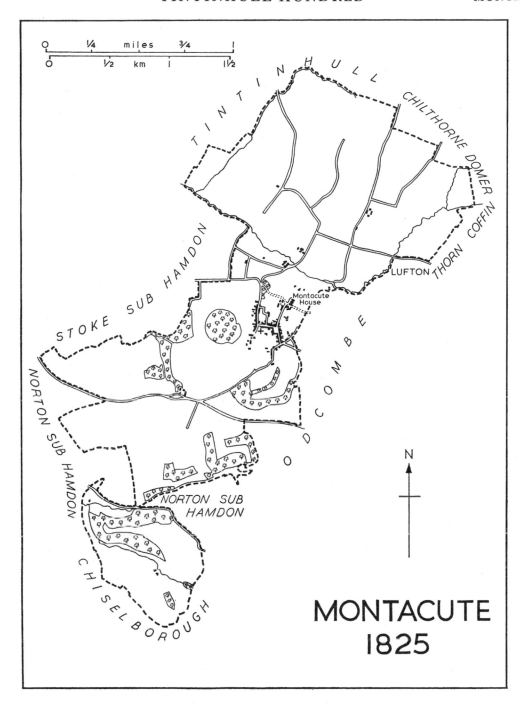

MONTACUTE
1825

or Witcombe Lane, runs south towards the site of Witcombe.[26]

The Iron Age camp on Ham Hill, usually associated with either Stoke or Norton, lies largely in Montacute parish, although most of the archaeological material has come from the quarry workings in Stoke.[27] Neolithic pottery and other material has been found 'in sufficient quantity to indicate permanent settlement'.[28] The site was fortified

probably in the 1st century B.C. as a stronghold of the Durotriges, but shortly after A.D. 43 appears to have been sacked by the Roman army. It may possibly have been used by the Romans as a fort,[29] but during the 3rd and 4th centuries part of it was probably under agriculture,[30] and much of the rest used for quarrying.[31] A hollow track running between Hedgecock hill and St. Michael's hill to Batemoor Barn and then southwards through the valley

[26] S.R.O., DD/SAS, H/528, map of Montacute, 1825; S.R.O., tithe award, 1838: O.S. Map 6", Som. LXXXII. SW., SE.; LXXXIX. NW., NE. (1886 and later edns.).
[27] *V.C.H. Som.* ii. 496–9, regards it as in Norton. For the large collection of archaeological finds from the site see *Proc. Som. Arch. Soc.* xlviii. 24–78.

[28] *Proc. Som. Arch. Soc.* cix. 51.
[29] *Jnl. Royal Arch. Inst.* cxv. 54. See *Proc. Som. Arch. Soc.* lviii. 49; lxix. 49–53; lxx. 104–16; lxxi. 57–76; lxxii. 55–68.
[30] *Proc. Som. Arch. Soc.* lviii. 49.
[31] *Medieval Arch.* viii. 103, 105.

bottom has been described as a Roman road.[32] It is certainly more ancient than the present field pattern of the south of the parish.

The origin of the settlement at Montacute is in the estate known as Logworesbeorh in the 7th century.[33] The name is probably of personal origin,[34] and William of Malmesbury linked it with one Logor, one of the original twelve monks of Glastonbury when Patrick arrived, who was commemorated on one of the two 'pyramids' outside the abbey.[35] Some time in the 9th century, apparently, the name was changed to Bishopston, possibly in connexion with Tunbeorht, who may have been both abbot of Glastonbury and bishop of Winchester.[36] The construction of the castle on St. Michael's hill to dominate the surrounding area brought about the introduction of the third name of the settlement, after the conical hill, the *mons acutus*, upon which it was built.[37] The name Bishopston, however, was retained as the name of a tithing, and is still given to part of the main street of the village, running northwards from the church. The strong connexion of the settlement with English influences was intensified in the legend of the Invention of the Holy Cross on St. Michael's hill; and the foundation of the Norman castle on the spot was seen as a final insult to the defeated race whose battle cry at Hastings, the object of Harold's particular veneration, had been that precious relic.[38] The siege of the castle in 1068 was an attempt at English independence.[39]

Place-name evidence thus suggests that the village originated north of the church at Bishopston. The borough, planted *ante* 1102,[40] and extended in the 13th century, continued the built-up area of the village eastwards from the church, around the precinct wall of the priory through Middle Street, the Borough, and part of South Street. Until after 1838 the road through Bishopston continued northwards past Smith's Row to the gates of Montacute House, and then turned sharply westwards;[41] but by 1853 this corner had been cut and the road took its present course.[42] Wash Lane, so called by 1766,[43] runs eastwards from Bishopston and emerges on the north side of Middle Street. Bowtell Street occurs in 1551; it contained a burgage and may therefore be an earlier name for either Middle Street or South Street.[44] Fleet Street occurs by 1760 until 1818,[45] New Lane, off Townsend, by 1780, and Pig Street 'next the Town Gate' between 1755 and 1797.[46]

The two-storeyed houses in the Borough, all constructed of local stone, with tiled or stone roofs, are mostly of the 18th and early 19th centuries. Near the entrance to Montacute House, however,

is an earlier building comprising two dwellings. The northern end, known as Montacute Cottage, is a two-storeyed house of c. 1500, having two- and three-light mullioned windows with traceried heads and a doorway with a four-centred arch. The house may once have contained an open hall. The southern end of the range, known as the Chantry, was formerly called the Old Chantry, and has housed successively a school and a post office. The house appears to have been a later addition to the range, but the bay window at the gable-end carries a carved panel, bearing the initials of Robert Shirborne, the last prior of Montacute (1532–9), probably re-set.[47] Now largely residential some of these properties in the Borough were originally used for commerce and manufacture in the 18th and 19th centuries. They, and the similar dwellings in Middle and South streets, were let to weavers and other craftsmen.[48] The Gables has smoke-blackened timbers in its former open hall and probably dates from the 16th century. Nos. 7–9 South Street represent a substantial L-shaped building of the 16th or 17th centuries, with a massive external chimney on the rear wing, a traceried three-light window in one gable-end, and an internal stud and panel partition with wide moulded studs. There is a tradition that this was the former manor-house of Montacute.[49]

North of the Borough, in its own extensive grounds, stands Montacute House, built probably by a Somerset mason, William Arnold, for Sir Edward Phelips.[50] The house, 'the most magnificent house of its time in Somerset',[51] was built probably in the 1590s, and had evidently been completed by 1601. It is of three storeys, in local Ham Hill stone. On plan it is H-shaped. The ground floor comprises a screened hall and a dining room, formerly a buttery and pantry, flanked on the north by a drawing room and a parlour. The southern wing housed the kitchen and servants' quarters. On the floor above is the great chamber in the north wing, now the library, and various bed- and dressing-rooms including the Garden Chamber, adapted by Lord Curzon when tenant of the house as his bedroom, and incorporating a bath camouflaged in a cupboard. On the second floor is the long gallery, running the whole length of the house. It is more than 180 ft. long, the longest surviving gallery in the country.[52]

The main entrance to the house was on the east side. In 1786, however, Edward Phelips built a two-storeyed addition between the two wings on the west side, thus providing corridors for easier access to all the rooms. The materials came from Clifton Maybank House (Dors.), and included the present porch and the ornamental stone front.[53]

[32] O.S. Map 6″, Som. LXXXII. SW. (1886 edn.).
[33] *Proc. Som. Arch. Soc.* xcv. 120–1.
[34] Ibid.
[35] William of Malmesbury, *De Gestis Regum* (Rolls Ser.), i. 25–6.
[36] *Proc. Som. Arch. Soc.* xcv. 120–1.
[37] *V.C.H. Som.* i. 483; Darby and Finn, *Dom. Geog. S.W. Eng.* 211.
[38] *Foundation of Waltham Abbey*, ed. W. Stubbs, 1–10; E. A. Freeman, *Norman Conquest*, iii. 478–9; iv. 170.
[39] *Norman Conquest*, iv. 271, 276; *V.C.H. Som.* ii. 180.
[40] See p. 215.
[41] S.R.O., tithe award.
[42] S.R.O., Q/SR, Spring 1853.
[43] S.R.O., DD/PH 68.
[44] *S.R.S.* li. 41.

[45] S.R.O., DD/PH 68, 72.
[46] Ibid. 69; par. rec., chwdns'. accts.
[47] Shirborne, otherwise Whitlocke or Gibbes, was appointed in 1532; the priory was dissolved in 1539: *V.C.H. Som.* i. 115. It was restored for a short time under Mary: E 134/5 Jas. I East. 6. For a colour drawing of the panel before recent decay see Taunton Castle, Braikenridge Colln.
[48] S.R.O., DD/PH 63–70; ex inf. Mr. W. H. Osborne.
[49] S.R.O., DD/SAS PR 54/5, p. 11. It is more likely to have been near the present house: Devon R.O. 123 M/E 92.
[50] M. Girouard, *Montacute House, Somerset* (Nat. Trust Guide, 1966).
[51] Ibid. 5.
[52] Ibid. 20.
[53] Ibid. 10–11.

The present layout of the extensive grounds dates from the 19th century, the gardens at the north end of the house replacing a pond and a mount. The former east entrance is now an enclosed court with balustraded walls and finials and pavilions at the outer corners. Other out-buildings include an arcaded garden house at the end of a yew walk on the south side of the house, and stables dating from the late 18th century.[54]

The relative prosperity of the village as a centre of small home industries, and its position on the Exeter–London coach road allowed several inns to flourish. The Guildhall and its shops had been converted to that purpose by 1612,[55] and Richard Hodder is described as an innholder in 1649.[56] The Red Lion, held by William Hodder in 1697, occurs until 1750; the George had a continuous history from 1698[57] and from at least 1726 until closure in 1822 was kept by members of the Isaac family.[58] The King's Arms in Bishopston had been established under that name by 1780; Francis Hann, its owner, had been an innkeeper since 1763.[59] The 18th-century house was altered in the 19th century and given a 'Tudor' frontage in ashlar. The Phelips Arms, perhaps successor to the George, was so named by 1835.[60]

The Durston–Yeovil branch of the Bristol and Exeter Railway was constructed through the centre of the parish in 1853, and was taken over by the Great Western Railway Company in 1876.[61] The line and station were closed in 1964.[62]

The Montacute Benevolent Friendly Society was founded in 1802, and had 48 members by the following year. Female friendly societies were founded at the King's Arms in 1811 and 1836, and at the Phelips Arms in 1835; a further female society was approved in 1843. A Guardian Friendly Society met at the Phelips Arms from 1836 and still flourished in 1844.[63] The Provident and Mutual Benefit Society was active by 1881, and a club festival was still held in 1933 with side shows and roundabouts in the Borough.[64] In 1876 a Working Men's Reading Room and Library was opened, and in 1892 the Constitutional Hall. Cricket and football clubs had been founded by 1903.[65]

Montacute, probably at the height of its prosperity in the 14th century,[66] had a taxable population of 87 in 1377.[67] The figure rose from 827 in 1801 to a peak of 1,047 in 1841. There was a gradual fall to 713 in 1911, and then a recovery to 867 in 1951. With the alteration of the parish boundary in 1957 the figure fell to 806 in 1961.[68]

Thomas Shoel, said to have been a labourer in the parish, was the author of a number of poems published between 1786 and 1821, largely by subscription, and composer of three volumes of church music.[69]

MANORS. Between 676 and 685 Baldred gave to Glastonbury abbey an estate of 16 hides at Logworesbeorh, identified as Montacute.[70] In 854 Athelwulf allowed half a hide of the abbey's estate there to be exempt from secular dues.[71] A holding, of unknown size, was the subject of a grant to Glastonbury by Bishop Tunbeorht of Winchester between 871 and 879;[72] this may not have been a further accretion of property, but rather a confirmation by the bishop who may previously have been abbot of Glastonbury.[73] Presumably with the virtual collapse of Glastonbury during the Danish invasions[74] the abbey lost these lands. Athelney abbey had certainly acquired them before 1066,[75] though in the legend of the Invention of the Holy Cross it is implied that the owner in Cnut's time was Tofig, the sheriff.[76] By 1086, however, Athelney had exchanged its estate, known as the manor of *BISHOPSTON*, with the count of Mortain, for his manor of Purse Caundle (Dors.).[77]

On his manor of Bishopston Robert, count of Mortain, built his castle and established a borough.[78] The castle became the head of an honor and two of its porters held land in serjeanty at Steart in Babcary.[79] Thenceforward the settlements and the manor were known as *MONTACUTE*.[80] About 1102 William, count of Mortain, gave the manor, castle, and borough, with other properties, to his newly-founded house of Cluniac monks established there.[81] The manor remained in monastic hands, save when seized as alien property during time of war, until the monastery was dissolved in 1539.[82]

Shortly after the surrender of the monastic estates, the Crown granted a lease of the property to Dr. William (later Sir William) Petre. The grant included the site of the monastery, the borough of Montacute, and the manors of *MONTACUTE*, *MONTACUTE BOROUGH*, and *MONTACUTE 'FORREN'*, later known as *MONTACUTE FORUM*. These divisions of the original estates were probably no more than simple administrative units, and do not seem to have been manors in the strict sense of the term. In 1542 Sir Thomas Wyatt (d. 1542) of Allington (Kent) acquired the reversion of Petre's lease, and granted

[54] Pevsner, *South and West Som.* 248.
[55] S.R.O., DD/PH 235.
[56] Ibid. 63, lease to Richard Hodder.
[57] Ibid. 64, 67, 144, 225/80.
[58] Par. rec., chwdns'. accts.
[59] Ibid. Its history may date from a century earlier: S.R.O., DD/PH 225/46.
[60] S.R.O., Q/R, Friendly Soc. rtns.
[61] Macdermott, *Hist. G.W.R.* ii. 601, 603, 617–18.
[62] C. R. Clinker and J. M. Firth, *Reg. Closed Stations*, ii.
[63] *Poor Law Abstract, 1804*; S.R.O., Q/R, Friendly Soc. rtns.; Margaret Fuller, *West-Country Friendly Soc.* 144.
[64] Taunton Castle, Tite Colln., *Rules*; S.R.O., DD/SAS PR 54/5, pp. 24–5.
[65] *Kelly's Dir. Som.* (1883, 1897); S.R.O., C/E 27.
[66] *S. & D. N. & Q.* xxix. 10–13.
[67] J. C. Russell, *Medieval Population*, 141.
[68] *V.C.H. Som.* ii. 349; *Census*, 1911–61.

[69] *Weekly Entertainer*, 20 Feb. 1786, p. 191, *Mileshill, a poem* (1803), *Glastonbury Tor* (1818), *Miscellaneous Pieces* (1819), *Poems* (1821), *Psalms, Tunes*, etc.
[70] Finberg, *Early Charters of Wessex*, p. 110.
[71] Ibid. p. 122; see below, p. 220.
[72] Finberg, op. cit. p. 123.
[73] Tumbert was abbot of Glastonbury: *V.C.H. Som.* ii. 98.
[74] *V.C.H. Som.* ii. 84, 98.
[75] Ibid. i. 483.
[76] *Foundation of Waltham Abbey*, ed. W. Stubbs, 1–10; Freeman, *Norman Conquest*, i. 529.
[77] *V.C.H. Som.* i. 483.
[78] M. W. Beresford, *New Towns of Middle Ages*, 483; see below, p. 215.
[79] *V.C.H. Som.* i. 478; ii. 181; *Bk. of Fees*, i. 79.
[80] *Proc. Som. Arch. Soc.* xcv. 120–1.
[81] *S.R.S.* viii. 119; *Reg. Regum Anglo-Norm.* ii, p. 50.
[82] S.C. 6/Hen. VIII/3137 mm. 24–5.

copyholds there. He bequeathed his interest to Elizabeth Darrell of Littlecote (Wilts.), with remainder, failing heirs, to his own son Thomas.[83] After the attainder of the younger Thomas in 1554 the reversion fell to the Crown and was given to Sir William Petre.[84] Petre continued in possession until his death in 1572. It is possible that his son John succeeded to the lease, which still had over twenty years to run, for he was certainly granting sub-leases of parts of the estate by 1580, and so continued until 1590.[85] Meanwhile in 1574 Robert Dudley, earl of Leicester, acquired the reversion of the manor in fee,[86] and at once sold it to Robert Freke of Iwerne Courtnay (Dors.).[87] Freke succeeded to the manor in fee before his death in 1592,[88] and his son Thomas was still lord of the manor in 1607.[89] By the end of the following year he had been succeeded by Sir Edward Phelips.[90]

The Phelips family, first settled in the parish by 1479,[91] thus began their reign as lords of the manor of Montacute which lasted until the 20th century. Sir Edward Phelips (d. 1614)[92] was followed successively by his son, Robert (d. 1638), by his grandson, Col. Edward (d. 1679), and by his great-grandson, Sir Edward (d. 1699). Through Sir Edward's daughter Elizabeth (d. 1750), who married Edward Phelips of Preston Plucknett, the estate descended to her son Edward (d. 1797). Edward was succeeded by his second son William (d. 1806), a clergyman. John Phelips, William's son (d. 1834), died without children, and the estate passed to a nephew William (d. 1889). On the death of his son William Robert in 1919, the property passed successively to his grandsons Edward Frederick (d. 1928) and Gerald Almarus. The latter made over the estate to the Society for the Protection of Ancient Buildings, who transferred it to the National Trust in 1931.[93] Several farms had earlier been sold, and the estate in 1931 amounted to less than 300 a.[94]

The grant of the former priory lands to William Petre in 1539 included the site of the monastery and its immediate grounds, including the monks' graveyard.[95] There is no mention of the monastic church, which was evidently demolished immediately. Surviving conventual buildings, including the gateway of the priory, were leased by Petre and his son as a farm-house to John Burt, who farmed some of the adjoining land for some fifty years until c. 1600.[96] Sir Edward Phelips had completed Montacute House before purchasing the manor, so the Abbey House, as it was called, became virtually redundant. By 1633 it was said to be 'almost desolate' because Sir Robert Phelips 'seldom makes use of it'.[97] In 1638 the site of the

old house of Montacute formed part of Sir Robert's estate,[98] and later in the century it became the residence of Col. Edward Phelips (d. 1679) after he had made over Montacute House and the estate to his son in 1668.[99] On Col. Phelips' death his widow retained the Abbey House and orchards.[1] About 1700 it was let to a Mr. Bone.[2] By 1782 the house had become a farm-house again, serving as the residence of John Wilton, who worked Abbey farm, the largest in the parish.[3] The farm remained part of the Phelips estate until it was sold to the occupier, Mr. Charles Dare, in 1918.[4] It then amounted to about 434 a.[5]

The former priory gatehouse, which stands south-west of the parish church, has thus been a residence since the 16th century. It comprises a tall embattled gatehouse with lower two-storeyed ranges to east and west of it. The arched gateway has a fan vault and the room above has oriel windows, enriched with quatrefoil bands, on two faces. At the centre of the parapet on the north or entrance front is a carved portcullis and the initials of Thomas Chard (prior 1514–32). On its inner side the gatehouse has two polygonal stair turrets, one higher and one lower than the main structure. Both east and west ranges, the former of three bays, the latter incomplete, have buttresses and embattled parapets. The least altered façade is on the south side of the east range; here the merlons of the parapet are carved with quatrefoils and there is a doorway with a four-centred head and carved spandrels. The square-headed windows have mullions and transomes. There was formerly an eastward continuation of the range, lower in height and possibly earlier in date, which had medieval features; it had been demolished by 1864.[6] Alterations were made to the building after it became a dwelling-house, including the addition of a 17th-century porch wing on the north side of the east range; this also disappeared in the mid 19th century. Earlier in the century the gateway arch had been blocked by a two-storeyed structure which was later removed. There are no other remains of the priory buildings except a square dovecot standing east of the gatehouse. The field behind the house, however, contains evidence of former buildings in the uneven surface of the pasture.[7]

Half the manor of Bishopston in 1086 was in the hands of four knights, Alfred the butler, Drew, Bretel de St. Clair, and Donecan.[8] The first three were substantial tenants of the count of Mortain elsewhere, but Donecan does not seem to have held other land in Somerset. Alfred held $1\frac{1}{2}$ hide and the other three 1 hide each. The descent of these properties

[83] L. & P. Hen. VIII, xvii, p. 107; xviii(1), p. 541; Devon R.O. 123 M/E 91, survey 1566.
[84] Cal. Pat. 1555–7, 57–8.
[85] S.R.O., DD/PH 144, survey 1608.
[86] C 66/1115 mm. 19–20.
[87] S.R.O., DD/PH 235.
[88] C 142/234/75.
[89] S.R.O., DD/PH 144.
[90] Ibid.
[91] Ibid. 5.
[92] Burke, Land. Gent. (1906), 1327.
[93] Ibid. (1952), 2019.
[94] S.R.O., DD/PH 249, sale cat. 1929; see below, p. 218.
[95] S.C. 6/Hen. VIII/3137 m. 24; Cal. Pat. 1555–7, 57–8.
[96] E 134/15 Jas. I Trin./6.
[97] S.R.S. xv. 99.
[98] C 142/486/151.

[99] S. & D. N. & Q. xxviii. 107.
[1] S.R.O., DD/PH 229/12.
[2] Ibid. 144, survey c. 1700.
[3] Ibid. 159, bk. of reference, 1782. The farm was then 612 a.
[4] S.R.O., D/G/Y 160.
[5] Ibid.
[6] Taunton Castle, Tite Colln., view by Alfred Clarke (1864). There are earlier views by J. Buckler (1826 and 1827) in the Pigott Colln., and by J. C. Buckler (1811) and W. W. Wheatley (1848) in the Braikenridge Colln., both in Taunton Castle. For modern photos. see Country Life, 19 June 1915.
[7] The remains of an archway, possibly an entrance into the monastic precinct, was found in Townsend in 1863: par. rec. burial reg. 1857–1926 (flyleaf).
[8] V.C.H. Som. i. 412, 483.

is obscure. According to Henry I's confirmation of the foundation charter of Montacute priory, the count's men as well as the count himself gave their property in the manor of Bishopston to the priory.[9] It is possible, therefore, that some of these small holdings became absorbed in the priory estate, but they are unlikely to have become part of the demesne lands, and were transferred, with the sitting tenants, from one landlord to another.

Two independent estates which emerged in the later Middle Ages may be the lineal descendants of these four Domesday holdings. The reputed manor of *HIDE* was distinct from other holdings in the parish in that all its tithes, not simply the tithes of hay and hemp, were payable to the vicar.[10] Often referred to as la Hyde[11] or Hyde,[12] it was first described as a manor at the end of the 16th century. By 1576 it was in the hands of Thomas Phelips (d. 1590), who settled it on his wife.[13] John, his son, held it from 1588[14] and was still in occupation in 1596.[15] The property formed part of the lands settled by Sir Robert Phelips in 1632 on his son's wife,[16] but at Sir Robert's death in 1638 it was still a separate unit.[17] In 1656 it was known as Hyde farm when mortgaged by Edward Phelips.[18] The farm appears to have remained in hand during much of the 17th and 18th centuries[19] though it was leased from 1797.[20] It did not survive as a farming unit, and by 1838 had been absorbed into other farms.[21]

The other independent medieval holding was the reputed manor of *BROOK MONTACUTE*. John Dudding and his wife made over a small estate to Sir Thomas Brook and Joan his wife in 1400.[22] Joan did fealty for the estate on the death of her husband in 1418.[23] Her son, Edward Brook, Lord Cobham (d. 1464), succeeded on her death.[24] John, Lord Cobham (d. 1512), was in possession in 1469.[25] His daughter Mary took it to her husband, Robert Blagg (d. 1522), and it descended to their son George.[26] John Bevyn had at his death in 1554 a lease of the property, which he left to his daughter Dorothy.[27] She was holding 'Brokes Lande' of William, Lord Cobham (d. 1597), in 1566.[28] Sir Edward Phelips acquired the estate, then amounting to 87 a., before 1607.[29] With Hyde farm it was mortgaged in 1656, and in 1685 it was described as the manor or reputed manor of Brooke alias Brooke Montacute alias Montacute.[30] In 1838 Brook

farm, still owned by the Phelips family and held by Jeremiah Hallett, measured just over 92 a.[31]

CASTLE. Montacute castle was built on an isolated conical hill, known as St. Michael's hill, dominating the village and visible from a wide area. The hill was scarped to form an oval motte, with an upper bailey on the south-east and a lower bailey on a plateau encircling the hill.[32] It was constructed by Robert, count of Mortain, by 1068 when it was besieged during a revolt against the Conqueror.[33] It presumably ceased to have any military importance after William, count of Mortain, gave it to his newly-founded Cluniac priory in the village c. 1102.[34] Leland declared that the castle 'partly fell to ruin, and partly was taken down to make the priory'.[35] In 1518–19 the churchwardens of Tintinhull paid for two loads of stone from it, suggesting that the remains were still being used as a quarry.[36]

There was a chapel in the castle, dedicated to St. Michael, by c. 1102.[37] It was still in use in 1315.[38] It stood on the castle mound, and was reached by a flight of stone steps.[39] In the 1630s it was described as 'a fine piece of work built with arched work, and an embowned roof, overlaid all of stone, very artificially'.[40] The site of the chapel is occupied by a tower built in 1760.[41] The castle mound has been wooded since the late 18th century.[42]

BOROUGH. The borough of Montacute seems to have been formed as an addition to the Domesday village of Bishopston at some date between 1086 and c. 1102.[43] Its founder was presumably Robert, count of Mortain (d. 1090), or his son William. About 1102 the latter gave the borough as part of the foundation estate of Montacute priory.[44] Durand (I), prior of Montacute in the reign of Henry I,[45] gave to the burgage tenants liberties and free customs of other Somerset burgesses.[46] About a century later Prior Mark[47] extended the area of the borough to provide additional rents for the support of the convent kitchen. His grant to the new extension (novo burgo) implies an already established settlement, including a merchant's house.[48]

The nature of the liberties enjoyed by the burgesses of Montacute is not known, though it is unlikely that they had any great measure of autonomy.

9 *Reg. Regum Anglo-Norm.* ii, p. 180.
10 S.R.O., D/D/Rg 225.
11 S.R.O., DD/CC 110025 39/44; C.P. 25(1)/31/19.
12 C 142/46/19. Also known as Hude in 1412 when held by Alice Sylveyn: *Feud. Aids*, vi. 507.
13 C 142/228/6.
14 S.R.O., DD/PH 164.
15 C 60/423, no. 56.
16 C.P. 25(2)/479/7 Chas. I Hil.
17 C 142/486/151.
18 S.R.O., DD/PH 1.
19 Ibid. 144, 159, 163.
20 Ibid. 75.
21 S.R.O., tithe award.
22 C.P. 25(1)/201/33/2.
23 *Cal. Close*, 1413–19, 478.
24 Ibid. 1435–41, 87, 189–90; *Cal. Inq. p.m.* (Rec. Com.), iv. 180.
25 S.R.O., DD/PH 112, quitclaim by Christopher Worsley, Lady Cobham's second husband.
26 C 142/40/50.
27 *S.R.S.* xxi. 164.
28 Devon R.O. 123 M/E 94.

29 S.R.O., DD/PH 144.
30 Ibid. 1.
31 S.R.O., tithe award.
32 *V.C.H. Som.* i. 515.
33 Ibid. ii. 180; Freeman, *Norman Conquest*, iv. 271, 276.
34 *E.H.R.* xix (1904), 238–9; *Reg. Regum Anglo-Norm.* ii, p. 50.
35 Leland, *Itin.* ed. Toulmin Smith, i. 157–8.
36 *S.R.S.* iv. 200.
37 Ibid. viii. 119.
38 Ibid. i. 100.
39 Ibid. xv. 98.
40 Ibid.
41 Date on doorway.
42 *Gent. Mag.* lxxxvi(2), 577.
43 M. W. Beresford, *New Towns of Middle Ages*, 483.
44 *S.R.S.* viii. 119; *Reg. Regum Anglo-Norm.* ii, p. 50.
45 G. Oliver, *Monasticon Diœcesis Exoniensis* (1896), 312; *V.C.H. Som.* ii. 114.
46 *S.R.S.* viii. 210.
47 He occurs as prior in 1237 and 1245: *V.C.H. Som.* ii. 115.
48 *S.R.S.* viii. 210–11.

The borough answered independently of the manor at 13th-century eyres, and writs were sent summoning two members to Parliament from the borough in 1306.[49] The summons was not repeated.

By 1302–3 the priory was receiving an income of 16d. from each of 51 burgages in Montacute.[50] By 1540 some of these had been consolidated and others divided, giving a total of 55¾ burgages, in addition to two shambles and two shops. These properties were held at rents varying from the original 16d. to 6s. 8d., and were held by tenures ranging from socage to copyhold and life leasehold.[51] By 1566 there were 81 separate holdings in the borough, ranging from a sixteenth of a burgage to 1½ burgage, besides a guildhall, 9 shambles, and 2 shops. Fifty separate holdings amounting to 36 burgages, were freehold, 29 copyhold for lives, 1 copyhold at will, and 1 'free leasehold'.[52] By 1608 the total number of burgage tenures had been halved, and many were held for high rents.[53] The area of the borough remained a unit of local administration throughout the 18th century.[54]

By 1540 a guildhall stood in the borough.[55] It was still there in 1608.[56] It may be the 'town house and shire hall' described in 1703.[57] There was a lock-up in the Borough until 1845.[58]

ECONOMIC HISTORY. The estate at Bishopston in 1086 represents only a section of the 16 hides given by Baldred to Glastonbury abbey in the 7th century.[59] Measuring 9 hides, half the estate was held directly by the count of Mortain, the rest held of him by four knights. This division remained a reality until the 17th century, since the grant of the demesne lands of the count to Montacute priory preserved the estate intact until after the Dissolution. The Phelips estate, formed gradually from the end of the 16th century onwards, absorbed this unit, which was not finally dispersed until the 20th century. This physical division, indicated by the tithe-free area of the former priory demesne, comprised all lands south and west of the Yeovil–Stoke road, together with some scattered fields in the north-west of the parish.[60]

The estate of the count of Mortain at the time of the Domesday survey comprised 2½ hides in demesne, cultivated by 4 serfs with 2 ploughs, and 4 villeins and 3 bordars with 2 ploughs had a hide between them. Since the tenants of the other part of the estate shared 4½ hides, a hide is thus not accounted for. There are said to have been, therefore, only 4 ploughs, on land for 7; this suggests a recent contraction of arable. Only 15 a. of meadow are recorded, although the estate supported a riding horse and 100 sheep.

Together the knights held 4½ hides, cultivated with a total of 5 ploughs. The largest farm was that of Alfred the butler, with 1½ hide, worked by 6 bordars and a serf, and supporting 80 sheep. Drew, Bretel de St. Clair, and Donecan each held a hide, worked by 5, 2, and 6 bordars respectively. No other stock is recorded. Together these holdings were worth £3 3s., as compared with the valuation of £6 put upon the count's estate.[61]

The creation of the borough in the late 11th century, and the consequent alteration in the balance of the economy, was accompanied by a similar change in the tenurial pattern of the priory estate. By 1303 the demesne lands amounted to just over 100 a. of arable, a small amount of pasture, and gardens worth together 79s. 5½d.[62] The orchards and vineyards forming part of the original grant from the count of Mortain had disappeared,[63] though the monks had acquired the park in 1192, a property apparently not reckoned in the 1302–3 survey.[64] By far the largest part of the estate had been let: apart from the borough,[65] with its 51 burgesses, there were 50 free tenements, 2 of a virgate, 9 of a half-virgate, 9 of a ferling, and 30 of a messuage and curtilage. There were also 25 villein holdings, 7 of a half-virgate, 11 of a ferling, and the rest cottar holdings. These properties, all let for rents alone, were worth a total of £16 10s. 10¾d., nearly half the income from the whole estate.[66] The monks continued their policy of leasing their demesne under licence from the Crown in 1319.[67]

Further leasing of the demesnes in the early 16th century[68] foreshadowed the end of the hamlet of Witcombe, on the demesne originally attached to the manor of Bishopston.[69] The hamlet may perhaps be identified as the settlement of the four villeins and three bordars of 1086.[70] This hamlet was still in existence in 1566, when twelve 'poor tenants' there each held 10 a. of land on lease.[71] Its end was even then in view, since the reversion of these leases had already been granted to the tenant of much of the surrounding land, which was under grass, supporting sheep.[72] By 1614 most of these holdings has been absorbed.[73]

The creation of the borough added a further dimension to the economy of Montacute. Little is known of trade there in the medieval period, though there are occasional references to shops and shambles.[74] Montacute was of sufficient importance to have been visited by Henry III in 1250.[75] It was taxed as a borough in 1316, 1319, 1332, 1334, and 1336,[76] and in 1340, for the tax on towns levied

[49] Ibid. xi. 33, 67, 290; V.C.H. Som. ii. 184.
[50] S.C. 11/798.
[51] S.R.O., DD/PH 228/24.
[52] Devon R.O. 123 M/E 94.
[53] S.R.O., DD/PH 144.
[54] See p. 220.
[55] S.R.O., DD/PH 228/24.
[56] Ibid. 144.
[57] Ibid. 64.
[58] S.R.O., DD/SAS PR 54/5, p. 23.
[59] V.C.H. Som. i. 483; Finberg, Early Charters of Wessex, p. 110.
[60] S.R.O., tithe award.
[61] V.C.H. Som. i. 483.
[62] S.C. 11/798.
[63] S.R.S. viii. 119; Reg. Regum Anglo-Norm., ii, p. 180; Cal. Chart. R. 1257–1300, 136.
[64] S.R.S. viii. 128–30.

[65] See p. 215.
[66] S.C. 11/798.
[67] Cal. Pat. 1317–21, 340.
[68] L. & P. Hen. VIII, xiv(1), p. 193.
[69] S.R.S. viii. 128; S. & D. N. & Q. xxix. 27–8.
[70] V.C.H. Som. i. 483.
[71] Devon R.O. 123 M/E 91.
[72] Ibid.; E 134/15 Jas. I East./6.
[73] S.R.O., DD/PH 235. There was still at least one house there in 1671: DD/PH 80.
[74] Cal. Pat. 1361–4, 193; S.R.O., DD/PH 228/24; Cal. Close, 1413–19, 29.
[75] Cal. Close, 1247–51, 310.
[76] Hist. Essays in Honour of James Tait, ed. J. G. Edwards, V. H. Galbraith, and E. F. Jacob, 434. It was marked on Matthew Paris's map of Great Britain: B.M. Cott. Jul. D. vii.

in that year, was ranked ninth in the county.[77] There are slight traces of trades later to be of importance in the parish in the occurrence of two drapers and dyers in the 14th century, a mercer in 1489, and a tanner in 1547;[78] but the general decline of the town in the 16th century is suggested by the disappearance of the fair and the poverty of the market.[79]

Apart from some slight evidence for the continuation of open-field cultivation on Hide manor[80] and for opposition to inclosure on Brook manor[81] the overwhelming weight of evidence for the economic history of Montacute for the 16th century comes from the former monastic estate, concentrated largely in the southern half of the parish. In 1535 the priory enjoyed rents of free and customary tenants, presumably in the borough and in the 'manor' of Montacute Forum, amounting to £53 19s. 4d.[82] The demesne lands were also let in small parcels, for which the Crown tenant in 1539 paid £14.[83] In terms of holdings there were at least sixteen on the former demesne; the borough comprised 79 separate holdings, and Montacute Forum was divided between 38 tenants, some leaseholders, some copyholders, and some tenants at will. Borough and Forum together were worth just over £48.[84] Seventy years later, when the estates had come into the hands of Sir Edward Phelips, the total income, including Brook manor, was only slightly increased.[85] More than half the rent came from life tenancies, known as tenancies 'by agreement'.

The fragmentation of the former monastic demesne, presumably brought about by letting to already established tenants, and the large number of separate holdings in other parts of the estate, was countered by a certain amount of consolidation by individual tenants. The most substantial tenant to emerge by 1540 was William Browne, former bailiff of the manor.[86] He held 'Estlonde' and 'Chaunts close' as his share of the demesne, and several holdings, mostly copyhold, in Montacute Forum.[87] Thomas Cogan or Cogayne, a local mercer[88] and from 1549 farmer of the rectory, was another substantial tenant, holding pasture grounds in the demesne, closes in Montacute Forum, and several burgages.[89] Thomas Phelips the elder was then among several much less wealthy inhabitants, and in 1540 was holding only three burgages and a watercourse.[90] At the same time Thomas Phelips the younger, his nephew, held 10¾ burgages, his own house being sited upon two of them, and another house, but apparently no land.[91] By 1566 Thomas the younger had outstripped the other tenants in wealth: he held 20½ burgages, two shambles, and a house in the borough, and was the largest tenant

of the former monastic demesne, with 226 a. leased from Wyatt from 1542 and 16 a. from Petre from 1560.[92] He died in 1590 leaving to his youngest son Edward his house in Montacute, a property which he had in fact conveyed to Edward two years earlier.[93] Possibly this was the manor-house of Hide: the identifiable lands of that manor lay in the area where Montacute House stands, and tradition places the site of the old house near the present stable block.[94]

During the 16th century changes had occurred in the husbandry of the parish, partly related to the tenurial changes of the period. Until shortly before the Dissolution, much of the priory's demesne lands had been devoted to sheep-farming,[95] but when they were divided between individual tenants some of the pasture grounds were ploughed to grow corn. Several lawsuits ensued when the lay impropriator claimed tithe, as anciently due from corn crops.[96] Some of the former demesne was evidently still under arable about 1632 and the then owner, Sir Robert Phelips, was being encouraged to plough more in order to increase his income.[97]

Including Hide manor and rents in Yeovil it was worth over £341 a year. 'Pyte' and 'Shortegrove' were worth £65 a year and could support 400 sheep. St. Michael's hill, Batemoor, Hamdon, and other lands were worth £100 a year, and 120 a. were cultivated, half producing rye and wheat, and half barley, beans, and oats. The surveyor considered that a further £300 could be made by putting more down to corn. The old monastic pastures including 'Witcombes', and others near the abbey site, were worth £83 and more, and could be put to better use to support oxen, cows, horses, and young stock. Costs of manuring and husbandry were put at 100 marks.[98]

Little material has survived for the next two centuries to show how the Phelipses farmed their estates, but there are rentals from 1705.[99] These strongly suggest that most of the property was farmed directly or by under-tenants: rents in 1705 came from a large number of small tenants, the most substantial paying only £2 8s. By 1756 the rental totalled £44 13s. 3d., from 77 tenants, and in 1801 both rental and the number of tenants had decreased slightly, to £39 7s. from 74 tenants. But by this time it is clear from other sources that most of the Phelips estate was being farmed in large units, some of it by leasehold tenants. By 1782 the estate was over 1,748 a. in extent. The largest unit, later Abbey farm, was technically in hand, but was let to John Wilton, as under-tenant, and comprised 612 a. John Hooper and John Trask held the later Windmill (133 a.) and Gaundle (123 a.) farms by similar tenure. Bagnell farm, measuring 98 a., was leased to

[77] E 179/169/14.
[78] S.R.S. iii. 225; xvi. 283; Cal. Pat. 1391–6, 678; 1548–9, 164; Winchester Coll. Mun. 14373–4.
[79] See p. 219.
[80] S.R.S. xvi. 216; xl. 175.
[81] C 47/7/4, no. 15.
[82] Valor Eccl. (Rec. Com.), i. 195.
[83] L. & P. Hen. VIII, xiv(1), p. 193; S.C. 6/Hen. VIII/3137 m. 24.
[84] S.R.O., DD/PH 228/24.
[85] Ibid. 144, survey 1608.
[86] Ibid. 228/24. Browne was also collector of rectory rents: S.C. 6/Hen. VIII/3137 m. 24d.
[87] S.C. 6/Hen. VIII/3137 m. 24; S.R.O., DD/PH 228/24.

[88] S.R.S. li. 41.
[89] Ibid.; S.C. 6/Hen. VIII/3137 m. 24; S.R.O., DD/PH 228/24.
[90] S.R.O., DD/PH 228/24.
[91] Ibid.
[92] Devon R.O. 123 M/E 91, survey 1566.
[93] Som. Wills, ed. Brown, i. 77; S.R.S. xxvii. 274n.
[94] H. A. Tipping, Story of Montacute and its House (Nat. Trust Guide, 1947), 18.
[95] E 134/15 Jas. I East./6.
[96] Ibid.; S.R.O., DD/PH 125, 159, 228/3.
[97] S.R.O., DD/PH 163.
[98] Ibid.
[99] Ibid. 143, rentals for 1705–26, 1734–6, 1752–5, 1756, 1758, 1801–4; ibid. 159, rental for 1843.

William Rodbard for lives. The lord of the manor had 218 a. in hand which he farmed direct. There were several other holdings of 20–30 a. which were held on leases for lives or for annual rents.[1] From 1797 onwards this tenurial pattern was somewhat changed, holdings formerly in hand, such as Gaundle and Hide farms, being leased to the tenants for terms of years.[2] This process continued so that by 1836 William Phelips had only Abbey and Bagnell farms and some scattered lands in hand.[3] Less than thirty years later these, too, were let.[4] The Phelips family gradually sold their estates in the parish in the first decades of the 20th century. Abbey farm, the largest unit, was sold in 1918[5] and by 1929 the estate amounted to only 303 a., including two small farms and scattered lands.[6]

The dominance of one landowner in the parish in the 18th century and later allowed inclosure to be made privately. Grazing in the common fields was mentioned in 1734,[7] but the rapid emergence of consolidated farms towards the end of the century indicates the disappearance of such rights. The names of the large open fields still survived at the end of the century, their number indicating a system of agriculture still practised at the time in Tintinhull.[8] The balance of cultivation in the parish, at least by 1825, was in favour of grassland, the southern half being almost exclusively such.[9] By 1905 964 a. were devoted to grass, 477 a. to arable, and 94 a. to woodland.[10] This pattern has continued into the 1970s.

Agriculture, however, was not the predominant interest in Montacute, either in the early 19th century or probably for the previous two centuries. Of 237 families in the parish in 1821, only 92 were engaged in it.[11] Others were quarrymen and clothworkers.

Sandstone from Hamdon or Ham Hill has been quarried for building and other purposes at least since Roman times, though most of the workings were in the parishes of Stoke and Norton.[12] Local stone was used almost exclusively for building until the 20th century.[13] No express reference to medieval quarries in Montacute has been found, though a freemason from the parish occurs in 1499,[14] and Thomas Wilkins of Montacute in 1540 left to John Morley, mason, his workshop in the quarries at Hamdon.[15] More specific information occurs in the 17th century. In 1625 Sir Robert Phelips leased land measuring 20 ft. by 40 ft., 'newly bounded out' on Ham Hill, within the parish, adjoining the 'east part of the quarrs', to make two quarries.[16] The lessee, Richard Frye of Stoke, who paid 12d. a year, was given 'liberty to lay his rubbish in the waste

ground of Norton Hill.' By 1697 nine quarries were being worked in the manor. John Clarke had three and three were in hand. These all seem to have been 18ft. square, and the annual rent was usually £6.[17]

There was a succession of masons in the village in the 18th century, notably three generations of the Hann family, and two each of the Newtons and the Geards.[18] In 1838 there seems to have been only one quarry, occupied by John Trask, tenant of of Abbey farm,[19] but there was evidently a considerable expansion of stone-working in the later 19th century. In 1861 there were four stone-masons resident in the village, and two years later six quarries were being worked, five belonging to the lord of the manor.[20] Three years later two more had been opened,[21] and a total of twelve was in production by 1875.[22] Eli Williams, tenant of one of Phelips's quarries in 1863, had in twelve years become a quarry-owner himself.[23] A decline set in fairly rapidly at the end of the century. There were four stone-masons in the parish in 1897, but only one by 1902.[24] By 1910 the surviving quarries were being worked by the Ham Hill and Doulting Stone Co., who themselves were taken over by the United Stone Firms Ltd. before 1914. One quarry owner and stone-merchant was still in business in 1919, supplying several kinds of stone in addition to that found locally.[25] Clearly the quarries themselves had largely been worked out and by 1968 were virtually closed.

From about 1592 until 1641 Montacute was the home of two generations of bell-founders, Robert Wiseman and his son William. Robert evidently began his work at Thorn Coffin, but died as 'of Montacute' in 1619.[26] Thirty-four of his bells survive in Somerset, mostly in the south of the county, and examples are also found in Devon, Dorset, Gloucestershire, and Monmouthshire. His son, William, was active as a bell-founder between 1622 and 1641. Twelve of his bells survive in Somerset and others in Dorset and Wiltshire.[27]

At least two traders issued tokens in the parish during the 17th century,[28] one, John Clothier, probably being related to the Anthony Clothier, pewterer, who occurs in 1664.[29] John Fathers, brazier and potfounder, occurs in 1659 and a namesake, either son or grandson, with the same occupation in 1742.[30] Throughout the 18th century various branches of the cloth industry were to be found in the parish, notably makers of saddle-girths, known as 'girt web weavers'. The trade was apparently dominated by the Geard family. John Geard or Gard occurs in 1705.[31] A descendant

[1] DD/PH 159, bk. of reference 1782.
[2] DD/PH 75.
[3] S.R.O., tithe award. Part of this award is missing, but a complete copy is in S.R.O., DD/PLE, box 18.
[4] S.R.O., D/G/Y 160.
[5] Ibid.
[6] S.R.O., DD/PH 249, sale cat. 1929.
[7] Ibid. 142.
[8] See pp. 210, 260.
[9] S.R.O., DD/SAS, H/528, map, 1825.
[10] Statistics supplied by the then Bd. of Agric. (1905).
[11] C. & J. Greenwood, Som. Delineated, 143.
[12] See p. 244.
[13] Leland, Itin. ed. Toulmin Smith, i. 157–8.
[14] Cal. Pat. 1494–1509, 152.
[15] Proc. Som. Arch. Soc. lxi. 97.
[16] S.R.O., DD/PH 229/6.

[17] Ibid. 144, 166.
[18] Ibid. 64–70.
[19] S.R.O., tithe award.
[20] P.O. Dir. Som. (1861); S.R.O., D/G/Y 160.
[21] S.R.O., D/G/Y 160.
[22] Ibid.
[23] Ibid.; P.O. Dir. Som. (1875).
[24] Kelly's Dir. Som. (1897, 1902).
[25] Ibid. (1910, 1914, 1919).
[26] D. M. Ross, Hist. Langport, 272; Prob. 11/134 (P.C.C. 80 Parker).
[27] S.R.O., DD/SAS CH 16; Proc. Som. Arch. Soc. lxvi. 131; V.C.H. Som. ii. 432.
[28] Trade Tokens of 17th Cent., ed. G. C. Williamson, ii. 984; Proc. Som. Arch. Soc. lxiii. 130.
[29] S.R.O., DD/PH 63.
[30] Ibid. 63, 66.
[31] Ibid. 64–5, 68–9.

Jesse Geard sailcloth-maker, was one of the leading Baptists in the parish.[32] Linen-weavers, clothiers, flaxdressers, leather-traders, and glovers were also at work in Montacute throughout the 18th century.[33] Thomas Shoel wrote in 1803 of 'nimble spinners', the 'neat gloveress', the leather-dresser, cooper, and cobbler in the parish where 'trade in various shapes her fingers plies'.[34] It is clear, however, that in the 19th century the manufactures of Montacute declined. There was still a canvas-maker in 1875 and a rope manufacturer in 1883; a chamois-leather-dresser worked there at least until 1927, and a glove-knife-maker until 1919.[35] Messrs. Taunton and Thorne, glove manufacturers, were established in the village by 1923 and were still in production in 1968, and some gloving is still practised in private homes. The village, however, by the end of the 19th century was predominantly agricultural. It lay in a fairly prosperous district[36] but was the scene of the first and several subsequent annual demonstrations of agricultural workers organized from 1872 by a local worker, George Mitchell, in support of the activities of Joseph Arch.[37]

Poverty, according to Shoel, 'here seldom holds her melancholy reign'.[38] This was a romantic rather than a realistic statement. Evidence of regular payments to paupers has survived from 1636.[39] In 1662 the overseers disbursed £18 6s. 6d. to eleven paupers. By 1707 £28 18s. was paid out in sums usually of a shilling a week. In 1732 £69 19s. 2d. was raised and nearly £48 spent; eight years later over £56 had to be found. By 1750 the rate had fallen, but within the next quarter-century the figure for expenditure had doubled, in 1776 standing at over £110. The figure rose to nearly £367 by 1803,[40] though there were violent fluctuations during the period. In 1797-8, for example, over £354 was spent, but in the following year only £179.[41] In 1803 41 people were being permanently relieved, all in their own homes, and 47 were relieved occasionally.[42] The highest figure was achieved in 1819 when £783 was spent on the poor. Thereafter the figure fluctuated between £340 and £450.[43]

A fair on Hamdon Hill and a market in the borough formed part of the count of Mortain's foundation grant to the priory.[44] The fair still existed in the early 12th century, but its subsequent history belongs more properly to Stoke.[45]

In 1246 the Crown granted the priory an annual three-day fair at St. Michael's chapel, on the site of the castle, to be held on the eve, feast, and morrow of St. Edward's Day (13th October).[46] This fair was worth 5s. in 1302-3,[47] but apparently lapsed in the 16th century.[48] During the 18th century a fair was held annually on 6 May; it was widely known as a market for leather, but sheep and cattle were also sold there.[49] Known as the 'May Fair', it was still held as late as 1936, but at least from the later 19th century had been organized largely to raise funds for local charities.[50]

The count of Mortain granted his market to Montacute priory c. 1102.[51] In 1302-3 it was worth only 13s. 4d.[52] Leland described it as a 'poor market'.[53] There were two shops and two separate shambles in the market-place in 1540,[54] two shops and three shambles in 1566.[55] By 1608 there was only one set of shambles and the shops were soon afterwards converted to an inn.[56] A market was apparently held as late as 1732.[57]

There was a mill in Montacute in 1086 paying 50d.[58] It was presumably the same as that granted to the priory c. 1102.[59] This may be identified with Park mill, on the priory demesne, which stood on a small stream at the north-western end of High wood, near the junction of streams from Pit wood and Bagnell farm.[60] In 1539 the property passed out of the hands of the monks and in the following year was held by Joan Frensshe as a copyhold tenement of the 'manor' of Montacute Forum.[61] The mill was subsequently tenanted from 1559 by John Alford, by 1608 by William Baron,[62] and by 1655 at least until 1662 by Edward Bayly.[63] In 1663 Richard Cox was tenant, from 1690 Anne Cox, and a Mr. Cox in 1706.[64] William Dibble occupied the mill in 1764.[65] It was then one of the three water-grist-mills which were part of the manorial estate.[66] The mill had apparently gone out of use by 1825, though the name was retained in Park Mill House,[67] later known as Park Mill Cottages.[68]

There was evidently at least one other water-mill in Montacute in the Middle Ages. In 1350 it was leased out by the owners, James Husee and his wife.[69] A grist mill, known as Clarc's mill, and pasture called Mill Ham were held as of Montacute Forum from 1534 at least until 1566 by Thomas

[32] See p. 223.
[33] S.R.O., DD/PH 64–70.
[34] T. Shoel, *Mileshill, a poem* (1803). For gloving see *V.C.H. Som.* ii. 427; *Rep. Com. Children and Women in Agric.* [4202–I] H.C. pp. 473–4 (1868–9), xiii.
[35] *Kelly's Dir. Som.* (1883, 1909, 1927); *P.O. Dir. Som.* (1875).
[36] *V.C.H. Som.* ii. 334n.
[37] *Bibliotheca Somersetensis*, ed. E. Green, ii. 99; iii. 52; *Proc. Som. Arch. Soc.* lvi. 62; Llewelyn Powys, *Som. and Dors. Essays*, 117.
[38] *Mileshill*, a poem.
[39] S.R.O., DD/S/PN: overseers' accts. 1636–1752; par. rec., overseers' rates and accts. 1794–1806.
[40] *Poor Law Abstract, 1804*.
[41] Par. rec., overseers' rates and accts. 1794–1806.
[42] *Poor Law Abstract, 1804*.
[43] *Poor Rate Rtns.* H.C. 556 (1822), v; *Poor Rel. Rtns.* H.C. 83 (1830–1), xi; ibid. H.C. 444 (1835), xlvii.
[44] *S.R.S.* viii. 119; *Reg. Regum Anglo-Norm.* ii, pp. 50, 348.
[45] See p. 245.
[46] *S.R.S.* viii. 131; *Cal. Chart. R.* 1226–57, 304.
[47] S.C. 11/798.
[48] There is no mention of the fair in post-Reformation

grants, but the bailiff received unspecified profits therefrom in 1566: Devon R.O. 123 M/E 94.
[49] *Bk. of Fairs*; *Proc. Som. Arch. Soc.* lxxxii. 124; Collinson, *Hist. Som.* iii. 314; *V.C.H. Som.* ii. 359.
[50] *Proc. Som. Arch. Soc.* lxxxii. 124; *Royal Com. on Market Rights Rep.* i. p. 200.
[51] *Plac. de Quo Warr.* (Rec. Com.), 696.
[52] S.C. 11/798.
[53] Leland, *Itin.* ed. Toulmin Smith, i. 157–8.
[54] S.R.O., DD/PH 228/24, rental 1540.
[55] Devon R.O. 123 M/E 91. Six other shambles produced no rent.
[56] S.R.O., DD/PH 144, 235.
[57] C.P. 43/596 rot. 247.
[58] *V.C.H. Som.* i. 483.
[59] *S.R.S.* viii. 119.
[60] O.S. Nat. Grid. 481156.
[61] S.R.O., DD/PH 228/24.
[62] Ibid. 144, 225/1, Devon R.O. 123 M/E 91.
[63] S.R.O., DD/S/PN: overseers' accts., *sub anno*.
[64] Ibid.; S.R.O., DD/PH 255/80.
[65] Ibid. S.R.O., DD/PH 68.
[66] C.P. 43/586 rot. 244; 596 rot. 247.
[67] S.R.O., DD/SAS, H/528, map, 1825.
[68] S.R.O., tithe award.   [69] Ibid.

Norman.[70] It was still part of the same estate in 1608.[71] About 1631 a mill was attached to the manor of Hide; it was evidently near the farm buildings, since about 1700 Mill close was associated with the farm-house.[72] In 1638 Brook mill was also part of that manor.[73] Both were presumably still in existence in 1732, and with Park mill made up the three water-grist-mills on the estate.[74]

In 1560 Thomas Phelips held a windmill of Montacute manor.[75] About 1700 three fields forming part of Hide farm were called respectively Little, Lower, and Higher Windmill.[76] The name Windmill farm is still retained, and may point to a windmill on the higher ground to the north of the village.

LOCAL GOVERNMENT. The convent of Montacute was quit of both shire and hundred courts at least from Henry II's time, and by 1275–6 their jurisdiction was described as a free manor.[77] No court rolls have survived for the Middle Ages but by 1566 two courts baron and two lawdays were held separately for the borough and the manor in the guildhall.[78] By the mid 18th century, when court papers survive for 1734–40, 1755, and 1778,[79] one court was held annually, described as court leet and baron. The court had jurisdiction over the borough and over the tithings of Bishopston, Witcombe, and Hide, and appointed a constable, bailiff, and water bailiff for the manor. The tithingmen held office in rotation. The borough appointed its own constable, bailiff, and water bailiff. Two waywardens and a hayward were answerable to the manor court. Courts survived at least until c. 1790.[80]

Early in the 19th century a select vestry of 7 or 8 members took over the functions of the manor court. In 1829 one man was assistant overseer, surveyor of the highways, and vestry clerk.[81] His functions were later divided, two surveyors being appointed in 1851. There were two surveyors until 1863 and one elected annually at least until 1882.

Accounts of the overseers of the poor have survived from 1636. By 1741 the parish was supporting a poorhouse for which, two years later, the overseers provided bedsteads.[82] By 1780 the house was in New Lane;[83] it was still there in 1838, divided into several tenements.[84] Since only out-relief was given by 1803 it is likely that these tenements had for long been leased to paupers at low rents.[85] The

parish became part of the Yeovil poor-law union in 1836.[86]

CHURCH. Exemption from payment of secular dues for ½ hide of land in Montacute in 854 may be an indication that the abbey of Glastonbury, the owners, had established a church there.[87] No church is mentioned in Domesday, though the later story of the Invention of the Holy Cross refers to a priest and a sexton.[88] A church, dedicated to St. Peter, had certainly been established by c. 1102, when it became the church of the newly-founded Cluniac priory there.[89] The monastic church, c. 1155 dedicated to Saint Peter and Saint Paul,[90] is the only one mentioned in a charter no later than 1166.[91] Between 1174 and 1180 a chapel dedicated to St. Catherine in the monks' burial place, was confirmed to the priory.[92] It subsequently became the parish church and the chaplains who served the cure paid the monks a pension of a mark.[93] Subsequently, rectors were apparently appointed until the church was appropriated and a vicarage ordained in 1238.[94] Either the monastic church or the parish church was burned c. 1207.[95]

The advowson of the rectory and subsequently of the vicarage belonged to Montacute priory until the Dissolution. The French wars and the consequent seizure of their estates brought the advowson temporarily into the hands of William Montacute, earl of Salisbury, who presented in 1349 and 1350.[96] The Crown presented in similar circumstances in 1371, 1374, and 1399.[97] After the Dissolution the advowson presumably passed to the Crown. In 1549 William Perye of Membury (Devon) and John Kyte of Stockland (Devon), probably acting as Crown agents, granted the advowson to Thomas Cogan, a Montacute merchant.[98] Thomas Cogan of Manchester in 1598 settled the property on his cousin Robert Cogan the younger, a London clothworker, though Robert's father apparently took it over, and settled the advowson with the rectory income on his younger son, John.[99] It seems likely that Robert's father won the Chancery suit which ensued:[1] Robert Cogan presented in 1618, Richard Prigg, clerk, by grant from Cogan in 1639.[2] Meanwhile, in the previous year, Cogan, then of Gillingham (Dors.), sold both rectory and advowson to Roger Norton, a London stationer.[3] Norton's widow

[70] S.R.O., DD/PH 228/24; Devon R.O. 123 M/E 91.
[71] S.R.O., DD/PH 144.
[72] Ibid.
[73] C 142/486/151.
[74] C.P. 43/596 rot. 247.
[75] S.R.O., DD/PH 225/1.
[76] Ibid. 144.
[77] Cal. Chart. R. 1257–1300, 136–7; S.R.S. viii. 129; Rot. Hund. (Rec. Com.), ii. 138.
[78] Devon R.O. 123 M/E 94.
[79] S.R.O., DD/PH 141–2.
[80] Collinson, Hist. Som. iii. 310.
[81] Par. rec., select vestry mins. 1819–82.
[82] S.R.O., DD/S/PN: overseers' rates and accts. 1636–1752; par. rec., overseers' rates and accts. 1794–1806. Other civil rec. of the parish, recorded in 1939 (Som. Par. Doc. ed. J. E. King), were not found.
[83] S.R.O., DD/PH 69.
[84] S.R.O., tithe award.
[85] Poor Law Abstract, 1804.
[86] Poor Law Com. 2nd Rep. p. 550.
[87] Finberg, Early Charters of Wessex, p. 122.

[88] Foundation of Waltham Abbey, ed. W. Stubbs, 4.
[89] Reg. Regum Anglo-Norm. ii, p. 50; S.R.S. viii. 119.
[90] S.R.S. viii. 123.
[91] Ibid. 191.
[92] Ibid. 191–2.
[93] Ibid.
[94] S.R.O., DD/CC 110025 39/44, partially calendared in S.R.S. viii. 194. The original grant to the bishop is S.R.O., DD/CC 110025 42/44, and the ordination was ratified in 1239: DD/CC 110025 18/44.
[95] Pipe R. 1207 (P.R.S. n.s. xxii), 60.
[96] Rot. Parl. iii. 189; Cal. Pat. 1338–40, 393, 435; 1343–5, 435; 1345–8, 444; Cal. Inq. p.m. viii, p. 388; S.R.S. viii. 213–14; x. 573, 592, 641.
[97] Rot. Parl. iv. 27; Cal. Pat. 1370–4, 38; 1374–7, 14; 1396–9, 523.
[98] Cal. Pat. 1548–9, 404; S.R.O., DD/PH 3.
[99] S.R.O., DD/PH 3; C 3/264/15; C.P. 25(2)/207/40 Eliz. I East.
[1] C 3/264/15; C.P. 43/131 rot. 146.
[2] Som. Incumbents, ed. Weaver, 147.
[3] S.R.O., DD/PH 3.

presented in 1665.[4] Their son, also Roger, made over the property to his brother Ambrose in 1676. Ambrose sold it in the same year to Thomas (later Sir Thomas) Fowle, a London goldsmith.[5] Fowle's son, Edward, of Manningford Abbots (Wilts.), sold his interest to Thomas Fowle of Charlton by Upavon (Wilts.) in 1698.[6] It remained in the Fowle family for the next eighty years, though the bishop presented in 1750.[7] In 1781 Edward Phelips, lord of the manor, purchased the rectory and advowson,[8] and it thereafter descended with the manor. From 1928 it was vested in trustees, and since 1967–8 has been in the gift of the bishop.[9]

The value of the rectory in 1291 was £10,[10] and in 1302–3 and 1428 it was assessed at the same sum.[11] By 1535, however, this had fallen to £6, of which tithes and casuals produced £5.[12] About 1625 the parsonage was valued at about £57, a rise partly due to the conversion of pasture to arable in the parish,[13] since the income was derived entirely from tithes of corn on all lands except the former priory demesne and the manor of Hide.[14] The parsonage was divided about 1644, and remained in the hands of several individuals until acquired by Sir Edward Phelips in 1682.[15] The Phelips estate was still charged with over £51 in rectorial tithe in 1929.[16]

The income of the vicarage under the ordination of 1238 comprised the small tithes of the priory demesne, oblations and obventions in the dependent chapels in the castle and on Hamdon Hill,[17] a corrody in the priory, obventions from the whole parish, and the tithes of corn and all other produce on the estate called 'la Hyde'.[18] The income so produced was assessed at £5 in 1291[19] and 1428.[20] By 1535 this had risen to £8 9s. 11d. clear, and included a pension of £4 from the prior, probably in lieu of the corrody.[21] This pension was still payable from the parsonage estate in 1638.[22] During the Interregnum there was a plan to augment the benefice by £60,[23] and to unite it with Lufton and part of Sock Dennis.[24] By 1668 the value was said to be £30.[25] The living was augmented in 1784,[26] and by 1809 its value was £127 2s. 7d.[27] In 1831 it was returned as £186[28] and by 1851 £202.[29]

Tithes and oblations of the vicarage were valued together in 1535 at £5 1s. 11d.[30] The tithes in 1626

were described as all those from Hide manor, and hay, hemp, and small tithes from the rest of the parish, except the former demesne lands of the priory.[31] In 1838 these were converted to a rent-charge of £191 10s.[32] The income from this source averaged £126 about 1910.[33]

In 1238 the vicar was assigned a barn formerly belonging to the rector, together with half the site between the wall of an old barn and the end wall of a house next the gateway into the rector's yard. The grant of a corrody in the priory indicates that no other residence was provided.[34] The land held by the vicar in 1626, the only glebe then held apart from the vicarage house and buildings, was probably acquired later.[35] There were just over 4 a. of glebe in 1838,[36] valued a little later at £10.[37] By 1948 3 a. of glebe were still held.[38]

In 1626 the vicar had a house, barn, and stable.[39] About 1705 the house was 'tumbling quite down', and for some time previously had been used to house the poor during a long sequestration.[40] It was replaced in 1715 by the then vicar, John Mowrie.[41] In 1827 it was said to be 'very dilapidated', and the vicar could not live there.[42] A faculty for its removal was granted in the following year, though it was not demolished, and still stands, opposite the church, on the corner of Bishopston and Middle Street.[43] It is a symmetrical two-storeyed Ham stone building of five bays, reached through a gateway with ball finials. The present vicarage house was evidently built in 1828, complete with stables and gig house, at the northern end of the village.[44]

Only one of the medieval incumbents of Montacute, Thomas Chard (vicar 1504–7), has any claim to distinction, as prior of Montacute and bishop of Selymbria.[45] Thomas Freke, instituted in 1520, survived successive crises during the Reformation period, and was still vicar in 1554.[46] Thomas Budd (vicar from 1639)[47] was evidently removed from the living after 1651.[48] In 1657, while resident at Ash, he was accused of organizing treasonable meetings.[49] Charles Darby and John Oliver[50] are said to have been ejected from the benefice. Darby was described as an 'after conformist', and later taught at Martock.[51] For several years before 1699 Henry Gifford (vicar 1677–1708) absented himself from the parish because of the small income of the benefice, and the

[4] Som. Incumbents, 147.
[5] S.R.O., DD/PH 3.
[6] Ibid.
[7] S.R.O., D/D/Bp.
[8] S.R.O., DD/PH 3.
[9] Dioc. Dir. (1928–70).
[10] Tax. Eccl. (Rec. Com.), 198.
[11] S.C. 11/798; Feud. Aids, iv. 403.
[12] Valor Eccl. (Rec. Com.), i. 196. There were 10 a. of glebe in 1334: E 179/169/14.
[13] S.R.O., DD/PH 159, certif. of value of parsonage; see above, p. 217.
[14] S.R.O., D/D/Rg 225.
[15] S.R.O., DD/S/PN: overseers' rates and accts. 1636–1752.
[16] S.R.O., DD/PH 249, sale cat. 1929.
[17] See p. 248.
[18] S.R.O., DD/CC 110025 39/44.
[19] Tax. Eccl. (Rec. Com.), 198.
[20] Feud. Aids, iv. 403.
[21] Valor Eccl. (Rec. Com.), i. 201.
[22] S.R.O., D/D/Rg 225.
[23] Lambeth Palace MSS. COMM VIb/2 ff. 132, 134.
[24] Cal. S.P. Dom. 1657–8, 81.
[25] S.R.O., D/D/Vc 24.
[26] Hodgson, Queen Anne's Bounty.

[27] Augmentation of Livings, 1703–1815, H.C. 115 (1814–15), xii.
[28] Rep. Com. Eccl. Revenues, pp. 172–3.
[29] H.O. 129/319/3/4/11.
[30] Valor Eccl. (Rec. Com.), i. 201.
[31] S.R.O., D/D/Rg 225.
[32] S.R.O., tithe award (part). Complete draft in S.R.O., DD/PLE, box 18.
[33] Crockford.
[34] S.R.O., DD/CC 110025 39/44.
[35] S.R.O., D/D/Rg 225.
[36] S.R.O., tithe award.
[37] H.O. 129/319/3/4/11.   [38] Crockford.
[39] S.R.O., D/D/Rg 225.
[40] S.R.O., DD/PH 140.
[41] Par. rec., burial reg. 1725.
[42] S.R.O., D/D/V rtns. 1827.
[43] S.R.O., D/D/faculties, 1827.   [44] Ibid.
[45] Emden, Biog. Reg. Univ. Oxford.
[46] S.R.S. xl. 175; lv. 12.
[47] Som. Incumbents, ed. Weaver, 147.
[48] S.R.O., DD/S/PN.
[49] S.R.S. xxviii. 339–40; see also V.C.H. Som. ii. 44.
[50] S.R.O., DD/PH 205 contains a letter bk. of John Oliver.
[51] Calamy Revised, ed. Matthews.

vicar of Mudford was paid by Lady Phelips to take the Sunday service.[52] In 1815 the vicar, William Langdon, was only occasionally resident, because of illness. His curate, who had two other charges, held one service each Sunday at Montacute.[53] By 1827 there were services at 11 o'clock and 2 o'clock each Sunday.[54] Holy Communion was celebrated six times a year by 1840, and two sermons were preached every Sunday. The vicar catechized the children in Sunday school.[55] On Census Sunday, 1851, the congregation numbered 270 in the morning and 375 in the afternoon, each service being attended by 200 Sunday-school pupils.[56] Two sermons each Sunday were still the rule, but Holy Communion was celebrated eight times a year.[57]

The revenues of a ½ burgage and a dovecot supported a light in the parish church by 1548.[58] The church rented 2¾ burgages in the borough in 1566, some of which perhaps served as the church house.[59] The church house still existed in 1614.[60] The parishioners held a burgage in 1649, together with the parish barn.[61]

The parish church of *ST. CATHERINE* consists of a chancel with south vestry, nave, with north and south transepts, a two-storeyed north porch, a 'curious extra porch or lobby'[62] between porch and north transept, and a west tower. The only recognizable features which survive from the first church, built perhaps *c.* 1170, are the Norman chancel arch, one of the brackets supporting the present organ loft, and the re-set voussoirs of an enriched arch in the north wall of the nave. The chancel arch is of three unmoulded orders resting on shafts with scalloped capitals. The church was evidently enlarged at the end of the 13th century, the chancel, transepts, and north porch being of this date; the porch has a later vault. The side walls and east end of the chancel contain three-light windows with much-restored plate tracery. There is a similar but less altered window in the south wall of the south transept, and both transepts contain single-light lancets. South of the chancel arch is a squint between chancel and transept, and there are blocked rood-loft openings at a higher level. The nave, of four bays with Perpendicular windows, was evidently remodelled in the 15th or early 16th century. The west tower is of three stages with carved quatrefoil bands between them, as well as to the plinth and parapet. These bands, the buttresses, and the west doorway have much in common with similar features at the priory gatehouse, suggesting that the tower may date from the first quarter of the 16th century.[63] The windows have Perpendicular tracery with pierced stonework of the Somerset type at the belfry stage. The tower arch is lined with carved panelling. The lobby between the porch and the north transept, which has similar panelling, may have been built to give separate access to the transept after it became a Phelips chapel; in 1969 the lobby was used as a baptistry and contained the 15th-century font. A square-headed window in the east wall of the south transept carries a carved bracket on its central mullion, perhaps connected with the light which was endowed in the church by 1548.

The north transept contains monuments to the Phelips family, including four recumbent effigies. The earliest is claimed to represent David Phelips (d. 1484). Two are unidentified and the fourth, which is surmounted by a canopy, has effigies of Thomas Phelips (d. 1590) and his wife. A classical wall monument commemorates Sir Edward Phelips (d. 1699) and his wife (d. 1728).

A vestry was built on the south side of the chancel in 1864. In 1870–1 the church was much restored by Henry Hall of London.[64] The chancel received particular attention and it was probably at this time that the 16th-century texts which adorn the reredos and flanking niches were re-set and partly re-cut. In the churchyard are the remains of a 15th-century cross, with tapered shaft and square base, and also what appears to be the base of a stone pulpit of similar date, perhaps removed in 1870–1 when the present stone and brass pulpit was erected.[65]

The oldest piece of plate is a cup and cover of silver gilt, dated 1573 and made by 'I.P.' A pair of silver gilt candlesticks, dated 1691, was presented to the church in 1796; and there are two patens of 1713 and an oblong salver and ewer of 1724.[66] There are six bells: (i) 1901, Mears and Stainbank; (ii) 1619, Robert Wiseman of Montacute;[67] (iii) 1610, Wiseman; (iv) 1614, Wiseman; (v) 1810, Mears; (vi) 1733, William Knight.[68] The registers begin in 1558 but are incomplete.[69]

NONCONFORMITY. The tradition of nonconformity in Montacute is closely linked both with the artisan community in the village, and also with several ejected ministers who settled in the area. A group of Baptists was meeting in the village as early as 1656.[70] Josiah Banger, ejected from Broadhembury (Devon), settled at Montacute, and another ejected minister, Thomas Willis, formerly rector of Heathfield, was minister of a Congregational group licensed to meet at Montacute in 1672.[71] A group of Presbyterians, meeting at the house of William Hooper, was licensed in the same year.[72] A few years earlier, in *c.* 1668, a Roman Catholic priest is said to have been active in the parish.[73]

Six licences for nonconformist meetings issued between 1698 and 1720 do not specify a denomination,

[52] S.R.O., DD/PH 140.
[53] S.R.O., D/D/V rtns. 1815.
[54] Ibid. 1827.   [55] Ibid. 1840, 1843.
[56] H.O. 129/319/3/4/11.
[57] S.R.O., D/D/V rtns. 1870.
[58] *S.R.S.* ii. 105, 289.
[59] Devon R.O. 123 M/E 94.   [60] S.R.O., DD/PH 235.
[61] Ibid. 63. The parish barn occurs in 1697: DD/PH 80.
[62] Pevsner, *South and West Som.* 244.
[63] There are two views of the church by J. Buckler (1836) in the Pigott Colln., Taunton Castle, and by W. W. Wheatley (1848) in the Braikenridge Colln. there. The churchyard cross and the font are illustrated by Wheatley and Buckler respectively.

[64] Par. rec., note on flyleaf of burial reg. 1857.
[65] Ibid. acct. of restoration.
[66] *Proc. Som. Arch. Soc.* xliii. 20–2.
[67] See p. 218.
[68] S.R.O., DD/SAS CH 16; ex inf. Mr. G. W. Rendell.
[69] In vestry safe.
[70] *Confessions of Faith of several Churches of Christ in Somerset* (1656); *V.C.H. Som.* ii. 51.
[71] *Calamy Revised*, ed. Matthews; G. L. Turner, *Rec. Early Nonconf.* ii. 1109, 1121; *Cal. S.P. Dom.*, 1672, 234.
[72] *Rec. Early Nonconf.* ii. 1109; *Cal. S.P. Dom.*, 1672, 402.
[73] Ralph Wallis, *Room for the Cobler of Gloucester etc.* (1668).

but they indicate continuity until a flourishing Presbyterian cause emerged from 1752. Six licences for Presbyterian meetings were issued in the next ten years. In addition, in 1733, William Isaac was allowed to use his house for Quaker meetings.[74]

From 1758 onwards meetings of Baptists were revived. The first, described as Anabaptist, was in the house of Samuel Geard, weaver, and the second, in 1760, in that of John Harris, mason.[75] Baptists in Montacute now formed their own church, having previously been members of South Street church, Yeovil.[76] About 1770 a barn was fitted up as a place for worship, and services were conducted by the deacons of the Yeovil Baptist church.[77] No further licences have survived until the 19th century, but continuity was probably maintained through the Geard family. In 1815 a barn, tenanted by Samuel Geard, was 'newly fitted up' for Particular Baptists.[78]

In 1822 fourteen Montacute people were baptized at Yeovil with a view to the foundation of a new church at Montacute.[79] Jesse Geard, a sail-cloth manufacturer, obtained a lease on a cottage in Townsend in 1824 for Particular Baptists.[80] In 1830 the cottage was demolished and the first chapel was built on its site.[81] An adjoining property, later the Shoemakers Arms, was acquired as a manse.[82] In 1851 this chapel accommodated 350, of which 280 seats were free. The average congregation was 180 for morning and afternoon services and 300 for evening meetings. Sunday-school children numbered 90, 90, and 40 at these respective services. Attendances were said to depend a good deal on the weather, since some of the congregation came from a distance.[83]

The foundation stone of the Baptist chapel used in 1968, on the east side of South Street, was laid in 1879, and the building, designed by Morgan H. Davies, was opened in the following year.[84] The chapel accommodates 250, and there are 13 members.[85]

Wesleyan Methodism came to Montacute in 1814 when the house of Joseph Fowler, glover, was licensed through the minister of South Petherton.[86] A chapel was thought later to have been erected about 1817;[87] a licence issued for a chapel in 1843 may have been for a new chapel, or for an altered building.[88] The site of the chapel is not exactly known, though it may possibly be identified with the meeting-house on the west side of South Street held by Thomas Isaac in 1838.[89] In 1851 the chapel

seated 86 people, with standing room for a further 40. On Census Sunday there were services in the morning attended by 40 and in the evening by 60. Normally only one service was held, in the evening, with Sunday school in the afternoon.[90] The chapel was still in use in 1875, but by 1883 the Methodist cause in the village had apparently been abandoned.[91]

EDUCATION. In 1603 William Pester was licensed to teach Latin grammar and English in the parish.[92] By 1818 about 200 poor children were taught at a Sunday school established and supported by Mrs. Phelips of Montacute House, who also provided money to help clothe the pupils.[93] This school was still in existence in 1835, when 160 children attended,[94] and was still wholly supported by Mrs. Phelips.[95] A second Sunday school, supported by the Baptist chapel, was established in 1825, and was open ten years later.[96] By 1835 there were also two small day-schools, both supported by pupils' parents; one was for 28 boys, the other for 25 boys and girls.[97] One of these presumably occupied the building at the north end of the Borough, now known as the Chantry and in 1835 as the School House.[98] Another school was held in Smith's Row.[99]

By 1846 two schools, one held on Sundays the other in the evenings, were being supported by the National Society. The Sunday school had 79 boys and 111 girls on its books, the evening school 29 boys and 32 girls. Both schools were under the same paid master, and 9 male and 11 female teachers gave their services.[1] The Sunday school continued, having 200 pupils in 1851.[2]

In 1847 the main part of the present school was opened under the auspices of the National Society.[3] The original building comprised only two classrooms. A playground and offices were added in 1893 and a new classroom in 1895–6.[4] Further property was purchased in 1928, and gardens were held on lease from 1935.[5] In 1883 there were 147 children on the books, with an average attendance of 112.[6] After the extension of the buildings there was accommodation for 190 children.[7] In 1903, however, it was stated that 100 boys and girls and 48 infants could be taken, though there were only 68 and 48 respectively on the roll, with an average attendance of 109.[8] By 1938 average attendance

[74] S.R.O., Q/RR, meeting-house lics. Samuel Isaac, clothier, a Quaker, flourished in Montacute 1752–66: S.R.O., Q/R 9/2, jurors' books.
[75] S.R.O., Q/RR, meeting-house lics.
[76] Ex inf. Mr. W. H. Osborne, Secretary, Baptist ch.
[77] Ibid.; D. Jackman, *Baptists in the West Country*, 34–6.
[78] S.R.O., D/D/Rm, box 2.
[79] Ex inf. Mr. W. H. Osborne.
[80] S.R.O., DD/PH 7, deed of trust for settlement of the Baptist chapel, 1830, recites deed of 14 June 1824.
[81] Ibid.
[82] Ex inf. Mr. W. H. Osborne.
[83] H.O. 129/319/3/4/12.
[84] Stone on building.
[85] *Baptist Handbk.* (1968).
[86] S.R.O., D/D/Rm, box 2.
[87] H.O. 129/319/3/4/13.
[88] S.R.O., D/D/Rm, box. 2.
[89] S.R.O., tithe award.
[90] H.O. 129/319/3/4/13.
[91] *Kelly's Dir. Som.* (1875, 1883).

[92] S.R.O., D/D/Vc 68.
[93] *Digest of Returns to Sel. Cttee. on Educ. of Poor*, H.C. 224 (1819), ix(2).
[94] *Educ. Enquiry Abstract*, H.C. 62 (1835), xlii.
[95] Ibid.
[96] Ibid.
[97] Ibid.
[98] Drawing by Buckler in the Pigott Colln., Taunton Castle. By 1848 it was simply described as an 'ancient building' in a view by W. W. Wheatley in the Braikenridge Colln., Taunton Castle.
[99] S.R.O., DD/SAS PR 54/5, 22.
[1] *Church Sch. Inquiry, 1846–7.*
[2] H.O. 129/319/3/4/11.
[3] S.R.O., C/E 27; *Kelly's Dir. Som.* (1883).
[4] Par. rec., school deeds; S.R.O., DD/EDS, plans for enlargement.
[5] Par. rec., school deeds.
[6] *Kelly's Dir. Som.* (1883).
[7] Ibid. (1897).
[8] S.R.O., C/E 27.

was 85, and two years later senior pupils were transferred to Stoke sub Hamdon.[9] In 1969 there were 58 children on the books.[10]

Evening continuation classes under the headmaster were being held by 1903 on two nights each week during the winter months, at a cost to the pupils of 1d. per night. In the class, which was still held in 1921 and catered for young workers employed at the Tintinhull glove factory, arithmetic, reading, writing, drawing, and singing were at first taught. In 1907 singing was replaced by Geography.[11]

In 1868 it was reported that education was 'generally very well taken care of in the parish'. The vicar declared he had 'an excellent school in the parish, so good as to attract artizans' children from other parishes'. Very few children had never been to school at all.[12] The first inspector's report (1903) described the school as 'well up to date', and the infants in particular were 'skilfully handled and taught'. In that year the school was absorbed into the local education authority system, and from 1907 has been known as Montacute C. of E. School.[13]

CHARITIES FOR THE POOR. In 1565 there was an alms-house near the church then called 'Julian Kymer's house', adjoining the 'almarye barn'.[14] In the following year there were two properties, one described as 'a house formerly (in the time of the prior) used as the alms-house' and the other as the 'former alms-house once held by Thomas Kymer'.[15]

Sir Edward Phelips, who had acted as paymaster for money given to the parish by Richard Sherwin (d. *ante* 1679) to bind two girls in domestic service, by will dated 1699 bequeathed £50 for binding out two poor children. The accrued interest was paid in 1714 and three children were bound apprentice. The interest was paid until 1719[16] but there is no trace thereafter.

By deed of trust dated 1882 a capital sum of £50 bequeathed to the Female Friendly Society of Montacute, by then defunct, by Robert Donne of Odcombe, was invested by the vicar and churchwardens to support any Friendly Society in the parish or to provide clothing, fuel, medicine, or food.[17] By 1891 the endowment was just under £100 and the interest in 1966 was £2 9s. 8d.[18] Until 1919 the distributions were usually in coal and for some few years afterwards in tea.[19] In 1971 it was distributed in cash.[20]

Miss Edith Ellen Phelips of Cheltenham, sister of W. R. Phelips, by will proved 1920, left £100 in trust for the Anglican poor.[21] A capital sum of nearly £146 was invested, yielding £5 16s. 10d. each year. The first distribution was made in vouchers for goods to the value of 10s. and 5s.[22] In 1971 it was distributed in cash.

NORTHOVER

THE ancient parish of Northover was 438 a. in extent in 1838.[1] Part of Somerton mead was transferred to Kingsdon in 1885 and a small detached part of Somerton to Northover.[2] The civil and ecclesiastical parishes were coterminous in 1901 and measured 440 a.[3] The civil parish was united with Ilchester in 1933.[4]

The parish lies on the north bank of the Yeo or Ivel, and may have formed the northern half of a bridgehead settlement, Ilchester forming the southern half. The settlement apparently remained a single unit until Domesday and the northern section seems to have comprised the estate and probably the site of St. Andrew's church.[5] Like Ilchester it was connected with the Saxon royal estate of Somerton, and survived as 'North Tone' in a perambulation of Somerton warren in Edward I's reign.[6] Subsequently Northover became divided from Ilchester, and the Yeo formed the boundary between them until the county gaol was established within the parish in the late 16th century. Ilchester parish was then slightly extended to embrace the gaol buildings.[7] The eastern boundary of Northover, following the Foss Way and then curving northwards to the Cary, was probably also the eastern boundary of Somerton warren. The irregularity of the western boundary resulted from the inclosure of Somerton mead.

The parish lies on the alluvium of the Yeo flood plain. The ground rises gently to the north to just over 80 ft., where clay loam predominates.[8] The triangle between the Somerton road, the Foss Way, and the northern boundary of the parish comprised the largest tract of land. Originally the whole area was probably one field in open cultivation, but by the beginning of the 17th century inclosures had been made in the north.[9] Most of the remainder was formally inclosed in 1839, though consolidation

9 *Bd. of Educ., List 21*, [*1938*] (H.M.S.O.), 349; par. rec., managers' min. bk.
10 Som. C.C. Educ. Cttee. *Schs. List*.
11 Par. rec., managers' min. bk.
12 *Rep. Com. Children and Women in Agric.* [4202–I] H.C. pp. 473–4 (1868–9), xiii.
13 S.R.O., C/E 27; par. rec., managers' min. bk. The school now has voluntary controlled status.
14 Exeter City R.O., DD/49/26/4/3.
15 Devon R.O. 123 M/E 91. 'Aumary Barn' was still standing in 1677: S.R.O., DD/PH 80.
16 S.R.O., DD/S/PN: overseers' rates and accts. 1636–1752, *sub annis*.
17 Char. Com. files.
18 *Dig. End. Chars. 1891*, H.C. 69 (1892), lix; Char. Com. files.

19 Par. rec., charity papers.
20 Ex inf. the vicar, the Revd. R. M. Bevan.
21 Char. Com. files.
22 Par. rec., charity papers.
1 S.R.O., tithe award. This article was completed in 1971.
2 *Local Govt. Bd. Prov. Orders Conf. Order (Poor Law) (No. 2)*, Act (1885), 48 & 49 Vict. c. 5.
3 *V.C.H. Som.* ii. 349.
4 *Som. Review Order, 1933*.
5 See p. 228.
6 *V.C.H. Som.* ii. 552.
7 S.R.O., tithe award.
8 Geol. Surv. Map 1", solid and drift, sheet 312 (1958 edn.).
9 See p. 227.

of holdings had long since obliterated most of the strips.[10] By 1838 the 'open' area was divided between North field and Worth field. The latter was known in the early 17th century as Woorth furlong,[11] an indication that originally both belonged to the same large field. In the same way Northover field and Witch furlong,[12] in the other arable area of the parish to the south-west of the Somerton road, were parts of a second open arable field, the southern parts of which were inclosed for pasture from the 17th century onwards.[13] Further south, between Conygar Lane and the river, lay the common pasture lands of the parish. Common rights were still enjoyed there in the early 17th century, but had been extinguished before 1838.[14]

Northover shared with Ilchester a significant position as an important crossing-place of the Yeo, where several ancient roads, two of them Roman, converged. The Foss Way, from Bath, and a road from the Bristol Channel joined a route from the east just north of the village.[15] This 'thoroughfare and travelling highway' was, by 1630, repairable by the parish.[16] All three roads were turnpiked in 1753 by the Ilchester Trust, and a toll-house was built at the first junction to the north of the village.[17] Besides these three roads a drove leading westwards, north of the church and the former manor-house, originally served Northover field and Somerton mead. Its early stretches were called Conygar Lane in the 19th century; further west it is known as South Mead drove.[18] There is much evidence of Roman occupation in the parish including many burials to the west of the village.[19]

As a suburb largely dependent on the prosperity of Ilchester the parish was probably most populous in the 13th century. By the end of the 14th century it was certainly larger than its declining neighbour, having a taxable population of 64, compared with Ilchester's 50 in 1377.[20] In 1801 there were 56 inhabitants; within twenty years this figure had doubled to 121 and reached 138 in 1831. The number then fluctuated between 90 and c. 120 until 1891 when only 79 were recorded. Ten years later this had fallen to 46. There followed a gradual recovery, the number reaching 67 by 1931.[21] Thenceforward no separate figures are available, though it is clear that the population has increased rapidly since 1949 with the erection first of the Admiralty houses and flats and then with Local Authority dwellings in Taranto Hill, Great Orchard, and Troubridge Park.

Apart from the manor-house and the 'Old Vicarage', described elsewhere,[22] the so-called 'Northover Manor', Darlington House, and North-over House are the only structures of any age in the village. The first is a late-18th-century house of stone, of two storeys and six bays. The ground-floor windows have wood casements with 'Gothick' glazing. Darlington House, nearer Ilchester, on the other side of the street, is a two-storey building of rubble, with brick window-surrounds, probably of the 18th century. It has a five-window front, dominated by a Roman Doric porch, and deep eaves. Northover House adjoining is somewhat larger; its seven bay ashlar front, with angle pilasters and porch, probably dates from the early 19th century, though the south wall contains a mullioned window somewhat earlier in date. The house was certainly standing in 1802 when George Tuson, solicitor, moved there, though its proximity to the gaol was thought by his clerk to render it 'not in a very desirable situation'.[23]

MANOR. The manor of *NORTHOVER* is not mentioned *eo nomine* in the Domesday survey, but seems to have been the estate of the church of St. Andrew held by Brictric of Glastonbury abbey T.R.E., and by Maurice, bishop of London, of the Crown in 1086.[24] By the beginning of the 13th century the manor evidently formed part of the barony of Great Torrington (Devon): William de Torrington held it in 1221 and was succeeded on his death in 1224 by his uncle, Matthew.[25] On Matthew's death in 1227 the barony was divided between his five sisters, Sibyl, wife of Richard de Umfraville, having, *inter alia*, a ⅓ fee in Northover.[26] By 1242–3 this holding was described as part of the honor of Gloucester;[27] it was held of the Clares until the partition of their estates in 1314, and then passed to the Despensers through Eleanor, youngest daughter of Gilbert de Clare.[28] Hugh le Despenser was overlord at his death in 1349, but by 1361 it was among the fees of Henry, late duke of Lancaster.[29] By 1375 it had reverted to the Despensers, and was confiscated by attainder in 1400.[30] It was parcel of the duchy of Lancaster in 1401–2, but Isabel, wife of Richard Beauchamp, earl of Warwick, the Despenser heir, died as overlord in 1439.[31] The overlordship probably lapsed on the death of her grand-daughter, Anne, in 1449.[32]

In 1219 or earlier William de Torrington granted part of his holding, including the church, to William Brewer (I). This gift was confirmed in 1221.[33] Brewer had, by 1219, given the property, later described as ½ fee, to his newly-founded hospital of St. John the Baptist at Bridgwater.[34] Though later described as half the manor, it was usually assessed

[10] Exceptions were strips in the extreme NE. corner, part of the glebe.
[11] S.R.O., D/D/Rg 227.
[12] S.R.O., tithe award; CR 32.
[13] See p. 227.   [14] Ibid.
[15] I. D. Margary, *Roman Roads in Britain*, i. 114–15; *Proc. Som. Arch. Soc.* xcvi. 189. The London road is thought by Mr. Stevens Cox to have been Roman, as the result of so far unpublished excavations.
[16] *S.R.S.* xxiv. 122–3.
[17] J. S. Cox, *Hist. Ilch.* opp. 211, 214.
[18] O.S. Map 6″, Som. LXXII. SE. (1886 edn.); S.R.O., tithe award.
[19] Ex inf. Mr. J. Stevens Cox. There are some Roman specimens in the County Museum, Taunton.
[20] *S. & D. N. & Q.* xxix. 12.
[21] *V.C.H. Som.* ii. 349.

[22] See pp. 226, 229.   [23] S.R.O., DD/SAS FA 185.
[24] *V.C.H. Som.* i. 467.
[25] *Pat. R.* 1216–25, 292; DL 42/2 f. 96; Sanders, *Eng. Baronies*, 48.
[26] *Bk. of Fees*, i. 400, where it is rendered Northwere.
[27] Ibid. ii. 750.
[28] *Rot. Hund.* (Rec. Com.), ii. 122, 127, 139; *Cal. Inq. p.m.* iii, p. 249; *Complete Peerage*, s.v. Despenser; *V.C.H. Glos.* vi. 187.
[29] *Cal. Inq. p.m.* ix, p. 340; xi, p. 108; *Cal. Close, 1360–4*, 209.
[30] *Cal. Inq. p.m.* xiv, p. 225; *Cal. Inq. Misc.* vii, p. 271.
[31] *Feud. Aids*, vi. 630; *Cal. Inq. p.m.* (Rec. Com.), iv. 194.
[32] *Cal. Inq. p.m.* (Rec. Com.), iv. 228.
[33] *S.R.S.* xlix. 288; *Pat. R.* 1216–25, 292.
[34] *S.R.S.* xlix. 288; *V.C.H. Som.* ii. 154–6.

at ¼ fee.[35] It seems likely that the hospital acquired parts of the other holdings in the parish by the Dissolution,[36] and from 1539 the hospital's successors were regarded as lords.

William de Torrington's heirs retained the other portion of his estate: Sibyl de Umfraville was the recorded holder in 1234, though she may already have been succeeded by her son Gilbert (I).[37] In 1295 the estate was said to be held of Gilbert's heirs.[38] A return, perhaps of 1330, gives the tenant as Henry de Umfraville, who was said to hold of a mesne tenant, Patrick de Chaworth.[39] Gilbert (II) de Umfraville (d. 1349) was tenant in 1349, holding directly of Hugh le Despenser.[40] Patrick de Chaworth was again mentioned in 1361, but by that year the Umfravilles had been succeeded by Roger Cammell.[41] Richard Brice of Ilchester[42] held the estate by 1376.[43] William Story was returned as tenant in 1401–2, though he apparently disclaimed the tenancy.[44] No further evidence of this estate has been found.

The holding of the dissolved hospital of St. John, Bridgwater, was granted by the Crown in fee to John Leygh in 1544.[45] In the same year Leygh alienated both manor and advowson to John Soper of Speckington.[46] Soper sold both of them in 1546 to William Lyte (d. 1558) of Lillesdon in North Curry. Lyte's eldest son John in turn sold them to Thomas Raymond of Chard in 1566.[47] Another Thomas Raymond, his grandson or nephew,[48] died in 1605 leaving Northover to his eldest son John.[49] By 1620 John had been succeeded by Thomas Raymond (d. 1650), probably his brother.[50] Thomas's daughter Mary, who succeeded to her father's sequestrated estates,[51] probably married Col. John Hody (d. 1702).[52] John Hody, the colonel's son, succeeded on his death in 1729, two years after his own son, the manor passed to his son-in-law, the Revd. Edward Chichester, who had married his daughter Elizabeth.[53] Chichester, who was both lord of the manor and incumbent, died in 1730, leaving as his heir his infant son Henry.[54] Henry Chichester was lord of the manor and the dominant figure in parish administration until his death in 1799.[55] He was succeeded by his son John Hody Chichester (d. 1834), and by his grandson J. H. W. Chichester (d. 1846), who left Northover to live at Stoke St. Michael.[56] The heir in 1846 was Charlotte, daughter of Chichester's sister Caroline, and wife of J. L. Burnard of Bath (d. 1873).[57] Mrs. Burnard

retained the property at least until 1895,[58] but her son the Revd. A. C. Burnard, was described as lord of the manor in 1897.[59] The Chichester family, in the person of F. E. Chichester, retained the title at least until 1910.[60]

The former manor-house stood to the north-west of the church. It appears to have been an irregular building of stone, with a stone tiled roof topped by a kind of cupola.[61] During the early 19th century it was let to successive vicars of the parish; it was subsequently pulled down and replaced by the present house, which from 1871 was the official residence of the incumbent.[62] A medieval barn of ten bays stood to the south of the manor-house; it was burnt down in 1876.[63]

ECONOMIC HISTORY. The estate of St. Andrew's church, Ilchester, identifiable as the later parish of Northover, included 3 hides of arable and 30 a. of meadow in 1086. The demesne estate comprised a hide and 3 virgates, worked with 2 ploughs by 2 serfs; one villein and 6 bordars with a plough cultivated the remainder of the arable. Stock included 2 pack-horses, 9 'beasts', and 50 sheep. The whole estate, including a mill worth 20s., was valued at 100s.[64]

There is virtually no direct evidence for the agrarian history of the parish from the 11th to the 16th centuries, though an indirect suggestion, in 1347, that a two-field system of cultivation was being practised,[65] is confirmed by the open-field system which survived into the 19th century.[66] Surviving property transactions usually involved houses rather than land, and indicate Northover's status as a suburb of Ilchester. People resident in the parish, such as Thurstan the goldsmith and William the smith in the 13th century, almost certainly had their business premises in the town and lived in the quieter suburb.[67] Northover's decline, however, did not immediately follow that of Ilchester: the manor was assessed at 20s. 2d. in 1327, compared with 24s. 3d. for Ilchester; by 1377 the town's taxable population was smaller than that of Northover.[68]

At the Dissolution the rectorial estate held by St. John's hospital was clearly the largest holding in the parish. The demesne farm and the tithes were leased to members of the Golde family for £5 6s. 8d.; the rest of the estate brought in rents of £6 15s. 10½d.[69]

[35] Close R. 1261–4, 285; Rot. Hund. (Rec. Com.), ii. 122, 134.
[36] e.g. Cal. Pat. 1343–5, 131; S.C. 6/Hen. VIII/3137.
[37] Bk. of Fees, i. 400; Sanders, Eng. Baronies, 49.
[38] Cal. Inq. p.m. iii, p. 249.
[39] Feud. Aids, vi. 577.
[40] Cal. Inq. p.m. ix, p. 340; Sanders, Eng. Baronies, 49.
[41] Cal. Close, 1360–4, 209; Cal. Inq. p.m. xi, p. 108.
[42] See p. 135.
[43] Cal. Close, 1374–7, 307.
[44] Feud. Aids, vi. 630.
[45] L. & P. Hen. VIII, xix, p. 39.
[46] Ibid. p. 507.
[47] Ibid. xxi(2), p. 246; C 142/119/165; Cal. Pat. 1563–6, p. 401; Proc. Som. Arch. Soc. xxxviii. 94–5.
[48] Visit. Som. 1623 (Harl. Soc. xi), 90.
[49] C 142/282/49.
[50] Som. Incumbents, ed. Weaver, 152; Cal. Cttee. for Money, iii. 1385.
[51] Cal. Cttee. for Money, iii. 1385; S.R.S. xxviii. 86.
[52] S.R.O., D/P/north. 2/1/1, 4/1/1; C.P. 25 (2)/1651 Trin.

[53] S.R.O., D/P/north. 2/1/2; M.I. in Northover church; Bath and Wells Marriage Lics., ed. A. J. Jewers, 74.
[54] M.I. in Northover church.
[55] Ibid.; see p. 228.
[56] S.R.O., DD/X/KC.
[57] Ibid.
[58] S.R.O., D/G/Y 160.
[59] S.R.O., DD/X/KC; Kelly's Dir. Som. (1897).
[60] Kelly's Dir. Som. (1910).
[61] Drawing by Buckler in Pigott Colln., Taunton Castle, of the medieval barn shows part of the house.
[62] S.R.O., D/P/north. 3/3/1, 4/1/1, 13/2/1.
[63] Drawing by Buckler in Pigott Colln.; S.R.O., DD/X/KC. Part of the wall, of seven bays, still remained in 1971.
[64] V.C.H. Som. ii. 470.
[65] S.R.S. ix. 341.
[66] S.R.O., tithe award.
[67] Ilchester Almshouse Deeds, ed. W. Buckler, no. 11; S.R.S. iii. 263; vi. 238, 241; xli. 116, 142–3.
[68] S.R.S. iii. 263, 273; S. & D. N. & Q. xxix. 12.
[69] S.C. 6/Hen. VIII/3137.

The demesne farm, known as Upper farm, comprised in 1601 several closes of pasture and large tracts of arable, described as a virgate and 89 a.[70]

By c. 1600 the field boundaries had reached a stage from which they had changed little by the mid 19th century. There were inclosed pasture grounds in the north of the parish at Saundhyll (later Swanhills) and Oxenlease, and also nearer to the village at Boughthayes (later Batthays) and Bonny's or Bonne's (later Bum's) Close. Madlands was in 1605 still common pasture, and Somerton mead was apparently divided for grazing into acre and half-acre strips. The rest of the parish was still in open-field cultivation.[71] Inclosure of the south-western portion of the ancient parish, the former Somerton mead, was made in 1806 under an Act of 1797. This involved nearly 75 a. of meadow and pasture lying between South Mead drove and the river.[72] Inclosure of the remaining open fields was made in 1839, and involved about 170 a. Most of this property was in the hands of two landowners, and the Act only gave legality to an arrangement of property which had prevailed for at least a year before the award was made.[73] In terms of land use the parish was equally divided between arable and pasture in 1834 but by 1905 only a quarter of the parish was arable.[74]

The largest holding in the parish, Northover farm, ceased to be the 'home farm' of the manor about 1805, and was let as a unit, with a farmhouse, from that time. The house, now a restaurant and known as Northover Manor Hotel, was before that time a private residence, and by 1861 had again ceased to be connected with Northover farm.[75] The farm itself was let to Messrs. Phelps and Ireland from 1805; by 1811 J. H. Crocker was tenant. James Crocker succeeded George Drew about 1821, and his family farmed the property until 1876. The farm was then just over 312 a., nearly three-quarters of the parish. At the end of J. B. Crocker's tenancy, in 1876, it was said to be 'well known to be one of the finest farms in the county'.[76] The holding was continued for some years, but had been divided by 1912.[77]

The only other substantial property in the parish was that built up by George Tuson, solicitor, in the early 19th century. In 1838 Frances Bailey Tuson and the Revd. William Wilkins Gale held an estate of just over 67 a.; by the following year Henry Tuson and Gale shared the property.[78] This was the nucleus of Southmead farm, the house and buildings of which were erected about 1842.[79] It remained in the Tuson family until after 1897.[80]

Agriculture was always the most prominent occupation in the parish. Twelve families out of 21, for example, were so employed in 1821.[81] In more recent times the presence of a main road through the parish, once considered a financial burden,[82] has been recognized as a source of income. Public houses, such as the Dolphin in the period 1716–23, or the Darlington Arms, now Darlington House, built in 1835, had comparatively short periods of existence, owing probably to the competition from Ilchester.[83] The popularity of the motor car, however, and greater space for expansion than Ilchester possessed, allowed Northover to take the lead in establishing garages and restaurants. The first garage was opened by 1931, and within the next four years two refreshment rooms, a trading company, and an antique dealer were in business. Four years later, by 1939, a café and a boarding house provided further accommodation for travellers;[84] more facilities, including a restaurant and two garages, have been added since the Second World War. About a quarter of the parish was under arable in 1971, the remainder used for grazing.

Parish expenditure on poor relief can be studied in detail from the beginning of the 18th century until 1836.[85] Out-relief was normally given: between 1740 and 1750, for example, the parish spent on average just over £17 a year. One year, 1747, was abnormally high, many children suffering from sickness, but the number of adults relieved varied between three and four. Towards the end of the 18th century, the average expenditure rose, not because of an increased number of paupers on regular relief, but as a result of a growing number of extraordinary payments for clothing, house rent, and administration. Expenditure in 1776, for example, was nearly £33; in 1797–8 only three paupers were relieved, for the sum of 18 guineas, but total expenditure was almost twice that sum. The highest payments were made in the periods 1803–6 and 1830–1.[86] In 1834 there were 14 labourers in the parish, all employed. Piece-work was general and the average wage was £20 a year. Women and children were employed either in a factory at Ilchester, or in gloving at home.[87]

There was a mill in Northover in 1086, valued at 20s.[88] A miller occurs in the 13th century,[89] but there is no further trace of a mill until 1538–9, when it was let by the lords of the manor.[90] In 1561 it was conveyed by Thomas Phelips to Thomas Gould, and seems to have remained with the Goulds until 1694, when Bernard Gould made it over to Katherine Webb, widow.[91] Its ownership has not been traced in the 18th century, though John Skreen occurs as miller in 1756–8.[92] Mrs. Alice Stuckey owned the mill by 1805 and retained it until 1809. She was followed in quick succession

[70] C 66/1585; S.R.O., D/D/Rg 227.
[71] C 66/1585; S.R.O., D/D/Rg 227; S.R.S. lxvii. 116–17.
[72] S.R.O., CR 43–5; now in Kingsdon parish.
[73] S.R.O., CR 32; S.R.O., tithe award.
[74] Rep. Com. Poor Laws, H.C. 44 (1834), xxx–xxxiv; statistics supplied by the then Bd. of Agric. (1905).
[75] P.O. Dir. Som. (1861).
[76] S.R.O., D/P/north. 4/1/1, 13/2/1; DD/X/KC; tithe award.   [77] S.R.O., D/G/Y 160.
[78] S.R.O., D/P/north. 4/1/1, 13/2/1; CR 32.
[79] Acct. bk. of James Webb, penes J. Stevens Cox, St. Peter Port, Guernsey. The farm was then known as South Mead New farm.
[80] S.R.O., D/G/Y 160; Kelly's Dir. Som. (1897).
[81] C. & J. Greenwood, Som. Delineated.

[82] S.R.S. xxiv. 122–3.
[83] S.R.O., D/P/north. 4/1/1, 13/2/1.
[84] Kelly's Dir. Som. (1931, 1935, 1939).
[85] S.R.O., D/P/north. 4/1/1, 13/2/1.
[86] Ibid. 13/2/1; Poor Law Abstract, 1804; Poor Rate Rtns. H.C. 556 (1822), v; Poor Rel. Rtns. H.C. 83 (1830–1), xi; ibid. H.C. 444 (1835), xlvii.
[87] Rep. Com. Poor Laws, H.C. 44 (1834), xxx–xxxiv.
[88] V.C.H. Som. ii. 470.
[89] Ilchester Almshouse Deeds, ed. W. Buckler, no. 11; S.R.S. xi. 165, 433.
[90] S.C. 6/Hen. VIII/3137.
[91] C.P. 25(2)/204/3 Eliz. I Mich.; C.P. 25(2)/869/6 Wm. & Mary Mich.; S.R.S. xxiii. 58–9.
[92] S.R.O., Q/R jurors' bk. 1697–1766.

by Miss Underwood in 1810 and Thomas Lockyer in 1811. George Tuson bought it in 1812; he sold it about 1826 to the earl of Darlington, and he in turn, about 1834, to James Peddle Bond. Mrs. Chard bought the property in 1846.[93] A succession of millers can be traced from 1816 until the early 20th century, some of whom were owners as well as occupiers. Probably the last to work the mill was Herbert Parker: he was in occupation throughout the First World War, but between 1919 and 1923 the mill became a private house.[94]

The mill, known as Northover Flour Mill in 1838,[95] was fed by a race, constructed behind the gardens of the houses flanking the east side of the main street. The mill-house and some of its buildings still stand, though the race has been almost completely filled in.

LOCAL GOVERNMENT. By 1273–4 Gilbert de Clare, earl of Gloucester, had a view of frankpledge on his 'free manor' of Northover, enjoyed the assize of bread and ale, and claimed the return of writs and right of tumbrel.[96] St. John's hospital, Bridgwater, appropriators of the benefice, held some kind of court until 1539.[97] There is no evidence that this court continued when the property came into lay hands.

From the 18th century and probably earlier the vestry was exercising wide powers. The appointment of the tithingman, an office reluctantly undertaken by the inhabitants in rotation in the 17th century,[98] had by 1733 become the responsibility of the overseers, who at least until 1749 paid a man £1 a year to hold the office, and provided him with clothing.[99] Until the 1730s normal parish affairs were conducted by two men, appointed annually as churchwardens and overseers,[1] though on occasion one accounted only for the church, the other only for the poor. From 1735 until 1750, however, the lord of the manor, Henry Chichester, was the sole churchwarden and overseer. In 1748–9 he combined these offices with that of waywarden, and for that year received £2 to cover expenses for the three offices. From 1753 until the end of the century the churchwardenship was held by one man only. Henry Chichester, who held it jointly, 1750–3, was sole warden from 1760 until 1774, and was followed by three members of the Culliford family. From 1787 onwards two overseers were appointed annually, one of whom was usually the churchwarden. Since 1804 two churchwardens have normally been appointed; the incumbent's custom of choosing one dates from 1827.[2]

Until the division of accounts after 1753 the same rate supported both the church and the poor, though separate accounts of expenditure were usually kept. The rate also supported the general expendi-ture on roads and gates in the common meadow lands, paid by the overseers. There is, however, evidence of a surveyor of highways by 1719. In 1743 the churchwardens made a payment to waywardens covering the period from 1735, and in 1744 there was clearly a separate account kept by the waywardens. During the period 1749–52 the offices of waywarden, churchwarden, and overseer were exercised by one man, and an account for the repair of roads has survived for 1751–2.[3]

Apart from direct payments to the poor[4] the overseers made occasional contributions for clothing, and more regularly paid rents for paupers. In 1739 they bought beef and beans because of the hard winter; for several years from 1808 they supported a parish mole-catcher; and in 1803–4 paid for drilling the Ilchester Volunteers.[5] Between 1801 and 1804 they rented several houses for the use of the poor, and in 1810–11 rented a poorhouse.[6] No other trace of such a house has been found, and there was certainly none in 1834.[7] The parish was incorporated in the Yeovil poor-law union in 1836.[8] The vestry appointed a parish constable in 1842–5.[9]

CHURCH. The church at Northover, judging by the size of its estate probably in origin a Saxon minster, occurs in the Confessor's time. It was then held by Brictric of Glastonbury abbey, but by 1086 was held by Maurice, bishop of London, of the Crown.[10] The benefice was appropriated by St. John's hospital, Bridgwater, in 1219,[11] and a vicarage was subsequently ordained at an unknown date. The income of the vicarage was augmented in 1337, possibly by a pension of £2 from the appropriators.[12] The rectorial tithes were added to the benefice probably early in the 18th century,[13] and the living was therefore occasionally described as a rectory, or as a rectory and vicarage.[14] Approval was given in 1656 to unite the parish with Ilchester and part of Sock Dennis,[15] but it retained its independent status until 1936, when the living was annexed to Ilchester rectory and the two parishes were united.[16]

The advowson lay with the appropriators until 1539. It then descended with the manor, though John Iverey in 1569, Giles Hodges in 1579, and Humphrey Drake, a relative of the patron, in 1627, each presented by grant of the lord of the manor.[17] George Hilborne and James Sampson, who presented in 1731, did so as trustees for the infant Henry Chichester.[18] Col. F. E. Chichester, the last to be described as lord of the manor, retained the patronage until his death; his executors and later his widow then held it. In 1961–2 the patron was Miss V. M. Newington 'by representation of Col. F. E. Chichester, deceased', in 1969 E. Chichester Everitt, and in 1971 Everitt's executors.[19]

93 S.R.O., D/P/north. 4/1/1, 13/2/1.
94 *Kelly's Dir. Som.* (1919, 1923).
95 S.R.O., tithe award.
96 *Rot. Hund.* (Rec. Com.), ii. 122, 127, 139.
97 S.C. 6/Hen. VIII/3137.
98 *S.R.S.* xxiv. 192–3.
99 S.R.O., D/P/north. 4/1/1.
1 Wardens and posts occur in 1554: S.R.O., D/D/Ca 22.
2 S.R.O., D/P/north. 4/1/1, 13/2/1.
3 Ibid. 4/1/1.   4 See p. 227.
5 S.R.O., D/P/north. 4/1/1, 13/2/1.
6 Ibid. 13/2/1.

7 *Rep. Com. Poor Laws*, H.C. 44 (1834), xxx–xxxiv.
8 *Poor Law Com. 2nd Rep.* p. 550.
9 S.R.O., D/P/north. 4/1/1.
10 *V.C.H. Som.* i. 467, 470.
11 *S.R.S.* xlix. 288.
12 Ibid. ix. 341; *Valor Eccl.* (Rec. Com.) i. 208.
13 See below.
14 S.R.O., D/D/Bp, 1760; *Crockford* (1902).
15 S.R.O., DD/LV 3/3; *Cal. S.P. Dom.* 1655–6, 329.
16 *Dioc. Dir.*; *Lond. Gaz.* 1 July 1924.
17 *Som. Incumbents*, ed. Weaver, 151–2.   18 Ibid.
19 *Crockford*; *Dioc. Dir.*

The patron of Northover presents to the united benefice one turn in three.[20]

It is not possible to separate the former rectorial estate from the rest of the holding of St. John's hospital, though the complete holding was said to be worth £20 in 1426,[21] and the rectory, including tithes, was let in 1515 for £5 6s. 8d.[22] Both before and after augmentation the income of the vicarage was small; the benefice was not normally taxed and was known for its poverty.[23] It was assessed at 20s. in 1426[24] and £3 6s. 8d. in 1445, but by 1535 it was worth £8 12s. 11d.[25] By the mid 17th century its value was £40, in 1786 £43, and in 1835 £106.[26] The benefice was augmented in 1859.[27]

The rector had predial tithes in the parish worth £3 in 1535.[28] By 1606 these were computed as the tithe corn of the 'Upper farm'; the occupier of the farm was regarded as the rector and had to maintain the chancel.[29] Probably when this farm and the benefice were in the hands of Edward Chichester in 1729–30, the rectorial tithes were merged with the vicarial.[30]

Under the augmentation of 1337 the vicar was given the tithe of hay, lambs, and ale in the whole parish, together with oblations.[31] These tithes and oblations were worth £5 6s. 4d. in 1535.[32] By 1606 the vicar received tithe of hay, except from 18 a. of 'Upper farm', tithe peas and onions throughout the parish, and tithe corn from all but 'Upper farm'. The occupier of the farm could compound for all other tithes; the rest were paid in kind except 'kyne white', a payment of 3d. for each milking cow, offerings, and 'garden pence'.[33] The consolidation of the tithes of rectory and vicarage simplified these arrangements. By 1838, in lieu of a modus of 2d. an acre on lands in Somerton mead, just over 33½ a. were awarded to the vicar. By that time tithes from gardens were no longer payable but the gross rent-charge which replaced all tithes was still worth £123.[34]

The size of the rectorial glebe is not known, and there is no separate valuation in 1535. From 1337 the vicarage was endowed with 9½ a. of arable and an area of meadow, 2 a. in one year and 1¾ a. in the next. This exchange of meadow was said to be by ancient custom.[35] The glebe was worth £1 14s. in 1535;[36] it was described in 1606 as a close, part arable and part pasture, 3 a. in the arable fields, and just under 2 a. of meadow, the meadow in lieu of the tithe hay of the 18 a. of 'Upper farm'. This meadow was in Somerton mead, and was cut for the vicar by the occupier of the farm.[37] By 1838 the glebe measured just over 10 a.[38] A strip in North field was exchanged in 1870 for the lower part of the grounds of the manor-house and a withy bed, presumably in connexion with the rebuilding of the house as a vicarage house.[39] By 1897 the glebe had increased to 14 a.; the sale of the vicarage house and grounds has reduced the acreage to just over 8½ a.[40]

A house and yard were assigned to the vicar, presumably soon after the rectory was appropriated.[41] By 1606 the vicar had a house, backside, and garden, which probably occupied the site of the present 'Old Vicarage', south-east of the church, between the road and the river.[42] The present house was built probably in the late 18th century; it is of two storeys, of rubble, with a thatched roof. Its wooden casements have 'Gothick' glazing, and there is a central rustic porch. The house was said to be in good repair in 1815, but twenty years later was considered by the then incumbent to be 'unfit'.[43] In fact, the vicars rarely lived in the house; from 1805 at least until 1838 it was let, and incumbents or their curates lived at the 'Old Mansion' as the manor-house was called.[44] William Harbin (vicar 1857–64) was living in Church Street, Ilchester, in 1859; and his successor, Sydney East, also lived in the town until he purchased from his father-in-law, J. L. Burnard, either the 'old mansion' itself or its site. There, about 1871, he built a new vicarage house; this remained the incumbent's home until the parish was united with Ilchester in 1936.[45]

At least two of the vicars of Northover in the late 15th century, Thomas Spencer (1497–8) and Robert Walsh (1506–9), were brethren of St. John's hospital, Bridgwater.[46] Thomas Master (vicar 1509–56) apparently survived the changes of the period unscathed;[47] in old age he evidently appointed a succession of curates, one of whom was reported in 1554 as 'not sufficient to have the cure'.[48] Master himself was accused in the same year of allowing the churchyard to decay and of failing to keep hospitality in his house.[49] From about 1575 the vicars were non-resident for at least five years.[50] George Drake, appointed vicar in 1627, was the son of Richard Drake of Donyatt, and a relative of the patron.[51] He held the benefice at least until 1650.[52] A Public Register was appointed in the parish in 1654.[53]

Between 1672 and 1713 three vicars in succession were also rectors of Ilchester. The second, Richard

[20] *Dioc. Dir.*
[21] *S.R.S.* xxxi. 24.
[22] S.C. 6/Hen. VIII/3137.
[23] E 179/169/14; *S.R.S.* xxxii. 246; xlix. 32.
[24] *S.R.S.* xxxi. 24.
[25] Ibid. xlix. 32; *Valor Eccl.* (Rec. Com.), i. 200, 208.
[26] S.R.O., DD/LV 3/3; D/D/Vc 24; *Rep. Com. Eccl. Revenues*, pp. 172–3.
[27] *Livings Aug. by Queen Anne's Bounty*, H.C. 122 (1867), liv.
[28] *Valor Eccl.* (Rec. Com.), i. 208.
[29] S.R.O., D/D/Rg 227.
[30] *Rep. Com. Eccl. Revenues*, pp. 172–3; see above, p. 226.
[31] *S.R.S.* ix. 341.
[32] *Valor Eccl.* (Rec. Com.), i. 200.
[33] S.R.O., D/D/Rg 227.
[34] S.R.O., tithe award.
[35] S.R.O., D/D/B, Reg. Shrewsbury f. 191.
[36] *Valor Eccl.* (Rec. Com.), i. 200.
[37] S.R.O., D/D/Rg 227.
[38] S.R.O., tithe award.
[39] S.R.O., D/P/north. 3/1/1.
[40] *Kelly's Dir. Som.* (1897); ex inf. the Rector, the Revd. A. G. Martin.
[41] *S.R.S.* ix. 341; xlix. 288.
[42] S.R.O., D/D/Rg 227.
[43] S.R.O., D/D/V rtns. 1815; *Rep. Com. Eccl. Revenues*, pp. 172–3.
[44] S.R.O., D/P/north. 4/1/1, 13/2/1; tithe award.
[45] Harrison, Harrod, & Co. *Dir. Som.* (1859); *P.O. Dir. Som.* (1861, 1866); S.R.O., D/P/north. 3/1/2, 3/3/1.
[46] *S.R.S.* liv. 5, 14, 116–17, 133; *V.C.H. Som.* ii. 156.
[47] *S.R.S.* liv. 133; lv. 144–5.
[48] S.R.O., D/D/Vc 20; D/D/Ca 22; *S.R.S.* xl. 107.
[49] S.R.O., D/D/Ca 22.
[50] *S. & D. N. & Q.* xiv. 105.
[51] *Som. Incumbents*, ed. Weaver, 152; Foster, *Alumni Oxon.*
[52] S.R.O., D/P/north. 2/1/1, memo. on flyleaf.
[53] Ibid.

Hody (1686–90), was a relative of the patron of Northover.[54] Edward Chichester combined Northover with the living of Berrynarbor (Devon) from 1714 until 1730, and married the heir of the lord of the manor.[55] Nathaniel Bartlett the younger (vicar 1785–1828) was in 1815 rector of Closworth with Bubdown and lived at Closworth.[56] Northover was then served by Thomas Ebrey, rector of Ilchester.[57] In 1827 Bartlett's curate also served Limington.[58] Bartlett's successor was John Maber Munden, the patron's son-in-law, who combined the living with that of Corscombe (Dors.).[59] Sydney East (vicar 1851–7, 1865–72) was also son-in-law of the patron.[60]

By 1815 one service was held each Sunday; some years later it was the practice to hold them alternately morning and afternoon.[61] This remained the pattern at least until 1870.[62] On Census Sunday 1851 the congregation in the afternoon was 129; the average attendance was about 70 at a morning service and 120 in the afternoon.[63] Holy Communion was celebrated four times a year by 1843 and six times by 1870.[64]

By 1548 half an acre of meadow was held by the churchwardens for the maintenance of a light.[65] This was still in their hands in 1554, although the light was not maintained.[66]

The church of *ST. ANDREW*, on high ground at the northern end of the village where the Shepton Mallet and London roads join, consists of a chancel and nave, with two shallow transepts and a western tower which serves as the entrance porch. The tower is plain, with diagonal buttresses at the foot and a plain parapet. The nave and chancel were completely rebuilt in 1821, when a porch was apparently demolished.[67] The south transept was added as an organ chamber upon restoration in 1878.[68] A gallery was erected in 1758, but was presumably dismantled in 1821.[69]

The marriage registers begin in 1531, baptisms in 1534, and burials in 1543 but the series is incomplete.[70] The plate includes a cup and salver presented to Ilchester church, and given to Northover in 1849, and a silver salver of 1722.[71] There are four bells: (i) 1636, by Roger Purdue of Bristol, cracked and lying on the tower floor; (ii) 1765, by Thomas Bayley of Bridgwater, (iii) 1751, by Thomas Elery of Closworth; (iv) 1450–80, Bristol.[72]

NONCONFORMITY. The house of Jasper Butt or Batt, a leading Quaker, was licensed as a meeting-house in 1689. This may have been for a group which had abandoned meetings in Ilchester.[73] The houses of John Sugg and John Miller were apparently used for religious meetings in 1815 and 1820 respectively. Their denominational connexions are unknown.[74]

EDUCATION. A number of private schools were conducted in the parish during the 19th century, though none was attached to the church.[75] A boy's boarding-school was held in Northover House in 1822–3.[76] By 1859 there was a girls' school which took boarders; and in 1870 a Miss Simpson conducted a day-school. By 1897 at least until 1910 a girls' preparatory school was held, at first in the Manor and later elsewhere.[77]

Northover was made contributory to the Ilchester School Board formed in 1875, and the children attended the Board School.[78] Infants also attended the National School in Ilchester. Both schools were closed in 1962 and were replaced by Ilchester County Primary School, situated in Northover parish.[79] In 1969 Ilchester County Junior School, also in Northover, was opened, taking pupils from the former Primary School and from Yeovilton and Limington. Infants from these two villages joined with the infants in the former Primary School, which was renamed Ilchester County Infants School. In 1971 there were 123 children in the infants' school and 168 in the junior school.[80]

CHARITIES FOR THE POOR. Robert Browne (d. 1610) gave £8 to be used as a stock for the poor 'at the discretion of the chief of the parish'.[81] There is no further evidence of the payment or investment of this money.

SOCK DENNIS

THE ancient parish of Sock Dennis, described as a 'district' in 1839,[1] was 880 a. in extent. It seems to have lost its parochial status in the ecclesiastical sense during the 16th century, for the church had disappeared by 1575[2] and the area was described c. 1585 as 'a manor of itself with a parsonage ap-

[54] Foster, *Alumni Oxon.*
[55] *Bath and Wells Marriage Licences*, ed. A. J. Jewers, 74; M.I. in Northover church; see p. 224.
[56] S.R.O., D/D/V rtns. 1815.
[57] He still served Northover in 1818: *Digest of Returns to Sel. Cttee. on Educ. of Poor*, H.C. 224 (1819), ix (2).
[58] S.R.O., D/D/V rtns. 1827.
[59] *Rep. Com. Eccles. Revenues*, pp. 172–3; S.R.O., DD/X/KC. [60] S.R.O., DD/X/KC.
[61] S.R.O., D/D/V rtns. 1815, 1827.
[62] Ibid. 1870. [63] H.O. 129/319/5/4/4.
[64] S.R.O., D/D/V rtns. 1843, 1870.
[65] *S.R.S.* ii. 106, 290.
[66] *Cal. Pat.* 1553–4, 96; S.R.O., D/D/Ca 22.
[67] S.R.O., D/P/north. 4/1/1. The architect was a Mr. Beard, and the work cost nearly £149.
[68] Transcript of accepted estimate *penes* Mr. J. Stevens Cox, St. Peter Port, Guernsey.

[69] S.R.O., D/P/north. 4/1/1.
[70] Ibid. 2/1/1–4; *S. & D. N. & Q.* vii. 113–14.
[71] *Proc. Som. Arch. Soc.* xlv. 136.
[72] S.R.O., DD/SAS CH 16.
[73] S.R.O., Q/RR, meeting-house lics.
[74] S.R.O., D/D/Rm, box 2.
[75] *Ann. Rep. B. & W. Dioc. Assoc. S.P.C.K.* (1825–6), 67; *Church Sch. Inquiry, 1846–7.*
[76] Pigot, *Nat. Com. Dir.* (1822–3).
[77] *P.O. Dir. Som.* (1859); *Kelly's Dir. Som.* (1897, 1902, 1910); J. S. Cox, *Hist. Ilchester*, 238.
[78] *Lond. Gaz.* 12 Mar. 1875, p. 158.
[79] *Som. C.C. Educ. Cttee. Schs. List.*
[80] Ibid.
[81] S.R.O., D/P/north. 2/1/1, burials, *sub anno* 1610.
[1] S.R.O., tithe award. This article was completed in 1968.
[2] See p. 235.

purtenant'.[3] Sock remained extra-parochial until 1883, when the Sock Dennis Rectory Act[4] transferred just over 117 a. of land at Chestermead to Tintinhull and the rest to Ilchester for ecclesiastical purposes. The civil parish, with the same boundaries as the ecclesiastical, was retained until 1957, when it was divided between Tintinhull and Ilchester in the same proportions.[5]

The parish lay immediately to the south of Ilchester, its northern boundary only five hundred yards from the town's defences. The two Roman roads leading south and south-west from the town formed part of its eastern and western boundaries. Chestermead, providing the meadow land for the parish, forms a detached area on the banks of the Yeo to the north-west of the main settlement.[6]

Most of the parish lay on alluvium in the Yeo flood plain, and the name Sock is considered to indicate an area of marsh or streams.[7] The suffix Dennis derives from the Dane family. Towards the south-west the land rises from 50 ft. to 150 ft. and clay predominates.[8] Outcrops of lias occur on Sock Dennis farm, and slabs are used in both farm and domestic buildings.

The present road system consists of tracks to the two remaining farms in the parish from the main boundary roads. A more ancient track, known in Tintinhull as Sock Lane and traceable further south as Kissmedown Lane in Montacute, bisects the angle between these two roads. Its present route, approaching Sock Dennis Farm from the south-east, may not be its original course. There is evidence of a track to the south-west of the farm buildings, aligned on a substantial stone bridge over Bearley brook north-west of the farm.[9]

The relationship between Ilchester and Sock was evidently close. Gerard of Trent, writing in the 17th century, tells of King John wresting Sock and Bearley from the men of Ilchester to give them to William the Dane in exchange for Petherton park.[10] An exchange of land called 'Deneysesdone' in Petherton forest was certainly made with a 'haywardwyk' in Ilchester, and Nicholas Bonville was still holding the Ilchester or Sock property in 1294.[11] Chestermead may once have been part of Ilchester West field: two small plots of land were certainly in dispute between the borough and Sock manor at the end of the 13th century,[12] and a piece of meadow in Ilchester West field was referred to in 1387 as de tenura de Sooke Denys.[13] The whole parish was regarded as part of Ilchester for taxation purposes in 1327,[14] but it was separately rated in 1377 and thereafter.[15]

There are remains of Roman occupation in the parish including a site immediately to the west of Sock Dennis farm-house.[16] The leper hospital of St. Margaret, founded by 1212, evidently stood in the parish.[17] John the Dane in 1227 gave to three brethren of the house of lepers at 'Socford' 7 a. of land, three of which were in 'Casteler', just north of their house.[18] 'Socford' may have been on the Foss Way; the regalem viam de Shotford occurs in 1276 in association with Sock manor.[19] There is no further trace of the hospital after 1268, but a chapel at 'Sokford by Ilchester' was in 1340 occupied by a hermit.[20] A building called the 'spytell' was apparently still standing in the early 16th century, and land in the same area still bore the name 'chastell'.[21] The present settlement in the parish comprises three farms, their cottages, and farm buildings.

There were 7 taxpayers in Sock in 1327[22] and 13 in 1377.[23] There were fewer than ten people by 1428,[24] and the disappearance of the church followed in little more than a century. By the end of the 18th century Sock was 'an obliterated place',[25] and had long comprised only two farms.[26] No individual return was made in the censuses of 1801 and 1811, but in 1821 the population was ten. By 1891 the number had risen to 33, but it fell to 18 in 1931. In 1951, when the last separate figure was given, the population was 23.[27]

Richard of Ilchester or de Toclive (d. 1188) is said to have been a native of Sock, and certainly held land there.[28] After a career as a government official he held the bishopric of Winchester from 1173 until his death.[29]

MANORS. The seven thegns who held Sock 'in parage' in the time of the Confessor were succeeded, after the Conquest, by Robert son of Ives, sometimes called 'the Constable', who held the estate from the count of Mortain.[30] The property continued to be held of Mortain until the second count's lands were confiscated in 1106, when the overlordship of Sock was resumed by the Crown. Robert son of Ives was the direct ancestor of the family of Beauchamp of Hatch,[31] and by 1236 the mesne tenant was Robert de Beauchamp (III).[32] The mesne lordship then passed to his son Robert (IV), his grandson John (I) (d. 1283), and John's heirs successively to John (IV) (d. 1361).[33] Part of it then passed to Alice, widow of John (IV), in dower.[34] The Beauchamp inheritance having then devolved on two coheirs, the mesne lordship seems to have lapsed.[35]

³ S.P. 12/clxxxv, no. 93.
⁴ 46 & 47 Vict. c. 173 (local act).
⁵ Somerset (Parishes in the Rural District of Yeovil) Confirmation Order, 1957.
⁶ Bearley formed a similar area of meadow in Tintinhull parish: see p. 256.
⁷ E. Ekwall, Dict. Eng. Place Names (4th edn.), 429.
⁸ Geol. Surv. Map 1", solid and drift, sheet 312 (1958 edn.).
⁹ Ex inf. Mr. R. S. White, owner of Sock Dennis fm.
¹⁰ S.R.S. xv. 207.
¹¹ Cal. Inq. p.m. iii, p. 121.
¹² Rot. Hund. (Rec. Com.), ii. 126.
¹³ Ilchester Almshouse Deeds, ed. W. Buckler, no. 74.
¹⁴ S.R.S. iii. 273.
¹⁵ E 179/169/31; S.R.S. iii. 307.
¹⁶ S. & D. N. & Q. xxv. 109.
¹⁷ V.C.H. Som. ii. 156.
¹⁸ S.R.S. vi. 57.

¹⁹ Rot. Hund. (Rec. Com.), ii. 126.
²⁰ Cal. Pat. 1338–40, 347.
²¹ E 315/385 f. 48v; S.R.O., DD/PH 52, rental etc. f. 6v.
²² S.R.S. iii. 273.
²³ E 179/169/31.
²⁴ Feud. Aids, iv. 403.
²⁵ Collinson, Hist. Som. iii. 307.
²⁶ See p. 234.
²⁷ V.C.H. Som. ii. 349; Census 1911–51.
²⁸ See p. 232.
²⁹ D.N.B.
³⁰ V.C.H. Som. i. 483.
³¹ Proc. Som. Arch. Soc. xxxvi. 20; R. W. Eyton, Dom. Studies Som. i. 97, 140.
³² S.R.S. xxxv. 2.
³³ Cal. Inq. p.m. i, p. 189; ii, p. 369; viii, pp. 322, 324; xi, pp. 25–6.
³⁴ Cal. Close, 1360–4, 449.
³⁵ Cal. Inq. p.m. xi, pp. 25–6.

Richard of Ilchester, bishop of Winchester 1174–88, held a hide of land there by grant of Robert de Beauchamp.[36] John the Dane,[37] his heir, brought an action in 1224 concerning a carucate which Richard had conveyed to William son of Ralph.[38] William the Dane, perhaps John's father, was the founder of the Whitehall in Ilchester between 1217 and 1220.[39] John the Dane held two fees in Sock of the Beauchamps in 1236.[40]

Between 1256 and 1268 the holding, described as a manor and divided into smaller fees, was disputed between the Bonvilles, the Pauncefoots, and Brice, son and heir of William Deneys, evidently successor to John the Dane. In 1256 Nicholas de Bonville established a claim to $2\frac{1}{4}$ fees which were said to form the manor.[41] Two years later the estate was settled on Nicholas's heir William, and was then said to comprise $2\frac{1}{5}$ fees.[42] At the death of Nicholas in 1264 the estate was held partly for $\frac{1}{4}$ fee of the king, and the rest for 2 fees of Mortain of Robert Beauchamp.[43] In 1268, however, Brice Deneys, a minor in the custody of the Crown, successfully recovered seisin against William Bonville and Isabel Pauncefoot, who were said to have acquired the estate during the civil war.[44]

In 1283 Grimbald Pauncefoot unsuccessfully challenged Brice's right to the manor, and three years later the holding, described as $1\frac{1}{2}$ fee, was in Deneys's hands.[45] Ten days earlier than this inquisition Brice enfeoffed Grimbald Pauncefoot with two thirds of the manor.[46] The grant represented half the manor except the capital messuage, and half the advowson.[47] Between 1292 and 1294 Nicholas Bonville acquired from Brice not only the mesne lordship of the Pauncefoot moiety, but also the ownership of the other moiety, including the capital messuage, part of the transaction being the purchase of a messuage and three carucates of land for 200 marks in 1293.[48]

Nicholas Bonville died in 1294 in possession of what later became known as the manor of *SOCK DENNIS*.[49] His son, also Nicholas, was holding the property for 2 fees of Mortain in 1337.[50] After failure to repay a debt contracted in 1345 he lost possession, and Sir Richard Abberbury was owner in 1361.[51] Abberbury lost possession in 1375 to Sir Thomas Brooke.[52] The Bonvilles retained some interest, however, and in 1388 the manor was settled on Nicholas Botiler, with remainder to William (later Sir William) Bonville.[53] Two years later Bonville had apparently taken possession.[54] At his

death in 1408 he was succeeded by his grandson, also William.[55]

Bonville came of age in 1416;[56] he was created Lord Bonville in 1449 and died in 1461.[57] His heir was his great-granddaughter Cecily (d. 1530), wife successively of Thomas Grey, marquess of Dorset (d. 1501), and of Henry Stafford, earl of Wiltshire (d. 1523).[58] Cecily's son by her first marriage, Thomas Grey, survived her by only six months, and was succeeded by his son Henry (cr. duke of Suffolk, 1551), though Sock seems to have been settled originally on his younger son Thomas.[59] On the attainder of the duke in 1554 the lands reverted to the Crown, but were settled on another brother, Sir John Grey, in 1559.[60] John's son Henry (cr. Lord Grey of Groby, 1603), sold the manor, together with lands in Ilchester and Yeovilton, to Edward Phelips of Montacute in 1594.[61]

The property remained in the Phelips family, sometimes forming part of the jointure of Phelips wives, until 1753.[62] In that year Edward Phelips sold both manor and advowson to Henry Hele, M.D., of the Close, Salisbury.[63] Hele's devizees, Thomas Phipps of Westbury Leigh (Wilts.) and Thomas Hele Phipps, his son and heir, sold the estate in 1818 to John Heathcote Wyndham (d. 1852). He was succeeded by his son J. E. Wyndham of Exeter.[64] The manor had by this time ceased to be anything more than a farm, known in 1968 as Sock Dennis farm.

Sock Dennis farm-house is a three-storeyed building of lias with Ham stone dressings. Originally of two storeys, it dates from the 17th century[65] and has round-headed mullioned windows on the ground floor. The front portion and the third storey were added early in the 19th century.

The estate later known as *SIR JOHN BERKELEY'S MANOR* or *WYNDHAM'S SOCK* originated in the holding of Grimbald Pauncefoot.[66] In a lawsuit in 1329 Clemence, widow of Grimbald Pauncefoot (II) (d. 1314), claimed that Grimbald (I) had enfeoffed Bishop Robert Burnell (d. 1292) of this property.[67] It had then descended to the bishop's nephew Philip (d. 1294), and then to Philip's son Edward. Edward then demised the estate to Clemence and Grimbald for her life, with remainder to Amaury, Grimbald's brother and heir.[68] Amaury Pauncefoot was returned as tenant for half the manor for a fee Mortain in 1316,[69] though Clemence was actual tenant in 1327.[70] Amaury seems to have succeeded by 1343,[71]

[36] B.M. Harl. Ch. 58 G 6.
[37] Or Daneis.
[38] *Curia Reg. R.* xi, pp. 344, 505.
[39] *S.R.S.* i. 68.
[40] *Bk. of Fees*, ii. 1469; *S.R.S.* xxxv. 2.
[41] *S.R.S.* vi. 179.
[42] Ibid. 180–1.
[43] *Cal. Inq. p.m.* i, p. 189.
[44] *Abbrev. Plac.* (Rec. Com.), 176; *Close R.* 1268–72, 8–9, 91; *Cal. Inq. p.m.* ii, p. 1.
[45] C.P. 40/51, rot. 80; *Cal. Inq. p.m.* ii, p. 369. The I.p.m. says the occupier was John Deneys.
[46] Hook Manor, Donhead St. Andrew, Arundell MSS. G/1440, no. 316.
[47] *S.R.S.* vi. 268.
[48] *Cal. Inq. p.m.* iii, pp. 49, 125; *S.R.S.* vi. 289.
[49] *Cal. Inq. p.m.* iii, p. 125.
[50] *S.R.S.* xxxv. 88; Devon R.O. 123 M/TB 475–6.
[51] C 260/73/10; *Cal. Inq. p.m.* xi, pp. 25–6.
[52] C 260/73/10.

[53] *S.R.S.* xvii. 204; *Cal. Close*, 1385–9, 666.
[54] *S.R.S.* xvii. 142; Devon R.O. 123 M/TB 487b, 493, 495.
[55] *Feud. Aids*, vi. 507–8.
[56] *Complete Peerage*, s.v. Bonville.
[57] Ibid.   [58] Ibid.
[59] *L. & P. Hen. VIII*, xv, p. 219.
[60] *Cal. Pat.* 1558–60, 82; *Cal. S.P. Dom.* 1547–80, 128.
[61] C.P. 25(2)/207/36 & 37 Eliz. I Mich.
[62] C 142/486/151; S.R.O., DD/PH 26, 163, 229/12.
[63] S.R.O., DD/PH 26.
[64] Burke, *Land. Gent.* (1910), 2809; Sock Dennis Rectory Act, 46 & 47 Vict. c. 173 (local act).
[65] The date 1623 appears on a rainwater-head.
[66] *S.R.S.* vi. 268; see above.
[67] C.P. 40/277 rot. 51.
[68] Ibid.
[69] *S.R.S.* xxxv. 70.
[70] Ibid. iii. 273.
[71] *Cal. Inq. p.m.* viii, pp. 322, 324; *S.R.S.* xxxv. 94.

but his son Grimbald (III) granted the estate before 1361 to Thomas, Lord Berkeley.[72]

Sir John Berkeley, successor to Thomas, let the estate for his life to Sir William Bonville in 1389.[73] In 1411, after Bonville's death, Sir John Berkeley (d. 1428) and Elizabeth his wife settled the property on their son Maurice (later Sir Maurice), of Bisterne (Hants), and Beverstone (Glos.).[74] Sir Maurice died in 1458 leaving Sock and other lands in trust for his grandson, William (d. 1485). Sock was held by William's widow for her life, and then passed to his uncle, Sir Edward Berkeley (d. 1506), of Avon (Hants).[75] It descended to his son Thomas, his grandson John, and his great grandson Sir William (d. 1551)[76] and then to Sir John Berkeley of North Hinton (Hants), who in 1568 sold the estate to Sir John Danvers of Dauntsey (Wilts.).[77] In 1585 Danvers sold Sock to Sir Matthew Arundell,[78] who was succeeded in 1598 by his son Thomas (cr. Lord Arundell of Wardour, 1605).[79] The trustees of Thomas, Lord Arundell (d. 1643), sold it to Wadham Wyndham of Dinton (Wilts.) in 1655.[80]

The property then descended in the Wyndham family through William (d. 1734), his son William (d. 1762), his grandson William (d. 1786), and his great-grandson, also William (d. 1841).[81] The property was still described as a manor in the early 18th century, but in the 19th was considered only a farm.[82]

The farm-house of Wyndham's Sock, known as Sock House in 1657, was then occupied by the tenant of half the land.[83] The present Ham stone house was built to the design of Joseph Beard of Kingsdon in the 1820s.[84] In 1968 the farm was known as Sock Manor farm.

ECONOMIC HISTORY. The estate at Sock in the 11th century was predominantly arable, though the four ploughs on land for five may perhaps indicate some then recent contraction of the cultivated area.[85] Thereafter, at least until the late 13th century, the arable remained constant in size, and in 1294 measured 480 a.[86] Grassland was evidently recovered from what was waste or marsh in the 11th century. In 1086 the manor had 70 a. of meadow, but no recorded pasture, though the demesne farm alone supported 5 beasts (*animalia*), 35 pigs, and 25 sheep.[87] By the late 13th century the two moieties of the original estate comprised between them 120 a. of meadow and the same amount of pasture, with

additional meadow in Chestermead, rented out for £6 3s. a year, and pasture, probably in common, worth £4.[88] Chestermead, sometimes divided into sesters, was obviously valuable and sought after, especially for grazing cattle.[89] One tenant in Sock in 1328 possessed a bull, 24 oxen, and 20 cows there; and another had at least 16 oxen in 1374.[90]

In the time of the Confessor the whole estate had been held by seven thegns 'in parage'.[91] Robert son of Ives's farm of 2½ hides was worked with one serf, and 8 villeins and 2 bordars held the rest of the land, amounting at the old valuation to one hide. By the late 13th century an unspecified number of both free and customary tenants were paying rents in cash.[92] The total value of the two parts of the parish in 1294 was returned as £69 11s., though in the following year the figure was £37 11s.[93] The estate of Cecily Bonville was farmed for £22 in 1527–8 and 1539–40.[94]

The farm of the manor of Sock Dennis by 1527 comprised rents of both free and customary tenants,[95] but it must be assumed that many of these were resident outside the manor and parish. Certainly the surviving medieval evidence suggests outside ownership and non-resident landlords. The decline in resident population evidently continued during the 16th century,[96] probably the result of change from arable to pasture. Such change had certainly occurred on Wyndham's Sock by the mid 17th century, the 500-a. holding having only 18½ a. of mixed arable and pasture and the remainder grass.[97] The manor included the meadows of Chestermead which the lessee in 1566–8 reseeded, thereby considerably increasing the value of his cattle.[98] There was a consequent rise in rents in the manor, from just over £57 in the 1580s to over £86 in the 1630s.[99]

In the later 17th century the two manors provided a contrast in estate management. By 1680 the Phelips estate, amounting to some 340 a., was divided between 117 a. in hand and 223 a. leased to George Hilborne of Ilchester.[1] The holding was gradually increased in size: c. 1700 there were over 429 a.[2] and by 1752 470 a.[3] In contrast the Wyndham estate covered c. 509 a. in 1657, divided into fourteen holdings.[4] In 1746 it was still split between five,[5] and was seriously fragmented by leases for lives as late as 1819.[6] One farm, known as Upper Sock farm, of c. 230 a., had then emerged in a total acreage of 496 a.[7]

[72] *Cal. Close*, 1360–4, 232; Hook Manor, Arundell MSS. G/1439, no. 29.
[73] B.M. Harl. Ch. 46 A 45.
[74] *S.R.S.* xxii. 38; *Cal. Close*, 1422–9, 373.
[75] J. C. Wedgwood, *Hist. Parl.*, Biogs. s.v.; *Cal. Inq. p.m. Hen. VII*, iii, p. 546.
[76] *V.C.H. Hants*, iv. 580.
[77] S.R.O., DD/WY, box 84.
[78] C.P. 25(2)/206/27 Eliz. I East.
[79] C 142/257/83.
[80] S.R.O., DD/LV 3 (ii); DD/WY, box 84.
[81] Burke, *Land. Gent.* (1910), 2809.
[82] S.R.O., DD/WY, box 84.
[83] S.R.O., DD/LV 3 (ii).
[84] S.R.O., DD/WY, box 84, undated specification. The tenant there mentioned had left by 1828 (DD/WY, box 130).
[85] *V.C.H. Som.* i. 483.
[86] C 133/68/10/44.
[87] *V.C.H. Som.* i. 483.
[88] C 133/68/10/44.
[89] E 326/5344–5, 9426; B.M. Harl. Ch. 50 H 44; *Cal.*

Inq. p.m. vi, p. 376; *Ilchester Almshouse Deeds*, ed. W. Buckler, pp. 23, 75–6; S.R.O., DD/TB, box 20, transcript of St. John's hosp. Bath, charters, pp. 56–7; *S.R.S.* viii. 147.
[90] *Cal. Pat.* 1327–30, 287; C 88/46/80.
[91] *V.C.H. Som.* i. 483.
[92] C 133/68/10/44.
[93] *Cal. Pat.* 1292–1301, 133.
[94] S.C. 6/Hen. VIII/6214–15.
[95] S.C. 6/Hen. VIII/6214.
[96] See p. 231.
[97] S.R.O., DD/WY, box 84, schedule of estate, 1657; DD/LV 3 (ii), survey, 1657.
[98] C 3/157/36.
[99] Hook Manor, Donhead St. Andrew, Arundell MSS. ct. bk. 9 f. 1; receivers'-general accts. 17–18.
[1] S.R.O., DD/PH 229/12.
[2] Ibid. 144.   [3] Ibid.
[4] S.R.O., DD/LV 3 (ii).
[5] S.R.O., DD/WY, box 84, survey, 1746.
[6] Ibid., survey, 1819, rental 1820–3.
[7] Ibid., survey, 1819; DD/LV 3 (i).

The Wyndhams carried out a number of improvements in the 1820s and 1830s, though they found it difficult to secure suitable tenants, particularly after severe flooding in 1828.[8] Wyndham's Sock farm, as it was then called, was said to be in a 'bad state' and lacked a tenant, although the farmhouse had recently been rebuilt.[9] Alterations at Burlinghams by 1838 had made the house 'very convenient', and other buildings had been made 'very perfect' according to the owner. When a few other old buildings had been attended to he hoped to 'have a truce from building'.[10]

By 1839 there were only four holdings in Sock. The largest, Sock Dennis farm, was 415 a.; Wyndham's Sock measured 314 a. and Chestermead 117 a. Just over 130 a. were then under arable cultivation and 747 a. under meadow or pasture.[11] In the early 1860s many of the workers on Sock farms had to live in Ilchester, but cottages were being provided later in the decade.[12] In 1968 three farms shared the land of the ancient parish between them and were predominantly pastoral.[13]

LOCAL GOVERNMENT. In 1327 Sock was described as the 'foreign' of the borough of Ilchester.[14] No court rolls survive for either manor, and certainly in 1527–8 and 1539–40 no courts were held.[15] By the end of the 18th century Sock tithing was considered part of Tintinhull parish.[16] It was incorporated in the Yeovil poor-law union in 1836.[17]

CHURCH. There was a church at Sock in 1286.[18] In origin it was evidently a daughter church of Yeovil, and a pension was still paid by the rector of Sock to the rector of Yeovil in 1428.[19] The church itself had disappeared by 1575 but the benefice, thereafter a sinecure, remained until suppressed in 1883.[20] An attempt to unite part of the parish with Ilchester and part with Lufton and Montacute proved unsuccessful in 1656–7.[21] In 1883 the ecclesiastical parish was divided between Ilchester and Tintinhull and the rectory dissolved.[22]

The advowson lay with the holders of the manor. In 1286, when the manor was divided, the right of patronage was to be exercised alternately.[23] Subsequently, despite the division of the holding, the advowson lay with the lord of Sock Dennis manor,

though the Crown presented in 1306 and 1318 during minorities,[24] and the bishop collated in 1409, apparently by lapse.[25] Thomas Phelips presented the rector in 1577, by grant of the patron;[26] and in 1766 and 1767 Sir Alexander Powell acted as joint patron with Henry Hele.[27] John Heathcote Wyndham was patron from 1818 until his death in 1852; his son, J. E. Wyndham of Exeter, succeeded him.[28]

In 1297 the church was worth £7 15s.[29] By 1334 the rector had 66 a. of glebe worth 44s. 8d., pasture for his cattle,[30] and oblations and small tithes worth 26s. 8d.[31] The rectory was assessed at £7 6s. 8d. in 1428,[32] but its real value was clearly smaller, since it was several times exempted from taxation, provided that the curate remained in residence.[33] In 1523–6 it was worth £6,[34] and £5 10s. 1½d. in 1535.[35] Its 'common reputed value' c. 1668 was £12.[36] By 1831 the income was £188. The tithes were commuted in 1839 for £254 19s. gross.[37]

The most distinguished medieval rector was Nicholas Halswell, M.D. (rector 1492–1500), a foundation fellow of the Royal College of Physicians in 1518.[38] Attempts to enforce residence on the rectors by tax exemption during the 15th century[39] appear on the whole to have been successful. A century earlier Walter Gerard (rector 1338–47) was allowed to serve in a private household provided he returned to his church for two days each fortnight in Lent.[40] Roger Hyllary (rector 1531–77) apparently held the benefice when the church itself went out of use.[41] In 1571–2, during a dispute with Thomas Phelips over a lease of the rectory lands, he described himself as 'a poor, aged, impotent, and blind person'.[42] Most of the rectors from the end of the 16th century held other benefices: John Beale (rector 1638–83) was vicar of Yeovil from 1660 until 1683; Thomas Brickenden (rector 1688–97) was rector of Corton Denham 1660–1701, and his successor at Sock, Edmund Brickenden (rector 1697–1706), was also his successor at Corton. This pattern continued throughout the 18th century. John Manning Hazeland (rector 1785–1819) was curate at Bishop's Cannings (Wilts.) 1779–95 and vicar of Bigbury (Devon) 1785–1819.[43] John Heathcote Wyndham (rector 1819–52) was rector of Corton Denham 1813–52, and patron of Sock. His successor as rector, William Pyne, held no other cure, but lived at Charlton Mackrell.[44]

The church of St. John the Baptist[45] had dis-

8 S.R.O., DD/WY, box 130, Fisher to Wyndham.
9 Ibid. box 84, undated specifications.
10 S.R.O., DD/BT 6/26. The farm-house, named after land known in the 13th century as Berligeham, is located in Tintinhull ancient parish, but most of its land was in Sock: S.R.O., DD/TB, box 20 (St. John's hosp. charters, p. 57); DD/LV 3 (i).
11 S.R.O., tithe award.
12 Rep. Com. Children and Women in Agric. [4202–I] H.C. (1868–9), xiii.   13 Local information.
14 E 179/169/5 m. 56d.
15 S.C. 6/Hen. VIII/6214–15.
16 S.R.O., D/P/tin 13/2/1.
17 Poor Law Com. 2nd Rep. p. 550.
18 S.R.S. vi. 268.
19 Feud. Aids, iv. 403; see also Tax. Eccl. (Rec. Com.), 197; E 326/6438.
20 S. & D. N. & Q. xiv. 107; Sock Dennis Rectory Act, 46 & 47 Vict., c. 173 (local act).
21 Cal. S. P. Dom. 1655–6, 329; 1656–8, 81; S.R.O., DD/LV 3 (iii).
22 Sock Dennis Rectory Act.   23 S.R.S. vi. 268.

24 Cal. Pat. 1301–7, 462; 1317–21, 67.
25 S.R.S. xxix. 65.
26 Som. Incumbents, ed. Weaver, 183.
27 S.R.O., D/D/Bp.
28 Sock Dennis Rectory Act.
29 Tax. Eccl. (Rec. Com.), 197.
30 The exact sum is illegible.
31 E 179/169/14.
32 Feud. Aids, iv. 403.
33 S.R.S. xxxii. 250; lii. 93, 144; liv. 172, 187.
34 E 315/385.
35 Valor Eccl. (Rec. Com.), i. 200.
36 S.R.O., D/D/Vc 24.
37 Rep. Com. Eccl. Revenues, pp. 178–9; S.R.O., tithe award.
38 Emden, Biog. Reg. Univ. Oxford.
39 S.R.S. xxxii. 250; lii. 93, 144; liv. 172, 187.
40 Ibid. x. 443.   41 See below.
42 Req. 2/40/39.
43 Foster, Alumni Oxon.; Som. Incumbents, ed. Weaver.
44 See p. 103.
45 B.M. Harl. Ch. 46 F 16.

appeared by 1575.[46] There had formerly been lights, supported by rents, before the altar of St. John the Baptist in the chancel and also before the altar of the Virgin.[47] A doorway, probably of the early 16th century and perhaps formerly part of the fabric of the church, is incorporated in one of the buildings of Sock Dennis farm.

NONCONFORMITY. None known.

EDUCATION. No evidence.

CHARITIES FOR THE POOR. None known.

STOKE SUB HAMDON

THE ancient parish of Stoke sub Hamdon, commonly called Stoke under Ham, covers 1,381 a.[1] It lies 5 miles west of Yeovil, between Montacute and the Foss Way, and measures nearly 3 miles from east to west, and 1½ mile from north to south. The Foss Way forms the whole of its north-western boundary, and Trutts brook and Wellham's brook bound the parish on the north-east. Its southern limits are less easily defined, though they follow a lane from the Yeovil road up Hedgecock hill. This boundary was marked at its northern end by a stone,[2] and the hill itself was divided from neighbouring Montacute by a ditch, and from the time of Sir Edward Phelips (d. 1614) by a wall,[3] 'ruinous' by 1786.[4] It then follows the northern defences of the encampment on Ham or Hamdon Hill. From there the boundary runs westwards, a stream dividing Stoke from Norton sub Hamdon until it reaches the Parrett.[5] The original course of the river to Petherton Bridge forms Stoke's south-western boundary.

The dominant physical feature of the parish is Ham Hill, rising abruptly some 200 ft. immediately south of the village, to a total height of 400 ft. The hill itself is of Yeovil sands, capped by shelly limestone known as Ham stone, widely used in the district and elsewhere for building.[6] The steep sides and worked-out quarries formed the largest area of common land in the parish. The land falls away gently from the settlement at the foot of the scarp: westwards, towards the Parrett, a junction bed of limestone is followed by Pennard sands, reaching the river below 75 ft. Northwards, too, the land falls away, with a similar geological sequence of limestone, junction bed, and Pennard sands, followed by silts and marls which formed the main area of meadow in the parish. To the north-west alluvium is encountered near Wellham's brook.[7]

The main artery of the parish is the east–west road from Yeovil and Montacute, which follows the 200-ft. contour below Ham Hill through East and West Stoke and joins the Foss Way just short of Petherton Bridge. This is now variously called along its course East Stoke, High Street, and West Street, though in the late 18th century it was known as Church, Upper, and West streets.[8] From this a number of roads and lanes lead north and south, the most important of which is North Street, from the centre of West Stoke to Cartgate on the Foss Way. This was known as Lower Street in 1776 and a cross stood at its junction with Upper Street.[9] Castle Street, formerly Stone or Stone's Lane,[10] runs eastwards from North Street, parallel with High Street, passing the site of the castle. Wherlygog Lane was so named in 1776.[11]

Eastwards from the Vicarage the road divides, forming an island around which the settlement of East Stoke is situated. The southern and higher branch is the course of the Yeovil road, passing the church. The by-road to the church itself marks the original course, which was abandoned for the present one in 1841.[12] The northern branch of the road, known as Lower East Stoke Street in 1776, and in 1968 as Windsor Lane, originally ran further eastwards past East Stoke Farm and directly beside East Stoke House. It was diverted to its present course in 1883, the original road becoming a private driveway.[13] Since 1883 Marsh Lane has been joined to Mulberry Lane to divert traffic from East Stoke House.[14] South of the main artery the road to Odcombe, climbing from High Street to the summit of Ham Hill, was in the 18th century the London–Exeter coach road.[15] There was a plan c. 1822 to adopt a narrow strip of land parallel to and west of this road as part of a projected turnpike road from Cartgate to Merriott.[16] The plan did not then materialize, but a road was made there in 1898, known first as New Road and later as Norton Road, linking Stoke with Norton sub Hamdon.[17] Further west, at Holy Tree Cross, is a road to Chiselborough and Norton from the Foss Way. It is known at its northern end as Prophets Lane (Provost Lane in 1838),[18] and south of the cross roads as Holy Field Lane where it borders the former arable Holloway field.[19]

---

[46] S. & D. N. & Q. xiv. 107.
[47] B.M. Harl. Ch. 46 F 16.
[1] Census, 1961. This article was completed in 1969.
[2] O.S. Nat. Grid 492173; removed by 1968.
[3] S.R.O., DD/PH 225/78.
[4] D.C.O., ct. roll 1785–6.
[5] Boundary stone at O.S. Nat. Grid 462163.
[6] A. Clifton Taylor, Pattern of Eng. Bldg. 104, 131–2.
[7] Geol. Surv. Map 1″, solid and drift, sheet 312 (1958 edn.).
[8] D.C.O., survey and map by William Simpson of Chippenham, 1775–6 (photocopy in S.R.O., T/PH/dcl). See map, p. 236.
[9] Ibid.
[10] Bonnies Lane was known as Stone Lane in 1776;

Castle Street was Stone's Lane in 1886: D.C.O., Simpson's map, 1776; O.S. Map 6″, Som. LXXXII. SE., SW. (1886 edn.).
[11] D.C.O., map, 1776.
[12] Ibid. rental, 1850.
[13] Ibid. map, 1776; S.R.O., tithe award; Q/SR, Spring 1883; HB/Y 112.
[14] S.R.O., Q/SR, Spring 1883.
[15] See p. 210.
[16] S.R.O., DD/WY, maps.
[17] S.R.O., Q/SR, Midsummer 1898.
[18] S.R.O., D/PC/st. u. ham 1/1.
[19] Corrupted to Holy Field by 1840: S.R.O., tithe award. See S. & D. N. & Q. xxii. 237, 264, 277–9 for suggested and clearly erroneous derivations.

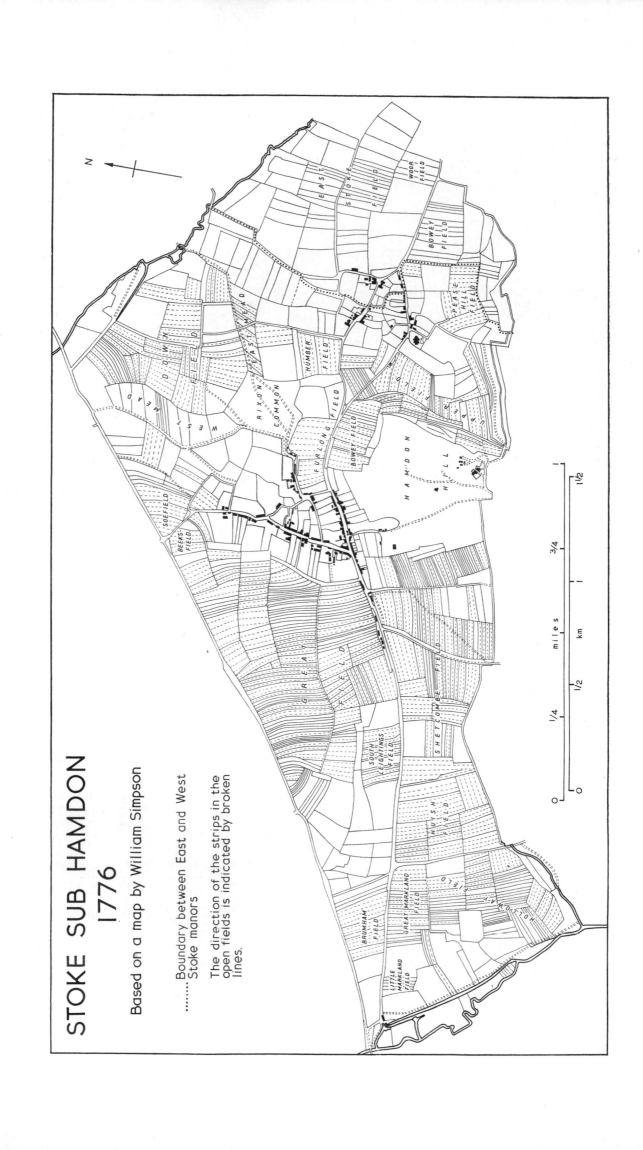

STOKE SUB HAMDON
1776

Based on a map by William Simpson

······· Boundary between East and West
Stoke manors

The direction of the strips in the
open fields is indicated by broken
lines.

N

EAST STOKE FIELD

WOOR HILL FIELD

BOWEY HILL FIELD

PEASE HILL FIELD

HUMBER FIELD

RIXON EAST MEAD

COMMON

BOWEY FIELD

SOUTH HILL FIELD

DOWN FIELD

WEST MEAD

SOEFIELD

BEEKS FIELD

HAMDON HILL

FURLONG FIELD

GREAT FIELD

SOUTH LEIGHTINGS FIELD

SHETCOMBE FIELD

HULSH FIELD

HOLLOWAY FIELD

BRUMHAM FIELD

GREAT MARKLAND FIELD

LITTLE MARKLAND FIELD

miles
km

0   1/4   1/2   3/4   1
0   1/2   1

Most of the small tracks serving the open fields disappeared after inclosure.[20] One right of way traceable in the later 18th century was the procession way, the route taken by the triennial manorial perambulation. Field names such as Procession Orchard mark its course. The perambulation was still walked in 1775, but by 1809 it had lapsed. Land in Rixon Common was held in return for supplying beer and victuals for the perambulation, and closes on the parish boundary adjoining Holloway field were known as Victuals Hams.[21]

The Iron Age encampment on Ham Hill, part of which protrudes into the southern edge of the parish, is apparently the oldest settlement site in Stoke, though any direct relationship between it and the village below the scarp is not proved.[22] The proximity of the Foss Way accounts for the presence of a Roman inscribed column found at Venn bridge,[23] and probably for the remains at Stanchester in the north of the parish.[24] The Domesday division of property between the holdings of Robert son of Ives and Mauger de Cartrai, which may reflect an earlier division of settlement, accounts for the two distinct centres of population at East and West Stoke. West Stoke, the settlement of Stoke manor, was more populous at least from the 14th century.[25] East Stoke, formerly the centre of Stokett manor, was by the later 18th century partially absorbed into Stoke manor.[26] In 1315–16 there was another hamlet in the parish, known as South Ameldon or Suth Meldon.[27] This may have been a small settlement on Ham Hill, associated with the chapel there.[28]

A feature of the settlement pattern of the parish is the remoteness of the church from the main village. East Stoke may therefore have been the original settlement. The foundation of a chapel within the precincts of the manor-house by the beginning of the 14th century may suggest such development.[29] The expansion of West Stoke in the 19th century and later has accentuated the isolation of the church, a fact which several 19th-century incumbents deplored.[30]

Open arable fields and common meadow and pasture survived more completely in Stoke than in any other parish in the hundred.[31] Arable not only covered the undulating parts of Stoke but also pushed up the scarp of Ham Hill, entirely dominating the western half of the parish. Thirteenth-century field names survived until the 19th century in Shetcombe (Shepcombe) and Huish (Helfhuwys) fields, Stanchester (Stonchester) furlong, and Rixon (Ryxe) common.[32] Inclosure was a gradual process, taking place by private agreement during the 19th century.[33]

The almost universal use of Ham stone as a building material gives a homogeneous appearance to the village although its houses are of widely different periods. At the end of the 18th century North and High streets were fairly continuously

occupied, with scattered houses in Wherlygog Lane and at the eastern end of the present Castle Street. There were also rows of cottages on the waste at the western end of the village and along the track to Rixon Common opposite the site of the former manor-house. East Stoke was a scattered settlement north and east of the parish church. High and West streets are now closely built up with houses on both sides, many of them dating from the 19th century. The oldest building in West Street is the Fleur de Lis inn, which is of 15th-century origin, considerably altered in the last hundred years.[34] The principal doorway, giving access to a cross-passage, has a pointed head and carved spandrels; a second 15th-century doorway, originally at the rear of the passage, has been incorporated in the street frontage. Behind the inn is an 18th-century fives court with a shaped parapet and ball finials.

High Street has several late-17th-century houses, including no. 47, of 1674, which has a two-storey splayed bay with a flat gable corbelled out above it. Pranketts, a little to the west, is dated 1693, and has a three-gabled front with a central arched entrance and mullioned windows with cavetto moulding. No. 37 also dates from the 17th century. No. 13 is an early-18th-century house, having a pulvinated frieze and a bull's-eye window above the central door. No. 17, Tan-y-Bryn, is a substantial house of the 18th century, with swept-up parapet to flanking wings and an Ionic porch.

In North Street the frontages are less regular than those of High Street and, particularly towards the northern end, the houses are more widely spaced. A dominating feature of the street is the large Congregational chapel of 1866[35] which looks like a Victorian parish church. The most notable of the buildings is the Priory, parts of which may date from the 14th century.[36] Further north is the Gables. The house, of two storeys and attics, was probably built c. 1600, confirming the date '1615' scratched in the porch. It has a symmetrical Ham stone front with a central gabled porch rising to the full height, flanked by canted bay windows corbelled square at eaves level to form attic gables. The porch opening is semi-circular and the doorway-head four-centred. The original house, three bays wide and one room deep, had a central staircase projection at the back and perhaps a small service wing. The drawing room contains a ceiling of c. 1600 with a geometrical design of moulded ribs and floral motifs in the panels; there is a vine frieze in the room above. A new south-east room with an adjoining stair was added early in the 18th century. Alterations of 1911 included a southern extension of the drawing room in which a doorway dated 1726 was re-set. In the grounds are the remains of what was probably an 18th-century swimming bath.[37] Further south stands Hoods, no. 34, a five-bay house of the later 17th century.[38]

The late 17th century is also represented at East

[20] D.C.O., map, 1776; S.R.O., tithe award; HB/Y 112.
[21] D.C.O., survey, 1775, amended 1809.
[22] See below.
[23] S. & D. N. & Q. xx. 73–5.
[24] Proc. Som. Arch. Soc. iv. 88; lxv. 86–7; V.C.H. Som. i. 366.
[25] S.R.S. iii. 223.
[26] D.C.O., map, 1776.
[27] Feud. Aids, iv. 327.
[28] See p. 248.
[29] V.C.H. Som. i. 161.
[30] S.R.O., DD/HW 17.

[31] See map, p. 236. For field names in 1615 see L.R. 2/207 f. 20v.; Royal Libr., Windsor, survey by John Norden, 1615 (microfilm in S.R.O., T/PH/vch).
[32] S.R.S. xxxv. 11–12.
[33] See p. 243.
[34] See plate facing p. 144.
[35] See p. 249.
[36] See p. 241.
[37] S.R.O., DD/SAS PR 36.
[38] Said to be 1695 and by the same builders who erected Pranketts: A. V. Richards, Hist. Stoke sub Hamdon (1971), 58.

Stoke: East Stoke Cottage is dated 1696, and East Stoke Farm, though considerably altered in the 1860s, has the date 1698 over an internal doorway. Several other small houses there date from the late 17th or early 18th century. West Street is largely a later development. Apart from no. 1, of 1679,[39] the private dwellings date from the 19th century, though most of the buildings further west belong to the 20th century.

By 1861 there were three inns in the parish, together with five beer retailers.[40] The oldest inn is the Fleur de Lis.[41] On the Foss Way stood the Cartgate inn, so called by 1828 but earlier known as the Prince of Wales Arms.[42] The Rose and Crown, also built to attract business from the Foss Way, was closed c. 1828; the Prince of Wales on Ham Hill served the quarrymen.[43] The new Rose and Crown was opened by 1876 and the Duke of Cornwall by 1883.[44] The former was closed in 1969, and the Cartgate inn was demolished in 1970.[45]

Fives-playing and cricket were popular in the village, the Ham Hill Cricket Club transferring from Hinton St. George in 1832.[46] Stoke Friendly Society, based at the Fleur de Lis, and a female friendly society were both registered in 1812.[47] The Royal George Seven Year Male Friendly Society, also based at the Fleur, was founded in 1829 and, as the Royal George Benefit Society, still existed c. 1890.[48] By 1877 the parish had a free library, and coal, clothing, blanket, and shoe clubs.[49] A working men's institute was established in 1883.[50]

Since Stoke was less dependent on agriculture than its neighbours its population pattern during the 19th century is not typical of the area. There was an increase, at first rapid and then slower, between 1801 and 1851, rising from 766 to a peak of 1,401. Only two families were helped to emigrate, both to Australia, in 1840.[51] Two very slight falls in the next two decades were followed by a rise to 1,726 in 1891. Fairly violent fluctuations took the total down to 1,553 in 1921, largely through the difficulties experienced by the glove trade, but since then there has been steady growth, to 1,782 in 1961.[52]

MANORS AND OTHER ESTATES. The count of Mortain held three estates in Stoke in 1086. Two of these had formerly been thegnland, held of Glastonbury abbey T.R.E.,[53] and part at least may earlier have been royal property. Between 924 and 939 Athelstan gave land at Stoke to Aelfric,

and Aelfric is said to have given it to the abbey. An estate of 5 hides at Stoke was also said to have been given to Glastonbury by Uffa, a widow.[54] In addition, a lost charter recorded the gift of land at Stoke made by Ethelred to his thegn Godric, which also passed to Glastonbury.[55] The overlordship of all these properties passed to the Crown in 1106 on the confiscation of the count of Mortain's estates.

Two of the three estates of the count, amounting to 7½ hides and a ½-virgate, were held of him by Robert son of Ives, ancestor of the family of Beauchamp of Hatch.[56] It is likely that his holding became known as the manor of *STOKE* or *STOKE BEAU-CHAMP*.[57] Robert son of Ives was succeeded by Robert (I) (fl. 1092), by Robert (II) (fl. 1150–8), and probably by a Robert (III) (fl. 1185, d. 1195). Robert (III)'s only daughter married Simon Vautort (d. before 1199) leaving a son, Robert, known as Robert son of Simon or Robert Beauchamp (IV).[58] During his minority his estates, which included two fees of Mortain at Stoke, were held by Hubert de Burgh.[59] Robert (IV) died about 1250–1, and his son Robert (V) before 1265–6.[60] He was succeeded by John (I) (d. 1283), and his heirs successively: John (II) (d. 1336), John (III) (d. 1343), and John (IV) (d. 1361).[61] The manor of Stoke was assigned to Alice, widow of John (IV), in dower, the heirs being her late husband's sister Cecily, widow of Roger Seymour, and his nephew, John de Meriet.[62] Meriet quitclaimed his reversionary interest to Alice's feoffees, and it was assigned to Sir Matthew Gournay, Alice's second husband, and to Alice, in tail.[63] On the death of Alice in 1383 the estate was divided, one half passing to William Beauchamp of Warwick, her brother and surviving feoffee, and the other to Cecily,[64] though it was not delivered to her until 1386.[65] By 1389 Sir Matthew Gournay acquired reversionary interests in the whole manor.[66] Both halves were settled on him and his second wife, Philippe, for their lives,[67] and after his death in 1406 on his widow and her third husband, Sir John Tiptoft, for the life of Philippe.[68] This settlement was altered in favour of Tiptoft, who retained the manor until his death in 1443.[69]

During Tiptoft's tenure, in 1421, the Crown acquired a reversionary interest in favour of the duchy of Cornwall, and on Tiptoft's death the manor passed to the duchy.[70] For a short period the Crown appointed keepers of the castle and

[39] A plaster overmantle, dated 1688, was destroyed in 1963.
[40] *P.O. Dir. Som.* (1861).
[41] See p. 247.
[42] D.C.O., 'Bk. of Extracts, 1794 etc.'; S.R.O., D/PC/st. u. ham 1/2.
[43] See p. 244.
[44] *Kelly's Dir. Som.* (1883).
[45] Richards, *Hist. Stoke*, 75–6.
[46] S.R.O., DD/HW 1; S.R.O., DD/LV 7; Richards, op. cit. 50.
[47] S.R.O., Q/R, Friendly Soc. rtns.
[48] Margaret Fuller, *West Country Friendly Socs.* 141; S.R.O., DD/X/BRI, cash bk. 1829–59; D/P/st. u. ham 23/1, vol. of photographs.
[49] S.R.O., DD/HW 17/4.
[50] *Kelly's Dir. Som.* (1883).
[51] S.R.O., D/PC/st. u. ham 1/1.
[52] *V.C.H. Som.* ii. 349; *Census*, 1911–61.
[53] *V.C.H. Som.* i. 467.

[54] Finberg, *Early Charters of Wessex*, p. 129.
[55] Ibid. p. 148.
[56] *V.C.H. Som.* i. 475; *Proc. Som. Arch. Soc.* xxxvi. 20–59; Sanders, *Eng. Baronies*, 51.
[57] C.P. 40/281 rot. 64; *Feud. Aids*, iv. 286.
[58] *Proc. Som. Arch. Soc.* xxxvi. 22–3.
[59] *Pipe R.* 1206 (P.R.S. n.s. xx), 135; *Bk. of Fees*, i. 85.
[60] *Cal. Inq. p.m.* i, p. 295; *Proc. Som. Arch. Soc.* xxxvi. 29–30; Sanders, *Eng. Baronies*, 51.
[61] *Complete Peerage*, s.v. Beauchamp of Hatch.
[62] *Cal. Close, 1360–4*, 308.
[63] *Cal. Pat. 1374–7*, 35.
[64] C 136/31/23; *Cal. Fine R. 1383–91*, 36–7. Cecily married a Turberville as her second husband: *Complete Peerage*, ii. 51 n.
[65] *Cal. Fine R. 1383–91*, 140–1.
[66] *Cal. Pat. 1388–92*, 158.
[67] C 143/408/1; *S.R.S.* xxii. 108.
[68] *S.R.S.* xxii. 171.
[69] C 139/110/45.   [70] *Rot. Parl.* iv. 141.

manor,[71] but in 1444 it was granted to Edmund Beaufort, marquess of Dorset, in tail male.[72] Under an Act of Resumption in 1449 the Crown regained the manor,[73] and Henry Holand, duke of Exeter, was appointed keeper in 1450.[74] Edmund Beaufort, duke of Somerset (d. 1455), regained Stoke in 1452,[75] and was holding it at his death.[76] Although the manor was resumed by the Crown in the same year, the duke's widow was granted the keepership for seven years in 1456, but surrendered it a year later to her son Henry, duke of Somerset (d. 1464).[77] On Henry's death the manor was granted to George, duke of Clarence, for his life.[78] This grant was apparently surrendered, for by 1472 Stoke had been reunited to the duchy of Cornwall.[79] In 1482 an Act of Parliament allowed Stoke and other manors of the duchy to be exchanged for lands belonging to William Herbert, earl of Huntingdon,[80] but the Act was declared void in 1495, Stoke becoming part of the estates of Prince Arthur.[81] The lands, however, were referred to as 'late Huntingdon's' as late as 1574.[82]

The manor was administered directly under the Crown until 1545.[83] Part was then leased to Paul Gressham,[84] and the reversion of this and the rest of the manor to Christopher Perne in 1557.[85] The reversion of the second lease was granted to Helen, marchioness of Northampton (d. 1635), and in 1606 to her second husband, Sir Thomas Gorges (d. 1610), to be effective after her death.[86] The manor was formally settled on Charles, prince of Wales, in 1615,[87] but in the following year Sir Edward Gorges (cr. Lord Gorges of Dundalk, 1620) received a lease for three lives after the death of his mother.[88] Gorges therefore succeeded his mother in 1635, and was himself succeeded by his son Richard in 1650.[89] The projected sale of the duchy lands including Stoke in 1652 did not apparently disturb Gorges's lease,[90] and he remained in possession until 1660. From that time the duchy has been in direct control of the manor, though the lands have always been leased in smaller units.[91]

John Beauchamp (II) received licence to crenellate his manor-house at Stoke in 1333,[92] but, apart from Sir Matthew Gournay (d. 1406), the lords of Stoke after the extinction of the Beauchamps were not resident.[93] The house probably fell into decay

during the 15th century. Leland saw 'very notable ruins of a great manor place or castle', together with St. Nicholas's chapel,[94] but by the early 17th century only the site was known, 'none of the buildings remaining but the place where it [the castle] stood and certain lands known by [sic] the castle gardens'.[95] Part of the perimeter wall and two blocked gateways still survive; an examination of the site made c. 1887 revealed a gatehouse, the sites of the chapel, a dovecot, and two ponds, together with many unidentified foundations.[96]

The manor of *EAST STOKE* or *STOKETT* was held by Alwin T.R.E. In 1086 Mauger de Cartrai held it of the count of Mortain.[97] By c. 1284 Ralph de Huppehull or Opehulle held it of Maud de Multon, lady of Ashill, and she of the countess of Aumale.[98] Mauger was also Domesday tenant of Ashill, and it is therefore probable that his holding at East Stoke may have descended like Ashill.

The origin and descent of the mesne tenancy of Isabel de Forz, countess of Aumale, has not been traced. Maud de Multon, however, succeeded at Ashill the family of Vaux, who had probably settled in the county by Henry II's reign.[99] Robert Vaux was certainly in possession of Ashill by 1214.[1] By 1235 he had been succeeded by Hubert, probably his son,[2] and he in turn, by 1253, by Maud, wife of Thomas de Multon, probably his daughter.[3] Thomas was evidently dead by c. 1284, when his widow was holding East Stoke and other properties.[4] Maud died in 1293, and her heir was her son Thomas.[5] John, his eldest son, appears to have succeeded c. 1317.[6] John's son Thomas probably died young, and the property passed to his sister Margaret, wife of Sir John Streche, of Wambrook (Dors. later Som.).[7] Sir John held the mesne tenancy in 1381,[8] but it has not been traced thereafter.[9] In 1627 the manor was said to be held of the lord of Tintinhull hundred.[10]

Ralph de Huppehull's estate at Stokett c. 1284 was ¼ fee.[11] By 1297 Ralph de Hull, possibly the same man, had apparently leased his lands there which became the subject of a legal dispute.[12] The property seems to have descended like the manor of Child Okeford (Dors.), to the Latimer family. Robert de Hull held that manor in 1317.[13] His daughter and heir Catherine married as her first husband Sir Andrew Turberville, who was in possession of

[71] S.C. 6/974/9; Cal. Pat. 1441–6, 283; Cal. Close, 1441–7, 111, 171.
[72] Cal. Pat. 1441–6, 324; Rot. Parl. v. 446.
[73] Cal. Pat. 1452–61, 18, 28.
[74] Cal. Fine R. 1445–52, 175, 182, 238.
[75] Cal. Pat. 1452–61, 18, 28.
[76] C 139/160/38.
[77] Cal. Fine R. 1452–61, 154; Cal. Pat. 1452–61, 390.
[78] Cal. Pat. 1461–7, 23, 214, 362; Cal. Close, 1461–8, 129; S.R.S. xlix. 337.
[79] S.R.S. lii. 43, 53.
[80] Rot. Parl. vi. 203.
[81] Ibid. 468, 469.
[82] C 66/1108.
[83] Cal. Pat. 1494–1509, 349; L. & P. Hen. VIII, i (1), p. 331; i (2), p. 1172; iv, p. 2035; xiii, p. 413.
[84] L. & P. Hen. VIII, xx, p. 423.
[85] Cal. Pat. 1557–8, 19.
[86] C 66/1108, 1678; Cal. S.P. Dom. 1603–10, 291.
[87] C 66/2060 no. 6.
[88] D.C.O., Bk. of Compositions; 'Inrollments, Prince Charles, 1617–20', i, f. 97 and v.
[89] D.C.O., survey, 1660.
[90] C 54/3677 no. 3.
[91] See p. 243.
[92] Cal. Pat. 1330–4, 494.
[93] Gournay was buried there: Leland, Itin. ed. Toulmin Smith, i. 159.
[94] Ibid. i. 158–9.
[95] L.R. 2/207 f. 20v.
[96] Proc. Som. Arch. Soc. xxxv.127–37; the site is centred on O.S. Nat. Grid 477177, and there is a plan based on the late-19th-century examination in Taunton Castle.
[97] V.C.H. Som. i. 474–5.
[98] Feud. Aids, iv. 286; S.R.S. iii. 22.
[99] S.R.S. viii. 136.
[1] H.M.C. Wells, i. 42, 44.
[2] S.R.S. vi. 367.
[3] Cal. Chart. R. 1226–57, 406.
[4] Feud. Aids, iv. 286; S.R.S. iii. 22.
[5] Cal. Inq. p.m. iii, p. 64; Cal. Close, 1288–96, 291.
[6] Cal. Chart. R. 1300–26, 335; S.R.S. iii. 71.
[7] S.R.S. xii. 171; Hutchins, Hist. Dors. iv. 197.
[8] Cal. Inq. p.m. xv, p. 212.
[9] Hutchins, Hist. Dors. iv. 197.
[10] C 142/750/122.
[11] Feud. Aids, iv. 286.
[12] Abbrev. Plac. (Rec. Com.), 294; Placita Coram Rege, 1297 (Ind. Libr.), 2.
[13] Hutchins, Hist. Dors. iv. 77.

Stokett by 1350.[14] As her second husband Catherine married Sir Robert Latimer of Duntish (Dors.).[15] When she died in 1361, shortly after her second husband, she was succeeded by her son William Turberville.[16] By 1381, however, William had died without male issue, and Robert Latimer, his half-brother, succeeding John Rocheford, had taken possession of the property.[17]

The estate then descended through the Latimer family. Sir John, son of Catherine's son Robert, died in 1460, and was succeeded by his son Sir Nicholas (d. 1505).[18] Nicholas's daughter and heir Edith married Sir John Mordaunt (d. 1504), of Turvey (Beds.), speaker of the House of Commons, and Stokett and other lands were settled on them.[19] By 1560 it was held by John, eldest son of John, Lord Mordaunt (d. 1562),[20] though the capital messuage was in the hands of John Buckland of West Harptree.[21] John's heir Lewis, Lord Mordaunt (1538–1601), sold the property to Thomas Freke in 1597.[22] In 1627 John Seward died holding the manor, described as a capital messuage, a farm called the farm of East Stokett, and named lands. He was succeeded by his infant son, also John.[23] John Seward and Elizabeth his wife made over the manor in 1649 to two feoffees.[24] From that time no trace has been found of the manor; the estate centred upon East Stoke House, created in the late 18th century by the Chaffey family,[25] never claimed manorial status, but was built up piecemeal from scattered holdings in the area of the original manor.

The only other substantial estate in Stoke was the parsonage. This came into lay hands in 1548 on the dissolution of the secular college, when it was leased to Elizabeth Darrell, already tenant of Montacute and Tintinhull.[26] Elizabeth married Robert Strode, who was living in the provost's house in 1560.[27] Cuthbert Vaughan, the queen's servant, acquired the reversion of the lease in 1560,[28] which he sold two years later to Richard Spryngham.[29] Spryngham and his wife Mary sold the reversion to William Burde in 1565, and he, his wife, and son, transferred it to the Crown in 1579.[30] Thomas Strode received a lease from the Crown in 1582[31] and in 1591 John Robinson and Lawrence Singleton were given the reversion of Strode's estate.[32] Strode died in 1595, leaving his tenancy to his widow during her widowhood and then to his eldest son John (d. 1621).[33] A Thomas Strode was living in the house about 1633,[34] and the family still lived in Stoke, probably on the parsonage estate, in 1652.[35]

By the time of his death in 1610 John Robinson, a London mercer, held both the advowson and the rectorial estate, but only the reversionary interest in the capital house of the parsonage. To his second son John, of Gravesend (Kent), he left the rectory, and to his elder son Robert, a London merchant, the reversion of the house, then held by his wife for life. This interest John bought from his brother in 1612 for £800.[36] The property passed to John's grandson Sir John, of Denston (Suff.), as part of his marriage settlement in 1677.[37] Sir John died in 1704, and his trustees sold the site of the college and the rectorial estate in 1712 to Thomas Rodbard, a London fishmonger.[38] Rodbard, who died in 1716, left much of his property, including that at Stoke, to his great-nephew, John Rodbard, son of his nephew William, of Middle Chinnock. John died in 1744, leaving the parsonage to his second son, also John, a London linen-draper (d. 1780). By will dated 1774 he left his property jointly to Sarah and Elizabeth Ellis. Sarah, later the wife of Sir Eyre Coote, sold her half in 1787 to her sister Elizabeth, then known as Elizabeth Rodbard of Hackney, and later of West Coker House. Elizabeth married Dr. Andrew Bain in 1793 and died in 1799. Dr. Bain later settled at Heffleton in East Stoke (Dors.), where he died in 1827.[39]

Dr. Bain's younger daughter and coheir, Sarah Frances, in 1831 married Thomas Hawkesworth of Forest (Leix, Ireland) and Weymouth (Dors.). Their son John William Bain Hawkesworth, of Stokeland, Wareham (Dors.), became patron of the living and owner of the estate on his father's death in 1881.[40] He sold most of the property in 1897, retaining only the house and 34 a. of land.[41] On his death in 1915 he was succeeded by his two sons C. E. M. and T. A. Hawkesworth.[42] The latter died in 1939 and the former in 1945.[43] The National Trust purchased the property of Charles Peter Hawkesworth in 1946.[44]

The Robinsons, the Rodbards, and the Hawkesworths were all absentee landlords, and the parsonage estate was farmed by a succession of tenants. Members of the Chaffey family held it from 1762 at least until 1815,[45] followed by Francis Stroud, 1818–20,[46] Charles Cave, 1820–47,[47] and William Darby, 1848 at least until 1875.[48] After the division of the holding in 1897, and a second sale in 1910,[49] the house and some land were occupied variously

[14] B.M. Harl. Ch. 57 B 10.
[15] Hutchins, *Hist. Dors.* iii. 705; iv. 78.
[16] *Cal. Inq. p.m.* xv, p. 212; Hutchins, *Hist. Dors.* iii. 705.
[17] *Cal. Inq. p.m.* xv, p. 212.
[18] Hutchins, *Hist. Dors.* iii. 705.
[19] *Cal. Pat.* 1476–85, 527.
[20] C.P. 40/1183 rot. 820.
[21] C 142/124/167.
[22] C.P. 25(2)/207/39 Eliz. I East.; *Cal. Proc. in Chanc. Eliz. I* (Rec. Com.), i. 320.
[23] C 142/750/122.
[24] C.P. 25(2)/610/1649 Mich.
[25] See below.
[26] E 310/23/126/34; *Cal. Pat.* 1560–3, 2.
[27] E 310/23/126/34.
[28] *Cal. Pat.* 1560–3, 2.
[29] C.P. 25(2)/204/4 Eliz. I East.
[30] Feet of Fines, 7 Eliz. I Hil. (calendar only); C.P. 25(2)/205/21 & 22 Eliz. I Mich.

[31] C 66/1212.
[32] C 66/1372.
[33] *S. & D. N. & Q.* xxiii. 145–7.
[34] *S.R.S.* xv. 100.
[35] *Cal. Cttee. for Money,* ii. 1106.
[36] S.R.O., DD/HW 1.
[37] Ibid.; C.P. 25(2)/762/29 Chas. II Mich.
[38] S.R.O., DD/HW 1, 14.
[39] Hutchins, *Hist. Dors.* i. 443; S.R.O., DD/HW 1.
[40] Gravestone in Stoke churchyard.
[41] S.R.O., D/G/Y 159, 160.
[42] Gravestone in Stoke churchyard; *Dioc. Dir.* (1915–45).
[43] Correspondence relating to patronage, *penes* the vicar.
[44] *Properties of the National Trust* (1969), 148.
[45] S.R.O., DD/HW 1, 14–15.
[46] Ibid. 11, 14–15.
[47] Ibid. 16.
[48] Ibid. 9–10; *P.O. Dir. Som.* (1875).
[49] S.R.O., D/G/Y 159, 160.

by small farmers, a 'fancy-box manufacturer',[50] and a glove manufacturer.[51]

The value of the rectorial tithes in 1545 was about £30.[52] By the end of the 18th century they were worth over £206, in 1814 £202, and in 1823–4 £282.[53] The gross rent-charge in lieu of tithes was assessed in 1840 at £447 10s.[54] By 1793 the tithe on arable land and orchards was reckoned at 5s. an acre, on mowing at 1s. 6d. an acre, on apples in the hedgerows at 4 guineas. A modus was claimed by the impropriator, but later disputed, of 8d. for every cow in milk, 1d. for every sheep, ½d. for lambs, and 1s. for colts.[55] The tenant of the property in 1814 claimed for his landlord 1d. for each old sheep, ½d. for lambs, 6d. for each calf, and 2d. for each cow in milk and each barren bullock.[56] In 1839 the modus of 8d. for each cow in lieu of calf or milk, 1d. for each sheep and its wool, and ½d. for each lamb was accepted.[57]

In 1545 the glebe lands of the rectory seem largely to have been let for rent, producing £11 5s. 8½d.; only land worth £1 19s. 4d. was held in demesne.[58] In addition there were lands and tenements attached to St. Nicholas's chapel, amounting to over 164 a. of arable and over 30 a. of meadow and pasture.[59] In 1814 the glebe land in Stoke amounted to just over 149 a.[60] and in 1839 to just over 151 a.[61]

The 'large house in the village' which in Leland's time was the lodging of the provost of the college and formerly housed the priests of the community, was one of the properties granted to the chantry priests in 1304, and may perhaps have been the rectory house.[62] For a hundred years from the mid 18th century the property was simply known as the Farm, and then as the Parsonage or Parsonage Farm. Its present name, the Priory, was first used in 1902.[63] The buildings, which include a dwelling-house, two large barns, and a dovecot, are grouped round a yard bounded along North Street by a high wall.[64] The wall is pierced by a postern (now blocked) and an arched gateway. Much of the house dates from the 15th century, although the presence of several ogee-headed openings suggests that parts may be of 14th-century origin. Structural alterations were made in the 16th and 17th centuries but the almost continuous occupation of the house by tenant farmers since that time has resulted in few subsequent changes. The building is L-shaped, consisting of a south wing along the street frontage and a principal range at right angles to it. A buttressed two-storeyed chapel block, surmounted by a bellcot, and a buttressed two-storeyed porch project from the principal range on its north or entrance front. The three west bays of the range comprise a single-storeyed open hall with an arch-braced collar-beam roof, the trusses of which were repaired and reinstated c. 1961. To the south of the most westerly bay is a small projecting room or recess which may have been the priests' parlour. Its end

wall, like that of the hall, is not medieval and the house may originally have extended further west. A large pointed window in the south wall of the parlour was blocked in the 17th century when floors, fire-places, and new windows were inserted and both hall and parlour became two-storeyed. Until c. 1960 this end of the house was used for farm storage.

Across the east end of the hall the former screens-passage is entered from the porch and has a 15th-century doorway at each end; the gallery above is a modern replacement. The partition truss at the back of the gallery was exposed during restoration in 1966–7. At its south end a jointed cruck has survived but at the north end the structural evidence had already been destroyed by decay. Also revealed at this time were the two sockets which had contained the feet of the former truss across the two-storeyed east end of the range.[65] Further east the two remaining bays of the range may originally have contained service rooms on the ground floor and the priests' dormitory above. From the upper room a door leads to the former chapel which has an original piscina. The small room below the chapel has an ogee-headed external doorway and both a doorway and a hatch communicating with the former service rooms. In the 16th century these service rooms were converted into a living room, probably by Thomas Strode, whose initials and the date 1585 appear on part of what remains of the panelling.

The three bays at the south end of the rear wing are medieval and may represent the single-storeyed kitchen of the priests' dwelling, originally detached from the principal range. The structure which now joins the two ranges was probably built in the 16th century. Its roof extends over the east end of the principal range but traces of the former medieval roof are visible internally. Nearly all the stone-mullioned windows in the house are insertions of the 16th and 17th centuries but original windows survive in the chapel and in the room above the porch.

The circular dovecot, west of the farmyard, has a pointed doorway and once had a conical roof. One of the two barns, both probably built in the 18th century, was gutted by fire in 1969.

ECONOMIC HISTORY. In 1086 there were three estates in Stoke; two held by Robert son of Ives became the manor of Stoke, and one by Mauger de Cartrai became the manor of Stokett. Together the estates measured 10 hides, and the demesne holdings 6 hides and a virgate. The demesnes on Robert's two estates amounted to 4½ hides; 5 serfs with two ploughs worked the larger part, but neither serfs nor ploughs are recorded on the smaller demesne. Mauger's demesne of 1¾ hide was worked by 7 serfs with 2 ploughs. Two villeins[66] and 18 bordars tenanted Robert's estates, and there was

[50] *Kelly's Dir. Som.* (1897).
[51] Ibid. (1910, 1915).
[52] *Valor Eccl.* (Rec. Com.), i. 199. The total figure included unspecified casual offerings.
[53] S.R.O., DD/HW 4, 14.
[54] S.R.O., tithe award.   [55] S.R.O., DD/HW 14.
[56] Ibid.   [57] S.R.O., tithe award.
[58] *Valor Eccl.* (Rec. Com.), i. 199.
[59] Collinson, *Hist. Som.* iii. 318.
[60] S.R.O., DD/HW 14.
[61] S.R.O., tithe award.

[62] Leland, *Itin.* ed. Toulmin Smith, i. 159; Collinson, *Hist. Som.* iii. 316–18; *Cal. Pat.* 1334–8, 254.
[63] S.R.O., D/P/st. u. ham 4/1/1: chwdns'. accts. 1728–1853, sub anno 1743; *Kelly's Dir. Som., passim*; *S. & D. N. & Q.* xxiv. 9.
[64] See plate facing p. 145.
[65] Ex inf. Sir R. de Z. Hall and Mr. F. L. Hannam of Messrs. Burrough and Hannam (architects of the 1966–7 restoration).
[66] The Exon Domesday says 9: *V.C.H. Som.* i. 475; Darby and Finn, *Dom. Geog. S.W. Eng.* 402.

a villein and a bordar at Stokett. The recorded area was predominantly arable, having only 45 a. of meadow, 15¼ a. of pasture, and 7 a. of wood. Between them, however, the estates supported 2 riding-horses, 14 beasts, 10 pigs, 6 cows, and 40 sheep, suggesting a large amount of unrecorded pasture. The value of Robert's holdings was given as £7 for the larger and 40s. for the smaller; Mauger's land was worth 60s. when the count acquired it, but in 1086 only 40s.[67]

By 1287 the value of the Beauchamp holding had increased nominally to nearly £102, including a cash assessment of services. In practice the income varied between about £83 and £89 depending on which fields lay fallow. The demesne farm, worth £71 14s. 1d., comprised 385 a. of arable, 48½ a. of meadow, and just over 113 a. of pasture, including 80 a. on Ham Hill, some of which was woodland. There were also woods round the hill, of unknown value and extent. The tenants already held in three different ways: 13 virgaters held in villeinage and one for two lives, and 4 half-virgaters were freeholders. Two tenants with 1½ 'ferling' held for their lives; 20 with a 'ferling' were in villeinage, but 2 others were freeholders, and 1 held for his life. Tenants of messuages and curtilages, totalling 8, held variously, but all 8 cottagers were customary.[68]

On the woodland and pasture of Ham Hill in 1248 the Beauchamps established a warren.[69] In 1339 a thousand rabbits were stolen from it.[70] In 1456–7 it was unstocked and valueless, though it remained part of the demesne estate until the end of the 16th century.[71]

The abandonment of the warren was but one result of the absence of the lords of the manor, most noticeable after the death of Sir Matthew Gournay in 1406. A more important effect was the gradual disappearance of the demesne estate. The Beauchamps had a holding of nearly 500 a. in 1287[72] and of over 350 a. in 1361.[73] By the mid 15th century all the demesnes were let, over 230 a. being arable and over 110 a. meadow and pasture.[74] The demesnes of Stokett manor had almost certainly disappeared by the end of the 14th century also.[75] In 1456–7 the Stoke demesnes were described as being farmed; in practice they were granted out as copyholds, and by the early 17th century could not be distinguished from ancient customary land.[76] In 1456 arable lands thus let were described as 'overland, formerly demesne';[77] all that remained of

the Beauchamp holding in 1615 was the site of the fortified manor-house and some gardens.[78]

The increase in customary holdings in the manor of Stoke further accentuated the financial insignificance of freeholds. In 1456–7 only 27s. rent was payable by freehold tenants, compared with over £24 from the farm of the former demesne and over £22 from ancient customary holdings.[79] Only one freehold existed by the mid 17th century.[80] In contrast in 1456–7 there were 14 customary tenants holding half a virgate, 19 holding a 'ferdell' or fardel, 8 half a 'ferdell', and 19 a cottage.[81] By the mid 17th century there were 107 separate copyholds held by 72 tenants.[82] In terms of acreage 417 a. were freehold and 946 a. copyhold by 1775.[83] Increasingly during the 19th century copyholds were surrendered in order to be replaced by leaseholds.[84]

In 1442 holders of half virgates and 'ferdells' paid £12 in lieu of services due from 1 February to 10 September,[85] but subsequent accounts, based at first on a rental made in 1447, omit this item, free and customary tenants thereafter paying only rent for their holdings.[86] The reorganization produced an income from Stoke varying from £42 to £57 according to surviving accounts up to 1545.[87] Other tenurial traditions survived longer. In the mid 17th century tenants held by copyhold for three lives, with a widow's estate. Entry fines were arbitrary, but sitting tenants could renew 'upon such reasonable prices' as others would give. Heriots were payable on most holdings, though some compounding had taken place. An heir on the death of a tenant had the option of paying an acre of his best wheat in lieu of best beast or goods.[88] Heriots were sporadically paid until the manorial court ceased to sit after 1889.[89]

In 1615 customary holdings were variously described, according to the size of the heriot payable, as 'whole places', 'half places', 'tofts', and 'cottages'.[90] Some of these terms were still applied at the end of the 18th century in reckoning the share of common pasture attached to each holding. The largest was then known as a 'leaze'. A 'place' was half a 'leaze', a 'leg' a quarter, and a 'claw' or 'toft' an eighth.[91]

A three-field system of cultivation was in operation in West Stoke in the later 13th century, apparently involving eight separate fields,[92] and a similar system obtained at East Stoke at the end of

[67] V.C.H. Som. i. 474–5.
[68] S.R.S. xxxv. 10–24.
[69] Cal. Chart. R. 1226–57, 330.
[70] Cal. Pat. 1338–40, 369.
[71] S.C. 6/1095/7; C 66/1108.
[72] See n. 87, below.
[73] S.R.S. xxxv. 10 sqq.; Cal. Inq. p.m. xi, pp. 24–5.
[74] S.C. 6/1095/7. Parts of the manor lay outside the parish of Stoke, in Ilchester, Kingsdon, and Chilthorne Domer.
[75] This is assumed from the existence of a substantial non-manorial estate there by 1389: Cal. Inq. Misc. v, p. 142.
[76] S.C. 6/1095/7; L.R. 2/207 f. 20v.
[77] S.C. 6/1095/7.
[78] L.R. 2/207 f. 20v. In 1574 a dovehouse in the court and two small pieces of land also survived: C 66/1108. They are given in detail in E 310/23/128/27 and Cal. Pat. 1557–8, 19.
[79] S.C. 6/1095/7.
[80] E 317/Somerset 38 pp. 3, 30 (Parliamentary survey

1650); D.C.O., misc. bound vol. including rental, 1661. The glebe holding was, of course, also freehold.
[81] S.C. 6/1095/7.
[82] D.C.O., rental, 1661. See also E 317/Somerset 38.
[83] D.C.O., survey and map, 1775–6.
[84] Ibid. ct. bks. 1793–1889.
[85] S.C. 6/1123/1.
[86] S.C. 6/1123/3; /1095/7; D.C.O., roll 300.
[87] S.C. 6/974/9 (1443); /1095/7 (1456–7); /1123/3 (1476–7); /Hen. VIII/3030 (1514–15); /Hen. VIII/3031 (1515–16); /Hen. VIII/3032 (1517–18); /Hen. VIII/345 m. 10 (1518–19); /Hen. VIII/3033 (1520–1); /Hen. VIII/ 3034 (1542–3); /Hen. VIII/3037 (1543–4); /Hen. VIII/ 3036 (1544–5); E 310/23/128/27 (1557); D.C.O., roll 300 (1474–5).
[88] E 317/Somerset 38 p. 30.
[89] D.C.O., ct. rolls and ct. bks. 1661–1889.
[90] L.R. 2/207 f. 20v.; Royal Libr., Windsor, survey by John Norden, 1615.
[91] D.C.O., survey, 1775.
[92] S.R.S. xxxv. 11–12, 23.

the 14th century.[93] Wheat, oats, barley, beans, and peas were grown at West Stoke in the 15th century.[94] By 1615 there were 15 common arable fields in the parish, of which 12 were at West Stoke.[95] They were farmed by a three-course rotation of Lent cornfields, wheat fields, and fallow.[96] The same number of fields survived until the early 19th century.[97] In 1814 some 372 a. were devoted to wheat, 273 a. to Lent corn, hemp, and flax, and 325 a. to small crops and fallow.[98]

Stoke manor also included a common arable close called Quantie,[99] two common meadows, East and West mead, and common pastures called Rixon or Rexon, Ham, and Islehams.[1] Rixon was stinted according to the size of heriot, a 'whole place', for example, being allowed 10 rother beasts or a horse and 60 sheep. Ham was let to the highest bidders, in 1672 to pay for fencing the corn fields.[2] Common on Ham Hill (c. 100 a.), for sheep only, could be used by the parish all the year.[3] Areas around the open fields, either closes[4] or common 'wayles', walls, or landshares,[5] were also available at certain times of the year.[6] Clarkum Walls, for example, was to be common to the parish after the first acre of grain had been cut in Upfield until the first acre had been sown in the same field. It was to lie common all the time Upfield remained fallow.[7]

Attempts were made to have the parish inclosed in the later 18th century. Some tenants were said in 1798 to be 'so extremely ill natured, that sooner than others should reap any advantage they would forego their own'.[8] The 'common field state'[9] of Stoke remained unchanged in 1809, though it was then considered 'peculiarly adapted for inclosure at a small expense'.[10] By 1840 two of the smaller open fields, Huish's and Humbershill, had been wholly inclosed, and only small strips remained of several others. West mead was also permanently divided.[11] The pace then quickened, though Great field was still being cultivated traditionally in the 1890s,[12] and vestiges of both Great and Furlong fields were visible in the 1960s.

Despite such conservatism the standard of farming was high in Stoke at the end of the 18th century. The arable land was 'kindly and pretty well managed, the Stoke farmers being very industrious and esteemed some of the best husbandmen in those parts'.[13] Pasture land was considered good,

though the method of watering the meadow was 'somewhat peculiar'. Drowning the meadow from Autumn to Spring as deep as possible often produced a good grass crop but only if land were naturally dry. In 1798 a surveyor thought Stoke was 'one of the best cultivated manors' within his memory, and he was particularly struck by the apple trees planted round the fields, which presented 'the idea of gardens or orchards rather than farms'.[14] By 1809, however, the report was less favourable. Rixon common was 'daily getting worse for want of a few strong drains which are not likely to be made whilst in a state of commonage', and the inclosed lands were little improved.[15]

More than half the parish, some 703 a., was arable in 1840, a proportion probably little changed since medieval times.[16] Wheat, Lent corn, hemp, and flax were the main crops in the early 19th century.[17] The seed wheat came from Taunton Deane. No break was used in making hemp, the poor stripping the stalks by hand in winter. The stalks were then used as fuel.[18] The acreage under flax was said to have been increased c. 1824.[19] No very large orchards existed in 1776, but cider was 'tolerable'; by 1809 the orchards were 'much attended to' and the local cider bore 'a good name in the county'.[20] About 400 sheep and 200 lambs were kept in the parish c. 1814.[21] Many changes occurred in land use in the later 19th century, since by 1905 grassland was more than double the area of arable.[22]

Although with the advent of gloving and other manufactures the balance of the economy was altered, agriculture still played an important part. As many as 167 families out of 240 were engaged in it in 1821 despite the rapid rise in population that gloving had produced.[23] The value of the duchy of Cornwall property improved markedly: from £857 in 1775 it rose to £1,044 in 1784, £1,269 in 1798, £1,410 in 1809, and £1,581 in 1837.[24] Individual farming units, however, remained small. The largest was Parsonage farm, the former glebe estate, comprising 151 a. in 1840.[25] It was followed by the 111 a. in the hands of John Chaffey, then attached to East Stoke House. Chaffey also had a farm of 91 a. Lower East Stoke farm, formerly Lower farm,[26] measured 84 a. There were four other holdings between 43 a. and 53 a.[27] A century later much

[93] *Cal. Inq. Misc.* vi, p. 228.
[94] S.C. 6/1123/1.
[95] L.R. 2/207 f. 20v.; Windsor Castle, Norden's survey, 1615.
[96] D.C.O., ct. rolls, *passim*.
[97] See below.
[98] S.R.O., DD/HW 4.
[99] In 1776 it was known as Quantick or Quanty, and lay by the Foss Way, south-west of Venn bridge: D.C.O., map, 1776.
[1] In 1287 it was known as Eham and in 1775 as Yahams or Yeams, and was the island formed between the original course of the Parrett and the mill race: *S.R.S.* xxxv. 12; D.C.O., survey, 1775.
[2] D.C.O., ct. rolls, Oct. 1663, Oct. 1672. See also new regulations for Ham and Rixon in ct. roll, Oct. 1748.
[3] L.R. 2/207 f. 21.
[4] e.g. Lydemead Close, which was common to Lydens Field: D.C.O., ct. roll, Oct. 1748.
[5] e.g. Landshare furlong in Holloway (Holy) field, adjacent to Landshareswell mead, and Landshare Hither, Middle, and Further crofts: map, 1776. Lanschovewyl occurs in 1287: *S.R.S.* xxxv. 12.
[6] e.g. D.C.O., ct. roll, Apr. 1661.

[7] D.C.O., ct. roll, Oct. 1748.
[8] Ibid. survey, 1798.
[9] Ibid. survey, 1775.
[10] Ibid. emendations (1809) to survey, 1775.
[11] S.R.O., tithe award.
[12] S.R.O., D/P/st. u. ham 23/1: volume of photographs.
[13] D.C.O., survey, 1775.
[14] Ibid. survey, 1798.
[15] Ibid. survey, 1809.
[16] S.R.O., tithe award.
[17] S.R.O., DD/HW 4.
[18] D.C.O., survey, 1775.
[19] S.R.O., DD/HW 15.
[20] D.C.O., surveys, 1775 and 1809.
[21] S.R.O., DD/HW 14.
[22] Statistics supplied by the then Bd. of Agric. (1905).
[23] C. & J. Greenwood, *Som. Delineated.*
[24] D.C.O., surveys, 1775, 1784, 1798, 1809; valuation, 1837.
[25] S.R.O., tithe award.
[26] Lower farm in 1840 was known as Staplehurst farm in 1886: O.S. Map 6", Som. LXXXII. SW., SE. (1888 edn.).
[27] S.R.O., tithe award.

consolidation had taken place, four holdings being over 150 a. each.[28]

The outcrop of shelly limestone known as Ham Hill occurs in the three parishes of Stoke, Norton sub Hamdon, and Montacute. Quarrying has taken place since Roman times at several points on the hill. Quarries in Stoke are known to have been used by the end of the Middle Ages, ten on lease in 1456–7.[29] Twenty years later 14 more had been opened, let for 4d. each. The abbot of Ford (Dors.) was a lessee. One quarry was then worked out, and another was described as a 'hoterell' quarraria petrarum', called Jopesboure. One of the fourteen was a 'quarraria lapidarum', 24 ft. square, for which a new tenant, Arnold Craftman, had paid an entry fine of 6s. 8d.[30]

The total income from the quarries was 3s. 4d. in 1515 and remained at this figure at least until 1545.[31] By the early 17th century the quarries in Stoke had evidently given place to those in Norton, though 'very famous far'.[32] Gerard wrote in 1633 of 'the goodliest quarry of freestone' he ever saw, where masons tried cases of trespass in their own court in a 'pretty kind of commonwealth'. The quarries themselves were then 'rather little parishes than quarries, so many buildings have they under the vast works to shelter themselves in wet weather, and their wrought stone in winter'.[33]

By the end of the 18th century Stoke's quarries were leased by the duchy of Cornwall to the Phelipses of Montacute. Though 'greatly exhausted' they still showed a profit. Quarries 20 ft. square were let each year at 6d. a square foot and 10s. a year lord's rent. Tile as well as freestone was taken, the tilers paying 1d. a cwt. The whole was valued in 1776 at £41 10s.[34] By 1798 the quarry was 'already run over in such a manner that the workmen scarcely know where to look for another'.[35]

By 1850 the quarries were being worked by nine tenants, paying at rates varying between 5d. and 1s. a foot.[36] In 1863 a tramway to carry stone from Stoke to Watergore was proposed.[37] Two masons were active in Stoke in the 1860s,[38] and by 1875 there were three small firms of stone merchants.[39] Expansion was short-lived, though the Ham Hill and Doulting Stone Co. apparently had business in the parish by 1908 at least until the Second World War.[40] A little stone was still taken in 1968, but quarrying had long ceased to be significant to the economy of the parish.

For more than a century Stoke was one of the most important gloving centres in the county. The beginning of the industry is obscure, but by 1798 some 'very poor huts' on the waste on Ham Hill housed many people employed in the industry.[41] The villagers did not like the settlers for they tried to pull down their dwellings and frighten them away.[42] The rapid increase in population between 1801 and 1821 was attributed to the growth of the industry.[43] By 1836 Amos Ashford had established a factory in the village,[44] and by 1844 there were four factories.[45] The firm of Southcombe Brothers began on the initiative of Richard Southcombe,[46] and by 1861 he, John Walter, and James Slade were in business.[47] Southcombe expanded his business, becoming also a linen- and woollen-draper and silk-mercer, presumably in connexion with the silk and taffeta gloves he manufactured.[48] By the late 1860s his firm was producing some 3,000 dozen pairs of fabric gloves each week. In 1873 Richard Southcombe built a new factory for leather gloves in Cole Lane, and with the serious slump in the fabric glove trade, his firm introduced the manufacture of gaiters and spats.[49] In 1897 and 1902 four firms were in business in Stoke, but by 1910 only three, that of William Brooks concentrating on housemaids' gloves.[50] There were five firms in 1923, and seven at the beginning of the Second World War. There were in 1968 four, only Southcombe's and Walter's dating from the 19th century.[51]

Stoke has also been the scene of other small industries, including the manufacture of fancy-boxes by 1875, of ginger beer by 1897, and of radio receivers by 1939.[52] The firm of Waterman and Son, box manufacturers and printers, of West Street, had been founded by 1897.[53] By 1844 there were six shops in the village.[54] At the beginning of the Second World War Stoke had taken on its present appearance, with some twenty shops including a house-furnisher's and refreshment rooms, two banks, and other commercial enterprises.[55]

In the Domesday survey there were two mills on Stoke manor, paying together 9s., and a mill on the later manor of Stokett worth 40d.[56] Nothing further is known of Stokett's mill, which was probably sited on Wellham's brook. By 1284 the rent of a mill near Petherton Bridge on the Parrett, worth 100s., had been temporarily alienated from the manor, but the other water-mill produced a rent of 30s.[57] Both were still part of the demesne in 1361.[58]

A century later Petherton Mill, as it was called,

28 Kelly's Dir. Som. (1939).
29 S.C. 6/1095/7; see L. F. Salzman, Building in Eng. 133.
30 S.C. 6/1123/3; D.C.O., roll 300 (1474–5) gives similar information. Apart from the abbot of Ford, tenants included Richard Typper, who held three quarries, Thomas Vestmentmaker, and Thomas Trevilian. These men do not occur as tenants of the manor.
31 S.C. 6/Hen. VIII/3030–2, 3034–6.
32 L.R. 2/207 f. 21.
33 S.R.S. xv. 102.
34 D.C.O., survey, 1775.
35 Ibid. survey, 1798.
36 Ibid. rental, 1850.
37 S.R.O., DD/HW 14.
38 P.O. Dir. Som. (1861, 1866).   39 Ibid. (1875).
40 Kelly's Dir. Som. (1908, 1939).
41 D.C.O., survey, 1798; Joseph Winter, glover, occurs 1747–66: S.R.O., D/B/il 6 ('Manor of Stocklinch'), p. 26; Q/R jurors' bk. 1697–1766.
42 D.C.O., survey, 1798.

43 C. & J. Greenwood, Som. Delineated.
44 S.R.O., DD/HW 12.
45 Ibid. 6: poor rate bk.
46 R. E. Southcombe, 'Southcombe Brothers Limited, Stoke under Ham' (TS. in S.R.O.).
47 P.O. Dir. Som. (1861).
48 Morris & Co. Dir. Som. (1872).
49 Southcombe, 'Southcombe Brothers Limited'; Kelly's Dir. Som. (1897, 1910). They also made shirts and sailor suits for boys.
50 Kelly's Dir. Som. (1897, 1902, 1910).
51 Local information.
52 P.O. Dir. Som. (1875); Kelly's Dir. Som. (1897, 1939).
53 Kelly's Dir. Som. (1897).
54 S.R.O., DD/HW 6: poor rate bk.
55 Kelly's Dir. Som. (1939).
56 V.C.H. Som. i. 474–5.
57 Cal. Inq. p.m. ii, p. 327; S.R.S. xxxv. 14.
58 Cal. Inq. p.m. xi, pp. 24–5.

was let for £4 17s. 5d. and an adjoining fulling mill for a mark.[59] Roger Garland held Petherton Mill in 1514–15, and John Axe the elder the fulling mill,[60] and rent was still paid for both at least until 1545.[61] Only one mill, the corn-mill, was mentioned in 1557.[62] In 1650 it was held by Mary Carter for the lives of her children and was called Stoke Mill.[63] A custom of the manor stated that tenants were to grind their corn at that mill 'so long as they are used well'.[64] In 1809 there was trouble with the water-supply. Petherton Bridge Mill, as it was then called, had an undershot wheel. Joylers Mill, next down the river, penned up the water and prevented it from working.[65] The family of Shore held the mill by 1759, and continued to have an interest until the end of the 19th century when the mill was abandoned.[66]

A fair on Hamdon formed part of the count of Mortain's foundation grant to Montacute priory c. 1102.[67] By 1118 the fair lasted for thirteen days,[68] but there is no further trace of it in medieval times. By c. 1615 a fair was held on Ham Hill on St. Mark's Day (25 April), but no profits were taken from it.[69] By 1767 there was a market for 'all sorts of cattle and pedlary',[70] evidently held in and around a building called the fairhouse.[71] By 1775 the tolls were 'scarcely worth collecting', largely because Mr. Phelips of Montacute was exercising 'great pains' to encourage Montacute's fair on the same day.[72] The tolls of the fair and the fair royalty were then let for 5 guineas.[73] By 1798 the fair had 'very little left besides the name', and the fair house was in 'a decaying state'.[74] The fair royalty and house, with a total rental of 14s. 4d., were leased to John Phelips for 31 years from 1810,[75] but no fair was apparently held. By 1841 the house was used as a poorhouse, though the fair, for pedlary, was said to be still held in 1861 and 1866.[76] It was described as a pleasure fair by 1872, and a stock fair by 1897.[77] A pleasure fair continued in 1969, but was held on the Recreation Ground.

LOCAL GOVERNMENT. In 1275–6 John Beauchamp (I) (d. 1283) claimed free warren and the assize of bread and ale, the former by charter, the latter by usage.[78] His claim to take strays, probably also in Stoke, was then challenged.[79] No court rolls have survived from the period of the Beauchamp tenure, and indeed not until the manor came into Crown hands. At a court described as curia legalis

held in 1540 the lord was exercising the assize of bread and ale and holding a view of frankpledge.[80] Court rolls survive from the time the duchy of Cornwall resumed the property in 1661 until 1792, and court books from then until 1889.[81]

Stokett was considered a tithing of Tintinhull manor at the end of the 16th century. About 1597 three freeholders there all owed suit of court to the manor,[82] and one of the holdings, that of Sir Thomas Freke, had rights of common in Tintinhull West field.[83] Neither the origin nor the subsequent history of this connexion has been traced, though doubt was raised in 1566 about the legal status of the tithing.[84] In 1627 Stokett was still held of the lord of Tintinhull hundred.[85]

By 1540 the courts for Stoke manor were held twice a year, in the spring and autumn; from the mid 17th century they were usually described as curia legalis, view of frankpledge, and court baron at each session, though by the 19th century this had been modified to 'general court baron and customary court'. Courts baron were held at other times as occasion required. The two main manorial officers, the tithingman and the hayward, were in evidence by 1540, the former being elected at the spring or Hockday court.[86] By the mid 17th century their elections were usually held at the October court, and by that time the number of officers had increased. The senior was the tithingman, who continued to be appointed until 1843. With him was the hayward, who served until the court ceased to meet after 1889. In 1661 there were two haywards and two 'viewers of fences' to sell and dispose of the common 'wayles' or verges.[87] In 1663, in addition to the hayward, later known as the 'town hayward',[88] there were two 'grass haywards' and also two men to supervise the letting of the common on Ham Hill.[89] These offices were still in existence in 1672, when there was an additional man to oversee the work of the two grass haywards or grass reeves.[90] The hayward was sometimes known as the reeve during the earlier 18th century, and the term 'hayward and bailiff' occurs in 1748. A separate officer, a bailiff, was mentioned as late as 1856, though he was not a servant of the court.[91] The hayward and the tithingman were chosen from those holding a unit of common known as a leaze.

Despite the dominance of a single landowner in Stoke the business of the manorial court was almost exclusively agricultural. By 1728 there was an open vestry which appointed both churchwardens and

[59] S.C. 6/1095/7. In 1442 the income from the fulling mill was described as 'new rent': S.C. 6/1123/1. In 1456–7 the weir had been damaged by floods, and iron-work was required to repair the mill.
[60] S.C. 6/Hen. VIII/3030.
[61] S.C. 6/Hen. VIII/3036.
[62] E 310/23/128/27; Cal. Pat. 1557–8, 19.
[63] L.R. 2/207 f. 21; E 317/Somerset 38 p. 16.
[64] E 317/Somerset 38 p. 31.
[65] D.C.O., surveys, 1775 and 1809.
[66] Ibid. survey of leasehold and copyhold estates, 1783; Kelly's Dir. Som. (1883, 1897); S.R.O., tithe award. S.R.O., D/P/st. u. ham 23/1 includes a photograph of the mill when derelict.
[67] S.R.S. viii. 119; Reg. Regum Anglo-Norm. ii, pp. 50, 348.
[68] S.R.S. viii. 120.
[69] L.R. 2/207 f. 21.
[70] Bk. of Fairs, 69.
[71] The remains of this building were visible in 1968 at the rear of the Prince of Wales inn.

[72] D.C.O., survey, 1775.
[73] Ibid.
[74] Ibid. survey, 1798.
[75] Ibid. 'Book of Extracts, 1794 etc.'.
[76] Ibid., valuation, 1841; P.O. Dir. Som. (1861, 1866).
[77] Morris and Co. Dir. Som. (1872); Kelly's Dir. Som. (1897).
[78] Plac. de Quo Warr. (Rec. Com.), 691–2.
[79] Rot. Hund. (Rec. Com.), ii. 140.
[80] S.C. 2/198/61.
[81] D.C.O.
[82] Devon R.O. 123 M/E 33.
[83] Ibid. E 35.
[84] Ibid. E 91.
[85] C 142/750/122.
[86] S.C. 2/198/61.
[87] D.C.O., ct. roll, 1661.
[88] Ibid. 1663, 1672.
[89] Ibid. 1672. There was a return to this system by 1736 until 1748.
[90] D.C.O., ct. rolls, 1672, 1681.
[91] Ibid. ct. bk. 1855–89.

presumably levied the poor-rate.[92] A select vestry was formed in 1826 by order of a local magistrate.[93] Two overseers were nominated until 1896, two, and later one, surveyor or waywarden until 1893, and a parish constable, paid only in the first year, between 1842 and 1872, were appointed by the vestry. A paid assistant overseer, acting for a time also as surveyor and rate collector, was employed for a short period from 1827 and also in the 1860s; and there was a paid vestry clerk from 1873. The only other employee was the parish molecatcher.

Until 1836 the vestry concerned itself mainly with poor-relief, and subsequently with the repair of roads. A nuisance committee was formed in 1872 and a sanitary committee in 1890. Lighting in the village was installed by the vestry in 1892. The strength of nonconformity in the parish was evident in the attempt to appoint a nonconformist as churchwarden in 1887, and in the pressure upon the vestry to subject the voluntary school to the school board in 1899.

A poorhouse was built by the parishioners by 1615, but in 1625 was not properly used.[94] By 1776 the parish poorhouse stood at the western end of the village, almost opposite the end of the present road to Norton.[95] The parish also owned a house in Castle Street.[96] Neither, apparently, was in use to house paupers in 1803.[97] The parish became part of the Yeovil poor-law union in 1836, but it still owned twelve cottages in 1839, including the poorhouse, the most westerly of the group of houses opposite the church.[98] There were four others in Castle Street, with the site of a fifth, and one in West Stoke. These were sold in 1840–1.[99] The parish officers also used the fair house, behind the present Prince of Wales inn on Ham Hill, to house paupers. By 1841 it was 'a very poor building' consisting 'merely of a room on the ground floor where the paupers have been stowed in a very uncomfortable manner'.[1]

CHURCH. Architectural evidence places the foundation of the church in Norman times or earlier.[2] The first known rector was recorded in 1174 × 1180,[3] and the benefice, valued at £20 in 1291,[4] remained a rectory, presumably in the patronage of the lords of Stoke manor,[5] until 1304. In that year it was appropriated to the new college of priests attached to St. Nicholas's chapel in the courtyard of Stoke

manor-house,[6] and a vicarage was ordained. The arrangement was to take effect on the death of the then rector. The vicarage was endowed with a house, land, and a third of the tithes, and its advowson belonged to the college.[7] In 1375, however, after disputes about the vicar's income, it was agreed that on the next vacancy the vicarage itself should be appropriated to the college,[8] whose provosts thereafter either served the cure themselves or appointed chaplains.[9]

After the dissolution of the college in 1548 the lessees, and later the owners, of the rectory estate were charged with paying the stipend of a curate.[10] In the 17th century the stipend was usually £30 a year,[11] and by 1796 had been increased *ex gratia* to £42.[12] In 1826 the lay rector agreed to a permanent charge on his estate and an augmentation from Queen Anne's Bounty[13] raised the curate's living to £89.[14] The perpetual curacy was further augmented in 1842 with money raised for building a glebe house:[15] the living was estimated at £109 gross in 1851.[16] The curacy had no glebe until 1877 when 2 a. were given as the site for a house,[17] which was built the following year.[18] The patronage of the perpetual curacy remained with the lay rectors until 1947, when it was transferred to the Church Patronage Trust.[19]

The provosts of the college who were also rectors of Stoke are unlikely to have taken more than a nominal share in parish work, and parochial chaplains such as Thomas Cox in 1450 and 1468 served the cure.[20] In 1532 Master John Glynne (provost 1508–34) employed both a curate and a chaplain;[21] his successor in 1548 did the same.[22] Little is known of later incumbents, the small income evidently not attracting prominent clergy. Thomas Tintiney was reported in 1623 for omitting prayers on the Monday in Whitsun week and for incontinence with his wife before marriage.[23] John Limberley's income was sequestrated during the Interregnum.[24] Reginald Bean relinquished the cure in 1775 because of the smallness of the stipend, and apologized to the patron that Stoke had 'been but badly supplied since I have not been able to officiate myself through an ill state of health'. He added that since the tithe estate was so large in comparison with the small benefice income, 'scarce any clergyman will choose to accept it upon the present footing'.[25] This comment was made on a number of occasions until the living was augmented.[26] Most of

[92] S.R.O., D/P/st. u. ham 4/1/1: chwdns.' accts. 1728–1853.
[93] S.R.O., D/PC/st. u. ham 1/1–3: vestry min. bks. 1826–94 (continued as parish meeting mins. until 1964).
[94] L.R. 2/207 f. 19v; *S.R.S.* xxiv. 3.
[95] D.C.O., survey and map, 1775–6.
[96] Ibid.
[97] *Poor Law Abstract, 1804.*
[98] S.R.O., tithe award; *Poor Law Com. 2nd. Rep.* p. 550.
[99] S.R.O., D/PC/st. u. ham 1/1.
[1] D.C.O., rep. on estates, Somerset, by Edward Driver. The use of the house had been recommended in 1798: ibid. survey, 1798.
[2] See below.
[3] *S.R.S.* viii. 192.
[4] *Tax. Eccl.* (Rec. Com.), 198.
[5] See p. 238.   [6] *V.C.H. Som.* ii. 161–2.
[7] Collinson, *Hist. Som.* iii. 316–18; *S.R.S.* i. 292; *Cal. Papal Regs.* ii. 63; *Cal. Pat.* 1334–8, 254.
[8] *H.M.C. Wells,* i. 278–9.
[9] *S.R.S.* ii. 117; xxx. 391; xxxii. 198; xlix. 18, 137; lii. 25; S.R.O., D/D/Vc 20.

[10] E 310/23/126/34; *Cal. Pat.* 1560–3, 2.
[11] S.R.O., D/D/Vc 24. Attempts to augment the stipend by 48s. a month were made in 1647: *Cal. Cttee. for Compounding,* ii. 1495.
[12] S.R.O., DD/HW 15, 17.
[13] Ibid. 13.
[14] *Rep. Com. Eccl. Revenues,* pp. 178–9.
[15] *Livings Aug. by Queen Anne's Bounty,* H.C. 122 (1867), liv; S.R.O., DD/HW 17.
[16] H.O. 129/319/3/3/8.
[17] S.R.O., DD/HW 17/4.
[18] Ibid. 17/1, 3, 4.
[19] Correspondence *penes* the vicar. Sir John Thynne presented by Crown grant in 1558: *S.R.S.* lv. 152.
[20] *S.R.S.* xlix. 137; lii. 25.
[21] Ibid. liv. 126; S.R.O., D/D/Vc 20.
[22] *S.R.S.* ii. 117.
[23] S.R.O., D/D/Ca 236.
[24] *Walker Revised,* ed. A. G. Matthews, 316.
[25] S.R.O., DD/HW 17/1.
[26] Ibid. 17: collection of letters from incumbents to patrons.

the early-19th-century clergy were non-resident. William Langdon (curate 1802–25) was also rector of Pylle and vicar of Montacute.[27] He only performed occasional duties at Stoke in 1815 as well as at Montacute, largely on account of blindness. His curate, T. G. Rees, who lived at Montacute, performed services at Stoke.[28] John Jarrett (curate 1826–36) lived in the parish in the early years of his curacy. By 1832, however, he was living on another benefice at North Cave (Yorks E.R.); the patron was unwilling to accept his resignation of Stoke, and he was obliged to employ curates until 1836.[29]

in 1544.[37] The property still retained its name until the late 18th century, when it became the Fleur de Lis inn.[38]

An iron mission church, dedicated to St. Nicholas, was built on a site on Ham Hill given by the duchy of Cornwall in 1905. It was closed in 1926 and services since then have been held at All Saints mission church, formerly the school. The former church is known as the Hamdon Hall.[39]

The parish church of *ST. MARY THE VIRGIN*, a mile east of the main village of West Stoke, was said in 1840 and 1859 to be dedicated to

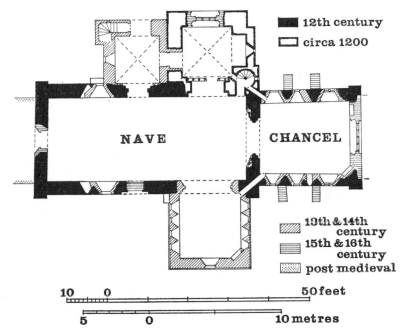

12th century
circa 1200

13th & 14th
century
15th & 16th
century
post medieval

10   0   50 feet

5   0   10 metres

THE CHURCH OF ST. MARY THE VIRGIN, STOKE SUB HAMDON

William Truell (curate 1837–52) was a relative of the patron;[30] his combative successor, William Greenslade, brought an unsuccessful action against the tenant of the lay rector for pasturing sheep in the churchyard,[31] which remained the lay rector's property until it was conveyed to the Church Commissioners in 1950.[32]

By 1815 services were held at Stoke alternately morning and afternoon;[33] just over a decade later there were two services and two sermons each Sunday.[34] This was still the pattern in 1851: on Census Sunday there was a general congregation of 73 in the morning, with 82 Sunday-school children, and 216 in the afternoon with 104 children.[35] Holy Communion was celebrated 'more than three times a year' in 1840, and ten times by 1870.[36]

A church house was evidently under construction

St. Denys.[40] In 1861 the dedication was said to be unknown.[41] From at least 1866 until about 1891 the dedication was to St. Andrew and thereafter to the Virgin.[42] The church consists of a chancel and nave, north and south transepts, the north forming the base of the tower, and a two-storeyed north porch. Vestries were added at the west end in 1916.[43] The nave and chancel are Norman and both retain pilaster buttresses at their angles. The chancel may originally have had an apsidal east end. The corbel-table below the chancel eaves survives. There are two small round-headed windows near the west end of the nave, that on the north side having its head cut from a single stone. Externally the head is carved with a man, a dragon, and interlacing orna-ment; it has been suggested that this may be Saxon work.[44] A blocked 12th-century window in the

[27] M.I. in Montacute ch.; see p. 222.
[28] S.R.O., D/D/V rtns. 1815, Stoke and Montacute.
[29] S.R.O., DD/HW 17.
[30] Foster, *Alumni Oxon.*
[31] S.R.O., DD/HW 17.
[32] MSS. *penes* the vicar.
[33] S.R.O., D/D/V rtns. 1815.
[34] Ibid. 1827.
[35] H.O. 129/319/3/3/8.
[36] S.R.O., D/D/V rtns. 1840, 1870.
[37] *S.R.S.* xl. 36, 52.
[38] D.C.O., map of Stoke (1776), leasehold and copyhold survey (1783), contracts for land tax redemption (p. 67),

rental (1850). The house was still used by parishioners in 1650: E 317/Somerset 38.
[39] MSS. *penes* the vicar, including deed poll (1905) and licence for All Saints mission ch. 1926; Char. Com. file. S.R.O., D/P/st. u. ham 2/5/1 is the service bk. of St. Nicholas's 1905–26.
[40] *County Gazette Dir. Som.* (1840); *P.O. Dir. Som.* (1859). The chapel in the north transept is dedicated to St. Denys. See plate facing p. 209.
[41] *P.O. Dir. Som.* (1861).
[42] Ibid. (1866); *Kelly's Dir. Som.* (1883); *Dioc. Kal.*
[43] By C. E. Ponting: MSS. *penes* the vicar.
[44] Pevsner, *South and West Som.* 304.

chancel is visible externally. Both north and south doorways of the nave, the latter now blocked, are of the 12th century and have flanking shafts with spiral, lozenge, and scale ornaments. On the tympanum of the north door is a relief carving of a tree of life carrying three birds, flanked on the right by a lamb and cross and an animal labelled LEO; a figure on the left is labelled SAGITARIUS [sic]. The fine 12th-century chancel arch is of three orders carved with billet, zig-zag, and lozenge ornament, the restored supporting shafts having scale and zigzag decoration.

The first addition to the Norman church was the base of the north tower which forms a stone-vaulted north transept, now used as the chapel of St. Denys. It was built c. 1200, the carved corbels from which the vaulting shafts spring being fine examples of Transitional work. A former stair projection on the east wall of the tower has been adapted as an altar recess. At the south-east angle of the transept is a combined piscina and hagioscope, the latter interrupted by a rood-loft stair. The upper part of the tower, which has twin lancets at the belfry stage, was built in the 13th century, and the parapet is a 15th-century addition.

The end of the 13th century saw the insertion of many new windows and probably the building of the south transept. Cusped lancets on both sides of the chancel near its west end are carried down as 'low side' windows. Further east two-light windows, one with later tracery, have cusped rear-arches supported on shafts. A large double piscina across the south-east angle of the chancel is of the same period. One of the two cusped lancets in the nave partly obscures the Norman window in the north wall. The south transept has four such lancets grouped together in each of its side walls, an angle piscina, and a hagioscope. A tomb recess in the south wall contains an effigy which may represent Reynold de Monkton (d. 1307), first provost of the secular college.

Later in the 14th century a window with reticulated tracery was inserted in the west wall of the nave. There is a window of similar type in the upper stage of the vaulted north porch. Externally, to the west of the porch, a canopy, the function of which is obscure, is built into the nave wall. In the 15th century the walls of the nave and south transept were raised in height and roofs of shallow pitch were constructed over them. Perpendicular windows were inserted at the east end of the chancel, above the south doorway, and in the north wall of the north transept.

The large circular font is Norman and has a moulded base and two boldly projecting bands of cable ornament, one combined with lozenges. There are fragments of 15th-century glass in the head of the east window; below is glass installed in 1949 depicting local industries. A 15th-century stone screen in the north transept arch may have been the former rood-screen. There is a canopied tomb of carved Ham stone bearing an effigy of Thomas Strode (d. 1595). The pulpit and communion rails date from the 17th century. In the churchyard is a 15th-century cross with a Crucifixion and a Madonna.

The church has six bells: (i) 1949, Taylor of Loughborough; (ii) 1787, G. Davis of Bridgwater; (iii) 1910, Taylor; (iv) 1949, Taylor; (v) 1530–70, Roger Semson of Ash Priors; (vi) 1688, Thomas Purdue of Closworth.[45] The plate includes a cup and cover inscribed with the date 1635.[46] The registers begin in 1558 but are incomplete.[47]

The free chapel of St. Nicholas, founded by 1287 and from 1304 the chapel of St. Nicholas's college, lay within the manor-house complex, on a site now occupied by the buildings of Castle farm.[48] It was evidently substantial, with more than one altar.[49] By the 16th century, although in some decay, it was still impressive; it had a nave large enough to hold seven tombs on the south-west side, five of them with recumbent effigies. There was also a wall tomb on the north side of the nave. The choir, separated from the nave by a screen, had a tomb on its north side; at the entrance to the choir was the brass over the tomb of Sir Matthew Gournay (d. 1406). The windows were filled with heraldic glass, and the floor decorated with heraldic tiles.[50] Fragments thought to have been part of the fabric are built into the walls of several houses in the village.

In the early 16th century mass was said there three times a week, though when the college was founded its members were to say fives masses daily as well as the canonical hours and the office for the dead.[51] Despite the pleas of the inhabitants that the chapel should be retained, the two bells and the lead from the roof were evidently sold,[52] and the building let with the parsonage estate.[53]

In 1535 there was a chapel on Ham Hill dedicated to the Holy Cross; oblations offered there belonged to Montacute priory as owner of Montacute rectory.[54] It probably stood near the Prince of Wales inn, where a piece of land was called Hanging Chapple in 1666,[55] and Ham Chapel in 1840.[56] Its connexion with Montacute may suggest an association with the fair on Ham Hill given by the count of Mortain to Montacute priory c. 1102.[57]

NONCONFORMITY. From 1689 onwards licences were issued for meetings in private houses, but usually the denomination was not specified.[58] By 1710, however, Henry Parsons, who in 1703 had been active in Montacute, was licensed to use his house in Stoke for meetings. Five years later he was described as the preacher in a Presbyterian meeting at Stoke, a group which was then receiving a grant from the Presbyterian Fund.[59] It is not clear

45 S.R.O., DD/SAS CH 16; Richards, Hist. Stoke, 38–9.
46 Proc. Som. Arch. Soc. xliv. 185.
47 S.R.O., D/P/st. u. ham 2/1/1–14.
48 Proc. Som. Arch. Soc. xxxv. 132–7; plan of excavation in Taunton Castle.
49 S.R.S. xxxv. 71 refers to the high altar.
50 Leland, Itin. ed. Toulmin Smith, i. 158–9. See S.R.O., DD/SAS PR 36 for details of Purbeck capitals in the chapel.

51 Collinson, Hist. Som. iii. 316–18, text of foundation deed.
52 E 117/12/21; S.R.S. ii. 116–17.
53 E 310/23/126/34.
54 Valor Eccl. (Rec. Com.), i. 196.
55 D.C.O., ct. roll, Oct. 1666.
56 S.R.O., tithe award.   57 See p. 219.
58 S.R.O., D/D/Rm, box 2; Q/RR, meeting-house lics.
59 London, Dr. Williams' Libr., Evans MS., p. 101.

whether the group survived, but in 1751 and 1753 licences for Presbyterian meetings were issued to Mary Clarke and Thomas Clothier respectively.[60] The house of Samuel Clark, 'lately used as a barn', was licensed, presumably for the same group, in 1773.[61] It may be identified with the Barn Chapel, possibly in High Street, founded before 1800 and used by Congregationalists by 1851.[62] In that year it was described as having 150 seats. Services were held on Sunday evenings and occasionally on week-days. On Census Sunday 1851 the congregation numbered 106.[63] The present Congregational chapel in North Street was opened in 1866. The infant school was added and the chapel enlarged in 1875.[64]

Quakers appear to have used a room in the village by 1715.[65] There was no established meeting there, though in 1771 unsuccessful application was made to the quarterly meeting for a monthly meeting to be held there.[66] Stoke seems for a time to have been a member of a circular monthly meeting, in existence by 1786, though at that date it was 'in a declining state'.[67] By 1799 the meeting had evidently been abandoned and the meeting-house was not used for worship.[68]

The house of Unity Richards was licensed for use by Methodists in 1812,[69] but two years later it had been replaced by a Wesleyan chapel.[70] By 1851 two services were held each Sunday; in the afternoon the average attendance was 140, including 40 Sunday school children, and in the evening 170, including 30 children. The total congregations on Census Sunday 1851 were 110 in the afternoon and 140 in the evening.[71] The present chapel was erected in 1909, very near the original site.

A group of Bible Christians, founded in 1826, was using a chapel called Zion, erected in 1844 on the slopes of Ham Hill.[72] There were 123 sittings and on Census Sunday 1851 there were congregations of 43 in the morning, 45 in the after-noon, and 50 in the evening.[73] The chapel was closed c. 1882,[74] and was in 1968 a private house.

A group of Plymouth Brethren is thought to have succeeded the Congregationalists at the Barn Chapel.[75]

EDUCATION. John Tachell, schoolmaster, was buried in Stoke in 1595, though whether he taught in the parish is not certain.[76] By 1819 the Sunday school had been established but was 'not properly attended to by the teachers in consequence of the smallness of their pay'. There was 'no parish in the neighbourhood where a good school' was 'more wanted'.[77] By 1825–6 the Sunday school catered

for 61 boys and 62 girls.[78] By 1833 Stoke had nine schools: six small ones for infants, taking between them 48 boys and 72 girls; a day-school for 30 boys, supported by parents' contributions; and two Sunday schools, the larger, for 100 boys and 100 girls, attached to the church, the smaller, for 22 boys and 23 girls, to the Methodist chapel.[79] The church Sunday school was housed in a room built in 1831 on the site of the village pound, opposite the Fleur de Lis inn.[80] It is a small rectangular stone building with a four-bay front and central door, in the Gothic style, with a clock over the door. By 1847 the numbers in this school had fallen to 77 boys and 93 girls, under 16 teachers, all housed in the single room.[81]

It is not clear how long this school survived, but when the elementary day-school was opened in Castle Street in 1876 the children were said to be 'in wretched order . . . very ignorant . . . very back-ward'.[82] The school was administered by a committee, elected annually by subscribers, and was supported by school pence and a government grant. From the beginning an evening school was held in the same building. By 1877 there were 41 day and 74 evening pupils under three teachers. The pressure on accom-modation became serious in the next twenty years: in 1895 there were 307 children in rooms for 223, but extension was evidently beyond the resources of the subscribers. A school board was therefore established and the school transferred to it in 1899. The premises were extended in 1900–1 to provide six rooms, with accommodation for 423. In 1903 there were 408 children on the books, with an average attendance of 313.[83] Evening classes, however, had been abandoned in 1899.[84] Attendances at the day-school continued to rise; in 1908 there were 240 in the mixed department and 103 infants.[85] By 1938, however, the numbers had fallen to a total of 241.[86] The school, now known as Stoke Castle County Primary School, ceased to take senior pupils in 1940, and in 1969 there were 129 junior pupils on the books.[87]

In 1940 a new school was opened at the eastern end of the parish for senior pupils from Stoke and surrounding villages. It was at first known as Stoke Senior School and, from 1956, has been called Stanchester Secondary School. In 1969 there were 403 pupils on its registers.[88]

CHARITIES FOR THE POOR. By will proved 1903 John Winter Walter gave an annual rent-charge of £5 for the benefit of the poor of the village.[89] The sum was distributed to forty widows in 1969.[90]

[60] S.R.O., Q/RR, meeting-house lics.
[61] Ibid.
[62] H.O. 129/319/3/3/9.
[63] Ibid.
[64] Rep. Som. Cong. Union (1896), 74–5; Morris & Co. Dir. Som. (1872).
[65] Street Meeting-house, monthly meeting min. bk. 1687–1723, min. 29 Oct. 1715.
[66] Ibid. 1767–83, min. 30 May 1771.
[67] Ibid. 1740–93, mins. 4 Oct. 1786, 7 Nov. 1787.
[68] Ibid. 1793–1835, min. 3 Apr. 1799.
[69] S.R.O., D/D/Rm, box 2.   [70] Ibid.
[71] H.O. 129/319/3/3/4. 33 members in 1841: S.R.O., D/N/sp.c. 2.
[72] S.R.O., D/N/sp.c. 31–2; D/D/Rm, box 2.
[73] H.O. 129/319/3/3/10.
[74] S.R.O., D/N/sp.c. 34. It had closed c. 1861–75.

[75] A. V. Richards, Hist. Stoke, 67.
[76] S.R.O., D/P/st. u. ham 2/1/1.
[77] Digest of Returns to Sel. Cttee. on Educ. of Poor, H.C. 224 (1819), ix(2).
[78] Rep. B. & W. Dioc. Assoc. S.P.C.K. (1825–6), 67.
[79] Educ. Enquiry Abstract, H.C. 62 (1835), xlii.
[80] S.R.O., DD/HW 17/1. Now used as All Saints mission church.
[81] Church Sch. Inquiry, 1846–7.
[82] Castle School, log bks. 1876–1939.
[83] Ibid.; S.R.O., C/E 28.
[84] S.R.O., C/E 28.
[85] Bd. of Educ., List 21, [1908] (H.M.S.O.), 417.
[86] Ibid. [1938] (H.M.S.O.), 352.
[87] Som. C.C. Educ. Cttee. Schs. List.   [88] Ibid.
[89] Char. Com. file.
[90] Ex inf. the Revd. F. W. Thomas, vicar.

THORNE

THE ancient parish of Thorn Coffin, known since 1884 as Thorne,[1] lies 2 miles north-west of Yeovil. It measured 413 a. in 1901,[2] and since 1933 has formed part of the civil parish of Brympton.[3] It is irregular in shape: its northern boundary with Chilthorne Domer follows, with slight deviations, the Yeovil–Tintinhull road, and was marked c. 1300 by Thorn Ditch.[4] Part of its southern boundary with Brympton and Lufton is aligned with Thorn Lane, the road from the hundred stone of Stone to Montacute. At the Oaks, however, it leaves the road and runs[5] southwards towards Lufton, field boundaries at that point suggesting the line of an earlier road or track. The western limit of the parish has a protrusion reaching Montacute and including meadow land known as Castle Leasne in the 17th century[6] and Castle Leaze in the nineteenth.[7] The name is a possible indication of an early attachment to Montacute castle.

The north-western part of the parish, about a third of the total area, lies on silts and marls below 200 ft., and is watered by a stream called Balls water, which rises in the east of the parish and flows through the middle of the village. The land rises sharply to the south-east, to 300 ft., through Pennard sands, Yeovil sands, and a junction bed of limestone.[8] The church stands on this rising ground above the village.

The road system is a single north–south road joining the east–west roads of the northern and southern boundaries. The village is scattered along this central route, and comprises a few cottages, some farms, and Thorne House. The church and former Rectory stood at its southern end, on a track serving the fields in the south-west of the parish. Higher Farm, like the other buildings in the village in the local Ham stone, is of 17th-century origin, and Middle Farm probably dates from the middle of that century. Manor Farm, with a symmetrical five-bay front and rusticated quoins, was built in the early 18th century.

The population of Thorne has always been small. Thirteen inhabitants were recorded in 1086,[9] but only four contributed to the subsidy of 1327.[10] In 1811 there were 97 people in the village, and throughout the 19th century the number fluctuated between 87 and 110. The figure then fell sharply, to only 50 in 1951.[11] Ten years later it had recovered to 75.[12]

MANORS. The estate later known as the manor of THORN was held in 1066 by Cheneve.[13] By 1086 he had been succeeded by Drew, who held it of the count of Mortain.[14] Drew's descendants, the de Montagues or Montacutes, later earls of Salisbury, held it in chief for ¼ knight's fee as of their manor of Shepton Montague.[15] It seems to have passed for a short time to the Despensers, probably on the marriage, c. 1341, of Elizabeth, daughter of William, earl of Salisbury (d. 1344), to Hugh, Lord le Despenser (d. 1349).[16] In 1381 the manor was held of the heir of Edward, Lord le Despenser (d. 1375).[17] By the time of his death in 1397 William, earl of Salisbury, was again lord of Thorn.[18] The property passed to Thomas, earl of Salisbury, in 1409, but the family's claims to overlordship seem to have lapsed after his death in 1428.[19]

In 1198 William de Montague (d. 1217) exchanged Thorn for Long Sutton with William, son of Robert de Montague.[20] This arrangement was subsequently disputed, evidently as the result of a grant of lands by William in two places to his son-in-law, Matthew of Clevedon.[21] Thus began the mesne tenancy of the Clevedons. Matthew was still alive in 1226 and had then a son, William.[22] There is no further reference to the family in connexion with Thorn until 1340, though it is probable that the holding descended with the elder branch of the family.[23] Sir Edmund of Clevedon (d. 1375) was certainly mesne lord in 1340, and presented to the rectory during the minorities of successive resident tenants.[24] Sir Edmund's heir was his grandson, Edmund Hogshaw, a minor.[25] On his death, still under age, in 1388, the inheritance was divided between his older sisters: Joan, wife of Thomas Lovel, received Thorn, Milton Clevedon, and other properties.[26] Thomas Lovel held ¼ fee in Thorn in 1409,[27] but the grant of three parts of the manor to Stavordale priory in 1442[28] eliminated most of the mesne lord's rights. Some land in Thorn, however, continued to be associated with the manor of Milton Clevedon as late as 1619.[29]

The occupiers of the manor of Thorn, by 1303 at the latest, were members of the Coffin family. It is not clear where they originated, though an Ellis Coffin occurs in the county in 1224,[30] and a Ralph Coffin at Northover in 1263.[31] In 1279 Ellis, son and heir of John Coffin, was concerned in a plea of land at Thorn, which already bore the

---

[1] S.R.O., GP/D 22/122; Local Govt. Bd. Order 17,533. The benefice is still known as Thorn Coffin. This article was completed in 1968.
[2] V.C.H. Som. ii. 348.
[3] S.R.O., GP/D 19/85; Som. Review Order.
[4] Ilchester Almshouse Deeds, ed. W. Buckler, no. 8.
[5] O.S. Nat. Grid, 522173.
[6] S.R.O., DD/HN, box 11, 29 Jan. 1672–3.
[7] S.R.O., tithe award.
[8] Geol. Surv. Map 1″, solid and drift, sheet 312 (1958 edn.).
[9] V.C.H. Som. i. 482–3.
[10] S.R.S. iii. 211.
[11] V.C.H. Som. ii. 349; Census, 1911–51.
[12] Dioc. Dir. (1961).
[13] V.C.H. Som. i. 482.
[14] Ibid.
[15] Complete Peerage, s.v. Salisbury.
[16] Ibid.
[17] Cal. Close, 1377–81, 438–9.
[18] C 136/94/35.
[19] Cal. Close, 1405–9, 213; Complete Peerage, s.v. Salisbury.
[20] Feet of Fines, 1197–8 (Pipe R. Soc. xxiii), 128–9; S.R.S. vi. 3.
[21] Cur. Reg. R. v. 299; xii. 424–5; Abbrev. Plac. (Rec. Com.), 56.
[22] Cur. Reg. R. v. 299.
[23] For the Clevedons see Proc. Som. Arch. Soc. xli. 1–37.
[24] See p. 251.
[25] C 135/255/14.
[26] Cal. Close, 1389–92, 80.
[27] Ibid. 1405–9, 456.
[28] See below.
[29] Cal. Pat. 1494–1509, 574; C 142/414/9; Wards 7/29/117.
[30] S.R.S. vi. 47.
[31] Ibid. 203.

suffix Coffin.[32] Probably the same Ellis was tenant of ⅛ fee there in 1303, though the holding had then been sub-let to Adam de Waltham.[33] By 1320 he had been succeeded by Robert Coffin, who held Long Sutton and Thorn jointly with Robert de Montague, the whole comprising one fee.[34] This joint holding seems to explain why Coffin's estate was referred to as only half a manor.[35] Robert Coffin was patron of the church[36] and the most prosperous resident at Thorn in 1327.[37] He was dead by 1340 and then and in 1341 the property was in the hands of Sir Edmund of Clevedon during a minority.[38] By 1346, however, William Coffin was returned as tenant of ⅛ fee.[39] Five years later he was dead and his son, also William, was still a minor.[40] There was a further minority in 1362, that of Robert son of William Coffin, probably brother of the previous tenant.[41] Before 1376 the estate had descended to Emme and Isabel, daughters of Richard Coffin, but both sisters died in that year and the estate, described as half the manor and the advowson, was divided between eight co-heirs, descendants of the four sisters of Richard Coffin.[42]

At least two of these heirs died childless before 1405,[43] allowing some small consolidation, but in 1414 five persons presented to the living. One of these was Margaret Retherdone or Rotherden, widow of one of the original heirs.[44] Another of the joint patrons was John Credy, who devised his part of the manor and the advowson in 1426 to Richard Burdon and his wife.[45] A Richard Burdene had been one of the original heirs,[46] and this suggests a further re-forming of the estate. In 1428 John Stourton of Preston Plucknett presented,[47] and probably by then the Stourtons had acquired a major interest in the manor. A number of feoffees, including the Stourtons, certainly presented in 1435 and 1441.[48] In 1441 John Stourton of Preston, at the head of a group of trustees, received licence to grant an estate, described as three parts of the manor of Thorn, just over 130 a. of land, to Stavordale priory,[49] united with Taunton priory in 1533.[50]

After the dissolution of Taunton priory in 1539 Thorn seems to have been retained by the Crown until 1554, when it formed part of a grant to Sir Edmund Peckham, Master of the Mint.[51] By 1558, however, the advowson, and most probably the manor, had come to Robert Hyett,[52] and had passed

to Thomas Hyett by 1575.[53] In that year Hyett and his wife made over the property to Edward Dyer.[54] Four years later Andrew Dyer granted the properties to Giles Penney.[55] By 1595 the manor, at least, had come to Sir Edward Phelips of Montacute;[56] his son, Sir Robert, settled both manor and advowson on his second son, Robert.[57] Robert Phelips sold them in 1673 to Thomas Napper of Tintinhull,[58] and the manor descended from this Thomas (d. 1700) to his grandson, Thomas (d. 1736), and to his great-grandson, also Thomas.[59] At the latter's death in 1760 the manor passed to Andrew, his brother; and at Andrew's death in 1781 to his nephew, John.[60] By this date, however, the manor of Thorn had virtually lost its identity by merger with the other manor in the parish.

A second estate in Thorn, later known as the manor of *THORN PRIOR*, belonged to Ralph the priest in 1086, having been held before the Conquest by two thegns 'in parage'.[61] Ranulph the chancellor is said to have given this estate to the abbey of Cluny, and it became part of the endowment of Montacute priory between 1091 and 1104.[62] Richard son of Drew is also said to have given his estate at Thorn to the priory, but its subsequent descent proves this grant to have been ineffective.[63] The estate, known as Thorn Prior by 1376,[64] was retained by the priory until the Dissolution in 1539.[65] It was considered part of the manor of Montacute Forum, and descended with that manor until 1566 or later.[66]

This holding was already known as Thorn farm well before the Dissolution, when it was let to the Salmon family. Elizabeth Darrell of Littlecote (Wilts.) attempted to gain 'forcible entry' in 1546,[67] but the Salmons continued in occupation at least until 1574.[68] At some date probably after 1574 Thorn was sold to one Downing.[69]

Leasing obscures the descent thereafter, but what must have represented a substantial portion of the former Montacute holding in succession to the Salmons became the property of Edward Alford of Hamsey (Suss.) and later of Offington (Suss.). By 1601 he was holding some 300 a. in Thorn Coffin and Thorn Prior.[70] Alford leased the estate in that year to Thomas (later Sir Thomas) Freke of Cerne (Dors.), and subsequently to the Fettiplace family.[71] The division of the manor-house of Thorn

[32] Ibid. xi. 159.
[33] *Feud. Aids*, iv. 316.
[34] *Cal. Inq. p.m.* vi, p. 143.
[35] See below.
[36] *S.R.S.* i. 255.
[37] Ibid. iii. 211.
[38] Ibid. ix. 367; x. 424.
[39] *Feud. Aids*, iv. 339.
[40] *S.R.S.* x. 689.
[41] Ibid. 762.
[42] *Cal. Inq. p.m.* xiv, p. 323; *Cal. Close*, 1377–81, 438–9; *Cal. Fine R.* 1369–77, 406.
[43] C 136/53/4; C 137/57/10.
[44] *S.R.S.* xxix. 196–7; *Cal. Close*, 1377–81, 438–9.
[45] *S.R.S.* xvi. 115–16.
[46] *Cal. Close*, 1377–81, 438–9.
[47] *S.R.S.* xxxi. 64.
[48] Ibid. xxxii. 183, 266.
[49] *Cal. Pat.* 1441–6, 27.
[50] *V.C.H. Som.* ii. 144.
[51] *Cal. Pat.* 1553–4, 473–4.
[52] *S.R.S.* lv. 154. This may be Robert Hyett of Street; *Visit. Som.* 1531, 1573, ed. Weaver, 38.
[53] C.P. 25(2)/204/17 Eliz. I East.
[54] Ibid.

[55] C.P. 25(2)/205/21 Eliz. I Hil.
[56] S.R.O., DD/PH 30.
[57] C 142/486/151.
[58] S.R.O., DD/PH 30; MS. notes by Henry Warry based on deeds then (1903) in family custody; ex inf. Mrs. S. W. Rawlins.
[59] *S. & D. N. & Q.* xxviii. 279; see below, p. 258.
[60] *Som. Wills*, ed. Brown, iii. 99–100.
[61] *V.C.H. Som.* i. 482–3.
[62] Ibid. ii. 111, 114; *S.R.S.* viii. 119–20, 125; *Reg. Regum Anglo-Norm.* ii, p. 348. Most of the Montacute charters are, however, regarded as spurious: *Reg. Regum Anglo-Norm.* ii, p. 50.
[63] *S.R.S.* viii. 125. Richard died between 1161 and 1166: *Complete Peerage*, s.v. Montacute.
[64] *S.R.S.* xvii. 93.
[65] *V.C.H. Som.* ii. 113.
[66] S.R.O., DD/PH 228/24; Devon R.O. 123 M/E 91; Sta. Cha. 2/29/152; *L. & P. Hen. VIII*, xviii (1), p. 541 (where it is called Thorney in error).
[67] Sta. Cha. 2/29/152.
[68] C 66/1115 mm. 19–20.
[69] Devon R.O. 123 M/E 91.
[70] B.M. Harl. Ch. 77 H 11, 79 F 28.
[71] S.R.O., DD/HN, box 11; B.M. Harl. Ch. 77 H 11.

Prior in 1635[72] suggests further and radical fragmentation of the estate, though there are indications that the Hawker family of Chilthorne Vagg reformed at least part of the holding.[73] Charles Hawker died in 1740 as occupier of a house and lands called Thorn Prior, evidently held in trust by him for his nieces and heirs, Sarah and Mary Hawker.[74] The Misses Hawker were succeeded by Thomas Napper in 1756,[75] and the estate was absorbed into the larger Napper holding. By 1785 the whole was known as Thorn Prior, though it evidently comprised parts of both former manors.[76]

The manor of 'Thorn *alias* Thorn Prior' was sold by John Napper in 1785 to his second cousin, Edward Berkeley Napier. Much of the land seems to have passed, with the manor-house, to the Revd. T. H. Pearson, but the lordship and some land belonged in 1840 to the Revd. George Bale.[77] Capt. Charles Pearson, R.N. (d. 1864), owned Thorn House by 1839; in 1843 he also held Manor farm, the largest single unit of the Napper estate of Thorn Prior.[78] He was succeeded by a Major Pearson[79] who, in 1869, sold the property to J. J. (later Judge) Hooper.[80] Hooper subsequently purchased a number of isolated holdings in the parish to form a consolidated estate, which came to be known as the manor of Thorne. At his death in 1895 the manor passed to his widow and, on her death in 1913, to her daughter by her first marriage, Miss M. E. Warry.[81] G. F. C. Warry (d. 1959) succeeded her in 1930.[82] The estate was sold, mostly to the tenants, about 1947.[83]

In 1635 the manor-house of Thorn Prior was divided into two parts, Hugh Donne acquiring the hall, kitchens and rooms above, and a room 'within the hall', together with part of the barn.[84] In 1740 the house, considerably enlarged if not rebuilt, and in sole occupation, comprised a hall, parlour, pantry, and kitchen, with six rooms above, and cellars.[85] By 1785 this 'good dwelling house' had 'pleasure grounds disposed and planted with flower shrubs by the modern taste' and was 'a fit residence for a gentleman'.[86] In 1839 the road which passed directly in front of the house was diverted to the west to improve the grounds.[87] The present house, built in the neo-Elizabethan style for Judge Hooper in 1882, was designed by Sir Thomas Jackson.[88] Some walls and outbuildings from its predecessor have survived.

ECONOMIC HISTORY. Before the Conquest there were two estates at Thorne, one held 'in parage' by two thegns. The whole comprised 3 hides and 1 virgate, with land for 5 ploughs, though only 3 seem to have been in use. There were 24 a. of meadow. Three-quarters of the larger estate, that of Ralph the priest, was in demesne, cultivated by 5 villeins and 2 bordars. These also shared a plough and worked the rest of the land. One hide of the other estate was in demesne, worked by 3 bordars and 3 serfs. Ralph's estate, worth 32s. in 1086, had been worth 40s. T.R.E.; the other had increased in value from 10s. to 20s.[89]

Montacute priory, Ralph's successor, had an estate described as half the vill in 1302–3, worth £4 10s. 5d.[90] It then comprised 83 a. of arable, 6 a. of meadow, and 6 bovates of pasture in demesne. There was one free tenant holding half a virgate. Villein tenures seems to have increased in number, but no services were demanded; two ½-virgate, two furlong, and five cottar tenements were held for rents in lieu of all services. The priory also owned the estovers of all the houses and a dovecot.[91]

At the Dissolution the priory estate, known as Thorn farm, was entirely let. The Salmon family, sole tenants from 1533[92] until at least 1574,[93] by 1539 held 150 a. and attached tenements for a rent of £9 6s. 8d.[94] The other estate in the parish was also let entirely, and rents, some of which were described as customary, amounted to £4 0s. 4d.[95]

There are no direct references to open fields, but in 1302–3 there were tenants known as *ferlingarii*, holding furlongs in villeinage.[96] By 1566 the manor of Thorn Prior was entirely in closes.[97] So late as 1717 common pasture is mentioned, though this formed part of the glebe, and probably was a close, shared with other tenants, known as Little New Close, of which the rector possessed half in 1639.[98]

The nature of the soil suggests that arable has always been less important than grazing. The 4 swine and 30 sheep of Domesday compared with the 3 ploughs on the combined estates probably represented the balance of farming throughout the Middle Ages and later.[99] In 1834 about a third of the parish was arable[1] and in 1905 about a sixth.[2] This ratio continues.

The division of the two manors into small leaseholds, particularly during the 17th century, included the physical division of the manor-house of Thorn Prior,[3] though by the middle of the 18th century the house was again in single occupation,[4] and by c. 1785 the estate had been so far consolidated as to include two farms, one of over 173 a.[5] The whole of this estate, in the hands of the Nappers,

[72] S.R.O., DD/HN, box 11.   [73] Ibid.
[74] S.R.O., DD/SF 3148.
[75] S.R.O., D/P/th.co. 4/1/3.
[76] S.R.O., DD/HN, box 11, survey of manor prior to possible sale, 1781–5.
[77] C.P. 25(2)/1400/25 Geo. III Hil; MS. notes by Henry Warry; Yeovil, Messrs. Marsh, Warry, & Arrow, deeds.
[78] S.R.O., tithe award; Q/SR, Spring 1839.
[79] P.O. Dir. Som. (1866).
[80] MS. notes of Henry Warry.
[81] Ex inf. Mrs. S. W. Rawlins.
[82] Ex inf. Mrs. S. W. Rawlins and Messrs. Marsh, Warry, & Arrow.
[83] Ibid.
[84] S.R.O., DD/HN, box 11.
[85] S.R.O., DD/SF 3148, inventory.
[86] S.R.O., DD/HN, box 11.

[87] S.R.O., Q/SR, Spring 1839.
[88] Pevsner, South and West Som.; datestone over porch.
[89] V.C.H. Som. i. 482–3.
[90] S.C. 11/798.   [91] Ibid.
[92] Sta. Cha. 2/29/152.   [93] C 66/1115 m. 20.
[94] S.R.O., DD/PH 228/24.
[95] Valor Eccl. (Rec. Com.), i. 169; S.C. 6/Hen. VIII/3137 m. 3d.
[96] S.C. 11/798.
[97] Devon R.O. 123 M/E 91. See also S.R.O., DD/HN, box 11.
[98] S.R.O., DD/SF 3148; C.P. 25(2)/1064/4 Geo. I Mich.
[99] V.C.H. Som. i. 482–3; S.R.O., DD/SF 3148.
[1] Rep. Com. Poor Law, H.C. 44(1834), xxx–xxxiv.
[2] Statistics supplied by the then Bd. of Agric. 1905.
[3] S.R.O., DD/HN, box 11.
[4] S.R.O., DD/SF 3148.
[5] S.R.O., DD/HN, box 11.

included 11 houses or cottages, held on leases for 99 years or three lives.[6] The rest of the parish was still in many small holdings, and the ownership was still 'much divided' in 1834.[7] In 1843 Manor farm, the nucleus of the Thorn Prior estate, comprised over 130 a., and was held with Thorn House by Capt. Charles Pearson. There were three other farms of c. 50 a., and one of 33 a.[8] There were three farmers in the parish in 1861,[9] four in 1875,[10] and five in 1878,[11] but most were tenants, the lord of the manor having purchased most of the property between 1869 and 1878.[12] Apart from farming the only other important occupation in the parish in the 19th century was glove-sewing, in which most of the women and girls were employed in their homes.[13]

LOCAL GOVERNMENT. Throughout the Middle Ages two courts had jurisdiction in Thorne. The prior of Montacute's court governed his holding, together with lands in Mudford,[14] for which he owed suit to Stone hundred.[15] The prior of Taunton, successor to the Coffins and to the prior of Stavordale, administered as one bailiwick his holding in Thorne and property in Bruton.[16] Thorn Prior by 1539 was considered part of Bishopston tithing in the manor of Montacute Forum,[17] and continued to be so regarded for fiscal purposes and for local administration in the 17th and 18th centuries.[18] Parts of Thorn Coffin were still in the 19th century outside this jurisdiction, and in 1837 constituted part of the out-hundred of Tintinhull manor.[19] There was, therefore, in 1841, doubt whether the parish was in Stone or Tintinhull hundred.[20]

There was a poorhouse in the parish c. 1785,[21] but it was probably closed by 1802–3, when only out-relief was given.[22] There was certainly no workhouse in 1834.[23] The parish became part of the Yeovil poor-law union in 1836.[24]

CHURCH. There was a church at Thorne in 1327.[25] Its omission from the Taxatio of 1291, where the prior of Montacute's estate in the village, but no church, is noted,[26] suggests a foundation after that date. At least from 1327 the advowson of the rectory was in the hands of the Coffin family, the resident lords of the manor, and it is possible

that the church was founded by them between these two dates. The present building is of that period. Since c. 1926 the rectory has been combined with Yeovil Marsh, and from 1937 has been held with Chilthorne Domer, where the incumbent lives.[27]

The advowson of Thorn Coffin was held by the Coffin family at least from 1327 until 1376,[28] although the mesne lords, the Clevedons, presented during minorities in 1340, 1341, and 1351,[29] and Alice Borde in 1362.[30] The Crown presented in 1384, 1385, 1392, and 1398, because of the fragmentation of the Coffin inheritance.[31] John Credy presented in 1412, but two years later he headed a group of patrons, some of whom were evidently co-heirs of the estate.[32] By his will, dated 1426, Credy gave the advowson to Richard Burdon and his wife.[33] By 1428, however, the whole advowson had passed to John Stourton of Preston Plucknett who, with other feoffees, was concerned to reunite the divided estate before granting it, with the advowson, to Stavordale priory about 1442.[34] At the next vacancies, in 1454 and 1465, the bishop and the vicar-general respectively collated to the benefice by lapse.[35] The priory presented between 1468 and 1510.[36] The Crown presented in 1552 and again in 1554 after a deprivation,[37] followed in 1558 by Robert Hyett.[38] Thomas Hyett sold the advowson, with the manor, to Edward Dyer in 1575.[39] Andrew Dyer transferred it to Giles Penney in 1579.[40] In or before 1622 John Wilkinson (rector 1622–66) acquired the patronage and presented himself,[41] but it subsequently passed to Sir Robert Phelips of Montacute, lord of Thorn manor. He settled both properties on his second son Robert, who presented in 1666 and 1673.[42] The advowson was sold to Thomas Napper in 1673, and descended with the manor until the death of Thomas Napper in 1760.[43] Napper left the advowson to his brother John (d. 1774), whose son, also John (d. 1791), conveyed it to his second cousin, Edward Berkeley Napier (d. 1798).[44] In 1804 it was sold to the Revd. John Hawkes Mules,[45] whose son and namesake presented himself in 1812.[46] Subsequently there were frequent changes of ownership: the Revd. Alfred Tooke was patron and rector from 1824 at least until 1840; by 1853 the patronage had been acquired by the Revd. Philip Rufford, rector of Great Alne (Warws.), himself shortly afterwards incumbent.[47] The Revd. Williams Sabine (rector

[6] Ibid.
[7] Rep. Com. Poor Law, H.C. 44 (1834), xxx–xxxiv.
[8] S.R.O., tithe award.
[9] P.O. Dir. Som. (1861).
[10] Ibid. (1875).
[11] Owen's Dir. Som. (1878).
[12] MS. notes by Henry Warry; ex inf. Mrs. S. W. Rawlins and Messrs. Marsh, Warry, & Arrow, Yeovil.
[13] Rep. Com. Poor Law, H.C. 44 (1834), xxx–xxxiv.
[14] S.C. 11/798.
[15] Rot. Hund. (Rec. Com.), ii. 131; Plac. de Quo Warr. (Rec. Com.), 696; S.R.S. viii. 207–8.
[16] S.C. 6/Hen. VIII/3137 m. 3d.
[17] S.R.O., DD/PH 228/24.
[18] Ibid. 142; DD/S/PN: Montacute overseers' accts.; Collinson, Hist. Som. iii. 314.
[19] S.R.O., DD/X/HO; Proc. Som. Arch. Soc. lxxvi, p. li.
[20] Census, 1841.
[21] S.R.O., DD/HN, box 11.
[22] Poor Law Abstract, 1804.
[23] Rep. Com. Poor Law, H.C. 44 (1834), xxx–xxxiv.
[24] Poor Law Com. 2nd Rep. p. 550.
[25] S.R.S. i. 255.
[26] Tax. Eccl. (Rec. Com.), 200, 204.

[27] Dioc. Dir. (1937–68).
[28] S.R.S. i. 255; Cal. Inq. p.m. xiv, p. 323.
[29] S.R.S. ix. 367, 424; x. 689.
[30] Ibid. x. 762.
[31] Cal. Pat. 1381–5, 378, 564, 577; 1391–6, 157; 1396–9, 455.
[32] S.R.S. xxix. 125, 196–7; Cal. Close, 1377–81, 438–9.
[33] S.R.S. xvi. 115–16; see above, p. 251.
[34] S.R.S. xxxi. 64, 183, 266; see above, p. 251.
[35] S.R.S. xlix. 230–1; lii, p. xxiii.
[36] Ibid. lii. 18, 130, 154; liv. 59–60, 121, 142.
[37] Cal. Pat. 1550–3, 436; 1553–4, 40; S.R.S. lv. 131.
[38] S.R.S. lv. 154.
[39] C.P. 25(2)/204/17 Eliz. I East.
[40] C.P. 25(2)/205/21 Eliz. I Hil.
[41] Som. Incumbents, ed. Weaver, 199.
[42] Ibid.
[43] See p. 251.
[44] Som. Wills, ed. Brown, iii. 99; C.P. 25(2)/1400/26 Geo. III Hil; S. & D. N. & Q. xxviii. 279.
[45] MS. notes by Henry Warry based on deeds then (1903) in family custody; ex inf. Mrs. S. W. Rawlins.
[46] C. & J. Greenwood, Som. Delineated.
[47] Rep. Com. Eccl. Revenues, pp. 180–1; County Gazette Dir. Som. (1840); S.R.O., tithe award, glebe exchange, 1853.

1846–53) was patron in 1857.[48] From 1859 until at least 1883 the Revd. Hugh Helyar, rector of Sutton Bingham, held the advowson;[49] from 1889 until 1892 it was held by W. Hargreaves,[50] who was succeeded by J. H. Hargreaves. By 1902 it passed to Mrs. Simpson,[51] and by 1906 to Miss M. E. Warry, who was patron until her death in 1930.[52] Her nephew, G. F. C. Warry, was patron from 1932 until 1934 and from 1940 until 1959. H. C. Warry, his father, was patron from 1935 until 1940.[53] The executors of G. F. C. Warry presented in 1965 and 1971.[54]

The benefice was small and was not taxed in 1334.[55] In 1535 its net value was £5 5s. 0½d.[56] By about 1668 it was said to be worth £30.[57] It was augmented in 1749 by Andrew Napper, son of the patron, and by a grant from the Pincombe trustees.[58] In 1774 the incumbent received a number of 'leazes' in the common fields of Tintinhull.[59] Further augmentations were made in 1811 and 1813 by the Revd. J. H. Mules, patron and rector, and by a further grant from the Pincombe trustees.[60] Thus in 1831 the net income was said to be £200[61] and in 1851 £210.[62]

In 1535 the tithes were valued at £4 18s. 8d.[63] By 1639 the rector claimed tithe corn and hay throughout the parish, and 3d. for a cow's milk, 2d. for a heifer's milk the first year; tithes of wool, lambs, and calves, hemp and flax, apples and pears, honey and pigs; 1d. for the fall of a colt, ½d. for every weaned calf, and 1d. for a garden. Outsiders who rented land in the parish were to pay these charges at the rector's discretion.[64] In 1842 a rent-charge of £135 was assigned to the rector.[65]

The glebe was valued at 8s. in 1535.[66] In 1639 the rector possessed 9½ a., of which 7½ a. were arable.[67] At the time of the tithe award in 1843 the rector had only 8½ a.,[68] but by 1861 he had 30 a., and by 1894 32 a.[69] Most of this was sold between 1919 and 1923.[70]

The parsonage house needed thatching in 1554 and required 'other needful reparations'.[71] In 1623 and 1629 it was reported to be 'very decayed'.[72] By 1815 the rector could not live there because the house was 'poor, mean and very small and greatly dilapidated'.[73] It was later used as a labourer's cottage, but by 1840 was unoccupied.[74] In 1847 it

was depicted in that condition, and was evidently a small, three-bay thatched house with a central door and gables to the first floor.[75] The present Old Rectory, probably erected on the same site, was described in 1861 as 'a good residence'.[76]

William Brett (rector 1412–14), then only in minor orders, combined his benefice with the office of registrar of the consistory court at Wells.[77] Edward Fletcher (rector 1435–41) was only in sub-deacon's orders when appointed.[78] William Grayner (rector 1507–10) was a brother of St. John's Hospital, Bridgwater.[79] Besides the rector there was a curate and a chaplain in the parish in 1532.[80] Like several of his neighbours Bartholomew Stare was deprived in 1554, leaving the church without parson or curate.[81] In 1608 the justices ordered John Hearne (rector 1579–1622) to be gaoled without bail in a paternity suit.[82] Four years later he was still 'in danger of process for debt and other trouble' and had been absent from his cure for several months. He promised, however, that he would 'perform to the uttermost his duty in the parish'.[83] His wife was accused of brawling in 1606.[84] Hearne's successor, John Wilkinson (rector 1622–66), remained in his benefice without interruption during the Interregnum, though in 1629 he was reported for non-residence and for failure to catechize.[85] Edward Napier (rector 1772–1812) combined the living with the perpetual curacy of Tintinhull and the rectory of Sutton Waldren (Dors.), where he lived. The rectory house was let in his time.[86] John Mules the younger (rector 1812–24) lived with his father at Ilminster and was employing a curate in 1818.[87] He probably resigned the rectory on succeeding his father at Ilminster.[88] Alfred Tooke, rector from 1824, was living at Grove House, near Yeovil, in 1827 and at Alvington in 1833 because the rectory-house was uninhabitable.[89]

At a visitation in 1612 it was reported that the absence of the rector deprived the parish of its usual monthly sermons; at the same time the warden was presented for not providing Jewel's *Works*.[90] There was no Bible 'of the new translation' in 1623, and the surplice was 'very insufficient'.[91] In the early 19th century services were held alternately morning and evening,[92] but by 1827 two services were held each Sunday from March until

[48] *Clergy List* (1857).
[49] Ibid. (1859); *Kelly's Dir. Som.* (1883).
[50] *Dioc. Kal.* (1889, 1892); *Kelly's Dir. Som.* (1889, 1892).
[51] *Dioc. Kal.* (1893, 1902).
[52] Ibid. (1906).
[53] *Dioc. Dir.* (1932–59).
[54] *Crockford*.
[55] E 179/169/14.
[56] *Valor Eccl.* (Rec. Com.), i. 200.
[57] S.R.O., D/D/Vc 24.
[58] Hodgson, *Queen Anne's Bounty*.
[59] S.R.O., DD/X/HO, Tintinhull ct. bk. 1770–1878, sub anno 1774.
[60] Hodgson, *Queen Anne's Bounty*.
[61] *Rep. Com. Eccl. Revenues*, pp. 180–1.
[62] H.O. 129/319/4/1/1.
[63] *Valor Eccl.* (Rec. Com.), i. 200.
[64] S.R.O., DD/SF 3148.
[65] S.R.O., tithe award.
[66] *Valor Eccl.* (Rec. Com.), i. 200.
[67] S.R.O., DD/SF 3148.
[68] S.R.O., tithe award.
[69] *P.O. Dir. Som.* (1861); *Kelly's Dir. Som.* (1894).
[70] *Kelly's Dir. Som.* (1919, 1923).

[71] S.R.O., D/D/Ca 22.
[72] Ibid. 236, 267.
[73] S.R.O., D/D/V rtns. 1815.
[74] Ibid. 1827, 1840.
[75] See plate facing p. 33.
[76] *P.O. Dir. Som.* (1861).
[77] *S.R.S.* xxix. 93, 117, 125, 196–7; xxx. 372, 408, 424.
[78] Ibid. xxxi. 183.
[79] Ibid. liv. 121, 142.
[80] S.R.O., D/D/Vc 20.
[81] *S.R.S.* lv. 131 and n.; *Cal. Pat.* 1550–3, 436; S.R.O., D/D/Ca 22. *V.C.H. Som.* ii. 66 is in error.
[82] *S.R.S.* xxiii. 10.
[83] S.R.O., D/D/Ca 177.
[84] Ibid. 150, p. 32.
[85] Ibid. 267.
[86] *S. & D. N. & Q.* xxviii. 284. Napier let the parsonage by 1781: S.R.O., Q/RE, land tax assessments. He was still rector in 1791: Collinson, *Hist. Som.* iii. 322.
[87] S.R.O., D/D/V rtns. 1815; *Digest of Returns to Sel. Cttee. on Educ. of Poor*, H.C. 224 (1819), ix (2).
[88] A. J. Street, *Mynster of the Ile*, 278.
[89] S.R.O., D/D/V rtns. 1827, 1833.
[90] S.R.O., D/D/Ca 177.
[91] Ibid. 236.
[92] S.R.O., D/D/V rtns. 1815.

September.[93] By 1833 the second service had been abandoned because the rector 'could not raise a congregation on account of the small population and other churches close at hand'.[94] Still in 1840 only one service was held and the rector did not catechize.[95] Three years later, however, two services had become the rule,[96] and in 1851 the average congregation was 44 in the morning and 50 in the afternoon.[97] By 1870 only one service was again being held every Sunday, with celebrations of the Holy Communion four times a year.[98] By 1914 Matins and Evensong were said daily, Communion was celebrated every Sunday, with Matins and Evensong alternately.[99]

The church of *ST. ANDREW*, on a hillside with a commanding view north over the village, consists of a chancel with south vestry, a nave with a north porch and a double bellcot in the west gable-end, all in the Decorated style. The church was much restored and partially rebuilt in 1895. The porch is dated 1613, and the vestry was added by public subscription in 1913.[1] The pulpit, dated 1624, was evidently provided after a presentment in the previous year that its predecessor was 'much decayed'.[2] The oak altar rails, in which figure carving has been incorporated, also date from the 17th century.

The plate includes a chalice and paten of 1573 by 'I.P.'[3] There are two bells, dated 1673 and 1679, both by Thomas Purdue.[4] The registers begin in 1695 and appear to be complete.[5]

NONCONFORMITY. The house of Hugh Donne, possibly the manor-house of Thorn Prior, was licensed for use by dissenters of unknown denomination in 1705, and the houses of William and Alice Marks in 1718.[6] About 1745 'parson Marks', described as a dissenting teacher, was still living in the village.[7]

EDUCATION. In 1818 there was a Sunday school in the parish supported by the curate and attended by 10 boys and 15 girls.[8] The poorer classes were then said to be 'very desirous' of having their children educated but were 'deficient in the means'.[9] This school had been abandoned by 1833,[10] but was revived by 1847, when it was held in the church.[11] Eight boys and 5 girls were then taught by 3 voluntary teachers, and the school was supported by subscriptions. There was also a dame school in the village by 1847, with 6 boys and 7 girls.[12] By 1861 the Sunday school was still being held in the church,[13] but by 1883 was held in the rectory house.[14]

CHARITIES FOR THE POOR. None known.

TINTINHULL

THE ancient parish of Tintinhull, 1,828 a. in extent,[1] was formed by two irregularly-shaped areas lying north-west and south-east of the Foss Way, two miles south-west of Ilchester. The Foss formed the boundary of each part, but was common for only about one tenth of a mile, the two parts of the parish being thus almost separated. The gradual dismemberment of the parish of Sock Dennis added land to Tintinhull between 1883 and 1957[2] so that the area of the parish in 1968 was 2,370 a.[3] The two parts of the parish now meet for a mile along the Foss.

The north-western section of the ancient parish may originally have been part of the Saxon royal estate of Martock:[4] physically it forms part of a triangular tract of land wedged between the Foss Way and the rivers Parrett and Yeo, and may be the area given by King Edmund to Wilfric before 946.[5] The other part of the parish has less easily-defined boundaries, though Wellhams brook forms its southern limit towards Stoke sub Hamdon and Sock Lane its division from Chilthorne Domer. This part of the parish contains the village and almost the whole population, but the northern part has produced evidence of Roman occupation near Bearley Farm.[6]

Almost the entire northern part of the parish lies on alluvium and clays below the 100 ft. contour. Clays continue in the gently rising ground of the southern part, though the relatively high points of 180 ft. on the Yeovil road and 167 ft. at Perren's hill are formed of Pennard sands. Further south the land falls away slightly to Wellhams brook.[7]

In consequence meadow and 'moor' land were to be found on the northern extremity of the parish, with meadow also at Wellhams. Common meadow

93 Ibid. 1827.
94 Ibid. 1833.
95 Ibid. 1840.
96 Ibid. 1843.
97 H.O. 129/319/4/1/1.
98 S.R.O., D/D/V rtns. 1870.
99 S.R.O., D/P/th. co. 2/5/1.
1 *Kelly's Dir. Som.* (1919).
2 S.R.O., D/D/Ca 236.
3 *Proc. Som. Arch. Soc.* xliii. 26–7.
4 S.R.O., DD/SAS CH 16.
5 S.R.O., D/P/th. co. 2/1/1–4.
6 S.R.O., Q/RR, rtns. of places certified, 1852–3.
7 *Life and Adventures of Mr. Bampfylde Moore Carew* (1785 edn.), 205–7.
8 *Digest of Returns to Sel. Cttee. on Educ. of Poor*, H.C. 224 (1819), ix (2).

9 Ibid.
10 *Educ. Enquiry Abstract*, H.C. 62 (1835), xlii.
11 *Church Sch. Inquiry, 1846–7*.
12 Ibid.
13 *P.O. Dir. Som.* (1861).
14 *Kelly's Dir. Som.* (1883).
1 S.R.O., tithe award. This article was completed in 1968.
2 See p. 231.
3 *Census, 1961; Somerset (Parishes in the Rural District of Yeovil) Confirmation Order, 1957.*
4 See p. 38.
5 See p. 257.
6 *Proc. Som. Arch. Soc.* xcvi. 51 and the refs. there cited.
7 Geol. Surv. Map 1″, solid and drift, sheet 312 (1956 edn.).

in Tintinhull mead, nearly 78 a. in extent in 1796,[8] lay along Bearley brook, and Tintinhull moor was further north-west, in the flood plain of the Yeo. The course of this river was ill-defined until comparatively recent years, a fact which often gave rise to grazing disputes.[9]

Further south, on the clays, lay the inclosed arable and pasture grounds of Bearley farm, already a consolidated unit in the 16th century,[10] and the open arable field called Socksam or Soxams, west of Bearley Lane.[11] The other five open fields lay in the southern section of the parish, around the village. The largest, Great or Broad East field, was over 109 a. in extent by the end of the 18th century, and beyond it lay Bottom or New field and Little East field. Further south, below the Yeovil road, was a small field called Southover. Marsh field (the 'marsh' in the 16th century) comprised the south-western part of the parish. These fields were inclosed in 1796.[12] In medieval times there had also been a North field, but it measured only 1 a. by c. 1580. West field, immediately to the west of the village, was common pasture, and measured 120 a. in the later 16th century. Together with Tintinhull moor (70 a.) it formed the common pasturage of the parish.[13]

The road system of the northern part of the parish consists of a spine road running from Town's End, the northern extremity of the village on the Foss Way, to Bearley Farm and thence to Tintinhull moor. This was known in 1787 as Green Lane.[14] Stone Lane and Shermoor Lane each ran westwards from this spine. A way from Ilchester to Martock via Bearley entered the parish from Chestermead across Hackum bridge, passed just south of Bearley farm-house and led directly to Ash.[15] Part of the route is still followed by a footpath, part by a double hedge.[16] The Foss Way acted as a boundary rather than as a thoroughfare for the parish, though by 1611 the parishioners were responsible for its repair from Tintinhull Forts to Ilchester meadow,[17] presumably the same stretch for which they were charged after the road was turnpiked in 1753.[18]

In the southern section of the parish the roads radiate from a large triangular area formed by Head Street, Vicarage Street, and St. Margaret's Road (formerly Hedge Street), the base forming part of the Yeovil–Martock road. At the apex is a green on which stand stocks.[19] From this apex three roads radiate: Farm Street, later becoming Bottomfield Lane,[20] runs eastwards past Tintinhull House and served the former Great East and Bottom fields; Queen Street runs north-north-west to join the Foss Way at Town's End; Church Street, becoming West Field drove, runs along the northern

side of the churchyard towards the former West field. Willey Lane connects the former parish pound at the end of the churchyard with Queen Street.[21]

Although most of the houses appear to be of stone and to date from the 17th century, timber and wattle-and-daub were earlier used.[22] Traces of similar construction still survive in Westfield Cottage, Queen Street, an L-shaped house with a steeply-pitched thatched roof. Its walls were subsequently faced with stone and brick, and there is an attached stone barn. Another similar cottage with attached barn, apparently all under one roof, was demolished c. 1847. It was described as of mud, and had a timber-framed gable-end and wattle-and-daub panels.[23]

The earliest dated building in the village, Francis Farm, on the east side of the green, was built by Richard Smith, gentleman, in 1603. It is a two-storeyed house of Ham stone ashlar with a projecting wing at its southern end. The principal range has a central door with four-centred head, ovolo-moulded mullions, and a string-course below the ground-floor sill level which is returned vertically at each side of the doorway. There is a continuous hood-mould over the door and an adjacent window, and contemporary panelling in the parlour, to the north of the screens-passage. The hall chimney backs on the passage to the south.

At the northern end of the green is the Dower House, probably that referred to about 1687 as Mrs. Napper's 'new house'.[24] It is of two storeys and attics with a symmetrical seven-bay front of Ham stone ashlar and a tile and stone slate roof. The two-light stone-mullioned windows, surmounted on each floor by a continuous hood-mould, appear to be 20th-century replacements, the former windows having been of wood.[25] The central doorway has a four-centred arch and a segmental-headed porch; above it is an oval window. Internally the range consists of three rooms with a fourth room in a rear wing. Also at the rear is a central staircase projection, now enclosed by a later addition to the house. The original chimney in the kitchen has the remains of a smoke chamber beside it. The gate piers to the forecourt are crowned with stone balls; further east is an arched and pedimented carriage entrance brought from elsewhere.[26]

Queen, Farm, and Vicarage Streets contain 17th- and 18th-century farm-houses, the most important of which, Tintinhull House, now bears the appearance of a much more sophisticated dwelling. Part of that building, the original farm-house, dates from 1630, but it was extensively altered and enlarged early in the 18th century.[27] It had evidently

8 S.R.O., CR 31.
9 S.R.S. lxix. 29.
10 See p. 258.
11 S.R.O., tithe award.
12 S.R.O., CR 31.
13 Devon R.O. 123 M/E 31–3.
14 S.R.O., DD/PLE box 89, map of Bearley fm. 1787.
15 Ibid. The owner of Burlinghams was ordered to repair the bridge in 1719: S.R.O., DD/X/HO, ct. bk. 1662–1723.
16 O.S. Map 1/25,000, ST 42 (1959 edn.).
17 S.R.S. xxiii. 55.
18 S.R.O., DD/X/BNL; D/T/ilch.: map of turnpike roads, 1826.
19 New stocks were erected in 1721: S.R.O., DD/X/HO, ct. bk. 1662–1723.

20 O.S. Map 6″, Som. LXXXII. NW. (1886 edn.).
21 Ibid.
22 S.R.S. iv. 196; see below, p. 264.
23 Taunton Castle, Braikenridge Colln.
24 S.R.O., DD/X/HO, Thomas Napper's Easter bk.
25 Old photograph penes Mr. J. R. E. Hindson in the house.
26 Country Life, 12 April 1956, 739.
27 Pevsner, South and West Som. 324, says c. 1700; a date of c. 1724 is favoured by Mr. Arthur Oswald, who thinks the alternative of 1690–5 is unlikely: Country Life, 19 April 1956, 800; S. & D. N. & Q. xxvii (but numbered xxviii), 283. From 1722 until the end of the century the property was rated at the same sum, a strong indication that no substantial alterations were made after that date: S.R.O., D/P/tin 13/2/1: overseers' rates and accts. 1721–89.

taken its present form by 1722, when it was occupied by Andrew Napper, younger brother of Thomas Napper (V), lord of the manor, who lived at Tintinhull Court.[28] By 1746 the property was known as the Farm, and part was let to the Pitt family.[29] Pitt Farm was the name by which it was known in 1790.[30] Throughout the 19th century it was called the Mansion. The Nappers still retained it after they had disposed of the manor, but in 1835 it passed to a local farmer, Jeremiah Penny. One of his sons sold it in 1898, and it became the residence of the Revd. Dr. S. J. M. Price,[31] a distinguished botanist, who laid out the formal gardens to the west of the house.[32] In 1933 it was purchased by Mr. and Mrs. F. E. Reiss, and Mrs. Reiss was largely responsible for creating the present gardens. The property was transferred to the National Trust in 1954.[33]

The 17th-century house, of which the east front with its mullioned windows still survives, evidently consisted of a long range, one room deep, with a cross-wing at its south end. The gable-end of the wing carries a date-stone of 1630 with the initial 'N' (for Napper). Internally a massive stone fireplace in the present entrance hall and an altered staircase in the wing belong to this building. In the early 18th century the west side was extended westward by three rooms and a new entrance front of five bays built facing west. The symmetrical two-storeyed elevation of Ham stone ashlar is considered to be an unusually perfect example of its size and period.[34] It has rusticated angle pilasters, stone-mullioned and transomed windows, and a hipped roof of stone slates with attic dormers. The three central bays are flanked by pilasters and surmounted by a pediment containing a circular window. The central doorway, which has Tuscan columns and a segmental pediment, is entered from what was originally a walled forecourt but is now part of the garden; angle piers to the forecourt are crowned by stone eagles. The present central staircase was evidently inserted in the old range when the extension was built. The west rooms contain contemporary fittings except the drawing room at the north end, which was remodelled later in the 18th century.

In 1777 a substantial L-shaped building on the south-west corner of the junction of the Yeovil and Montacute roads was known as the White Hart inn.[35] It was apparently in use as an inn between 1776 and 1791.[36] By 1839 it had been converted into five dwellings.[37]

A seven-year Friendly Society and a Female Friendly Society were both founded in 1843.[38] An Institute and Working Men's Club was opened in 1907.[39]

The population of the parish in 1716 was said to be 196.[40] By 1801 the figure had risen to 333, and by 1841 to 553. The subsequent decline in agriculture is reflected in the fall to 403 by 1881, accounted for at least in part by emigration to Australia.[41] There was a recovery during the first three decades of the 20th century, and since 1951 the increase has been rapid. In 1961 it was 694.[42] Most of the new housing development has taken place south of Head Street, around the glove factory and in the central triangle. This reflects the growing popularity of the village as a dormitory for Yeovil workers.

MANOR AND OTHER ESTATES. Two estates granted to Glastonbury abbey during the 10th century formed the nucleus of the present parish of Tintinhull. Five hides, probably once part of the Saxon royal estate of Martock, were granted between 939 and 946 by King Edmund to Wilfric. Wilfric left this property to Glastonbury for his soul-scot.[43] Between 959 and 975 Aelfswith granted another five hides of land there to Glastonbury.[44] The abbey retained these two holdings until Robert, count of Mortain, to consolidate his estates around his castle at Montacute,[45] exchanged them for his manor of Camerton.[46] About 1102 Robert's son, William, count of Mortain, gave the manor of *TINTINHULL* as part of the endowment of Montacute priory.[47] The priory retained the manor until the Dissolution in 1539, though not without a serious challenge to its rights from the Lovels of Castle Cary and their successor, Richard Seymour, who seem to have claimed a mesne lordship. The claim was first made by Hugh Lovel (d. 1291) in 1276, and again in 1280, though the prior was returned as holding the manor in chief in 1284–5 and 1316.[48] The claim was revived by Richard Lovel (d. 1351), who regarded Tintinhull as part of his barony, and in 1318 settled the manor on himself in fee.[49] This transaction was repudiated in 1319, but was used as the basis for a claim, revived before 1379 by Richard Seymour, husband of Lovel's grand-daughter. This dispute was not, apparently, settled until 1406.[50]

In 1539 the Crown leased the manor to Dr. William (later Sir William) Petre.[51] Sir Thomas Wyatt (d. 1542) of Allington (Kent) acquired the

[28] S.R.O., D/P/tin 13/2/1.
[29] Ibid.
[30] S.R.O., DD/X/HO, marr. settlement of E. B. Napier and Miss Martin, 1790.
[31] See Llewelyn Powys, *A Baker's Dozen* (1941), 80–1.
[32] National Trust, *Guide*, 4.
[33] *Country Life*, 19 April 1956, 801.
[34] Ibid. 798, 800. The façade was reproduced at Somerset House, Atlanta, Georgia, U.S.A. in 1918.
[35] S.R.O., DD/SAS PR 454, map of part of Tintinhull, 1777.
[36] S.R.O., Q/RL, victuallers' recogs.
[37] S.R.O., tithe award.
[38] S.R.O., Q/R Friendly Soc. rtns.; Margaret Fuller, *West-Country Friendly Soc.* 140.
[39] *Kelly's Dir. Som.* (1910).
[40] S.R.O., D/P/tin 2/1/2: inside back cover.
[41] *V.C.H. Som.* ii. 349; ex inf. Mr. R. G. Booker of Brisbane.

[42] *Census*, 1911–61. The alteration of the area of the parish accounts for only a small proportion of this increase.
[43] Finberg, *Early Charters of Wessex*, p. 134.
[44] Ibid. p. 143.
[45] See p. 215.
[46] *V.C.H. Som.* i. 409, 466, 474.
[47] *S.R.S.* viii. 119–26, 128; *Cal. Chart. R. 1257–1300*, 139; *Reg. Regum Anglo-Norm.* ii, p. 50.
[48] C 260/95/16, 96/25; *Sel. Cases in King's Bench, I* (Selden Soc.), 71; *S.R.S.* xlv. 148–9; *Feud. Aids*, iv. 286, 327.
[49] C 260/94/46; *Cal. Inq. ad quod damnum* (Rec. Com.), 253; *S.R.S.* xii. 69.
[50] C 47/77/3/82; C 260/94/46, 95/16, 96/4, 96/25, 118/27; *Plac. Abbrev.* (Rec. Com.), 334; *Cal. Inq. Misc.* iv, p. 55; *Rot. Parl.* iii. 172–3, 181, 186, 188, 190, 194, 197; *S.R.S.* viii. 211–12, 215–36; xvii. 176.
[51] *L. & P. Hen. VIII*, xvii, p. 107.

reversion in the year of his death, although he was in effectual control in the previous year.[52] By his will he left it to Elizabeth Darrell of Littlecote (Wilts.) with remainder, failing heirs, to his son Thomas.[53] She was in possession in 1547.[54] The attainder of the younger Thomas in 1554 gave the Crown the reversion after Elizabeth's death, but this was granted to Petre. He received a further lease to run from the death of Elizabeth, and he was certainly in occupation by 1556.[55] On his death in 1572 his son continued in occupation, and grants of the reversion of the manor to Robert Dudley, earl of Leicester, in 1574, and to Alexander Seton, Lord Fyvie, in 1605, did not disturb his tenure.[56] By 1612 John, Lord Petre (d. 1613), was holding the manor for life, with remainder to his third son Thomas. Thomas died in 1625 leaving his son Francis, a minor.[57] Early in 1626 the wardship of the heir was sold to Dr. William Smith, Warden of Wadham College, Oxford, and to Simon Baskerville, M.D.[58] They held courts in the manor until 1628, when it is probable that Thomas Napper, already owner of the parsonage, leased the property from them.[59] Francis Petre came of age in 1636 and recovered his inheritance from his former guardian, Baskerville.[60] Nathaniel Wright, merchant, was described as lord of the manor in 1649, though he was evidently Petre's tenant.[61] Petre (cr. Bt. 1642–4) died probably in 1660, and was succeeded by his son, also Francis.[62] By 1662 he and William Herris or Harrys were holding the manor court jointly, and continued to do so until 1669.[63] From 1670, however, the courts were held in the name of Thomas Napper (III) (d. 1700), and the final transfer from Petre to Napper was made in 1673.[64]

The manor descended in the Napper family, passing successively to Thomas Napper (V) (d. 1736) and Thomas Napper (VI) (d. 1760).[65] From Thomas (VI) it passed to his brother John (d. 1774), whose son, also John, died in 1791 heavily in debt.[66] His widow, Mary, held the manor court in 1791,[67] but sold the property in the following year to Admiral Marriott Arbuthnott (d. 1794).[68]

The Arbuthnotts, who were not resident in Tintinhull, held the manor until 1913. Admiral Arbuthnott was succeeded by John Arbuthnott, who held courts until 1809.[69] By 1811 the lord of the manor was Hugh (later Gen. Sir Hugh) Arbuthnott

(d. 1868).[70] He was succeeded by his brother Gen. William (d. 1876), and then by his nephew John, Viscount Arbuthnott (d. 1891). By 1885 there was only one acre of land in hand, and Viscount Arbuthnott was advised to discontinue the manor court.[71] A revival was contemplated in 1897.[72] The Arbuthnott estate, amounting to 476 a., was sold in 1913; the Ecclesiastical Commissioners became the appropriators, and the other properties were sold to the occupiers.[73] Mr. H. S. Howard, owner of Tintinhull Court from c. 1930, regarded himself as lord of the manor, but no courts were held.[74]

Part of the demesne land, or barton land as it was called, amounting to c. 300 a., was leased as a single unit by Sir William Petre in 1560.[75] With some additions, amounting to 200 a.,[76] the land was sold to John Lavyson or Lovyson, a London goldsmith (d. 1582).[77] By 1602–3 the original 300 a., called Belly or Belheighe and Berecrofte, were occupied by Romayn Sprackley.[78] By 1604 the lands had passed to Sir Thomas Freke, lord of Montacute,[79] who in 1612 settled them on Sir Joseph Killigrew and his wife.[80] Killigrew's son, Henry, made the estate over to William Bassett of Claverton in 1644.[81] Bassett's son, Sir William, sold the northern part, then called Bellheigh or Bewley farm, to Henry Seymour of St. Giles in the Fields, London, for £6,500 in 1676.[82] Seymour's son retained his interest until 1705, when he sold the farm to John Poulett, Earl Poulett (d. 1743), for £5,800.[83] The earl's widow retained the farm until 1750, when it passed to Thomas Lockyer, owner at least until 1783.[84] Lockyer was dead two years later, and by 1786 Bearley had become the property of Edward Phelips of Montacute.[85] By 1787 the farm was a compact unit of just over 409 a., including c. 117 a. of Chestermead in Sock Dennis.[86] It is said to have been sold to meet gambling debts.[87] By 1839 it was owned by Mrs. Brittenham or Brettingham.[88] Robert Brittingham was succeeded there by E. J. Bradshaw c. 1863,[89] and by 1871 the owner was J. T. Nicholetts of South Petherton.[90] The Ecclesiastical Commissioners purchased the farm in 1877.[91] Since the break-up of the Tintinhull Court Estate in 1913, they have been the largest landowners in the parish.

Bearley farm-house is of stone, brick, and tile; it has a five-bay front of two storeys with attics. The date 1658 occurs twice on the building, carrying

[52] Devon R.O. 123 M/E 91.
[53] L. & P. Hen. VIII, xvii, p. 107; xviii, p. 541.
[54] Devon R.O. 123 M/E 91.
[55] L. & P. Hen. VIII, xix, p. 86; Cal. Pat. 1555–7, 57–8; C 66/1421 m. 7.
[56] C 66/1115 mm. 19–20; Cal. S.P. Dom. 1591–4, 527; 603–10, 188.
[57] S.R.O., DD/X/HO, ct. roll, 28 Oct. 1612; S.R.S. lxvii. 191–2.
[58] S.R.S. lxvii. 191–2.
[59] C.P. 43/183 rot. 18.
[60] Ibid. 216 rot. 71.
[61] S.R.O., DD/X/HO, ct. roll, 6 July 1649.
[62] G.E.C. Baronetage, ii. 247.
[63] S.R.O., DD/X/HO, ct. rolls and bks.
[64] Ibid. ct. bk. 1662–1723; C.P. 25(2)/717/25 Chas. II Mich.
[65] S. & D. N. & Q. xxvii. 277–85.
[66] Ibid. 284.
[67] S.R.O., DD/X/HO, ct. bk. 1770–1878.
[68] S. & D. N. & Q. xxvii. 284; S.R.O., DD/X/HO, ct. bk. 1770–1878; D.N.B.
[69] S.R.O., DD/X/HO, ct. bk. 1770–1878.
[70] Ibid.; Burke, Peerage (1910), 108–9.

[71] S.R.O., DD/X/HO, ct. bk. 1878–85, letter enclosed.
[72] Ibid.
[73] S.R.O., DD/CC maps, box 4, sale partics. Tintinhull Court Estate.
[74] S.R.O., DD/X/HO, letter of Mr. Howard; Proc. Som. Arch. Soc. lxxvi, p. li.
[75] Devon R.O. 123 M/E 91, lease to Thomas Hurde.
[76] Devon R.O. 123 M/E 34, 91.
[77] C 142/197/48.
[78] S.R.O., D/P/tin 4/1/1, p. 203.
[79] Ibid. p. 212.
[80] S.R.O., DD/PH 59.
[81] Ibid.
[82] Ibid.
[83] Ibid.
[84] S.R.O., D/P/tin 4/1/2.
[85] Ibid.
[86] S.R.O., DD/PLE, box 89, map of Bearley fm. 1787.
[87] Llewelyn Powys, Som. and Dors. Essays, 18.
[88] S.R.O., DD/BT 3/7/5; tithe awards, Sock Dennis, Tintinhull.
[89] S.R.O., D/G/Y 160.
[90] Ibid.
[91] Ex inf. Trust Officer, Church Commrs.

the initials of Sir William Bassett, but at least part of the house was rebuilt after a fire in 1818.[92]

A thegn held a virgate of the count of Mortain T.R.E., which in 1086 was occupied by Drew.[93] The subsequent descent of the land has not been traced and it was evidently absorbed into the main manor. Freeholds in Stokett with rights in Tintinhull West field in the 16th century may indicate the position of the earlier estate.[94]

The estate formed when Montacute priory appropriated the rectory in 1528 or 1529[95] remained a separate unit at the Dissolution. It was leased for 21 years from the Crown by Sir William Petre from 1545.[96] The property was subject to several reversionary interests, though it remained in Petre's hands until 1559.[97] He is said to have assigned his lease to Edward Napper in 1546[98] but this is more likely to have been a short under-tenancy.[99] The property was sold by the Crown to Nicholas Napper in 1559 and the reversion in 1560.[1] The land was conveyed by Nicholas (d. 1579) to his second and third sons, James and Lancelot, for the payment of his debts,[2] but on his death it passed to his eldest son Thomas, the first of six successive sons and heirs bearing that name. Thomas (I) (d. 1626) and Thomas (II) (d. 1650) held the parsonage only, but under Thomas (III) (d. 1700) it was combined with the manor, and descended in the same way.

The parsonage estate consisted of tithes and small scattered pieces of glebe[3] including, presumably, a close of pasture to the west of the church still known as Parson's Close in 1839.[4] This, like the rest of the land, became indistinguishable from the remainder of the manorial property when Thomas Napper (III) became lord of the manor. The estates remained so united until 1913.[5]

The parsonage house, until appropriation the residence of the rector, was let at the Dissolution to Sir John Cuffe, farmer of the tithes.[6] His son still held it in 1559.[7] It subsequently became the home of the Nappers, the elder branch living there until its sale to Admiral Arbuthnott in 1793.[8] Tenant farmers then lived in the house until 1913.[9] Known as Tintinhull Manor Farm in 1819[10] and 1883,[11] it became known as Court Farm by 1897[12] and as Tintinhull Court by 1913.[13]

The present house is of two storeys and attics, built of coursed rubble and ashlar with a slate roof and coped gables. It consists of a principal range with a cross-wing to the south and a rear service wing to the north. The principal range preserves a basically medieval plan with a hall and cross-passage, but most of the structure was built or remodelled in the 17th and 18th centuries. An exception is an embattled and buttressed projection

at the front of the hall dating from c. 1500, which retains part of an original ground-floor window. It was formerly two-storeyed with a small room on each floor communicating with the hall and the room above by stone doorways. In the 20th century it was converted into a stair-well and a panelled ceiling was taken out and re-fixed beneath the roof.[14] A 'great chamber' and an 'oriel chamber' are mentioned by the occupier in his will dated 1552.[15] The only other early feature is a small two-light window re-set in the front wall of the house. Extensive rebuilding was carried out in the 17th century by the Nappers, whose arms appear above the round arch of the main doorway. A weather vane on the south wing is dated 1673 with the initials of Thomas Napper (III), who may have been responsible for most of the work. The stone windows, surmounted by hood-moulds, are mullioned and transomed. Those at the northern end of the front are hollow-chamfered while those in the hall and south wing, perhaps slightly later in date, are ovolo-moulded. In the angle between the principal range and the rear wing is a stair projection with an altered 17th-century staircase. The hall appears to have been refitted internally c. 1700 when it was given bolection-moulded panelling and an enriched plaster ceiling. There is earlier panelling in the room above. The rear wing is dated 1777. The curious north windows have wide round-headed lights and slender mullions, perhaps an example of 18th-century antiquarianism. Various additions at the rear of the house were the work of Mr. H. S. Howard. The wall between the garden and the churchyard is pierced by an 18th-century gateway with square piers and ball finials.

ECONOMIC HISTORY. The 10-hide estate of Glastonbury abbey in Tintinhull before the Conquest was rated for geld at only half that number in 1086.[16] There were, however, admitted to be 7 hides and 1 virgate of arable, together with 60 a. of meadow, 200 a. of pasture, and 57 a. of wood, which indicates that the estate had not changed significantly in area since the mid 10th century. The demesne arable of the count of Mortain amounted to 4 hides, farmed by 5 serfs with 2 ploughs. Nineteen villeins and 9 bordars with 8 ploughs worked the 'rest of the land', save 1 virgate held by Drew. The significant pasture and meadow land was stocked in 1086 with 2 riding-horses, 5 cows, 30 pigs, and 94 sheep. The whole estate was worth £16, a considerable increase on the £10 when the count acquired the property. In addition, Drew's estate was worth a mark.

By 1302–3[17] the arable demesne of Montacute

[92] Inscr. on building. A sketch of the house in 1787 (S.R.O. DD/PLE, box 89) shows a building of three bays with smaller, flanking, three-bay wings, and a large central stack.
[93] V.C.H. Som. i. 474.
[94] Devon R.O. 123 M/E 91.
[95] See p. 263.
[96] L. & P. Hen. VIII, xx(1), p. 679.
[97] Ibid. xx(2), pp. 543–4; xxi(1), p. 78; E 318/box 47/2483.
[98] Proc. Som. Arch. Soc. xxxii. 88.
[99] E 318/box 47/2483.
[1] Ibid.; Cal. Pat. 1558–60, 315.
[2] C.P. 25(2)/205/23 Eliz. I East.; Req. 2/245/1; Cal. Proc. in Chanc. Eliz. I (Rec. Com.), ii. 263, 274.
[3] E 315/398 f. 39.

[4] S.R.O., tithe award.
[5] See p. 258.
[6] E 315/398 f. 39.
[7] E 318/box 47/2483.
[8] S. & D. N. & Q. xxvii. 282–4.
[9] S.R.O., DD/CC maps, box 4, sale partics. Tintinhull Court Estate.
[10] S.R.O., DD/X/HO, sale poster 1819, in ct. bk. 1878–85.
[11] Kelly's Dir. Som. (1883).
[12] Ibid. (1897).
[13] S.R.O., DD/CC maps, box 4, sale partics. Tintinhull Court Estate.
[14] Country Life, 12 April 1956, 739.
[15] S.R.S. xxi. 137–8.
[16] V.C.H. Som. i. 474.
[17] S.C. 11/798.

priory, successor to the count of Mortain, amounted to 498 a., probably little changed from the 4 hides the count held. The monks also had 76 a. of meadow, 36 bovates of pasture, and pasture for 4 cows worth 6s. The change from two centuries earlier appeared in the tenant holdings: 17 free tenants had emerged, 7 holding a virgate each, 4 a ½-virgate, 5 a furlong, and 1 five acres. The number of villeins had risen from the 1086 figure: 13 *customarii*, 14 *ferlongarii*, and 16 cottars. All tenants, however, both free and villein, paid rent, as all services were commuted. The whole estate, including a fair, courts, and rents of gardens, amounted to £41 8s.

By the end of the 13th century at least part of the demesne in the south of the parish, around Wellhams, was held under a lease containing a marling clause.[18] A larger unit, comprising 60 a. of arable, 17 a. of meadow, and 8 bovates of pasture, was being held by a single tenant during the life of another party by 1399. The property included a messuage in the village called the woolhouse, perhaps a central collecting place for wool.[19]

By 1535, after appropriating the parsonage, the holding of Montacute priory in Tintinhull was valued at £88 13s. 3¾d.[20] Over £64 came from the rents of free and customary tenants, of whom there were 2 free and 58 customary in 1538–9.[21] In that year both demesne and rectory were let to farm, the former for £23 17s.[22] Twenty years later the total regular income had increased to just over £77, augmented in 1560 by entry fines totalling over £606 for new leases of demesne, notably for 300 a. at Bearley and Barcroft.[23] Six years later, when all the demesne or barton land was let, the total income had fallen to just over £65.[24] The tenancy structure was also changing. By 1597 there were 9 freehold estates attached to the manor, including five in Montacute and Stokett. Exeter College, Oxford, the largest tenant in Tintinhull, held just over 33 a., and Richard Mawdlen 30 a. The total income from the four freeholds in the parish was 25s. 6½d.[25] At the same time there were 40 customary holdings, and pieces of demesne or barton land held by customary tenure. The largest such holding was just over 51 a. Among these holdings was some property in Ilchester, including the site of a chapel.[26] A third group of properties, also barton land, was held mostly by leases for 21 years; there were 9 of these in Tintinhull and one in Babcary, and they ranged from 12 a. to 26 a.[27]

By the end of the 16th century the husbandry of the parish was based on five open arable fields, Great or Broad East field, the marsh or Marsh field, Little East field, Southover, and Socksam. In the early years of the 17th century the last three were worked together, and Great and Marsh fields together, growing alternately corn and beans.[28] Until *c.* 1596–7 there were two large areas of common

pasture in the parish, West field (120 a.) and the moor (70 a.). The former was also used by the tenants of Stokett, and both were described as 'very fruitful and commodious'.[29] About 1597 the moor was divided into 25 shares each attached to an already-established holding or bargain.[30]

This was not the beginning of inclosure. Closes of pasture and meadow already existed around Wellhams in the south and there were closes of arable in the northern part of Socksam by 1560.[31] The demesnes of Bearley and Barcroft were also inclosed, evidently for pasturage, for the estate was let in 1560 complete with shippens at both Tintinhull and Bearley.[32] The lessee undertook to 'feed and stall feed' with grass and hay four oxen belonging to the lessor from fifteen days before Michaelmas until fifteen days after Easter.[33]

A prosperous yeoman farmer and former bailiff of the manor,[34] Thomas Predell (d. 1546), probably reflected the general pattern of farming in the area when he left stock including 4 oxen, 5 cows, 3 heifers, 3 steers, 4 calves, 2 colts, and a flock of ewes and lambs.[35] The short leasing of the demesne or barton lands from 1560 onwards allowed the landlord to make detailed demands of his tenants for the maintenance of buildings, ditches, and hedges. The tenant of Bearley in 1560 was to 'plant for every timber tree to be delivered to him [for repairs] three other trees of the nature of oaks, ashes or elms'. This measure was, perhaps, in answer to a report still current in 1566, that there were 'no woods, but elms growing in hedgerows'. A lease of 1603 stipulated the annual planting of 'three apple, pear, or walnut, and three oak, ash, or elm'.[36]

Perhaps the most striking feature of the economy of the parish in the 16th and 17th centuries is the rise of the Napper family. Nicholas Napper (d. 1579) purchased the rectorial lands from the Crown in 1559 for £237,[37] to which he added the tenancy of some meadow land from the former manorial demesne and fishing and fowling rights.[38] By the end of the century Thomas Napper (I) (d. 1626) was holding by lease 48 a. of former demesne.[39] Within two generations the head of the family had acquired the lordship of the manor,[40] and the three largest houses in the village. Tintinhull Court, the Dower House, and Tintinhull House all witness to the prosperity of the family.

Until the inclosure of the parish in 1796 the only significant consolidated holding was Bearley farm. By 1787 it comprised 409 a., and stretched across the meadows into Sock Dennis.[41] The farm included some 'new inclosures' made at the northern end of Tintinhull mead. By the end of the 18th century other former commonable areas had been inclosed, notably West field, Perren's Hill, Broad Leaze, and Trent's Leazes. Pitte farm was still

[18] B.M. Harl. Ch. 44 G 11.
[19] *Cal. Inq. Misc.* vi, p. 228.
[20] *Valor Eccl.* (Rec. Com.), i. 195–6.
[21] S.C. 6/Hen. VIII/3137 mm. 26d–27d; E 315/398 f. 39.
[22] E 315/398 f. 39.
[23] S.R.O., DD/PH 225/1; Devon R.O. 123 M/E 91.
[24] Devon R.O. 123 M/E 91.
[25] Ibid. E 33.
[26] Ibid.
[27] Ibid.
[28] S.R.O., DD/X/HO, ct. rolls.
[29] Devon R.O. 123 M/E 91.

[30] Ibid.
[31] Ibid.
[32] Ibid.
[33] Ibid.
[34] *Valor Eccl.* (Rec. Com.), i. 195.
[35] *S.R.S.* xl. 152.
[36] Devon R.O. 123 M/E 91, 1561.
[37] E 318/box 47/2483.
[38] S.R.O., DD/PH 225/1.
[39] Devon R.O. 123 M/E 35.
[40] See p. 258.
[41] S.R.O., DD/PLE, box 89, map of Bearley farm, 1787.

almost entirely dispersed in the common fields, and included 20 a. of arable divided between three fields in fourteen separate parcels.[42] The parish was inclosed under an Act of 1794. The award, dated 1796,[43] regulated 310 a. of arable and 77 a. of meadow, just over one fifth of the total area of the parish, and divided it between 18 allottees.

By 1839 a number of farms, more or less consolidated units, had been created.[44] The largest, Manor farm of 456 a., was in fact the most scattered, having changed little since the time of inclosure. There were three farms of just over 100 a. each, including Perren's Hill and Leaches, four between 50 a. and 90 a., including Broad Leaze.[45] Eleven men were described as farmers in the village in 1859,[46] 19 in 1883,[47] but only 9 in 1902.[48] By 1931 only Bearley and Perren's Hill farms were said to be more than 150 a., but by 1939 four had reached that figure, Bearley, Perren's Hill, Winter's, and Higher farms.[49]

Like several of its neighbours Tintinhull still had a small gloving industry in 1968. Robert Southcombe, whose brother Richard had already established a factory at Stoke, opened his premises at the southern end of the village in 1875.[50] The factory then made fabric gloves,[51] though by the early 20th century leather ones. The firm, known from 1900 as Ensor and Southcombe, joined the larger concern of Southcombe Brothers in 1965, and has since been called the Tintinhull Glove Co. Ltd. It makes all types of gloves in both leather and fabric.[52]

There was a mill at Tintinhull in 1086, valued at 30d.[53] The name Wellhams, by which the mill was later known, occurs as a personal name by 1273,[54] and meadows lying east of the former mill-house were still so called in the 19th century.[55] The site of the mill, on a race constructed within the southern parish boundary, may well have been that of the Domesday mill. The mill formed part of Montacute priory demesne at least until the late 14th century. The priory had the tithes of the area by 1334,[56] but had apparently leased the mill to Walter and Maud de Welnham in or after 1319. The lessees had rights to carry millstones and large timbers for its repair.[57] By 1374 the mill, together with a messuage, presumably the mill-house, and a carucate of land, had been acquired for life by John Bondeman, and was the subject of a Chancery action.[58] In 1381 Bondeman and his wife sold the

mill, together with 120 a. of land, meadow, and pasture in 'West Welham' and Stokett to John Breynton and his wife.[59] By 1541 the mill was held again directly of the manor, and was let to Robert Stybbes;[60] by 1605 the tenant was Ambrose Bishop.[61]

By 1629 the mills at Wellhams were the freehold property of Sampson Burr, who was succeeded by his widow in 1644.[62] From 1650 one Hann was acting as her miller. John Bishop was owner from 1654 at least until 1670,[63] when the mill was said to be in decay.[64] During the 19th and early 20th centuries a succession of millers can be traced, the last being Esau Saunders in 1902.[65] In 1968 the mill-house was in private occupation.

William, count of Mortain, granted a fair at Tintinhull to Montacute priory as part of his foundation gift c. 1102.[66] Before 1122 it was held for thirteen days around St. Margaret's day (20 July).[67] In 1242–3 the prior of Montacute was challenged for taking tolls there from the men of Exeter,[68] and in 1280 the burgesses of Ilchester complained that it was detrimental to their trade.[69] The fair was worth £2 in 1302–3,[70] but was not mentioned among Montacute's assets in 1535, and was worth nothing by 1559–60.[71]

LOCAL GOVERNMENT. Montacute priory held courts in Tintinhull and owned the assizes of bread and ale.[72] Court rolls, books, and extracts, however, survive only from after the Dissolution, for 1586–7, 1612–23, 1624–38, 1649, 1662–1723, 1770–1878, and 1879–85.[73] They reveal, among other things, that the hundred and the manor were administered by the same court from at least the 1580s until 1885.[74]

By 1586 two courts were held annually before a steward, usually in April and October. They seem to have become annual, held in October or November, by the late 17th century.[75] From 1612 the court was described as *curia legalis* and view of frankpledge, with court baron occasionally added in the heading without any change being apparent in the character of the proceedings.[76] The term court leet alone was introduced in 1675 and was usual thereafter. The court ceased to meet after 1885.[77]

As the governing body of the manor the court elected a tithingman annually in the autumn. The office was held in rotation by the owners or occupiers of freehold 'places' or tenements, but could

[42] S.R.O., DD/X/HO, marr. settlement of E. B. Napier, 1790.
[43] S.R.O., CR 31.
[44] S.R.O., tithe award.
[45] Broad Leaze was known as Mount Hunger farm in 1826: S.R.O., D/T/ilch.
[46] P.O. Dir. Som. (1859).
[47] Kelly's Dir. Som. (1883).
[48] Ibid. (1902).
[49] Ibid. (1931, 1939).
[50] S.R.O., D/G/Y 160 shows the factory first rated in that year. See R. E. Southcombe, 'Southcombe Brothers Limited, Stoke under Ham' (TS. in S.R.O.).
[51] Kelly's Dir. Som. (1897).
[52] Ex inf. Mr. R. E. Southcombe. See also V.C.H. Som. ii. 428; Proc. Som. Arch. Soc. lviii. 111.
[53] V.C.H. Som. i. 474.
[54] B.M. Harl. Ch. 44 G 11.
[55] S.R.O., tithe award.
[56] E 179/169/14.
[57] Cal. Pat. 1343–5, 271.
[58] C 44/7/11; C 260/87/50.

[59] S.R.S. xvii. 108–9.
[60] Devon R.O. 123 M/E 91.   [61] Ibid. E 33.
[62] S.R.O., DD/X/HO, Thomas Napper's Easter bk.
[63] Ibid. Thomas Napper's Easter bk. and ct. bk. 1662–1723.
[64] Ibid. ct. bk. 1662–1723, Oct. 1670.
[65] S.R.O., tithe award; P.O. Dir. Som. (1866, 1875); Kelly's Dir. Som. (1883, 1897, 1902).
[66] S.R.S. viii. 119; Cal. Chart. R. 1257–1300, 314.
[67] Reg. Regum Anglo-Norm. ii. pp. 180–1; S.C. 11/798.
[68] S.R.S. xi. 325.
[69] Plac. de Quo Warr. (Rec. Com.), 696; S.R.S. viii. 207.
[70] S.C. 11/798.
[71] S.R.O., DD/PH 225/1.
[72] S.R.S. viii. 207.
[73] Devon R.O. 123 M/M 108–9; S.R.O., DD/X/HO.
[74] See p. 177.
[75] S.R.O., DD/X/HO.
[76] The one exception is a court baron in 1649.
[77] S.R.O., DD/X/HO, ct. bk. 1662–1723, Oct. 1675; ct. bk. 1878–85.

be executed by deputy.[78] The last election to the office took place in 1842. Haywards occur irregularly from 1620 onwards. Until the late 17th century the court does not seem to have been concerned in their appointment. By 'ancient custom', however, they were paid a levy of 5s. on every 'place'.[79] From 1774 two haywards were appointed each year by the court; in return for three leazes in the common fields and three in Tintinhull mead they were made responsible for maintaining droves and floodgates.[80] By 1860 a distinction was made between the parish hayward, an office thenceforward held by the village policeman, and the manorial hayward, who was elected by the manor court.[81] These offices continued at least until 1885.[82]

Two surveyors of the common fields were appointed annually at the spring court to supervise the execution of inclosure and drainage regulations. They ceased to act regularly after 1624 when they were replaced by the haywards. Two 'viewers of fences' occurred in 1701, probably with the same functions.[83] From 1772 until 1869 a manorial constable as well as the older officer, the hundred constable, was chosen yearly.

The activities of the court in the general administration of agriculture in the parish included the supervision of crop rotation and grazing rights, the maintenance of banks, ditches, and bridges, and the control of water meadows in the north of the parish. Thus in 1623 an old order was quoted whereby freehold 'places' were charged with the upkeep of gates in the temporary inclosures in the open fields. Each freeholder was thenceforward required to find locks for the gates until the grass or corn was taken, and then to re-lock until the whole field was breached.[84] Of particular importance in the north of the parish were the water meadows, regulated by floodgates or 'shittles'. One of these, Tintinhull moor shittle, was maintained under the court's supervision until 1885 out of land called 'landacre' and by occasional rates charged on the occupiers of the meadows.

The court still clearly controlled parish affairs in the late 17th century, ordering the waywardens, for example, to repair gutters in the village street, and the churchwardens and overseers to erect stocks.[85] The churchwardens and overseers, however, managed the poor. In 1610 two wardens and three overseers leased from the lord some waste land between the pound and the church house on which to build a poorhouse.[86] There were already three houses near the site 'lately' erected for the poor at the request of the parish officers.[87] By 1722 the overseers were renting five houses, normally known

as 'poor houses' or 'parish houses', which they in turn let at higher rents to increase their income. Only on rare occasions, for example in 1745, were paupers temporarily lodged in one of these houses.[88] The tenements, under a single thatched roof, came to be regarded as one house, though divided into separate dwellings. In 1762–3 the house was rebuilt as six tenements of two storeys, each 14 ft. square.[89]

Tintinhull became part of the Yeovil poor-law union in 1836, and the tenements were sold c. 1839.[90] The school and private dwellings occupied the site in 1968.

The parish vestry emerged in the mid 18th century. In 1743 a group of parishioners met at the church house, then parish property,[91] and ordered the overseers to make payments to certain paupers. In the following year the same body was described as a vestry, when it superintended the placing of parish apprentices.[92] Further activities have not been traced until the mid 19th century.[93] They were then regularly appointing two overseers and two waywardens, whose duties were little more than nominal, and from 1874 they levied a school rate.[94] Overseers and waywardens were appointed annually at least until 1892.[95]

CHURCH. There was a church at Tintinhull by c. 1102 when it was granted by William, count of Mortain, as part of Montacute priory's foundation estate.[96] It was charged until 1174–80 simply with a pension to the monks, a payment which continued at least until 1428.[97] From 1180 a further charge was made on the church for the benefit of the sacristan at Montacute, who was allowed to hold the church annually from the tenth day before the patronal feast (20 July) until its morrow, and was to have any revenues then accruing except tithes.[98] This arrangement seems to have been superseded by 1334 when the prior of Montacute was receiving tithes from Wellhams, in the south of the parish.[99] In 1528 the convent was licensed to appropriate the remaining revenues provided that a vicarage was established, served by a secular priest.[1] The vicarage was ordained in 1529,[2] though the cure was still being served by the monks in 1532.[3] Doubt is therefore cast on the validity of the ordination and, although the incumbent was called a vicar in 1535, the legal status of the benefice was a perpetual curacy until 1968.[4]

Until the Dissolution the advowson belonged to Montacute priory.[5] As a Cluniac house, however, its property was seized several times during the 14th century by the Crown, which then exercised

[78] e.g. courts for Oct. 1633 and Oct. 1667.
[79] S.R.O., DD/X/HO, ct. bk. 1662–1723, Apr. 1697.
[80] Ibid. ct. bk. 1770–1878.   [81] Ibid.
[82] Ibid. ct. bk. 1878–85.
[83] Ibid. ct. bk. 1662–1723.
[84] Ibid. ct. roll 26 Apr. 1623.
[85] Ibid. ct. bk. 1662–1723, 17 May 1690.
[86] Devon R.O. 123 M/E 34, 91.
[87] Ibid. E 34.
[88] S.R.O., D/P/tin 13/2/1: overseers' rate and acct. bk. 1721–89.
[89] Ibid. Three tenements are depicted on a map of 1777: S.R.O., DD/SAS PR 454.
[90] Poor Law Com. 2nd Rep., p. 550; S.R.O., D/P/tin 13/8/1; tithe award.
[91] S.R.O., D/P/tin 4/1/1, pp. 206, 227; 13/2/1. Probably demolished c. 1763: 13/2/1.

[92] S.R.O., D/P/tin 13/2/1.
[93] Ibid. 9/1/1: vestry min. bk. 1857–1944.
[94] Ibid. 13/1/1; 13/2/2–5; 14/5/1: overseers' payments and accts. from 1796; surveyors accts. and rates, from 1750.
[95] S.R.O., DD/X/HO.
[96] S.R.S. viii. 119–20.
[97] Tax. Eccl. (Rec. Com.), 197; Feud. Aids, iv. 402.
[98] S.R.S. viii. 191–2.
[99] E 179/169/14.
[1] L. & P. Hen. VIII, iv(2), p. 1896.
[2] Proc. Som. Arch. Soc. xxxii. 87, quoting abstract of title of parsonage.
[3] S.R.O., D/D/Vc 20.
[4] Valor Eccl. (Rec. Com.), i. 198.
[5] S.R.S. i. 163; xxix. 261; xxxi. 61, 73; xxxii. 156; lii, pp. xxiii, 13, 53, 70–1, 84, 87; liv. 53.

the patronage itself,[6] or granted it to the earls of Salisbury.[7] The abbot of Glastonbury presented in 1521 by grant of Montacute priory, the presentee being the prior of Montacute himself.[8] Between the Dissolution and 1566 the Crown presumably retained the advowson, and certainly presented in 1566 and 1571,[9] the advowson having been expressly excepted from the grant of the parsonage estate in 1559.[10] By 1576 Nicholas Napper had acquired the patronage,[11] which thenceforward descended with the parsonage estate and, from 1673, with the manor, to the Arbuthnotts.[12] In 1913 the patronage passed from Viscount Arbuthnot to the Revd. S. J. M. Price, D.D., of Tintinhull House (d. 1926).[13] His trustees presented up to 1941 and thereafter the Guild of All Souls.[14]

The rectory was valued at £16 in 1291[15] and 1428;[16] by about 1539 the net value was only about £9 9s.[17] By 1559 the net income enjoyed by the impropriator was £7 8s. 1½d.[18] The rector had glebe lands, tithe corn, rents, oblations, and small tithes amounting to £7 in 1334, and Montacute priory had tithes at Wellhams worth £3.[19] In 1535 the tithes and other dues were valued at £18 net[20] and were farmed for that sum. Glebe lands were let to various tenants for £5 8s.[21] Tithes and glebe emerged as a separate estate after the Dissolution,[22] although the tithes were farmed separately in 1535.[23] The glebe subsequently lost its identity in the other holdings of the lay impropriators, but the tithes remained distinct: in 1634, for example, Thomas Napper collected £30 16s. 11d.[24] The tithes were commuted in 1838 for a rent-charge of £396 10s.[25]

By the ordination of 1529 the vicar was to receive from the impropriator £10 gross and £9 8s. 7d. net.[26] The impropriator continued to pay this sum throughout the 17th century,[27] though in 1571 the vicar claimed to have suffered 'open wrong' because the impropriator would not pay tenths and subsidies as originally agreed.[28] By about 1668 the reputed value of the benefice was £30.[29] The living was augmented by the impropriator in 1729 and 1761, in the second year £100 being made available by the Pincombe trustees.[30] In 1819 the incumbent, John Valentine, and the Pincombe trustees further augmented the benefice,[31] which by 1809 had risen to £77 18s. 6d.,[32] though it was given as only £60 in 1815.[33] The income was said to be £90 in 1831.[34]

An acre of meadow in New mead was allotted to the vicar in 1529, with an orchard, garden, and close.[35] In 1774 the vicar was assigned a number of leazes in the common fields.[36] There was one acre of glebe in 1840,[37] but by 1851 the income of £91 was said to be almost entirely from glebe.[38] In 1902 the income of the benefice included a tithe rent-charge of £31, 42 a. of glebe, and other items, making £89 in all.[39]

A house was assigned to the vicar in 1529;[40] it possessed an 'outhouse called a kitchen' in 1633.[41] In 1815 the glebe house, 'a small tenement', was thought unfit for the vicar.[42] In 1827 it was called a 'mean cottage', and the vicar lived elsewhere in the village.[43] In 1831 it was again styled 'unfit',[44] and in 1840 was 'let as a cottage'.[45] A new house was built in 1871;[46] it was still in use in 1968, and stands at the south-east corner of the village.

During the Middle Ages the Crown took advantage of its occasional patronage rights to appoint government clerks such as John of Chester (occurs 1294),[47] clerk of the King's Bench,[48] or the diplomat Richard de Saham (unsuccessfully intruded 1346).[49] Non-residence was therefore not uncommon.[50] During the 15th century several eminent ecclesiastics held the benefice, including John Hornse (rector 1480–1), bishop of Ross and a Cistercian monk, suffragan in the diocese of Bath and Wells 1479–81;[51] John Wyche (rector 1501–21), fellow and sub-warden of New College, Oxford;[52] and Thomas Chard (rector from 1521), prior of Montacute and of Carswell (Devon), bishop of Selymbria and suffragan to the bishops of Bath and Wells and Exeter.[53] John Heth (rector 1434–64) was licensed to be absent for two years for study,[54] and at his death in 1464 was also rector of Chiselborough;[55] and Robert Newton (rector 1465–7),

[6] *Cal. Pat.* 1343–5, 435, 472; 1345–8, 39; 1354–8, 48; 1381–5, 159; 1388–92, 477; 1391–6, 657; 1396–9, 41.
[7] *S.R.S.* x. 625; *Cal. Pat.* 1343–5, 435, 472; 1345–8, 39.
[8] *S.R.S.* lv. 17.
[9] S.R.O., D/D/Bp; *Som. Incumbents*, ed. Weaver, 200.
[10] E 318/box 47/2483.
[11] *Som. Incumbents*, 200.
[12] Giles Flint presented in 1609 by virtue of a grant from Thomas Napper: *Som. Incumbents*, 200.
[13] *Dioc. Dir.* (1913, 1927).
[14] Ibid. (1941–70).
[15] *Tax. Eccl.* (Rec. Com.), 197.
[16] *Feud. Aids*, iv. 402.
[17] E 315/398 f. 39.
[18] E 318/box 47/2483.
[19] E 179/169/14.
[20] *Valor Eccl.* (Rec. Com.), i. 198.
[21] E 315/398 f. 39.
[22] See p. 259.
[23] E 315/398 f. 39.
[24] S.R.O., DD/X/HO, Thomas Napper's Easter bk., which records 'donations and tithes due at Easter yearly' 1629–87.
[25] S.R.O., DD/X/HO, tithe apportionment.
[26] *Proc. Som. Arch. Soc.* xxxii. 87; *Valor. Eccl.* (Rec. Com.), i. 198.
[27] E 318/box 47/2483; S.R.O., D/D/Rg 234; DD/X/HO, Thomas Napper's Easter bk.
[28] S.R.O., D/D/Rg 234.

[29] S.R.O., D/D/Vc 24.
[30] Hodgson, *Queen Anne's Bounty.*   [31] Ibid.
[32] *Augmentation of Livings, 1703–1815*, H. C. 115 (1814–15), xii.
[33] S.R.O., D/D/V rtns. 1815.
[34] *Rep. Com. Eccl. Revenues*, pp. 182–3.
[35] *Proc. Som. Arch. Soc.* xxxii. 87.
[36] S.R.O., DD/X/HO, ct. bk. 1770–1878, *sub anno* 1774.
[37] *County Gazette Dir. Som.* (1840).
[38] H.O. 129/319/3/2/7.
[39] *Crockford* (1902).
[40] *Proc. Som. Arch. Soc.* xxxii. 87.
[41] S.R.O., D/D/Rg 234.
[42] S.R.O., D/D/V rtns. 1815. The house was on the east side of Vicarage St.: S.R.O., tithe award.
[43] S.R.O., D/D/V rtns. 1827.
[44] *Rep. Com. Eccl. Revenues*, pp. 182–3.
[45] S.R.O., D/D/V rtns. 1840.
[46] *Lond. Gaz.* 24 Nov. 1871, p. 4910.
[47] *Cal. Pat.* 1292–1301, 122.
[48] *Sel. Cases King's Bench, I* (Selden Soc.), lxxxvii.
[49] *Cal. Pat.* 1345–8, 39; Emden, *Biog. Reg. Univ. Cambridge.*
[50] e.g. *S.R.S.* i. 43.
[51] Emden, *Biog. Reg. Univ. Oxford*; *Handbk. of Brit. Chron.* ed. F. M. Powicke and E. B. Fryde, 271.
[52] Emden, *Biog. Reg. Univ. Oxford.*
[53] Ibid.; *Handbk. of Brit. Chron.* 278.
[54] *S.R.S.* xxxii. 169.
[55] *Proc. Som. Arch. Soc.* lxxi, opp. p. 108.

apparently a monk, died at Rome while still holding the cure.[56] The church was presumably served during their absences by chaplains: two occur in 1434–5,[57] and one in 1437–8, 1450,[58] and 1468.[59]

In 1554 the lay rector was presented for allowing the chancel to decay, and for failing to maintain a light on the altar.[60] Richard Loughe, vicar, was reported non-resident in 1568; no quarterly sermons had been preached, and the fabric needed attention.[61] One of Loughe's successors, John Lorrimer, was crushed to death under a collapsed 'linhay' in 1593.[62] In 1612 the churchwardens were presented for not having a copy of Jewel's *Works*; they had acquired one by the following year.[63] Further criticisms were evidently made at the next visitation, including the need for a stall for the vicar. The churchwardens paid a fine 'for a longer time for amending of those defaults'.[64]

The church was served from 1609 until his death in 1646 by Adam Farnham. During his time, probably in 1642, Parliamentary troops visited the church and took away two surplices, cutting them up and distributing the pieces to the poor.[65] It is not clear how the church was served after Farnham's death. The record of the Register survives, but no clergyman is found until Thomas Farnham, who died as incumbent in 1661.[66] For most of the 18th century the benefice was combined with Thorn Coffin rectory and, in the persons of Edward Napper or Napier (vicar from 1741 until at least 1752) and of his son Edward (vicar 1772–1816) was held by members of the patron's family.[67] The last was an absentee, living in 1815 on a third cure at Sutton Waldren (Dors.).[68] At least eleven assistant curates successively served the church during the younger Napper's incumbency.[69] John Valentine, one of these and vicar 1816–44, was also chaplain of Ilchester gaol.[70]

By 1827 one service with sermon was held every Sunday, alternately morning and afternoon.[71] Two sermons were preached every Sunday by 1843, Holy Communion was celebrated each quarter, and children were catechized weekly.[72] In 1851 there was no resident minister, and in consequence there was only one service on Census Sunday, when 159 people attended in the afternoon. The average congregation was said to be 100 in the morning and 150 in the afternoon, with Sunday-school pupils numbering 56 in the morning and 76 in the afternoon.[73] Two services with sermons were the rule in 1870, the second service having been moved to the evening. Holy Communion was celebrated eight times a year.[74]

Churchwardens' accounts survive from 1433 until 1678.[75] They show that income was derived during the 15th and 16th centuries from the proceeds of church ales and the rent of the parish bakehouse and brewhouse. In 1497 a church house was built to house both, replaced by a more substantial stone house in 1531–2.[76] Parts of the house were let by the mid 16th century,[77] but it continued in use by the parish until c. 1763, when it was demolished and its site incorporated in the rebuilt poorhouses.[78] Church ales provided an income for the parish until 1609;[79] the churchwardens also let the grass in the droves, often called 'lane acres', and from 1596–7 an acre in Tintinhull moor was assigned to the church house.[80]

The church of *ST. MARGARET* consists of a chancel and nave, with north tower and south porch, and modern vestries at the west end. The original early-13th-century building was not divided by a chancel arch, a fact demonstrated by the roll-moulded string-course surviving almost continuously around the whole structure and rising to form hood-moulds above doors and other original openings; and by the common width of the present chancel and nave. Externally the level of the corbel-table was later broken when the nave roof was raised. The lighting of the original building survives in the blocked window between nave and tower; it is a lancet, with depressed trefoil head in a deeply splayed surround flanked with shafted rear-arches.[81] Rear-arches also survive around the three two-light windows on each side of the chancel. The tracery was inserted later, possibly when the church was remodelled and the chancel arch inserted in the 14th century. The double piscina, which belongs to the original structure, is of two trefoiled arches on shafts which are evidently replacements of originals in Purbeck marble.

The north tower is slightly later than the main structure. It is now of four stages with lancet windows and a plain parapet. The top stage and the north-east stair turret were added in 1516–17.[82] In the 15th century large Perpendicular windows were inserted in the nave, one in each of the side walls and one at the west end. That on the north nave wall incorporates a light bracket. The south porch, originally thatched, and now capped by a sundial, was built in 1441–2;[83] it has a ribbed barrel vault, the central rib springing from wall-shafts. Part of the stone base of the rood screen is preserved, perhaps belonging to the new screen and loft constructed in 1451–2.[84] Bench-ends, carved with panels and flowers, were made in 1511–12.[85] Still attached to some of them are hinged flaps which, when raised, could be used as extra seats in the central aisle. The

[56] *S.R.S.* lii. 13–14.
[57] Ibid. iv. 176.
[58] Ibid. 178; xlix. 137.
[59] Ibid. lii. 25.
[60] S.R.O., D/D/Ca 22.
[61] Ibid. 40.
[62] S.R.O., D/P/tin 4/1/1, p. 185.
[63] S.R.O., D/D/Ca 177; D/P/tin 4/1/2, p. 3.
[64] S.R.O., D/P/tin 4/1/2, p. 2.
[65] Ibid. p. 102.
[66] S.R.O., D/P/tin 2/1/1, burials.
[67] S.R.O., D/D/Vc 9, 27–9, 31–2, 35–6; *S. & D. N. & Q.* xxvii. 284.
[68] S.R.O., D/D/V rtns. 1815.
[69] S.R.O., D/D/Rr 419; D/D/V rtns. 1815.
[70] S.R.O., D/D/V rtns. 1827; *Rep. Com. Ilchester Gaol, App.* H.C. 54 (1822), xi.

[71] S.R.O., D/D/V rtns. 1827.
[72] Ibid. 1843.
[73] H.O. 129/319/3/2/7.
[74] S.R.O., D/D/V rtns. 1870.
[75] S.R.O., D/P/tin 4/1/1–2; extracts from 1433 to 1569 printed in *S.R.S.* iv. 175–207.
[76] *S.R.S.* iv. 173, 195–6, 201; S.R.O., D/P/tin 4/1/1, pp. 115–16.
[77] S.R.O., D/P/tin 4/1/1, p. 206.
[78] Ibid. p. 227; D/P/tin 13/2/1; see above, p. 262.
[79] S.R.O., D/P/tin 4/1/1, p. 227.
[80] Ibid. *passim*. A church rate was levied from 1602–3.
[81] See plate facing p. 209.
[82] *S.R.S.* iv. 202.
[83] Ibid. 180.
[84] Ibid. 185.
[85] Ibid. 199.

pulpit and sounding board date from the early 17th century. The church contains a brass to John Stone (d. 1416) and one with a figure of rector John Heth (d. 1464). The east window, which has a four-centred head and contains glass by F. C. Eden, is said to date from the 19th century.[86] Outside the church, at the end of the original churchyard, is the 'stonyn' door, incorporating a doorhead made in 1517 as part of the west entrance to the churchyard.[87] The churchyard cross was designed by Sir Ninian Comper c. 1920.[88]

The church has five bells: (i) 1617, Robert Wiseman of Montacute; (ii) 1787, Thomas Pyke of Bridgwater; (iii) 1799, George Davis of Bridgwater; (iv) 1602, Robert Wiseman of Montacute; (v) 1629, William Wiseman.[89] The plate includes a chalice and cover of 1635, maker 'R.W.'[90] The registers date from 1561, but there is a gap in baptisms between 1607 and 1610.[91]

NONCONFORMITY. In 1669 forty people were meeting regularly in William Webb's house under the leadership of a Presbyterian teacher.[92] This group does not seem to have survived. In 1826 Methodists applied to use a house in the parish and a group of Bible Christians was formed for a few months in 1835.[93] In 1840 some Baptists were licensed to use what had once been the poor-houses.[94] Part of the site was used for the village school in 1848.[95] There is no record of a chapel in 1851, but by 1875 Montacute Baptist church had a 'preaching station' in the parish.[96] This was probably the room at the side of Walters's Farm at the northern end of the green which by 1897 had 100 sittings.[97] From about 1898 Yeovil Baptist church became responsible for the chapel 'as a help to some young men belonging to a preacher's training class'.[98] By 1902 the building had been handed over to a group of Brethren from the Martock Assembly, who continued to hold services there at least until 1951.[99]

EDUCATION. John Priddle, described as a schoolmaster, lived in the village in 1752.[1] By 1818 there was a day-school for c. 30 boys and girls and a Sunday school for c. 70.[2] The Sunday school was supported by the church and had 33 boys and 31 girls on its register in 1825–6.[3] There were two schools in the village in 1833: a day-school for 12 boys and 20 girls, taught at their parents' expense, and a Sunday school for 33 boys and 47 girls, supported by subscriptions.[4] The second was evidently held in the church.[5] By 1846–7 there were four schools.[6] The largest, the Church school, had 60 boys and 61 girls under four teachers, and accommodation consisted of two rooms and a teacher's house. It was supported by subscriptions. A Miss Morey kept a day-school for 4 boys and 19 girls under two teachers. There were also two dame schools, between them taking 28 boys and 25 girls. The last three schools were supported by payment of school pence.

The building used in 1969 was erected in 1848 and extended in 1854.[7] By 1872 there were four classes under one teacher and two monitresses, though the low average attendance, 40, was partly explained by children being absent for bean planting. Twenty years later a new teacher found the school 'in a very backward state', but a year later 'very satisfactory progress' had been made.[8] By 1894 there was accommodation for 83, with an average attendance of 57.[9] There were two classrooms for 77 children by 1903, with a staff of three. Evening continuation classes had been held until that year, and the inspector's report was favourable.[10] Average attendance had fallen to 53 by 1938, and fell still further in the 1940s when senior pupils were sent elsewhere. In 1969, however, Tintinhull C. of E. (V.A.) School had 71 registered pupils.[11]

CHARITIES FOR THE POOR. By will dated 1862 William Wilson gave a rent-charge of £5, payable yearly on 24 December for a dinner of roast beef and plum pudding on Christmas Day to 'deserving' pupils in the Sunday school[12]. In 1972 the income was still used for the benefit of children connected with the church.[13]

[86] Pevsner, *South and West Som.* 323.
[87] *Proc. Som. Arch. Soc.* xxxii. 73–4.
[88] Pevsner, *South and West Som.* 324.
[89] S.R.O., DD/SAS CH 16.
[90] *Proc. Som. Arch. Soc.* xliv. 186.
[91] S.R.O., D/P/tin 2/1/1–8.
[92] G. L. Turner, *Rec. Early Nonconf.* ii. 1106.
[93] S.R.O., D/D/Rm, box 2; D/N/sp.c. 31.
[94] S.R.O., D/D/Rm, box 2.
[95] See below and p. 262.
[96] Ex inf. Mr. W. H. Osborne, Sec. Montacute Baptist chapel.
[97] *Kelly's Dir. Som.* (1897).
[98] Ex inf. Mr. Osborne.
[99] *Kelly's Dir. Som.* (1902); ex inf. Mr. Osborne.

[1] S.R.O., Q/R jurors' bk. 1697–1766.
[2] *Digest of Returns to Sel. Cttee on Educ. of Poor*, II.C. 224 (1819), ix(2).
[3] *Rep. B. & W. Dioc. Assoc. S.P.C.K.* (1825–6), 67.
[4] *Educ. Enquiry Abstract*, H.C. (1835), xlii.
[5] S.R.O., D/D/V rtns. 1840, 1843.
[6] *Church Sch. Inquiry, 1846–7.*
[7] S.R.O., C/E 28; D/P/tin 18/8/1.
[8] S.R.O., D/P/tin 18/7/1, log bk. 1872–1906.
[9] *Rtns. of Schs.* [C 7529] H.C. (1894), lxv.
[10] S.R.O., C/E 28.
[11] *Bd. of Educ., List 21*, [*1938*] (H.M.S.O.), 352; Som. C.C. Educ. Cttee. *Schs. List.*
[12] S.R.O., D/P/tin 17/1/1.
[13] Ex inf. the Revd. R. I. H. Brown, vicar.

INDEX

INDEX